RELATED BOOKS FOR STUDENTS OF ENGLISH AND/OR SPANISH

Dictionary of the Spanish Language/Diccionario del Idioma Español
Edited by Edwin B. Williams

A new all-Spanish dictionary, the most concise, modern, and up-to-date volume of its kind, including 35,000 entries, modern scientific terminology, guides to the conjugation of irregular verbs, and a comprehensive English-Spanish word list.

Williams' Handbook of Modern Spanish
Edited by Edwin B. Williams

A complete reference guide to all aspects of the Spanish language. Pronunciation, punctuation, grammar, verb forms, idioms, word usage, sentence structure, etc.

Language Through Pictures Series
Edited by I. A. Richards and Christine Gibson

A famous and widely tested method of learning a language without a teacher.
FIRST STEPS IN READING ENGLISH
ENGLISH THROUGH PICTURES BOOK I and
  A FIRST WORKBOOK OF ENGLISH
ENGLISH THROUGH PICTURES BOOK II and
  A SECOND WORKBOOK OF ENGLISH
ENGLISH THROUGH PICTURES BOOK III
FRENCH THROUGH PICTURES BOOK I
  A First Workbook of French
  A Second Workbook of French
GERMAN THROUGH PICTURES BOOK I
SPANISH THROUGH PICTURES BOOK I and
  A FIRST WORKBOOK OF SPANISH
SPANISH THROUGH PICTURES BOOK II and
  A SECOND WORKBOOK OF SPANISH

Published by POCKET BOOKS

UNIVERSIDAD DE CHICAGO

DICCIONARIO

ESPAÑOL-INGLÉS e INGLÉS-ESPAÑOL

*Un Nuevo y Conciso Diccionario Que Contiene las Voces
y Locuciones Básicas de Ambos Idiomas*

RECOPILACIÓN
DE
CARLOS CASTILLO *y* **OTTO F. BOND**

Universidad de Chicago

CON LA AYUDA DE

BARBARA M. GARCÍA

Mills College

Con una tercera sección de las expresiones idiomáticas obtenidas de *The Traveler's Phrase Book: English-Spanish, Español-Inglés*, redactado por Lester G. Crocker y Enrique Noble.

PUBLISHED BY POCKET BOOKS NEW YORK

THE UNIVERSITY OF CHICAGO

SPANISH-ENGLISH, ENGLISH-SPANISH

DICTIONARY

*A New Concise Dictionary of Words and Phrases Basic
to the Written and Spoken Languages of Today*

COMPILED BY
CARLOS CASTILLO & OTTO F. BOND
The University of Chicago

WITH THE ASSISTANCE OF
BARBARA M. GARCÍA
Mills College

With a new third section of idiomatic phrases taken from
*The Traveler's Phrase Book: English-Spanish, Español-
Inglés*, edited by Lester G. Crocker and Enrique Noble

PUBLISHED BY POCKET BOOKS NEW YORK

THE UNIVERSITY OF CHICAGO SPANISH-ENGLISH,
ENGLISH-SPANISH DICTIONARY

University of Chicago edition published 1948

POCKET BOOK edition published November, 1950
115th printing.........April, 1973

The University of Chicago Spanish-English, English-Spanish Dictionary
was formerly published under the imprint of WASHINGTON SQUARE
PRESS, a division of Simon & Schuster, Inc.

This POCKET BOOK edition includes every word
contained in the original, higher-priced edition. It is printed
from brand-new plates made from completely reset, clear, easy-to-read
type. POCKET BOOK editions are published by POCKET BOOKS, a division
of Simon & Schuster, Inc., 630 Fifth Avenue, New York, N.Y. 10020.
Trademarks registered in the United States and other countries.

L

FOREWORD

THE *University of Chicago Spanish-English, English-Spanish Dictionary* has been compiled for the general use of the American learner of Spanish and the Spanish learner of English, with special reference in either case to New World usages as found in the United States and in Latin America.

With this particular purpose in mind, the editors have selected the words to be defined according to the relative frequency of their occurrence. The Spanish-English section, therefore, contains all the items listed in Buchanan's *Graded Spanish Word Book* (Toronto: University of Toronto Press, 1929); all the idioms found in Keniston's *Standard List of Spanish Words and Idioms* (Boston: D. C. Heath & Co., 1941); and the words and idioms used in the Heath-Chicago series of *Graded Spanish Readers* (Boston: D. C. Heath & Co., 1936——), supplemented by many words occurring in a number of textbooks used in the United States at the elementary and intermediate levels of Spanish instruction, in Spanish-American newspapers and commercial correspondence, and in technical use by the average layman.

Similarly, in the English-Spanish section the words selected for definition have been taken from the first nine thousand entries in Thorndike and Lorge's *Teacher's Word Book of 30,000 Words* (New York: Bureau of Publications, Teachers College, Columbia University, 1944), supplemented by residual words in the combined word lists of Eaton, Buckingham-Dolch, and the *Interim Report on Vocabulary Selection* (London: P. S. King & Co., 1936).

In order to equalize the two parts and not leave undefined words used in a definition, it has been necessary to introduce into each section a number of secondary entries which are a by-product of the primary definitions, bringing the total number of entries for the *Dictionary* to approximately 30,000 words.

The New World application of the *Dictionary* is further emphasized by its acceptance of American standards of speech in indicating the pronunciation of the English entries and by the inclusion of American and Latin-American equivalents and usages throughout. The latter values have been identified by the use of the abbreviation *"Am."*

It should be noted, however, that the abbreviation *"Am."* may mean that the word is exclusively Spanish American or that a certain meaning is exclusively Spanish American or that the word is relatively common in Spanish America but is obsolete or obsolescent in Spain or that the word or meaning may be known locally or regionally in Spain, as well as in Spanish America, although the *Dictionary* of the Spanish Academy fails to recognize it.

Certain auxiliary data have been provided at the beginning of each section, such as a list of abbreviations; an explanation of speech sounds; a summary of the use and value of suffixes; a list of numerals; a brief treatment of nouns, adjectives, and adverbs; and a table of irregular verb forms. In the Spanish-English section a superior number following a verb entry refers to a similarly numbered verb listed in the table preceding the section.

A dictionary should be an instrument for the better understanding between peoples. It is the earnest wish of the editors of this one that it may serve to that end.

THE EDITORS

In its first decade, nearly three million copies of this very useful dictionary were sold. At that time we were able to secure the right to add a new section of idiomatic phrases, both Spanish and English taken from *The Traveler's Phrase Book: English-Spanish, Español-Inglés* by Lester G. Crocker and Enrique Noble. Sales have now passed seven million, making this standard reference work the best-selling book of its kind throughout the world.

THE PUBLISHERS

PART ONE
SPANISH-ENGLISH

PART ONE

SPANISH-ENGLISH

LIST OF ABBREVIATIONS

adj.	adjective	*m.*	masculine noun
adv.	adverb	*math.*	mathematics
Am.[1]	Americanism	*neut.*	neuter
arith.	arithmetic	*num.*	numeral
conj.	conjunction	*p.p.*	past participle
contr.	contraction	*pers.*	personal
def.	definite	*pers. pron.*	personal pronoun
def. art.	definite article	*pl.*	plural
dem.	demonstrative	*poss.*	possessive
dem. adj.	demonstrative adjective	*prep.*	preposition
dem. pron.	demonstrative pronoun	*pron.*	pronoun
etc.	et cetera	*refl.*	reflexive
f.	feminine noun	*refl. pron.*	reflexive pronoun
fam.	familiar	*rel.*	relative
indef.	indefinite	*rel. adv.*	relative adverb
indef. art.	indefinite article	*rel. pron.*	relative pronoun
inf.	infinitive	*sing.*	singular
interj.	interjection	*subj.*	subjunctive
interr.	interrogative	*v.*	verb
irr.	irregular	*v. irr.*	irregular verb

SPANISH PRONUNCIATION

The Spanish alphabet consists of twenty-eight letters: *a, b, c, ch, d, e, f, g, h, i, j, l, ll, m, n, ñ, o, p, q, r, rr, s, t, u, v, x, y, z* (*k* and *w* are found only in words of foreign origin).

I. THE VOWELS AND DIPHTHONGS

Each Spanish vowel has one *fundamental* sound.

1. i, like *i* in *police*. Examples: **hilo, camino, piso.**

   a) When i is the first member of a diphthong, it is a semicon-

---

[1] This abbreviation placed before a word or phrase *does not apply* to definitions beyond the semicolon.

sonant and is pronounced like the English *y* in *year, yes*: **ie, ia, io, iu.** Examples: **bien, diablo, sabio, ciudad.**

   b) When **i** is the second member of a diphthong, it is a semivowel: **ei, ai, oi, ui.** (At the end of a word the first three diphthongs are written: **ey, ay, oy.**) They have the following approximate English equivalents: **ei,** like the *ey* in *they*; **ai,** like the *i* in *wife*; **oi,** like the *oy* in *toy*; **ui,** like *we*. Note that the **i** in these diphthongs is closer and more tense than in English. Examples: **aceite, ley; baile, hay; heroico, hoy; cuida.**

2. e, like *e* in *they*, but without diphthongal glide. Examples: **tela, mesa, este.** However, it is more open before **rr** and before **r** plus consonant: **perro, terco, cerdo.**

3. a, like the first *a* in *mama* (if accented on first syllable). Examples: **caso, cano; ¡ah!**

4. o, like the *o* in *low*, but without diphthongal glide. Examples: **boda, hablo, modo.** However, it is more open before **rr** and before **r** plus consonant: **corro, porte, torpe.**

5. u, like the *u* in *rude*, or *oo* in *fool*. Examples: **cura, agudo, uno.**
   a) Note that the **u** is silent in the following combinations: **qui, que, gui, gue.**
   b) When **u** is the first member of a diphthong, it is a semiconsonant and is pronounced like the English *w* in *wet*: **ui, ue, ua, uo.** Examples: **cuida, cuento, cuadro, cuota.**
   c) When **u** is the second member of a diphthong, it is a semivowel and has the following approximate English equivalents: **iu,** like the *ew* in *few*; **au,** like the *ou* in *foul*; **eu** has no equivalent. Note that the **u** in these diphthongs is closer and more tense than in English. Examples: **ciudad, deuda, causa.**

II. THE CONSONANTS

  1. p

Spanish **p** has *approximately* the same sound as in English, but it is weaker and less explosive. It is similar to the English *p* in *open, April*. Examples: **padre, capa, apuro, punto.**

NOTE—
   a) In ordinary speech **p** is generally omitted in **septiembre, séptimo, suscriptor.**
   b) It is not pronounced, except in affected speech, in the initial group **ps: psicología.**

  2. b and v

These two letters have identically the same sound in Spanish.

a) When initial in a breath group,[1] or when preceded by **m** or **n**, Spanish **b** or **v** is pronounced by bringing the lips lightly together. In English the lips are tightly pressed in pronouncing the *b*, but in Spanish there is only a slight pressure, except in emphatic utterance. It is similar to the English *b* in an unstressed syllable, as in *abolition*. Examples: **bomba, en vez de, vine, invierno.**

b) When not initial in a breath group, and when within a word (except after **m** or **n**), Spanish **b** or **v** is like neither English *b* nor English *v*. It is pronounced by bringing the lips as near together as possible without completely closing them. Examples: **hablar, haba, la vaca, la bella, hervir.**

3. m

Spanish **m** has approximately the same sound as the English *m* in *much*. Examples: **madre, mano, cama.** Final **m** is generally pronounced as an **n** in such foreign or learned words as: **álbum, memorándum.**

4. f

Spanish **f** is similar to the English *f* in *few, floor*. Examples: **fuente, afán, flor.**

5. t

In the articulation of Spanish **t** the tongue touches the inner surface of the upper front teeth, while in English the tongue touches slightly above the gums. The *t*-sound in Spanish is more vigorous, tense, and precise and is not pronounced with audible breath as in English. It is similar to the English *t* in *stun, astonish, stupid*. Examples: **tela, tino, tinta.**

6. d

Spanish **d** has three sounds:

a) When initial in a breath group, or when preceded by **l** or **n**, Spanish **d** is somewhat like English *d*, but it is less explosive. It is similar to the *d* in *colder, elude, idle, yesterday*. Examples: **donde, falda, conde.**

b) When not initial in a breath group, and when within a word (except after **l** or **n**), **d** is like the English *th* in *then*, but it is pronounced by projecting the tongue out between the teeth, leaving a small opening for the air to escape so that the ar-

---

[1] A "breath group" is a word or group of words pronounced between pauses or breaths.

ticulation is very feeble. Examples: **hado, cuerda, hablado.**
Note that **d** has this sound also in intervocalic **dr: padre,**
cuadro.

c) When at the end of a word, it has the same sound as intervocalic **d,** but it is pronounced weakly and half-whispered.
Examples: **abad, Madrid.**

7. z

In Castilian Spanish **z** is similar to the *th* in *thin;* but in Spanish
America it is commonly pronounced as the *s* in *sane.* This sound is
represented in Spanish by **z** before **a, o, u,** and **c** before **e** and **i:**
ci, ce, za, zo, zu. The letter **z** is very seldom used before **e** or **i.**
Examples: **ciento, cerro, zagal, zorro, azul.**

8. s

Spanish **s** has two sounds:

a) When initial or intervocalic, **s** is approximately the same as
the English *s* in *son* or the *ss* in *essence,* but the articulation is
more feeble. When final in a syllable or word, **s** is weak and
brief; in certain regions it is hardly pronounced. Examples:
sonido, sano, cosa, casas, hasta.

b) When **s** is followed by a voiced consonant (**b, v, d, m, n, l, g, r**),
it is similar to the English *s* in *rose,* but it is only half-voiced
and brief and is never prolonged as in English. In certain regions this Spanish voiced **s** is reduced to a breath sound or *h.*
Examples: **mismo, desde, es verde, los labios.**

9. l

Spanish **l** has practically one sound, whether it is initial, intervocalic, or final. It is similar to the English *l* when initial, as in
late, light, but it is pronounced more precisely and forcefully.
Examples: **lado, ala, farol.**

10. n

Spanish **n** has four sounds:

a) Spanish **n,** except in the cases listed below, has approximately
the same sound as the English *n* in *no* or *enter;* however, the
intervocalic **n** is more tense and precise in Spanish than in
English. Examples: **no, nada, mano.**

b) Before **b, v,** or **p** it is pronounced like an **m: envidia, en vez**
de, en Barcelona, en paz.

c) Before **f** it is similar to the English *m* in *comfort.* Examples:
enfermo, confiado.

d) Before **ca, co, cu, que, qui, g** and **j** it is similar to the English *n* in *ankle, angle.* Examples: **anca, banco, aunque, tengo, mango, conjugar.**

11. ll

This symbol represents one sound. The nearest English equivalent is a blending of *l* and *y* as in *will you*, pronounced rapidly. This sound is often reduced to a *y* as in *York*. Examples: **calle, pillo.** In certain regions **ll** is pronounced like the *y* in paragraph 14,*b.*

12. ñ

Spanish **ñ** is formed by the blending of *n* and *y* as in *can you.* The tongue must be placed in the *y* position and the *n* and *y* sounded at the same time. Examples: **cañón, año.**

13. ch

Spanish **ch** has approximately the same sound as the English *ch* in *choose, choice, cheek.* Examples: **chato, chaleco, mucho.**

14. y

a) Spanish *y* is similar to the English *y* in *yawn*, but it is pronounced with a stronger palatal friction. Examples: **ayer, leyes.** The combination **hie** is equal to **ye: hierba (yerba).**

b) In some regions the **y** is similar to a sound midway between the *j* in *joy* and the *z* in *azure.* This tendency is especially noticeable in Argentina and Uruguay.

c) For the pronunciation of final *y* see paragraph 1,*b.*

15. x

a) Spanish **x** between vowels in emphatic pronunciation is similar to the English *x* in *axle.* Note that the **x** in **México** is pronounced like a **j**. See paragraph 20.

b) Before a consonant **x** is given the sound of *gss* by careful speakers. In ordinary speech it is pronounced like the *s* in *sane.* Examples: **explicar, exterminar.**

16. c

Spanish **c** has two sounds:

a) Spanish **c** before **a, o, u** (or before **l** or **r**) is similar to the English *k* sound, but it is less explosive. Examples: **casa, cosa, cuna, aclamar, crudo.** This *k* sound before **e** and **i** is represented by **qu: quinto, queso.** Before **t** or **c** in ordinary speech, **c** is pronounced like a soft *k*, so that **acto** sounds like *agto*, **recto** like *regto.*

b) For the pronunciation of the **c** before **e** and **i** see paragraph 7.

17. k

There is no letter **k** in Spanish except in words of foreign derivation: **kilo, kilómetro.** This sound is represented in Spanish by **c** before **a, o, u,** and by **qu** before **e** and **i: ca, co, cu, qui, que.** See paragraph 16,*a*.

18. q

This letter is used only in the combinations **qui, que.** See paragraph 16,*a*.

19. g

Spanish **g** has three sounds:

a) g before **a, o, u,** when initial in a breath group, or after **n,** has approximately the sound of the English *g* in *agony*: **gato, goma, guarda, mango, tengo.** The **u** is not sounded in **gue** or **gui** unless these syllables are written **güe, güi: guerra, guitarra; agüero, argüir.**

b) When not initial of a breath group and when within a word (except after **n**), the Spanish **g** has no equivalent in English. The articulation of this sound is similar to the initial **g,** but the contact of the tongue with the palate is loose, and the breath passing through the narrow passage produces a slight friction. Examples: **la guerra, agua, lago, averigüe, fragua.**

c) For the pronunciation of **g** before **e** or **i** see paragraph 20.

20. j

Spanish **j** has no exact equivalent in English. It is a strongly aspirated *h* or a guttural sound, produced by forcing voiceless breath through a loose contact of the back of the tongue with the soft palate. The sound is represented by **j** before **a, o, u,** (and occasionally before **e** or **i**) and by **g** before **e** and **i: gi, ge, ja, jo, ju.** Examples: **giro, gema, jalar, jovial, jugo.**

21. h

This letter is not pronounced in Spanish.

22. r and rr

Spanish **r** has little in common with English *r*. It has two sounds:

a) Within a word (when not preceded by **l, n,** or **s**), **r** is similar in articulation to English **tt** as in **kitty** pronounced rapidly. The articulation requires one single flip of the tongue tip against the ridge of the gums. Examples: **caro, farol, mero.**

b) Single **r** at the beginning of a word, **rr** within a word, and **r** preceded by **l, n,** or **s** have the same position of formation as the **r** described above, but they are strongly trilled. Examples: **rico, ronda, alrededor, honra, Enrique, correr.**

III. ACCENT OR STRESS

1. *Syllabic stress*

a) Words ending in a vowel, or in **n** or **s**, are accented on the next to the last syllable: **madre, hablan, campos.**

b) Words ending in a consonant other than **n** or **s** are accented on the last syllable: **farol, calidad, hablar.**

c) Words that do not conform to the above rules must have the written accent over the vowel to be stressed: **café, cortés, acción, alemán, teléfono, último, cónsul.**

d) The written accent is also used to distinguish words that are written alike but have different meanings: **de** (the preposition "of"), **dé** (subjunctive of **dar**); **este** (the demonstrative adjective "this"), **éste** (the demonstrative pronoun "this one", "the latter"); **el** (the definite article "the"), **él** (the pronoun "he").

2. *Syllable division*

a) When consonant and vowel alternate, the division is always after the vowel: **ma-má, ca-lle, ni-ño, ca-mi-no, mu-cho.**

b) Generally, two consonants within a word are divided as follows: **cal-ma, cos-ta, pal-co, ac-ción.** (Note that **s** plus a consonant cannot begin a syllable in Spanish). These groups, however, are pronounced with the following vowel: **pl, pr, bl, br, fl, fr, tl, tr, dr, cl, cr, gl, gr.** Examples: **a-fli-gir, co-fre, a-pla-nar, pa-dre, a-bra-zo.**[1]

c) Three adjacent consonants are always divided, the last two going with the following vowel whenever possible: **hom-bre, com-pren-der, cons-tan-te.** (Note that **s** plus a consonant cannot begin a syllable in Spanish.)

THE NOUN

I. GENDER[2]

A. *Masculine Gender*

1. Names of male beings are naturally masculine: **el hombre** the

---

[1] In printing it is customary to avoid leaving a lone vowel at the end of a line Divide thus: **afli-gir, apla-nar, abra-zo.**

[2] There is no general rule for the gender of nouns that are not treated in this section.

man; **el muchacho** the boy; **el tío** the uncle; **el rey** the king; **el buey** the ox.

2. Nouns ending in **-o** are masculine: **el libro** the book; **el banco** the bank. *Exception*: **la mano** the hand.

3. Days of the week, months, rivers, oceans, and mountains are masculine: **el martes** Tuesday; **enero** January; **el Pacífico** the Pacific; **el Rin** the Rhine; **los Andes** the Andes.

4. Many nouns ending in **-l** or **-r**, and nouns of Greek origin ending in **-ma** are masculine: **el papel** the paper; **el azúcar** the sugar; **el favor** the favor; **el drama** the drama. *Common exceptions*: **la miel** the honey; **la sal** the salt; **la catedral** the cathedral; **la flor** the flower. Note that **mar** is both masculine and feminine.

B. *Feminine Gender*

1. Names of female persons or animals are naturally feminine: **la mujer** the woman; **la muchacha** the girl; **la tía** the aunt; **la vaca** the cow.

2. Nouns ending in **-a** are feminine: **la pluma** the pen; **la carta** the letter; **la casa** the house. *Common exceptions*: **el día** the day; **el mapa** the map; nouns of Greek origin ending in **-ma:** **el dogma** the dogma; **el programa** the program.

3. Letters of the alphabet are feminine: **la *e*, la *s*, la *t*.**

4. Nouns ending in **-ión, -tad, -dad, -tud, -umbre** are feminine: **la canción** the song; **la facultad** the faculty; **la ciudad** the city; **la virtud** the virtue; **la muchedumbre** the crowd. *Exceptions:* **el gorrión** the sparrow; **el sarampión** the measles.

C. *Formation of the Feminine*

1. Nouns ending in **-o** change **o** to **a: tío** uncle, **tía** aunt; **niño** boy, **niña** girl.

2. Nouns ending in **-ón, -or,** and **-án** add **a: patrón** patron, **patrona** patroness; **pastor** shepherd, **pastora** shepherdess; **holgazán** lazy man, **holgazana** lazy woman.

3. Certain nouns have a special form for the feminine: **el poeta, la poetisa; el cantante, la cantatriz; el sacerdote, la sacerdotisa; el emperador, la emperatriz; el abad, la abadesa; el conde, la condesa; el duque, la duquesa.**

Note that (a) some nouns have different genders according to their meanings: **el corte** the cut or the cutting edge; **la corte** the court; **el guía** the guide; **la guía** the guidebook; **el capital** the capital (money); **la capital** the capital (city); (b) some nouns have invariable endings which are used for both the masculine and the feminine: **artista** (and all nouns ending in

-ista), amante, mártir, testigo, reo, demócrata, aristócrata, intérprete, consorte, comensal, homicida, suicida, indígena, cómplice,
cliente.

II. PLURAL OF NOUNS[1]

1. Nouns ending in an unaccented vowel add -s to form the plural:
el libro, los libros; la casa, las casas.

2. Nouns ending in a consonant, in -y, or in an accented vowel
add -es: **el papel, los papeles; la canción, las canciones: la
ley, las leyes; el rubí, los rubíes.** The accepted plural, however, of **papá** is **papás,** and of **mamá** is **mamás.**

3. Nouns ending in unaccented -es and -is do not change in the
plural: **el lunes** Monday, **los lunes** Mondays; **la tesis** the
thesis, **las tesis** the theses.

Note that (a) nouns ending in -z change z to c before -es: **lápiz, lápices;**
(b) nouns ending in -ión lose the written accent in the plural: **canción,
canciones.**

THE ADJECTIVE AND ADVERB

I. THE ADJECTIVE

A. *Agreement.* The adjective in Spanish agrees in gender and number
with the noun it modifies: **el lápiz rojo** the red pencil; **la casa blanca**
the white house; **los libros interesantes** the interesting books; **las
muchachas hermosas** the beautiful girls.

B. *Formation of the plural.* Adjectives follow the same rules as nouns
for the formation of the plural: **pálido, pálidos** pale; **fácil, fáciles**
easy; **cortés, corteses** courteous; **capaz, capaces** capable.

C. *Formation of the feminine.*

1. Adjectives ending in -o change o to a: **blanco, blanca.**

2. Adjectives ending in other vowels are invariable: **verde** green;
fuerte strong; **indígena** indigenous, native; **pesimista** pessimistic;
baladí trivial.

3. Adjectives ending in a consonant are invariable: **fácil** easy; **cortés**
courteous. *Exceptions:* (a) adjectives ending in -ón, -án, -or (except comparatives) add a to form the feminine: **holgazán, holgazana** lazy; **preguntón, preguntona** inquisitive; **hablador, habladora** talkative (Note that **mayor, mejor, menor, peor, superior, inferior, exterior, interior, anterior,** and **posterior** are
invariable. **Superior** adds an **a** when it is used as a noun meaning

[1] The plurals of certain masculine nouns may include the masculine and
feminine genders: **los padres** the father(s) and mother(s), the parents; **los tíos**
the uncle(s) and aunt(s); **los reyes** the king(s) and queen(s).

"mother superior.") (b) adjectives of nationality ending in a consonant add **a** to form the feminine: **francés, francesa** French; **español, española** Spanish; **alemán, alemana** German; **inglés, inglesa** English.

II. THE ADVERB

Many adverbs are formed by adding **-mente** to the feminine form of the adjective: **claro, claramente; lento, lentamente; fácil, fácilmente.**

III. COMPARISON OF ADJECTIVES AND ADVERBS

A. *Comparative of inequality.* The comparative of inequality is formed by placing **más** or **menos** before the positive form of the adjective or adverb: **más rico que** richer than; **menos rico que** less rich than; **más tarde** later; **menos tarde** less late. The superlative is formed by placing the definite article **el** before the comparative: **el más rico** the richest; **el menos rico** the least rich. Note the position of the article in the following examples: **la niña más linda** or **la más linda niña** the prettiest girl.

The following adjectives and adverbs have in addition irregular forms of comparison:

Positive	Comparative	Superlative
bueno	mejor	el (la) mejor
malo	peor	el (la) peor
grande	mayor	el (la) mayor
pequeño	menor	el (la) menor
alto	superior	supremo
bajo	inferior	ínfimo
mucho	más	
poco	menos	

B. *Comparative of equality.* With adjectives and adverbs the comparative of equality is formed with **tan ... como: tan fácil como** as easy as; **tan bien como** as well as; with nouns the comparative of equality is formed with **tanto (tanta, tantos, tantas) ... como: tanto dinero como** as much money as; **tantas personas como** as many people as.

C. *Absolute superlative of adjectives.* The absolute superlative of adjectives is formed by placing **muy** (very) before the adjective or by adding the suffix **-ísimo:**

Positive	Absolute Superlative
feliz	muy feliz, felicísimo
fácil	muy fácil, facilísimo
importante	muy importante, importantísimo

Positive	*Absolute Superlative*
limpio	muy limpio, limpísimo
feo	muy feo, feísimo
rico	muy rico, riquísimo
largo	muy largo, larguísimo
notable	muy notable, notabilísimo

A few adjectives have, in addition, other forms derived from the Latin superlatives:

bueno	muy bueno, bonísimo[1], óptimo
malo	muy malo, malísimo, pésimo
grande	muy grande, grandísimo, máximo
pequeño	muy pequeño, pequeñísimo, mínimo

Some adjectives ending in -ro or -re revert to the corresponding Latin superlative:

acre	muy acre, acérrimo
célebre	muy célebre, celebérrimo
mísero	muy mísero, misérrimo
salubre	muy salubre, salubérrimo

D. *Absolute superlative of adverbs.* The absolute superlative of adverbs not ending in -mente is formed in the same manner as that of adjectives:

tarde	muy tarde, tardísimo
pronto	muy pronto, prontísimo
mucho	muchísimo
poco	poquísimo
cerca	muy cerca, cerquísima
lejos	muy lejos, lejísimos

Superlative adverbs ending in -mente are formed by adding the suffix -ísima to the corresponding feminine adjective:

claramente	muy claramente, clarísimamente
noblemente	muy noblemente, nobilísimamente

COMMON SPANISH SUFFIXES

I. Diminutives

The most common diminutive endings in Spanish are:

-ito, -ita	(-cito, -cita, -ecito, -ecita). Examples: librito (from libro), casita (from casa), corazoncito (from corazón), mujercita (from mujer), cochecito (from coche), florecita (from flor).
-illo, -illa	(-cillo, -cilla, -ecillo, -ecilla). Examples: corderillo (from cordero), dolorcillo (from dolor), viejecillo (from viejo), piedrecilla (from piedra).

[1] Also buenísimo.

-ico, -ica	(-cico, -cica, -ecico, -ecica). Examples: **niñico** (from **niño**), **hermanica** (from **hermana**), **corazoncico** (from **corazón**), **mujercica** (from **mujer**), **pobrecico** (from **pobre**).
-uelo, -uela	(-zuelo, -zuela, -ezuelo, -ezuela). Examples: **arroyuelo** (from **arroyo**), **mozuela** (from **moza**), **mujerzuela** (from **mujer**), **reyezuelo** (from **rey**), **piedrezuela** (from **piedra**).
-ete, -eta.	Examples: **vejete** (from **viejo**), **vejeta** (from **vieja**).
-uco, -uca.	Example: **casuca** (from **casa**).
-ucho, -ucha.	Examples: **serrucho** (from **sierra**), **casucha** (from **casa**).

II. AUGMENTATIVES

The most common augmentative endings in Spanish are:

-acho, -acha.	Example: **ricacho** (from **rico**).
-azo, -aza.	Examples: **gigantazo** (from **gigante**), **bribonazo** (from **bribón**, **manaza** (from **mano**), **bocaza** (from **boca**).
-ón, -ona.	Examples: **hombrón** (from **hombre**), **mujerona** (from **mujer**), **almohadón** (from **almohada**), **borrachón** (from **borracho**).
-ote, -ota.	Examples: **grandote** (from **grande**), **muchachote** (from **muchacho**), **muchachota** (from **muchacha**).

III. DEPRECIATIVES

The most common depreciative endings in Spanish are:

-aco, -aca.	Example: **pajarraco** ugly bird.
-ejo, -eja.	Example: **librejo** old, worthless book.

Note that a depreciative or ironic connotation is often conveyed by many of the augmentatives and by the diminutive endings **-uelo, -ete, -uco, -ucho, -illo.**

IV. OTHER SUFFIXES

-ada	*a)* is sometimes equal to the English suffix *-ful:* **cucharada** spoonful; **palada** shovelful;
	b) often indicates a blow: **puñada** blow with the fist; **puñalada** stab or blow with a dagger; **topetada** butt, blow with the head;

c) indicates a group or a crowd of: **peonada** a group or crowd of peons; **indiada** a group or crowd of Indians.

-al, -ar   denote a grove, field, plantation or orchard: **naranjal** orange grove; **cauchal** rubber plantation; **pinar** pine grove.

indicates a blow or explosion: **puñetazo** blow with the fist; **topetazo** butt, blow with the head; **escobazo** blow with a broom; **cañonazo** cannon shot.

-dad, -tad   are suffixes forming many abstract nouns and are usually equivalent to the English suffix *-ty*: **fraternidad** fraternity; **facultad** faculty; **cantidad** quantity; **calidad** quality.

-dizo   is an adjective-forming suffix which means sometimes *tending to*, or *in the habit of*: **resbaladizo** slippery; **olvidadizo** forgetful; **enojadizo** irritable, easily angered; **asustadizo** easily frightened, scary, timid; **movedizo** movable.

-ería   *a*) denotes a place where something is made or sold: **panadería** bakery; **librería** bookstore; **zapatería** shoestore; **pastelería** pastry shop;
b) indicates a profession, business or occupation: **carpintería** carpentry; **ingeniería** engineering;
c) means sometimes a collection: **pastelería** pastry, pastries;
d) is sometimes equivalent to English suffix *-ness*; it also suggests a single act or action: **tontería** foolishness; foolish act; **niñería** childishness; childish act.

-ero   *a*) indicates a person who makes, sells, or is in charge of: **panadero** baker; **librero** bookseller; **zapatero** shoemaker; **carcelero** jailer; **cajero** cashier;
b) is an adjective-forming suffix: **parlero** talkative; **guerrero** warlike.

-ez, -eza   are used to make abstract nouns: **vejez** old age; **niñez** childhood; **viudez** widowhood; **grandeza** greatness.

-ía   *a*) is the ending of the names of many arts and

sciences: **geología** geology; **geometría** geometry; **biología** biology;

b) see **-ería.**

-iento indicates a *resemblance*, or a *tendency to*: **ceniciento** ashlike; **soñoliento** sleepy, drowsy.

-ísimo is the ending of the absolute superlative: **hermosísimo** very beautiful.

-izo is a suffix meaning *tending to* or *somewhat*: **rojizo** reddish. See **-dizo.**

-mente is the adverbial ending attached to the feminine form of the adjective: **generosamente** generously; **claramente** clearly.

-ón a) is an augmentative suffix;

b) is also a suffix without an augmentative force, meaning *in the habit of*, or *full of*: **juguetón** playful; **preguntón** full of questions, inquisitive; **llorón** tearful; crybaby;

c) indicates suddenness or violence of an action: **estirón** pull, tug, jerk; **apretón** squeeze.

-or, -dor a) are equivalent to the English suffixes *-or*, *-er*, and indicate the agent or doer: **hablador** talker; **regulador** regulator;

b) may also be used as adjectives: **hablador** talkative; **regulador** regulating.

-oso is an adjective-forming suffix which usually means *having*, *full of*, or *characterized by*: **rocoso** rocky; **tormentoso** stormy; **fangoso** muddy; **herboso** grassy; **lluvioso** rainy; **maravilloso** marvelous; **famoso** famous.

-udo is an adjective-forming suffix meaning *having* or *characterized by*: **zancudo** long-legged; **peludo** hairy; **panzudo** big-bellied; **caprichudo** stubborn.

-ura is a suffix forming many abstract nouns: **negrura** blackness; **blancura** whiteness; **altura** height; **lisura** smoothness.

-uzco indicates *resemblance* or *a tendency to*; it is akin to the English suffix *-ish*: **blancuzco** whitish; **negruzco** blackish.

SPANISH IRREGULAR AND ORTHOGRAPHIC CHANGING VERBS

The superior number, or numbers, after a verb entry indicate that it is conjugated like the model verb in this section which has the corresponding number. Only the tenses which have irregular forms or spelling changes are given. The irregular forms and spelling changes are shown in bold-face type.

1. pensar (if stressed, the stem vowel **e** becomes **ie**)

    Pres. Indic. **pienso, piensas, piensa,** pensamos, pensáis, **piensan.**

    Pres. Subj. **piense, pienses, piense,** pensemos, penséis, **piensen.**

    Imper. **piensa** tú, **piense** Vd., pensemos nosotros, pensad vosotros, **piensen** Vds.

2. contar (if stressed, the stem vowel **o** becomes **ue**)

    Pres. Indic. **cuento, cuentas, cuenta,** contamos, contáis, **cuentan.**

    Pres. Subj. **cuente, cuentes, cuente,** contemos, contéis, **cuenten.**

    Imper. **cuenta** tú, **cuente** Vd. contemos nosotros, contad vosotros, **cuenten** Vds.

3. *a)* sentir (if stressed, the stem vowel **e** becomes **ie**; if unstressed, the stem vowel **e** becomes **i** when the following syllable contains stressed **a, ie,** or **ió**)

    Pres. Indic. **siento, sientes, siente,** sentimos, sentís, **sienten.**

    Pres. Subj. **sienta, sientas, sienta, sintamos, sintáis, sientan.**

    Pret. Indic. sentí, **sentiste, sintió,** sentimos, sentisteis, **sintieron.**

    Imp. Subj. **sintiera** or **sintiese, sintieras** or **sintieses, sintiera** or **sintiese, sintiéramos** or **sintiésemos, sintierais** or **sintieseis, sintieran** or **sintiesen.**

    Imper. **siente** tú, **sienta** Vd., **sintamos** nosotros, sentid vosotros, **sientan** Vds.

    Pres. Part. **sintiendo.**

    b) erguir (this verb has same vowel changes as *sentir*, but the initial **i** of the diphthong **ie** is changed to **y**. For regular spelling changes see No. 12,*a*)

    Pres. Indic. **yergo, yergues, yergue,** erguimos, erguís, **yerguen.**

    Pres. Subj. **yerga, yergas, yerga,** irgamos, irgáis, **yergan.**

    Pret. Indic. erguí, erguiste, **irguió,** erguimos, erguisteis, **irguieron.**

    Imp. Subj. **irguiera** or **irguiese, irguieras** or **irguieses, irguiera** or **irguiese, irguiéramos** or **irguiésemos, irguierais** or **irguieseis, irguieran** or **irguiesen.**

Imper. **yergue tú, yerga** Vd., **irgamos** nosotros, erguid vosotros, **yergan** Vds.
Pres. Part. **irguiendo.**

4. dormir (if stressed, the stem vowel **o** becomes **ue**; if unstressed,
   the stem vowel **o** becomes **u** when the following syllable contains
   stressed **a, ie,** or **ió**)
Pres. Indic. **duermo, duermes, duerme,** dormimos, dormís,
   duermen.
Pres. Subj. **duerma, duermas, duerma, durmamos, durmáis,
   duerman.**
Pret. Indic. dormí, dormiste, **durmió,** dormimos, dormisteis,
   durmieron.
Imp. Subj. **durmiera** or **durmiese, durmieras** or **durmieses,
   durmiera** or **durmiese, durmiéramos** or **durmié-
   semos, durmierais** or **durmieseis, durmieran** or
   durmiesen.
Imper. **duerme** tú, **duerma** Vd., **durmamos** nosotros, dormid
   vosotros, **duerman** Vds.
Pres. Part. **durmiendo.**

5. pedir (if stressed, the stem vowel **e** becomes **i;** if unstressed, the
   stem vowel **e** becomes **i** when the following syllable contains
   stressed **a, ie,** or **ió**)
Pres. Indic. **pido, pides, pide,** pedimos, pedís, **piden.**
Pres. Subj. **pida, pidas, pida, pidamos, pidáis, pidan.**
Pret. Indic. pedí, pediste, **pidió,** pedimos, pedisteis, **pidieron.**
Imp. Subj. **pidiera** or **pidiese, pidieras** or **pidieses, pidiera** or
   pidiese, pidiéramos or **pidiésemos, pidierais** or
   pidieseis, pidieran or **pidiesen.**
Imper. **pide** tú, **pida** Vd., **pidamos** nosotros, pedid vosotros,
   pidan Vds.
Pres. Part. **pidiendo.**

6. buscar (verbs ending in **car** change **c** to **qu** before **e**)
Pres. Subj. **busque, busques, busque, busquemos, bus-
   quéis, busquen.**
Pret. Indic. **busqué,** buscaste, buscó, buscamos, buscasteis,
   buscaron.
Imper. busca tú, **busque** Vd., **busquemos** nosotros, buscad
   vosotros, **busquen** Vds.

7. **llegar** (verbs ending in **gar** change the g to **gu** before **e**)

  Pres. Subj. **llegue, llegues, llegue, lleguemos, lleguéis, lleguen.**

  Pret. Indic.: llegué, llegaste, llegó, llegamos, llegasteis, llegaron.

  Imper. llega tú, **llegue** Vd., **lleguemos** nosotros, llegad vosotros, **lleguen** Vds.

8. **averiguar** (verbs ending in **guar** change the gu to **gü** before **e**)

  Pres. Subj. **averigüe, averigües, averigüe, averigüemos, averigüéis, averigüen.**

  Pret. Indic. **averigüé,** averiguaste, averiguó, averiguamos, averiguasteis, averiguaron.

  Imper. averigua tú, **averigüe** Vd., **averigüemos** nosotros, averiguad vosotros, **averigüen** Vds.

9. **abrazar** (verbs ending in **zar** change z to **c** before **e**)

  Pres. Subj. **abrace, abraces, abrace, abracemos, abracéis, abracen.**

  Pret. Indic. **abracé,** abrazaste, abrazó, abrazamos, abrazasteis, abrazaron.

  Imper. abraza tú, **abrace** Vd., **abracemos** nosotros, abrazad vosotros, **abracen** Vds.

10. *a)* convencer (verbs ending in **cer** preceded by a consonant change **c** to **z** before **a** and **o**)

  Pres. Indic. **convenzo,** convences, convence, convencemos, convencéis, convencen.

  Pres. Subj. **convenza, convenzas, convenza, convenzamos, convenzáis, convenzan.**

  Imper. convence tú, **convenza** Vd., **convenzamos** nosotros, convenced vosotros, **convenzan** Vds.

  b) esparcir (verbs ending in **cir** preceded by a consonant change **c** to **z** before **a** and **o**)

  Pres. Indic. **esparzo,** esparces, esparce, esparcimos, esparcís, esparcen.

  Pres. Subj. **esparza, esparzas, esparza, esparzamos, esparzáis, esparzan.**

  Imper. esparce tú, **esparza** Vd., **esparzamos** nosotros, esparcid vosotros, **esparzan** Vds.

  c) mecer (some verbs ending in **cer** preceded by a vowel change **c** to **z** before **a** and **o**; see No. 13)

  Pres. Indic. **mezo,** meces, mece, mecemos, mecéis, mecen.

Pres. Subj. meza, mezas, meza, mezamos, mezáis, mezan.

Imper. mece tú, meza Vd., mezamos nosotros, meced vosotros, mezan Vds.

11. *a*) dirigir (verbs ending in **gir** change g to j before a and o)

Pres. Indic. dirijo, diriges, dirige, dirigimos, dirigís, dirigen.

Pres. Subj. dirija, dirijas, dirija, dirijamos, dirijáis, dirijan.

Imper. dirige tú, dirija Vd., dirijamos nosotros, dirigid vosotros, dirijan Vds.

  b) coger (verbs ending in **ger** change g to j before o and a)

Pres. Indic. cojo, coges, coge, cogemos, cogéis, cogen.

Pres. Subj. coja, cojas, coja, cojamos, cojáis, cojan.

Imper. coge tú, coja Vd., cojamos nosotros, coged vosotros, cojan Vds.

12. *a*) distinguir (verbs ending in **guir** drop the u before o and a)

Pres. Indic. distingo, distingues, distingue, distinguimos, distinguís, distinguen.

Pres. Subj. distinga, distingas, distinga, distingamos, distingáis, distingan.

Imper. distingue tú, distinga Vd., distingamos nosotros, distinguid vosotros, distingan Vds.

  b) delinquir (verbs ending in **quir** change qu to c before o and a)

Pres. Indic. delinco, delinques, delinque, delinquimos, delinquís, delinquen.

Pres. Subj. delinca, delincas, delinca, delincamos, delincáis, delincan.

13. *a*) conocer (verbs ending in **cer** when preceded by a vowel insert z before c when c is followed by o or a; see No. 10,*c*)

Pres. Indic. conozco, conoces, conoce, conocemos, conocéis, conocen.

Pres. Subj. conozca, conozcas, conozca, conozcamos, conozcáis, conozcan.

Imper. conoce tú, conozca Vd., conozcamos nosotros, conoced vosotros, conozcan Vds.

  b) lucir (verbs ending in **cir** when preceded by a vowel insert z before c when c is followed by o or a; see No. 25)

Pres. Indic. luzco, luces, luce, lucimos, lucís, lucen.

Pres. Subj. luzca, luzcas, luzca, luzcamos, luzcáis, luzcan.

Imper. luce tú, luzca Vd., luzcamos nosotros, lucid vosotros, luzcan Vds.

14. creer (unstressed **i** between vowels is regularly changed to **y**)
Pret. Indic. creí, creíste, crey6, creímos, creísteis, **creyeron.**
Imp. Subj. **creyera** or **creyese, creyeras** or **creyeses, creyera**
or **creyese, creyéramos** or **creyésemos, creyerais**
or **creyeseis, creyeran** or **creyesen.**
Pres. Part. **creyendo.**

15. reír (like No. 5, except that when the **i** of the stem would be
followed by **ie** or **i6** the two **i**'s are reduced to one)
Pres. Indic. **río, ríes, ríe,** reímos, reís, **ríen.**
Pres. Subj. **ría, rías, ría, riamos, riáis, rían.**
Pret. Indic. reí, reíste, rió, reímos, reísteis, **rieron.**
Imp. Subj. **riera,** or **riese, rieras** or **rieses, riera,** or **riese, riéra-**
mos or **riésemos, rierais** or **rieseis, rieran** or **riesen.**
Imper. **ríe** tú, **ría** Vd., **ríamos** nosotros, reíd vosotros, **rían** Vds.
Pres. Part. **riendo.**

16. podrir or **pudrir**
Pres. Indic. **pudro, pudres, pudre,** podrimos or pudrimos, po-
drís or pudrís, **pudren.**
Pres. Subj. **pudra, pudras, pudra, pudramos, pudráis,**
pudran.
Imp. Indic. pudría or podría, etc. (Seldom *podría* because of con-
fusion with *poder*)
Pret. Indic. podrí or pudrí, podriste or pudriste, **pudrió,** podri-
mos or pudrimos, podristeis or pudristeis, **pudrieron.**
Imp. Subj. **pudriera** or **pudriese, pudrieras** or **pudrieses,**
pudriera or **pudriese, pudriéramos** or **pudriése-**
mos, pudrierais or **pudrieseis, pudrieran** or
pudriesen.
Fut. Indic. pudriré or podriré, etc.
Cond. pudriría or podriría, etc.
Pres. Part. **pudriendo.**
Past. Part. podrido or pudrido.

17. enviar
Pres. Indic. envío, envías, envía, enviamos, enviáis, envían.
Pres. Subj. envíe, envíes, enviemos, enviéis, envíen.
Imper. envía tú, envíe Vd., enviemos nosotros, enviad vosotros,
envíen Vds.

18. continuar

    Pres. Indic. continúo, continúas, continúa, continuamos, continuáis, continúan.

    Pres. Subj. continúe, continúes, continúe, continuemos, continuéis, continúen.

    Imper. continúa tú, continúe Vd., continuemos nosotros, continuad vosotros, continúen Vds.

19. gruñir (i of the diphthong ie or ió is lost after ñ)

    Pret. Indic. gruñí, gruñiste, **gruñó**, gruñimos, gruñisteis, **gruñeron.**

    Imp. Subj. **gruñera** or **gruñese, gruñeras** or **gruñeses, gruñera** or **gruñese, gruñéramos** or **gruñésemos, gruñerais** or **gruñeseis, gruñeran** or **gruñesen.**

    Pres. Part. **gruñendo.**

20. bullir (i of the diphthong ie or ió is lost after ll)

    Pret. Indic. bullí, bulliste, **bulló,** bullimos, bullisteis, **bulleron.**

    Imp. Subj. **bullera** or **bullese, bulleras** or **bulleses, bullera** or **bullese, bulléramos** or **bullésemos, bullerais** or **bulleseis, bulleran** or **bullesen.**

    Pres. Part. **bullendo.**

21. andar

    Pret. Indic. **anduve, anduviste, anduvo, anduvimos, anduvisteis, anduvieron.**

    Imp. Subj. **anduviera** or **anduviese, anduvieras** or **anduvieses, anduviera** or **anduviese, anduviéramos** or **anduviésemos, anduvierais** or **anduvieseis, anduvieran** or **anduviesen.**

22. asir

    Pres. Indic. **asgo,** ases, ase, asimos, asís, asen.

    Pres. Subj. **asga, asgas, asga, asgamos, asgáis, asgan.**

    Imper. ase tú, **asga** Vd., **asgamos** nosotros, asid vosotros, **asgan** Vds.

23. caber

    Pres. Indic. **quepo,** cabes, cabe, cabemos, cabéis, caben.

    Pres. Subj. **quepa, quepas, quepa, quepamos, quepáis, quepan.**

    Pret. Indic. **cupe, cupiste, cupo, cupimos, cupisteis, cupieron.**

Imp. Subj. · **cupiera** or **cupiese, cupieras** or **cupieses, cupiera
  or cupiese, cupiéramos** or **cupiésemos, cupierais
  or cupieseis, cupieran** or **cupiesen.**
Fut. Indic. **cabré, cabrás, cabrá, cabremos, cabréis, cabrán.**
Cond. **cabría, cabrías, cabría, cabríamos, cabríais, cabrían.**
Imper. **cabe tú, quepa Vd., quepamos** nosotros, **cabed** vosotros, **quepan Vds.**

24. caer
  Pres. Indic. **caigo, caes, cae, caemos, caéis, caen.**
  Pres. Subj. **caiga, caigas, caiga, caigamos, caigáis, caigan.**
  Pret. Indic. **caí, caiste, cayó, caímos, caísteis, cayeron.**
  Imp. Subj. · **cayera** or **cayese, cayeras** or **cayeses, cayera** or
    cayese, cayéramos or **cayésemos, cayerais** or
    cayeseis, cayeran or **cayesen.**
  Imper. **cae tú, caiga Vd., caigamos** nosotros, **caed** vosotros,
    caigan Vds.
  Pres. Part. **cayendo.**

25. conducir (all verbs ending in **ducir** have the irregularities of
    conducir)
  Pres. Indic. **conduzco,** conduces, conduce, conducimos, con-
    ducís, conducen.
  Pres. Subj. **conduzca, conduzcas, conduzca, conduzcamos,
    conduzcáis, conduzcan.**
  Pret. Indic. **conduje, condujiste, condujo, condujimos, con-
    dujisteis, condujeron.**
  Imp. Subj. **condujera** or **condujese, condujeras** or **condu-
    jeses, condujera** or **condujese, condujéramos** or
    condujésemos, condujerais or **condujeseis, con-
    dujeran** or **condujesen.**
  Imp. conduce tú, **conduzca Vd., conduzcamos** nosotros, con-
    ducid vosotros, **conduzcan Vds.**

26. dar
  Pres. Indic. **doy, das, da, damos, dais, dan.**
  Pres. Subj. **dé, des, dé, demos, deis, den.**
  Pret. Indic. **dí, diste, dió, dimos, disteis, dieron.**
  Imp. Subj. **diera** or **diese, dieras** or **dieses, diera** or **diese, dié-
    ramos** or **diésemos, dierais** or **dieseis, dieran** or
    diesen.

27. decir

Pres. Indic. digo, dices, dice, decimos, decís, dicen.
Pres. Subj. diga, digas, diga, digamos, digáis, digan.
Pret. Indic. dije, dijiste, dijo, dijimos, dijisteis, dijeron.
Imp. Subj. dijera or dijese, dijeras or dijeses, dijera or dijese,
    dijéramos or dijésemos, dijerais or dijeseis, di-
    jeran or dijesen.
Fut. Indic. diré, dirás, dirá, diremos, diréis, dirán.
Cond. diría, dirías, diría, diríamos, diríais, dirían.
Imper. di tú, diga Vd., digamos nosotros, decid vosotros, di-
    gan Vds.
Pres. Part. diciendo.
Past. Part. dicho.

NOTE. The compound verbs of *decir* have the same irregularities with the
exception of the following:

a) The future and conditional of the compound verbs *bendecir* and *maldecir*
   are regular: *bendeciré, maldeciré,* etc.; *bendeciría, maldeciría,* etc.
b) The familiar imperative is regular: *bendice tu, maldice tu, contradice tu,* etc.
c) The past participles of *bendecir* and *maldecir* are regular when used with
   haber: *bendecido, maldecido;* when used as an adjective with *estar,* the
   forms are: *bendito, maldito.*

28. errar (like No. 1, except that the initial *ie* is spelled *ye*)

Pres. Indic. yerro, yerras, yerra, erramos, erráis, yerran.
Pres. Subj. yerre, yerres, yerre, erremos, erréis, yerren.
Imper. yerra tu, yerre Vd., erremos nosotros, errad vosotros,
    yerren Vds.

29. estar

Pres. Indic. estoy, estás, está, estamos, estáis, están.
Pres. Subj. esté, estés, esté, estemos, estéis, estén.
Pret. Indic. estuve, estuviste, estuvo, estuvimos, estuvisteis,
    estuvieron.
Imp. Subj. estuviera or estuviese, estuvieras or estuvieses,
    estuviera or estuviese, estuviéramos or estuviése-
    mos, estuvierais or estuvieseis, estuvieran or es-
    tuviesen.
Imper. está tú, esté Vd., estemos nosotros, estad vosotros, estén
    Vds.

30. haber

Pres. Indic. he, has, ha, hemos, habéis, han.
Pres. Subj. haya, hayas, haya, hayamos, hayáis, hayan.

Pret. Indic. **hube, hubiste, hubo, hubimos, hubisteis, hu-**
  bieron.
Imp. Subj. **hubiera** or **hubiese, hubieras** or **hubieses, hubiera**
  or **hubiese, hubiéramos** or **hubiésemos, hubierais**
  or **hubieseis, hubieran** or **hubiesen.**
Fut. Indic. **habré, habrás, habrá, habremos, habréis, habrán.**
Cond. **habría, habrías, habría, habríamos, habríais, habrían.**

31. hacer
Pres. Indic. **hago, haces, hace, hacemos, hacéis, hacen.**
Pres. Subj. **haga, hagas, haga, hagamos, hagáis, hagan.**
Pret. Indic. **hice, hiciste, hizo, hicimos, hicisteis, hicieron.**
Imp. Subj. **hiciera** or **hiciese, hicieras** or **hicieses, hiciera** or
  hiciese, hiciéramos or **hiciésemos, hicierais** or
  hicieseis, hicieran or **hiciesem.**
Fut. Indic. **haré, harás, hará, haremos, haréis, harán.**
Cond. **haría, harías, haría, haríamos, haríais, harían.**
Imper. **haz** tú, **haga** Vd., **hagamos** nosotros, **haced** vosotros,
  hagan Vds.
Past. Part. **hecho.**

32. a) huir
Pres. Indic. **huyo, huyes, huye,** huimos, huís, **huyen.**
Pres. Subj. **huya, huyas, huya, huyamos, huyáis, huyan.**
Pret. Indic. huí, huiste, **huyó,** huimos, huisteis, **huyeron.**
Imp. Subj. **huyera** or **huyese, huyeras** or **huyeses, huyera**
  or **huyese, huyéramos** or **huyésemos, huyerais**
  or **huyeseis, huyeran** or **huyesen.**
Imper. **huye** tú, **huya** Vd., **huyamos** nosotros, **huid** vosotros,
  huyan Vds.
Pres. Part. **huyendo.**

b) argüir
Pres. Indic. **arguyo, arguyes, arguye,** argüimos, argüís, **ar-**
  guyen.
Pres. Subj. **arguya, arguyas, arguya, arguyamos, arguyáis,**
  arguyan.
Pret. Indic. argüí, argüiste, **arguyó,** argüimos, argüisteis, **ar-**
  guyeron.
Imp. Subj. **arguyera** or **arguyese, arguyeras** or **arguyeses,**
  arguyera or **arguyese, arguyéramos** or **arguyé-**

semos, **arguyerais** or **arguyeseis, arguyeran** or
arguyesen.

Imper. **arguye** tú, **arguya** Vd., **arguyamos** nosotros, argüid
vosotros, **arguyan** Vds.

Pres. Part. **arguyendo.**

33. ir

Pres. Indic. **voy, vas, va, vamos, vais, van.**

Pres. Subj. **vaya, vayas, vaya, vayamos, vayáis, vayan.**

Imp. Indic. **iba, ibas, iba, íbamos, ibais, iban.**

Pret. Indic. **fuí, fuiste, fué, fuimos, fuisteis, fueron.**

Imp. Subj. **fuera** or **fuese, fueras** or **fueses, fuera** or **fuese,
fuéramos** or **fuésemos, fuerais** or **fueseis, fueran**
or **fuesen.**

Imper. **ve** tú, **vaya** Vd., **vayamos (vamos)** nosotros, id vosotros,
vayan Vds.

Pres. Part. **yendo.**

34. jugar (cf. Nos. 2 and 7)

Pres. Indic. **juego, juegas, juega,** jugamos, jugáis, **juegan.**

Pres. Subj. **juegue, juegues, juegue,** juguemos, juguéis,
jueguen.

Pret. Indic. jugué, jugaste, jugó, jugamos, jugasteis, jugaron.

Imper. **juega** tú, **juegue** Vd., **juguemos** nosotros, jugad vosotros, **jueguen** Vds.

35. adquirir

Pres. Indic. **adquiero, adquieres, adquiere,** adquirimos, ad-
quirís, **adquieren.**

Pres. Subj. **adquiera, adquieras, adquiera,** adquiramos, ad-
quiráis, **adquieran.**

Imper. **adquiere** tú, **adquiera** Vd., adquiramos nosotros, ad-
quirid vosotros, **adquieran** .Vds.

36. oír

Pres. Indic. **oigo, oyes, oye,** oímos, oís, **oyen.**

Pres. Subj. **oiga, oigas, oiga, oigamos, oigáis, oigan.**

Pret. Indic. oí, oíste, oỹó, oímos, oísteis, **oyeron.**

Imp. Subj. **oyera** or **oyese, oyeras** or **oyeses, oyera** or **oyese,
oyéramos** or **oyésemos, oyerais** or **oyeseis, oyeran**
or **oyesen.**

Imper. **oye** tú, **oiga** Vd., **oigamos** nosotros, oíd vosotros, **oigan**
Vds.

Pres. Part. **oyendo.**

37. oler (like No. 2, except that initial ue is spelled hue)
   Pres. Indic. huelo, hueles, huele, olemos, oléis, huelen.
   Pres. Subj. huela, huelas, huela, olamos, oláis, huelan.
   Imper. huele tú, huela Vd., olamos nosotros, oled vosotros, huelan Vds.

38. placer
   Pres. Indic.: plazco, places, place, placemos, placéis, placen.
   Pres. Subj.: plazca, plazcas, plazca, plazcamos, plazcáis, plazcan. (There are also the antiquated forms, plegue and plega, used now only in the third person in poetic language.)
   Pret. Indic. In addition to the regular forms, there is the antiquated form plugo, used now only in poetic language.
   Imp. Subj. In addition to the regular forms, there are the antiquated forms, pluguiera and pluguiese, used now only in poetic language.

39. poder
   Pres. Indic. puedo, puedes, puede, podemos, podéis, pueden.
   Pres. Subj. pueda, puedas, pueda, podamos, podáis, puedan.
   Pret. Indic. pude, pudiste, pudo, pudimos, pudisteis, pudieron.
   Imp. Subj. pudiera or pudiese, pudieras or pudieses, pudiera or pudiese, pudiéramos or pudiésemos, pudierais or pudieseis, pudieran or pudiesen.
   Fut. Indic. podré, podrás, podrá, podremos, podréis, podrán.
   Cond. podría, podrías, podría, podríamos, podríais, podrían.
   Pres. Part. pudiendo.

40. poner
   Pres. Indic. pongo, pones, pone, ponemos, ponéis, ponen.
   Pres. Subj. ponga, pongas, ponga, pongamos, pongáis, pongan.
   Pret. Indic. puse, pusiste, puso, pusimos, pusisteis, pusieron.
   Imp. Subj. pusiera or pusiese, pusieras or pusieses, pusiera or pusiese, pusiéramos or pusiésemos, pusierais or pusieseis, pusieran or pusiesen.
   Fut. Indic. pondré, pondrás, pondrá, pondremos, pondréis, pondrán.
   Cond. pondría, pondrías, pondría, pondríamos, pondríais, pondrían.

Imper. pon tú, ponga Vd., **pongamos** nosotros, poned vosotros, **pongan** Vds.

Past Part. puesto.

41. querer

Pres. Indic. quiero, quieres, quiere, queremos, queréis, quieren.

Pres. Subj. quiera, quieras, quiera, queramos, queráis, quieren.

Pret. Indic. quise, quisiste, quiso, quisimos, quisisteis, quisieron.

Imp. Subj. quisiera or quisiese, quisieras or quisieses, quisiera or quisiese, quisiéramos or quisiémos, quisierais or quisieseis, quisieran or quisiesen.

Fut. Indic. querré, querrás, querrá, querremos, querréis, querrán.

Cond. querría, querrías, querría, querríamos, querríais, querrían.

Imper. quiere tú, quiera Vd., queramos nosotros, quered vosotros, quieran Vds.

42. saber

Pres. Indic. sé, sabes, sabe, sabemos, sabéis, saben.

Pres. Subj. sepa, sepas, sepa, sepamos, sepáis, sepan.

Pret. Indic. supe, supiste, supo, supimos, supisteis, supieron.

Imp. Subj. supiera or supiese, supieras or supieses, supiera or supiese, supiéramos or supiésemos, supierais or supieseis, supieran or supiesen.

Fut. Indic. sabré, sabrás, sabrá, sabremos, sabréis, sabrán.

Cond. sabría, sabrías, sabría, sabríamos, sabríais, sabrían.

Imper. sabe tú, sepa Vd., sepamos ñosotros, sabed vosotros, sepan Vds.

43. salir

Pres. Indic. salgo, sales, sale, salimos, salís, salen.

Pres. Subj. salga, salgas, salga, salgamos, salgáis, salgan.

Fut. Indic. saldré, saldrás, saldrá, saldremos, saldréis, saldrán.

Cond. saldría, saldrías, saldría, saldríamos, saldríais, saldrían.

Imper. sal tú, salga Vd., salgamos nosotros, salid vosotros, salgan Vds.

NOTE. The compound *sobresalir* is regular in the familiar imperative: so-bresale tú.

44. ser
> *Pres. Indic.* soy, eres, es, somos, sois, son.
> *Pres. Subj.* sea, seas, sea, seamos, seáis, sean.
> *Imp. Indic.* era, eras, era, éramos, erais, eran.
> *Pret. Indic.* fuí, fuiste, fué, fuimos, fuisteis, fueron.
> *Imp. Subj.* fuera or fuese, fueras or fueses, fuera or fuese, fuéramos or fuésemos, fuerais or fueseis, fueran or fuesen.
> *Imper.* sé tú, sea Vd., seamos nosotros, sed vosotros, sean Vds.

45. tener
> *Pres. Indic.* tengo, tienes, tiene, tenemos, tenéis, tienen.
> *Pres. Subj.* tenga, tengas, tenga, tengamos, tengáis, tengan.
> *Pret. Indic.* tuve, tuviste, tuvo, tuvimos, tuvisteis, tuvieron.
> *Imp. Subj* tuviera or tuviese, tuvieras or tuvieses, tuviera or tuviese, tuviéramos or tuviésemos, tuvierais or or tuvieseis, tuvieran or tuviesen.
> *Fut. Indic.* tendré, tendrás, tendrá, tendremos, tendréis, tendrán.
> *Cond.* tendría, tendrías, tendría, tendríamos, tendríais, tendrían.
> *Imper.* ten tú, tenga Vd., tengamos nosotros, tened vosotros, tengan Vds.

46. traer
> *Pres. Indic.* traigo, traes, trae, traemos, traéis, traen.
> *Pres. Subj.* traiga, traigas, traiga, traigamos, traigáis, traigan.
> *Pret. Indic.* traje, trajiste, trajo, trajimos, trajisteis, trajeron.
> *Imp. Subj.* trajera or trajese, trajeras or trajeses, trajera or trajese, trajéramos or trajésemos, trajerais or trajeseis, trajeran or trajesen.
> *Imper.* trae tú, traiga Vd., traigamos nosotros, traed vosotros, traigan Vds.
> *Prés. Part.* trayendo.

47. valer
> *Pres. Indic.* valgo, vales, vale, valemos, valéis, valen.
> *Pres. Subj.* valga, valgas, valga, valgamos, valgáis, valgan.
> *Fut. Indic.* valdré, valdrás, valdrá, valdremos, valdréis, valdrán.

Cond. **valdría, valdrías, valdría, valdríamos, valdríais, val-**
    drían.
Imper. **val** or **vale tú, valga Vd., valgamos** nosotros, **valed** voso-
    tros, **valgan Vds.**

48. **venir**
    Pres. Indic. **vengo, vienes, viene,** venimos, venís, **vienen.**
    Pres. Subj. **venga, vengas, venga, vengamos, vengáis, vengan.**
    Pret. Indic. **vine, viniste, vino, vinimos, vinisteis, vinieron.**
    Imp. Subj. **viniera** or **viniese, vinieras** or **vinieses, viniera** or
        viniese, viniéramos or **viniésemos, vinierais** or
        vinieseis, vinieran or **viniesen.**
    Fut. Indic. **vendré, vendrás, vendrá, vendremos, vendréis,**
        vendrán.
    Cond. **vendría, vendrías, vendría, vendríamos, vendríais,**
        vendrían.
    Imper. **ven tú, venga Vd., vengamos** nosotros, **venid** vosotros,
        vengan Vds.
    Pres. Part. **viniendo.**

49. **ver**
    Pres. Indic. **veo,** ves, ve, vemos, veis, ven.
    Pres. Subj. **vea, veas, vea, veamos, veáis, vean.**
    Imp. Indic. **veía, veías, veía, veíamos, veíais, veían.**
    Imper. **ve tú, vea Vd., veamos** nosotros, **ved** vosotros, **vean Vds.**
    Past Part. **visto.**

50. **yacer**
    Pres. Indic. **yazco** or **yazgo, yaces, yace,** yacemos, **yacéis, yacen.**
    Pres. Subj. **yazca** or **yazga, yazcas** or **yazgas, yazca** or **yazga,**
        yazcamos or **yazgamos, yazcáis** or **yazgáis, yaz-**
        can or **yazgan.**
    Imper. **yace tú, yazca** or **yazga Vd., yazcamos** or **yazgamos**
        nosotros, **yaced** vosotros, **yazcan** or **yazgan Vds.**

51. **DEFECTIVE VERBS**
    a) The following verbs are used only in the forms that have an **i**
        in the ending: abolir, agredir, aterirse, empedernir, transgredir.
    b) atañer
        This verb is used only in the third person. It is most frequently
        used in the present indicative: atañe, atañen.
    c) concernir

This verb is used only in the third person of the following tenses:

Pres. Indic. **concierne, conciernen.**

Pres. Subj. **concierna, conciernan.**

Imp. Indic. concernía, concernían.

Imp. Subj. concerniera or concerniese, concernieran or concerniesen.

Pres. Part. concerniendo.

d) soler

This verb is used most frequently in the present and imperfect indicative. It is less frequently used in the present subjunctive.

Pres. Indic. **suelo, sueles, suele,** solemos, soléis, **suelen.**

Pres. Subj. **suela, suelas, suela,** solamos, soláis, **suelan.**

Imp. Indic. solía, solías, solía, solíamos, solíais, solían.

The preterit is seldom used. Of the compound tenses, only the present perfect is commonly used: he solido, etc. The other tenses are very rare.

e) roer

This verb has three forms in the first person of the present indicative: **roo, royo, roigo,** all of which are infrequently used. In the present subjunctive the preferable form is **roa, roas, roa,** etc., although the forms **roya** and **roiga** are found.

52. **IRREGULAR PAST PARTICIPLES**

abrir—**abierto**

absorber—absorbido, **absorto**

bendecir—bendecido, **bendito**

componer—**compuesto**

cubrir—**cubierto**

decir—**dicho**

deponer—**depuesto**

descomponer—**descompuesto**

describir—**descrito**

descubrir—**descubierto**

desenvolver—**desenvuelto**

deshacer—**deshecho**

devolver—**devuelto**

disolver—**disuelto**

encubrir—**encubierto**

entreabrir—**entreabierto**

entrever—**entrevisto**

envolver—**envuelto**

escribir—**escrito**

freir—**frito,** freído

hacer—**hecho**

imprimir—**impreso**

inscribir—**inscrito, inscripto**

maldecir—maldecido, **maldito**

morir—**muerto**

poner—**puesto**

prescribir—**prescrito, prescripto**

proscribir—**proscrito, proscripto**

proveer—proveído, **provisto**

resolver—**resuelto**

revolver—**revuelto**

romper—rompido, **roto**

satisfacer—**satisfecho**

subscribir—**subscrito**

ver—**visto**

volver—**vuelto**

NUMERALS—NUMEROS

Cardinal Numbers		Números Cardinales	Ordinal Numbers	Números Ordinales[1]
1	one	uno, una	first	primero
2	two	dos	second	segundo
3	three	tres	third	tercero
4	four	cuatro	fourth	cuarto
5	five	cinco	fifth	quinto
6	six	seis	sixth	sexto
7	seven	siete	seventh	séptimo
8	eight	ocho	eighth	octavo
9	nine	nueve	ninth	noveno, nono
10	ten	diez	tenth	décimo
11	eleven	once	eleventh	undécimo
12	twelve	doce	twelfth	duodécimo
13	thirteen	trece	thirteenth	décimotercio
14	fourteen	catorce	fourteenth	décimocuarto
15	fifteen	quince	fifteenth	décimoquinto
16	sixteen	dieciseis, diez y seis	sixteenth	décimosexto
17	seventeen	diecisiete, diez y siete	seventeenth	décimoséptimo
18	eighteen	dieciocho, diez y ocho	eighteenth	décimoctavo
19	nineteen	diecinueve, diez y nueve	nineteenth	décimonono
20	twenty	veinte	twentieth	vigésimo
21	twenty-one	veintiuno, veinte y uno	twenty-first	vigésimo primero
30	thirty	treinta	thirtieth	trigésimo
40	forty	cuarenta	fortieth	cuadragésimo
50	fifty	cincuenta	fiftieth	quincuagésimo
60	sixty	sesenta	sixtieth	sexagésimo
70	seventy	setenta	seventieth	septuagésimo
80	eighty	ochenta	eightieth	octogésimo
90	ninety	noventa	ninetieth	nonagésimo
100	one hundred	ciento	(one) hundredth	centésimo
101	one hundred and one	ciento (y) uno	(one) hundred and first	centésimo primo
200	two hundred	doscientos	two-hundredth	ducentésimo
300	three hundred	trescientos	three-hundredth	tricentésimo
400	four hundred	cuatrocientos	four-hundredth	cuadringentésimo
500	five hundred	quinientos	five-hundredth	quingentésimo
600	six hundred	seiscientos	six-hundredth	sexagésimo
700	seven hundred	setecientos	seven-hundredth	septingentésimo
800	eight hundred	ochocientos	eight-hundredth	octingentésimo
900	nine hundred	novecientos	nine-hundredth	noningentésimo
1000	one thousand	mil	(one) thousandth	milésimo
100,000	one hundred thousand	cien mil	(one) hundred thousandth	cienmilésimo
1,000,000	one million	un millón	(one) millionth	millonésimo

1. The ordinals beyond the "tenth" are less used in Spanish than in English. They are often replaced by the cardinals: *Alfonso the Thirteenth* Alfonso trece.

A

a *prep.* to; in, into; on; by.

abacería *f.* grocery; grocery store; **abacero** *m.* grocer.

abad *m.* abbot; **abadía** *f.* abbey.

abajarse *v.* to lower oneself, humiliate oneself.

abajo *adv.* down, below; downstairs.

abalanzar⁹ *v.* to balance; to hurl, impel; **-se** to hurl oneself; to rush (upon), swoop down (upon); *Am.* to rear, balk.

abandonamiento = **abandono**.

abandonar *v.* to abandon, desert; to give up.

abandono *m.* abandon; desertion; neglect.

abanicar⁶ *v.* to fan.

abanico *m.* fan.

abaratar *v.* to cheapen, lower the price of.

abarcar⁶ *v.* to embrace, contain, include; *Am.* to buy up, monopolize.

abarrotería *f. Am.* grocery, grocery store; **abarrotero** *m. Am.* grocer.

abarrotes *m. pl.* small packages (*in hold of a ship*); *Am.* groceries; **tienda de** — *Am.* grocery store.

abastecer¹³ *v. irr.* to supply.

abastecimiento *m.* supply; provisions.

abasto *m.* supply; **no dar** — **a** to be unable to cope with.

abatido *adj.* dejected, depressed, crestfallen, humbled; fallen; lowered.

abatimiento *m.* discouragement, dejection, depression; descent, swoop, drop.

abatir *v.* to lower; to knock down; to depress; to humble; **-se** to become discouraged; to swoop down.

abdicar⁶ *v.* to abdicate.

abdomen *m.* abdomen.

abecedario *m.* alphabet; primer.

abedul *m.* birch.

abeja *f.* bee; **abejera** *f.* beehive; **abejón** *m.* drone; bumblebee; **abejorro** *m.* bumblebee.

aberración *f.* aberration, mental or moral deviation.

abertura *f.* aperture, opening, hole, slit.

abeto *m.* fir (*tree and wood*).

abierto *p.p. of* **abrir** opened; *adj.* open; frank; *Am.* proud, self-satisfied; *Am.* generous.

abigarrado *adj.* motley; multicolored; variegated.

abismado *p.p.* absorbed, buried in thought; overwhelmed.

abismar *v.* to overwhelm; to depress; **-se** to be plunged (into); to bury oneself (*in thought, grief, etc.*).

abismo *m.* abyss, precipice, chasm.

ablandar *v.* to soften.

abnegación *f.* abnegation, self-denial, self-sacrifice.

abnegado *adj.* self-sacrificing.

abnegarse⁷ *v.* to deny oneself, sacrifice oneself.

abobado *adj.* stupid, silly.

abochornar *v.* to overheat; to embarrass; **-se** to get overheated; to blush; to be embarrassed.

abofetear *v.* to slap.

abogado *m.* lawyer.

abogar⁷ *v.* to advocate, plead in favor of; to intercede.

abolengo *m.* lineage, ancestry; inheritance, patrimony.

abolición *f.* abolition.

abolir⁵¹. *v.* to abolish; to repeal.

abolsarse *v.* to bag (*said of trousers, skirts, etc.*).

abollado *p.p. & adj.* dented; bumped; bruised.

abolladura *f.* dent, bump.

abollar *v.* to dent; to bump; to crush, crumple; to bruise.

abominable *adj.* abominable, detestable.

abominar *v.* to abominate, abhor, detest.

abonado *m.* subscriber; *p.p. of* **abonar**.

abonar *v.* to credit with; to make a payment; to indorse, back (*a person*); to fertilize (*soil*); **-se** to subscribe.

abonaré *m.* promissory note; I.O.U.

abono *m.* payment; installment; indorsement, guarantee; fertilizer; subscription.

abordar *v.* to board (*a ship*); to dock, put into port; to approach; to undertake, take up (*a matter, problem, etc.*).

aborigen *adj.* aboriginal, indigenous, native; **aborígenes** *m. pl.* aborigines, primitive inhabitants.

aborrascarse⁶ *v.* to become stormy.

aborrecer¹³ *v. irr.* to abhor, hate, detest.

aborrecible *adj.* abominable, hateful.

aborrecimiento *m.* abhorrence; hatred.

abortar *v.* to miscarry, have a miscarriage; to give birth prematurely; to fail.

aborto *m.* abortion, miscarriage; monster.

abotagarse⁷ *v.* to bloat; to swell.

abotonador *m.* buttonhook.

abotonar *v.* to button, button up; to bud; **-se** to button up.

abovedar *v.* to vault, cover with a vault; to arch.

abozalar *v.* to muzzle.

abra *f.* cove; mountain gap or pass; dale; *Am.* breach (*in the jungle*); *Am.* leaf (*of a door*).

abrasador *adj.* burning, very hot.

abrasar *v.* to burn; to parch; **-se** to

1

burn up, be consumed.

abrazar[9] v. to hug, embrace; to include.

abrazo m. hug, embrace.

abrelatas m. can opener.

abrevadero m. drinking trough; watering place for cattle.

abrevar v. to water (*livestock*).

abreviación f. abbreviation.

abreviar v. to abbreviate, shorten, condense.

abreviatura f. abbreviation.

abrigar[7] v. to shelter, cover, protect; to wrap up; to harbor (*fear*), cherish (*hope*); -se to find shelter; to wrap oneself up.

abrigo m. shelter, cover, protection; wrap; overcoat.

abril m. April.

abrillantar v. to polish, shine; to glaze.

abrir[52] v. to open; to unlock.

abrochar v. to button; to clasp; to fasten.

abrogación f. repeal.

abrogar[7] v. to abrogate, repeal, annul.

abrojo m. thistle, thorn; -s reef.

abrumador adj. crushing, overwhelming; oppressive; fatiguing.

abrumar v. to crush, overwhelm; to trouble, annoy; -se to become foggy.

abrupto adj. abrupt, steep.

absceso m. abscess.

absolución f. absolution; acquittal.

absoluto adj. absolute; unconditional.

absolver[2,52] v. irr. to absolve, free from guilt; to pardon, acquit.

absorbente adj. & m. absorbent.

absorber[52] v. to absorb.

absorción f. absorption.

absorto p.p. irr. of **absorber** & adj. absorbed, engrossed; amazed.

abstenerse[45] v. irr. to abstain, refrain.

abstinencia f. abstinence; fasting.

abstracción f. abstraction; reverie.

abstracto adj. abstract.

abstraer[46] v. irr. to abstract; to withdraw, remove; -se to be lost in thought.

abstraído adj. lost in thought, absentminded; aloof.

absuelto p.p. of **absolver** absolved, acquitted.

absurdo adj. absurd, ridiculous, senseless; m. absurdity.

abuela f. grandmother.

abuelo m. grandfather; -s grandparents; ancestors.

abulia f. abulia, loss of will power.

abultado adj. bulky, bulgy.

abultar v. to bulge; to be bulky; to enlarge.

abundancia f. abundance, plenty.

abundante adj. abundant, plentiful.

abundar v. to abound, be plentiful.

aburrido p.p. & adj. bored; boring, tiresome; weary.

aburrimiento m. weariness, dullness, boredom.

aburrir v. to bore, vex; -se to become bored or vexed.

abusar v. to abuse, mistreat; to misuse; —de to take unfair advantage of; to impose upon.

abuso m. abuse; misuse.

acá adv. here, over here; this way, hither.

acabamiento m. finish, completion, end; death; Am. exhaustion, physical decline.

acabar v. to end, finish, complete; —de (+ inf.) to have just; —por (+ inf.) to end by; —con to put an end to, make short work of; to destroy; -se to be over, finished; to be consumed; Am. to wear oneself out; Am. to age or decline in health.

academia f. academy; a special school; a scientific, literary, or artistic society.

académico adj. academic; m. academician, member of an academy.

acaecer[13] v. irr. to happen, occur.

acaecimiento m. event, happening.

acalorado adj. heated, excited, angry.

acaloramiento m. heat, ardor, excitement.

acalorar v. to heat, warm; to excite; -se to get overheated, get excited.

acallar v. to silence; to calm, quiet.

acampar v. to encamp; to camp.

acanalar v. to groove; to flute (as a column); to form a channel in.

acantilado adj. sheer, steep (cliff); m. bluff, cliff.

acantonar v. to quarter (troops).

acaparar v. to corner (the market); to monopolize; to gather in (for one's gain or profit).

acariciar v. to caress, pet; to cherish (a hope or illusion).

acarreador m. carter; carrier.

acarrear v. to cart, transport; to bring about (harm, disaster).

acarreo m. cartage, carriage, transport, haul.

acaso adv. perhaps; by chance; por si — just in case; m. chance, accident.

acatamiento m. homage, reverence, respect.

acatar v. to revere, respect; to pay homage to; Am. to realize; Am. to notice, pay attention.

acatarrar v. to chill; Am. to bother, annoy; -se to get chilled, catch cold; Am. to get tipsy.

acaudillar v. to lead, command.
acceso m. access; entrance, admittance; attack; fit (*of madness, anger, etc.*).
accesorio adj. & m. accessory.
accidentado adj. seized with a fit; in a swoon; rough, uneven (*ground*).
accidental adj. accidental, casual.
accidentarse v. to have a seizure or fit; to swoon, faint.
accidente m. accident, mishap; chance; sudden fit, swoon.
acción f. action; act; gesture; battle; stock, share; — **de gracias** thanksgiving.
accionar v. to gesticulate, make gestures; *Am.* to act, be active.
accionista m. & f. shareholder, stockholder.
acechanza f. snare; ambush.
acechar v. to lurk; to spy.
acecho m. ambush; spying; **al** (*or* **en**) — waiting in ambush, lying in wait.
acedo adj. rancid; acid; sour; harsh, disagreeable.
aceitar v. to oil, grease.
aceite m. oil; — **alcanforado** camphorated oil; — **de hígado de bacalao** cod-liver oil; — **de oliva** olive oil; — **de ricino** castor oil.
aceitera f. oil can; oil cruet (*bottle for the table*).
aceitoso adj. oily.
aceituna f. olive; **aceitunado** adj. olive green.
aceleración f. acceleration.
acelerador m. accelerator.
acelerar v. to accelerate, speed up; to quicken; to hurry, hasten.
acémila f. pack mule.
acendrado adj. pure, without blemish; purified.
acendrar v. to refine (*metals*); to purify, cleanse.
acento m. accent; emphasis.
acentuar[18] v. to accentuate, emphasize; to accent; **-se** to become worse (*as an illness*).
acepción f. acceptation, usual meaning.
acepillar v. to brush; to plane.
aceptación f. acceptance; approval.
aceptar v. to accept; to approve; to admit.
acequia f. irrigation canal or ditch; *Am.* small stream; *Am.* sewer.
acera f. sidewalk.
acerado adj. steely, made of steel; steel-like; sharp.
acerar v. to steel.
acerbo adj. bitter; harsh, cruel.
acerca de prep. about, concerning.

acercamiento m. approach; approaching; rapprochement (*coming together*).
acercar[6] v. to bring near, draw up; **-se** to get near, approach.
acero m. steel.
acérrimo adj. very sour, very tart; very harsh; very strong, stanch, stalwart, steadfast.
acertar[1] v. irr. to hit (*the mark*); to hit upon, find by chance; to guess right; — **a** (+ *inf.*) to happen to.
acertijo m. riddle.
aciago adj. ill-fated, unlucky.
acicalado p.p. & adj. polished; dressed up; adorned; trim, neat.
acicalar v. to polish; to adorn; **-se** to dress up, doll up.
acicate m. spur; incentive.
acidez f. acidity, sourness.
ácido m. acid; adj. acid, sour.
acierto m. right guess; lucky hit; good aim; good judgment; **con** — effectively, successfully.
aclamación f. acclamation, applause.
aclamar v. to acclaim, cheer, hail, applaud.
aclaración f. explanation.
aclarar v. to clarify, explain; to clear up; to rinse; to dawn.
aclimatar v. to acclimatize, accustom to a climate or new environment.
acobardar v. to frighten, intimidate.
acoger[11] v. to receive; to give shelter; **-se** to take refuge.
acogida f. reception, welcome; refuge.
acogimiento m. reception, welcome.
acojinar v. to cushion; to quilt.
acolchar v. to quilt.
acólito m. acolyte, altar boy.
acometer v. to attack; to undertake.
acometida f., **acometimiento** m. attack, assault.
acomodado adj. well-off, wealthy; suitable, convenient; p.p. of **acomodar**.
acomodador m. usher (*in a theater*).
acomodar v. to arrange, adjust; to accommodate, lodge; to place; to give employment to; **-se** to make oneself comfortable; to adapt oneself.
acomodo m. occupation, employment; arrangement.
acompañador m. companion; accompanist.
acompañamiento m. accompaniment; retinue, company.
acompañante m. companion; escort; attendant; accompanist.
acompañar v. to accompany; to escort; to enclose (*in a letter*).
acompasado adj. rhythmical; measured;

3

slow, deliberate.

acondicionado *adj.* conditioned; comfortable; air-conditioned; *Am.* adequate, suitable.

acondicionar *v.* to condition; to prepare; to arrange; -se to become conditioned or prepared.

acongojar *v.* to grieve; -se to grieve; to be distressed.

aconsejar *v.* to advise, counsel.

acontecer[13] *v. irr.* to happen, occur.

acontecimiento *m.* event, happening.

acopiar *v.* to gather, accumulate, store up.

acopio *m.* storing; accumulation; stock, store, supply.

acoplamiento *m.* coupling; joint, connection.

acoplar *v.* to couple, connect; to fit or join together; to yoke; to pair, mate.

acorazado *m.* armored ship, battleship.

acorazar[9] *v.* to armor.

acordar[3] *v. irr.* to agree; to decide; to tune, put in harmony (*stringed instruments*); *Am.* to grant; -se to remember.

acorde *adj.* in harmony; in tune; *m.* chord.

acordelar *v.* to measure with a cord; to rope off, put a cord around.

acordonar *v.* to tie with a cord, string or rope; to rope off, tie a rope around (*a place*); to mill (*a coin*).

acornear *v.* to gore, wound with a horn; to butt.

acorralar *v.* to corral; to surround.

acortamiento *m.* shortening.

acortar *v.* to shorten, diminish; -se to shrink; to be shy, bashful.

acosar *v.* to pursue, harass.

acostado *adj.* reclining, lying down, in bed; tilted.

acostar[3] *v. irr.* to put to bed; to lay down; -se to lie down, go to bed; to tilt.

acostumbrado *adj.* accustomed, used; usual, habitual.

acostumbrar *v.* to accustom, train; to be used to, be accustomed to; -se to get accustomed.

acotación *f.* marginal note; stage directions (*for a play*); boundary mark; mark on a map showing altitude.

acotar *v.* to mark off (*with boundary marks*); to make marginal notes or citations; to put the elevation marks on (*maps*).

acre *adj.* sour, tart, sharp; rude, harsh; *m.* acre.

acrecentamiento *m.* growth, increase.

acrecentar[1] *v. irr.* to increase; to advance, promote.

acreditar *v.* to credit; to bring fame or credit to; to accredit, authorize; -se to win credit or fame.

acreedor *adj.* worthy, deserving; *m.* creditor.

acribillar *v.* to riddle; to perforate; to pierce.

acróbata *m. & f.* acrobat.

acta *f.* minutes (*of a meeting*); document; **levantar** — to write the minutes.

actitud *f.* attitude; posture, pose.

activar *v.* to activate, make active; to speed up, hasten.

actividad *f.* activity; energy.

activo *adj.* active, lively; *m.* assets.

acto *m.* act; action, deed; ceremony; — **continuo** (*or* **seguido**) immediately after; **en el** — immediately.

actor *m.* actor; **actriz** *f.* actress.

actuación *f.* action; intervention, participation, performance; -es legal proceedings.

actual *adj.* present (*time*); of the present month; -mente *adv.* at present, nowadays.

actualidad *f.* present time; -es latest news, fashions, or events; **de** — current, up-to-date.

actuar[18] *v.* to act, perform a function or act; to set in motion, cause to act.

acuarela *f.* water color.

acuario *m.* aquarium.

acuartelar *v.* to quarter (*troops*).

acuático *adj.* aquatic; **deportes** -s water sports.

acuchillar *v.* to knife; to stab; to slash.

acudir *v.* to go or come (*to aid, or in response to a call*); to attend, be present; to resort or turn to for help.

acueducto *m.* aqueduct, water channel or pipe.

acuerdo *m.* agreement; decision, resolution; opinion; remembrance; **estar de** — to be in agreement; **ponerse de** — to come to an agreement; **tomar un** — to take a decision.

acullá *adv.* yonder, over there.

acumulación *f.* accumulation.

acumulador *m.* storage battery.

acumular *v.* to accumulate, gather, pile up.

acuñación *f.* coinage, minting; wedging.

acuñar *v.* to mint, coin; to wedge.

acuoso *adj.* watery.

acurrucarse[6] *v.* to cuddle, nestle; to huddle.

acusación *f.* accusation, charge.

acusado *p.p. & adj.* accused; *m.* defendant.

acusar v. to accuse, denounce; to acknowledge (*receipt*).
acuse m. acknowledgment (*of receipt*).
acústica f. acoustics (*science of sound*).
achacar⁶ v. to impute, attribute.
achacoso adj. sickly.
achaparrado adj. scrub, of shrub size; squat, squatty.
achaque m. slight chronic illness; excuse; pretext; infirmity.
achicar⁶ v. to shorten; to make small; to bail (*water*); to humiliate; *Am.* to kill; *Am.* to tie, fasten; -se to get smaller; to shrink.
adagio m. adage, proverb, wise saying; adagio (*musical Spanish America*).
adaptar v. to adapt, fit, adjust.
adecuado adj. adequate, fit, suitable.
adecuar v. to fit, adapt.
adefesio m. absurdity, nonsense; ridiculous sight, dress, or person.
adelantado p.p. & adj. anticipated; advanced; ahead; forward, bold; **por —** in advance; m. governor of a province (*in colonial Spanish America*).
adelantamiento m. advancement, progress, betterment.
adelantar v. to advance; to move forward; to progress; to better; -se to get ahead.
adelante adv. forward, ahead; **en —** from now on.
adelanto m. advance; advancement, progress; betterment.
adelgazar⁹ v. to thin out, taper; -se to get thin, slender.
ademán m. gesture, gesticulation; attitude.
además adv. moreover, besides; **— de** prep. in addition to, besides.
adentro adv. within, inside; **tierra —** inland; **mar —** out to sea; **hablar para sus -s** to talk to oneself.
aderezamiento m. dressing; adornment, decoration.
aderezar⁹ v. to fix up, adorn, beautify; to garnish (*food*); to season; to prepare; to starch, stiffen.
aderezo m. adornment; garnish; trappings; finery; set of jewels; dressing; seasoning; starch, stiffener, filler (*used in cloth*).
adestrado adj. trained, skilled.
adestrar¹ v. irr. to train; to guide.
adeudado adj. indebted; in debt; p.p. of adeudar.
adeudar v. to owe; to debit, charge; -se to run into debt.
adeudo m. debt, indebtedness; duty (*on imports*); debit, charge.

adherencia f. adherence; attachment.
adherir³ v. irr. to adhere, stick.
adhesión f. adhesion; attachment.
adicto adj. addicted; devoted; m. addict; follower.
adiestrado = adestrado.
adiestramiento m. training; drill.
adiestrar = adestrar.
adinerado adj. wealthy.
¡adiós! interj. good-bye!; farewell! *Am.* you don't say!
aditamento m. addition; annex.
adivinación f. divination, prediction; guess.
adivinanza f. conundrum, riddle.
adivinar v. to guess.
adivino m. fortuneteller; soothsayer.
adjetivo m. & adj. adjective.
adjudicar⁶ v. to adjudge, award, assign; -se to appropriate.
adjunto adj. adjoining; attached, enclosed.
adminículo m. accessory; gadget.
administración f. administration, management; headquarters; *Am.* extreme unction, last sacrament.
administrador m. administrator, manager.
administrar v. to administer; to manage; -se *Am.* to receive the extreme unction or last sacrament.
administrativo adj. administrative.
admirable adj. admirable, wonderful.
admiración f. admiration, wonder; **punto de —** exclamation point.
admirador m. admirer.
admirar v. to admire; -se to be astonished or amazed; to wonder.
admisión f. admission; acceptance; acknowledgment.
admitir v. to admit; to let in; to accept; to allow, permit.
adobar v. to fix, cook, prepare (*food*); to tan (*hides*); to pickle (*meats, fish*).
adobe m. adobe, sun-dried mud brick.
adobo m. mending; sauce for seasoning or pickling; mixture for dressing skins or cloth; rouge.
adoctrinamiento m. indoctrination, teaching, instruction.
adoctrinar v. to indoctrinate, teach, instruct.
adolecer¹³ v. irr. to suffer (*from an illness, defect, etc.*).
adolescencia f. adolescence.
adolescente adj. adolescent.
adonde rel. adv. where; **¿adónde?** interr. adv. where to?; where?
adoptar v. to adopt; to accept (*an opinion*).

5

adoptivo *adj.* adoptive, related by adoption; adopted.

adoración *f.* adoration, worship.

adorar *v.* to adore, worship.

adormecer[13] *v. irr.* to make sleepy or drowsy; to lull; **-se** to get sleepy; to get numb; to fall asleep.

adormilado *adj.* drowsy.

adornar *v.* to adorn, decorate, ornament.

adorno *m.* adornment, ornament, decoration.

adquirir[35] *v. irr.* to acquire, gain, win, obtain.

adquisición *f.* acquisition; attainment.

adrede *adv.* on purpose, intentionally.

aduana *f.* customhouse.

aduanero *m.* customhouse officer; *adj.* customhouse.

aduar *m.* gypsy camp; *Am.* Indian camp or ranch.

aducir[25] *v. irr.* to cite, allege, offer as proof.

adueñarse *v.* to take possession.

adulación *f.* flattery.

adulador *m.* flatterer.

adular *v.* to flatter.

adulterar *v.* to adulterate, corrupt, make impure.

adulterio *m.* adultery.

adúltero *m.* adulterer.

adulto *m. & adj.* adult.

adusto *adj.* stern, severe, austere.

advenedizo *m.* newcomer, stranger; upstart; *Am.* novice, beginner; *adj.* newly arrived; upstart; *Am.* inexperienced.

advenimiento *m.* advent, arrival, coming.

adverbio *m.* adverb.

adversario *m.* adversary, opponent; foe.

adversidad *f.* adversity; calamity.

adverso *adj.* adverse; contrary; unfavorable.

advertencia *f.* notice; warning; advice.

advertir[3] *v. irr.* to notice; to warn; to advise.

adyacente *adj.* adjacent.

aéreo *adj.* aerial; airy; **correo —** air mail.

aeródromo *m.* airport.

aeronave *f.* airship.

aeroplano *m.* airplane.

aeropuerto *m.* airport.

afabilidad *f.* friendliness, pleasantness, courtesy; **afable** *adj.* affable, pleasant, courteous.

afamado *adj.* famous.

afán *m.* eagerness, anxiety, ardor.

afanar *v.* to urge, press; **-se** to hurry; to worry; to work eagerly; to toil.

afear *v.* to make ugly; to disfigure; to blame, censure, condemn.

afección *f.* affection, fondness; disease.

afectado *p.p. & adj.* affected; *Am.* hurt, harmed; *Am.* **estar — del corazón** to have heart trouble.

afectar *v.* to affect, move; to pretend to have or feel; *Am.* to injure, hurt, harm.

afecto *m.* affection; *adj.* fond; **— a** fond of; given to, prone to.

afectuoso *adj.* affectionate, tender.

afeitada *f. Am.* shave, shaving.

afeitar *v.* to shave; **-se** to shave oneself; to put on make-up.

afeite *m.* make-up, cosmetics.

afeminado *adj.* effeminate.

aferrado *adj.* stubborn, obstinate; *p.p.* of **aferrar.**

aferramiento *m.* grasping, seizing; attachment; stubbornness; tenacity.

aferrar *v.* to seize, grasp, grapple; **-se** to take or seize hold of; to cling; **-se a una opinión** to cling to an opinion.

afianzar[9] *v.* to fasten, secure; to steady; to give bail or bond.

afición *f.* taste, inclination; fondness, affection.

aficionado *adj.* fond; *m.* amateur, fan.

aficionar *v.* to inspire a liking or fondness; **-se a** to become fond of.

afilador *m.* grinder, sharpener.

afilar *v.* to sharpen; to grind; *Am.* to make love to, woo; *Am.* to flatter; *Am.* **— con** to flirt with.

afín *adj.* kindred, related; **ideas afines** related ideas.

afinador *m.* piano tuner.

afinar *v.* to refine, polish; to tune.

afinidad *f.* affinity; similarity; relationship.

afirmación *f.* affirmation, assertion.

afirmar *v.* to affirm, assert; to make firm; *Am.* **— un golpe** to deal a blow.

afirmativa *f.* affirmative.

afirmativo *adj.* affirmative.

aflicción *f.* affliction, trouble, pain, grief.

afligir[11] *v.* to afflict, trouble, grieve; *Am.* to mistreat, harm, beat, strike; **-se** to worry, grieve.

aflojar *v.* to slacken; to loosen, unfasten; to let go; *Am.* to let go of money, spend easily; *Am.* **— un golpe** to give a blow.

afluente *m.* tributary; *adj.* abundant.

afluir[32] *v. irr.* to flow (into).

afortunado *adj.* fortunate; lucky.

afrenta *f.* affront, offense, insult.

afrentar *v.* to insult, offend, dishonor.

afrentoso *adj.* outrageous, shameful, disgraceful.

africano *adj. & m.* African.

afrontar *v.* to face; to confront.

afuera *adv.* out, outside; **-s** *f. pl.* outskirts.

agachar *v.* to lower; to bend down; **-se** to stoop, bend down, duck; to crouch; *Am.* to give in, yield; *Am.* **-se con algo** to make away with or steal something.

agalla *f.* gill; tonsil; *Am.* greed; **tener -s** to have guts, have courage; *Am.* to be unscrupulous and bold in business deals; *Am.* to be greedy or stingy; *Am.* to be smart, astute, cunning.

agarrar *v.* to seize, grasp, grab; **-se** to cling, hold on.

agarro *m.* clench, clutch, grasp, grip, grab; **agarrón** *m.* tight clench, sudden grasp, grab; *Am.* pull, tug.

agasajar *v.* to entertain; to flatter.

agasajo *m.* entertainment, kind reception; friendliness; flattery.

agazapar *v.* to nab, seize (*a person*); **-se** to crouch; to squat.

agencia *f.* agency; *Am.* pawnshop.

agenciar *v.* to negotiate; to procure by negotiation; to promote.

agente *m.* agent; *Am.* officer, official.

ágil *adj.* agile, nimble, limber.

agilidad *f.* agility, nimbleness.

agitación *f.* agitation; excitement.

agitador *m.* agitator; *adj.* agitating; stirring.

agitar *v.* to agitate, excite; to stir; to wave; to shake.

aglomeración *f.* conglomeration, heap, pile, mass.

aglomerar *v.* to mass together; to cluster; **-se** to crowd together, pile up.

agobiar *v.* to oppress, weigh down; to overwhelm.

agolparse *v.* to crowd together, jam.

agonía *f.* agony.

agonizante *adj.* dying; *m.* dying person.

agonizar[9] *v.* to be dying.

agorero *adj.* ominous, of bad omen; prophetic; *m.* augur, prophet, fortuneteller.

agostar *v.* to parch, dry up; to pasture; to plow (*in August*).

agosto *m.* August; harvest; **hacer su —** to make hay while the sun shines.

agotado *adj. & p.p.* exhausted; out-of-print.

agotamiento *m.* exhaustion; draining.

agotar *v.* to exhaust, use up; to drain off; **-se** to be exhausted, used up.

agraciado *adj.* graceful; *m.* winner (*of a favor, prize, etc.*).

agraciar *v.* to grace; to adorn.

agradable *adj.* agreeable, pleasant.

agradar *v.* to please, be agreeable (to).

agradecer[13] *v. irr.* to thank for; to be grateful for.

agradecido *adj.* thankful, grateful.

agradecimiento *m.* gratitude, thankfulness.

agrado *m.* agreeableness; liking, pleasure; **de su —** to his liking.

agrandar *v.* to enlarge; to aggrandize, make greater.

agravar *v.* to aggravate, make worse; to make heavier; to oppress; **-se** to get worse.

agraviar *v.* to offend, insult, affront.

agravio *m.* offense, insult, affront.

agredir[51] *v.* to assail, assault, attack.

agregado *m.* attaché, person attached to a staff; aggregate, collection.

agregar[7] *v.* to add; to join; to attach.

agresivo *adj.* aggressive, offensive.

agresor *m.* aggressor; assailant.

agreste *adj.* rustic; wild (*fruit, flower, etc.*).

agriar[17] *v.* to sour, make sour; **-se** to sour, turn sour, become sour.

agrícola *adj.* agricultural.

agricultor *m.* agriculturist, farmer.

agricultura *f.* agriculture.

agridulce *adj.* bittersweet, tart.

agrietarse *v.* to crack; to chap (*said of the skin*).

agrimensura *f.* survey, surveying (*of land*).

agrio *adj.* sour; disagreeable.

agrupación *f.* group; bunch; grouping; gathering.

agrupar *v.* to group, bunch up.

agrura *f.* sourness.

agua *f.* water; rain; **— abajo** downstream; **— arriba** upstream.

aguacate *m.* *Am.* avocado, alligator pear, *Am.* avocado tree; *Am.* phlegmatic person.

aguacero *m.* shower.

aguada *f.* watering place; supply of drinking water; flood in a mine; wall wash; water color.

aguadero *m.* watering place.

aguado *adj.* watery; watered; *Am.* soft, unstarched; *Am.* weak, limp; *Am.* insipid, uninteresting, dull; **sopa aguada** thin soup; *p.p. of* **aguar.**

aguantar *v.* to endure, bear; to resist; **-se** to be silent, restrain oneself.

aguante *m.* endurance, fortitude, resistance.

aguar[9] *v.* to water, dilute with water; to spoil (*pleasure*); *Am.* to water (*livestock*); **-se** to become diluted; to get watery; to fill up with water; **se aguó**

7

la fiesta the party was spoiled.

aguardar v. to wait; to wait for.

aguardentoso adj. alcoholic; hoarse, raucous.

aguardiente m. brandy, hard liquor; — de caña rum.

aguarrás m. turpentine, oil of turpentine.

aguazal m. marsh, swamp.

agudeza f. sharpness; keenness; wit; witty remark or saying.

agudo adj. sharp; sharp-pointed; keen, witty; acute; shrill.

agüero m. augury, prediction; sign, omen; Am. fortuneteller.

aguijar v. to prick, spur, goad; to encourage, incite.

aguijón m. prick; sting; spur, goad.

aguijonear v. to goad; to prick.

águila f. eagle; es un — he is a shark.

aguileño adj. aquiline; eaglelike.

aguinaldo m. Christmas or New Year's gift.

aguja f. needle; crochet hook; watch hand; church spire; railroad switch.

agujerear v. to pierce, perforate; to riddle.

agujero m. hole; needle peddler; needle box; pincushion.

aguzar[6] v. to sharpen; to goad, stimulate; — las orejas to prick up one's ears.

ahí adv. there; por — over there.

ahijado m. godchild.

ahinco m. effort, eagerness, zeal.

ahogar[7] v. to drown; to choke, strangle; to smother; to quench, extinguish.

ahogo m. suffocation; breathlessness; anguish, grief.

ahondar v. to deepen; to dig; to penetrate, go deep into.

ahora adv. now; — mismo right now; por — for the present; — que Am. as soon as; ahorita instantly, this very minute; ahoritica, ahoritita Am. this very second, in a jiffy.

ahorcar[6] v. to hang, kill by hanging.

ahorrar v. to save; to spare; to avoid.

ahorro m. saving, economy; caja de -s savings bank.

ahuecar[6] v. to make hollow; to hollow out; — la voz to speak in a hollow voice; Am. ¡ahueca! get out of here!; -se to become puffed up, get conceited.

ahuehuete m. Am. a Mexican cypress.

ahumado adj. smoked; smoky.

ahumar v. to smoke; to fume.

ahuyentar v. to drive away; to scare away; -se to go away, flee; Am. to stop frequenting a place.

aindiado adj. Indian-like.

airar v. to annoy, irritate; -se to get angry.

aire m. air; wind; tune; appearance; conceit; -cito m. breeze; a little tune; a certain air or appearance.

airear v. to air, ventilate.

airoso adj. windy; airy; graceful, elegant; lively, spirited.

aislador m. insulator; isolator; adj. insulating; isolating.

aislamiento m. isolation; insulation.

aislar v. to isolate, place apart; to insulate.

ajar v. to crumple, wither.

ajedrez m. chess

ajeno adj. another's; unaware; oblivious; alien; — a mi voluntad beyond my control; —de cuidados free from cares.

ajetrearse v. to hustle and bustle; to get tired out.

ajetreo m. bustle, hustle; hubbub; fuss; fatigue.

ají m. Am. chili pepper, chili sauce.

ajo m. garlic; garlic clove; garlic sauce swear word.

ajuar m. furniture set; trousseau, bride's outfit; bride's portion or dowry.

ajustado adj. tight, fitting tight; agreed upon (as a price); — a la ley in accordance with the law; p.p. of ajustar.

ajustamiento m. adjustment.

ajustar v. to adjust; to fit tight; to regulate; to tighten; to settle (accounts); to hire (a person); Am. to stint, scrimp, save; Am. — una bofetada to give a good slap; Am. hoy ajusta quince años he is just fifteen years old today; -se to come to an agreement.

ajuste m. adjustment, fit; agreement; settlement (of accounts).

ajusticiar v. to execute, put to death.

al = a + el to the.

ala f. wing; hat brim.

alabanza f. praise.

alabar v. to praise.

alacena f. cupboard; closet; Am. booth, stall, market stand.

alacrán m. scorpion.

alado adj. winged.

alambicado p.p. & adj. distilled; over-refined, over-subtle (applied to style).

alambique m. still.

alambrada f. wire entanglement.

alambrado m. wire fence; wire screening; wiring.

alambre m. wire.

alameda f. poplar grove; park.

álamo m. poplar.

alancear v. to lance, spear.

alano m. mastiff.

alarde m. boast, bluff, brag.

alardear *v.* to boast, brag.

alargar[7] *v.* to lengthen; to prolong; to stretch out, extend.

alarido *m.* shout, scream, howl.

alarma *f.* alarm.

alarmar *v.* to alarm.

alazán *adj.* chestnut-colored; sorrel.

alba *f.* dawn; alb (*white robe worn by priest*).

albacea *m.* executor.

albañal *m.* sewer.

albañil *m.* mason, brickmason; **albañilería** *f.* masonry.

albaricoque *m.* apricot; **albaricoquero** *m.* apricot tree.

albayalde *m.* white lead.

albazo *m. Am.* early morning serenade; *Am.* bad surprise, surprise attack at dawn.

albear *v.* to show white (*in the distance*); *Am.* to rise at dawn.

albedrío *m.* free will.

albéitar *m.* veterinary.

alberca *f.* water reservoir, tank; pool.

albergar[7] *v.* to house, shelter, lodge; **-se** to take shelter; to lodge.

albo *adj.* white; *Am.* white-footed (*horse*).

albóndiga *f.* meat ball; fish ball.

albor *f.* dawn; whiteness.

alborada *f.* dawn; reveille (*morning bugle call*).

alborear *v.* to dawn.

alborotador *m.* agitator, troublemaker.

alborotar *v.* to disturb, upset; *Am.* to excite, arouse enthusiasm; **-se** to get upset; to mutiny; to riot; *Am.* to get excited; *Am.* to rear, balk (*said of a horse*).

alboroto *m.* uproar, disturbance; riot; *Am.* excitement, enthusiasm; *Am.* popcorn, candied popcorn ball.

alborozado *adj.* elated, excited.

alborozar[9] *v.* to gladden; **-se** to rejoice.

alborozo *m.* joy, delight.

albricias *f. pl.* good news; reward (*for good news*).

alcachofa *f.* artichoke; *Am.* sock, blow.

alcahuete *m.* procurer, pander; go-between; **alcahueta** *f.* bawd, procuress, go-between.

alcaide *m.* warden (*of a fortress, prison, etc.*).

alcalde *m.* mayor; justice of the peace; **— mayor** mayor.

alcance *m.* reach; scope; talent, capacity; last minute news, newspaper extra; **cortos -s** meagre intellect; **dar — a** to catch up with.

alcancía *f.* money box (*with slit for coin*); savings bank.

alcanfor *m.* camphor.

alcanzado *adj.* needy; broke, short of funds.

alcanzar[9] *v.* to reach; to overtake; to obtain; to befall; to be enough; *Am.* to hand, pass, put within reach.

alcayata *f.* wall hook; meat hook.

alcázar *m.* castle, fortress.

alcoba *f.* alcove, bedroom.

alcohol *m.* alcohol; **alcohólico** *adj.* alcoholic.

alcor *m.* hill.

alcornoque *m.* cork tree; cork wood; blockhead, dunce.

alcuza *f.* oil can; cruet, oil bottle.

aldaba *f.* knocker (*of a door*); crossbar, bolt, latch; handle (*of a door, chest, etc.*); **tener buenas -s** to have "pull," influential connections.

aldabón *m.* large iron knocker; large handle; **aldabonazo** *m.* knock, knocking.

aldea *f.* village; **aldehuela** *f.* little village, hamlet.

aldeano *adj.* rustic, countrified; *m.* villager; peasant.

aleación *f.* alloy; alloying.

alear *v.* to alloy, mix (*metals*); to flutter; to flap (*wings, arms, etc.*).

aleccionar *v.* to coach; to teach, instruct; to train; to drill.

aledaños *m. pl.* borders, frontiers.

alegar[7] *v.* to allege, assert; *Am.* to argue, dispute.

alegato *m.* allegation; assertion.

alegrar *v.* to cheer up, gladden; to brighten; **-se** to be glad, rejoice; to get tipsy.

alegre *adj.* merry, gay, joyful, cheerful, bright; tipsy.

alegría *f.* joy, mirth, gaiety, merriment.

alejamiento *m.* withdrawal; retirement; aloofness.

alejar *v.* to remove, move away from; **-se** to move away; to withdraw, be aloof.

alelado *adj.* stupefied, open-mouthed; silly.

alemán *adj. & m.* German.

alentar[1] *v. irr.* to breathe; to encourage, cheer, cheer up; **-se** to take heart; *Am.* to recover (*from illness*).

alergia *f.* allergy.

alero *m.* eaves; projecting edge.

alerto *adj.* alert, watchful; **¡alerta!** attention! look out!; **estar alerta** to be on the alert.

aleta *f.* small wing; flap; fin (*of a fish*).

aletargado *adj.* drowsy, sluggish.

aletargarse[7] *v.* to fall into a state of

9

lethargy; to become drowsy.

aletazo *m.* flap, blow with a wing.

aletear *v.* to flap, flutter.

aleteo *m.* flapping, flutter (*of wings*).

aleve *adj.* treacherous.

alevosía *f.* treachery.

alevoso *adj.* treacherous.

alfabeto *m.* alphabet.

alfalfa *f.* alfalfa; **alfalfar** *m.* alfalfa field.

alfarería *f.* pottery; **alfarero** *m.* potter.

alfeñicar⁰ *v.* to frost with sugar (*a cake, cookie, etc.*); **-se** to get frail, delicate; to act affectedly.

alfeñique *m.* sugar paste; delicate person.

alférez *m.* ensign; second lieutenant.

alfil *m.* bishop (*in chess*).

alfiler *m.* pin; brooch; **-es** pin money; **ponerse de veinticinco -es** to doll up, dress up.

alfombra *f.* carpet; **alfombrilla** *f.* small carpet, rug; measles; *Am.* plant of the vervain family; *Am.* black smallpox; *Am.* skin eruption.

alforja *f.* saddlebag; knapsack; food provisions for a trip; *Am.* **pasarse a la otra —** to take undue liberties.

alforza *f.* tuck, fold, pleat; scar.

algarabía *f.* jargon; chatter; uproar.

algarrobo *m.* locust tree; carob tree.

algazara *f.* clamor; shouting; uproar.

álgebra *f.* algebra.

algo *pron.* something; *adv.* somewhat.

algodón *m.* cotton; **algodonal** *m.* cotton plantation.

alguacil *m.* policeman, constable.

alguien *pron.* somebody, someone.

algún(o) *adj.* some; any; *pron.* someone.

alhaja *f.* jewel.

alharaca *f.* rumpus, clamor, racket.

aliado *adj.* allied; *m.* ally.

alianza *f.* alliance, union; *Am.* wedding ring; *Am.* mixture of liquors.

aliar¹⁷ *v.* to ally; to unite; **-se** to form an alliance; to unite.

alicaído *adj.* crestfallen, downcast, discouraged; drooping.

alicates *m. pl.* pliers, small pincers.

aliciente *m.* inducement, incentive, attraction.

alienista *m.* alienist (*doctor who treats mental diseases*).

aliento *m.* breath; encouragement.

aligerar *v.* to lighten; to hasten.

alimentación *f.* nourishment, food, nutrition; feeding.

alimentar *v.* to feed, nourish.

alimenticio *adj.* nutritious, nourishing.

alimento *m.* food.

alinear *v.* to line up, put into line; to

range; **-se** to fall in line, form into a line.

aliño *m.* ornament, decoration; neatness; condiment, dressing, seasoning.

alisar *v.* to smooth; to polish; to plane.

alistamiento *m.* enlistment; enrollment.

alistar *v.* to enlist; to enroll; to make ready; **-se** to enlist; to get ready; *Am.* to dress up.

aliviar *v.* to lighten; to alleviate, relieve, remedy, soothe; **-se** to get better, recover.

alivio *m.* relief, remedy; aid, help; improvement.

aljibe *m.* cistern, reservoir, tank; water tanker; *Am.* well, artesian well, spring.

alma *f.* soul, spirit; inhabitant.

almacén *m.* warehouse; department store; store.

almacenaje *m.* storage.

almacenar *v.* to store, store up; to put in storage.

almacenista *m. & f.* department store owner; warehouse owner or manager; wholesale merchant.

almanaque *m.* almanac, calendar.

almeja *f.* clam.

almendra *f.* almond; **almendrado** *m.* almond paste; **almendro** *m.* almond tree.

almíbar *m.* syrup.

almidón *m.* starch; *Am.* paste (*for gluing*).

almidonar *v.* to starch.

alminar *m.* turret.

almirante *m.* admiral.

almirez *m.* metal mortar.

almohada *f.* pillow; **almohadón** *m.* large cushion or pillow.

almohaza *f.* currycomb (*for grooming horses*).

almoneda *f.* auction.

almorzar²,⁹ *v.* *irr.* to lunch, eat lunch.

almuerzo *m.* lunch.

alojamiento *m.* lodging.

alojar *v.* to lodge; to house; to quarter (*troops*); **-se** to lodge, room.

alondra *f.* lark.

alpaca *f.* alpaca (*sheeplike animal of South America*); alpaca wool; alpaca cloth.

alpargata *f.* sandal (*usually of canvas and with hemp sole*).

alquería *f.* farmhouse.

alquilar *v.* to rent; to hire; **-se** to hire out.

alquiler *m.* rent, rental; **de —** for rent, for hire.

alquitrán *m.* tar.

alrededor *adv.* about, around; **— de**

prep. around; **-es** *m. pl.* environs, outskirts.

altanería *f.* haughtiness.

altanero *adj.* haughty, proud.

altar *m.* altar; — **mayor** high altar.

altavoz *m.* loud-speaker.

alteración *f.* alteration, change; disturbance.

alterar *v.* to alter, change; to disturb.

altercar[6] *v.* to argue, dispute; to quarrel.

alternar *v.* to alternate; to take turns; — **con** to rub elbows with, be friendly with.

alternativa *f.* alternative, choice, option.

alternativo *adj.* alternating, alternative.

alterno *adj.* alternate.

alteza *f.* highness (*title*); lofty height.

altibajo *m.* downward thrust (*in fencing*); **-s** ups and downs; uneven ground.

altiplanicie *f.* upland; high plateau.

altiplano *m. Am.* high plateau.

altisonante *adj.* high-sounding.

altitud *f.* altitude.

altivez *f.* haughtiness, arrogance.

altivo *adj.* haughty, proud, arrogant.

alto *adj.* high; tall; loud; *adv.* loud; *m.* height; story (*of a building*); halt; *Am.* heap, pile: **-s** *Am.* upper floors; **hacer —** to halt, stop; **pasar por —** to omit, overlook; ¡ — ! halt!

altoparlante *m.* loud-speaker.

altura *f.* height, altitude.

alud *m.* avalanche.

aludir *v.* to allude, refer indirectly.

alumbrado *m.* lighting; *adj.* lit, lighted; tipsy.

alumbramiento *m.* childbirth; lighting.

alumbrar *v.* to light, give light; to enlighten; to give birth; **-se** to get tipsy.

aluminio *m.* aluminum.

alumno *m.* student.

alusión *f.* allusion.

alza *f.* rise; lift (*for shoes*).

alzada *f.* height (*of a horse*).

alzamiento *m.* raising, lifting; uprising, insurrection.

alzar[9] *v.* to lift, raise; to cut (*cards*); **-se** to rebel, rise up in arms; *Am.* to puff up with pride; **-se con algo** to run off with something, steal something.

allá *adv.* there, over there; **más —** farther.

allanar *v.* to level, even off; to invade, break into (*a house*); to raid; — **una dificultad** to smooth out a difficulty.

allegado *adj.* near; related; allied; *m.* relative; partisan, follower.

allegar[7] *v.* to accumulate, heap up, gather.

allende *adv.* on the other side; beyond; — **el mar** across the sea, overseas.

allí *adv.* there; **por —** through that place, around there.

ama *f.* mistress, owner; — **de leche** wet nurse; — **de llaves** housekeeper.

amabilidad *f.* kindness, courtesy.

amable *adj.* kind, amiable.

amador *m.* lover.

amaestrar *v.* to teach, coach, train.

amagar[7] *v.* to threaten; to feint, make a threatening motion; to strike at.

amago *m.* threat; indication.

amalgamar *v.* to amalgamate, combine, mix, blend.

amamantar *v.* to nurse, suckle.

amanecer[13] *v. irr.* to dawn; — **malo** to wake up ill; *m.* dawn, sunrise.

amanecida *f.* dawn, sunrise.

amansar *v.* to tame; to subdue; to pacify.

amante *m.* lover; — **de** fond of.

amapola *f.* poppy.

amar *v.* to love.

amargar[7] *v.* to embitter, make bitter.

amargo *adj.* bitter; *m.* bitters; *Am.* mate (*Paraguayan tea*) without sugar.

amargor *m.* bitterness.

amargura *f.* bitterness; grief.

amarillear *v.* to show or have a yellowish tinge; to turn yellow.

amarillento *adj.* yellowish.

amarillo *adj.* yellow.

amarra *f.* cable; rope; strap.

amarrar *v.* to tie, fasten, rope; to moor (*a ship*); *Am.* 'amarrárselas to get "tight," drunk.

amasar *v.* to knead, mix; to mash; *Am.* to amass, accumulate (*a fortune*).

amatista *f.* amethyst.

ambages *m. pl.* circumlocutions; **hablar sin —** to go straight to the point, speak plainly, not to beat about the bush.

ámbar *m.* amber; **ambarino** *adj.* amber; like amber.

ambición *f.* ambition; aspiration.

ambicionar *v.* to seek, aspire after; to covet.

ambicioso *adj.* ambitious, eager; greedy, grasping.

ambiente *m.* atmosphere, environment.

ambigüedad *f.* ambiguity.

ambiguo *adj.* ambiguous; uncertain, doubtful.

ámbito *m.* precinct, enclosure.

ambos *adj. & pron.* both.

ambulancia *f.* ambulance; field hospital.

ambulante *adj.* walking; itinerant; moving; wandering.

amedrentar v. to scare, frighten.

amenaza f. menace, threat.

amenazador, amenazante adj. threatening.

amenazar[9] v. to menace, threaten.

amenguar[8] v. to lessen, diminish; to defame, dishonor.

amenidad f. pleasantness.

amenizar[9] v. to make pleasant, cheer, brighten.

ameno adj. pleasant, agreeable.

americana f. suit coat.

americano adj. & m. American.

ametrallador m. gunner; **ametralladora** f. machine gun.

amigable adj. friendly; affable, pleasant.

amígdala f. tonsil; **amigdalitis** f. tonsilitis.

amigo m. friend; — de fond of.

aminorar v. to lessen.

amistad f. friendship; friendliness.

amistoso adj. friendly.

amo m. master, owner, boss.

amodorrado adj. drowsy.

amodorrar v. to make drowsy; -se to become drowsy.

amolador m. grinder, sharpener; adj. grinding, sharpening.

amolar[2] v. irr. to hone, sharpen, grind; to annoy; Am. to ruin, harm; -se Am. to go to rack and ruin.

amoldar v. to mold; to shape; to adjust; to adapt.

amonestación f. admonition, advice, warning; -es marriage bans (or banns).

amonestar v. to admonish, advise, warn.

amoníaco m. ammonia.

amontonamiento m. accumulation, pile, heap.

amontonar v. to heap up, pile up, crowd up.

amor m. love; — propio self-esteem.

amoratado adj. livid, bluish, purplish.

amordazar[9] v. to gag; to muzzle.

amorío m. love affair; love-making.

amoroso adj. loving, tender, affectionate.

amortajar v. to shroud.

amortiguador m. shock absorber; silencer, muffler.

amortiguar[9] v. to muffle; to deafen (a sound); to deaden (a blow or sound); to soften, tone down (a color or sound).

amortizar[9] v. to pay on account; to liquidate, pay (a debt); to provide a sinking fund.

amoscarse[6] v. to get peeved, annoyed; Am. to blush, be inhibited or embarrassed.

amostazar[9] v. to anger, irritate; -se to get angry or irritated.

amotinar v. to incite to rebellion; -se to mutiny; to riot.

amparar v. to protect; to defend; Am. to grant mining rights; -se to seek protection or refuge; to protect oneself.

amparo m. protection; habeas corpus (protection against imprisonment); Am. mining rights.

ampliación f. enlargement, widening.

ampliar[17] v. to enlarge, widen.

amplificar[6] v. to amplify, expand, extend, enlarge; to magnify.

amplio adj. ample; wide, large, roomy.

amplitud f. breadth, extent, width.

ampolla f. blister; water bubble; narrow-necked bottle or vase; cruet; electric-light bulb; **ampolleta** f. small vial; small cruet.

ampollar v. to blister; -se to blister.

ampuloso adj. inflated, wordy, bombastic, pompous.

amputar v. to amputate, cut off.

amueblar v. to furnish (with furniture).

ánade m. & f. duck; **anadeja** f. duckling.

anadear v. to waddle.

anales m. pl. annals, historical records.

analfabeto adj. & m. illiterate; **analfabetismo** m. illiteracy.

análisis m. analysis.

analizar[9] v. to analyze, examine.

analogía f. analogy, similarity.

análogo adj. analogous, similar, comparable.

ananá, ananás f. pineapple. See piña.

anaquel m. shelf; bookshelf; **anaquelería** f. shelves, bookshelves, library stacks.

anaranjado adj. orange-colored; m. orange color.

anarquía f. anarchy.

anatomía f. anatomy.

anca f. haunch, hind quarter, rump; Am. popcorn.

ancianidad f. old age.

anciano adj. old, aged; m. old man.

ancla f. anchor.

anclar v. to anchor.

ancho adj. wide; broad; loose; roomy; Am. self-satisfied, conceited; a sus anchas at one's ease; comfortable; leisurely; m. width.

anchoa, anchova f. anchovy.

anchura f. width, breadth; comfort, ease.

anchuroso adj. vast, extensive; spacious.

andada f. Am. walk, stroll; -s track,

footprints; **volver a las -s** to fall back into one's old ways or habits.
andadura f. gait, pace.
andaluz adj. Andalusian, of or pertaining to Andalusia, Spain; m. Andalusian, native of Andalusia.
andamiada f., **andamiaje** m. scaffolding; framework.
andamio m. scaffold, scaffolding.
andanada f. grandstand; broadside (discharge of the guns on one side of a ship); **soltar una —** to discharge a broadside; to reprimand.
andante adj. walking; errant, wandering; moderately slow (music); **caballero —** knight-errant.
andanzas f. pl. rambles, wanderings.
andar[21] v. irr. to walk; to go, go about; to run (as a watch or machinery); **— con cuidado** to be careful; **anda en quince años** he is about fifteen; **a todo —** at full (walking) speed; **a más —** walking briskly; **¡anda!** move on!; **¿qué andas haciendo?** what are you doing?; Am. **— andando** to be walking around; Am. **¡ándale!** hurry!
andariego adj. fond of walking; roving; m. walker.
andas f. pl. portable platform; litter.
andén m. railway station platform.
andino adj. Andean, of or from the Andes.
andrajo m. rag.
andrajoso adj. ragged, in rags.
anécdota f. anecdote, story.
anegar[7] v. to drown; to flood.
anejo adj. annexed, attached.
anestésico m. & adj. anesthetic.
anexar v. to annex.
anexo m. annex; adj. annexed, joined.
anfiteatro m. amphitheater.
anfitrión m. generous host.
ángel m. angel.
angélico adj. angelic.
angina f. angina, inflammation of the throat; Am. tonsil; **— del pecho** angina pectoris.
anglosajón adj. & m. Anglo-Saxon.
angostar v. to narrow; -se to narrow, become narrow; to contract.
angosto adj. narrow.
angostura f. narrowness; narrows (narrow part of a river, valley, strait, etc.)
anguila f. eel.
angular adj. angular; **piedra —** cornerstone.
ángulo m. angle, corner.
anguloso adj. angular, sharp-cornered.
angustia f. anguish, sorrow, grief, worry.
angustiar v. to distress, grieve, worry.

angustioso adj. anguished, worried, grievous; distressing.
anhelante adj. anxious, desirous, longing; panting.
anhelar v. to long for; to breathe hard; to pant.
anhelo m. longing.
anheloso adj. anxious; eager.
anidar v. to nest; to nestle; to dwell; to shelter.
anillo m. ring.
ánima f. soul, spirit.
animación f. animation, liveliness, life.
animal m. animal; adj. animal; stupid; beastly; **animalejo** m. little animal; **animalucho** m. insignificant animal; hideous little beast.
animar v. to animate, give life to; to inspire, encourage.
ánimo m. spirit, mind; courage, valor; intention.
animosidad f. animosity, ill will; courage, energy.
animoso adj. spirited; courageous.
aniñado adj. boyish; childish; **aniñada** girlish.
aniquilar v. to annihilate, wipe out, destroy completely.
aniversario m. anniversary.
anoche adv. last night.
anochecer[13] v. irr. to grow dark; to be or arrive at nightfall; m. nightfall.
anochecida f. nightfall.
anonadar v. to annihilate; to humiliate.
anónimo adj. anonymous; nameless; m. anonymous letter or note.
anormal adj. abnormal.
anotación f. annotation; note.
anotar v. to annotate, provide with notes; to write down.
anquilosado adj. stiff-jointed; gnarled.
anquilosarse v. to become stiff in the joints; to become mentally stagnant.
ansia f. anxiety, anguish; longing, eagerness; -s anguish; Am. nausea.
ansiar[17] v. to long for, desire eagerly.
ansiedad f. anxiety; worry.
ansioso adj. anxious, troubled; eager.
antagonismo m. antagonism.
antagonista m. & f. antagonist, adversary, opponent.
antaño adv. yesteryear, formerly; **días de —** days of old.
ante prep. before, in the presence of; **— todo** above all; m. elk; buckskin.
anteanoche adv. night before last.
anteayer adv. day before yesterday.
antebrazo m. forearm.
antecámara f. antechamber, waiting room.

13

antecedente *m.* antecedent; *adj.* antecedent, preceding.

antecesor *m.* ancestor; predecessor.

antedicho *adj.* aforesaid.

antelación *f.* precedence, priority (*in time*).

antemano: de — beforehand.

antena *f.* antenna (*of a radio or wireless*); lateen yard (*of a ship*); **-s** antennae, feelers.

antenoche = anteanoche.

anteojera *f.* blinder.

anteojo *m.* spyglass; small telescope; cyeglass; **-s** spectacles; **-s de larga vista** field glasses.

antepasado *adj.* passed; **año —** year before last; *m.* ancestor.

antepecho *m.* sill, railing.

anteponer[10] *v. irr.* to place before; to prefer.

antepuesto *p.p. of* **anteponer.**

anterior *adj.* front, toward the front; earlier, previous; **el día —** the day before.

antes *adv.* before, formerly; **— de** *prep.* before; **— (de) que** *conj.* before.

antesala *f.* anteroom, waiting room.

antiaéreo *adj.* antiaircraft.

anticipación *f.* anticipation, expectation; **con —** in advance.

anticipado *adj.* early, ahead of time; advanced (*payment*); **por —** in advance; *p.p. of* **anticipar** anticipated.

anticipar *v.* to anticipate; to advance, pay in advance; **-se** to get ahead (of).

anticipo *m.* advance, advance payment.

anticlericalismo *m.* anticlericalism (*opposition or antagonism to the clergy*).

anticuado *adj.* antiquated, out-of-date.

antídoto *m.* antidote.

antigualla *f.* antique; anything old.

antigüedad *f.* antiquity, ancient times; **-es** antique objects, antiques.

antiguo *adj.* ancient, old; antique.

antílope *m.* antelope.

antiparras *f. pl.* goggles; spectacles.

antipatía *f.* antipathy, dislike; mutual antagonism.

antipático *adj.* disagreeable; unlikeable, unpleasant.

antiséptico *adj. & m.* antiseptic.

antojadizo *adj.* fanciful, whimsical.

antojarse *v. :* **antojársele a uno** to take a notion or fancy to; to strike one's fancy; to want, desire.

antojo *m.* whim, notion, fancy.

antorcha *f.* torch.

antracita *f.* anthracite, hard coal.

anual *adj.* annual, yearly.

anuario *m.* annual, yearbook.

anublar *v.* to cloud; to dim, obscure; **-se** to become cloudy.

anudar *v.* to knot; **anudársele a uno la garganta** to choke up with emotion.

anulación *f.* voiding, cancellation.

anular *v.* to annul, void, cancel, abolish.

anunciador *m.* announcer; advertiser; *adj.* announcing; advertising.

anunciante *m. & f.* announcer, advertiser.

anunciar *v.* to announce; to advertise.

anuncio *m.* announcement; advertisement.

anzuelo *m.* fishhook; lure, attraction.

añadidura *f.* addition.

añadir *v.* to add.

añejado *adj.* aged (*wine, cheese, etc.*).

añejo *adj.* old; of old vintage; stale.

añicos *m. pl.* bits, shatters, fragments; **hacer(se) —** to shatter, break into a thousand pieces.

añil *m.* indigo (*plant*); indigo blue.

año *m.* year; **— bisiesto** leap year; **¿cuántos -s tiene Vd.?** how old are you?

añoranza *f.* nostalgia, longing.

añorar *v.* to long for, yearn for, be homesick for; to make reminiscences.

añoso *adj.* old, aged.

aojar *v.* to bewitch; to cast the evil eye.

apabullar *v.* to crush, crumple.

apacentar[1] *v. irr.* to graze, pasture; to feed (*the spirit, desires, passions, etc.*); **-se** to graze, pasture.

apacibilidad *f.* gentleness, mildness, pleasantness; **apacible** *adj.* pleasant, quiet, gentle.

apaciguamiento *m.* appeasement.

apaciguar[8] *v.* to pacify, calm, appease; **-se** to calm down.

apachurrar *v. Am.* to crush. *See* **despachurrar.**

apadrinar *v.* to sponsor; to act as a godfather; to act as a second in a duel.

apagar[7] *v.* to put out, extinguish; to deafen (*a sound*).

apalabrar *v.* to speak for, engage, reserve; **-se con** to make a verbal agreement with.

apalear *v.* to beat up, thrash; to thresh.

aparador *m.* sideboard; cupboard; showcase; show window; workshop.

aparato *m.* apparatus; pomp.

aparatoso *adj.* pompous, ostentatious.

aparcero *m.* co-owner of land; *Am.* pal, comrade.

aparear *v.* to mate; to match; to pair. **-se** to mate; to match; to pair.

aparecer[13] *v. irr.* to appear, show up.

aparecido *m.* ghost, specter, phantom.

aparejar *v.* to prepare; to harness; to rig; to equip.

aparejo *m.* harness; packsaddle; rigging (*of a boat*); preparation; fishing tackle; -s equipment, tools.

aparentar *v.* to appear, seem; to pretend, feign, affect.

aparente *adj.* apparent.

aparición *f.* apparition, ghost; appearance.

apariencia *f.* appearance.

apartado *adj.* compartment; — postal post office letter box; *p.p.* of **apartar.**

apartamento *m.* apartment.

apartamiento *m.* separation; retirement; aloofness; retreat, refuge; *Am.* apartment, flat.

apartar *v.* to set apart, separate; to remove; *Am.* — **las reses** to sort out cattle; -se to withdraw; to step aside; to go away.

aparte *adv.* apart; aside; *m.* aside (*in a play*); new paragraph; *Am.* sorting out of cattle.

apasionado *adj.* passionate; very fond (of); impassioned, emotional.

apasionar *v.* to arouse passion; to fill with passion; -se to become impassioned; to fall ardently in love.

apatía *f.* apathy, indolence, indifference.

apático *adj.* apathetic, indifferent, indolent.

apear *v.* to dismount; to lower, take down; to shackle (*a horse*); to fell (*a tree*); *Am.* to fire, dismiss from a position; — **el tratamiento** to omit the title (*in addressing a person*); -se to get off, alight; *Am.* -se por la cola (*or* por las orejas) to go off at a tangent, make an irrelevant remark.

apechugar[7] *v.* to push with the chest; to push ahead; — **con** to accept reluctantly; to go through with (*something*) courageously; *Am.* to snatch, take possession of.

apedrear *v.* to stone, hit with stones.

apegado *adj.* devoted, attached; *p.p.* of **apegarse.**

apegarse[7] *v.* to become attached (to); to become fond (of).

apego *m.* attachment, fondness.

apelación *f.* appeal.

apelar *v.* to appeal.

apelotonar *v.* to form or roll into a ball; to pile up, bunch together.

apellidar *v.* to call, name; -se to be named; to have the surname of.

apellido *m.* surname.

apenar *v.* to grieve, afflict; -se to be grieved, *Am.* to feel embarrassed,

feel ashamed.

apenas *adv.* hardly, scarcely; *conj.* as soon as.

apéndice *m.* appendix.

apercibir *v.* to prepare beforehand; to supply; to warn, advise; to perceive; -se a la pelea to get ready to fight; *Am.* -se de to notice.

apergaminado *adj.* parchment-like; dried up.

aperitivo *m.* aperitif, appetizer; cocktail.

aperlado *adj.* pearly, pearl-colored.

apero *m.* farm equipment; -s tools, implements; *Am.* saddle and trappings.

apertura *f.* opening (*act of opening or beginning*).

apestar *v.* to infect; to corrupt; to sicken; to stink; -se to turn putrid, become corrupted; *Am.* to catch cold.

apestoso *adj.* putrid, foul-smelling.

apetecer[13] *v. irr.* to desire, crave.

apetecible *adj.* desirable; appetizing.

apetencia *f.* hunger, appetite; desire.

apetito *m.* appetite; hunger.

apetitoso *adj.* appetizing; gluttonous.

apiadarse *v.* to pity; — de to pity, take pity on.

ápice *m.* apex, top, summit.

apilar *v.* to pile up, stack, heap.

apiñado *p.p.* of **apiñar** & *adj.* crowded, jammed; cone-shaped, shaped like a pine cone.

apiñamiento *m.* crowd, jam (*of people or animals*); crowding together.

apiñar *v.* to cram together; to crowd; -se to pile up, crowd together.

apio *m.* celery.

apisonar *v.* to pack down, flatten by pounding.

aplacar[6] *v.* to appease, pacify, soothe.

aplanamiento *m.* flattening, leveling; dejection, depression.

aplanar *v.* to level; to flatten; to astonish, *Am.* — las calles to tramp the streets; -se to be flattened out; to be leveled to the ground; to lose one's strength; *Am.* to give in, yield.

aplastar *v.* to squash, crush, flatten; *Am.* to tire out, break (*a horse*); -se *Am.* to plump oneself down; *Am.* to overstay a call (*remaining seated*).

aplaudir *v.* to applaud, clap; to approve, praise.

aplauso *m.* applause; praise, approval.

aplazamiento *m.* postponement; adjournment.

aplazar[9] *v.* to postpone; to adjourn.

aplicable *adj.* applicable, suitable, fitting.

aplicación *f.* application; effort, dili-

15

gence; -es appliqué (*trimming laid on a dress*).

aplicado *adj.* industrious, diligent.

aplicar[6] *v.* to apply; to put on, lay on; -se to apply oneself, work hard.

aplomado *adj.* gray, lead-colored; *p.p.* of aplomar.

aplomar *v.* to plumb (*a wall*); to make vertical; to make heavier; -se *Am.* to become ashamed or embarrassed; *Am.* to be slow

aplomo *m.* assurance, confidence, self-possession, serenity; **estar** — to be plumb, vertical.

apocado *adj.* cowardly; timid; *p.p.* of apocar.

apocamiento *m.* timidity; bashfulness; belittling.

apocar[6] *v.* to lessen; to belittle, give little importance to; -se to humble oneself.

apodar *v.* to nickname.

apoderado *m.* attorney; proxy, substitute.

apoderar *v.* to empower, give power of attorney; -se de to take possession of, seize.

apodo *m.* nickname.

apogeo *m.* apogee (*point at which a planet is at the greatest distance from the earth*); highest point, height (*of glory, fame, etc.*).

apolillado *adj.* moth-eaten; worm-eaten.

apología *f.* apology

apoplejía *f.* apoplexy, stroke.

aporrear *v.* to beat; to maul; *Am.* to beat (*in a game*), defeat.

aportación *f.* contribution.

aportar *v.* to bring; to contribute; to arrive in port; to reach an unexpected place (*after having gone astray*); -se *Am.* to appear, approach.

aporte *m.* contribution

aposento *m.* room; lodging.

apostar[2] *v* *irr.* to bet; to post, station.

apóstol *m.* apostle; religious leader.

apostólico *adj.* apostolic (*pertaining to the apostles, or to the Pope and his authority*).

apostura *f.* elegant bearing, graceful carriage.

apoyar *v.* to lean, rest; to back, support; to aid, favor; to confirm; -se to lean (on)

apoyo *m.* support; favor, protection.

apreciable *adj.* appreciable, noticeable; estimable, esteemed; valuable; appraisable.

apreciación *f.* appreciation, valuation; estimation.

apreciar *v.* to appreciate, value, esteem; to price, fix the price of; to appraise.

aprecio *m.* esteem, high regard; appraisal, valuation, estimate; *Am.* **hacer** — to notice, pay attention.

aprehender *v.* to apprehend, seize, arrest.

aprehensión, aprensión *f.* apprehension; fear, dread; seizure, arrest; *Am.* prejudice.

aprehensor, aprensor *m.* captor.

apremiante *adj.* pressing, urgent.

apremiar *v.* to press, urge onward, hurry.

apremio *m.* pressure; urgency

aprender *v.* to learn.

aprendiz *m.* apprentice.

aprendizaje *m.* apprenticeship; learning (*act of learning*).

apresar *v.* to seize, grab; to capture; to imprison.

aprestar *v.* to prepare, make ready; -se to get ready.

apresto *m.* preparation; readiness.

apresurado *adj.* hasty.

apresurar *v.* to hurry, hasten; -se to hurry, hasten.

apretado *adj.* tight; compact; stingy, miserly; difficult, dangerous; *p.p.* of apretar.

apretar[1] *v.* *irr.* to press, squeeze, tighten; to urge on; *Am.* to increase in strength or intensity (*as rain, wind, etc.*); *Am.* to redouble one's effort; — **a correr** to start to run; -se *Am.* to gorge, overeat.

apretón *m.* sudden pressure; squeeze; dash, short run; — **de manos** handshake.

apretura *f.* jam, crush; tight squeeze, narrow place; difficulty, predicament; dire poverty.

aprieto *m.* tight spot, difficulty.

aprisa *adv.* quickly, fast, speedily

aprisco *m.* sheepfold.

aprisionar *v.* to imprison; to tie, fasten.

aprobación *f.* approbation, approval; consent; pass, passing grade.

aprobar[2] *v.* *irr.* to approve; to pass (*in an examination*).

aprontar *v.* to make ready; to expedite; to hand over without delay; *Am.* to pay in advance.

apropiación *f.* appropriation; confiscation.

apropiado *adj.* appropriate, proper, fitting, suitable; *p.p.* of apropiar.

apropiar *v.* to fit; to adapt; -se to take possession (of); to confiscate.

aprovechable *adj.* available; usable, fit

16

to use.

aprovechado *adj.* diligent, industrious; *p.p. of* aprovechar.

aprovechamiento *m.* use, utilization; exploitation; profit, benefit; progress.

aprovechar *v.* to profit, be profitable; to progress, get ahead; to utilize; -se de to take advantage of; ¡que aproveche! may you enjoy it!

aproximado *adj.* approximate; near; nearly correct.

aproximar *v.* to place or bring near; to approximate; -se to get near, approach.

aproximativo *adj.* approximate.

aptitud *f.* aptitude, capacity, ability.

apto *adj.* apt; competent.

apuesta *f.* bet, wager.

apuesto *adj.* smart, stylish; good-looking.

apuntación *f.* note; memorandum; musical notation, set of musical symbols or signs.

apuntalar *v.* to prop; to shore up.

apuntar *v.* to point; to aim; to write down; to prompt (*an actor*); to sharpen; to stitch, mend; to begin to show (*as a mustache or beard on a young face*); — el día to begin to dawn; -se *Am.* to sprout (*said of wheat, corn, etc.*)

apunte *m.* note, memorandum.

apuñalar *v.* to stab.

apuración *f.* worry; trouble.

apurado *adj.* worried; needy, difficult; dangerous; in a hurry.

apurar *v.* to drain to the last drop; to exhaust (*a subject*); to press, hurry; to worry, annoy; -se to be or get worried; to hurry up.

apuro *m.* need; worry; predicament; *Am.* rush, hurry.

aquejar *v.* to grieve, afflict.

aquel, aquella *dem. adj.* that (*at a distance*); **aquellos, aquellas** those; **aquél, aquélla** *m., f. dem. pron.* that one; the former; **aquello** that, that thing; **aquéllos, aquéllas** *m., f. pl.* those; the former.

aquí *adv.* here; por — this way; through here; around here.

aquietar *v.* to quiet, calm, to hush; -se to calm down, become calm.

aquilón *m.* north wind.

ara *f.* altar.

árabe *adj. & m.* Arab; Arabic.

arado *m.* plow; *Am.* plowed land, piece of cultivated land.

aragonés *adj.* Aragonese, of or from Aragón, Spain; *m.* Aragonese.

arancel *m.* tariff; — de aduanas customs, duties; **arancelario** *adj.* pertaining to tariff.

araña *f.* spider; chandelier.

arañar *v.* to scratch; to claw.

araño *m.* scratch; **arañazo** *m.* big scratch.

arar *v.* to plow.

arbitración *f.* arbitration.

arbitrador *m.* arbitrator, referee, umpire.

arbitraje *m.* arbitration.

arbitrar *v.* to arbitrate, to umpire.

arbitrario *adj.* arbitrary.

arbitrio *m.* free will; scheme, means, compromise, arbitration; sentence (*of a judge*); judgment.

árbitro *m.* arbitrator, sole judge, umpire.

árbol *m.* tree; mast; **arbolado** *adj.* wooded; *m.* grove of trees.

arboleda *f.* grove.

arbusto *m.* shrub.

arca *f.* ark; chest, coffer, **arcón** *m.* large coffer or chest, bin.

arcada *f.* arcade; archway.

arcaico *adj.* archaic.

arcano *adj.* hidden, secret; *m.* secret, mystery.

arce *m.* maple, maple tree.

arcilla *f.* clay.

arco *m.* arc; arch; bow; violin bow, — iris rainbow.

archipiélago *m.* archipelago (*group of many islands*).

archisabido *adj.* very well-known.

archivo *m.* archives; file; public records; *Am.* office, business office; **archivero** *m.* keeper of archives; city clerk.

arder *v.* to burn; to be consumed (*with fever or passion*); *Am.* to smart, sting.

ardid *m.* trick, scheme.

ardiente *adj.* ardent, burning, fervent; passionate; fiery.

ardilla *f.* squirrel.

ardite *m.* ancient coin of small value; bit, trifle; no valer un — not to be worth a penny.

ardor *m.* ardor; heat; fervor, eagerness.

ardoroso *adj.* ardent, fiery.

arduo *adj.* arduous, hard, difficult.

área *f.* area.

arena *f.* sand; arena; -s kidney stones, **arenal** *m.* sand pit.

arenga *f.* address, speech.

arenisco *adj.* sandy; gritty; **piedra arenisca** sandstone.

arenoso *adj.* sandy; gritty.

arenque *m.* herring.

arete *m.* earring.

argamasa *f.* mortar.

argentar *v.* to plate (*with silver*); to polish.

17

argentino adj. silvery; Argentine; m. Argentine; Argentine gold coin worth 5 pesos.

argolla f. large iron ring, Am. plain finger ring, engagement ring; Am. **tener —** to be lucky.

argucia f. cunning, astuteness; scheme; subtlety.

argüir⁴² v. irr. to argue; to deduce, infer.

argumentación f. argumentation, argument, reasoning.

argumento m. argument, reasoning; subject matter, resumé (of a play or story).

aridez f. barrenness; dryness; drought.

árido adj. arid, dry, barren; **-s** m. pl. grains and dry vegetables; **medida para -s** dry measure.

ariete m. ram, battering ram; — **hidráulico** hydraulic ram.

arisco adj. gruff, harsh, unsociable; Am. shy, distrustful.

arista f. sharp edge; ridge; beard (of wheat or corn).

aristocracia f. aristocracy.

aristócrata m. & f. aristocrat.

aristocrático adj. aristocratic.

aritmética f. arithmetic.

arma f. arm, weapon; branch (of the army); **-s armed forces; — arrojadiza** missile weapon; — **blanca** sword; **de -s tomar** ready for any emergency; ready to fight.

armada f. armada, fleet.

armador m. shipbuilder; assembler.

armadura f. armor; armature (of a generator or dynamo); framework; mounting.

armamento m. armament; equipment.

armar v. to arm; to set up, assemble, rig up; — **una pendencia** to start a quarrel; Am. — **un trique** to lay a snare, set a trap; Am. **-se** to balk; to be stubborn; Am. **-se con alguna cosa** to refuse to return something.

armario m. wardrobe, clothes closet; cabinet.

armatoste m. unwieldy object or machine; clumsy thing; heavy, clumsy fellow.

armazón f. framework, skeleton; m. skeleton (of an animal); Am. shelf, set of shelves.

armella f. staple; screw eye.

armiño m. ermine.

armisticio m. armistice.

armonía f. harmony.

armónico adj. harmonic; harmonious.

armonioso adj. harmonious, musical.

armonizar⁹ v. to harmonize.

arnés m. harness; coat of mail; **-es** harness and trappings; equipment, outfit.

aro m. hoop; rim (of a wheel); Am. finger ring; Am. earring.

aroma f. aroma, scent, perfume.

aromático adj. aromatic, fragrant, spicy; **sales aromáticas** smelling salts.

arpa f. harp.

arpía f. shrew.

arpón m. harpoon, spear.

arqueado adj. arched.

arquear v. to arch.

arquitecto m. architect.

arquitectónico adj. architectural.

arquitectura f. architecture.

arrabal m. outlying district; **-es** outskirts, suburbs.

arracada f. earring.

arraigar⁷ v. to root, take root; **-se** to become rooted, attached.

arrancar⁶ v. to uproot; to pull out; to start, start out; Am. to flee, run away.

arranque m. start; pull; uprooting; automobile starter; — **de ira** fit or outburst of anger; **punto de —** starting point.

arrasar v. to level; to tear down, raze; to fill to the brim; **-se** to clear up (said of the sky); **-se de lágrimas** to fill up with tears.

arrastrado adj. poor, destitute; mean, vile; wretched; rascally; Am. **llevar una vida arrastrada** to lead a dog's life.

arrastrar v. to drag, haul; Am. to harrow (land); **-se** to drag along, crawl.

arrayán m. myrtle.

¡arre! interj. gee! get up there!

arrear v. to drive (mules, cattle); Am. to rustle, steal cattle; Am. **-le a uno una bofetada** to give a person a slap.

arrebatamiento m. snatch; ecstasy; rage.

arrebatar v. to snatch away; **-se de cólera** to have a fit of anger.

arrebatiña f. grab, snatch; scramble; arrebatón m. quick or violent grab.

arrebato m. rage; rapture, ecstacy; fit.

arrebol m. red color of the sky; rouge; **-es** red clouds.

arreciar v. to increase in intensity, get stronger.

arrecife m. reef.

arredrar v. to frighten, intimidate; **-se** to be or get scared.

arreglar v. to arrange, put in order; to regulate; to fix; to adjust, settle; Am. to pay (a debt); Am. to correct, punish; **-se** to doll up, fix oneself up; to settle differences, come to an agreement.

arreglo m. arrangement; adjustment;

settlement; conformity, agreement; con — a according to the.

arrellanarse *v.* to sprawl, lounge; to be self-satisfied.

arremangado *adj. & p.p.* turned up; **nariz arremangada** turned up nose.

arremangar[7] *v.* to tuck up, turn up, roll up (*the sleeves, trousers, etc.*); **-se** to roll up one's sleeves; **-se los pantalones** to roll up one's trousers.

arremeter *v.* to attack, assail, assault.

arremetida *f.* thrust, push, attack.

arremolinarse *v.* to whirl, swirl; to eddy; to mill around.

arrendamiento *m.* renting; lease; rental, rent.

arrendar[1] *v. irr.* to rent, lease, let; to hire; to tie (*a horse*); to bridle; *Am.* to head for.

arrendatario *m.* renter, tenant.

arreo *m.* raiment; ornament; *Am.* driving of horses or mules; *Am.* drove of horses or mules; **-s** trappings; equipment; finery; *adv.* uninterruptedly, without interruption.

arrepentido *adj* repentant; *p.p.* of **arrepentirse**.

arrepentimiento *m.* repentance, regret.

arrepentirse[3] *v. irr.* to repent, regret.

arrestado *adj.* daring, rash; *p.p.* of **arrestar**.

arrestar *v.* to arrest; *Am.* to return, strike back (*a ball*); *Am.* to reprimand; **-se** to dare, venture.

arresto *m.* arrest, imprisonment; detention; daring, rashness; rash act.

arriar[17] *v.* to haul down, lower (*the flag*); to lower (*the sails*); to slacken (*a rope*).

arriba *adv.* above; upstairs; **de — abajo** from top to bottom; up and down; **río — upstream; ¡ — !** hurrah!

arribada *f.* arrival; *Am.* back talk, impudent answer.

arribar *v.* to arrive; to put into port; *Am.* to prosper, better one's lot.

arribo *m.* arrival.

arriendo = **arrendamiento.**

arriero *m.* muleteer.

arriesgado *adj.* risky, daring.

arriesgar[7] *v.* to risk; **-se** to dare, run a risk.

arrimar *v.* to bring or place near; to lay aside; to strike (*a blow*); **-se** to lean (on); to get near; to seek shelter.

arrinconar *v.* to corner; to put in a corner; to lay aside; to slight, neglect; **-se** to retire; to live a secluded life.

arriscado *adj.* bold; daring; brisk; spirited (*horse*); craggy, rugged.

arriscar[6] *v.* to risk, venture; *Am.* to roll up, curl up, tuck up, fold back; *Am.* to have vim and vigor; *Am.* — a to reach, amount to; **-se** to get angry; *Am.* to dress up, doll up.

arroba *f.* weight of 25 pounds.

arrobamiento *m.* trance, rapture.

arrobarse *v.* to be entranced; to be in a trance; to be enraptured.

arrodillarse *v.* to kneel.

arrogancia *f.* arrogance, pride.

arrogante *adj.* arrogant, haughty, proud.

arrogarse[7] *v.* to appropriate, usurp, assume (*power or rights*).

arrojadizo *adj.* missile; **arma arrojadiza** missile weapon.

arrojado *adj.* daring, rash, fearless; *p.p.* of **arrojar**.

arrojar *v.* to throw, hurl, cast; to expel; *Am.* to throw up, vomit; **— un saldo de** to show a balance of; **-se a** to hurl oneself upon or at; to dare to.

arrojo *m.* boldness, daring.

arrollador *adj.* sweeping, overwhelming, violent; winding (*that serves to wind or roll up*).

arrollar *v.* to roll up; to sweep away; to trample upon; to destroy.

arropar *v.* to wrap, cover; *Am.* to snap up, accept on the spot (*a deal*); **-se** to wrap up, cover up.

arrostrar *v.* to face, defy; **-se a** to dare, dare to fight face to face.

arroyada *f.* gully, valley of a stream; bed (*formed by a stream*); river flood.

arroyo *m.* brook, small stream, rivulet; gutter; **arroyuelo** *m.* rivulet.

arroz *m.* rice; **arrozal** *m.* rice field.

arruga *f.* wrinkle.

arrugar[7] *v.* to wrinkle; *Am.* to bother, annoy; **-se** to get wrinkled; *Am.* to crouch with fear, be afraid.

arruinar *v.* to ruin, destroy; **-se** to become ruined; *Am.* to go "broke", lose all one's fortune.

arrullar *v.* to lull; to coo.

arrullo *m.* lullaby; cooing.

arrumbar *v.* to lay aside (*as useless*), put away in a corner, discard; to dismiss, remove (*from office or a position of trust*); to take bearings; **— a su adversario** to corner one's opponent, overpower him.

arsenal *m.* arsenal; navy yard.

arsénico *m.* arsenic.

arte *m. & f.* art; skill, ability; cunning; craft; **por — de** by way or means of; **bellas -s** fine arts.

artefacto *m.* piece of workmanship, manufactured object; handiwork; contrivance.

arteria f. artery.

artero adj. crafty, astute.

artesa f. trough.

artesano m. artisan, craftsman; artesanía f. arts and crafts; workmanship, craftsmanship.

artesonado m. ceiling decorated with carved panels.

ártico adj. arctic.

articulación f. articulation; pronunciation; joint.

articular v. to articulate; to join, unite.

artículo m. article; — de fondo editorial.

artífice m. artisan, craftsman.

artificial adj. artificial.

artificio m. artifice, clever device; craft, skill; cunning, deceit.

artificioso adj. cunning, astute, deceitful; skilful.

artillería f. artillery, gunnery; — de plaza (or de sitio) heavy artillery; — de montaña light mountain artillery.

artillero m. artilleryman, gunner.

artimaña f. trick.

artista m. & f. artist.

artístico adj. artistic.

arzobispo m. archbishop.

arzón m. saddletree.

as m. ace.

asa f handle.

asado m. roast; p.p. & adj. roasted.

asador m. spit (for roasting).

asaltador m. assailant; highway robber.

asaltar v to assault, attack; -le a uno una idea to be struck by an idea; Am — la casa de un amigo to give a surprise party.

asalto m. assault, attack; Am. surprise party.

asamblea f assembly, legislature; meeting.

asar v. to roast; -se to roast; to feel hot.

asaz adv. enough, very

ascendencia f. ancestry; origin.

ascendente adj. ascendent, ascending, upward, rising.

ascender[1] v.irr. to ascend, climb; to promote; to amount (to).

ascendiente m. ancestor; influence.

ascensión f ascension; ascent.

ascenso m. ascent, rise; promotion.

ascensor m. elevator

asco m. disgust, loathing; nausea, me da — it makes me sick; it disgusts me; Am. poner a uno del — to call a person all kinds of bad names; to soil.

ascua f ember

aseado adj. clean, neat; p.p. of asear.

asear v. to adorn; to make neat and clean; -se to clean oneself up.

asechanza = acechanza.

asediar v. to besiege, attack.

asedio m. siege.

asegurar v. to assure; to secure; to affirm; to insure; -se to make sure; to hold on; to get insured.

asemejar v. to liken, compare; -se a to resemble.

asentaderas f. pl. buttocks.

asentador m. razor strop.

asentar[1] v. irr. to set; to put down in writing; to assert; to iron out; to hone, strop; to establish, -se to settle.

asentimiento m. assent, acquiescence, agreement.

asentir[3] v. irr. to assent, agree.

aseo m. neatness, cleanliness.

asequible adj. obtainable, available.

aserción f. assertion, affirmation.

aserradero m. sawmill.

aserrar[1] v. irr. to saw.

aserrín m. sawdust.

aserto m. assertion.

asesinar v. to assassinate, murder.

asesinato m. assassination, murder.

asesino m. assassin, murderer; adj. murderous.

asestar v. to point, aim, direct; — un golpe to deal a blow; — un tiro to fire a shot.

aseveración f. assertion, affirmation, contention.

aseverar v. to assert, affirm.

asfalto m. asphalt.

asfixia f. suffocation.

asfixiar v. to suffocate, smother.

así adv. so, thus, like this; therefore; — — so-so; — que so that; — que (or como) conj. as soon as; Am. — no más so-so; just so

asiático adj. & m. Asiatic

asidero m. handle; hold

asiduo adj assiduous, diligent, persevering.

asiento m. seat; site, location; bottom; entry (in bookkeeping), -s dregs, sediment.

asignación f assignment, allowance

asignar v. to assign; to allot, to attribute; to appoint.

asilado m. inmate (of an asylum).

asilar v. to house, shelter; to put in an asylum.

asilo m. asylum, refuge, shelter

asimilar v to assimilate, digest, absorb; to liken, compare.

asimismo adv. likewise, also

asir[22] v. irr to seize, take hold of.

asistencia *f.* presence; attendance; assistance, help; *Am.* sitting room; **-s** allowance; *Am.* **casa de —** boarding house.

asistente *m.* assistant; helper; military orderly; *Am.* servant; **los -s** those present.

asistir *v.* to attend, be present; to help; *Am.* to board, serve meals.

asno *m.* ass, donkey.

asociación *f.* association.

asociado *m.* associate.

asociar *v.* to associate; **-se** to join; to associate.

asolamiento *m.* devastation, ravage, havoc, destruction.

asolar[2] *v. irr.* to raze; to lay waste; to parch; **-se** to dry up, become parched; to settle (*as liquids*).

asoleado *adj.* sunny; *p.p. of* asolear.

asolear *v.* to sun; **-se** to bask in the sun; to get sunburnt.

asomar *v.* to show, appear; **— la cabeza** to stick one's head out; **-se** to look out (*of a window*); to peep out (*or* into); *Am.* to draw near, approach.

asombrar *v.* to astonish, amaze; to frighten; to cast a shadow; to darken; **-se** to be astonished, be amazed.

asombro *m.* astonishment, amazement; fright.

asombroso *adj.* astonishing, amazing.

asomo *m.* sign, indication; conjecture, suspicion; **ni por —** by no means.

aspa *f.* wing of a windmill; blade (*of a propeller*); reel (*for winding yarn*).

aspecto *m.* aspect, look, appearance.

aspereza *f.* roughness, ruggedness; harshness; severity.

áspero *adj.* rough, uneven, harsh; gruff.

aspiración *f.* aspiration, ambition, longing; inhalation, breathing in.

aspirante *m. & f.* applicant; candidate.

aspirar *v.* to aspire, long for, seek, to inhale, breathe in; to aspirate (*pronounce an* h *sound*).

asquear *v.* to disgust, nauseate, sicken.

asqueroso *adj.* loathsome, disgusting, sickening, filthy.

asta *f.* horn; antler; mast, pole, staff, flagstaff; lance; **a media —** at half mast.

asterisco *m.* asterisk, star (*used in printing*).

astilla *f.* chip; splinter; splint.

astillar *v.* to chip; to splinter; **-se** to splinter, break into splinters.

astillero *m.* dry dock; shipyard; lumber yard; rack (*for lances or spears*)

astro *m.* star; planet.

astronomía *f.* astronomy; **astrónomo** *m.* astronomer.

astucia *f.* shrewdness, cunning; trick.

asturiano *adj.* Asturian, of or from Asturias, Spain; *m.* Asturian.

astuto *adj.* astute, shrewd, wily, crafty.

asueto *m.* recess, vacation; **día de —** holiday.

asumir *v.* to assume.

asunto *m.* topic, subject matter; business; affair.

asustadizo *adj.* shy, scary, easily frightened, jumpy.

asustar *v.* to frighten, scare.

atacante *m.* attacker; *adj.* attacking.

atacar[6] *v.* to attack; to tighten, fasten; to ram; to plug, wad (*a gun*).

atadura *f.* tie, knot; fastening.

atajar *v.* to intercept; to interrupt, cut off; to take a short cut; to cross out.

atajo *m.* short cut; interception; *Am.* drove. *See* hatajo.

atalaya *f.* lookout, watchtower; *m.* lookout, watchman, guard.

atañer[19, 51] *v.* to concern.

ataque *m.* attack; fit.

atar *v.* to tie, fasten; **-se** to get tied up, to be puzzled or perplexed.

atareado *adj.* busy, over-worked.

atarear *v.* to overwork, load with work; **-se** to toil, work hard; to be very busy.

atascadero *m.* muddy place; obstruction.

atascar[6] *v.* to stop up; to jam, obstruct; **-se** to get stuck; to stick; to jam, get obstructed; to stall.

ataúd *m.* coffin.

ataviar[17] *v.* to attire, deck, adorn; **-se** to dress up, doll up.

atavío *m.* attire, costume; ornaments, finery.

atemorizar[9] *v.* to frighten, scare.

atención *f.* attention, care, thought; courtesy; **-es** business, affairs; **en —** a having in mind, considering.

atender[1] *v. irr.* to heed, pay attention, to attend to, take care of; to take into account or consideration.

atendido *adj. Am.* attentive, courteous.

atenerse[45] *v. irr.* to rely (on); to accept, abide (by).

atenido *adj. Am.* habitually dependent on another; *p.p. of* atenerse.

atentado *m.* offense, violation, crime, violence.

atentar[1] *v. irr.* to attempt, try; **— contra la vida de alguien** to attempt the life of someone.

atento *adj.* attentive; courteous, polite.

atenuar[18] *v.* to attenuate, lessen; to tone down; to dim; to make thin or slender.

ateo *m.* atheist; *adj.* atheistic.

aterciopelado *adj.* velvety.

aterido *adj.* stiff, numb from cold.

aterirse[3,51] *v. irr.* to become numb with cold.

aterrador *adj.* terrifying, appalling.

aterrar *v.* to terrify, frighten.

aterrizaje *m.* landing (*of a plane*); **pista de —** landing strip.

aterrizar[9] *v.* to land (*said of a plane*).

aterronar *v.* to make lumpy, form into lumps; **-se** to lump, form into lumps, become lumpy.

aterrorizar[9] *v.* to terrify, frighten, appall.

atesorar *v.* to treasure; to hoard, lay up, accumulate.

atestado *adj.* crowded, jammed, stuffed; witnessed; *p.p. of* **atestar**.

atestar *v.* to attest, testify, witness; to fill up, cram, stuff, crowd; **-se de** to stuff oneself with; to get stuffed with.

atestiguar[8] *v.* to testify, witness; to attest.

atiborrar *v.* to stuff; **-se** to stuff oneself.

atiesar *v.* to stiffen.

atildado *adj.* spruce, trim; painstaking in dress or style.

atinar *v.* to hit the mark; to guess right.

atisbar *v.* to spy, look cautiously; to watch, pry; to catch a glimpse of; to peek.

atisbo *m.* glimpse; insight; peek; spying.

atizar[9] *v.* to poke, stir (*the fire*); to kindle, rouse; to trim (*a wick*); **— un bofetón** to give a wallop.

atlántico *adj.* Atlantic; **el Atlántico** the Atlantic.

atlas *m.* atlas.

atleta *m. & f.* athlete.

atlético *adj.* athletic.

atletismo *m.* athletics.

atmósfera *f.* atmosphere, air.

atmosférico *adj.* atmospheric.

atole *m. Am.* Mexican drink made of corn meal.

atolondrado *p.p. & adj.* confused, muddled; stunned; heedless, harebrained, thoughtless.

atolondramiento *m.* thoughtlessness, recklessness; confusion, perplexity.

atolondrar *v.* to confuse, muddle, perplex; to stun; **-se** to get muddled, confused; to get stunned.

átomo *m.* atom; small particle, tiny bit.

atónito *adj.* astonished, amazed.

atontado *adj.* stupefied, stupid, stunned.

atontar *v.* to stupefy, stun, to confuse.

atorar *v.* to jam; to stop up, clog; *Am.* to hold up, stop; **-se** to get stuck (*in*

the mud*); to get clogged; to get jammed; to choke (*with food*).

atormentar *v.* to torment; to worry, afflict; to tease, bother, vex.

atornasolado = **tornasolado.**

atornillar *v.* to screw, *Am.* to bother, torment.

atorrante *m. & f. Am.* vagabond, tramp.

atrabancar[6] *v.* to rush awkwardly; to run over; **-se** *Am.* to get involved in difficulties; *Am.* to rush into things.

atrabiliario *adj.* melancholy; bad-tempered.

atracar[6] *v.* to cram, stuff; to moor; to approach land; to hold up, assault; *Am.* to seize; *Am.* to pursue, harass; *Am.* to treat severely; *Am.* to thrash, beat; **— al muelle** to dock, moor to the wharf; **-se** to stuff oneself, overeat; *Am.* to have a fist fight; *Am.* to falter, stutter; **-se a** to come alongside of (*a ship*).

atracción *f.* attraction.

atraco *m.* holdup, assault; *Am.* **darse un — de comida** to stuff oneself, gorge.

atracón *m.* stuffing, gorging; *Am.* violent quarrel; **darse un — de comida** to stuff oneself, gorge.

atractivo *adj.* attractive; *m.* attractiveness, charm.

atraer[46] *v. irr.* to attract.

atragantarse *v.* to gobble up; to choke (*with food*).

atrancar[6] *v.* to bolt, fasten with a bolt; *Am.* **-le a una cosa** to face something, stand up against something; **-se** to get crammed, obstructed; *Am.* to be stubborn, stick to one's opinion; *Am.* to stuff oneself, choke (*with food*).

atrapar *v.* to trap, ensnare; to seize, grab; to overtake.

atrás *adv.* back; behind; backward; *Am.* **echarse — (or para —)** to back out, go back on one's word.

atrasado *adj.* late; behind time; backward; behind (*in one's work, payments, etc.*); slow (*said of a clock*); *p.p. of* **atrasar.**

atrasar *v.* to delay; to be slow or behind time; **-se** to get behind, lose time; *Am.* to suffer a setback (*in one's health or fortune*).

atraso *m.* backwardness; delay; setback; **-s** arrears.

atravesar[1] *v. irr.* to cross; to walk across; to go through; to pierce; *Am.* to buy wholesale.

atreverse *v.* to dare, risk; to be insolent, saucy.

atrevido *adj.* bold, daring; insolent.
atrevimiento *m.* boldness, daring; insolence.
atribuir [32] *v. irr.* to attribute, ascribe, impute.
atribular *v.* to grieve, distress; -se to grieve; to be distressed.
atributo *m.* attribute, quality.
atril *m.* lectern, reading desk, book stand; music stand.
atrincherar *v.* to intrench, fortify with trenches; -se to intrench oneself.
atrio *m.* court, patio in front of a church; entrance hall.
atrocidad *f.* atrocity.
atronador *adj.* thunderous, deafening.
atronar [2] *v. irr.* to deafen; to stun.
atropellar *v.* to run over, run down, knock down; to trample upon; to insult; — por to knock down, overcome with violence; -se to rush.
atropello *m.* violent act; insult; outrage; trampling.
atroz *adj.* atrocious, awful; inhuman.
atún *m.* tunny fish, tuna fish.
aturdido *adj. & p.p.* stupid, awkward; stunned, bewildered.
aturdimiento *m.* daze, bewilderment, confusion.
aturdir *v.* to stun; to deafen; to bewilder.
audacia *f.* daring, boldness.
audaz *adj.* daring, bold.
audiencia *f.* audience, hearing; court of justice.
audifor *m.* judge advocate.
auditorio *m.* audience.
auge *f.* boom (*in the market*); boost (*in prices*); topmost height (*of fortune, fame, dignity, etc.*); estar (*or* ir) en — to be on the increase.
augurar *v.* to foretell, predict.
augusto *adj.* venerable; majestic.
aula *f.* schoolroom, classroom; lecture hall.
aullar *v.* to howl; to shriek; to bawl.
aullido *m.* howl.
aumentar *v.* to augment, increase.
aumento *m.* increase, advance, rise.
aun (**aún**) *adv.* even, still, yet.
aunque *conj.* though, although.
aura *f.* breeze; favor, applause; *Am.* bird of prey, buzzard, vulture.
áureo *adj.* golden.
aureola *f.* aureole, halo.
aurora *f.* dawn; beginning; — **boreal** aurora borealis, northern lights.
auscultar *v.* to sound, examine by listening to (*the chest, lungs, heart, etc.*).
ausencia *f.* absence.
ausentarse *v.* to absent oneself; to be

absent; to leave
ausente *adj.* absent.
auspicios *m. pl.* auspices, patronage; omens.
austeridad *f.* austerity, severity, sternness, harshness.
austero *adj.* austere, stern, strict, harsh.
austral *adj.* southern.
austríaco *adj. & m.* Austrian.
austro *m.* south wind.
auténtico *adj.* authentic, true, genuine
auto *m.* auto, automobile; one-act play, writ, order; — **sacramental** one-act religious play; -s proceedings.
autobús *m.* bus, autobus.
autóctono *adj.* indigenous, native.
automático *adj.* automatic.
automotriz *adj.* automotive, self-moving.
automóvil *m.* automobile, auto
automovilista *m. & f.* motorist.
autonomía *f.* autonomy.
autor *m.* author.
autoridad *f.* authority.
autoritario *adj.* authoritative; authoritarian, domineering; bossy.
autorización *f.* authorization, sanction
autorizar [9] *v.* to authorize, give power (to).
auxiliar *v.* to aid, help; *adj.* auxiliary, helping, assisting; *m.* assistant.
auxilio *m.* aid, help.
avaluación *f.* valuation, appraisal, assessment.
avaluar [18] *v.* to value, appraise
avalúo *m.* valuation, appraisal.
avance *m.* advance, progress, headway; advanced payment; attack.
avanzada *f.* advance guard; outpost; advanced unit, spearhead.
avanzar [9] *v.* to advance.
avaricia *f.* avarice, greed.
avariento *adj.* avaricious, miserly; *m* miser.
avaro *adj.* miserly, greedy; *m.* miser.
avasallar *v.* to subject, dominate, subdue.
ave *f.* bird; fowl; — **de corral** domestic fowl; — **de rapiña** bird of prey.
avecindarse *v.* to settle, locate, establish oneself, take up residence (*in a community*)
avellana *f.* hazelnut; **avellano** *m.* hazel; hazelnut tree; **avellanado** *adj.* hazel, light brown.
avena *f.* oats.
avenencia *f.* harmony, agreement; conformity
avenida *f.* avenue; flood.
avenir [48] *v. irr.* to adjust; to reconcile;

-se a to adapt oneself to; -se con alguien to get along with someone.

aventador m. fan (for fanning a fire); ventilator; winnower (machine for separating wheat from chaff).

aventajar v. to excel; to be ahead (of), -se a to get ahead of.

aventar[1] v. irr. to fan, to winnow, blow chaff from grain; to throw out, expel; Am. to pitch, throw; Am. to dry sugar (in the open); Am. to rouse (game); -se to be full of wind; to flee, run away; Am. to attack, hurl oneself (on someone)

aventura f. adventure, risk, danger; chance.

aventurado adj. adventurous, risky; bold, daring

aventurar v. to venture, risk, -se a to risk, run the risk of; to dare

aventurero adj. adventurous, m adventurer.

avergonzar[2,9] v. irr to shame, -se to feel ashamed.

avería f. damage; aviary, birdhouse; Am. misfortune; Am. mischief.

averiar[17] v. to damage, spoil, hurt; -se to become damaged; to spoil.

averiguar[8] v. to find out; to investigate.

aversión f. aversion, dislike, reluctance.

avestruz m. ostrich.

avezado p.p. & adj accustomed; trained, practiced.

aviación f. aviation

aviador m. aviator, flyer, purveyor, provider, Am moneylender (to miners or laborers), promoter

aviar[17] v. to equip, to supply, to prepare, make ready, Am. to lend money or equipment, estar aviado to be surrounded by difficulties; to be in a fix

ávido adj. eager, greedy

avinagrado adj. sour, acid, cross.

avinagrar v. to sour, make sour or acid; -se to sour, become sour

avío m. provision, supply; preparation; Am. loan of money or equipment; -s equipment; -s de pescar fishing tackle.

avión m. airplane; martin (a bird similar to a swallow).

avisar v. to inform, give notice, advise; to announce, to warn.

aviso m. notice, advice, announcement; warning.

avispa f. wasp; **avispero** m. wasp's nest; **avispón** m. hornet.

avispado adj lively, keen, clever, wideawake; Am. frightened, scared

avispar v. to spur, incite; -se to be on the alert; to be uneasy; Am. to become

frightened, scared

avistar v. to glimpse, catch sight of, -se to see each other, meet.

avivar v. to enliven, give life to, to revive; to brighten; to quicken.

avizor adj. alert, watchful.

avizorar v. to spy, watch closely.

aya f. child's nurse, governess, **ayo** m. tutor, guardian.

ayer adv. yesterday.

ayuda f. aid, help.

ayudante m. assistant.

ayudar v. to aid, help.

ayunar v. to fast.

ayunas: en — fasting, en — de totally ignorant of

ayuno m fast, **— de** wholly ignorant of

ayuntamiento m municipal government; town hall.

azabache m. jet; -s jet ornaments.

azada f. spade; hoe, **azadón** m. hoe.

azafrán m. saffron.

azahar m. orange or lemon blossom.

azar m. hazard; chance; accident; disaster

azogue m. quicksilver.

azolvar v. to clog, obstruct, -se to clog, get clogged

azorar v. to disturb, startle, to bewilder; -se to be startled, astonished, to be bewildered, perplexed; to be uneasy

azotaina f flogging, lashing, beating

azotar v. to whip, lash, beat, Am to thresh (rice); — **las calles** to "beat the pavement," walk the streets

azote m. whip; lash with a whip; scourge; affliction, calamity

azotea f. flat roof.

azteca adj., m. & f Aztec

azúcar m. sugar

azucarar v. to sugar, to sweeten, -se to become sweet, Am. to crystallize, turn to sugar.

azucarera f. sugar bowl; sugar mill.

azucarero adj. sugar (used as adj.); m. sugar manufacturer, producer or dealer; sugar bowl.

azucena f. white lily.

azufre m. sulphur.

azul adj. blue; — **celeste** sky-blue; — **marino** navy blue; — **turquí** indigo; Am. **tiempos** -es hard times.

azulado adj. bluish.

azular v. to dye or color blue.

azulejo m. glazed tile, Am. bluebird; adj. bluish.

azuzar[9] v. to urge, egg on, to incite.

B

baba f drivel, slaver, saliva; slime, slimy secretion, Am. small alligator.

babear v. to drivel; to slobber

babero m. baby's bib.

babor m. port, port side (of a ship)

babosear v. to slaver, drivel; to keep one's mouth open; to act like a fool.

baboso adj. driveling, slobbering; slimy; foolishly sentimental; Am. silly, idiotic, foolish; **babosa** f. slug (creature like a snail, but without a shell).

babucha f. slipper; Am. **a —** pickaback, on the back or shoulders.

bacalao, bacallao m. codfish

bacilo m. bacillus.

bacín m. pot, chamber pot; **bacinica** f. chamber pot.

bacteria f. bacterium; **-s** bacteria.

bacteriología f. bacteriology.

bacteriológico adj. bacteriological, pertaining to bacteriology.

báculo m. staff, cane; aid, support.

bache m. rut, hole in the road.

bachiller m. bachelor (one who holds degree); talkative person; **bachillerato** m. bachelor's degree; studies for the bachelor's degree.

badajo m. clapper of a bell, foolish talker.

badana f. sheepskin.

bagaje m. baggage, army pack mule.

bagatela f. trifle.

bagazo m. waste pulp (of sugarcane, olives, grapes, etc.)

bagual adj. Am. wild, untamed, unruly; Am. rude, discourteous; Am. lanky, awkward; m. Am. wild horse.

bahía f. bay, harbor.

bailador m. dancer; adj. dancing.

bailar v. to dance, to spin around

bailarín m. dancer, **bailarina** f. dancer.

baile m. dance, ball; ballet.

bailotear v. to jig, jiggle; to dance poorly; to dance around.

baja f. fall (of prices), war casualty, **dar de —** to discharge, muster out.

bajada f. descent; slope, dip (on a road); **de —** on the way down; **subidas y -s** ups and downs.

bajar v. to go down, to drop (as price or value); to lower; to take or carry down; to humble; **-se** to get down or off; to alight; Am. to stop at a hotel.

bajel m. boat, ship.

bajeza f. vile act or remark, meanness, baseness; degradation.

bajío m. shoal, sand bank; Am. lowland.

bajo adj. low; short; soft, bass (tone or voice); shallow (water); subdued (color); humble; base; **piso —** first floor, ground floor; prep. under, underneath;

m. bass.

bala f. bullet, shot, ball; bale (of cotton).

balada f. ballad.

baladí adj. trivial; flimsy.

balance m. balance; equilibrium; balance sheet; rocking, rolling.

balancear v. to balance; to rock, roll, to swing, sway; to waver.

balanceo m. rocking, rolling, swinging, balancing; wavering; wabbling.

balanza f. balance, scale.

balar v. to bleat.

balaustrada f. balustrade, banisters, railing.

balaustre m. banister

balazo m. shot; bullet wound; adj. Am clever, cunning.

balbucear v. to stammer, stutter, to babble.

balbuceo m. babble.

balcón m. balcony.

baldado m. cripple; adj. & p.p. crippled.

baldar v. to cripple; to trump (a card).

balde m. pail; bucket; **de —** free of charge; **en —** in vain.

baldío adj. barren; fallow, uncultivated; m. fallow land; wasteland

baldón m. infamy, insult.

baldosa f. floor tile; paving stone

balido m. bleat, bleating.

balneario m. bathing resort, adj. pertaining to bathing resorts or medicinal springs.

balompié m. football

balota f. ballot.

balotar v. to ballot, vote.

balsa f. pond, pool, raft, Am. marsh, Am. a species of ceiba (a tropical tree).

bálsamo m. balsam, balm.

baluarte m. bulwark.

ballena f. whale, whalebone.

bambolear v. to sway, swing, rock, **-se** to stagger; to sway

bambú m. bamboo.

banana f. banana, **banano** m. banana tree.

banasta f. large basket.

banca f. bench; card game, banking, banking house.

bancario adj. bank, pertaining to a bank.

bancarrota f. bankruptcy, failure, collapse.

banco m. bank; bench, stool; school (of fish); Am. pile of grain; Am. small hill on a plain.

banda f. band; ribbon, sash, gang, group, party; flock; side, edge, border.

bandada f. flock of birds; Am. gang.

bandeja f. tray; Am. bowl.

bandera *f.* banner, flag; *Am.* **parar uno — to** take the lead, be a gangleader.

banderilla *f.* dart with a small flag or streamers (*used in bullfights*); **clavar a tino una — to** goad or taunt someone; *Am.* **pegar una—** to touch for a loan.

banderillero *m.* bullfighter who sticks the **banderillas** into the bull.

banderín *m.* small flag; signal flag; recruiting office.

banderola *f.* streamer, small banner or flag; pennant.

bandidaje *m.* banditry, highway robbery; bandits.

bandido *m.* bandit, gangster.

bando *m.* decree, proclamation; party, faction.

bandolero *m.* bandit.

bandurria *f.* bandore (*stringed instrument*); *Am.* a species of wading bird.

banquero *m.* banker.

banqueta *f.* bench (*without a back*), stool, footstool; *Am.* sidewalk.

banquete *m.* banquet.

banquetear *v.* to banquet, feast.

banquillo *m.* bench, stool.

bañada *f.* shower, spray; dip, bath.

bañar *v.* to bathe, wash, to dip; **-se** to take a bath.

bañera *f.* bathtub.

bañista *m & f.* bather.

baño *m.* bath, bathtub, cover, coating; **— de María** double boiler, *Am.* **— ruso** steam bath.

baqueta *f.* rod; whip, **-s** drumsticks; **tratar a la — to** treat scornfully, despotically

baquiano, baqueano, *m. Am.* native guide (*through the wilderness, Pampas, etc.*); *adj. Am.* having an instinctive sense of direction.

bar *m.* bar, taproom, tavern.

baraja *f.* pack of cards.

barajar *v.* to shuffle, to mix, jumble together; to scuffle, wrangle; *Am.* to hinder, obstruct.

baranda *f.* railing; **barandal** *m.* banister, railing.

barandilla *f.* balustrade, rail, railing.

barata *f.* barter, exchange, *Am.* bargain sale; *Am.* cockroach.

baratear *v.* to sell cheap; to cheapen; to cut the price of.

baratija *f.* trinket, trifle.

barato *adj.* cheap; *m.* bargain sale; money given by the winning gambler.

baratura *f.* cheapness.

baraúnda *f.* clamor, uproar, clatter.

barba *f.* chin; beard; **-s** whiskers.

barbacoa *f. Am.* barbecue; barbecued meat.

barbado *adj.* bearded.

barbaridad *f.* cruelty, brutality, rudeness; **una — de** a lot of; **¡que — !** what nonsense!; what an atrocity!

barbarie *f.* barbarousness; savagery; lack of culture, ignorance; cruelty, brutality.

bárbaro *adj.* barbarous, cruel, savage; crude, coarse; *m.* barbarian.

barbechar *v.* to plow; to fallow.

barbecho *m.* first plowing; plowed land; fallow, fallow land.

barbería *f.* barbershop.

barbero *m.* barber; *Am.* flatterer.

barbilla *f.* point of the chin.

barbón, barbudo *adj.* bearded.

barca *f.* boat, launch, barge.

barco *m.* boat, ship.

bardo *m.* bard, minstrel, poet.

barniz *m.* varnish; glaze; printer's ink.

barnizar[9] *v.* to varnish; to glaze.

barómetro *m.* barometer.

barquero *m.* boatman; bargeman.

barquillo *m.* rolled wafer.

barquinazo *m.* tumble, bad fall, hard bump, somersault; *Am.* lurch (*of a vehicle or boat*).

barra *f.* bar; rod; railing; sand bar; **— de jabón** bar of soap.

barrabasada *f.* mischief, mean prank; rash, hasty act.

barraca *f.* hut, cabin, *Am.* large shed, warehouse.

barranca *f.,* **barranco** *m.* ravine, gorge, *Am.* cliff.

barreminas *m.* mine-sweeper.

barrena *f.* auger, drill; gimlet (*small tool for boring holes*); spinning dive (*of a plane*)

barrenar *v.* to drill, bore; to scuttle (*a ship*), to blast (*a rock*).

barrendero *m.* sweeper.

barrer *v.* to sweep, to sweep away; *Am.* to defeat; *Am.* **al — altogether,** as a whole.

barrera *f.* barrier, obstacle.

barreta *f.* small iron bar; *Am.* pick, pickaxe.

barrica *f.* cask, keg.

barrida *f. Am.* sweep, sweeping.

barrido *m.* sweep, sweeping; sweepings, *p.p. of* **barrer.**

barriga *f.* belly; bulge.

barrigón, barrigudo *adj.* big-bellied.

barril *m.* barrel, keg.

barrio *m.* district, neighborhood, quarter; **-s bajos** slums.

barro *m.* mud, clay; pimple; *Am.* **hacer** (*or* **cometer**) **un — to** commit a blunder.

barroso *adj.* muddy; pimply; reddish.

barrote *m.* short, thick bar; brace; rung (*of a ladder or chair*).

barruntar *v.* to foresee; to have a presentiment; to conjecture.

barrunto *m.* foreboding, presentiment; guess; hint, indication, sign.

bártulos *m. pl.* household goods; implements, tools.

barullo *m.* hubbub, racket, disorder.

basa *f.* base, pedestal; basis, foundation.

basar *v.* to base; to put on a base.

basca *f.* nausea, sickness to one's stomach; **tener -s** to be nauseated, sick to one's stomach.

báscula *f.* scale (*for weighing*), platform scale.

base *f.* base, basis, foundation.

básico *adj.* basic.

basquear *v.* to heave, try to vomit; to be nauseated, sick to one's stomach.

basquetbol *m.* basketball.

bastante *adj.* enough, sufficient; *adv.* enough.

bastar *v.* to be enough; to suffice.

bastardilla *f.* italic type, italics.

bastardo *adj.* bastard.

bastidor *m.* wing (*of a stage*); frame; embroidery frame; window sash; easel (*support for a picture, blackboard, etc.*); **entre -es** behind the scenes, off stage.

bastilla *f.* hem.

bastimento *m.* supply, provisions; vessel, ship.

basto *adj.* coarse; *m.* club (*in cards*); *Am.* saddle pad.

bastón *m.* cane, walking stick.

basura *f.* rubbish, scraps; garbage; refuse.

basurero *m.* garbage or rubbish dump; manure pile; garbage man, rubbish man; street cleaner.

bata *f.* lounging robe; housecoat, wrapper, dressing gown; smock; **batín** *m.* smock.

batahola *f.* hubbub, racket, uproar.

batalla *f.* battle; struggle.

batallar *v.* to battle, fight, struggle.

batallón *m.* battalion.

batata *f.* sweet potato.

bate *m. Am.* baseball bat.

batea *f.* tray; trough; bowl; barge; *Am.* washtub.

bateador *m. Am.* batter (*in baseball*).

batear *v. Am.* to bat.

batería *f.* battery (*military, naval, or electric*); **— de cocina** set of kitchen utensils; *Am.* **dar —** to raise a rumpus; to plod, work hard.

batidor *m.* beater; scout.

batintín *m.* gong.

batir *v.* to beat, whip; to defeat; to reconnoiter, explore; to flap; *Am.* to rinse (*clothes*); *Am.* to denounce; **-se** to fight; **— palmas** to clap, applaud.

baturrillo *m.* medley, mixture; hodgepodge.

batuta *f.* orchestra conductor's baton or wand; **llevar la —** to lead; to be the leader.

baúl *m.* trunk, chest; **— mundo** large trunk.

bautismo *m.* baptism, christening; **nombre de —** Christian name.

bautista *m. & f.* Baptist; baptizer.

bautizar⁹ *v.* to baptize, christen.

bautizo *m.* christening, baptism.

baya *f.* berry.

bayeta *f.* flannel; flannelette; **bayetón** *m.* thick wool cloth; *Am.* long poncho lined with flannel.

bayo *adj.* bay, reddish-brown.

baza *f.* trick (*cards played in one round*); **meter —** to meddle; to butt into a conversation; **no dejar meter —** not to let a person put a word in edgewise.

bazar *m.* bazaar; department store.

bazo *m.* spleen.

bazofia *f.* scraps, refuse, garbage; dregs.

beatitud *f.* bliss, blessedness.

beato *adj.* blessed; beatified; devout; overpious; hypocritical.

bebé *m.* baby.

bebedero *m.* drinking trough; watering place; spout.

bebedor *m.* drinker; drunkard.

beber *v.* to drink; to drink in, absorb.

bebida *f.* drink, beverage; **dado a la —** given to drink.

beca *f.* scholarship, fellowship; sash worn over the academic gown.

becario *m.* scholar, fellow, holder of a scholarship.

becerro *m.* young bull; calf; calfskin.

becuadro *m.* natural sign (*in music*).

befa *f.* scoff, jeer.

befar *v.* to scoff, jeer at, mock.

bejuco *m.* cane; **silla de —** cane chair.

beldad *f.* beauty.

belga *adj., m. & f.* Belgian.

bélico *adj.* warlike.

beligerante *adj., m. & f.* belligerent.

bellaco *adj.* sly, deceitful; *m.* villain; rascal.

bellaquear *v.* to cheat; to play tricks; *Am.* to rear, stand up on the hind legs; *Am.* to balk; *Am.* to be touchy, over-sensitive.

bellaquería *f.* cunning, trickery; sly

act or remark.

belleza *f.* beauty.

bello *adj.* beautiful.

bellota *f.* acorn.

bendecir[27,52] *v. irr.* to bless.

bendición *f.* benediction, blessing; *Am.* **echarle la — a una cosa** to give something up for lost.

bendito *adj.* blessed; saintly; **es un —** he is a saint, he is a simple soul; *p.p.* of **bendecir.**

benefactor *m.* benefactor; patron.

beneficencia *f.* beneficence, kindness, charity.

beneficiar *v.* to benefit, do good; to cultivate (*land*); to exploit (*a mine*); to treat (*metals*); *Am.* to slaughter (*cattle*) for marketing.

beneficio *m.* benefit; profit; exploitation of a mine; land cultivation; *Am.* fertilizer; *Am.* slaughtering (*of-cattle*).

benéfico *adj.* beneficent, good, kind.

benemérito *m.* worthy, notable; *adj.* worthy.

benevolencia *f.* benevolence, kindness.

benévolo *adj.* benevolent, good, kindly.

benigno *adj.* benign, gentle, mild, kind.

beodo *adj.* drunk; *m.* drunkard.

berenjena *f.* eggplant; *Am.* kind of squash; **berenjenal** *m.* eggplant patch; **meterse uno en un —** to get into a mess.

bergantín *m.* brigantine, brig (*square-rigged ship with two masts*).

bermejo *adj.* crimson, bright red.

bermellón *adj.* vermilion (*bright red*).

berrear *v.* to bellow; to scream; to sing off key.

berrido *m.* bellow, bellowing; scream.

berrinche *m.* fit of anger; tantrum.

berza *f.* cabbage.

besar *v.* to kiss.

beso *m.* kiss.

bestia *f.* beast.

bestialidad *f.* bestiality, brutality.

besugo *m.* sea bream (*a fish*).

besuquear *v.* to kiss repeatedly.

betabel *f. Am.* beet.

betún *m.* bitumen (*combustible mineral*); black pitch; shoeblacking.

Biblia *f.* Bible.

bíblico *adj.* Biblical.

biblioteca *f.* library; set of volumes; bookcase.

bibliotecario *m.* librarian.

bicicleta *f.* bicycle; **biciclista, bicicletista** *m. & f.* bicyclist, bicycle rider.

bicho *m.* insect, bug; any small animal; an insignificant person.

bien *adv.* well; **— que** although; **ahora**
— now then; **más —** rather; **si —** although; *m.* good, benefit; **-es** property; **-es inmuebles** real estate; **-es raíces** real estate.

bienaventurado *adj.* blessed, happy.

bienaventuranza *f.* blessedness; beatitude; bliss.

bienestar *m.* well-being, comfort, welfare.

bienhechor *m.* benefactor.

bienvenida *f.* welcome.

bienvenido *adj.* welcome.

biftec, bistec, bisté *m.* beefsteak.

bifurcación *f.* fork, forking, branching out; railway junction; branch railroad.

bifurcarse[6] *v.* to fork, branch off, divide into two branches.

bigamía *f.* bigamy.

bigote *m.* mustache.

bilis *f.* bile.

billar *m.* billiards; billiard room.

billete *m.* ticket; note; bill, banknote.

billón *m.* billion.

bimestre *m.* two-month period; bimonthly salary, rent, etc; *adj.* bimonthly; **bimestral** *adj.* bimonthly.

biografía *f.* biography.

biología *f.* biology.

biombo *m.* folding screen.

birlar *v.* to snatch away; to steal; to kill or knock down with one blow.

bisabuelo *m.* great-grandfather; **bisabuela** *f.* great-grandmother.

bisagra *f.* hinge.

bisiesto *adj.* leap (*year*).

bisojo *adj.* squint-eyed.

bisturí *m.* bistoury, surgical knife.

bitoque *m.* barrel plug, stopper; *Am.* faucet; *Am.* injection point (*of a syringe*).

bizarría *f.* gallantry, bravery; generosity.

bizarro *adj.* gallant, brave; generous.

bizco *adj.* cross-eyed.

bizcocho *m.* hardtack, hard biscuit; cooky; **— borracho** cake dipped in wine.

biznieto *m.* great-grandson; **biznieta** *f.* great-granddaughter.

blanco *adj.* white; *m.* white man; blank; blank sheet; target, aim, goal; **— del ojo** white of the eye.

blancura *f.* whiteness.

blancuzco, blanquecino, blanquizco *adj.* whitish.

blandir *v.* to brandish, flourish, swing.

blando *adj.* bland, smooth; soft; **blanducho** *adj.* flabby; soft.

blandura *f.* softness; mildness, gentleness.

blanquear v. to whiten, bleach; to white-wash; to show white; to begin to turn white.

blanqueo m. whitening, bleach, bleaching.

blanquillo adj. whitish; white (flour); m. Am. egg; Am. white peach.

blasfemar v. to blaspheme, curse, swear.

blasfemia f. blasphemy.

blasón m. coat of arms; honor, glory.

blasonar v. to boast.

blindaje m. armor, armor plating.

blindar v. to armor.

bloc m. Am. tablet, pad of paper.

blondo adj. blond.

bloque m. block (of stone, wood, etc.); Am. tablet, pad of paper; Am. political block.

bloquear v. to blockade.

bloqueo m. blockade.

blusa f. blouse.

boato m. pomp, ostentation.

bobada f. foolishness, folly.

bobalicón adj. foolish, silly; m. simpleton, blockhead, dunce.

bobear v. to act like a fool; to fool around; to gawk, stare foolishly.

bobería f. foolishness, folly; nonsense; foolish remark.

bobina f. bobbin (spool or reel for holding thread); electric coil.

bobo adj. simple, foolish, stupid; m. booby, fool, dunce.

boca f. mouth; opening; — abajo face downward; — arriba face upward; a — de jarro at close range; **bocaza** f. large mouth.

bocacalle f. street intersection.

bocado m. mouthful, morsel, bite; bit (of a bridle); **bocadillo, bocadito** m. snack; sandwich; tidbit; Am. piece of candy.

bocanada f. mouthful; puff (of smoke).

boceto m. sketch; outline; skit.

bocina f. horn; trumpet; automobile horn; speaking tube; megaphone.

bochorno m. sultry weather; suffocating heat; blush, flush; embarrassment.

bochornoso adj. sultry; embarrassing.

boda f. marriage, wedding: — de negros a noisy party; -s de Camacho lavish feast, banquet.

bodega f. cellar; wine cellar; storeroom; warehouse; Am. grocery store; **bodeguero** m. keeper of a wine cellar; liquor dealer; Am. grocer.

bodoque m. wad; lump; dunce; Am. bump, swelling.

bofe m. lung; Am. easy job; **echar uno los -s** to throw oneself into a job;

to work hard; Am. **ser un —** to be a bore; to be repulsive

bofetada f. slap; **bofetón** m. big slap, blow, hard sock, wallop.

boga f. vogue, fashion; rowing; m. rower.

bogar v. to row.

bohemio adj. & m. Bohemian.

bohío m. Am. cabin, shack, hut.

boina f. cap.

bola f. ball; game of bowling; fib, lie; shoe polish; Am. brawl, disturbance, riot, revolution; **no dar pie con —** not to do things right; not to hit the mark; to make mistakes; Am. **darle a la —** to hit the mark.

boleada f. Am. lassoing with **boleadoras**; Am. hunting expedition (with **boleadoras**); Am. shoeshine; Am. affront, insult.

boleadoras f. pl. Am. lasso with balls at the ends.

bolear v. to play billiards; to bowl; to lie, fib; Am. to lasso with **boleadoras**; Am. to entangle; Am. to polish (shoes); Am. to dismiss; Am. to blackball, vote against; Am. to flunk; -se Am. to rear, balk (said of a horse); Am. to blush, be ashamed.

boleta f. certificate; pass; pay order; Am. ballot; Am. first draft of a deed.

boletín m. bulletin.

boleto m. Am. ticket; **boletería** f. Am. ticket office.

boliche m. bowl (wooden ball for bowling); bowling alley; Am. cheap tavern; Am. gambling joint; Am. cheap store or shop, notions' store, variety store.

bolita f. small ball; Am. ballot (small ball used in voting); Am. marble; Am. armadillo.

bolo m. one of the ninepins (used in bowling); dunce, stupid fellow; -s bowls, bowling; **jugar a los -s** to bowl.

bolsa f. bag, purse; stock exchange; Am. pocket.

bolsillo m. pocket; pocketbook.

bolsista m. stockbroker, market operator.

bollo m. bun, muffin; bump, lump; puff (in a dress); tuft (on upholstery); Am. loaf of bread; Am. a kind of tamale; -s Am. difficulties, troubles.

bomba f. bomb; pump; lamp globe; Am. false news; Am. stanza improvised by a dancer; Am. firecracker, skyrocket; Am. satirical remark; Am. large drum; — para incendios fire engine; Am. **estar con una —** to be drunk; **bombita** f. soap bubble; Am. shame, embarrassment.

bombachas *f. pl. Am.* loose-fitting breeches.

bombacho *adj.* loose-fitting (*trousers or breeches*).

bombardear *v.* to bomb.

bombardeo *m.* bombardment, bombing; **avión de —** bomber, bombing plane.

bombardero *m.* bombardier; bomber.

bombear *v.* to bomb; to praise, extol; *Am.* to pump; *Am.* to fire, dismiss; *Am.* to puff hard on a cigar or cigarette.

bombero *m.* fireman; pumper.

bombilla *f.* electric-light bulb; *Am.* kerosene lamp tube; *Am.* small tube for drinking mate.

bombo *m.* large drum; base drum; player on a bass drum; *Am.* pomp, ostentation; *Am.* buttocks, rump; **dar —** to praise, extol (*in the press or newspapers*); *Am.* **darse —** to put on airs; *Am.* **irse uno al —** to fail; *adj.* stunned; *Am.* lukewarm; *Am.* slightly rotten; *Am.* stupid, silly, simple; *Am.* **fruta bomba** papaya (*tropical fruit*).

bombón *m.* bonbon, candy; **— de altea** marshmallow.

bonachón *adj.* good-natured; naive, simple.

bonanza *f.* fair weather; prosperity; rich vein of ore.

bondad *f.* goodness.

bondadoso *adj.* good, kind.

boniato *m. Am.* sweet potato.

bonito *adj.* pretty; *m.* striped tunny (*a fish*).

bono *m.* certificate; bond.

boñiga *f.* dung, manure.

boqueada *f.* gape, gasp.

boquear *v.* to open one's mouth; to gape, gasp; to be dying.

boquete *m.* breach, gap, hole, opening.

boquiabierto *adj.* openmouthed.

boquilla *f.* little mouth; small opening; cigarette or cigar holder; mouthpiece (*of a wind instrument*).

borbollón, borbotón *m.* spurt; spurting; big bubble; bubbling up; **a -es** in spurts.

borbotar *v.* to bubble up; to spurt, gush forth; to boil over.

bordado *m.* embroidery.

bordadura *f.* embroidery.

bordar *v.* to embroider.

borde *m.* border, edge.

bordear *v.* to skirt, go along the edge of; *Am.* to trim with a border; *Am.* to make a **bordo** (*small, temporary dam*); **-se** *Am.* to approach, get near.

bordo *m.* board, side of a ship; tack (*of a ship*); *Am.* ridge (*of a furrow*); *Am.* small dam; **a —** on board.

borla *f.* tassel; doctor's cap; doctor's degree; tuft; powder puff; **tomar uno la —** to get a doctor's degree.

borlarse *v. Am.* to get a doctor's degree.

borrachera *f.* drunkenness; drunken spree.

borrachín *m.* toper.

borracho *adj.* drunk; *m.* drunkard; **borrachón** *m.* drunkard, heavy drinker.

borrador *m.* rough draft; *Am.* rubber eraser.

borrar *v.* to blot out; to erase.

borrasca *f.* storm, tempest.

borrascoso *adj.* stormy.

borrego *m.* lamb; fool, simpleton; *Am.* false news.

borrico *m.* donkey, ass; fool; sawhorse.

borrón *m.* blotch (*of ink*), blot.

borronear *v.* to blot, blotch; to scribble; to blur; to make a rough sketch.

boruca *f.* racket, noise.

boscaje *m.* grove, thicket, woods; landscape (*picture of natural scenery*).

bosque *m.* forest, woods; **bosquecillo** *m.* small forest, grove.

bosquejar *v.* to sketch; to outline.

bosquejo *m.* sketch, plan, outline, rough draft.

bostezar[9] *v.* to yawn.

bostezo *m.* yawn.

bota *f.* leather wine bag; boot; *adj. Am.* stupid, clumsy; *Am.* drunk.

botar *v.* to launch; to fling; to throw away; to bounce; *Am.* to waste, squander; *Am.* to fire, dismiss; **-se** *Am.* to lie down.

botarate *m.* fool; braggart; *Am.* spendthrift.

bote *m.* small jar; boat; bounce; blow; jump; *Am.* liquor bottle; *Am.* jail; **estar de — en —** to be crowded, completely filled up.

botella *f.* bottle.

botica *f.* drugstore.

boticario *m.* druggist.

botija *f.* earthern jug; fat person; *Am.* buried treasure; *Am.* belly; *Am.* **poner a uno como — verde** to dress down, scold, insult a person.

botín *m.* booty, plunder; high shoe; *Am.* sock.

botiquín *m.* medicine cabinet; medicine kit; *Am.* liquor store, wine shop.

botón *m.* bud; button; knob; handle; **-es** bellboy.

bóveda *f.* arched roof; vault, underground cellar; burial place.

boxeador *m.* boxer.

boxear *v.* to box, fight with the fists.
boxeo *m.* boxing.
boya *f.* buoy; float net; *Am.* crease, dent; *Am.* rich mineral vein; *Am.* **estar en la buena** — to be in good humor.
bozal *m.* muzzle; bells on a harness; novice, beginner; negro native of Africa; *Am.* headstall (*of a halter*); *Am.* person (*especially a negro*) who speaks broken Spanish; *Am.* coarse, crude individual; *adj.* green, inexperienced; wild, untamed; stupid.
bozo *m.* down (*on the upper lip*); mustache; outside part of the mouth; headstall (*of a halter*).
bracear *v.* to swing one's arms; to struggle; to crawl, swim with a crawl.
bracero *m.* laborer; **de** — arm in arm; **servir de** — **a una señora** to serve as an escort, give a lady one's arm.
bracete: de — arm in arm.
bramante *m.* hemp cord, hemp string; Brabant linen; *adj.* roaring, bellowing.
bramar *v.* to bellow, roar, howl; to rage.
bramido *m.* roar; howl; bellow.
brasa *f.* red-hot coal.
brasero *m.* brazier (*pan for burning coal*), grate; hearth; *Am.* brick cooking stove.
bravata *f.* bravado, boastfulness, defiance.
bravear *v.* to bluster; to bully.
bravío *adj.* savage, wild; rustic.
bravo *adj.* brave; wild, ferocious; harsh; ill-tempered; *Am.* angry; *Am.* hot, highly seasoned.
bravura *f.* fierceness; courage; bravado, show of boldness.
braza *f.* fathom.
brazada *f.* armful; movement of the arms; **a una** — at arm's length.
brazalete *m.* bracelet.
brazo *m.* arm; branch; -s day laborers; *Am.* **de** — arm in arm; **luchar a** — **partido** to wrestle; to fight hand to hand.
brea *f.* pitch; tar; canvas.
brecha *f.* breach, gap.
bregar [7] *v.* to struggle; to fight.
breña *f.* rough, craggy ground covered with brambles; bramble; **breñal** *m.* brambles; bush country.
breve *adj.* brief, short; **en** — shortly.
brevedad *f.* brevity; shortness.
bribón *adj.* idle, indolent; *m.* rascal, rogue; **bribonazo** *m.* scoundrel, cheat.
brida *f.* bridle; rein.
brigada *f.* brigade.
brillante *adj.* brilliant, bright; *m.* diamond.

brillantez *f.* brilliance, dazzle.
brillar *v.* to shine.
brillo *m.* luster, sparkle, shine.
brincar [6] *v.* to hop, skip, jump, bounce.
brinco *m.* hop, skip, bounce, leap.
brindar *v.* to toast, drink to the health of; to offer.
brindis *m.* toast (*to a person's health*).
brío *m.* vigor, liveliness; valor, courage.
brioso *adj.* lively; brave.
brisa *f.* breeze.
británico *adj.* British.
brizna *f.* particle, chip, fragment; blade of grass.
brocal *m.* curb, curbstone (*of a well*).
brocha *f.* painter's brush; loaded dice; **cuadro de** — **gorda** badly done painting; **pintor de** — **gorda** house painter; **brochada** *f.* stroke of the brush, brush stroke; **brochazo** *m.* blow with a brush; brush stroke.
broche *m.* brooch; clasp, clip, fastener; hook and eye.
broma *f.* jest, joke; fun, merriment; *Am.* disappointment, irritation; **de** — in jest; **fuera de** — all joking aside.
bromear *v.* to joke, jest.
bronca *f.* quarrel, dispute, wrangle; **armar una** — to cause a disturbance, raise a rumpus.
bronce *m.* bronze.
bronceado *adj.* bronzed; bronze-colored; *m.* bronze finish.
bronco *adj.* hoarse; raspy, harsh; coarse, rough; uncouth; wild, untamed (*horse*).
broquel *m.* buckler, shield (*worn on the arm*).
brotar *v.* to shoot forth; to bud; to break out (*on the skin*); to gush, flow; to spring forth.
broza *f.* brushwood, underbrush; rubbish, refuse, trash; coarse, hard brush.
bruces: de — face downward.
bruja *f.* witch; hag; owl; *adj. Am.* broke, poor; **brujo** *m.* sorcerer, magician, wizard.
brújula *f.* compass; magnetic needle; peephole; gun sight.
bruma *f.* mist, fog; **brumoso** *adj.* foggy, misty, hazy.
bruñir [19] *v. irr.* to burnish, polish; to put on make-up.
brusco *adj.* blunt, rude, abrupt.
brutal *adj.* brutal, beastly, savage.
brutalidad *f.* brutality.
bruto *adj.* brutal; stupid; coarse, rough; **peso** — gross weight; **diamante en** — diamond in the rough, unpolished diamond; *m.* brute, beast.

31

bucal adj. oral, pertaining to the mouth.

bucear v. to dive; to dive into, plunge into; to explore thoroughly a subject.

bucle m. curl, ringlet.

buche m. crop (of a bird); mouthful (of water); wrinkle, bag (in clothes); Am. goiter.

budín m. pudding.

buen(o) adj. good; kind; useful; well, in good health; **de buenas a primeras** all of a sudden, unexpectedly, on the spur of the moment; **por la(s) buena(s) o por la(s) mala(s)** willingly or unwillingly, by hook or crook.

buey m. ox.

búfalo m. buffalo.

bufanda f. muffler, scarf.

bufar v. to snort; to puff with anger; **-se** Am. to swell, bulge (as a wall).

bufete m. desk, writing table; lawyer's office.

bufido m. snort.

bufón m. buffoon, jester, clown; adj. comical, funny; **bufonada** f. wisecrack; jest.

bufonear v. to clown; to jest.

buhardilla f. garret, attic; skylight.

buho m. owl.

buhonero m. peddler.

buitre m. vulture.

bujía f. candle; candle power; candlestick; spark plug.

bula f. bull (papal document); papal seal.

bulevar m. boulevard.

bulto m. bulk, volume; lump, swelling; shadow, body; bundle; Am. briefcase; **a —** haphazardly, by guess; **escurrir el —** to dodge; **imagen de —** statue, sculpture; **una verdad de —** an evident truth.

bulla f. shouting, uproar; noisy crowd.

bullicio m. noise, uproar.

bullicioso adj. boisterous, noisy; gay, lively; turbulent, stormy.

bullir[20] v. irr. to boil; to buzz about; to bustle; to stir, move; Am. to deride.

buñuelo m. fritter; botch, poor piece of work.

buque m. ship, boat.

burbuja f. bubble.

burdo adj. coarse.

burgués adj. bourgeois, middle-class.

burla f. jest, mockery; **de — in** jest.

burlador m. practical joker; jester; scoffer; seducer.

burlar v. to mock, ridicule, deceive; **-se de** to scoff at; to make fun of.

burlón m. jester, teaser.

burro m. ass, donkey; Am. stepladder; adj. stupid; **burrito** m. small donkey;

Am. saddle rack.

busca f. search; hunting party; Am. **-s** profit on the side; graft.

buscar[6] v. to seek, search, look for; Am. to provoke.

búsqueda f. search.

busto m. bust (upper part of body).

butaca f. armchair; orchestra seat; **butacón** m. large armchair.

buzo m. diver.

buzón m. mailbox; letter drop.

C

cabal adj. complete, entire; exact; **estar uno en sus -es** to be in one's right mind.

cabalgar[7] v. to ride, mount (a horse); to ride horseback.

caballa f. horse mackerel.

caballada f. herd of horses; Am. nonsense, stupidity, blunder.

caballejo m. nag; poor horse.

caballeresco adj. gentlemanly; knightly; chivalrous, gallant.

caballería f. cavalry; horsemanship; mount, horse; knighthood; chivalry.

caballeriza f. stable; horses of a stable.

caballerizo m. groom, stableman.

caballero m. gentleman; knight, horseman; adj. gentlemanly.

caballerosidad f. chivalry, gentlemanly conduct.

caballeroso adj. chivalrous, gentlemanly.

caballete m. small horse; sawhorse; easel; ridge of a roof; bridge of the nose; Am. knife and fork rest.

caballo m. horse; knight (in chess); Am. stupid or brutal person; **a —** on horseback; **caballuco** m. nag.

cabaña f. hut, cabin; Am. cattle ranch.

cabecear v. to nod; to shake the head; to pitch (as a boat); Am. to begin to rise or fall (said of a river).

cabeceo m. nodding; pitching (of a boat).

cabecera f. head (of bed or table); seat, chief city (of a district).

cabecilla f. small head; m. ringleader.

cabellera f. head of hair, long hair; wig; tail of a comet.

cabello m. hair; **traer algo por los -s** to bring in a far-fetched fact or quotation; **-s de angel** cotton candy.

cabelludo adj. hairy; **cuero —** scalp.

caber[23] v. irr. to fit into, go into; to have enough room for; to befall; **no cabe duda** there is no doubt; **no cabe más** there is no room for more; **no — uno en sí** to be puffed up with pride; **no cabe en lo posible** it is absolutely impossible.

cabestro *m.* halter; leading ox; *Am.* rope, cord; *Am.* advance payment; **cabestrillo** *m.* sling (*for an arm*).

cabeza *f.* head; chief, leader; upper part; capital (*of a district*); *Am.* source (*of a river*); **— de playa** beachhead; **— de puente** bridgehead.

cabezada *f.* butt (*with the head*); bump on the head; nod; shake of the head; pitching (*of a ship*); headgear (*of a harness*).

cabezazo *m.* butt (*with the head*); bump on the head.

cabezudo *adj.* big-headed; hard-headed, pig-headed, stubborn, headstrong.

cabezón *adj.* big-headed; pig-headed, stubborn; *Am.* strong (*liquor*); *m.* large head; cavesson (*iron noseband used in breaking a horse*); *Am.* rapids or whirl-pool in a river.

cabida *f.* space, room, capacity; **tener — con alguien** to have influence with someone.

cabildo *m.* cathedral chapter; municipal council; council room; town hall.

cabina *f.* cabin (*of an airplane*).

cabizbajo *adj.* crestfallen, downcast; pensive.

cable *m.* cable.

cablegrafiar[17] *v.* to cable.

cablegrama *m.* cablegram.

cabo *m.* end, tip, handle; piece of rope; cape, headland; corporal; **al —** finally; **al fin y al —** anyway, in the long run; **de — a rabo** from beginning to end; **estar al — de** to be well informed about; **llevar a —** to carry out, finish.

cabra *f.* goat; *Am.* fraud, trick; *Am.* loaded dice; *Am.* light two-wheeled carriage; **cabrillas** *f. pl.* whitecaps (*small waves with white crests*); Pleiades (*constellation*); game of skipping stones on the water.

cabrío *adj.* goatish; **macho —** he-goat; *m.* herd of goats.

cabriola *f.* caper, leap, hop, skip; somersault; **hacer -s** to cut capers; to prance.

cabriolar *v.* to prance; to caper; to romp, frolic, frisk.

cabrito *m.* kid; **cabritilla** *f.* kid, kid-skin.

cabrón *m.* he-goat; cuckold (*man whose wife is unfaithful*).

cacahuate *m.* peanut.

cacao *m.* cocoa.

cacarear *v.* to cackle; to boast; *Am.* to run away from a fight.

cacareo *m.* cackle.

cacería *f.* hunt, hunting.

cacerola *f.* saucepan.

cacique *m.* chief; political boss; *Am.* tyrant; *Am.* one who leads an easy life.

caciquismo *m.* political bossism (*rule by political bosses*).

cacto *m.* cactus.

cacumen *m.* acumen, keen insight.

cacharro *m.* earthen pot or vase; broken piece of a pot; crude utensil; *Am.* cheap trinket.

cachaza *f.* slowness; calm; rum.

cachazudo *adj.* slow, easy going.

cachetada *f. Am.* slap on the face.

cachete *m.* cheek; slap on the cheek.

cachivache *m.* piece of junk; worthless fellow; *Am.* trinket.

cachorro *m.* cub; small pistol; *Am.* rude, ill-bred person.

cachucha *f.* cap; rowboat; popular Andalusian dance, song and music; *Am.* slap.

cada *adj.* each, every; **— uno** each one; **— y cuando que** whenever; *Am.* **a — nada** every second.

cadalso *m.* gallows; scaffold, platform.

cadáver *m.* corpse; **cadavérico** *adj.* deadly, ghastly, pale, like a corpse.

cadena *f.* chain.

cadencia *f.* cadence.

cadencioso *adj.* rhythmical.

cadera *f.* hip.

cadete *m.* cadet.

caducar[6] *v.* to dote, be in one's dotage; to lapse, expire; to become extinct, fall into disuse.

caduco *adj.* decrepit, very old, feeble; perishable.

caer[24] *v. irr.* to fall; to fall down; to fall off; **-se** to fall down, tumble; **— a** to face, overlook; **— bien a fit**, be becoming; **— en cama** to fall ill; **— en la cuenta** to catch on, get the point; **— en gracia** to please; **al — de la noche** at nightfall; **dejar —** to drop.

café *m.* coffee; café; *Am.* annoyance, bad time.

cafeína *f.* caffein.

cafetal *m.* coffee plantation.

cafetera *f.* coffeepot; woman café owner, coffee vendor or merchant; coffee-bean picker.

cafetero *adj.* pertaining to coffee; *m.* coffee grower; coffee merchant; owner of a café or coffee-house; *Am.* coffee drinker.

cafeto *m.* coffee tree.

caída *f.* fall, drop; descent; **a la — del sol** (*or* **de la tarde**) at sunset.

caimán m. cayman, alligator.

caja f. case, box; — **de ahorros** savings bank; — **de píldora** pillbox; — **fuerte** safe; **echar a uno con -s destempladas** to give someone the gate.

cajero m. cashier; box maker.

cajetilla f. small box; package of cigarettes.

cajón m. large box, chest; drawer; vendor's booth or stand; *Am.* narrow canyon; — **de muerto** coffin; *Am.* — **de ropa** dry-goods and clothing store.

cal f. lime (*mineral*).

calabaza f. pumpkin, squash; gourd; an ignorant person; **dar -s** to jilt, turn down (*a suitor*); to flunk, fail.

calabozo m. dungeon; prison cell.

calado m. drawn work; openwork (*in wood, metal, linen, etc.*), fretwork; draft (*of a ship*).

calamar m. squid, cuttlefish.

calambre m. cramp.

calamidad f. calamity, misfortune.

calandria f. lark, skylark.

calar v. to pierce, penetrate; to soak through; to make openwork (*in cloth, metal*); to cut out a sample of; to probe, search into; **-se el sombrero** to put on one's hat; to pull down one's hat.

calavera f. skull; *Am.* tail light; m. madcap, reckless fellow.

calcar⁶ v. to trace; to copy, imitate.

calceta f. hose, stocking; **hacer —** to knit; **calcetería** f. hosiery shop; hosiery (*business of making hose*).

calcetín m. sock.

calcinar v. to burn, char, heat.

calcio m. calcium.

calco m. tracing, traced copy; exact copy; imitation.

calcular v. to calculate, figure, estimate.

cálculo m. calculation, estimate; calculus; gravel (*in the gall bladder, kidney, etc.*).

caldear v. to heat; to weld; **-se** *Am.* to become overheated, excited; *Am.* to get "lit up", get drunk.

caldera f. boiler; caldron, kettle; **calderilla** f. copper coin.

caldo m. broth; gravy.

calefacción f. heat, heating.

calendario m. calendar; almanac.

caléndula f. marigold.

calentador m. heater.

calentar¹ v. irr. to warm, heat; to spank; *Am.* to annoy, bother; **-se** to warm oneself; to become heated, excited; to be in heat; *Am.* to become angry.

calentura f. fever; *Am.* fit of temper; — **de pollo** feigned illness; **calenturón** m. high fever.

calenturiento adj. feverish; *Am.* tubercular.

caletre m. judgment, acumen, keen insight.

calibrar v. to gauge, measure; to measure the caliber of.

calibre m. caliber; bore, gauge (*of a gun*); diameter (*of a pipe, tube, wire*).

calicanto m. stone masonry.

calicó m. calico, cotton cloth.

calidad f. quality.

cálido adj. warm, hot.

caliente adj. warm, hot; heated; fiery; *Am.* angry; *Am.* bold, brave; m. *Am.* brandy in hot water; **calientito** adj. nice and warm.

calificación f. qualification; grade, mark (*in a course or examination*); judgment.

calificar⁶ v. to qualify; to rate, consider, judge; to grade; *Am.* to compute (*election returns*); **-se** *Am.* to qualify or register (*as a voter*).

caligrafía f. penmanship.

calina f. haze, mist.

cáliz m. chalice; communion cup; cup, goblet; calyx (*of a flower*).

calma f. calm, quiet.

calmante adj. soothing; m. sedative.

calmar v. to calm, quiet, soothe.

calmo adj. calm, quiet.

calmoso adj. calm; soothing; phlegmatic, slow.

calor m. heat, warmth; ardor.

calorífero m. heater, radiator.

calosfrío, calofrío m. chill.

calumnia f. slander.

calumniar v. to slander.

caluroso adj. hot, warm; heated, excited; cordial, enthusiastic.

calva f. bald head; bald spot; barren spot.

calvario m. Calvary, place of the Cross; suffering, tribulation.

calvo adj. bald; barren.

calza f. wedge; shoehorn; *Am.* gold inlay, tooth filling; **-s** breeches.

calzada f. paved road; highway; *Am.* wide avenue.

calzado m. footwear.

calzador m. shoehorn.

calzar⁹ v. to put on (*shoes, gloves, spurs*); to put a wedge under a wheel; *Am.* to fill (*a tooth*).

calzón m. (or **calzones**) breeches, short trousers; *Am.* drawers; *Am.* white cotton trousers; **calzoncillos** m. pl. drawers, men's shorts.

callado adj. silent, quiet.

callar v. to be silent; to hush; **-se** to be or keep silent.

calle f. street.

calleja f. small street, alley, lane; **callejuela** f. small, narrow street; lane.

callejear v. to walk the streets, ramble.

callejero m. street-rambler, street-stroller; street-loiterer; adj. fond of walking the streets; rambling.

callejón m. alley; lane; narrow pass; — **sin salida** blind alley.

callo m. callus, corn; **-s** tripe (food).

calloso adj. callous, hard.

cama f. bed, couch, cot; litter; **caer en— to fall ill; guardar — to be confined to bed;** Am. **tenderle uno la — a otro** to help one in his love affairs; to set a trap for someone; **camastro** m. poor, uncomfortable bed.

camada f. litter; brood.

cámara f. chamber, hall, parlor; house (of a legislative body); cabin, stateroom; chamber (of a gun); — **de aire** inner tube; — **fotográfica** camera.

camarada f. comrade; **camaradería** f. comradeship, companionship.

camarera f. waitress; chambermaid; stewardess.

camarero m. waiter; chamberlain; steward; valet.

camarilla f. political lobby; small group of politicians; "kitchen cabinet," group of unofficial advisers; small room.

camarón m. shrimp.

camarote m. cabin, stateroom.

cambalache m. swap, barter, exchange.

cambalachear v. to swap, barter, exchange.

cambiador m. barterer; money changer; Am. switchman.

cambiante adj. changing; exchanging; **-s** m. pl. iridescent-colors.

cambiar v. to change; to exchange; to shift; — **de marcha** to shift gears.

cambiavía m. Am. railway switchman. See **guardagujas** and **cambiador.**

cambio m. change; exchange; railway switch, **libre —** free trade; **en —** on the other hand; in exchange.

cambista m. exchange broker, banker; Am. railway switchman.

camello m. camel.

camilla f. stretcher; cot; **camillero** m. stretcher bearer.

caminante m. & f. walker, traveler.

caminar v. to travel; to walk; Am. to progress, prosper.

caminata f. long walk; hike; jaunt.

camino m. road; course; Am. table runner; Am. hall-runner; — **de hierro**

railroad; — **real** highway; **de —** on the way.

camión m. truck; wagon; Am. bus; **camionero** m. truck driver; **camioneta** f. small truck; Am. bus.

camisa f. shirt; — **de fuerza** strait jacket; **meterse en — de once varas** to attempt more than one can manage, bite off more than one can chew; **camiseta** f. undershirt.

camisón m. long shirt; Am. nightgown; Am. gown, dress.

camote m. Am. a kind of sweet potato.

campamento m. encampment; camp.

campana f. bell; Am. spy, lookout (for thieves); **campanada** f. stroke of a bell; Am. **por — de vacante** once in a blue moon, very seldom.

campanario m. bell tower.

campanilla f. small bell; bubble; uvula; tassel; bell-flower.

campanillazo m. loud ring of a bell.

campanilleo m. ringing; tinkling.

campaña f. level, open country; campaign; period of active service.

campear v. to pasture; to grow green (said of the fields); to excel; to be prominent, stand out; to be in the field; Am. to search the plains for lost cattle; Am. to act the bully.

campechano adj. frank, open.

campeón m. champion; defender.

campeonato m. championship.

campesino adj. rural, rustic; m. peasant, countryman; farmer.

campestre adj. rural, rustic.

campiña f. large field; open country.

campo m. country; field; camp; **a — raso** in the open; **a — traviesa** (or **travieso**) cross-country.

camposanto m. churchyard, cemetery.

camuesa f. pippin (a variety of apple).

camuflaje m. camouflage.

can m. dog; trigger (of a gun).

cana f. white hair, grey hair; Am. a kind of palm; **echar una — al aire** to go out for a good time; to go out on a fling.

canadiense adj., m. & f. Canadian.

canal m. canal, channel; f. eaves trough.

canalla f. rabble, mob; m. mean fellow.

canana f. cartridge belt; **-s** Am. handcuffs.

canapé m. couch, lounge, sofa; settee.

canario m. canary; native of the Canary Islands; interj. great Scott!

canasta f. basket; crate.

cancelación f. cancellation.

cancelar v. to cancel.

canciller m. chancellor.

canción f. song; a kind of lyric poem; **volver a la misma —** to repeat, harp on the same thing.

cancha f. court (for tennis, etc.); sports ground or field; cockpit, enclosure for cockfights; Am. roasted corn or beans; Am. ¡abran — ! gangway!; make room!

candado m. padlock; Am. goatee.

candela f. candle; fire, forest fire; light.

candelero m. candlestick.

candente adj. incandescent, white-hot, red-hot.

candidato m. candidate.

candidatura f. candidacy.

candidez f. candor, simplicity.

cándido adj. candid, simple, innocent; white.

candil m. lamp; Am. chandelier; **candileja** f. small oil lamp; oil receptacle (of a lamp); -s footlights (of a stage).

candor m. candor, simplicity, innocence; frankness, sincerity.

canela f. cinnamon; an exquisite thing.

cangrejo m. crab.

canguro m. kangaroo.

caníbal m. cannibal.

canica f. marble (small glass or marble ball).

canilla f. long bone (of the arm or leg); cock (of a barrel), faucet; spool (for a sewing maching); Am. slender leg; Am. calf (of the leg); Am. **tener —** to have physical strength; **canillita** m. Am. newspaper boy.

canino adj. canine; **tener un hambre canina** to be ravenous; to be hungry as a dog.

canje m. interchange, exchange.

canjear v. to exchange, interchange.

cano adj. grey-headed, grey-haired.

canoa f. canoe.

canon m. canon; precept, rule, principle.

canónigo m. canon (churchman).

canonizar[9] v. to canonize, saint.

canoso adj. grey, grey-haired.

cansado adj. tired; tiresome, boring.

cansancio m. fatigue, weariness.

cansar v. to tire, fatigue; -se to get tired.

cantar v. to sing; to squeal, confess; Am. — **alto** to ask a high price; — **claro** (or -las claras) to speak with brutal frankness; m. song, epic poem.

cántaro m. pitcher, jug.

cantatriz f. singer.

cantera f. quarry; Am. stone block.

cántico m. canticle, religious song.

cantidad f. quantity.

cantilena f. song, ballad; monotonous repetition.

cantimplora f. canteen; metal vessel for cooling water; Am. flask for carrying gunpowder.

cantina f. mess hall; wine cellar; wine shop; canteen; Am. barroom, tavern; Am. saddlebag.

cantinela = cantilena.

cantinero m. bartender; tavern keeper.

canto m. song; singing; canto (division of a long poem); stone; edge; Am. lap; Am. piece.

cantón m. canton, region; corner; Am. cotton cloth.

cantor m. singer; song bird.

canturrear, canturriar v. to hum, sing softly.

canturreo m. hum, humming.

caña f. cane, reed; tall, thin glass; stem; Am. sugar-cane brandy; Am. a kind of dance; Am. bluff, boast.

cañada f. narrow canyon, dale, dell, gully, ravine; Am. brook.

cáñamo m. hemp; hemp cloth; Am. hemp cord, rope; **cañamazo** m. canvas.

cañaveral m. cane field; reed patch; sugar-cane plantation.

cañería f. conduit, pipe line; tubing, piping; gas or water main.

caño m. pipe, tube; spout; sewer; narrow channel; Am. branch of a river, stream.

cañón m. cannon, gun; barrel (of a gun); ravine, gorge, canyon; tube, pipe; beard stubble; pinfeather; quill (of a feather); chimney shaft; **cañonazo** m. cannon shot.

cañonear v. to cannonade, bombard.

cañoneo m. cannonade; bombardment.

cañonero m. gunboat; gunner; **lancha cañonera** gunboat.

caoba f. mahogany.

caos m. chaos, confusion.

capa f. cape, cloak; covering, coating; layer; scum; **so —** under the guise of, under pretense of.

capacidad f. capacity; ability

capacitar v. to enable, prepare, fit, qualify; Am. to empower, authorize.

capataz m. boss, foreman, overseer.

capaz adj. capable, able, competent; spacious, roomy.

capellán m. chaplain, priest, clergyman.

caperuza f. pointed hood.

capilla f. chapel; hood.

capirote m. hood; **tonto de —** dunce, plain fool.

capital m. capital, funds; f. capital, capital city; adj. capital; **capitalismo** m. capitalism; **capitalista** m. & f.

36

capitalist; adj. capitalistic.

capitalizar[9] v. to capitalize.

capitán m. captain.

capitanear v. to command, lead.

capitolio m. capitol.

capitular v. to surrender; to come to an agreement.

capítulo m. chapter.

caporal m. boss, leader; Am. foreman in a cattle ranch.

capote m. cloak (with sleeves); bullfighter's cloak; Am. thrashing, beating; decir para su — to say to oneself; Am. de — in an underhanded way; Am. dar — to get ahead; to deceive.

capricho m. caprice, whim, notion.

caprichoso adj. capricious, whimsical; changeable, fickle.

caprichudo adj. whimsical; stubborn, willful.

cápsula f. capsule; percussion cap, cartridge shell; metal cap (on bottles).

captar v. to win, attract; to captivate; Am. to get, tune in on (a radio station).

captura f. capture.

capturar v. to capture, arrest.

capucha f. hood.

capullo m. cocoon, bud; acorn cup.

cara f. face; expression, countenance; front; de — opposite; echar (or dar) en — to reproach, blame; sacar la — por alguien to take someone's part, defend him.

carabina f. carbine, rifle.

caracol m. snail; winding stairs; Am. embroidered blouse; Am. curl.

caracolear v. to caper, prance around (said of horses); Am. to muddle, entangle; Am. to sidestep an obligation.

caracoleo m. prancing around; winding, turn.

carácter m. character; temper.

característico adj. characteristic; característica f. characteristic, trait.

caracterizar[9] v. to characterize.

¡caramba! interj. great guns! great Scott!

carámbano m. icicle.

caramelo m. caramel

caramillo m. reed pipe, small flute; armar un — to raise a rumpus, create a disturbance.

carancho m. Am. hawk, buzzard.

carátula f. mask; Am. title page of a book; Am. dial, face of a watch.

caravana f. caravan.

carbólico adj. carbolic.

carbón m. carbon; coal; — de leña charcoal; carbono m. carbon.

carbonera f. coal bin; coal cellar; woman coal or charcoal vendor; Am. coal

mine; carbonero m. coal dealer; charcoal vendor; adj. coal, relating to coal or charcoal.

carburador m. carburetor.

carcajada f. loud laughter, peal of laughter.

cárcel f. jail, prison.

carcelero m. jailer; adj. relating to a jail.

carcomido adj. worm-eaten; decayed.

cardar v. to card, comb (wool).

cardenal m. cardinal; cardinal bird; bruise.

cárdeno adj. dark-purple.

cardo m. thistle; a kind of cactus.

carear v. to confront, bring face to face; to compare; -se to meet face to face.

carecer[13] v. irr. to lack, be in need of.

carencia f. lack, want.

carente adj. lacking.

carero adj. overcharging; profiteering; m. profiteer.

carestía f. dearth, scarcity; high price.

careta f. mask.

carga f. load, burden; freight; cargo; charge of gunpowder; volver a la — to insist again and again.

cargado p.p. & adj. loaded; strong (as tea or coffee); cloudy, sultry; — de espaldas round-shouldered, stoop-shouldered.

cargador m. loader; stevedore; Am. carrier, errand boy, mover.

cargamento m. cargo.

cargar[7] v. to load; to charge; to bother, annoy; Am. to carry, lug; Am. to punish; — con to carry away; to assume (responsibility); — con el muerto to get the blame (unjustly).

cargo m. charge, position, duty, burden, loading; accusation; hacerse — de to take charge of; to realize.

carguero adj. load-carrying; freight-carrying; m. Am. beast of burden; Am. skilled loader of pack animals; Am. patient, long-suffering person.

caribe adj. Caribbean; m. Carib, Caribbean Indian; cannibal; savage.

caricatura f. caricature; cartoon.

caricia f. caress.

caridad f. charity; alms.

caries f. decay (of a bone), tooth decay.

cariño m. affection, love; Am. gift.

cariñoso adj. affectionate, loving.

caritativo adj. charitable.

carmesí adj. & m. crimson.

carmín m. crimson.

carnal adj. carnal, sensual.

carnaval m. carnival.

carne *f.* meat; flesh; — **de gallina** "goose flesh", "goose pimples"; **echar -s** to put on weight, get fat; *Am.* — **de res** beef.

carneada *f. Am.* butchering, slaughtering.

carnear *v. Am.* to butcher; *Am.* to kill.

carnero *m.* ram, male sheep; mutton; *Am.* a weak-willed person; *Am.* waste basket; *Am.* — **de la tierra llama** (*or any fleece-bearing animal*); *Am.* **cantar uno el** — to die.

carnicería *f.* meat market; butchery, slaughter; *Am.* slaughterhouse.

carnicero *m.* butcher; *adj.* carnivorous, flesh-eating; cruel.

carnívoro *adj.* carnivorous.

carnosidad *f.* fleshiness, fatness; abnormal growth (*on animal or plant tissues*).

carnoso *adj.* fleshy, meaty; pulpy

caro *adj.* expensive; dear; *adv.* at a high price.

carona *f.* saddle pad.

carozo *m.* cob, corncob.

carpa *f.* carp (*fresh-water fish*), *Am.* canvas tent, circus tent; — **dorada** goldfish.

carpeta *f.* table cover; desk pad, portfolio, letter case or file; *Am.* office desk; *Am.* bookkeeping department; **carpetazo: dar** — to table (*a motion*); to set aside, pigeonhole or dismiss.

carpintería *f.* carpentry; carpénter's workshop.

carpintero *m.* carpenter, **pájaro** — woodpecker.

carraspear *v.* to cough up, to clear one's throat; to be hoarse.

carraspera *f.* hoarseness.

carrera *f.* career; race, run, course; stocking run.

carreta *f.* long, narrow wagon; cart; *Am.* wheelbarrow

carretaje *m.* cartage (*transporting by cart, truck, etc.*); price paid for cartage.

carrete *m.* spool; reel.

carretel *m.* reel, spool, bobbin, fishing reel; log reel (*of a boat*).

carretera *f.* highway.

carretero *m.* carter, teamster, cart maker; **camino** — highway.

carretilla *f.* wheelbarrow; small cart, baggage truck; *Am.* wagon; *Am.* jaw; *Am.* string, series (*of lies, blunders, etc.*); *Am.* firecracker; **repetir de** — to rattle off, repeat mechanically.

carretón *m.* truck; wagon, cart.

carril *m.* rail; rut; furrow.

carrillo *m.* cheek; pulley; small cart.

carro *m.* cart; cartload *Am.* car, auto, streetcar, coach; *Am.* **pararle a uno el** — to restrain someone; *Am.* **pasarle a uno el** — to suffer an injury or misfortune; **carroza** *f.* large and luxurious carriage; chariot.

carroña *f.* dead and decaying flesh, putrid, decaying carcass.

carruaje *m.* carriage, vehicle.

carta *f.* letter; playing card; charter; map; — **blanca** full authority, freedom to act; — **de naturaleza** naturalization papers; — **de venta** bill of sale; *Am.* **retirar** — to repent, back down; *Am.* **ser la última** — **de la baraja** to be the worst or most insignificant person or thing.

cartearse *v.* to correspond, write to each other.

cartel *m.* poster, handbill; cartel, written agreement; **cartela** *f.* tag, slip of paper, small card, piece of cardboard; **cartelera** *f.* billboard; **cartelón** *m.* large poster.

cartera *f.* wallet, briefcase, desk pad, portfolio, position of a minister or cabinet member.

cartero *m.* mailman, letter carrier, postman.

cartilla *f.* primer; note, short letter; **leerle a uno la** — to scold, lecture someone concerning his duties.

cartografiar[17] *v.* to chart; to make charts.

cartón *m.* cardboard, pasteboard; **cartulina** *f.* fine cardboard.

cartuchera *f.* cartridge belt.

cartucho *m.* cartridge; roll of coins; paper cone or bag.

casa *f.* house, home; household; business firm; square (*of a chessboard*); *Am.* bet, wager; — **de empeños** pawnshop; — **de huéspedes** boardinghouse; **echar la** — **por la ventana** to spend recklessly, squander everything; **poner** — to set up housekeeping.

casabe, cazabe *m. Am.* cassava; *Am.* cassava bread.

casaca *f.* long military coat; **volver** — to be a turncoat, change sides or parties.

casamiento *m.* wedding; marriage.

casar *v.* to marry; to match; *Am.* to graft (*trees*); **-se** to get married.

cascabel *m.* jingle bell, tinkle bell; snake's rattle; *Am.* rattlesnake; **cascabela** *f. Am.* rattlesnake.

cascada *f.* cascade, waterfall.

cascajo *m.* coarse gravel; crushed stone;

pebble; fragment; rubbish.

cascanueces *m.* nutcracker.

cascar[6] *v.* to crack, break; **-se** to crack or break open.

cáscara *f.* shell, husk, hull, rind; bark of a tree; *Am.* **dar a uno — de novillo** to give someone a whipping; **cascarudo** *adj.* having a thick husk; having a thick rind.

cascarrabias *m.* & *f* crab, grouch, ill-tempered person; *adj.* grouchy, cranky, irritable.

casco *m.* helmet, hoof; skull; broken piece of earthenware; cask; empty bottle; hull of a ship; *Am.* compound, main buildings of a farm; **caliente de -s** hot-headed; **ligero de -s** light-headed, frivolous; **romperse los -s** to rack one's brain.

caserío *m.* hamlet, small settlement.

casero *adj.* domestic; homemade; *m.* landlord; janitor, caretaker; *Am.* customer; *Am.* delivery boy; **casera** *f.* landlady; housekeeper.

caseta *f* small house, cottage; booth, stall

casi *adv.* almost.

casilla *f.* stall, booth; square (*of a checkerboard*); pigeonhole; post-office box; **sacarle a uno de sus -s** to change someone's way of life or habits; to irritate, annoy, try someone's patience; **salirse de sus -s** to lose one's temper; to do something out of the way.

casino *m.* club, society, clubhouse; recreation hall.

caso *m.* case; point; matter; event; **— que** (*or* **en — de que**) in case that; **dado** — supposing; **hacer — de** to pay attention to; **hacer — omiso de** to omit; **no viene al —** that is not to the point.

casorio *m.* wedding, marriage.

caspa *f.* dandruff.

casta *f.* race, breed; caste, distinct class; quality, kind.

castaña *f.* chestnut; jug; knot or roll of hair; *Am.* small barrel; *Am.* trunk, large suitcase.

castañetear *v.* to rattle the castanets; to chatter (*said of the teeth*); to crackle (*said of the knees or joints*); **— con los dedos** to snap one's fingers.

castañeteo *m.* rattle or sound of castanets; chatter, chattering (*of the teeth*).

castaño *m.* chestnut (*tree and wood*); *adj.* chestnut-colored.

castañuela *f.* castanet.

castellano *adj.* & *m.* Castilian.

castidad *f.* chastity.

castigar[7] *v.* to chastise, punish.

castigo *m.* punishment; correction.

castillo *m.* castle.

castizo *adj.* pure, correct (*language*); pure-blooded.

casto *adj.* chaste, pure.

castor *m.* beaver; beaver cloth.

casual *adj.* casual, accidental.

casualidad *f.* chance, accident.

casuca *f.* little house; hut, shanty.

casucha *f.* hut, hovel, shack.

catadura *f.* aspect, appearance.

catalán *adj.* Catalan, Catalonian, or of from Catalonia, Spain; *m.* Catalan.

catalogar[7] *v.* to catalogue.

catálogo *m.* catalogue.

catar *v.* to look at, examine; to taste, sample.

catarata *f.* cataract; waterfall.

catarro *m.* catarrh, cold.

catástrofe *f.* catastrophe, mishap.

catear *v.* to explore, look around; *Am.* to search or raid (*a home*); *Am.* to explore for ore; *Am.* to test, try.

catecismo *m.* catechism.

cátedra *f.* class; subject; chair, professorship.

catedral *f.* cathedral.

catedrático *m.* professor.

categoría *f* category, rank; kind, class.

categórico *adj.* categorical, positive.

catequizar[9] *v.* to catechize, give religious instruction (to); to induce, persuade.

católico *adj.* Catholic; universal; *m.* Catholic; **catolicismo** *m.* Catholicism.

catre *m.* cot, small bed; *Am.* raft, float; *Am.* camp stool, folding stool; **— de tijera** folding cot.

catrín *m.* *Am.* dandy; *adj.* *Am.* over-elegant, dressy.

cauce *m.* river bed.

caución *f.* precaution; security, guarantee; bail.

cauchero *m.* *Am.* rubber gatherer; *Am.* rubber producer; *adj.* *Am.* rubber, pertaining to rubber.

caucho *m.* rubber; *Am.* rubber tree; *Am.* rubber raincoat or cloak; **cauchal** *m.* rubber grove or plantation.

caudal *m.* wealth; river current; volume of water.

caudaloso *adj.* wealthy; abundant.

caudillaje *m.* military leadership; *Am.* political bossism; *Am.* tyranny.

caudillo *m.* leader, chief; *Am.* political boss.

causa *f.* cause; case, lawsuit; *Am.* light lunch, snack.

causar v. to cause.

cautela f. caution; cunning, craftiness; trick, deception.

cauteloso adj. cautious; crafty.

cautivar v. to capture; to charm, fascinate.

cautiverio m captivity.

cautivo m. captive, war prisoner.

cauto adj. cautious.

cavar v. to dig, spade; to excavate.

caverna f. cavern, cave.

cavernoso adj. cavernous, like a cavern, hollow; **voz cavernosa** deep, hollow voice.

cavidad f. cavity.

cayado m. shepherd's crook, staff

cayo m. key, island reef.

caza f. hunt, hunting; wild game; **dar —** to pursue, track down.

cazador adj. hunting; m. hunter.

cazar[9] v. to chase, hunt; to track down.

cazatorpedero m. destroyer, torpedo-boat.

cazo m. dipper; pot, pan.

cazuela f. stewing pan; earthenware cooking pan; topmost theatre gallery; Am. stewed hen; Am. candied sweet potatoes with spices.

cebada f. barley; Am. brewing of **mate**; **cebadal** m. barley field.

cebar v. to feed, fatten (animals); to encourage, nourish (a passion); to prime (a gun, pump, etc.); to bait (a fishhook); Am. to brew and serve mate or tea; **-se** to vent one's fury.

cebo m. feed (for animals); bait; incentive.

cebolla f. onion.

cecear v. to lisp.

ceceo m. lisp, lisping.

cecina f. dried beef, jerked beef.

cedazo m. sieve.

ceder v. to cede, transfer; to yield, surrender, submit; to diminish, abate.

cedro m. cedar.

cédula f. slip of paper; certificate; **— de vecindad** (or **— personal**) official identification card.

céfiro m. zephyr, soft breeze; Am. fine muslin.

cegar[1],[7] v. irr. to blind; to become blind; to confuse; to fill up, stop up (a hole).

ceguedad, ceguera f. blindness.

ceiba f. Am. ceiba, silk-cotton tree.

ceja f. eyebrow; brow of a hill.

cejar v. to go backward; to back; to back down, give in, yield; to slacken.

cejijunto adj. frowning; with knitted eyebrows.

celada f. ambush, snare, trap.

celaje m. colored clouds; skylight; presage, portent; Am. shadow, ghost; Am. **como un —** like lightning.

celar v. to guard, watch; to watch over jealously; to conceal.

celda f. cell.

celebración f. celebration.

celebrar v. to celebrate; to praise, honor; to be glad.

célebre adj. famous; funny, witty; Am. graceful, pretty (woman).

celebridad f. fame, renown; celebrity, famous person; celebration.

celeridad f. swiftness, speed.

celeste adj. celestial, heavenly.

celestial adj. celestial, heavenly, divine.

célibe adj. unmarried; m. & f. unmarried person.

celo m. zeal, ardor; envy; heat (sexual excitement in animals); **-s** jealousy, suspicion, **tener -s** to be jealous.

celosía f. window lattice; Venetian blind.

celoso adj. jealous; zealous, eager; suspicious.

célula f. cell.

celuloide m. celluloid.

cellisca f. sleet; rain and snow.

cementar v. to cement.

cementerio m. cemetery.

cemento m. cement; **— armado** reinforced concrete.

cena f. supper.

cenagal m. quagmire, muddy ground, swamp.

cenagoso adj. muddy, miry.

cenar v. to eat supper.

cencerrada f. racket, noise (with cowbells, tin cans, etc.); tin pan serenade.

cencerrear v. to make a racket (with cowbells, tin cans, etc.).

cencerro m. cowbell.

cendal m. gauze; thin veil.

cenicero m. ash tray; ash pit; ash pan.

ceniciento adj. ashen, ash-colored.

cenit m. zenith.

ceniza f. ashes, cinders.

cenizo adj. ash-colored.

censo m. census.

censor m. censor.

censura f. censure, criticism, disapproval; censorship.

censurador m. censor, critic; critical person; adj. critical.

censurar v. to censure, criticize, reprove; to censor.

centavo m. cent.

centella f. lightning, flash; spark.

centelleante adj. sparkling; flashing.

centellear v. to twinkle; to sparkle,

glitter; to flash.

centelleo *m.* glitter, sparkle.

centenar *m.* one hundred; field of rye.

centenario *m.* centennial, one hundredth anniversary; *adj.* centennial; old ancient.

centeno *m.* rye.

centésimo *adj.* & *m.* hundredth.

centímetro *m.* centimeter (*one hundredth part of a meter*).

céntimo *m.* one hundredth part of a peseta.

centinela *m.* sentry, sentinel.

central *adj.* central; *f.* main office; headquarters; *Am.* main sugar mill or refinery.

centrar *v.* to center.

céntrico *adj.* central.

centro *m.* center, middle.

ceñidor *m.* girdle, belt, sash.

ceñir[5, 19] *v. irr.* to gird, girdle; to tighten; to encircle; to diminish; to limit; **-se a** to limit oneself to.

ceño *m.* frown; scowl; **fruncir el —** to frown; to scowl.

cepa *f.* stump, stub (*of a tree or plant*); vinestock; origin, stock (*of a family*); *Am.* mass of plants growing from a common root; *Am.* excavation (*for a building*), hole, pit (*for planting trees*); **de buena —** of good stock.

cepillo *m.* brush; alms box; carpenter's plane; *Am.* flatterer; **— de dientes** toothbrush.

cera *f.* wax.

cerámica *f.* ceramics, pottery.

cerca *adv.* near, near by; **— de** *prep.* near, nearly; *f.* fence, low wall.

cercado *m.* enclosure; fenced-in garden; fence; *Am.* Peruvian political division; *p.p.* of **cercar.**

cercanía *f.* proximity; **-s** surroundings, vicinity.

cercano *adj.* near; neighboring.

cercar[6] *v.* to fence, enclose; to surround; to besiege.

cercenar *v.* to clip off; to curtail, diminish, reduce.

cerciorar *v.* to assure, affirm; **-se** to ascertain, find out.

cerco *m.* fence, enclosure; siege; circle; *Am.* small farm or orchard.

cerda *f.* bristle; *Am.* **ir en -s** to go halves or share in a deal.

cerdo *m.* hog, pig; pork.

cerdoso *adj.* bristly.

cereal *m.* cereal, grain.

cerebro *m.* brain.

ceremonia *f.* ceremony.

ceremonial *adj.* & *m.* ceremonial.

ceremonioso *adj.* ceremonious.

cereza *f.* cherry; **cerezo** *m.* cherry tree; cherry wood.

cerilla *f.* wax taper; wax match; earwax.

cerillo *m. Am.* match.

cerner[1] *v. irr.* to sift; to drizzle; *Am.* to strain through a sieve; **-se** to hover (*as a bird or plane*).

cero *m.* zero; nothing.

cerquita *adv.* quite near, nice and near.

cerrado *adj.* closed; cloudy; thick (*beard*); reserved (*person*); dull; *Am.* stubborn.

cerradura *f.* locking, closing; lock; **— de golpe** spring lock.

cerrajería *f.* locksmith's shop; locksmith's trade.

cerrajero *m.* locksmith.

cerrar[1] *v. irr.* to close, shut, lock; **-se** to close; **-se el cielo** to become overcast or cloudy.

cerrazón *f.* cloudiness, darkness.

cerro *m.* hill.

cerrojo *m.* latch, bolt.

certamen *m.* contest, literary contest; debate; competition.

certero *adj.* accurate, exact; well-aimed; **tirador —** good shot.

certeza *f.* certainty.

certidumbre *f.* certainty.

certificado *adj.* certified, registered; *m.* certificate.

certificar[6] *v.* to certify; to register (*a letter*).

cervato *m.* fawn, young deer.

cerveza *f.* beer; **cervecería** *f.* beer tavern; brewery.

cesante *adj.* unemployed.

cesar *v.* to cease, stop; to quit.

cesta *f.* basket; a kind of racket for playing jai alai (*Basque ball game*).

cesto *m.* large basket, hamper.

cetrino *adj.* greenish-yellow, lemon-colored; citronlike; melancholy, gloomy.

cetro *m.* scepter, staff.

cicatero *adj.* miserly, stingy.

cicatriz *f.* scar.

cicatrizar[9] *v.* to heal, close (*a wound*).

ciclo *m.* cycle; period of time; school term.

ciclón *m.* cyclone.

ciego *adj.* blind; **a ciegas** blindly; *m.* blindman.

cielo *m.* sky; heaven; **— de la boca** palate; **poner en el —** to praise, extol; **poner el grito en el —** to "hit the ceiling"; **cielito** *m. Am.* gaucho group dance and tune.

ciempiés, cientopiés *m.* centipede.

ciénaga f. swamp, bog, quagmire, marsh.
ciencia f. science; learning; skill; a (or de) — cierta with certainty.
cieno m. mud, mire.
científico adj. scientific; m. scientist.
cierre m. clasp, fastener; closing, fastening, locking; method of closing.
cierto adj. certain, true, sure; por — certainly; Am. ciertas hierbas so-and-so (person not named).
ciervo m. deer; cierva f. doe, hind, female deer.
cierzo m. north wind.
cifra f. cipher, number; abridgment, summary; code; monogram; emblem.
cifrar v. to write in code; to summarize; — la esperanza en to place one's hope in.
cigarra f. cicada, locust.
cigarrera f. cigar or cigarette case; woman cigar maker or vendor.
cigarrillo m. cigarette.
cigarro m. cigar; cigarette.
cigüeña f. stork; crank, handle (for turning).
cilíndrico adj. cylindrical.
cilindro m. cylinder; Am. hand organ.
cima f. peak, summit, top; dar — to complete, carry out.
cimarrón adj. Am. wild, untamed; Am. mate — black, bitter mate.
cimarronear v. Am. to drink mate without sugar.
cimbrar, cimbrear v. to 'brandish, flourish, swing; to shake; to bend; Am. to swing around, change suddenly one's direction; — a uno de un golpe to knock a person down with a blow; -se to swing, sway; to vibrate, shake.
cimiento m. foundation, base; source, root; abrir los -s to break ground for a building.
cinc m. zinc.
cincel m. chisel.
cincelar v. to chisel; to engrave.
cincha f. cinch, girth; Am. blows with the flat of a sword; Am. a revienta -s unwillingly; hurriedly; at breakneck speed.
cinchar v. to cinch, tighten the saddle girth; Am. to hit with the flat of a sword.
cine, cínema m. cinema, motion picture, movie; cinematógrafo m. motion picture.
cíngulo m. girdle, cord, belt.
cínico adj. cynical, sarcastic, sneering; m. cynic.
cinta f. ribbon, band; tape; strip; movie film; coarse fishing net; Am. tin can.

cintarada f. beating, flogging; cintarazo m. blow with the flat of a sword.
cintilar v. to sparkle, twinkle; to glimmer.
cinto m. belt; girdle.
cintura f. waist; meter en — to subdue, subject.
cinturón m. belt, — de seguridad safety belt.
ciprés m. cypress.
circo m. circus.
circuito m. circuit.
circulación f. circulation; traffic.
circular v. to circulate; to circle; adj. circular; f. circular letter, notice.
círculo m. circle; group; club; clubhouse.
circundante adj. surrounding.
circundar v. to surround.
circunferencia f. circumference.
circunlocución f. circumlocution, roundabout expression.
circunspección f. circumspection, decorum, prudence, restraint.
circunspecto adj. circumspect, prudent.
circunstancia f. circumstance.
circunstante adj. surrounding; present; -s m. pl. bystanders, onlookers, audience.
circunvecino adj. neighboring, surrounding.
cirio m. wax candle.
ciruela f. plum; prune; — pasa prune, dried prune; ciruelo m. plum tree.
cirugía f. surgery.
cirujano m. surgeon.
cisne m. swan; Am. powder puff.
cisterna f. cistern.
cita f. date, appointment; citation, summons; quotation.
citación f. citation, quotation; summons.
citar v. to make a date or appointment with; to cite, quote; to summon; to incite, provoke (a bull).
ciudad f. city.
ciudadano m. citizen; resident of a city; adj. of or pertaining to a city; ciudadanía f. citizenship.
ciudadela f. citadel.
cívico adj. civic.
civil adj. civil; polite, courteous.
civilidad f. civility, courtesy.
civilización f. civilization.
civilizador adj. civilizing; m. civilizer.
civilizar⁹ v. to civilize.
cizaña f. weed; vice; discord; sembrar — to sow discord.
clamar v. to clamor, shout; to whine.
clamor m. clamor, shout; whine; knell.
clamoreo m. clamoring; shouting.

clamorear v. to clamor, shout; to toll, knell.

clandestino adj. clandestine, underhanded, secret.

clara f. white of egg; bald spot; thin spot (in a fabric); **a las -s** clearly, openly, frankly.

claraboya f. skylight.

clarear v. to clarify, make clear; to grow light, begin to dawn; to clear up; Am. to pierce through and through; **-se** to become transparent; to reveal oneself.

claridad f. clarity, clearness; blunt remark, slam; fame.

claridoso adj. Am. blunt, outspoken, plainspoken.

clarificar⁶ v. to clarify, make clear.

clarín m. bugle; bugler; organ stop; Am. song bird.

clarinete m. clarinet; clarinet player.

clarito adj. & adv. quite clear, nice and clear.

clarividencia f. clairvoyance; keen insight.

claro adj. clear; light (color); illustrious; adv. clearly; m. skylight; space, gap; clearing (in a forest); **pasar la noche de — en — ** not to sleep a wink; Am. **en —** without eating or sleeping; Am. **poner en —** to copy (a rough draft).

clase f. class; classroom; kind, sort.

clásico adj. classic, classical.

clasificación f. classification.

clasificar⁶ v. to classify.

claustro m. cloister; meeting of a university faculty; **— de profesores** university faculty.

cláusula f. clause.

clausura f. closing; seclusion, monastic life.

clavar v. to nail; to fix; to deceive, cheat; **-se** to be deceived; Am. to fall into a trap.

clave f. key, code; keystone; clef.

clavel m. carnation, pink.

clavetear v. to nail; to stud with nails.

clavija f. peg; electric plug; peg (of a stringed instrument).

clavijero m. hat or clothes rack.

clavo m. nail; clove (spice); sharp pain or grief; sick headache; Am. rich mineral vein; Am. bother, worry; Am. surprise, disappointment; Am. drug on the market (unsaleable article); **dar en el —** to hit the nail on the head; Am. **meter a uno en un —** to put a person in a predicament; Am. **ser un —** to be punctual, exact.

clemencia f. mercy; **clemente** adj. merciful.

clerical adj. clerical, of a clergyman or the clergy.

clérigo m. clergyman.

clero m. clergy.

cliente m. & f. client; customer; **clientela** f. clientele, clients; customers.

clima m. climate.

clímax m. climax.

clínica f. clinic.

clíper m. clipper.

cloaca f. sewer.

cloquear v. to cluck.

cloqueo m. cluck, clucking.

cloro m. chlorine.

club m. club, society.

clueca f. brooding hen.

coacción f. compulsion, force; enforcement.

coagular v. to coagulate, thicken, clot; to curd, curdle; **-se** to coagulate, clot; to curd, curdle.

coágulo m. coagulation, clot.

coartar v. to restrain, limit.

coba f. flattery; fib; **dar —** to flatter; to tease.

cobarde adj. cowardly; timid; weak; m. coward.

cobardía f. cowardice.

cobertizo m. shed; shanty.

cobertor m. bedcover, quilt.

cobertura f. cover, covering.

cobija f. cover; shelter; roof; Am. blanket; Am. shawl, serape, poncho; **-s** Am. bedclothes.

cobijar v. to cover; to shelter.

cobrador m. collector; ticket collector.

cobranza f. collection (of a sum of money); cashing.

cobrar v. to collect (bills, debts); to charge; to cash (a draft, check, etc.); to recover, regain; to gain, acquire; Am. to demand payment; **— cariño a** to take a liking to.

cobre m. copper; copper kitchen utensils; Am. copper coin; **-s** brass musical instruments; **batir el —** to hustle, work with energy; Am. **mostrar el —** to show one's worse side.

cobrizo adj. coppery, copper-colored.

cobro m. collection (of bills); **poner en — ** to put in a safe place; **ponerse en —** to take refuge, get to a safe place.

coca f. Am. coca (South American shrub and its leaves); Am. cocaine; Am. coca tea; Am. eggshell; Am. fruit skin or rind; Am. **de —** free of charge; in vain.

cocaína f. cocaine.

43

cocear v. to kick.

cocer[2,10] v. irr. to cook; to boil; to bake.

cocido m. Spanish stew; p.p. of **cocer**.

cociente m. quotient.

cocimiento m. cooking; baking; liquid concoction (generally made of medicinal herbs).

cocina f. kitchen; cuisine, cooking; — económica stove, range.

cocinar v. to cook.

cocinero m. cook.

coco m. coconut; coconut palm; bogyman, goblin; Am. derby hat; Am. head; Am. blow on the head; **hacer -s** a to make eyes at, flirt with; Am. **pelar a** — to crop the hair; **cocotal** m. grove of coconut palms; coconut plantation; **cocotero** m. coconut palm.

cocodrilo m. crocodile.

coche m. coach; car; taxi.

cochero m. coachman; cabman; taxi driver.

cochinada f. filth, filthiness; filthy act or remark; dirty trick; herd of swine.

cochino m. hog, pig; dirty person; Am. stingy person; Am. — de monte wild boar; adj. filthy, dirty; Am. miserly, stingy.

codazo m. nudge; poke (with the elbow).

codear v. to elbow; to nudge; **-se con alguien** to rub elbows with someone.

codicia f. greed; greediness.

codiciar v. to covet.

codicioso adj. covetous, greedy.

código m. code of laws.

codo m. elbow; bend; **alzar** (or empinar) **el** — to drink too much; **hablar por los -s** to talk too much; **meterse** (or **estar metido**) **hasta los -s** to be up to the elbows, be very busy.

codorniz f. partridge.

coetáneo adj. contemporary.

cofrade m. & f. fellow member (of a brotherhood, club, society, etc.).

cofradía f. brotherhood; sisterhood; guild; trade union.

cofre m. coffer, jewel box; chest, trunk.

coger[11] v. to seize; to catch; to grasp; to gather; Am. **-se una cosa** to steal something.

cogote m. nape, back of the neck.

cohechar v. to bribe.

coheredero m. joint heir.

coherente adj. coherent; connected.

cohete m. skyrocket; rocket; Am. **al** — in vain, uselessly.

cohibición f. repression, inhibition, restraint.

cohibido p.p. & adj. inhibited; embarrassed, uneasy.

cohibir v. to restrain, repress; to inhibit.

coincidencia f. coincidence.

coincidir v. to coincide.

cojear v. to limp; **cojeamos del mismo pie** we both have the same weakness.

cojera f. limp, lameness.

cojín m. cushion; pad; **cojincillo** m. pad.

cojinete m. small pillow or cushion, pad; bearing, ball bearing.

cojo adj. lame, crippled; one-legged.

col f. cabbage; — de Bruselas Brussels sprouts.

cola f. tail; line of people; train of a dress; glue; **hacer** — to stand in line; Am. **comer** — to be the last one in a contest.

colaboración f. collaboration, mutual help.

colaborar v. to collaborate, work together.

coladera f. colander, strainer, sieve; Am. drain.

colar[3] v. irr. to strain, filter; to bleach with lye; **-se** to slip in or out, sneak in.

colcha f. quilt; bedspread; **-s** Am. saddle and trappings; Am. gaucho clothing.

colchón m. mattress.

colear v. to wag the tail; to grab a bull by the tail and throw him over; Am. to flunk (a student); Am. to trail, tag behind (a person); Am. to bother, nag, harass; Am. to smoke one cigarette after another.

colección f. collection; set; gathering.

coleccionista m. & f. collector (of stamps, curios, etc.).

coleccionar v. to collect, make a collection.

colecta f. collection of voluntary gifts; assessment; collect (a short prayer of the mass).

colectivo adj. collective; m. Am. small bus.

colector m. collector; water pipe, drain.

colega m. & f. colleague, fellow worker.

colegiatura f. college fellowship or scholarship; Am. tuition in a college.

colegio m. boarding school; school, academy; college, body of professional men.

colegir[5,11] v. to gather; to conclude, infer.

cólera f. anger, rage; m. cholera (disease).

colérico adj. irritable; angry.

coleto m. leather jacket; one's inner self; Am. impudence, shamelessness; **decir**

para su — to say to oneself; **echarse al** — to drink down; to devour.

colgadero m. hanger; hook, peg; hat or clothes rack.

colgadura f. drape, hanging; drapery; tapestry.

colgante adj. hanging; dangling; **puente** — suspension bridge.

colgar[2, 7] v. irr. to hang, suspend; to dangle; to drape (walls); to impute, attribute; Am. to flunk, fail (a student); Am. -se to fall behind.

colibrí m. hummingbird.

coliflor f. cauliflower.

coligarse[7] v. to league together, band together.

colilla f. small tail; butt (of a cigarette), stub (of a cigar).

colina f. hill.

colindante adj. contiguous, neighboring, adjacent.

colindar v. to border (on); to be adjoining.

colisión f. collision, clash.

colmar v. to fill to the brim; — **de** to fill with; to shower with (gifts, favors, etc.); **-le a uno el plato** to exhaust one's patience.

colmena f. beehive; Am. bee.

colmillo m. eyetooth, canine tooth; tusk; fang.

colmo m. overfullness; limit; — **de la locura** height of folly; ¡ **eso es el** — ! that's the limit! adj. overfull, filled to the brim.

colocación f. placing, arrangement; position, job.

colocar[6] v. to place; to put in place, arrange; to give employment to.

colombiano adj. Colombian, of or pertaining to Colombia, South America.

colon m. colon (of the large intestine).

colonia f. colony; silk ribbon; Am. city district; Am. sugar plantation.

coloniaje m. Am. colonial period.

colonial adj. colonial.

colonización f. colonization.

colonizador m. colonizer, colonist; adj. colonizing.

colonizar[9] v. to colonize.

colono m. colonist, settler; tenant farmer; Am. owner of a sugar plantation; Am. bootlicker, flatterer.

coloquio m. conversation, talk; literary dialogue; Am. street comedy, farce.

color m. color; coloring; paint; rouge; **so — de** under the pretext of.

coloración f. coloring.

colorado adj. red, reddish; colored; **ponerse** — to blush.

colorante adj. & m. coloring.

colorar v. to color; to stain; to dye.

colorear v. to color; to redden; to give color to.

colorete m. rouge.

colorido m. coloring; color; adj. colored; colorful.

colosal adj. colossal, huge.

columbrar v. to see faintly; to glimpse.

columna f. column.

columpiar v. to swing; **-se** to swing; to sway.

columpio m. swing.

collado m. hillock, knoll.

collar m. necklace; dog collar; Am. collar (of a draft horse); **collera** f. collar (for draft animals).

coma f. comma; m. coma, stupor, prolonged unconsciousness.

comadre f. gossip; woman friend; midwife; name used to express kinship between mother and godmother; **comadrona** f. midwife.

comadreja f. weasel.

comandancia f. command; position and headquarters of a commander.

comandante m. major; commander.

comandar v. to command (troops).

comandita f. silent partnership; **sociedad en** — limited company.

comando m. military command.

comarca f. district, region.

comba f. bulge, warp.

combar v. to warp, bend, twist; **-se** to warp; to sag; to bulge.

combate m. combat, battle, fight.

combatiente m. combatant, fighter.

combatir v. to combat; to fight.

combinación f. combination.

combinar v. to combine, unite.

combustible adj. combustible; m. fuel.

combustión f. combustion.

comedero m. trough (for feeding animals); adj. edible, eatable.

comedia f. comedy; farce.

comediante m. actor, comedian.

comedido adj. courteous, polite; obliging; p.p. of comedirse.

comedirse[5] v. irr. to be civil, polite, obliging; Am. to meddle; Am. — **a hacer algo** to volunteer to do something.

comedor m. dining room; great eater.

comelón m. Am. big eater. See comilón.

comendador m. commander (of certain military orders).

comensal m. & f. table companion; dinner guest.

comentador m. commentator.

comentar v. to comment.

comentario *m.* commentary, explanation.

comentarista *m.* & *f.* commentator.

comenzar[1, 9] *v. irr.* to begin.

comer *v.* to eat; to dine; to take (*in chess or checkers*); **dar de —** to feed; **ganar de —** to earn a living; **-se** to eat; to eat up; to skip (*a letter, syllable, word, etc.*); *Am.* **-se uno a otro** to deceive each other.

comercial *adj.* commercial.

comerciante *m.* merchant; storekeeper.

comerciar *v.* to trade; to have dealings (with).

comercio *m.* commerce, trade.

comestible *adj.* edible, eatable; **-s** *m. pl.* food, groceries.

cometa *m.* comet; *Am.* person seldom seen; *f.* kite.

cometer *v.* to commit; to entrust; to use (*a figure of speech*).

cometido *m.* commission, assignment, charge; task, duty.

comezón *f.* itch.

comicios *m., pl.* primaries, elections.

cómico *adj.* comic, of comedy; comical, funny, amusing; *m.* comedian, actor.

comida *f.* meal; dinner; food; **comidilla** *f.* small meal; gossip; **la comidilla de la vecindad** the talk of the town.

comienzo *m.* beginning; origin.

comilitona *f.* spread, big feast.

comilón *m.* big eater.

comillas *f. pl.* quotation marks.

comisario *m.* commissary, deputy, delegate; manager; *Am.* police inspector.

comisión *f.* commission; committee.

comisionado *adj.* commissioned, charged, delegated; *m.* commissioner; *Am.* constable.

comisionar *v.* to commission.

comistrajo *m.* mess, strange food concoction, mixture.

comité *m.* committee, commission.

comitiva *f.* retinue, group of attendants or followers.

como *adv.* & *conj.* as, like, such as; if, provided that, since, when; *Am.* about, approximately; **¿cómo?** *interr. adv.* how?; what (did you say)?; *Am.* **¡cómo no!** yes, of course!

cómoda *f.* bureau, chest of drawers.

comodidad *f.* comfort; convenience.

cómodo *adj.* comfortable; convenient; *m. Am.* bedpan.

compacto *adj.* compact

compadecer[13] *v. irr.* to pity, sympathize with; **-se con** to be in harmony with; **-se de** to take pity on.

compadrazgo *m.* compaternity (*spirit-*

ual affinity between the godfather and the parents of a child); friendship; relationship; clique, group of friends.

compadre *m.* co-sponsor; crony, pal, comrade; *name used to express kinship between father and godfather.*

compañero *m.* companion; partner; mate; **compañerismo** *m.* companionship.

compañía *f.* company; *Am.* **— del ahorcado** silent companion, poor company.

comparación *f.* comparison.

comparar *v.* to compare.

comparativo *adj.* comparative.

comparecer[13] *v. irr.* to appear (*before a judge or tribunal*).

compartimento *m.* compartment.

compartir *v.* to share; to divide into shares.

compás *m.* compass; measure; beat; **llevar el —** to beat time.

compasión *f.* compassion, pity.

compasivo *adj.* compassionate, sympathetic.

compatible *adj.* compatible, in harmony

compatriota *m.* & *f.* compatriot, fellow countryman.

compeler *v.* to compel, force.

compendiar *v.* to abstract, summarize, condense.

compendio *m.* summary, condensation.

compensación *f.* compensation; recompense.

compensar *v.* to balance; to make equal; to compensate, recompense.

competencia *f.* competition, rivalry; competence, ability.

competente *adj.* competent; capable; adequate.

competidor *m.* competitor; rival; *adj.* competing.

competir[5] *v. irr.* to compete, vie.

compilar *v.* to compile.

compinche *m.* chum, pal, comrade.

complacencia *f.* complacency, satisfaction, contentment.

complacer[38] *v. irr.* to please, humor; to comply; **-se** to take pleasure or satisfaction (in).

complaciente *adj.* obliging, agreeable, willing to please.

complejidad *f.* complexity.

complejo *adj.* & *m.* complex.

complemento *m.* complement; object (*of a verb*).

completamiento *m.* completion.

completar *v.* to complete; to finish.

completo *adj.* complete, full, perfect.

complicar[6] *v.* to complicate.

cómplice *m. & f.* accomplice, companion in crime.

complot *m.* plot, conspiracy; intrigue.

componenda *f.* adjustment; compromise.

componente *adj.* component, constituent; *m.* component, essential part.

componer[40] *v. irr.* to fix, repair; to fix up; to adorn, trim; to compose; to set up (*type*); to settle (*a dispute*); *Am.* to set (*bones*).

comportamiento *m.* conduct, behavior.

composición *f.* composition; settlement.

compositor *m.* composer.

compostura *f.* repair; composure, dignity; neatness; composition; settlement, adjustment.

compota *f.* fruit preserves; — **de manzana** applesauce.

compra *f.* purchase; buying; **ir de -s** to go shopping.

comprador *m.* buyer, purchaser.

comprar *v.* to buy, purchase.

comprender *v.* to understand, grasp, comprehend; to comprise, embrace.

comprensible *adj.* comprehensible, understandable.

comprensión *f.* understanding; comprehension); keenness.

comprensivo *adj.* comprehensive; understanding.

compresión *f.* compression.

comprimir *v.* to compress; to repress.

comprobación *f.* confirmation, check, proof, test.

comprobante *adj.* proving, verifying; *m.* proof; evidence; certificate; voucher; warrant.

comprobar[2] *v. irr.* to verify; to check; to prove.

comprometer *v.* to compromise; to endanger; to bind; **-se** to promise, bind oneself; to become engaged; to compromise oneself.

compromiso *f.* compromise; engagement; appointment; predicament, trouble.

compuerta *f.* sluice (*gate to control the flow of water*), floodgate.

compuesto *p.p. of* **componer** & *adj.* repaired; fixed, adorned; composed; composite; compound; *m.* composite; compound.

compungirse[11] *v.* to feel regret or remorse.

computar *v.* to compute, calculate.

cómputo *m.* computation, calculation.

comulgar[7] *v.* to commune, take communion.

común *adj.* common; **por lo —** generally; *m.* toilet; **el — de las gentes** the majority of the people; the average person.

comunero *adj.* common, popular; *Am.* pertaining to a community; *m.* commoner (*one of the common people*); *Am.* member of an Indian community.

comunicación *f.* communication.

comunicar[6] *v.* to communicate; to notify; **-se** to communicate; to correspond; to be in touch (with); to connect.

comunicativo *adj.* communicative, talkative.

comunidad *f.* community; commonwealth; the common people; commonness; guild.

comunión *f.* communion; political party.

comunismo *m.* communism; **comunista** *m. & f.* communist; *adj.* communistic, communist.

con *prep.* with; — **ser** in spite of being; — **tal que** provided that; — **todo** however.

concavidad *f.* hollow, cavity; hollowness.

cóncavo *adj.* concave, hollow.

concebible *adj.* conceivable.

concebir[5] *v. irr.* to conceive; to imagine; to understand, grasp.

conceder *v.* to concede, grant; to admit.

concejal *m.* councilman, alderman.

concentración *f.* concentration.

concentrar *v.* to concentrate.

concepción *f.* conception.

concepto *m.* concept, idea, thought.

concernir[51] *v. irr.* to concern.

concertar[1] *v. irr.* to arrange, plan, settle; to conclude (*a treaty or business deal*); to harmonize; to agree.

concesión *f.* concession, grant; granting; acknowledgment.

conciencia *f.* conscience.

concienzudo *adj.* conscientious.

concierto *m.* concert; harmony; agreement; **de —** by common agreement.

conciliar *v.* to conciliate, win over; to reconcile, bring into harmony; — **el sueño** to get to sleep.

concilio *m.* council.

concisión *f.* conciseness, brevity.

conciso *adj.* concise, brief.

conciudadano *m.* fellow citizen, fellow countryman.

concluir[32] *v. irr.* to conclude, finish; to infer.

conclusión *f.* conclusion.

concordancia *f.* concord, agreement, harmony.

concordar² v. irr. to agree; to be in harmony; to put in harmony.

concordia f. concord, harmony, agreement.

concretar v. to summarize, condense; to limit; **-se a** to limit oneself to.

concreto adj. concrete, real, specific; **en —** concretely; to sum up; m. Am. concrete.

concupiscente adj. sensual.

concurrencia f. gathering, audience; concurrence, simultaneous meeting or happening; competition.

concurrido adj. well-patronized, well-attended, much frequented.

concurrir v. to concur, meet together; to happen at the same time or place; to attend; to agree.

concurso m. gathering; contest; competitive examination; assistance.

concha f. shell; shellfish; prompter's box; Am. **tener —** to be indifferent, unruffled, tough.

conchabar v. to unite, join; Am. to hire (labor); **-se** to join, gang together; to conspire; Am. to hire oneself out, get a job.

conchabo m. Am. hiring of a laborer or servant; Am. job, menial job.

conde m. count; **condesa** f. countess.

condecoración f. decoration; badge, medal.

condecorar v. to decorate (with a badge or medal).

condena f. term in prison, sentence, penalty.

condenación f. condemnation; conviction (of a prisoner or criminal); damnation.

condenar v. to condemn; to sentence; Am. to annoy, irritate; **-se** to be damned, go to hell.

condensar v. to condense.

condescendencia f. condescension, patronizing attitude.

condescender¹ v. irr. to condescend; to comply, yield.

condición f. condition.

condimentar v. to season.

condimento m. condiment, seasoning.

condolerse² v. irr. to condole (with), sympathize (with), be sorry (for).

cóndor m. Am. condor, vulture; Am. gold coin of Ecuador, Chile and Colombia.

conducir²⁵ v. irr. to conduct, lead; to drive (an auto); **-se** to behave, act.

conducta f. conduct; behavior; convoy, escort; management.

conducto m. conduit, pipe, channel;

por — de through.

conductor adj. conducting; m. leader, guide; conductor (electrical); Am. conductor, ticket collector (on trains, buses, streetcars); Am. teamster, driver.

conectar v. to connect.

condiscípulo m. schoolmate, classmate.

conejera f. burrow; rabbit warren (piece of land for breeding rabbits); den, joint, dive (of ill repute).

conejo m. rabbit; Am. guinea pig; **conejillo de Indias** guinea pig.

conexión f. connection.

conexo adj. connected; coherent.

confección f. making; confection; manufactured article; workmanship; concoction, compound.

confeccionar v. to make; to manufacture; to mix, put up (a prescription).

confederación f. confederation, alliance, league.

confederar v. to confederate; **-se** to confederate, form into a confederacy.

conferencia f. lecture; conference, meeting.

conferenciante m. & f. lecturer.

conferencista m. & f. lecturer.

conferir³ v. irr. to confer; to give, bestow.

confesar¹ v. irr. to confess.

confesión f. confession.

confesionario m. confessional, confessional box.

confesor m. confessor.

confiado adj. confident, trusting, credulous; presumptuous, self-confident.

confianza f. confidence, trust; familiarity; informality; **reunión de —** informal gathering or party.

confianzudo adj. over-friendly, over-familiar; Am. meddlesome.

confiar¹⁷ v. to confide, entrust; to trust, hope firmly.

confidencia f. confidence, trust; secret, confidential remark; **confidencial** adj. confidential.

confidente m. confidant; spy, secret agent; settee or sofa for two people, love seat; adj. faithful, trustworthy.

confín m. limit, border, boundary; adj. bordering, limiting.

confinar v. to border (upon); to confine, exile to a specific place.

confirmación f. confirmation.

confirmar v. to confirm.

confiscar⁶ v. to confiscate.

confitar v. to candy (with sugar syrup); to make into candy or preserves; to sweeten.

confite m. candy, bonbon; **confitería** f. confectionery; candy shop; **confitura**

f. confection.

conflicto *m.* conflict.

confluencia *f.* junction (*of two rivers*).

conformar *v.* to adapt, adjust; -se to conform, comply; to agree; to be resigned (to); to be satisfied.

conforme *adj.* in agreement; resigned, satisfied; alike, similar; — a in accordance with.

conformidad *f.* conformity; agreement, harmony; compliance; — con la voluntad de Dios resignation to the will of God; en — con in compliance with; estar de — con to be in accordance or agreement with.

confortar *v.* to comfort, console.

confraternidad *f.* brotherhood.

confrontar *v.* to confront; to face; to compare, check.

confundir *v.* to confound, confuse, mix up; to bewilder; to shame.

confusión *f.* confusion.

confuso *adj.* confused, bewildered; blurred; vague.

congelado *p.p. & adj.* frozen; icy.

congelar *v.* to congeal, freeze.

congenial *adj.* congenial.

congeniar *v.* to be congenial (with); to harmonize, be in harmony (with).

congoja *f.* anguish, grief, anxiety.

congratular *v.* to congratulate.

congregación *f.* congregation, assembly; religious fraternity.

congregar[7] *v.* to congregate, call together; to assemble, -se to congregate, assemble.

congresista *m.* congressman; *f.* congresswoman.

congreso *m.* congress, assembly; — de los Diputados House of Representatives.

conjetura *f.* conjecture, guess, surmise.

conjeturar *v.* to conjecture, guess, surmise.

conjugación *f.* conjugation; coupling, joining together.

conjugar[7] *v.* to conjugate.

conjunción *f.* conjunction; union, combination.

conjunto *m.* total, whole, entirety; en — as a whole; *adj.* joined; related, allied.

conjuración *f.* conspiracy, plot.

conjurado *m.* conspirator.

conjurar *v.* to conspire, plot; to join a conspiracy; to entreat; to conjure; to ward off.

conmemorar *v.* to commemorate.

conmemorativo *adj.* memorial, serving to commemorate.

conmigo with me.

conminación *f.* threat.

conminatorio *adj.* threatening.

conmoción *f.* commotion.

conmovedor *adj.* moving, touching; stirring.

conmover[2] *v. irr.* to move, touch, affect (*with emotion*); to stir (*emotions*).

conmutador *m.* electric switch; cuadro — switchboard.

connatural *adj.* inborn.

cono *m.* cone; pine cone.

conocedor *adj.* knowing, aware, expert; *m.* connoisseur, judge, expert; ser — de to be judge of.

conocer[13] *v. irr.* to know, be acquainted with; to recognize; to meet; se conoce que it is clear or evident that.

conocido *p.p. & adj.* known; well-known; *m.* acquaintance.

conocimiento *m.* knowledge, understanding; acquaintance; bill of lading; -s knowledge, learning; poner en — to inform.

conque *conj.* so then, well then, and so.

conquista *f.* conquest.

conquistador *m.* conqueror; *adj.* conquering, victorious.

conquistar *v.* to conquer, defeat; to win.

consabido *adj.* aforementioned, aforesaid.

consagración *f.* consecration.

consagrar *v.* to consecrate.

consciencia *f.* consciousness.

consciente *adj.* conscious.

consecución *f.* attainment.

consecuencia *f.* consequence; result; a — de as a result of; por (*or* en) — therefore; consequently.

consecuente *adj.* consequent, logical; consistent; *m.* consequence, result.

consecutivo *adj.* consecutive, successive.

conseguir[5, 12] *v. irr.* to get, obtain; to reach, attain.

conseja *f.* old wives' tale, fable.

consejero *m.* adviser, counselor.

consejo *m.* counsel, advice; council; council hall.

consentimiento *m.* consent.

consentir[3] *v. irr.* to consent, permit; to pamper, spoil.

conserje *m.* janitor, caretaker

conserva *f.* preserve; pickled fruit or vegetables; *Am.* filling (*for tarts or candy*).

conservación *f.* conservation.

conservador *m.* conservative; preserver; guardian; *adj.* conservative.

conservar v. to conserve, keep; to preserve.

considerable adj. considerable.

consideración f. consideration.

considerado adj. considerate, thoughtful; respected; prudent.

considerar v. to consider; to treat with consideration.

consigna f. watchword, password; Am. checkroom.

consignar v. to consign; to deliver; to deposit; to assign; to check (baggage).

consigo with oneself; with himself (herself, themselves).

consiguiente adj. consequent; m. consequence; **por — consequently.**

consistente adj. firm, substantial.

consistir v. to consist; to be based on; ¿en qué consiste? why?; what is the explanation for it?

consocio m. associate, partner.

consolación f. consolation.

consolar[2] v. irr. to console, cheer.

consolidar v. to consolidate, make solid; to unite, combine.

consonante m. perfect rhyme; f. consonant; adj. in harmony.

consorte m. & f. consort; mate; companion.

conspicuo adj. conspicuous.

conspiración f. conspiracy, plot.

conspirador m. conspirator, plotter.

conspirar v. to conspire, plot.

constancia f. constancy; perseverance; evidence, certainty; Am. documentary proof, record.

constante adj. constant; continual; firm, faithful.

constar v. to be evident, clear; to consist (of), be composed (of); to be on record.

constatación f. Am. proof, check, evidence.

constelación f. constellation.

constipado adj. suffering from a cold; m. cold in the head.

constipar v. to stop up (the nasal passages); to cause a cold; -se to catch cold.

constitución f. constitution.

constitucional adj. constitutional.

constituir[32] v. irr. to constitute, form; to set up, establish; -se en to set oneself up as.

constitutivo = constituyente.

constituyente adj. constituent.

constreñir[5, 19] v. irr. to constrain; to compel, oblige.

construcción f. construction; structure; building.

construir[32] v. irr. to construct, build

consuelo m. consolation, comfort; relief; cheer.

consuetudinario adj. habitual, customary; **derecho — common law.**

cónsul m. consul.

consulado m. consulate.

consulta f. consultation; opinion.

consultar v. to consult.

consultorio m. office for consultation; doctor's office or clinic.

consumado p.p. of consumar; adj. consummate, perfect, complete; accomplished.

consumar v. to consummate, complete.

consumidor m. consumer; adj. consuming.

consumir v. to consume; to waste; -se to be consumed; to burn out; to be exhausted; to waste away.

consumo m. consumption (of food, provisions, etc).

consunción f. consumption (illness).

contabilidad f. accounting; bookkeeping.

contacto m. contact.

contado : al — in cash; de — immediately; **por de — of course; contados** adj. few, scarce, rare.

contador m. accountant; purser; cashier; counter; meter (for water, gas, or electricity).

contaduría f. accountant's or auditor's office; box office; cashier's office; accounting.

contagiar v. to infect; to corrupt; to contaminate.

contagio m. contagion; infection.

contagioso adj. contagious; infectious.

contaminar v. to contaminate, defile; to corrupt.

contar[2] v. irr. to count; to tell, relate; **— con** to count on, rely on; **a —** desde starting from, beginning with.

contemplación f. contemplation; gazing; meditation.

contemplar v. to contemplate, gaze at; to examine; to meditate.

contemporáneo adj. contemporary.

contender[1] v. irr. to contend, fight; to compete.

contener[45] v. irr. to contain; to restrain, check; -se to refrain; to restrain oneself.

contenido m. contents; adj. restrained, moderate.

contentamiento m. contentment, joy.

contentar v. to give pleasure, make happy; -se to be satisfied, pleased; Am. to make up, renew friendship.

contento *adj.* content, contented, satisfied, glad; *m.* gladness, contentment.

contera *f.* metal tip (*of a cane, umbrella, etc.*); tip, end; refrain of a song; **por —** as a finishing touch.

contertulio *m.* fellow-member.

contestación *f.* answer, reply; argument.

contestar *v.* to answer, reply.

contextura *f.* texture, composition; structure (*of animal or vegetable tissues*).

contienda *f.* fight; dispute; contest.

contigo with you (with thee).

contiguo *adj.* contiguous, next, neighboring.

continental *adj.* continental.

continente *m.* continent; countenance; *adj.* continent, moderate, sober.

contingencia *f.* contingency, possibility; risk.

contingente *adj.* contingent, accidental; *m.* quota; military contingent.

continuación *f.* continuation; continuance; **a —** below, as follows.

continuar[18] *v.* to continue; to last.

continuidad *f.* continuity.

continuo *adj.* continuous, connected; continual; steady, constant.

contonearse *v.* to strut, swagger; to waddle.

contoneo *m.* strut; waddle.

contorno *m.* environs, surrounding country; contour, outline.

contra *prep.* against; **el pro y el —** the pro and con; *f.* opposition; *Am.* antidote, remedy; **-s** *Am.* play-off, final game (*to determine the winner*); **llevar a uno la —** to contradict a person, take the opposite view.

contraalmirante *m.* rear admiral.

contrabandear *v.* to smuggle.

contrabandista *m.* smuggler.

contrabando *m.* contraband; smuggled goods; smuggling.

contracción *f.* contraction; *Am.* diligence, application, devotion.

contradecir[27] *v. irr.* to contradict.

contradicción *f.* contradiction.

contradictorio *adj.* contradictory, contrary, opposing.

contradicho *p.p.* of **contradecir.**

contraer[46] *v. irr.* to contract; **— matrimonio** to get married; **-se** to shrink; to contract.

contrafuerte *m.* buttress; spur (*of a mountain*); **-s** secondary chain of mountains.

contrahacer[31] *v. irr.* to counterfeit; to forge; to copy, imitate; to mimic.

contrahecho *p.p.* of **contrahacer** & *adj.* counterfeit; forged; deformed.

contralor *m.* *Am.* controller or comptroller (*of accounts or expenditures*). See **controlador.**

contraorden *f.* countermand; cancellation of an order.

contrapelo : a — against the grain.

contrapesar *v.* to counterbalance, balance; to offset.

contrapeso *m.* counterpoise, counterweight, counterbalance; *Am.* fear, uneasiness.

contrariar[17] *v.* to oppose; to contradict; to irritate, vex.

contrariedad *f.* opposition; contradiction; bother, irritation; disappointment.

contrario *adj.* contrary; opposite; *m.* opponent.

contrarrestar *v.* to counteract; to resist, oppose; to strike back (*a ball*).

contraseña *f.* password, watchword; mark; check (*for baggage*); **— de salida** theatre check (*to re-enter during the performance*).

contrastar *v.* to contrast; to resist, oppose; to test (*scales, weights, measures, etc.*); to assay (*metals*).

contraste *m.* contrast; assay, test; assayer, tester; assayer's office.

contrata *f.* contract, bargain, agreement.

contratar *v.* to contract for; to trade; to engage, hire (*men*); **-se** to come to, or make, an agreement.

contratiempo *m.* accident, mishap.

contratista *m.* & *f.* contractor.

contrato *m.* contract.

contraventana *f.* shutter.

contribución *f.* contribution; tax.

contribuir[32] *v. irr.* to contribute.

contribuyente *m.* contributor; taxpayer; *adj.* contributing.

control *m.* *Am.* control.

controlador *m.* *Am.* controller.

controlar *v.* *Am.* to control.

controversia *f.* controversy.

contumacia *f.* stubbornness, obstinacy; contempt of court, failure to appear in court; rebelliousness.

contumaz *adj.* stubborn; rebellious.

contusión *f.* bruise.

convalecer[13] *v. irr.* to convalesce, recover from an illness.

convecino *adj.* near, neighboring; *m.* neighbor.

convencedor *adj.* convincing.

convencer[10] *v.* to convince.

convencimiento *m.* conviction, belief; convincing.

convención *f.* convention, assembly; pact, agreement; *Am.* political convention; **convencional** *adj.* conventional.

convenido *adj.* agreed; O.K., all right; *p.p.* of **convenir**.

conveniencia *f.* convenience; comfort; utility, profit.

conveniente *adj.* convenient, useful, profitable; fit, proper, suitable; opportune.

convenio *m.* pact, agreement.

convenir[48] *v. irr.* to agree; to convene, assemble; to be suitable, proper, advisable; to suit, fit; **-se** to agree.

conventillo *m. Am.* tenement house.

convento *m.* convent.

convergente *adj.* convergent, coming together.

converger,[II] **convergir**[II] *v.* to converge.

conversación *f.* conversation.

conversar *v.* to converse.

conversión *f.* conversion.

convertir[3] *v. irr.* to convert.

convicción *f.* conviction.

convicto *p.p. irr.* of **convencer**; convicted, guilty.

convidado *m.* guest; *Am.* — y con ollita guest who abuses hospitality.

convidar *v.* to invite; **-se** to volunteer one's services; to invite oneself.

convincente *adj.* convincing.

convite *m.* invitation; banquet.

convocación *f.* convocation.

convocar[6] *v.* to convoke, call together.

convoyar *v.* to convoy, escort.

convulsión *f.* convulsion.

convulsivo *adj.* convulsive; **tos convulsiva** whooping cough.

conyugal *adj.* conjugal, pertaining to marriage or a married couple; **vida —** married life.

cónyuge *m.* husband; *f.* wife.

cooperación *f.* cooperation.

cooperador *adj.* cooperating, cooperative; *m.* cooperator, co-worker.

cooperar *v.* to cooperate.

cooperativo *adj.* cooperative; **cooperativa** *f.* cooperative, cooperative society.

coordinación *f.* coordination.

coordinar *v.* to coordinate.

copa *f.* goblet; treetop; crown of a hat; card in the suit of **copas** (*in Spanish cards*); *Am.* **empinar la —** to drink, get drunk.

copartícipe *adj.* participant; *m. & f.* joint partner.

copete *m.* tuft; crest; top, summit; ornamental top on furniture; **de —** of high rank, important; proud; **estar uno hasta el —** to be stuffed; to be fed up; **tener mucho —** to be arrogant, haughty.

copia *f.* copy; imitation; abundance.

copiar *v.* to copy.

copioso *adj.* copious, abundant.

copita *f.* little glass; little drink.

copla *f.* couplet; stanza (*of variable length and meter*); popular song.

copo *m.* snowflake; wad, tuft (*of wool or cotton*).

coqueta *f.* coquette, flirt.

coquetear *v.* to flirt.

coquetería *f.* coquetry, flirting.

coraje *m.* courage, valor; anger.

coral *m.* coral; *Am.* red poisonous snake; **-es** coral beads; *adj.* choral, pertaining to a choir; **coralino** *adj.* coral, like coral.

coraza *f.* cuirass, armor; armor plate or plating; shell (*of a turtle*).

corazón *m.* heart; core, center.

corazonada *f.* presentiment, foreboding; hunch.

corbata *f.* necktie; cravat; *Am.* colorful kerchief, scarf.

corcel *m.* charger, steed.

corcova *f.* hump, hunch; **corcovado** *adj.* hunchbacked; *m.* hunchback.

corcovear *v.* to prance about, leap; *Am.* to kick, protest against.

corcho *m.* cork; beehive; *adj. Am.* corklike, spongy.

cordel *m.* cord, rope.

cordero *m.* lamb; lambskin.

cordial *adj.* cordial, friendly; **dedo —** middle finger.

cordialidad *f.* cordiality, friendliness, warmth.

cordillera *f.* mountain range.

cordobés *adj.* Cordovan, of or pertaining to Cordova; *m.* native of Cordova.

cordón *m.* cord; braid; cordon, line of soldiers; *Am.* — de la acera curb, curbstone of the sidewalk; **cordonería** *f.* lace or cord maker's shop; collection of cords and laces; cord maker's work; braiding.

cordoncillo *m.* small cord, drawstring, lace, lacing; braid; mill (*ridged edge of a coin*); ridge, rib (*of certain fabrics*).

cordura *f.* good judgment, wisdom; sanity.

cornada *f.* goring; butt with the horns; **dar -s** to gore, horn, butt with the horns.

corneta *f.* cornet; bugle; horn; *m.* bugler.

cornisa *f.* cornice.

coro *m.* choir; chorus.

corona *f.* crown; wreath.

coronar *v.* to crown; to top.

coronel *m.* colonel.

coronilla *f.* small crown; crown of the head; **estar uno hasta la —** to be fed up, be satiated.

corpanchón *m.* large body; carcass.

corpiño *m.* bodice.

corporación *f.* corporation.

corporal *adj.* corporal, of the body; *m.* corporal (*small piece of linen used at Mass*).

corpóreo *adj.* corporeal, bodily; tangible, material.

corpulento *adj.* corpulent, fat, stout.

corral *m.* yard; corral, cattle yard; **corralón** *m.* large corral; *Am.* lumber warehouse.

correa *f.* leather strap; resistance; *Am.* -s leather blanket carrier; *Am.* **tener muchas -s** to be phlegmatic, calm.

corrección *f.* correction; correctness.

correcto *adj.* correct, proper.

corredizo *adj.* sliding, slipping; **nudo — slip knot.**

corredor *m.* runner; racer; corridor; gallery around a patio; broker; *Am.* covered porch; *Am.* beater of wild game; *adj.* running; speedy.

corregidor *m.* corrector; Spanish magistrate.

corregir[5, 11] *v. irr.* to correct; to reprove; to punish; **-se** to mend one's ways.

correligionario *adj.* of the same religion; of the same political party or sympathies; *m.* coreligionist.

correntada *f. Am.* strong river current.

correo *m.* mail; mail service; postman; post office; **— aéreo** air mail.

correón *m.* large strap.

correoso *adj.* flexible; leathery; tough; **correosidad** *f.* toughness; flexibility.

correr *v.* to run; to blow (*said of the wind*); to pass, elapse; to draw (*a curtain*); to race; to chase; *Am.* to dismiss, throw out; **-se** to slip through; to slide; to be embarrassed.

correría *f.* foray, raid for plunder; excursion, short trip; **-s** wanderings, travels; raids.

correspondencia *f.* correspondence; letters, mail; agreement; interchange.

corresponder *v.* to reciprocate, return (*love, favors*); to belong; to concern; to correspond (*one thing with another*).

correspondiente *adj.* corresponding, agreeing; respective; *m.* correspondent.

corresponsal *m.* correspondent; agent; newspaper reporter.

corretear *v.* to run around; to roam, rove; *Am.* to pursue, chase.

corrida *f.* race; *Am.* row, file; *Am.* night spree; *Am.* beating up of game; **— del tiempo** swiftness of time; **— de toros** bullfight; **de —** without stopping.

corrido *adj.* embarrassed, ashamed; worldly-wise; flowing, fluent; **de —** without stopping; *m. Am.* popular ballad.

corriente *adj.* running; flowing, fluent; usual, common, ordinary; *Am.* frank, open; **¡—!** all right! O.K.!; **el ocho del — the eighth of the current month; estar al — to be up-to-date; to be well-informed** (*about current news*); **poner a uno al — to keep someone posted or well informed;** *f.* current; flow; course; *Am.* **hay que llevarle la — one must humor him.**

corrillo *m.* circle or group of gossipers.

corro *m.* group of talkers or spectators.

corroer[51] *v. irr.* to corrode.

corromper *v.* to corrupt; to seduce; to bribe; **-se** to rot; to become corrupted.

corrompido *adj.* corrupt; rotten, spoiled; degenerate; *p.p. of* **corromper.**

corrupción *f.* corruption.

corrupto *adj.* corrupt, rotten.

corsé *m.* corset.

cortada *f. Am.* cut, slash.

cortador *m.* cutter.

cortadura *f.* cut; gash; slash.

cortante *adj.* cutting; sharp.

cortaplumas *m.* penknife.

cortar *v.* to cut; to cut off; to cut out; to cut down; to interrupt; *Am.* to harvest, pick (*fruit*); to gossip, speak ill of someone; **-se** to be embarrassed, ashamed; to sour, curdle (*said of milk*); *Am.* to become separated, cut off; *Am.* to leave in a hurry; *Am.* to die.

corte *m.* cut; cutting; cutting edge; fit, style; *Am.* cut (*in cards*); *Am.* harvest; *Am.* weeding; *Am.* gracefulness in dancing; *f.* royal court; retinue; *Am.* court of justice; **-s** Spanish parliament; **hacer la —** to court, woo; *Am.* **darse uno —** to put on airs.

cortedad *f.* smallness; timidity; bashfulness, shyness.

cortejar *v.* to court, woo.

cortejo *m.* cortege, procession; retinue; courtship; suitor.

cortés *adj.* courteous, polite.

cortesana *f.* courtesan, prostitute.

cortesano *m.* courtier; *adj.* courtlike; courteous.

cortesía f. courtesy, politeness.
corteza f. bark; crust; peel.
cortijo m. farmhouse.
cortina m. curtain.
corto adj. short; scanty; bashful.
corveta f. buck, leap, bound (of a horse); **hacer -s** to prance.
corvo adj. see **curvo**.
cosa f. thing; **— de** approximately, about; **no es —** it is not worth anything; **otra —** something else; **como si tal —** serene, as if nothing had happened; **Am. ni por una de estas nueve -s** absolutely not, not for anything in the world.
cosecha f. crop; harvest.
cosechar v. to reap; to harvest.
coser v. to sew; to stitch.
cosmético m. & adj. cosmetic.
cosquillas f. pl. ticklishness; tickling; **hacer —** to tickle; to excite (one's desire or curiosity); **tener —** to be ticklish.
cosquillear v. to tickle; to excite (one's curiosity or desire).
cosquilleo m. tickle, tickling sensation.
cosquilloso adj. ticklish; touchy.
costa f. coast; cost, expense, price; a **toda —** at all costs, by all means.
costado m. side; flank.
costal m. sack; **estar hecho un — de huesos** to be nothing but skin and bones; to be very thin.
costanero adj. coastal, relating to a coast; sloping.
costar[2] v. irr. to cost; **— trabajo** to be difficult.
costarricense adj., m. & f. Costa Rican.
coste, costo m. cost; expense.
costear v. to defray or pay costs; to pay, be profitable; to navigate along the coast; to go along the edge of; **no costea** it does not pay.
costero adj. coastal; **navegación costera** coastal navigation.
costilla f. rib; chop, cutlet.
costoso adj. costly, expensive.
costra f. crust; scab.
costroso adj. crusty, scabby.
costumbre f. custom, habit.
costura f. sewing; stitching; seam.
costurera f. seamstress.
costurero m. sewing table or cabinet; sewing box; sewing room.
costurón m. coarse stitching; large seam; patch, mend; big scar.
cotejar v. to confront, compare.
cotejo m. comparison.
cotense m. Am. burlap.
cotidiano adj. daily.

cotizable adj. quotable (price).
cotización f. quotation of prices; current price.
cotizar[9] v. to quote (prices); Am. to contribute one's share or quota; Am. to prorate, distribute proportionally.
coto m. enclosure; landmark; limitation; limit, boundary; **poner — a** to set a limit to; to put an end to.
cotorra f. small parrot; magpie; talkative person, chatterbox.
cotorrear v. to chatter; to gossip.
covacha f. small cave; grotto; Am. hut, shanty; Am. cubbyhole, small dark room.
coyote m. Am. coyote, prairie wolf; Am. shyster, tricky lawyer; Am. agent, broker (often illegal).
coyuntura f. joint; articulation; occasion; precise moment.
coz f. kick; recoil of a gun; butt of a firearm; **dar** (or **tirar**) **coces** to kick.
cráneo m. cranium, skull.
craso adj. fat; thick, coarse, gross; **ignorancia crasa** gross ignorance.
cráter m. crater of a volcano.
creación f. creation.
creador m. creator; adj. creating, creative.
crear v. to create.
crecer[13] v. irr. to grow; to increase; **-se** to swell (as a river); to become or feel important.
crecida f. river flood.
crecido adj. grown, increased; large; swollen.
creciente adj. growing, increasing; crescent (moon); f. river flood; m. crescent.
crecimiento m. growth, increase.
credenciales f. pl. credentials.
crédito m. credit; credence, belief; fame, reputation; letter of credit; **dar a —** to loan on credit.
credo m. creed; **en un —** in a jiffy, in a minute.
crédulo adj. credulous, too ready to believe.
creencia f. belief, faith.
creer[14] v. to believe; to think, suppose; **¡ya lo creo!** I should say so!; yes, of course!
creíble adj. credible, believable.
crema f. cream; custard; cold cream.
crepitar v. to crackle, snap; to creak; to rattle.
crepuscular adj. twilight.
crepúsculo m. twilight.
crespo adj. curly; artificial (style); angry; crisp.
crespón m. crepe.

cresta *f.* crest; top, summit; tuft, comb (*of a bird*).

cretona *f.* cretonne.

creyente *m.* & *f.* believer; *adj.* believing.

creyón *m.* *Am.* crayon.

cría *f.* brood; suckling; breeding.

criadero *m.* tree nursery; breeding place; hotbed; rich mine.

criado *m.* servant; *adj.* bred; **mal —** ill-bred; **criada** *f.* maid, servant.

criador *m.* breeder, raiser, rearer; creator; *adj.* creating, creative; breeding; nourishing.

crianza *f.* breeding; nursing; manners.

criar[17] *v.* to breed; to bring up, rear, educate; to nurse.

criatura *f.* creature; baby, child.

criba *f.* sieve.

cribar *v.* to sift.

crimen *m.* crime.

criminal *adj.*, *m.* & *f.* criminal.

crin *f.* mane.

crinudo *adj.* *Am.* with a long or thick mane.

criollo *m.* *Am.* Creole; native of America (*especially Spanish America*); *adj.* *Am.* national, domestic (*not foreign to Spanish America*).

crisantema *f.*, **crisantemo** *m.* chrysanthemum.

crisis *f.* crisis.

crisol *m.* crucible, melting pot; hearth of a blast furnace.

crispar *v.* to contract (*muscles*); to clench (*fists*); to put (*nerves*) on edge.

cristal *m.* crystal; glass; mirror; lens.

cristalería *f.* glassware shop or factory; glassware.

cristalino *adj.* crystalline, transparent, clear; *m.* lens of the eye.

cristalizar[9] *v.* to crystallize.

cristiandad *f.* Christianity; Christendom.

cristianismo *m.* Christianity.

cristiano *m.* Christian; person; **hablar en —** to speak clearly; *adj.* Christian.

criterio *m.* criterion, rule, standard; judgment.

crítica *f.* criticism; censure; gossip.

criticador *adj.* critical; *m.* critic, fault-finder.

criticar[6] *v.* to criticize; to censure; to find fault with.

crítico *adj.* critical; *m.* critic, judge; *Am.* faultfinder, slanderer; **criticón** *m.* critic, knocker, faultfinder; *adj.* critical, over-critical, faultfinding.

croar *v.* to croak.

crónica *f.* chronicle, history; **cronista** *m.* & *f.* chronicler.

crónico *adj.* chronic.

cronómetro *m.* chronometer, timepiece.

croquis *m.* rough sketch.

cruce *m.* crossing; crossroads; cross-breeding.

crucero *m.* cross-bearer; crossing, crossroads; cruiser; transept (*of a church*); crossbeam; Cross (*a constellation*).

crucificar[6] *v.* to crucify.

crucifijo *m.* crucifix.

crucigrama *m.* crossword puzzle.

crudo *adj.* raw; uncooked; unripe; harsh; **agua cruda** hard water; **petróleo —** crude oil; *Am.* **estar —** to have a hang-over; **cruda** *f.* *Am.* hang-over.

cruel *adj.* cruel.

crueldad *f.* cruelty.

crujido *m.* creak, crack, creaking; rustle.

crujir *v.* to creak, crackle; to grate (*one's teeth*); to rustle; to crunch.

cruz *f.* cross.

cruzada *f.* crusade; holy war; campaign.

cruzado *m.* crusader; *adj.* crossed; cross, crosswise, transverse.

cruzamiento *m.* crossing; crossroads.

cruzar[9] *v.* to cross; *Am.* to fight, dispute; **-se con** to meet.

cuaco *m.* *Am.* horse; *Am.* cassava flour.

cuaderno *m.* notebook; memorandum book; booklet; *Am.* pamphlet.

cuadra *f.* hall, large room; stable; hospital or prison ward; *Am.* city block; *Am.* reception room.

cuadrado *adj.* square; *m.* square; square ruler; die, metal block or plate.

cuadrante *m.* dial, face of a clock or watch; sundial; quadrant (*fourth part of circle*; *instrument used in astronomy*).

cuadrar *v.* to square; to form into a square; to please; to conform, harmonize; *Am.* to be becoming (*said of clothes*); *Am.* to be ready; *Am.* to contribute a large sum; *Am.* to come out well, succeed; **-se** to stand at attention.

cuadricular *v.* to square off, divide into squares.

cuadrilla *f.* group, troupe, gang; armed band; quadrille, square dance.

cuadro *m.* square; picture; scene; frame; flower bed; *Am.* blackboard; *Am.* slaughterhouse.

cuajada *f.* curd.

cuajado *p.p.* & *adj.* coagulated, curdled; filled, covered; **— de** full or covered with (*flowers, dew, etc.*).

cuajar *v.* to coagulate, thicken, curd, curdle; to turn out well; to jell; to please; *Am.* to chatter, prattle; **-se** to coagulate, curd; to become crowded, be filled; **la cosa no cuajó** the thing did not work, did not jell.

cuajarón *m.*clot.

cual *rel. pron.* which; **cada —** each one; **— más, — menos** some people more, others less; **el —, la —, los -es, las -es** which; who; **lo —** which; *adv.* as, like; **¿cuál?** *interr. pron.* which one? what?

cualidad *f.* quality; trait.

cualquier(a) *indef. adj. & pron.* any, anyone; whichever; **un hombre cualquiera** any man whatever.

cuando *rel. adv. & conj.* when; **aun —** even though; **¿cuándo?** *interr. adv.* when?

cuantía *f.* quantity; rank, importance.

cuantioso *adj.* plentiful, abundant; numerous.

cuanto *rel. adj. & pron.* as much as, as many as; all that; **— antes** as soon as possible, immediately; **en — conj.** as soon as; **en — a** as for, with regard to; **unos -s** a few; **¿cuánto?** *interr. adj. & pron.* how much?; **¿cuántos?** how many?

cuarentena *f.* quarantine; forty units of anything; period of forty days, months, or years.

cuarentón *m.* man in his forties; **cuarentona** *f.* woman in her forties.

cuaresma *f.* Lent.

cuarta *f.* fourth, fourth part; span of a hand; *Am.* horse whip; *Am.* **echar —** to beat, flog.

cuartear *v.* to quarter, divide into quarters; *Am.* to whip; **-se** to crack, split (*said of walls or ceilings*); *Am.* to back down, go back on one's word.

cuartel *m.* quarter, one fourth; quarters, barracks; district; quarter, mercy; **no dar —** to give no quarter.

cuartelada *f.* military coup d'état, uprising, insurrection.

cuartelazo *m. Am.* military coup d'état, insurrection.

cuarterón *m.* quarter, fourth part; fourth of a pound; panel (*of a door or window*); *adj. & m.* quarter-breed (*one fourth Indian and three fourths Spanish*); quadroon (*person of quarter negro blood*).

cuarteto *m.* quartet; quatrain (*stanza of four lines*).

cuartilla *f.* sheet of paper; about 4 quarts; about 1½ pecks; fourth of an **arroba** (*about 6 pounds*); *Am.* three cents' worth; *Am.* **no valer uno —** not to be worth a penny.

cuartillo *m.* fourth of a peck; about a pint; fourth of a **real.**

cuarto *m.* room; quarter, one fourth; **tener -s** to have money; *adj.* fourth.

cuarzo *m.* quartz.

cuate *adj., m. & f. Am.* twin.

cuatrero *m.* horse thief, cattle thief; *Am.* Indian who speaks "broken" Spanish.

cuba *f.* cask, barrel; tub, vat; big-bellied person; drunkard.

cubano *adj. & m.* Cuban.·

cubeta *f.* small barrel or keg; bucket, pail.

cúbico *adj.* cubic.

cubierta *f.* cover; covering; envelope; deck (*of a ship*); *Am.* sheath.

cubierto *p.p. of* **cubrir;** *m.* cover; place setting for one person at a table.

cubo *m.* cube; bucket, pail; hub of a wheel; mill pond; *Am.* finger bowl.

cubremesa *f.* table cover.

cubrir[52] *v.* to cover; to hide; to coat; to settle, pay (*a bill*); **-se** to cover oneself; to put on one's hat.

cucaracha *f.* cockroach.

cuclillas : en — in a squatting position; **sentarse en —** to squat.

cuclillo *m.* cuckoo.

cuco *adj.* dainty, cute; sly, shrewd; *m.* cuckoo; a kind of caterpillar; card game; *Am.* peach, peach tree; *Am.* **hacer —** a to make fun of; to fool.

cucurucho *m.* paper cone; *Am.* peak, summit; *Am.* cowl, cloak with a hood (*worn by penitents in Holy Week processions*).

cuchara *f.* spoon; scoop; *Am.* mason's trowel; **media —** mediocre person; *Am.* mason's helper; *Am.* **hacer —** to pout; *Am.* **meter uno su —** to butt into a conversation; to meddle; **cucharada** *f.* spoonful; scoop; **cucharón** *m.* large spoon; ladle; dipper; scoop.

cuchichear *v.* to whisper.

cuchicheo *m.* whispering, whisper.

cuchilla *f.* large knife, cleaver; blade (*of any cutting instrument*); *Am.* penknife; *Am.* mountain ridge; *Am.* gore (*in a garment*); *Am.* narrow tract of land.

cuchillada *f.* thrust with a knife, stab, slash; cut, gash.

cuchillo *m.* knife; gore (*in a garment*); **— de monte** hunting knife; **cuchillería** *f.* cutlery; cutlery shop.

cueca *f. Am.* a Chilean dance.

cuello *m.* neck; collar.

cuenca *f.* river basin; narrow valley; wooden bowl; socket of the eye.

cuenco *m.* earthen bowl.

cuenta *f.* count, calculation; bill; account; bead (*of a rosary or necklace*); **a fin de -s** in the final analysis; **caer en la —** to see, get the point; **darse — to realize;** *Am.* **de toda —** anyway; **eso corre de mi —** that is my responsibility; I'll take charge of that; **eso no me tiene —** that does not pay me; it is of no profit to me; **en resumidas -s** in short; *Am.* **hacerle — una cosa a uno** to be useful or profitable for one; **tomar en —** to take into account; **tomar una cosa por su —** to take charge of something, take the responsibility for it; **vamos a -s** let's understand or settle this.

cuentagotas *m.* dropper (*for counting drops*).

cuento *m.* story, tale; **— de nunca acabar** never-ending tale; **déjese de -s** come to the point; **no viene a —** it is not opportune or to the point.

cuerda *f.* cord, string, rope; chord; watch spring; **dar — a** to wind (*a watch*).

cuerdo *adj.* sane; wise.

cuereada *f. Am.* flogging, whipping; *Am.* skinning of an animal.

cuerear *v. Am.* to flog, whip; *Am.* to harm, dishonor; *Am.* to beat (*in a game*); *Am.* to skin (*an animal*).

cuerno *m.* horn; antenna, feeler; **poner -s a** to be unfaithful to, deceive (*a husband*); *Am.* **mandar al —** to send to the devil.

cuero *m.* hide, skin; leather; wineskin; *Am.* whip; **en -s** naked.

cuerpeada *f Am.* dodge; evasion.

cuerpo *m.* body; bulk; corps; **en —** without hat or coat; **luchar — a —** to fight in single combat; *Am.* **sacar el —** to dodge; to escape, avoid doing something.

cuervo *m.* crow; raven; *Am.* buzzard; *Am.* dishonest priest; *Am.* **hacer uno la del —** to leave abruptly and not return.

cuesta *f.* hill, slope; **a -s** on one's shoulders or back; **in one's care; — abajo** downhill; **— arriba** uphill.

cuestión *f.* question; controversy, dispute; problem, matter.

cuestionario *m.* questionnaire, list of questions.

cueva *f.* cave, cavern; cellar.

cuico *m. Am.* cop, policeman; *Am.* gossiper, tattletale, "squealer"; *Am.* half-breed; *Am.* short, chubby person.

cuidado *m.* care, attention; worry, misgiving; **al — de** in care of; **tener —**

to be careful; **¡ — !** look out!; be careful! **¡cuidadito!** be very careful!

cuidadoso *adj.* careful; attentive; anxious.

cuidar *v.* to take care of, look after, keep; to make or do carefully.

cuita *f.* grief, care, anxiety; misfortune; *Am.* bird dung.

cuitado *adj.* unfortunate; timid, shy.

culata *f.* haunch, buttock; rear; butt (*of a firearm*).

culatazo *f.* blow with the butt of a rifle; recoil, kick of a firearm.

culebra *f.* snake; coil; *Am.* money belt.

culebrear *v.* to zigzag; to twist, wriggle.

culminación *f.* culmination, climax.

culminar *v.* to culminate; to come to a climax.

culpa *f.* fault; guilt; blame; **echar la — a** to blame; **tener la —** to be to blame.

culpabilidad *f.* guilt; **culpable** *adj.* guilty.

culpar *v.* to blame; to declare guilty.

cultivación *f.* cultivation.

cultivador *m.* cultivator; **máquina cultivadora** cultivator.

cultivar *v.* to cultivate.

cultivo *m.* cultivation, culture.

culto *adj.* cultured; *m.* cult, worship; religious sect; **rendir — a** to pay homage to; to worship.

cultura *f.* culture; cultivation.

cumbre *f.* summit; top.

cumpleaños *m.* birthday.

cumplido *adj.* complete, full; perfect; courteous; *p.p.* fulfilled; due, fallen due; **tiene tres años -s** he is just over three years old; *m.* courtesy, attention; compliment.

cumplimentar *v.* to compliment; to congratulate; to pay a courtesy visit.

cumplimiento *m.* fulfilment; courtesy; completion; compliment; **de — formal,** ceremonious.

cumplir *v.* to fulfill; to comply; to carry out; to fall due; **— años** to have a birthday; to be (*so many*) years old.

cúmulo *m.* pile, heap; accumulation; cumulus (*mass of clouds*).

cuna *f.* cradle; origin; *Am.* coffin for the poor; *Am.* dive, den (*for gambling and dancing*).

cundir *v.* to spread (*as news, disease, liquids*); to propagate, extend, multiply.

cuña *f.* wedge; splinter; *Am.* influential person.

cuñado *m.* brother-in-law; **cuñada** *f.* sister-in-law.

cuota *f.* quota; dues, fee; — **de entrada** admission fee.

cuotidiano *adj.* everyday, daily.

cupé *m.* coupé.

cupón *m.* coupon.

cúpula *f.* dome.

cura *f.* cure; *m.* curate, priest.

curación *f.* cure.

curandero *m.* healer (*not a doctor*); quack; medicine man (*among Indians*).

curar *v.* to cure, heal; to treat; to cure (*meats, tobacco*); to tan (*skins*); *Am.* to load (*dice*), fix (*cards*); — **de** to take care of; **-se** to cure oneself; to get well; *Am.* to get drunk.

curiosear *v.* to snoop, peek, peer, pry; to observe with curiosity.

curiosidad *f.* curiosity; neatness, daintiness.

curioso *adj.* curious; neat, dainty; **libros raros y -s** rare books.

curro *adj.* showy, gaudy, flashy; *m.* dandy.

currutaco *m.* fop, dandy; *adj.* affected (*in one's dress*).

cursi *adj.* common, in bad taste; cheap, ridiculous; **cursilería** *f.* bad taste, cheapness, false elegance; group of cheap, ridiculous people.

curso *m.* course, direction; scholastic year; course of study.

curtidor *m.* tanner.

curtiduría *f.* tannery.

curtir *v.* to tan; to harden, accustom to hardships; *Am.* to dirty, soil; **-se** to get tanned or sunburned; to become accustomed to hardships.

curva *f.* curve.

curvo *adj.* curved; bent, crooked; arched.

cúspide *f.* summit, peak, top; spire, steeple.

custodia *f.* custody; guard, guardian; monstrance (*vessel in which the consecrated Host is exposed*).

custodiar *v.* to guard, watch; to keep in custody.

custodio *m.* guardian, keeper.

cutícula *f.* cuticle.

cutis *m.* skin; complexion.

cuyo *rel. poss. adj.* whose, of whom, of which.

CH

chabacano *adj.* crude, unpolished; inartistic; cheap, in bad taste; *m. Am.* a variety of apricot.

chacota *f.* fun; jest; **echar a —** to take as a joke; **hacer — de** to make fun of.

chacotear *v.* to frolic, joke, make merry;

to be boisterous; to show off.

chacra *f. Am.* small farm; *Am.* cultivated field.

chagra *f. Am.* farm, piece of farm land; *m. & f. Am.* peasant; *adj.* uncivilized, unrefined.

chal *m.* shawl.

chalán *m.* horse trader; *Am.* broncobuster, horse breaker.

chaleco *m.* waistcoat, vest.

chalupa *f.* sloop, sailboat; launch; *Am.* canoe; *Am.* raft; *Am.* Mexican tortilla with sauce.

chamaco *m. Am.* boy; **chamaquito** *m. Am.* little boy.

chamarra *f.* coarse wool jacket or sweater; *Am.* sheepskin jacket, leather jacket; *Am.* heavy wool blanket.

chamarreta *f.* short loose jacket; *Am.* square poncho.

chambón *adj.* clumsy, awkward, unskillful; *m.* bungler, clumsy performer, awkward workman; clumsy player.

champaña *f.* champagne.

champú *m.* shampoo.

champurrado *m. Am.* a mixed drink of chocolate and **atole**; *Am.* a mixed alcoholic beverage.

champurrar, *Am.* **champurrear** *v.* to mix (*drinks*).

chamuscada, **chamuscadura** *f. Am.* singe, scorch.

chamuscar[6] *v.* to scorch; to singe; to sear; *Am.* to sell at a low cost; **-se** to get scorched, singed, or seared; *Am.* to get peeved, offended.

chamusquina *f.* singe, scorch.

chancear *v.* to fool, joke, jest.

chancero *m.* jester, joker; *adj.* jolly.

chancla *f.* slipper; old shoe; **chancleta** *f.* slipper; *m. Am.* good-for-nothing.

chanclo *m.* galosh, overshoe; clog; rubber overshoe; **-s** rubbers.

changador *m. Am.* carrier, porter; *Am.* handy man, person who does odd jobs.

chantaje *m.* blackmail, blackmailing.

chanza *f.* joke, jest.

chapa *f.* metal plate; veneer (*thin leaf of wood*); rosy spot on the cheeks; *Am.* lock; *Am.* Indian spy; **-s** game of tossing coins; **hombre de —** serious, reliable man.

chapado *adj.* veneered (*covered with a thin layer of wood or other material*); — **a la antigua** old-fashioned.

chapalear = **chapotear**.

chaparro *m.* scrub oak; short, chubby person; *Am.* a kind of tropical shrub with rough leaves; *Am.* short whip; *adj. Am.* short, squatty.

chaparrón m. downpour, heavy shower.

chapitel m. spire, steeple; capital (of a column).

chapotear v. to splash, paddle in the water.

chapoteo m. splash.

chapucear v. to fumble; to botch, bungle, do or make clumsily; Am. to deceive, trick.

chapulín m. Am. grasshopper.

chapurrar v. to speak (a language) brokenly; to mix (drinks).

chapuz m. dive, duck, ducking.

chapuza f. botch, clumsy piece of work; Am. foul trick, fraud.

chapuzar⁹ v. to duck; to dive.

chaqueta f. jacket; **chaquetón** m. long jacket, coat.

charamusca f. Am. twisted candy stick or cane; Am. brushwood, firewood; Am. hubbub, uproar.

charamusquero m. Am. candystick maker or vendor.

charca f. pond.

charco m. puddle, pool; **pasar el —** to cross the pond, cross the ocean.

charla f. chat, chatter, prattle.

charladuría f. chatter, gossip.

charlar v. to chat, chatter, prate.

charlatán m. chatterer, prater; gossiper; charlatan, quack.

charol m. varnish; patent leather; **charola** f. Am. tray.

charolar v. to varnish, polish.

charqui m. jerky, jerked beef.

charrúa m. & f. Am. Charruan Indian (Indian of Uruguay).

chascarrillo m. joke, funny story.

chasco m. joke, prank; surprise; disillusionment, disappointment; **llevarse —** to be disappointed, surprised or fooled; adj. Am. thick, curly (hair); Am. ruffled (plumage).

chasquear v. to play a trick on; to disappoint; to crack (a whip); to smack (the lips); to click (the tongue) to crack, snap; Am. to chatter (said of the teeth); Am. to munch (food); -se to be disappointed or disillusioned; to be tricked or fooled.

chasqui m. Am. courier, messenger.

chasquido m. crack of a whip; crackle; smack (of the lips); click (of the tongue).

chata f. bedpan; scow, barge, flat-bottomed boat; Am. platform wagon, platform car, flatcar; **chatita** f. Am. "honey," "cutie," "funny face."

chato adj. snub-nosed, flat-nosed; flat; flattened; squatty; Am. **quedarse uno —** to be left flat or in the lurch; to be disappointed.

chayote m. Am. vegetable pear (a tropical fruit growing on a vine); Am. dunce, silly fool.

che Am. word used in Argentina as a familiar form of address; **¡ — !** interj. Am. say! listen!

cheque m. check, bank check.

chica f. little girl; girl; maid, servant.

chicle m. Am. chicle; Am. chewing gum.

chico adj. small, little; m. child, boy; Am. each game of billiards; Am. = **chicozapote** (tropical fruit and tree from which chicle is extracted).

chicote m. cigar; piece of rope; Am. whip; Am. cigar butt.

chicotear v. Am. to lash, whip, flog; Am. to fight, quarrel; Am. to kill.

chicoteo m. Am. whipping; Am. shooting, killing; Am. crackling, rattling (as of machine guns); Am. quarreling.

chicha f. Am. chicha (a popular alcoholic beverage); Am. thick-soled shoe; **no ser ni — ni limonada** to be worth nothing, be neither fish nor fowl.

chícharo m. pea; Am. bad cigar; Am. apprentice.

chicharra f. cicada, locust; talkative person; Am. person with a shrill voice; Am. rickety, squeaky car; Am. harsh-sounding musical instrument or bell; Am. piece of fried pork skin.

chicharrón m. crackling, crisp piece of fried pork skin; burned piece of meat; sunburnt person; Am. dried-up, wrinkled person; Am. bootlicker, flatterer.

chichón m. bump, lump; Am. joker, jester; **chichona** adj. Am. large-breasted.

chiflado adj. "cracked", "touched", crazy; p.p. of chiflar.

chifladura f. craziness, mania; mockery, jest.

chiflar v. to whistle; to hiss; Am. to sing (said of birds); -se to lose one's head; to become unbalanced, crazy.

chiflido m. whistle; hiss; Am. **en un —** in a jiffy, in a second.

chile m. chili, red pepper.

chileno adj. & m. Chilean.

chillante adj. flashy, bright, showy, loud; shrieking.

chillar v. to shriek, scream; to hiss; Am. to shout, protest, moan; Am. to "squeal," turn informer; Am. **no — not to say a word**; Am. -se to be piqued, offended.

chillido m. shriek, scream.

chillón adj. shrieking, screaming; shrill;

59

loud, gaudy; *Am.* whining, discontented; *Am.* touchy.

chimenea *f.* chimney; fireplace, hearth.

china *f.* Chinese woman; pebble; porcelain; China silk or cotton; *Am.* girl,
young woman (*usually half-breed or
Indian*); *Am.* servant girl; *Am.* sweet
orange; *Am.* spinning top; **chinita** *f.*
Am. little Indian girl; darling.

chinche *f.* bedbug; thumbtack; tiresome
person, bore; *Am.* touchy or irritable
person; *Am.* plump, squatty person.

chino *adj.* Chinese; *Am.* curly; *m.*
Chinese; Chinaman; *Am.* pig; *Am.*
half-breed (*Negro and Indian, white
and Indian*); *Am.* Indian; *Am.* house
servant; *Am.* coarse, rough, ugly
person; *Am.* curl.

chiquero *m.* pigsty, pigpen; pen for
bulls; goat shelter.

chiquilín *m.* *Am.* tot, little boy;
chiquilina *f.* *Am.* little girl.

chiquito *adj.* tiny, very small; *m.* tiny
tot, tiny child; **chiquitico** *adj.* tiny.

chiripa *f.* stroke of good luck.

chiripá *m.* *Am.* loose riding trousers
(*square of cloth draped from the waist
and between the legs*).

chirola *f.* *Am.* "jug," jail; *Am.* coin of
low value.

chirona *f.* "jug," jail.

chirriar[17] *v.* to squeak, creak; to sizzle;
to chirp; to sing out of tune; *Am.* to
go on a spree.

chirrido *m.* creak, squeak; chirp;
squeaking, creaking; chirping.

chisguete *m.* squirt.

chisme *m.* gossip, piece of gossip; trifle,
trinket, knickknack, gadget.

chismear *v.* to gossip; to tattle.

chismería *f.* gossiping, talebearing.

chismero *adj.* gossiping; *m.* gossip.

chismoso *adj.* gossiping; *m.* gossip,
talebearer, tattletale.

chispa *f.* spark; small diamond; wit;
Am. false rumor, lie; *Am.* two-wheeled
cart; *Am.* brazen, shameless woman;
Am. **da** — it clicks, works, functions;
Am. **ponerse** — to get drunk.

chispeante *adj.* sparkling.

chispear *v.* to spark; to sparkle; to
twinkle; to drizzle.

chisporrotear *v.* to sputter, throw off
sparks.

chiste *m.* joke, jest; **dar en el** — to
guess right, hit the nail on the head.

chistera *f.* top hat; fish basket.

chistoso *adj.* funny, amusing, humorous.

¡chito! ¡chitón! *interj.* hush!

chiva *f.* female goat; *Am.* goatee; **chi-**

vo *m.* he-goat; *Am.* fit of anger; *Am.*
insulting remark; *Am.* **estar hecho
un** — to be very angry; *adj. Am.*
angry.

chocante *adj.* striking, surprising;
shocking; disgusting; *Am.* tiresome,
annoying, impertinent.

chocar[6] *v.* to bump, collide, clash; to
fight; to shock, surprise, disgust; **me
choca ese hombre** I loathe that man.

chocarrear *v.* to tell coarse jokes; to
clown.

chocarrería *f.* coarse joke; **chocarrero**
adj. coarse, vulgar; clownish.

choclo *m.* overshoe; clog; *Am.* low shoe
or slipper; *Am.* ear of corn; *Am.* corn
stew; *Am.* spike, ear of wheat.

chocolate *m.* chocolate.

chochear *v.* to be in one's dotage, act
senile.

chochera, chochez *f.* senility, dotage;
chocheras, chocheces senile actions
or habits.

chocho *adj.* doting; *m.* childish old
man.

chófer *m.* chauffeur.

cholo *m.* *Am.* half-breed; *Am.* half-
civilized Indian; *adj. Am.* coarse, rude;
Am. dark-skinned; *Am.* black (*dog*).

chopo *m.* black poplar; *adj. Am.* stupid.

choque *m.* collision, bump; shock;
clash, conflict; dispute.

chorizo *m.* sausage; *Am.* string of things;
Am. fool.

chorrazo *m.* spurt, large stream or jet.

chorrear *v.* to drip; to spout.

chorro *m.* spurt, jet; stream, flow; *Am.*
strand of a whip; *Am.* river rapids.

choteador *m.* *Am.* joker, jester.

chotear *v.* *Am.* to make fun of, jeer,
jest, mock, kid; *Am.* to idle, fool
around; *Am.* to pamper.

choteo *m.* *Am.* joking, jeering, kidding.

choza *f.* hut, cabin.

chubasco *m.* squall, sudden shower;
aguantar el — to weather the storm.

chuchería *f.* trifle, trinket; knickknack;
tidbit.

chueco *adj.* *Am.* crooked, bent; *Am.*
crook-legged, bow-legged, knock-
kneed; *Am.* worn-out, dejected; *Am.*
disgusted, annoyed; *Am.* **comerciar
en** — to trade in stolen goods.

chuleta *f.* cutlet, chop; blow, slap.

chulo *m.* dandy; effeminate man;
clownish fellow; bullfighter's assistant; *Am.* buzzard; *Am.* coarse, thick
brush; *adj. Am.* good-looking, pretty.

chupada *f.* sucking; suction; suck, sip;
Am. puff from a cigarette; *Am.*

big swallow of liquor.

chupador *m.* sucker; teething ring; *Am.* toper, heavy drinker; *Am.* smoker.

chupaflor, chuparrosa *m. Am.* hummingbird.

chupar *v.* to suck; to sip; to absorb, take in; *Am.* to smoke; *Am.* to drink, get drunk; -se to shrivel up.

churrasco *m. Am.* roasted meat; *Am.* barbecued meat; *Am.* large piece of meat for barbecuing.

churrasquear *v. Am.* to barbecue, roast over coals; *Am.* to prepare (*meat*) for barbecuing; *Am.* to eat barbecued meat.

churrasquito *m.* small piece of roast.

churrigueresco *adj.* baroque, ornate (*architecture*).

chuscada *f.* jest, joke.

chusco *adj.* funny, witty; ridiculous; *Am.* **perro** — mongrel dog.

chusma *f.* rabble, mob.

D

dable *adj.* feasible, possible.

daca = **da acá.**

dádiva *f.* gift.

dadivoso *adj.* liberal, generous.

dado *m.* die; -s dice.

dador *m.* giver.

daga *f.* dagger.

dama *f.* lady; **jugar a las -s** to play checkers.

damisela *f.* damsel, girl.

danza *f.* dance.

danzante *m. & f.* dancer.

danzar[9] *v.* to dance.

danzarina *f.* dancer.

dañar *v.* to harm, hurt, damage; -se to spoil, rot; to get hurt; to get damaged.

dañino *adj.* harmful; destructive.

daño *m.* damage, harm, loss.

dañoso *adj.* harmful.

dar[26] *v. irr.* to give; to strike, hit; to emit, give off; — **a luz** to give birth to; to publish; — **con** to encounter, find; — **de comer** to feed; — **de sí** to give, stretch; — **en** to hit upon; to persist in; — **largas a un asunto** to prolong or postpone a matter; *Am.* — **cuero (guasca, puños)** to beat, thrash, lash; **lo mismo da** it makes no difference; -se to give up; **dárselas de** to boast of.

dardo *m.* dart, arrow.

dares y tomares *m. pl.* give-and-take, dispute; dealings.

dársena *f.* dock, wharf.

datar *v.* to date; — **de** to date from.

dátil *m.* date (*fruit of the date palm*).

dato *m.* datum, fact; -s data.

de *prep.* of, from; about, concerning; in (*after a superlative*); if (*before inf.*); — **no llegar** if he does not arrive; **el** — **la gorra azul** the one with the blue cap; **el mejor** — **América** the best in America; **más** — **lo que dice** more than he says.

debajo *adv.* under, underneath; — **de** *prep.* under.

debate *m.* debate; dispute, quarrel.

debatir *v.* to debate, argue, discuss; to fight; -se to struggle.

debe *m.* debit.

debelar *v.* to subdue, defeat.

deber *v.* to owe; to have to (must, should, ought); **debe de ser** it must be, probably is; ¡**me la debes!** I have an account to settle with you!

deber *m.* duty, obligation; debt; debit, debit side (*in bookkeeping*).

debido *adj.* due, owing; just, appropriate.

débil *adj.* weak, feeble.

debilidad *f.* debility, weakness.

debilitación *f.,* **debilitamiento** *m.* weakening; weakness.

debilitar *v.* to weaken.

débito *m.* debt; debit.

debutar *v.* to make a debut, make a first public appearance.

década *f.* decade, ten years; series of ten.

decadencia *f.* decadence, decline, falling off.

decaer[24] *v. irr.* to decay, decline, wither, fade; to fall to leeward.

decaimiento *m.* decline, decay; dejection; weakness.

decano *m.* dean; senior member of a group.

decantado *p.p. & adj.* much talked about; overrated.

decapitar *v.* to behead.

decencia *f.* decency; **decente** *adj.* decent; respectable; fair.

decenio *m.* decade.

decepción *f.* disillusion, disappointment.

decepcionante *adj.* disappointing.

decepcionar *v.* to disillusion, disappoint.

decidir *v.* to decide, resolve; -se a to make up one's mind to; to decide to.

décima *f.* tenth; tithe; stanza of ten octosyllabic lines.

décimo *adj.* tenth.

decir[27] *v. irr.* to say; to tell; to speak; **es** — that is; **querer** — to mean, signify.

decisión *f.* decision.

decisivo *adj.* decisive, final.

declamar v. to declaim, recite.
declaración f. declaration; statement; deposition, testimony.
declarar v. to declare, state, affirm; to testify; -se to propose, declare one's love; to give one's views or opinion.
declinar v. to decline; to go down; to lose vigor, decay; to bend down.
declive m. declivity, slope.
decoración f. decoration, ornament; stage setting.
decorar v. to decorate, adorn.
decorativo adj. decorative, ornamental.
decoro m. decorum, propriety, dignity; honor.
decoroso adj. decorous, becoming, proper, decent.
decrépito adj. decrepit, old, feeble.
decretar v. to decree.
decreto m. decree; decision, order.
dechado m. model, pattern, example.
dedal m. thimble.
dedicar⁶ v. to dedicate; to devote; -se to apply oneself.
dedicatoria f. dedication, inscription.
dedo m. finger; toe; — del corazón middle finger; — meñique little finger; — pulgar thumb; no mamarse el — not to be easily fooled; dedillo m. small finger; saber al dedillo to know perfectly, know by heart.
deducción f. deduction; inference.
deducir²⁵ v. irr. to deduce, conclude; to deduct.
defecto m. defect, fault.
defectuoso adj. defective, faulty.
defender¹ v. irr. to defend.
defensa f. defense; Am. automobile bumper.
defensivo adj. defensive; m. defense, safeguard; defensiva f. defensive.
defensor m. defender.
deficiencia f. deficiency; deficiente adj. deficient.
déficit m. deficit, shortage.
definición f. definition.
definido adj. definite; p.p. of definir.
definir v. to define, explain; to determine.
definitivo adj. definitive, conclusive, final; en definitiva in short, in conclusion; definitely.
deformación f. deformation, deformity.
deformar v. to deform; -se to become deformed; to lose its shape or form.
deforme adj. deformed; ugly.
deformidad f. deformity.
defraudar v. to defraud, cheat, rob of.
defunción f. death, decease.
degenerado adj. & m. degenerate.

degenerar v. to degenerate.
deglución f. swallowing.
deglutir v. to swallow.
degollar² v. irr. to behead; to slash the throat; to cut (a dress) low in the neck.
degradar v. to degrade; to debase.
degüello m. beheading; throat-slashing.
dehesa f. pasture, grazing ground.
deidad f. deity.
dejadez f. lassitude, languor, listlessness; self-neglect, slovenliness.
dejado adj. indolent, listless; slovenly.
dejar v. to leave; to quit; to let go; to omit; to let, permit; to abandon; — de to stop, cease; — caer to drop; Am. no -se not to be an easy mark, not to let others pick on one.
dejo m. aftertaste; slight accent, peculiar inflection; slight taste.
del = de + el of the.
delantal m. apron.
delante adv. before, in front; — de prep. in front of.
delantera f. lead, forepart, front.
delantero adj. front, foremost, first.
delatar v. to denounce, accuse, inform against.
delator m. accuser, informer.
delegación f. delegation.
delegado m. delegate.
delegar⁷ v. to delegate.
deleitable adj. delightful, enjoyable.
deleitar v. to delight, please.
deleite m. delight, joy, pleasure.
deleitoso adj. delightful.
deletrear v. to spell.
deleznable adj. perishable; brittle.
delgadez f. thinness; slimness; fineness.
delgado adj. thin, slender, slim.
deliberado adj. deliberate; p.p. of deliberar.
deliberar v. to deliberate, consider, ponder.
delicadeza f. fineness; delicacy; softness, exquisiteness.
delicado adj. delicate; weak, frail; exquisite, dainty; tender.
delicia f. delight.
delicioso adj. delicious, delightful.
delincuente adj., m. & f. delinquent.
delineación f., delineamiento m. delineation, design, outline, drawing; portrayal.
delinear v. to delineate, sketch, outline.
delirante adj. delirious, raving.
delirar v. to be delirious; to rave, talk wildly or foolishly.
delirio m. delirium, temporary madness; wild excitement; foolishness.
delito m. crime; misdemeanor.

demacrado *adj.* scrawny, emaciated, thin.

demanda *f.* demand; petition; question; claim; complaint; lawsuit.

demandado *m.* defendant; *p.p. of* **demandar.**

demandante *m. & f.* plaintiff.

demandar *v.* to demand; to petition; to sue, file a suit; to indict.

demás *indef. adj. & pron.*: **los —** the rest; the others; **las — personas** the other people; **lo —** the rest; **por —** useless; uselessly; **por lo —** as to the rest; moreover.

demasía *f.* excess; boldness, insolence; offense, outrage; **en —** excessively.

demasiado *adv.* too much, excessively; too; *adj.* too much, excessive.

demente *adj.* demented, insane, crazy.

democracia *f.* democracy; **demócrata** *m. & f.* democrat; **democrático** *adj.* democratic.

demoler[2] *v.irr.* to demolish, tear down.

demonio *m.* demon, devil; evil spirit.

demontre *m.* devil; **¡ — !** the deuce!

demora *f.* delay.

demorar *v.* to delay; to retard; **-se** to linger; to be delayed.

demostración *f.* demonstration; proof, explanation.

demostrar[2] *v. irr.* to demonstrate, show, prove, explain.

demostrativo *adj.* demonstrative.

demovilizar[9] *v.* to demobilize.

demudar *v.* to change, alter; to disguise; **-se** to change color or one's facial expression; to turn pale.

dengoso, denguero *adj.* affected; finicky.

dengue *m.* primness; coyness, affectation; dengue, breakbone fever; *Am.* marigold; *Am.* zigzag; *Am.* swagger; **hacer -s** to act coy, make grimaces.

denigrar *v.* to blacken, defame, revile, insult.

denodado *adj.* dauntless, daring.

denominación *f.* denomination; name, title, designation.

denominar *v.* to name, call, entitle.

denostar[2] *v. irr.* to insult, outrage, revile.

denotar *v.* to denote, indicate, mean.

densidad *f.* density.

denso *adj.* dense, compact; thick.

dentado *adj.* toothed, notched.

dentadura *f.* set of teeth.

dentar[1] *v. irr.* to tooth, furnish (*a saw*) with teeth; to indent; to cut teeth, grow teeth (*referring to a child*).

dentellada *f.* bite; tooth mark; **a -s** with big bites.

dentición *f.* teething.

dentífrico *m.* dentifrice, tooth cleanser; **pasta dentífrica** toothpaste; **polvos dentífricos** toothpowder.

dentista *m.* dentist.

dentro *adv.* inside, within; **— de** *prep.* inside of; **por —** on the inside.

denuedo *m.* spirit, courage, daring.

denuesto *m.* affront, insult.

denuncia *f.* denunciation, condemnation, accusation; miner's claim.

denunciar *v.* to denounce, accuse; to proclaim, advise, give notice; to claim (*a mine*).

deparar *v.* to furnish, offer, supply.

departamento *m.* department; compartment; apartment.

departir *v.* to talk, converse.

dependencia *f.* dependence; dependency; branch office.

depender *v.* to depend, rely (on).

dependiente *m.* clerk; dependent, subordinate; *adj.* dependent.

deplorar *v.* to deplore, lament, regret.

deponer[40] *v. irr.* to set aside; to depose, remove (*an official*); to testify, declare; to have a bowel movement; *Am.* to vomit.

deportar *v.* to deport, banish.

deporte *m.* sport; pastime, recreation.

deportista *m.* sportsman; *f.* sportswoman.

deportivo *adj.* sport, sports (*used as an adj.*); **copa deportiva** loving cup.

deposición *f.* declaration, assertion; testimony; dismissal, removal (*from office or power*); bowel movement.

depositar *v.* to deposit; to deliver, intrust.

depositario *m.* receiver, trustee.

depósito *m.* deposit; storage; warehouse; **— de agua** reservoir.

depravado *adj.* depraved, corrupt, degenerate.

depravar *v.* to corrupt, pervert, contaminate.

depreciar *v.* to depreciate, lessen the value of.

depresión *f.* depression; dip, sag.

deprimente *adj.* depressing.

deprimir *v.* to depress; to press down; to humiliate, belittle.

depuesto *p.p. of* **deponer.**

depurar *v.* to purify.

derecha *f.* right hand; right side; **right wing** (*in politics*); **a la —** to the right.

derecho *adj.* right; straight; *m.* law; duty, tax; fee.

derechura *f.* straightness.

deriva *f.* drift (*of a boat or plane*); **irse** (*or* **andar) a la —** to drift, be drifting.

derivar *v.* to derive; to come (from).

derogar[7] *v.* to revoke, repeal, abolish.

derramamiento *m.* spill, spilling, shedding; overflow; scattering; — **de sangre** bloodshed.

derramar *v.* to spill; to spread, scatter; to shed.

derrame *m.* spill, spilling, shedding; overflow; discharge (*of secretion, blood, etc.*); slope.

derredor *m.* circuit; contour; **al —** around; **en —** around.

derrengado *p.p. & adj.* lame, crippled; dislocated (*said of hip or spine*).

derrengar[1, 7] *v. irr.* to dislocate or sprain (*hip or spine*); to cripple; to bend.

derretimiento *m.* thaw, thawing, melting.

derretir[5] *v. irr.* to melt, dissolve; **-se** to be consumed; to melt.

derribar *v.* to demolish, knock down, fell; to overthrow; **-se** to lie down, throw oneself down.

derrocamiento *m.* overthrow.

derrocar[6] *v.* to fling down; to fell; to overthrow.

derrochador *m.* squanderer, spendthrift; *adj.* wasteful, extravagant.

derrochar *v.* to waste; to squander.

derroche *m.* waste; dissipation, lavish spending.

derrota *f.* rout, defeat; ship's route or course.

derrotar *v.* to defeat; to squander; to destroy, ruin; to lose or shift its course (*said of a ship*).

derrotero *m.* course, direction; ship's course; book of marine charts.

derrumbadero *m.* precipice.

derrumbamiento *m.* landslide; collapse.

derrumbar *v.* to fling down; *Am.* to knock down; *Am.* to go down in a hurry; **-se** to crumble away; to topple over; *Am.* to dwindle (*as a business*).

derrumbe *m.* landslide; collapse.

desabotonar *v.* to unbutton.

desabrido *adj.* tasteless, insipid; harsh; sour.

desabrigar[7] *v.* to uncover; **-se** to uncover oneself.

desabrimiento *m.* tastelessness; harshness; sourness.

desabrochar *v.* to unfasten, unbutton, unclasp; **-se** to unbutton oneself, unfasten one's clothes.

desacato *m.* irreverence, disrespect; profanation.

desacierto *m.* mistake, error.

desacostumbrado *adj.* unaccustomed; unusual; *p.p. of* **desacostumbrar**.

desacostumbrar *v.* to disaccustom, rid of a habit; **-se** to become unaccustomed; to lose a custom.

desacreditar *v.* to discredit; to disgrace.

desacuerdo *m.* disagreement; discord; blunder; forgetfulness.

desafiar[17] *v.* to challenge; to compete; to defy.

desafinado *adj.* out of tune.

desafinar *v.* to be discordant; to be out of tune; **-se** to get out of tune.

desafío *m.* challenge, defiance; duel; contest.

desafortunado *adj.* unfortunate, unlucky.

desafuero *m.* violation; outrage, abuse.

desagradable *adj.* disagreeable, unpleasant.

desagradar *v.* to displease.

desagradecido *adj.* ungrateful

desagrado *m.* displeasure; discontent.

desagraviar *v.* to make amends; to compensate for a damage or injury; to right a wrong; to apologize; to vindicate.

desagravio *m.* reparation; compensation for a wrong or injury; vindication; apology.

desaguadero *m.* drain, drain pipe, water outlet.

desaguar[8] *v.* to drain, draw off; to flow (into); *Am.* to wash (*something*) two or more times; *Am.* to extract the juice from; *Am.* to urinate; **-se** to drain.

desagüe *m.* drainage; drain.

desaguisado *m.* outrage, violence, wrong.

desahogado *p.p. & adj.* relieved; roomy, spacious; **estar —** to be in easy or comfortable circumstances; to be well-off.

desahogar[7] *v.* to relieve from pain or trouble; **-se** to find relief or release; to unbosom oneself, disclose one's feelings.

desahogo *m.* relief from pain or trouble; release; ease, comfort, relaxation; freedom, unrestraint.

desairar *v.* to slight, snub, disdain; to rebuff; to disappoint; to neglect.

desaire *m.* rebuff, snub, slight, disdain.

desalentar[1] *v. irr.* to put out of breath; to discourage; **-se** to get discouraged.

desaliento *m.* discouragement, dejection.

desaliñado *adj.* disheveled, slovenly, unkempt, untidy; disorderly.

desaliño *m.* slovenliness, untidiness; neglect, carelessness; disorder.

desalmado *adj.* soulless, cruel, inhuman.
desalojar *v.* to dislodge; to evict, expel from a lodging; to vacate.
desamarrar *v.* to untie, unfasten; to unmoor (*a ship*).
desamparar *v.* to abandon, forsake.
desamparo *m.* desertion, abandonment.
desamueblado *adj.* unfurnished.
desangrar *v.* to bleed, draw blood from; to drain; -se to bleed, lose blood.
desanimado *adj.* discouraged; lifeless; dull (*said of a party, meeting, etc.*).
desanimar *v.* to dishearten, discourage.
desaparecer[13] *v. irr.* to disappear; to hide; -se to disappear, vanish.
desaparición *f.* disappearance.
desapasionado *adj.* dispassionate; free from passion; calm; impartial.
desapego *m.* aloofness, indifference; detachment.
desapercibido *adj.* unprepared; unprovided; unnoticed.
desaprobación *f.* disapproval.
desaprobar[2] *v. irr.* to disapprove.
desarmar *v.* to disarm; to dismount, take apart.
desarme *m.* disarmament.
desarraigar[7] *v.* to root out, uproot.
desarreglado *p.p.* & *adj.* disordered; disorderly; slovenly.
desarreglar *v.* to disarrange, disorder, disturb, upset.
desarreglo *m.* disorder, confusion.
desarrollar *v.* to unroll, unfold; to develop, explain; -se to develop; to unfold.
desarrollo *m.* development.
desaseado *adj.* unkempt, untidy.
desaseo *m.* slover liness, untidiness.
desasir[22] *v. irr.* to loosen, unfasten; -se to get loose (from); to let go (of).
desasosiego *m.* unrest, uneasiness, restlessness.
desastrado *adj.* unfortunate, unhappy; ragged, dirty, untidy.
desastre *m.* disaster.
desastroso *adj.* disastrous, unfortunate.
desatar *v.* to untie, loosen; to dissolve; to unravel, clear up; -se to let loose, let go; to break loose; -se en improperios to let out a string of insults.
desatención *f.* inattention, lack of attention; discourtesy.
desatender[1] *v. irr.* to disregard, pay no attention (to); to slight, neglect.
desatento *adj.* inattentive; discourteous.
desatinado *adj.* senseless; reckless.
desatinar *v.* to act foolishly; to talk nonsense; to blunder; to rave; to lose one's bearings.

desatino *m.* blunder, error; folly, nonsense.
desatracar[6] *v.* to push off (*from shore or from another ship*); to cast off, unmoor.
desavenencia *f.* disagreement, discord; dispute, misunderstanding.
desayunarse *v.* to eat breakfast; — con la noticia to hear a piece of news for the first time.
desayuno *m.* breakfast.
desazón *f.* uneasiness, anxiety; insipidity, flatness, tastelessness; displeasure.
desbandarse *v.* to disband, scatter, disperse; to desert the army or a party.
desbaratar *v.* to destroy, ruin; to upset, disturb; to disperse, put to flight; to talk nonsense; -se to be upset, be in disorder; to fall to pieces.
desbocado *adj.* runaway (*horse*), dashing headlong; foul-mouthed, abusive; broken-mouthed (*jar, pitcher, etc.*).
desbordamiento *m.* overflow, flood.
desbordante *adj.* overflowing; *Am.* frantic.
desbordar *v.* to overflow, flood; -se to spill over; to get overexcited.
descabalar *v.* to break (*a given amount, making it thereby incomplete*).
descabezado *p.p.* beheaded; *adj.* headless; harebrained, thoughtless.
descabezar[9] *v.* to behead; to chop off the head or tip of; — el sueño to take a nap; -se to break one's head; to rack one's brain.
descaecido *adj.* feeble, weak; — de ánimo depressed, dejected, despondent.
descaecimiento *m.* languor, weakness; depression, dejection.
descalabradura *f.* blow or wound on the head; scar on the head.
descalabrar *v.* to wound on the head; to hurt, injure; to damage; -se to suffer a head wound or skull fracture.
descalabro *m.* loss, misfortune.
descalzar[9] *v.* to take off (*someone's*) shoes or (and) stockings; -se to take off one's shoes or (and) stockings; to lose a shoe (*said of horses*).
descalzo *adj.* barefoot; shoeless.
descaminar *v.* to mislead, lead astray; -se to go astray.
descamisado *adj.* shirtless; in rags; *m.* ragamuffin, ragged fellow.
descansar *v.* to rest.
descanso *m.* rest; staircase landing.
descarado *adj.* shameless, impudent, brazen.
descarga *f.* discharge; unloading.
descargar[7] *v.* to discharge; to unload.

descargo m. discharge (of a duty or obligation); unloading; relief.

descargue m. unloading; discharge.

descarnado adj. fleshless, scrawny.

descarnar v. to pull the flesh from the bone; to corrode, eat away; -se to become thin, emaciated.

descaro m. effrontery, shamelessness, impudence, audacity.

descarriar[17] v. to mislead, lead astray; to separate (cattle) from the herd; -se to stray; to go astray.

descarrilar v. to derail (cause a train to run off the track); to wreck (a train); -se to get or run off the track; to go astray.

descartar v. to discard; to put aside.

descascarado p.p. & adj. peeled off; chipped off.

descascarar v. to shell, hull, husk; to peel; to chip off (plaster); Am. to defame, discredit; Am. to flay; -se to chip off, peel off.

descendencia f. descent, lineage; descendants, offspring.

descendente adj. descending, downward.

descender[1] v. irr. to descend, go down; to get down; to come (from), originate.

descendiente m. & f. descendant; adj. descending.

descendimiento m. descent.

descenso m. descent; fall.

descifrar v. to decipher, puzzle out, figure out.

descolgar[2,7] v. irr. to unhang, take down; to let down; -se to climb down (a rope, tree, etc.); -se to drop in, appear unexpectedly.

descolorar v. to discolor; to fade; -se to fade, lose its color; to discolor.

descolorido adj. pale.

descollar[2] v. irr. to excel; to stand out, tower (above).

descomedido adj. rude, discourteous, impolite; unobliging.

descompletar v. to make incomplete, break (a unit, sum, set, etc.).

descomponer[40] v. irr. to upset, disturb; to put out of order; to decompose; -se to decompose, rot; to become upset, ill; to get out of order; Am. se me descompuso el brazo I dislocated my arm, my arm got out of joint.

descomposición f. decomposition; decay, corruption; disorder, confusion.

descompuesto p.p. of **descomponer**; adj. out of order; insolent; brazen; immodest.

descomunal adj. colossal, enormous, monstrous.

desconcertante adj. disconcerting, disturbing, confusing, baffling, embarrassing.

desconcertar[1] v. irr. to disconcert, bewilder, confuse; to disturb; -se to be confused, perplexed.

desconcierto m. disorder; confusion; disagreement; feeling of discomfort.

desconchadura f. chip (chipped off place); chipping off, peeling off (of plaster, varnish, etc.).

desconchar v. to scrape off (plaster or stucco); -se to peel off, chip off (as plaster).

desconectar v. to disconnect.

desconfiado adj. distrustful, suspicious.

desconfianza f. mistrust, distrust.

desconfiar[17] v. to distrust; to lose confidence.

desconocer[13] v. irr. to fail to recognize or remember; to disown; to disregard, slight; not to know.

desconocido adj. unknown; unrecognizable; m. stranger.

desconocimiento m. disregard; ignorance.

desconsolado p.p. & adj. disconsolate, forlorn; disheartened, grieved.

desconsolador adj. disheartening, saddening.

desconsolar[2] v. irr. to sadden, grieve; to discourage; -se to become disheartened, grieved.

desconsuelo m. dejection, sadness, distress.

descontar[2] v. irr. to discount, deduct; to allow for.

descontentadizo adj. discontented, fretful, hard to please.

descontentar v. to displease.

descontento adj. discontent, displeased; m. discontent, displeasure.

descorazonado adj. disheartened, discouraged, depressed.

descorchar v. to uncork; to remove the bark from (a cork tree); to force or break open.

descortés adj. discourteous, rude, impolite.

descortesía f. discourtesy, rudeness, impoliteness.

descortezar[9] v. to bark, strip the bark from (trees); to remove the crust or shell from; to peel; to civilize, remove the rough manners from.

descoser v. to rip, unsew, unstitch; -se to rip, come unstitched; to talk too much or indiscreetly.

descosido m. rip; adj. too talkative, indiscreet; disorderly, *p.p. of* **descoser.**

descostrar *v.* to flake; to scale off; to remove the crust from; **-se** to flake, scale off.

descoyuntado *p.p. & adj.* dislocated, out of joint.

descoyuntar *v.* to dislocate, put out of joint; **-se** to get out of joint.

descrédito *m.* discredit.

descreído *adj.* incredulous, unbelieving; *m.* unbeliever.

descreimiento *m.* unbelief, lack of faith.

describir[52] *v.* to describe.

descripción *f.* description.

descriptivo *adj.* descriptive.

descrito *p.p. irr. of* **describir.**

descuartizar[9] *v.* to quarter (*an animal*); to tear or cut into parts.

descubierto *p.p. of* **descubrir** *& adj.* discovered; uncovered; hatless; bareheaded; *m.* deficit, shortage; **al —** openly, in the open; **en —** uncovered, unpaid.

descubridor *m.* discoverer.

descubrimiento *m.* discovery; find; invention.

descubrir[52] *v.* to discover; to uncover; **-se** to uncover; to take off one's hat.

descuento *m.* discount; deduction.

descuidado *adj.* careless, negligent; untidy, slovenly; unaware; thoughtless.

descuidar *v.* to neglect; to overlook; to be careless or negligent; **-se** to be careless or negligent.

descuido *m.* carelessness; neglect; oversight; disregard; inattention; slip, error.

desde *prep.* from; since; **— luego** immediately; of course; **— que** *conj.* since, ever since.

desdecir[27] *v. irr.* to be out of harmony (with); to detract (from); **-se** to retract; to contradict oneself.

desdén *m.* disdain, scorn.

desdentado *adj.* toothless.

desdeñar *v.* to disdain, scorn.

desdeñoso *adj.* disdainful, scornful.

desdicha *f.* misfortune; misery, poverty.

desdichado *adj.* unfortunate; unhappy, wretched; miserable; *m.* wretch.

desdoblamiento *m.* unfolding.

desdoblar *v.* to unfold; to spread out.

desdorar *v.* to remove the gilt from; to tarnish; to dishonor.

desdoro *m.* tarnish, blemish; dishonor.

deseable *adj.* desirable.

desear *v.* to desire, want.

desecación *f.*, **desecamiento** *m.* drying; drainage.

desecar[6] *v.* to dry; to dry up; to drain

(*land*).

desechar *v.* to discard; to reject; to refuse, decline; *Am.* to cut across, take a short cut.

desecho *m.* remainder, residue; waste material; piece of junk; discard; **-s** refuse, scraps, junk; **hierro de —** scrap iron; **papel de —** wastepaper, scraps of paper.

desembalar *v.* to unpack.

desembarazar[9] *v.* to rid, free, clear; *Am.* to give birth; **-se** to get rid of.

desembarazo *m.* freedom, case, naturalness; *Am.* childbirth.

desembarcadero *m.* dock, wharf, pier.

desembarcar[6] *v.* to disembark, land; to unload; to go ashore.

desembarco, desembarque *m.* landing; unloading.

desembocadura *f.* mouth (*of a river, canal, etc.*); outlet.

desembocar[6] *v.* to flow (into); to lead (to).

desembolsar *v.* to disburse, pay out.

desembolso *m.* disbursement, outlay, expenditure.

desembragar[7] *v.* to throw out the clutch; to disconnect.

desemejante *adj.* unlike.

desempacar[6] *v.* to unpack.

desempeñar *v.* to recover, redeem, take out of pawn; **— un cargo** to perform the duties of a position; **— un papel** to play a part; **-se** to get out of debt.

desempeño *m.* fulfilment, carrying out, discharge; performance (*of a duty*); acting (*of a role*); redeeming (*of a thing pawned*).

desempleado *adj.* unemployed.

desempleo *m.* unemployment.

desempolvar *v.* to dust, remove the dust from.

desencadenar *v.* to unchain, free from chains; to loosen, set free; **-se** to free oneself; to break loose.

desencajado *p.p.. & adj.* disjointed; disfigured; sunken (*eyes*); emaciated.

desencantar *v.* to disillusion, disappoint.

desencanto *m.* disillusion, disappointment.

desenfado *m.* ease, freedom; calmness.

desenfrenado *p.p. & adj.* unbridled; wanton, reckless; loose, immoral.

desenganchar *v.* to unhitch; to unhook; to unfasten.

desengañador *adj.* disappointing, disillusioning.

desengañar *v.* to undeceive, disillusion, disappoint.

desengaño m. disillusion, disappointment, blighted hope.

desengranar v. to throw out of gear.

desenmarañar v. to untangle; to unravel.

desenmascarar v. to unmask.

desenredar v. to disentangle, unravel.

desenrollar v. to unroll.

desensartar v. to unstring; to unthread; to unfasten from a ring.

desensillar v. to unsaddle.

desentenderse[1] v. irr. to neglect, ignore, pay no attention to; to pretend not to see, hear or understand.

desentendido adj. unmindful, heedless; p.p. of **desentenderse**; **hacerse el —** to pretend not to notice.

desenterrar[1] v. irr. to unearth, dig up.

desentonado adj. inharmonious, out of tune.

desentonar v. to be out of tune; to be out of harmony; to sing off key, play out of tune.

desenvoltura f. freedom, ease, abandon; boldness, impudence.

desenvolver[2, 52] v. irr. to unroll, unfold; to unwrap; to develop.

desenvolvimiento m. development, unfolding.

desenvuelto adj. free, easy; forward, bold; shameless, brazen; p.p. of **desenvolver**.

deseo m. desire, wish.

deseoso adj. desirous, eager.

desequilibrado adj. unbalanced; p.p. of **desequilibrar**.

desequilibrar v. to unbalance; to derange.

desequilibrio m. lack of balance; derangement, mental disorder.

deserción f. desertion.

desertar v. to desert; to abandon; -se de to desert.

desertor m. deserter; quitter.

desesperación f. despair; desperation; fury.

desesperado adj. desperate; despairing; hopeless, p.p.. of **desesperar**.

desesperanzado p.p. & adj. discouraged; hopeless; desperate, in despair.

desesperanzar[9] v. to discourage, deprive of hope; -se to be discouraged; to despair, lose one's hope.

desesperar v. to despair, lose hope; to make (someone) despair; -se to despair, be desperate; to be furious.

desfachatez f. shamelessness, effrontery, impudence.

desfalcar[6] v. to embezzle; to remove a part of.

desfalco m. embezzlement; diminution, decrease.

desfallecer[13] v. irr. to grow weak; to faint.

desfallecimiento m. faintness; weakness; languor; swoon, faint.

desfavorable adj. unfavorable.

desfigurar v. to disfigure; to deface; to distort.

desfiladero m. narrow passage, narrow gorge; road on the edge of a precipice.

desfilar v. to march, parade, pass by.

desfile m. parade.

desgana f. lack of appetite; reluctance.

desgarrado p.p. torn; adj. shameless; impudent.

desgarradura f. tear.

desgarrar v. to tear, rend; to expectorate, cough up; -se to tear; to separate oneself (from).

desgastar v. to waste, consume, wear away; -se to waste away, lose one's strength or vigor; to wear off.

desgaste m. waste; wear and tear.

desgracia f. misfortune, mishap; disgrace.

desgraciado adj. unfortunate, wretched.

desgranar v. to thrash, thresh (grain); to remove the grain from; to shell (peas, beans, etc.).

desgreñado adj. disheveled.

deshabitado adj. uninhabited, deserted; empty, vacant.

deshacer[31] v. irr. to undo; to dissolve; to destroy; to untie; -se to dissolve; to melt; to waste away; -se de to get rid of.

desharrapado, desarrapado adj. ragged, shabby, tattered.

deshecha f. simulation, pretense; **hacer la —** to feign, pretend.

deshecho p.p. of **deshacer** & adj. undone; ruined, destroyed, in pieces; violent (said of rainstorms); worn-out, fatigued; Am. disorderly, untidy.

deshelar[1] v. irr. to melt; to thaw; -se to melt; to thaw.

desherbar[1] v. irr. to weed.

deshielo m. thaw.

deshierbe m. weeding.

deshilachar v. to ravel, fray.

deshilar v. to unravel; -se to unravel; to fray.

deshojar v. to strip off the leaves, petals, or pages; -se to lose its leaves (said of a plant or book); to lose petals.

deshollejar v. to husk, hull; to peel, pare, skin; to shell (beans).

deshonesto adj. immodest; unchaste, lewd.

deshonra *f.* dishonor; disgrace.

deshonrar *v.* to dishonor, disgrace; to insult, offend; to seduce.

deshonroso *adj.* dishonorable; shameful.

deshora *f.* inopportune time; **a —** (*or a* **-s**) unexpectedly; **comer a —** to piece, eat between meals.

deshuesar *v.* to stone, remove the pits or stones from (*fruits*); to bone, remove the bones from (*an animal*).

desidia *f.* indolence, laziness.

desidioso *adj.* indolent, negligent, lazy; listless.

desierto *adj.* deserted, uninhabited; alone, lonely; *m.* desert, wilderness.

designación *f.* designation; appointment.

designar *v.* to designate, appoint, select; to design, plan, intend.

designio *m.* design, plan, purpose.

desigual *adj.* unequal; uneven; variable, changeable.

desigualdad *f.* inequality; unevenness; roughness (*of the ground*).

desilusión *f.* disillusion, disappointment.

desilusionar *v.* to disillusion, disappoint; **-se** to become disillusioned; to lose one's illusions.

desinencia *f.* termination, ending (*of a word*).

desinfectante *adj.* disinfecting; *m.* disinfectant.

desinfectar *v.* to disinfect.

desinflado *adj.* deflated, not inflated, flat.

desinterés *m.* disinterestedness, unselfishness, impartiality.

desinteresado *adj.* disinterested, unselfish, fair, impartial.

desistir *v.* to desist, stop, cease.

deslavado *p.p. & adj.* half-washed; weakened; faded; pale; saucy.

deslavar *v.* to wash away; to fade; to wash superficially.

desleal *adj.* disloyal, faithless.

desleír[15] *v. irr.* to dissolve; to dilute, make thin or weak; **-se** to become diluted.

deslindar *v.* to mark off, mark the boundaries of.

desliz *m.* slip, slide; error.

deslizador *m.* glider.

deslizamiento *m.* slip, slipping; glide; sliding, skidding.

deslizar[9] *v.* to slip, slide; **-se** to slip; to skid; to glide; to slip out.

deslucido *p.p. & adj.* tarnished; dull; discredited; dingy, shabby; awkward, ungraceful; inelegant.

deslucir[13] *v. irr.* to tarnish, dull the lustre of; to discredit.

deslumbrador *adj.* dazzling, glaring.

deslumbramiento *m.* dazzle, glare; daze, confusion.

deslumbrar *v.* to dazzle.

deslustrado *adj. & p.p.* tarnished; dim, dull; opaque.

deslustrar *v.* to tarnish; to soil, stain (*one's honor or reputation*).

deslustre *m.* tarnish; disgrace.

desmadejado *p.p. & adj.* enervated, exhausted; depressed.

desmadejar *v.* to enervate, weaken.

desmán *m.* misconduct, abuse, insult; calamity, disaster.

desmantelar *v.* to dismantle, strip of furniture, equipment, etc.

desmañado *adj.* unskilful, awkward, clumsy.

desmayar *v.* to dismay; to lose strength, courage; **-se** to faint.

desmayo *m.* faint, swoon; dismay, discouragement.

desmazalado *adj.* dejected, depressed.

desmejorar *v.* to impair; to make worse; **-se** to grow worse; to waste away, lose one's health.

desmentir[3] *v. irr.* to contradict; to give the lie; **-se** to contradict oneself; to retract, take back one's word.

desmenuzar[9] *v.* to crumble, break into bits; to mince; to shred; **-se** to crumble, fall to pieces.

desmerecer[13] *v. irr.* to become unworthy of; to deteriorate, lose merit or value; to be inferior to.

desmigajar *v.* to crumb (*bread*); to crumble; **-se** to crumble.

desmochar *v.* to cut off, chop off (*the top or tip*).

desmolado *adj.* toothless, without molars.

desmontar *v.* to dismount; to cut down (*a forest*); to clear or level off (*ground*); to dismantle, take apart; to tear down **-se** to dismount, alight, get off.

desmoronar *v.* to crumble; **-se** to crumble down, fall gradually to pieces.

desnatar *v.* to skim, take the cream from (*milk*).

desnaturalizado *adj.* unnatural, cruel; **alcohol —** denatured alcohol (*made unfit for drinking*); **madre desnaturalizada** unnatural mother (*one without motherly instincts*).

desnudar *v.* to undress, uncover; **-se** to undress.

desnudez *f.* nudity, nakedness.

desnudo *adj.* nude, naked, bare.

desobedecer[13] *v. irr.* to disobey.

desobediencia *f.* disobedience; **desobediente** *adj.* disobedient.

desocupación *f.* unemployment; idleness; vacationing.

desocupado *adj.* unoccupied; unemployed, idle; empty, vacant.

desocupar *v.* to empty, vacate; **-se de un negocio** to get rid of, or not pay attention to, a business.

desoír[36] *v. irr.* to turn a deaf ear to, not to heed; to refuse (*a petition*).

desolación *f.* desolation; ruin; loneliness; anguish, affliction, grief.

desolado *adj.* desolate; *p.p. of* **desolar.**

desolar[2] *v. irr.* to lay waste, ruin; **-se** to be in anguish; to grieve.

desollar[2] *v. irr.* to skin, flay; to fleece, extort money from.

desorbitado *adj.* out of its orbit; out of place or proportion; decentered; *Am.* popeyed, with bulging eyes; *Am.* crazy, eccentric.

desorden *m.* disorder, confusion.

desordenado *adj.* disorderly; lawless; unsettled; *p.p. of* **desordenar.**

desordenar *v.* to disturb, confuse, upset.

desorientar *v.* to throw off one's bearings; to lead astray; to misdirect, mislead; to confuse; **-se** to lose one's bearings; to go astray, get lost.

despabilado *adj.* wakeful; wide-awake; bright, lively.

despabilar *v.* to snuff, trim the wick of (*a candle*); to enliven, awaken (*the mind*), sharpen (*the wits*); **-se** to wake up, rouse oneself, shake off drowsiness.

despacio *adv.* slowly.

despacioso *adj.* slow.

despachar *v.* to despatch; to send; to facilitate; to ship.

despacho *m.* dispatch; office, bureau; salesroom; message; official communication; sending, shipment; promptness; *Am.* country store, farm store.

despachurrar *v.* to crush, squash.

desparejo *adj.* unequal, uneven.

desparpajar *v.* to upset, disarrange; to rant, talk too much; *Am.* to disperse, scatter.

desparpajo *m.* ease, freedom of manner; freshness, pertness; *Am.* dispersion, scattering; *Am.* disorder, jumble.

desparramar *v.* to scatter, spread; to spill; to squander; **-se** to "spread" oneself, spend lavishly; to scatter; to spill.

desparramo *m. Am.* scattering, spreading, spilling; *Am.* disorder, commotion.

despatarrarse *v.* to sprawl; to fall sprawling to the ground.

despecho *m.* spite; grudge; despair; weaning; **a — de** in spite of.

despedazar[9] *v.* to break, cut, tear into pieces.

despedida *f.* farewell; departure; dismissal.

despedir[5] *v. irr.* to discharge, dismiss; to emit, throw off, give off; to see (*a person*) off (*at a station, airport, etc.*); **-se** to take leave, say good-bye.

despegar[7] *v.* to detach; to unfasten; to take off (*said of a plane*); *Am.* to unhitch; **no — los labios** not to say a word, not to open one's mouth; **-se to** grow apart; to come loose or detached.

despego = **desapego.**

despegue *m.* take-off (*of an airplane*).

despejado *adj.* clear, cloudless; smart, bright; *p.p. of* **despejar.**

despejar *v.* to clear; to remove obstacles from; **-se** to clear up (*as the sky*); to clear one's mind.

despellejar *v.* to skin, flay.

despensa *f.* pantry; storeroom (*for food*); food provisions.

despensero *m.* butler; steward.

despeñadero *m.* steep cliff, precipice.

despeñar *v.* to fling down a precipice; **-se** to fall down a precipice; to throw oneself down a cliff.

despepitar *v.* to seed, remove the seeds from; **-se** to talk or shout vehemently; to rave, talk wildly; **-se por una cosa** to long for something; to be crazy about something.

desperdiciado *adj.* wasteful; *p.p. of* **desperdiciar.**

desperdiciar *v.* to squander; to waste.

desperdicio *m.* waste; extravagance; **-s** leftovers, garbage; residue.

desperdigar[7] *v.* to disperse; to scatter; to strew.

desperezarse[9] *v.* to stretch oneself.

desperfecto *m.* damage; flaw, defect.

despertador *m.* alarm clock.

despertar[1] *v. irr.* to awaken; to wake up; **-se** to wake up.

despiadado *adj.* pitiless, heartless, cruel.

despierto *adj.* awake; wide-awake.

despilfarrado *adj.* wasteful, extravagant; ragged; *p.p. of* **despilfarrar.**

despilfarrar *v.* to squander; to waste.

despilfarro *m.* extravagance, squandering; waste.

despistar *v.* to throw off the track.

desplante *m.* arrogance; impudent remark or act.

desplazar[9] *v.* to displace.

desplegar[1,7] *v. irr.* to unfold; to unfurl; to show, manifest.

desplomar *v.* to cause (*a wall*) to lean; **-se** to slump; to topple over, tumble down, collapse.

desplome *m.* collapse; toppling over; landslide.

desplumar *v.* to pick, pluck (*a fowl*); to fleece, skin, rob, strip; **-se** to molt, shed the feathers.

despoblado *adj.* uninhabited, desolate; **— de árboles** treeless; *m.* open country; uninhabited place; wilderness.

despojar *v.* to despoil, rob; to strip (of), deprive (of); **-se** to undress; to deprive oneself.

despojo *m.* plundering, robbery; spoil, booty; leftover, scrap; **-s** remains.

desportilladura *f.* chip; nick.

desportillar *v.* to chip; to nick.

desposar *v.* to marry; **-se** to become formally engaged; to get married.

déspota *m. & f.* despot, tyrant.

despótico *adj.* despotic, tyrannical.

despotismo *m.* despotism, tyranny.

despreciable *adj.* contemptible; worthless; insignificant, negligible.

despreciar *v.* to despise, scorn.

desprecio *m.* scorn, contempt.

desprender *v.* to unfasten, loosen; to detach; **-se** to get loose, come unfastened; to climb down; to get rid (of); to be inferred, be deduced.

desprendimiento *m.* detachment; generosity; unfastening; landslide.

despreocupado *p.p. & adj.* unbiased; liberal, broadminded; unconventional, carefree; *Am.* careless, slovenly; *Am.* indifferent to criticism.

desprestigiar *v.* to discredit, harm the reputation of; **-se** to lose one's prestige.

desprestigio *m.* discredit, loss of prestige.

desprevenido *adj.* unprepared; unaware.

despropósito *m.* absurdity, nonsense.

después *adv.* after, afterward; then, later; **— de** *prep.* after; **— (de) que** *conj.* after.

despuntado *adj.* blunt, dull; *p.p. of* **despuntar.**

despuntar *v.* to blunt; to cut off (*a point*), nip; to bud or sprout; to be clever, witty; to excel; **— el alba** to begin to dawn.

desprovisto *adj.* destitute; lacking; devoid.

desquitar *v.* to retrieve, restore (*a loss*); **-se** to get even, take revenge; to win

back one's money; to make up (for).

desquite *m.* retaliation, revenge; getting even; recovery of a loss; return game or match.

desrazonable *adj.* unreasonable.

destacado *adj.* outstanding; *p.p. of* **destacar.**

destacamento *m.* military detachment.

destacar[6] *v.* to detach (*troops*); to make stand out; to stand out; **hacer —** to emphasize; to make stand out; **-se** to stand out.

destapar *v.* to uncover; to uncork; *Am.* to start running; **-se** to uncover, get uncovered; to get uncorked; *Am.* to burst out talking.

destartalado *adj.* in disorder; in rack and ruin; dismantled, stripped of furniture.

destechado *adj.* roofless.

destellar *v.* to flash; to sparkle, twinkle; to gleam.

destello *m.* flash, sparkle, gleam.

destemplado *adj.* out of tune, out of harmony; immoderate; **sentirse —** not to feel well; to feel feverish.

desteñir[5, 19] *v. irr.* to discolor; to fade; to bleach; **-se** to become discolored; to fade.

desternillarse *v.* **— de risa** to split one's sides with laughter.

desterrado *m.* exile; outcast; *p.p. & adj.* exiled, banished.

desterrar[1] *v. irr.* to exile, banish; to remove earth (from).

destetar *v.* to wean.

destierro *m.* exile.

destilación *f.* distillation.

destiladera *f.* still; *Am.* filter.

destilar *v.* to distill; to drip, trickle; to filter.

destilería *f.* distillery.

destinación *f.* destination.

destinar *v.* to destine; to employ.

destinatario *m.* addressee.

destino *m.* destiny, fate; destination; employment, job.

destituido *adj.* destitute; *p.p. of* **destituir.**

destituir[32] *v. irr.* to deprive.

destornillador *m.* screwdriver.

destornillar *v.* to unscrew.

destrabar *v.* to unlock, unfasten; to untie; to separate; to unfetter.

destreza *f.* dexterity, skill, ability.

destronar *v.* to dethrone, depose, overthrow.

destrozar[9] *v.* to shatter, cut to pieces; to destroy; to squander.

destrozo *m.* destruction; ruin.

destrucción *f.* destruction.

destructivo *adj.* destructive.

destructor *adj.* destructive; *m.* destroyer.

destruir[32] *v. irr.* to destroy; to ruin.

desunir *v.* to divide, separate.

desusado *adj.* unusual, unaccustomed; obsolete, out of use.

desuso *m.* disuse; obsoleteness.

desvaído *adj.* lanky, tall and awkward; gaunt; dull, faded.

desvainar *v.* to shell (*peas, beans, etc.*).

desvalido *adj.* abandoned; destitute; helpless.

desvalijar *v.* to ransack the contents of a valise; to rob.

desván *m.* garret, attic.

desvanecer[13] *v. irr.* to fade, dissolve; to make vain; to make dizzy; -se to evaporate; to vanish; to fade out, disappear; to get dizzy.

desvanecido *adj.* dizzy, faint; proud, haughty; *p.p. of* desvanecer.

desvanecimiento *m.* dizziness, faintness; vanity.

desvariar[17] *v.* to rave, be delirious; to rant, talk excitedly; to talk nonsense.

desvarío *m.* raving; delirium; madness; inconstancy.

desvelado *adj.* sleepless, awake; watchful; *p.p. of* desvelar.

desvelar *v.* to keep (*another*) awake; -se to keep awake; to have insomnia, lose sleep; to be worried, anxious.

desvelo *m.* lack of sleep; restlessness; vigilance, watchfulness; worry, anxiety.

desvencijado *adj.* tottering, rickety, shaky, falling apart.

desventaja *f.* disadvantage.

desventura *f.* misfortune, unhappiness.

desventurado *adj.* unfortunate, unhappy, miserable, wretched.

desvergonzado *adj.* shameless, brazen.

desvergüenza *f.* shamelessness; disgrace; shame; insolence; impudent word.

desvestir[5] *v. irr.* to undress; -se to undress.

desviación *f.* deviation, turning aside, shift; detour.

desviar[17] *v.* to deviate, turn aside; to swerve; -se to shift direction; to branch off, turn off the main road; to swerve.

desvío *m.* deviation, turning aside; indifference, coldness; side track, railroad siding; detour.

desvirtuar[18] *v.* to impair, diminish the value or quality of.

desvivirse *v.* — por to long for; to be excessively fond of, be crazy about,

make a fuss over; to do one's best for; **ella se desvive por complacerme** she does her utmost to please me.

desyerbar = **desherbar**.

detallar *v.* to detail, report in detail; to retail.

detalle *m.* detail; retail; ¡ahí está el — ! that's the point.

detallista *m. & f.* retailer; detailer, person fond of detail.

detective, detectivo *m.* detective.

detención *f.* detention, arrest; stop, halt; delay.

detener[45] *v. irr.* to detain, stop; to arrest; -se to halt; to delay oneself, stay.

detenimiento *m.* detention; delay; care, deliberation.

deteriorar *v.* to deteriorate, damage; -se to deteriorate, become impaired or damaged; to wear out.

deterioro *m.* deterioration, impairment.

determinación *f.* determination; firmness.

determinar *v.* to determine; to decide; -se to resolve, decide.

detestable *adj.* detestable; hateful.

detestar *v.* to detest.

detonación *f.* detonation, report (*of a gun*), loud explosion; pop.

detonar *v.* to detonate, explode with a loud noise; to pop.

detrás *adv.* behind; — de *prep.* behind; **por** — from the rear, by the rear, from behind.

deuda *f.* debt; indebtedness.

deudo *m.* relative, kinsman.

deudor *m.* debtor; *adj.* indebted, obligated.

devanar *v.* to spool, wind on a spool; -se los sesos to rack one's brain.

devaneo *m.* frenzy; dissipation; wandering; idle pursuit; giddiness.

devastar *v.* to devastate, lay waste, destroy.

devenir[48] *v. irr.* to befall; to become, be transformed into.

devoción *f.* devotion; piety; attachment.

devocionario *m.* prayer book.

devolución *f.* return, giving back; replacement.

devolver[2, 52] *v. irr.* to return, give back, pay back.

devorador *adj.* devouring; absorbing; ravenous; *m.* devourer.

devorar *v.* to devour, gobble up.

devoto *adj.* devout, religious, pious; very fond (of).

devuelto *p.p. of* devolver.

día *m.* day; al otro — on the next day; hoy — nowadays; un — sí y otro no every other day.

diablo *m.* devil, demon.

diablura *f.* deviltry, mischief, devilish prank.

diabólico *adj.* diabolic, devilish, fiendish.

diácono *m.* deacon.

diadema *f.* diadem, crown.

diáfano *adj.* transparent, clear; sheer.

diagnosticar[6] *v.* to diagnose.

diagrama *m.* diagram; graph.

dialecto *m.* dialect.

dialogar[7] *v.* to dialogue.

diálogo *m.* dialogue.

diamante *m.* diamond.

diámetro *m.* diameter.

diantre *m.* devil.

diapasón *m.* pitch (*of a sound*); tuning fork.

diario *adj.* daily; *m.* newspaper; daily expense; journal, diary.

diarrea *f.* diarrhea.

dibujante *m. & f.* draftsman; designer.

dibujar *v.* to draw, make a drawing; to delineate, depict, portray; to describe; -se to appear, show.

dibujo *m.* drawing; delineation, portrayal, picture; — natural drawing of the human figure, drawing from life.

dicción *f.* diction; word; choice of words, style.

diciembre *m.* December.

dictado *m.* dictation; title; dictate; escribir al — to take dictation.

dictador *m.* dictator.

dictadura *f.* dictatorship.

dictamen *m.* opinion, judgment.

dictaminar *v.* to give an opinion or judgment.

dictar *v.* to dictate.

dicha *f.* happiness; good luck.

dicharachero *adj.* fond of making wisecracks; witty.

dicharacho *m.* wisecrack, smart remark; malicious remark.

dicho *p.p. of* decir said; — y hecho no sooner said than done; *m.* saying, popular proverb.

dichoso *adj.* happy, lucky.

diente *m.* tooth; tusk; — de león dandelion; de -s afuera insincerely; *Am.* pelar el — to smile affectedly.

diestra *f.* right hand.

diestro *adj.* skilful; right; *m.* matador; skilful swordsman; halter.

dieta *f.* diet; assembly; salary, fee.

diezmo *m.* tithe.

difamación *f.* libel, slander.

difamador *m.* slanderer.

difamar *v.* to defame, libel, malign, slander.

difamatorio *adj.* scandalous, slandering.

diferencia *f.* difference.

diferenciar *v.* to differentiate, distinguish; to differ, disagree; -se to distinguish oneself; to become different.

diferente *adj.* different.

diferir[3] *v. irr.* to defer, put off, delay; to differ, disagree; to be different.

difícil *adj.* difficult.

dificultad *f.* difficulty.

dificultar *v.* to make difficult; — el paso to impede or obstruct the passage; -se to become difficult.

dificultoso *adj.* difficult, hard.

difteria *f.* diphtheria.

difundir *v.* to diffuse, spread out, scatter; to broadcast by radio.

difunto *adj.* deceased, dead; *m.* corpse.

difusión *f.* diffusion, spreading, scattering; wordiness; broadcasting.

difuso *adj.* diffuse; diffused, widespread.

digerible *adj.* digestible.

digerir[3] *v. irr.* to digest.

dignarse *v.* to deign, condescend.

dignatario *m.* dignitary (*person in a high office*).

dignidad *f.* dignity.

digno *adj.* worthy; dignified.

digresión *f.* digression.

dije *m.* trinket, small piece of jewelry; locket; woman of fine qualities, a "jewel"; *Am.* locket or charm of a watch chain.

dilación *f.* delay.

dilatado *adj.* vast, spacious; extensive; *p.p. of* dilatar.

dilatar *v.* to dilate, widen, enlarge; to expand; to lengthen, extend; to spread out; to defer, put off, retard; -se to expand; to be diffuse, wordy; *Am.* to delay oneself, take long.

diligencia *f.* diligence, care, industry; speed; stagecoach; business, errand.

diligente *adj.* diligent; quick, speedy.

diluir[32] *v. irr.* to dilute.

diluvio *m.* flood.

dimensión *f.* dimension.

dimes: — y diretes quibbling, arguing; andar en — y diretes to quibble, argue.

diminución *f.* diminution, decrease.

diminutivo *adj.* diminutive, tiny; diminishing; *m.* diminutive.

diminuto *adj.* tiny, little.

dimisión *f.* resignation (*from an office*).

dimitir *v.* to resign, give up (*a position, office, etc.*).

dinámica *f.* dynamics; dinámico *adj.* dynamic.

dinamismo *m.* vigor, forcefulness; dynamic force or energy.

dinamita *f.* dynamite.

dínamo *m.* dynamo.

dinastía *f.* dynasty.

dineral *m.* a lot of money.

dinero *m.* money; currency; *Am.* Peruvian silver coin equivalent to about ten cents; — contante y sonante ready cash, hard cash.

dios *m.* god; Dios God; a la buena de — without malice; without plan, haphazard, at random.

diosa *f.* goddess.

diplomacia *f.* diplomacy; tact.

diplomático *adj.* diplomatic; tactful; *m.* diplomat.

diputación *f.* deputation; committee.

diputado *m.* deputy; representative.

diputar *v.* to depute, delegate, commission.

dique *m.* dike; barrier; — de carena dry dock.

dirección *f.* direction, course; advice, guidance; management; board of directors; office of the board of directors; address.

directivo *adj.* directive, directing, guiding; mesa directiva board of directors.

directo *adj.* direct, straight.

director *m.* director, manager; *adj.* directing.

directorio *adj.* directory, directive, directing; *m.* directory, book of instructions; directorate, board of directors.

dirigente *adj.* directing, leading; *m.* leader, director.

dirigir[11] *v.* to direct, manage, govern; to guide; to address (*letters, packages*); to dedicate; -se a to address (*a person*); to go to or toward.

discernimiento *m.* discernment, keen judgment, insight, discrimination.

discernir[3] *v. irr.* to discern; to distinguish; to discriminate.

disciplina *f.* discipline, training; rule of conduct; order; any art or science; scourge, whip.

disciplinar *v.* to discipline, train; to drill; -se to discipline oneself; to scourge oneself.

discípulo *m.* pupil; disciple.

disco *m.* disk; discus; phonograph record.

díscolo *adj.* unruly, disobedient; unfriendly.

discordancia *f.* discord, disagreement.

discordia *f.* discord.

discreción *f.* discretion; keenness; wit; darse (*or* rendirse) a — to surrender unconditionally; discrecional *adj.* optional.

discrepancia *f.* discrepancy.

discreto *adj.* discreet, prudent; clever.

disculpa *f.* excuse; apology.

disculpable *adj.* excusable.

disculpar *v.* to excuse, free from blame; -se to excuse oneself, apologize.

discurrir *v.* to ramble about; to reason, think over; to invent, think out; to discuss.

discursear *v.* to make speeches.

discurso *m.* discourse; speech; reasoning; lapse of time.

discusión *f.* discussion.

discutible *adj.* debatable, questionable.

discutir *v.* to discuss.

disecar[6] *v.* to dissect; to stuff and mount (*the skins of animals*).

diseminación *f.* dissemination, spread, scattering.

diseminar *v.* to disseminate, scatter, spread.

disensión *f.* dissension, dissent, disagreement.

disentería *f.* dysentery.

disentir[3] *v. irr.* to dissent, differ, disagree.

diseñador *m.* designer.

diseñar *v.* to design; to sketch, outline.

diseño *m.* design; sketch, outline.

disertar *v.* to discourse, discuss.

disforme *adj.* deformed; ugly, hideous; out of proportion.

disfraz *m.* disguise, mask; masquerade costume.

disfrazar[9] *v.* to disguise, conceal; -se to disguise oneself; to masquerade.

disfrutar *v.* to enjoy; to reap benefit or advantage; to make use of.

disfrute *m.* enjoyment, benefit, use.

disgustar *v.* to disgust, displease; -se to get angry; to get bored.

disgusto *m.* displeasure; unpleasantness; annoyance; quarrel; grief; disgust.

disimulado *adj.* underhanded, sly, cunning; *p.p. of* disimular.

disimular *v.* to feign, hide, mask; to overlook, excuse.

disimulo *m.* dissimulation, feigning, pretense; slyness; reserve.

disipación *f.* dissipation; waste, extravagance.

disipar *v.* to dissipate, scatter; to squander; -se to vanish.

dislocar[6] *v.* to dislocate, put out of joint; -se to become dislocated, get out of joint.

disminución = diminución.

disminuir[32] *v. irr.* to diminish, decrease, lessen.

disociación *f.* dissociation, separation.

disociar *v.* to dissociate, separate.

disolución *f.* dissolution, breaking up; dissoluteness, lewdness.

disoluto *adj.* dissolute, loose, immoral, dissipated.

disolver[2, 52] *v. irr.* to dissolve; to melt.

disonancia *f.* discord.

disparada *f. Am.* rush, run.

disparar *v.* to shoot, fire, discharge; to throw; -se to run away, dart out.

disparatado *adj.* absurd, foolish, senseless.

disparatar *v.* to talk nonsense; to blunder; to act foolishly.

disparate *m.* nonsense, blunder.

disparidad *f.* inequality.

disparo *m.* shooting, discharge, explosion; shot; sudden dash, run.

dispensa *f.* dispensation; exemption.

dispensar *v.* to excuse, absolve, pardon; to grant, give.

dispensario *m.* dispensary; pharmaceutical laboratory; pharmacopoeia (*book containing list and description of drugs*).

dispersar *v.* to disperse, scatter.

dispersión *f.* dispersion, dispersal.

displicencia *f.* displeasure, discontent, dislike.

displicente *adj.* unpleasant, disagreeable, cross.

disponer[40] *v. irr.* to dispose; to arrange, put in order; to prepare; to order, command; -se to get ready; to make one's will and testament.

disponible *adj.* spare, available; on hand.

disposición *f.* disposition; arrangement; order, command; aptitude; disposal.

dispuesto *p.p. of* **disponer** & *adj.* disposed; ready; fit; smart, clever.

disputa *f.* dispute.

disputar *v.* to dispute.

distancia *f.* distance.

distante *adj.* distant.

distar *v.* to be distant, far (from).

distender[1] *v. irr.* to distend, stretch; to inflate; -se to distend, expand.

distinción *f.* distinction.

distinguido *adj. & p.p.* distinguished.

distinguir[12] *v.* to distinguish; -se to distinguish oneself, excel; to differ, be different.

distintivo *adj.* distinctive, distinguishing; *m.* distinguishing characteristic;

mark, sign; badge.

distinto *adj.* distinct, plain, clear; different.

distracción *f.* distraction; diversion, amusement; lack of attention.

distraer[46] *v. irr.* to distract; to divert, amuse; to lead astray; to divert (*funds*); -se to have a good time; to be absent-minded; to be inattentive.

distraído *adj.* distracted; inattentive; absent-minded; *Am.* slovenly, untidy.

distribución *f.* distribution, apportionment.

distribuidor *m.* distributor; *adj.* distributing.

distribuir[32] *v. irr.* to distribute; to sort, classify.

distrito *m.* district; region.

disturbio *m.* disturbance.

disuelto *p.p. of* disolver.

divagación *f.* rambling, digression.

divagar[7] *v.* to ramble; to digress.

diván *m.* divan, sofa.

divergencia *f.* divergence; difference (*of opinion*).

divergir[11] *v.* to diverge; to differ.

diversidad *f.* diversity; variety.

diversión *f.* amusement.

diverso *adj.* diverse; different; -s several, various.

divertido *adj.* amusing, funny.

divertir[3] *v. irr.* to amuse, entertain; to divert, turn aside; -se to have a good time, amuse oneself.

dividendo *m.* dividend.

dividir *v.* to divide, split.

divinidad *f.* divinity, deity; ¡qué — ! what a beauty!

divino *adj.* divine.

divisa *f.* device, emblem.

divisar *v.* to sight; to make out, distinguish.

división *f.* division.

divorciar *v.* to divorce; to separate.

divorcio *m.* divorce.

divulgar[7] *v.* to divulge, spread, make public, give out.

diz = dice; dizque they say that . . .

dobladillar *v.* to hem.

dobladillo *m.* hem; — de ojo hemstitch.

doblar *v.* to bend, fold; to double; to toll, knell; *Am.* to knock down; — la esquina to turn the corner; -se to stoop; to bend down; to give in.

doble *adj.* double, twofold; double-faced, hypocritical; *Am.* broke, poor; *m.* fold; toll, tolling of bells, knell.

doblegar[7] *v.* to bend; to fold; -se to bend over; to stoop; to submit, yield.

doblez *m.* fold, crease; duplicity, hypocrisy.

docena *f.* dozen.

docente *adj.* teaching; educational.

dócil *adj.* docile, obedient, manageable, meek; flexible; **docilidad** *f.* obedience, meekness, gentleness; flexibility.

docto *adj.* learned; expert.

doctor *m.* doctor.

doctorar *v.* to grant a doctor's degree to; -se to get a doctor's degree.

doctrina *f.* doctrine.

documentar *v.* to document.

documento *m.* document.

dogal *m.* halter; noose.

dogma *m.* dogma; **dogmático** *adj.* dogmatic, pertaining to dogma; positive.

dolencia *f.* ailment; ache, aching.

doler² *v. irr.* to ache, hurt, cause pain; to cause grief; -se de to feel pity for, feel sorry for; to repent from.

doliente *adj.* sorrowful; suffering; aching; *m.* sick person, patient; mourner.

dolor *m.* pain, ache; sorrow, grief.

dolorido *adj.* aching, sore; afflicted; repentant; doleful.

doloroso *adj.* painful; sorrowful.

doma *f.* breaking of horses.

domador *m.* horsebreaker, broncobuster.

domar *v.* to tame, subdue.

domeñar *v.* to tame; to subdue; to dominate.

domesticar⁶ *v.* to domesticate, tame.

doméstico *adj.* domestic; *m.* house servant.

domiciliar *v.* to house, lodge; *Am.* to address (*a letter*); -se to take up residence; to settle down; to dwell, reside.

domicilio *m.* home, dwelling.

dominación *f.* domination, rule, authority.

dominador *adj.* dominant, dominating; domineering, bossy; *m.* ruler, boss.

dominante *adj.* dominant; domineering; tyrannical; prevailing, predominant.

dominar *v.* to dominate, rule, lead; to stand out, tower above; to master.

dómine *m.* teacher; pedagogue; pedant.

domingo *m.* Sunday; — de ramos Palm Sunday.

dominio *m.* domain; dominion; authority; mastery (*of a science, art, language, etc.*).

dominó *m.* domino.

don *m.* gift; ability, knack; Don (*title used only before Christian names of men*).

donación *f.* donation; grant.

donador *m.* donor, giver.

donaire *m.* grace, elegance; wit; humor witty remark.

donairoso *adj.* elegant, graceful; witty.

donar *v.* to donate.

doncella *f.* virgin, maiden; maid servant; *Am.* felon (*sore or inflammation near a finger or toe nail*).

donde *rel. adv.* where, in which; a — (adonde) where, to which; *Am.* to the house of; de — from where, from which; en — where, in which; por — where, through which; wherefore; — no otherwise; if not; ¿dónde? *interr. adv.* where?; ¿por — ? which way?

dondequiera *adv.* wherever; anywhere.

donoso *adj.* witty, gay; graceful.

doña *f.* Doña (*title used only before Christian names of women*).

dorado *p.p.* & *adj.* gilded, gilt; golden; *m.* gilding; de — from where, *Am.* a kind of hummingbird; **doradillo** *adj.* *Am.* honey-colored, golden (*applied to horses*).

dorar *v.* to gild.

dormir⁴ *v. irr.* to sleep; -se to go to sleep, fall asleep; to become numb.

dormitar *v.* to doze.

dormitorio *m.* dormitory; bedroom.

dorso *m.* back, reverse.

dosel *m.* canopy.

dosis *f.* dose.

dotación *f.* endowment, endowing; donation, foundation; dowry; complement (*personnel of a warship*); office force.

dotar *v.* to endow; to provide with a dowry.

dote *m.* & *f.* dowry; *f.* natural gift, talent, or quality.

draga *f.* dredge, dredging machine.

dragado *m.* dredging.

dragaminas *m.* mine sweeper.

dragar⁷ *v.* to dredge.

dragón *m.* dragon.

drama *m.* drama.

dramático *adj.* dramatic; *m.* dramatic actor; playwright, dramatist.

dramatizar⁹ *v.* to dramatize.

dramaturgo *m.* playwright, dramatist.

drenaje *m.* *Am.* drainage.

drenar *v.* *Am.* to drain.

dril *m.* drill (*strong cotton or linen cloth*).

droga *f.* drug, medicine; lie, fib; trick; bother, nuisance; *Am.* bad debt; *Am.* drug on the market, unsaleable article.

droguería *f.* drugstore; drug business.

droguero *m.* druggist; *Am.* cheat, debt evader.

droguista *m.* & *f.* druggist; cheat, crook.

ducha *f.* shower bath; douche.

ducho *adj.* expert, skilful.

duda f. doubt.
dudable adj. doubtful.
dudar v. to doubt; to hesitate.
dudoso adj. doubtful; uncertain.
duela f. stave (of a barrel); Am. long, narrow floor board.
duelo m. grief, sorrow; mourning; mourners; duel; **estar de —** to be in mourning; to mourn.
duende m. goblin.
dueña f. owner, landlady; duenna, chaperon or governess.
dueño m. owner; master.
dueto, duo m. duet.
dulce adj. sweet; pleasant, agreeable; fresh (water); soft (metal); m. sweet-meat; candy; preserves; Am. sugar, honey; **dulcería** f. candy shop.
dulcificar⁶ v. to sweeten; to soften.
dulzón adj. over-sweet, sickeningly sweet.
dulzura f. sweetness; meekness.
duplicado adj. & m. duplicate; **por —** in duplicate; p.p. of duplicar.
duplicar⁶ v. to duplicate, double; to repeat.
duplicidad f. duplicity, deceit, deceitfulness, treachery.
duque m. duke.
duquesa f. duchess.
durabilidad f. durability, durable quality, wear.
durable adj. durable.
duración f. duration.
duradero adj. durable, lasting.
durante prep. during, for.
durar v. to last, endure; to wear well.
durazno m. peach; peach tree; **duraznero** m. peach tree.
dureza f. hardness; harshness.
durmiente adj. sleeping; m. sleeper; crossbeam; Am. railroad tie.
duro adj. hard; firm, solid; strong, untiring; harsh; rigid; cruel; stubborn; stingy; **a duras penas** with difficulty; Am. **— y parejo** eagerly, tenaciously; Am. **hacer —** to resist stubbornly; m. **duro** (Spanish dollar).

E

e conj. and (before words beginning with i or hi).
ébano m. ebony.
ebrio adj. drunk.
ebullición f. boiling, bubbling up.
eclesiástico adj. ecclesiastic, belonging to the church; m. clergyman.
eclipsar v. to eclipse; to outshine, surpass.
écloga f. eclogue, pastoral poem, idyll.

eco m. echo.
economía f. economy; **— política** economics, political economy.
económico adj. economic; economical, saving; **economista** m. economist.
economizar⁹ v. to economize, save.
ecuación f. equation.
ecuador m. equator.
echar v. to throw, cast; to expel, throw out; to give off; to sprout; **— a correr** to run away; **-(se) a perder** to spoil; **— a pique** to sink; **-(se) a reír** to burst out laughing; **— carnes** to get fat; **— de menos** to miss; **— de ver** to notice; to make out; **— mano** to seize; **— papas** to fib; **— raíces** to take root; **— suertes** to draw lots; **-se** to lie down; Am. **echársela** to boast.
edad f. age.
edén m. Eden, paradise.
edición f. edition; publication.
edificación f. edification (moral or spiritual uplift); construction.
edificar⁶ v. to construct, build; to edify, uplift.
edificio m. edifice, building.
editar v. to publish.
editor m. publisher; adj. publishing.
editorial adj. publishing, editorial; m. editorial; f. publishing house.
edredón m. down quilt, comforter, quilted blanket.
educación f. education, training; breeding, manners.
educador m. educator; adj. educating.
educando m. pupil; inmate (of an orphanage, boarding school, etc.).
educar⁶ v. to educate, teach, train, raise, bring up.
educativo adj. educational.
efectivo adj. effective; real; in operation, active; m. cash.
efecto m. effect, result; end, purpose; **-s** goods, personal property; **en —** in fact, actually; **llevar a —** to carry out; **surtir —** to come out as expected; to give good results.
efectuar¹⁸ v. to effect, bring about.
eficacia f. efficacy; efficiency; effectiveness.
eficaz adj. effective; active; efficient.
eficiencia f. efficiency; **eficiente** adj. efficient.
efímero adj. ephemeral, short-lived, brief.
efluvio m. emanation, exhalation, vapors.
efusión f. effusion, unrestrained expression of feeling, gushy manner; **—**

de sangre bloodshed.

efusivo adj. effusive, too demonstrative, over-emotional.

egipcio adj. & m. Egyptian.

egocéntrico adj. egocentric, self-centered.

egoísmo m. selfishness.

egoísta adj. selfish; m. & f. selfish person.

egolatría f. self-worship.

eje m. axis; axle.

ejecución f. execution; carrying out.

ejecutar v. to execute; to carry out; to perform, do.

ejecutivo adj. executive; active; m. executive.

ejecutor m. executor; — de la justicia executioner.

ejemplar adj. exemplary, model; m. copy; specimen.

ejemplo m. example; model, pattern.

ejercer[10] v. to practice (a profession); to exert.

ejercicio m. exercise; practice; military drill; exercise (of authority); hacer — to take exercise.

ejercitar v. to practice, exercise; to drill, train; -se to train oneself; to practice.

ejército m. army.

ejido m. public land, common.

ejote m. Am. string bean.

el def. art. m. the; — de the one with, that one with; — que rel. pron. he who, the one that; él pers. pron. he; him, it (after a prep.).

elaborar v. to elaborate.

elasticidad f. elasticity.

elástico adj. elastic; flexible; m. elastic; elastic tape; wire spring; -s Am. suspenders.

elección f. election; choice.

electo adj. elect, chosen; m. elect, person chosen.

elector m. elector, voter; adj. electoral, electing.

electoral adj. electoral.

electricidad f. electricity.

electricista m. electrician; electrical engineer.

eléctrico adj. electric, electrical.

electrizar[9] v. to electrify; to thrill, excite; Am. to anger, irritate.

elefante m. elephant.

elegancia f. elegance, grace, distinguished manner.

elegante adj. elegant, graceful, polished; stylish.

elegir[5, 11] v. irr. to elect, choose.

elemental adj. elementary; elemental, fundamental.

elemento m. element; -s elements, fundamentals; Am. ser (or estar) hecho un — to be an idiot, a fool.

elevación f. elevation; height; rise; rapture.

elevador m. Am. elevator, hoist.

elevar v. to elevate, raise, lift; -se to go up; to soar.

eliminación f. elimination, removal

eliminar v. to eliminate.

elocuencia f. eloquence.

elocuente adj. eloquent.

elogiar v. to praise.

elogio m. praise.

elote m. Am. ear of corn, corn on the cob.

elucidación f. elucidation, explanation.

elucidar v. to elucidate, illustrate, explain.

eludir v. to elude, avoid, dodge.

ella pers. pron. she; her, it (after a prep.).

ello pron. it; — es que the fact is that.

emanación f. emanation, flow; fumes, vapor, odor; manifestation.

emanar v. to emanate, spring, issue.

emancipación f. emancipation.

emancipar v. to emancipate, set free; -se to become free.

embajada f. embassy; errand, mission.

embajador m. ambassador.

embalador m. packer.

embalaje m. packing.

embalar v. to pack; to bale, crate.

embaldosar v. to pave with flagstones or tiles.

embalsamar v. to embalm; to scent, perfume.

embarazar[9] v. to embarrass, hinder; to obstruct; to make pregnant; -se to become pregnant; to become embarrassed.

embarazo m. impediment, obstacle; pregnancy; embarrassment; bashfulness, awkwardness.

embarazoso adj. embarrassing; cumbersome, unwieldly.

embarcación f. ship, boat; embarkation.

embarcadero m. wharf, pier.

embarcador m. shipper.

embarcar[6] v. to embark; to ship; Am. to ship by train or any vehicle; -se to embark, sail; to engage (in); Am. to board, get on a train.

embarco m. embarkation.

embargar[7] v. to impede; to restrain; to attach, confiscate; to lay an embargo on; estar embargado de emoción to be overcome with emotion.

embargo m. embargo, restriction on commerce; attachment, confiscation;

sin — nevertheless.

embarque *m.* shipment.

embarrado *p.p. & adj.* smeared; plastered; muddy.

embarrar *v.* to smear, daub.

embaucador *m.* cheat, impostor.

embaucar[6] *v.* to fool, trick, swindle, deceive.

embebecido *p.p. & adj.* absorbed; amazed.

embebecimiento *m.* absorption; rapture.

embeber *v.* to imbibe, absorb; to soak; to shrink; -se to be fascinated; to be absorbed.

embelesar *v.* to enrapture, delight, charm.

embeleso *m.* delight, ecstasy.

embellecer[13] *v. irr.* to embellish, beautify, adorn.

embestida *f.* sudden attack, onset, assault.

embestir[5] *v. irr.* to attack, assail.

embetunar *v.* to cover with pitch; to black.

emblanquecer[13] *v. irr.* to whiten; to bleach; to become white; -se to whiten, become white.

emblema *m.* emblem.

embobar *v.* to fool; to amuse; to fascinate; to amaze; -se to be amazed; to be fascinated.

embocadura *f.* mouth (*of a river*); entrance (*through a narrow passage*); mouthpiece (*of a wind instrument*); bit (*of a bridle*); taste, flavor (*said of wines*).

embolado *m.* bull whose horns have been tipped with balls; impotent, ineffectual person; *p.p. of* embolar.

embolar *v.* to tip a bull's horns with balls; to black, polish; -se *Am.* to get drunk.

émbolo *m.* piston; plunger (*of a pump*); embolus (*clot in a blood vessel*).

embolsar *v.* to put into a pocket or purse; -se to pocket, put into one's pocket.

emborrachar *v.* to intoxicate; -se to get drunk.

emborronar *v.* to blot; to scribble.

emboscada *f.* ambush.

emboscar[6] *v.* to ambush; -se to lie in ambush; to go into a forest.

embotado *adj.* dull, blunt; *p.p. of* embotar.

embotamiento *m.* dullness, bluntness; dulling, blunting.

embotar *v.* to dull, blunt; to enervate, weaken.

embotellar *v.* to bottle; to bottle up; *Am.* to jail.

embozado *adj.* cloaked; muffled, covered up to the face.

embozar[7] *v.* to muffle; to cloak, conceal, disguise; to muzzle; -se to muffle oneself, wrap oneself.

embragar[7] *v.* to engage or throw in the clutch.

embrague *m.* clutch (*of a machine*); coupling.

embriagar[7] *v.* to intoxicate; -se to get drunk, intoxicated.

embriaguez *f.* intoxication; drunkenness.

embrollar *v.* to involve, ensnare, entangle; to confuse.

embrollo *m.* confusion, tangle; trickery, lie, deception.

embromar *v.* to chaff, make fun of, "kid"; *Am.* to bother, molest; *Am.* to delay unnecessarily; *Am.* to ruin, harm; -se *Am.* to be bothered, disgusted; *Am.* to get delayed.

embrujar *v.* to bewitch, enchant.

embrujo *m.* charm, enchantment; glamour.

embrutecer[13] *v. irr.* to stupefy, render brutish; to dull the mind, make insensible.

embudo *m.* funnel; trick.

embuste *m.* lie, fraud; trinket.

embustero *m.* liar; *adj.* deceitful, tricky.

embutido *m.* sausage; inlaid work; *Am.* insertion of embroidery or lace; *p.p. of* embutir.

embutir *v.* to insert, inlay; to stuff.

emerger[11] *v.* to emerge, come out.

emigración *f.* emigration.

emigrante *m. & f.* emigrant.

emigrar *v.* to emigrate; to migrate.

eminencia *f.* eminence; height.

eminente *adj.* eminent, high, lofty.

emisión *f.* issue (*of bonds, money, etc.*); radio broadcast.

emisor *adj.* emitting; broadcasting; *m.* radio transmitter; **emisora** *f.* broadcasting station.

emitir *v.* to emit, give off; to utter; to send forth; to issue; to broadcast.

emoción *f.* emotion.

emocional *adj.* emotional.

emocionante *adj.* moving, touching, thrilling.

emocionar *v.* to cause emotion, touch, move; -se to be touched, moved, stirred.

emotivo *adj.* emotional.

empacador *m.* packer.

empacar[6] *v.* to pack up, wrap up, bale,

crate; *Am.* to goad, irritate (*an animal*); -se to be stubborn; to get angry; *Am.* to balk; *Am.* to put on airs.

empachado *p.p.* & *adj.* clogged; stuffed; upset from indigestion; embarrassed; bashful.

empachar *v.* to stuff, cram; to cause indigestion; -se to get upset; to get clogged; to be stuffed; to suffer indigestion; to get embarrassed.

empacho *m.* indigestion; bashfulness; no tener — en to have no objection to; to feel free to.

empalagar[7] *v.* to cloy; to pall on, become distasteful; to disgust.

empalagoso *adj.* cloying; sickeningly sweet; boring, wearisome.

empalizada *f.* stockade, palisade.

empalmar *v.* to splice; to join; — con to join (*as railroads or highways*).

empalme *m.* junction; joint, connection; splice.

empanada *f.* pie, meat pie; swindle, fraud.

empanizar[9] *v. Am.* to bread.

empañado *adj.* & *p.p.* tarnished; dim, blurred.

empañar *v.* to blur, dim, tarnish.

empapada *f. Am.* drench, soaking.

empapar *v.* to soak, drench, saturate.

empapelador *m.* paper hanger.

empapelar *v.* to paper; to wrap in paper.

empaque *m.* packing; looks, appearance, air; airs, importance; *Am.* impudence.

empaquetar *v.* to pack; to pack in; to make a package; -se to dress up, doll up.

emparedado *adj.* shut up, confined between walls; *m.* sandwich; prisoner confined in a narrow cell.

emparejar *v.* to even up, level off; to match; to pair off; to overtake, catch up with.

emparentado *adj.* & *p.p.* related by marriage.

emparentar *v.* to become related by marriage.

emparrado *m.* vine arbor.

empastar *v.* to paste; to fill (*a tooth*); to bind (*books*); -se *Am.* to get lost in the pasture; *Am.* to become overgrown with grass.

empaste *m.* tooth filling; binding (*of a book*).

empatar *v.* to tie (*in a game*), have an equal score; to have an equal number of votes; to hinder, obstruct; *Am.* to tie, join.

empate *m.* tie, draw, equal score, equal number of votes; hindrance, obstruction; *Am.* joint, junction.

empecinado *adj. Am.* stubborn.

empedernido *adj.* hardened, hard-hearted.

empedernir[51] *v.* to harden, toughen; -se to become hardened.

empedrado *m.* cobblestone pavement; *p.p.* & *adj.* paved with stones.

empedrar[1] *v. irr.* to pave with stones.

empeine *m.* instep; groin (*hollow between lower part of abdomen and thigh*).

empellón *m.* push, shove; a -es by pushing.

empeñar *v.* to pawn; to oblige, compel; -se to persist, insist; to apply oneself; to go into debt; -se por to plead for, intercede for; se empeñaron en una lucha they engaged in a fight.

empeño *m.* pledge, pawn; persistence, insistence; perseverance; eagerness; *Am.* pawnshop; tener — en to be eager to.

empeorar *v.* to impair; to make worse; to grow worse; -se to grow worse.

empequeñecer[13] *v. irr.* to diminish, make smaller; to belittle.

emperador *m.* emperor; **emperatriz** *f.* empress.

emperifollar *v.* to decorate, adorn; -se to dress up, deck out, doll up.

empero *conj.* however, nevertheless.

empezar[1, 9] *v. irr.* to begin.

empiezo *m. Am.* beginning.

empinado *adj.* steep; lofty.

empinar *v.* to raise, lift; to incline, bend; — el codo to drink; -se to stand on tiptoes; to rear (*said of horses*); to rise high; *Am.* to overeat.

empiojado *adj.* lousy, full of lice.

emplasto *m.* plaster, poultice.

empleado *m.* employee; *p.p.* of **emplear**.

emplear *v.* to employ; to invest, spend; -se en to be employed in.

empleo *m.* employment, position, job; employ; occupation; aim; investment.

emplumar *v.* to feather; to adorn with feathers; to tar and feather; *Am.* to deceive; *Am.* to send away to a house of correction or prison; *Am.* — con algo to run away with something, steal it; *Am.* -las (*or* emplumárselas) to take to one's heels, flee, escape.

empobrecer[13] *v. irr.* to impoverish; -se to become poor.

empobrecimiento *m.* impoverishment.

empolvado *adj.* dusty, covered with dust or powder.

empolvar v. to sprinkle powder; to cover with dust; -se to get dusty; to powder one's face.

empollar v. to hatch, brood.

emponzoñar v. to poison.

emprendedor adj. enterprising.

emprender v. to undertake.

empreñar v. to impregnate, make pregnant.

empresa f. enterprise, undertaking; symbol; company, management.

empresario m. manager; impresario, promoter.

empréstito m. loan.

empujar v. to push, shove.

empuje m. push; shove; impulse; energy.

empujón m. shove, push.

empuñar v. to grasp, grab, clutch, seize.

émulo m. rival, competitor.

en prep. in, on, upon.

enaguas f. pl. underskirt, petticoat; short skirt.

enajenamiento m. trance; abstraction, absence of mind; transfer (of properly); — mental mental disorder; — de los sentidos loss of consciousness.

enajenar v. to dispossess, transfer property; to enrapture, charm; to deprive (of one's senses); — el afecto de to alienate the affection of; -se to be enraptured, be in a trance.

enaltecer[13] v. to extol, exalt.

enamorado adj. in love; m. lover.

enamorar v. to make love, woo, court; to enamor; -se to fall in love.

enano m. dwarf; adj. dwarfish, tiny, little.

enarbolar v. to hoist, lift, raise on high; to brandish (a sword, cane, etc.); -se to rear, balk.

enarcado p.p. arched.

enarcar[6] v. to arch; to hoop (barrels, kegs, etc.); — las cejas to arch one's eyebrows.

enardecer[13] v. irr. to excite, kindle, fire with passion; -se to become excited; to become passionate; to get angry.

enardecimiento m. ardor, passion, unbridled enthusiasm; inflaming.

encabezado m. headline; heading.

encabezamiento m. heading; headline; list or roll of taxpayers; registration of taxpayers.

encabezar[9] v. to give a heading or title to; to head; to lead; to make up (a list or tax roll); to strengthen (wine).

encabritarse v. to rear, rise up on the hind legs.

encadenar v. to chain; to link together.

encajar v. to thrust in, fit into, insert; -se to squeeze into; to intrude, meddle.

encaje m. lace; adjustment; fitting together; socket, groove, hole; inlaid work.

encajonar v. to box (put or pack in a box).

encallar v. to strand, run aground; to get stuck.

encamado p.p. confined in bed.

encaminar v. to direct, guide; -se to betake oneself, go (toward); to start out on a road.

encanecer[13] v. irr. to get grey, get grey-haired.

encanijado adj. emaciated, thin, sickly.

encanijarse v. to get thin, emaciated.

encantado p.p. & adj. delighted, charmed; enchanted.

encantador adj. charming; m. charmer, enchanter.

encantamiento m. enchantment.

encantar v. to charm, enchant.

encanto m. charm, enchantment, delight.

encapillar v. Am. to confine in the death cell.

encapotado p.p. & adj. cloaked; overcast, cloudy; in a bad humor.

encapotarse v. to become overcast, cloudy; to cover up, put on a cloak or raincoat; to frown.

encapricharse v. to persist in one's whims; to get stubborn.

encaramar v. to raise; to elevate; to extol; -se to climb; to climb upon, get upon, perch upon; Am. to be ashamed. Am. to go to one's head (said of liquor).

encarar v. to face; to aim; -se con to face; to confront.

encarcelación f. imprisonment.

encarcelamiento = encarcelación.

encarcelar v. to imprison, jail.

encarecer[13] v. irr. to go up in value; to make dear, raise the price of; to exaggerate; to extol; to recommend highly; to enhance.

encarecidamente adv. earnestly.

encargar[7] v. to put in charge; to entrust; to recommend, advise; to order; to commission; to beg; -se de to take charge of.

encargo m. recommendation, advice; charge; order; commission; errand.

encariñado adj. & p.p. attached, fond, enamored.

encariñamiento m. affection, fondness, attachment.

encariñar v. to awaken love or affec-

81

tion; -se to become fond (of), attached (to).

encarnado *adj.* flesh-colored; red; *p.p.* of encarnar.

encarnar *v.* to incarnate, embody; to bait (*a fishhook*).

encarnizado *adj.* bloody; hard-fought, fierce.

encarnizar[9] *v.* to infuriate, enrage; -se to get furious, enraged; to fight with fury.

encasillar *v.* to pigeonhole, put in a pigeonhole or compartment; to put in a stall; to classify, sort out.

encender[1] *v. irr.* to light, kindle; to set on fire; -se to take fire, be on fire; to get red.

encendido *adj.* red; *p.p.* of encender; *m.* ignition (*of a motor*).

encerado *m.* blackboard; oilcloth; wax coating; *p.p. & adj.* waxed; wax-colored; **papel —** wax paper.

encerar *v.* to wax; to thicken (*lime*).

encerramiento *m.* enclosure, confinement; locking up; retreat; prison.

encerrar[1] *v. irr.* to enclose; to lock up; to contain; -se to lock oneself up, go into seclusion.

encía *f.* gum (*of the teeth*).

enciclopedia *f.* encyclopedia.

encierro *m.* confinement; retreat; prison.

encima *adv.* above, overhead, over, on top; besides, in addition; **— de** on top of; **por — de** over; **A m. de —** besides, in addition; **A m. echárselo todo —** to spend everything on clothes.

encina *f.* live oak.

encinta *adj.* pregnant.

encintado *m.* curb (*of a sidewalk*).

enclaustrar *v.* to cloister.

enclavar *v.* to nail, fix, fasten.

enclenque *adj.* sickly, wan; weak, feeble.

encoger[11] *v.* to shrink, shrivel, shorten, contract; -se to shrink; to shrivel; **-se de hombros** to shrug one's shoulders.

encogido *p.p. & adj.* shrunk, shrivelled; timid, shy.

encogimiento *m.* shrinking; timidity; **— de hombros** shrug.

encolerizar[9] *v.* to anger; -se to get angry.

encomendar[1] *v. irr.* to charge, advise; to entrust; to recommend, commend; -se to put oneself in the hands (of); to send regards; to pray (to).

encomiar *v.* to extol, praise.

encomienda *f.* charge, commission; recommendation; royal land grant (*in-cluding Indian inhabitants*); *Am.* warehouse (*for agricultural products*); *Am.* parcel-post package.

encomio *m.* encomium, high praise.

enconado *p.p. & adj.* inflamed; infected; sore; angry.

enconar *v.* to inflame; to infect; to irritate; -se to become inflamed, infected; to get irritated.

encono *m.* rancor, animosity, ill will; *Am.* inflammation, swelling.

encontrado *adj.* opposite; opposing; contrary; *p.p.* of encontrar.

encontrar[2] *v. irr.* to encounter, meet; to find ; -se to meet; to coincide; to be; to be found, be situated; to collide; to conflict; -se con to come across, meet up with.

encontrón, encontronazo *m.* bump, collision; **darse un —** to collide (with), bump (into); to bump into each other.

encordelar *v.* to string; to tie with strings.

encorvar *v.* to curve, bend; -se to bend down; to stoop.

encrespar *v.* to curl; to ruffle; to irritate; -se to curl; to get ruffled; to become involved or entangled (*a matter or affair*); to become rough (*said of the sea*).

encrucijada *f.* crossroads, street intersection; ambush.

encuadernación *f.* binding (*of books*).

encuadernar *v.* to bind (*books*).

encuadrar *v.* to enclose in a frame; to encompass; to fit (into); *Am.* to suit; *Am.* to summarize briefly, give a synthesis of.

encubierto *p.p.* of encubrir.

encubrir[52] *v.* to cover, hide.

encuentro *m.* encounter, meeting; find, finding; conflict, clash; collision; **salir al — de** to go out to meet; to make a stand against, oppose; *Am.* **llevarse de —** to run over, knock down; to drag along.

encuerado *adj. Am.* naked; *Am.* ragged.

encuerar *v. Am.* to strip of clothes; *Am.* to skin, fleece, strip of money; -se *Am.* to strip, get undressed.

encuesta *f.* search, inquiry, investigation.

encumbrado *p.p. & adj.* elevated; exalted; high, lofty.

encumbramiento *m.* elevation; exaltation; height; eminence.

encumbrar *v.* to elevate; to exalt, extol; -se to climb to the top; to rise up; to hold oneself high; to soar.

encurtido *m.* pickle; *p.p. of* encurtir.
encurtir *v.* to pickle.
enchilada *f. Am.* rolled **tortilla** served with chili.
enchuecar[6] *v.* to bend, twist; **-se** *Am.* to get bent or twisted.
enchufar *v.* to plug in; to telescope; to fit (*a tube or pipe*) into another.
enchufe *m.* socket; plug; electric outlet.
ende : por — hence, therefore.
endeble *adj.* weak, feeble; flimsy.
endemoniado *adj.* possessed by the devil; devilish, fiendish; mischievous.
endentar[1] *v. irr.* to indent, form notches in; to furnish (*a saw, wheel, etc.*) with teeth; to mesh.
enderezar[9] *v.* to straighten; to set upright; to right, correct; to direct; to address; **-se** to go straight (to); to straighten up.
endeudado *p.p. & adj.* indebted; in debt.
endeudarse *v.* to get into debt, become indebted.
endiablado *adj.* devilish; possessed by the devil; ugly; mean, wicked; *Am.* dangerous, risky.
endomingado *p.p. & adj.* dressed up in one's Sunday, or best, clothes.
endosante *m.* indorser.
endosar *v.* to indorse (*a check, draft, etc.*).
endose, endoso *m.* indorsement.
endulzar[9] *v.* to sweeten; to soften.
endurecer[13] *v. irr.* to harden; **-se** to get hardened; to get cruel.
enemigo *m.* enemy; devil; *adj.* hostile; unfriendly; **ser — de una cosa** to dislike a thing.
enemistad *f.* enmity, hatred.
enemistar *v.* to cause enmity between; **-se con** to become an enemy of.
energía *f.* energy.
enérgico *adj.* energetic.
enero *m.* January.
enervar *v.* to enervate, weaken.
enfadar *v.* to anger; **-se** to get angry.
enfado *m.* anger, disgust.
enfadoso *adj.* annoying.
enfardar *v.* to bale, pack.
énfasis *m.* emphasis; **enfático** *adj.* emphatic.
enfermar *v.* to become ill; to make ill; to weaken; **-se** to become ill.
enfermedad *f.* sickness, illness.
enfermería *f.* infirmary.
enfermero *m.* male nurse; **enfermera** *f.* nurse (*for the sick*).
enfermizo *adj.* sickly; unhealthy.
enfermo *adj.* sick, ill; feeble; *m.* patient.

enflaquecer[13] *v. irr.* to become thin; to make thin; to weaken.
enfocar[6] *v.* to focus.
enfrenar *v.* to bridle; to brake, put the brake on; to check, curb.
enfrentar *v.* to put face to face; **-se con** to confront, face, meet face to face.
enfrente *adv.* in front, opposite; **— de** in front of, opposite.
enfriamiento *m.* cooling; chill; refrigeration.
enfriar[17] *v.* to cool, chill; *Am.* to kill; **-se** to cool, cool off; to get chilled.
enfurecer[13] *v.irr.* to infuriate, enrage; **-se** to rage; to get furious; to get rough, stormy (*said of the sea*).
enfurruñarse *v.* to get angry; to grumble.
engalanar *v.* to adorn, decorate; **-se** to dress up, primp.
enganchamiento = **enganche.**
enganchar *v.* to hitch; to hook; to ensnare; to draft; to attract into the army; *Am.* to hire (*labor with false promises*); **-se** to engage, interlock; to get hooked; to enlist in the army.
enganche *m.* hooking; coupling; draft (*into the army*); *Am.* enrolling of laborers (*for a rubber plantation or other risky business under false promises.*).
engañador *adj.* deceitful, deceiving; *m.* deceiver.
engañar *v.* to deceive; to while away (*time*); to ward off (*hunger or sleep*); **-se** to deceive oneself; to be mistaken.
engaño *m.* deceit, trick, fraud; mistake, misunderstanding; *Am.* bribe.
engañoso *adj.* deceitful; tricky; misleading.
engastar *v.* to mount, set (*jewels*).
engaste *m.* setting (*for a gem or stone*).
engatusar *v.* to coax, entice; to fool.
engendrar *v.* to engender, beget, produce; to cause.
engolfarse *v.* to get deep (into); to go deeply (into); to become absorbed, lost in thought.
engomar *v.* to gum; to glue.
engordar *v.* to fatten; to get fat; to get rich.
engorroso *adj.* cumbersome; bothersome.
engranaje *m.* gear, gears, gearing.
engranar *v.* to gear, throw in gear; to mesh gears.
engrandecer[13] *v. irr.* to aggrandize, make greater; to magnify; to exalt.
engrane *m.* engagement (*of gears*); gear.
engrasar *v.* to lubricate, grease; to stain with grease; to fertilize, manure; to

dress (cloth).

engreído adj. & p.p. conceited, vain; Am. attached, fond.

engreír[15] v. irr. to make vain, conceited; -se to puff up, get conceited; Am. to become fond (of), become attached (to).

engrosar[2] v. irr. to enlarge; to thicken; to fatten; to get fat.

engrudo m. paste (for gluing).

engullir[20] v. to gobble, devour; to gorge.

enhebrar v. to thread (a needle); to string (beads).

enhiesto adj. straight, upright, erect.

enhorabuena f. congratulation; adv. safely; well and good; all right; with much pleasure.

enigma m. enigma, riddle, puzzle.

enjabonar v. to soap; to soft-soap, flatter.

enjaezar[9] v. to harness.

enjalbegar[7] v. to whitewash; -se to paint (one's face).

enjambre m. swarm of bees; crowd.

enjaular v. to cage; to confine; to jail.

enjuagar[7] v. to rinse, rinse out.

enjuague m. mouth wash; rinse; rinsing; scheme, plot.

enjugar[7] v. to dry; to wipe; -se to dry oneself.

enjuiciar v. to indict; to prosecute, bring suit against; to try (a case); to judge.

enjundia f. substance, essence; fat; force, strength.

enjuto adj. dried; thin, skinny; -s m. pl. dry kindling.

enlace m. link; tie, bond; marriage.

enladrillado m. brick pavement or floor.

enladrillar v. to pave with bricks.

enlatar v. to can; Am. to roof with tin.

enlazar[9] v. to join, bind, tie; to rope; Am. to lasso; -se to join; to marry; to become related through marriage.

enlodar v. to cover with mud; to smear, sully, soil, dirty; -se to get in the mud; to get muddy.

enloquecer[13] v. irr. to make crazy; to drive mad; to lose one's mind; -se to go crazy.

enlosado m. flagstone pavement; p.p. of enlosar.

enlosar v. to pave with flagstones.

enmantecado m. Am. ice cream. See mantecado.

enmantecar[6] v. to butter; to grease (with lard or butter).

enmarañar v. to entangle; to snarl; to confuse, mix up.

enmascarar v. to mask; -se to put on a mask; to masquerade.

enmendar[1] v. irr. to amend, correct; to indemnify, compensate; -se to reform, mend one's ways.

enmienda f. correction; amendment; reform; indemnity, compensation.

enmohecer[13] v. to rust; to mold; -se to rust, become rusty; to mold.

enmudecer[13] v. irr. to silence; to remain silent; to lose one's voice; to become dumb.

ennegrecer[13] v.irr. to blacken; to darken; -se to become dark; to get cloudy.

ennoblecer[13] v. irr. to ennoble, dignify.

enojadizo adj. irritable, ill-tempered.

enojado adj. angry.

enojar v. to make angry, vex, annoy; -se to get angry.

enojo m. anger; annoyance.

enojoso adj. annoying, bothersome.

enorgullecer[13] v. irr. to fill with pride; -se to swell up with pride; to be proud.

enorme adj. enormous.

enramada f. arbor, bower; shady grove.

enrarecer[13] v. irr. to rarefy, thin, make less dense (as air); -se to become rarefied; to become scarce.

enrarecimiento m. rarity, thinness (of the air); rarefaction (act of making thin, rare or less dense).

enredadera f. climbing vine.

enredar v. to entangle, snare; to snarl; to mix up; to raise a rumpus; to wind (on a spool); -se to get tangled up, mixed up; to get trapped; -se con to have an affair with.

enredista m. Am. liar; Am. talebearer.

enredo m. tangle; confusion; lie; plot.

enredoso adj. tangled up; Am. tattler.

enrejado m. trellis; grating.

enrevesado adj. turned around; intricate, complicated; unruly.

enriquecer[13] v. irr. to enrich; to become rich; -se to become rich.

enrojecer[13] v. irr. to redden; -se to get red, blush.

enrollar v. to roll, roll up; to coil.

enronquecer[13] v. irr. to make hoarse; to become hoarse; -se to become hoarse.

enroscar[6] v. to coil; to twist, twine; -se to coil; to curl up.

ensacar[6] v. to sack, bag, put in a bag or sack.

ensalada f. salad; hodgepodge, mixture.

ensalzar[9] v. to exalt, praise.

ensanchar v. to widen, enlarge; -se to expand; to puff up.

ensanche m. widening, expansion, extension.

ensangrentado *adj.* gory, bloody; *p.p. of* ensangrentar.

ensangrentar *v.* to stain with blood; -se to be covered with blood; to get red with anger.

ensartar *v.* to string; to thread; to link; to rattle off (*tales, stories, etc.*); *Am.* to tie to a ring; *Am.* to swindle, trick; -se *Am.* to fall into a trap.

ensayar *v.* to try; to attempt; to test; to rehearse; -se to practice, train oneself.

ensayo *m.* trial, attempt; rehearsal; test; experiment; essay.

ensenada *f.* small bay, cove.

enseñanza *f.* teaching; education, training.

enseñar *v.* to show; to teach; to train; to point out.

enseres *m. pl.* household goods; utensils; implements; equipment.

ensillar *v.* to saddle; *Am.* to abuse, mistreat, domineer; *Am.* — **el picazo** to get angry.

ensimismarse *v.* to become absorbed in thought; *Am.* to become conceited or vain.

ensoberbecer[13] *v. irr.* to make proud or haughty; -se to puff up with pride; to become haughty; to get rough, choppy (*said of the sea*).

ensordecer[13] *v. irr.* to deafen; to become deaf.

ensortijar *v.* to curl; to ring the nose of (*an animal*); -se to curl.

ensuciar *v.* to dirty, soil; to stain; -se to get dirty; to soil oneself.

ensueño *m.* illusion, dream.

entablar *v.* to board up; to plank; to splint; — **una conversación** to start a conversation; — **un pleito** to bring a lawsuit.

entablillar *v.* to splint; *Am.* to cut (*chocolate*) into tablets or squares.

entallar *v.* to fit closely (*a dress*); to carve.

entapizar[9] *v.* to cover with tapestry; to drape with tapestries; to upholster.

entarimar *v.* to floor (*with boards*).

ente *m.* entity, being; queer fellow.

enteco *adj.* sickly, skinny.

entender[1] *v. irr.* to understand; — **de** to know, be an expert in; — **en** to take care of; to deal with; -se **con** to have dealings or relations with; to have an understanding with.

entendido *p.p.* understood; *adj.* wise, prudent; well-informed; able, skilful; **no darse por** — to pretend not to hear or understand; not to take the hint.

entendimiento *m.* understanding; intellect; mind.

enterado *p.p. & adj.* informed; aware.

enterar *v.* to inform, acquaint; -se to know, learn, find out; to understand, get the idea.

entereza *f.* entirety; integrity; fortitude; serenity; firmness; perfection.

enternecedor *adj.* touching, moving, pitiful.

enternecer[13] *v. irr.* to soften, touch, stir, move; -se to become tender; to be touched, stirred.

entero *adj.* entire, whole; just, right; firm; *m.* integer, whole number; *Am.* payment, reimbursement; *Am.* balance of an account; **caballo** — stallion.

enterramiento *m.* burial.

enterrar[1] *v. irr.* to bury; *Am.* to sink, stick into.

entibiar *v.* to make lukewarm; -se to become lukewarm.

entidad *f.* entity; unit, group, organization; **de** — of value or importance.

entierro *m.* burial; funeral; grave; *Am.* hidden treasure.

entintar *v.* to ink; to stain with ink; to dye.

entoldar *v.* to cover with an awning; -se to puff up with pride; to become overcast, cloudy.

entonación *f.* intonation.

entonar *v.* to sing in tune; to start a song (*for others to follow*); to be in tune; to harmonize; -se to put on airs.

entonces *adv.* then, at that time; **pues** — well then.

entornado *adj.* half-open; half-closed, ajar.

entornar *v.* to half-open.

entorpecer[13] *v. irr.* to stupefy; to benumb, make numb; to delay, obstruct; to thwart, frustrate.

entorpecimiento *m.* numbness; dullness; delay, obstruction.

entrada *f.* entrance; entry; gate; opening; entering; admission; entrée (*dish or dinner course*); *Am.* attack, assault, goring; *Am.* beating; -s cash receipts.

entrambos *adj. & pron.* both.

entrampar *v.* to trap, ensnare; to trick; to burden with debts; -se to get trapped or entangled; to run into debt.

entrante *adj.* entering; incoming; **el año** — next year.

entraña *f.* entrail; innermost recess; heart; disposition, temper; -s entrails, "innards", insides; **hijo de mis -s** child of my heart; **no tener -s** to be cruel.

entrar *v.* to enter, go in, come in; to attack; **me entró miedo I became afraid; -se** to slip in, get in, sneak in; to enter.

entre *prep.* between; among: **dijo — sí** he said to himself; **— tanto** meanwhile; *Am.* **— más habla menos dice** the more he talks the less he says.

entreabierto *p.p. of* **entreabrir;** *adj.* ajar, half-open, partly open.

entreabrir[52] *v.* to half-open.

entreacto *m.* intermission; **intermezzo** (*entertainment between the acts*); small cigar.

entrecano *adj.* greyish.

entrecejo *m.* space between the eyebrows; **fruncir el —** to wrinkle one's brow.

entrecortado *adj.* hesitating, **faltering** (*speech*); breathless, choking; *p.p.* interrupted.

entrecortar *v.* to cut halfway through or in between; to interrupt at intervals.

entrecruzar[9] *v.* to intercross, cross; to interlace; **-se** to cross.

entredicho *m.* prohibition, **injunction.**

entrega *f.* delivery; surrender; instalment · (*of a book*); **novela por -s** serial novel.

entregar[7] to deliver, hand over; **-se** to surrender, submit, give up; to devote oneself (to); to abandon oneself (to).

entrelazar[9] *v.* to interlace; to weave together.

entremés *m.* relish, side dish (*of olives, pickles, etc.*); one-act farce (*formerly presented between the acts of a play.*)

entremeter *v.* to insert; to place between; **-se** to meddle; to intrude.

entremetido *adj.* meddlesome; *m.* meddler; intruder.

entremetimiento *m.* intrusion, meddling.

entremezclar *v.* to intermix, intermingle.

entrenador *m. Am.* trainer.

entrenamiento *m. Am.* training, drill.

entrenar *v. Am.* to train, drill; **-se** *Am.* to train.

entresacar[6] *v.* to pick out, select.

entresuelo *m.* mezzanine; second floor.

entretanto *adv.* meanwhile.

entretejer *v.* to weave together; to intertwine.

entretener[45] *v. irr.* to delay, detain; to amuse, entertain; **-se** to amuse one-

self; to delay oneself; **— el tiempo** to while away the time.

entretenido *adj.* entertaining, amusing; *p.p. of* **entretener.**

entretenimiento *m.* entertainment; pastime; delay.

entrever[49] *v.* to glimpse, catch a glimpse of; to half-see, see vaguely.

entreverar *v.* to intermingle, intermix.

entrevista *f.* interview; date, appointment.

entrevistar *v.* to interview; **-se con** to have an interview with.

entrevisto *p.p. of* **entrever.**

entristecer[13] *v. irr.* to sadden, make sad; **-se** to become sad.

entrometer = **entremeter.**

entrometido = **entremetido.**

entumecer[13] *v. irr.* to make numb; **-se** to get numb; to surge; to swell.

entumido *adj.* numb, stiff; *Am.* timid, shy, awkward.

entumirse *v.* to get numb.

enturbiar *v.* to make muddy; to muddle; to disturb; to obscure; **-se** to get muddy; to get muddled.

entusiasmar *v.* to excite, fill with enthusiasm; **-se** to get enthusiastic, excited.

entusiasmo *m.* enthusiasm.

entusiasta *m. & f.* enthusiast; **entusiástico** *adj.* enthusiastic.

enumeración *f.* enumeration, counting.

enumerar *v.* to enumerate.

enunciar *v.* to express, state, declare.

envainar *v.* to sheathe.

envalentonar *v.* to make bold or haughty; **-se** to get bold; to brag, swagger.

envanecer[13] *v. irr.* to make vain; **-se** to become vain.

envasar *v.* to pack, put up in any container; to bottle; to can.

envase *m.* packing; container, jar, bottle, can (*for packing*).

envejecer[13] *v. irr.* to make old; to grow old, get old; **-se** to grow old, get old.

envenenamiento *m.* poisoning.

envenenar *v.* to poison; to infect.

envergadura *f.* span (*of an airplane*); spread (*of a bird's wings*); breadth (*of sails*).

envés *m.* back or wrong side.

enviado *m.* envoy.

enviar[17] *v.* to send; **— a uno a paseo** to give someone his walking papers.

enviciar *v.* to vitiate, corrupt; **-se** to become addicted (to), overly fond (of).

envidar *v.* to bid (*in cards*); to bet.

envidia *f.* envy.

envidiable *adj.* enviable, desirable.

envidiar v. to envy.

envidioso adj. envious.

envilecer[13] v. irr. to revile, malign, degrade; -se to degrade or lower oneself.

envilecimiento m. degradation, humiliation, shame.

envío m. remittance, sending; shipment.

envite m. bid; stake (*in cards*); offer; push.

envoltorio m. bundle, package.

envoltura f. wrapping, cover; wrapper.

envolver[2, 52] v. irr. to involve, entangle; to wrap; to wind (*a thread, rope, etc.*); to surround; -se to become involved, entangled; to cover up, wrap up.

envuelto p.p. of **envolver**.

enyesar v. to plaster; to chalk.

enzolvar v. *Am.* to clog, obstruct; *Am.* -se to clog, get clogged. *See* **azolvar**.

¡epa! *interj. Am.* hey! listen! stop! look out!

épico adj. epic.

epidemia f. epidemic.

episodio m. episode.

epístola f. epistle; letter.

epitafio m. epitaph.

época f. epoch.

epopeya f. epic poem.

equidad f. equity, justice, fairness.

equidistante adj. equidistant, equally distant, halfway, midway.

equilibrar v. to balance, poise.

equilibrio m. equilibrium, balance; poise.

equipaje m. baggage, luggage; equipment, outfit; crew.

equipar v. to equip, fit out; to man, equip and provision (*a ship*).

equipo m. equipment, equipping; outfit; work crew; sport team; — de novia trousseau.

equitación f. horsemanship; horseback riding.

equitativo adj. fair, just.

equivalente adj. equivalent.

equivaler[47] v. irr. to be equivalent.

equivocación f. error, mistake.

equivocado p.p. & adj. mistaken.

equivocar[6] v. to mistake; -se to be mistaken; to make a mistake.

equívoco adj. equivocal, ambiguous, vague; *Am.* mistaken; m. pun, play on words; *Am.* mistake, error.

era f. era, age; threshing floor.

erario m. public treasury.

erguido adj. erect; p.p. of **erguir**.

erguir[3] v. irr. to erect, set upright; to lift (*the head*); -se to sit up or stand erect; to become proud and haughty.

erial m. uncultivated land; adj. unplowed, untilled.

erigir[11] v. to erect, build; to found.

erizado adj. bristly, prickly; — de bristling with.

erizar[9] v. to set on end, make bristle; -se to bristle; to stand on end (*hair*).

erizo m. hedgehog, porcupine; thistle; — de mar sea urchin; ser un — to be irritable, harsh.

ermitaño m. hermit.

erosión f. erosion.

errabundo adj. wandering.

errado adj. mistaken, wrong, in error; p.p. of **errar**.

errante adj. errant, roving, wandering.

errar[28] v. irr. to err, make mistakes; to miss (*target, road*); to rove, wander.

errata f. misprint, printer's error.

erróneo adj. erroneous, mistaken, wrong, incorrect.

error m. error, fault, mistake.

eructar v. to belch.

eructo m. belch.

erudición f. erudition, learning.

erudito adj. erudite, scholarly, learned; m. scholar.

erupción f. eruption; outburst; rash.

esbelto adj. slender.

esbozar[9] v. to sketch, outline.

esbozo m. sketch, outline.

escabechar v. to pickle.

escabeche m. pickled fish; pickle (*solution for pickling*).

escabel m. stool; footstool.

escabrosidad f. roughness, unevenness; harshness; improper word or phrase.

escabroso adj. rough; rugged; scabrous, rather indecent.

escabullirse[20] v. irr. to slip away; to slip through; to scoot, scamper, scurry.

escala f. ladder; scale; port of call; stopover; hacer — en to stop over at; **escalafón** m. army register.

escalar v. to scale; to climb.

escaldar v. to scald; to make red-hot; -se to get scalded.

escalera f. stairs, staircase; ladder.

escalfar v. to poach (*eggs*).

escalinata f. flight of stairs (*usually on the outside*).

escalofriarse[17] v. to become chilled.

escalofrío m. chill; -s chills and fever.

escalón m. step (*of a ladder or staircase*); stepping stone; *Am.* -es tribe of quichua Indians.

escalonar v. to echelon (*arrange in step-like formation*); to terrace; -se to rise in terraces.

escama f. scale, fish scale; flake.

escamoso adj. scaly.

escamotear v. to whisk out of sight; to steal or snatch away with cunning; to conceal by a trick or sleight of hand.

escandalizar[9] v. to scandalize, shock; **-se** to be shocked.

escándalo m. scandal; bad example.

escandaloso adj. scandalous, shocking; Am. showy, loud (color).

escapada f. escape, flight.

escapar v. to escape, flee, avoid; **-se** to run away, escape.

escaparate m. show window; glass case, glass cabinet or cupboard.

escapatoria f. escape, loophole, excuse.

escape m. escape; vent, outlet; exhaust; **a —** rapidly, at full speed.

escarabajo m. black beetle.

escaramuza f. skirmish; quarrel.

escarbar v. to scrape, scratch; to dig out; to pry into, investigate.

escarcear v. Am. to prance.

escarcha f. frost; frosting.

escarchar v. to frost; to freeze.

escardar v. to weed; to weed out.

escarlata f. scarlet; scarlet fever; scarlet cloth; **escarlatina** f. scarlet fever

escarmentar[1] v. irr. to punish (as an example or warning); to profit by one's misfortunes, punishment, etc.; **— en cabeza ajena** to profit by another's mistake or misfortune.

escarmiento m. lesson, example, warning; punishment.

escarnecer[13] v. irr. to jeer, insult, mock.

escarnio m. scoff, jeer.

escarpa f. steep slope, bluff, cliff; scarp (of a fortification).

escarpado adj. steep; rugged.

escarpia f. hook (for hanging something).

escasear v. to be scarce; to grow less, become scarce; to stint.

escasez f. scarcity, lack, scantiness.

escaso adj. scarce, limited; scant; scanty; stingy.

escatimar v. to stint, skimp; to curtail.

escena f. scene; scenery; theatre, stage.

escenario m. stage.

escenificación f. dramatization, stage adaptation.

escepticismo m. scepticism; doubt, unbelief.

escéptico m. & adj. sceptic.

esclarecer[13] v. irr. to lighten, illuminate; to elucidate, make clear, explain.

esclarecimiento m. clarification, illumination, illustration; worth, nobility.

esclavitud f. slavery.

esclavizar[9] v. to enslave.

esclavo m. slave.

esclusa f. lock (of a canal); sluice, flood-gate.

escoba f. broom.

escobazo m. blow with a broom.

escobilla f. whisk broom; small broom.

escocer[2, 10] v. irr. to sting, smart.

escocés adj. Scotch; m. Scotch; Scotchman.

escoger[11] v. to choose, select, pick out.

escolar adj. scholastic, academic; m. scholar, student.

escolástico adj. & m. scholastic.

escolta f. escort; convoy.

escoltar v. to escort; to convoy.

escollo m. reef; danger; obstacle.

escombro m. debris, rubbish; mackerel.

esconder v. to hide, conceal; **-se** to hide, go into hiding.

escondidas : a — on the sly, under cover; Am. **jugar a las —** to play hide-and-seek.

escondite m. hiding place; **jugar al —** to play hide-and-seek.

escondrijo m. hiding place.

escopeta f. shotgun.

escopetazo m. gunshot; gunshot wound; sudden bad news; Am. offensive or ironic remark.

escoplo m. chisel.

escoria f. slag; scum; **escorial** m. dump, dumping place; pile of slag.

escorpión m. scorpion.

escote m. low neck; **convite a —** Dutch treat (where everyone pays his share).

escotilla f. hatchway; **escotillón** m. hatch, hatchway; trap door.

escozor m. smarting sensation, sting.

escribano m. court clerk; lawyer's clerk; notary.

escribiente m. clerk, office clerk.

escribir[52] v. to write.

escrito p.p. of **escribir** written; m. writing, manuscript.

escritor m. writer.

escritorio m. desk; office.

escritura f. writing, handwriting; deed, document; **Sagrada Escritura** Holy Scripture.

escrúpulo m. scruple, doubt.

escrupuloso adj. scrupulous; particular, exact.

escrutador adj. scrutinizing, examining; peering; penetrating; m. scrutinizer, examiner; inspector of election returns.

escrutar v. to scrutinize.

escrutinio m. scrutiny, careful inspection.

escuadra f. squadron; fleet; square (instrument for drawing or testing right angles).

escuadrón m. squadron.

escualidez f. squalor.

escuálido adj. squalid, filthy; thin, emaciated.

escuchar v. to listen; to heed.

escudar v. to shield.

escudero m. squire.

escudo m. shield; escutcheon, coat of arms; gold crown (ancient coin); Am. Chilean gold coin.

escudriñar v. to scrutinize, search, pry into.

escuela f. school.

escuelante m. & f. Am. schoolboy; schoolgirl.

escueto adj. plain, unadorned; bare.

esculcar[6] v. Am. to search; Am. to frisk (a person's pockets).

esculpir v. to sculpture; to engrave.

escultor m. sculptor.

escultura f. sculpture.

escupir v. to spit.

escurrir v. to drip; to drain; to trickle; -se to ooze out, trickle; to slip out, sneak out.

ese, esa dem. adj. that; **esos, esas** those; **ése, ésa** m., f. dem. pron. that one; **ésos, ésas** m., f. pl. those.

esencia f. essence.

esencial adj. essential.

esfera f. sphere; clock dial.

esférico adj. spherical.

esforzado adj. strong; valiant; courageous.

esforzar[2, 9] v. irr. to give or inspire strength; to encourage; -se to make an effort; to strive, try hard.

esfuerzo m. effort; spirit, courage, vigor; stress.

esfumar v. to shade, tone down; -se to vanish, disappear.

esgrima f. fencing.

esgrimir v. to fence; to brandish; to wield (the sword or pen).

eslabón m. link of a chain; steel knife sharpener; black scorpion; Am. a kind of lizard.

eslabonar v. to link; to join; to connect.

esmaltar v. to enamel; to beautify, adorn.

esmalte m. enamel; enamel work; smalt (a blue pigment).

esmerado adj. painstaking, careful, conscientious; p.p. of **esmerar**.

esmeralda f. emerald; Am. an eel-like fish; Am. hummingbird; Am. variety of pineapple.

esmerar v. to polish, clean; -se to strive, take special pains, use great care.

esmero m. care, precision.

esmoquin m. tuxedo, dinner coat.

eso dem. pron. that, that thing, that fact; — es that is it; a — de at about (referring to time); Am. ¡eso! that's right!

espaciar[17] v. to space; to spread; to expand; -se to enlarge (upon a subject); to relax, amuse oneself.

espacio m. space; interval; slowness, delay; adv. Am. slowly.

espacioso adj. spacious; slow.

espada f. sword; skilled swordsman; matador (bull-fighter who kills the bull); -s swords (Spanish card suit).

espalda f. back, shoulders; -s back, back part; a -s behind one's back; de -s on one's back; dar la — a to turn one's back on; **espaldilla** f. shoulder blade.

espaldar m. back (of a chair); trellis (for plants); backplate of a cuirass (armor).

espantadizo adj. scary, shy, timid.

espantajo m. scarecrow.

espantapájaros m. scarecrow.

espantar v. to frighten, scare; to scare away; Am. to haunt; -se to be scared; to be astonished; Am. **espantárselas** to be wide-awake, catch on quickly.

espanto m. fright, terror; astonishment; Am. ghost.

espantoso adj. frightful, terrifying; wonderful.

español adj. Spanish; m. Spaniard; Spanish language.

esparadrapo m. court plaster, adhesive tape. See **tela adhesiva.**

esparcir[10] v. to scatter, spread; -se to relax, amuse oneself.

espárrago m. asparagus.

esparto m. esparto grass (used for making ropes, mats, etc.).

espasmo m. spasm; horror.

especia f. spice.

especial adj. special; **en** — in particular, specially.

especialidad f. specialty.

especialista m. & f. specialist.

especializar[9] v. to specialize; -se en to specialize in.

especie f. species; kind, sort; pretext; idea.

especificar[6] v. to specify; to name.

específico adj. specific; m. specific (medicine).

espécimen m. specimen, sample.

espectacular adj. spectacular.

espectáculo m. spectacle.

espectador m. spectator.

espectro m. spectre, ghost; spectrum.

especulación f. speculation.

especulador m. speculator.

especular v. to speculate.

especulativo adj. speculative.

espejismo m. mirage; illusion.

espejo m. mirror; model; — de cuerpo entero full-length mirror.

espeluznante adj. hair-raising, terrifying.

espeluznarse v. to be terrified; to bristle with fear.

espera f. wait; stay (granted by judge), delay; extension of time (for payment); **sala de** — waiting room; **estar en** — **de** to be waiting for; to be expecting.

esperanza f. hope; expectation.

esperanzado adj. hopeful.

esperanzar[9] to give hope to.

esperar v. to hope; to expect; to trust; to wait; to await, wait for; — **en alguien** to place hope or confidence in someone.

esperezarse = desperezarse.

esperpento m. ugly thing; nonsense.

espesar v. to thicken; to make dense; -se to thicken; to become thick or dense.

espeso adj. thick, dense; compact; slovenly; Am. bothersome, boring.

espesor m. thickness.

espesura f. density, thickness; thicket; thickest part (of a forest).

espetar v. to spring (a joke, story, etc.) on (a person), surprise with (a joke, speech, story, etc.); to pop (a question); to run a spit through (meat, fish, etc. for roasting); to pierce; -se to be stiff, pompous.

espía m. & f. spy.

espiar[17] v. to spy; Am. -se to bruise the hoofs, get lame (said of horses).

espiga f. ear of wheat; peg; spike.

espigar[7] v. to glean; to grow spikes (said of corn or grain); -se to grow tall and slender.

espina f. thorn; sharp splinter; fish bone; spine; fear, suspicion; **darle a uno mala** — to arouse one's suspicion.

espinaca f. spinach.

espinazo m. spine, backbone.

espinilla f. shin (front part of leg); blackhead (on the skin).

espino m. hawthorn; thorny shrub; thorny branch.

espinoso adj. thorny; difficult, dangerous.

espionaje m. espionage, spying.

espiral adj. & f. spiral.

espirar v. to exhale; to emit, give off; to die. See expirar.

espíritu m. spirit; soul; courage; vigor; essence; ghost.

espiritual adj. spiritual.

espita f. spigot, faucet, tap; toper, drunkard

esplendidez f. splendor.

espléndido adj. splendid.

esplendor m. splendor.

esplendoroso adj. resplendent, shining.

espliego m. lavender (plant).

espolear v. to spur; to incite.

espolón m. spur (on a cock's leg); ram (of a boat); spur, buttress.

espolvorear v. to powder, sprinkle with powder.

esponja f. sponge; sponger, parasite; Am. souse, habitual drunkard.

esponjado adj. fluffy; spongy; puffed up; p.p. of esponjar.

esponjar v. to fluff; to make spongy or porous; -se to fluff up; to become spongy or porous; to swell, puff up; to puff up with pride.

esponjoso adj. spongy.

esponsales m. pl. betrothal.

espontaneidad f. spontaneity, ease, naturalness.

espontáneo adj. spontaneous.

esposa f. wife; -s handcuffs.

esposo m. husband.

espuela f. spur.

espulgar[7] v. to delouse, remove lice or fleas from; to scrutinize.

espuma f. foam, froth; scum; — de jabón suds.

espumar v. to skim; to froth, foam.

espumarajo m. froth, foam (from the mouth); echar -s to froth at the mouth; to be very angry.

espumoso adj. foamy.

esputo m. sputum, spit, saliva.

esquela f. note, letter; announcement

esqueleto m. skeleton; carcass; framework; Am. blank (to fill out); Am. outline.

esquema f. scheme, outline.

esquí m. ski.

esquiar[17] v. to ski.

esquila f. small bell; cow bell; sheepshearing.

esquilar v. to shear; to clip; to crop.

esquina f. corner, angle; **esquinazo** m. corner; Am. serenade; **dar esquinazo** to avoid meeting someone; to "ditch" someone.

esquivar v. to avoid, dodge; to shun; -se to withdraw, shy away.

esquivez f. shyness; aloofness; disdain.

90

esquivo *adv.* reserved, unsociable; shy; disdainful, aloof.

estabilidad *f.* stability.

estable *adj.* stable, firm, steady.

establecer[13] *v. irr.* to establish; to found; to decree, ordain.

establecimiento *m.* establishment; foundation; statute, law.

establo *m.* stable; **establero** *m.* groom.

estaca *f.* stake, club; stick; picket.

estacada *f.* stockade; picket fence; *Am.* predicament.

estacar[6] *v.* to stake; to tie to a stake; to stake off, mark off with stakes; *Am.* to fasten down with stakes; -se to remain stiff or rigid.

estación *f.* station; season; railway station.

estacionar *v.* to station; to place; to park (*a car*); -se to remain stationary; to park.

estacionario *adj.* stationary; motionless.

estada *f.* sojourn, stay.

estadía *f.* detention, stay; stay in port (*beyond time allowed for loading and unloading*); *Am.* sojourn, stay (*in any sense*).

estadio *m.* stadium.

estadista *m.* statesman.

estadística *f.* statistics.

estado *m.* state, condition; station, rank; estate; — **mayor** army staff; **hombre de** — statesman; *Am.* **en** — **interesante** pregnant.

estadounidense *adj.* from the United States, American.

estafa *f.* swindle, fraud, trick.

estafador *m.* swindler, crook.

estafar *v.* to swindle, defraud, cheat.

estallar *v.* to explode, burst; to creak, crackle.

estallido *m.* explosion, outburst; crash; creaking; crack (*of a gun*), report (*of a gun or cannon*).

estambre *m.* woolen yarn; stamen (*of a flower*).

estampa *f.* image; print; stamp; cut, picture; footprint; figure, appearance.

estampado *m.* print, printed fabric; printing.

estampar *v.* to stamp, print.

estampida *f.* crack, sharp sound; *Am.* stampede (*sudden scattering of a herd of cattle or horses*).

estampido *m.* crack, sharp sound; report of a gun.

estampilla *f.* stamp, seal; *Am.* postage stamp.

estancar[6] *v.* to stem; to stanch; to stop the flow of; to corner (*a market*); -se to stagnate, become stagnant.

estancia *f.* stay; hall, room; mansion; *Am.* farm, cattle ranch; *Am.* main building of a farm or ranch.

estanciero *m. Am.* rancher, ranch-owner, cattle raiser; *adj.* pertaining to an **estancia**.

estanco *m.* monopoly; government store (*for sale of monopolized goods such as tobacco, stamps and matches*); tank, reservoir; *Am.* liquor store.

estándar *m. Am.* standard, norm.

estandardizar, estandarizar[9] *v. Am* to standardize.

estandarte *m.* standard, flag, banner.

estanque *m.* pond, pool, reservoir.

estanquillo *m.* tobacco store; *Am.* small store; *Am.* small liquor store, tavern.

estante *m.* shelf; bookshelf; *Am.* prop, support; **estantería** *f.* shelves; bookcases.

estaño *m.* tin.

estaquilla *f.* peg; spike.

estar[29] *v. irr.* to be; **-le bien a uno** to be becoming to one; — **de prisa** to be in a hurry; **¿a cuántos estamos?** what day of the month is it today?; -se to keep, remain.

estático *adj.* static; **estática** *f.* statics; radio static.

estatua *f.* statue.

estatura *f.* stature, height.

estatuto *m.* statute.

este, esta *dem. adj.* this; **estos, estas** these; **éste, ésta** *m., f. dem. pron.* this one, this thing; the latter; **esto** this, this thing; **éstos, éstas** *m., f. pl.* these; the latter.

este *m.* east; east wind.

estela *f.* wake of a ship.

estenógrafo *m.* stenographer.

estentóreo *adj.* loud, thundering (*voice*).

estepa *f.* steppe, treeless plain.

estera *f.* matting; mat.

estercolar *v.* to manure, fertilize with manure.

estercolero *m.* manure pile, manure dump; manure collector.

estéril *adj.* sterile, barren.

esterilidad *f.* sterility, barrenness.

esterilizar[9] *v.* to sterilize.

esterlina *adj.* sterling; **libra** — **pound** sterling.

estero *m.* estuary.

estertor *m.* death-rattle; snort.

estético *adj.* aesthetic; **estética** *f.* aesthetics.

91

estetoscopio *m.* stethoscope.

estibador *m.* stevedore, longshoreman.

estibar *v.* to stow (*in a boat*); to pack down, compress.

estiércol *m.* manure; fertilizer.

estigma *m.* stigma; brand, mark of disgrace; birthmark.

estilar *v.* to use, be accustomed to using;-se to be in style (*said of clothes*).

estilete *m.* stiletto, narrow-bladed dagger; stylet (*instrument for probing wounds*); long, narrow sword.

estilo *m.* style; fashion.

estima *f.* esteem.

estimación *f.* esteem, regard; valuation.

estimar *v.* to esteem, regard highly; to estimate, appraise; to judge, think.

estimulante *adj.* stimulant, stimulating; *m.* stimulant.

estimular *v.* to stimulate, excite, goad.

estímulo *m.* stimulation, incitement; stimulus.

estío *m.* summer.

estipulación *f.* stipulation, specification, provision, proviso.

estipular *v.* to stipulate, specify.

estirado *p.p.* & *adj.* stretched; extended, drawn out; stuck-up, conceited.

estirar *v.* to stretch, extend; — la pata to die; -se to stretch out; *Am.* to die.

estirón *m.* hard pull, tug; stretch; dar un — to grow suddenly (*said of a child*).

estirpe *f.* lineage, family, race.

estival *adj.* summer, relating to the summer.

estocada *f.* thrust, stab; stab wound.

estofa *f.* stuff, cloth; class, quality; gente de baja — low class people, rabble.

estofado *m.* stew, stewed meat; *p.p.* of **estofar.**

estofar *v.* to quilt; to stew.

estoico *adj.* & *m.* stoic.

estómago *m.* stomach.

estopa *f.* burlap; oakum (*loose fiber of old ropes*).

estoque *m.* long, narrow sword.

estorbar *v.* to hinder; to obstruct.

estorbo *m.* hindrance; nuisance, bother.

estornudar *v.* to sneeze.

estornudo *m.* sneeze.

estrado *m.* dais (*platform for a throne, seats of honor, etc.*); main part of a parlor or drawing room.

estragado *p.p.* & *adj.* corrupted; spoiled; ruined; tired, worn out.

estragar[7] *v.* to corrupt, contaminate; to spoil; to ruin.

estrago *m.* havoc, ruin; massacre.

estrangulador *m.* strangler, choke (*of an automobile*); *adj.* strangling.

estrangular *v.* to strangle; to choke, throttle.

estratagema *f.* stratagem, scheme.

estrategia *f.* strategy.

estratégico *adj.* strategic; *m.* strategist, person trained or skilled in strategy.

estrato *m.* stratum, layer (*of mineral*).

estratosfera *f.* stratosphere.

estrechar *v.* to tighten; to narrow down; to embrace, hug; — la mano to squeeze, grasp another's hand; to shake hands.

estrechez, estrechura *f.* narrowness; tightness; austerity; dire straits; poverty; closeness.

estrecho *adj.* narrow; tight; *m.* strait, narrow passage.

estrella *f.* star; — de mar starfish.

estrellado *adj.* starry; spangled with stars; huevos -s fried eggs.

estrellar *v.* to shatter; to dash to pieces; to star, spangle with stars; -se to shatter, break into pieces; to fail.

estremecer[13] *v. irr.* to shake; -se to shiver, shudder; to vibrate.

estremecimiento *m.* shiver, shudder; vibration; shaking.

estrenar *v.* to wear for the first time; to perform (*a play*) for the first time; to inaugurate; to begin.

estreno *m.* début, first appearance or performance.

estreñimiento *m.* constipation.

estreñir[5, 19] *v. irr.* to constipate; -se to become constipated.

estrépito *m.* racket, noise, crash.

estrepitoso *adj.* noisy; boisterous.

estriado *p.p.* & *adj.* fluted, grooved; streaked.

estriar[17] *v.* to groove; to flute (*as a column*).

estribación *f.* spur (*of a mountain or mountain range*).

estribar *v.* to rest (upon); eso estriba en que . . . the basis or reason for it is that . . .

estribillo *m.* refrain.

estribo *m.* stirrup; footboard, running board; support; brace; spur (*of a mountain*); perder los -s to lose one's balance; to lose control of oneself.

estribor *m.* starboard.

estricto *adj.* strict.

estrofa *f.* strophe, stanza.

estropajo *m.* fibrous mass (*for scrubbing*); **tratar a uno como un —** to treat someone scornfully.

estropear *v.* to spoil, ruin, damage; to cripple.

estructura *f.* structure.

estructural *adj.* structural.

estruendo *m.* clatter; clamor, din, racket.

estruendoso *adj.* thunderous, uproarious, deafening.

estrujamiento *m.* crushing, squeezing.

estrujar *v.* to squeeze, press, crush.

estrujón *m.* squeeze, crush; smashing.

estuario *m.* estuary.

estuco *m.* stucco.

estuche *m.* jewel box; instrument case, kit; small casket; sheath.

estudiante *m. & f.* student.

estudiar *v.* to study.

estudio *m.* study; studio.

estudioso *adj.* studious; *m.* learner.

estufa *f.* heater; stove; hothouse; steam room; steam cabinet.

estupefacto *adj.* stunned; speechless.

estupendo *adj.* stupendous, marvelous.

estupidez *f.* stupidity.

estúpido *adj.* stupid.

etapa *f.* stage, lap (*of a journey or race*); army food rations; epoch, period.

éter *m.* ether.

etéreo *adj.* ethereal; heavenly.

eternidad *f.* eternity.

eternizar[9] *v.* to prolong excessively; to perpetuate, make eternal.

eterno *adj.* eternal, everlasting.

ética *f.* ethics; **ético** *adj.* ethical, moral.

etiqueta *f.* etiquette; formality; tag; **de —** formal (*dress, function, etc.*).

eucalipto *m.* eucalyptus.

europeo *adj. & m.* European.

evacuación *f.* evacuation; bowel movement.

evacuar[18] *v.* to evacuate, empty; to vacate.

evadir *v.* to evade, elude; **-se** to slip away, escape.

evaluar[18] *v.* to evaluate, appraise.

evangelio *m.* gospel.

evaporar *v.* to evaporate; **-se** to evaporate; to vanish, disappear.

evasión *f.* evasion, dodge, escape.

evasiva *f.* evasion, dodge, escape.

evasivo *adj.* evasive.

evasor *m.* evader, dodger.

evento *m.* event.

evidencia *f.* evidence.

evidenciar *v.* to prove, show, make evident.

evidente *adj.* evident.

evitable *adj.* avoidable.

evitar *v.* to avoid, shun.

evocar[6] *v.* to evoke, call forth.

evolución *f.* evolution.

evolucionar *v.* to evolve; to perform maneuvers; to go through changes.

exacerbar *v.* to exasperate, irritate; to aggravate, make worse.

exactitud *f.* exactness, precision; punctuality.

exacto *adj.* exact, precise; punctual.

exagerar *v.* to exaggerate.

exaltación *f.* exaltation; excitement.

exaltado *adj.* elated; excited; hotheaded.

exaltar *v.* to exalt, elevate, glorify; to praise; **-se** to get excited; to become upset emotionally.

examen *m.* examination; inspection.

examinar *v.* to examine; to inspect.

exánime *adj.* lifeless, motionless; weak, faint.

exasperar *v.* to exasperate, irritate, annoy.

excavar *v.* to excavate, dig, dig out.

excedente *m.* surplus; *adj.* exceeding, extra.

exceder *v.* to exceed, surpass; to overdo; **-se** to go beyond the proper limit; to misbehave.

excelencia *f.* excellence, superiority; excellency (*title*).

excelente *adj.* excellent.

excelso *adj.* lofty, elevated; sublime; **El Excelso** the Most High.

excéntrico *adj.* eccentric; queer, odd.

excepción *f.* exception.

excepcional *adj.* exceptional, unusual.

excepto *adv.* except, with the exception of.

exceptuar[18] *v.* to except.

excesivo *adj.* excessive.

exceso *m.* excess; crime; **— de equipaje** excess baggage; **en —** in excess, excessively.

excitación *f.* excitement.

excitante *adj.* exciting; stimulating.

excitar *v.* to excite, stir; **-se** to get excited.

exclamación *f.* exclamation.

exclamar *v.* to exclaim.

excluir[32] *v. irr.* to exclude.

exclusivo *adj.* exclusive.

excomunicar[6] *v.* to excommunicate.

excomunión *f.* excommunication.

excrecencia, excrescencia *f.* excrescence (*abnormal growth or tumor*).

excremento *m.* excrement.

excursión *f.* excursion, tour, outing.

excusa *f.* excuse.

excusado *p.p. & adj.* excused; exempt; superfluous; unnecessary; reserved, private; *m.* toilet.

excusar *v.* to excuse; to avoid, shun; to exempt; -se to excuse oneself, apologize; to decline.

exención *f.* exemption.

exentar *v.* to exempt. *See* **eximir.**

exento *adj.* exempt, freed; free, unobstructed.

exequias *f. pl.* obsequies, funeral rites.

exhalar *v.* to exhale; to emit, give off; to breathe forth; -se to evaporate; to run away.

exhibición *f.* exhibition; exposition; *Am.* payment of an installment.

exhibir *v.* to exhibit; *Am.* to pay for in installments (*stocks, policies, etc.*); -se to exhibit oneself, show off.

exhortar *v.* to exhort, admonish.

exigencia *f.* demand; urgent want; emergency.

exigente *adj.* demanding, exacting; urgent.

exigir[11] *v.* to require; to demand; to exact.

exiguo *adj.* scanty, meager.

eximio *adj.* very distinguished.

eximir *v.* to exempt, except, excuse; -se de to avoid, shun.

existencia *f.* existence; -s stock on hand, goods; en — in stock, on hand.

existente *adj.* existent, existing; in stock.

existir *v.* to exist.

éxito *m.* outcome, result; success; tener buen (mal) — to be successful (unsuccessful).

éxodo *m.* exodus, emigration.

exonerar *v.* to exonerate, free from blame; to relieve of a burden or position; to dismiss.

exorbitante *adj.* exorbitant, excessive, extravagant.

exótico *adj.* exotic, foreign, strange; quaint.

expansión *f.* expansion; relaxation; recreation.

expansivo *adj.* expansive; demonstrative, effusive.

expatriar *v.* to expatriate, exile; -se to expatriate oneself, renounce one's citizenship; to emigrate.

expectación *f.* expectation.

expectativa *f.* expectation; hope, prospect; estar en — de algo to be expecting, or on the lookout for, something.

expectorar *v.* to expectorate, cough up.

expedición *f.* expedition; dispatch,

promptness; papal dispatch or bull.

expedicionario *adj.* expeditionary; *m.* member of an expedition; explorer.

expediente *m.* certificate; papers pertaining to a business matter; expedient, means; dispatch, promptness.

expedir[5] *v. irr.* to dispatch; to issue officially; to remit, send.

expeler *v.* to expel, eject.

experiencia *f.* experience; experiment.

experimentado *adj. & p.p.* experienced.

experimental *adj.* experimental.

experimentar *v.* to experiment, try, test; to experience, feel.

experimento *m.* experiment, trial.

experto *adj.* expert, skilful; *m.* expert.

expiación *f.* expiation, atonement.

expiar[17] *v.* to atone for; to make amends for; to purify.

expirar *v.* to die; to expire, come to an end.

explayar *v.* to extend; -se to become extended; to relax in the open air; to enlarge upon a subject; -se con un amigo to unbosom oneself, speak with utmost frankness with a friend.

explicable *adj.* explainable.

explicación *f.* explanation.

explicar[6] *v.* to explain; — una cátedra to teach a course; -se to explain oneself; to account for one's conduct.

explicativo *adj.* explanatory, explaining.

explícito *adj.* explicit, express, clear, definite.

exploración *f.* exploration.

explorador *m.* explorer, scout; *adj.* exploring.

explorar *v.* to explore.

explosión *f.* explosion.

explosivo *adj. & m.* explosive.

explotación *f.* exploitation; operation of a mine; development of a business; plant.

explotar *v.* to exploit, operate, develop; to utilize, profit by; to make unfair use of; *Am.* to explode.

exponer[40] *v. irr.* to expose, reveal; to show, exhibit; to display; to expose, leave unprotected; to explain, expound; -se a to expose oneself to; to run the risk of.

exportación *f.* exportation; export.

exportar *v.* to export.

exposición *f.* exposition; exhibition; explanation; exposure.

exprés *m. Am.* express; *Am.* express company.

expresar *v.* to express; -se to express oneself, speak.

expresión *f.* expression; utterance; -es

regards.

expresivo *adj.* expressive; affectionate.

expreso *adj.* expressed; express, clear, exact; fast; *m.* express train.

exprimir *v.* to squeeze, extract (*juice*); to wring out; to express, utter.

expuesto *p.p. of* **exponer** & *adj.* exposed; expressed; displayed; risky, dangerous; **lo —** what has been said.

expulsar *v.* to expel, eject.

expulsión *f.* expulsion, expelling.

exquisitez *f.* exquisiteness.

exquisito *adj.* exquisite.

extasiado *adj.* rapt, in ecstasy; *p.p. of* **extasiar.**

extasiar[17] *v.* to delight; **-se** to be in ecstasy; to be entranced.

éxtasis *m.* ecstasy.

extender[1] *v. irr.* to extend; to spread; to unfold; to draw up (*a document*); **-se** to extend, spread; to expatiate, be too wordy.

extensión *f.* extension; extent; expanse; expansion.

extensivo *adj.* extensive.

extenso *p.p. irr. of* **extender** extended; *adj.* extensive, vast, spacious; **por —** extensively, in detail.

extenuado *adj.* wasted, weak, emaciated.

exterior *adj.* exterior, outer; *m.* exterior; outside; outward appearance.

exterminar *v.* to exterminate.

exterminio *m.* extermination, destruction.

externo *adj.* external, outward.

extinguir[12] *v.* to extinguish, put out; to destroy.

extinto *adj.* extinct.

extirpar *v.* to eradicate, pull out by the roots, root out, remove completely; to destroy completely.

extorsión *f.* extortion.

extorsionar *v. Am.* to extort, extract money, blackmail.

extorsionista *m. Am.* extortioner, profiteer, racketeer.

extracto *m.* extract; abstract, summary.

extraer[46] *v. irr.* to extract.

extranjero *adj.* foreign; *m.* foreigner.

extrañamiento *m.* wonder, surprise, amazement.

extrañar *v.* to wonder at; to banish; *Am.* to miss (*a person or thing*); **-se** to marvel, be astonished.

extrañeza *f.* strangeness; surprise, astonishment; oddity, odd thing.

extraño *adj.* strange; rare; odd; *m.* stranger.

extraordinario *adj.* extraordinary.

extravagancia *f.* extravagance; folly.

extravagante *adj.* extravagant, fantastic; queer, odd.

extraviar[17] *v.* to lead astray; to strand; to misplace; **-se** to lose one's way; to get stranded; to get lost; to miss the road.

extravío *m.* deviation, straying; error; misconduct; damage.

extremado *adj.* extreme; extremely good or extremely bad; *p.p. of* **extremar.**

extremar *v.* to carry to an extreme; **-se** to take great pains, exert great effort.

extremidad *f.* extremity; extreme degree; remotest part; **-es** extremities, hands and feet.

extremo *adj.* extreme, last; farthest; excessive; utmost; *m.* extreme, highest degree or point; end, extremity; extreme care; **con (en** *or* **por) —** very much, extremely.

exuberante *adj.* exuberant; luxuriant.

F

fábrica *f.* manufacture; factory, mill; structure.

fabricación *f.* manufacture.

fabricante *m.* manufacturer, maker.

fabricar[6] *v.* to manufacture, make; to construct, build; to fabricate, make up, invent.

fabril *adj.* manufacturing.

fábula *f.* fable, tale; falsehood.

fabuloso *adj.* fabulous; false, imaginary.

facción *f.* faction, band, party; battle; **-es** features; **estar de —** to be on duty.

faceto *adj. Am.* cute, funny; *Am.* affected.

fácil *adj.* easy; docile, yielding, manageable; likely; probable.

facilidad *f.* facility, ease; opportunity.

facilitar *v.* to facilitate, make easy; to furnish, give; **— todos los datos** to furnish all the data.

facón *m. Am.* dagger, large knife; **faconazo** *m. Am.* stab.

factible *adj.* feasible.

factor *m.* factor; element, joint cause; commercial agent; baggage man.

factura *f.* invoice, itemized bill; make; workmanship, form; *Am.* roll, biscuit, muffin; **— simulada** temporary invoice, memorandum.

facturar *v.* to invoice, bill; to check (*baggage*).

facultad *f.* faculty; ability, aptitude; power, right; permission; branch of learning.

facultativo *m.* doctor, physician.

facundia *f.* eloquence, fluency, facility in speaking, gift of expression.

facha *f.* appearance, figure, aspect, looks.

fachada *f.* façade, front (*of a building*); title page.

fachenda *f.* ostentation, vanity.

fachendoso *adj.* vain, boastful, ostentatious.

faena *f.* task, job, duty; *Am.* extra job; *Am.* work crew, labor gang.

faja *f.* sash; girdle; band; *Am.* belt, waist band.

fajar *v.* to girdle; to bind, wrap, or bandage with a strip of cloth; *Am.* to beat, strike, thrash; *Am.* — **un latigazo a uno** to whip, thrash someone; **-se** to put on a sash or belt; to tighten one's sash or belt; *Am.* **-se con** to have a fight with, come to blows with.

fajo *m.* bundle; sheaf.

falaz *adj.* illusive, illusory; deceitful, deceiving.

falda *f.* skirt; lap; hat brim; foothill, slope; **faldón** *m.* coattail; shirttail.

faldear *v.* to skirt (*a hill*).

falsario *m.* crook, forger; liar.

falsear *v.* to falsify, misrepresent; to counterfeit; to forge; to pick (*a lock*); to flag, grow weak; to hit a wrong note.

falsedad *f.* falsehood, lie; deceit.

falsificación *f.* falsification, forgery; counterfeit.

falsificar[6] *v.* to falsify, make false; to counterfeit; to forge.

falso *adj.* false; untrue, unreal; deceitful; counterfeit; sham; *Am.* cowardly; *m.* inside facing of a dress; lining; *Am.* false testimony, slander; **en — upon a false foundation; without proper security; *Am.* **coger a uno en — to catch one lying.

falta *f.* lack, want; fault, mistake; defect; absence; misdemeanor, offense; a **— de** for want of; **hacer — to be necessary; to be missing; **me hace — I need it; **sin — without fail.

faltar *v.* to be lacking, wanting; to be absent or missing; to fail, be of no use or help; to fail to fulfill (*a promise or duty*); to die; *Am.* to insult; — **poco para las cinco** to be almost five o'clock; **¡no faltaba más!** that's the last straw!; why, the very idea!

falto *adj.* lacking; deficient, short; *Am.* foolish, stupid.

faltriquera *f.* pocket.

falla *f.* fault, defect; failure; fault (*fracture in the earth's crust*); *Am.* baby's bonnet.

fallar *v.* to render a verdict; to fail, be deficient; to default; to miss, fail to hit; to give way, break; to trump.

fallecer[15] *v. irr.* to die.

fallecimiento *m.* decease, death.

fallido *adj.* frustrated; bankrupt.

fallo *m.* verdict, judgment; decision; *adj.* lacking (*a card, or suit, in card games*); *Am.* silly, foolish.

fama *f.* fame, reputation; rumor, report; *Am.* bull's-eye, center of a target.

famélico *adj.* ravenous, hungry, starved.

familia *f.* family.

familiar *adj.* domestic, homelike; familiar, well-known; friendly, informal; colloquial (*phrase or expression*); *m.* intimate friend; member of a household; domestic servant; familiar spirit, demon; *Am.* relative.

familiaridad *f.* familiarity, informality.

familiarizar[9] *v.* to familiarize, acquaint; **-se** to acquaint oneself, become familiar (with).

famoso *adj.* famous; excellent.

fanal *m.* beacon, lighthouse; lantern; headlight; bell jar, glass cover.

fanático *adj.* & *m.* fanatic.

fanatismo *m.* fanaticism.

fanega *f.* Spanish bushel; — **de tierra** land measure (*variable according to region*).

fanfarrón *m.* braggart, boaster; bluffer.

fanfarronada *f.* boast, brag, swagger, bluff.

fanfarronear *v.* to bluff, brag; to swagger.

fango *m.* mud, mire.

fangoso *adj.* muddy, miry.

fantasear *v.* to fancy; to imagine.

fantasía *f.* fantasy, imagination, fancy, whim; **-s** string of pearls; *Am.* **tocar por — to play by ear.

fantasma *m.* phantom, image; vision, ghost; *f.* scarecrow.

fantasmagórico *adj.* fantastic, unreal, illusory.

fantástico *adj.* fantastic.

fardel *m.* knapsack, bag; bundle.

fardo *m.* bundle; bale; *Am.* **pasar el — to "pass the buck", shift the responsibility to someone else.

farmacéutico *m.* pharmacist, druggist; *adj.* pharmaceutical (*pertaining to a pharmacy or pharmacists*).

farmacia *f.* pharmacy; drugstore.

faro *m.* lighthouse; beacon; *Am.* headlight.

farol *m.* lantern; street lamp; conceit, self-importance; *Am.* balcony; *Am.* presumptuous man; *Am.* bluff; **darse — to show off; to put on airs.

farolero *adj.* vain, ostentatious; *m.* lamp maker or vendor; lamplighter (*person*).

farra *f.* *Am.* spree, revelry, wild party, noisy merrymaking; *Am.* **ir de —** to go on a spree.

farsa *f.* farce; company of actors; sham, fraud.

farsante *m.* charlatan, bluffer; quack; comedian; wag.

fascinación *f.* fascination; glamour.

fascinador *adj.* fascinating, glamorous, charming,

fascinar *v.* to fascinate, bewitch, charm; to allure.

fase *f.* phase, aspect.

fastidiar *v.* to annoy, bother; to bore; *Am.* to hurt, harm, ruin.

fastidio *m.* boredom; disgust; nuisance, annoyance.

fastidioso *adj.* annoying, bothersome; boring, tiresome.

fatal *adj.* fatal; mortal, deadly; unfortunate.

fatalidad *f.* fatality, destiny; calamity, misfortune.

fatiga *f.* fatigue, weariness; toil; **-s** hardships.

fatigar[7] *v.* to fatigue, weary; to bother.

fatigoso *adj.* fatiguing, tiring.

fatuo *adj.* foolish, stupid; vain; **fuego — will-o'-the-wisp.**

favor *m.* favor; kindness; help, aid; protection; *Am.* ribbon bow; **a — de** in favor of; **hágame el —** please.

favorable *adj.* favorable.

favorecer[13] *v. irr.* to favor, help, protect.

favoritismo *m.* favoritism.

favorito *adj.* & *m.* favorite.

faz *f.* face.

fe *f.* faith; **— de bautismo** baptismal certificate.

fealdad *f.* ugliness, homeliness; foulness, foul or immoral action.

febrero *m.* February.

febril *adj.* feverish.

fécula *f.* starch.

fecundar *v.* to fertilize.

fecundo *adj.* fruitful, fertile, productive.

fecha *f.* date.

fechar *v.* to date.

fechoría *f.* misdeed, misdemeanor.

federación *f.* federation, union.

federal *adj.* federal.

felicidad *f.* happiness; **¡-es!** congratulations!

felicitación *f.* congratulation.

felicitar *v.* to congratulate.

feligrés *m.* parishioner.

feliz *adj.* happy; lucky.

felpudo *adj.* plushy, like plush; *m.* small plushlike mat; door mat.

femenil *adj.* womanly, feminine.

femenino *adj.* feminine.

fementido *adj.* false; treacherous.

fenecer[13] *v. irr.* to die; to finish, end.

fénix *m.* phoenix (*mythical bird*).

fenómeno *m.* phenomenon.

feo *adj.* ugly, homely; *Am.* bad (*referring to taste or odor*); **feote** *adj.* hideous, very ugly.

féretro *m.* bier; coffin.

feria *f.* fair; market; *Am.* change (*money*); *Am.* tip; **-s** *Am.* present given to servants or the poor during holidays.

feriante *m.* & *f.* trader at fairs; trader; peddler.

fermentar *v.* to ferment.

fermento *m.* ferment; yeast, leaven.

ferocidad *f.* ferocity, fierceness.

feroz *adj.* ferocious, wild, fierce.

férreo *adj.* ferrous (*pertaining to or derived from iron*); ironlike; harsh; **vía férrea** railroad.

ferretería *f.* hardware shop; hardware.

ferrocarril *m.* railroad.

ferroviario *adj.* railway, railroad (*used as adj.*); *m.* railroad man; railroad employee.

fértil *adj.* fertile, productive; **fertilidad** *f.* fertility.

fertilizar[9] *v.* to fertilize.

ferviente *adj.* fervent, ardent.

fervor *m.* fervor, zeal, devotion.

fervoroso *adj.* fervent, ardent; pious, devout; zealous.

festejar *v.* to feast, entertain; to celebrate; to woo; *Am.* to thrash, beat.

festejo *m.* entertainment, festival, celebration; courtship; *Am.* revelry.

festín *m.* feast; banquet.

festividad *f.* festival; holiday; holy day; festivity, gaiety, rejoicing.

festivo *adj.* festive, gay; **día —** holiday.

fétido *adj.* foul, foul-smelling.

fiado *p.p.* of **fiar**; **al —** on credit.

fiador *m.* guarantor, backer, bondsman; *Am.* chin strap, hat guard.

fiambre *m.* cold meat; cold or late news; *Am.* cold meat salad; *Am.* flop, failure (*referring to a party*).

fianza *f.* bond, security, surety, guarantee; bail.

fiar[17] to trust; to guarantee, back; *Am.* to borrow on credit; **-se de** to place confidence in.

fibra *f.* fiber; **fibroso** *adj.* fibrous.

ficción *f.* fiction.

ficticio *adj.* fictitious.

ficha f. chip; token; domino; file card; Am. check (used in barbershops and stores); Am. rascal, scamp; **fichero** m. file, card index, filing cabinet.

fidedigno adj. trustworthy, reliable.

fidelidad f. fidelity, faithfulness.

fideo m. vermicelli, thin noodle; thin person.

fiebre f. fever; excitement, agitation; Am. astute person.

fiel adj. faithful; true, accurate; m. public inspector; pointer of a balance or scale; pin of the scissors; **los -es** the worshipers, the congregation.

fieltro m. felt; felt hat; felt rug.

fiera f. wild beast; Am. go-getter, hustler; **ser una — para el trabajo** to be a demon for work.

fiereza f. ferocity, fierceness; cruelty; ugliness.

fiero adj. fierce, ferocious, wild; cruel; ugly, horrible; huge; m. threat; **echar (or hacer) -s** to threaten; to boast.

fierro m. Am. iron; Am. iron bar; Am. cattle brand; **-s** Am. tools, implements. See **hierro**.

fiesta f. festivity, celebration, entertainment; holiday; **estar de —** to be in a holiday mood; **hacer -s a uno** to fawn on a person.

fiestero adj. fond of parties, fond of entertaining; gay, festive; playful; m. merrymaker.

figón m. cheap eating house, "joint."

figura f. figure; shape, form; countenance; face card.

figurado adj. figurative.

figurar v. to figure; to form; to represent, symbolize; **-se** to imagine; **se me figura** I think, guess, or imagine.

figurín m. fashion plate; dandy.

fijar v. to fix, fasten; to establish; **-se** to settle; **-se en** to notice, pay attention to.

fijeza f. firmness, solidity, steadiness.

fijo adj. fixed; firm; secure.

fila f. row, tier; rank.

filamento m. filament.

filete m. edge, rim; fillet, tenderloin; snaffle bit (for horses); hem; screw thread.

filial adj. filial.

filmar v. to film, screen (a play or novel).

filo m. cutting edge; Am. hunger; **por — exactly**; Am. de — resolutely.

filón m. seam, layer (of metallic ore).

filoso adj. Am. sharp, sharp-edged.

filosofía f. philosophy.

filosófico adj. philosophic, philosoph-

ical.

filósofo m. philosopher.

filtrar v. to filter; **-se** to leak through, leak out; to filter.

filtro m. filter.

filudo adj. Am. sharp, sharp-edged.

fin m. end, ending; purpose; **al — at last**; **al — y al cabo** at last; anyway; **in the end**; **a — de que** so that; **a -es del mes** toward the end of the month; **en —** in conclusion; well; in short.

final adj. final; m. end.

finalizar[9] v. to finish; to end.

financiamiento m. Am. financing.

financiar v. Am. to finance.

financiero adj. financial; m. financier.

financista m. Am. financier.

finanza f. Am. finance; **-s** Am. public treasury, government funds.

finca f. real estate; property; country house; Am. ranch, farm.

fincar v. to buy real estate; Am. to rest (on), be based (on); Am. to build a farmhouse or country house.

fineza f. fineness; nicety; courtesy; favor, kindness; present.

fingimiento m. pretense, sham.

fingir[11] v. to feign, pretend, fake; to imagine.

finiquito m. settlement (of an account); quittance, final receipt; **dar —** to finish up.

fino adj. fine; nice; delicate; sharp; subtle; refined.

finura f. fineness; nicety; subtlety; courtesy, good manners.

firma f. signature; firm, firm name.

firmamento m. firmament, sky.

firmante m. & f. signer.

firmar v. to sign.

firme adj. firm; solid; hard; **de — without** stopping, hard, steadily.

firmeza f. firmness.

fiscal m. public prosecutor, district attorney; adj. fiscal.

fisgar[7] v. to pry; to snoop; to spy on.

fisgón m. snoop, snooper; adj. snooping; curious.

fisgonear v. to pry about; to snoop.

física f. physics.

físico adj. physical; Am. vain, prudish, affected; Am. real; m. physicist.

fisiología f. physiology.

fisiológico adj. physiological.

fisonomía f. face, features.

flaco adj. lean, skinny; frail, weak; **su lado —** his weak side, his weakness.

flacura f. thinness.

flama f. flame.

flamante *adj.* bright, shiny; brand-new.

flameante *adj.* flaming, flashing.

flamear *v.* to flame; to flap, flutter (*in the wind*).

flamenco *adj.* Flemish; *Am.* skinny; *m.* Flemish, Flemish language; flamingo.

flan *m.* custard.

flanco *m.* flank, side.

flanquear *v.* to flank.

flaquear *v.* to weaken, flag.

flaqueza *f.* thinness, leanness; weakness, frailty.

flauta *f.* flute; **flautista** *m.* & *f.* flute player.

fleco *m.* fringe; bangs, fringe of hair.

flecha *f.* arrow, dart.

flechar *v.* to dart, shoot (*an arrow*); to strike, wound or kill with an arrow; to cast an amorous or ardent glance; *Am.* to prick, sting; *Am.* to burn (*said of the sun*).

fletamento *m.* charter, charter party (*of a ship*).

fletar *v.* to charter (*a ship*); to freight; *Am.* to hire (*pack animals*); *Am.* to let loose (*strong words*); *Am.* to scatter (*false rumors*); **-se** *Am.* to run away, slip away; *Am.* to slip in uninvited; *Am.* **salir fletado** to leave on the run.

flete *m.* freight, freightage; cargo; load; *Am.* fine horse, race horse; *Am.* bother, nuisance; *Am.* **salir sin -s** to leave in a hurry.

flexibilidad *f.* flexibility; **flexible** *adj.* flexible.

flexión *f.* bending, bend; sag.

flojear *v.* to slacken; to weaken; to idle, be lazy.

flojedad *f.* laxity, looseness; slackness; laziness; slack.

flojera = **flojedad**.

flojo *adj.* lax; loose, slack; lazy; weak; *Am.* timid.

flor *f.* flower, blossom; compliment; **— de la edad** prime; **— de lis** iris (*flower*); **— y nata** the best, the cream, the chosen few; **a — de** flush with; **echar -es** to throw a bouquet; to compliment, flatter.

floreado *p.p.* & *adj.* flowered; made of the finest wheat.

florear *v.* to decorate with flowers; to brandish, flourish; to make a flourish on the guitar; to flatter, compliment; to bolt, sift out (*the finest flour*); *Am.* to flower, bloom; *Am.* to choose the best; **-se** *Am.* to shine, excel; *Am.* to burst open like a flower.

florecer[13] *v. irr.* to flower, bloom; to flourish, thrive.

floreciente *adj.* flourishing, thriving; prosperous.

florecimiento *m.* flourishing, flowering, bloom.

floreo *m.* flourish; idle talk; flattery, compliment.

florería *f.* florist's shop.

florero *m.* florist; flower vase; flatterer; *adj.* flattering.

floresta *f.* wooded place, grove; arbor.

florete *m.* fencing foil.

florido *adj.* flowery.

flota *f.* fleet; *Am.* **echar -s** to brag, boast.

flotador *m.* floater; float; pontoon (*of a hydroplane*); *adj.* floating.

flotante *adj.* floating; *m. Am.* bluffer, braggart.

flotar *v.* to float.

flote : a — afloat.

fluctuación *f.* fluctuation; wavering, hesitation.

fluctuar[18] *v.* to fluctuate; to waver; to hesitate.

fluente *adj.* fluent, flowing.

fluidez *f.* fluidity, easy flow, fluency.

fluido *adj.* fluid, flowing, fluent; *m.* fluid.

fluir[32] *v. irr.* to flow.

flujo *m.* flux; flow; flood tide.

flux *f.* flush (*in cards*); *Am.* suit of clothes; **hacer —** to use up one's funds, lose everything; *Am.* **tener uno —** to be lucky.

foca *f.* seal, sea lion.

foco *m.* focus, center; *Am.* electric-light bulb.

fofo *adj.* spongy, porous; light (*in weight*); soft.

fogata *f.* fire, blaze, bonfire.

fogón *m.* hearth, fireplace; grill (*for cooking*); vent of a gun; *Am.* fire, bonfire; **fogonazo** *m.* flash (*of gun-powder*).

fogoso *adj.* fiery, ardent; lively, spirited.

follaje *m.* foliage.

folletín *m.* small pamphlet; serial story.

folleto *m.* pamphlet.

fomentar *v.* to foment, encourage, promote, foster.

fomento *m.* promotion, encouragement; development; aid.

fonda *f.* inn; restaurant.

fondear *v.* to cast anchor; to sound, make soundings; to search (*a ship*); to sound out; **-se** *Am.* to save up for the future.

fondero *m. Am.* innkeeper.

fondillos *m. pl.* seat of trousers.

fondista *m.* & *f.* innkeeper.

99

fondo *m.* bottom; depth; background; back, rear end; nature, heart, inner self; fund; *Am.* underskirt; -s funds; a — thoroughly; echar a — to sink.

fonducho *m.* cheap eating place.

fonética *f.* phonetics, study of pronunciation.

fonógrafo *m..* phonograph.

forajido *m.* outlaw, fugitive; highwayman, bandit.

foráneo *adj.* foreign; *m.* outsider, stranger.

forastero *m.* stranger; foreigner; outsider; *adj.* foreign.

forcejear, forcejar *v.* to struggle; to strive; to oppose, resist.

forja *f.* forge; forging; blacksmith's shop.

forjador *m.* forger (*of metals*); smith, blacksmith; inventor (*of lies, stories, tricks, etc.*).

forjar *v.* to forge; to form, shape; to invent, feign, fake.

forma *f.* form, shape, figure; manner; format (*size and shape of a book*); host (*unleavened bread for communion*).

formación *f.* formation.

formal *adj.* formal; serious, trustworthy, punctual; reliable.

formalidad *f.* formality; seriousness, reliability; gravity, dignity; punctuality; red tape.

formalismo *m.* formality, red tape (*excess of formalities*); **formalista** *adj.* fond of excessive formalities, fond of red tape.

formalizar[9] *v.* to give proper form to; to legalize; to make official; -se to settle down, become serious.

formar *v.* to form; to shape, mold; -se to get into line; to be molded, educated; to take form.

formidable *adj.* formidable; fearful.

formón *m.* wide chisel.

fórmula *f.* formula.

formular *v.* to formulate, word.

fornido *adj.* stout, strong, sturdy.

foro *m.* stage; back, rear (*of a stage*); forum, court; bar (*profession of law*).

forraje *m.* forage, green grass, fodder, feed.

forrajear *v.* to forage, gather forage.

forrar *v.* to line; to cover, put a sheath, case, or covering on; -se *Am.* to eat well; *Am.* to supply oneself with provisions; *Am.* to save money.

forro *m.* lining; sheathing; casing; covering; book cover.

fortalecer[13] *v. irr.* to fortify; to strengthen.

fortaleza *f.* fortress; fortitude; strength, vigor; *Am.* stench, stink.

fortificación *f.* fortification; fort.

fortificar[6] *v.* to fortify.

fortuito *adj.* fortuitous, accidental, unexpected.

fortuna *f.* fortune; fate, chance; wealth; por — fortunately.

forzar[9] *v. irr.* to force; to compel; to take (*a fort*); to rape; — la entrada en to break into.

forzozo *adj.* compulsory; necessary.

fosa *f.* grave; cavity.

fosco *adj.* dark; cross, irritable, frowning.

fosfato *m.* phosphate.

fosforecer[13], **fosforescer** *v.* to glow.

fósforo *m.* phosphorus; match.

fósil *adj. & m.* fossil.

foso *m.* hole, pit; stage pit; ditch.

fotografía *f.* photograph; photography.

fotografiar[17] *v.* to photograph.

fotógrafo *m.* photographer.

fracasado *adj.* failed; *m.* failure.

fracasar *v.* to fail; to come to ruin; to crumble to pieces.

fracaso *m.* failure, ruin; calamity; crash.

fracción *f.* fraction.

fractura *f.* fracture; break, crack.

fracturar *v.* to fracture, break.

fragancia *f.* fragrance, scent, perfume.

fragante *adj.* fragrant; en — in the act.

fragata *f.* frigate.

frágil *adj.* fragile, breakable; frail, weak.

fragmento *m.* fragment.

fragor *m.* clang, din; crash.

fragoroso *adj.* deafening, thunderous.

fragoso *adj.* rugged, craggy, rough, uneven; noisy.

fragua *f.* forge; blacksmith's shop.

fraguar *v.* to forge; to scheme, hatch (*a plot*).

fraile *m.* friar; priest; **frailuco** *m.* little old friar.

frambuesa *f.* raspberry; **frambueso** *m.* raspberry bush.

francés *adj.* French; *m.* Frenchman; French language.

franco *adj.* frank, open, candid, sincere; free; exempt; *m.* franc; **francote** *adj.* very frank, blunt, outspoken.

franela *f.* flannel.

franja *f.* fringe, border; stripe; braid.

franquear *v.* to exempt; to free; to frank (*a letter*); to dispatch, send; to make grants; — el paso to permit the passage (of); -se to unbosom oneself, disclose one's innermost thoughts and feelings.

franqueo *m.* postage; franking (*of a*

letter); freeing (*of slaves or prisoners*).
franqueza *f.* frankness; freedom.
franquicia *f.* franchise, grant, privilege; freedom or exemption (*from fees*).
frasco *m.* flask, vial, small bottle.
frase *f.* phrase; sentence.
fraternal *adj.* fraternal, brotherly.
fraternidad *f.* fraternity; brotherhood.
fraude *m.* fraud.
fraudulento *adj.* fraudulent, tricky, deceitful, dishonest.
fray *m.* (*contr. of* **fraile**, *used before Christian name*) friar.
frazada *f.* blanket.
frecuencia *f.* frequency; **con —** frequently.
frecuentar *v.* to frequent.
frecuente *adj.* frequent.
fregadero *m.* sink.
fregado *m.* scrub, scrubbing; *p.p. of* **fregar**; *adj. Am.* bothersome, annoying; *Am.* stubborn; *Am.* brazen.
fregar[1] *v. irr.* to scour; to scrub; to rub; to wash (*dishes*); *Am.* to molest, annoy.
fregona *f.* scrub woman; dishwasher, kitchen maid.
freír[15] *v. irr.* to fry; to tease, bother.
frenesí *m.* frenzy, madness.
frenético *adj.* frantic; furious; in a frenzy.·
freno *m.* bridle; brake; control; bit (*for horses*).
frente *f.* forehead; countenance; *m.* front; **en — de** in front of; **— a** in front of, facing; **hacer —** to face.
fresa *f.* strawberry.
fresca *f.* fresh air; fresh remark.
fresco *adj.* fresh; cool; calm, serene; forward, bold; *m.* coolness; cool air; **fresco** (*painting*); *Am.* refreshment; **al — in** the open air; **pintura al —** painting in fresco.
frescor *m.* freshness, coolness.
frescura *f.* freshness; coolness; calm; freedom, ease; boldness, impudence; impudent remark.
fresno *m.* ash, ash tree.
fresquecillo *adj.* nice and cool; *m.* cool air, fresh breeze; **fresquecito, fresquito** *adj.* nice and cool.
frialdad *f.* coldness; coolness, indifference.
fricción *f.* friction, rub, rubbing.
friccionar *v.* to rub; to massage.
friega *f.* rub, rubbing; *Am.* bother, nuisance, irritation; *Am.* flogging, beating.
frigorífico *adj.* freezing; *m.* refrigerator, icebox; *Am.* meat-packing house.
frijol *m.* bean; kidney bean, navy bean.

frío *adj.* cold; frigid; cool, indifferent; *m.* cold; **-s** *Am.* chills and fever; *Am.* malaria.
friolento *adj.* cold-blooded, sensitive to cold; chilly.
friolera *f.* trifle.
fritada *f.* dish of fried food.
frito *p.p. irr. of* **freír** fried; *m.* fry, dish of fried food.
fritura *f.* fry, dish of fried food; fritter.
frivolidad *f.* frivolity; **frívolo** *adj.* frivolous.
fronda *f.* leaf; fern leaf; foliage.
frondoso *adj.* leafy.
frontera *f.* frontier, border; **fronterizo** *adj.* frontier (*used as an adj.*); opposite, facing.
frontero *adj.* facing, opposite.
frontis *m.* façade, front (*of a building*).
frontispicio *m.* front, façade (*front of a building*); title page.
frontón *m.* main wall of a handball court; handball court.
frotación *f.* friction, rubbing.
frotar *v.* to rub; to scour.
frote *m.* rubbing; friction.
fructificar[6] *v.* to fruit, bear or produce fruit; to yield profit.
fructuoso *adj.* fruitful.
frugal *adj.* frugal, economical, saving, thrifty; **frugalidad** *f.* frugality, thrift.
fruncir[10] *v.* to wrinkle; to gather in pleats; to contract, shrivel; **— las cejas** to frown; to knit the eyebrows; **— los labios** to purse or curl the lips.
fruslería *f.* trifle, trinket.
frustración *f.* frustration; failure.
frustrar *v.* to frustrate, thwart, foil; **-se** to fail, be thwarted.
fruta *f.* fruit (*not a vegetable*); **frutería** *f.* fruit store.
frutero *m.* fruit vendor; fruit dish; *adj.* fruit (*used as an adj.*); **buque —** fruit boat; **plato —** fruit dish.
fruto *m.* fruit (*any organic product of the earth*); result; benefit, profit.
¡fuche! *interj. Am.* phew! ugh! pew! phooey!
fuego *m.* fire; passion; skin eruption; *Am.* cold sore; **-s artificiales** fireworks; **hacer —** to fire, shoot; **estar hecho un —** to be very angry; **romper —** to begin to fire, start shooting.
fuelle *m.* bellows; pucker, wrinkle, fold; tattletale, windbag, gossiper.
fuente *f.* fountain; source, origin; spring; platter, serving dish.
fuera *adv.* outside, out; **— de** *prep* outside of; in addition to.

fuereño *m. Am.* outsider, stranger.
fuero *m.* law, statute; power, jurisdiction; code of laws; exemption, privilege.
fuerte *adj.* strong; loud; secure, fortified; grave, serious; excessive; *Am.* stinking; *m.* fort; forte, strong point; forte (*music*); *Am.* alcohol, liquor; *adv.* strongly; excessively; loud; hard.
fuerza *f.* force; power, strength; violence, compulsion; a — de by dint of; a la — (por —, por la —, de por —, *Am.* de —) by force, forcibly; necessarily; ser — to be necessary.
fuete *m. Am.* whip; **fuetazo** *m. Am.* lash.
fuga *f.* flight, escape; leak, leakage; fugue (*musical composition*).
fugarse[7] *v.* to flee, escape.
fugaz *adj.* fleeing, fleeting, brief, passing.
fugitivo *adj.* fugitive; fleeting, passing; perishable; *m.* fugitive.
fulano *m.* so-and-so (*referring to person*).
fulgor *m.* radiance, brilliance.
fulgurar *v.* to gleam, flash, shine.
fulminar *v.* to thunder, thunder forth; to utter (*threats*).
fullero *m.* cardsharp; crooked gambler; cheat.
fumada *f.* puff, whiff (*of smoke*).
fumadero *m.* smoking room.
fumador *m.* smoker, habitual smoker.
fumar *v.* to smoke (*tobacco*); *Am.* **-se a uno** to swindle or cheat someone.
fumigar[7] *v.* to fumigate.
función *f.* function; functioning; office, occupation; show, performance; religious festival.
funcionamiento *m.* functioning, action, working, operation.
funcionar *v.* to function; to work, run (*said of machines*).
funcionario *m.* public employee, officer or official.
funda *f.* cover, case; *Am.* skirt; — de almohada pillowcase.
fundación *f.* foundation.
fundador *m.* founder.
fundamental *adj.* fundamental.
fundamento *m.* foundation, groundwork; basis; *Am.* skirt.
fundar *v.* to found, establish; to erect; to base, ground.
fundir *v.* to smelt, fuse, melt; to cast, mold; *Am.* to ruin; **-se** to fuse, melt together; to unite; *Am.* to be ruined.
fundo *m.* farm, country estate; property, land.
fúnebre *adj.* funeral; funereal, gloomy,

dismal.
funeral *adj. & m.* funeral.
funeraria *f.* undertaking establishment, funeral parlor.
funesto *adj.* ill-fated, unlucky; sad, unfortunate.
fungosidad *f.* fungus, fungous growth.
furgón *m.* freight car, boxcar; **furgonada** *f.* carload.
furia *f.* fury, rage; speed.
furibundo *adj.* furious.
furioso *adj.* furious.
furor *m.* fury, rage, anger; frenzy.
furtivo *adj.* furtive, sly, secret.
fuselaje *m.* fuselage (*of an airplane*).
fusible *adj.* fusible; *m.* electric fuse.
fusil *m.* gun, rifle.
fusilar *v.* to shoot, execute.
fustigar[7] *v.* to lash, whip; to censure severely, scold sharply.
fútil *adj.* futile, useless; trivial; **futilidad** *f.* futility, uselessness.
futuro *adj.* future; *m.* fiancé, future husband; future.

G

gabacho *adj.* from or of the Pyrenees; Frenchlike; *Am.* me salió — it turned out wrong; *m.* Frenchman (*used depreciatively*).
gabán *m.* overcoat.
gabeta = gaveta.
gabinete *m.* cabinet (*of a government*); studio; study, library room; dressing room; sitting room; private room; dentist's office; laboratory; *Am.* glassed-in mirador.
gaceta *f.* gazette, official newspaper; professional periodical; *Am.* any newspaper.
gacetilla *f.* short newspaper article; column of short news items; gossip column; *m. &. f.* newsmonger, tattletale; **gacetillero** *m.* newspaper reporter; newsmonger.
gacha *f.* watery mass or mush; *Am.* china or earthenware bowl; **-s** porridge, mush; caresses; **-s de avena** oatmeal.
gacho *adj.* drooping; bent downward; turned down; stooping; slouching; with horns curved downward; **sombrero** — slouch hat; a gachas on all fours; **con las orejas gachas** with drooping ears; crestfallen, discouraged.
gafas *f. pl.* spectacles; grappling hooks.
gaita *f.* flageolet, a kind of flute; *Am.* good-for-nothing, lazy bum;— **gallega** bagpipe; **sacar la** — to stick out one's neck; **gaitero** *m.* piper, bagpipe

player.

gaje m. fee; -s wages, salary; fees.

gala f. elegance; full dress or uniform; ostentation; Am. award, prize, tip; -s finery, regalia, best clothes; -s de novia trousseau; hacer — de to boast of.

galán m. gallant, lover; leading man (in a play).

galante adj gallant, attentive to ladies; polite.

galanteador m. gallant, lady's man; flatterer.

galantear v. to court, woo; to make love.

galanteo m. wooing, courtship.

galantería f. gallantry, compliment, attention to ladies; courtesy; gracefulness; generosity.

galardón m. recompense, reward.

galeote m. galley slave.

galera f. galley; large wagon; women's jail; printer's galley; Am. jail; Am. tall hat.

galerada f. galley, galley proof; wagon load, van load.

galería f. gallery; corridor.

galgo m. greyhound; adj. Am. gluttonous, always hungry.

galillo m. uvula.

galón m. galloon, braid, trimming; gallon.

galoneado adj. gallooned, trimmed with braid.

galopada f. gallop; pegar una — to break into a gallop.

galopar v. to gallop.

galope m. gallop; a (al or de) — at a gallop; speedily.

galopear = galopar.

galpón m. Am. large open shed.

gallardete m. streamer.

gallardía f. elegance; gracefulness; bravery.

gallardo adj. elegant, graceful; brave.

gallego adj. Galician, from or of Galicia, Spain; m. Galician; Am. Spaniard (used as a nickname).

galleta f. cracker; hardtack, hard biscuit; hard cookie; blow, slap; small pot; Am. bread of coarse meal or bran; Am. reproof; Am. colgarle la — a uno to fire, dismiss someone; Am. tener — to have strength, muscle.

gallina f. hen; m. & f. chickenhearted person.

gallinero m. chicken coop, house, or yard; flock of chickens; basket for carrying chickens; poultryman; noisy gathering; top gallery of a theatre.

gallo m. cock, rooster; aggressive, bossy

person; cork float; false note (in singing); frog (in one's throat); Am. secondhand clothing; Am. fire wagon; Am. serenade.

gamo m. buck, male deer.

gamuza f. chamois, chamois skin (soft leather made from the skin of sheep, goats, deer, etc.).

gana f. desire, appetite; de buena (mala) — willingly (unwillingly); tener — (or -s) to feel like, want to; no me da la — I don't want to.

ganadero m. cattleman; cattle dealer; adj. cattle, pertaining to cattle.

ganado m. cattle; herd; livestock; — mayor cattle; horses; mules; — menor sheep; — de cerda swine.

ganador m. winner; adj. winning.

ganancia f. profit, gain; Am. something to boot, something extra.

ganancioso adj. winning; profitable; m. winner.

ganar v. to win; to profit, gain; to earn; to get ahead of.

gancho m. hook; hooked staff; Am. hairpin; Am. bait, lure, trick; aguja de — crochet hook; echar a uno el — to hook someone; tener — to be attractive, alluring.

gandul m. bum, loafer.

ganga f. bargain; snap, easy job; kind of prairie hen.

gangoso adj. twangy, nasal (voice).

gangrena f. gangrene.

gangrenar v. to gangrene, cause gangrene; -se to gangrene.

ganoso adj. desirous; Am. lively, spirited (horse).

ganso m. goose, gander; lazy, slovenly person; dunce.

ganzúa f. hook; picklock (tool for picking locks); m. & f. burglar.

garabato m. hook; scrawl, scribble; hacer -s to scribble, write poorly.

garaje m. garage.

garantía f. guaranty; security; bail, bond.

garantizar[9] v. to guarantee, vouch for.

garañón m. jackass, male ass; male camel (for breeding); Am. stallion.

garapiñar v. to candy (almonds, fruits, etc.).

garbanzo m. chickpea.

garbo m. elegance, graceful air, good carriage.

garboso adj. graceful; elegant; sprightly.

garfio m. hook.

garganta f. throat, neck; gorge, ravine; gargantilla f. necklace.

gárgara f. gargling; -s Am. gargle, gargling solution; **hacer -s** to gargle.

gargarear v. Am. to gargle.

gargarismo m. gargling; gargle, gargling solution.

gargarizar[9] v. to gargle.

garita f. sentry box; watchman's booth; Am. vendor's booth.

garito m. gambling house, gambling joint; gambler's winnings.

garra f. claw, paw; hook; Am. strength; Am. leather or cloth remnant; Am. skinny person or animal; Am. margin of profit in a business deal; **echar la — to arrest; to grab; Am. hacer -s** to tear to pieces.

garrafa f. decanter; **garrafón** m. large decanter.

garrapata f. tick (an insect).

garrapatear v. to scribble, scrawl, write poorly.

garrocha f. pole; iron-pointed staff; Am. goad (for goading oxen).

garrote m. club, cudgel, heavy stick; Am. brake; **dar — to strangle;** Am. to brake, set the brakes; **garrotazo** m. blow with a club; huge stick.

garrotero m. Am. brakeman; Am. beater (one who beats with a club); adj. Am. stingy.

garrucha f. pulley.

garúa f. Am. drizzle.

garza f. heron.

garzo adj. blue, bluish; blue-eyed.

gas m. gas, vapor; Am. gasoline.

gasa f. gauze.

gascosa f. soda water; soda pop.

gaseoso adj. gaseous.

gasolina f. gasoline.

gastador adj. lavish, extravagant, wasteful; m. spendthrift, lavish spender.

gastar v. to spend; to wear; to use; to waste; **-se** to wear out; to get old.

gasto m. expense, expenditure; wear.

gatas : **a — on all fours; andar a —** to creep, crawl; **salir a — to crawl out of a difficulty.**

gateado adj. catlike; veined, streaked; m. Am. light-colored horse with black streaks.

gatear v. to creep, crawl; to walk on all fours; to claw, scratch; to steal.

gatillo m. kitten; trigger; forceps (for extracting teeth); petty thief.

gato m. cat; moneybag; jack (for lifting weights); sneak thief; sly fellow; Am. trigger; Am. outdoor market; Am. hot-water bottle; Am. a gaucho song and tap dance (by extension, the dancer); Am. blunder.

gatuperio m. fraud, intrigue.

gauchada f. Am. gaucho deed or exploit.

gauchaje m. Am. band of Gauchos, Gaucho folk.

gauchesco adj. Am. relating to Gauchos.

gaucho m. Am. Gaucho, Argentine and Uruguayan cowboy; Am. good horseman; adj. Am. relating to Gauchos, Gaucho-like; Am. sly, crafty

gaveta f. drawer.

gavilla f. sheaf; gang, band (of rogues, thieves, etc.).

gaviota f. sea gull.

gaza f. loop; Am. noose of a lasso.

gazmoñería f. prudery, affected modesty; **gazmoño** adj. prudish, affected, coy.

gaznate m. windpipe, a kind of fritter; Am. a sweetmeat made of pineapple or coconut.

gelatina f. gelatin; jelly.

gema f. gem, jewel; bud.

gemelo m. twin, **-s** twins; binoculars, opera glasses, field glasses; cuff links.

gemido m. moan; wail, cry.

gemir[5] v. irr. to moan; to wail, cry.

gendarme m. Am. policeman.

generación f. generation.

general adj. & m. general; **por lo —** generally.

generalidad f. generality; majority.

generalizar[9] v. to generalize; **-se** to spread, become general.

género m. kind, sort, class, gender; goods, material, cloth, **— humano** human race.

generosidad f. generosity.

generoso adj. generous; best (wine).

genial adj. genial, jovial, pleasant.

genio m. genius; temperament, disposition; spirit.

gente f. people; crowd; race, nation; clan; Am. **— bien upper-class or important person;** Am. **ser — to be a somebody; to be cultured; to be socially important.**

gentil adj. graceful; genteel; courteous; gentile; m. pagan; gentile.

gentileza f. grace, courtesy; nobility; favor.

gentío m. crowd, throng.

gentuza f. rabble.

genuino adj. genuine.

geografía f. geography; **geográfico** adj. geographical.

geología f. geology; **geológico** adj. geological.

geometría f. geometry; **geométrico** adj. geometric.

geranio m. geranium.

gerencia f. management, administration.

gerente *m.* manager.

germen *m.* germ; origin, source.

germinar *v.* to germinate.

gerundio *m.* gerund; present participle.

gesticular *v.* to gesticulate.

gestión *f.* action, step, maneuver; intervention; -es negotiations.

gestionar *v.* to manage; to take steps; to negotiate or carry out (*a deal, transaction, etc.*).

gesto *m.* face, expression; grimace; gesture; **estar de buen** (*or* **mal**) — to be in a good (*or* bad) humor; **hacer -s a** to make faces at.

giba *f.* hump, hunch.

gigante *adj.* gigantic; *m.* giant.

gigantesco *adj.* gigantic.

gimnasia *f.* gymnastics; **gimnasio** *m.* gymnasium; German institute (*for secondary instruction*).

gimotear *v.* to whimper, whine.

gimoteo *m.* whimper, whining.

ginebra *f.* gin (*liquor*).

gira *f.* excursion, tour; outing, picnic.

girador *m.* drawer (*of a check or draft*).

girar *v.* to revolve, rotate, whirl; to send, issue, or draw (*checks, drafts, etc.*); to manage (*a business*).

girasol *m.* sunflower.

giratorio *adj.* rotary, revolving.

giro *m.* rotation; trend, bend, direction, turn; turn of phrase; line of business; draft; — **postal** money order; *adj.* yellowish (*rooster*); *Am.* black and white (*rooster*); *Am.* cocky.

gitano *adj.* gypsy; gypsylike; sly, clever, *m.* gypsy.

gitomate *Am.* = **jitomate**.

glacial *adj.* glacial, icy, very cold.

glaciar *m.* glacier.

glándula *f.* gland.

glasear *v.* to glaze (*paper, fruits, etc.*), make glossy.

globo *m.* globe, sphere; world; balloon.

gloria *f.* glory; gloria (*song of praise to God*).

gloriarse[17] *v.* to glory (in), delight (in), be proud (of); to boast (of).

glorieta *f.* arbor, bower; secluded nook in a park (*with benches*).

glorificar[6] *v.* to glorify; -se to glory (in), take great pride (in).

glorioso *adj.* glorious.

glosar *v.* to gloss, comment upon, explain (*a text*).

glosario *m.* glossary.

glotón *adj.* gluttonous; *m.* glutton.

glotonería *f.* gluttony.

gobernador *m.* governing; *m.* governor, ruler.

gobernante *adj.* governing, ruling; *m.* governor, ruler.

gobernar[1] *v. irr.* to govern, rule; to lead, direct; to steer (*a boat*).

gobierno *m.* government; management; control; helm, rudder.

goce *m.* enjoyment; joy.

goleta *f.* schooner, sailing vessel.

golfo *m.* gulf; open sea; faro (*gambling game*); vagabond, bum, ragamuffin.

golondrina *f.* swallow; swallow fish.

golosina *f.* sweet, dainty, tidbit; trifle; appetite, desire.

goloso *adj.* sweet-toothed, fond of sweets; gluttonous.

golpazo *m.* bang, whack, heavy blow, hard knock.

golpe *m.* blow, hit, stroke; knock; beat; *A m.* facing (*of a garment*); *Am.* sledge hammer; — **de fortuna** stroke of good luck; — **de gente** crowd, throng; — **de gracia** death blow; finishing stroke; **de** — suddenly; **de un** — all at once; **pestillo de** — spring latch; *Am.* **al** — instantly, at once; *Am.* **al** — **de vista** at one glance.

golpear *v.* to strike, hit; to knock; to beat; *Am.* to knock at a door.

golpetear *v.* to tap, knock or pound continuously; to flap; to rattle.

golpeteo *m.* tapping, pounding, knocking; flapping; rattling.

gollería *f.* dainty, delicacy; superfluous thing.

goma *f.* gum; rubber; elastic; eraser; tire; — **de repuesto** spare tire; *Am.* **estar de** — to have a hang-over (*after excessive drinking*).

gomero *adj.* rubber, pertaining to rubber; *m.* gum or rubber tree; *Am.* rubber producer; *Am.* rubber-plantation worker; *Am.* glue container or bottle.

gomífero *adj.* rubber-bearing, rubber-producing.

gomoso *adj.* gummy, sticky; *m.* dandy.

gordiflón *adj.* fat; chubby.

gordo *adj.* fat; plump; *m.* suet, fat; **gorda** *f. Am.* thick tortilla or cornmeal cake; **se armó la gorda** all hell broke loose; there was a big rumpus.

gordura *f.* fatness; stoutness; fat.

gorgojo *m.* weevil; puny person; *Am.* wood borer, wood louse; **gorgojoso** *adj.* infested with weevils.

gorila *m.* gorilla.

gorjeador *m.* warbler; *adj.* warbling; **pájaro** — warbler.

gorjear *v.* to warble; to chirp.

gorjeo *m.* warble; warbling.

gorra *f.* cap; bonnet; **de —** at another's expense; **vivir de —** to sponge, live at another's expense.

gorrión *m.* sparrow.

gorro *m.* cap; bonnet.

gorrón *m.* sponge, parasite; bum; rake (*dissolute fellow*).

gota *f.* drop; gout; **sudar la — gorda** to sweat profusely, toil, work hard.

gotear *v.* to drip; to leak; to dribble, trickle; to sprinkle, begin to rain; **-se** to leak.

goteo *m.* trickle, drip.

gotera *f.* leak, hole (*in the roof*); eaves trough; **-s** *Am.* surroundings, outskirts.

gotero *m. Am.* dropper (*for counting drops*).

gótico *adj.* Gothic; *m.* Goth; Gothic language.

gozar[9] *v.* to enjoy; to possess, have; **-se** to rejoice.

gozne *m.* hinge.

gozo *m.* pleasure, joy.

gozoso *adj.* joyful, glad, merry.

gozque, gozquejo, gozquecillo *m.* a small dog.

grabado *adj.* engraved; *m.* engraving; woodcut, print; **— al agua fuerte** etching.

grabar *v.* to engrave; to carve; to fix, impress; **— al agua fuerte** to etch.

gracejada *f. Am.* clownish act or expression.

gracejo *m.* grace; cuteness; humor, wit.

gracia *f.* grace; gracious act; favor; pardon; joke, witty remark; **caer en —** to please; **hacer —** to amuse, make (*someone*) laugh; **¡-s!** thanks!; **dar -s** to thank.

gracioso *adj.* graceful, attractive; witty, amusing; gracious; *m.* comedian, clown.

grada *f.* step of a staircase; harrow; **-s** steps; seats of an amphitheatre; bleachers.

gradación *f* gradation.

gradería *f.* series of steps; rows of seats (*in an amphitheater or stadium*); **— cubierta** grandstand; **-s** bleachers.

grado *m.* degree; step; **de (buen) —** willingly, with pleasure; **de mal —** unwillingly; **de — en —** by degrees, gradually.

graduación *f.* graduation; military rank.

gradual *adj.* gradual; *m.* response sung at mass.

graduar[18] *v.* to graduate, give a diploma, rank or degree to; to gauge; to classify;

grade; **-se** to graduate, take a degree.

gráfico *adj.* graphic; vivid, lifelike; **gráfica** *f.* graph, diagram, chart.

grafito *m.* graphite.

grajo *m.* jay.

grama *f.* grama grass.

gramática *f.* grammar; **gramatical** *adj.* grammatical; **gramático** *adj.* grammatical; *m.* grammarian.

gramo *m.* gram.

gran *contr.* of **grande**.

grana *f.* cochineal, kermes (*insects used for producing a red dye*); scarlet color; scarlet cloth; any small seed.

granada *f.* pomegranate; grenade, shell, small bomb; **— de mano** hand grenade.

granado *m.* pomegranate tree; *adj.* notable; illustrious; select.

grande *adj.* large, big; great, grand; *Am.* **mamá (papá) —** grandmother (grandfather); *m.* grandee (*Spanish or Portuguese nobleman*); **en —** on a large scale.

grandeza *f.* greatness; grandeur, splendor; bigness; size; grandeeship; body of grandees.

grandiosidad *f.* grandeur, grandness; greatness; **grandioso** *adj.* grandiose, great, grand, magnificent.

granero *m.* granary; grain bin; country or region rich in grain.

granito *m.* granite; small grain; small pimple.

granizada *f.* hailstorm; shower, volley.

granizar[9] *v.* to hail.

granizo *m.* hail; hailstorm; web or film in the eye; *adj. Am.* spotted (*horse*).

granja *f.* grange, farm; country house.

granjear *v.* to earn, gain; to acquire, obtain; *Am.* to steal; **-se** to win for oneself (*favor, goodwill, esteem, etc.*).

granjería *f.* farming; business profit.

granjero *m.* farmer.

grano *m.* grain; seed; pimple; grain (*unit of measure*); **ir al —** to come to the point.

granuja *m.* ragamuffin, urchin; scamp.

granular *v.* to granulate; **-se** to become granulated; to break out with pimples.

grapa *f.* clamp.

grasa *f.* grease; fat; tallow; *Am.* shoe polish; *Am.* **dar —** to polish (*shoes*).

grasiento *adj.* greasy, oily.

grasoso *adj.* greasy, oily.

gratificación *f.* gratuity, bonus, tip; recompense, reward.

gratis *adv.* gratis, for nothing, free of charge.

gratitud *f.* gratitude.

grato *adj.* pleasing, pleasant; gratuitous; **su grata** your favor, your letter.

gratuito *adj.* gratuitous, free, free of charge.

grava *f.* gravel.

gravamen *m.* burden; mortgage.

grave *adj.* grave; serious; weighty, heavy; grievous; deep, low (*in pitch*).

gravedad *f.* gravity; seriousness; depth (*of a sound*).

gravoso *adj.* burdensome; **serle a uno** — to be burdensome; to weigh on one's conscience.

graznar *v.* to caw, croak, squawk, cackle, quack.

graznido *m.* caw, croak, squawk, cackle, quack.

greda *f.* clay, chalk; chalk cleaner.

gremio *m.* guild, society, brotherhood; trade union; fold (*referring to the Church*).

greña *f.* shock of hair, tangled mop of hair (*usually* **greñas**); **greñudo** *adj.* shaggy, with long, unkempt hair.

grey *f.* flock; congregation (*of a church*).

griego *adj.* Greek, Grecian; *m.* Greek.

grieta *f.* crevice; crack; fissure.

grifo *m.* faucet; *Am.* cheap tavern (*where* **chicha** *is sold*); *Am.* gas station; *Am.* colored person; *Am.* drug addict; *Am.* drunkard; *adj.* curly, kinky, woolly (*hair*); *Am.* vain, conceited; **letra grifa** script; **ponerse** — to bristle, stand on end (*said of hair*).

grillo *m.* cricket; sprout, shoot; **-s** fetters; obstacle, hindrance.

grima *f.* uneasiness; displeasure, disgust; *Am.* sadness, compassion, pity; *Am.* bit, small particle; **dar** — to disgust; to make uneasy; *Am.* to make sad, inspire pity.

gringo *adj. Am.* foreign (*not Spanish*); *m. Am.* foreigner (*not Spanish*); *Am.* Yankee or English-speaking person.

gripe *f.* grippe, flu, influenza.

gris *adj.* grey; **grisáceo** *adj.* greyish.

grita *f.* shouting, hooting; clamor, uproar.

gritar *v.* to shout, cry.

gritería *f.* shouting, clamor, uproar.

grito *m.* shout, cry; **poner el** — **en el cielo** to complain loudly, "hit the ceiling".

grosella *f.* currant; — **blanca** gooseberry; **grosellero** *m.* currant bush.

grosería *f.* rudeness; coarseness; crudeness; insult.

grosero *adj.* rough, coarse; rude, impolite.

grosor *m.* thickness.

grotesco *adj.* grotesque, fantastic; absurd.

grúa *f.* crane, derrick.

gruesa *f.* gross, twelve dozen.

grueso *adj.* fat, stout; thick; coarse; bulky, big, heavy; gross, dense; *m.* thickness; bulk; density; main part; **en** — in gross, in bulk, by wholesale.

grulla *f.* crane (*bird*).

gruñido *m.* growl, grumble; grunt.

gruñir[19] *v. irr.* to grunt; to growl; to snarl; to grumble.

gruñón *adj.* growling; grunting; grumbly; *m.* growler; grumbler.

grupa *f.* rump; **volver -s** to turn around (*usually on horseback*).

grupo *m.* group; set.

gruta *f.* grotto, cavern.

guacal *m. Am.* crate (*for transporting fruit, vegetables, etc.*). *Also* **huacal**.

guacamayo *m. Am.* macaw (*large parrot*); *Am.* flashily dressed person.

guacho *m.* birdling, chick; young animal; *Am.* orphan; *Am.* foundling, abandoned child; *adj. Am.* odd, not paired; *Am.* forlorn, alone, abandoned.

guadal *m. Am.* small dune, sand hill; *Am.* quagmire, bog, swamp; *Am.* growth of bamboo grass.

guadaña *f.* scythe.

guagua *f. Am.* bus; trifle, insignificant thing; *m. & f. Am.* baby; **de** — for nothing, gratis, free.

guaje *m. Am.* a species of gourd; *Am.* vessel or bowl made of a gourd; *Am.* simpleton, fool; *Am.* trifle, trinket, piece of junk; *adj. Am.* foolish; *Am.* **hacerse uno** — to play the fool; *Am.* **hacer a uno** — to fool, deceive someone.

guajiro *m.* Indian of the Guajira peninsula (*in Venezuela and Colombia*); *Am.* rustic, peasant.

guajolote *m. Am.* turkey; *Am.* fool.

guanaco *m. Am.* guanaco (*a kind of llama*); *Am.* tall, lanky, gawky person; *Am.* fool, simpleton.

guanajo *m. Am.* turkey; *Am.* fool, dunce.

guano *m. Am.* palm tree; *Am.* palm leaves (*used for thatching*); *Am.* guano, bird dung, fertilizer.

guantada *f.* wallop, blow, slap.

guante *m.* glove; *Am.* whip, scourge; **echar el** — **a uno** to seize or grab a person; **guantelete** *m.* gauntlet.

guapo *adj.* handsome, good-looking; ostentatious, showy; daring, brave; *Am.* harsh, severe; *Am.* angry; *m.* brawler, quarreler, bully.

guarache *m. Am.* Mexican leather sandal; *Am.* tire patch. *Also* **huarache**.

guaraní *adj.* pertaining to the Guarani Indians of Paraguay; *m. & f.* Guarani Indian.

guarapo *m. Am.* juice of the sugar cane; *Am.* sugar-cane liquor; *Am.* low grade brandy.

guarda *m. & f.* guard; keeper; *Am.* ticket collector on a streetcar; *f.* custody, care, keeping; observance of a law; -s outside ribs of a fan; flyleaves.

guardabarros, guardafango *m.* fender.

guardabosques *m.* forest ranger, forester, forest keeper.

guardabrisa *f.* windshield.

guardafrenos *m.* brakeman.

guardagujas *m.* switchman.

guardapapeles *m.* file, filing cabinet or box.

guardapelo *m.* locket.

guardar *v.* to guard, watch over; to keep; to store; to observe (*laws, customs*); -se de to guard against, keep from, avoid.

guardarropa *m.* wardrobe; cloakroom; keeper of a cloakroom.

guardia *f.* guard, body of guards; defense, protection; *m.* guard, guardsman.

guardiamarina *f.* midshipman.

guardián *m.* guardian, keeper; guardian, superior of a Franciscan monastery.

guarecer[13] *v. irr.* to protect, shelter; -se to take shelter.

guarida *f.* den, cave, lair.

guarismo *m.* number.

guarnecer[13] *v. irr.* to garnish, decorate; to adorn; to trim; to harness; to garrison; to set (*jewels*).

guarnición *f.* adornment; trimming; setting of a jewel; guard of a sword; garrison; -es trappings, harness.

guasca *f. Am.* leather thong; *Am.* rope, cord; *Am.* whip; *Am.* dar — to whip, beat, thrash.

guaso *m. Am.* stag, male deer; *Am.* peasant; *Am.* half-breed; *Am.* lasso; *adj.* rustic, peasantlike.

guasón *adj.* funny, comical; *m.* joker, jester.

guata *f. Am.* padding; *Am.* fib; *Am.* a species of potato; *Am.* paunch, belly; *Am.* echar — to get fat.

guatemalteco *m. & adj.* Guatemalan.

guayaba *f.* guava (*pear-shaped tropical fruit*); guayabo *m.* guava tree; *Am.* lie, fraud, trick.

gubernativo *adj.* governmental, administrative.

guedeja *f.* forelock; lock of hair; lion's mane.

güero *adj. Am.* blond; *m. Am.* cassava liquor. *See* huero.

guerra *f.* war; — a muerte war to the finish; dar — to bother, trouble.

guerrear *v.* to war; *Am.* to do mischief or to bother (*said of children*).

guerrero *adj.* warlike, martial; *m.* warrior, soldier.

guerrilla *f.* small war; skirmish; body of soldiers; band of fighters.

guerrillero *m.* guerrilla fighter.

guía *m. & f.* guide, leader; *f.* guidebook, directory; signpost; shoot, sprout; *Am.* garland of flowers.

guiar[17] *v.* to guide; to drive (*a car*).

guija *f.* pebble; guijarro *m.* pebble.

guijo *m.* gravel.

guinda *f.* a kind of cherry.

guiñada *f.* wink.

guiñapo *m.* tag, tatter, rag; ragamuffin, ragged person.

guiñar *v.* to wink.

guiño *m.* wink.

guión *m.* hyphen; repeat sign (*in music*); cross (*carried before a prelate in a procession*); guide, leader (*among birds and animals*); leader in a dance.

guirnalda *f.* garland, wreath.

guisa *f.* way, manner; a — de like, in the manner of.

guisado *m.* stew.

guisante *m.* pea; — de olor sweet pea.

guisar *v.* to cook; to prepare, arrange.

guiso *m.* dish, dish of food.

guitarra *f.* guitar.

gula *f.* gluttony.

gusano *m.* worm; caterpillar; — de la conciencia remorse; — de luz glowworm; *Am.* matar el — to satisfy a need or desire (*particularly hunger or thirst*).

gustar *v.* to taste; to experience; to please, be pleasing; -le a uno una cosa to like something — de to have a liking for, be fond of.

gusto *m.* taste; flavor; pleasure; whim, fancy; dar — to please; estar a — to be comfortable, contented; tener — en to be glad to; tomar el — a una cosa to become fond of something.

gustoso *adj.* tasty; pleasant; glad, merry; willing; *adv.* willingly.

H

haba *f.* large bean; Lima bean.

haber[30] *v. irr.* to have (*auxiliary verb*); habérselas con to have it out with; ha de llegar mañana he is to arrive tomorrow; ha de ser verdad it must be true; **hay** (**había, hubo,** *etc.*) there is, there are (there was, there were, *etc.*); **hay que** (+ *inf.*) it is necessary; **no hay de qué** you are welcome; **¿qué hay?** what's the matter?

haber *m.* credit, credit side (*in bookkeeping*); **-es** property, goods, cash, assets.

habichuela *f.* bean; — **verde** string bean.

hábil *adj.* skilful, capable, able.

habilidad *f.* ability, skill.

habilitar *v.* to enable; to equip; to qualify.

habitación *f.* apartment; room; lodging.

habitante *m.* inhabitant; resident.

habitar *v.* to inhabit; to live, reside.

hábito *m.* habit; custom.

habitual *adj.* habitual, customary.

habituar[18] *v.* to accustom; **-se** to get used, accustomed.

habla *f.* speech; language, dialect; **al** — within speaking distance; in communication (with).

hablador *m.* talker; gossip; *adj.* talkative.

habladuría *f.* gossip, rumor; empty talk; impertinent remark.

hablar *v.* to speak; to talk; — **alto** (*or* **en voz alta**) to speak loud; — **bajo** (**quedo** *or* **en voz baja**) to speak softly; — **por los codos** to chatter constantly.

hablilla *f.* gossip, rumor, malicious tale.

hacedero *adj.* feasible.

hacedor *m.* maker; **el Supremo Hacedor** the Maker.

hacendado *m.* landholder; *Am.* owner of a farm, plantation, or ranch.

hacendoso *adj.* industrious, diligent.

hacer[31] *v. irr.* to do; to make; to form; to accustom; to cause, order (*followed by inf.*); — **caso** to mind, pay attention; — **frío** (**calor**) to be cold (warm); — **la maleta** to pack one's suitcase; — **un papel** to play a part; *Am.* — **aprecio** to pay attention; *Am.* — **caras** (*or* **caritas**) to flirt; **no le hace** it makes no difference; **-se** to become, grow, get to be; **-se a** to get used to; **-se de rogar** to want to be coaxed.

hacia *prep.* toward; about; — **adelante** forward; — **atrás** backward.

hacienda *f.* estate; property; finance; large farm; *Am.* cattle, livestock.

hacina *f.* shock (*of grain*), stack, pile.

hacinar *v.* to shock (*grain*); to stack, pile up; to accumulate.

hacha *f.* ax; hatchet; torch.

hachero *m.* axman, woodcutter.

hada *f.* fairy.

hado *m.* fate, fortune, destiny.

halagar[7] *v.* to coax; to flatter; to allure, attract.

halago *m.* flattery; caress; allurement.

halagüeño *adj.* alluring, attractive; flattering; promising.

halar = **jalar.**

halcón *m.* falcon.

hálito *m.* breath; vapor.

hallar *v.* to find; to discover, find out; **-se** to be; to fare, get along.

hallazgo *m.* find; discovery; reward (*for finding something*).

hamaca *f.* hammock.

hambre *f.* hunger; famine; appetite; **tener** — to be hungry; **hambruna** *f. Am.* great hunger, starvation.

hambrear *v.* to starve; to be hungry.

hambriento *adj.* hungry; greedy; *Am.* stingy.

hampa *f.* underworld.

hangar *m.* hangar.

haragán *adj.* lazy, indolent; *m.* loafer, idler.

haraganear *v.* to lounge, loaf, be lazy.

haraganería *f.* laziness.

harapiento *adj.* tattered, ragged.

harapo *m.* rag, tatter; **andar hecho un** — to be in tatters.

haraposo *adj.* tattered, ragged.

harina *f.* flour; **eso es** — **de otro costal** that is something entirely different; **harinoso** *adj.* floury; flourlike.

harmonía *f.* harmony.

hartar *v.* to fill up, gorge; to sate, satiate; **-se** to have one's fill; to overeat, eat too much.

harto *adj.* full; sated, satiated; fed up; too much; *adv.* too much; *Am.* much, very much.

hasta *prep.* till, until; up to; — **luego** good-bye, see you later; *conj.* even; — **que** until.

hastiar[17] *v.* to surfeit; to cloy; to disgust.

hastío *m.* surfeit, excess; boredom; loathing, disgust.

hato *m.* herd; flock; sheepfold; shepherd's hut; gang, crowd; pile; *Am.* cattle ranch.

haya *f.* beech; **hayuco** *m.* beechnut.

haz *f.* face; surface; *m.* fagot, bundle, bunch.

hazaña *f.* deed, exploit, feat.

he (*used with* **aquí** *or* **allí**) behold, here is, here you have; **heme aquí** here I am; **helo aquí** here it is.

hebilla *f.* buckle.

hebra f. thread; fiber; fine string; *Am.* **de una —** all at once, at one stroke, *Am.* **ni —** absolutely nothing; **hebroso** *adj.* fibrous, stringy.

hecatombe m. massacre, great slaughter; **hecatomb** (*sacrifice of* 100 *oxen*).

hechicera f. witch, enchantress; hag.

hechicería f. witchcraft; magic; charm; enchantment.

hechicero *adj.* bewitching, charming; *m.* magician; charmer; sorcerer.

hechizar[9] *v.* to bewitch; to charm.

hechizo m. charm; enchantment.

hecho m. fact; act, deed; **de —** in fact; *p.p. of* **hacer** done, made.

hechura f. make; shape, cut; workmanship.

heder[1] *v. irr.* to stink; to reek.

hediondez f. stink, stench.

hediondo *adj.* foul-smelling, stinking; filthy; m. *Am.* skunk.

hedor m. stink, stench.

helada f. frost.

helado *adj.* frozen; freezing; frosty; icy; m. ice cream; ice, sherbet; **heladería** f. *Am.* ice-cream parlor.

heladora f. freezer.

helar[1] *v. irr.* to freeze.

helecho m. fern.

hélice f. screw propeller; helix, spiral.

hembra f. female; staple; nut (*of a screw*); **macho y —** hook and eye.

hemisferio m. hemisphere.

henchir[5] *v. irr.* to swell, stuff, fill.

hendedura, hendidura f. crack, crevice, fissure.

hender[1] *v. irr.* to split, crack, cleave.

henequén m. *Am.* sisal, sisal hemp.

heno m. hay; **henil** m. hayloft.

heraldo m. herald.

herbazal m. field of grass.

herboso *adj.* grassy; weedy.

heredad f. parcel of land; rural property; estate.

heredar *v.* to inherit; to bequeath, leave in a will.

heredero m. heir; successor; **heredera** f. heiress.

hereditario *adj.* hereditary.

hereje m. heretic; **cara de —** hideous face.

herejía f. heresy; offensive remark.

herencia f. inheritance; heritage; heredity.

herida f. wound; injury.

herido *adj.* wounded; m. wounded man; *Am.* small drainage channel.

herir[3] *v. irr.* to wound; to hurt; to strike; to offend.

hermana f. sister.

hermanastro m. stepbrother, half brother; **hermanastra** f. stepsister, half sister.

hermandad f. brotherhood, fraternity.

hermano m. brother.

hermético *adj.* hermetic; airtight; tight-lipped; close-mouthed; **hermetismo** m. complete silence.

hermosear *v.* to beautify, adorn.

hermoso *adj.* beautiful, handsome.

hermosura f. beauty.

héroe m. hero; **heroína** f. heroine.

heroico *adj.* heroic.

heroísmo m. heroism.

herradura f. horseshoe.

herraje m. ironwork; iron trimmings; horseshoes and nails; *Am.* silver saddle trimmings; *Am.* horseshoe.

herramienta f. set of tools; iron tool.

herrar[1] *v. irr.* to shoe (*a horse*); to brand; to trim with iron.

herrería f. blacksmith's shop or trade; forge; ironworks.

herrero m. blacksmith.

hervidero m. bubbling sound (*of boiling water*); bubbling spring; swarm, crowd; **un — de gente** a swarm of people.

hervir[3] *v. irr.* to boil; **— de gente** to swarm with people.

hervor m. boiling; boiling point; **soltar el —** to come to a boil.

hez f. scum; **la — del pueblo** the scum of society; **heces** dregs, sediment.

hidalgo m. hidalgo (*Spanish nobleman*); *adj.* noble, courteous.

hidalguía f. nobility; generosity; courtesy.

hidráulico *adj.* hydraulic; **fuerza hidráulica** water power; **ingeniero —** hydraulic engineer.

hidroavión m. hydroplane, seaplane.

hidrógeno m. hydrogen.

hidroplano m. hydroplane.

hiedra f. ivy.

hiel f. gall, bile; bitterness.

hielo m. ice; frost.

hierba f. grass; herb; weed; *Am.* **mate** (*Paraguayan tea*); *Am.* marihuana (*a narcotic*); *Am.* **ciertas -s** so-and-so (*person not named*).

hierbabuena f. mint. *Also* **yerbabuena**.

hierro m. iron; brand; iron tool, instrument, or weapon; **-s** irons, chains, handcuffs.

hígado m. liver; courage, valor; **malos -s** ill will.

higiene f. hygiene; **higiénico** *adj.* hygienic, sanitary.

higo m. fig; **higuera** f. fig tree; **hi-**

guerilla f. Am. castor-oil plant.

hija f. daughter; native daughter.

hijo m. son; native son; offspring; fruit, result.

hilachas f. pl. lint; **mostrar uno la hilacha** to show one's worst side or nature; **hilachos** m. pl. Am. rags, tatters.

hilado m. yarn; p.p. of **hilar**.

hilandera f. spinner.

hilandería f. spinning mill; art of spinning; spinning.

hilandero m. spinner; spinning room.

hilar v. to spin, make into thread; — **muy delgado** to be very subtle.

hilas f. pl. lint, fine ravelings (for dressing wounds).

hilaza f. coarse thread; yarn.

hilera f. file, row, line; — **de perlas** strand or string of pearls.

hilo m. thread; fine yarn; string; filament; thin wire; linen; **a** — **without** interruption; **al** — along the thread; Am. very well, all right; **de** —straight, without stopping; Am. **de un** — constantly, without stopping; **tener el alma en un** — to be frightened to death; to be in great anxiety or suspense.

hilván m. basting stitch; basting; Am. hem.

hilvanar v. to baste; to put together; connect; to do hastily; Am. to hem.

himno m. hymn.

hincapié : hacer — to emphasize, stress; to insist (upon).

hincar [6] v. to drive, thrust (into); -**se** (or -**se de rodillas**) to kneel down.

hinchado adj. & p.p. swollen; inflated; presumptuous.

hinchar v. to swell; -**se** to swell; to swell up, puff up.

hinchazón f. swelling; inflation; conceit; bombast, inflated style.

hinojos : de — on one's knees.

hipo m. hiccough; sob; longing; grudge, ill will.

hipocresía f. hypocrisy.

hipócrita adj. hypocritical, insincere; m. & f. hypocrite.

hipódromo m. race track.

hipoteca f. mortgage.

hipotecar [6] v. to mortgage.

hipótesis f. hypothesis, theory.

hirviente adj. boiling.

hispano adj. Hispanic, Spanish; m. Spaniard.

hispanoamericano adj. Spanish-American.

histérico adj. hysterical.

historia f. history; story; tale, fable; **dejarse de** -**s** to stop fooling and come to the point; **historieta** f. story, anecdote.

historiador m. historian.

historial m. record, data (concerning a person or firm); adj. historic.

histórico adj. historic, historical.

hocico m. snout; **caer de** -**s** to fall on one's face; **meter el** — **en todo** to meddle, stick one's nose in everything.

hogaño adv. nowadays.

hogar m. hearth, fireplace; home.

hogareño adj. home-loving, domestic; homelike.

hoguera f. bonfire.

hoja f. leaf; petal; sheet of paper or metal; blade; — **de lata** tin plate.

hojalata f. tin plate.

hojaldre m. & f. puff pastry.

hojarasca f. fallen leaves; dry foliage; superfluous ornament; trash; useless words.

hojear v. to leaf, turn the pages of; to browse.

hojuela f. leaflet, small leaf; thin leaf (of metal); flake; thin pancake; — **de estaño** tin foil.

¡hola! interj. hello!; ho!; ah!

holandés adj. Dutch; m. Dutchman; Dutch language.

holgado adj. loose, wide; roomy, spacious; comfortable; free, at leisure; p.p. of **holgar**.

holgar [2,7] v. irr. to rest; to loaf; -**se** to be glad; to relax, have a good time; **huelga decir** needless to say.

holgazán m. idler, loafer; adj. lazy, idle.

holgazanear v. to loiter, lounge, idle, bum around.

holgazanería f. idleness, laziness.

holgorio m. spree.

holgura f. ease; rest, comfort; roominess, plenty of room.

holocausto m. holocaust, burnt offering, sacrifice.

hollar v. to tread, trample upon.

hollejo m. skin, peel; husk.

hollín m. soot.

hombrada f. manly act; show of bravery.

hombre m. man; **hombría** f. manliness, manly strength; — **de bien** honesty.

hombro m. shoulder; **arrimar** (or **meter**) **el** — to help.

hombruno adj. mannish, masculine.

homenaje m. homage, honor.

homicida m. murderer; f. murderess; adj. homicidal, murderous.

homicidio m. homicide, murder.

homogéneo adj. homogeneous, of the

same kind or nature.

honda f. sling, slingshot.

hondo adj. deep; low; m. bottom, depth.

hondonada f. hollow, dip, gully, ravine.

hondura f. depth; **meterse en -s** to go beyond one's depth; to get into trouble.

honestidad f. chastity, modesty, decency; decorum, propriety.

honesto adj. chaste, modest, decent; just; honest.

hongo m. mushroom; fungus; derby hat.

honor m. honor; glory; dignity.

honorario m. fee (for professional services); adj. honorary.

honorífico adj. honorary; **mención honorífica** honorable mention.

honra f. honor; reputation; **-s obsequias**, funeral rites.

honradez f. honesty, honor, integrity.

honrado adj. honest, honorable; honored.

honrar v. to honor; **-se** to be honored; to consider it an honor.

honroso adj. honorable; honoring.

hora f. hour; time; **-s canonical** hours, office (required daily prayers for priests and nuns); **es — de** it is time to; **no ver la — de** (+ inf.) to be anxious to; **¿qué — es?** what time is it?

horadar v. to pierce, bore, perforate.

horario m. schedule, timetable; hour hand.

horca f. gallows; pitchfork; forked prop; Am. birthday present; **— de ajos** string of garlic.

horcajadas: a — astride (with one leg on each side); **ponerse a — to** straddle.

horcón m. forked pole, forked prop; Am. post, roof support; Am. roof.

horda f. horde.

horizontal adj. horizontal.

horizonte m. horizon.

horma f. form, mold; block (for shaping a hat); shoe last; shoe tree.

hormiga f. ant.

hormigón m. concrete.

hormiguear v. to swarm; to be crawling with ants; **me hormiguea el cuerpo** I itch all over.

hormigueo m. itching, creeping sensation; tingle, tingling sensation.

hormiguero m. ant hill; ant nest; swarm; **oso — anteater**.

hornada f. batch of bread, baking.

hornear v. to bake (in an oven).

hornilla f. burner; grate (of a stove).

horno m. furnace; oven; kiln (for baking bricks).

horquilla f. hairpin; forked pole;

small pitchfork.

horrendo adj. horrible, hideous.

horrible adj. horrible.

horripilante adj. horrifying.

horror m. horror; atrocity; **dar — to** cause fright; to horrify; **tenerle — a uno** to feel a strong dislike for one.

horrorizar[9] v. to horrify, shock, terrify.

horroroso adj. horrid; frightful, hideous.

hortaliza f. vegetables; vegetable garden.

hortelano m. gardener.

hosco = **fosco**.

hospedaje m. board and lodging; lodging.

hospedar v. to lodge, give lodging; **-se** to take lodging; to room; to stop (at a hotel).

hospedero m. innkeeper.

hospicio m. asylum; orphanage, orphan asylum; poorhouse; **hospiciano** m. inmate of a poorhouse or asylum.

hospital m. hospital; **— de primera sangre** first-aid station.

hospitalidad f. hospitality.

hostia f. host (consecrated wafer).

hostigar[7] v. to harass, vex; to beat, lash; Am. to cloy.

hostil adj. hostile; **hostilidad** f. hostility.

hotel m. hotel; villa; **hotelero** m. hotel-keeper.

hoy adv. today; **— día** nowadays; **de — en adelante** from now on; **— por — at** present; **de — más** henceforth.

hoya f. pit, hole; grave; valley; Am. river basin.

hoyo m. hole; pit; grave; Am. dimple.

hoyuelo m. dimple; tiny hole.

hoz f. sickle; narrow ravine.

hozar[9] v. to root, turn up the earth with the snout (as hogs).

huacal = **guacal**.

huarache = **guarache**.

huaso = **guaso**.

hueco adj. hollow; empty; vain, affected; puffed up; high-sounding; m. gap, space, hole.

huelga f. labor strike; rest; leisure; **declararse en — to** strike.

huelguista m. striker.

huella f. trace; footprint.

huérfano adj. & m. orphan.

huero adj. empty; rotten, spoiled (egg). See **güero**.

huerta f. orchard and vegetable garden; irrigated land.

huerto m. small orchard and vegetable garden; garden patch.

hueso m. bone; stone, pit; **la sin — the** tongue; **soltar la sin — to** talk too much; **no dejarle un — sano** to pick him to pieces.

huésped *m.* guest; host; **ser — en su casa** to be seldom at home.

hueste *f.* host, army, multitude.

huesudo *adj.* bony.

huevo *m.* egg; **— duro** hard-boiled egg; **— estrellado** fried egg; **— pasado por agua** soft-boiled egg; **-s revueltos** scrambled eggs; *Am.* **-s tibios** soft-boiled eggs; *Am.* **-s pericos** scrambled eggs; *Am.* **costar un —** to be very expensive.

huída *f.* flight; escape.

huir[32] *v. irr.* to flee, escape; to avoid, shun.

huizache *m. Am.* huisache (*a species of acacia*).

hule *m.* rubber; oilcloth; *Am.* rubber tree.

hulla *f.* soft coal.

humanidad *f.* humanity, mankind; humaneness; **-es** humanities, letters.

humanitario *adj.* humanitarian, humane, kind, charitable.

humano *adj.* human; humane; *m.* man, human being.

humareda *f.* cloud of smoke.

humeante *adj.* smoking, smoky; steaming.

humear *v.* to smoke, give off smoke; to steam; *Am.* to fumigate.

humedad *f.* humidity, moisture, dampness.

humedecer[13] *v. irr.* to moisten, wet, dampen.

húmedo *adj.* humid, moist, wet, damp.

humildad *f.* humility; humbleness; meekness.

humilde *adj.* humble, lowly, meek.

humillación *f.* humiliation; submission.

humillar *v.* to humiliate, humble, lower, crush; **-se** to humiliate oneself; to bow humbly.

humillos *m. pl.* airs, conceit, vanity.

humo *m.* smoke, fume, vapor; **-s** conceit, vanity.

humor *m.* humor; mood, disposition.

humorada *f.* pleasantry, witty remark; caprice, notion.

humorismo *m.* humor, humorous style.

humorístico *adj.* humorous.

humoso *adj.* smoky.

hundimiento *m.* sinking, collapse, cave-in.

hundir *v.* to sink, submerge; to crush, oppress; to destroy; **-se** to sink; to collapse, cave in.

huracán *m.* hurricane.

huraño *adj.* diffident, shy, bashful; unsociable.

¡hurra! *interj.* hurrah!

hurtadillas : a — on the sly, secretly, stealthily.

hurtar *v.* to steal, rob; **-se** to withdraw, slip away; to hide; **— el cuerpo** to dodge; to flee.

hurto *m.* robbery, theft; stolen article; **a —** stealthily, on the sly.

husmear *v.* to scent, smell, follow the track of; to nose, pry (into).

husmeo *m.* sniff, sniffing, smelling; prying.

huso *m.* spindle.

I

ibérico, ibero *adj.* Iberian; **iberoamericano** *adj.* Ibero-American (*Spanish or Portuguese American*).

ida *f.* departure; sally; **billete de — y vuelta** round-trip ticket; **-s y venidas** goings and comings.

idea *f.* idea; notion.

ideal *m. & adj.* ideal.

idealismo *m.* idealism.

idealista *adj.* idealistic; *m. & f.* idealist; dreamer.

idear *v.* to form an idea of; to devise, think out, plan.

ídem idem (*abbreviation*: id.), ditto, the same.

idéntico *adj.* identical.

identidad *f.* identity.

identificar[6] *v.* to identify.

idilio *m.* idyl.

idioma *m.* language, tongue.

idiota *m. & f.* idiot; *adj.* idiotic, foolish.

idiotismo *m.* idiom; idiocy.

idolatrar *v.* to idolize, worship.

ídolo *m.* idol.

idóneo *adj.* fit, suitable; qualified.

iglesia *f.* church.

ignición *f.* ignition.

ignominia *f.* infamy, shame, disgrace.

ignominioso *adj.* ignominious; infamous, shameful, disgraceful.

ignorancia *f.* ignorance.

ignorante *adj.* ignorant.

ignorar *v.* to be ignorant of, not to know.

ignoto *adj.* unknown, undiscovered.

igual *adj.* equal; even, smooth; uniform; constant; **serle — a uno** to be all the same to one, make no difference to one; *m.* equal; **al —** equally.

igualar *v.* to equal; to equalize; to match; to level, smooth; to adjust; to be equal.

igualdad *f.* equality.

igualitario *adj.* equalitarian (*promoting the doctrine of equality*).

ijada *f.* loin; flank (*of an animal*); pain

in the side; **ijar** m. flank (of an animal).
ilegal adj. illegal, unlawful.
ilegítimo adj. illegitimate; illegal.
ileso adj. unharmed, uninjured, unhurt, safe and sound.
ilícito adj. illicit, unlawful.
ilimitado adj. unlimited.
iluminación f. illumination.
iluminar v. to illuminate; to light; to enlighten.
ilusión f. illusion.
ilusivo adj. illusive.
iluso adj. deluded; m. visionary, dreamer.
ilusorio adj. illusive; deceptive; worthless.
ilustración f. illustration; elucidation, explanation.
ilustrador m. illustrator.
ilustrar v. to illustrate.
ilustre adj. illustrious, distinguished.
imagen f. image.
imaginable adj. imaginable, conceivable.
imaginación f. imagination.
imaginar v. to imagine.
imaginario adj. imaginary.
imaginativo adj. imaginative; **imaginativa** f. imagination.
imán m. magnet; attraction.
imbécil adj. imbecile, stupid.
imborrable adj. indelible, not erasable; unforgettable.
imbuir[32] v. irr. to imbue; to instill, infuse, inspire (with).
imitación f. imitation.
imitador m. imitator; follower; adj. imitative, imitating.
imitar v. to imitate.
impaciencia f. impatience.
impaciente adj. impatient.
impar adj. odd; **número — odd** number.
imparcial adj. impartial; **imparcialidad** f. impartiality, fairness, justice.
impasible adj. impassive, insensitive, insensible, unfeeling, unmoved.
impávido adj. fearless; calm; Am. impudent, brazen.
impedimento m. impediment, hindrance, obstacle.
impedir[5] v. irr. to impede, prevent, hinder.
impeler v. to impel, push; to incite, spur.
impenetrable adj. impenetrable; impervious; incomprehensible.
impensado adj. unforeseen, unexpected; offhand, done without thinking; **impensadamente** adv. offhand, without thinking; unexpectedly.
imperar v. to rule, command, dominate.

imperativo adj. imperative; urgent, compelling; m. imperative mood.
imperceptible adj. imperceptible.
imperdible m. safety pin; adj. safe, that cannot be lost.
imperecedero adj. imperishable, enduring, everlasting.
imperfecto adj. imperfect; m. imperfect tense.
imperial adj. imperial; f. coach top; top seats on a coach or bus.
impericia f. inexperience.
imperio m. empire; command, rule; sway, influence.
imperioso adj. imperious, arrogant, domineering; urgent.
impermeable adj. waterproof, impervious, rainproof; m. raincoat.
impersonal adj. impersonal.
impertinencia f. impertinence; impudence; insolent remark or act; **decir -s** to talk nonsense; to make insolent remarks.
impertinente adj. impertinent, impudent; meddlesome; irrelevant, not to the point; **-s** m. pl. lorgnette (eyeglasses mounted on a handle).
ímpetu m. impetus; violent force; impulse; Am. vehement desire; **— de ira** fit of anger.
impetuoso adj. impetuous, violent.
impío adj. impious, irreligious; profane.
implacable adj. implacable, relentless.
implantación f. implantation, establishment, introduction (of a system).
implantar v. to implant, establish, introduce.
implicar[6] v. to imply; to implicate, involve.
implorar v. to implore, entreat, beg.
imponente adj. imposing.
imponer[40] v. irr. to impose; to invest (money); **— miedo** to inspire fear; **— respeto** to inspire or command respect; **-se** to inspire fear or respect; to dominate; Am. **-se a** to get accustomed or used to.
importancia f. importance.
importante adj. important.
importar v. to be important; to matter; to amount to; to be necessary; to concern; to import.
importe m. amount, price, value.
importunar v. to importune, nag, tease, pester.
importuno adj. annoying, persistent.
imposibilidad f. impossibility.
imposibilitado p.p. & adj. disabled, unfit; helpless.
imposibilitar v. to make impossible; to

disable.

imposible *adj.* impossible; intolerable, unbearable; *Am.* disabled (*because of illness*); *Am.* slovenly, untidy.

imposición *f.* imposition; burden; tax.

impostor *m.* impostor, cheat; **impostura** *f.* imposture, fraud, deceit.

impotencia *f.* impotence.

impotente *adj.* impotent, powerless.

impreciso *adj.* vague, indefinite; inaccurate.

impregnar *v.* to impregnate, saturate.

imprenta *f.* press; printing shop; printing.

imprescindible *adj.* essential, indispensable.

impresión *f.* impression; printing; mark; footprint.

impresionante *adj.* impressive.

impresionar *v.* to impress; to move, affect, stir; -se to be stirred, moved.

impreso *p.p. irr. of* **imprimir** printed; impressed, imprinted; *m.* printed matter.

impresor *m.* printer.

imprevisión *f.* carelessness, lack of foresight.

imprevisto *adj.* unforeseen, unexpected.

imprimir *v.* to print; to imprint, impress.

improbable *adj.* improbable, unlikely.

improperio *m.* affront, insult.

impropio *adj.* improper; unsuitable.

improvisar *v.* to improvise.

improviso *adj.* unforeseen; **de — **suddenly; *Am.* **en un — **in a moment, in the twinkling of an eye.

imprudencia *f.* imprudence, indiscretion, rash act.

imprudente *adj.* imprudent; unwise; indiscreet.

impuesto *p.p. of* **imponer** imposed; informed; *Am.* **estar — a** to be used or accustomed to; *m.* tax, duty.

impulsar *v.* to impel, push, move; to force.

impulso *m.* impulse; push.

impureza *f.* impurity.

impuro *adj.* impure.

imputar *v.* to impute, attribute.

inacabable *adj.* unending, endless.

inacabado *adj.* unfinished.

inaccesible *adj.* inaccessible, unobtainable.

inacción *f.* inaction, inactivity, idleness.

inaceptable *adj.* unacceptable, unsatisfactory.

inactividad *f.* inactivity.

inactivo *adj.* inactive.

inadecuado *adj.* inadequate.

inadvertencia *f.* oversight; inattention, heedlessness.

inadvertido *adj.* careless, heedless; unnoticed.

inafectado *adj.* unaffected.

inagotable *adj.* inexhaustible.

inaguantable *adj.* insufferable, unbearable.

inalámbrico *adj.* wireless.

inalterable *adj.* unalterable, unchangeable.

inalterado *adj.* unchanged.

inamovible = **inmovible.**

inanición *f.* starvation.

inanimado *adj.* inanimate, lifeless.

inapetencia *f.* lack of appetite.

inaplicable *adj.* inapplicable, unsuitable; **— al caso** irrelevant.

inapreciable *adj.* invaluable; inappreciable, too small to be perceived, very slight.

inasequible *adj.* inaccessible, not obtainable; hard to attain or obtain.

inaudito *adj.* unheard-of; unprecedented.

inauguración *f.* inauguration.

inaugurar *v.* to inaugurate, begin, open.

incaico, incásico *adj.* Incan (*of or pertaining to the Incas*).

incalculable *adj.* incalculable; innumerable, untold.

incandescente *adj.* incandescent.

incansable *adj.* untiring, tireless.

incapacidad *f.* incompetence, inability, unfitness.

incapacitar *v.* to cripple, disable, handicap, unfit, make unfit.

incapaz *adj.* incapable, unable.

incauto *adj.* unwary, heedless, reckless.

incendiar *v.* to set fire to; -se to catch fire.

incendio *m.* conflagration, fire.

incentivo *m.* incentive, inducement.

incertidumbre *f.* uncertainty, doubt.

incesante *adj.* incessant.

incidental *adj.* incidental.

incidente *adj.* incidental; *m.* incident.

incienso *m.* incense.

incierto *adj.* uncertain, doubtful; unstable; unknown; untrue.

incisión *f.* incision, cut, slit, gash.

incitamiento *m.* incitement, inducement, incentive.

incitar *v.* to incite, rouse, stir up.

incivil *adj.* uncivil, rude, impolite.

inclemencia *f.* inclemency, severity, harshness; **inclemente** *adj.* unmerciful, merciless.

inclinación *f.* inclination, affection; tendency, bent; bow; incline, slope.

inclinar *v.* to incline; to persuade; **-se** to bow; to stoop; to incline, slope, slant; to lean, bend.

incluir[32] *v. irr.* to include; to inclose.

inclusive *adv.* inclusive, including; **inclusivo** *adj.* inclusive; comprehensive.

incluso *adj.* inclosed; included; including; even.

incógnito *adj.* unknown; **de —** incognito (*with one's name or rank unknown*); **incógnita** *f.* unknown quantity (*in mathematics*).

incoherente *adj.* incoherent, disconnected, rambling.

incoloro *adj.* colorless.

incombustible *adj.* incombustible; fireproof.

incomodar *v.* to inconvenience, disturb, trouble, annoy.

incomodidad *f.* inconvenience, discomfort; bother, annoyance.

incómodo *adj.* inconvenient, bothersome; uncomfortable.

incomparable *adj.* incomparable.

incompasivo *adj.* merciless, pitiless.

incompatible *adj.* incompatible; unsuitable, uncongenial.

incompetencia *f.* incompetence, inability, unfitness; **incompetente** *adj.* incompetent, unfit.

incompleto *adj.* incomplete.

incomprensible *adj.* incomprehensible.

incondicional *adj.* unconditional.

inconexo *adj.* unconnected; incoherent, disconnected.

inconfundible *adj.* unmistakable.

incongruente *adj.* unsuitable, not appropriate; not harmonious.

inconquistable *adj.* unconquerable.

inconsciencia *f.* unconsciousness; unawareness.

inconsciente *adj.* unconscious; unaware.

inconsecuente *adj.* inconsistent; illogical.

inconsiderado *adj.* inconsiderate, thoughtless.

inconstancia *f.* inconstancy, changeableness, fickleness.

inconstante *adj.* inconstant, fickle, changeable, variable.

incontable *adj.* countless, innumerable.

inconveniencia *f.* inconvenience; trouble.

inconveniente *adj.* inconvenient; improper; *m.* obstacle; objection.

incorporar *v.* to incorporate, unite; to embody; to include; **-se** to sit up; **-se** a to join.

incorrecto *adj.* incorrect.

incredulidad *f.* incredulity, unbelief.

incrédulo *adj.* incredulous, unbelieving; *m.* unbeliever.

increíble *adj.* incredible, unbelievable.

incremento *m.* increment, increase.

incrustar *v.* to inlay; to encrust (*cover with a crust or hard coating*); **-se en** to penetrate, impress itself deeply into.

inculcar[6] *v.* to inculcate, instill, impress.

inculto *adj.* uncultured; uncultivated; unrefined.

incumbencia *f.* concern, duty, obligation; **no es de mi —** it does not concern me, it is not within my province.

incurable *adj.* incurable.

incurrir *v.* to incur, fall (into); **— en un error** to fall into or commit an error; **— en el odio de** to incur the hatred of.

incursión *f.* raid, invasion.

indagación *f.* investigation, inquiry.

indagador *m.* investigator; inquirer; *adj.* investigating; inquiring.

indagar[7] *v.* to find out, investigate; to inquire.

indebido *adj.* undue, improper; illegal; **indebidamente** *adv.* unduly; illegally.

indecencia *f.* indecency, obscenity, indecent act or remark.

indecente *adj.* indecent, improper.

indecible *adj.* inexpressible, untold.

indeciso *adj.* undecided; doubtful, uncertain.

indefectible *adj.* unfailing; **-mente** unfailingly.

indefenso *adj.* defenseless, unprotected.

indefinible *adj.* indefinable.

indefinido *adj.* indefinite.

indeleble *adj.* indelible.

indemnización *f.* indemnity, compensation.

indemnizar[9] *v.* to indemnify, compensate.

independencia *f.* independence.

independiente *adj.* independent.

indescriptible *adj.* indescribable.

indeseable *adj.* undesirable, unwelcome.

indiada *f. Am.* community, group, or crowd of Indians; *Am.* an Indian-like remark or act; *Am.* an uncontrollable fit of anger.

indianista *m. & f.* student of Indian culture; *adj.* pertaining to Indian culture.

indiano *adj.* of or pertaining to the West or East Indies; *m.* Spaniard who goes back to settle in his country after having lived for some time in Spanish America.

indicación *f.* indication.

indicar[6] *v.* to indicate, show, point out.

indicativo adj. indicative; m. indicative, indicative mood.
índice m. index; catalogue; sign; pointer; forefinger.
indicio m. indication, sign.
indiferencia f. indifference.
indiferente adj. indifferent.
indígena adj. indigenous, native; m. & f. native inhabitant; Am. Indian.
indignación f. indignation.
indignado p.p. & adj. indignant, irritated, angry.
indignar v. to irritate, anger; -se to become indignant, angry.
indignidad f. indignity, affront, insult; unworthy or disgraceful act.
indigno adj. unworthy; low, contemptible.
indio adj. & m. Indian; Hindu.
indirecta f. hint, indirect remark, innuendo, insinuation.
indirecto adj. indirect.
indisciplinado adj. undisciplined, untrained.
indiscreto adj. indiscreet, imprudent, unwise, rash.
indiscutible adj. indisputable, unquestionable.
indispensable adj. indispensable.
indisponer[40] v. irr. to indispose; to make ill; — a uno con otro to prejudice someone against another; -se to become ill; -se con to fall out with, quarrel with.
indisposición f. indisposition, upset, slight illness; reluctance, unwillingness.
indispuesto p.p. of **indisponer** & adj. indisposed, unwilling; ill.
indisputable adj. unquestionable.
indistinto adj. indistinct, dim, vague, not clear.
individual adj. individual.
individualidad f. individuality.
individuo adj. individual; indivisible; m. individual; person; member.
indócil adj. unruly, disobedient, headstrong.
indocto adj. uneducated, ignorant.
índole f. disposition, temper; kind, class.
indolencia f. indolence, laziness; insensitiveness, indifference.
indolente adj. indolent, lazy; insensitive, indifferent.
indomable adj. indomitable, unconquerable; unmanageable; untamable.
indómito adj. untamed; uncontrollable, unruly.
inducir[25] v. irr. to induce; to persuade.
indudable adj. unquestionable, certain.

indulgencia f. indulgence, tolerance, forgiveness; remission of sins.
indulgente adj. indulgent, lenient.
indultar v. to pardon, set free; to exempt.
indulto m. pardon, forgiveness; exemption; privilege.
indumentaria f. costume, dress; manner of dressing.
industria f. industry; cleverness, skill; de — intentionally, on purpose.
industrial adj. industrial; m. industrialist; manufacturer.
industrioso adj. industrious.
inédito adj. unpublished.
inefable adj. ineffable, inexpressible.
ineficaz adj. ineffective; inefficient.
inepto adj. incompetent; unsuitable.
inequívoco adj. unmistakable.
inercia f. inertia, lifelessness; inactivity.
inerme adj. unarmed, defenseless.
inerte adj. inert; inactive, sluggish, slow.
inesperado adj. unexpected.
inestable adj. unstable; unsettled; unsteady.
inestimable adj. inestimable, invaluable.
inevitable adj. inevitable, unavoidable.
inexacto adj. inexact, inaccurate.
inexperiencia f. inexperience.
inexperto adj. unskilful, unskilled, inexperienced.
inexplicable adj. inexplicable.
inextinguible adj. inextinguishable, unquenchable.
infalible adj. infallible.
infame adj. infamous; m. scoundrel.
infamia f. infamy, dishonor; wickedness.
infancia f. infancy.
infante m. infant; infante (royal prince of Spain, except the heir to the throne); infantryman.
infantería f. infantry.
infantil adj. infantile, childlike, childish.
infatigable adj. tireless, untiring.
infausto adj. unfortunate; unhappy.
infección f. infection; **infeccioso** adj. infectious.
infectar v. to infect; to corrupt; -se to become infected.
infeliz adj. unhappy, unfortunate; m. poor wretch.
inferior adj. inferior; lower; m. inferior.
inferioridad f. inferiority.
inferir[3] v. irr. to infer; to imply; to inflict.
infernal adj. infernal.
infestar v. to infest, invade, overrun, plague; to corrupt, infect.

117

inficionar *v.* to infect; to contaminate.

infiel *adj.* unfaithful, faithless; infidel; inaccurate.

infierno *m.* hell; **en el quinto —** very far away.

infiltrar *v.* to filter through; **-se** to leak (into), filter (through), infiltrate.

infinidad *f.* infinity; **una — de** a large number of.

infinito *adj.* infinite; *adv.* infinitely; *m.* infinity.

inflamación *f.* inflammation.

inflamado *p.p.* & *adj.* inflamed; sore.

inflamar *v.* to inflame, excite; to kindle, set on fire; **-se** to become inflamed.

inflar *v.* to inflate; to exaggerate; **-se** to become inflated; to swell up with pride.

inflexible *adj.* inflexible, stiff, rigid; unbending.

inflexión *f.* inflection.

infligir[11] *v.* to inflict.

influencia *f.* influence.

influenza *f.* influenza, grippe, flu.

influir[32] *v. irr.* to influence.

influjo *m.* influence; influx, inward flow.

influyente *adj.* influential.

información *f.* information.

informal *adj.* informal; unconventional; unreliable, not dependable, not punctual; brief.

informar *v.* to inform; to give form to; to give a report; to present a case; **-se** to find out.

informe *m.* report, account; information; brief; *adj.* formless, shapeless.

infortunio *m.* misfortune, mishap; misery.

infracción *f.* infraction, breach, violation (*of a law, treaty, etc.*).

infractor *m.* transgressor, lawbreaker, violator (*of a law*).

infrascrito *m.* undersigned, subscriber, signer (*of a letter, document, etc.*); **el — secretario** the secretary whose signature appears below.

infringir[11] *v.* to infringe, break, violate.

infructuoso *adj.* fruitless.

ínfulas *f. pl.* airs, false importance; **darse —** to put on airs.

infundado *adj.* groundless, without foundation.

infundir *v.* to infuse, inspire; to instill.

infusión *f.* infusion (*liquid extract obtained by steeping*); infusion, inspiration; **poner en —** to steep (*as tea leaves*).

ingeniería *f.* engineering.

ingeniero *m.* engineer.

ingenio *m.* genius; talent; ingenuity;

mentality, mental power, mind; wit; **— de azúcar** sugar refinery; sugar plantation.

ingeniosidad *f.* ingenuity, cleverness.

ingenioso *adj.* ingenious, clever.

ingenuidad *f.* candor, frankness; unaffected simplicity.

ingenuo *adj.* frank, sincere; simple, unaffected.

ingerir = injerir.

inglés *adj.* English; **a la inglesa** in the English fashion; *Am.* **ir a la inglesa** to go Dutch treat; *m.* Englishman; the English language.

ingobernable *adj.* ungovernable, unruly, uncontrollable.

ingratitud *f.* ingratitude.

ingrato *adj.* ungrateful, thankless; harsh; cruel; disdainful.

ingrediente *m.* ingredient.

ingresar *v.* to enter; **— en** to join (*a society, club, etc.*).

ingreso *m.* entrance; entry; **-s** receipts, profits; revenue.

inhábil *adj.* unskilled; unskilful; unfit.

inhabilidad *f.* inability; unfitness.

inhabilitar *v.* to disqualify; to unfit, disable.

inherente *adj.* inherent.

inhospitalario *adj.* inhospitable.

inhumano *adj.* inhuman, cruel.

iniciador *m.* initiator; pioneer; *adj.* initiating.

inicial *adj.* & *f.* initial.

iniciar *v.* to initiate; to begin.

iniciativa *f.* initiative.

inicuo *adj.* wicked.

iniquidad *f.* iniquity, wickedness; sin.

injerir[3] *v. irr.* to inject, insert; **-se** to interfere, meddle.

injertar *v.* to graft.

injuria *f.* affront, insult; harm, damage.

injuriar *v.* to insult, offend; to harm, damage.

injurioso *adj.* insulting, offensive; harmful.

injusticia *f.* injustice.

injustificado *adj.* unjustified; unjustifiable.

injusto *adj.* unjust, unfair.

inmaculado *adj.* immaculate, clean; pure.

inmediación *f.* vicinity; nearness; **-es** environs, outskirts.

inmediato *adj.* near, close; *Am.* **de —** immediately; suddenly; **inmediatamente** *adv.* immediately, at once.

inmensidad *f.* immensity, vastness; vast number.

inmenso *adj.* immense, vast, huge;

boundless.

inmersión f. immersion, dip.

inmigración f. immigration.

inmigrante adj., m. & f. immigrant.

inmigrar v. to immigrate.

inminente adj. imminent.

inmiscuir[32] v. irr. to mix; -se to meddle, interfere.

inmoble adj. motionless; unshaken.

inmoral adj. immoral; **inmoralidad** f. immorality.

inmortal adj. immortal; **inmortalidad** f. immortality.

inmovible adj. immovable, fixed; steadfast.

inmóvil adj. motionless, still; immovable.

inmundicia f. filth, dirt; nastiness.

inmundo adj. filthy, dirty; impure; nasty.

inmune adj. immune; exempt.

inmunidad f. immunity.

inmutable adj. unchangeable, invariable.

inmutar v. to alter, change; -se to show emotion (either by turning pale or blushing).

innato adj. innate, natural, inborn.

innecesario adj. unnecessary.

innegable adj. undeniable, not to be denied.

innocuo adj. innocuous, harmless; **innocuidad** f. harmlessness.

innovación f. innovation; novelty.

innumerable adj. innumerable.

inobservancia f. nonobservance, violation (of a law), lack of observance (of a law, rule, or custom).

inocencia f. innocence.

inocente adj. innocent; m. innocent person; **inocentón** adj. quite foolish or simple; easily fooled; m. dupe, unsuspecting victim.

inocular v. to inoculate.

inodoro adj. odorless; m. Am. toilet, water closet.

inofensivo adj. inoffensive; harmless.

inolvidable adj. unforgettable.

inopinado adj. unexpected.

inoportuno adj. inopportune, untimely, unsuitable.

inquietar v. to worry, disturb, make uneasy; -se to become disturbed, uneasy.

inquieto adj. restless; uneasy, anxious.

inquietud f. restlessness; anxiety, uneasiness; fear.

inquilino m. tenant, renter; lodger.

inquina f. aversion, grudge, dislike.

inquirir[35] v. irr. to inquire, investigate;

to find out.

inquisición f. inquisition; inquiry, investigation.

insaciable adj. insatiable, never satisfied, greedy.

insalubre adj. unhealthy, unhealthful, unwholesome.

insano adj. insane, crazy; unhealthy.

inscribir[52] v. to inscribe; to register, enroll; to record; -se to register.

inscripción f. inscription; registration.

inscripto, inscrito p.p. of **inscribir.**

insecto m. insect.

inseguro adj. insecure; unsafe; doubtful, uncertain.

insensato adj. senseless; foolish.

insensibilidad f. insensibility, unconsciousness; lack of feeling.

insensible adj. insensible; unfeeling; imperceptible.

inseparable adj. inseparable.

inserción f. insertion; insert.

insertar v. to insert.

inserto adj. inserted.

inservible adj. useless.

insidioso adj. insidious; sly, crafty.

insigne adj. famous.

insignia f. badge, medal, decoration; flag, pennant; -s insignia.

insignificante adj. insignificant.

insinuación f. insinuation; intimation, hint.

insinuar[18] v. to insinuate, hint; -se to insinuate oneself (into another's friendship); to creep (into) gradually.

insipidez f. flatness, tastelessness, dullness; **insípido** adj. insipid; tasteless.

insistencia f. insistence, persistence, obstinacy; **insistente** adj. insistent, persistent.

insistir v. to insist; to persist.

insociable adj. unsociable.

insolación f. sunstroke.

insolencia f. insolence.

insolentarse v. to sauce, become insolent, act with insolence.

insolente adj. insolent.

insólito adj. unusual; uncommon.

insolvente adj. insolvent, bankrupt.

insomne adj. sleepless.

insondable adj. fathomless, deep; impenetrable.

insoportable adj. unbearable.

insospechado adj. unsuspected.

inspección f. inspection.

inspeccionar v. to inspect.

inspector m. inspector; overseer.

inspiración f. inspiration; inhalation, breathing in.

inspirar v. to inspire; to inhale.

instalación f. installation.

instalar v. to install.

instancia f. instance, urgent request; petition; **a -s de** at the request of.

instantánea f. snapshot.

instantáneo adj. instantaneous; sudden.

instante m. instant, moment; **al — at once**, immediately; **por -s** continually; from one moment to another; adj. instant, urgent.

instar v. to urge, press; to be urgent.

instigar[7] v. to instigate, urge on, incite.

instintivo adj. instinctive.

instinto m. instinct.

institución f. institution; establishment, foundation; **-es** institutes, collection of precepts and principles.

instituir[32] v. irr. to institute; **— por heredero** to appoint as heir.

instituto m. institute; established principle, law, or custom; **— de segunda enseñanza** high school.

institutriz f. governess.

instrucción f. instruction; education.

instructivo adj. instructive.

instruir[32] v. irr. to instruct, teach; to inform.

instrumento m. instrument.

insuficiencia f. insufficiency, deficiency; incompetence; dearth, scarcity, lack.

insuficiente adj. insufficient.

insufrible adj. insufferable, unbearable.

ínsula f. island.

insultante adj. insulting, abusive.

insultar v. to insult, **-se** to be seized with a fit.

insulto m. insult; sudden fit or attack.

insuperable adj. insuperable; insurmountable.

insurgente adj., m. & f. insurgent.

insurrección f. insurrection, uprising, revolt.

insurrecto m. insurgent, rebel; adj. rebellious.

intacto adj. intact.

intachable adj. faultless, irreproachable.

integral adj. integral; f. integral (math).

integrante adj. integral; integrating.

integridad f. integrity; wholeness; honesty; purity.

íntegro adj. whole, complete; honest, upright.

intelecto m. intellect.

intelectual adj. intellectual.

inteligencia f. intelligence.

inteligente adj. intelligent.

intemperancia f. intemperance, excess.

intemperie f. open air; bad weather; **a la —** unsheltered, outdoors, in the open air; exposed to the weather.

intención f. intention; **intencional** adj. intentional.

intendente m. manager, superintendent, supervisor; Am. governor of a province; Am. police commissioner.

intensidad f. intensity.

intenso adj. intense; intensive; ardent, vehement.

intentar v. to attempt, try; to intend.

intento m. intent, purpose, intention; **de —** on purpose.

intercalar v. to insert, place between.

intercambio m. interchange; exchange.

interceder v. to intercede.

interceptar v. to intercept.

intercesión f. intercession, mediation.

interés m. interest.

interesante adj. interesting.

interesar v. to interest; to give an interest or share; **-se** to be or become interested.

interferencia f. interference.

ínterin m. interim, meantime; **en el —** in the meantime.

interino adj. acting, temporary.

interior adj. interior; inner; internal; m. interior, inside.

interjección f. interjection, exclamation.

interlocutor m. participant in a dialogue.

intermedio adj. intermediate; intervening; m. intermission; interval; **por — de** by means of, through the intervention of.

interminable adj. interminable, unending, endless.

intermisión f. intermission, interruption, pause, interval.

intermitente adj. intermittent, occurring at intervals; **calentura (or fiebre) —** intermittent fever.

internacional adj. international.

internar v. to intern, confine; **-se** to penetrate, go into the interior.

interno adj. internal; interior; m. boarding-school student.

interoceánico adj. interoceanic; transcontinental.

interpelar v. to interrogate, question, demand explanations; to ask the aid of.

interponer[40] v. irr. to interpose, put between, insert; to place as a mediator; **-se** to intervene, mediate.

interpretación f. interpretation.

interpretar v. to interpret.

intérprete m. & f. interpreter.

interpuesto p.p. of **interponer**.

interrogación f. interrogation, question; **signo de —** question mark.

120

interrogador *m.* questioner; *adj.* questioning.
interrogar[7] *v.* to interrogate, question.
interrogativo *adj.* interrogative.
interrogatorio *m.* interrogation, questioning.
interrumpir *v.* to interrupt.
interrupción *f.* interruption.
interruptor *m.* interrupter; electric switch.
intersección *f.* intersection.
intervalo *m.* interval.
intervención *f.* intervention; mediation; participation; auditing of accounts.
intervenir[48] *v. irr.* to intervene; to mediate; to audit (*accounts*).
interventor *m.* inspector; controller, comptroller; auditor.
intestino *m.* intestine; *adj.* intestine, internal.
intimación *f.* intimation; hint, insinuation, suggestion.
intimar *v.* to announce, notify; to intimate, hint; to become intimate, become friendly.
intimidad *f.* intimacy.
intimidar *v.* to intimidate.
íntimo *adj.* intimate.
intitular *v.* to entitle; to give a title to (*a person or a thing*); -se to be entitled, be called; to call oneself (*by a certain name*).
intolerable *adj.* intolerable.
intolerancia *f.* intolerance; **intolerante** *adj.* intolerant, narrow-minded.
intranquilo *adj.* disturbed, uneasy.
intranquilidad *f.* uneasiness, restlessness.
intransigencia *f.* uncompromising act or attitude; intolerance.
intransigente *adj.* uncompromising, unwilling to compromise or yield; intolerant.
intratable *adj.* unsociable; rude; unruly.
intravenoso *adj.* intravenous (*within a vein or the veins; into a vein*).
intrepidez *f.* fearlessness, courage.
intrépido *adj.* intrepid, fearless.
intriga *f.* intrigue; scheme; plot.
intrigante *m. & f.* intriguer, plotter; *adj.* intriguing.
intrigar[7] *v.* to intrigue.
intrincado *adj.* intricate, complicated, entangled.
introducción *f.* introduction.
introducir[25] *v. irr.* to introduce; -se to introduce oneself; to get in; to penetrate.
intromisión *f.* meddling; insertion.
intruso *adj.* intrusive, intruding; *m.* intruder.
intuición *f.* intuition.
intuir[32] *v. irr.* to sense, feel by intuition.
inundación *f.* inundation, flood.
inundar *v.* to inundate, flood.
inusitado *adj.* unusual, rare.
inútil *adj.* useless.
inutilidad *f.* uselessness.
inutilizar[9] *v.* to make useless, put out of commission; to disable; to ruin, spoil.
invadir *v.* to invade.
invalidar *v.* to render invalid; to void, annul.
inválido *adj.* invalid; void, null; sickly, weak; *m.* invalid.
invariable *adj.* invariable.
invasión *f.* invasion.
invasor *m.* invader; *adj.* invading; **ejército —** invading army.
invencible *adj.* invincible, unconquerable.
invención *f.* invention.
invendible *adj.* unsaleable.
inventar *v.* to invent.
inventariar[17] *v.* to inventory, take an inventory of.
inventario *m.* inventory.
inventiva *f.* inventiveness, power of inventing, ingenuity.
inventivo *adj.* inventive.
invento *m.* invention.
inventor *m.* inventor; storyteller; fibber.
invernáculo *m.* greenhouse, hothouse.
invernadero *m.* winter quarters; winter resort; winter pasture; greenhouse, hothouse.
invernal *adj.* wintry, winter.
invernar[1] *v. irr.* to winter, spend the winter.
inverosímil, inverisímil *adj.* unlikely, improbable.
inversión *f.* inversion; investment.
inverso *adj.* inverse, inverted; reverse; **a** (*or* **por**) **la inversa** on the contrary.
invertir[3] *v. irr.* to invert; to reverse; to invest; to employ, spend (*time*).
investigación *f.* investigation.
investigador *m.* investigator; *adj.* investigating.
investigar[7] *v.* to investigate.
invicto *adj.* unconquered; always victorious.
invierno *m.* winter.
invisible *adj.* invisible.
invitación *f.* invitation.
invitar *v.* to invite.
invocar[6] *v.* to invoke.
involuntario *adj.* involuntary.
inyección *f.* injection.

inyectado p.p. injected; *adj.* bloodshot, inflamed.

inyectar *v.* to inject.

ir[35] *v. irr.* to go; to walk; — **corriendo** to be running; — **entendiendo** to understand gradually; to begin to understand; — **a caballo** to ride horseback; — **a pie** to walk; — **en automóvil** to drive, ride in an automobile; **no irle ni venirle a uno** to make no difference to one; ¿**cómo le va?** how are you?; **no me va nada en eso** that doesn't concern me; ¡**vamos!** let's go! come on!; ¡**vaya!** well now!; ¡**vaya un hombre!** what a man!; **-se** to go, go away; to escape; **-se abajo** to fall down, topple over; to collapse; **-se a pique** to founder, sink.

ira *f.* ire, anger.

iracundo *adj.* irritable; angry.

iris *m.* iris (*of the eye*); **arco** — rainbow.

irisado *adj.* iridescent, rainbow-hued.

ironía *f.* irony.

irónico *adj.* ironic, ironical.

irracional *adj.* irrational, unreasonable.

irradiar *v.* to radiate.

irreal *adj.* unreal.

irreflexión *f.* thoughtlessness.

irreflexivo *adj.* thoughtless.

irrefrenable *adj.* uncontrollable.

irregular *adj.* irregular.

irreligioso *adj.* irreligious.

irremediable *adj.* irremediable; hopeless, incurable.

irreprochable *adj.* irreproachable, flawless.

irresistible *adj.* irresistible.

irresoluto *adj.* irresolute, undecided, hesitating.

irrespetuoso *adj.* disrespectful.

irreverencia *f.* irreverence.

irreverente *adj.* irreverent.

irrigación *f.* irrigation.

irrigar[7] *v.* to irrigate.

irrisión *f.* mockery, ridicule, derision.

irritación *f.* irritation.

irritante *adj.* irritating.

irritar *v.* to irritate.

irrupción *f.* sudden attack, raid, invasion.

isla *f.* island.

isleño *m.* islander.

islote *m.* islet, small rocky island.

istmo *m.* isthmus.

italiano *adj.* & *m.* Italian.

itinerario *m.* itinerary; timetable, schedule; railroad guide.

izar[9] *v.* to hoist; to heave.

izquierda *f.* left hand; left side; left wing (*in politics*); **a la** — to the left;

izquierdista *m.* & *f.* leftist, radical.

izquierdo *adj.* left; left-handed.

J

jabalí *m.* wild boar.

jabón *m.* soap; *Am.* fright, fear; **dar** — to soft-soap, flatter; **dar un** — to give a good scolding; to beat, thrash.

jabonadura *f.* washing, soaping; **-s** suds, lather; **dar a uno una** — to reprimand or scold someone.

jabonar *v.* to lather, soap; to scold, reprimand.

jabonera *f.* soap dish; woman soap vendor or maker.

jaca *f.* pony; small horse; **jaco** *m.* small nag; poor horse.

jacal *m. Am.* shack, adobe hut; **jacalucho** *m. Am.* poor, ugly shack.

jacinto *m.* hyacinth.

jactancia *f.* boast, brag; boasting.

jactancioso *adj.* braggart, boastful.

jactarse *v.* to brag, boast.

jaculatoria *f.* short, fervent prayer.

jadeante *adj.* breathless, panting, out of breath.

jadear *v.* to pant.

jadeo *m.* pant, panting.

jaez *m.* harness; kind, sort; **jaeces** trappings.

jalar *v.* to pull; to haul; to jerk; *Am.* to court, make love; *Am.* to flunk (*a student*); *Am.* ¡**jala** (or **jálale**)! get going! get a move on there!; **-se** *Am.* to get drunk; *Am.* to go away, move away.

jalea *f.* jelly.

jalear *v.* to shout (*to hunting dogs*); to rouse, beat up (*game*); to shout and clap (*to encourage dancers*).

jaleo *m.* shouting and clapping (*to encourage dancers*); an Andalusian dance; revelry, merrymaking; jesting; gracefulness.

jaletina *f.* gelatin.

jalón *m.* marker (*for boundaries*); *Am.* pull, jerk, tug; *Am.* swallow of liquor; *Am.* stretch, distance.

jalonear *v. Am.* to pull, jerk.

jamás *adv.* never.

jamón *m.* ham; *Am.* fix, difficulty.

japonés *adj.* & *m.* Japanese.

jaque *m.* check (*in chess*); braggart, bully; — **mate** checkmate (*in chess*); **tener a uno en** — to hold someone under a threat.

jaqueca *f.* headache; sick headache.

jara *f.* rockrose (*shrub*); *Am.* reed; **jaral** *m.* bramble of rockroses; *Am.* reeds, clump of reeds.

jarabe *m.* syrup; sweet beverage; *Am.* a kind of tap dance; *Am.* song and musical accompaniment of the jarabe.

jarana *f.* merrymaking, revelry; trick; fib; jest; *Am.* small guitar; **ir de** — to go on a spree.

jarcia *f.* rigging (*ropes, chains, etc. for the masts, yards and sails of a ship*); fishing tackle; pile, heap; jumble of things.

jardín *m.* flower garden.

jardinero *m.* gardener.

jarra *f.* jar, vase, pitcher; **de** (*or* **en**) **-s akimbo** (*with hands on the hips*).

jarro *m.* jar, jug, pitcher.

jarrón *m.* large vase or jar.

jaspe *m.* jasper; veined marble; **jaspeado** *adj.* veined, streaked, mottled.

jaula *f.* cage; cagelike cell or prison; *Am.* roofless cattle car or freight car.

jauría *f.* pack of hounds.

jazmín *m.* jasmine.

jefatura *f.* position of chief; headquarters of a chief.

jefe *m.* chief, leader, head.

jengibre *m.* ginger.

jerez *m.* sherry wine.

jerga *f.* thick coarse cloth; straw mattress; jargon; slang; *Am.* saddle pad; *Am.* poncho made of coarse cloth.

jergón *m.* straw mattress; ill-fitting suit or dress; big clumsy fellow; *Am.* cheap coarse rug.

jerigonza *f.* jargon; slang.

jeringa *f.* syringe; **jeringazo** *m.* injection; squirt.

jeringar *v.* to inject; to squirt; to bother, molest, vex, annoy.

jesuita *m.* Jesuit.

jeta *f.* snout; thick lips.

jiba = **giba.**

jíbaro *adj. Am.* rustic, rural, rude, uncultured; *m. Am.* bumpkin, peasant.

jícara *f.* chocolate cup; *Am.* small bowl made out of a gourd; *Am.* any small bowl; *Am.* bald head.

jilguero *m.* linnet.

jinete *m.* horseman, rider.

jineteada *f. Am.* roughriding, horsebreaking.

jinetear *v.* to ride horseback; to perform on horseback; *Am.* to break in (*a horse*); *Am.* to ride a bronco or bull.

jira *f.* excursion, tour; outing, picnic; strip of cloth.

jirafa *f.* giraffe.

jitomate *m. Am.* tomato. *Also* **gitomate.**

jofaina *f.* basin, washbowl.

jolgorio = **holgorio.**

jornada *f.* day's journey; military expedition; working day; act (*of a Spanish play*).

jornal *m.* day's wages; bookkeeping journal; **a** — by the day.

jornalero *m.* day laborer.

joroba *f.* hump; nuisance, annoyance.

jorobado *adj.* hunchbacked; annoyed, bothered, in a bad fix; *m.* hunchback.

jorobar *v.* to bother, pester, annoy.

jorongo *m. Am.* Mexican poncho.

jota *f.* name of the letter *j*; iota (*anything insignificant*); Aragonese and Valencian dance and music; *Am.* (= **ojota**) leather sandal; **no saber una** — not to know anything.

joven *adj.* young; *m. & f.* youth; young man; young woman.

jovial *adj.* jovial, jolly, merry; **jovialidad** *f.* gaiety, merriment, fun.

joya *f.* jewel; piece of jewelry; **-s jewels**; trousseau.

joyería *f.* jeweler's shop.

joyero *m.* jeweler; jewel box.

juanete *m.* bunion.

jubilación *f.* retirement (*from a position or office*); pension.

jubilar *v.* to pension; to retire; **-se** to be pensioned or retired; to rejoice; *Am.* to decline, fall into decline; *Am.* to play hooky or truant.

jubileo *m.* jubilee; time of rejoicing; concession by the Pope of plenary (*complete*) indulgence.

júbilo *m.* joy, glee.

jubiloso *adj.* jubilant, joyful.

jubón *m.* jacket; bodice.

judía *f.* bean; string bean; Jewess; **-s tiernas** (*or* **verdes**) string beans.

judicial *adj.* judicial; **-mente** *adv.* judicially.

judío *adj.* Jewish; *m.* Jew.

juego *m.* game; play; sport; gambling; pack of cards; set; — **de palabras** pun, play on words; — **de te tea set**; **hacer** — to match; **poner en** — to coordinate; to set in motion.

juerga *f.* spree, revelry, wild festivity; **irse de** — to go out on a spree; **juerguista** *m. & f.* merrymaker.

jueves *m.* Thursday.

juez *m.* judge; juror, member of a jury; — **arbitrador** (*or* **árbitro**) arbitrator, umpire.

jugada *f.* play, move; stroke; trick.

jugador *m.* player; gambler; — **de manos** juggler.

jugar [34] *v. irr.* to play; to gamble; to toy; — **a la pelota** to play ball; *Am.* — **a dos cartas** to be double-faced.

jugarreta f. bad play, wrong play; mean trick; tricky deal; *Am.* noisy game.

ugo m. juice; sap.

ugosidad f. juiciness; **jugoso** adj. juicy.

juguete m. plaything, toy; jest, joke; — cómico skit; por (or de) — jokingly.

juguetear v. to play around, romp, frolic; to toy; to tamper (with), fool (with).

juguetón adj. playful.

juicio m. judgment; sense, wisdom; opinion; trial; **perder el —** to lose one's mind, go crazy.

juicioso adj. judicious, wise; sensible.

julio m. July.

jumento m. ass, donkey.

junco m. rush, reed; junk (*Chinese sailboat*).

jungla f. *Am.* jungle.

junio m. June.

junquillo m. reed; jonquil (*yellow flower similar to the daffodil*), species of narcissus.

junta f. meeting, conference; board, council.

juntar v. to join, unite; to connect; to assemble; to collect; **-se** to assemble, gather; to be closely united; to associate (with).

junto adj. joined, united; **-s together**; adv. near; — a near to, close to; **en —** all together, in all; **por —** all together, in a lump; wholesale.

juntura f. juncture; junction; joint, seam.

jurado m. jury; juror, juryman; adj. & p.p. sworn.

juramentar v. to swear in; **-se** to take an oath, be sworn in.

juramento m. oath; vow; curse.

jurar v. to swear, vow; to take oath; to curse.

jurisconsulto m. jurist, expert in law; lawyer.

jurisdicción f. jurisdiction.

jurisprudencia f. jurisprudence, law.

juro: de — adv. certainly, of course.

justa f. joust, tournament, combat (*between horsemen with lances*); contest.

justicia f. justice; court of justice; judge; police.

justiciero adj. strictly just, austere (*in matters of justice*).

justificación f. justification.

justificante adj. justifying; m. voucher; written excuse; proof.

justificar[6] v. to justify; to vindicate, clear of blame.

justo adj. just; pious; exact, correct;

tight; adv. duly; exactly; tightly; m. just man; **los -s** the just.

juvenil adj. juvenile, young, youthful.

juventud f. youth; young people.

juzgado m. court, tribunal.

juzgar[7] v. to judge.

K

kerosena f. kerosene, coal oil.

kilo m. kilo, kilogram.

kilogramo m. kilogram.

kilometraje m. number of kilometers.

kilómetro m. kilometer.

L

la def. art. f. the; — de the one with, that one with; obj. pron. her; it; — que rel. pron. she who, the one that; which.

laberinto m. labyrinth, maze; labyrinth, internal ear.

labia f. fluency, talkativeness, gift of gab; **tener mucha —** to be a good talker.

labio m. lip.

labor f. labor, work; embroidery; needlework; tillage; — de punto knitting; **laborable** adj. workable; tillable; **día laborable** work day; **laboral** adj. pertaining to labor.

laboratorio m. laboratory.

laboriosidad f. laboriousness, industry.

laborioso adj. laborious; industrious.

labrado p.p. & adj. tilled, cultivated; wrought; carved; manufactured; m. carving; — en madera woodwork, carving; **-s** cultivated lands.

labrador m. farmer; peasant.

labranza f. farming, tillage, plowing; cultivated land, farm.

labrar v. to till, cultivate, farm; to plow; to carve; to embroider; to work (*metals*); to build (*a monument*).

labriego m. peasant.

laca f. lacquer; shellac.

lacayo m. lackey, footman, flunky.

lacio adj. withered; languid; limp; straight (*hair*).

lacra f. trace of an illness; blemish, defect; *Am.* sore, ulcer, scab, scar.

lacre m. red sealing wax; adj. *Am.* red.

lactar v. to nurse, suckle; to feed with milk.

lácteo adj. milky; **fiebre láctea** milk fever; **régimen —** milk diet; **Vía Láctea** Milky Way.

ladear v. to tilt, tip; to go along the slope or side of; to turn aside (*from a way or course*); **-se** to tilt; to sway; to incline or lean (towards); to move

to one side; *Am.* to fall in love.

ladeo *m.* inclination, tilt.

ladera *f.* slope.

ladino *adj.* crafty, sly, shrewd; conversant with two or three languages; *m. Am.* Spanish-speaking person (*as opposed to one who speaks an Indian language*); *Am.* mestizo, half-breed; *Am.* talker, talkative person.

lado *m.* side; **al —** near, at hand, at one's side; **de —** tilted, obliquely; sideways; **— a —** side by side; **¡a un —!** gangway! **hacerse a un —** to move over, step aside, move to one side; *Am.* **echársela de —** to boast.

ladrar *v.* to bark.

ladrido *m.* bark, barking.

ladrillo *m.* brick.

ladrón *m.* thief, robber; **ladronzuelo** *m.* petty thief.

lagartija *f.* small lizard.

lagarto *m.* lizard; rascal, sly fellow.

lago *m.* lake.

lágrima *f.* tear; **llorar a —** viva to weep abundantly.

lagrimear *v.* to weep, shed tears.

laguna *f.* lagoon; gap, blank space.

laico *adj.* lay; *m.* layman.

laja *f.* slab; flat stone.

lamedero *m.* salt lick (*for cattle*).

lamentable *adj.* lamentable, pitiful.

lamentación *f.* lamentation.

lamentar *v.* to lament, deplore; **-se** to moan, complain, wail.

lamento *m.* lament, moan, cry.

lamer *v.* to lick; to lap.

lamida *f. Am.* lick.

lámina *f.* metal plate; sheet of metal; engraving; book illustration.

lámpara *f.* lamp.

lampiño *adj.* hairless; beardless.

lana *f.* wool; *Am.* tramp, vagabond.

lanar *adj.* wool-bearing; of wool.

lance *m.* occurrence, event; cast, throw, move, turn; accident; quarrel; predicament.

lancear *v.* to lance, spear.

lancha *f.* launch; boat; slab; **lanchón** *m.* barge.

langosta *f.* lobster; locust.

languidecer[13] *v. irr.* to languish.

languidez *f.* languor, faintness, weakness.

lánguido *adj.* languid.

lanudo *adj.* wooly; *Am.* coarse, crude, ill-bred; *Am.* dull, slow, weak-willed.

lanza *f.* lance, spear; *Am.* swindler, cheat.

lanzada *f.* thrust (*with a spear*).

lanzadera *f.* shuttle.

lanzar[9] *v.* to fling, throw; to eject; to launch; **-se** to rush, fling oneself; to dart out.

lanzazo *m.* thrust with a lance.

lapicero *m.* pencil (*a mechanical pencil, one with an adjustable lead*).

lápida *f.* slab, tombstone; stone tablet.

lapidar *v.* to stone; *Am.* to cut precious stones.

lápiz *m.* pencil; crayon; **— para los labios** lipstick.

lapso *m.* lapse.

lardo *m.* lard.

largar[7] *v.* to loosen; to let go; to set free; to unfold (*a flag or sails*); *Am.* to hurl, throw; *Am.* to strike (*a blow*); *Am.* to give, hand over; **-se** to go away, slip away; to leave.

largo *adj.* long; generous; *m.* length; largo (*music*); **a la larga** in the long run; slowly; **a lo —** along; lengthwise; **¡ — de aquí!** get out of here!

largor *m.* length.

largucho *adj.* lanky.

largueza *f.* generosity, liberality; length.

larguísimo *adj.* very long.

largura *f.* length.

laringe *f.* larynx.

larva *f.* larva.

las *def. art. f. pl.* the; *obj. pron.* them; **— que** *rel. pron.* those which; which.

lascivia *f.* lewdness.

lascivo *adj.* lascivious, lewd.

lástima *f.* pity; compassion, grief.

lastimadura *f.* sore, hurt.

lastimar *v.* to hurt; to offend; **-se** to get hurt; **-se de** to feel pity for.

lastimero *adj.* pitiful; mournful.

lastimoso *adj.* pitiful.

lastre *m.* ballast, weight.

lata *f.* tin plate; tin can, can; thin board; small log; boring speech; annoyance; embarrassment; *Am.* gaucho saber; *Am.* prop.

latente *adj.* latent.

lateral *adj.* lateral, side.

latido *m.* palpitation, throb, beat; bark, howl.

latifundio *m.* large landed estate.

latigazo *m.* lash, stroke with a whip; crack of a whip; harsh reprimand; unexpected blow or offense.

látigo *m.* whip; *Am.* whipping, beating; *Am.* end or goal of a horse race.

latín *m.* Latin language.

latino *adj.* Latin; *m.* Latinist, Latin scholar; Latin.

latir *v.* to throb, beat, palpitate; to bark.

latitud *f.* latitude; extent, breadth.

latón *m.* brass.

latrocinio *m.* larceny, theft, robbery.
laúd *m.* lute; catboat (*long, narrow boat with a lateen sail*).
laudable *adj.* laudable, praiseworthy.
laurel *m.* laurel; laurel wreath.
lauro *m.* laurel; glory, fame.
lava *f.* lava; washing of minerals.
lavable *adj.* washable.
lavabo *m.* lavatory, washroom; washstand; washbowl.
lavadero *m.* washing place.
lavado *m.* wash, washing; laundry, laundry work.
lavador *m.* washer; cleaner; *adj.* washing; cleaning; lavadora *f.* washer, washing machine.
lavadura *f.* washing; slops, dirty water.
lavamanos *m.* lavatory, washbowl, washstand.
lavandera *f.* laundress, washerwoman.
lavandería *f.* laundry.
lavar *v.* to wash; to launder; to whitewash.
lavativa *f.* enema; syringe; bother, nuisance.
lavatorio *m.* washing (*act of washing*); wash (*liquid or solution for washing*); lavatory (*ceremonial act of washing*); washbowl, washstand; *Am.* washroom.
lavazas *f. pl.* slops, dirty water.
lazada *f.* bow, bowknot; *Am.* throwing of the lasso, lassoing.
lazar[9] *v.* to rope, lasso; to noose.
lazarillo *m.* blindman's guide.
lazo *m.* bow, knot; slipknot; lasso, lariat; tie, bond; snare, trap; trick.
le *obj. pron.* him; you (*formal*); to him; to her; to you (*formal*).
leal *adj.* loyal.
lealtad *f.* loyalty.
lebrel *m.* greyhound.
lebrillo *m.* earthenware basin or tub.
lección *f.* lesson; reading; dar la — to recite the lesson; dar — to teach; tomarle a uno la — to have someone recite his lesson.
lector *m.* reader; lecturer.
lectura *f.* reading; libro de — reader.
lechada *f.* whitewash; *Am.* milking.
leche *f.* milk; *Am.* luck (*in games*).
lechería *f.* dairy, creamery; lechero *adj.* milk; milch, giving milk (*applied to animals*); *Am.* lucky (*in games of chance*); *m.* milkman; lechera *f.* milkmaid; milk can; milk pitcher.
lecho *m.* bed; river bed.
lechón *m.* suckling pig; pig.
lechoso *adj.* milky; *m.* papaya tree; lechosa *f.* papaya (*tropical fruit*).
lechuga *f.* lettuce.

lechuza *f.* screech owl, barn owl.
leer[14] *v.* to read.
legación *f.* legation.
legado *m.* legacy; legate, representative, ambassador.
legal *adj.* legal, lawful; truthful; reliable; *Am.* excellent, best; *Am.* just, honest.
legalizar[9] *v.* to legalize.
legar[7] *v.* to will, bequeath; to send as a delegate.
legendario *adj.* legendary.
legión *f.* legion.
legislación *f.* legislation.
legislador *m.* legislator; *adj.* legislating, legislative.
legislar *v.* to legislate.
legislativo *adj.* legislative.
legislatura *f.* legislature, legislative assembly.
legítimo *adj.* legitimate; real, genuine.
lego *adj.* lay; ignorant; *m.* layman.
legua *f.* league (*about 3 miles*).
leguleyo *m.* shyster.
legumbre *f.* vegetable.
leída *f. Am.* reading. *See* lectura.
lejanía *f.* distance; distant place.
lejano *adj.* distant; remote.
lejía *f.* lye; harsh reprimand.
lejos *adv.* far, far away; a lo — in the distance; *Am.* a un — in the distance; de (o desde) — from afar; *m.* view, perspective; background.
lelo *adj.* silly, stupid, foolish.
lema *m.* motto; theme; slogan.
lencería *f.* dry goods; dry-goods store; linen room or closet.
lengua *f.* tongue; language; interpreter; — de tierra point, neck of land.
lenguado *m.* flounder, sole (*a fish*).
lenguaje *m.* language (*manner of expression*).
lenguaraz *adj.* talkative, loose-tongued.
lengüeta *f.* small tongue; lengüetada *f.* lick.
lente *m. & f.* lens; -s *m. pl.* eyeglasses.
lenteja *f.* lentil; lentil seed; lentejuela *f.* spangle.
lentitud *f.* slowness.
lento *adj.* slow; dull.
leña *f.* firewood; kindling; beating; leñera *f.* woodshed; woodbox.
leñador *m.* woodcutter, woodman.
leño *m.* log; timber; piece of firewood.
león *m.* lion; leona *f.* lioness; leonera *f.* lion's den or cage; dive, gambling joint; disorderly room.
leontina *f. Am.* watch chain.
leopardo *m.* leopard.
leopoldina *f. Am.* watch chain.
lerdo *adj.* dull, heavy, stupid, slow.

les *obj. pron.* to them; to you (*formal*).

lesión *f.* wound, injury.

lesionar *v.* to injure; to wound; to hurt; to damage.

lesna = **lezna.**

letargo *m.* lethargy, stupor, drowsiness.

letra *f.* letter (*of the alphabet*); printing type; hand, handwriting; letter (*exact wording or meaning*); words of a song; — **abierta** letter of credit; — **de cambio** draft, bill of exchange; — **mayúscula** capital letter; — **minúscula** small letter; **al pie de la** — literally; **-s** letters, learning.

letrado *adj.* learned; *m.* lawyer.

letrero *m.* notice, poster, sign; legend (*under an illustration*).

leva *f.* levy, draft; weighing anchor, setting sail; **echar** — to draft, conscript; *Am.* **echar -s** to boast.

levadura *f.* leaven, yeast.

levantamiento *m.* uprising, revolt, insurrection; elevation; lifting, raising; adjournment (*of a meeting*); — **de un plano** surveying.

levantar *v.* to raise, lift; to set up; to erect; to rouse, stir up; to recruit; *Am.* to break land, plow; — **el campo** to break camp; — **la mesa** to clear the table; — **la sesión** to adjourn the meeting; — **un plano** to survey, map out; — **falso testimonio** to bear false witness; **-se** to stand up, get up, rise; to rebel.

levante *m.* east; east wind.

levantisco *adj.* turbulent; rebellious.

levar *v.* to weigh (*anchor*); — **el ancla** to weigh anchor, **-se** to weigh anchor, set sail.

leve *adj.* light; slight, unimportant.

levita *f.* frock coat; *m.* Levite, member of the tribe of Levi.

léxico *m.* lexicon, dictionary; vocabulary; glossary.

ley *f.* law; rule; loyalty; standard quality; **de buena** — of good quality; **plata de** — sterling silver; **-es** jurisprudence, law; system of laws.

leyenda *f.* legend; reading; inscription.

lezna *f.* awl.

liar[17] *v.* to tie, bind; to roll up; to deceive; **-se** to bind oneself; to get tangled up.

libelo *m.* libel.

libélula *f.* dragon fly.

liberación *f.* liberation; deliverance.

liberal *adj.* liberal; generous; **liberalidad** *f.* liberality; generosity.

libertad *f.* liberty.

libertador *m.* liberator, deliverer.

libertar *v.* to liberate, free, set free; **-se** to get free; to escape.

libertinaje *m.* license, licentiousness, lack of moral restraint.

libertino *m.* libertine (*person without moral restraint*).

libra *f.* pound; Libra (*sign of the Zodiac*).

librador *m.* drawer (*of a bill, draft, etc.*); deliverer, liberator; measuring scoop.

libranza *f.* bill of exchange, draft.

librar *v.* to free, set free; to issue; to draw (*a draft*); — **guerra** to wage war; **-se** to save oneself; to escape; **-se de** to get rid of, escape from.

libre *adj.* free; unmarried; loose; vacant.

librea *f.* livery (*uniform*).

librería *f.* bookstore.

librero *m.* bookseller; *Am.* bookcase, bookshelves.

libreta *f.* notebook, memorandum book.

libro *m.* book; — **de caja** cashbook; — **mayor** ledger.

licencia *f.* license; permission; furlough, leave; looseness; license to practice.

licenciado *m.* licenciate (*person having a degree approximately equivalent to a master's degree*); *Am.* lawyer.

licenciar *v.* to license; to give a license or permit; to dismiss, discharge (*from the army*); to confer the degree of **licenciado**; **-se** to get the degree of **licenciado**.

licenciatura *f.* degree of **licenciado.**

licencioso *adj.* licentious, lewd.

lícito *adj.* lawful; permissible, allowable.

licor *m.* liquid; liquor.

lid *f.* fight; contest.

líder *m. Am.* leader.

lidiar *v.* to fight; to combat; to contend.

liebre *f.* hare; coward.

lienzo *m.* cotton or linen cloth; canvas; painting.

liga *f.* league; alliance; garter; alloy (*mixture of metals*); birdlime.

ligadura *f.* binding; tie, bond.

ligar[7] *v.* to bind, tie, unite; to alloy (*combine metals*); **-se** to unite, combine, form an alliance.

ligereza *f.* lightness; swiftness; flippancy; frivolity.

ligero *adj.* light; swift; nimble; flippant; *adv. Am.* quickly; **a la ligera** quickly, superficially.

lija *f.* sandpaper.

lijar *v.* to sandpaper.

lila *f.* lilac; pinkish-purple.

lima *f.* file; lime (*fruit*); finishing, polishing.

limar *v.* to file; to file down; to smooth, polish.

limeño adj. of or from Lima, Peru.
limitación f. limitation; district.
limitar v. to limit; to restrict; to bound.
límite m. limit; boundary.
limo m. slime.
limón m. lemon; lemon tree; **limonada** f. lemonade; **limonero** m. lemon tree; lemon dealer or vendor.
limosna f. alms, charity.
limpiabotas m. bootblack; Am. bootlicker, flatterer.
limpiadientes m. toothpick.
limpiar v. to clean; to wipe; to cleanse, purify; Am. to beat up, whip, lash.
límpido adj. limpid, clear.
limpieza f. cleanliness, neatness; purity; honesty.
limpio adj. clean; neat; pure; **poner en** — to make a clean copy; Am. — y **soplado** absolutely broke, wiped out.
linaje m. lineage, family, race.
linaza f. linseed.
lince m. lynx; sharp-sighted person.
linchar v. to lynch.
lindar v. to border, adjoin.
linde m. & f. limit, border, boundary; landmark.
lindero adj. bordering upon; m. Am. landmark; boundary.
lindeza f. prettiness; exquisiteness; neatness; witty act or remark.
lindo adj. pretty; de lo — wonderfully; very much; to the utmost.
línea f. line; limit.
lineal adj. lineal, linear.
lino m. linen; flax; **linón** m. lawn, thin linen or cotton.
linterna f. lantern.
lío m. bundle; fib; mess, confusion; **armar un** — to raise a rumpus; to cause confusion; **hacerse un** — to be confused, get tangled up; **meterse en un** — to get oneself into a mess.
liquidación f. liquidation; settlement (of an account).
liquidar v. to liquidate; to settle (an account).
líquido m. liquid.
lira f. lyre, small harp; a type of metrical composition; lira (Italian coin).
lírico adj. lyric, lyrical; Am. fantastic; m. Am. visionary, dreamer.
lirio m. lily.
lirismo m. lyricism (lyric quality); Am. idle dream, fantasy.
lisiado adj. lame, hurt, injured
liso adj. smooth, even; flat; evident, clear; Am. crafty, sly; Am. fresh, impudent.
lisonja f. flattery.

lisonjear v. to flatter; to fawn on; to please.
lisonjero adj. flattering, pleasing; m. flatterer.
lista f. list; strip; stripe; **pasar** — to call the roll.
listado adj. striped.
listar v. to register, enter in a list; Am. to stripe, streak.
listo adj. ready, prompt; clever; Am. mischievous.
listón m. ribbon, tape; strip.
lisura f. smoothness; sincerity, frankness; Am. freshness, impudence; insulting or filthy remark.
litera f. berth (on a boat or train); litter (for carrying a person).
literario adj. literary.
literato adj. literary, learned; m. literary man, writer.
literatura f. literature.
litigio m. litigation, lawsuit.
litoral adj. seaboard, coastal; m. coast, shore.
litro m. liter (about 1.05 quarts).
liviandad f. lightness; frivolity; lewdness.
liviano adj. light; slight, unimportant; frivolous, fickle; lewd; unchaste.
lívido adj. livid, having a dull-bluish color; pale.
lo obj. pron. him; you (formal); it; so; dem. pron. — de that of, that affair of, that matter of; — **bueno** the good, what is good; **sé** — **bueno que Vd. es** I know how good you are; — **que** that which, what.
loable adj. laudable, worthy of praise.
loar v. to praise.
lobanillo m. growth, tumor.
lobo m. wolf.
lóbrego adj. dark, gloomy.
lobreguez f. darkness, gloominess.
local adj. local; m. place, quarters; site; premises.
localidad f. location; locality, town; place; seat (in a theatre).
localización f. localization, localizing.
localizar v. to localize.
loco adj. insane, mad, crazy; — de **remate** stark mad; m. lunatic, insane person.
locomotor adj. locomotive.
locomotora f. locomotive.
locuaz adj. loquacious, talkative.
locución f. phrase; diction.
locura f. madness, insanity.
locutor m. radio announcer.
lodazal m. muddy place; mire.
lodo m. mud; **lodoso** adj. muddy, miry.

128

logia f. lodge (*secret society*).

lógica f. logic; reasoning.

lógico adj. logical.

lograr v. to gain, obtain, accomplish; — (+ inf.) to succeed in; -se to succeed; to turn out well.

logrero m. usurer; profiteer.

logro m. profit, gain; usury; attainment; realization.

loma f. small hill; **lomerío** m. Am. group of hills.

lombriz f. earthworm.

lomo m. back (*of an animal, book, knife, etc.*); loin; ridge between two furrows; Am. hacer — to bear with patience, resign oneself.

lona f. canvas.

lonche m. Am. lunch; **lonchería** f. Am. lunchroom.

longaniza f. pork sausage.

longevidad f. longevity, long life; span of life, length of life.

longitud f. longitude; length.

longitudinal adj. longitudinal, lengthwise; **-mente** adv. longitudinally, lengthwise.

lonja f. exchange; market; slice of meat; leather strap; Am. raw hide.

lontananza f. background; **en —** in the distance, in the background.

loro m. parrot.

los def. art. m. pl. the; obj. pron. them; — que rel. pron. those which; which.

losa f. flagstone; slab; gravestone.

lote m. lot, share, part; Am. remnant lot; Am. swallow of liquor; Am. blockhead, dunce.

lotear v. Am. to subdivide into lots; Am. to divide into portions.

lotería f. lottery; raffle.

loza f. fine earthenware; crockery; — fina chinaware.

lozanía f. luxuriance (*rich foliage or growth*); vigor.

lozano adj. luxuriant; exuberant, vigorous, lusty.

lubricar[6] v. to lubricate, oil, grease.

lucero m. morning star; any bright star; star on the forehead of certain animals; splendor, brightness.

lúcido adj. lucid, clear; shining, bright.

luciente adj. shining, bright.

luciérnaga f. firefly; glowworm.

lucimiento m. splendor; brilliance; success.

lucir[13] v. irr. to shine; to excel; to illuminate; to brighten; to show off; -se to shine, be brilliant; to show off; to be successful.

lucrativo adj. lucrative, profitable.

lucro m. profit, gain.

luctuoso adj. sad, mournful, dismal.

lucha f. fight, struggle; dispute; wrestling match.

luchador m. fighter; wrestler.

luchar v. to fight; to wrestle; to struggle; to dispute.

luego adv. soon, presently; afterwards, then, next; **desde —** immediately, at once; naturally; **— de** after; **— que** as soon as; **hasta —** good-bye, so long; **— —** right away.

luengo adj. long; -s años many years.

lugar m. place; site; town; space; position, employment; time, occasion, opportunity; **dar — a** to give cause or occasion for; **hacer (or dar) —** to make room; **en — de** instead of.

lúgubre adj. mournful, gloomy.

lujo m. luxury, extravagance.

lujoso adj. luxurious; elegant; showy.

lujuria f. lust, lewdness, sensuality.

lujurioso adj. lustful, lewd, sensual.

lumbre f. fire; brightness.

luminoso adj. luminous, bright, shining.

luna f. moon; mirror, glass for mirrors.

lunar adj. lunar; m. mole; blemish, spot.

lunático adj. & m. lunatic.

lunes m. Monday; Am. hacer San Lunes to lay off on Monday.

lustre m. luster, shine; glory.

lustroso adj. lustrous, glossy, shining.

luto m. mourning; sorrow, grief.

luz f. light; clarity; hint, guidance; dar a — to give birth; to publish; **entre dos luces** at twilight.

LL

llaga f. wound; ulcer, sore.

llama f. flame; llama (a *South American beast of burden*).

llamada f. call; beckon, sign; knock; reference mark (*as an asterisk*).

llamador m. knocker (*of a door*); caller.

llamamiento m. call, calling; calling together; appeal.

llamar v. to call; to summon; to name; to invoke; **— a la puerta** to knock at the door; -se to be called, named; Am. to break one's word or promise.

llamarada f. flash; sudden flame or blaze; sudden flush, blush.

llamativo adj. showy, loud, gaudy, flashy; thirst-exciting.

llameante adj. flaming.

llana f. mason's trowel.

llanero m. Am. plainsman.

llaneza f. simplicity; frankness; sincerity; plainness.

llano adj. plain, simple; even, smooth,

level; frank; *m.* plain, flat ground.

llanta *f.* tire; tire casing; rim of a wheel; *Am.* large sunshade (*used in Peruvian markets*).

llanto *m.* crying, weeping; tears.

llanura *f.* extensive plain; prairie; evenness, flatness.

llave *f.* key; faucet; clef; — **de tuercas** wrench; — **inglesa** monkey wrench; — **maestra** master key.

llavera *f. Am.* housekeeper.

llavero *m.* key ring; key maker; keeper of the keys.

llavín *m.* small key.

llegada *f.* arrival.

llegar[7] *v.* to arrive; to reach; to amount; — **a ser** to get or come to be; — **a las manos** to come to blows; **-se** to approach, get near.

llenar *v.* to fill; to stuff; **-se** to fill up; to overeat; **-se de** to get filled with; to get covered with, spattered with.

lleno *adj.* full; *m.* fullness, completeness; **de** — totally, completely; **un** — **completo** a full house (*said of a theater*).

llenura *f.* fullness; abundance.

llevadero *adj.* bearable, tolerable.

llevar *v.* to carry; to bear; to transport; to wear; to keep (*accounts*); to charge, ask a certain price; to take, lead; — **ventaja** to be ahead, have the advantage; — **un año a** to be one year older than; — **un mes aquí** to have been here one month; — **un castigo** to suffer punishment; **-se** to carry away; **-se bien con** to get along with.

llorar *v.* to cry, weep.

lloriquear *v.* to whimper, whine, weep.

lloriqueo *m.* whimper, whining.

lloro *m.* weeping.

llorón *adj.* weeping; **sauce** — weeping willow; *m.* weeper, crybaby, whiner.

llorona *f.* weeping woman; **-s** *Am.* large spurs.

lloroso *adj.* tearful; weeping.

llovedizo *adj.* rain (*used as adj.*); **agua llovediza** rain water.

llover[2] *v. irr.* to rain, shower.

llovizna *f.* drizzle.

lloviznar *v.* to drizzle, sprinkle.

lluvia *f.* rain; shower.

lluvioso *adj.* rainy.

M

macana *f. Am.* club, cudgel, stick; *Am.* lie, absurdity, nonsense.

macarrón *m.* macaroon; **-es** macaroni.

maceta *f.* flowerpot; small mallet; stonecutter's hammer; handle of tools; *Am.* head; *adj. Am.* slow.

macilento *adj.* thin, emaciated; pale.

macizo *adj.* solid, firm; massive; *m.* massiveness; firmness; thicket; clump.

machacar[6] *v.* to pound, crush; to insist, harp on.

machacón *adj.* persistent; tenacious.

machete *m.* machete, large heavy knife; **machetazo** *m.* large machete; blow with a machete.

macho *m.* male; he-mule; hook (*of a hook and eye*); abutment; pillar; stupid fellow; sledge hammer; *Am.* **pararle a uno el** — to halt or repress a person; *adj.* masculine, male; strong.

machucar[6] *v.* to pound, beat, bruise; *Am.* to crush; *Am.* to break (*a horse*).

machucón *m.* smash; bruise.

madeja *f.* skein; mass of hair; limp, listless person.

madera *f.* wood; timber; lumber; **maderero** *m.* lumberman, lumber dealer.

maderaje *m.* timber, lumber; timber work; woodwork.

maderamen *m.* timber; timber work; woodwork.

madero *m.* beam; plank; timber, piece of lumber; blockhead, dunce.

madrastra *f.* stepmother.

madre *f.* mother; womb; root, origin; river bed; **salirse de** — to overflow (*said of rivers*).

madrepeña *f. Am.* moss.

madreperla *f.* mother-of-pearl.

madreselva *f.* honeysuckle.

madriguera *f.* burrow; den, lair.

madrileño *adj.* Madrilenian, from or pertaining to Madrid; *m.* Madrilenian.

madrina *f.* godmother; bridesmaid; sponsor; prop; strap for yoking two horses; leading mare; *Am.* small herd of tame cattle (*used for leading wild cattle*).

madrugada *f.* dawn; early morning; **de** — at daybreak.

madrugador *m.* early riser.

madrugar[7] *v.* to rise early; to be ahead of others.

madurar *v.* to mature; to ripen.

madurez *f.* maturity; ripeness.

maduro *adj.* ripe; mature; prudent, wise; *Am.* bruised, sore.

maestría *f.* mastery; great skill.

maestro *m.* master, teacher; chief craftsman; *adj.* master; masterly, skilful; **llave maestra** master key; **obra maestra** masterpiece.

magia *f.* magic; charm.

mágico *adj.* magic; *m.* magician.

magín *m.* imagination, fancy.

magisterio *m.* teaching profession.

magistrado *m.* magistrate, judge.
magistral *adj.* masterly; masterful; authoritative.
magnánimo *adj.* magnanimous, noble, generous.
magnético *adj.* magnetic; attractive.
magnificencia *f.* magnificence, splendor.
magnífico *adj.* magnificent, splendid.
magnitud *f.* magnitude, greatness.
mago *m.* magician, wizard; **los tres Reyes Magos** the Three Wise Men.
magra *f.* slice of ham.
magro *adj.* lean.
maguey *m.* maguey, century plant.
magullar *v.* to bruise; to maul; to mangle; *Am.* to crumple.
mahometano *adj.* & *m.* Mohammedan.
maíz *m.* corn; **maizal** *m.* cornfield.
majada *f.* sheepfold; dung, manure; *Am.* flock of sheep or goats.
majadería *f.* foolishness, nonsense.
majadero *adj.* foolish; bothersome.
majar *v.* to pound; to crush; to bruise; to crumple; to mash; to annoy, bother.
majestad *f.* majesty; dignity.
majestuoso *adj.* majestic, stately.
majo *adj.* gaudy, showy; gaily attired; pretty; *m.* dandy; **maja** *f.* belle.
mal *m.* evil; illness; harm; wrong. *See* **malo.**
malabarista *m.* & *f.* juggler; *Am.* sly thief.
malacate *m.* hoist, hoisting machine; winch; *Am.* spindle (*for cotton*); *Am.* **parecer uno un —** to be constantly on the go, be in constant motion.
malandanza *f.* misfortune.
malaventura *f.* misfortune, disaster.
malazo *adj.* perverse, evil, wicked; vicious.
malbaratar *v.* to undersell, sell at a loss; to squander.
malcontento *adj.* discontented; *m.* malcontent, troublemaker.
malcriado *adj.* ill-bred, rude.
maldad *f.* badness, evil, wickedness.
maldecir[27, 52] *v. irr.* to curse; to damn.
maldición *f.* curse.
maldispuesto *adj.* unwilling, not inclined.
maldito *p.p. of* **maldecir** & *adj.* cursed; wicked; damned; *Am.* tricky; *Am.* bold, boastful.
maleante *m.* crook, rogue, rascal, villain.
malecón *m.* mole, dike.
maledicencia *f.* slander.
maleficio *m.* spell, charm, witchery.
maléfico *adj.* evil, harmful.
malestar *m.* indisposition; slight illness; discomfort.

maleta *f.* travelling bag; suitcase; *Am.* bundle of clothes; *Am.* hump (*on the back*); *Am.* saddlebag; *Am.* rogue, rascal; *Am.* lazy fellow.
maletín *m.* small valise, satchel.
malevo *adj. Am.* bad, wicked.
malévolo *adj.* bad, evil, wicked.
maleza *f.* underbrush; thicket; weeds.
malgastar *v.* to squander, waste.
malhechor *m.* malefactor, evildoer, criminal.
malhora *f. Am.* trouble, misfortune.
malhumorado *adj.* ill-humored.
malicia *f.* malice; wickedness; shrewdness; suspicion; *Am.* bit of brandy or cognac added to another drink.
maliciar *v.* to suspect.
malicioso *adj.* malicious; wicked; shrewd; suspicious.
maligno *adj.* malign, malignant; pernicious, harmful.
malmandado *adj.* disobedient; stubborn.
mal(o) *adj.* bad, evil; wicked; ill; difficult; *Am.* **a la mala** treacherously; *Am.* **de malas** by force; **estar de malas** to be out of luck; **por la mala** unwillingly, by force; **venir de malas** to come with evil intentions; **mal** *adv.* badly; poorly; wrongly.
malograr *v.* to waste, lose; **-se** to turn out badly; to fail.
malón *m.* mean trick; *Am.* surprise Indian raid; *Am.* tin-pan serenade, boisterous surprise party.
malpagar[7] *v.* to underpay, pay poorly.
malparto *m.* miscarriage, abortion.
malquerencia *f.* aversion, dislike, ill will.
malsano *adj.* unhealthy; sickly.
malta *f.* malt.
maltratar *v.* to treat badly; to misuse, abuse.
maltrato *m.* mistreatment, abuse.
maltrecho *adj.* battered, bruised, injured.
malvado *adj.* wicked; malicious.
malversación *f.* graft, corruption, misuse of public funds.
malversar *v.* to misuse (*funds in one's trust*); to embezzle.
malla *f.* mesh; coat of mail; *Am.* species of potato; **hacer —** to knit.
mamá *f.* mamma.
mamada *f.* suck, sucking.
mamar *v.* to suckle; to suck; to gorge; **-se** *Am.* to get drunk; *Am.* to go back on one's promise; *Am.* to fold up, crack up; **-se a uno** to get the best of someone, deceive someone;

Am. to kill someone.

mamífero *m.* mammal; *adj.* mammalian, of mammals.

mamón *adj.* suckling; *m.* suckling (*very young animal or child*); shoot, sucker (*of a tree*); *Am.* cherimoya (*tree and fruit*); *Am.* papaya (*tree and fruit*); *Am.* a kind of cake.

mampara *f.* screen.

mampostería *f.* masonry, stone masonry.

manada *f.* herd; drove; pack; flock.

manantial *m.* spring; source, origin.

manar *v.* to spring, flow (from); to abound.

manaza *f.* large hand.

manazo *m. Am.* slap. *See* **manotazo.**

mancarrón *m.* one-armed or one-handed man; cripple; old nag; *Am.* crude, clumsy fellow; *Am.* disabled workman; *Am.* dike, small dam.

mancebo *m.* youth, young man; bachelor.

mancera *f.* handle of a plough.

mancilla *f.* stain, spot; dishonor.

manco *adj.* one-armed; one-handed; maimed; lame (*referring to an arm or the front leg of an animal*); faulty, defective; *m. Am.* nag.

mancha *f.* spot, stain, blemish; *Am.* cloud, swarm; *Am.* roving herd of cattle.

manchar *v.* to stain, soil, spot; to tarnish.

manchego *adj.* of or belonging to La Mancha (*region of Spain*); *m.* inhabitant of la Mancha.

manchón *m.* large stain; large patch.

mandadero *m.* messenger, errand boy.

mandado *m.* command, order; errand; *p.p. of* **mandar; bien — well-behaved; mal — ill-behaved.**

mandamiento *m.* command, order; writ; commandment.

mandar *v.* to command, order; to send; to bequeath, will; to rule; *Am.* to throw, hurl; **— hacer** to have made, order; *Am.* **— una bofetada** to give a slap; *Am.* **— una pedrada** to throw a stone; **-se** *Am.* to be impudent; **-se mudar** *Am.* to go away.

mandatario *m.* attorney, representative; *Am.* magistrate, chief.

mandato *m.* mandate; order, command.

mandíbula *f.* jaw, jawbone.

mando *m.* command, authority, power.

mandón *adj.* bossy, domineering; *m.* bossy person; *Am.* boss or foreman of a mine; *Am.* race starter.

maneador *m. Am.* hobble, leather lasso

(*for the legs of an animal*); *Am.* whip; *Am.* halter.

manear *v.* to hobble, lasso, tie the legs of (*an animal*); **-se** *Am.* to get tangled up.

manecilla *f.* small hand; hand of a watch or clock.

manejable *adj.* manageable.

manejar *v.* to manage, handle; to drive (*a car*); **-se** to move about, get around (*after an illness or accident*); *Am.* to behave oneself.

manejo *m.* handling; management; trick, intrigue.

manera *f.* manner, way, mode; side opening in a skirt; front opening in breeches; **-s** customs; manners, behavior; **a — de** (*or* **a la — de**) like, in the style of; **de — que** so that; **sobre —** exceedingly; extremely.

manga *f.* sleeve; bag; hose (*for watering*); body of troops; *Am.* multitude, herd, swarm; *Am.* cattle chute (*narrow passageway*); *Am.* corral; **— de agua** waterspout, whirlwind over the ocean; *Am.* **— de hule** raincape; **por angas o por -s** by hook or crook, in one way or another.

mangana *f.* lariat, lasso.

manganeso *m.* manganese.

mango *m.* handle; *Am.* mango (*tropical tree and its fruit*).

manguera *f.* hose (*for water*); waterspout; *Am.* large corral (*for livestock*).

manguito *m.* muff; knitted half-sleeve (*worn on the forearm*); oversleeve.

maní *m. Am.* peanut; **manicero** *m. Am.* peanut vendor.

manía *f.* mania, frenzy; craze, whim.

maniatar *v.* to tie the hands; to handcuff; to hobble (*an animal*).

maniático *m.* crank, queer fellow; *adj.* cranky, queer, odd.

manicomio *m.* insane asylum.

manicura *f.* manicure; manicurist.

manicurar *v.* to manicure.

manido *adj.* rotting; *Am.* trite, commonplace.

manifestación *f.* manifestation; demonstration.

manifestar[1] *v. irr.* to manifest; to show.

manifiesto *adj.* manifest, clear, plain; *m.* manifesto, public declaration; customhouse manifest.

manigua *f. Am.* Cuban jungle or thicket; *Am.* **coger —** to get feverish; *Am.* **irse a la —** to rise up in rebellion.

manija *f.* handle; crank; fetter.

manilla *f.* small hand; bracelet; **-s de hierro** handcuffs.

132

maniobra *f.* maneuver; operation.

maniobrar *v.* to maneuver.

manipulación *f.* manipulation.

manipular *v.* to manipulate, handle.

maniquí *m.* manikin, model, dummy, figure of a person; puppet.

manivela *f.* crank.

manjar *m.* dish, food; choice bit of food.

mano *f.* hand; forefoot; clock hand; coat of paint or varnish; quire (25 *sheets*) of paper; *Am.* adventure, mishap; *Am.* handful; — **de obra** workmanship; labor; **a** — at hand; by hand; *Am.* **estamos a** — we are even, we are quits; *Am.* **doblar las -s** to give up; **ser** — to be first (*in a game*); to lead (*in a game*); **venir a las -s** to come to blows.

manojo *m.* handful; bunch.

manopla *f.* gauntlet; heavy glove; huge hand.

manosear *v.* to handle, touch, feel with the hand; *Am.* to fondle, pet, caress.

manotada *f.* slap, blow; sweep of the hand; *Am.* handful, fistful; **manotazo** *m.* slap.

manotear *v.* to gesticulate; to strike with the hands; *Am.* to embezzle, steal; *Am.* to snatch away (*what is given*).

mansalva: a — without danger or risk; treacherously; **matar a** — to kill without warning or without giving a person a chance to defend himself.

mansedumbre *f.* meekness; gentleness.

mansión *f.* sojourn, stay; abode, dwelling.

manso *adj.* meek; mild, gentle; tame; *Am.* cultivated (*plant*), civilized (*Indian*); *m.* leading sheep, goat, or ox.

manta *f.* blanket; large shawl; tossing in a blanket; *Am.* coarse cotton cloth; *Am.* poncho; *Am.* — **mojada** dull person, dunce; **darle a uno una** — to toss someone in a blanket.

mantear *v.* to toss (*someone*) in a blanket.

manteca *f.* fat; lard; butter; *Am.* — **de cacao** cocoa butter; *Am.* — **de coco** coconut oil; **mantequera** *f.* churn; butter dish; woman who makes or sells butter.

mantecado *m.* ice cream.

mantel *m.* tablecloth; altar cloth; *Am.* **estar de -es largos** to dine in style.

mantener[45] *v. irr.* to maintain; to support; to sustain; to defend; **-se** to continue, remain; to support oneself; **-se firme** to remain firm; **-se quieto** to stay or keep quiet.

mantenimiento *m.* maintenance, support; sustenance; livelihood.

mantequilla *f.* butter; **mantequillería** *f. Am.* creamery, dairy (*for making butter*).

mantilla *f.* mantilla (*Spanish veil or scarf for the head*); saddlecloth.

manto *m.* mantle, cloak; cape; large mantilla; mantel, mantelpiece.

mantón *m.* large shawl; — **de Manila** embroidered silk shawl.

manuable *adj.* handy, easy to handle.

manual *adj.* manual; handy; *m.* manual, handbook.

manubrio *m.* crank; handle.

manufacturar *v.* to manufacture.

manufacturero *adj.* manufacturing; *m.* manufacturer.

manuscrito *adj.* written by hand; *m.* manuscript.

manutención *f.* maintenance; support; conservation.

manzana *f.* apple; block of houses; *Am.* Adam's apple; **manzano** *m.* apple tree.

maña *f.* skill, knack; cunning; **malas -s** bad tricks or habits.

mañana *f.* morning; *Am.* **media** — mid-morning snack; *adv.* tomorrow, in the near future; **pasado** — day after tomorrow; **muy de** — very early in the morning; *m.* morrow; **mañanitas** *f. pl. Am.* popular song sung early in the morning to celebrate a birthday, saint's day, etc.

mañanero *m.* early riser; *adj.* early rising; **mañanista** *m. & f. Am.* procrastinator, one who puts things off until tomorrow.

mañero *adj.* astute, artful, clever; *Am.* tricky; *Am.* shy (*animal*); *Am.* indolent, lazy (*child*).

mañoso *adj.* skilful; clever; sly; tricky; *Am.* slow, lazy; *Am.* greedy, gluttonous (*child*).

mapa *m.* map, chart.

mapache *m. Am.* raccoon.

mapurite, mapurito *m. Am.* skunk. See **zorrino, zorrillo.**

máquina *f.* machine; engine; — **de coser** sewing machine; — **de escribir** typewriter.

maquinación *f.* machination, scheming, plotting; plot, scheme.

maquinador *m.* schemer, plotter.

maquinal *adj.* mechanical, automatic; **-mente** *adv.* mechanically, automatically, in a mechanical manner.

maquinar *v.* to plot, scheme.

maquinaria *f.* machinery; mechanism; mechanics.

maquinista *m.* engineer, locomotive

engineer; machinist; mechanic.

mar *m. & f.* sea; — **alta** rough sea; — **llena** high tide (*see* **pleamar**); — **de fondo** swell; **a -es** abundantly; **baja** — low tide; **en alta** — on the high seas; **la** — **de cosas** a lot of things.

maraña *f.* tangle; snarl; thicket; maze; plot, intrigue.

maravedí *m.* maravedi (*an old Spanish coin*).

maravilla *f.* wonder, marvel; marigold; **a las mil -s** wonderfully, perfectly.

maravillar *v.* to astonish, dazzle; **-se** to wonder, marvel.

maravilloso *adj.* marvellous, wonderful.

marbete *m.* label, stamp; baggage tag or check.

marca *f.* mark, stamp; sign; brand, make; gauge, rule; march, frontier province; — **de fábrica** trademark; **de** — of excellent quality.

marcar[6] *v.* to mark, stamp, brand; to note, observe.

marcial *adj.* martial, warlike; frank, abrupt.

marco *m.* frame; mark (*German coin*); mark (*unit of weight, equal to 8 ounces*).

marcha *f.* march; course, progress; speed; gait; running, functioning; movement of a watch.

marchamo *m.* customhouse mark; *Am.* tax on each slaughtered animal.

marchante *m.* merchant, dealer; customer, regular client.

marchar *v.* to march, mark step; to walk; to parade; to run (*said of machinery*); **-se** to go away.

marchitar *v.* to wither; **-se** to wither; to fade; to shrivel up.

marchito *adj.* withered; faded; shrivel-ed up.

marea *f.* tide; *Am.* sea fog.

mareado *adj.* seasick; dizzy.

marear *v.* to navigate, sail; to annoy, upset (*a person*); **-se** to get sea-sick, nauseated.

mareo *m.* seasickness; nausea; vexa-tion, annoyance.

marfil *m.* ivory; *Am.* fine-toothed comb.

margarita *f.* marguerite, daisy; pearl.

margen *m. & f.* margin, border; river bank; **dar** — **a** to give an occasion to.

maricón *adj.* sissy, effeminate; *m.* sissy.

marido *m.* husband.

marina *f.* sea coast, shore; marine, fleet; navy; seamanship; seascape; — **de guerra** navy; — **mercante** mer-chant marine.

marinero *m.* mariner, seaman, sailor.

marino *adj.* marine; *m.* mariner, sea-man, sailor.

mariposa *f.* butterfly; moth; *Am.* blind-man's buff (*a game*).

mariscal *m.* marshal; blacksmith; — **de campo** field marshal.

marisco *m.* shellfish.

marítimo *adj.* maritime, marine.

marmita *f.* kettle, boiler, teakettle.

mármol *m.* marble.

marmóreo *adj.* marble, of marble, like marble.

maroma *f.* rope; *Am.* somersault; *Am.* acrobatic performance; *Am.* sudden change of political views; **andar en la** — to walk the tightrope; **maro-mero** *m. Am.* acrobat.

marqués *m.* marquis.

marquesa *f.* marquise; *Am.* couch.

marrano *m.* pig, hog; filthy person.

marrazo *m. Am.* bayonet, dagger.

marrullero *adj.* sly, wily.

martes *m.* Tuesday; — **de carnes-tolendas** Shrove Tuesday (*Tuesday before Lent*).

martillar *v.* to hammer, pound.

martillo *m.* hammer.

martinete *m.* pile driver; drop hammer; hammer of a piano.

mártir *m. & f.* martyr.

martirio *m.* martyrdom; torture, tor-ment.

martirizar[9] *v.* to martyr; to torture, torment.

marzo *m.* March.

mas *conj.* but.

más *adj.* more; most; *adv.* more; most; plus; — **bien** rather; — **de** more than, over; — **que** more than; **no . . . —** **que** only; **a — de** in addition to; **a lo** — at the most; **está de — it is super-fluous, unnecessary; *Am.* no — only; *Am.* no quiero — nada (*instead of* no quiero nada —) I don't want anything more.

masa *f.* mass; volume; crowd; dough, paste; mortar; — **coral** glee club, choral society; **agarrarle a uno con las manos en la** — to catch some-one in the act; **masilla** *f.* putty.

masaje *m.* massage.

mascada *f.* chewing; *Am.* mouthful; *Am.* chew or quid of tobacco; *Am.* reprimand, scolding; *Am.* silk hand-kerchief, scarf.

mascar[6] *v.* to chew.

máscara *f.* mask; **-s** masquerade; *m. & f.* masquerader; **mascarada** *f.* masquerade.

masculino *adj.* masculine.

mascullar *v.* to mumble; to munch.

mason *m.* mason, freemason; **masoneria** *f.* masonry, freemasonry.
masticar[6] *v.* to chew.
mástil *m.* mast; post.
mastín *m.* mastiff.
mastuerzo *m.* nasturtium; simpleton, fool.
mata *f.* shrub, plant, bush; grove; clump of trees; *Am.* thicket, jungle; **— de pelo** head of hair.
matadero *m.* slaughterhouse; hard work.
matador *m.* killer, murderer; bullfighter who kills the bull.
matanza *f.* massacre, butchery; slaughter of livestock; *Am.* slaughterhouse.
matar *v.* to kill; to murder; **-se** to commit suicide; to overwork; **-se con alguien** to fight with somebody.
matasanos *m.* quack, quack doctor.
mate *m.* checkmate (*winning move in chess*); *Am.* Paraguayan tea (*used also in Argentina and Uruguay*); *Am.* teapot (*for mate*), any small pot; *Am.* bald head; *adj.* unpolished, dull (*surface*).
matear *v.* to plant seeds or shoots; to hunt among the bushes; *Am.* to drink mate; *Am.* to checkmate (*make the winning move in chess*).
matemáticas *f. pl.* mathematics.
matemático *adj.* mathematical; *m.* mathematician.
materia *f.* matter; material; subject; pus; **— prima** (*or* **primera —**) raw material.
material *adj.* material; rude, coarse; *m.* ingredient; material; equipment; *Am.* **de —** made of adobe.
maternal *adj.* maternal.
maternidad *f.* maternity, motherhood.
materno *adj.* maternal.
matinal *adj.* morning, of the morning.
matiné *m. Am.* matinée.
matiz *m.* tint, shade, color, hue; shading.
matizar[9] *v.* to blend (*colors*); to tint; to shade, tone down.
matón *m.* bully.
matorral *m.* thicket.
matoso *adj.* bushy; weedy, full of weeds.
matrero *adj.* astute, shrewd; cunning, sly; *m. Am.* trickster, swindler; *Am.* bandit, outlaw, cattle thief.
matrícula *f.* register, list; matriculation, registration; certificate of registration.
matricular *v.* to matriculate, enroll, register.
matrimonio *m.* matrimony, marriage; married couple.
matriz *f.* matrix, mold, form; womb;

screw nut; *adj.* main, principal, first.
matungo *m. Am.* nag, old worn-out horse.
matutino *adj.* morning, of the morning.
maullar *v.* to mew.
maullido, maúllo *m.* mew.
máxima *f.* maxim, rule; proverb.
máxime *adj.* principally, especially.
máximo *adj. & m.* maximum.
maya *f.* daisy; May queen; *m. & f.* Maya, Mayan Indian; *m.* Mayan language.
mayo *m.* May; Maypole; *Am.* Mayo Indian (*from Sonora, Mexico*); *Am.* language of the Mayo Indian.
mayonesa *f.* mayonnaise; dish served with mayonnaise.
mayor *adj.* greater; larger; older; greatest; largest; oldest; main; major; high (*altar, mass*); *m.* major; chief; **-es** elders; ancestors; **— de edad** of age; **por —** (*or* **al por —**) wholesale; *f.* major premise (*of a syllogism*).
mayoral *m.* head shepherd; stagecoach driver; foreman; overseer, boss.
mayorazgo *m.* primogeniture (*right of inheritance by the first-born*); firstborn son and heir; family estate left to the eldest son.
mayordomo *m.* majordomo, steward, butler; manager of an estate.
mayorear *v. Am.* to wholesale, sell at wholesale.
mayoreo *m. Am.* wholesale.
mayoría *f.* majority.
mayorista *m. Am.* wholesale dealer.
mazmorra *f.* dungeon.
mazo *m.* mallet; sledge hammer; bunch, handful.
mazorca *f.* ear of corn; *Am.* tyrannical government; *Am.* cruel torture (*imposed by tyrants*).
me *obj. pron.* me; to me; for me; myself.
mecánico *adj.* mechanical; *m.* mechanic, machinist, repairman; driver, chauffeur.
mecanismo *m.* mechanism.
mecanografía *f.* stenography, typewriting.
mecanógrafo *m.* stenographer, typist.
mecate *m. Am.* rope, cord.
mecedor *m.* swing; *adj.* swinging, rocking.
mecedora *f.* rocking chair.
mecer[10] *v.* to swing, rock, sway; to shake.
mecha *f.* wick; lock of hair; fuse; strip of salt pork or bacon (*for larding meat*); *Am.* tip of a whip; *Am.* scare, fright; *Am.* fib; *Am.* jest, joke; *Am.* trifle,

worthless thing.

mechar v. to lard (*meat or fowl*).

mechero m. lamp burner; gas jet; candlestick socket; pocket lighter; large wick; *Am.* disheveled hair; *Am.* joker, jester.

mechón m. large wick; large lock of hair.

medalla f. medal.

médano m. dune, sand hill, sand bank; *Am.* sandy marshland.

media f. stocking; *Am.* — **corta** (*or* — —) sock.

mediación f. mediation.

mediador m. mediator.

mediados : a — **de** about the middle of.

medianero m. mediator; go-between; adj. mediating; intermediate; **pared medianera** partition wall.

medianía f. mediocrity; average; middle ground; moderate circumstances; moderation; *Am.* partition wall.

mediano adj. medium; moderate; middle-sized; average; mediocre.

medianoche f. midnight.

mediante adj. intervening; **Dios** — God willing; prep. by means of, through, with the help of.

mediar v. to mediate, intervene; to intercede; to arrive at, or be in, the middle.

medible adj. measurable.

medicamento m. medicament, medicine.

medicastro m. quack, quack doctor.

medicina f. medicine.

medicinar v. to doctor, treat, prescribe medicine for; -se to take medicine.

medición f. measurement; measuring.

médico m. doctor, physician; adj. medical.

medida f. measure; measurement; gauge, rule; — **para áridos** dry measure; a — **del deseo** according to one's desire; a — **que** as, in proportion as; **al same time as.**

medio adj. half; middle; intermediate; medium, average; **media noche** midnight; **hacer una cosa a medias** to do something halfway; **ir a medias** to go halves; adv. half, not completely; m. middle; means, way; medium; environment; -s means, resources; **meterse de por** — to intervene, meddle in a dispute.

mediocre adj. mediocre; **mediocridad** f. mediocrity.

mediodía m. midday, noon; south.

medioeval, medieval adj. medieval.

medir[5] v. irr. to measure; to scan (ver-

ses); *Am.* — **las calles** to walk the streets, be out of a job; -se to measure one's words or actions; *Am.* -se con otro to try one's strength or ability against another; to fight with another.

meditación f. meditation.

meditar v. to meditate; to muse.

medrar v. to flourish, thrive; to prosper.

medroso adj. timid, faint-hearted; fearful, dreadful.

médula f. marrow; pith; — **oblongada** medulla oblongata (*the posterior part of the brain tapering off into the spinal cord*).

megáfono m. megaphone.

mejicano adj. Mexican; m. Mexican; the Aztec language; inhabitant of Mexico City. Also **mexicano**.

mejilla f. cheek.

mejor adj. better; **el** — the best; adv. better; **a lo** — suddenly, unexpectedly; **tanto** — so much the better.

mejora f. betterment; improvement.

mejoramiento m. improvement.

mejorar v. to better, improve; to get better, recover; -se to get better, recover.

mejoría f. betterment, improvement; superiority.

melado adj. honey-colored; m. sugarcane syrup; honey cake.

melancolía f. melancholy, gloom.

melancólico adj. melancholy, gloomy.

melaza f. molasses.

melena f. mane.

melindre m. affectation; affected act or gesture; whim; fritter; marzipan (*sweetmeat made of almond paste*).

melindroso adj. affected; too particular, finicky, fussy.

melocotón m. peach; **melocotonero** m. peach tree.

melodía f. melody; **melodioso** adj. melodious.

melón m. melon; cantaloupe; muskmelon; melon vine.

melosidad f. sweetness; softness, gentleness.

meloso adj. honeyed; soft, sweet; m. *Am.* honey-voiced person; *Am.* over-affectionate person.

mella f. nick; dent; **hacer** — to make a dent or impression; to cause pain, worry, or suffering.

mellar v. to notch; to nick; to dent; to impair, damage.

mellizo adj. & m. twin.

membrete m. heading; letterhead; memorandum.

membrillo m. quince (*tree and its fruit*).

membrudo *adj.* sinewy, robust, strong, muscular.

memorable *adj.* memorable, notable.

memorándum *m.* memorandum, note; memorandum book, notebook.

memoria *f.* memory; remembrance; reminiscence; memoir, note, account; memorandum; **de** — by heart; **hacer** — to remember, recollect; — **de gallo** poor memory; **-s** regards; memoirs.

memorial *m.* memorandum book; memorial, brief, petition.

mención *f.* mention.

mencionar *v.* to mention.

mendigar[7] *v.* to beg; to ask alms.

mendigo *m.* beggar.

mendrugo *m.* crumb of bread.

menear *v.* to move, shake, stir; to wiggle; to wag; **-se** to hustle about; to wag; to wiggle.

meneo *m.* shaking; swaying; wagging; wiggle; wiggling.

menester *m.* need; job, occupation; **-es** bodily needs; implements, tools; tasks, chores; **ser** — to be necessary.

menesteroso *adj.* needy, in want.

mengua *f.* diminution, decrease; waning; poverty, want; discredit.

menguar[9] *v.* to diminish, decrease; to wane.

menjurje *m.* stuff, mixture.

menor *adj.* smaller, lesser, younger; smallest, least, youngest; minor; *m. & f.* — **de edad** minor; *m.* minor (*music*); Minorite, Franciscan; *f.* minor premise (*of a syllogism*); **por** — (**al por** —) at retail; in small quantities.

menoría = **minoría**

menos *adv.* less; least; except; *adj. & pron.* less, least; *m.* minus; — **de** (*or* — **que**) less than; **a lo** — (**al** —, *or* **por lo** —) at least; **a** — **que** unless; **echar de** — to miss, feel or notice the absence of; **no puede** — **de hacerlo** he cannot help doing it; **venir a** — to decline; to become weak or poor.

menoscabar *v.* to diminish, lessen; to impair, damage; — **la honra de** to undermine the reputation of.

menoscabo *m.* impairment; damage; diminution, lessening.

menospreciar *v.* to despise, scorn; to underestimate.

menosprecio *m.* scorn, contempt; underestimation.

mensaje *m.* message.

mensajero *m.* messenger.

menstruo *m.* menstruation.

mensual *adj.* monthly.

mensualidad *f.* monthly allowance; monthly payment.

mensurable *adj.* measurable.

menta *f.* mint; peppermint; *Am.* rumor, hearsay; *Am.* **por -s** by hearsay; *Am.* **persona de** — famous person.

mentado *adj.* famous; *p.p.* mentioned.

mental *adj.* mental.

mentalidad *f.* mentality.

mentar[1] *v. irr.* to mention; to call, name.

mente *f.* mind; intellect.

mentecato *adj.* foolish, simple; *m.* fool.

mentir[3] *v. irr.* to lie, tell lies.

mentira *f.* lie, falsehood, fib; white spot on the fingernails.

mentiroso *adj.* lying; deceptive, false; *m.* liar, fibber; **mentirosillo** *m.* little fibber.

mentís: **dar un** — to give the lie (to).

mentón *m.* chin.

menú *m.* menu.

menudear *v.* to occur frequently; to repeat over and over; to fall incessantly (*as rain, stones, projectiles, etc.*); to tell in detail; *Am.* to retail, sell at retail; *Am.* to meet together often.

menudeo *m.* retail; **vender al** — to retail, sell at retail.

menudo *adj.* minute, small; insignificant; exact, detailed; **dinero** — change; **a** — often; **por** — in detail; retail; *m.* entrails, "innards"; change, small coins.

meñique *adj.* tiny, wee; **dedo** — little finger.

meollo *m.* marrow; pith; kernel; substance; brain; brains.

meple *m. Am.* maple.

merca *f.* purchase.

mercachifle *m.* peddler, vendor; cheap merchant; cheap fellow.

mercader *m.* trader, merchant.

mercadería *f.* merchandise; trade.

mercado *m.* market; mart.

mercancía *f.* merchandise; goods.

mercantil *adj.* mercantile, commercial.

mercar[6] *v.* to purchase, buy.

merced *f.* favor; present, gift; mercy; **Vuestra Merced** Your Honor; **a** — **de** at the mercy of; at the expense of.

mercería *f.* notions (*pins, buttons, etc.*); notions store; *Am.* drygoods store.

mercurio *m.* mercury; quicksilver.

merecedor *adj.* worthy, deserving.

merecer[13] *v. irr.* to deserve.

merecido *adj. & p.p.* deserved; *m.* deserved punishment.

merecimiento *m.* merit.

merendar[1] *v. irr.* to have an afternoon

snack or refreshment; *Am.* -se uno a alguien to fleece or skin someone (*in a game or business deal*); to kill someone.

merendero *m.* lunchroom.

meridional *adj.* southern; *m.* southerner.

meridiano *adj. & m.* meridian.

merienda *f.* light afternoon meal; afternoon refreshments.

mérito *m.* merit; de — notable.

merito *dim. of* mero.

meritorio *adj.* meritorious, worthy, deserving; *m.* employee without salary (*learning trade or profession*).

merluza *f.* hake (*species of codfish*); drunken state.

merma *f.* reduction, decrease.

mermar *v.* to dwindle; to decrease, reduce.

mermelada *f.* marmalade.

mero *adj.* mere, pure; *Am.* exact, real; la mera verdad the real truth; *adv. Am.* very, very same, exactly; *Am.* soon; *Am.* only; *Am.* una mera de las tres only one of the three; *Am.* ya — (*or* merito) very soon; *Am.* allí — (*or* merito) right there; *m.* species of perch; *Am.* species of thrush.

merodear *v.* to rove in search of plunder.

mes *m.* month.

mesa *f.* table; executive board; staircase landing; mesa, plateau; levantar la — to clear the table; poner la — to set the table; *Am.* quitar la — to clear the table.

mesada *f.* monthly salary or allowance.

mesarse *v.* to tear (*one's hair or beard*).

mesero *m. Am.* waiter.

meseta *f.* plateau; staircase landing.

mesón *m.* inn (*usually a large one-story shelter for men and pack animals*).

mesonero *m.* innkeeper.

mestizo *adj.* half-breed; hybrid; perro — mongrel dog; *m.* mestizo, half-breed.

mesura *f.* moderation; composure; dignity; politeness.

mesurado *adj.* moderate, temperate; dignified.

meta *f.* goal; objective.

metáfora *f.* metaphor.

metal *m.* metal.

metálico *adj.* metallic, metal; *m.* specie, coined money; cash in coin.

metalurgia *f.* metallurgy.

metate *m. Am.* flat stone (*used for grinding corn, etc.*).

meteoro *m.* meteor.

meteorología *f.* meteorology; **meteoro-**

lógico *adj.* meteorological; oficina meteorológica weather bureau.

meter *v.* to put (in); to get (in); to insert; to smuggle; to make (*noise, trouble, etc.*); to cause (*fear*); *Am.* to strike (*a blow*); *Am.* -le to hurry up; -se to meddle, interfere; to plunge (into); -se monja (*Am.* -se de monja*) to become a nun; -se con to pick a quarrel with.

metódico *adj.* methodical.

método *m.* method.

métrico *adj.* metric.

metro *m.* meter; subway.

metrópoli *f.* metropolis.

metropolitano *adj.* metropolitan; *m.* archbishop.

mexicano = mejicano. (*Pronounced identically*).

mezcal *m. Am.* mescal (*a species of maguey and an alcoholic beverage made from it*).

mezcla *f.* mixture; mortar; mixed cloth; **mezclilla** *f.* mixed cloth (*generally black and white*); tweed.

mezclar *v.* to mix, blend; -se to mix, mingle; to meddle.

mezcolanza *f.* jumble, mess, mixture.

mezquindad *f.* meanness; stinginess; dire poverty.

mezquino *adj.* poor, needy; mean, stingy; meager; small, tiny; *m. Am.* wart (*usually on a finger*).

mi *adj.* my.

mí *pers. pron.* (*used after prep.*) me, myself.

miaja = migaja.

miau *m.* mew.

microbio *m.* microbe.

micrófono *m.* microphone

microscopio *m.* microscope; **microscópico** *adj.* microscopic.

miedo *m.* fear; dread; tener — to be afraid.

miedoso *adj.* afraid, fearful, timid.

miel *m.* honey; molasses.

miembro *m.* member; limb.

mientes *f. pl.* thought, mind; parar — en to consider, reflect on; traer a las — to recall; venírsele a uno a las — to occur to one, come to one's mind.

mientras *conj.* while; — que while; — tanto in the meantime, meanwhile; — más . . . — menos . . . the more . . . the less . . .

miércoles *m.* Wednesday.

mies *f.* ripe grain; harvest; -es fields of grain.

miga *f.* crumb; soft part of bread; substance; -s crumbs; fried crumbs of bread; **hacer buenas -s** (*or* **malas -s**) **con** to get along well (*or* badly) with.

migaja *f.* crumb; bit, fragment, small particle.

migración *f.* migration.

milagro *m.* miracle; wonder.

milagroso *adj.* miraculous.

milicia *f.* militia; military science; military profession.

militar *adj.* military; *m.* soldier, military man; *v.* to serve in the army; to militate, fight (against).

milpa *f. Am.* cornfield.

milla *f.* mile.

millar *m.* thousand; **-es** thousands, a great number.

millón *m.* million; **millonario** *adj.* & *m.* millionaire; **millonésimo** *adj.* & *m.* millionth.

mimar *v.* to pamper, spoil, humor; to pet.

mimbre *m.* wicker; **mimbrera** *f.* willow.

mímico *adj.* mimic.

mimo *m.* pampering, caress; coaxing.

mimoso *adj.* tender, sensitive; delicate; finicky, fussy.

mina *f.* mine; source; fortune.

minar *v.* to mine; to undermine; to sow with explosive mines.

mineral *m.* mineral; mine; wealth, fortune; *adj.* mineral.

minería *f.* mining; miners.

minero *m.* miner; wealth, fortune; source; *adj.* mining; **compañía minera** mining company.

miniatura *f.* miniature.

mínimo *adj.* least, smallest; *m.* minimum.

minino *m.* kitten, kitty, pussy.

ministerio *m.* ministry; administration, ministering; portfolio (*office of a cabinet member*); minister's office.

ministrar *v.* to minister; to give (*money, aid, etc.*).

ministro *m.* minister; cabinet member; officer of justice.

minoría *f.* minority.

minoridad *f.* minority (*in age*).

minucioso *adj.* minute, detailed; scrupulous.

minúsculo *adj.* small; **letra minúscula** small letter.

minuta *f.* minutes; memorandum; first draft (*of a contract, deed, etc.*); memorandum list; lawyer's bill; *Am.* **a la —** breaded and fried (*said of meat or fish*).

minuto *m.* minute; **minutero** *m.* minute hand.

mío *poss. adj.* my, of mine; *poss. pron.*

mine; *Am.* **detrás —** behind me.

miope *adj.* shortsighted, nearsighted; *m.* & *f.* nearsighted person.

mira *f.* gun sight; guiding point; intention, design; lookout; **estar a la —** **de** to be on the lookout for; to be on the alert for; **poner la — en** to fix one's eyes on; to aim at.

mirada *f.* glance, gaze, look.

mirador *m.* mirador, enclosed balcony (*commanding an extensive view*); watchtower; onlooker, spectator; *Am.* penthouse (*small house built on a roof for recreation*).

miramiento *m.* consideration, respect, regard; reverence; circumspection, prudence.

mirar *v.* to look; to glance; to behold; to see; **— por alguien** to take care of someone; ¡**mira (tú)**! look!

miríada *f.* myriad, multitude, great number.

mirlo *m.* blackbird.

mirón *m.* bystander, onlooker, spectator; *adj.* curious.

mirto *m.* myrtle.

misa *f.* mass; **— del gallo** midnight mass.

misceláneo *adj.* miscellaneous.

miserable *adj.* miserable, unhappy; forlorn; miserly, stingy; mean.

miseria *f.* misery; poverty; stinginess; bit, trifle.

misericordia *f.* mercy, compassion, pity.

misericordioso *adj.* merciful, compassionate.

mísero *adj.* miserable, unhappy; forlorn; stingy.

misión *f.* mission.

misionero *m.* missionary.

mismo *adj.* same; self, very; **ahora —** right away.

misterio *m.* mystery; secret.

misterioso *adj.* mysterious.

místico *adj.* mystical, mystic; *m.* mystic.

mitad *f.* half; middle.

mitigar *v.* to mitigate, soften, soothe.

mitin *m.* meeting.

mito *m.* myth; **mitología** *f.* mythology.

mitra *f.* bishop's miter.

mixto *adj.* mixed; half-breed; *m.* composite; match; explosive compound.

mobiliario *m.* furniture.

moblaje = **mueblaje**

mocedad *f.* youth; youthfulness; youthful prank.

mocetón *m.* tall, robust lad.

moción *f.* motion.

mocoso *adj.* sniffling; *m.* brat, scamp;

sniffling boy

mochar v. *Am.* to cut off, chop off, cut, trim (*see* desmochar); *Am.* to snitch, pilfer; *Am.* to depose, dismiss, put out of a job.

mochila f. knapsack; soldier's kit.

mocho *adj.* cut off; cropped, shorn; *Am.* maimed, mutilated; *Am.* reactionary, conservative; *m.* butt of a firearm; *Am.* nag; *Am.* cigar butt.

moda f. mode, custom, style, fashion; de — fashionable.

modelar v. to model.

modelo m. model, copy, pattern; m. & f. life model.

moderación f. moderation.

moderado *adj.* moderate; conservative.

moderar v. to moderate, temper; to regulate; to restrain.

moderno *adj.* modern.

modestia f. modesty.

modesto *adj.* modest.

módico *adj.* moderate, reasonable (*price*).

modificación f. modification.

modificar v. to modify.

modismo m. idiom.

modista f. dressmaker; milliner.

modo m. mode, manner, way; mood (*grammar*); a (*or* al) — de like, in the manner of; de — que so that; and so; de todos -s at any rate, anyway.

modorra f. drowsiness; gid (*a disease of sheep*).

modular v. to modulate, tone down.

mofa f. scoff, jeer, taunt; mockery.

mofar v. to mock, scoff, jeer; -se de to make fun of, scoff at.

moflete m. fat cheek; **mofletudo** *adj.* fat-cheeked.

mohín m. grimace; wry face.

mohíno *adj.* moody, discontented, sad, melancholy; black (*referring to a horse, cow, or bull*).

moho m. rust; mold.

mohoso *adj.* musty, moldy; rusty.

mojada f. drench, drenching, wetting.

mojado *adj.* wet, damp, moist; *p.p. of* mojar.

mojadura f. wetting, dampening, drenching.

mojar v. to dampen, wet, moisten; *Am.* to accompany (*a song*); *Am.* to bribe; *Am.* to celebrate by drinking; *Am.* mojársele a uno los papeles to get things mixed up.

mojicón m. punch, blow; muffin, bun.

mojigatería f. prudery; false humility; affected piety.

mojigato *adj.* prudish; affectedly pious, overzealous (*in matters of religion*); hypocritical; *m.* prude; hypocrite.

mojón m. landmark; milestone; heap, pile.

molde m. mold, cast; form; pattern, model; venir de — to come pat, be to the point; letras de — printed letters; print.

moldear v. to mold; to cast; to decorate with moldings.

moldura f. molding.

mole f. mass, bulk; *adj.* soft, mild; *m. Am.* — de guajolote a Mexican dish of turkey served with a chili gravy.

molécula f. molecule.

moler v. *irr.* to mill; to grind; to tire, fatigue; to wear out, destroy; to bother; — a palos to give a thorough beating.

molestar v. to molest, disturb; to bother, annoy.

molestia f. bother, annoyance; discomfort.

molesto *adj.* bothersome, annoying; uncomfortable.

molicie f. softness; fondness for luxury.

molienda f. grind, grinding, milling; portion to be, or that has been, ground; grinding season (*for sugar cane or olives*); fatigue, weariness; bother.

molinero m. miller.

molinete m. small mill; ventilating fan; pin wheel; twirl, whirl, flourish.

molinillo m. small mill or grinder; chocolate beater; restless person.

molino m. mill; restless person; — de viento windmill.

mollera f. crown of the head; judgment, good sense; ser duro de — to be stubborn; no tener sal en la — to be dull, stupid.

momentáneo *adj.* momentary; sudden, quick.

momento m. moment; importance; momentum; al — immediately, without delay; a cada — continually, frequently.

mona f. female monkey; mimic; drunkenness; dormir la — to sleep it off; pillar una — to get drunk.

monada f. monkeyshine; monkey face; cute little thing; cute gesture; nonsense; flattery.

monarca m. monarch.

monarquía f. monarchy.

monasterio m. monastery.

mondadientes m. toothpick.

mondar v. to pare; to peel; to prune;

to clean out; *Am.* to beat, thrash; *Am.* to beat, defeat; **-se los dientes** to pick one's teeth.

moneda *f.* coin; money; **— corriente** currency; **— menuda** (*or* **suelta**) change, small coins; **casa de —** mint.

monería *f.* monkeyshine, antic; trifle, trinket; cute little thing.

monetario *adj.* monetary, pertaining to money; financial.

monigote *m.* puppet, ridiculous figure; dunce.

monje *m.* monk.

monja *f.* nun.

mono *m.* monkey; silly fool; mimic; *Am.* pile of fruit or vegetables (*in a market*); **-s** *Am.* worthless household utensils and furniture; *Am.* **meterle a uno los -s en el cuerpo** to frighten, terrify someone; *adj.* pretty, neat, cute; *Am.* sorrel, reddish-brown; *Am.* blond.

monologar⁷ *v.* to soliloquize, talk to oneself; to recite monologues; to monopolize the conversation.

monólogo *m.* monologue.

monopolio *m.* monopoly.

monopolizar⁹ *v.* to monopolize; to corner (*a market*).

monosílabo *adj.* monosyllabic, of one syllable; *m.* monosyllable.

monotonía *f.* monotony; **monótono** *adj.* monotonous.

monserga *f.* gabble.

monstruo *m.* monster.

monstruosidad *f.* monstrosity; **monster, freak.**

monstruoso *adj.* monstrous.

monta *f.* amount, sum; value, importance; **de poca —** of little value or importance.

montaje *m.* assembly, assembling (*of machinery*); mount, support for a cannon.

montante *m.* broadsword; transom; upright; post; *Am.* sum, amount, cost; *f.* high tide.

montaña *f.* mountain; **—.rusa** roller coaster.

montañés *adj.* mountain (*used as adj.*), of, from or pertaining to the mountains; *m.* mountaineer; native of the province of Santander, Spain.

montañoso *adj.* mountainous.

montar *v.* to mount; to ride horseback; to amount (to); to set (*jewels*); to cock (*a gun*); to assemble, set up (*machinery*); *Am.* to organize, establish.

montaraz *adj.* wild, primitive, uncivilized; *m.* forester.

monte *m.* mount, mountain; forest; thicket; monte (*a card game*); *Am.* grass, pasture; *Am.* country, outskirts; **montecillo** *m.* mound, small hill; **montepío** *m.* pawnshop.

montera *f.* cap; *Am.* Bolivian cone-shaped hat (*worn by Indians*).

montés *adj.* wild, mountain (*used as as adj.*); **cabra —** mountain goat; **gato —** wildcat.

montículo *m.* mound.

montón *m.* pile, heap; mass, great number; **a -es** in abundance, in heaps, by heaps.

montonera *f.* *Am.* band of mounted rebels or guerrilla fighters; *Am.* pile of wheat, hay, straw, etc.; *Am.* pile, heap (*of anything*).

montuoso *adj.* hilly; mountainous.

montura *f.* mount, horse; saddle and trappings.

monumento *m.* monument; **monumental** *adj.* monumental.

moño *m.* knot or roll of hair; bow of ribbon; crest, tuft of feathers; *Am.* forelock (*lock of hair on the fore part of the head*); *Am.* crest, peak (*of anything*); *Am.* whim; *Am.* a Colombian popular dance; **-s** frippery, gaudy ornaments; *Am.* **estar con el — torcido** to be in an ugly humor.

mora *f.* blackberry; mulberry; brambleberry; *Am.* blood pudding, sausage.

morada *f.* dwelling, residence; stay.

morado *adj.* purple.

morador *m.* dweller, resident.

moral *adj.* moral; *f.* ethics, moral philosophy; morale; *m.* mulberry tree; blackberry bush.

moraleja *f.* moral, lesson, maxim.

moralidad *f.* morality.

moralista *m.* & *f.* moralist.

morar *v.* to live, dwell, reside.

morbidez *f.* softness; mellowness.

mórbido *adj.* morbid; soft.

morboso *adj.* morbid, unhealthy, diseased.

morcilla *f.* blood pudding, blood sausage; gag (*an amusing remark by a comedian*).

mordacidad *f.* sharpness (*of tongue*).

mordaz *adj.* biting, cutting, sarcastic.

mordaza *f.* gag (*for the mouth*).

mordedor *adj.* biting; snappy *m.* biter; slanderer.

mordedura *f.* bite; sting.

mordelón *adj.* *Am.* biting, snappy; *m.* *Am.* biter; *Am.* public official who accepts a bribe.

morder² *v. irr.* to bite; to nip; to gnaw; to corrode; to backbite, slander; *Am.* to swindle; *Am.* to "shake down", exact a bribe.

mordida *f. Am.* bite; *Am.* graft, money obtained by graft.

mordiscar⁶, mordisquear *v.* to nibble; to gnaw.

mordisco *m.* bite; nibble.

moreno *adj.* brown; dark, brunette; *m. Am.* colored person.

moretón *m.* bruise, black-and-blue mark.

morfina *f.* morphine; **morfinómano** *m.* morphine addict, drug fiend.

moribundo *adj.* dying.

morir⁴·⁵² *v. irr.* to die; **-se** to die; to die out, be extinguished.

morisco *adj.* Moorish; Moresque, in the Moorish style; *m.* Morisco (*Christianized Moor*); language of the Moriscos.

moro *adj.* Moorish; *Am.* dappled, spotted (*horse*); *Am.* unbaptized; *m.* Moor; *Am.* frosted cookie. ·

morral *m.* nose bag; knapsack; hunter's bag.

morriña *f.* melancholy, blues, sadness.

mortaja *f.* shroud; *Am.* cigarette paper.

mortal *adj.* mortal; fatal; deadly; *m.* mortal; **mortalidad** *f.* mortality; death rate.

mortandad *f.* mortality, death rate; massacre, slaughter.

mortecino *adj.* deathly pale; dying; **hacer la mortecina** to pretend to be dead.

morterete *m.* small mortar, small cannon.

mortero *m.* mortar (*for grinding*).

mortífero *adj.* deadly, fatal.

mortificar⁶ *v.* to mortify; to torment; to vex, annoy; **-se** to do penance; to be grieved; *Am.* to be embarrassed.

mortuorio *adj.* funeral; funereal, mournful; *m.* funeral, burial.

mosaico *adj. & m.* mosaic.

mosca *f.* fly; bore; bother; *Am.* sponger, parasite; *Am.* bull's-eye, center of a target; **moscón** *m.* large fly; *Am.* **ir de moscón** to go along as a chaperone.

mosquear *v.* to brush off or drive away flies; to whip, beat; *Am.* to rage, be furious; **-se** to show pique or resentment; *Am.* to go away.

mosquito *m.* mosquito; gnat; *Am.* Mosquito Indian of Nicaragua; **mosquitero** *m.* mosquito net.

mostacho *m.* mustache.

mostaza *f.* mustard; mustard seed;

bird shot.

mostrador *m.* demonstrator; store counter; clock dial.

mostrar² *v. irr.* to show; to demonstrate; to exhibit.

mostrenco *adj.* ownerless; homeless; stray (*animal*); slow, dull; fat, heavy; *m.* dunce; *Am.* worthless animal.

mota *f.* mote, speck; knot in cloth; slight defect; mound, knoll; *Am.* powder puff; *Am.* tuft.

mote *m.* motto; slogan; nickname; *Am.* stewed corn; *Am.* grammatical error (*made by illiterate people and children*); *Am.* **— pelado** hominy.

motear *v.* to speck, speckle; to spot; *Am.* to mispronounce, enunciate badly.

motejar *v.* to jeer at; to call bad names; to insult; to censure; **— de** to brand as.

motín *m.* mutiny; riot.

motivar *v.* to cause; to give a cause for.

motivo *m.* motive, reason; motif, theme; *m.* **con —** de because of; on the occasion of; *adj.* motive.

motocicleta *f.* motorcycle; **motociclista** *m. & f.* motorcyclist, motorcycle rider.

motor *m.* motor; *adj.* motor, causing motion.

motorista *m. & f.* motorist; motorman, motorwoman.

motriz *adj.* motive, impelling, driving; **fuerza —** power, driving force.

movedizo *adj.* movable; shaky; shifting; **arena movediza** quicksand.

mover² *v. irr.* to move; to persuade; to stir, excite; to touch, affect; **-se** to move.

movible *adj.* movable; mobile; fickle.

móvil *m.* motive, inducement, incentive; *adj.* mobile, movable; unstable.

movilización *f.* mobilization.

movilizar⁹ *v.* to mobilize.

movimiento *m.* movement; motion; commotion, disturbance.

moza *f.* maid; girl; last hand of a game; *Am.* last song or dance of a fiesta.

mozalbete *m.* youth, lad.

mozo *adj.* young; unmarried; *m.* youth; manservant; waiter; porter; errand boy; **buen —** handsome man.

mozuela *f.* lass, young girl.

mozuelo *m.* lad, young boy.

mucama *f. Am.* servant girl; **mucamo** *m. Am.* servant.

mucoso *adj.* mucous; slimy; **membrana mucosa** mucous membrane.

muchacha *f.* child; girl; servant, maid.

muchacho *m.* child; boy, lad.

muchedumbre *f.* multitude; crowd.

mucho *adj.* much, a lot of; long (*referring to time*); **-s** many; *adv.* much; a great deal; **ni con —** not by far, not by a long shot; **ni — menos** not by any means, nor anything like it; **por — que** no matter how much; **no es — que** it is no wonder that.

muda *f.* change; change of clothes; molt (*act or time of shedding feathers*); *Am.* relay of draft animals.

mudable *adj.* changeable; fickle.

mudanza *f.* change; removal; inconstancy.

mudar *v.* to change; to remove; to molt; **— de casa** to move; **— de traje** to change one's suit or costume; **-se** to change one's clothes; to change one's habits; to move, change one's abode.

mudez *f.* muteness, dumbness.

mudo *adj.* mute, dumb; silent; *m.* dumb person.

mueblaje *m.* furniture.

mueble *m.* piece of furniture; **-s** furniture, household goods; *adj.* movable; **bienes -s** chattels, movable possessions.

mueca *f.* grimace; wry face.

muela *f.* molar tooth; millstone; grindstone; **— cordal** (*or* **— del juicio**) wisdom tooth.

muelle *adj.* soft; voluptuous; *m.* spring; wharf; loading platform; **— real** main spring of a watch.

muerte *f.* death.

muerto *p.p.* of **morir** & *adj.* dead; withered; faded; **naturaleza muerta** still life; *m.* corpse.

muesca *f.* notch; groove.

muestra *f.* sample; pattern, model; shop sign; sign, indication; presence, bearing; face, dial (*of a clock or watch*); **muestrario** *m.* book or collection of samples.

mugido *m.* moo; mooing, lowing of cattle.

mugir[11] *v.* to moo, low.

mugre *f.* dirt, grime.

mugriento *adj.* grimy, dirty.

mujer *f.* woman; wife.

mujeril *adj.* womanly, feminine; womanish, like a woman.

mula *f.* mule; *Am.* cushion for carrying loads; *Am.* worthless merchandise; *Am.* cruel, treacherous person; *Am.* **echar a uno la —** to give someone the dickens, scold someone.

muladar *m.* rubbish pile or dump;

dunghill, pile of manure.

mulato *adj.* & *m.* mulatto.

muleta *f.* crutch; red cloth draped over a rod (*used by bullfighters*).

muletilla *f.* cane with a crutchlike handle; red cloth draped over a rod (*used by bullfighters*); cliché (*hackneyed or trite phrase*); refrain; repetitious word or phrase; braid frog (*fastener for a coat*).

mulo *m.* mule.

multa *f.* fine.

multicolor *adj.* many-colored, motley.

múltiple *adj.* multiple.

multiplicación *f.* multiplication.

multiplicar[6] *v.* to multiply.

multiplicidad *f.* multiplicity, manifold variety.

múltiplo *m.* multiple number.

multitud *f.* multitude; crowd.

mullido *adj.* soft; fluffy; *m.* stuffing for mattresses or pillows; soft cushion or mattress.

mullir[20] *v.* to fluff; to soften.

mundanal *adj.* worldly.

mundano *adj.* mundane, worldly.

mundial *adj.* universal; **la guerra —** the World War.

mundo *m.* world; trunk; **todo el —** everybody.

munición *f.* ammunition; buckshot; **-es de guerra** war supplies.

municipal *adj.* municipal; **municipalidad** *f.* municipality; town hall; city government.

municipio *m.* municipality.

muñeca *f.* doll; wrist; manikin (*figure for displaying clothes*); **muñeco** *m.* boy doll; dummy, puppet.

muñón *m.* stump (*of an arm or leg*).

muralla *f.* surrounding wall; rampart.

murciano *adj.* of or from Murcia, Spain; *m.* native of Murcia.

murciélago *m.* bat.

murga *f.* brass band.

murmullo *m.* murmur, rumor; whisper; muttering.

murmuración *f.* slander, gossip; grumbling.

murmurar *v.* to murmur; to slander, gossip; to whisper; to grumble.

muro *m.* wall.

murria *f.* sulkiness, sullenness, melancholy, blues; **tener —** to be sulky; to have the blues.

musa *f.* Muse; muse, poetic inspiration; poetry; **-s** fine arts.

muscular *adj.* muscular.

musculatura *f.* muscles; muscular system.

músculo m. muscle.
musculoso adj. muscular; sinewy.
muselina f. muslin.
museo m. museum.
musgo m. moss.
musgoso adj. mossy.
música f. music.
musical adj. musical.
músico adj. musical; m. musician.
musitar v. to mutter, mumble; to whisper.
muslo m. thigh.
mustio adj. sad; withered; humble.
mutilar v. to mutilate; to butcher; to mar.
mutismo m. muteness, silence.
mutuo adj. mutual; reciprocal.
muy adv. very; greatly; most.

N

nabo m. turnip.
nácar m. mother-of-pearl; pearl color.
nacarado adj. pearly.
nacer[13] v. irr. to be born; to spring, originate; to bud; to sprout, grow (said of plants); — de pie (or — de pies) to be born lucky.
naciente adj. rising (sun); m. orient, east.
nacimiento m. birth; origin; beginning; descent; source; crèche (representation of the Nativity).
nación f. nation.
nacional adj. national; m. national, citizen.
nacionalidad f. nationality.
nada f. nothingness; indef. pron. nothing, not . . . anything; adv. not at all; de — you are welcome, don't mention it (as a reply to « gracias »); Am. a cada — constantly; una nadita a trifle, just a little.
nadada f. swim.
nadador m. swimmer; Am. fish-net float.
nadar v. to swim; to float.
nadería f. a mere nothing, trifle, worthless thing.
nadie indef. pron. nobody, no one, not . . . anyone.
nafta f. naphtha.
naguas = enaguas.
naipe m. playing card.
nalgas f. pl. buttocks; rump; **nalgada** f. spank; -s spanking.
nana f. grandma; lullaby; Am. child's nurse; Am. nice old lady.
naranja f. orange; — tangerina tangerine; **naranjada** f. orangeade; orange juice; orange marmalade;

naranjal m. orange grove; **naranjo** m. orange tree.
narciso m. narcissus; daffodil; fop, dandy.
narcótico adj. & m. narcotic.
narcotizar[9] v. to dope, drug with narcotics.
nariz f. nose; nostril; **narices** nostrils.
narración f. narration, account, story.
narrar v. to narrate, tell, relate.
narrativo adj. narrative; **narrativa** f. narrative.
nata f. cream; best part; scum; -s whipped cream with sugar; custard; **natoso** adj. creamy.
natal adj. natal; native; **natalicio** m. birthday; **natalidad** f. birth rate.
natillas f. pl. custard.
nativo adj. native.
natural adj. natural; native; simple, unaffected; m. & f. native; m. nature, disposition; al — without affectation; del — from nature, from life.
naturaleza f. nature; disposition; nationality; naturalization; — muerta still life.
naturalidad f. naturalness; simplicity; birthright.
naturalista adj. naturalistic; m. & f. naturalist.
naturalización f. naturalization.
naturalizar[9] v. to naturalize; to acclimatize, accustom to a new climate; -se to become naturalized.
naufragar[7] v. to be shipwrecked; to fail.
naufragio m. shipwreck; failure, ruin.
náufrago m. shipwrecked person.
náusea f. nausea; dar -s to nauseate, sicken; to disgust; **tener** -s to be nauseated, be sick to one's stomach.
nauseabundo adj. nauseating, sickening.
nauseado adj. nauseated, sick to one's stomach.
náutica f. navigation (science of navigation).
navaja f. jackknife, pocketknife; penknife; razor.
navajazo m. stab with a jackknife or razor; stab wound.
naval adj. naval.
navarro adj. Navarrese, of or pertaining to Navarre, Spain; m. Navarrese.
nave f. ship, boat; nave.
navegable adj. navigable.
navegación f. navigation; sea voyage; — aérea aviation.
navegador, navegante m. navigator; adj. navigating.
navegar[7] v. to navigate; to sail.

navidad f. Nativity; Christmas; **-es** Christmas season.

navío m. vessel, ship; **— de guerra** warship.

neblina f. fog, mist.

necedad f. foolishness, nonsense.

necesario adj. necessary.

neceser m. toilet case; sewing kit.

necesidad f. necessity, need, want.

necesitado adj. needy; in need, destitute, poor; p.p. of **necesitar**; m. needy person.

necesitar v. to need; to necessitate.

necio adj. stupid, ignorant; foolish; stubborn; Am. touchy.

nefando adj. abominable; wicked.

negación f. negation, denial; negative (negative particle).

negar[1, 7] v. irr. to deny; to refuse; to prohibit; to disown; **-se** to refuse, decline.

negativa f. negative; denial, refusal.

negativo adj. negative.

negligencia f. negligence, neglect, carelessness.

negligente adj. negligent, neglectful, careless.

negociación f. negotiation; business; business house; management; transaction, deal.

negociante m. merchant, trader, dealer; businessman; adj. negotiating.

negociar v. to negotiate; to trade; to transact.

negocio m. business; business deal; negotiation, transaction; Am. store; **hombre de -s** businessman.

negrear v. to become black; to appear black, look black (in the distance).

negro adj. black; dark; sad, gloomy; unfortunate; m. black color; negro; Am. dear, darling; **negra** f. negress; Am. dear, darling.

negrura f. blackness.

negruzco adj. blackish.

nena f. baby girl; **nene** m. baby boy.

nervio m. nerve.

nervioso, nervoso adj. nervous; sinewy, strong.

nerviosidad, nervosidad f. nervousness; flexibility; vigor.

nervudo adj. sinewy, tough, powerful.

neto adj. clear, pure; net (profit, price, etc); **netamente** adv. clearly, distinctly.

neumático m. tire; adj. pneumatic.

neutralidad f. neutrality.

neutralizar[9] v. to neutralize, counteract.

neutro adj. neutral; neuter; sexless.

nevada f. snowfall.

nevado adj. snowy, white as snow; covered with snow.

nevar[1] v. irr. to snow.

nevasca f. snowstorm.

nevera f. icebox; refrigerator; ice store-house; ice or ice-cream vendor (woman).

ni conj. & adv. nor; not even; neither; **— siquiera** not even.

nicho m. niche; recess, hollow in a wall.

nidada f. nestful of eggs; brood of chicks; hatch, brood.

nido m. nest; abode; Am. **patearle el — a alguien** to "upset the apple-cart", upset someone's plans.

niebla f. fog, mist; confusion.

nieto m. grandson, grandchild; **nieta** f. granddaughter.

nieve f. snow; Am. sherbet, ice cream; **tiempo de -s** snowy season.

nimio adj. miserly, stingy; Am. very small, insignificant.

ninfa f. nymph.

ningun(o) indef. adj. & pron. no one, none, not . . . any; nobody.

niña f. girl; baby girl; Am. lady, mistress (title of respect and endearment given to adults); **— del ojo** pupil of the eye.

niñada f. childishness, childish act or remark.

niñera f. child's nurse.

niñería f. childish act; child's play; trifle; foolishness.

niñez f. infancy; childhood.

niño m. child, boy; infant; Am. master (title of respect given to a young man by his servants); adj. childlike, childish; very young, immature.

níquel m. nickel.

niquelado adj. nickel-plated; m. nickel plating; nickel plate.

nitidez f. clarity, clearness.

nítido adj. clear.

nitrato m. nitrate; saltpeter.

nitro m. niter, saltpeter.

nitrógeno m. nitrogen.

nivel m. level.

nivelar v. to level; to grade; to equalize.

no adv. no; not; nay; **— bien** as soon as; **un —** sé qué something indefinable; **por sí o por —** just in case, anyway.

noble adj. noble; m. nobleman.

nobleza f. nobility; nobleness.

noción f. notion, idea.

nocivo adj. noxious, harmful, injurious.

nocturno adj. nocturnal, night, nightly; m. nocturne (musical or lyrical composition).

noche f. night; darkness; **a la —** to-night; **de —** by (at) night; **por (en)**

la — at night, in the evening; **dejar a uno a buenas -s** to leave a person in the lurch.

Nochebuena f. Christmas Eve.

nocherniego m. night owl (person).

nodriza f. child's nurse; wet nurse.

nogal m. walnut (tree and wood).

nomás Am. = no más just; only.

nombradía f. renown, fame.

nombramiento m. nomination; appointment; naming.

nombrar v. to nominate; to name; to appoint.

nombre m. name; fame; noun; watchword; — **de pila** (or — **de bautismo**) Christian name.

nomeolvides f. forget-me-not.

nómina f. list (of names); pay roll.

nominación f. nomination; appointment.

nominal adj. nominal; **valor** — small, insignificant value.

nominar v. to nominate.

non adj. odd, uneven; m. odd number, uneven number; **estar** (or **quedar**) **de** — to be left alone, be left without a partner or companion.

nonada f. trifle, mere nothing.

nopal m. nopal, prickly pear tree (species of cactus).

nordeste adj. & m. northeast.

noria f. draw well; chain pump.

norma f. norm, standard, model.

normal adj. normal; standard; f. perpendicular line.

normalizar v. to normalize, make normal; to standardize.

noroeste adj. & m. northwest.

nortada f. strong north wind.

nortazo m. Am. sudden gust of wind, strong north wind.

norte m. north; north wind; guide; North Star; direction.

norteamericano adj. North American; American (from or of the United States).

norteño adj. northern; m. northerner.

noruego adj. & m. Norwegian.

nostalgia f. nostalgia, longing, homesickness.

nostálgico adj. homesick; lonesome; longing.

nota f. note; mark; fame.

notable adj. notable; noticeable.

notar v. to note, observe; to mark; to write down.

notario m. notary.

noticia f. notice, information; news; **recibir -s** to receive word, hear (from).

noticiario m. news sheet, news column,

news bulletin; **noticiero** m. = **noticiario**; adj. news (used as adj.); newsy, full of news.

noticioso adj. newsy, full of news; well-informed.

notificación f. notification, notifying; notice; summons.

notificar v. to notify.

notorio adj. well-known; obvious, evident.

novato m. novice, beginner.

novedad f. novelty; latest news, event, or fashion; change; newness; **hacerle a uno** — to seem strange or new to one; to excite one's curiosity or interest; **sin** — as usual; well.

novel adj. new, inexperienced.

novela f. novel; fiction.

novelesco adj. novelistic, fictional; fantastic.

novelista m. & f. novelist.

novia f. fiancée; sweetheart; bride.

noviazgo m. betrothal, engagement; courtship.

novicio m. novice; beginner; apprentice; adj. inexperienced.

noviembre m. November.

novilla f. heifer, young cow.

novillada f. herd of young bulls; bullfight (using young bulls).

novillo m. young bull; steer; **-s** bullfight (using young bulls); **hacer -s** to play hooky, cut classes; to play truant.

novio m. fiancé; sweetheart; bridegroom.

nubarrón m. large storm cloud.

nube f. cloud; film on the eyeball; **poner por las -s** to praise to the skies.

nublado m. storm cloud; imminent danger; adj. cloudy.

nublar v. to cloud; to darken, obscure; **-se** to grow cloudy.

nubloso adj. cloudy; gloomy.

nuca f. nape.

núcleo m. nucleus; kernel.

nudillo m. small knot; knuckle; loop, knitted stitch.

nudo m. knot; joint; union, bond, tie; crisis, turning point (of a play); knot, nautical mile; — **ciego** hard knot.

nudoso adj. knotty, gnarled, knotted.

nuera f. daughter-in-law.

nueva f. news.

nuevecito adj. nice and new, brand-new.

nuevo adj. new; newly arrived; **de** — again; ¿ **qué hay de** —? what's new? what's the news?

nuez f. walnut; nut; — (or — **de Adán**) Adam's apple; — **moscada** (or — **de especia**) nutmeg.

nulidad f. nullity (state or quality of

being null); incompetence; nonentity, a nobody.
nulo *adj.* null, void; useless.
numeral *adj. & m.* numeral.
numerar *v.* to number; to calculate; to enumerate.
numérico *adj.* numerical.
número *m.* number; numeral.
numeroso *adj.* numerous.
nunca *adv.* never; **no . . . — not . . .** ever; **más que —** more than ever.
nuncio *m.* herald, messenger; nuncio, Papal envoy.
nupcial *adj.* nuptial, relating to marriage or weddings.
nupcias *f. pl.* nuptials, wedding.
nutria *f.* otter.
nutrición *f.* nutrition; nourishment.
nutrido *adj.* full, abundant; substantial; *p.p. of* **nutrir.**
nutrimento, nutrimiento *m.* nutrition; nourishment, food.
nutrir *v.* to nourish, feed.
nutritivo *adj.* nutritious, nourishing.

Ñ

ñapa *f. Am.* additional amount, something extra; *Am.* **de —** to boot, in addition, besides.
ñato *adj. Am.* flat-nosed, pug-nosed, snub-nosed; *Am.* ugly, deformed; *Am.* insignificant.
ñoñería *f.* silly remark or action; *Am.* dotage.
ñoño *adj.* feeble-minded; silly; *Am.* old, decrepit, feeble; *Am.* old-fashioned, out of style.

O

o *conj.* or, either.
oasis *m.* oasis.
obedecer[13] *v. irr.* to obey; **— a cierta causa** to arise from, be due to, a certain cause; **esto obedece a que . . .** this is due to the fact that . . .
obediencia *f.* obedience.
obediente *adj.* obedient.
obertura *f.* musical overture.
obispo *m.* bishop; *Am.* **a cada muerte de** (*or* **por la muerte de un**) **—** once in a blue moon.
objeción *f.* objection.
objetar *v.* to object.
objetivo *adj.* objective; *m.* objective (*lens of a microscope*); objective.
objeto *m.* object, purpose, aim; thing.
oblea *f.* wafer.
oblicuo *adj.* oblique, slanting, bias.
obligación *f.* obligation; duty; bond, security; engagement.

obligar[7] *v.* to oblige; to obligate, bind, compel, put under obligation; **-se** to bind oneself, obligate oneself.
obligatorio *adj.* obligatory, compulsory; binding.
óbolo *m.* mite, small contribution.
obra *f.* work; act; labor, toil; book; building (*under construction*); repair; **— de** approximately; **por — de** through, by virtue of power of; **hacer mala —** to interfere, hinder; **poner por —** to undertake, begin; to put into practice.
obrar *v.* to work; to act; to operate; to function; to perform; to make; to do; **obra en nuestro poder** we are in receipt of; **la carta que obra en su poder** the letter that is in his possession.
obrero *m.* workman, laborer.
obscenidad *f.* obscenity.
obsceno *adj.* obscene.
obscurecer[13] *v. irr.* to obscure, darken; to tarnish; to grow dark; **-se** to get dark or cloudy.
obscuridad *f.* obscurity; darkness; dimness.
obscuro *adj.* obscure; dark; dim; **a obscuras** (= **a oscuras**) in the dark; *m.* shade (*in painting*).
obsequiar *v.* to regale, entertain; to court; *Am.* to give, make a present of.
obsequio *m.* attention, courtesy; gift; **en — de** for the sake of, in honor of.
obsequioso *adj.* attentive, courteous, obliging; obsequious, servile.
observación *f.* observation; remark.
observador *m.* observer; *adj.* observing.
observancia *f.* observance (*of a law, rule, custom, etc.*).
observante *adj.* observant (*of a law, custom, or rule*).
observar *v.* to observe; to watch; to remark.
observatorio *m.* observatory.
obsesión *f.* obsession.
obsesionar *v.* to obsess.
obstáculo *m.* obstacle.
obstante: no — notwithstanding; nevertheless.
obstar *v.* to hinder, impede, obstruct.
obstinación *f.* obstinacy, stubbornness.
obstinado *adj.* obstinate, stubborn.
obstinarse *v.* to persist (in); to be obstinate, stubborn (about).
obstrucción *f.* obstruction.
obstruir[32] *v. irr.* to obstruct, block.
obtener[45] *v. irr.* to obtain, get; to attain.
obtenible *adj.* obtainable, available.
obturador *m.* choke (*of an automobile*);

throttle; plug, stopper; shutter (*of a camera*).

obviar *v.* to obviate, clear away, remove.

obvio *adj.* obvious.

ocasión *f.* occasion, opportunity; cause; danger, risk; **de** — reduced, bargain; **avisos de** — want "ads" (*advertisements*); *Am.* **esta** — this time.

ocasional *adj.* occasional.

ocasionar *v.* to occasion, cause.

ocaso *m.* sunset; setting (*of any star or planet*); west; decadence, decline, end.

occidental *adj.* occidental, western.

occidente *m.* occident, west.

océano *m.* ocean.

ocio *m.* leisure, idleness; recreation, pastime.

ociosidad *f.* idleness, leisure.

ocioso *adj.* idle; useless.

octubre *m.* October.

ocular *adj.* ocular; **testigo** — eye witness; *m.* eyepiece, lens (*for the eye in a microscope or telescope*).

oculista *m. & f.* oculist; *Am.* flatterer.

ocultar *v.* to hide, conceal.

oculto *adj.* hidden, concealed; *m. Am.* species of mole (*small animal*).

ocupación *f.* occupation; employment.

ocupante *m. & f.* occupant.

ocupar *v.* to occupy; to employ; **-se en** (*Am.* **-se de**) to be engaged in; to pay attention to, be interested in.

ocurrencia *f.* occurrence, event; witticism, joke; bright or funny idea.

ocurrente *adj.* witty, funny, humorous; occurring.

ocurrir *v.* to occur.

ocurso *m. Am.* petition, application.

oda *f.* ode.

odiar *v.* to hate.

odio *m.* hatred.

odioso *adj.* odious, hateful.

oeste *m.* west; west wind.

ofender *v.* to offend; to displease; **-se** to get offended; to become angry, take offense.

ofensa *f.* offense.

ofensivo *adj.* offensive; obnoxious; attacking; **ofensiva** *f.* offensive.

ofensor *m.* offender; *adj.* offending

oferta *f.* offer; promise.

oficial *m.* official, officer; skilled workman; *adj.* official.

oficiar *v.* to officiate, serve, minister, perform the duties of a priest or minister; to communicate officially; — **de** to serve as, act as.

oficina *f.* office; shop; **oficinesco** *adj.* clerical, pertaining to an office.

oficio *m.* office, position; trade; function; official communication; religious office (*prayers*).

oficioso *adj.* officious, meddlesome.

ofrecer[13] *v. irr.* to offer; to promise; **-se** to offer, occur, present itself; to offer oneself, volunteer; ¿**qué se le ofrece a Vd?** what do you wish?

ofrecimiento *m.* offer; offering.

ofrenda *f.* offering, gift.

ofuscamiento *m.* clouded vision, blindness; cloudiness of the mind, bewilderment, mental confusion.

ofuscar[6] *v.* to darken, cast a shadow on; to blind; to cloud; to bewilder, confuse.

ogro *m.* ogre.

oído *m.* hearing; ear; **al** — confidentially; **de** (*or* **al**) — by ear; **de -s** (*or de* **oídas**) by hearsay or rumor.

oidor *m.* hearer, listener; judge.

oír[36] *v. irr.* to hear; to listen; to understand; — **misa** to attend mass; — **decir que** to hear that; — **hablar de** to hear about.

ojal *m.* buttonhole; hole.

¡**ojalá!** *interj.* God grant!; I hope so!; — **que** would that, I hope that.

ojazo *m.* large eye.

ojeada *f.* glimpse, quick glance.

ojear *v.* to eye, stare; to bewitch; to beat up, rouse (*wild game*).

ojera *f.* dark circle under the eye; eyecup.

ojeriza *f.* grudge, spite.

ojeroso *adj.* with dark circles under the eyes.

ojiva *f.* pointed arch; **ojival** *adj.* pointed (*arch*); **ventana ojival** window with a pointed arch.

ojo *m.* eye; keyhole; hole; ¡ — ! careful! look out!; **a** — by sight, by guess; **a -s vistas** visibly, clearly; **mal** (*or* **mal de**) — evil eye; *Am.* **hacer** — to cast the evil eye; *Am.* **pelar el** — to be alert, keep one's eye peeled; *Am.* **poner a uno los -s verdes** to deceive someone; **tener entre -s a** to have ill will toward, have a grudge against.

ojota *f. Am.* leather sandal.

ola *f.* wave.

oleada *f.* big wave; swell; surge; abundant yield of oil.

oleaje, olaje *m.* swell, surge, succession of waves.

oleo *m.* oil; holy oil; **pintura al** — oil painting.

oleoso *adj.* oily.

oler[37] *v. irr.* to smell; to scent; — **a** to smack of; to smell like; *Am.* **olérselas** to suspect it, "smell a rat".

148

olfatear *v.* to scent, sniff, smell.

olfateo *m.* sniff, sniffing.

olfato *m.* sense of smell.

oliva *f.* olive; olive tree; owl; **olivar** *m.* olive grove; **olivo** *m.* olive tree.

olmo *m.* elm.

olor *m.* smell, odor, fragrance; smack, trace, suspicion; *Am.* spice; **olorcillo** *m.* faint odor.

oloroso *adj.* fragrant.

olote *m.* *Am.* cob, corncob.

olvidadizo *adj.* forgetful.

olvidar *v.* to forget; to neglect; **-se de** to forget; **olvidársele a uno algo to** forget something.

olvido *m.* forgetfulness; oblivion; neglect; **echar al —** to cast into oblivion; to forget on purpose.

olla *f.* pot, kettle; olla (*vegetable and meat stew*); **— podrida** Spanish stew of mixed vegetables and meat.

ombligo *m.* navel; middle, center.

omisión *f.* omission; oversight, neglect.

omiso *adj.* careless, neglectful; *Am.* guilty; **hacer caso —** to omit.

omitir *v.* to omit; to overlook.

ómnibus *m.* omnibus, bus.

omnipotente *adj.* omnipotent, ˋalmighty.

onda *f.* wave; ripple; sound wave; scallop.

ondear *v.* to wave; to waver; to ripple; to sway, swing.

ondulación *f.* undulation, waving motion; wave; **— permanente** permanent wave.

ondulado *p.p.* & *adj.* wavy; scalloped (*edge*).

ondulante *adj.* wavy, waving.

ondular *v.* to undulate, wave.

onza *f.* ounce; ounce, wildcat; *Am.* small tiger.

opaco *adj.* opaque, dim, dull.

ópalo *m.* opal.

ópera *f.* opera.

operación *f.* operation; business transaction.

operador *m.* operator, surgeon.

operar *v.* to operate; to take effect, work; to speculate (*in business*); to manipulate, handle.

operario *m.* operator, workman, worker.

opereta *f.* operetta.

opinar *v.* to express an opinion; to think; to judge; to argue.

opinión *f.* opinion; reputation.

opio *m.* opium.

oponer[40] *v.* *irr.* to oppose; **-se** to disapprove; **-se a** to. oppose, be against.

oporto *m.* port wine.

oportunidad *f.* opportunity.

oportuno *adj.* opportune; convenient, timely.

oposición *f.* opposition; competition; **-es** competitive examinations.

opositor *m.* opponent; competitor.

opresión *f.* oppression.

opresivo *adj.* oppressive.

opresor *m.* oppressor.

oprimir *v.* to oppress; to crush; to press down.

oprobio *m.* infamy; insult; shame; dishonor.

optar *v.* to choose, select; **— por** to decide upon; to choose.

óptica *f.* optics.

óptico *adj.* optical, optic; *m.* optician.

optimismo *m.* optimism; **optimista** *m.* & *f.* optimist; *adj.* optimistic.

óptimo *adj.* very good, very best.

opuesto *p.p.* *of* **oponer** opposed; *adj.* opposite; contrary.

opulencia *f.* opulence, abundance, wealth.

opulento *adj.* opulent, wealthy.

oquedad *f.* cavity, hollow; chasm.

ora *conj.* now, then; whether; either.

oración *f.* oration; prayer; sentence.

oráculo *m.* oracle.

orador *m.* orator, speaker.

oral *adj.* oral.

orar *v.* to pray.

oratoria *f.* oratory, eloquence.

oratorio *m.* oratory, private chapel; oratorio (*a religious musical composition*); *adj.* oratorical, pertaining to oratory.

orbe *m.* orb, sphere, globe; the earth; world, universe.

órbita *f.* orbit; eye socket.

orden *m.* order; succession, series; class, group; relation; proportion; *f.* order, command; honorary or religious order; *m.* & *f.* sacrament of ordination; **a sus órdenes** at your service.

ordenado *p.p.* & *adj.* ordered; ordained; orderly; neat.

ordenanza *f.* ordinance, decree, law; command, order; *m.* orderly (*military*).

ordenar *v.* to arrange, put in order; to order, command; to ordain; **-se** to become ordained.

ordeña *f.* milking.

ordeñar *v.* to milk.

ordinariez *f.* commonness, lack of manners.

ordinario *adj.* ordinary; usual; common, coarse; *m.* ordinary (*a bishop or judge*); ordinary mail; daily household expense; **de —** usually, ordinarily.

orear *v.* to air; -se to be exposed to the air; to dry in the air.

oreja *f.* ear; hearing; loop; small flap; *Am.* handle (*shaped like an ear*);.

orejano *adj.* unbranded (*cattle*); *Am.* cautious; *m. Am.* aloof, unsociable person; **orejera** *f.* ear muff, ear flap; **orejón** *m.* pull by the ear; *Am.* rancher or inhabitant of the **sabana**; *adj. Am.* long-eared, long-horned; *Am.* unbranded (*cattle*); *Am.* coarse, crude, uncouth.

orfandad *f.* orphanage (*state of being an orphan*).

orfanato *m.* orphanage, orphan asylum.

orfanatorio *Am.* = **orfanato.**

orfebre *m.* goldsmith; silversmith.

orfeón *m.* glee club, choir.

orgánico *adj.* organic.

organismo *m.* organism.

organización *f.* organization.

organizador *m.* organizer.

organizar[9] *v.* to organize; to arrange.

órgano *m.* organ; **organillo** *m.* hand organ.

orgía *f.* orgy, wild revel.

orgullo *m.* pride; haughtiness, arrogance.

orgulloso *adj.* proud; haughty, arrogant.

oriental *adj.* oriental, eastern.

orientar *v.* to orientate, orient; -se to orient oneself, find one's bearings.

oriente *m.* orient, east; east wind; source, origin.

orificación *f.* gold filling.

orificio *m.* orifice, small hole, aperture, outlet.

origen *m.* origin; source.

original *adj.* original; strange, quaint; *m.* original; manuscript, copy; queer person; **originalidad** *f.* originality.

originar *v.* to originate, cause to be; -se originate, arise.

orilla *f.* shore, bank; beach; edge, border; -s *Am.* outskirts, environs.

orillar *v.* to border, trim the edge of; to skirt, go along the edge of; to reach the edge or shore.

orín *m.* rust; **orines** *m. pl.* urine.

orina *f.* urine.

orinar *v.* to urinate.

oriol *m.* oriole.

oriundo *adj.* native; **ser — de** to hail from, come from.

orla *f.* border; trimming, fringe.

orlar *v.* to border, edge, trim with a border or fringe.

ornado *adj.* ornate; *p.p.* adorned, orna-

mented.

ornamentar *v.* to ornament, adorn.

ornamento *m.* ornament; decoration; -s sacred vestments.

ornar *v.* to adorn.

oro *m.* gold; gold ornament; -s "gold coins" (*Spanish card suit*).

orondo *adj.* self-satisfied, puffed up, vain; *Am.* serene, calm.

oropel *m.* tinsel.

orquesta *f.* orchestra.

orquídea *f.* orchid.

ortiga *f.* nettle.

ortografía *f.* orthography, spelling.

ortográfico *adj.* orthographic (*pertaining to orthography or spelling*).

oruga *f.* caterpillar.

orzuelo *m.* sty (*on the eyelid*).

osadía *f.* boldness, daring.

osado *adj.* bold, daring.

osar *v.* to dare, venture.

oscilación *f.* oscillation, sway; fluctuation, wavering.

oscilar *v.* to oscillate, swing, sway; to waver.

oscurecer = obscurecer.

oscuridad = obsuridad.

oscuro = obscuro.

oso *m.* bear; **— blanco** polar bear; **— hormiguero** anteater; **— marino** seal.

ostentación *f.* ostentation, show, display.

ostentar *v.* to display, show; to show off; to boast.

ostentoso *adj.* ostentatious, showy.

ostión *m.* large oyster.

ostra *f.* oyster.

otate *m. Am.* species of bamboo; *Am.* bamboo stick or cane.

otero *m.* hillock, small hill, knoll.

otoñal *adj.* autumnal, of autumn.

otoño *m.* autumn, fall.

otorgar[7] *v.* to grant; to promise; to consent to.

otro *adj.* another; **otra vez** again; *Am.* **como dijo el —** as someone said.

otrora *adv.* formerly, in other times.

ovación *f.* ovation, enthusiastic applause.

oval, ovalado *adj.* oval; **óvalo** *m.* oval.

oveja *f.* sheep.

ovejero *m.* shepherd; sheep dog.

ovejuno *adj.* sheep, pertaining or relating to sheep.

overo *adj.* peach-colored (*applied to horses and cattle*); *Am.* mottled, spotted; *Am.* multicolored; *Am.* **ponerle a uno —** to insult someone.

overol, overoles *m. Am.* overalls.

ovillar *v.* to ball, wind or form into a ball; **-se** to curl up into a ball.

ovillo *m.* ball of yarn or thread; tangle; **hacerse uno un —** to curl up into a ball; to become entangled, confused.

oxidado *p.p.* rusted; *adj.* rusty.

oxidar *v.* to oxidize; to rust; **-se** to become oxidized; to rust.

oxígeno *m.* oxygen.

oyente *m. & f.* listener, auditor, hearer; *adj.* listening.

P

pabellón *m.* pavilion; canopy; banner, flag; shelter, covering; external ear.

pabilo *m.* wick; snuff (*of a candle*).

pacer[13] *v. irr.* to pasture; to graze.

paciencia *f.* patience.

paciente *adj.* patient; *m. & f.* patient.

pacienzudo *adj.* patient, long-suffering.

pacificar[6] *v.* to pacify; to appease.

pacífico *adj.* pacific, peaceful, calm.

pacto *m.* pact, agreement.

padecer[13] *v. irr.* to suffer.

padecimiento *m.* suffering.

padrastro *m.* stepfather; hangnail.

padre *m.* father; **-s** parents; ancestors; *adj. Am.* very great, stupendous.

padrenuestro *m.* paternoster, the Lord's Prayer.

padrino *m.* godfather; sponsor, patron; second in a duel; best man (*at a wedding*).

paella *f.* a popular rice dish with chicken, vegetables, etc.

paga *f.* payment; pay, salary.

pagadero *adj.* payable.

pagado *p.p. & adj.* paid; self-satisfied, conceited; **— de sí mismo** pleased with oneself.

pagador *m.* payer; paymaster; paying teller (*in a bank*).

paganismo *m.* paganism, heathenism.

pagano *adj.* pagan; *m.* pagan; payer; dupe, sucker.

pagar[7] *v.* to pay; to pay for; to requite, return (*love*); **-se de** to be proud of; to boast of; to be pleased with; *Am.* **-se de palabras** to let oneself be tricked; *Am.* **— a nueve** to pay in excess.

pagaré *m.* promissory note; I.O.U.

página *f.* page.

paginar *v.* to page.

pago *m.* payment; prize, reward; country district; *Am.* one's native farm land or district; *adj.* paid; *Am.* **estar -s** to be quits.

país *m.* nation, country; region.

paisaje *m.* landscape.

paisanaje *m.* peasantry, country people; civilians; *Am.* gang of farm laborers.

paisano *m.* countryman; peasant; fellow countryman; civilian.

paja *f.* straw; chaff; rubbish; *Am.* grass for pasture; **echar -s** to draw lots; **por quítame allá esas -s** for an insignificant reason or pretext; **en un quítame allá esas -s** in a jiffy, in a second; **a humo de -s** thoughtlessly; lightly; **no lo hizo a humo de -s** he did not do it without a special reason or intention.

pajar *m.* straw loft, barn.

pájaro *m.* bird; shrewd, cautious person; *Am.* absent-minded person; *Am.* person of suspicious conduct; **— carpintero** woodpecker; **— mosca** hummingbird.

paje *m.* page, valet, attendant.

pajizo *adj.* made of straw; covered with straw; straw-colored.

pajonal *m.* plain or field of tall coarse grass.

pala *f.* shovel; trowel; scoop; paddle; blade of an oar; racket; upper (*of a shoe*); cunning, craftiness; **meter la —** to deceive with cunning; *Am.* **hacer la —** to deceive with cunning; to stall, pretend to work; to flatter; **palada** *f.* scoop, shovelful; stroke of an oar.

palabra *f.* word; promise; **de —** by word of mouth; **cuatro -s** a few words; **empeñar la —** to promise, pledge; **tener la —** to have the floor; *Am.* **¡ — !** I mean it, it is true!

palabrero *adj.* wordy, talkative.

palabrita *f.* a little word, a few words; a word of advice.

palacio *m.* palace; **palaciego** *m.* courtier; *adj.* relating to a palace or court; court (*used as an adj.*).

paladar *m.* palate; taste, relish.

paladear *v.* to relish, taste with relish.

paladín *m.* knight; champion, defender.

palanca *f.* lever; crowbar; bar used for carrying a load.

palangana *f.* washbowl, basin; *Am.* platter; *Am.* large wooden bowl; *m. Am.* bluffer, charlatan.

palco *m.* theatre box; **— escénico** stage.

palenque *m.* palisade, fence; enclosure; *Am.* hitching post or plank.

paleta *f.* small flat shovel; mason's trowel; shoulder blade; blade (*of a rudder, of a ventilating fan*); paddle (*of a paddle wheel*); painter's palette; *Am.* candy, sweetmeat or ice cream attached to a stick; *Am.* a wooden paddle to stir with, or for beating clothes; **en dos -s** in a jiffy, in a second; **paletilla** *f.* shoulder blade.

palidecer[18] *v. irr.* to turn pale.

palidez *f.* pallor, paleness.

pálido *adj.* pallid, pale.

palillo *m.* small stick; toothpick; **tocar todos los -s** (*Am.* **menear uno los -s**) to try every possible means.

paliza *f.* beating (*with a stick*), thrashing.

palizada *f.* palisade; stockade.

palma *f.* palm tree; palm leaf; palm of the hand; **batir -s** to clap, applaud; **llevarse la —** to triumph, win, carry off the honors; to be the best.

palmada *f.* slap; clap.

palmario *adj.* clear, evident.

palmatoria *f.* small candlestick with handle.

palmear *v.* to clap, applaud; *Am.* to pat, clap on the back; *Am.* to flatter.

palmera *f.* palm tree.

palmo *m.* span (*about 9 inches*); **— a —** slowly, foot by foot.

palmotear *v.* to clap, applaud.

palo *m.* stick; pole; log; mast; wood; blow with a stick; suit (*in a deck of cards*); *Am.* tree; *Am.* reprimand, reproof; *Am.* large swallow of liquor; **— del Brasil** Brazil wood; *Am.* **— a pique** rail fence, barbed wire fence; *Am.* **a medio —** half-done; half-drunk; *Am.* **a — entero** drunk.

paloma *f.* dove, pigeon; pleasant, mild person; **-s** whitecaps.

palomar *m.* dovecot (*shelter for doves or pigeons*).

palomilla *f.* little dove; moth; small butterfly; **-s** small whitecaps.

palomita *f.* little dove; **-s** *Am.* popcorn.

palpable *adj.* palpable (*that can be felt or touched*); clear, obvious, evident.

palpar *v.* to feel; to touch; to grope.

palpitación *f.* palpitation; beat, throb.

palpitante *adj.* palpitating, throbbing, trembling; exciting; **la cuestión —** the burning question.

palpitar *v.* to palpitate; to throb, beat.

palta *f. Am.* avocado, alligator pear; **palto** *m. Am.* avocado tree. *See* **aguacate**.

palúdico *adj.* marshy; **fiebre palúdica** malarial, or marsh, fever; malaria; **paludismo** *m.* malaria.

pampa *f. Am.* pampa (*vast treeless plain of South America*); *Am.* prairie; *Am.* drill field (*military*); *m. & f.* pampa Indian of Argentina; *m. Am.* language of the pampa Indian; *adj. Am.* pertaining to the pampa Indian; *Am.* **caballo**

— horse with head and body of different colors; *Am.* **trato —** dubious or dishonest deal; *Am.* **estar a la —** to be in the open; *Am.* **tener todo a la —** to be ragged or to be indecently exposed; *Am.* **quedar en —** to be left without clothes; to be left in the lurch.

pampeano *adj. Am.* of, or pertaining to, the pampa.

pampero *adj. Am.* of, or pertaining to, the pampas; *m. Am.* inhabitant of the pampas; *Am.* violent wind of the pampa.

pan *m.* bread; loaf of bread; wheat; **-es** fields of grain; breadstuffs; *Am.* **echar -es** to brag, boast.

pana *f.* corduroy.

panadería *f.* bakery.

panadero *m.* baker; *Am.* flatterer.

panal *m.* honeycomb; sweetmeat (*made of sugar, egg white, and lemon*).

panamericano *adj.* Pan-American.

pandearse *v.* to bulge, warp; to sag.

pandeo *m.* sag; bulge.

pandilla *f.* gang, band.

panfleto *m. Am.* pamphlet.

pánico *m.* panic; *adj.* panic, panicky.

panne *f.* accident, car trouble.

panocha *f.* ear of corn; *Am.* Mexican raw sugar; *Am.* a kind of tamale.

panqué *m. Am.* small cake, cup cake; *Am.* pancake.

pantalón *m.* trousers; pants; **un par de -es** a pair of trousers.

pantalla *f.* light shade; screen; fireplace screen; motion-picture screen; *Am.* fan, palm leaf fan.

pantano *m.* swamp; dam; difficulty.

pantanoso *adj.* swampy, marshy; muddy.

pantera *f.* panther.

pantorrilla *f.* calf (*of the leg*).

pantufla *f.* bedroom slipper.

panza *f.* paunch, belly.

panzón, panzudo *adj.* big-bellied.

pañal *m.* diaper; **estar en -es** to be in one's infancy; to have little or no knowledge of a thing.

paño *m.* cloth (*any cloth, especially woolen*); blotch or spot on the skin; film on the eyeball; *Am.* parcel of tillable land; *Am.* kerchief, shawl; **— de manos** towel; **— de mesa** tablecloth; **al —** off-stage; **-s clothes,** garments; **-s menores** underwear; **pañero** *m.* clothier.

pañolón *m.* scarf, large kerchief; shawl.

pañuelo *m.* handkerchief.

papa *m.* Pope; *f.* potato; fib, lie; *Am.* snap, easy job; **-s** pap (*soft food for* *babies*); soup; *Am.* **cosa —** something good to eat; excellent thing; **echar -s** to fib, lie; *Am.* **importarle a uno una —** not to matter to one a bit; *Am.* **no saber ni —** not to a know a thing; to be completely ignorant.

papá *m.* papa; *Am.* **— grande** grandfather.

papagayo *m.* parrot; talker, chatterer.

papal *adj.* papal.

papalote, papelote *m. Am.* kite.

papamoscas *m.* flycatcher (*a bird*); simpleton, half-wit, dunce.

papanatas *m.* simpleton, fool, dunce.

paparrucha *f.* fib, lie; **paparruchero** *m.* fibber.

papel *m.* paper; sheet of paper; document; role; **— de estraza** brown wrapping paper; **— de lija** sandpaper; **— de seda** tissue paper; **— moneda** paper money; **— secante** blotting. paper; **hacer el — de** to play the role of; **hacer buen** (*or* **mal**) **—** to cut a good (*or* bad) figure.

papelera *f.* folder, file, case or device for keeping papers; *Am.* wastepaper basket; **papelero** *m.* paper manufacturer; *adj.* pertaining to paper; vain, ostentatious.

papelería *f.* stationery store; stationery; lot of papers.

papeleta *f.* card, file card, slip of paper.

papelucho *m.* worthless piece of paper.

papera *f.* goiter; **-s** mumps.

paquete *m.* package; bundle; dandy; packet boat (*mail boat*); *adj. Am.* dolled up, dressed up; *Am.* important, pompous; *Am.* insincere.

par *adj.* even; *m.* pair, couple; peer; **a la —** at par; jointly; at the same time; **al — de** on a par with; **bajo —** below par; **sin —** peerless, without an equal, having no equal; **sobre —** above par; **de — en —** wide-open.

para *prep.* for; to; toward; in order to; **¿ — qué?** what for; **— que** so that; **— siempre** forever; **— mis adentros** to myself; **sin qué ni — qué** without rhyme or reason; *m. Am.* Paraguayan tobacco; *Am.* Paraguayan (*used as nickname*).

parabién *m.* congratulation; **dar el —** to congratulate.

parabrisa *m.* windshield.

paracaídas *m.* parachute; **paracaidista** *m. & f.* parachutist.

parachoques *m.* bumper.

parada *f.* stop; stopping place; bet, stake; military review; *Am.* parade; *Am.* boastfulness; *Am.* **tener mucha**

— to dress very well.

paradero *m.* stopping place; whereabouts; end.

parado *p.p. & adj.* stopped; unoccupied, unemployed; fixed, motionless; *Am.* standing, erect, straight up; *Am.* stiff, proud; *Am.* cold, unenthusiastic; *Am.* **caer uno —** to land on one's feet; to be lucky; *Am.* **estar bien —** to be well-fixed, well-established; to be lucky; *m.·Am.* air, appearance.

paradoja *f.* paradox.

parafina *f.* paraffin.

paraguas *m.* umbrella; **paragüero** *m.* umbrella stand; umbrella maker or seller.

paraguayo *adj. & m.* Paraguayan.

paraíso *m.* paradise, heaven; upper gallery (*in a theater*).

paraje *m.* place; spot; situation.

paralelo *adj.* parallel; similar; *m.* parallel; similarity; **paralela** *f.* parallel line; **paralelismo** *m.* parallelism.

parálisis *f.* paralysis.

paralizar[9] *v.* to paralyze; to stop.

páramo *m.* high, bleak plain; cold region; *Am.* blizzard or a cold drizzle.

parangón *m.* comparison.

parangonar *v.* to compare.

paraninfo *m.* assembly hall, lecture hall, auditorium.

parapeto *m.* parapet.

parar *v.* to stop; to end, end up, come to an end; to parry (*in fencing*); to set up (*type*); *Am.* to stand, place in upright position; **— atención** to notice; **— mientes en** to observe, notice; *Am.* **— las orejas** to prick up one's ears; to pay close attention; **-se** to stop; *Am.* to stand up, get up.

pararrayos *m.* lightning rod.

parásito *m.* parasite; *adj.* parasitic.

parasol *m.* parasol.

parcela *f.* parcel of land; particle, small piece.

parcial *adj.* partial; *m.* follower, partisan; **parcialidad** *f.* partiality; faction, party.

parche *m.* mending patch; sticking plaster; medicated plaster; drum.

pardal *m.* sparrow; linnet; sly fellow.

pardear *v.* to grow dusky; to appear brownish-grey.

pardo *adj.* dark-grey; brown; dark; cloudy; *m.* leopard; *Am.* mulatto; **pardusco** *adj.* greyish; brownish.

parear *v.* to pair, couple, match, mate.

parecer[13] *v. irr.* to seem; to appear, show up; **-se** to resemble each other, look alike; *m.* opinion; appearance,

PAR—PAR

looks; **al —** apparently, seemingly.
parecido *adj.* alike, similar; **bien —** good-looking; *p.p. of* **parecer;** *m.* similarity, likeness, resemblance.
pared *f.* wall; **— maestra** main wall; **— medianera** partition wall.
pareja *f.* pair; couple; match; partner; *Am.* team of two horses; *Am.* horse race.
parejero *m. Am.* race horse; *Am.* over-familiar person, backslapper, hail-fellow-well-met.
parejo *adj.* even; smooth; equal; *adv. Am.* hard.
parentela *f.* relatives, kin.
parentesco *m.* kinship, relationship.
paréntesis *m.* parenthesis; digression; **entre —** by the way.
paria *m. & f.* outcast.
paridad *f.* par, equality.
pariente *m. & f.* relative, relation.
parir *v.* to give birth; to bear *(children).*
parlamentar *v.* to converse; to parley, discuss terms with an enemy.
parlamentario *adj.* parliamentary; *m.* member of parliament; envoy to a parley.
parlamento *m.* speech *(of a character in a play);* parley; parliament, legislative assembly.
parlanchín *adj.* talkative; *m.* talker, chatterer.
parlero *adj.* talkative; gossipy; chattering, chirping.
parlotear *v.* to prate, prattle, chatter, chat.
parloteo *m.* chatter, prattle, idle talk.
paro *m.* work stoppage; lockout; *Am.* throw *(in the game of dice);* **Am. — y pinta** game of dice.
parodia *f.* parody, take-off, humorous imitation.
parodiar *v.* to parody, take off, imitate.
parótidas *f. pl.* mumps.
parpadear *v.* to wink; to blink; to flutter the eyelids; to twinkle.
parpadeo *m.* winking; blinking; fluttering of the eyelids; twinkling.
párpado *m.* eyelid.
parque *m.* park; *Am.* ammunition.
parra *f.* grapevine; earthenware jug.
parrafada *f.* chat.
párrafo *m.* paragraph; **echar un — con** to have a chat with.
parranda *f.* revel, orgy, spree; *Am.* gang, band; **andar** *(or* **ir)** **de —** to go on a spree.
parrandear *v.* to revel, make merry, go on a spree.
parrilla *f.* grill, gridiron, broiler; grate.

párroco *m.* parish priest.
parroquia *f.* parish; parish church; clientele, customers.
parroquiano *m.* client, customer; parishioner; *adj.* parochial, of a parish.
parsimonia *f.* thrift, economy; moderation; prudence.
parsimonioso *adj.* thrifty; stingy; cautious; slow.
parte *f.* part; share; place; party *(legal term);* **-s** qualities; *Am.* unnecessary excuses or explanations; **de algún tiempo a esta —** for some time past; **de — de** on behalf of; in favor of; **de — a —** through, from one side to the other; **dar —** to inform; **echar a mala —** to take amiss; **en —** partly; **por todas -s** everywhere; *m.* telegram; message.
partera *f.* midwife.
partición *f.* partition, division.
participación *f.* participation, share; notice.
participante *m. & f.* participant; *adj.* participating, sharing.
participar *v.* to participate, share; to inform, notify.
partícipe *m. & f.* participant; *adj.* participating.
participio *m.* participle.
partícula *f.* particle.
particular *adj.* particular, special; peculiar; private, personal; odd, strange; **en —** specially; **lecciones -es** private lessons; *m.* private citizen; individual; point, detail; matter.
partida *f.* departure, leave; item, entry; record; band, group; squad; shipment; game; set *(in tennis);* *Am.* part in the hair; **— de bautismo (de matrimonio** *or* **de defunción)** birth (marriage, *or* death) certificate; **— de campo** picnic; **— de caza** hunting party; **— doble** double-entry bookkeeping; *Am.* **confesar la —** to tell the truth, speak plainly; **jugar una mala —** to play a mean trick.
partidario *m.* partisan, follower, supporter.
partido *m.* party, faction, group; contest, game; profit; district; *Am.* **a** *(or* **al) —** in equal shares; *Am.* **dar —** to give a handicap or advantage *(in certain games);* **darse a —** to yield, give up; **sacar — de** to derive advantage from, make the best of; **tomar un —** to decide, make a decision.
partir *v.* to split, divide; to crack, break; to depart, leave; **a — de hoy**

154

starting today; from this day on; *Am.* **a** (*or* **al**) — in equal parts; *Am.* **— a uno por el eje** to ruin someone.

partitura *f.* musical score.

parto *m.* childbirth, delivery; product, offspring; **estar de** — to be in labor.

parvada *f.* pile of unthreshed grain; brood; *Am.* flock (*of birds or children*).

parvedad *f.* smallness; trifle; snack, bit of food.

párvulo *m.* child; *adj.* small; innocent.

pasa *f.* raisin; woolly hair of negroes.

pasada *f.* passing, passage; *Am.* stay; *Am.* embarrassment, shame; **una mala** — a mean trick; **de** — on the way; incidentally, by the way; **dar una** — **por** to pass by, walk by.

pasadizo *m.* aisle; narrow hall; narrow passageway.

pasado *m.* past; *p.p.* past, gone; *adj.* overripe, spoiled; *Am.* dried (*fruits*); *Am.* thin, bony (*animal*); — **mañana** day after tomorrow; **el año** — last year; **en días -s** in days gone by.

pasaje *m.* passage; fare, ticket; total number of passengers; *Am.* private alley; *Am.* anecdote.

pasajero *adj.* passing, temporary, fleeting, transitory; *m.* passenger.

pasamano *m.* railing, hand rail; gangplank; gangway (*of a ship*).

pasaporte *m.* passport.

pasar *v.* to pass; to cross; to surpass, exceed; to pierce; to go forward; to go over (in, by, to); to enter; to carry over, take across; to happen; to get along; to swallow; to overlook; to tolerate; to suffer; — **las de Caín** to have a hard time; — **por alto** to omit, overlook; — **por las armas** to execute; **-se** to transfer, change over; to get overripe, spoiled; to exceed, go beyond; **se me pasó decirte** I forgot to tell you; *Am.* **pasársela a uno** to deceive someone, break someone's confidence; **un buen** — enough to live on.

pasarela *f.* gangplank.

pasatiempo *m.* pastime; *Am.* cookie.

pascua *f.* Easter; Jewish Passover; — **florida** (*or* **de resurrección**) Easter Sunday; — **de Navidad** Christmas.

pase *m.* pass, permit; thrust (*in fencing*).

pasear *v.* to walk; to take a walk; to ride; **-se** to take a walk; to parade; **-se en automóvil** to take an automobile ride; **-se a caballo** to go horseback riding.

paseo *m.* walk, ride; parade; public park; boulevard; — **en automóvil** automobile ride; **dar un** — to take a walk.

pasillo *m.* aisle; hallway, corridor; short step; short skit; *Am.* a type of dance music; *Am.* runner, hall carpet.

pasión *f.* passion; suffering.

pasivo *adj.* passive; inactive; *m.* liabilities, debts; debit, debit side (*in bookkeeping*).

pasmar *v.* to astound, stun; **-se** to be amazed, stunned; to marvel; to get a sudden chill; to get frostbitten; *Am.* to become dried up, shriveled up; *Am.* to get bruised by the saddle or pack (*said of horses and mules*).

pasmo *m.* amazement, astonishment; wonder, awe.

pasmoso *adj.* astonishing, astounding; marvellous.

paso *m.* pass; step; pace; gait; passage; passing; skit; incident; *Am.* ford; *Am.* ferry, ferryboat wharf; *adv.* slowly; **de** — by the way, in passing; **al** — **que** while; **salir del** — to get out of a difficulty; *Am.* **marcar el** — to mark step, obey humbly; *adj.* dried (*figs, grapes, prunes, etc.*).

pasta *f.* paste; dough; noodles; book cover, binding; *Am.* cookie, cracker; **de buena** — of good temper or disposition.

pastal *m.* *Am.* range, grazing land, large pasture.

pastar *v.* to pasture, graze.

pastear *v.* *Am.* to graze, pasture.

pastel *m.* pie; pastry roll; filled pastry; trick, fraud; secret pact, plot; pastel crayon; **pintura al** — pastel painting.

pastelería *f.* pastry shop, bakery; pastry.

pastelero *m.* pastry cook; *Am.* turncoat (*person who changes easily from one political party to another*); *Am.* political intriguer.

pasterizar[9], **pasteurizar[9]** *v.* to pasteurize.

pastilla *f.* tablet (*of medicine, candy, etc.*); bar (*of chocolate*); cake (*of soap*).

pastizal *m.* pasture, grassland.

pasto *m.* pasture; grassland; grazing; nourishment; *Am.* grass; **a todo** — without restraint.

pastor *m.* shepherd; pastor.

pastoral *adj.* pastoral; *f.* pastoral play; idyll; pastoral letter; **pastorela** *f.* pastoral, pastoral play; **pastoril** *adj.* pastoral.

pastoso *adj.* pasty, soft; mellow (*said of the voice*); *Am.* grassy.

pastura *f.* pasture; fodder, feed.

pata *f.* foot, leg (*of an animal, table,*

155

chair, etc.); female duck; **— de gallo** crow's-foot (*wrinkle at the corner of the eye*); *Am.* **— de perro** wanderer; *Am.* **hacer — ancha** to stand firm, face a danger; **meter la —** to put one's foot in it, make an embarrassing blunder; **-s arriba** upside down, head over heels.

patacón *m. Am.* silver coin worth about one peso.

patada *f.* kick; stamp (*with the foot*); footprint; "kick," intoxicating effect; **a -s** with kicks; in great abundance; *Am.* **en dos -s** in a jiffy, in a second.

patalear *v.* to kick around; to stamp.

pataleo *m.* kicking; stamping.

pataleta *f.* convulsion; fainting fit.

patán *m.* boor, ill-mannered person; rustic; *adj.* rude, boorish, ill-mannered.

patata *f.* potato.

patear *v.* to kick; to stamp the foot; to tramp about; to trample on; to humiliate; *Am.* to kick, spring back (*as a gun*); *Am.* to have a kick or intoxicating effect.

patentar *v.* to patent.

patente *adj.* patent, evident, clear; *f.* patent; grant; privilege; *Am.* **de —** excellent, of best quality.

patentizar² *v.* to evidence, reveal, show.

paternal *adj.* paternal; fatherly.

paternidad *f.* paternity, fatherhood; authorship.

paterno *adj.* paternal, fatherly.

patético *adj.* pathetic.

patibulario *adj.* harrowing, frightful, hair-raising; criminal.

patíbulo *m.* scaffold, gallows.

patilla *f.* small foot or paw; *Am.* watermelon; *Am.* stone or brick bench (*near a wall*); *Am.* railing of a balcony; *Am.* slip from a plant; **-s** side whiskers; **Patillas** the Devil.

patín *m.* skate; a small patio; goosander (*a kind of duck*); **— de ruedas** roller skate; **patinadero** *m.* skating rink.

patinar *v.* to skate; to skid.

patio *m.* patio, open court, courtyard; *Am.* railway switchyard; *Am.* **pasarse uno el —** to take undue liberties.

patituerto *adj.* crook-legged; knock-kneed; bow-legged.

patizambo *adj.* knock-kneed.

pato *m.* duck; **pagar el —** to be the goat; to get the blame; *Am.* **andar —** to be flat broke, penniless; *Am.* **hacerse —** to play the fool; *Am.* **pasarse de — a ganso** to take undue liberties; *Am.* **ser el — de la boda** to be the life of the party; **patito** *m.* duckling.

patochada *f.* stupidity, blunder, nonsense.

patraña *f.* fabulous tale; lie, falsehood.

patria *f.* fatherland, native country.

patriarca *m.* patriarch; **patriarcal** *adj.* patriarchal.

patrimonio *m.* patrimony; inheritance.

patrio *adj.* native, of one's native country; paternal, belonging to the father.

patriota *m. & f.* patriot.

patriótico *adj.* patriotic.

patriotismo *m.* patriotism. .

patrocinar *v.* to patronize, favor, sponsor.

patrocinio *m.* patronage, protection.

patrón *m.* patron; patron saint; sponsor; master, boss; proprietor, landlord; host; skipper; pattern, standard, model; **patrona** *f.* landlady; patroness; hostess.

patronato *m.* board of trustees; foundation (*for educational, cultural, or charitable purposes*).

patrono *m.* patron, protector; trustee; patron saint.

patrulla *f.* patrol; squad, gang.

patrullar *v.* to patrol.

pausa *f.* pause, stop, rest.

pausar *v.* to pause.

pauta *f.* norm, rule, standard; guide lines (*for writing*).

pava *f.* turkey hen; *Am.* kettle, teapot, teakettle; *Am.* jest, coarse joke; **pelar la —** to talk by night at the window (*said of lovers*).

pavesa *f.* cinder; small firebrand; burnt wick or snuff of a candle; **-s** cinders.

pavimentar *v.* to pave.

pavimento *m.* pavement.

pavo *m.* turkey; *Am.* sponger, parasite; **— real** peacock; **comer —** to be a wallflower at a dance; *adj.* silly, foolish; vain.

pavón *m.* peacock.

pavonearse *v.* to strut, swagger.

pavoneo *m.* strut, swagger.

pavor *m.* awe, dread, terror.

pavoroso *adj.* frightful, dreadful.

payasada *f.* clownish act or remark.

payasear *v.* to clown, play the fool.

payaso *m.* clown.

paz *f.* peace.

pazguato *adj.* simple, dumb, stupid; *m.* simpleton.

peaje *m.* toll (*for crossing a bridge or ferry*).

pealar = **pialar.**

peal = **pial.**

peatón *m.* pedestrian.

peca f. freckle.
pecado m. sin.
pecador m. sinner; adj. sinful.
pecaminoso adj. sinful.
pecar[6] v. to sin; — **de bueno** to be too
· good; — **de oscuro** to be exceedingly
unclear, too complicated.
pecera f. fish bowl.
pecoso adj. freckly, freckled.
peculado m. embezzlement.
peculiar adj. peculiar; **peculiaridad** f.
peculiarity.
pechada f. Am. bump, push, shove
with the chest; Am. bumping contest
between two riders; Am. overthrow-
·ing an animal (by bumping it with the
chest of a horse).
pechar v. Am. to bump, push, shove
with the chest; Am. to drive one's
horse against; Am. to borrow, strike
(someone) for a loan.
pechera f. shirtfront; chest protector;
bib (of an apron).
pecho m. chest; breast; bosom; heart;
courage; **dar el** — to nurse; **tomar a**
-s to take to heart; Am. **a todo** —
shouting; Am. **en -s de camisa**
in shirt sleeves.
pechuga f. breast, breast meat of a
fowl; bosom; Am. courage, nerve,
audacity, impudence.
pedagogía f. pedagogy, science of education.
pedagógico adj. pedagogic, relating to
education or teaching.
pedagogo m. pedagogue, teacher, educator.
pedal m. pedal.
pedalear v. to pedal.
pedante adj. pedantic, affected, vain,
superficial; m. pedant; **pedantesco**
adj. pedantic.
pedazo m. piece, portion, bit; **hacer -s**
to tear or break into pieces; **caerse a**
-s to fall into pieces.
pedernal m. flint.
pedestal m. pedestal, base.
pedestre adj. pedestrian, walking, going on foot; commonplace, vulgar, low.
pedido m. commercial order; request,
petition; p.p. of **pedir**.
pedigüeño adj. begging, demanding.
pedir[5] v. irr. to ask, beg, petition; to
ask for; to demand; to require; to
order (merchandise); **a** — **de boca**
exactly as desired.
pedrada f. hit or blow with a stone;
throw with a stone; mark or bruise
made by a stone (thrown); **a -s** by
stoning; with stones; **dar una** — to hit

with a stone; **echar a alguien a -s**
to stone someone out; **matar a -s** to
stone to death.
pedregal m. rocky ground, ground
strewn with rocks.
pedregoso adj. rocky, stony, pebbly.
pedrería f. precious stones; precious
stone ornament; jewelry.
pedrusco m. boulder.
pedúnculo m. stem (of a leaf, flower or
fruit), stalk.
pegajoso adj. sticky; contagious.
pegar[7] v. to hit, strike, slap, beat; to
stick, paste, glue; to sew on (a button);
to infect; to be becoming; to be fitting, opportune, to the point; Am. to
tie, fasten; Am. to yoke; — **fuego** to
set on fire; — **un chasco** to play a
trick; to surprise, disappoint; — **un
susto** to give a scare; — **un salto**
(**una carrera**) to take a jump (a run);
-se to stick, cling; **pegársela a uno**
to fool somebody.
pegote m. sticky thing; sticking plaster;
clumsy patch; sponger; thick, sticky
concoction; clumsy addition or insertion (in a literary or artistic work).
peinado m. coiffure, hairdo; hairdressing;
p.p. combed; groomed; adj. effeminate;
bien — spruce, trim.
peinador m. hairdresser; short wrapper
or dressing gown; **peinadora** f. woman hairdresser.
peinar v. to comb; Am. to flatter.
peine m. comb.
peineta f. large ornamental comb.
peladilla f. small pebble.
pelado p.p. & adj. peeled; plucked; skin-
ned; hairless; featherless; barren, treeless, bare; penniless, broke; m. Am.
ragged fellow (generally a peon); Am.
ill-bred person.
pelafustán m. tramp, vagabond.
pelagatos m. ragged fellow, tramp.
pelaje m. animal's coat, fur; external
appearance.
pelar v. to cut the hair of; to pluck the
feathers or hair from; to peel, shell,
skin, husk; to fleece, rob; Am. to beat,
thrash; Am. to slander; Am. — **los
dientes** to show one's teeth; to smile
affectedly; Am. — **los ojos** to keep
one's eyes peeled; to open one's eyes
wide; **-se el pelo** off; to lose one's hair;
Am. to be confused; Am. to be careless, unaware; Am. to slip away; Am.
to die; **pelárselas por algo** to be
dying for something, want something
very much.
peldaño m. step (of a staircase).

pelea *f.* fight, quarrel.
pelear *v.* to fight; to quarrel.
peletería *f.* fur store; fur trade; furs; *Am.* leather goods, leather shop; *Am.* shoe store.
película *f.* thin skin; membrane; film; motion-picture film.
peligrar *v.* to be in danger.
peligro *m.* danger.
peligroso *adj.* dangerous.
pelillo *m.* short, fine hair; -s trouble, nuisance; **echar -s a la mar** to "bury the hatchet", become reconciled; **no pararse en -s** not to stop at small details, not to bother about trifles; **no tener -s en la lengua** to speak frankly.
pelirrojo *adj.* redheaded, red-haired.
pelo *m.* hair; nap (*of cloth*); grain (*in wood*); **al —** perfectly; agreed; apropos, to the point; along the grain; **eso me viene al —** that suits me perfectly; **con todos sus -s y señales** with every possible detail; *Am.* **por** (*or* **en**) **un —** on the point of, almost, by a hair's breadth; **montar en —** to ride bareback; **tomar el — a** to kid, make fun of; *Am.* **no aflojar un —** not to yield an inch.
pelota *f.* ball; ball game; *Am.* boat made of cowhide; **en —** (*or* **en -s**) naked; *Am.* **darle a la —** to hit upon by chance; **pelotilla** *f.* pellet, little ball.
pelotera *f.* brawl, row, riot; *Am.* crowd.
pelotón *m.* large ball; crowd, gang; heap, pile; platoon of soldiers.
peluca *f.* wig.
peludo *adj.* hairy; shaggy; *m.* plush carpet with shaggy pile; *Am.* a species of armadillo; *Am.* **agarrar un —** to get drunk.
peluquería *f.* barbershop, hairdresser's shop.
peluquero *m.* hairdresser, barber.
pelusa *f.* down; fuzz; nap (*of cloth*).
pellejo *m.* hide; skin; peel; **salvar el —** to save one's skin, escape punishment; *Am.* **jugarse el —** to gamble one's life.
pellizcar[6] *v.* to pinch, nip.
pellizco *m.* pinching, nipping; pinch, nip.
pena *f.* penalty; grief, worry; hardship; toil; *Am.* embarrassment; **a duras -s** with great difficulty; hardly; **me da — it** grieves me; *Am.* it embarrasses me; **valer la —** to be worth while; **tener** (*or* **estar con**) **mucha —** to be terribly sorry; *Am.* to be greatly embarrassed.

penacho *m.* tuft, crest; plume.
penal *adj.* penal; **código —** penal code.
penalidad *f.* hardship; trouble; penalty.
penar *v.* to suffer; to worry, fret; to impose a penalty; **— por** to long for; to suffer because of.
penca *f.* leaf of a cactus plant; *Am.* sweetheart; *Am.* **coger una —** to get drunk.
penco *m.* nag, horse; *Am.* boor.
pendencia *f.* quarrel; scuffle, fight.
pendenciero *adj.* quarrelsome.
pender *v.* to hang; to dangle; to depend.
pendiente *f.* slope; *m.* earring; pendant; *Am.* watch chain; *adj.* hanging, dangling; pending.
pendón *m.* banner.
péndulo *m.* pendulum.
penetración *f.* penetration; acuteness; keen judgment.
penetrante *adj.* penetrating; acute; keen.
penetrar *v.* to penetrate; to pierce; to fathom, comprehend.
península *f.* peninsula.
peninsular *adj.* peninsular.
penitencia *f.* penance.
penitenciaría *f.* penitentiary.
penitente *adj.* repentant, penitent; *m.* & *f.* penitent.
penoso *adj.* painful; hard, difficult; embarrassing; fatiguing; *Am.* timid, shy.
pensador *m.* thinker; *adj.* thinking.
pensamiento *m.* thought; mind; pansy.
pensar[1] *v. irr.* to think; to think over; to intend.
pensativo *adj.* pensive.
pensión *f.* pension; board; scholarship for study; boardinghouse; *Am.* apprehension, anxiety; **— completa** room and board.
pensionado *m.* pensioner (*person receiving a pension*); *adj.* & *p.p.* pensioned.
pensionar *v.* to pension.
pensionista *m.* & *f.* boarder; pensioner (*person receiving a pension*).
pentagrama *m.* musical staff.
penúltimo *adj.* next to the last.
penumbra *f.* partial shadow, dimness.
penumbroso *adj.* dim.
peña *f.* rock, large stone.
peñasco *m.* large rock; crag.
peñascoso *adj.* rocky.
peón *m.* unskilled laborer; foot soldier; spinning top; pawn (*in chess*); *Am.* farm hand; *Am.* apprentice; *Am.* **— de albañil** mason's helper.
peonada *f.* gang of laborers or peons.

peor *adj. & adv.* worse; worst; — **que** worse than; — **que** — that is even worse; **tanto** — so much the worse.

pepa *f. Am.* seed (*of an apple, melon, etc.*); *Am.* marble (*to play with*); **Pepa** *nickname for* **Josefa.**

pepenar *v. Am.* to pick up; *Am.* to seize, grab.

pepino *m.* cucumber.

pepita *f.* seed (*of an apple, melon, etc.*); pip (*a disease of birds*); nugget (*lump of gold or other minerals*); *Am.* fruit stone, pit; **Pepita** = **Josefita** *dim. of* **Josefa.**

pequeñez *f.* smallness; childhood; trifle; meanness.

pequeño *adj.* small, little; young; low, humble; *m.* child.

pera *f.* pear; goatee; sinecure, easy job; *Am.* Peruvian alligator pear (*see* **aguacate**); *Am.* **hacerle a uno la** — to play a trick on someone; **peral** *m.* pear tree; pear orchard.

percal *m.* percale (*fine cotton cloth*).

percance *m.* misfortune, accident; occurrence.

percepción *f.* perception; idea.

perceptible *adj.* perceptible, noticeable.

percibir *v.* to perceive; to collect, receive.

percudido *adj.* dirty, grimy.

percudir *v.* to soil, make dirty or grimy; -**se** to get grimy.

percha *f.* clothes or hat rack; pole; perch, roost; perch (*a fish*); **perchero** *m.* clothes or hat rack.

perder[1] *v. irr.* to lose; to squander; to ruin, harm; to miss (*a train*); — **de vista** to lose sight of; -**se** to lose one's way; to get lost; to go astray; to get spoiled; to become ruined.

perdición *f.* perdition, damnation, hell, ruin.

pérdida *f.* loss; damage.

perdidamente *adv.* excessively.

perdido *p.p. & adj.* lost; strayed; mislaid; ruined; **estar** — **por alguien** to be crazy about, to be very fond of, someone; *m.* rake, dissolute fellow; bum, vagabond.

perdigón *m.* young partridge; bird shot, buckshot; losing gambler.

perdiz *f.* partridge.

perdón *m.* pardon; forgiveness; remission.

perdonar *v.* to pardon; to forgive.

perdulario *m.* rake, dissolute person; reckless fellow; good-for-nothing; tramp.

perdurable *adj.* lasting, everlasting.

perdurar *v.* to last, endure.

perecedero *adj.* perishable.

perecer[13] *v. irr.* to perish; to die; -**se** to long (for), pine (for).

peregrinación *f.* pilgrimage; long journey.

peregrino *m.* pilgrim, *adj.* foreign, strange; rare, beautiful, perfect; travelling, wandering; **ave peregrina** migratory bird, bird of passage.

perejil *m.* parsley; -**es** frippery, showy clothes or ornaments.

perenne *adj.* perennial, enduring, perpetual.

pereza *f.* laziness; idleness.

perezoso *adj.* lazy; *m. Am.* sloth (*an animal*); *Am.* safety pin; *Am.* bed cushion.

perfección *f.* perfection; **a la** — to perfection, perfectly.

perfeccionamiento *m.* perfecting, perfection; completion.

perfeccionar *v.* to perfect, finish, complete.

perfecto *adj.* perfect.

perfidia *f.* perfidy, treachery.

pérfido *adj.* perfidious, treacherous, faithless.

perfil *m.* profile; outline; *Am.* pen or pen point.

perfilar *v.* to silhouette; to outline; -**se** to show one's profile; to be silhouetted.

perforación *f.* perforation, hole; puncture; perforating, boring, drilling.

perforar *v.* to perforate, pierce; to drill, bore.

perfumar *v.* to perfume, scent.

perfume *m.* perfume; fragrance.

perfumería *f.* perfumery; perfume shop.

pergamino *m.* parchment.

pericia *f.* expertness, skill.

perico *m.* parakeet, small parrot.

perifollos *m. pl.* frippery, finery, showy ornaments.

perifrasear *v.* to paraphrase.

perilla *f.* small pear; pear-shaped ornament, knob; pommel of a saddle; goatee, **de** — apropos, to the point.

perímetro *m.* perimeter.

periódico *m.* newspaper; periodical; *adj.* periodic, periodical.

periodismo *m.* journalism; **periodista** *m. & f.* journalist; newspaper editor or publisher; **periodístico** *adj.* journalistic.

período *m.* period; cycle; sentence.

peripecia *f.* vicissitude, change in fortune; unforeseen incident.

peripuesto *adj.* dressed up, dolled up, decked out.

perito *adj.* learned; experienced; skilful; skilled; *m.* expert.

perjudicar[6] *v.* to damage, impair, harm.

perjudicial *adj.* harmful, injurious.

perjuicio *m.* damage, ruin, mischief; harm.

perjurar *v.* to perjure oneself; to commit perjury; to curse, swear.

perjurio *m.* perjury.

perla *f.* pearl; **de -s** perfectly, just right, to the point.

perlino *adj.* pearly, pearl-colored.

permanecer[13] *v. irr.* to remain, stay.

permanencia *f.* permanence, duration; stability; stay, sojourn.

permanente *adj.* permanent.

permiso *m.* permission; permit.

permitir[6] *v.* to permit, let; to grant.

permuta *f.* exchange, barter.

permutar *v.* to exchange; to barter; to change around.

pernetas : en — barelegged, with bare legs.

pernicioso *adj.* pernicious, harmful.

perno *m.* bolt; spike; **-s** *Am.* tricks, frauds.

pero *conj.* but, except, yet; *m.* objection, exception; defect; a variety of apple tree; a variety of apple; **perón** *m. Am.* a variety of apple.

perogrullada *f.* platitude, trite or commonplace remark.

peroración *f.* peroration, speech, harangue.

perorar *v.* to make an impassioned speech; to declaim, harangue; to plea, make a plea.

perorata *f.* harangue, speech.

perpendicular *adj.*, *m.* & *f.* perpendicular.

perpetuar[18] *v.* to perpetuate.

perpetuo *adj.* perpetual; **perpetua** *f.* everlasting.

perplejidad *f.* perplexity.

perplejo *adj.* perplexed, bewildered.

perra *f.* bitch, female dog; drunkenness; **— chica** five-centime copper coin; **— grande** (*or* **gorda**) ten-centime copper coin.

perrada *f.* pack of dogs; **hacer una —** to play a mean trick.

perrera *f.* kennel; toil, hard work, hard job; tantrum; *Am.* brawl, dispute.

perrilla *f. Am.* sty (*on the eyelid*). See **orzuelo.**

perro *m.* dog; **— de busca** hunting dog; **— dogo** bulldog; **— de lanas** poodle; *adj.* dogged, tenacious; *Am.* hard, selfish, mean, stingy.

perruno *adj.* canine, doglike.

persecución *f.* persecution; pursuit.

perseguidor *m.* pursuer; persecutor.

perseguimiento *m.* pursuit; persecution.

perseguir[5, 12] *v. irr.* to pursue; to persecute; to harass, annoy.

perseverancia *f.* perseverance.

perseverar *v.* to persevere.

persiana *f.* Venetian blind; window shade.

persistencia *f.* persistence; **persistente** *adj.* persistent.

persistir *v.* to persist.

persona *f.* person; personage.

personaje *m.* personage; character (*in a book or play*).

personal *adj.* personal; *m.* personnel.

personalidad *f.* personality; individuality; person, personage.

perspectiva *f.* perspective; view; appearance; outlook; prospect.

perspicacia *f.* keenness of mind, penetration, keen insight.

perspicaz *adj.* keen, shrewd.

persuadir . to persuade.

persuasión *f.* persuasion.

persuasivo *adj.* persuasive.

pertenecer[13] *v. irr.* to belong; to pertain; to concern.

perteneciente *adj.* pertaining, belonging, concerning.

pértiga *f.* pole, bar, rod.

pertinente *adj.* pertinent, to the point, apt, fitting.

pertrechos *m. pl.* military supplies; tools, implements.

perturbación *f.* uneasiness, agitation, disturbance.

perturbar *v.* to perturb, disturb.

peruano *adj.* & *m.* Peruvian.

perversidad *f.* perversity, wickedness.

perverso *adj.* perverse, wicked; *m.* pervert.

pervertir[3] *v. irr.* to pervert; to corrupt; to distort; **-se** to become perverted; to go wrong.

pesa *f.* weight (*for scales*); **— de reloj** clock weight; **-s y medidas** weights and measures.

pesadez *f.* heaviness; dullness, drowsiness; slowness; bother; stubbornness.

pesadilla *f.* nightmare.

pesado *adj.* heavy; sound (*sleep*); tiresome, boring; annoying; slow; dull.

pesadumbre *f.* grief, sorrow; weight, heaviness.

pésame *m.* condolence, expression of sympathy.

pesantez *f.* gravity; heaviness.

pesar *v.* to weigh; to consider; to have

weight, value, or importance; to cause grief, sorrow, or regret; *m.* grief, sorrow; **a — de** in spite of.

pesaroso *adj.* grieved, sad; repentant.

pesca *f.* fishing; catch, fish caught.

pescadería *f.* fish market; **pescadero** *m.* fishmonger, dealer in fish.

pescado *m.* fish (*especially after being caught*); salted codfish.

pescador *m.* fisherman.

pescar[6] *v.* to fish; to catch; to catch unaware, catch in the act.

pescozón *m.* blow on the back of the head or neck.

pescuezo *m.* neck.

pesebre *m.* manger.

peseta *f.* peseta (*monetary unit of Spain*).

pesimismo *m.* pessimism; **pesimista** *m. & f.* pessimist; *adj.* pessimistic.

pésimo *adj.* very bad.

peso *m.* weight; weighing; burden; importance; *Am.* peso (*monetary unit of several Spanish American countries*).

pesquera *f.* fishery (*place for catching fish*); **pesquería** *f.* fishery; fishing.

pesquero *adj.* fishing; **buque —** fishing boat; **industria pesquera** fishing industry.

pesquisa *f.* investigation, inquiry; *m. Am.* police investigator.

pestaña *f.* eyelash; edging, fringe; **quemarse las -s** to burn the midnight oil, study hard at night.

pestañear *v.* to blink; to wink; to flicker.

peste *f.* pest, pestilence, plague; epidemic; stench, stink, foul odor; overabundance, excess; *Am.* smallpox; *Am.* head cold; **echar -s** to utter insults.

pestillo *m.* bolt; latch; lock.

petaca *f.* tobacco pouch; cigar case; leather covered hamper (*used as a pack*); *Am.* leather covered trunk, suitcase; *adj. Am.* heavy, clumsy.

pétalo *m.* petal.

petate *m.* bundle; impostor; *Am.* mat (*of straw or palm leaves*); *Am.* dunce; *Am.* coward; **liar el —** to pack up and go; *Am.* to die; *Am.* **dejar a uno en un —** to ruin a person, leave him penniless.

petición *f.* petition, request.

petirrojo *m.* robin, robin redbreast.

petiso *adj. Am.* small, short, dwarfish; *m. Am.* small horse, pony.

pétreo *adj.* stone, stony.

petróleo *m.* petroleum.

petrolero *m.* oil man; dealer in petroleum; **compañía petrolera** oil company.

petulancia *f.* flippancy; insolence; **petulante** *adj.* pert, impertinent, flippant.

pez *m.* fish; *f.* pitch, tar.

pezón *m.* nipple; stem, stalk (*of a fruit, leaf or flower*); small point of land.

pezuña *f.* hoof.

piadoso *adj.* pious; kind, merciful.

pial *m. Am.* lasso, lariat (*thrown in order to trip an animal*); *Am.* snare, trap.

pialar *v.* to lasso — by tripping with a **pial.**

piano *m.* piano; **— de cola** grand piano; **—** vertical upright piano.

piar[17] *v.* to peep, chirp; to cry, whine.

pica *f.* pike, spear; picador's goad or lance; stonecutter's hammer; *Am.* tapping of rubber trees; *Am.* trail; *Am.* pique, resentment; *Am.* cockfight.

picada *f.* prick; bite (*as of an insect or fish*); puncture; sharp pain; dive (*of a plane*); *Am.* path, trail (*cut through a forest*); *Am.* narrow ford; *Am.* peck.

picadillo *m.* meat and vegetable hash; minced meat, mincemeat.

picador *m.* picador (*mounted bullfighter armed with a goad*); horse-breaker; chopping block; *Am.* tree tapper.

picadura *f.* biting; pricking; bite; prick; sting; puncture; cut tobacco.

picante *adj.* pricking, biting, stinging; spicy; highly seasoned; *m.* strong seasoning; *Am.* highly seasoned sauce (*usually containing chili pepper*).

picapleitos *m.* quarrelsome person (*one who likes to pick a fight*); shyster.

picaporte *m.* latch; latchkey; door knocker.

picar[6] *v.* to prick; to pierce; to bite (*said of fish or insects*); to sting; to peck; to nibble; to mince, chop up; to goad; to stick, poke; to hew, chisel; to pique, vex; to itch, smart, burn; *Am.* to chop (*wood*); *Am.* to open a trail; *Am.* to tap (*a tree*); *Am.* to slaughter (*cattle*); **— muy alto** to aim very high; **— en** to border on, be somewhat of; *Am.* **¡pícale!** hurry! **-se** to be piqued, angry; to be moth-eaten; to begin to sour; to begin to rot; *Am.* to get tipsy; **-se de** to boast of.

picardía *f.* roguishness; offensive act or remark; roguish trick; mischief.

picaresco *adj.* picaresque, roguish.

pícaro *m.* rogue, rascal; *adj.* roguish; mischievous; crafty, sly; low, vile; **picarón** *m.* big rascal.

picazón *f.* itch, itching.

pico *m.* beak, bill; sharp point, peak;

pickaxe, pick; spout; mouth; additional amount, a little over; *Am.* a small balance; *Am.* a goodly sum; **tener el — de oro** to be very eloquent; **tener mucho —** to be very talkative.

picotada *f.*, **picotazo** *m.* peck.

picotear *v.* to peck; to chatter; *Am.* to mince, cut into small pieces.

pichel *m.* pitcher; mug.

pichón *m.* pigeon; *Am.* any male bird (*except a rooster*); *Am.* dupe, easy mark, *Am.* novice, inexperienced person, apprentice; *adj. Am.* timid, shy.

pie *m.* foot; leg; stand; stem; base; *Am.* down payment; *Am.* strophe, stanza; *Am.* — **de amigo** wedge; prop; — **de banco** silly remark; **a — juntillas** steadfastly, firmly; **al — de la letra** to the letter, exactly; **de —** (*or* **en —**) standing; **a cuatro -s** on all fours; **dar —** to give an opportunity or occasion; *Am.* **estar a — en** to be ignorant of; **ir a —** to walk.

piececito, piecito *m.* little foot.

piedad *f.* piety; pity; mercy; **monte de —** pawnshop.

piedra *f.* stone; gravel; hailstone; *Am.* piece of a domino set; — **angular** (*or* **fundamental**) cornerstone; — **caliza** limestone; — **pómez** pumice, pumice stone; **a — y lodo** shut tight; **ser — de escándalo** to be an object of scandal.

piel *f.* skin; hide; leather; fur.

piélago *m.* high sea; sea; great abundance, great plenty.

pienso *m.* feed; thought; **ni por —** not even in thought.

pierna *f.* leg; **dormir a — suelta** to sleep like a log, sleep soundly; *Am.* **ser una buena — ** to be a good fellow, be always in a good mood.

pieza *f.* piece; part; room; play; **de una —** solid, in one piece; *Am.* **ser de una — ** to be an honest, upright man.

pigmento *m.* pigment.

pijama *m.* pajamas.

pila *f.* basin; baptismal font; trough; pile; heap; electric battery; *Am.* fountain; *Am.* hairless dog; *Am.* bald head; **nombre de —** Christian name; *Am.* **andar —** to go naked; *Am.* **tener las -s** (*or* **tener por -s**) to have a lot, have heaps.

pilar *m.* pillar, column; basin of a have fountain.

pilcha *f. Am.* any article of clothing; *Am.* mistress; **-s** *Am.* belongings.

píldora *f.* pill.

pilmama *f. Am.* child's nurse, wet nurse.

pilón *m.* basin (*of a fountain*); watering trough; sugar loaf; large wooden or metal mortar (*for grinding grain*); counterpoise; *Am.* an additional amount, premium (*given to a buyer*); *Am.* **de —** to boot, in addition, besides; **piloncillo** *m. Am.* unrefined sugar loaf.

pilotar, pilotear *v.* to pilot.

pilote *m.* pile (*for building*).

piloto *m.* pilot; *Am.* generous entertainer or host.

pillaje *m.* pillage, plunder.

pillar *v.* to pillage, plunder; to pilfer; to seize, snatch, grasp; to catch; *Am.* to surprise, catch in the act.

pillo *adj.* roguish; sly, crafty; *m.* rogue, rascal; *Am.* a species of heron; *Am.* long-legged person; **pilluelo** *m.* little rascal, scamp.

pimentero *m.* pepper plant; pepperbox, pepper shaker.

pimentón *m.* large pepper; cayenne, red pepper; paprika.

pimienta *f.* black pepper.

pimiento *m.* green pepper; red pepper.

pimpollo *m.* rosebud; bud; shoot, sprout; attractive youth.

pináculo *m.* pinnacle, top, summit.

pinar *m.* pine grove.

pincel *m.* artist's brush; **pincelada** *f.* stroke of the brush.

pinchar *v.* to prick; to puncture.

pinchazo *m.* prick; puncture; stab.

pingajo *m.* tag, tatter, rag.

pingo *m. Am.* saddle horse; *Am.* devil.

pingüe *adj.* abundant, copious; fat, greasy.

pino *m.* pine; *Am.* filling for a meat pie; **hacer -s** (*or* **hacer pinitos**) to begin to walk (*said of a baby*); to begin to do things (*said of a novice*).

pinta *f.* spot, mark; outward sign, aspect; pint; *Am.* **hacer —** to play hooky, cut class.

pintar *v.* to paint; to describe, depict; to feign; to begin to turn red, begin to ripen (*said of fruit*); to fancy, imagine; *Am.* to play hooky, play truant; *Am.* to fawn, flatter; **no — nada** to be worth nothing, count for nothing; **las cosas no pintaban bien** things did not look well; *Am.* **— venados** to play hooky; **-se** to put on make-up; *Am.* to excel (in); *Am.* to praise oneself.

pintarrajear *v.* to daub; to smear with paint or rouge.

pinto *adj. Am.* spotted, speckled.

162

pintor *m.* painter, artist; — **de brocha gorda** house painter; poor artist; *adj. Am.* boastful, conceited.

pintoresco *adj.* picturesque.

pintura *f.* painting; picture; paint, color; description

pinzas *f. pl.* pincers· tweezers· claws (*of lobsters, crabs, etc.*); *Am.* pliers, tongs.

piña *f.* pineapple; pine cone; piña cloth; cluster; *Am.* pool (*a billiard game*).

piñata *f.* pot; hanging pot or other container (*filled with candies, fruit, etc.*).

piñón *m.* pine nut; nut pine; pinion.

pío *adj.* pious, devout; kind, merciful; dappled, spotted (*horse*), **obras pías** pious works, charitable deeds.

piojo *m.* louse

piojoso *adj.* lousy; mean, stingy.

pipa *f.* tobacco pipe keg, barrel; reed pipe (*musical instrument*); fruit seed (*of a lemon, orange, melon*); *Am.* green coconut; *Am.* potato; *Am.* **estar —** to be drunk; *m. Am.* species of green frog.

pipiar[17] *v.* to peep, chirp.

pipiolo *m.* novice, beginner; *Am.* child, youngster

pique *m.* pique, resentment; chigger (*insect*), flea; *Am.* small chili pepper; *Am.* trail: **a — de** in danger of, on the point of; **echar a —** to sink (*a ship*); to destroy; **irse a —** to capsize; to sink.

piquete *m.* prick, bite, sting (*of insects*), small hole, picket, stake; picket (*military*), *Am.* small band of musicians; *Am.* small corral. *Am.* cutting edge of scissors

piragua *f Am.* Indian canoe.

pirámide *f.* pyramid.

pirata *m.* pirate

piratear *v* to pirate

piropo *m.* flattery compliment; a variety of garnet (*a precious stone*); **echar un —** to "throw a bouquet", to compliment

pirueta *f* whirl· somersault, caper; **hacer -s** to cut capers, to turn somersaults. to do stunts.

pisada *f.* footstep, footprint, **dar una —** to step on, stamp on; **seguir las -s de** to follow in the footsteps of, to imitate.

pisapapeles *n.* paperweight.

pisar *v.* to step on, tread upon, to trample under foot; to pound; to cover (*said of a male bird*).

piscina *f* swimming pool, swimming tank, fish pond.

pise *m. Am.* rut. *Am.* tread (*of a wheel*).

See **rodadura**

piso *m* floor; story; pavement; apartment, flat; tread, *Am.* fee for pasturage rights; *Am* table scarf; *Am.* stool, footstool; *Am.* small rug.

pisón *m* heavy mallet (*for pounding, flattening, crushing*)

pisotear *v.* to tramp tramp on, trample; to tread

pisotón *m* hard step, stamp (*of the foot*); **dar un —** to step hard, stamp (upon)

pista *f* track, trace, trail; clew; race track; — **de aterrizaje** landing field.

pistola *f* pistol, **pistolera** *f* holster

pistón *m* piston, *Am.* cornet

pita *f. Am.* agave or century plant; *Am.* fiber, or thread made from the fiber, of the agave or maguey.

pitar *v.* to toot; to whistle, *Am.* to smoke, *Am.* to hiss; *Am.* to slip away, escape; *Am.* **-se una cosa** to steal something; *Am* **salir pitando** to leave on the run.

pitazo *m.* toot, whistle, blast.

pitillo *m.* cigarette; **pitillera** *f* cigarette case.

pito *m.* whistle; cigarette; *Am* tick (*an insect*); **no vale un —** it is not worth a straw, *Am.* **no saber ni — de una cosa** not to know anything about a subject.

pizarra *f* slate, blackboard· **pizarrín** *m.* slate pencil· **pizarrón** *m* blackboard.

pizca *f* pinch small bit, *Am.* harvest.

placa *f.* badge insignia, plaque, tablet, metal plate; photographic plate; license plate· *Am.* scab or skin blemish

placentero *adj.* pleasant agreeable.

placer[33] *v irr* to please, content, *m.* pleasure; sand bank, shoal; placer (*place where gold is obtained by washing*), *Am.* pearl fishing.

placero *m.,* **placera** *f* market vendor

plácido *adj.* placid, calm.

plaga *f* plague, calamity

plagar[7] *v.* to plague, infest, **-se de** to become plagued or infested with

plagiar *v.* to plagiarize, steal and use as one's own (*the writings, ideas. etc. of another*); to kidnap, abduct.

plan *m.* plan; design, project, drawing, mine floor; *Am.* clearing; *Am* building grounds of a ranch.

plana *f* page; plain, flat country; mason's trowel, tally sheet, **enmendar la — a uno** to correct a person's mistakes.

plancha *f.* flatiron, metal plate; gangplank. blunder, *Am.* railway flatcar;

Am. dental plate; — **de blindaje** armor plate; **hacer una** — to make a ridiculous blunder; **tirarse una** — to place oneself in a ridiculous situation.

planchado *m.* ironing; clothes ironed or to be ironed; *adj Am.* smart, clever; *Am.* brave; *Am* dolled up, dressed up; *Am.* broke, penniless.

planchar *v.* to iron; to smooth out; *Am.* to leave (*someone*) waiting; *Am.* to strike with the flat of a blade; *Am.* to flatter; *Am.* — **el asiento** to be a wallflower at a dance.

planeador *m* glider airplane.

planear *v.* to plan; to glide (*said of an airplane or bird*).

planeo *m* planning; glide, gliding (*of an airplane*)

planeta *m.* planet.

plano *adj.* plane, flat, level; *m.* plane; plan; map; **de** — flatly, clearly, openly; **dar de** — to hit with the flat of anything.

planta *f* plant; plantation; plan; ground plan; sole of the foot; — **baja** ground floor; **buena** — good looks; **echar -s** to brag.

plantación *f* plantation; planting.

plantar *v.* to plant; to strike (*a blow*); **-se** to stand firm; to balk; *Am.* to doll up, dress up; **dejar a uno plantado** to "stand someone up," keep someone waiting indefinitely.

plantear *v.* to plan; to establish; to carry out, to state, present (*a problem*); to try

plantío *m.* planting; plantation; recently planted garden; tree nursery

plasma *m.* plasma.

plástico *adj.* plastic.

plata *f.* silver; silver money; **hablar en** — to speak in plain language.

plataforma *f.* platform.

platanal, platanar *m.* grove of banana trees; banana plantation.

plátano *m.* banana; banana tree; plane tree.

platea *f.* main floor of a theatre.

plateado *adj.* silver-plated; silvery.

platear *v* to silver, plate, cover with silver.

platel *m* platter; tray

platero *m.* silversmith; jeweler

plática *f.* conversation, talk, chat; informal lecture.

platicador *m.* talker; *adj.* talkative.

platicar[6] *v.* to converse, talk, chat.

platillo *m.* saucer; pan (*of a pair of scales*); cymbal; stew.

plato *m.* plate; dish; dinner course.

platón *m.* large plate; platter.

platudo *adj. Am.* wealthy, rich.

playa *f.* beach, shore; *Am.* wide, open space in front of a ranch house; *Am.* — **de estacionamiento** parking lot.

plaza *f* plaza, public square; public market, job, employment; *Am.* park, promenade; — **de armas** parade ground; public square; fortress; — **fuerte** fortress; — **de gallos** cockpit (*for cockfights*); — **de toros** bull ring; **sacar a** — to bring out into the open, make public; **sentar** — to enlist; **plazoleta, plazuela** *f.* small square, court.

plazo *m* term, time; **a** — on credit; in installments.

pleamar *m.* flood tide, high tide.

plebe *f* rabble; masses

plebeyo *adj.* plebeian.

plebiscito *m.* plebiscite, direct vote.

plegadizo *adj.* folding; pliable, easily bent.

plegar[1,7] *v* to fold; to pleat; to crease; **-se** to bend, yield, submit.

plegaria *f* supplication, prayer; prayer hour.

pleito *m.* litigation, lawsuit; dispute; debate; — **de acreedores** bankruptcy proceedings; **pleitista** *m.* & *f.* quarrelsome person.

plenipotenciario *m.* plenipotentiary (*diplomatic agent having full power or authority*); *adj.* plenipotentiary, having full power.

plenitud *f* plenitude, fullness, completeness; abundance.

pleno *adj.* full, complete; **sesión plena** joint session, **en** — **día** in broad daylight, openly; **en** — **rostro** (*or* **en plena cara**) right on the face.

pliego *m.* sheet of paper; sealed letter or document.

pliegue *m.* fold, crease, pleat.

plomada *f* plumb, lead weight, plumb bob.

plomazo *m. Am.* shot, bullet.

plomería *f.* plumbing; plumber's shop; lead roof.

plomero *m.* plumber.

plomizo *adj.* leaden, lead-colored.

plomo *m.* lead; plumb, lead weight; bullet; boring person; **a** — vertical; vertically; *adj. Am.* lead-colored.

pluma *f.* feather; plume; quill; pen; — **estilográfica** (*or* — **fuente**) fountain pen, **plumada** *f* dash, stroke of the pen, flourish; **plumaje** *m.* plumage; plume; **plumero** *m.* feather duster; box for feathers; feather ornament (*on* *hats, helmets, etc.*); **plumón** *m.* down; feather mattress; **plumoso** *adj.* downy, feathery.

plural *adj.* plural.

pluvial *adj.* rain (*used as adj.*); **capa —** cope (*long cape used by priests during certain religious ceremonies*).

población *f.* population; populating; town, city; *Am.* house.

poblado *m.* inhabited place; village; *p.p.* populated; covered with growth.

poblador *m.* settler (*of a colony*).

poblar[2] *v. irr.* to populate, people; to to colonize, settle; to stock (*a farm*); to breed; **-se** to become covered (*with leaves or buds*).

pobre *adj.* poor; *m.* poor man; beggar; **pobrete** *m.* poor devil, poor wretch; **pobretón** *m.* poor old fellow, poor wretch.

pobreza *f.* poverty; need; lack, scarcity; barrenness.

pocilga *f.* pigsty, pigpen.

pocillo *m.* cup.

poco *adj.* little, scanty; small; short (*time*); **-s** few, some; *m.* a little, a bit; *adv.* little; **a —** presently, after a short time; **a — rato** (*or* **al — rato**) after a short while, **— a —** slowly, little by little; **a los -s meses** after a few months; **por — me caigo** I almost fell; **tener en — a** to hold in low esteem.

podar *v.* to prune, trim, cut off.

podenco *m.* hound.

poder[39] *v. irr* to be able; can; may; **él puede mucho** (*or poco*) he has much (*or little*) power; **puede que** it is possible that, it may be that, perhaps; **hasta más no —** to the utmost, to the limit; **no — más** not to be able to do more; **to be exhausted; no puede menos de hacerlo** he cannot help doing it; **no — con la carga** not to be equal to the burden, not to be able to lift the load; *Am.* **-le a uno algo to** be worried or affected by something; *m.* power, authority

poderío *m.* power, dominion; might; wealth.

poderoso *adj.* powerful, wealthy.

podre *f.* pus; decayed matter; **podredumbre** *f.* corruption, decay; pus; rotten matter

podrido *adj.* rotten, *p.p. of* **podrir**.

podrir[16] = **pudrir**[16].

poema *m.* poem.

poesía *f.* poetry; poem.

poeta *m.* poet; **poetastro** *m.* bad poet.

poético *adj.* poetic; **poética** *f.* poetics.

poetisa *f.* poetess.

polaco *adj.* Polish; *m.* Polish, Polish language; Pole.

polaina *f.* legging.

polar *adj.* polar.

polea *f.* pulley

polen *m.* pollen.

policía *f.* police; *m.* policeman.

policial *m. Am.* policeman.

polilla *f.* moth, larva of the moth.

política *f.* politics; policy; *Am.* **— de campanario** politics of a clique.

politicastro *m.* bad or incapable politician.

político *adj.* political; politic; polite; **madre política** mother-in-law; *m.* politician.

póliza *f.* policy, written contract, draft; customhouse certificate, **— de seguros** insurance policy

polizonte *m.* policeman.

polo *m.* pole (*of a magnet or of an axis*), polo (*a game*).

poltrón *adj.* lazy, idle, **silla poltrona** easy chair.

polvareda *f.* cloud of dust; **armar** (*or* **levantar**) **una —** to kick up the dust; to raise a rumpus.

polvera *f.* powder box; compact; powder puff.

polvo *m.* dust, powder; pinch of snuff or powder; **-s** toilet powder; **-s para dientes** tooth powder; **limpio de — y paja** entirely free; net; *Am.* cleaned out, without a penny; *Am.* innocent, ignorant, unaware; *Am.* **tomar el —** to escape, "beat it."

pólvora *f.* gunpowder; fireworks.

polvorear *v.* to powder, sprinkle with powder.

polvoriento *adj.* dusty

polvorín *m.* powder magazine; priming powder; powder flask; *Am.* tick (*parasitic insect*); *Am.* spitfire, quick-tempered person.

polla *f.* pullet (*young hen*); young lass, pool (*in cards*).

pollada *f.* hatch, brood; flock of chicks.

pollera *f.* woman who raises and sells chickens; chicken coop; a bell-shaped basket for chickens; petticoat; *Am.* skirt.

pollino *m.* young donkey, ass.

pollo *m.* young chicken; nestling, young bird; young man; **polluelo** *m.* chick.

pompa *f.* pomp, pageant, procession; bubble; pump.

pomposo *adj.* pompous.

pómulo *m.* cheek bone.

ponche *m.* punch (*a beverage*); **ponchera** *f.* punch bowl.

ponderación *f.* pondering, careful consideration, weighing; exaggeration.

ponderar *v.* to ponder, consider, weigh; to exaggerate; to extol.

ponderoso *adj.* ponderous, heavy

poner[10] *v. irr.* to put; to place; to set; to lay; to suppose; — **como nuevo a alguien** to cover someone with insults; — **en claro** to clarify; — **en limpio** to recopy, make a clean copy; — **todo de su parte** to do one's best; **pongamos que** let us suppose that , -**se** to place oneself; to become; -**se a** to begin to; -**se al corriente** to become informed; -**se de pie** to stand up; *Am.* -**se bien con alguien** to ingratiate oneself with someone, get on his good side; *Am.* **ponérsela** to get drunk.

poniente *m.* west; west wind; **el sol** — the setting sun.

pontón *m.* pontoon; scow, flat-bottomed boat; log bridge; pontoon bridge.

ponzoña *f.* venom, poison.

ponzoñoso *adj.* venomous, poisonous.

popa *f.* poop, stern; **viento en** — speedily; going well.

popote *m. Am.* straw for brooms; *Am.* drinking straw or tube.

populacho *m.* populace, rabble.

popular *adj.* popular.

popularidad *f.* popularity.

populoso *adj.* populous, densely populated.

poquito *adj.* very little; *Am.* timid, shy; *m.* a small bit; **a -s** in small quantities.

por *prep.* by; for; for the sake of, on account of, in behalf of; because of; through; along; in exchange for; in the place of; during; about, around; to, with the idea of; — **ciento** percent; — **consiguiente** consequently; — **entre** among, between; — **escrito** in writing; — **poco se muere** he almost died; **está** — **hacer** it is yet to be done; **él está** — **hacerlo** he is in favor of doing it; **recibir** — **esposa** to receive as a wife; **tener** — to consider, think of as; ¿ — **qué?** *interr. adv.* why? for what reason?

porcelana *f.* porcelain, china; enamel.

porcentaje *m.* percentage.

porción *f.* portion; part, share, **una** — **de gente** a lot of people.

porche *m.* porch.

pordiosear *v.* to beg.

pordiosero *m.* beggar.

porfía *f.* stubbornness, obstinacy; persistence, insistence; **a** — in competition; with great insistence.

porfiado *adj.* stubborn, obstinate, persistent.

porfiar[17] *v.* to persist; to insist; to dispute obstinately, to argue.

pormenor *m.* detail.

pormenorizar[9] *v.* to detail, tell in detail; to itemize.

poro *m.* pore.

poroso *adj.* porous.

poroto *m. Am.* bean, *Am.* runt.

porque *conj.* because, so that.

porqué *m.* cause, reason, motive.

porquería *f.* filth, filthy act or word; nasty piece of food, trifle, worthless object.

porra *f.* club, stick; *Am.* **mandar a uno a la** — to send someone to the devil; **porrazo** *m.* blow; knock; bump.

porta *f.* porthole; cover for a porthole; goal (*in football*).

portaaviones *m.* airplane carrier.

portada *f.* façade, front (*of a building*); title page.

portador *m.* carrier; bearer; tray

portal *m.* portal; entrance, vestibule; portico, porch; *Am.* Christmas crèche; -**es** arcades, galleries; **portalón** *m.* large portal; gangway (*of a ship*).

portamonedas *m.* pocketbook, coin purse.

portapapeles *m.* briefcase.

portaplumas *m.* penholder.

portar *v. Am.* to carry; -**se** to behave.

portátil *adj.* portable.

portavoz *m.* megaphone; mouthpiece.

portazgo *m.* toll.

portazo *m.* bang or slam of a door; **dar un** — to bang or slam the door.

porte *m.* portage, cost of carriage; freight; postage; manner, bearing; size, capacity; *Am.* birthday present.

portear *v.* to carry on one's back; *Am.* to get out in a hurry.

portento *m.* portent; wonder, marvel.

portentoso *adj.* marvelous, extraordinary, amazing, terrifying.

porteño *adj.* from a port; *Am.* from Buenos Aires.

portero *m.* doorkeeper, doorman; janitor.

pórtico *m.* portico, porch.

portilla *f.* porthole; small gate or passageway

portón *m.* gate.

portugués *adj.* Portuguese; *m.* Portuguese, Portuguese language.

porvenir *m.* future.

pos : en — **de** after; in pursuit of.

posada *f.* lodging; inn; boardinghouse,

dwelling, home; *Am.* las -s a Christmas festivity lasting nine days; **posadero** *m.* innkeeper.

posaderas *f. pl.* posterior, buttocks, rump.

posar *v.* to lodge; to rest; to sit down; to pose (*as a model*); to perch (*said of birds*); -se to settle (*said of sediment*); to perch (*said of birds*).

posdata *f.* postscript.

poseedor *m.* possessor, owner.

poseer[14] *v.* to possess, own; to master, know well; -se to have control of oneself.

posesión *f.* possession.

posesivo *adj. & m.* possessive.

posesor *m.* possessor, owner.

posibilidad *f.* possibility.

posible *adj.* possible; hacer lo — to do one's best; -s *m. pl.* goods, property, means.

posición *f.* position; posture; status, rank, standing; placing.

positivo *adj.* positive; effective; true; practical.

posponer[40] *v. irr.* to postpone, put off; to put after; to subordinate.

pospuesto *p.p.* of **posponer.**

posta *f.* small bullet; bet, wager; relay (*of post horses*); post station; -s buckshot; por la — posthaste; fast, speedily; *m.* postboy, courier, messenger.

postal *adj.* postal; tarjeta — postcard.

postdata = **posdata.**

poste *m.* post, pillar.

postergar[7] *v.* to delay; to postpone; to disregard someone's right.

posteridad *f.* posterity.

posterior *adj.* posterior, back, rear; later.

postigo *m.* wicket, small door or gate; shutter; peep window.

postizo *adj.* false, artificial; *m.* switch, false hair.

postración *f.* prostration, collapse, exhaustion; dejection, lowness of spirits.

postrar *v.* to prostrate; to humiliate; to throw down; to weaken, exhaust; -se to kneel to the ground; to be weakened, exhausted; to collapse.

postre *m.* dessert; a la — at last.

postrer(o) *adj.* last; hindmost, nearest the rear.

postulante *m. & f.* petitioner; applicant, candidate.

póstumo *adj.* posthumous, after one's death.

postura *f.* posture, position; bid; wager; pact, agreement; egg-laying.

potable *adj.* drinkable; agua — drinking water.

potaje *m.* pottage, thick soup; porridge; mixed drink.

pote *m.* pot; jar; jug; *Am.* flask; *Am.* buzzard.

potencia *f.* potency; power; faculty, ability; powerful nation.

potente *adj.* potent, powerful, strong.

potestad *f.* power; dominion, authority.

potranca *f.* filly, young mare.

potrero *m.* herdsman of colts; fenced-in pasture land; *Am.* cattle ranch, stock farm.

potro *m.* colt; rack, torture; *Am.* wild horse; *Am.* stallion.

poyo *m.* stone or brick bench (*usually built against a wall*).

pozo *m.* well; hole, pit; mine shaft; hold of a ship; *Am.* pool, puddle; *Am.* spring, fountain.

práctica *f.* practice; exercise; custom, habit; method.

practicante *m. & f.* doctor's assistant; hospital intern.

practicar[6] *v.* to practice; to put into practice.

práctico *adj.* practical; experienced, skilful; *m.* — de puerto harbor pilot.

pradera *f.* prairie; meadow.

prado *m.* meadow, field; lawn.

preámbulo *m.* preamble, introduction, prologue.

precario *adj.* precarious.

precaución *f.* precaution.

precaver *v.* to guard (against), keep (from); to warn, caution; -se to guard oneself (against); to take precautions.

precavido *adj.* cautious, on guard.

precedencia *f.* precedence; priority.

precedente *adj.* preceding; *m.* precedent.

preceder *v.* to precede; to have precedence.

precepto *m.* precept; rule; order.

preceptor *m.* teacher, tutor.

preciado *adj.* prized, esteemed; precious, valuable.

preciar *v.* to appraise; to value; -se de to boast of, be proud of.

precio *m.* price; value, worth; esteem.

precioso *adj.* precious, valuable; fine, exquisite; beautiful.

precipicio *m.* precipice; ruin.

precipitación *f.* precipitation; rush, haste, hurry.

precipitado *adj.* precipitate, hasty, rash; *m.* precipitate (*chemical term*).

precipitar *v.* to precipitate; to hasten, rush; to hurl, throw headlong; -se to throw oneself headlong; to rush (into).

precipitoso adj. precipitous, steep; rash.
precisar v. to determine precisely; to force, compel, make necessary; Am. to be necessary or urgent; Am. to need.
precisión f. precision, exactness; accuracy; compulsion, force, necessity; Am. haste.
preciso adj. necessary; precise, exact; clear; m. Am. small travelling bag.
precoz adj. precocious.
precursor m. precursor, forerunner.
predecir[27] v. irr. to predict, prophesy, forecast, foretell.
predestinar v. to predestine.
predicación f. preaching.
predicado adj. & m. predicate; p.p. of **predicar**.
predicador m. preacher.
predicar[6] v. to preach.
predicción f. prediction.
predilección f. predilection, preference, liking.
predilecto adj. favorite, preferred.
predisponer[40] v. irr to predispose, bias, prejudice.
predispuesto p.p. of **predisponer** & adj. predisposed, prejudiced, biased.
predominante adj. predominant; prevailing, ruling.
predominar v. to predominate, prevail.
predominio m. predominance; sway, influence.
prefacio m. preface.
prefecto m. prefect (military or civil chief; sometimes a mayor, sometimes governor of a province, as in Peru).
preferencia f. preference; de — with preference; preferably.
preferente adj. preferable; preferred; preferential; **acciones -s** preferred shares.
preferible adj. preferable.
preferir[3] v. irr. to prefer.
prefijar v. to prefix; to set beforehand (as a date).
prefijo m. prefix.
pregonar v. to proclaim, cry out; to make known.
pregunta f. question; **hacer una —** to ask a question.
preguntar v. to ask, inquire.
preguntón adj. inquisitive.
prejuicio m. prejudice.
prelado m. prelate.
preliminar adj. & m. preliminary.
preludiar v. to be the prelude or beginning of; to initiate, introduce; to try out (a musical instrument).
preludio m. prelude; introduction.
prematuro adj. premature, untimely.

premeditado adj. premeditated, deliberate.
premiar v. to reward.
premio m. prize; reward; recompense; premium; **a —** with interest, at interest.
premisa f. premise (either of the first two propositions of a syllogism).
premura f. pressure, urgency, haste.
prenda f. pawn, pledge, security; token; article of clothing; anything valuable; jewel; loved person; **-s** good qualities, gifts, talents; **— de vestir** garment; **juego de -s** game of forfeits; **en — de** as a proof of, as a pledge of.
prendar v. to pawn, pledge; to charm, please; **-se de** to get attached to; to fall in love with.
prendedor m. clasp; stickpin; tie pin; brooch; Am. lighter.
prender v. to seize, catch; to bite (said of an insect); to fasten, clasp; to arrest, imprison; to take root; to begin to burn, catch fire; Am. to light (a lamp); Am. to start, begin, undertake; **— el fuego** to start the fire; Am. **-las** to take to one's heels; **-se** to dress up.
prendero m. pawnbroker; second-hand dealer.
prensa f. press; printing press.
prensar v. to press.
preñado adj. pregnant; full.
preñez f. pregnancy.
preocupación f. preoccupation; worry; bias, prejudice.
preocupar v. to preoccupy; to worry; to prejudice; **-se** to be preoccupied; to worry; to be prejudiced.
preparación f. preparation.
preparar v. to prepare; **-se** to get ready; to be prepared.
preparativo adj. preparatory; m. preparation.
preparatorio adj. preparatory.
preposición f. preposition.
prerrogativa f. prerogative, right, privilege.
presa f. prey; dam; fang, tusk; claw; **hacer —** to seize.
presagiar v. to foretell.
presagio m. presage, omen, sign.
presbítero m. priest.
prescindir v. to disregard, set aside, leave aside; to omit; to dispense (with).
prescribir[52] v. to prescribe.
prescrito p.p. of **prescribir**.
presencia f. presence; figure, bearing; **— de ánimo** presence of mind, serenity.
presenciar v. to see, witness; to be

168

present at.

presentación *f.* presentation; personal introduction; *Am.* petition.

presentar *v.* to present; to introduce; -se to appear, present oneself; to introduce oneself; to offer one's services; *Am.* to have recourse to justice, file suit.

presente *adj.* present; *m.* present, gift; **al** — now, at the present time; **por el (la,** *or* **lo)** — for the present; **mejorando lo** — present company excepted; **tener** — to bear in mind.

presentimiento *m.* presentiment, foreboding.

presentir⁵ *v. irr.* to have a presentiment, foreboding or hunch.

preservación *f.* preservation.

preservar *v.* to preserve, guard, protect, keep.

presidencia *f.* presidency; office of president; presidential term; chairmanship.

presidencial *adj.* presidential.

presidente *m.* president; chairman; presiding judge.

presidiario *m.* prisoner, convict.

presidio *m.* garrison; fortress; penitentiary, prison; **diez años de** — ten years at hard labor (*in a prison*).

presidir *v.* to preside; to direct.

presilla *f.* loop, fastener; clip.

presión *f.* pressure.

preso *m.* prisoner; *p.p. irr.* of **prender** imprisoned.

prestado *adj.* & *p.p.* loaned, lent; **dar** — to lend; **pedir** — to borrow.

prestamista. *m.* & *f.* moneylender.

préstamo *m.* loan.

prestar *v.* to loan, lend; *Am.* to borrow; — **ayuda** to give help; — **atención** to pay attention; *Am.* **presta acá** give it here, give it to me; -se to lend oneself or itself.

presteza *f.* promptness, speed.

prestidigitación *f.* juggling, sleight of hand.

prestidigitador *m.* juggler.

prestigio *m.* prestige; influence, authority; good reputation.

presto *adj.* quick; nimble; prompt; ready; *adv.* soon, at once; **de** — quickly, promptly.

presumido *adj.* conceited, presumptuous; *p.p. of* **presumir.**

presumir *v.* to presume; to boast; to show off; *Am.* to court, woo; — **de valiente** to boast of one's valor.

presunción *f.* presumption, assumption; conceit, arrogance.

presunto *adj.* presumed; supposed; prospective; **heredero** — heir apparent.

presuntuoso *adj.* presumptuous, conceited.

presuponer⁴⁰ *v. irr.* to presuppose, take for granted, imply; to estimate.

presupuesto *p.p. of* **presuponer** presupposed; estimated; *m.* budget, estimate.

presuroso *adj.* quick, prompt; hasty.

pretencioso *adj.* presumptuous; conceited.

pretender *v.* to pretend; to solicit, seek; to claim; to try; to court.

pretendiente *m.* pretender, claimant; suitor; office seeker.

pretensión *f.* pretension; claim; presumption; pretense.

pretérito *adj.* preterite, past; *m.* preterite, the past tense.

pretexto *m.* pretext, pretense, excuse.

pretil *m.* stone or brick railing; *Am.* ledge; *Am.* stone or brick bench (*built against a wall*).

pretina *f.* belt, girdle; waistband.

prevalecer¹³ *v. irr.* to prevail.

prevaleciente *adj.* prevalent, current.

prevención *f.* prevention; foresight, preparedness; bias, prejudice; provision, supply; admonition, warning; police station; guardhouse.

prevenido *adj.* & *p.p.* prepared, ready; forewarned; cautious; supplied.

prevenir⁴⁸ *v. irr.* to prevent, avoid; to prepare beforehand; to foresee; to warn; to predispose; -se to get prepared, get ready.

prever⁴⁹ *v. irr.* to foresee.

previo *adj.* previous; *m. Am.* preliminary examination.

previsión *f.* foresight.

previsto *p.p. of* **prever.**

prieto *adj.* dark, black; tight; compact; *Am.* dark-complexioned, swarthy.

prima *f.* female cousin; premium; prime (*first of the canonical hours*).

primacía *f.* priority, precedence; superiority.

primario *adj.* primary, principal.

primavera *f.* spring; primrose; print, flowered silk cloth.

primaveral *adj.* spring, pertaining to spring.

primer(o) *adj.* first; former; leading, principal; **primera enseñanza** primary education; **primera materia** raw material; **de buenas a primeras** all of a sudden, unexpectedly; **a primera luz** at dawn; *adv.* first; rather.

primicia f. first fruit; first profit; **-s** first fruits.

primitivo adj. primitive; primary; original.

primo m. cousin; simpleton, sucker, dupe; — **hermano** (or — **carnal**) first cousin; Am. **coger a uno de** — to deceive someone easily; adj. first; **número** — prime number.

primogénito adj. & m. first-born; **primogenitura** f. birthright; rights of the first-born.

primor m. beauty; excellence; exquisiteness; skill, ability.

primoroso adj. excellent, fine, exquisite; skilful.

prímula f. primrose.

princesa f. princess.

principal adj. principal; renowned, famous; **piso** — main floor (usually, the second floor); m. principal, capital sum; chief, head.

príncipe m. prince; adj. princeps, first (edition).

principiante m. beginner.

principiar v. to begin.

principio m. principle; beginning; origin, source; entrée (main dinner course); a - **-s de** towards the beginning of.

prioridad f. priority; precedence.

prisa f. speed, haste; **de** (or a) — quickly, speedily; a **toda** — with the greatest speed; **eso corre** — that is urgent; **dar** — a to hurry; **darse** — to hurry; **tener** (or **estar de**) — to be in a hurry.

prisión f. prison; imprisonment; seizure; shackle; **-es** shackles, fetters, chains.

prisionero m. prisoner.

prisma f. prism.

pristino adj. first, early, former, primitive.

privación f. privation; want, lack; loss.

privado adj. private; personal; unconscious; p.p. deprived; m. favorite.

privar v. to deprive; to enjoy the favor of someone; to be in vogue; **-le a uno del sentido** to stun, daze; **ya no privan esas costumbres** those customs are no longer in vogue or in existence; **-se** to lose consciousness; **-se de** to deprive oneself of.

privativo adj. exclusive; particular, distinctive.

privilegiado adj. privileged.

privilegiar v. to favor; to give a privilege to.

privilegio m. privilege; exemption; patent; copyright; — **de invención** patent on an invention.

pro m. & f. profit, advantage; **en** — **de** in behalf of; **en** — **y en contra** pro and con, for and against; **hombre de** — man of worth.

proa f. prow.

probabilidad f. probability.

probable adj. probable.

probar[2] v. irr. to prove; to taste; to test; to try; to try on; to suit, agree with; **no me prueba el clima** the climate does not agree with me.

probeta f. test tube; pressure gauge.

probidad f. integrity, uprightness, honesty.

problema m. problem.

procedente adj. proceeding (from), originating; according to law.

proceder v. to proceed; to originate; to behave; to take action (against); m. behavior, conduct.

procedimiento m. procedure; method; process; conduct.

prócer m. distinguished person; hero; great statesman.

procesado p.p. & adj. relating to, or included in, a lawsuit; accused, prosecuted; m. defendant.

procesar v. to prosecute; to accuse; to indict; to sue.

procesión f. procession; parade.

proceso m. process; lawsuit, legal proceedings; lapse of time; — **verbal** minutes, record.

proclama f. proclamation, ban; marriage banns.

proclamación f. proclamation.

proclamar v. to proclaim.

procurador m. attorney.

procurar v. to procure, obtain, get, acquire; to try, endeavor.

prodigar[7] v. to lavish; to bestow upon; to squander, waste.

prodigio m. prodigy, wonder, marvel; miracle.

prodigioso adj. prodigious, marvelous; fine, exquisite.

pródigo adj. prodigal, wasteful; lavish; generous; m. spendthrift.

producción f. production; produce.

producir[25] v. irr. to produce; to bring about; to yield; **-se** to express oneself, explain oneself; Am. to occur, happen.

productivo adj. productive; fruitful; profitable.

producto m. product; yield; result.

productor m. producer; adj. producing, productive.

proeza f. prowess; Am. boast, exaggeration.

profanación f. profanation.

profanar v. to profane; to defile.

profano adj. profane, not sacred; irreverent; lay, uninformed (about a branch of learning).

profecía f. prophecy; prediction.

proferir[3] v. irr. to utter, express, speak.

profesar v. to profess; to avow, confess.

profesión f. profession; avowal, declaration.

profesional adj., m. & f. professional.

profesionista m. & f. Am. professional.

profesor m. professor, teacher; **profesorado** m. professorship; faculty; body of teachers; teaching profession.

profeta m. prophet.

profético adj. prophetic.

profetizar[9] v. to prophesy.

proficiente adj. proficient, skilled.

profilaxis f. prophylaxis (disease prevention).

prófugo adj. & m. fugitive.

profundidad f. profundity, depth.

profundizar[9] v. to deepen; to go deep into.

profundo adj. profound; deep; low.

profuso adj. profuse; lavish.

programa m. program; plan.

progresar v. to progress.

progresista m., f. & adj. progressive.

progresivo adj. progressive.

progreso m. progress.

prohibición f. prohibition; ban.

prohibir v. to prohibit, forbid.

prójimo m. neighbor, fellow being; Am. **ese —** that fellow.

prole f. progeny, offspring.

proletariado m. proletariat, working class.

proletario adj. proletarian, belonging to the working class; plebeian; m. proletarian.

prolijo adj. prolix, too long, drawn out, too detailed; boring, tedious.

prologar[7] v. to preface, write a preface for.

prólogo m. prologue.

prolongación f. prolongation, extension; lengthening.

prolongar[7] v. to prolong, lengthen, extend.

promediar v. to average; to divide or distribute into two equal parts; to mediate; **antes de — el mes** before the middle of the month.

promedio m. middle; average.

promesa f. promise.

prometedor adj. promising hopeful.

prometer v. to promise; to show promise; Am. to affirm, assure; **-se** to become engaged, betrothed.

prometido adj. & p.p. betrothed; m. fiancé, betrothed; promise.

prominente adj. prominent.

promisorio adj. promissory.

promoción f. promotion, advancement.

promontorio m. promontory, headland, cape; anything bulky; bulge.

promotor m. promoter.

promovedor m. promoter.

promover[2] v. irr. to promote; to advance.

promulgación f. promulgation, publication, proclamation (of a law).

promulgar[7] v. to promulgate, proclaim, announce publicly.

pronombre m. pronoun.

pronosticar[6] v. to prophesy, predict.

pronóstico m. forecast; prediction; omen.

prontitud f. promptness; quickness.

pronto adj. quick, speedy; ready; prompt; adv. soon; quickly; **de —** suddenly; **al —** at first; **por de (or por lo) —** for the present; m. sudden impulse.

pronunciación f. pronunciation.

pronunciar v. to pronounce; to utter; **-se** to rise up in rebellion.

propagación f. propagation, spread, spreading.

propaganda f. propaganda.

propagar[7] v. to propagate, reproduce; to spread.

propalar v. to spread (news).

propasarse v. to overstep one's bounds; to exceed one's authority, go too far.

propensión f. tendency, inclination; bent, natural tendency or ability.

propenso adj. prone, susceptible, inclined.

propicio adj. propitious, favorable.

propiedad f. property; ownership; attribute, quality; propriety, appropriateness.

propietario m. proprietor, owner.

propina f. tip (voluntary gift of money for service).

propinar v. to give (something to drink); to give (a beating, kick, slap); Am. to tip, give a tip to; **— una paliza** to give a beating.

propio adj. proper; suitable; own; same; **amor —** vanity, pride, self-esteem; m. messenger.

proponer[40] v. irr. to propose; to resolve; to present; **-se** to resolve, make a resolution.

proporción f. proportion; dimension; ratio; opportunity, chance.

proporcionar v. to proportion; to

adapt, adjust; to furnish, supply; give.

proposición *f.* proposition; proposal; assertion.

propósito *m.* purpose, aim, design; **a —** apropos, suitable, fitting; by the way; **de —** on purpose; **fuera de —** irrelevant, beside the point.

propuesta *f.* proposal, offer; proposition.

propuesto *p.p.* of **proponer.**

propulsar *v.* to propel.

propulsor *m.* propeller; *adj.* propelling.

prorratear *v.* to prorate, distribute or assess proportionally; to average.

prorrateo *m.* apportionment, proportional distribution.

prórroga *f.* renewal, extension of time.

prorrogar[1] *v.* to put off, postpone; to adjourn; to extend (*time limit*).

prorrumpir *v.* to break forth; **— en llanto** to burst into tears; **— en una carcajada** to let out a big laugh.

prosa *f.* prose.

prosaico *adj.* prosaic; dull; tedious.

proscribir[52] *v.* to proscribe, banish; to outlaw.

proscripción *f.* banishment.

proscripto, proscrito *p.p..* of **proscribir**; *m.* exile, outlaw.

proseguir[5, 12] *v. irr.* to continue; to follow.

prosperar *v.* to prosper.

prosperidad *f.* prosperity; success.

próspero *adj.* prosperous; successful.

prostituir[32] *v.* to prostitute, corrupt.

prostituta *f.* prostitute.

protagonista *m.* & *f.* protagonist (*main character or actor*).

protección *f.* protection; support.

proteccionista *adj.* protective; **tarifa —** protective tariff; *m.* & *f.* protectionist (*follower of the economic principles of protection*).

protector *m.* protector, guardian; *adj.* protecting, protective.

protectorado *m.* protectorate.

proteger[11] *v.* to protect; to shelter; to defend.

proteína *f.* protein.

protesta *f.* protest; protestation.

protestación *f.* protestation, solemn declaration; protest.

protestar *v.* to protest; to assert, assure; to avow publicly; **— una letra** to protest a draft.

protoplasma *m.* protoplasm.

protuberancia *f.* protuberance, bulge.

protuberante *adj.* protuberant, prominent, bulging.

provecho *m.* profit; benefit; utility; advantage; **hombre de —** worthy, useful man.

provechoso *adj.* profitable; useful; beneficial; advantageous.

proveedor *m.* provisioner, provider; supply man.

proveer[14, 52] *v. irr.* to provide; to supply; to confer, bestow; to decide; **-se de** to supply oneself with.

provenir[48] *v. irr.* to originate, arise, come (from).

proverbio *m.* proverb.

providencia *f.* providence; foresight; Providence, God; legal decision, sentence; provision, measure; **tomar una —** to take a step or measure.

providencial *adj.* providential.

provincia *f.* province.

provincial *adj.* provincial.

provinciano *adj.* & *m.* provincial.

provisión *f.* provision; supply, stock.

provisorio *adj.* provisional, temporary.

provisto *p.p.* of **proveer.**

provocación *f.* provocation; dare, defiance.

provocador *adj.* provoking; — provoker.

provocar[6] *v.* to provoke; to excite, rouse; to stimulate.

proximidad *f.* proximity, nearness.

próximo *adj.* next; neighboring; near; **del — pasado** of last month.

proyección *f.* projection; jut.

proyectar *v.* to project; to plan; to throw; to cast; **-se** to be cast (*as a shadow*).

proyectil *m.* projectile.

proyectista *m.* & *f.* designer; schemer, planner.

proyecto *m.* project; plan; **— de ley** bill (*in a legislature*).

prudencia *f.* prudence, practical wisdom, discretion.

prudente *adj.* prudent, wise, discreet.

prueba *f.* proof; trial; test; fitting; sample; evidence; *Am.* acrobatic performance, stunt, trick, sleight of hand; **a — de incendio** fireproof.

prurito *m.* itch; keen desire.

psicología *f.* psychology.

psicológico *adj.* psychological.

psicólogo *m.* psychologist.

psiquiatra *m.* & *f.* psychiatrist, alienist.

psiquiatría *f.* psychiatry.

púa *f.* prick; barb; prong; thorn; quill (*of a porcupine, etc.*); sharp, cunning person; *Am.* cock's spur; **alambre de -s** barbed wire.

publicación *f.* publication.

publicar[6] *v.* to publish; to reveal; to announce.

publicidad *f.* publicity.

público adj. & m. public.
puchero m. pot, kettle; meat and vegetable stew; pout; **hacer -s** to pout.
pudiente adj. powerful; rich, wealthy; m. man of means.
pudín m. pudding.
pudor m. modesty; shyness.
pudrir[16] v. to rot; to vex, annoy; **-se** to rot.
pueblero m. Am. townsman (as opposed to countryman).
pueblo m. town, village; people, race, nation; populace; common people.
puente m. bridge; Am. dental bridge; Am. knife and fork rest; **— colgante** suspension bridge; **— levadizo** drawbridge.
puerca f. sow.
puerco m. pig, hog; **— espín** porcupine; **— jabalí** wild boar; adj. filthy, dirty; coarse, ill-bred.
pueril adj. puerile, childish.
puerta f. door; gate; entrance; **— accesoria (excusada**, or **falsa)** side door; **— de golpe** spring door; trap door; **— franca** open door; free entrance or entry; **— trasera** back door; **a — cerrada** secretly, behind closed doors; Am. **en —** in view, in sight, very near.
puerto m. port; harbor; refuge; mountain pass; **— franco** free port.
pues conj. since, because, for, inasmuch as; then; adv. then; well; **— bien** well then, well; **— que** since.
puesta f. set, setting (of a star or planet); stake at cards; **— de sol** sunset.
puestero m. Am. vendor, seller (at a stand or stall); Am. man in charge of livestock on Argentine ranches.
puesto p.p. of **poner** placed, put, set; **mal (or bien) —** badly (or well) dressed; m. place; vendor's booth or stand; post, position, office; military post; Am. station for watching and taking care of cattle on a ranch; **— de socorros** first-aid station; **— que** conj. since.
pugilato m. boxing.
pugilista m. boxer, prize fighter.
pugna f. struggle; conflict; **estar en — con** to be in conflict with; to be opposed to.
pugnar v. to fight; to struggle; to strive; to persist.
pujanza f. push, force, power.
pujar v. to make a strenuous effort; to grope for words; to falter; to outbid (offer a higher bid than); Am. to grunt; Am. to reject; Am. to dismiss; Am. **—**

para adentro to forbear, keep silent; Am. **andar pujado** to go around crestfallen; to be in disgrace.
pujido m. Am. grunt (due to strenuous effort).
pulcritud f. neatness, trimness; excellence, perfection.
pulcro adj. neat, trim; beautiful.
pulga f. flea; Am. small and insignificant person; **tener malas -s** to be ill-tempered; Am. **ser de pocas -s** to be touchy, oversensitive; **pulgón** m. blight, plant louse.
pulgada f. inch.
pulgar m. thumb.
pulido adj. polished, refined; polite; neat; exquisite.
pulimentar v. to polish.
pulimento m. polish; gloss.
pulir v. to polish.
pulmón m. lung.
pulmonar adj. pulmonary, pertaining to the lungs.
pulmonía f. pneumonia.
pulpa f. pulp.
pulpería f. Am. country general store; Am. tavern.
pulpero m. Am. owner of a country store or tavern.
púlpito m. pulpit.
pulque m. Am. pulque (fermented juice of the maguey).
pulsación f. pulsation, beat, throb; pulse, beating.
pulsar v. to pulsate, throb, beat; to feel the pulse of; to sound out, examine; to play (the harp); Am. to judge or try the weight of (by lifting).
pulsera f. bracelet; wrist bandage; **reloj de —** wrist watch.
pulso m. pulse; steadiness; tact; Am. bracelet, wrist watch; **un hombre de —** a prudent, steady man; Am. **beber a —** to drink straight down, gulp down; **levantar a —** to lift with the strength of the wrist or hand; **sacar a — un negocio** to carry out a deal by sheer perseverance.
pulular v. to swarm; to multiply rapidly; to sprout, bud.
pulverizar[9] v. to pulverize.
pulla f. taunt; mean dig, quip, cutting remark; filthy word or remark.
puma f. puma, mountain lion.
puna f. Am. cold, arid tableland of the Andes; Am. desert; Am. sickness caused by high altitude.
pundonor m. point of honor.
punta f. point, tip; bull's horn; cigar or cigarette butt; Am. gang, band,

herd, a lot (of things, people, etc.); Am. small leaf of fine tobacco; Am. jeer, cutting remark; **-s** point lace; scallops; **de — on** end; **de -s** (or **de puntillas**) on tiptoe; Am. **a — de** by dint of, by means of; **estar de — con** to be on bad terms with; **sacar — a un lápiz** to sharpen a pencil; **tener sus -s de poeta** to be something of a poet.

puntada f. stitch; hint; Am. prick, pricking, sting, sharp pain; **no he dado — en este asunto** I have left this matter completely untouched.

puntal m. prop; support, basis; bull's horn; Am. snack (between meals).

puntapié m. kick (with the toe of the shoe).

puntazo m. Am. stab, jab.

puntear v. to pluck (the strings of a guitar); to play (a guitar); to make dots; to engrave, draw or paint by means of dots; to stitch; to tack (said of a boat).

puntería f. aim.

puntero m. pointer; chisel; blacksmith's punch; Am. clock or watch hand; Am. leader of a parade; Am. leading ox (or other animal); Am. guide.

puntiagudo adj. sharp, sharp-pointed.

puntilla f. small point; tip; small dagger; tracing point; point lace; Am. penknife; Am. toe rubber; Am. ridge (of a hill); **de -s** on tiptoe; **puntillazo** m. stab (with a dagger).

punto m. point; dot; period; stop; stitch; mesh; gun sight; place; moment; **— de admiración** exclamation mark; **— de interrogación** question mark; **— y coma** semicolon; **dos -s** colon; **al —** at once, immediately; **a — de** on the point of; **de —** knitted, porous knit, stockinet or jersey weave; **en —** exactly, on the dot; **a — fijo** with certainty; **subir de —** to increase or get worse.

puntuación f. punctuation.

puntual adj. punctual, prompt; exact.

puntualidad f. punctuality, promptness; certainty.

puntuar[18] v. to punctuate.

punzada f. puncture; prick; sharp pain.

punzante adj. sharp; pricking; piercing, penetrating.

punzar[9] v. to puncture; to sting; to prick; to punch, perforate.

punzón m. punch, puncher; pick; awl.

puñada f. punch, box, blow with the fist.

puñado m. fistful, handful; **a -s** abun-

dantly; by handfuls.

puñal m. dagger.

puñalada f. stab; sharp pain; **coser a -s** to stab to death.

puñetazo m. punch, blow with the fist.

puño m. fist; fistful, handful; cuff; hilt, handle; Am. blow with the fist; **a — cerrado** firmly; **ser como un —** to be stingy; **tener -s** to be strong, courageous.

pupila f. pupil (of the eye).

pupilo m. ward; boarding-school pupil; boarder.

pupitre m. desk, school desk.

puré m. purée, thick soup.

pureza f. purity; chastity.

purga f. purge, laxative, physic.

purgante adj. purgative, laxative; m. purgative, physic, laxative.

purgar[7] v. to purge; to purify; to atone for; **-se** to purge oneself; to take a laxative.

purgatorio m. purgatory.

purificar[6] v. to purify.

puro adj. pure; clean; chaste; mere, only, sheer; **a pura fuerza** by sheer force; **a puros gritos** by just shouting; m. cigar.

púrpura f. purple; purple cloth.

purpúreo adj. purple.

pus m. pus.

puta f. whore, prostitute.

putativo adj. reputed, supposed; **padre — foster father.**

putrefacción f. putrefaction, decay, rotting.

putrefacto adj. putrid, rotten, decayed.

Q

que rel. pron. that; which; who; whom; **el —** who; which; the one who; the one which; conj. that; for, because; **más (menos) —** more (less) than; **el mismo — the** same as; **—** (= subj.) let, may you, I hope that; **por mucho** no matter how much; **quieras — no** whether you wish or not.

qué interr. adj. & pron. what?; what a!; interr. adv. how; **¡ — bonito!** how beautiful!!; **¿ a — ?** what for?; **¿ para — ?** what for?; **¿ por — ?** why?; **¿ — tal?** how?; hello!; **¡ —más da!** what's the difference!; **¡a mí — !** so what! and what's that to me!

quebrada f. ravine; gorge; failure, bankruptcy; Am. brook.

quebradizo adj. breakable; brittle; fragile; delicate.

quebrado adj. broken; weakened; ruptured; bankrupt; rough or rugged

174

(*ground*); *m.* common fraction; *Am.* navigable waters between reefs.

quebrantar *v.* to break; to break open; to pound, crush; to violate (*a law*); to weaken; to vex; *Am.* to tame, break in (*a colt*); — **el agua** to take the chill off the water.

quebranto *m.* breaking; grief, affliction; discouragement; damage, loss.

quebrar[1] *v. irr.* to break; to crush; to interrupt; to wither (*said of the complexion*); to become bankrupt; **-se** to break; to get broken; to be ruptured; **-se uno la cabeza** to rack one's brain.

quebrazón *m. Am.* breakage, breaking.

quechua *adj. Am.* Quichuan; *m. & f.* Quichua, Quichuan Indian; *m.* Quichuan language.

quedar *v.* to stay; to remain; to be left over; to be left (*in a state or condition*); — **en** to agree to; *Am.* — **de** to agree to; — **bien** to acquit oneself well; to come out well; *Am.* to suit, become (*said of a dress, hat, etc.*); *Am.* — **bien con alguien** to please someone; **-se** to remain; **-se con una cosa** to keep something; to take something (*buy it*); *Am.* **-se como si tal cosa** to act as if nothing had happened.

quedo *adj.* quiet, still; gentle; *adv.* softly; in a low voice; **quedito** *adj.* nice and quiet; *adv.* very softly.

quehacer *m.* work, occupation; task, duty, chore.

queja *f.* complaint; groan, moan; grudge.

quejarse *v.* to complain; to grumble; to moan; to lament.

quejido *m.* moan; groan.

quejoso *adj.* complaining, whining.

quejumbre *f.* whine, moan; murmur, complaint; **-s** *m. Am.* grumbler, whiner; **quejumbroso** *adj.* whining, complaining.

quemada *f.* burned forest; *Am.* burn.

quemado *m.* burned portion of a forest; *Am.* burned field; *Am.* hot alcoholic drink; *adj.* dark, tan; *Am.* peeved, piqued; *Am.* ruined; *p p. of* **quemar.**

quemadura *f.* burn; scald; smut (*plant disease*).

quemar *v.* to burn; to scald; to scorch; to sell at a loss; to annoy; *Am.* to deceive, swindle; **-se** to burn; to be hot.

quemazón *f.* burn; burning; great heat; fire, conflagration; pique, anger; bargain sale; *Am.* mirage on the pampas.

querella *f.* quarrel; complaint; controversy.

querellarse *v.* to complain.

querencia *f.* affection; longing; favorite spot; haunt; stable.

querer[41] *v. irr.* to want, wish, desire; to will; to be willing; to love; — **decir** to mean; **sin** — unwillingly; **no quiso hacerlo** he refused to do it; **quiere llover** it is trying to rain, it is about to rain; **como quiera** in any way; **como quiera que** since; no matter how; **cuando quiera** whenever; **donde quiera** wherever; anywhere; **-se** to love each other; *Am.* to be on the point of, be about to; **se quiere caer esa pared** that wall is about to fall.

querido *p.p.* wanted, desired; *adj.* beloved, dear; *m.* lover; **querida** *f.* darling; mistress.

quesería *f.* dairy, creamery, cheese factory; **quesera** *f.* dairy, cheese factory; cheese dish; dairymaid, woman cheese vendor or cheesemaker; **quesero** *adj.* pertaining to cheese; *m.* cheesemaker.

queso *m.* cheese; *Am.* — **de higos** fig paste.

quicio *m.* hinge of a door; **sacar a uno de** — to exasperate someone.

quichua = **quechua.**

quiebra *f.* break; crack; fissure; fracture; damage, loss; bankruptcy.

quien *rel. pron.* who, whom; he who, she who; **quién** *interr. pron.* who? whom?

quienquiera *pron.* whoever, whosoever, whomsoever.

quieto *adj.* quiet, still; calm.

quietud *f.* quiet, stillness, calmness.

quijada *f.* jaw; jawbone.

quilate *m.* carat (*twenty-fourth part in weight and value of gold*); unit of weight for precious stones and pearls; **-s** qualities; degree of perfection or purity.

quilla *f.* keel.

quimera *f.* absurd idea, wild fancy.

química *f.* chemistry.

químico *adj.* chemical; *m.* chemist.

quina, quinina *f.* quinine.

quincalla *f.* hardware.

quincallería *f.* hardware; hardware store; hardware trade.

quincena *f.* fortnight; semimonthly pay.

quinta *f.* villa, country house; draft, military conscription; sequence of five cards.

quintaesencia *f.* quintessence, pure essence, purest form.

quiosco *m.* kiosk, small pavilion.

quirúrgico *adj.* surgical.

quisquilloso *adj.* touchy, oversensitive.

quisto : bien — well-liked, well-re-

175

ceived, welcome; **mal —** disliked; **un-**welcome.

quitamanchas *m.* cleaner, stain remover.

quitar *v.* to remove; to take away (off, *or* from); to rob of; to deprive of; to subtract; to parry (*in fencing*); **-se** to take off (*clothing*); to remove oneself, withdraw; **-se de una cosa** to give up something, get rid of something; **-se a alguien de encima** to get rid of someone; **¡quita allá!** don't tell me that!; **¡quítese de aquí!** get out of here!

quitasol *m.* large sunshade, parasol.

quite *m.* parry (*in fencing*); dodge, dodging; *Am.* **andar a los -s** to be on the defensive; to take offense easily; to be afraid of one's own shadow; **eso no tiene —** that can't be helped.

quizá, quizás *adv.* perhaps, maybe.

R

rabadilla *f.* end of the spinal column; tail of a fowl; rump.

rábano *m.* radish; **tomar el — por las hojas** to take one thing for another; to misinterpret something.

rabia *f.* rabies; rage; **tener — a alguien** to hate someone; *Am.* **volarse de —** to get furious, angry.

rabiar *v.* to have rabies; to rage; to rave; to suffer a severe pain; **— por** to be dying to or for, be very eager to; **quema que rabia** it burns terribly.

rabieta *f.* tantrum, fit of temper.

rabioso *adj.* rabid (*having rabies*), mad; furious, angry, violent.

rabo *m.* tail; de cabo a **—** from beginning to end; **mirar con el — del ojo** to look out of the corner of one's eye.

racimo *m.* bunch; cluster.

raciocinio *m.* reasoning.

ración *f.* ration; allowance; supply.

racional *adj.* rational; reasonable.

racionamiento *m.* rationing.

racionar *v.* to ration.

radiador *m.* radiator.

radiante *adj.* radiant; shining; beaming.

radiar *v.* to radiate; to radio; to broadcast.

radical *adj.* radical; fundamental; extreme; *m.* radical; root of a word.

radicar[6] *v.* to take root; to be, be found (*in a certain place*); **-se** to take root; to locate, settle.

radio *m.* radius; radium; *m. & f.* radio.

radiodifundir *v.* to broadcast by radio. *See* **difundir.**

radiodifusión *f.* broadcasting. *See* **difu-**sión.

radiodifusora, radioemisora *f.* broadcasting station.

radioescucha *m. & f.* radio listener.

radiofónico *adj.* radio (*used as adj.*); **estación radiofónica** radio station.

radiografía *f.* radiography, X-ray photography; X-ray picture.

radiografiar[17] *v.* to take X-ray pictures.

radiolocutor *m.* radio announcer. *See* **locutor.**

radiotelefonía *f.* radiotelephony, radio, wireless.

radiotelegrafía *f.* radiotelegraphy, radio, wireless telegraphy.

radioyente = **radioescucha.**

raer[24] *v. irr.* to scrape off; to rub off; to scratch off; to fray; to erase.

ráfaga *f.* gust of wind; flash of light.

raído *p.p. & adj.* scraped off; rubbed off; frayed; worn, threadbare.

raigón *m.* large root; root of a tooth.

raíz *f.* root; origin; foundation; a **— de** close to, right after; de **—** by the roots, completely; **echar raíces** to take root, become firmly fixed.

raja *f.* slice; splinter; crack; split, crevice; **hacer -s** to slice; to tear into strips; to cut into splinters; **hacerse uno -s** to wear oneself out (*by dancing, jumping or any violent exercise*).

rajadura *f.* crack, crevice.

rajar *v.* to split; to crack; to cleave; to slice; to chatter; to brag; *Am.* to defame, insult; *Am.* to flunk, fail (*a student*); **-se** to split open; to crack; *Am.* to get afraid, back down.

rajatablas *m. Am.* reprimand, scolding; a **—** in great haste.

ralea *f.* breed, race, stock; species, kind.

ralear *v.* to thin out, make less dense; to become less dense.

ralo *adj.* sparse, thin, thinly scattered.

rallador *m.* grater.

rallar *v.* to grate; to grate on, annoy; *Am.* to goad, spur.

rama *f.* branch, limb; en **—** crude, raw; **andarse por las -s** to beat about the bush, not to stick to the point.

ramada *f.* branches, foliage; arbor; *Am.* shed, tent.

ramaje *m.* foliage; branches.

ramal *m.* strand (*of a rope, etc.*); branch; branch railway line; halter.

ramera *f.* harlot, prostitute.

ramificarse[6] *v.* to branch off, divide into branches.

ramillete *m.* bouquet; flower cluster.

ramo *m.* bunch (*of flowers*), bouquet; line, branch (*of art, science, industry,* *etc.*); branch, bough; **domingo de -s** Palm Sunday.

ramonear *v.* to cut off twigs or tips of branches; to nibble grass, twigs, or leaves; *Am.* to eat scraps or left-overs.

ramplón *adj.* coarse; crude, uncouth; slovenly.

ramplonería *f.* coarse act or remark; crudeness, coarseness; slovenliness.

rana *f.* frog.

rancio *adj.* rancid, stale; old (*wine*); **linaje** — old, noble lineage.

ranchero *m. Am.* rancher, farmer; **ranchería** *f.* group of huts; *Am.* inn (*for arrieros*).

rancho *m.* camp; hamlet; mess (*meal for a group and the group itself*); *Am.* hut; *Am.* country house; *Am.* ranch, small farm (*usually for cattle raising*).

rango *m.* rank, position.

ranura *f.* groove; slot.

rapar *v.* to shave off; to crop (*hair*); to strip bare, rob of everything.

rapaz *adj.* rapacious, grasping, greedy; *m.* lad; **rapaza** *f.* lass, young girl.

rapé *m.* snuff (*pulverized tobacco*).

rapidez *f.* rapidity, speed.

rápido *adj.* rapid, swift; *m.* rapids.

rapiña *f.* plunder; **ave de** — bird of prey.

rapiñar *v.* to plunder; to steal.

raposa *f.* fox.

raptar *v.* to kidnap, abduct.

rapto *m.* abduction, kidnapping; ecstasy, rapture; outburst.

raqueta *f.* racket (*used in games*); tennis.

raquítico *adj.* rickety, feeble, weak, skinny, sickly.

rareza *f.* rarity; oddity; strangeness; freak; curiosity; queer act or remark; peculiarity; **por** — seldom.

raro *adj.* rare; thin, not dense; scarce; strange, odd; ridiculous; **rara vez** (*or* **raras veces**) rarely, seldom.

ras : a — **de** flush with, even with; **al** — **con** flush with; **estar** — **con** — to be flush, perfectly even.

rascacielos *m.* skyscraper.

rascar[6] *v.* to scratch; to scrape; *Am.* to dig up potatoes; *Am.* — **uno para adentro** to seek one's own advantage, look out for oneself.

rasete *m.* sateen.

rasgado *adj.* torn; open; *Am.* generous; *Am.* outspoken; **ojos -s** large, wide-open eyes.

rasgadura *f.* tear, rip, rent.

rasgar[7] *v.* to tear; to rip.

rasgo *m.* trait, characteristic; stroke of the pen, flourish; feat; *Am.* irrigation

ditch; *Am.* **un** — **de terreno** a parcel of land; **-s** features; traits.

rasgón *m.* large tear, rent, rip.

rasguñar *v.* to scratch; to claw.

rasguño *m.* scratch.

raso *adj.* plain; flat, smooth; clear, cloudless; *Am.* even, level (*when measuring wheat, corn, etc.*); *Am.* scarce, scanty; **soldado** — private; **al** — **in** the open air; *m.* satin.

raspadura *f.* scrape; scraping; erasure; shaving (*of wood or metal*).

raspar *v.* to scrape, scrape off; to steal; *Am.* to scold, upbraid.

rastra *f.* drag; sled; large rake; harrow; **a -s** dragging; unwillingly.

rastreador *m.* trailer, tracker, tracer.

rastrear *v.* to trail, track, trace; to rake, harrow; to drag (*a dragnet*); to skim, scrape the ground.

rastrero *adj.* low, vile.

rastrillar *v.* to rake; to comb (*flax or hemp*); *Am.* to scrape; *Am.* to shoot; *Am.* to barter, exchange; *Am.* to pilfer, steal (*in stores*).

rastrillo *m.* rake; *Am.* barter, exchange; *Am.* business deal.

rastro *m.* track, trail, scent; trace, sign; rake, harrow; slaughterhouse.

rastrojo *m.* stubble.

rasura *f.* shave, shaving.

rasurar *v.* to shave.

rata *f.* rat; *m.* pickpocket.

ratear *v.* to pilfer; to pick pockets; to creep, crawl.

ratería *f.* petty larceny; meanness.

ratero *m.* pickpocket; *adj.* contemptible, mean.

ratificar[6] *v.* to ratify.

rato *m.* short time, little while; **buen** — pleasant time; long time; **-s perdidos** leisure hours; **a -s** at intervals, from time to time; **pasar el** — to while away the time, kill time; *Am.* **¡hasta cada** — ! so long!; see you later!

ratón *m.* mouse; *Am.* **tener un** — to have a hang-over; **ratonera** *f.* mouse trap.

raudal *m.* torrent, downpour, flood; *Am.* rapids.

raudo *adj.* rapid, swift.

raya *f.* line; dash; stripe; boundary line; part in the hair; *Am.* pay, wage; *Am.* **día de** — pay day; **tener a** — to keep within bounds; to hold in check; **pasar de la** — to overstep one's bounds, take undue liberties; *m.* sting ray (*a species of fish*).

rayador *m. Am.* paymaster; *Am.* umpire in a game.

rayar v. to line, make lines on; to streak; to scratch, mark; to cross out; *Am.* to pay or collect wages; *Am.* to stop a horse all of a sudden; *Am.* to spur a horse to run at top speed; — **el alba** to dawn; — **en** to border on; *Am.* **-se uno** to help oneself; to get rich.

rayo m. ray, beam; lightning, thunder-bolt; spoke; **-s X** X-rays.

raza f. race; clan; breed; fissure, crevice; **caballo de** — thoroughbred horse.

razón f. reason; right, justice; ratio; account, information, word, message; — **social** firm, firm name; **a** — **de** at the rate of; ¡**con** — ! no wonder!; **dar** — to inform; **dar la** — **a una persona** to admit that a person is right; **perder la** — to lose one's mind; **poner en** — to pacify; **tener** — to be right.

razonable adj. reasonable.

razonamiento m. reasoning.

razonar v. to reason; to discourse, talk; to argue.

reabierto p.p. of **reabrir**.

reabrir[52] v. to reopen.

reacción f. reaction.

reaccionar v. to react.

reaccionario adj. & m. reactionary.

reacio adj. stubborn, obstinate.

reajustar v. to readjust.

reajuste m. readjustment.

real adj. real; royal; m. army camp; fair ground; real (*Spanish coin worth one fourth of a peseta*); **-es** *Am.* money (*in general*); **levantar el** — (*or* **los -es**) to break camp.

realce m. embossment, raised work, re-lief; prestige; lustre, splendour; **dar** — to enhance; to emphasize.

realeza f. royalty (*royal dignity*).

realidad f. reality; truth; fact; **en** — really, truly, in fact.

realismo m. realism; royalism.

realista adj. realistic; royalist; m. realist; royalist.

realización f. realization, fulfilment; conversion into money, sale.

realizar[9] v. to realize, fulfill, make real; to convert into money; to sell out.

realzar[9] v. to emboss; to raise; to en-hance; to make stand out; to empha-size.

reanimar v. to revive; to comfort; to cheer; to encourage.

reanudación f. renewal.

reanudar v. to renew, resume, begin again.

reaparecer[13] v. irr. to reappear.

reasumir v. to resume.

reata f. lariat, rope, lasso.

reavivar v. to revive.

rebaja f. deduction; reduction; dis-count.

rebajar v. to diminish; to lower, reduce; to tone down (*a painting*); to humil-iate; **-se** to lower or humble oneself.

rebanada f. slice.

rebanar v. to slice.

rebaño m. flock; herd.

rebatir v. to beat over and over; to repel, resist; to refute; to rebut (*come back with an argument*); to argue; to parry (*in fencing*).

rebato m. alarm, call to arms; surprise attack.

rebelarse v. to rebel.

rebelde adj. rebellious; m. rebel; de-faulter (*one who fails to appear in court*).

rebeldía f. rebelliousness; defiance; de-fault, failure to appear in court; **en** — in revolt.

rebelión f. rebellion, revolt.

rebencazo m. *Am.* crack of a whip; *Am.* lash, stroke with a whip.

rebenque m. rawhide whip.

reborde m. edge, border.

rebosante adj. brimming, overflowing.

rebosar v. to overflow, brim over; to abound.

rebotar v. to rebound, bounce back or again; to make rebound; to repel, re-ject; to annoy, vex; **-se** to become vexed, upset; *Am.* to become cloudy or muddy (*said of water*); *Am.* **rebotársele a uno la bilis** to get angry, become upset.

rebote m. rebound, bounce; **de** — on the rebound; indirectly.

rebozar[9] v. to muffle up; **-se** to muffle oneself up; to wrap oneself up.

rebozo m. shawl; **sin** — frankly, openly.

rebullir[20] v. irr. to stir, move; to boil up.

rebusca f. research; search; searching; gleaning; residue.

rebuscar[6] v. to search thoroughly; to pry into; to glean.

rebuznar v. to bray.

rebuzno m. bray.

recabar v. to obtain, gain by entreaty.

recado m. message; gift; daily food supply, daily marketing; precaution; equipment; *Am.* saddle and trappings; — **de escribir** writing materials; **-s a** regards to.

recaer[24] v. irr. to fall (upon); to fall again; to relapse; to have a relapse.

recaída f. relapse; falling again.

recalar v. to saturate, soak through; to reach port; to come within sight of land; to land, end up, stop at; *Am.* — **con alguien** to "land" on somebody, take it out on somebody.

recalcar⁶ v. to emphasize; to harp on; to press down.

recalcitrante *adj.* obstinate, disobedient, stubborn.

recalentar¹ v. *irr.* to reheat, warm over; to overheat, heat too much.

recamar v. to embroider (*usually with gold or silver*).

recámara f. dressing room; *Am.* bedroom; chamber for an explosive charge.

recapitular v. to recapitulate, sum up, tell briefly.

recargo m. overload; extra load; extra charge; increase (*of fever*); new charge, new accusation.

recatado *adj.* cautious, prudent; modest; *p.p.* concealed.

recatar v. to cover, conceal; **-se** to show timidity; to be cautious; to hide (from), shun.

recato m. caution, prudence; reserve, restraint, secrecy; modesty.

recaudación f. collection, collecting; office of tax collector.

recaudador m. tax collector.

recaudar v. to collect (*money, taxes, rents, etc.*).

recaudo m. collection, collecting; precaution; bond, security; *Am.* spices, seasonings; *Am.* daily supply of vegetables; **estar a buen —** to be afe; **poner a buen —** to place in safety.

recelar v. to suspect, fear; **-se de** to be suspicious or afraid of.

recelo m. suspicion, fear.

receloso *adj.* suspicious, distrustful, fearful.

recepción f. reception; admission.

receptáculo m. receptacle.

receptivo *adj.* receptive, capable of receiving, quick to receive.

receptor m. receiver; *adj.* receiving.

receta f. recipe; prescription.

recetar v. to prescribe (*a medicine*).

recibidor m. receiver; reception room.

recibimiento m. reception; welcome; reception room; parlor.

recibir v. to receive; to admit, accept; to go out to meet; — **noticias de** to hear from; **-se de** to receive a title or degree of

recibo m. reception; receipt; reception room; parlor; **sala de** — reception room; **estar de** — to be at home for receiving callers; **ser de** — to be

acceptable, be fit for use.

reciedumbre f. strength, force, vigor.

recién *adv.* recently, lately, newly (*used before a past participle*); *Am.* just now; *Am.* a short time ago; *Am.* — **entonces** just then.

reciente *adj.* recent, new.

recinto m. enclosure; precinct.

recio *adj.* strong, robust; harsh; hard, severe; *adv.* strongly; harshly; rapidly; hard; loud.

recipiente m. receptacle, container; recipient, receiver (*he who receives*).

recíproco *adj.* reciprocal, mutual.

recitación f. recitation, recital.

recital m. musical recital.

recitar v. to recite.

reclamación f. protest, complaint; claim, demand.

reclamador m. claimant; complainer.

reclamante m. & f. claimant; complainer; *adj.* complaining; claiming.

reclamar v. to claim, demand; to complain, protest (against); to lure, call back (*a bird*).

reclamo m. protest; claim; advertisement; call; bird call; decoy bird; lure.

reclinar v. to recline, lean; **-se** to recline, lean back.

recluir³² v. *irr.* to seclude, shut up; **-se** to isolate oneself.

recluso m. recluse, hermit; *adj.* shut in, shut up.

recluta f. recruiting; *Am.* roundup of cattle; m. recruit.

reclutamiento m. recruiting; levy, draft.

reclutar v. to recruit, enlist; *Am.* to round up (*cattle*).

recobrar v. to recover, regain; **-se** to recover; to recuperate.

recobro m. recovery.

recodo m. bend, turn; elbow (*of a road*).

recoger¹¹ v. to gather; to collect; to pick up; to take in, tighten; to shelter; **-se** to retire, go home; to withdraw; to seclude oneself; to take shelter.

recogimiento m. seclusion; concentration of thought, composure; retreat; collecting, gathering.

recolección f. collecting, gathering; harvest, crop; summary.

recolectar v. to harvest; to gather.

recomendable *adj.* praiseworthy, laudable; advisable.

recomendación f. recommendation; request.

recomendar¹ v. *irr.* to recommend; to commend, praise; to enjoin, urge; to advise.

recompensa *f.* recompense; compensation.

recompensar *v.* to recompense, reward; to compensate.

reconcentrar *v.* to concentrate, bring together; to hide in the depth of one's heart; -se to concentrate, become absorbed in thought, collect one's thoughts.

reconciliación *f.* reconciliation.

reconciliar *v.* to reconcile; -se to become reconciled.

recóndito *adj.* hidden, concealed; profound.

reconocer[13] *v. irr.* to recognize; to admit, acknowledge; to examine carefully; to reconnoiter, scout, explore.

reconocimiento *m.* recognition; acknowledgment; gratitude; examination; scouting, exploring.

reconstruir[32] *v. irr.* to reconstruct, rebuild.

recontar[2] *v. irr.* to recount; to tell, relate.

recopilar *v.* to compile; to digest, make a digest of.

recordación *f.* recollection; remembrance.

recordar[2] *v. irr.* to remember; to recall; to remind; *Am.* to rouse, awaken; -se to remember; to wake up.

recordativo *m.* reminder; *adj.* reminding.

recordatorio *m.* reminder.

recorrer *v.* to go over; to travel over; to read over; to look over; to overhaul.

recorrido *m.* trip, run; mileage, distance traveled.

recortar *v.* to trim, clip; to shorten; to cut out (*figures*); to pare off; -se to project itself (*as a shadow*); to outline itself.

recorte *m.* clipping; cutting; outline; *Am.* gossip, slander.

recostar *v.* to recline, lean; -se to recline, lean back.

recoveco *m.* turn, bend; nook; sly or underhanded manner.

recreación *f.* recreation.

recrear *v.* to entertain, amuse; to gratify, please; -se to amuse oneself; to take delight (in).

recreo *m.* recreation, entertainment; place of amusement.

recrudecer[13] *v.* to recur, break out again, flare up, become worse (*said of an illness or evil*).

rectángulo *m.* rectangle; *adj.* rectangular, right-angled.

rectificar[6] *v.* to rectify, correct, amend; to refine (*liquors*).

rectitud *f.* rectitude, uprightness, righteousness; straightness; accuracy.

recto *adj.* straight; right; just, honest; ángulo — right angle; *m.* rectum.

rector *m.* college or university president; principal; rector, curate, priest.

recua *f.* drove of pack animals; drove, crowd.

recuento *m.* recount.

recuerdo *m.* remembrance; recollection; souvenir, keepsake; memory; -s regards; *adj. Am.* awake.

reculada *f.* recoil.

recular *v.* to recoil, spring back; to fall back, go back, retreat; to yield, back down.

recuperación *f.* recovery.

recuperar *v.* to recuperate, recover, regain; -se to recuperate, recover one's health.

recurrir *v.* to resort (to); to have recourse (to).

recurso *m.* recourse, resort; petition, appeal; -s means, resources; sin — without remedy; without appeal.

recusar *v.* to reject, decline.

rechazar[9] *v.* to reject; to repel, drive back; to rebuff.

rechifla *f.* hooting; hissing; ridicule.

rechiflar *v.* to hoot; to hiss; to ridicule.

rechinamiento *m.* creak; squeak; squeaking; gnashing.

rechinar *v.* to squeak; to creak; *Am.* to be furious, angry; *Am.* to grumble, growl; — los dientes to gnash one's teeth.

rechino = **rechinamiento.**

rechoncho *adj.* plump, chubby; squat.

rechuparse *v.* to smack one's lips.

red *f.* net; netting; network; snare; **redecilla** *f.* small net; mesh; hair net.

redacción *f.* wording; editing; newspaper offices; editorial department; editorial staff.

redactar *v.* to word, compose; to edit.

redactor *m.* editor.

redargüir[32] *v. irr.* to retort, answer back; to contradict, call in question; to reargue.

rededor *m.* surroundings; al (*or* en) — around, about.

redención *f.* redemption.

redentor *m.* redeemer, savior; el Redentor the Savior.

redil *m.* sheepfold.

redimir *v.* to redeem; to ransom; to set free.

rédito *m.* interest, revenue, yield.

redituar[18] *v.* to produce, yield (*interest*).

redoblar v. to double; to clinch (a nail); to reiterate, repeat; to roll (a drum).

redoble m. roll (of a drum).

redoma f. flask, vial.

redomón m. Am. half-tame horse or bull; adj. Am. half-civilized, rustic.

redonda f. surrounding district, neighborhood; whole note (music); **a la —** all around, round-about.

redondear v. to round, make round; to round off; to round out.

redondel m. arena, bull ring; circle.

redondo adj. round; whole, entire; clear, evident; Am. stupid; Am. honest; **en — all around.**

redopelo : a — against the grain.

redor m. round mat; **en —** around.

reducción f. reduction; cut, discount; decrease.

reducido p.p. & adj. reduced; compact, small.

reducir[25] v. irr. to reduce; to diminish; to convert (into); to reset (a bone); **-se** to adapt oneself, adjust oneself; to be constrained, forced.

reedificar[6] v. to rebuild, reconstruct.

reelección f. re-election.

reelegir[11] v. to re-elect.

reembolsar v. to reimburse, refund, repay, pay back.

reembolso m. reimbursement, refund.

reemitir v. to emit again; to issue again; to rebroadcast; to relay (a broadcast).

reemplazable adj. replaceable.

reemplazar[9] v. to replace; to substitute.

reemplazo m. replacement; substitute, substitution.

refacción f. light lunch, refreshment; repair, reparation; Am. spare part; Am. help, aid, loan.

refajo m. underskirt; short skirt.

referencia f. reference; narration, account.

referente adj. referring.

referir[3] v. irr. to refer; to narrate; to relate; **-se** to refer (to), relate (to).

refinamiento m. refinement.

refinar v. to refine; to purify.

refinería f. refinery.

reflector m. reflector; floodlight.

reflejar v. to reflect; to think over; **-se** to be reflected.

reflejo m. reflection, image; reflex; adj. reflected; reflex.

reflexión f. reflection; meditation, consideration.

reflexionar v. to reflect, meditate, think over.

reflexivo adj. reflexive; reflective, thoughtful.

reflujo m. ebb; ebb tide.

reforma f. reform; reformation; improvement.

reformador m. reformer.

reformar v. to reform; to correct, amend; to improve; **-se** to reform.

reformista m. & f. reformer.

reforzar[2, 9] v. irr. to reinforce; to strengthen.

refracción f. refraction.

refractario adj. refractory; impervious; rebellious, unruly; stubborn.

refrán m. popular proverb or saying.

refrenar v. to restrain, keep in check; to curb; to rein.

refrendar v. to legalize by signing; to countersign (confirm by another signature); **— un pasaporte** to visé a passport.

refrescante adj. refreshing.

refrescar[6] v. to refresh, renew; to cool; to get cool (said of the weather); **-se** to cool off; to take the fresh air; to take a cooling drink or refreshment; Am. to take an afternoon refreshment.

refresco m. refreshment.

refresquería f. Am. refreshment shop, outdoor refreshment stand.

refriega f. strife, fray, scuffle.

refrigeración f. refrigeration; light meal or refreshment.

refrigerador m. Am. refrigerator, freezer; adj. refrigerating, freezing; refreshing.

refrigerio m., refreshment; relief, comfort; coolness.

refuerzo m. reinforcement.

refugiado m. refugee; p.p. of refugiar.

refugiar v. to shelter; **-se** to take shelter or refuge.

refugio m. refuge, shelter.

refulgente adj. refulgent, radiant, shining.

refundir v. to remelt, refound, recast (metals); to recast, rewrite, reconstruct.

refunfuñar v. to grumble, mumble, growl, mutter.

refunfuño m. grumble, growl; refunfuñón adj. grouchy; grumbly, grumbling.

refutar v. to refute.

regadío adj. irrigable, that can be irrigated; irrigated; m. irrigated land; **tierras de —** irrigable lands.

regalar v. to give, present as a gift; to regale, entertain; to delight, please; **-se** to treat oneself well, live a life of ease.

regalo m. present, gift; pleasure, delight; dainty, delicacy; luxury, comfort.

regañadientes : a — much against one's wishes; unwillingly.

regañar v. to growl; to grumble; to quarrel; to scold.

regaño m. scolding, reprimand.

regañón adj. grumbling; scolding; quarrelsome; m. growler, grumbler, scolder.

regar[1,7] v. irr. to irrigate; to water; to sprinkle, scatter; Am. to spill, throw off (said of a horse); **-se** Am. to scatter, disperse (said of a group, herd, etc.).

regatear v. to haggle, bargain; to dispute; to sell at retail; to race (in a regatta or boat race).

regazo m. lap.

regentar v. to direct, conduct, manage; **—** una cátedra to teach a course (at a university).

regente m. regent; manager; adj. ruling.

regidor m. councilman, alderman; adj. governing, ruling.

régimen m. regime; government, rule, management; **—** lácteo milk diet.

regimiento m. regiment; administration; municipal council; position of alderman.

regio adj. regal, royal; splendid, magnificent.

región f. region.

regir[5,11] v. irr. to rule, govern; to direct, manage; to be in force (said of a law); to move (said of the bowels).

registrador m. registrar, recorder; city clerk, official in charge of records; inspector (in a customhouse); searcher; adj. registering; **caja registradora** cash register.

registrar v. to examine, inspect, scrutinize; to register, record; **-se** to register, enroll.

registro m. search, inspection; registration; census; registration office; register; record; registration certificate; watch regulator; bookmark; organ stop; Am. wholesale textile store.

regla f. rule; ruler; order; precept, principle; measure, moderation; menstruation; **en —** in order, in due form; **por — general** as a general rule; usually.

reglamento m. regulations, rules; rule, bylaw.

regocijado adj. joyful, merry, gay; p.p. of regocijar.

regocijar v. to gladden, delight; **-se** to be glad; to rejoice.

regocijo m. joy; rejoicing.

regordete adj. plump.

regresar v. to return.

regreso m. return; **estar de —** to be back.

reguero m. stream, rivulet; trickle; irrigation ditch.

regulación f. regulation; adjustment.

regulador m. regulator; controller, governor (of a machine); adj. regulating.

regular v. to regulate; to adjust; adj. regular; ordinary; moderate; fair, medium; **por lo —** as a rule, usually; adv. fairly well.

regularidad f. regularity.

regularizar[9] v. to regulate, make regular.

rehacer[31] v. irr. to remake; to make over; to repair; **-se** to recover one's strength; to rally.

rehén m. hostage; **en rehenes as a** hostage.

rehuir[32] v. irr. to shun, avoid; to shrink (from).

rehusar v. to refuse; **-se a** to refuse to.

reina f. queen.

reinado m. reign.

reinante adj. reigning; prevailing.

reinar v. to reign; to rule; to prevail.

reincidir v. to relapse, slide back (into).

reino m. kingdom.

reintegro m. reimbursement, refund.

reír[15] v. irr. to laugh; **-se de** to laugh at; Am. **— de dientes para afuera** to laugh outwardly, laugh hypocritically.

reiterar v. to reiterate, repeat.

reja f. grate, grating; plowshare (blade of the plow); plowing; Am. jail.

rejilla f. small grating, lattice; small latticed window; fireplace grate; cane upholstery; Am. wire dish-cover.

rejuvenecer[13] v. irr. to rejuvenate, make young; **-se** to become rejuvenated.

relación f. relation; story, account; long speech in a play, Am. verse recited alternately by a couple in a folk dance; **-es** personal relations, connections; acquaintances.

relacionar v. to relate, connect; **-se** to be related, connected; to become acquainted, establish friendly connections.

relajación f., **relajamiento** m. relaxation; laxity; slackening; hernia.

relajar v. to relax; to slacken; to release from a vow or oath; **-se** to get a hernia or rupture; to become weakened; to become lax (said of laws, customs, etc.).

relamerse v. to lick one's lips; to gloat;

to boast; to slick oneself up.

relámpago m. lightning; flash.

relampaguear v. to lighten; to flash; to sparkle.

relampagueo m. flashing; sheet lightning.

relatar v. to relate, narrate.

relativo adj. relative; — a relative to, regarding.

relato m. narration, account, story.

relegar[1] v. to relegate, banish; to postpone; to set aside, put away.

relente m. night dampness; Am. fresh night breeze.

relevar v. to relieve; to release; to absolve; to replace, substitute; to emboss; to make stand out in relief.

relevo m. relief (from a post or military duty; person who relieves another from the performance of a duty).

relicario m. reliquary (small box or casket for keeping relics); Am. locket.

relieve m. relief, embossment, raised work; -s scraps, leftovers; de — in relief; prominent, outstanding; poner de — to make stand out; to emphasize.

religión f. religion.

religiosidad f. religiousness, piety; faithfulness.

religioso adj. religious; faithful; punctual; m. friar, monk.

relinchar v. to neigh.

relincho m. neigh.

reliquia f. relic; vestige; -s relics, remains.

reloj m. clock; watch; — de pulsera wrist watch; — de sol (or — solar) sundial; — despertador alarm clock.

reluciente adj. shining; sparkling.

relucir[13] v. irr. to glitter, sparkle; to shine.

relumbrante adj. brilliant, flashing, resplendent.

relumbrar v. to glare; to glitter.

relumbre m. glare, glitter.

rellenar v. to refill; to fill up; to pad; to stuff.

relleno adj. stuffed; m. meat stuffing; filling.

remachar v. to clinch; to hammer down; to flatten; to rivet; to fix firmly; -se Am. to be tight-lipped, stubbornly silent.

remache m. clinching; fastening, securing; riveting; rivet.

remanente m. remainder, balance; remnant; residue.

remar v. to row; to struggle.

rematado adj. & p.p. finished; sold at auction; loco — completely crazy.

rematar v. to finish; to end; to give the final or finishing stroke; to auction; to fasten (a stitch); Am. to stop (a horse) suddenly; Am. to buy or sell at auction; -se to be finished, be completely destroyed or ruined.

remate m. finish, end; highest bid at an auction; sale at auction; pinnacle, spire; Am. selvage, edge of a fabric; de — absolutely, without remedy; loco de — completely crazy, stark mad.

remedar v. to imitate; to mimic.

remediar v. to remedy; to help; to avoid.

remedio m. remedy; help; amendment; recourse, resort; sin — without help, unavoidable; no tiene — it can't be helped.

remedo m. imitation; mockery.

remembranza f. remembrance, memory.

rememorar v. to remember, call to mind.

remendar[1] v. irr. to mend, patch; to darn; to repair.

remendón m. cobbler, shoe repairman; mender, patcher.

remero m. rower.

remesa f. shipment; remittance, payment.

remesar v. to remit; to ship.

remiendo m. mend; mending; patch; darn; repair; a -s piecemeal, piece by piece.

remilgado adj. prudish, prim, affected.

remilgo m. prudery, primness, affectation.

reminiscencia f. reminiscence.

remisión f. remission; forgiveness; remittance, remitting; abatement, slackening; Am. anything shipped or sent.

remitente m. & f. sender; shipper.

remitir v. to remit; to send; to pardon; to defer; to refer; to abate; -se to defer, yield (to another's judgment).

remo m. oar; hard and long work; al — at the oar; at hard labor.

remojar v. to soak; to steep; Am. to tip, bribe.

remojo m. soaking; steeping; Am. tip, bribe.

remolacha f. beet.

remolcador m. towboat, tug, tugboat; lancha remolcadora tugboat.

remolcar[6] v. to tow, tug; to take (a person) in tow.

remolino m. swirl, whirl; whirlwind; whirlpool; commotion; Am. pin wheel; Am. ventilating wheel (fan); — de gente throng, crowd.

remolón adj. indolent, lazy.

remolque *m.* tow; towrope; **llevar a —** to tow; to take in tow.

remontar *v.* to elevate, raise; to resole; to revamp, patch up, repair; *Am.* to go up; *Am.* to go upstream; **-se** to rise; to soar, fly upward; to date (from), go back (to); *Am.* to take to the woods or hills.

rémora *f.* impediment, obstacle, hindrance.

remordimiento *m.* remorse.

remoto *adj.* remote, distant; improbable.

remover[2] *v. irr.* to remove; to dismiss; to stir.

rempujar *v.* to jostle, push.

rempujón *m.* jostle, push.

remuda *f.* change; substitution; replacement; change of clothes; spare tire; relay of horses; *Am.* spare horse, spare pack animal.

remudar *v.* to change; to replace.

remuneración *f.* remuneration, compensation, pay, reward.

remunerar *v.* to remunerate, compensate, pay, reward (*for services*).

renacer[13] *v. irr.* to be reborn; to spring up, grow up again.

renacimiento *m.* renascence, renaissance; revival; rebirth.

renco *adj.* lame.

rencor *m.* rancor, resentment, hatred, grudge.

rencoroso *adj.* resentful, spiteful.

rendición *f.* surrender; submission; yield, profit.

rendido *p.p. & adj.* tired out, fatigued; devoted; obsequious, servile.

rendija *f.* crack, crevice.

rendimiento *m.* yield, output, profit; surrender, submission; fatigue.

rendir[5] *v. irr.* to subdue; to surrender, hand over; to yield, produce; to fatigue; to render, do (*homage*); *Am.* **— la jornada** to end or suspend the day's work; **-se** to surrender, give up; to become fatigued, worn out.

renegado *m.* renegade, traitor; *adj.* renegade, disloyal; wicked.

renegar[1,7] *v. irr.* to deny insistently; to detest; to blaspheme, curse; **— de** to deny, renounce (*one's faith*); *Am.* to hate, protest against.

renglón *m.* line (*written or printed*); item; *Am.* line of business, specialty.

renombrado *adj.* renowned, famous.

renombre *m.* renown, fame.

renovación *f.* renovation, restoration; renewal.

renovar[2] *v. irr.* to renovate; to renew; to replace.

renquear *v.* to limp.

renta *f.* rent, rental; income; revenue.

renuencia *f.* reluctance, unwillingness.

renuente *adj.* reluctant, unwilling.

renuevo *m.* sprout, shoot; renovation, restoration.

renunciar *v.* to renounce; to resign; to refuse; to renege (*fail to follow suit in cards*).

reñidor *adj.* quarrelsome.

reñir[5,19] *v. irr.* to quarrel; to fight; to scold.

reo *adj.* guilty; *m.* culprit, criminal; defendant.

reojo : mirar de — to look out of the corner of one's eye; to look scornfully.

repantigarse[7] *v.* to lounge, stretch out (*in a chair*).

reparación *f.* reparation; repair; indemnity.

reparar *v.* to repair; to regain; to recover; to make amends for, atone for; to remedy; to ward off (*a blow*); *Am.* to rear, buck (*said of horses*); **— en** to observe, notice.

reparo *m.* repair; restoration; observation; notice; doubt, objection; protection; shelter; parry (*fencing*); *Am.* sudden bound or leap of a horse.

repartimiento *m.* distribution, division; assessment.

repartir *v.* to distribute; to allot.

reparto *m.* distribution; mail delivery; cast of characters.

repasar *v.* to review, look over, go over again; to mend (*clothes*); to pass by again.

repaso *m.* review; revision.

repelente *adj.* repellent, repulsive, repugnant.

repeler *v.* to repel; to reject.

repente *m.* sudden movement; *Am.* attack, fit; **de —** suddenly.

repentino *adj.* sudden.

repercutir *v.* to resound, echo back; to rebound; to reflect back (*as light*).

repetición *f.* repetition.

repetido *p.p.* repeated; **repetidas veces** repeatedly, often.

repetir[5] *v. irr.* to repeat; to belch.

repicar[6] *v.* to chime, ring; to mince, chop fine; to sting again, prick again; *Am.* to drum, tap (*with the fingers or heels*); **-se** to boast; to be conceited.

repique *m.* chime, ringing, peal; mincing, chopping.

repiquetear *v.* to chime, ring; to jingle; *Am.* to tap (*with fingers or heels*).

repiqueteo *m.* chiming, ringing; jingling, tinkling; *Am.* clicking sound of heels.

repisa *f.* shelf, ledge; sill; wall bracket; — de ventana window sill.

replegar[1,7] *v. irr.* to fold, pleat; -se to retreat, fall back.

réplica *f.* reply, answer, retort; replica, copy; *Am.* examiner.

replicar[6] *v.* to reply, answer back; to retort.

repliegue *m.* fold, crease; retreat (*of troops*).

repollo *m.* cabbage.

reponer[40] *v. irr.* to replace; to put back; to reply, retort; to restore; -se to recover one's health or fortune; to collect oneself, become calm.

reportaje *m.* newspaper report; reporting.

reportar *v.* to check, control, restrain; to attain, obtain; to bring; to carry; *Am.* to report; -se to control oneself.

reporte *m.* report, news.

repórter, reportero *m.* reporter.

reposado *p.p.* & *adj.* reposed; quiet, calm; restful.

reposar *v.* to repose; to rest; to lie buried; -se to settle (*said of sediment*).

reposición *f.* replacement; recovery (*of one's health*).

reposo *m.* repose, rest; calm.

repostada *f.* sharp answer, back talk.

reprender *v.* to reprimand, scold.

reprensible *adj.* reprehensible, deserving reproof.

reprensión *f.* reproof, rebuke.

represa *f.* dam; damming, stopping; *Am.* reservoir.

represalia *f.* reprisal.

represar *v.* to bank, dam; to recapture (*a ship*) from the enemy; to repress, check.

representación *f.* representation; play, performance; authority, dignity; petition, plea.

representante *adj.* representing; *m.* & *f.* representative; actor.

representar *v.* to represent; to declare, state; to express, show; to play, act, perform; -se to imagine, picture to oneself.

representativo *adj.* representative.

represión *f.* repression, control, restraint.

reprimenda *f.* reprimand, rebuke.

reprimir *v.* to repress, check, curb; -se to repress oneself; to refrain.

reprobar[2] *v. irr.* to reprove, blame; to condemn; to flunk, fail.

reprochar *v.* to reproach.

reproche *m.* reproach.

reproducción *f.* reproduction.

reproducir[25] *v. irr.* to reproduce.

reptil *m.* reptile.

república *f.* republic.

republicano *adj.* & *m.* republican.

repudiar *v.* to repudiate; to disown.

repuesto *m.* stock, supply, provisions; sideboard; **de** — spare, extra; *p.p. of* **reponer** & *adj.* recovered (*from an illness, loss, fright, etc.*); replaced; restored.

repugnancia *f.* repugnance, disgust; aversion; dislike, reluctance.

repugnante *adj.* repugnant, disgusting, loathsome.

repugnar *v.* to be repugnant; to disgust; to oppose, contradict.

repulido *adj.* polished up, slick; shiny; spruce.

repulsa *f.* repulse; rebuff; rebuke.

repulsar *v.* to repulse, repel, reject.

repulsivo *adj.* repulsive, repugnant.

reputación *f.* reputation.

reputar *v.* to repute.

requebrar[1] *v. irr.* to compliment; to flatter; to flirt with; to court, woo; to break again.

requemado *p.p.* & *adj.* burned; parched; tanned, sunburnt.

requemar *v.* to parch, dry up; to burn; to overcook; -se to become overheated; to burn inwardly; to get tanned, sunburnt.

requerimiento *m.* requisition; requirement; summons; -s amorous advances, insinuations.

requerir[3] *v. irr.* to require; to need; to summon; to notify; to examine, investigate; — de amores to court, woo.

requesón *m.* cottage cheese.

requiebro *m.* flattery; compliment.

requisito *m.* requirement, requisite; — previo prerequisite.

res *f.* head of cattle; any large animal.

resabio *m.* disagreeable aftertaste; bad habit.

resaca *f.* undertow; surge, surf; redraft (*of a bill of exchange*); *Am.* beating, thrashing; *Am.* mud and slime (*left by a flood*).

resaltar *v.* to stand out; to project, jut out; to rebound, bounce or spring back; to be evident, obvious.

resarcir[10] *v.* to indemnify, compensate, repay; to make amends for; -se de to make up for.

resbaladero *m.* slide, slippery place.

resbaladizo *adj.* slippery.

resbalar *v.* to slide; -se to slip; to slide; to skid; **resbalársele a uno una cosa** to let a thing slide off one's back, be impervious to a thing.

resbalón *m.* sudden or violent slip; slide; error; **darse un —** to slip.

resbaloso *adj.* slippery.

rescatar *v.* to ransom; to redeem; to barter, exchange, trade; *Am.* to resell.

rescate *m.* ransom; redemption; barter, exchange.

rescoldo *m.* embers, hot cinders, hot ashes; doubt, scruple.

resecar[6] *v.* to dry up; to parch.

reseco *adj.* very dry; dried up, parched; thin, skinny.

resentimiento *m.* resentment; impairment, damage (*to one's health*).

resentirse[3] *v. irr.* to show resentment, hurt, or grief; to resent; to weaken; to become worse.

reseña *f.* military review; book review; brief account; sign, signal.

reseñar *v.* to review (*a book*); to review (*troops*); to outline briefly, give a short account of.

resero *m. Am.* cowboy, herdsman; *Am.* dealer in livestock.

reserva *f.* reserve; reservation; exception; caution; **a — de** reserving the right to, intending to; **sin —** without reserve, frankly.

reservación *f.* reservation.

reservar *v.* to reserve; to put aside; to postpone; to exempt; to keep secret; **-se** to conserve one's strength, spare oneself (*for another time*).

resfriado *m.* cold (*illness*); *p.p. of* **resfriar**; *adj. Am.* indiscreet.

resfriar[17] *v.* to cool; to chill; **-se** to catch cold; to cool.

resfrío *m.* chill; cold.

resguardar *v.* to guard, defend; to shield; **-se de** to guard oneself against; to seek shelter from.

resguardo *m.* defense; security; guarantee; guard.

residencia *f.* residence; office or post of a resident foreign minister; *Am.* luxurious dwelling.

residente *adj.* resident, residing; *m. & f.* resident, dweller; resident foreign minister; *Am.* alien resident.

residir *v.* to reside; to live, dwell; to be inherent, belong (to).

residuo *m.* residue; remainder.

resignación *f.* resignation.

resignar *v.* to resign; to hand over; **-se** to resign oneself.

resina *f.* resin.

resistencia *f.* resistance.

resistente *adj.* resistant; resisting.

resistir *v.* to resist; to tolerate, endure;

-se to resist, struggle.

resolución *f.* resolution; courage, determination; solution; **en —** in brief.

resolver[2, 52] *v. irr.* to resolve, decide; to solve; to dissolve; **-se** to resolve, decide; to be reduced (to), dissolve (into).

resollar[2] *v. irr.* to breathe hard; to pant.

resonar[2] *v. irr.* to resound.

resoplar *v.* to puff, breathe hard; to snort.

resoplido *m.* puff, pant; snort.

resorte *m.* spring; elasticity; means (*to attain an object*); *Am.* elastic, rubber band; *Am.* **no es de mi —** it doesn't concern me.

respaldar *v.* to endorse; to guarantee; *Am.* to back, support; **-se** to lean back; *Am.* to protect one's rear.

respaldo *m.* back (*of a chair or sheet of paper*); protecting wall; endorsement; *Am.* protection, security, guarantee.

respectivo *adj.* respective.

respecto *m.* respect, relation, reference; point, matter; (**con**) **— a** (*or* **— de**) with respect to, with regard to.

respetable *adj.* respectable.

respetar *v.* to respect.

respeto *m.* respect; reverence, regard; consideration.

respetuoso *adj.* respectful; respectable.

respingar[7] *v.* to buck; to balk (*said of a horse*); to grumble; to curl up (*said of the edge of a garment*).

respingo *m.* buck, balking; muttering, grumbling.

respiración *f.* respiration, breathing.

respirar *v.* to breathe.

respiro *m.* breathing; breath; respite, pause, moment of rest; extension of time (*for payment*).

resplandecer[13] *v. irr.* to shine; to glitter.

resplandeciente *adj.* resplendent, shining.

resplandor *m.* splendor, brilliance, brightness; *Am.* sun's glare.

responder *v.* to respond; to answer; to correspond, harmonize; to answer (for), be responsible (for).

respondón *adj.* saucy, pert, insolent (*in answering*).

responsabilidad *f.* responsibility.

responsable *adj.* responsible.

respuesta *f.* response; answer, reply.

resquebradura, resquebrajadura *f.* fissure, crevice, crack.

resquebrajar = resquebrar.

resquebrar[1] *v. irr.* to crack; to split.

resquicio *m.* crack, slit, crevice; opening; *Am.* vestige, sign, trace.

resta *f.* subtraction (*as an arithmetical*

operation); remainder.

restablecer[13] *v. irr.* to re-establish; to restore; **-se** to recover.

restante *adj.* remaining; *m.* residue, remainder.

restañar *v.* to stanch (*a wound*); to check the flow of.

restar *v.* to deduct; to subtract; to remain, be left over; to strike back (*a ball*).

restauración *f.* restoration.

restaurante *m.* restaurant.

restaurar *v.* to restore; to recover; to re-establish; to repair.

restitución *f.* restitution, restoration, return.

restituir[32] *v. irr.* to return, give back; to restore.

resto *m.* rest, remainder; stakes at cards; return (*of a tennis ball*); player who returns the ball; **-s** remains.

restorán *m. Am.* restaurant.

restregar[1, 7] *v. irr.* to rub hard; to scrub.

restricción *f.* restriction; restraint; curb; limitation.

restringir[11] *v.* to restrict; to restrain; to limit.

resucitar *v.* to resuscitate, bring to life; to come to life; to revive.

resuelto *p.p. of* **resolver** resolved, determined; *adj.* resolute, bold; quick.

resuello *m.* breath; breathing, panting.

resulta *f.* result; effect, consequence; **de -s as a result**, in consequence.

resultado *m.* result, effect, consequence.

resultante *adj.* resulting; *f.* resultant (*force*).

resultar *v.* to result; to spring, arise as a consequence; to turn out to be; **resulta que** it turns out that.

resumen *m.* résumé, summary; **en —** summing up, in brief.

resumidero *m. Am.* = **sumidero**.

resumir *v.* to summarize, sum up; **-se** to be reduced or condensed.

resurgir[11] *v.* to arise again; to reappear.

retablo *m.* altarpiece; religious picture hung as a votive offering; series of pictures that tell a story.

retaguardia *f.* rear guard.

retal *m.* remnant.

retar *v.* to challenge, defy; to reprimand, scold; *Am.* to insult.

retardar *v.* to retard, delay.

retazo *m.* remnant; piece; fragment.

retener[45] *v. irr.* to retain; to keep; to withhold; to detain.

retintín *m.* jingle, tinkle; sarcastic tone or ring.

retirada *f.* retreat; withdrawal.

retirado *p.p. & adj.* retired; distant, remote; isolated; pensioned.

retirar *v.* to withdraw; to take away; **-se** to retire, withdraw; to retreat.

retiro *m.* retreat; retirement; withdrawal; place of refuge; pension of a retired officer.

reto *m.* challenge; defiance; *Am.* scolding; *Am.* insult.

retobado *adj. Am.* saucy; *Am.* stubborn, unruly; *Am.* peevish; *Am.* sly, astute.

retobar *v. Am.* to cover with leather; *Am.* to wrap with leather, oilcloth, or burlap; *Am.* to tan (*leather*); **-se** *Am.* to rebel, talk back, act saucy; *Am.* to become disagreeable and aloof.

retocar[6] *v.* to retouch, touch up; to finish, perfect.

retoñar *v.* to sprout; to bud; to sprout again; to reappear.

retoño *m.* sprout, shoot; bud.

retoque *m.* retouching; finishing touch.

retorcer[2, 10] *v. irr.* to twist; to retort; to distort; **-se** to wriggle; to squirm.

retorcimiento *m.* twisting; squirming.

retórica *f.* rhetoric.

retornar *v.* to return; to give back.

retorno *m.* return; repayment; barter.

retozar[9] *v.* to gambol, frisk about, frolic, romp; to stir within (*said of passions*).

retozo *m.* frolic; **retozón** *adj.* frisky, playful.

retractarse *v.* to retract, take back one's word.

retraer[46] *v. irr.* to withdraw, draw back, take back; **-se de** to withdraw from; to keep aloof or away from; to shun.

retraimiento *m.* retirement; reserve, aloofness, shyness.

retranca *f. Am.* brake; **retranquero** *m. Am.* brakeman.

retrancar[6] *v. Am.* to brake, put the brake on; *Am.* **se ha retrancado el asunto** the affair has come to a standstill.

retrasado *p.p. & adj.* behind, behind time; backward; postponed, delayed.

retrasar *v.* to delay, retard; to set back; to go backward; **-se** to fall behind; to be late, behind time.

retraso *m.* delay.

retratar *v.* to portray; to photograph; to copy, imitate; **-se** to be portrayed; to be photographed; to be reflected.

retrato *m.* portrait; photograph; copy, imitation; reflection.

retrete *m.* toilet, water closet; place of retreat.

retroceder *v.* to turn back; to fall back,

draw back; to recede.

retroceso *m.* retrogression, backward step; retreat; setback, relapse.

retruécano *m.* pun.

retumbar *v.* to resound; to rumble.

retumbo *m.* loud echo or sound; rumble (*of thunder, cannon, etc.*).

reuma *m. & f.*, **reumatismo** *m.* rheumatism.

reunión *f.* reunion; meeting.

reunir *v.* to reunite; to unite; to group; to gather; to assemble; to collect; -se to meet, assemble; to reunite.

revancha *f.* revenge; return game or match.

revelación *f.* revelation.

revelador *adj.* revealing; *m.* developer (*in photography*).

revelar *v.* to reveal; to develop (*a film*).

revendedor *m.* retailer; reseller; ticket scalper.

reventa *f.* resale.

reventar[1] *v. irr.* to burst; to burst forth; to explode; to smash; to fatigue, exhaust; to bother; -se to burst; to blow out, explode.

reventón *m.* burst, bursting; blowout; steep hill; hard work, toil; *adj.* bursting.

reverdecer[13] *v. irr.* to grow fresh and green again; to gain new strength and vigor.

reverencia *f.* reverence; bow.

reverenciar *v.* to revere, venerate.

reverendo *adj.* reverend; *Am.* large, big (*ironically*).

reverente *adj.* reverent.

reverso *m.* reverse; back side.

revertir[3] *v. irr.* to revert.

revés *m.* reverse; back, wrong side; back stroke or slap; backhanded thrust (*in fencing*); misfortune; **al — backwards;** wrong side out; in the opposite way; from left to right.

revestir[5] *v. irr.* to dress, clothe; to coat, cover with a coating; -se to dress, put on an outer garment or vestment; to be invested (*with power, authority, etc.*); -se de paciencia to arm oneself with patience.

revisar *v.* to revise; to review; to examine, inspect.

revisión *m.* revision; review (*of a case*), new trial.

revisor *m.* corrector; inspector; overseer.

revista *f.* review; inspection; magazine, journal; second trial or hearing; **pasar — to pass in review; to examine carefully; to review (*troops*).**

revistar *v.* to review, inspect (*troops*).

revivir *v.* to revive.

revocación *f.* repeal, cancellation.

revocar[6] *v.* to revoke, repeal.

revolcar[6] *v.* to knock down; to turn over and over; to floor, defeat; to flunk, fail; -se to wallow; to roll over and over; to flounder.

revolotear *v.* to fly about, flutter around; to hover; to circle around.

revoltijo, revoltillo *m.* jumble, mixture, mess; tangle, muddle; **revoltillo de huevos** scrambled eggs.

revoltoso *adj.* turbulent, unruly, rebellious; mischievous; intricate; *m.* agitator, troublemaker; rebel.

revolución *f.* revolution.

revolucionario *adj.* revolutionary; *m.* revolutionist, revolutionary.

revolver[2] *v. irr.* to revolve; to turn over; to stir up; to mix up; to turn around swiftly (*a horse*); -se to move back and forth; to roll over and over; to change (*said of the weather*).

revólver *m.* revolver, pistol.

revuelo *m.* whirl; stir, commotion; flying around.

revuelta *f.* revolt, revolution; second turn; turn, bend; quarrel, fight; *Am.* sudden turning of a horse.

revuelto *p.p. of* **revolver** & *adj.* confused; mixed up; intricate, complicated; choppy (*sea*); changeable (*weather*); **huevos -s** scrambled eggs.

rey *m.* king.

reyerta *f.* quarrel, dispute.

rezagado *adj.* back, behind; *m.* straggler, slow poke, latecomer.

rezagar[7] *v.* to leave behind; to separate (*the weak cattle*) from the herd; *Am.* to reserve, set aside; -se to lag behind.

rezar[9] *v.* to pray; to say or recite (*a prayer*); to mutter, grumble; **así lo reza el libro** so the book says; **eso no reza conmigo** that has nothing to do with me.

rezo *m.* prayer.

rezongar[7] *v.* to grumble, growl, mutter.

rezongón *adj.* growling, grumbling; *m.* grumbler, growler; scolder.

rezumar *v.* to ooze; to leak; **se rezuma** it oozes, it seeps through.

ría *f.* mouth of a river, estuary.

riachuelo *m.* rivulet; brook.

ribazo *m.* bank, ridge.

ribera *f.* shore, bank, beach.

ribereño *adj.* of, pertaining to, or living on, a river bank.

ribete *m.* trimming, border, edge, binding; addition; **tiene sus -s de poeta** he is something of a poet.

ribetear *v.* to bind, put a binding on; to border, trim the edge or border of.
ricacho *adj.* quite rich (*often said sarcastically*); ricachón *adj.* extremely rich, disgustingly rich.
rico *adj.* rich, wealthy; delicious; exquisite; ricote = ricacho.
ridiculizar[9] *v.* to ridicule, deride.
ridículo *adj.* ridiculous; queer, strange; *m.* ridicule; ridiculous situation; hacer el — to be ridiculous; to act the fool.
riego *m.* irrigation; watering.
riel *m.* rail; -es track, railroad track.
rienda *f.* rein, bridle; moderation, restraint; a — suelta with free rein, without restraint; violently, swiftly; soltar la — to let loose, act without restraint; tirar las -s to draw rein, tighten the reins; to restrain.
riente *adj.* laughing, smiling.
riesgo *m.* risk.
rifa *f.* raffle; scuffle, quarrel.
rifar *v.* to raffle; to scuffle, quarrel.
rifle *m.* rifle.
rigidez *f.* rigidity, stiffness; severity, strictness.
rígido *adj.* rigid, stiff; severe, strict.
rigor *m.* rigor; severity; harshness; rigidity, stiffness; en — in reality; strictly; ser de — to be absolutely indispensable, be required by custom.
rigoroso, riguroso *adj.* rigorous; harsh; severe; strict.
rima *f.* rhyme; -s poems.
rimar *v.* to rhyme.
rimbombante *adj.* high-sounding; resounding.
rimero *m.* pile, heap.
rincón *m.* corner; nook; *Am.* narrow valley.
rinconada *f.* corner; nook.
rinconera *f.* corner cupboard, corner table, corner bracket.
ringlera *f.* tier, row, line.
rinoceronte *m.* rhinoceros.
riña *f.* quarrel, dispute, fight.
riñón *m.* kidney; center, interior.
río *m.* river.
ripio *m.* rubble, stone or brick fragments; padding (*in a verse, speech, etc.*), useless word.
riqueza *f.* riches; wealth.
risa *f.* laugh; laughter; reventar de — to burst with laughter; tomar a — to take lightly; to laugh off.
risada *f.* gale of laughter, loud laugh.
risco *m.* rocky cliff, crag; honey fritter.
risible *adj.* laughable, ridiculous.
risotada *f.* guffaw, big laugh.
ristra *f.* string (*of onions, garlic, etc.*);

series, row.
risueño *adj.* smiling; pleasant; delightful.
rítmico *adj.* rhythmical.
ritmo *m.* rhythm.
rito *m.* rite, ceremony.
rival *m. & f.* rival, competitor; enemy.
rivalidad *f.* rivalry, competition; enmity.
rivalizar[9] *v.* to rival, compete.
rizado *p.p.* curled; *adj.* wavy, curly; *m.* curling; curls.
rizar[9] *v.* to curl; to ripple; to ruffle, gather into ruffles; -se to curl one's hair; to curl.
rizo *m.* curl; *adj.* curly; rizoso *adj.* curly.
roano *adj.* roan (*red, bay or chestnut-colored, mixed with white; applied to a horse*).
robar *v.* to rob, steal; to abduct, kidnap.
roble *m.* oak tree; oak wood; robledal, robledo *m.* oak grove.
robo *m.* robbery, theft; loot, plunder.
robusto *adj.* robust, vigorous.
roca *f.* rock, boulder; rocky cliff, crag.
rocalloso *adj.* rocky.
roce *m.* graze; friction; contact; no tener — con to have no contact with (*a person*).
rociada *f.* sprinkling; spray; dew; sprinkle, shower; volley of harsh words.
rociar[17] *v.* to sprinkle; to spray; to fall (*said of dew*).
rocín *m.* nag, hack; draft horse; coarse, ill-bred man; *Am.* riding horse.
rocío *m.* dew; sprinkle; shower; spray; *adj. Am.* reddish, roan (*horse*).
rocoso *adj.* rocky.
rodada *f.* rut, wheel track; *Am.* tumble, fall.
rodado *adj.* dapple (*horse*); *p.p. of* rodar.
rodadura *f.* rolling; rut; — del neumático tire tread.
rodaja *f.* disk; small wheel; round slice.
rodar[2] *v. irr.* to roll; to revolve; to roam, wander about; to fall down (*rolling*); *Am.* — a patadas to kick down.
rodear *v.* to go around; to go by a roundabout way; to surround, encircle; *Am.* to round up (*cattle*).
rodela *f.* round shield; *Am.* padded ring for carrying loads on the head; *Am.* round slice; *Am.* kettle lid; *Am.* hoop; *Am.* game of rolling a hoop.
rodeo *m.* detour, roundabout way; circumlocution, roundabout expression; dodge, evasion; corral, stockyard; rodeo, roundup.
rodilla *f.* knee; de -s on one's knees;

hincarse de -s to kneel down.

rodillo *m.* roller; rolling pin; road roller.

roer[51] *v. irr.* to gnaw; to corrode, eat away; to torment, harass.

rogar[2,7] *v. irr.* to pray, beg, beseech; **hacerse de —** to let oneself be coaxed.

rojez *f.* redness.

rojizo *adj.* reddish.

rojo *adj.* red; red, radical.

rojura *f.* redness.

rollizo *adj.* plump; *m.* log.

rollo *m.* roll; bundle; rolling pin; log.

romadizo *m.* nasal catarrh, head cold.

romance *adj.* Romance, Romanic (*language*); *m.* Romance language; Spanish language; romance, chivalric novel; ballad; eight-syllable meter with even verses rhyming in assonance; **en buen — in** plain language.

románico *adj.* Romanesque (*architecture*); Romance (*language*).

romano *adj. & m.* Roman.

romanticismo *m.* romanticism.

romántico *adj.* romantic; sentimental; *m.* sentimentalist.

romería *f.* pilgrimage.

romero *m.* pilgrim; rosemary (*shrub*).

romo *adj.* blunt; snub-nosed.

rompecabezas *m.* puzzle, riddle.

rompeolas *m.* breakwater, mole.

rompe: de — y rasga resolute, bold; **al —** *Am.* suddenly.

romper[52] *v.* to break; to shatter; to tear; to wear through; *Am.* to leave suddenly or on the run; **— el alba** to dawn; **— a** to start to; **-se** to break.

rompiente *m.* shoal, sand bank, reef; **-s** breakers, surf.

rompimiento *m.* rupture, break; crack; breach; quarrel.

ron *m.* rum.

roncar[6] *v.* to snore; to roar; to brag.

ronco *adj.* hoarse; harsh-sounding.

roncha *f.* hive; welt.

ronda *f.* patrol; night serenaders; round (*of a game, of drinks, etc.*); *Am.* ring-around-a-rosy (*a children's game*); **hacer la — a** to court; *Am.* to surround, trap (*an animal*).

rondar *v.* to go around, hover around; to patrol; to make the rounds; to serenade.

ronquera *f.* hoarseness.

ronquido *m.* snore; snort.

ronronear *v.* to purr.

ronroneo *m.* purr.

ronzal *m.* halter.

roña *f.* scab, mange; filth; infection; stinginess; trickery; *Am.* ill will, grudge; *Am.* **hacer —** to fake an illness.

roñoso *adj.* scabby, mangy; dirty; stingy; *Am.* spiteful; *Am.* faint-hearted, cowardly.

ropa *f.* clothing, clothes; **— blanca** linen; **— vieja** old clothes; stew made from leftover meat; **a quema —** at close range (*when shooting*); suddenly, without warning.

ropaje *m.* clothes, clothing, apparel; robe.

ropero *m.* clothier; wardrobe, clothes-press; wardrobe keeper; *Am.* clothes rack.

roqueño *adj.* rocky; hard, like rock.

rosa *f.* rose; red spot on the skin; rose color; *Am.* rosebush; **— de los vientos** (*or* **— náutica**) mariner's compass.

rosado *adj.* rosy, rose-colored; frosted (*drink*); *Am.* roan, reddish-brown (*horse*).

rosal *m.* rosebush.

rosario *m.* rosary; **— de desdichas** chain of misfortunes.

rosbif *m.* roast beef.

rosca *f.* screw and nut; screw thread; spiral, twist; ring-shaped roll; *Am.* ring-shaped cushion (*for carrying loads on the head*); *Am.* circle of card players.

roseta *f.* rosette; small rose; **-s** popcorn; **rosetón** *m.* large rosette; rose window.

rosillo *adj.* light red; roan (*horse*).

rostro *m.* face; **hacer —** to face.

rota *f.* rout, defeat; ship's course; Rota (*ecclesiastical court*); rattan palm tree.

rotación *f.* rotation.

rotatorio *adj.* rotary.

roto *p.p. irr.* of **romper** & *adj.* broken; shattered; torn; worn out, ragged; *m. Am.* person of the poorer class.

rotular *v.* to label; to letter.

rótulo *m.* title, inscription; label.

rotundo *adj.* round; sonorous; **una negativa rotunda** a flat denial.

rotura *f.* breach, opening; break; tear, rip; rupture; fracture.

roturar *v.* to break ground; to plow (*new ground*).

rozadura *f.* friction; chafe; chafing.

rozamiento *m.* friction; rubbing.

rozar[9] *v.* to graze; to scrape; to chafe; to clear of underbrush; **-se con alguien** to have connections, contact, or dealings with someone.

rozón *m.* graze, sudden or violent scrape; short, broad scythe.

ruano = roano.

rubí *m.* ruby.

rubicundo *adj.* reddish; ruddy, healthy red; reddish-blonde.

rubio *adj.* blond, blonde.

rubor *m.* blush; bashfulness, shyness.

ruborizarse[9] *v.* to blush; to feel ashamed.

rúbrica *f.* scroll, flourish (*added to a signature*); title, heading; **de —** according to ritual, rule or custom.

rucio *adj.* grey (*horse or donkey*); **— rodado** dapple-grey.

rudeza *f.* rudeness; coarseness; roughness.

rudo *adj.* rude; coarse; rough; stupid.

rueca *f.* distaff (*used for spinning*).

rueda *f.* wheel; circle, group; round slice; spread of a peacock's tail; **en —** in turn; in a circle; **hacer la — a** to court; to flatter.

ruedo *m.* circuit, tour; border, rim; circumference.

ruego *m.* prayer, supplication, request.

rufián *m.* ruffian; bully.

rugido *m.* roar; rumbling.

rugir[11] *v.* to roar; to bellow.

rugoso *adj.* wrinkled; furrowed.

ruibarbo *m.* rhubarb.

ruidazo *m.* big noise.

ruido *m.* noise; din; dispute; talk, rumor; **hacer** (*or* **meter**) **—** to make a noise; to create a sensation; to cause a disturbance.

ruidoso *adj.* noisy; loud; sensational.

ruin *adj.* vile, base, mean; small, petty; puny; stingy; vicious (*animal*).

ruina *f.* ruin; destruction; downfall.

ruindad *f.* baseness; meanness; stinginess; mean or vile act.

ruinoso *adj.* ruinous; in a state of ruin or decay.

ruiseñor *m.* nightingale.

rumba *f.* *Am.* rumba (*dance and music*); *Am.* spree; *Am.* **irse de —** to go on a spree.

rumbear *v. Am.* to head (towards), take a certain direction; *Am.* to cut a path through a forest; *Am.* to go on a spree.

rumbo *m.* direction, course; route; pomp; ostentation; *Am.* cut on the head; *Am.* revel, noisy spree; **hacer —** a to head or sail towards; *Am.* **ir al —** to be going in the right direction, be on the right track.

rumboso *adj.* pompous, ostentatious; generous.

rumiar *v.* to ruminate; to chew the cud; to ponder, meditate.

rumor *m.* rumor, report; murmur; rumble.

runfla *f.* series (*of things of the same kind*); sequence (*in cards*).

runrún *m.* rumor; murmur.

ruptura *f.* rupture; break; fracture.

rural *adj.* rural.

ruso *adj.* Russian; *m.* Russian; Russian language.

rústico *adj.* rustic, rural; crude, coarse; *m.* peasant; **en** (*or* **a la**) **rústica** unbound, paper-bound.

ruta *f.* route, course, way.

rutina *f.* routine.

S

sábado *m.* Saturday.

sábana *f.* bed sheet; altar cloth.

sabana *f. Am.* savanna, treeless plain; *Am.* **ponerse en la —** to become suddenly rich.

sabandija *f.* small reptile; small lizard.

sabañón *m.* chilblain.

sabedor *adj.* knowing; aware, informed.

saber[42] *v. irr.* to know; to know how to, be able to; to learn, find out; *Am.* to be in the habit of; **— a** to taste of, taste like; **sabe bien** it tastes good; **a —** namely; that is; *Am.* **¡a — si venga!** who knows whether he will come!; **un no sé qué** an indefinable something; **¿sabe Vd. a la plaza?** do you know the way to the square?; *m.* knowledge, learning.

sabiduría *f.* wisdom; knowledge.

sabiendas : a — consciously, knowingly.

sabio *adj.* wise; judicious; learned; *m.* savant, scholar; sage, wise man.

sable *m.* saber; **sablazo** *m.* blow with a saber; saber wound; **dar un sablazo** to strike for a loan.

sabor *m.* savor, taste, flavor.

saborear *v.* to savor, flavor, season; to relish, taste with pleasure; to enjoy; **-se** to eat or drink with relish; to smack one's lips.

sabotaje *m.* sabotage.

sabotear *v.* to sabotage.

sabroso *adj.* savory, tasty; delicious; delightful.

sabueso *m.* hound.

sacabocados *m.* punch (*tool*).

sacacorchos *m.* corkscrew.

sacamuelas *m. & f.* tooth puller; quack dentist.

sacar[6] *v.* to draw, draw out, pull out, get out, or take out; to get, obtain; to infer; to make (*a copy*); to take (*a snapshot or picture*); to stick out (*one's tongue*); to serve (*a ball*); **— a bailar** to ask to dance, lead on to the dance floor; **— a luz** to publish; **— el cuerpo** to dodge; **— en claro** (*or* **— en limpio**) to deduce, conclude; *Am.* **— el sombrero** to take off one's hat; *Am.* **¡sáquese de allí!** get out

191

of there!

sacerdocio *m.* priesthood.

sacerdote *m.* priest.

saciar *v.* to satiate, satisfy; **-se** to be satiated, satisfied completely.

saco *m.* sack, bag; sackful, bagful; loose-fitting coat; sack, plundering; *Am.* suit coat; — **de noche** overnight bag, satchel.

sacramento *m.* sacrament.

sacrificar[6] *v.* to sacrifice.

sacrificio *m.* sacrifice.

sacrilegio *m.* sacrilege.

sacrílego *adj.* sacrilegious.

sacristán *m.* sacristan, **sexton**; *Am.* busybody, meddler.

sacro *adj.* sacred.

sacrosanto *adj.* sacrosanct, holy and sacred.

sacudida *f.* shake, jolt, jerk.

sacudimiento *m.* shaking; shake, jerk; shock, jolt.

sacudir *v.* to shake; to jerk; to beat; to beat the dust from; to shake off; **-se** to shake oneself; to brush oneself off; **-se de alguien** to shake someone off, get rid of someone.

sádico *adj.* sadistic, cruel.

saeta *f.* arrow, dart.

sagacidad *f.* sagacity.

sagaz *adj.* sagacious, shrewd.

sagrado *adj.* sacred; consecrated; *m.* asylum, refuge.

sahumar *v.* to perfume with incense; to fumigate.

sahumerio *m.* vapor, fume; incense; burning of incense; fumigation.

sainete *m.* one-act comedy or farce; delicacy, tasty tidbit; flavor, relish; sauce.

sajón *adj. & m.* Saxon.

sal *f.* salt; wit, humor; grace; *Am.* misfortune, bad luck.

sala *f.* parlor; hall, large room; — **de justicia** courtroom.

salado *adj.* salty; salted; witty; charming; *Am.* costly; *Am.* **estar** — to be unlucky; *m. Am.* salt pit, salt mine.

salar *v.* to salt; to cure or preserve with salt; *Am.* to bring bad luck (to); *Am.* to dishonor; *Am.* to ruin, spoil; *Am.* to bribe; *Am.* to feed salt to cattle; *m. Am.* salt pit.

salario *m.* salary, wages.

salchicha *f.* sausage; **salchichón** *m.* large sausage.

saldar *v.* to balance, settle (*an account*).

saldo *m.* balance, settlement (*of an account*); bargain sale.

saledizo = salidizo.

salero *m.* saltcellar, saltshaker; place for storing salt; salt lick; wit, grace, charm; *Am.* salt dealer.

salida *f.* departure; exit; sally; outlet; way out; loophole; outskirts; outcome; jut, projection; outlay, expenditure; witty remark; — **de pie de banco** silly remark, nonsense; — **del sol** sunrise; *Am.* — **de teatro** evening wrap.

salidizo *m.* jut, ledge, projection; *adj.* salient, jutting, projecting.

saliente *adj.* salient, standing out; projecting; *m.* salient, salient angle; jut, projection.

salina *f.* salt mine or pit; salt works.

salir[43] *v. irr.* to go out; to leave, depart; to get out (of); to come out; to sprout; to come (from); to turn out to be; — **bien** to turn out well; to come out well; — **a su padre** to turn out to be or look like his father; *Am.* — **a mano** to come out even; **-se** to get out, slip out; to leak out; **-se con la suya** to get one's own way.

salitral *m.* saltpeter bed or mine.

salitre *m.* saltpeter; **salitrera** *f.* saltpeter mine or bed; **salitroso** *adj.* nitrous, abounding in saltpeter.

saliva *f.* saliva.

salmo *m.* psalm.

salmodiar *v.* to chant; to talk in a monotone or singsong.

salmón *m.* salmon.

salmuera *f.* brine.

salobre *adj.* briny, salty.

salón *m.* salon, hall, large room; salted meat or fish.

salpicadura *f.* spatter, splash.

salpicar[6] *v.* to sprinkle, spray, spatter.

salpimentar[1] *v. irr.* to salt and pepper.

salpimienta *f.* salt and pepper.

salpullido *m.* rash, skin eruption.

salsa *f.* sauce; gravy; *Am.* sound whipping or beating; **salsera** *f.* sauce dish.

saltamontes *m.* grasshopper.

saltar *v.* to jump; to jump over; to leap; to bounce; to skip; to burst, break into pieces; to come off; — **a la vista** to be obvious, evident; — **a tierra** to disembark, land; *Am.* — **las trancas** to lose one's patience; to lose one's head.

salteador *m.* bandit, highway robber.

saltear *v.* to assault, attack; to hold up, rob; to take by surprise; to jump or skip around.

salto *m.* jump; leap; precipice; gap; — **de agua** waterfall; **a -s** by jumps; **en un** (*or* **de un**) — in a jiffy, quickly; **dar un** — to jump, leap.

saltón adj. jumping, skipping, hopping; jumpy; protruding; Am. half-cooked; ojos -es popeyes, bulging. eyes; m. grasshopper.

salubre adj. healthy, healthful.

salubridad f. healthfulness, health; sanitation.

salud f. health; welfare; salvation; ¡ — ! greetings!; your health!

saludable adj. wholesome, healthful, beneficial.

saludador m. greeter; healer, quack.

saludar v. to salute, greet; to fire a salute.

saludo m. salute, nod, greeting.

salutación f. salutation; greeting.

salva f. salvo, salute with guns; greeting, welcome.

salvación f. salvation.

salvado m. bran.

salvador m. savior, rescuer; Savior; adj. saving.

salvaguardar v. to safeguard, defend, protect.

salvaguardia m. safeguard, protection; guard; f. safe-conduct paper, passport; password.

salvajada f. savage act or remark.

salvaje adj. savage; wild; m. savage.

salvajez f. wildness, savagery.

salvajismo m. savagery; Am. savage act or remark. See salvajada.

salvamento m. salvation, rescue; place of safety; salvage (rescue of property); bote de — lifeboat.

salvar v. to save; to clear, jump over; to except, exclude; -se to be saved; to save oneself, escape.

salvavidas m. life preserver; lancha — lifeboat.

¡salve! interj. hail!; Salve f. Salve Regina, prayer to the Virgin Mary.

salvia f. sage (a plant).

salvo adj. saved; safe; prep. save, except, but; a — safe, without injury; en — in safety; out of danger.

salvoconducto m. safe-conduct, pass.

san adj. (contr. of santo) saint.

sánalotodo m. cure-all.

sanar v. to heal, cure; to recover, get well.

sanatorio m. sanitarium.

sanción f. sanction.

sancionar v. to sanction; to authorize, ratify.

sandalia f. sandal.

sandez f. stupidity; folly; foolish remark.

sandía f. watermelon.

sandio adj. silly, foolish.

saneamiento m. sanitation; drainage of land.

sanear v. to make sanitary (land, property, etc.); to drain, dry up (land).

sangrar v. to bleed; to drain; to tap (a tree); to pilfer; to exploit (someone); to indent (a line).

sangre f. blood; — fría calmness, coolness of mind; a — fría in cold blood.

sangriento adj. bleeding; bloody; blood-stained; bloodthirsty, cruel.

sanguijuela f. leech.

sanguinario adj. bloody, cruel; bloodthirsty, murderous.

sanidad f. health; soundness; healthfulness; sanitation.

sanitario adj. sanitary.

sano adj. sound, healthy; healthful; safe; sane, sensible; whole, unbroken; undamaged; — y salvo safe and sound.

sanseacabó that's all; that's the end.

santiamén: en un — in a jiffy.

santidad f. sanctity, holiness, saintliness; su Santidad his Holiness.

santificar v. to sanctify; to consecrate.

santiguar v. to bless; to make the sign of the cross; to beat, hit, punish; -se to cross oneself; to show astonishment (by crossing oneself).

santísimo adj. most holy; m. the Holy Sacrament.

santo adj. saintly, holy; sacred; esperar todo el — día to wait the whole blessed day; — y bueno well and good; Am. ¡santa palabra! that's my final and last word!; m. saint; saint's day; Am. tener el — de espaldas to have a streak of bad luck; santurrón m. religious hypocrite, affectedly pious person.

santuario m. sanctuary; Am. buried treasure; Am. Indian idol.

saña f. fury, rage.

sañudo adj. furious, enraged.

sapo m. toad; Am. despicable little man; Am. chubby person; Am. sly person; echar -s y culebras to swear, curse.

saque m. serve, service (in tennis); server.

saquear v. to sack, plunder, pillage, loot.

saqueo m. sacking, pillaging, plunder; loot, booty.

saquillo m. small bag, handbag, satchel.

sarampión m. measles.

sarao m. soirée, evening party.

sarape m. Am. serape, blanket.

sarcasmo m. sarcasm.

sarcástico adj. sarcastic.

sardina f. sardine.

sargento m. sergeant.

sarmentoso *adj.* vinelike; full of vine shoots; gnarled, knotty.
sarmiento *m.* shoot or branch of a vine.
sarna *f.* itch; mange.
sarnoso *adj.* itchy, scabby, mangy.
sarpullido = **salpullido.**
sarro *m.* tartar (*on teeth*); crust, sediment (*in utensils*).
sarta *f.* string (*of beads*); series.
sartén *f.* frying pan.
sastre *m.* tailor.
satánico *adj.* satanic, devilish.
satélite *m.* satellite.
satén *m.* sateen.
sátira *f.* satire.
satírico *adj.* satirical.
satirizar⁹ *v.* to satirize.
satisfacción *f.* satisfaction; apology, excuse; **tomar —** to vindicate oneself; to take revenge; **dar una —** to offer an apology; to apologize.
satisfacer³¹ *v. irr.* to satisfy; to pay (*a debt*); **— una letra** to honor a draft; **-se** to be satisfied; to take satisfaction.
satisfactorio *adj.* satisfactory.
satisfecho *p.p.* of **satisfacer** satisfied, gratified; *adj.* content, contented.
saturar *v.* to saturate; to satiate.
sauce *m.* willow.
savia *f.* sap.
saxófono *m.* saxophone.
sazón *f.* season, opportune moment; ripeness; taste, flavor; **a la —** then, at that time; **en —** in season; ripe; opportunely; *adj. Am.* ripe.
sazonado *adj. & p.p.* seasoned; mellow, ripe; expressive (*said of a phrase*).
sazonar *v.* to season; to flavor; **-se** to become seasoned; to ripen, mature.
se *obj. pron.* (*before* **le, la, lo, las,** *and* **los**) to him, to her, to you (*formal*); to them; *refl. pron.* himself, herself, yourself (*formal*), yourselves (*formal*), themselves; *reciprocal pron.* each other, one another.
sebo *m.* tallow, fat.
secante *adj.* drying, blotting; **papel —** blotter; *f.* secant (*math.*).
secar⁶ *v.* to dry; to wipe dry; **-se** to dry or wipe oneself; to dry up; to wither; to get thin.
sección *f.* section; division; cutting.
seccionar *v.* to section.
seco *adj.* dry; dried; withered; harsh; abrupt; plain, unadorned; **en —** on dry land, out of the water; **parar en —** to stop short, stop suddenly; **a secas** plain; alone, without anything else; *Am.* simply, straight to the point; **comer pan a secas** to eat just bread;

Am. **bailar a secas** to dance without musical accompaniment.
secreción *f.* secretion.
secretar *v.* to secrete.
secretaría *f.* secretary's office; position of secretary.
secretario *m.* secretary; confidant; **secretaria** *f.* woman secretary; secretary's wife.
secretear *v.* to whisper; **-se** to whisper to each other.
secreto *adj.* secret, hidden; secretive; *m.* secret; secrecy; secret place; **— a voces** open secret; **en —** secretly; **hablar en —** to whisper.
secta *f.* sect.
secuaz *m.* partisan, follower.
secuela *f.* sequel, outcome, consequence.
secuencia *f.* sequence.
secuestrador *m.* kidnapper; confiscator.
secuestrar *v.* to seize; to kidnap; to confiscate.
secuestro *m.* kidnapping; seizure.
secular *adj.* secular; lay, worldly; centennial; *m.* secular, secular priest.
secundar *v.* to second, favor, back up.
secundario *adj.* secondary.
sed *f.* thirst; craving, desire; **tener —** to be thirsty.
seda *f.* silk; **como una —** soft as silk; sweet-tempered; smoothly, easily.
sedán *m.* sedan.
sedativo *adj. & m.* sedative.
sede *f.* seat, see; **Santa Sede** Holy See.
sedentario *adj.* sedentary.
sedeño *adj.* silky, silken.
sedería *f.* silk goods; silk shop.
sedero *m.* silk dealer or weaver; *adj.* silk, pertaining to silk; **industria sedera** silk industry.
sedición *f.* sedition.
sedicioso *adj.* seditious, turbulent.
sediento *adj.* thirsty; dry, parched; anxious, desirous.
sedimento *m.* sediment; dregs, grounds.
sedoso *adj.* silken, silky.
seducción *f.* seduction.
seducir²⁵ *v. irr.* to seduce; to entice; to charm.
seductivo *adj.* seductive, alluring; inviting, enticing.
seductor *adj.* tempting, fascinating; *m.* seducer; tempter; charming person.
segador *m.* harvester, reaper; **segadora** *f.* harvester, mowing machine; woman reaper.
segar¹·⁷ *v. irr.* to mow, reap; to cut off.
seglar *adj.* secular, lay; *m.* layman.
segmento *m.* segment.
seguida *f.* succession; series, contin-

uation; **de —** without interruption, continuously; **en —** at once, immediately.

seguido *p.p.* followed; continued; *adj.* continuous; straight, direct; *adv.* without interruption; *Am.* often; *Am.* **de — at** once, immediately.

seguidor *m.* follower.

seguimiento *m.* pursuit.

seguir[5,12] *v.irr.* to follow; to continue; to pursue; **-se** to follow as a consequence.

según *prep.* according to; *conj.* as; according to; **— y conforme** (*or* **— y como**) exactly as, just as; that depends.

segundar *v.* to repeat a second time; to second.

segundero *m.* second hand (*of a watch or clock*).

segundo *adj. & m.* second.

seguridad *f.* security; safety; certainty; **alfiler de —** safety pin.

seguro *adj.* secure; sure, certain; safe; *Am.* honest, trustworthy; *m.* assurance; insurance; safety device; **a buen — (al —** , *or* **de —**) truly, certainly; **en — in** safety; **sobre —** without risk; without taking a chance; *Am.* **irse uno del —** to lose one's temper; *Am.* **a la segura** without risk.

selección *f.* selection, choice.

seleccionar *v.* to select, choose.

selecto *adj.* select, choice.

selva *f.* forest; jungle.

sellar *v.* to seal; to stamp; to conclude; to seal, close tightly.

sello *m.* seal; stamp; *Am.* official stamped paper.

semana *f.* week; week's wages; **días de — week** days; **entre —** during the week.

semanal *adj.* weekly; **-mente** *adv.* weekly, every week.

semanario *m.* weekly publication; *adj.* weekly.

semblante *m.* countenance; facial expression; appearance.

semblanza *f.* portrait, literary sketch.

sembrado *m.* sown ground; cultivated field.

sembrar[1] *v. irr.* to sow; to scatter.

semejante *adj.* similar, like; such a; *m.* fellow man; **nuestros -s** our fellow men.

semejanza *f.* resemblance, similarity; simile; **a — de** in the manner of.

semejar *v.* to resemble, **-se** to resemble.

semilla *f.* seed.

semillero *m.* seed bed; plant nursery; **— de vicios** hotbed of vice.

seminario *m.* seminary; plant nursery, seed plot.

sempiterno *adj.* everlasting; evergreen.

senado *m.* senate.

senador *m.* senator.

sencillez *f.* simplicity; plainness.

sencillo *adj.* simple; easy; plain; unadorned; unaffected; *m.* loose change, small coins.

senda *f.* path; way, course.

sendero *m.* path.

senectud *f.* senility, old age.

senil *adj.* senile.

seno *m.* cavity, hollow; breast, bosom; womb; lap; cove, bay; innermost recess; sinus (*cavity in a bone*); sine (*math.*).

sensación *f.* sensation.

sensacional *adj.* sensational.

sensatez *f.* prudence, common sense.

sensato *adj.* sensible, wise, prudent.

sensibilidad *f.* sensibility; sensitiveness.

sensible *adj.* sensitive; perceptible; regrettable.

sensitivo *adj.* sensitive.

sensual *adj.* sensual; sensuous.

sensualidad *f.* sensuality; lewdness.

sentada *f.* sitting; **de una —** at one sitting.

sentado *adj.* seated, sitting; **dar por — to** take for granted.

sentar[1] *v. irr.* to seat; to set; to establish; to become, suit, fit; to agree with one (*as food or climate*); **-se** to sit down; to settle down; *Am.* **-se en la palabra** to do all the talking, monopolize the conversation.

sentencia *f.* sentence; verdict; judgment; maxim, proverb.

sentenciar *v.* to sentence; to pass judgment on; to decide.

sentido *p.p.* felt; experienced; *adj.* heartfelt, filled with feeling; sensitive; touchy; **darse por —** to take offense; to have one's feelings hurt; **estar — con alguien** to be offended or peeved at someone; *m.* sense; meaning; judgment; **aguzar el —** to prick up one's ears; **perder el —** to faint.

sentimental *adj.* sentimental.

sentimentalismo *m.* sentimentalism, sentimentality.

sentimiento *m.* sentiment; sensation, feeling; grief, regret.

sentir[3] *v. irr.* to feel; to sense; to hear; to regret; **-se** to feel (*well, strong, sad, etc.*); to feel oneself, consider oneself; to feel resentment; to feel a pain; **sin — without** being realized or felt; inadvertently; unnoticed; *m.* feeling; judgment, opinion.

señá *familiar contraction of* **señora.**

seña *f.* sign, mark; signal; password; **-s** address (*name and place of residence*); **por más -s** as an additional proof.

señal *f.* sign, mark; signal; reminder; indication; trace, vestige; scar; token, pledge; *Am.* earmark, brand (*on the ear of livestock*); **en — de** in proof of, in token of.

señalar *v.* to mark; to point out; to indicate; to determine, fix; to appoint; to signal; to assign; *Am.* to earmark, brand (*cattle*); **-se** to distinguish oneself.

señor *m.* mister; sir; owner; master, lord; gentleman; **el Señor** the Lord.

señora *f.* lady; madam; mistress; Mrs.

señorear *v.* to lord it over, domineer; to dominate; to master, control.

señoría *f.* lordship.

señoril *adj.* lordly.

señorío *m.* dominion, rule; domain of a lord; lordship; dignity; mastery, control; body of noblemen.

señorita *f.* miss; young lady.

señorito *m.* master, young gentleman.

señuelo *m.* decoy; lure, bait; *Am.* leading or guiding oxen.

separación *f.* separation.

separado *p.p.* & *adj.* separate; separated; **por —** separately.

separar *v.* to separate; to set aside; to remove (from); to dismiss (from); **-se** to separate; to retire, resign; to withdraw, leave.

septentrional *adj.* northern.

septiembre *m.* September.

sepulcral *adj.* sepulchral (*pertaining to sepulchers or tombs*); **lápida —** tombstone.

sepulcro *m.* sepulcher, tomb, grave.

sepultar *v.* to bury; to hide.

sepultura *f.* burial; grave; **dar — to** bury.

sequedad *f.* dryness; gruffness.

sequía *f.* drought.

séquito *m.* retinue, following.

ser[44] *v. irr.* to be; to exist; to happen, occur; **— de** (*or* **para**) **ver** to be worth seeing; *m.* being; essence, nature; existence; *Am.* **estar en un —** to be always in the same condition.

serenar *v.* to pacify; to calm down; *Am.* to drizzle, rain gently; **-se** to become serene, calm down; to clear up (*said of the weather*).

serenata *f.* serenade.

serenidad *f.* serenity, calm.

sereno *adj.* serene, calm; clear, cloudless; *m.* night humidity, dew; night watchman; **al — in** the night air.

serie *f.* series.

seriedad *f.* seriousness; gravity; earnestness; dignity.

serio *adj.* serious; grave; earnest; dignified; formal; **en — seriously.**

sermón *m.* sermon; reproof.

sermonear *v.* to preach; to admonish, reprimand.

serpentear *v.* to wind, twist, turn, zigzag.

serpiente *f.* serpent, snake.

serrado *adj.* toothed, notched (*like a saw*); jagged.

serrana *f.* mountain girl; **serranilla** *f.* lyric poem with a rustic theme.

serranía *f.* mountainous region; chain of mountains.

serrano *m.* mountaineer; *adj.* of, pertaining to, or from the mountains.

serrar = aserrar.

serrín *m.* sawdust.

serrucho *m.* handsaw.

servible *adj.* serviceable, useful.

servicial *adj.* helpful, obliging.

servicio *m.* service; table service; tea or coffee set; chamber pot; *Am.* toilet, water closet.

servidor *m.* servant; waiter; **— de Vd.** at your service; **su seguro —** yours truly.

servidumbre *f.* domestic help, servants; servitude, slavery; service.

servil *adj.* servile; **servilón** *adj.* very servile; *m.* bootlicker, great flatterer.

servilismo *m.* servility, servile behavior or attitude, servile submission.

servilleta *f.* napkin.

servir[5] *v. irr.* to serve; to be of use; **— de** to serve as, act as; to be used as; **— para** to be good for; to be used for; **-se** to serve or help oneself; to be pleased to; **-se de** to make use of; **sírvase Vd. hacerlo** please do it.

sesgado *adj.* slanting, oblique, bias.

sesgar[7] *v.* to slant; to cut on the bias; to follow an oblique line.

sesgo *m.* bias; slant; diagonal cut; turn; **al —** on the bias; diagonally, obliquely.

sesión *f.* session; meeting, conference.

seso *m.* brain; wisdom, intelligence; **devanarse los -s** to rack one's brain.

sestear *v.* to snooze, take a nap.

sesudo *adj.* sensible, wise, prudent; *Am.* stubborn.

seta *f.* mushroom.

seto *m.* fence; hedge.

seudónimo *m.* pseudonym, pen name.

severidad *f.* severity; strictness; seriousness.

severo adj. severe; strict; stern.
sevillano adj. of, from, or pertaining to Seville, Spain.
sexo m. sex.
sexual adj. sexual.
si conj. if; whether; ¡ — ya te lo dije! but I already told you!; — bien although; **por — acaso** just in case.
sí adv. yes; — que certainly, really; un — es no es a trifle, somewhat; m. assent, consent; refl. pron. (used after a prep.) himself, herself, yourself (formal), themselves; de por — separately, by itself; **estar sobre —** to be on the alert.
sidra f. cider.
siega f. reaping, mowing; harvesting; harvest, harvest season.
siembra f. sowing; seedtime, sowing time; sown field.
siempre adv. always; Am. in any case, anyway; **para** (or **por**) — forever, for always; **por — jamás** forever and ever; — **que** whenever; provided that; Am. — **sí me voy** I've decided to go anyway.
siempreviva f. evergreen; everlasting.
sien f. temple (of the forehead).
sierpe f. serpent, snake.
sierra f. saw; rocky mountain range.
siervo m. serf; slave; servant.
siesta f. siesta, afternoon nap; early afternoon; **dormir la —** to take an afternoon nap.
sifón m. siphon; siphon bottle.
sigilo m. secret; secrecy.
siglo m. century; period, epoch; the world, worldly matters.
significación f. meaning; significance.
significado m. significance, meaning.
significar [6] v. to signify; to mean; to make known, show; to matter, have importance.
significativo adj. significant.
signo m. sign; mark; symbol.
siguiente adj. following.
sílaba f. syllable.
silabario m. speller, spelling book.
silbar v. to whistle; to hiss.
silbato m. whistle.
silbido m. whistle; hiss.
silenciador m. silencer; muffler (of an automobile).
silencio m. silence; pause; adj. Am. silent, quiet, motionless.
silencioso adj. silent, quiet.
silueta f. silhouette.
silvestre adj. wild; uncultivated.
silvicultor m. forester; **silvicultura** f. forestry.

silla f. chair; saddle; — **de montar** saddle; Am. — **de balanza** rocking chair. See **mecedora**.
sillón m. large chair; easy chair; Am. — **de hamaca** rocking chair.
sima f. chasm, abyss.
simbólico adj. symbolic.
simbolismo m. symbolism.
símbolo m. symbol; — **de la fe** (or **de los Apóstoles**) the Apostle's creed.
simetría f. symmetry.
simétrico adj. symmetrical.
simiente f. seed.
símil m. simile; similarity; adj. similar.
simpatía f. sympathy; accord, harmony; liking.
simpático adj. sympathetic, congenial; pleasant, agreeable, nice.
simpatizar [9] v. to sympathize (with); to have a liking or sympathy (for); to be congenial (with); **no me simpatiza** I don't like him.
simple adj. simple; mere; plain; pure, unmixed; naive, innocent; silly, foolish; m. simpleton.
simpleza f. simplicity; simpleness, stupidity, foolishness.
simplicidad f. simplicity; candor.
simplificar [6] v. to simplify.
simplón m. simpleton.
simulacro m. mimic battle, sham or mock battle; image, vision.
simular v. to simulate, feign.
simultáneo adj. simultaneous.
sin prep. without; besides, not counting; — **que** conj. without; — **embargo** nevertheless, still, yet; — **qué ni para qué** without rhyme or reason.
sinapismo m. mustard plaster; irritating person, nuisance, pest, bore.
sincerar v. to square, justify, excuse; -**se** to square oneself (with), justify oneself (with).
sinceridad f. sincerity.
sincero adj. sincere.
sindicar [6] v. to syndicate; -**se** to syndicate, form a syndicate.
sindicato m. syndicate.
síndico m. receiver (person appointed to take charge of property under litigation or to liquidate a bankrupt business); trustee.
sinecura f. sinecure (easy and well paid position).
sinfonía f. symphony.
singular adj. singular; unique; striking; odd, strange.
singularizar [9] v. to single out, choose; to distinguish; -**se** to distinguish oneself; to be singled out.

siniestro *adj.* sinister; left (*side*); *m.* unforeseen loss, damage; **siniestra** *f.* left hand; left-hand side.

sinnúmero *m.* great number, endless number.

sino *conj.* but; *prep.* except; **no hace — lo que le mandan** he only does what he is told; **— que** *conj.* but; *m.* fate, destiny.

sinónimo *m.* synonym; *adj.* synonymous.

sinrazón *f.* injustice, wrong.

sinsabor *m.* displeasure; trouble, grief, distress.

sintaxis *f.* syntax.

síntesis *f.* synthesis; summary.

sintético *adj.* synthetic.

síntoma *m.* symptom; indication, sign.

sintonizar[9] *v.* to tune in (on).

sinuoso *adj.* sinuous, winding; wavy.

sinvergüenza *m. & f.* shameless person; scoundrel.

siquiera *adv.* at least; even; **ni —** not even; *conj.* even though.

sirena *f.* siren; whistle, foghorn.

sirviente *m.* servant; waiter; **sirvienta** *f.* housemaid; waitress.

sisa *f.* petty theft; dart (*made in a garment*).

sisal *m.* *Am.* sisal or sisal hemp (*fiber used in ropemaking*).

sisar *v.* to take in (*a garment*); to pilfer; to cheat out of, defraud.

sisear *v.* to hiss.

siseo *m.* hiss, hissing.

sistema *m.* system.

sistemático *adj.* systematic.

sitial *m.* chair of a presiding officer; place of honor.

sitiar *v.* to besiege; to surround.

sitio *m.* site, location; place, spot, space; siege; *Am.* cattle ranch; *Am.* taxicab station; **poner — a** to lay siege to.

sito *adj.* situated, located.

situación *f.* situation; position; location; state, condition; *Am.* **hombre de la —** man of the hour, man of influence.

situado *p.p.* situated; placed.

situar[18] *v.* to locate; to place; **-se** to station oneself, place oneself; to be located, placed, situated.

so : **— capa de** under the guise of; **— pena de** under penalty of; **— pretexto de** under the pretext of.

sobaco *m.* armpit.

sobar *v.* to rub; to touch, handle; to knead; to massage; to fondle, pet; to bother; to beat, slap; *Am.* to set bones; *Am.* to flay, skin; *Am.* to win (*in a*

fight); *Am.* to tire out (*a horse*).

soberanía *f.* sovereignty.

soberano *adj. & m.* sovereign.

soberbia *f.* pride, arrogance; ostentation, pomp.

soberbio *adj.* proud, haughty, arrogant; pompous; superb, magnificent; spirited (*horse*).

sobornar *v.* to bribe.

soborno *m.* bribery; bribe; *Am.* overload (*on a pack animal*), extra load.

sobra *f.* surplus, excess; **-s** leftovers, leavings; **de —** more than enough; superfluous, unnecessary.

sobrado *m.* attic; loft; *Am.* pantry shelf; **-s** *Am.* leftovers, leavings; *adj.* leftover; excessive; superfluous; forward, brazen; **sobradas veces** many times, repeatedly.

sobrante *adj.* leftover, surplus, excess, spare; *m.* surplus, excess, remainder.

sobrar *v.* to exceed; to remain, be left over; to be more than enough.

sobre *prep.* over; above; on, upon; about; approximately; besides; **— manera** excessively; **estar — sí** to be cautious, on the alert; **— que** besides, in addition to the fact that; *m.* envelope; address (*on an envelope*).

sobrecama *f.* bedspread.

sobrecarga *f.* overload; overburden.

sobrecargar[7] *v.* to overload; to overburden.

sobrecoger[11] *v.* to surprise, catch unaware; to startle; **-se** to be startled; **-se de miedo** to be seized with fear.

sobreexcitación *f.* overexcitement; thrill.

sobreexcitar *v.* to overexcite.

sobrehumano *adj.* superhuman.

sobrellevar *v.* to endure, bear; to tolerate; to lighten (*another's burden*).

sobremesa *f.* table runner; after dinner conversation at the table; **de —** during the after dinner conversation.

sobrenadar *v.* to float.

sobrenatural *adj.* supernatural.

sobrenombre *m.* surname; nickname.

sobrentender[1] *v. irr.* to assume, understand; **-se** to be assumed, be obvious, be understood.

sobrepasar *v.* to exceed; to excel; **-se** to overstep, go too far.

sobreponer[40] *v. irr.* to lay on top; **-se** to dominate oneself; **-se a** to overcome; to dominate.

sobrepuesto *p.p. of* **sobreponer**; *m.* appliqué (*trimming laid on a dress*); *Am.* mend, patch.

sobrepujar *v.* to exceed, excel, surpass;

to outweigh.

sobresaliente *adj.* outstanding; projecting; excellent; *m. & f.* substitute (*a person*); understudy (*substitute actor*).

sobresalir[43] *v. irr.* to stand out; to project, jut out; to excel.

sobresaltar *v.* to startle, frighten; to assail; to stand out clearly; -se to be startled, frightened.

sobresalto *m.* start, scare, fright, shock; **de —** suddenly.

sobrescrito *m.* address (*on an envelope*).

sobrestante *m.* overseer, boss, foreman.

sobresueldo *m.* overtime pay, extra pay or wages.

sobretodo *m.* overcoat.

sobrevenir[48] *v. irr.* to happen, occur, come unexpectedly; to follow, happen after.

sobreviviente *m. & f.* survivor; *adj.* surviving.

sobrevivir *v.* to survive.

sobriedad *f.* sobriety, soberness, temperance, moderation.

sobrina *f.* niece.

sobrino *m.* nephew.

sobrio *adj.* sober, temperate, moderate.

socarrón *adj.* cunning, sly, crafty.

socarronería *f.* craftiness, slyness, cunning.

socavar *v.* to dig under; to undermine.

socavón *m.* tunnel; cave, cavern; underground passageway.

social *adj.* social; sociable, friendly.

socialista *adj.* socialist, socialistic; *m. & f.* socialist.

sociedad *f.* society; partnership; company, firm, corporation; **— anónima** (*or* **— por acciones**) stock company.

socio *m.* associate, partner; member.

sociología *f.* sociology.

socorrer *v.* to help, aid, assist.

socorro *m.* help, aid, assistance, relief; *Am.* partial advance payment on a workman's wages.

sodio *m.* sodium.

soez *adj.* low, vile, vulgar; coarse, ill-mannered.

sofá *m.* sofa, davenport.

sofocante *adj.* suffocating, stifling.

sofocar[6] *v.* to suffocate, choke; to smother; to bother; to embarrass.

sofoco *m.* suffocation, choking; upset, annoyance; embarrassment.

sofrenar *v.* to check; to control; to reprimand.

soga *f.* rope; *Am.* leather lasso or rope.

sojuzgamiento *m.* subjugation, subjection.

sojuzgar[7] *v.* to subjugate, subdue, subject.

sol *m.* sun; sunshine; sol (*fifth note of the scale*); *Am.* sol (*monetary unit of Peru*); **de — a —** from sunrise to sunset; **hace —** it is sunny; **tomar el —** to bask in the sun; to enjoy the sunshine.

solana *f.* sunny place; sunroom; sun porch; intense sunlight; **solanera** *f.* sunburn; sunny place.

solapa *f.* lapel.

solapado *adj.* sly, crafty, cunning, deceitful, underhanded.

solar *m.* lot, plot of ground; ancestral mansion, manor; *Am.* tenement house; *Am.* back yard; *Am.* town lot, field (*for growing alfalfa, corn, etc.*); *adj.* solar, of the sun.

solar[2] *v. irr.* to sole (*shoes*); to pave, floor.

solariego *adj.* manorial, pertaining to a manor; **casa solariega** ancestral manor or mansion.

solaz *m.* solace, comfort; relaxation, recreation.

solazar[9] *v.* to console, cheer, comfort; -se to seek relaxation or pleasure; to enjoy oneself.

soldado *m.* soldier; **— raso** private; **— de línea** regular soldier.

soldadura *f.* soldering; welding; solder.

soldar[2] *v. irr.* to solder; to weld.

soleado *adj.* sunny; *p.p.* sunned.

solear = **asolear**.

soledad *f.* solitude; loneliness; homesickness; lonely retreat.

solemne *adj.* solemn; imposing; **— disparate** downright foolishness, huge blunder.

solemnidad *f.* solemnity; solemn ceremony.

soler[2, 51] *v. irr.* to have the custom of, be in the habit of.

solferino *adj.* reddish-purple.

solicitante *m. & f.* solicitor; applicant.

solicitar *v.* to solicit; to apply for; to beg, ask for; to court, woo.

solícito *adj.* solicitous, careful; anxious, concerned, diligent.

solicitud *f.* solicitude; care, concern, anxiety.

solidaridad *f.* solidarity; union; bond, community of interests.

solidez *f.* solidity; compactness.

solidificar[6] *v.* to solidify.

sólido *adj.* solid; firm; strong; *m.* solid.

soliloquio *m.* soliloquy, monologue.

solista *m. & f.* soloist.

solitaria *f.* tapeworm.

solitario *adj.* solitary; lonely; *m.* recluse, hermit; solitaire (*card game*);

solitaire (*gem set by itself*).

solo *adj.* sole, only; single; alone; lonely; a solas alone; *m.* solo; sólo *adv.* only.

solomillo, solomo *m.* sirloin; loin; loin of pork.

soltar² *v. irr.* to loosen, untie, unfasten; to let loose; to set free; to let go; to let out; to utter; -se to set oneself free; to come loose; to lose restraint; to loosen up; -se a to begin to, start to.

soltero *adj.* single, unmarried; *m.* bachelor; soltera *f.* spinster; solterón *m.* old bachelor; solterona *f.* old maid.

soltura *f.* looseness; freedom; facility, ease; agility, nimbleness; release (*of a prisoner*).

solución *f.* solution; loosening, untying.

solventar *v.* to pay (*a bill*), settle (*an account*); to solve (*a problem or difficulty*).

sollozar⁹ *v.* to sob.

sollozo *m.* sob.

sombra *f.* shadow; shade; darkness; shelter, protection; image, reflection (*in the water*); *Am.* guide lines (*under writing paper*); *Am.* awning, sunshade; hacer — to shade; to cast a shadow (on).

sombreado *adj.* shady; shaded.

sombrear *v.* to shade; -se *Am.* to seek the shade, stand in the shade.

sombrerería *f.* hat shop.

sombrero *m.* hat; — de copa top hat, high hat; — hongo derby; — de jipijapa Panama hat; *Am.* — de pelo top hat.

sombrilla *f.* parasol, sunshade.

sombrío *adj.* somber, gloomy; shady.

somero *adj.* superficial, shallow; summary, concise.

someter *v.* to submit; to subject; -se to submit.

sometimiento *m.* submission; subjection.

somnolencia *f.* drowsiness, sleepiness; con — sleepily.

son *m.* sound; tune; rumor; en — de guerra in a warlike manner; sin ton ni — without rhyme or reason.

sonaja *f.* jingles, tambourine (*to accompany certain dances*); rattle; sonajero *m.* child's rattle.

sonante *adj.* sounding; ringing; sonorous; en dinero — y contante in hard cash.

sonar² *v. irr.* to sound; to ring; to sound · familiar; — a to sound like, seem like; -se to blow one's nose; se suena que it is rumored that.

sonda *f.* plumb, string with lead weight

(*for sounding the depth of water*); sounding; surgeon's probe.

sondar = sondear.

sondear *v.* to sound, fathom; to sound out; to probe; to examine into.

sondeo *m.* sounding, fathoming.

soneto *m.* sonnet.

sonido *m.* sound.

sonoro *adj.* sonorous; consonante sonora voiced consonant.

sonreír¹⁵ *v. irr.* to smile; -se to smile.

sonriente *adj.* smiling, beaming, radiant.

sonrisa *f.* smile.

sonrojarse *v.* to blush.

sonrojo *m.* blush.

sonrosado *adj.* rosy.

sonsacar⁶ *v.* to lure away; to draw (*someone*) out; to extract (*a secret*); to take on the sly.

sonsonete *m.* singsong; rhythmical tapping sound.

soñador *m.* dreamer.

soñar² *v. irr.* to dream; — con (*or* — en) to dream of; — despierto to daydream.

soñoliento *adj.* sleepy, drowsy.

sopa *f.* soup; sop; estar hecho una — to be sopping wet; *Am.* es un -s he is a fool.

sopapo *m.* chuck, tap, pat (*under the chin*); slap.

sopetón *m.* box, slap; de — all of a sudden, unexpectedly.

soplar *v.* to blow; to blow away; to blow up, inflate; to swipe, steal; to prompt; to "squeal" on, inform against; *Am.* — una bofetada to strike a blow; -se to swell up, puff up; to eat up, gobble up; to gulp down; se sopló el pastel he gobbled up the pie; *Am.* -se a uno to deceive someone, get the best of someone.

soplete *m.* blow torch; blowpipe.

soplo *m.* blowing; puff, gust of wind; breath; whispered warning or advice; "squealing," informing; en un — in a jiffy, in a second.

soplón *m.* informer, "squealer" (*one who tells on someone*), tattletale.

soportal *m.* arcade.

soportar *v.* to support, hold up, bear; to stand, endure, tolerate.

soporte *m.* support.

sorber *v.* to sip; to suck; to swallow; to absorb; to snuff up one's nose.

sorbete *m.* sherbet; fruit ice; *Am.* cone, ice-cream cone; *Am.* silk top hat.

sorbo *m.* sip, swallow, gulp; sniff.

sordera, sordez *f.* deafness.

sórdido *adj.* sordid.

sordina f. mute (of a musical instrument).

sordo adj. deaf; silent, noiseless; dull; muffled; **consonante sorda** voiceless consonant; m. deaf person; **hacerse el** — to pretend not to hear; to turn a deaf ear.

sordomudo adj. deaf and dumb; m. deaf-mute.

sorna f. slyness, cunning; sneer.

soroche m. Am. shortness of breath, sickness caused by high altitude; Am. blush, flush.

sorprendente adj. surprising.

sorprender v. to surprise; **-se** to be surprised.

sorpresa f. surprise.

sortear v. to draw lots; to raffle; to dodge; to shun; to fight (bulls) skilfully.

sorteo m. drawing or casting of lots; raffle.

sortija f. ring; finger ring; ringlet, curl.

sosa f. soda.

sosegado adj. calm, quiet, peaceful.

sosegar[1,7] v. to calm, quiet; to be quiet; **-se** to quiet down.

sosiego m. calm, peace, quiet.

soslayo : al — obliquely; slanting; on the bias; **de** — oblique, slanting; at a slant; sideways; **mirada de** — side glance; **pegar de** — to glance, hit at a slant.

soso adj. flat, tasteless, insipid; dull; silly; awkward.

sospecha f. suspicion; mistrust.

sospechar v. to suspect; to mistrust.

sospechoso adj. suspicious; m. suspect.

sostén m. support; prop; supporter; brassière.

sostener[45] v. irr. to sustain; to hold; to support, maintain; to defend, uphold; to endure.

sostenido p.p. & adj. sustained; supported, held up; m. sharp (in music).

sota f. jack (at cards); m. Am. foreman, boss, overseer.

sotana f. cassock (black outer robe of a priest).

sótano m. cellar, basement.

soto m. grove; thicket.

sotreta m. Am. nag, old horse.

soviet m. soviet; **soviético** adj. soviet, of, or pertaining to, soviets.

suave adj. soft; smooth; mild; bland; gentle.

suavidad f. softness; smoothness; mildness; gentleness.

suavizar[9] v. to smooth; to soften.

subalterno adj. & m. subordinate.

subasta f. public auction.

subastar v. to sell at auction.

súbdito m. subject.

subida f. rise; ascent; carrying up; **de** — on the way up; **muchas -s y bajadas** many ups and downs; much going up and down.

subir v. to ascend, go up, climb; to raise, lift; to carry up; to mount; — **al tren** to board the train, get on the train.

súbito adj. sudden; **de** — suddenly.

sublevación f. revolt, uprising, insurrection.

sublevar v. to excite to rebellion; **-se** to revolt.

sublime adj. sublime.

submarino m. & adj. submarine.

subordinado adj. & m. subordinate.

subordinar v. to subordinate; to subdue.

subrayar v. to underline; to emphasize.

subsanar v. to mend, remedy, repair (a damage, error, defect, etc.); to make up for (an error, fault, etc.); to excuse (a fault or error).

subscribir = **suscribir**.

subscripción = **suscripción**.

subscriptor = **suscritor**.

subsecretario m. undersecretary.

subsecuente adj. subsequent.

subsiguiente adj. subsequent.

subsistencia f. living, livelihood; sustenance; permanence.

subsistir v. to subsist; to exist; to last.

substancia = **sustancia**.

substancial = **sustancial**.

substancioso = **sustancioso**.

substituíble = **sustituíble**.

substantivo = **sustantivo**.

substitución = **sustitución**.

substituir = **sustituir**.

substituto = **sustituto**.

substracción = **sustracción**.

substraer = **sustraer**.

subteniente m. second lieutenant.

subterráneo adj. subterranean, underground; m. underground; cave, tunnel, vault.

suburbano adj. suburban; m. suburban resident.

suburbio m. suburb.

subvención f. subsidy.

subvencionar v. to subsidize.

subyugar v. to subdue.

succión f. suction.

suceder v. to happen, occur; to succeed, follow.

sucesión f. succession; heirs, offspring.

sucesivo adj. successive; **en lo** — hereafter, in the future.

suceso m. event; outcome, result.

sucesor m. successor.

suciedad f. dirt, filth; filthiness; filthy act or remark.

sucinto adj. compact, concise, brief.

sucio adj. dirty; foul, filthy.

suculento adj. juicy.

sucumbir v. to succumb; to yield.

sucursal f. branch, branch office (of a post office, bank, etc.); adj. branch (used as an adj.)).

suche adj. Am. sour, unripe; m. Am. pimple; Am. office boy, insignificant employee; Am. suche (a tree).

sud m. south; south wind; **sudeste** m. & adj. southeast; **sudoeste** m. & adj. southwest.

sudamericano adj. & m. South American.

sudar v. to sweat, perspire; to ooze; to toil.

sudor m. sweat, perspiration; toil.

sudoroso adj. sweaty, sweating, perspiring.

sueco adj. Swedish; m. Swede; Swedish language; **hacerse el** — to pretend not to see or understand.

suegra f. mother-in-law.

suegro m. father-in-law.

suela f. sole of a shoe; shoe leather.

sueldo m. salary.

suelo m. soil, ground; floor; pavement; bottom.

suelto adj. loose; free, easy; agile, nimble; blank (verse); m. small change; short newspaper article, news item.

sueño m. sleep; dream; sleepiness, drowsiness; **en -s** in one's sleep; **conciliar el** — to get to sleep; **tener** — to be sleepy.

suero m. serum.

suerte f. fate; fortune; chance; luck; sort, kind; way, manner; trick; **de** — **que** so that, in such a way that; and so; **echar -s** to cast lots; **tener** — to be lucky; **tocarle a uno la** — to fall to one's lot; to be lucky.

suéter m. Am. sweater.

suficiente adj. sufficient; competent, able.

sufragar[7] v. to defray, pay; to help, aid; Am. — **por** to vote for.

sufragio m. suffrage; vote; help, aid.

sufrido adj. suffering, long-suffering, patient; **mal** — impatient.

sufridor m. sufferer; adj. suffering.

sufrimiento m. suffering; patience, endurance.

sufrir v. to suffer; to endure; to allow, permit; to sustain; to undergo; — **un**

examen to take an examination.

sugerencia f. Am. suggestion, hint.

sugerir[3] v. irr. to suggest; to hint.

sugestión f. suggestion; hint.

sugestivo adj. suggestive.

suicida m. & f. suicide (person who commits suicide).

suicidarse v. to commit suicide.

suicidio m. suicide (act of suicide).

suizo adj. & m. Swiss.

sujeción f. subjection; control; submission.

sujetapapeles m. paper clip.

sujetar v. to subject; to control; to subdue; to fasten; to grasp, hold; **-se** to subject oneself; to submit; to adhere (to).

sujeto adj. subject; liable; fastened; under control; m. subject matter; subject; fellow, individual.

sulfato m. sulphate.

sulfurarse v. to get angry.

sulfúrico adj. sulphuric.

sulfuro m. sulphide.

sultán m. sultan.

suma f. sum; addition; substance; summary; **en** — in short.

sumador adj. adding; **máquina sumadora** adding machine.

sumar v. to add; to add up (to), amount (to); to sum up; **-se a** to join.

sumario m. summary; indictment; adj. summary, brief, concise; swift (punishment).

sumergible adj. submergible; m. submarine.

sumergir[11] v. to submerge, plunge, sink; to immerse; **-se** to submerge; to sink.

sumidero m. sink; sewer, drain.

suministrar v. to give, supply with, provide with.

sumir v. to sink; to submerge; to immerse; Am. to dent; **-se** to sink; Am. to shrink, shrivel; Am. to cower, crouch in fear; Am. **-se el sombrero hasta las cejas** to pull one's hat over one's eyes.

sumisión f. submission; obedience.

sumiso adj. submissive; obedient; meek.

sumo adj. supreme, highest, high; greatest; — **pontífice** Sovereign Pontiff (the Pope); **a lo** — at the most.

suntuoso adj. sumptuous, magnificent, luxurious.

superabundancia f. superabundance, great abundance, overflow.

superar v. to surpass; to exceed; to overcome.

superávit m. surplus.

superficial adj. superficial; shallow;

frivolous; **superficialidad** f. superficiality, shallowness, frivolity.

superficie f. surface; area.

superfluo adj. superfluous.

superintendente m. superintendent; supervisor; overseer.

superior adj. superior; higher; better; upper; m. superior; father superior; **superiora** f. superior, mother superior.

superioridad f. superiority; excellence.

superlativo adj. & m. superlative.

superstición f. superstition.

supersticioso adj. superstitious.

supervivencia f. survival.

superviviente = **sobreviviente.**

suplantar v. to supplant; to forge (a document or check).

suplementar v. to supplement.

suplementario adj. supplementary, extra.

suplemento m. supplement; supply, supplying.

suplente adj., m. & f. substitute.

súplica f. entreaty; request; petition; prayer.

suplicante adj. suppliant, beseeching; m. & f. suppliant; petitioner.

suplicar[6] v. to beg, entreat, implore; to pray humbly; to appeal, petition.

suplicio m. torture; torment; anguish; execution; instrument of torture; scaffold, gallows.

suplir v. to supply; to make up for; to substitute, take the place of (temporarily).

suponer[40] v. irr. to suppose; to assume; to be important.

suposición f. supposition; assumption.

supremacía f. supremacy.

supremo adj. supreme; final, last.

supresión f. suppression; omission; elimination.

suprimir v. to suppress; to abolish; to omit.

supuesto p.p. of **suponer** supposed, assumed; — **que** supposing that; since; **por** — of course, naturally; m. supposition; assumption.

supuración f. formation or discharge of pus.

supurar v. to fester, form or discharge pus.

sur m. south; south wind; **sureste** m. southeast; **suroeste** m. southwest.

suramericano = **sudamericano.**

surcar[6] v. to furrow; to plow; to plow through; to cut through.

surco m. furrow; rut; groove; wrinkle.

sureño adj. southern, from the south.

surgir[11] v. to surge, rise; to spurt; spout;

to appear.

surtido m. stock, supply, assortment; adj. assorted.

surtidor m. supplier; spout, jet.

surtir v. to provide, supply, stock (with); to spout, spurt; — **efecto** to produce the desired result; — **un pedido** to fill an order.

susceptible adj. susceptible; sensitive; touchy.

suscitar v. to raise, stir up, provoke.

suscribir[52] v. to subscribe; to endorse; to agree (to); -se to subscribe.

suscripción f. subscription.

suscrito p.p. of **suscribir.**

suscritor m. subscriber.

susodicho adj. aforesaid, above-mentioned.

suspender v. to suspend; to hang; to stop; to defer; to astonish; to flunk, fail; to dismiss temporarily.

suspensión f. suspension; postponement, delay; uncertainty; cessation.

suspenso adj. suspended; hanging; pending; perplexed, astonished; **en** — in suspense; m. failure (in an examination).

suspicaz adj. suspicious.

suspirar v. to sigh; to sigh (for), long (for).

suspiro m. sigh; brief pause (in music).

sustancia f. substance; essence; Am. broth.

sustancial adj. substantial; nourishing.

sustancioso adj. substantial; nourishing.

sustantivo m. noun; adj. substantive; real; independent.

sustentar v. to sustain; to support; to feed, nourish; to maintain, uphold.

sustento m. sustenance; food; support.

sustitución f. substitution.

sustituible adj. replaceable.

sustituir[32] v. irr. to substitute.

sustituto m. substitute.

susto m. scare, fright.

sustracción f. subtraction.

sustraer[46] v. irr. to subtract; to remove, withdraw; -se a to evade, avoid, slip away from.

susurrar v. to whisper; to murmur; to rustle; -se to be whispered or rumored about.

susurro m. whisper; murmur; rustle.

sutil adj. subtle; keen; clever; crafty; thin, fine, delicate.

sutileza, sutilidad f. subtlety; keenness, cleverness; cunning; thinness, fineness.

suyo adj. his, of his; her, of hers; your,

of yours (*formal*); their, of theirs; *pron.* his, hers, yours (*formal*), theirs; **de — naturally**, by nature; **salirse con la suya to get one's own way; hacer de las suyas** to be up to one's tricks; **los -s** his (hers, theirs); his (her, their) own people.

T

tabaco *m.* tobacco; cigar; snuff; *Am.* blow with the fist; **tabaquería** *f.* tobacco store, cigar store.

tábano *m.* horsefly, gadfly.

taberna *f.* tavern, bar, liquor store.

tabernáculo *m.* tabernacle.

tabique *m.* partition, partition wall.

tabla *f.* board, plank; plate of metal; slab; table, list; strip of ground; *Am.* chocolate tablet; **-s** draw, tie (*in games*); stage boards, the stage; a **raja** — cost what it may; *Am.* in great haste; **hacer — rasa de algo** to disregard, omit, or ignore something; *Am.* to clear away all obstacles in the way of something.

tablado *m.* platform, stage; scaffold; floor boards.

tablero *m.* board; panel; timber, piece of lumber; chessboard, checkerboard; store counter; large work table; gambling table; *Am.* blackboard; **poner al —** to risk, endanger.

tableta *f.* tablet; small thin board; memorandum pad.

tabletear *v.* to rattle; to make a continuous rattling or tapping sound.

tableteo *m.* rattling sound; tapping.

tablilla *f.* tablet; slat, small thin board; splint; small bulletin board; **-s** wooden clappers.

tablón *m.* plank; large, thick board.

taburete *m.* stool; footstool.

tacañería *f.* stinginess, tightness, miserliness.

tacaño *adj.* stingy, tight, miserly; sly.

tácito *adj.* tacit, implied; silent.

taciturno *adj.* taciturn, silent, sullen, sad.

taco *m.* wad; roll; plug, stopper; billiard cue; bite, snack; swear word; *Am.* leather legging; *Am.* short, fat person; *Am.* heel of a shoe; *Am.* pile, heap; **echar -s** to curse, swear; *Am.* **darse uno —** to strut, put on airs.

tacón *m.* heel of a shoe.

taconear *v.* to click the heels, walk hard on one's heels.

taconeo *m.* click, clicking (*of the heels*).

táctica *f.* tactics.

tacto *m.* tact; touch, sense of touch.

tacha *f.* flaw, defect, blemish.

tachar *v.* to cross out; to scratch out; to blot out; to blame; to find fault with; to censure.

tachón *m.* stud; trimming, braid; blot.

tachonar *v.* to stud, ornament with studs; to adorn with trimming.

tachuela *f.* tack, small nail; *Am.* metal dipper; *Am.* runt, "shorty."

tafetán *m.* taffeta; **— inglés** court plaster.

tahur *m.* gambler; cardsharp.

taimado *adj.* sly, crafty; *Am.* sullen, gloomy, gruff.

taita = **tatita**. *See* **tata**.

tajada *f.* slice; cut.

tajalápiz *m.* pencil sharpener.

tajar *v.* to slice; to cut; to sharpen (*a pencil*).

tajo *m.* cut; gash; cutting edge; sheer cliff; chopping block.

tal *adj.* such; such a; **— cual** such as; **so-so**, fair; **— vez** perhaps; **el — Pedro** that fellow Peter; **un — García** a certain García; **— para cual** two of a kind; **un — por cual** a nobody; *adv.* just as, in such a way; **estaba — como le dejé** he was just as I left him; **con — (de) que** provided that; **¿qué — ?** how are you?; hello!

talabarte *m.* sword belt.

taladrar *v.* to bore, drill; to pierce; to penetrate.

taladro *m.* auger, drill; bore, drill hole; *Am.* mine tunnel.

tálamo *m.* bridal bed or chamber.

talante *m.* disposition; mood; appearance, manner.

talco *m.* talc (*a soft mineral*); **— en polvo** talcum powder.

talega *f.* money bag, sack.

talento *m.* talent; ability, natural gift.

talentoso *adj.* talented, gifted.

talismán *m.* talisman, charm.

talón *m.* heel; stub, check, coupon.

talonario *m.* stub book; **libro —** stub book.

talonear *v.* to tap with one's heel; to walk briskly.

taloneo *m.* tapping with the heel; loud footsteps.

talla *f.* stature, height; carving; round of a card game; ransom; *Am.* chat; *Am.* thrashing, beating.

tallar *v.* to carve; to cut (*stone*); to appraise; to deal (*cards*); *Am.* to court, make love; *Am.* to bother, disturb.

tallarín *m.* noodle.

talle *m.* figure, form; waist; fit (*of a

dress); looks, appearance; *Am.* bodice.
taller *m.* workshop; laboratory; studio; factory.
tallo *m.* stalk; stem; shoot, sprout.
tamal *m. Am.* tamale; *Am.* vile trick, intrigue; *Am.* clumsy bundle.
tamaño *m.* size; *adj.* such a; of the size of; — **disparate** such a (big) mistake; — **como un elefante** big as an elephant; **tamañito** *adj.* very small; **tamañito así** about this little; **se quedó tamañito** he was (left) astonished, amazed.
tambalearse *v.* to totter, stagger, sway, reel.
también *adv.* also, too; likewise.
tambor *m.* drum; drum-like object; drummer; pair of embroidery hoops; *Am.* bedspring, spring mattress; **tambora** *f.* bass drum; **tamboril** *m.* small drum; **tamborilero** *m.* drummer.
tamborilear *v.* to drum; to extol.
tamiz *m.* fine sieve.
tamizar *v.* to sift; to blend.
tampoco *conj.* either (*after a negative*); **no lo hizo tampoco** he did not do it either; **ni yo** — nor I either.
tan *adv.* (*contr. of tanto*) so, as; such a.
tanda *f.* turn; round, bout; task; gang, group; shift, relay; *Am.* section of a theatrical performance.
tangente *adj. & f.* tangent; **salirse por la** — to go off at a tangent; to avoid the issue.
tangible *adj.* tangible.
tango *m.* tango.
tanque *m.* tank; reservoir; *Am.* pond; *Am.* swimming pool.
tantán *m.* clang; knock! knock!; sound of a bell, drum, etc.
tantear *v.* to probe, test; to sound out, feel out; to estimate, calculate approximately; *Am.* to grope, feel one's way; *Am.* to lie in wait; *Am.* to fool, make a fool of; *Am.* ¡**tantee Vd.**! just imagine!
tanteo *m.* trial, test; calculation, estimate; score; **al** — by guess; hit or miss.
tanto *adj., pron. & adv.* so much, as much; so; **-s** so many, as many; *m.* certain amount; counter, chip (*to keep score*); **cuarenta y -s** forty odd; **el** — **por ciento** percentage, rate; **un** — (*or* **algún** —) somewhat; — **como** as well as; as much as; — ... **como** both ... and; — **en la ciudad como en el campo** both in the city and in the country; **entre** (*or* **mientras**) — meanwhile; **por lo** — therefore.
tañer *v.* to play (*an instrument*); to ring.

tañido *m.* sound, tune; ring; twang (*of a guitar*).
tapa *f.* cover; lid; book cover; heel lift.
tapadera *f.* cover, lid; one who shields another.
tapar *v.* to cover; to plug, stop up; to veil; to hide; *Am.* to fill (*a tooth*); *Am.* to crush, crumple; *Am.* to cover with insults; **-se** to cover up; to wrap oneself up.
tapera *f. Am.* ruins; *Am.* abandoned room or house.
tapete *m.* rug; table scarf.
tapia *f.* adobe wall; wall fence.
tapiar *v.* to wall up; to block up (*a door or window*).
tapicería *f.* tapestry; upholstery; tapestry shop; tapestry making.
tapiz *m.* tapestry.
tapón *m.* plug, stopper, cork; bottle cap.
taquigrafía *f.* shorthand.
taquígrafo *m.* stenographer.
taquilla *f.* ticket office; box office; file (*for letters, papers, etc.*); *Am.* tavern, liquor store.
tararear *v.* to hum.
tarareo *m.* hum, humming.
tarascada *f.* snap, bite; snappy or harsh answer.
tardanza *f.* delay; slowness.
tardar *v.* to delay; to be late; to be long (in); to take long (in); **-se** to delay oneself; to be delayed; **a más** — at the very latest.
tarde *f.* afternoon; *adv.* late; **de** — **en** — from time to time, now and then.
tardío *adj.* late; slow.
tardo *adj.* slow, lazy; tardy, late; stupid, dull; **tardón** *adj.* very slow; *m.* slow poke, slow person.
tarea *f.* task, job; anxiety, care.
tarifa *f.* tariff; list of duties, taxes, or prices; fare.
tarima *f.* wooden platform; low bench.
tarjeta *f.* card; — **postal** postcard.
tarro *m.* earthen jar; *Am.* horn (*of an animal*); *Am.* can; *Am.* top hat.
tarta *f.* tart.
tartamudear *v.* to stutter, stammer.
tartamudeo *m.* stammer, stammering.
tartamudo *m.* stutterer, stammerer; *adj.* stuttering, stammering.
tartera *f.* griddle; baking pan.
tarugo *m.* wooden block; wooden peg; blockhead, dunce; *adj. Am.* mischievous, devilish.
tasa *f.* measure; standard; rate; appraisal; valuation.
tasación *f.* assessment, valuation, appraisal.

tasajo *m.* piece of jerked beef.

tasar *v.* to measure; to appraise; to rate.

tata *f.* daddy, dad; *Am.* chief (*said by Indians to a superior*); **tatita** *m.* daddy; *Am.* dear chief or daddy (*said by Indians*).

tataranieto *m.* great-great-grandson.

taxear *v.* to taxi (*said of a plane*).

taxi, taxímetro *m.* taxi, taxicab.

taza *f.* cup; bowl; basin of a fountain.

tazón *m.* large cup; bowl; basin of a fountain.

té *m.* tea; *f.* T-square, T-shaped ruler.

te *obj. pron.* you (*fam. sing.*); to you; for you; yourself.

teatral *adj.* theatrical.

teatro *m.* theater; stage; scene, setting; **hacer** — to put on airs, show off.

tecla *f.* key (*of a piano, typewriter, etc.*); **dar uno en la** — to hit the nail on the head, find the right way to do something.

teclado *m.* keyboard.

técnica *f.* technique.

técnico *adj.* technical; *m.* technical expert, technician.

tecolote *m.* *Am.* owl.

techado *m.* roof; shed; *p.p. of* **techar.**

techar *v.* to roof.

techo *m.* roof; ceiling.

techumbre *f.* roof; ceiling.

tedio *m.* tediousness; boredom; bother.

tedioso *adj.* tedious, boring, tiresome.

teja *f.* tile; linden tree; *Am.* rear part of a saddle; **de -s abajo** here below, in this world.

tejado *m.* roof; shed.

tejamanil *m.* shingle; small thin board.

tejedor *m.* weaver.

tejer *v.* to weave; to interlace; to braid; to knit.

tejido *m.* textile, fabric; texture; weave; weaving; tissue.

tejón *m.* badger; bar of gold.

tela *f.* cloth; membrane; web; film (*on the surface of liquids*); — **adhesiva** adhesive tape; — **de cebolla** onion skin; flimsy fabric; *Am.* — **emplástica** court plaster; — **metálica** wire screen; **poner en** — **de juicio** to call in question.

telar *m.* loom.

telaraña *f.* cobweb, spider's web.

telefonear *v.* to telephone.

telefónico *adj.* telephonic, telephone (*used as adj.*); **receptor** — telephone receiver.

teléfono *m.* telephone; **telefonista** *m. & f.* telephone operator.

telegrafía *f.* telegraphy.

telegrafiar[17] *v.* to telegraph.

telegráfico *adj.* telegraphic.

telégrafo *m.* telegraph; — **sin hilos** (*or* — **inalámbrico**) wireless telegraph; **telegrafista** *m. & f.* telegraph operator.

telegrama *m.* telegram.

telescopio *m.* telescope.

televisión *f.* television.

telón *m.* theater curtain; — **de boca** drop curtain; — **de foro** drop scene.

tema *m.* theme; subject; *f.* fixed idea, mania.

temblar[1] *v. irr.* to tremble; to shake; to quiver.

temblón *adj.* tremulous, trembling, shaking, quivering.

temblor *m.* tremor, trembling; shiver; quake; — **de tierra** earthquake.

tembloroso *adj.* trembling, shaking.

temer *v.* to fear; to dread; to suspect.

temerario *adj.* rash, reckless.

temeridad *f.* temerity, recklessness; folly.

temeroso *adj.* fearful; suspicious; timid.

temible *adj.* terrible, dreadful.

temor *m.* fear; dread, suspicion.

témpano *m.* thick slice or chunk (*of anything*); kettledrum; drumhead (*parchment stretched over the end of a drum*); — **de hielo** block of ice; iceberg.

temperamento *m.* temperament; climate.

temperatura *f.* temperature.

tempestad *f.* tempest, storm.

tempestuoso *adj.* tempestuous, stormy.

templado *p.p.* tempered; tuned; *adj.* moderate; temperate; lukewarm; brave; *Am.* in love; *Am.* half-drunk; *Am.* hard, severe; **estar mal** — to be in a bad humor.

templanza *f.* temperance; moderation; mildness.

templar *v.* to temper; to moderate; to calm; to soften; to tune; **-se** to be tempered, moderate; to control oneself; *Am.* to fall in love; *Am.* to take to one's heels; *Am.* to stuff oneself.

temple *m.* temper; temperament; valor, courage; harmony (*of musical instruments*); *Am.* sweetheart; **de mal** — in a bad humor.

templo *m.* temple; church.

temporada *f.* period of time, season; — **de ópera** opera season.

temporal *adj.* temporal; secular, worldly; temporary; *m.* weather; storm; spell of rainy weather.

tempranero *adj.* habitually early or ahead of time; **ser** — to be an early riser.

temprano *adj.* early; premature; *adv.* early.

tenacidad *f.* tenacity; tenaciousness; perseverance.

tenacillas *f. pl.* small tongs; pincers, tweezers; sugar tongs; curling iron.

tenaz *adj.* tenacious; firm; strong, resistant; stubborn.

tenazas *f. pl.* pincers; pliers; tongs; forceps (*for pulling teeth*); **tenazuelas** *f. pl.* tweezers, small pincers.

tendedero *m.* place to hang or spread clothes; clothesline.

tendencia *f.* tendency, inclination.

tender[1] *v. irr.* to spread out; to stretch out; to lay out; to tend, have a tendency, move (toward); to hang to dry; *Am.* to make (*a bed*); **-se** to stretch oneself out; to lay all one's cards on the table; to run at full gallop.

ténder *m.* tender (*of a train*).

tendero *m.* storekeeper; tentmaker.

tendón *m.* tendon, sinew.

tenducho *m.* wretched little shop.

tenebroso *adj.* dark, shadowy; gloomy.

tenedor *m.* table fork; holder, possessor, keeper; **— de libros** bookkeeper.

teneduría *f.* office and position of bookkeeper; **— de libros** bookkeeping.

tener[45] *v. irr.* to have; to possess; to hold; **— en mucho** to esteem highly; **— por** to consider, judge; **— que** (+ *inf.*) to have to; **— gana** (*or* **— ganas**) **de** to desire, feel like; **— miedo** (**sueño, frío, hambre,** *etc.*) to be afraid (sleepy, cold, hungry, *etc.*); **— ... años** to be ... years old; **-se** to stand firm; to hold on.

tenería *f.* tannery.

teniente *m.* first lieutenant; substitute, deputy.

tenis *m.* tennis.

tenor *m.* tenor; text, literal meaning; kind, sort, nature.

tensión *f.* tension; strain.

tenso *adj.* tense; tight, taut.

tentación *f.* temptation.

tentáculo *m.* tentacle, feeler.

tentador *adj.* tempting; *m.* tempter; the devil.

tentalear *v.* to grope, feel around; to finger, touch; to fumble (*for something*).

tentar[1] *v. irr.* to tempt; to touch, feel with the fingers; to grope; to attempt, try; to test; to probe, examine with a probe.

tentativa *f.* attempt, trial.

tentativo *adj.* tentative.

tenue *adj.* delicate, thin; flimsy; worthless.

teñir[5,19] *v. irr.* to dye; to tinge; to darken (*the color of a painting*).

teologal, teológico *adj.* theological.

teología *f.* theology.

teoría *f.* theory.

teórico *adj.* theoretical.

tequila *m. Am.* tequila (*liquor made from the maguey plant*).

tercero *adj.* third; *m.* third person; mediator; go-between; tertiary (*member of the third order of St. Francis*).

terciar *v.* to sling across one's shoulders; to divide into three parts; to intervene, mediate; to meddle, join (in); to balance the load on a pack animal; *Am.* to load or carry on the back; *Am.* to adulterate, add water to; *Am.* to mix.

tercio *adj.* third; *m.* one third; half of a mule load; military regiment or division; *Am.* bale, bundle; **hacer uno mal —** to hinder, interfere.

terciopelo *m.* velvet.

terco *adj.* obstinate, stubborn; hard; *Am.* harsh, severe.

tergiversar *v.* to distort, twist.

terminación *f.* termination, end; ending.

terminal *adj.* terminal, final.

terminante *adj.* closing, ending; decisive, final.

terminar *v.* to terminate, end; to finish; **-se** to end.

término *m.* end; completion; goal, object; boundary, limit; terminal; term; word, phrase; **en otros -s** in other words; **por — medio** on an average; as a rule; **primer —** foreground.

termómetro *m.* thermometer.

Termos *f.* Thermos (trade mark).

ternera *f.* calf; veal.

terneza *f.* tenderness; softness; affection; affectionate word; caress.

terno *m.* group or combination of three; suit of clothes; *Am.* set of jewels (*earrings, necklace and brooch*); *Am.* cup and saucer; **echar** (*or* **soltar**) **un —** to utter a bad word; to curse, swear.

ternura *f.* tenderness.

terquedad *f.* obstinacy, stubbornness.

terrado *m.* terrace; flat roof.

terraplén *m.* railroad embankment.

terrateniente *m. & f.* landholder.

terraza *f.* terrace, veranda; flat roof.

terremoto *m.* earthquake.

terrenal *adj.* earthly, worldly.

terreno *m.* land; ground; field; *adj.* earthly, worldly.

terrestre *adj.* terrestrial; earthly.
terrible *adj.* terrible.
terrífico *adj.* terrific.
territorio *m.* territory.
terrón *m.* clod; lump.
terror *m.* terror.
terso *adj.* polished, smooth.
tertulia *f.* evening party; social gathering; club; conversation; *Am.* theater gallery.
tertuliano, tertulio *m.* member of a tertulia.
tesis *f.* thesis.
tesón *m.* grit, endurance, pluck, persistence.
tesonero *adj. Am.* tenacious, stubborn, persevering, persistent.
tesorería *f.* treasury; **tesorero** *m.* treasurer.
tesoro *m.* treasure; treasury.
testa *f.* head; crown of the head; front.
testamento *m.* testament; will.
testarudez *f.* stubbornness, obstinacy.
testarudo *adj.* stubborn.
testigo *m.* & *f.* witness; *m.* testimony, proof, evidence; — **de cargo** witness for the prosecution; — **de vista** eyewitness.
testimoniar *v.* to give testimony of; to serve as a witness.
testimonio *m.* testimony; proof, evidence; **levantar falso** — to bear false witness.
testuz *m.* nape; crown of the head (*of certain animals*).
teta *f.* teat, nipple; breast; udder.
tetera *f.* teapot; teakettle; *Am.* nursing bottle.
tétrico *adj.* sad, melancholy, gloomy.
textil *adj.* textile.
texto *m.* text; quotation; textbook.
tez *f.* complexion, skin.
ti *pers. pron.* (*used after prep.*) you; yourself (*fam. sing.*).
tía *f.* aunt; older woman; *Am.* — **rica** pawnshop; **no hay tu** — there is no use or hope; there is no way out of it; **quedarse una para** — to remain an old maid.
tibio *adj.* tepid, lukewarm; indifferent; *Am.* annoyed, angry.
tiburón *m.* shark.
tico *adj.* & *m. Am.* Costa Rican (*humorous nickname*).
tiempo *m.* time; weather; tense; **a** — in time, on time; **a su** — in due time, at the proper time; **a un** — at one and the same time; **andando el** — in time, as time goes on.
tienda *f.* store; tent; — **de campaña**

camping tent, army tent.
tienta *f.* probe (*surgical instrument*); **a -s** gropingly, feeling one's way; **andar a -s** to grope, feel one's way.
tiento *m.* touch; tact; blind man's stick; steady hand; blow; tentacle, feeler (*of an insect*); *Am.* saddle strap, leather strap, thong; *Am.* snack; *Am.* swallow of liquor; **dar un** — to make a trial or attempt; **hacer algo con mucho** — to do something with great care or caution; **perder el** — to lose one's skill; *Am.* **tener a uno a los -s** to keep someone within sight; *Am.* **tener la vida en un** — to be in great danger.
tierno *adj.* tender; soft; young; recent, new; sensitive; affectionate; *Am.* green, unripe.
tierra *f.* earth; land; ground; soil; native land; — **adentro** inland; — **firme** mainland; solid ground; **dar en** — **con alguien** to overthrow someone; **echar por** — to knock down; to demolish; **tomar** — to land.
tieso *adj.* stiff, rigid; stuck-up; firm; stubborn.
tiesto *m.* flowerpot; broken piece of earthenware; *Am.* pot.
tiesura *f.* stiffness.
tifo *m.* typhus; **tifoidea** *f.* typhoid fever.
tigre *m.* tiger.
tijera *f.* (*usually* **tijeras**) scissors; sawhorse; **silla de** — folding chair; **tener buena**— (*or* **tener buenas -s**) to have a sharp tongue; to be a gossip.
tijeretada *f.,* **tijeretazo** *m.* snip, cut, clip (*with the scissors*).
tijeretear *v.* to snip, cut, clip (*with scissors*); to criticize others, gossip.
tilde *f.* tilde (*mark over an* **n**); blemish; jot, bit, speck.
timbrar *v.* to stamp, mark with a seal.
timbre *m.* revenue stamp; seal; crest (*on a coat of arms*); call bell; timbre (*quality of tone, tone color*); merit, fame; glorious deed; *Am.* postage stamp.
timidez *f.* timidity; shyness.
tímido *adj.* timid; shy.
timón *m.* helm; rudder; beam of a plow.
timonear *v.* to steer (*a ship*).
timorato *adj.* timorous, timid.
tímpano *m.* eardrum; kettledrum.
tina *f.* large earthen jar; vat, tank; tub; bathtub.
tinaco *m.* tank, vat, tub.
tinaja *f.* large earthen jar.
tinieblas *f. pl.* darkness; obscurity; ignorance, confusion; Tenebrae (*Holy Week religious service*).
tino *m.* acumen, keen insight, good

208

judgment; tact; accurate aim; good sense of touch; tank, vat.

tinta f. ink; dye; tint, hue; -s paints; — simpática invisible ink; saber de buena — to know on good authority.

tinte m. tint, hue; tinge; color; dye; dyeing.

tinterillo m. shyster. *See* picapleitos.

tintero m. inkwell, inkstand; *Am.* writing materials, desk set.

tintinear v. to tinkle.

tintineo m. tinkle, tinkling.

tinto adj. tinged; red (*wine*); *Am.* dark-red; p.p. irr. of teñir.

tintorería f. cleaner's and dyer's shop.

tintorero m. dyer.

tintura f. tincture; tint, color; dye.

tinturar v. to tincture; to tinge; to dye.

tiñoso adj. scabby, mangy; stingy.

tío m. uncle; old man; good old man; fellow, guy; *Am.* el cuento del — deceitful story (*told to extract money*).

tiovivo m. merry-go-round.

típico adj. typical; *Am.* corrected (*edition*).

tiple m. & f. high soprano singer; m. treble; soprano voice; treble guitar.

tipo m. type; class; model, standard; fellow, guy; *Am.* rate of interest; *Am.* — de cambio rate of exchange; buen — good-looking fellow.

tipografía f. typography, printing; press, printing shop.

tira f. strip; stripe; *Am.* estar hecho -s to be in rags; *Am.* sacar a uno las -s to tan one's hide, beat one to pieces.

tirabuzón m. corkscrew.

tirada f. throw; issue, edition, printing; *Am.* tirade, long speech; *Am.* sly trick; *Am.* dash (*on horseback*); de una — all at once, at one fell swoop.

tirador m. shooter; thrower; slingshot; bell cord; handle; printer; *Am.* leather belt with pockets; — de goma slingshot.

tiranía f. tyranny.

tiránico adj. tyrannical.

tirano adj. tyrannical; m. tyrant.

tirante adj. pulling; stretched, taut; strained; m. trace (*of a harness*); brace; -s suspenders; supporters (*for stockings*).

tirantez f. tension, tightness; strain; pull.

tirar v. to throw; to throw away; to shoot, fire; to draw; to print; to attract; *Am.* to cart; — a to tend toward; to resemble; to aim at; — de to pull, tug; — bien a la espada to handle a sword well; ir tirando to get along;

a todo (*or* a más) — at the most; *Am.* al — haphazardly; -se to throw oneself; to lie down; *Am.* tirársela de to boast of.

tiritar v. to shiver.

tiro m. throw; shot; piece of artillery; range of a gun; shooting range; charge of a gun; team (*of horses*); chimney draft; mine shaft; *Am.* issue, printing; *Am.* cartage, transport; -s *Am.* suspenders; — al blanco target practice; *Am.* al — at once; *Am.* de a (*or* de al) — all at once; completely; caballo de — draft horse; ni a -s absolutely not (*not even if you shoot me*).

tirón m. jerk, sudden pull; de un — all at once, with one big pull.

tironear v. *Am.* to pull, jerk; *Am.* to attract.

tirotear v. to shoot around; to shoot at random; -se to exchange shots.

tiroteo m. shooting; exchange of shots; skirmish.

tirria f. aversion, grudge; tenerle — a una persona to have a strong dislike for someone; to hold a grudge against someone.

tísico adj. tubercular, consumptive.

tisis f. tuberculosis, consumption.

títere m. puppet; ridiculous little fellow; -s puppet show.

titilación f. flicker; twinkle; titileo m. flickering; twinkling; glimmer.

titilar v. to flicker; to twinkle.

titubear v. to hesitate; to totter, stagger; to grope; to stutter, stammer.

titubeo m. hesitation, wavering.

titular v. to entitle; to name; -se to be called or named; to call oneself; to receive a title; adj. titular, in name only.

título m. title; heading; sign; inscription; claim, legal right; degree, diploma; credential; titled person; merit; bond, certificate; a — de under the pretext of; in the capacity of.

tiza f. chalk.

tiznado adj. sooty, covered with soot; smutty; dirty; *Am.* drunk; p.p. of tiznar.

tiznar v. to smudge, smut; to smear with soot.

tizne m. soot; smut; tiznón m. smudge.

tizón m. firebrand (*piece of burning wood*); rust, blight (*on plants*); stain (*on one's honor*).

toalla f. towel.

tobillo m. ankle.

tocado m. headdress; hairdo, coiffure; adj. "touched", half-crazy; p.p. of

tocar.

tocador *m.* dressing table; boudoir, dressing room; dressing case; player (*of a musical instrument*).

tocar[6] *v.* to touch; to play (*an instrument*); to toll, ring; to knock, rap; **—en** to stop over in; **-le a uno** to fall to one's lot; to be one's share; to be one's turn; to concern one; **-se** to fix one's hair; to become "touched," go slightly crazy.

tocayo *m.* namesake.

tocino *m.* bacon; salt pork; lard.

tocón *m.* stub, stump (*of a tree, arm or leg*).

todavía *adv.* still; yet; even.

todo *adj.* all, whole; every, each; **—hombre** every man; **-s los días** every day; **a —** correr at full or top speed; *m.* whole; all; everything; **-s** everybody; **ante —** first of all; **así y —** in spite of that; **con —** in spite of that; **del —** wholly.

todopoderoso *adj.* almighty.

toga *f.* gown, robe (*worn by a judge, professor, etc.*); Roman toga:

toldería *f.* Am. Indian camp, Indian village.

toldo *m.* awning; pomp, vanity; Am. Indian hut.

tolerancia *f.* tolerance, toleration; **tolerante** *adj.* tolerant.

tolerar *v.* to tolerate; to allow; to overlook, let pass.

tolete *m.* Am. stick, club, cudgel; Am. raft.

toma *f.* taking; seizure, capture; dose; tap (*of a water main*); Am. irrigation ditch; **— de corriente** plug, electric outlet.

tomar *v.* to take; to grasp, catch; to capture; to drink; **— a pechos** to take to heart, take seriously; **-lo a mal** to take it amiss; **— el pelo a** to make fun of, make a fool of; **— por la derecha** to turn to the right; **-se con** to quarrel with.

tomate *m.* tomato.

tomillo *m.* thyme.

tomo *m.* tome, volume; Am. heavy person; Am. dull, silent person; Am. buen **— a** heavy drinker; de **— y lomo** bulky; important.

ton: sin — ni son without rhyme or reason.

tonada *f.* tune, song; Am. singsong; Am. local accent; **tonadilla** *f.* little tune; short popular song.

tonel *m.* keg, cask, barrel.

tonelada *f.* ton.

tonelaje *m.* tonnage.

tónico *adj. & m.* tonic.

tono *m.* tone; tune; key, pitch; accent; manner; vigor, strength; **de buen —** of good taste, stylish; **subirse de —** to put on airs.

tontera = **tontería.**

tontería *f.* foolishness; stupidity.

tonto *adj.* foolish; stupid; **a tontas y a locas** recklessly, without thought; *m.* fool; dunce; Am. a game of cards.

topar *v.* to collide with, run into, bump into; to encounter; to find; to run across; to butt; Am. to gamble; Am. to fight with the fists; Am. to meet, greet.

tope *m.* butt, bump, collision; encounter; bumper; **hasta el —** up to the top; **estar hasta los -s** to be filled up.

topetada *f.*, **topetazo** *m.* butt; bump, blow on the head; **topetón** *m.* hard bump, collision; butt.

topetear *v.* to butt; to bump.

tópico *m.* topic, subject.

topo *m.* mole (*small animal*); dunce; awkward person.

toque *m.* touch; ringing; beat (*of a drum*); tap; sound (*of a trumpet, clarinet, etc.*); assay; **piedra de —** touchstone; **¡allí está el —!** there is the difficulty! there is the real test!

torbellino *m.* whirlwind; rush, bustle, confusion.

torcedura *f.* twist; sprain, strain.

torcer[2.10] *v. irr.* to twist; to turn; to bend; to sprain; to distort; **-se** to become twisted, bent, or sprained; to get crooked; to go astray; to turn sour (*said of wine*); Am. to get offended, angry.

torcido *p.p. & adj.* twisted, turned, bent; crooked; angry, resentful; Am. unfortunate, unlucky; **estar — con** to be on unfriendly terms with; *m.* twisted roll of candied fruit; coarse silk twist; Am. gesture or look of disdain; Am. lasso made of twisted leather.

tordillo *adj.* greyish, dapple-grey.

tordo *adj.* dapple-grey; *m.* thrush; dapple-grey horse.

torear *v.* to perform in a bullfight; to incite, provoke (*a bull*); to tease.

torero *m.* bullfighter; *adj.* relating to bullfighting.

tormenta *f.* storm, tempest; misfortune.

tormento *m.* torment; torture; rack (*instrument of torture*); anguish; pain.

tornar *v.* to return; to turn; to change, alter; **— a hacerlo** to do it again.

tornasolado *adj.* iridescent, rainbow-colored; changeable (*silk*).

tornear *v.* to turn in a lathe; to do lathe work; to fight in a tournament.

torneo *m.* tournament.

tornillo *m.* screw; clamp, vise; **faltarle a uno un** — to have little sense, "have a screw loose."

torno *m.* turn; lathe; turnstile; revolving server; winch or windlass (*machine for lifting or pulling, turned by a crank*); — **de hilar** spinning wheel; **en** — around.

toro *m.* bull; *Am.* difficult question; **-s** bullfight; *Am.* **estar en las astas del** — to be in a predicament.

toronja *f.* grapefruit.

torpe *adj.* stupid, dull; clumsy; slow; lewd.

torpedear *v.* to torpedo.

torpedo *m.* torpedo; **torpedero** *m.* torpedo boat.

torpeza *f.* stupidity, dullness; clumsiness; slowness; moral turpitude, lewdness.

torre *f.* tower; turret; castle (*in chess*).

torrente *m.* torrent; flood; — **de voz** powerful voice.

torreón *m.* large tower (*of a fortress, castle, etc.*).

tórrido *adj.* torrid.

torsión *f.* twist; sprain.

torta *f.* torte, round cake; round loaf.

tortilla *f.* omelet; *Am.* tortilla (*flat, thin cornmeal cake*).

tórtola *f.* turtledove.

tortuga *f.* tortoise; turtle.

tortuoso *adj.* tortuous, twisting, winding; sly.

tortura *f.* torture; grief, affliction.

torturar *v.* to torture.

torvo *adj.* grim, stern, severe.

tos *f.* cough; — **ferina** whooping cough.

tosco *adj.* coarse, harsh, rough.

toser *v.* to cough; *Am.* to brag, boast.

tosquedad *f.* coarseness, crudeness, roughness; rudeness.

tostada *f.* toast, toasted bread; *Am.* boring visit or conversation; *Am.* toasted **tortilla; dar** (*or* **pegar**) **una** — **a uno** to play a mean trick on someone; *Am.* to make someone very angry.

tostado *p.p.* & *adj.* toasted; roasted; tanned; *Am.* worn out, tired out; *m.* toasting; *Am.* roasted corn.

tostador *m.* toaster.

tostar[2] *v. irr.* to toast; to tan; to overheat; to roast (*coffee*).

tostón *m.* toast dipped in oil: small roasted pig; *Am.* coin worth half a Mexican peso.

total *adj.* & *m.* total.

totalidad *f.* entirety, whole.

totalitario *adj.* totalitarian.

tóxico *adj.* toxic.

toxina *f.* toxin (*poison produced within animals and plants*).

toza *f.* wooden block; stump; log; piece of bark.

traba *f.* bond, tie; binding or locking device; fastener, fetter, shackle; hindrance, obstacle.

trabado *adj. Am.* tongue-tied; *p.p.* of **trabar.**

trabajador *adj.* industrious; *m.* worker, laborer.

trabajar *v.* to work; to labor; to strive.

trabajo *m.* work; labor; difficulty, obstacle; trouble; hardship.

trabajoso *adj.* laborious, difficult; troublesome; *Am.* unobliging; *Am.* demanding.

trabar *v.* to join, fasten; to clasp; to shackle; to brace; — **amistad con alguien** to become friends with someone; — **batalla** to join in battle; — **conversación** to be engaged in conversation; to engage in conversation; **-se** *Am.* to stammer; **-se de palabras** to get into an argument.

tracción *f.* traction.

tractor *m.* tractor.

tradición *f.* tradition.

tradicional *adj.* traditional.

traducción *f.* translation.

traducir[25] *v. irr.* to translate; to interpret.

traductor *m.* translator.

traer[46] *v. irr.* to bring; to carry; to lead, conduct; to have; to bring about; to wear; — **a uno inquieto** to keep one disturbed; — **a uno a mal** — to mistreat someone; to bother someone; **-se bien** to dress well; to carry oneself well.

trafagar[7] *v.* to traffic, trade; to roam about; to bustle, hustle; to toil.

tráfago *m.* trade, commerce; bustle, hustle; toil.

traficante *m.* trader; dealer; tradesman.

traficar[6] *v.* to traffic, trade; *Am.* to pass or move back and forth (*as traffic*). See **transitar.**

tráfico *m.* traffic; trade, commerce.

tragaluz *f.* skylight.

tragar[7] *v.* to swallow; to gulp; to engulf; swallow up.

tragedia *f.* tragedy.

trágico *adj.* tragic.

trago *m.* swallow, gulp; misfortune; *Am.*

brandy, hard liquor; **a -s** slowly, by degrees; **echar un —** to take a drink; **tragón** *m.* glutton; *adj.* gluttonous.

traición *f.* treason; treachery; **a —** treacherously; deceitfully.

traicionar *v.* to betray.

traicionero *adj.* treacherous; deceitful; *m.* traitor.

traído *adj.* used, old, worn out; **muy — y llevado** very worn out; *p.p. of* **traer.**

traidor *adj.* treacherous; *m.* traitor; betrayer.

traje *m.* dress; suit; gown; **— de etiqueta** (**— de ceremonia,** *or Am.* **— de parada)** formal gown; formal suit; dress uniform; **— de luces** bullfighter's costume; *Am.* **— sastre** woman's tailor-made suit.

trajeado *p.p. & adj.* dressed, clothed.

trajín *m.* traffic, going and coming; hustle, bustle, commotion.

trajinar *v.* to carry, cart back and forth; to go back and forth; to bustle, hustle.

trama *f.* plot; scheme; conspiracy; woof (*horizontal threads of a fabric*).

tramar *v.* to weave; to plot; to scheme.

tramitar *v.* to transact; to take legal steps; to negotiate.

trámite *m.* transaction, procedure, step, formality.

tramo *m.* stretch, lap, span; short distance; regular interval; flight of stairs.

trampa *f.* trap; snare; hatch, trap door; hinged section of a counter; spring door; fraud; trick.

trampear *v.* to trick, cheat, swindle.

trampista *m. & f.* cheat, crook, swindler.

trampolín *m.* springboard.

tramposo *adj.* deceitful, tricky; *m.* swindler, cheat.

tranca *f.* crossbar, bolt; pole, prop; club, stick; *Am.* rustic gate; *Am.* fence with gates; *Am.* **saltar las -s** to jump over the fence; to lose one's patience, rebel, get angry; *Am.* **tener una —** to be drunk.

trance *m.* critical moment; dangerous situation; **el último —** the last moment of life; **a todo —** at any cost, cost what it may.

tranco *m.* stride, long step; threshold; **a -s** hurriedly; **en dos -s** in a jiffy; *Am.* **al —** striding, with long steps.

tranquear *v.* to stride along.

tranquera *f.* stockade, wooden fence; *Am.* large gate (*made with* **trancas).**

tranquilidad *f.* tranquillity, peacefulness.

tranquilizar[9] *v.* to quiet, calm down; to

pacify; **-se** to become tranquil, calm down.

tranquilo *adj.* tranquil, peaceful.

transacción *f.* transaction, negotiation; compromise.

transar *v. Am.* to compromise, yield, give in.

transatlántico *adj.* transatlantic; *m.* transatlantic steamer.

transbordar = trasbordar.

transbordo = trasbordo.

transcendencia *f.* consequence, importance; penetration.

transcendental *adj.* consequential, important, far-reaching.

transcurrir *v.* to pass, elapse.

transcurso *m.* passing, lapse (*of time*).

transeúnte *m.* passer-by; pedestrian; transient; *adj.* transient.

transferencia *f.* transference, transfer.

transferir[3] *v. irr.* to transfer.

transformación *f.* transformation.

transformar *v.* to transform.

transgredir[51] *v.* to transgress.

transgresión *f.* transgression.

transgresor *m.* transgressor, offender.

transición *f.* transition.

transigente *adj.* compromising, yielding, pliable.

transigir[11] *v.* to compromise, yield, make concessions; to settle by compromise.

transitable *adj.* passable (*road*).

transitar *v.* to pass or move back and forth (*as traffic*).

tránsito *m.* transit; traffic; passing; passage; transition; **de — on the way, in transit, passing through.**

transitorio *adj.* transitory.

transmisión *f.* transmission.

transmisor *m.* transmitter; *adj.* transmitting.

transmitir *v.* to transmit.

transparencia *f.* transparency.

transparente *adj.* transparent; lucid, clear; *m.* window shade; stained-glass window.

transponer[40] *v. irr.* to transpose; to transfer; to transplant; to go beyond, go over to the other side; **-se** to hide from view, go behind; to set, go below the horizon.

transportación *f.* transportation, transport.

transportar *v.* to transport; to transpose (*music*); **-se** to be transported, carried away by strong feeling; to be in ecstasy.

transporte *m.* transport; transportation; transport vessel; ecstasy; **— de locura** fit of madness.

transpuesto *p.p. of* transponer.

transversal *adj.* transversal, transverse; sección — cross section.

transverso *adj.* transverse, cross.

tranvía *m.* streetcar; streetcar track.

trapacear *v.* to swindle, cheat; to racketeer.

trapacería *f.* racket, fraud, swindle.

trapacero *m.* racketeer; cheat, swindler; *adj.* cheating, deceiving.

trapacista *m. & f.* racketeer; swindler; cheat.

trapeador *m. Am.* mopper; *Am.* mop.

trapear *v. Am.* to mop; *Am.* to beat up, give·(*someone*) a licking.

trapiche *m.* sugar mill; press (*for extracting juices*); *Am.* grinding machine (*for pulverizing minerals*).

trapisonda *f.* escapade, prank; brawl; noisy spree.

trapo *m.* rag; *Am.* cloth; -s clothes; a todo — at full sail; speedily; poner a uno como un — to make one feel like a rag; sacarle a uno los -s al sol to exhibit somebody's dirty linen; soltar el — to burst out laughing or crying.

traposo *adj. Am.* ragged, tattered, in rags.

tráquea *f.* trachea, windpipe.

traquetear *v.* to rattle; to shake; to jolt; to crack, crackle.

traqueteo *m.* rattling; shaking; jolting; cracking, crackling; *Am.* uproar, din; *Am.* noisy, disorderly traffic.

tras *prep.* after; in search of; behind, in back of; — de behind, after; besides, in addition to; *interj.* ¡ — ! bang!

trasbordar *v.* to transfer.

trasbordo *m.* transfer.

trascendencia = transcendencia.

trascendental = transcendental.

trasegar[1,7] *v. irr.* to upset, overturn; to change from one place to another; to pour from one container to another.

trasero *adj.* rear, hind, back; *m.* rump.

trasladar *v.* to move, remove; to transfer; to postpone; to translate; to transcribe, copy.

traslado *m.* transfer; transcript, written copy.

traslucirse[13] *v. irr.* to be translucent; to be transparent, clear, evident.

trasnochar *v.* to sit up all night; to stay awake all night; to spend the night out.

traspalar *v.* to shovel.

traspapelar *v.* to mislay, misplace (*a paper, letter, document, etc.*); -se to become mislaid among other papers.

traspasar *v.* to pass over, cross over; to go beyond; to pass through; to pierce;

to transfer (*property*); to trespass.

traspaso *m.* transfer; transgression, trespass.

traspié *m.* stumble, slip; dar un — to stumble or trip.

trasponer[40] = transponer.

trasplantar *v.* to transplant.

trasquila, trasquiladura *f.* shearing, clip, clipping; bad haircut.

trasquilar *v.* to shear; to clip; to crop; to cut badly (*hair*).

trastazo *m.* thump, blow.

traste *m.* fret, stop (*of a guitar*); *Am.* utensil, implement; dar al — con to destroy, ruin.

trasto *m.* household utensil; piece of junk; rubbish, trash; -s utensils; implements; -s de pescar fishing tackle.

trastornar *v.* to overturn; to upset; to disturb.

trastorno *m.* upset; disorder; disturbance.

trastrocar[2,6] *v. irr.* to invert, change; to upset.

trasudar *v.* to perspire, sweat slightly.

trasudor *m.* slight perspiration or sweat.

tratable *adj.* friendly, sociable; manageable.

tratado *m.* treaty; treatise.

tratamiento *m.* treatment; title of courtesy; form of address.

tratante *m. & f.* dealer, tradesman, trader.

tratar *v.* to treat; to handle; to discuss; to have social relations with; — con to have dealings with; — de to try to; to treat of, deal with; -le a uno· de to address someone as; to treat someone as; — en to deal in; -se bien to treat oneself well; to behave well; -se de to be a question of; no se trata de eso that isn't the question, that isn't the point.

trato *m.* treatment; deal, pact; trade; manner, behavior; social relations; dealings; *Am.* — pampa unfair deal; ¡ — hecho! it's a deal!; tener buen — to be affable, sociable.

través *m.* crossbeam; reverse, misfortune; a (*or* al) — de through, across; de — across; dar al — con to ruin, destroy; to squander; mirar de — to squint in a sinister manner.

travesaño *m.* crosspiece, crossbar; bolster, long bedpillow; *Am.* railway tie.

travesear *v.* to romp, frisk, frolic; to fool around; to misbehave.

travesía *f.* crossing; sea voyage; wind blowing towards a coast; *Am.* wasteland, desert land; *Am.* partition wall or fence; *Am.* mid-year crop.

travesura *f.* mischief; prank; lively wit.

traviesa *f.* railway tie; rafter, crossbeam.

travieso *adv.* mischievous; lively; restless; **a campo —** (*or* **a campo traviesa**) cross-country.

trayecto *m.* run, stretch, lap, distance (*traveled over*).

trayectoria *f.* path (*of a bullet, missile, etc.*).

traza *f.* plan, design; scheme; plot, invention; appearance; semblance; aspect; indication, sign; **darse -s** to use one's wits or ingenuity; **tener -s de** to have the appearance or signs of; **tiene** (*or* **lleva**) **-s de no acabar nunca** it looks as if he would never end.

trazado *m.* draft, plan, sketch, outline; drawing; *p.p.* & *adj.* traced, sketched, outlined.

trazar[9] *v.* to trace, sketch; to draw, mark out; to plan.

trébol *m.* clover.

trecho *m.* space, distance; lap (*in a race*); **a -s** by or at intervals; **de — en — at** certain points or intervals; from time to time.

tregua *f.* truce; rest, respite.

tremedal *m.* quagmire, bog.

tremendo *adj.* tremendous, huge; terrible.

trementina *f.* turpentine.

tremolar *v.* to flutter, wave (*as a flag*).

trémolo *m.* tremolo (*of the voice*), quaver.

trémulo *adj.* tremulous, trembling, quivering; flickering.

tren *m.* train; *Am.* traffic; **— correo** mail train; **— de aterrizaje** landing gear; *Am.* **— de lavado** laundry; *Am.* **— de mudadas** moving company; **— de recreo** excursion train; **— mixto** freight and passenger train.

trenza *f.* tress; braid; *Am.* string (*of garlic, onions, etc.*); **trencilla** *f.* braid.

trenzar[9] *v.* to braid; **-se** to braid one's hair; *Am.* to fight hand to hand.

trepar *v.* to climb; to clamber; **-se** to climb; to clamber; to perch.

trepidación *f.* jar, vibration; trembling, shaking.

trepidar *v.* to shake, vibrate, tremble, jar.

treta *f.* trick, wile; **malas -s** bad tricks, bad habits.

triángulo *m.* triangle.

tribu *f.* tribe.

tribulación *f.* tribulation, trouble.

tribuna *f.* rostrum (*speaker's platform*).

tribunal *m.* tribunal; court of justice;

body of judges.

tributar *v.* to pay tribute, pay homage.

tributario *adj.* & *m.* tributary.

tributo *m.* tribute; contribution, tax.

trifulca *f.* fight, quarrel, wrangle, row.

trigo *m.* wheat.

trigueño *adj.* swarthy; brunet; dark.

trillado *p.p.* beaten; *adj.* trite, hackneyed, commonplace; **camino — beaten** path.

trillar *v.* to thresh; to beat, mistreat; *Am.* to cut a path.

trimestre *m.* quarter, period of three months; quarterly payment, income or salary; **trimestral** *adj.* quarterly.

trinar *v.* to trill (*in singing*); to warble; to quaver (*said of the voice*); to get furious.

trinchante *m.* carving fork; carving knife; carver.

trinchar *v.* to carve (*meat*).

trinche *m. Am.* fork; *Am.* carving table; *Am.* **plato —** carving platter.

trinchera *f.* trench; ditch; *Am.* stockade, fence; *Am.* curved knife.

trinchero *m.* carving table; **plato —** carving platter.

trineo *m.* sleigh; sled.

trino *m.* trill (*in singing*).

tripa *f.* intestine, bowel; paunch, belly; **-s** entrails, insides.

triple *adj.* & *m.* triple.

triplicar[6] *v.* to triplicate, triple, treble.

tripulación *f.* crew, ship's company.

tripular *v.* to man (*a ship*).

trique *m.* crack, snap; *Am.* utensil, trinket; *Am.* clever trick in a game; *Am.* drink made from barley; **-s** *Am.* poor household utensils, goods, etc.

triscar[6] *v.* to romp, frisk, frolic; to stamp or shuffle the feet; *Am.* to tease, make fun of.

triste *adj.* sad; sorrowful; *Am.* bashful, backward; *m. Am.* melancholy love song.

tristeza *f.* sadness; sorrow; *Am.* tick fever.

tristón *adj.* wistful, quite sad, melancholy.

triunfal *adj.* triumphal.

triunfante *adj.* triumphant.

triunfar *v.* to triumph; to trump (*at cards*).

triunfo *m.* triumph; trump card; trophy.

trivial *adj.* trivial, commonplace, trite.

triza *f.* shred, fragment, small piece; cord, rope (*for sails*); **hacer -s** to tear into shreds; to tear to pieces.

trocar[2,6] *v. irr.* to change; to barter, exchange; to do one thing instead of another; **-se** to change; to be transformed; to exchange.

trocha *f.* path, trail; *Am.* gauge (*of a railway*); *Am.* trot; *Am.* slice or serving of meat.

trofeo *m.* trophy; booty, spoils.

troj, troje *m.* barn, granary.

trole *m.* trolley.

tromba *f.* waterspout.

trombón *m.* trombone.

trompa *f.* trumpet; trunk of an elephant; large spinning top; *Am.* snout; *Am.* cowcatcher (*of a locomotive*).

trompada *f.* blow with the fist; bump.

trompeta *f.* trumpet; *m.* trumpeter; useless individual; *Am.* drunk, drunkard; *Am.* bold, shameless fellow.

trompetear *v.* to trumpet, blow the trumpet.

trompo *m.* spinning top; stupid fellow, dunce.

tronada *f.* thunderstorm.

tronar[2] *v. irr.* to thunder; to explode, burst; *Am.* to execute by shooting; — **los dedos** to snap one's fingers; **por lo que pueda** — just in case.

tronco *m.* tree trunk; log; stem; trunk (*of the human body*); team (*of horses*).

tronchar *v.* to bend or break (*a stalk or trunk*); to chop off; to break off; **-se** to break off or get bent (*said of a stalk or trunk*); *Am.* to get twisted or bent.

tronera *f.* opening; porthole (*through which to shoot*); small, narrow window; pocket of a billiard table; *m.* madcap, reckless fellow.

tronido *m.* thunder; detonation, sharp, sudden sound.

trono *m.* throne.

tropa *f.* troop; crowd; *Am.* herd of cattle, drove of horses (*often* **tropilla**).

tropel *m.* throng; bustle; rush; jumble, confusion.

tropezar[1,9] *v. irr.* to stumble; to blunder; — **con** to meet, come across, encounter.

tropezón *m.* stumbling; stumble; slip; **a -es** falteringly, stumbling along clumsily; **darse un** — to stumble, trip.

tropical *adj.* tropical.

trópico *m.* tropic.

tropiezo *m.* stumble; stumbling block; slip, fault; dispute.

tropilla *f.* small troop; *Am.* drove of horses guided by the **madrina**; *Am.* pack of dogs; *Am.* group of spare saddle horses.

tropillero *m.* *Am.* horse wrangler, herdsman.

trotar *v.* to trot; to hurry.

trote *m.* trot; **al** — quickly.

trovador *m.* troubadour, minstrel.

troza *f.* log.

trozar[9] *v.* to cut off, break off (*a piece*); to break or cut into pieces.

trozo *m.* piece, bit, fragment; passage, selection.

truco *m.* clever trick; pocketing of a ball (*in the game of pool*); *Am.* blow with the fist; *Am.* a card game; **-s** game of pool (*game similar to billiards*).

truculencia *f.* cruelty, ferocity, ruthlessness.

truculento *adj.* cruel, fierce, ruthless.

trucha *f.* trout; *Am.* vendor's portable stand.

trueno *m.* thunder; explosion, report of a gun; wild youth, troublemaker; *Am.* firecracker, rocket.

trueque, trueco *m.* exchange; barter; *Am.* change, small money; **a** (*or* **en**) — **de** in exchange for.

truhán *m.* scoundrel; swindler; cheat; buffoon, jester.

tu *adj.* thy; your (*fam. sing.*).

tú *pers. pron.* thou; you (*fam. sing.*).

tualet = **lavabo**.

tuberculosis *f.* tuberculosis; **tuberculoso** *adj.* tuberculous, tubercular.

tubería *f.* tubing, piping; pipe line.

tubo *m.* tube; pipe; lamp chimney; — **de ensayo** test tube.

tuerca *f.* nut (*of a screw*); **llave de -s** wrench.

tuerto *adj.* one-eyed; blind in one eye; *m.* wrong, injustice; **a** — **o a derecho** (*or* **a tuertas o a derechas**) rightly or wrongly; thoughtlessly.

tuétano *m.* marrow; pith; innermost part; **mojado hasta los -s** soaked through and through.

tufo *m.* vapor, fume; disagreeable odor; airs, conceit; **tufillo** *m.* whiff, pungent odor.

tul *m.* tulle (*a thin, fine net for veils*); **tul, tule** *m.* *Am.* a kind of reed or bulrush (*used in the manufacture of seats and backs of chairs*).

tulipán *m.* tulip.

tullido *p.p.* crippled; paralyzed; numb.

tullirse[20] *v. irr.* to become crippled; to become numb or paralyzed.

tumba *f.* tomb; grave; *Am.* felling of timber; *Am.* forest clearing.

tumbar *v.* to knock down; *Am.* to fell timber; **-se** to lie down.

tumbo *m.* tumble; somersault; **dar -s** to jump, bump along.

tumor *m.* tumor; **tumorcillo** *m.* boil; small tumor.

tumulto *m.* tumult, uproar; mob; throng.

tumultuoso *adj.* tumultuous.

tuna *f.* prickly pear.

tunante *m. & f.* rascal, rogue, scamp; loafer; *Am.* libertine, licentious or lewd person.

tunda *f.* whipping, thrashing; shearing (*the nap of cloth*).

tundir *v.* to lash, beat, whip; to shear (*the nap of cloth*).

túnel *m.* tunnel.

túnica *f.* tunic; gown, robe.

tupido *adj.* dense; compact, thick; blocked, obstructed.

tupir *v.* to press, pack, squeeze together; to stop up, clog; -se to get stopped up; to stuff oneself; to become dense (*as a forest*); *Am.* to get astonished or confused.

turba *f.* mob, throng.

turbación *f.* disturbance, confusion; embarrassment.

turbamulta *f.* throng, mob, crowd.

turbar *v.* to perturb; to disturb; to trouble; -se to get disturbed, confused, embarrassed.

turbio *adj.* muddy; muddled, confused.

turbulento *adj.* turbulent; restless; disorderly.

turco *adj.* Turkish; *m.* Turk; Turkish, Turkish language; *Am.* peddler.

turismo *m.* tourist travel; touring, sightseeing; **oficina de —** travel bureau; **turista** *m. & f.* tourist.

turnar *v.* to alternate; -se to alternate; to take turns.

turno *m.* turn, alternate order.

turrón *m.* nougat, nut confection; almond cake; *Am.* **romper el —** to decide to use the **tú** form of address (*as a mark of close friendship*).

tusa *f.* *Am.* corn, corncob; *Am.* corn husk; *Am.* corn silk, tassel of an ear of corn.

tusar *v.* *Am.* to shear; *Am.* to crop, cut badly (*hair*).

tutear *v.* to address familiarly (*using the tú form*).

tutela *f.* guardianship; guidance, protection.

tutelar *v.* to guide, coach, direct; *adj.* guiding, guardian (*used as adj.*).

tutor *m.* tutor; guardian.

tuyo *poss. adj.* your, of yours (*fam. sing.*); *poss. pron.* yours.

U

u *conj.* (*before words beginning with o or ho*) or.

ubicar[6] *v.* *Am.* to locate; -se to be situated or located.

ubre *f.* udder.

ufanarse *v.* to glory (in); to be proud (of).

ufano *adj.* proud; gay; self-satisfied.

ujier *m.* usher, doorman.

úlcera *f.* ulcer; sore.

ulterior *adj.* ulterior; further; later.

ultimar *v.* to put an end to; *Am.* to give the finishing blow, kill.

último *adj.* last, final; ultimate; latest; **estar en las últimas** to be on one's last legs; to be at the end of one's rope, be at the end of one's resources.

ultrajar *v.* to outrage, insult; to scorn.

ultraje *m.* outrage, insult.

ultramar *m.* country or place across the sea; **de —** overseas, from across the sea; **en** (or **a**) **—** overseas.

ulular *v.* to howl, shriek, hoot.

umbral *m.* threshold.

umbrío *adj.* shady.

un(o) *indef. art.* a, an; -s some, a few; -s **cuantos** a few; **uno** *pron. & num.* one.

unánime *adj.* unanimous.

unanimidad *f.* unanimity, complete accord.

unción *f.* unction (*anointing with oil*); religious fervor; spiritual grace; **Extremaunción** Extreme Unction (*the Last Sacrament of the Church*).

uncir[10] *v.* to yoke.

ungir[11] *v.* to anoint; to consecrate.

ungüento *m.* ointment; salve.

único *adj.* only, sole; unique, singular, rare.

unidad *f.* unity; unit.

unificar[6] *v.* to unify; to unite.

uniformar *v.* to standardize; to make uniform; to furnish with uniforms.

uniforme *adj. & m.* uniform.

uniformidad *f.* uniformity.

unilateral *adj.* unilateral, one-sided.

unión *f.* union.

unir *v.* to unite; to join; to bring together; -se to unite, join together; to wed.

universal *adj.* universal.

universidad *f.* university.

universo *m.* universe.

untar *v.* to anoint; to smear; to oil, grease; to bribe; to corrupt; -se to smear oneself; to get smeared.

unto *m.* grease, fat; ointment.

untuosidad *f.* greasiness; **untuoso** *adj.* unctuous; oily, greasy.

uña *f.* fingernail; toenail; claw; hoof; hook (*on a tool*); **a — de caballo** at full gallop, at full speed; **largo de -s** prone to stealing; *Am.* **largas -s** thief; **vivir de sus -s** to live by stealing; *Am.* **echar la — to steal; ser — y carne** to be inseparable friends.

urbanidad *f.* courtesy, politeness, refinement.

urbano *adj.* urban; courteous, polite.

urbe *f.* metropolis, large city.

urdimbre *f.* warp (*of a fabric*); scheme.

urdir *v.* to warp (*in weaving*); to plot, scheme; to invent (*a lie, story, etc.*).

urgencia *f.* urgency; pressing need.

urgente *adj.* urgent, pressing.

urgir[11] *v.* to urge; to be urgent.

urna *f.* urn; **— electoral** ballot box.

urraca *f.* magpie.

usado *p.p. & adj.* used; accustomed; worn; threadbare.

usanza *f.* usage, custom, habit.

usar *v.* to use; to wear; to wear out; to be accustomed; **-se** to be in use, be in vogue.

uso *m.* use; usage; wear; practice, habit; custom; **al — de la época** according to the custom or usage of the period; **estar en buen —** to be in good condition (*said of a thing*).

usted *pers. pron.* (*abbreviated as* **Vd., V.,** *or* **Ud.**) you.

usual *adj.* usual; ordinary, customary.

usufructo *m.* use, enjoyment; profit.

usufructuar[18] *v.* to enjoy the use of; to make use of.

usura *f.* usury.

usurero *m.* usurer, loan shark.

usurpar *v.* to usurp.

utensilio *m.* utensil; implement, tool.

útero *m.* uterus, womb.

útil *adj.* useful; profitable; **-es** *m. pl.* tools, instruments.

utilidad *f.* utility; profit; usefulness.

utilizar[9] *v.* to utilize; to use.

uva *f.* grape; **— espina** gooseberry; **— pasa** raisin; **estar hecho una —** to be tipsy, drunk.

V

vaca *f.* cow; **carne de —** beef; **cuero de — cowhide;** *Am.* **hacer —** to play hooky, play truant, cut class; to join in a quick business deal.

vacación *f.* vacation (*usually* **vacaciones**).

vacada *f.* herd of cows.

vacancia *f.* vacancy.

vacante *adj.* vacant, unfilled, unoccupied; *f.* vacancy.

vaciar[17] *v.* to empty; to drain; to cast into a mold; to hollow out; to flow

(into); **-se** to spill; to empty; to become empty; to flow (into).

vaciedad *f.* emptiness; nonsense, silliness.

vacilación *f.* hesitation; wavering; doubt.

vacilante *adj.* vacillating, hesitating, wavering; unsteady.

vacilar *v.* to vacillate, waver, hesitate; to sway.

vacío *adj.* empty; vacant; unoccupied; hollow; *m.* void; hollow; vacuum; vacancy; gap, blank.

vacuna *f.* vaccine; vaccination; cowpox (*eruptive disease of the cow*); **vacunación** *f.* vaccination.

vacunar *v.* to vaccinate.

vadear *v.* to ford; to wade; to avoid (*a difficulty*).

vado *m.* ford; **no hallar —** to find no way out.

vagabundear *v.* to tramp around, wander, rove; to loiter.

vagabundo *adj.* vagabond, wandering; *m.* vagabond, tramp; vagrant; wanderer.

vagar[7] *v.* to wander, roam; to loiter; to loaf; *m.* leisure; loitering.

vago *adj.* vague; roaming; idle; vagrant; *m.* vagrant, tramp.

vagón *m.* railway car or coach; **vagoneta** *f.* small railway car or tram (*used in mines*); **vagonada** *f.* carload.

vaguear = vagar.

vahído *m.* dizziness, dizzy spell.

vaho *m.* vapor, steam, fume, mist; odor.

vaina *f.* sheath, scabbard; case; pod, husk; *Am.* bother, nuisance; *Am.* luck.

vainilla *f.* vanilla.

vaivén *m.* sway; fluctuation, wavering; traffic, coming and going; **-es** comings and goings; ups and downs; inconstancy.

vajilla *f.* tableware; set of dishes; **— de plata** silverware; **— de porcelana** chinaware.

vale *m.* bond, promissory note; voucher; adieu, farewell; *m. & f. Am.* comrade, pal, chum.

valedero *adj.* valid, binding, effective.

valedor *m.* defender, protector; *Am.* pal, comrade.

valenciano *adj.* Valencian, of or from Valencia, Spain; *m.* Valencian.

valentía *f.* courage, valor; exploit; boast.

valentón *adj.* blustering, boastful; *m.* bully, braggart.

valer[47] *v. irr.* to favor, protect; to cost; to be worth; to be worthy; to be

217

equivalent to; to be valid; to prevail; to be useful; — **la pena** to be worth while; — **por** to be worth; **-se de** to avail oneself of, make use of; **más vale** it is better; **¡válgame Dios!** heaven help me! good heavens!

valeroso *adj.* valiant, brave; valuable.

valía *f.* worth, value; influence.

validez *f.* validity; stability, soundness.

válido *adj.* valid.

valiente *adj.* valiant, brave; powerful; *m.* brave man; bully.

valija *f.* valise, satchel; mailbag.

valimiento *m.* favor, protection; **gozar de** — to enjoy protection or favor.

valioso *adj.* valuable; worthy; wealthy.

valor *m.* value; worth; price; significance; valor, courage; boldness; efficacy, power; **-es** stocks, bonds.

valoración *f.* valuation, appraisal.

valorar *v.* to evaluate, value, appraise.

valorizar[9] *v. Am.* to value, appraise; *Am.* to realize, convert into money.

vals *m.* waltz.

valsar *v.* to waltz.

valuación *f.* valuation, appraisal.

valuar[18] *v.* to value, price, appraise; to rate.

válvula *f.* valve.

valla *f.* stockade, fence; barrier; obstacle; *Am.* cockpit (*for cockfights*).

vallado *m.* stockade, fenced-in place; fence.

valle *m.* valley; vale.

vanagloria *f.* vainglory, boastful vanity.

vanagloriarse[17] *v.* to glory, take great pride (in), boast (of).

vanaglorioso *adj.* vain, boastful, conceited.

vanguardia *f.* vanguard.

vanidad *f.* vanity; conceit; emptiness.

vanidoso *adj.* vain, conceited.

vano *adj.* vain; empty; hollow; *m.* opening in a wall (*for a door or window*).

vapor *m.* vapor, steam, mist; steamer, steamship.

vaporoso *adj.* vaporous, steamy, misty; vaporlike.

vapulear *v.* to beat, whip, thrash.

vapuleo *m.* beating, whipping, thrashing.

vaquería *f.* herd of cows; stable for cows; dairy.

vaquerizo *m.* herdsman; *adj.* pertaining to cows; **vaqueriza** *f.* stable for cows.

vaquero *m.* cowherd, herdsman; cowboy; *Am.* milkman; *adj.* relating to cowherds, cowboys, or cattle.

vaqueta *f.* sole leather; cowhide; *Am.* **zurrar a uno la** — to tan someone's hide, beat someone up.

vara *f.* twig; stick; rod; wand; staff; yard, yardstick; thrust with a picador's lance.

varadero *m.* shipyard.

varar *v.* to beach (*a boat*); to run aground; to stop, come to a standstill (*said of business*).

varear *v.* to beat; to whip; to sell by the yard; to measure with a **vara**; *Am.* to exercise (*a horse before a race*).

variable *adj.* variable, unstable, changeable; *f.* variable.

variación *f.* variation.

variado *p.p.* & *adj.* varied; variegated.

variar[17] *v.* to vary; to change; to shift; to differ.

variedad *f.* variety; variation, change.

varilla *f.* small rod; wand; long, flexible twig; rib (*of an umbrella or fan*); corset stay; *Am.* peddler's wares.

varillero *m. Am.* peddler.

vario *adj.* various; different; changeable; varied; **-s** various, several.

varón *m.* male, man; *Am.* long beam, timber.

varonil *adj.* manly; strong; brave.

vasallo *adj.* & *m.* vassal, subject.

vasco, vascongado *adj.* & *m.* Basque.

vasija *f.* vessel, container, receptacle.

vaso *m.* drinking glass; glassful; vase; vessel; hull of a ship; horse's hoof; — **de elección** person chosen by God.

vástago *m.* shoot, sprout, stem; scion, offspring; *Am.* stem, trunk of a banana tree.

vasto *adj.* vast, extensive, large.

vate *m.* bard, poet.

vaticinar *v.* to prophesy, predict, foretell.

vaticinio *m.* prophecy, prediction.

vecindad *f.* vicinity; neighborhood; neighborliness; **casa de** — tenement.

vecindario *m.* neighborhood, neighbors; vicinity.

vecino *m.* neighbor; resident; citizen; *adj.* neighboring; next, near.

vedar *v.* to prohibit; to impede.

vega *f.* fertile lowland or plain; *Am.* tobacco plantation.

vegetación *f.* vegetation.

vegetal *adj.* vegetable; *m.* vegetable, plant.

vegetar *v.* to vegetate.

vehemente *adj.* vehement, passionate, impetuous; violent.

vehículo *m.* vehicle.

veintena *f.* score, twenty.

vejestorio *m.* wrinkled old person.

vejete *m.* little old man.

vejez *f.* old age.

vejiga *f.* bladder; blister; smallpox sore; — **de la bilis** (*or* — **de la hiel**) gall bladder.

vela *f.* vigil, watch; night watch; candle; sail; **a toda** — under full sail; **at full speed; en** — on watch, without sleep; **hacerse a la** — to set sail.

velada *f.* watch, vigil; evening party; evening function or meeting.

velador *m.* night watchman; keeper, guard; lamp table; bedside table; candlestick; *Am.* lamp shade.

velar *v.* to keep vigil; to stay up at night; to be vigilant; to watch over; to veil; to cover, hide.

velatorio *m.* wake (*vigil over a corpse*). *See* **velorio.**

veleidoso *adj.* inconstant, fickle, changeable.

velero *m.* sailboat; sailmaker; candlemaker; *adj.* swift-sailing; **buque** — sailboat.

veleta *f.* weathervane, weathercock; *m.* & *f.* fickle person.

velís *m. Am.* valise.

velo *m.* veil; curtain, covering; — **del paladar** velum, soft palate.

velocidad *f.* velocity.

velocímetro *m.* speedometer.

velorio *m. Am.* wake (*vigil over a corpse*); *Am.* dull party.

veloz *adj.* swift, quick, fast.

vello *m.* hair (*on the body*); down, fuzz; nap (*of cloth*).

vellón *m.* fleece; tuft of wool; sheepskin with fleece; silver and copper alloy; an ancient copper coin.

velloso *adj.* hairy; downy, fuzzy.

velludo *adj.* hairy; downy; fuzzy; *m.* plush; velvet.

vena *f.* vein; lode, vein of metal ore; mood, disposition; **estar en** — to be in the mood; to be inspired.

venado *m.* deer; venison, deer meat; *Am.* **pintar** — to play hooky.

vencedor *adj.* conquering, winning, victorious; *m.* conqueror, winner, victor.

vencer[10] *v.* to conquer, vanquish; to defeat; to overcome; to surpass; to win; -se to control oneself; to mature, fall due; **se venció el plazo** the time limit expired.

vencido *p.p. & adj.* conquered; defeated; due, fallen due.

vencimiento *m.* conquering, defeat; maturity (*of a debt*), falling due; expiration (*of a period of time*).

venda *f.* bandage.

vendaje *m.* bandage.

vendar *v.* to bandage; to blindfold.

vendaval *m.* strong wind, gale.

vendedor *m.* vendor, seller, peddler.

vender *v.* to sell; to betray; -se to be sold; to sell oneself, accept a bribe.

vendimia *f.* vintage; profit.

venduta *f. Am.* auction; *Am.* small fruit and vegetable store.

veneno *m.* venom, poison.

venenoso *adj.* poisonous.

venerable *adj.* venerable.

veneración *f.* veneration, reverence.

venerando *adj.* venerable, worthy of respect.

venerar *v.* to venerate, revere; to worship.

venero *m.* water spring; source, origin; lode, layer, seam (*of mineral*).

venezolano *adj.* Venezuelan; *m.* Venezuelan; *Am.* Venezuelan silver coin.

vengador *adj.* avenging, revenging; *m.* avenger.

venganza *f.* vengeance, revenge.

vengar[7] *v.* to avenge, revenge; -se de to take revenge on.

vengativo *adj.* vindictive, revengeful.

venia *f.* pardon; permission, leave; bow, nod; *Am.* military salute.

venida *f.* arrival; return; river flood, onrush of water; attack (*in fencing*).

venidero *adj.* coming, future; **en lo** — in the future; -s *m. pl.* successors.

venir[48] *v. irr.* to come; to arrive; to fit; -**le a uno bien** (*or* **mal**) to be becoming (*or* unbecoming); — **a menos** to decline, decay; — **a pelo** to come just at the right moment; to suit perfectly; to be pat, opportune, to the point; — **en** to agree to; — **sobre** to fall upon; **¿a qué viene eso?** what is the point of that?; -**se abajo** to fall down; to collapse; to fail.

venoso *adj.* veined; venous (*of or pertaining to the veins; with veins*).

venta *f.* sale; roadside inn; *Am.* store, vendor's stand; — **pública** auction.

ventaja *f.* advantage; gain, profit; bonus; odds.

ventajoso *adj.* advantageous, beneficial, profitable; *Am.* self-seeking, profiteering.

ventana *f.* window; window shutter; *Am.* clearing (*in a forest*); — (*or* **ventanilla**) **de la nariz** nostril.

ventarrón *m.* gale, strong wind.

ventear *v.* to scent, sniff; to nose around; to air; to blow, be windy; *Am.* to toss in the wind; *Am.* to flee; *Am.* to outrun; -se to expel air, break wind; *Am.* to stay outdoors.

ventero *m.* innkeeper.

ventilación f. ventilation.

ventilador m. ventilator; fan (*for ventilation*).

ventilar v. to ventilate; to air.

ventisca f. blizzard, snowstorm; snowdrift.

ventiscar⁶ v. to snow hard and blow (*as in a blizzard*); to drift (*as snow in a blizzard*).

ventisquero m. blizzard, snowstorm; glacier; snowdrift; snow-capped mountain peak.

ventolera f. gust of wind; pride, vanity; whim; pin wheel; **darle a uno la —de** to take the notion to.

ventoso adj. windy.

ventura f. happiness; fortune, chance; risk, danger; **a la —** at random; **buena — fortune; por —** perchance.

venturoso adj. fortunate, lucky; happy.

ver⁴⁹ v. irr. to see; to look; to look at; to look into, examine; **— de** to try to, see to it that; **a más (or hasta más) — good-bye; no — la hora de to be anxious to; **no tener nada que —con** not to have anything to do with; **-se** to be seen; to be; **-se obligado a** to be obliged to, be forced to; **a mi modo de —** in my opinion; **de buen — good-looking; ser de —** to be worth seeing.

vera f. edge; **a la — del camino** at the edge of the road.

veracidad f. truthfulness.

veraneante m. & f. summer resorter, vacationist, or tourist.

veranear v. to spend the summer.

veraneo m. summering, summer vacation.

veraniego adj. summer, of summer.

verano m. summer.

veras f. pl. reality, truth; **de —** in truth; truly; in earnest.

veraz adj. truthful.

verbal adj. verbal; oral.

verbena f. verbena (*a plant*); festival or carnival (*on eve of a religious holiday*).

verbigracia adv. for instance, for example.

verbo m. verb; **el Verbo** the Word (*second person of the Trinity*).

verboso adj. verbose, wordy.

verdad f. truth; ¿ — ? really?; is that so?; isn't that so?; **— de Perogrullo** truism, evident truth; **de —** (*or a la —*) in truth, in earnest; **en —** really, truly.

verdadero adj. real; true; truthful; sincere.

verde adj. green; unripe; young; off-color, indecent; m. green; verdure; Am. country, countryside.

verdear v. to grow green; to look green.

verdinegro adj. dark-green.

verdor m. verdure, greenness.

verdoso adj. greenish.

verdugo m. executioner; cruel person; torment; rapier (*light sword*); lash, whip; welt; shoot of a tree; **verdugón** m. large welt.

verdulera f. woman „vendor of green vegetables; **verdulería** f. green vegetable store or stand.

verdura f. verdure; greenness; green vegetables.

vereda f. path; Am. sidewalk.

veredicto m. verdict.

vergonzoso adj. shameful, disgraceful; shy, bashful; m. species of armadillo.

vergüenza f. shame; disgrace; shyness, bashfulness; **tener —** to have shame; to be ashamed.

vericueto m. rugged, wild place (*often rocky*).

verídico adj. truthful; true.

verificar⁶ v. to verify; to confirm; to test, check; to carry out, fulfill; **-se** to be verified; to take place.

verijas f. pl. Am. groin (*hollow between lower part of abdomen and thigh*); Am. flanks of a horse.

verja f. grate, grating.

verruga f. wart; nuisance.

versado adj. versed, skilled, expert.

versar v. to deal (with), treat (of); **-se en** to become versed in.

versión f. version; translation.

verso m. verse; meter; **— suelto** (*or — libre*) free or blank verse.

verter¹ v. irr. to pour; to empty; to spill; to translate; to flow down.

vertical adj. vertical.

vértice m. top, apex, summit.

vertiente f. slope; watershed; adj. flowing.

vertiginoso adj. whirling, dizzy, giddy.

vértigo m. dizziness, giddiness; fit of madness.

vestíbulo m. vestibule; lobby.

vestido m. clothing, apparel; dress; garment; suit.

vestidura f. vestment; attire, apparel; raiment.

vestigio m. vestige, sign, trace.

vestir⁵ v. irr. to dress; to clothe; to wear; to put on; to adorn; to cover; **-se** to dress, get dressed; to be clothed; to be covered.

vestuario m. wardrobe, apparel; theatrical costumes; cloakroom; dressing room; vestry (*room for church vest-ments*).

veta *f.* vein, seam (*of mineral*); streak, grain (*in wood*); stripe; *Am.* rope.

veteado *adj.* veined; striped; streaked.

veterano *adj.* & *m.* veteran.

veterinario *m.* veterinary.

veto *m.* veto.

vetusto *adj.* old, ancient.

vez *f.* time, occasion; turn; **a la —** at the same time; **cada — más** more and more; **cada — que** whenever; **de — en cuando** from time to time; **de una —** all at once; **en — de** instead of; **otra —** again; **una que otra —** rarely, once in a while; **tal —** perhaps; **a veces** sometimes; **raras veces** seldom; **hacer las veces de** to take the place of.

vía *f.* way; road; track; railroad track; conduit; **Vía Crucis** the Way of the Cross; **Vía Láctea** the Milky Way.

viaducto *m.* viaduct.

viajante *m.* traveler; **— de comercio** traveling salesman.

viajar *v.* to travel.

viaje *m.* voyage; trip; travel; **— de ida y vuelta** (or **— redondo**) round trip.

viajero *m.* traveler; *adj.* traveling.

vianda *f.* viands, food; meal.

viandante *m.* & *f.* wayfarer, walker; pedestrian; passer-by; vagabond.

viático *m.* provisions for a journey; viaticum (*communion given to dying persons*).

víbora *f.* viper.

vibración *f.* vibration.

vibrante *adj.* vibrant, vibrating.

vibrar *v.* to vibrate.

vicepresidente *m.* vice-president.

viceversa *adv.* vice versa, conversely.

viciado *adj.* contaminated, foul; corrupt; *p.p. of* **viciar.**

viciar *v.* to vitiate, corrupt; to adulterate; to falsify; **-se** to become corrupt.

vicio *m.* vice; bad habit; fault; craving; **de — as** a habit; **hablar de —** to talk too much; **-s** *Am.* articles and ingredients used for serving **mate.**

vicioso *adj.* vicious, evil, wicked; having bad habits; licentious; faulty, incorrect (*grammatical construction, reasoning, etc.*).

vicisitud *f.* vicissitude; **-es** vicissitudes, ups and downs, changes of fortune or condition.

víctima *f.* victim.

victoria *f.* victory, triumph; victoria (*carriage*).

victorioso *adj.* victorious.

vicuña *f.* vicuña (*an Andean animal allied to the alpaca and llama*); vicuña wool; vicuña cloth.

vid *f.* vine, grapevine.

vida *f.* life; living; livelihood; **— mía** dearest; **hacer —** to live together; **pasar a mejor —** to die; **tener la — en un hilo** to be in great danger

vidalita *f.* *Am.* melancholy song of Argentina and Chile.

vidente *m.* seer, prophet; *adj.* seeing.

vidriado *m.* glaze; glazed earthenware; *p.p.* & *adj.* glazed.

vidriar[17] *v.* to glaze (*earthenware*).

vidriera *f.* glass window; glass door; *Am.* show case, show window; **— de colores** stained-glass window.

vidriero *m.* glazier (*one who installs windowpanes*); glass blower; glass maker; glass dealer.

vidrio *m.* glass; any glass article.

vidrioso *adj.* glassy; brittle; slippery, icy; touchy, irritable.

viejo *adj.* old; ancient; worn-out; *m.* old man; **— verde** old man who boasts of his youth and vigor; *Am.* **los -s** the old folks (*applied to one's parents*); **viejota** *f.* old hag.

viento *m.* wind; scent; **hace —** it is windy; **a los cuatro -s** in all directions; **vientecito** *m.* gentle breeze.

vientre *m.* abdomen; belly; bowels; entrails; womb.

viernes *m.* Friday.

viga *f.* beam; rafter.

vigencia *f.* operation (*of a law*); **entrar en —** to take effect (*said of a law*); **estar en —** to be in force (*said of a law*).

vigente *adj.* effective, in force (*as a law*).

vigía *f.* lookout, watchtower; watch (*act of watching*); reef; *m.* lookout, watchman.

vigilancia *f.* vigilance.

vigilante *adj.* vigilant, watchful; *m.* watchman.

vigilar *v.* to keep guard; to watch over.

vigilia *f.* vigil, watch; wakefulness, sleeplessness; night hours (*spent in study*); eve before certain church festivals; vesper service; **día de —** day of abstinence; **comer de —** to abstain from meat.

vigor *m.* vigor; **en — in** force (*said of a law*); **entrar en —** to become effective (*as a law, statute, etc.*).

vigorizar[9] *v.* to invigorate, tone up, give vigor to, strengthen.

vigoroso *adj.* vigorous.

vihuela *f.* guitar.

221

vil *adj.* vile, base, low, mean.

vileza *f.* villainy; baseness; vile act.

vilipendiar *v.* to revile.

vilo : en — in the air; suspended; undecided; in suspense; **llevar en — to** waft.

villa *f.* village; villa, country house.

villancico *m.* carol; Christmas carol.

villanía *f.* villainy; lowliness.

villano *adj.* rustic, uncouth; villainous, mean, base; *m.* villain; rustic, peasant.

villorrio *m.* small village, hamlet.

vinagre *m.* vinegar; **vinagrera** *f.* vinegar cruet.

vincular *v.* to tie, bind, unite; to entail (*limit the inheritance of property*); to found, base (on).

vínculo *m.* bond, tie, chain; entailed inheritance.

vindicar[6] *v.* to vindicate; to avenge; to defend, assert (*one's rights*); **-se** to avenge oneself; to defend oneself.

vino *m.* wine; **— amontillado** good grade of pale sherry (*originally from Montilla*); **— tinto** dark-red wine; **vinería** *f. Am.* wineshop; **vinero** *adj. Am.* pertaining to wine; **vinoso** *adj.* winy.

viña *f.* vineyard.

viñedo *m.* vineyard.

violación *f.* violation.

violado *adj.* violet; *m.* violet, violet color; *p.p.* violated.

violar *v.* to violate; to rape.

violencia *f.* violence.

violentar *v.* to force; to break into (*a house*); **-se** to force oneself; to get angry.

violento *adj.* violent; impetuous; forced; strained; unnatural.

violeta *f.* violet.

violín *m.* violin; *m. & f.* violinist; *Am.* **estar hecho un —** to be very thin.

violinista *m. & f.* violinist.

virada *f.* tack, change of direction, turn.

virar *v.* to turn, turn around, change direction; to tack (*said of a ship*).

virgen *adj. & f.* virgin.

virginal *adj.* virginal, virgin, pure.

viril *adj.* virile, manly.

virilidad *f.* virility, manhood, manly strength, vigor.

virreinato *m.* viceroyalty (*office or jurisdiction of a viceroy*).

virrey *m.* viceroy.

virtud *f.* virtue.

virtuoso *adj.* virtuous; *m.* virtuoso (*person skilled in an art*).

viruela *f.* smallpox; pock (*mark left by*

smallpox); **-s locas** (*or* **-s bastardas**) chicken pox.

viruta *f.* wood shaving.

visa *f.* visa, visé; **visado** *p.p. of* **visar;** *m.* visa, visé.

visaje *m.* grimace; wry face; **hacer -s** to make faces.

visar *v.* to visé; to approve; to O.K.

viscoso *adj.* slimy, sticky.

visera *f.* visor; eye shade; *Am.* blinder (*on a horse's bridle*).

visible *adj.* visible; evident; conspicuous, notable.

visillo *m.* window curtain.

visión *f.* vision; sight; fantasy; apparition; sight (*ridiculous-looking person or thing*).

visionario *adj. & m.* visionary.

visita *f.* visit, call; visitor; callers, company; **— de cumplimiento** (*or* **— de cumplido**) formal courtesy call; **— domiciliaria** police inspection of a house; home call (*of a social worker, doctor, etc.*).

visitación *f.* visitation, visit.

visitador *m.* visitor, caller; inspector.

visitante *m. & f.* caller, visitor; *adj.* visiting.

visitar *v.* to visit; to inspect.

vislumbrar *v.* to catch a glimpse of; to guess, surmise; **-se** to be faintly visible.

vislumbre *f.* glimmer; glimpse; vague idea; faint appearance.

viso *m.* appearance, semblance; pretense, pretext; luster, brilliance, glitter; glass curtain; **a dos -s** with a double view; with a double purpose.

víspera *f.* eve, evening or day before; time just before; **-s** vespers; **en -s de** on the eve of; about to.

vista *f.* sight; vision; view; landscape; look, glance; **a — de** in the presence of; in front of, within view of; **pagadero a la —** payable at sight or upon presentation; **¡hasta la — !** good-bye!; **bajar la —** to lower one's eyes; **conocer de —** to know by sight; **hacer la — gorda** to pretend not to see; **pasar la — por** to glance over; **perder de —** to lose sight of; **tener a la —** to have before one; to have received (*a letter*).

vistazo *m.* glance; **dar un — a** to glance over.

visto *p.p. of* **ver** seen; *adj.* evident, clear; **bien —** well thought of, proper; **mal — looked** down upon, improper; **— bueno** (V°.B° .) approved (O.K.); **dar el — bueno** to approve, O.K.; **— que** whereas, considering that.

vistoso *adj.* showy; colorful.
vital *adj.* vital; important, necessary.
vitalicio *adj.* for life; *m.* life-insurance policy; lifetime pension.
vitalidad *f.* vitality.
vitamina *f.* vitamin.
vítor *m.* cheer, applause; ¡ — ! hurrah!
vitorear *v.* to cheer, applaud.
vitrina *f.* glass case; show case; show window.
vituallas *f. pl.* victuals, food, provisions.
vituperar *v.* to revile, insult, call bad names.
vituperio *m.* affront, insult; reproach; censure.
viuda *f.* widow.
viudez *f.* widowhood.
viudo *m.* widower.
vivac, vivaque *m.* bivouac, military encampment; *Am.* police headquarters.
vivacidad *f.* vivacity; brightness; liveliness.
vivaracho *adj.* lively; vivacious, gay.
vivaz *adj.* vivacious, lively; bright, keen, witty.
víveres *m. pl.* food supplies, provisions.
vivero *m.* fish pond, fish hatchery, tree nursery.
viveza *f.* vivacity; animation, liveliness; quickness; brilliance, cleverness.
vívido *adj.* vivid; colorful.
vivienda *f.* dwelling; apartment.
viviente *adj.* living.
vivir *v.* to live; to endure, last; ¡viva! hurrah! long live!; ¿quién vive? who goes there?; *m.* existence, living.
vivo *adj.* alive; living; lively; quick; vivid; bright; clever, wide-awake; tío — merry-go-round; al — vividly; de viva voz by word of mouth; tocar en lo — to hurt to the quick, touch the most sensitive spot.
vizcacha *f. Am.* viscacha (*South American rodent about the size of a hare*).
vizcachera *f. Am.* viscacha burrow or hole; *Am.* room filled with junk; **vizcacheral** *m. Am.* ground full of viscacha burrows.
vizcaíno *adj.* Biscayan, of or from Biscay, Spain.
vocablo *m.* word, term.
vocabulario *m.* vocabulary.
vocación *f.* vocation; aptness, talent.
vocal *adj.* vocal; oral; vowel; *f.* vowel; *m.* voter (*in an assembly or council*).
vocear *v.* to shout; to cry out; to hail.
vocecita *f.* sweet little voice.
vocería *f.* clamor, shouting.
vocerío *m. Am.* clamor, shouting.
vocero *m.* spokesman.

vociferar *v.* to shout, clamor; to yell; to boast loudly of.
vodevil *m.* vaudeville.
volante *adj.* flying; floating; **papel** (or **hoja**) — handbill, circular; *m.* ruffle, frill; steering wheel; balance wheel; flywheel.
volar[2] *v. irr.* to fly; to fly away; to explode; to irritate, pique; to rouse (*bird game*); -se *Am.* to fly off the handle, lose one's temper.
volátil *adj.* volatile; fickle, changeable; flying.
volcán *m.* volcano; *Am.* precipice; *Am.* swift torrent.
volcánico *adj.* volcanic.
volcar[2,6] *v. irr.* to overturn; to capsize; to upset; to make dizzy; -se to upset, get upset.
volear *v.* to volley, hit (*a ball*) in the air.
volición *f.* volition.
voltaje *m.* voltage.
voltear *v.* to turn, turn around; to revolve; to turn inside out; to overturn; to tumble or roll over; to turn a somersault; *Am.* to go prying around; *Am.* — la espalda to turn one's back; -se to turn over; to change sides.
voltereta *f.* somersault, tumble.
voltio, volt *m.* volt.
voluble *adj.* fickle; moody; changeable; twining (*as a climbing vine*).
volumen *m.* volume.
voluminoso *adj.* voluminous, bulky, very large.
voluntad *f.* will; desire; determination; benevolence, good will; consent; última — last will, testament; de (or de buena) — willingly, with pleasure.
voluntario *adj.* voluntary; willful; *m.* volunteer.
voluntarioso *adj.* willful.
voluptuoso *adj.* voluptuous; sensual.
voluta *f.* scroll, spiral-like ornament; -s de humo spirals of smoke.
volver[2,52] *v. irr.* to return; to turn; to turn up, over, or inside out; to restore; — loco to drive crazy; — a (+*inf.*) to do again; — en sí to come to, recover one's senses; — por to return for; to defend; -se to become; to turn; to turn around; to change one's ideas; -se atrás to go back; to back out, go back on one's word; -se loco to go crazy.
vomitar *v.* to vomit.
vómito *m.* vomit; vomiting.
voracidad *f.* voraciousness, greediness.
vorágine *f.* vortex, whirlpool.
voraz *adj.* voracious, ravenous, greedy.

vórtice *m.* vortex, whirlpool; whirlwind, tornado; center of a cyclone.

votación *f.* voting; vote, total number of votes.

votante *m. & f.* voter.

votar *v.* to vote; to vow; to curse; ¡voto a tal! by Jove!

voto *m.* vote; vow; prayer; votive offering; oath; wish; — de confianza vote of confidence.

voz *f.* voice; sound; shout, outcry; word; rumor; — común common rumor or gossip; a — en cuello (*or* a — en grito) shouting; at the top of one's lungs; en — alta aloud; a voces shouting, with shouts; secreto a voces open secret; dar voces to shout, yell.

vozarrón *m.* loud, strong voice.

vuelco *m.* upset; overturning; capsizing; tumble.

vuelo *m.* flight; width, fulness (*of a dress or cloak*); frill, ruffle; jut, projection (*of a building*); al (*or* a) — on the fly; quickly; levantar (*or* alzar) el — to fly away; to soar.

vuelta *f.* turn; return; repetition; reverse side; cuff, facing of a sleeve; cloak lining; change (*money returned*); a la — around the corner; on returning; a la — de los años within a few years; *Am.* otra — again; dar -s to turn over and over; to wander about; dar una — to take a walk; estar de — to be back; no tiene — de hoja there are no two ways about it.

vuelto *p.p. of* volver; *m. Am.* change (*money returned*).

vuestro *poss. adj.* your, of yours (*fam. pl.*); *poss. pron.* yours.

vulgar *adj.* common, ordinary; in common use; low, vile, base.

vulgaridad *f.* vulgarity, coarseness, commonness.

vulgarismo *m.* slang, slang expression; vulgar or ungrammatical expression.

vulgo *m.* populace, the common people; *adv.* commonly, popularly.

Y

y *conj.* and.

ya *adv.* already; now; finally; soon, presently; in time; ¡ — ! now I see!; I understand; enough!; ¡ — lo creo! I should say so!; yes, of course!; — no no longer; — que since; although; — se ve of course; it is clear; — voy I am coming.

yacer[50] *v. irr.* to lie (*in the grave*); to be lying down; to lie, be situated.

yacimiento *m.* bed, layer (*of ore*); — de petróleo oil field.

yanqui *m. & f.* North American, native of the United States; Yankee.

yantar *v.* to eat; *m.* food, meal.

**yararᇠ*f. Am.* Argentine poisonous snake.

yarda *f.* yard (*unit of measure*).

yate *m.* yacht.

yedra = **hiedra.**

yegua *f.* mare; *Am.* cigar butt; *adj. Am.* big, large; **yeguada** *f.* herd of mares.

yelmo *m.* helmet.

yema *f.* egg yolk; bud, shoot; candied egg yolk; — del dedo finger tip.

yerba = **hierba.**

yerbabuena *f.* mint; peppermint.

yerbero *m. Am.* herb vendor.

yermo *m.* desert, wilderness; *adj.* desert, uninhabited; uncultivated.

yerno *m.* son-in-law.

yerro *m.* error, fault, mistake.

yerto *adj.* stiff, motionless, rigid.

yesca *f.* tinder; anything highly inflammable; incentive (*to passion*); *Am.* estar hecho una — to be in great anger.

yeso *m.* gypsum, chalk; plaster; chalk (*for blackboard*); — blanco whitewash; — mate plaster of Paris; **yesoso** *adj.* chalky.

yo *pers. pron.* I.

yodo *m.* iodine.

yugo *m.* yoke; marriage tie; burden.

yunque *f.* anvil.

yunta *f.* yoke of oxen; pair of draft animals.

yuyo *m. Am.* wild grass, weeds; *Am.* an herb sauce; *Am.* garden stuff; *Am.* estar — to be lifeless, insipid; *Am.* volverse uno — to faint.

Z

zacate *m. Am.* grass, forage; hay.

zafado *adj.* impudent, brazen, shameless; *Am.* smart, wide-awake, keen; *Am.* "touched", half-crazy; *p.p. of* zafar.

zafar *v.* to release, set free; to dislodge; *Am.* to exclude; -se to slip away; to dodge; to get rid (of); to get loose; *Am.* to get dislocated (*said of a bone*); *Am.* to go crazy; *Am.* to use foul language.

zafio *adj.* coarse, uncouth, rude.

zafir, zafiro *m.* sapphire.

zafra *f.* sugar-making season; sugar making; sugar crop.

zaga *f.* rear; a la — (a *or* en —) behind.

zagal *m.* young shepherd; lad; **zagala** *f.* young shepherdess; lass, maiden; **zagalejo** *m.* young shepherd; short

224

skirt; petticoat.

zaguán m. vestibule.

zaherir[3] v. irr. to hurt (feelings); to censure, reprove; to reproach.

zaino adj. treacherous; vicious; chestnut-colored (horse).

zalamero m. fawner, flatterer, servile person; **zalamería** f. flattery, scraping and bowing.

zalea f. pelt, undressed sheepskin.

zambo adj. knock-kneed; m. Am. Indian and negro half-breed; Am. a species of South American monkey.

zambullida f. dive, dip, plunge.

zambullir[20] v. to plunge, dip, duck; -se to dive; to plunge.

zambullón m. quick, sudden dip or dive.

zanahoria f. carrot.

zanca f. long leg of any fowl; long leg; long prop; **zancada** f. stride, long step.

zanco m. stilt; **andar en -s** to walk on stilts.

zancón adj. lanky, long-legged; Am. too short (skirt or dress).

zancudo adj. long-legged; m. Am. mosquito.

zángano m. drone; loafer, sponger; Am. rogue, rascal.

zangolotear v. to shake, jiggle; -se to shake; to waddle; to sway from side to side.

zangoloteo m. jiggle, jiggling; shaking; waddling.

zanguanga f. feigned illness; **hacer la — to** pretend to be ill; **zanguango** adj. lazy; silly; m. fool.

zanja f. ditch; trench; Am. irrigation ditch.

zanjar v. to excavate; to dig ditches in; to settle (disputes).

zapapico m. pickaxe.

zapateado m. a Spanish tap dance.

zapatear v. to tap with the feet; to tapdance.

zapateo m. tapping with the feet; Am. a popular tap dance.

zapatería f. shoe store; shoemaker's shop.

zapatero m. shoemaker; shoe dealer.

zapatilla f. slipper, pump.

zapato m. shoe.

zarandajas f. pl. trifles, trinkets, worthless things.

zarandear v. to winnow (separate the chaff from grain); to sift; to sift out; to move (something) quickly, wiggle, jiggle; Am. to whip, lash, mistreat, abuse; -se to wiggle, jiggle; to bump along; to waddle; to strut, swagger.

zarandeo m. jiggle, jiggling; sifting;

waddling; strutting.

zarcillo m. earring; tendril (coil of a climbing vine); Am. earmark (on the ear of an animal).

zarpa f. paw, claw; weighing anchor; **echar la — to** grasp, seize; **zarpada** f. pounce; blow with a paw; **zarpazo** m. blow with the paw; big blow, thud; hard fall.

zarpar v. to weigh anchor; to set sail.

zarza f. bramble; blackberry bush.

zarzamora f. blackberry.

zarzuela f. Spanish musical comedy.

zigzag m. zigzag.

zigzaguear v. to zigzag.

zinc = **cinc**.

zócalo m. base (of a pedestal); Am. public square.

zodíaco m. zodiac.

zona f. zone; band, girdle; shingles (a disease).

zonzo adj. dull, stupid, silly, foolish.

zoología f. zoology.

zoológico adj. zoological; **jardín — zoo.**

zopenco adj. stupid, dull, thick-headed; m. blockhead, dunce.

zopilote m. Am. buzzard.

zoquete m. block, chunk of wood; hunk of bread; blockhead, dunce, fool; ugly fat person; Am. grease, dirt, filth; Am. slap.

zorra f. fox; foxy person; drunkenness; prostitute; **pillar una — to** get drunk.

zorro m. fox; foxy person; -s fox skins; duster made of cloth or leather strips; **estar hecho un — to** be drowsy; **hacerse uno el — to** pretend to be stupid or not to hear; adj. foxy; **zorrillo, zorrino** m. Am. skunk; **zorruno** adj. foxy.

zorzal m. thrush; crafty fellow; Am. fool, scapegoat, dupe.

zozobra f. foundering; sinking; anxiety, worry.

zozobrar v. to founder; to capsize; to sink; to be in great danger; to fret, worry.

zumbar v. to buzz; to hum; to ring (said of the ears); to scoff at; to strike, hit; Am. to throw out or away; **— una bofetada** to give a slap; -se Am. to slip away, disappear.

zumbido m. buzzing, humming; ringing (in one's ears); hit, blow, whack.

zumbón adj. funny, playful; sarcastic; m. jester.

zumo m. juice; profit; **zumoso** adj. juicy.

zurcido m. darn; darning; p.p. of **zurcir.**

zurcir[10] *v.* to darn; to invent, make up (*lies*).

zurdo *adj.* left-handed; left; **a zurdas** with the left hand; clumsily.

zuro *m.* cob, corncob.

zurra *f.* beating, flogging; tanning (*of leather*).

zurrar *v.* to flog, thrash; to tan (*leather*).

zurrón *m.* pouch; bag; leather bag; *Am.* big coward.

Zutano *m.* so-and-so; a certain person. (*Used often with* **Fulano** *and* **Mengano**).

PARTE SEGUNDA
INGLES-ESPAÑOL

PARTE SEGUNDA
INGLES-ESPAÑOL

AL ESTUDIOSO

EL AUGE que desde el principio de la Guerra Mundial II viene cobrando en la América española el aprendizaje del inglés, nos ha movido a recopilar en este breve Diccionario las voces y locuciones más indispensables de esta lengua tal como se habla y escribe en los Estados Unidos de América.

Al igual que en la Sección española-inglesa hemos antepuesto la abreviatura *Am.* a aquellos vocablos o idiotismos que son de uso exclusivo en alguna región de la América española, o bien de uso frecuentísimo en ésta, aunque ya hayan caído en desuso en la Península. Todo lo cual no excluye la posibilidad de que alguna acepción así designada se oiga en labios de español o sea de uso esporádico en España.

Lo que sí hemos procurado con gran ahinco y anhelamos lograr, presentando al estudioso este caudal indispensable de palabras, es el acercamiento lingüístico de las Américas, como base para nuestra mutua comprensión y como instrumento poderosísimo para nuestra solidaridad.

LOS EDITORES

LISTA DE ABREVIATURAS

adj.	adjectivo	*interr.*	interrogativo
adv.	adverbio	*irr.*	irregular
Am.	Americanismo	*p.p.*	participio pasado o pasivo
art.	artículo	*pers.*	personal

i

art. indef.	artículo indefinido	*pl.*	plural
aux.	auxiliar	*pos.*	posesivo
comp.	comparativo	*prep.*	preposición
conj.	conjunción	*pron.*	pronombre
contr.	contracción	*pron. pers.*	pronombre personal
defect.	defectivo	*pron. pos.*	pronombre posesivo
etc.	etcétera	*s.*	sustantivo
ger.	gerundio	*sing.*	singular
gram.	gramatical, gramática	*subj.*	subjuntivo
imperf.	imperfecto	*v.*	verbo
indic.	indicativo	*v. defect.*	verbo defectivo
interj.	interjección	*v. irr.*	verbo irregular

PRONUNCIACION INGLESA[1]

I. VOCALES

Símbolo fonético	Ortografía inglesa	Ortografía fonética	Explicación de los sonidos
i	see pea	si pi	Equivale a la *i* in *hilo*.
ɪ	bit	bɪt	El sonido más aproximado es la *i* en *virtud*, pero la [ɪ] inglesa es una *i* más abierta tirando a *e* cerrada.
e	late they	let ðe	Equivale aproximadamente a *ei*; la *i* de este diptongo es muy relajada y más abierta que en español.
e	bet	bet	El sonido más aproximado en español es la *e* abierta de *perro*.
æ	sat	sæt	Es una vocal intermedia entre la *a* y la *e*.
a	car	kar	Equivale aproximadamente a la *a* en *corgo*.
ə	forge	fordʒ	Equivale aproximadamente a la *o* en *corto, corre*.
o	mode	mod	Equivale aproximademente a *ou*; la *u* de este diptongo es muy relajada y más abierta que en español.
ʊ	pull	puɪ	El sonido más aproximado en español es la *u* en *turrón*, pero la [ʊ] inglesa es todavía más abierta.

[1] El estudioso puede consultar el importante diccionario de pronunciación norteamericana: Kenyon and Knott, *A Pronouncing Dictionary of American English* (Springfield, Massachusetts: G. & C. Merriam Company, Publishers, 1944).

Símbolo fonético	Ortografía inglesa	Ortografía fonética	Explicación de los sonidos.
u	June moon	dʒuu mun	Equivale aproximadamente a la *u* en *uno*.
ə	cudgel apply	kʌdʒəl əplái	Es una *e* muy relajada. No tiene equivalente en español.
ə	teacher	títʃə	Es una *e* muy relajada, articulada simultáneamente con la *r*. No tiene equivalente en español.
ɜ	earth fur	ɜθ fɜ	Es un sonido intermedio entre la *e* y la *o* articulado simultáneamente con la *r*. Se acerca más a la *e* que a la *o*. No tiene equivalente en español.
ʌ	duck	dʌk	Es una vocal intermedia entre la *e* muy abierta y la *o*. Se acerca más a la *o* que a la *e*. No tiene equivalente en español.

II. DIPTONGOS

aɪ	aisle nice	aɪl naɪs	Equivale aproximadamente a *ai* en *aire*.
aʊ	now	naʊ	Equivale aproximadamente a *au* en *causa*.
ɔɪ	coy	kɔɪ	Equivale aproximadamente a *oy* en *hoy*. El segundo elemento del diptongo es más abierto y débil, tirando a *e*.
ju	used	juzd	Equivale aproximadamente a *iu* en *ciudad*.
jʊ	cure	kjʊr	Equivale aproximadamente al diptongo *iu*, pero la *u* es más abierta.

III. CONSONANTES

p	paper	pépə	Equivale aproximadamente a la *p* española, pero es mucho más explosiva.
b	bat	bæt	La *b* inglesa es semejante a la *b* inicial española, pero se pronuncia más explosivamente.

Símbolo fonético	Ortografía inglesa	Ortografía fonética	Explicación de los sonidos.
t	tea	ti	Es bastante diferente de la *t* española. Se articula colocando flojamente la lengua arriba de los dientes incisivos superiores.
d	day	de	Equivale a la *d* inicial española pronunciada con mayor énfasis.
k	cat kill	kæt kɪl	Equivale aproximadamente a la *c* española delante de *a,o,u* pronunciada con mayor énfasis.
g	go gum ago	go gʌm əgó	Equivale aproximadamente a la *g* inicial delante de *a,o,u*: *goma, guerra, gana*; sólo que la *g* inglesa se pronuncia con mayor explosión.
f	fun affair	fʌn əfér	Equivale aproximadamente a la *f* española.
v	very	véɪ	No tiene equivalente en español. Es una labiodental que se articula con el labio inferior y los dientes incisivos superiores.
o	thin	ɵɪn	Equivale aproximadamente a la *z* en el castellano *cazar*.
ð	then other	ðɛn ʌ̆ðə	Equivale aproximadamente a la *d* española en *pardo*.
s	send case cent	sɛnd kes sɛnt	Equivale aproximadamente a la *s* inicial española: *santo*.
z	rose these zero	roz ðiz zíro	Equivale aproximadamente a la *s* sonora en *mismo*, pero se pronuncia con más sonoridad en inglés.
ʃ	sheet machine nation	ʃit maʃín néʃən	Es una *s* palatal que no tiene equivalente en español. Suena como la *ch* francesa: *chapeau*.
ʒ	vision	víʒən	No tiene equivalente en español. Es una palatal fricativa sonora, semejante a la *y* argentina y uruguaya.
tʃ	chase	tʃes	Equivale aproximadamente a la *ch* en *charla*.

Símbolo fonético	Ortografía inglesa	Ortografía fonética	Explicación de los sonidos.
dʒ	judge gentle	dʒʌdʒ dʒéntļ	No tiene equivalente exacto en español. Se parece a la *y* de *inyectar* en la pronunciación de uruguayos y argentinos.
m	much	mʌtʃ	Equivale aproximadamente a la *m* española.
n	none any	nʌn éni	Equivale aproximadamente a la *n* española en *nada*.
ņ	eaten button lesson	ítņ bʌtņ lésņ	No tiene equivalente en español. Representa la *n* sin la articulación de la vocal anterior.
ŋ	ankle angle ring	ǽŋkļ ǽŋgļ rɪŋ	Equivale a la *n* española en *mango*, *banco*.
l	late altar fall folly	let ɔ́ltə fɔl fálɪ	La *l* inicial equivale aproximadamente a la *l* española en *lado*. La *l* en medio de palabra es más débil que la inicial. La *l* final se pronuncia a veces de una manera tan relajada en inglés que apenas la percibe el oído español.
ļ	able ankle	ébļ ǽŋkļ	No tiene equivalente en español. Se pronuncia como la *l* en *hábil*, pero omitiendo la *i*.
w	weed well wall	wid wɛl wɔl	Equivale a la *u* de los diptongos: *ui, ue, ua, uo.*
h	hat whole	hæt hol	No tiene equivalente exacto en español. Equivale aproximadamente a una *j* suave que se reduce a una simple aspiración.
hw	where	hwer	Equivale a una *j* suave seguida de una *w* arriba explicada.
j	year yawn yet	jɪr jɔn jɛt	Equivale a la *i* española en los diptongos *ie, ia, io, iu: hiena.*
r	rose bear	roz bɛr	No tiene equivalente en español. La punta de la lengua se arrolla hacia atrás sin tocar el paladar. A veces se pierde al grado de vocalizarse.

PRONUNCIACION DE LA S DEL PLURAL[1]

I. La **s** del plural es sorda cuando la palabra termina en las consonantes sordas representadas por los símbolos fonéticos [p], [t], [k], [f], [θ]. Pronúnciase como la *s* de *santo:* **caps** [kæps], **gates** [gets], **cats** [kæts], **books** [bʊks], **cliffs** [klɪfs], **lengths** [leŋkθs].

Las excepciones más comunes son: **oath** [oθ], **oaths** [oðz]; **leaf** [lif], **leaves** [livz]; **wife** [waɪf], **wives** [waɪvz]; **knife** [naɪf], **knives** [naɪvz]; **calf** [kæf], **calves** [kævz]; **half** [hæf], **halves** [hævz].

II. La **s** del plural es sonora cuando la palabra termina en vocal (incluyendo la **y** que se cambia en **ies**), o en las consonantes sonoras representadas por los símbolos fonéticos [b], [d], [g], [v], [ð], [m], [n], [ŋ], [l]: **cries** [kraɪz], **robes** [robz], **beds** [bɛdz], **logs** [lɔgz], **stoves** [stovz], **lathes** [leðz], **farms** [farmz], **bins** [bɪnz], **kings** [kɪŋz], **falls** [fɔlz], **furs** [fɝz], **papers** [pépɚz], **plows** [plaʊz].

III. Cuando la palabra termina en las consonantes representadas por los símbolos [s], [ʃ], [tʃ], [z], [ʒ], [dʒ], se añade es [ɪz], o s [ɪz], si la palabra termina en **-ce, -se, -dge, -ge: face** [fes], **faces** [fésɪz]; **kiss** [kɪs], **kisses** [kísɪz]; **ash** [æʃ], **ashes** [ǽʃɪz]; **lunch** [lʌntʃ], **lunches** [lʌ́ntʃɪz]; **rose** [roz], **roses** [rózɪz]; **judge** [dʒʌdʒ], **judges** [dʒʌ́dʒɪz].

EL SUSTANTIVO

I. Género

Son masculinos los nombres de varón o animal macho, y son femeninos los nombres de mujer o animal hembra. Los demás son neutros. El artículo definido **the** se aplica a todos los sustantivos, singular y plural: **the man** el hombre; **the men** los hombres; **the book** el libro; **the books** los libros; **the woman** la mujer; **the women** las mujeres.

En ciertos sustantivos se distingue el género femenino por medio del sufijo **-ess: poet** poeta; **poetess** poetisa. A veces es indispensable indicar el género por medio de las palabras **male** o **female, boy** o **girl, man** o **woman, she** o **he: baby boy** niño; **baby girl** niña; **woman writer** escritora; **she-bear** osa. En otros casos hay una palabra distinta para cada género; **uncle** tío; **aunt** tía.

[1] Las mismas reglas se aplican a la pronunciación del genitivo y de la tercera persona del presente de indicativo, singular: **keeps** [kips]; **Kate's** [kets]; **saves** [sevz]; **John's** [dʒanz]; **judges** [dʒʌ́dʒɪz]; **Alice's** [ǽlɪsɪz].

II. PLURAL DE LOS SUSTANTIVOS[1]

1. Generalmente se forma el plural añadiendo s al singular: **paper, papers** papel, papeles; **book, books** libro, libros; **chief, chiefs,** jefe, jefes.

2. Los sustantivos que terminan en ch (pronunciada como la *ch* española), ss, x, sh, z, y o añaden es para formar el plural: **arch, arches** arco, arcos; **kiss, kisses** beso, besos; **box, boxes** caja, cajas; **dish, dishes** plato, platos; **buzz, buzzes** zumbido, zumbidos; **hero, heroes** héroe, héroes. Nótese que los sustantivos terminados en ch (pronunciada [k]) forman el plural añadiendo s: **monarch, monarchs** monarca, monarcas.

3. Los sustantivos que terminan en fe, y ciertos sustantivos que terminan en f, cambian estas letras en v y añaden es: **leaf, leaves** hoja, hojas; **life, lives** vida, vidas; **wife, wives** esposa, esposas; **knife, knives** cuchillo, cuchillos.

4. Para formar el plural de los sustantivos terminados en y precedida de consonante cámbiase la y en ies: **fly, flies** mosca, moscas; **cry, cries** grito, gritos; **family, families** familia, familias; **quantity, quantities** cantidad, cantidades. Nótese que los sustantivos terminados en y precedida de vocal forman el plural añadiendo s al singular: **day, days** día, días.

5. Ciertos sustantivos forman el plural de una manera irregular: **man, men** hombre, hombres; **woman, women** mujer, mujeres; **mouse, mice** ratón, ratones; **louse, lice** piojo, piojos; **goose, geese** ganso, gansos; **tooth, teeth** diente, dientes; **foot, feet** pie, pies; **ox, oxen** buey, bueyes.

6. Ciertos sustantivos que terminan en is forman el plural cambiando la i de la terminación en e: **axis, axes** eje, ejes; **the crisis, the crises** la crisis, las crisis.

EL ADJETIVO

El adjetivo inglés es invariable en cuanto a género y número. Normalmente se coloca delante del sustantivo: **an interesting book** un libro interesante; **a large table** una mesa grande; **beautiful women** mujeres hermosas.

Los comparativos y superlativos. Aunque no hay una regla general, por lo común los adjetivos monosílabos, los adjetivos acentuados en la última sílaba y algunos bisílabos fácilmente pronunciados forman

[1] Véase las reglas para la pronunciación del plural.

el comparativo de aumento y el superlativo añadiendo **-er** y **-est**. Los demás adjetivos van precedidos de **more** y **most**. Nótese que (1) sólo se añaden **-r** y **-st** a los que terminan en **e** muda; (2) los adjetivos terminados en **-y** cambian esta letra en **i**; (3) los adjetivos terminados en consonante precedida de vocal doblan la consonante:

Positivo	*Comparativo*	*Superlativo*
tall alto	**taller** más alto	**the tallest** el más alto
wise sabio	**wiser** más sabio	**the wisest** el más sabio
polite cortés	**politer** más cortés	**the politest** el más cortés
happy feliz	**happier** más feliz	**the happiest** el más feliz
fat gordo	**fatter** más gordo	**the fattest** el más gordo
careful cuidadoso	**more careful** más cuidadoso	**the most careful** el más cuidadoso

El superlativo absoluto se forma anteponiendo **very** y a veces **most: very intelligent** muy inteligente; **she is a most beautiful woman** es una mujer hermosísima.

El comparativo y el superlativo de inferioridad se forman con los adverbios **less** y **least: less wise** menos sabio; **the least wise** el menos sabio.

El comparativo de igualdad se forma con el adverbio **as: as poor as** tan pobre como; **as much as** tanto como; **as much money as** tanto dinero como.

Los adjetivos siguientes forman el comparativo y el superlativo de una manera irregular:

good, well	**better**	**best**
bad, ill	**worse**	**worst**
little	**less, lesser**	**least**
far	**farther, further**	**farthest, furthest**
much, many	**more**	**most**
old	**older, elder**	**oldest, eldest**

EL ADVERBIO

Fórmanse muchos adverbios, añadiendo **-ly** al adjetivo: **courteous** cortés, **courteously** cortésmente; **bold** atrevido, **boldly** atrevidamente. Existen las irregularidades siguientes en la formación de los adverbios que terminan en **-ly**: (1) los adjetivos terminados en **-ble** cambian la **-e** en **-y: possible, possibly;** (2) los terminados en **-ic** añaden **-ally: poetic, poetically;** (3) los terminados en **-ll** añaden sólo la **-y: full, fully;** (4) los terminados en **-ue** pierden la e final: **true, truly;** (5) los terminados en **-y** cambian la **y** en **i: happy, happily.**

Como los adjetivos, la mayor parte de los adverbíos forman el *comparativo* y el *superlativo* con los adverbios **more** (más), **most** (más), y **very** (muy). Asimismo los adverbios monosílabos añaden **-er** y **-est:**

Positivo	Comparativo	Superlativo	Superlativo Absoluto
boldly	more boldly	most boldly	very boldly
generously	more generously	most generously	very generously
soon	sooner	soonest	very soon
early	earlier	earliest	very early
late	later	latest	very late
near	nearer	nearest	very near
fast	faster	fastest	very fast

Los adverbios siguientes forman el comparativo y el superlativo de una manera irregular:

well	better	best	very well
badly, ill	worse	worst	very badly
little	less	least	very little
much	more	most	very much
far	farther, further	farthest, furthest	very far

SUFIJOS COMUNES EN INGLES

-dom denota dominio, jurisdicción, estado, condición, etc.: **kingdom** reino; **martyrdom** martirio; **boredom** aburrimiento; **freedom** libertad.

-ed,-d es la terminación del pretérito y del participio pasivo o pasado de los verbos regulares: **I called** llamé; **called** llamado.

-ee indica la persona que recibe la acción: **addressee** destinatario; **employee** empleado.

-eer denota oficio u ocupación: **engineer** ingeniero; **auctioneer** subastador.

-en *a)* terminación del participio de muchos verbos irregulares: **fallen, broken, shaken;**
b) sufijo que significa *hecho de:* **golden** dorado, de oro; **wooden** de madera; **leaden** de plomo;
c) terminación verbal equivalente a *hacer:* **whiten** hacer blanco, emblanquecer; **darken** hacer obscuro, obscurecer.

-er *a)* indica la persona que hace o el agente de la acción del verbo: **player** jugador; **talker** hablador;
b) indica el residente de un lugar: **New Yorker** habitante o residente de Nueva York; **islander** isleño;

	c) denota ocupación: **carpenter** carpintero; **baker** panadero;
	d) es la terminación del comparativo de adjetivos y adverbios: **taller** más alto; **faster** más aprisa.
-est	terminación del superlativo: **tallest** el más alto.
-ess	úsase para formar el género femenino de ciertos sustantivos: **patroness** patrona; **poetess** poetisa; **countess** condesa.
-fold	sufijo que significa *veces*: **twofold** dos veces; **hundredfold** cien veces.
-ful	a) equivale a *lleno*, y tratándose de adjetivos es igual a *-oso*: **hopeful** lleno de esperanzas; **careful** cuidadoso; **wilful** voluntarioso; **merciful** misericordioso; **glassful** un vaso (*lleno*);
	b) indica a veces hábito o inclinación: **forgetful** olvidadizo;
	c) es a veces equivalente a los sufijos españoles *-ado*, *-ada*: **handful** puñado; **spoonful** cucharada.
-hood	indica estado, condición, carácter, grupo; a menudo equivale a *-dad*: **motherhood** maternidad; **brotherhood** fraternidad; **childhood** niñez; **falsehood** falsedad.
-ician	denota especialidad en cierto ramo: **musician** músico; **technician** técnico; **electrician** electricista.
-ie	sufijo diminutivo: **birdie** pajarito; **Annie** Anita.
-ing	a) sufijo del gerundio: **speaking** hablando;
	b) sufijo del participio activo; **threatening** amenazante; **surprising** sorprendente;
	c) úsase a menudo para formar adjetivos: **running water** agua corriente; **drinking water** agua potable; **waiting room** sala de espera; **washing machine** máquina lavadora;
	d) úsase para formar sustantivos: **understanding** entendimiento; **supplying** abastecimiento; **clothing** ropa; **covering** cobertura; equivale al infinitivo castellano: **swimming is good exercise** el nadar es buen ejercicio.
-ish	a) úsase para formar ciertos adjetivos de nacionalidad: **Spanish** español; **English** inglés; **Turkish** turco;
	b) indica semejanza: **boyish** como niño, aniñado;

womanish como mujer, mujeril, afeminado; **whitish** blancuzco, medio blanco, que tira a blanco.

-less   equivale a *sin, falto de*: **childless** sin hijos; **penniless** sin dinero; en ciertos casos el sufijo inglés se traduce por medio de un prefijo: **countless** innumerable, sin número; **endless** interminable, sin fin.

-like   significa *semejanza*, y equivale a *como, a manera de*: **lifelike** que parece vivo; **childlike** como niño, infantil; **tigerlike** como tigre.

-ly   *a)* sufijo adverbial: **slowly** lentamente; **happily** felizmente; **possibly** posiblemente;

b) añadido a ciertos sustantivos equivale a *como, a la manera de*: **motherly** como madre, materno; **gentlemanly** como caballero, caballeroso; **friendly** amigable; **manly** varonil;

c) equivale a *cada* en estos ejemplos: **daily** cada día; diario; **weekly** cada semana; semanal; **monthly** cada mes; mensual; **yearly** cada año; anual.

-ness   úsase para formar sustantivos abstractos: **goodness** bondad; **darkness** obscuridad; **foolishness** tontería; **shamelessness** desvergüenza.

-ship   *a)* úsase para formar sustantivos abstractos: **friendship** amistad; **relationship** relación; parentesco;

b) denota arte o destreza: **horsemanship** equitación;

c) expresa dignidad, oficio, cargo, o título: **professorship** profesorado o cátedra; **chairmanship** presidencia (*de un comité, asamblea, etc.*); **lordship** señoría;

d) a veces expresa tan sólo un estado y su duración: **courtship** galanteo, cortejo, noviazgo.

-some   expresa en alto grado la cualidad representada por el vocablo al cual se añade: **tiresome** que cansa, cansado; **quarrelsome** dado a riñas, pendenciero; **loathsome** que repugna, asqueroso; **burdensome** gravoso.

-th   úsase para formar números ordinales: **fifth** quinto; **tenth** décimo.

-ty   *a)* terminación de los múltiples de diez: **twenty** veinte; **thirty** treinta; **forty** cuarenta;

b) terminación de muchos sustantivos abstractos; equivale frecuentemente al sufijo español *-tad* o *-dad*:

beauty beldad; **paternity** paternidad; **falsity** falsedad.

-ward,-wards denotan *hacia*: **homeward** hacia casa; **downward** hacia abajo.

-ways, -wise expresan manera, dirección, posición, etc.: **edgewise** de lado; **sideways** de lado; **lengthwise** a lo largo.

-y   *a*) terminación equivalente a los sufijos españoles *-ia*, *-ía*: **victory** victoria; **glory** gloria; **courtesy** cortesía; **biology** biología. **astronomy** astronomía;
b) sufijo diminutivo: **doggy** perrito; **Johnny** Juanito;
c) denota abundancia, y es a menudo equivalente a *-udo, -oso, -ado*: **rocky** lleno de rocas, rocoso, pedregoso; **rainy** lluvioso; **hairy** lleno de pelo, peludo; **bulky** abultado; **wavy** ondulado; **angry** enojado;
d) expresa semejanza: **rosy** rosado, como una rosa color de rosa.

VERBOS IRREGULARES DE LA LENGUA INGLESA

Se denominan verbos irregulares los que no forman el pretérito o el participio pasivo con la adición de **-d** o **-ed** al presente. Obsérvese que en ciertos verbos coexiste la forma regular al lado de la irregular. En otros coexisten dos formas irregulares juntamente con la regular.

Presente	*Pretérito*	*Participio pasivo o pasado*
abide	abode	abode
am, is, are	was, were	been
arise	arose	arisen
awake	awoke, awaked	awaked, awoke
bear	bore	born, borne
beat	beat	beat, beaten
become	became	become
befall	befell	befallen
beget	begot	begotten
begin	began	begun
behold	beheld	beheld
bend	bent	bent
bereave	bereft, bereaved	bereft, bereaved
beseech	besought, beseeched	besought, beseeched
beset	beset	beset

Presente	*Pretérito*	*Participio pasivo o pasado*
bet	bet	bet
bid	bid, bade	bidden, bid
bind	bound	bound
bite	bit	bitten, bit
bleed	bled	bled
blow	blew	blown
break	broke	broken
breed	bred	bred
bring	brought	brought
build	built	built
burn	burnt, burned	burnt, burned
burst	burst	burst
buy	bought	bought
can (*verbo defectivo*)	could	—
cast	cast	cast
catch	caught	caught
chide	chided, chid	chided, chidden
choose	chose	chosen
cleave	cleft, clove, cleaved	cleft, cleaved, cloven
cling	clung	clung
clothe	clad, clothed	clad, clothed
come	came	come
cost	cost	cost
creep	crept	crept
crow	crew, crowed	crowed
cut	cut	cut
deal	dealt	dealt
dig	dug, digged	dug, digged
do	did	done
draw	drew	drawn
dream	dreamt, dreamed	dreamt, dreamed
drink	drank	drunk
drive	drove	driven
dwell	dwelt, dwelled	dwelt, dwelled
eat	ate	eaten
fall	fell	fallen
feed	fed	fed
feel	felt	felt
fight	fought	fought
find	found	found
flee	fled	fled
fling	flung	flung
fly	flew	flown
forbear	forbore	forborne
forbid	forbade	forbidden
foresee	foresaw	foreseen
foretell	foretold	foretold

Presente	Pretérito	Participio pasivo o pasado
forget	forgot	forgotten, forgot
forgive	forgave	forgiven
forsake	forsook	forsaken
freeze	froze	frozen
get	got	got, gotten
gild	gilt, gilded	gilt, gilded
gird	girt, girded	girt, girded
give	gave	given
go	went	gone
grind	ground	ground
grow	grew	grown
hang[1]	hung	hung
have, has	had	had
hear	heard	heard
heave	hove, heaved	hove, heaved
hew	hewed	hewn, hewed
hide	hid	hidden, hid
hit	hit	hit
hold	held	held
hurt	hurt	hurt
inlay	inlaid	inlaid
keep	kept	kept
kneel	knelt	knelt
knit	knit, knitted	knit, knitted
know	knew	known
lay	laid	laid
lead	led	led
lean	leaned, leant	leaned, leant
leap	leapt, leaped	leapt, leaped
learn	learned, learnt	learned, learnt
learn	learned, learnt	learned, learnt
leave	left	left
lend	lent	lent
let	let	let
lie[2] (yacer; echarse)	lay	lain
light	lit, lighted	lit, lighted
load	loaded	loaded, laden
lose	lost	lost
make	made	made
may (verbo defectivo)	might	—
mean	meant	meant
meet	met	met
melt	melted	melted, molten
mistake	mistook	mistaken

[1] Es regular cuando significa "ahorcar."
[2] Es regular cuando significa "mentir."

Presente	Pretérito	Participio pasivo o pasado
mow	mowed	mown, mowed
must (verbo defectivo)	—	—
ought (verbo defectivo)	ought	—
pay	paid	paid
put	put	put
quit	quit, quitted	quit, quitted
read [rid]	read [red]	read [red]
rend	rent	rent
rid	rid, ridded	rid, ridded
ride	rode	ridden
ring	rang, rung	rung
rise	rose	risen
run	ran	run
saw	sawed	sawn, sawed
say	said	said
see	saw	seen
seek	sought	sought
sell	sold	sold
send	sent	sent
set	set	set
sew	sewed	sewn, sewed
shake	shook	shaken
shall	should	—
shave	shaved	shaved, shaven
shear	sheared	shorn, sheared
shed	shed	shed
shine²	shone	shone
shoe	shod	shod
shoot	shot	shot
show	showed	shown, showed
shred	shred, shredded	shred, shredded
shrink	shrank, shrunk	shrunk, shrunken
shut	shut	shut
sing	sang, sung	sung
sink	sank	sunk
sit	sat	sat
slay	slew	slain
sleep	slept	slept
slide	slid	slid, slidden
sling	slung	slung
slink	slunk	slunk
slit	slit	slit
smell	smelt, smelled	smelt, smelled
smite	smote	smitten
sow	sowed	sown, sowed
speak	spoke	spoken

² Es por lo común regular cuando significa "pulir, dar brillo."

Presente	*Pretérito*	*Participio pasivo o pasado*
speed	sped, speeded	sped, speeded
spell	spelled, spelt	spelled, spelt
spend	spent	spent
spill	spilled, spilt	spilled, spilt
spin	spun	spun
spit	spit, spat	spit, spat
split	split	split
spread	spread	spread
spring	sprang, sprung	sprung
stand	stood	stood
stave	staved, stove	staved, stove
steal	stole	stolen
stick	stuck	stuck
sting	stung	stung
stink	stank, stunk	stunk
strew	strewed	strewn, strewed
stride	strode	stridden
strike	struck	struck, striken
string	strung	strung
strive	strove, strived	striven, strived
swear	swore	sworn
sweep	swept	swept
swell	swelled	swollen, swelled
swim	swam	swum
swing	swung	swung
take	took	taken
teach	taught	taught
tear	tore	torn
tell	told	told
think	thought	thought
thrive	throve, thrived	thriven, thrived
throw	threw	thrown
thrust	thrust	thrust
tread	trod	trod, trodden
understand	understood	understood
undertake	undertook	undertaken
undo	undid	undone
uphold	upheld	upheld
upset	upset	upset
wake	woke, waked	waked
wear	wore	worn
weave	wove	woven
wed	wedded	wedded, wed
weep	wept	wept
wet	wet, wetted	wet, wetted
will (*verbo auxiliar*)	would	—
win	won	won

Presente	*Pretérito*	*Participio pasivo o pasado*
wind	wound	wound
withdraw	withdrew	withdrawn
withhold	withheld	withheld
withstand	withstood	withstood
work	worked; wrought	worked; wrought
wring	wrung	wrung
write	wrote	written

NUMERALS—NUMEROS

Cardinal Numbers		Números Cardinales	Ordinal Numbers	Números Ordinales
1	one	uno, una	first	primero
2	two	dos	second	segundo
3	three	tres	third	tercero
4	four	cuatro	fourth	cuarto
5	five	cinco	fifth	quinto
6	six	seis	sixth	sexto
7	seven	siete	seventh	séptimo
8	eight	ocho	eighth	octavo
9	nine	nueve	ninth	noveno, nono
10	ten	diez	tenth	décimo
11	eleven	once	eleventh	undécimo
12	twelve	doce	twelfth	duodécimo
13	thirteen	trece	thirteenth	décimotercio
14	fourteen	catorce	fourteenth	décimocuarto
15	fifteen	quince	fifteenth	décimoquinto
16	sixteen	dieciseis, diez y seis	sixteenth	décimosexto
17	seventeen	diecisiete, diez y siete	seventeenth	décimoséptimo
18	eighteen	dieciocho, diez y ocho	eighteenth	décimoctavo
19	nineteen	diecinueve, diez y nueve	nineteenth	décimonono
20	twenty	veinte	twentieth	vigésimo
21	twenty-one	veintiuno, veinte y uno	twenty-first	vigésimo primero
30	thirty	treinta	thirtieth	trigésimo
40	forty	cuarenta	fortieth	cuadragésimo
50	fifty	cincuenta	fiftieth	quincuagésimo
60	sixty	sesenta	sixtieth	sexagésimo
70	seventy	setenta	seventieth	septuagésimo
80	eighty	ochenta	eightieth	octogésimo
90	ninety	noventa	ninetieth	nonagésimo
100	one hundred	ciento	(one) hundredth	centésimo
101	one hundred and one	ciento (y) uno	(one) hundred and first	centésimo primo
200	two hundred	doscientos	two-hundredth	ducentésimo
300	three hundred	trescientos	three-hundredth	tricentésimo
400	four hundred	cuatrocientos	four-hundredth	cuadringentésimo
500	five hundred	quinientos	five-hundredth	quingentésimo
600	six hundred	seiscientos	six-hundredth	sexagésimo
700	seven hundred	setecientos	seven-hundredth	septingentésimo
800	eight hundred	ochocientos	eight-hundredth	octingentésimo
900	nine hundred	novecientos	nine-hundredth	noningentésimo
1000	one thousand	mil	(one) thousandth	milésimo
100,000	one hundred thousand	cien mil	(one) hundred thousandth	cienmilésimo
1,000,000	one million	un millón	(one) millionth	millonésimo

A

a [ə, e] *art. indef.* un, una; **what —** . . . ! ¡qué . . . !; **such —** tal; tan.

abandon [əbǽndən] *v.* abandonar; dejar; *s.* abandono, desahogo, desenvoltura; entrega.

abandoned [əbǽndənd] *adj.* abandonado; dejado; perverso; inmoral.

abandonment [əbǽndənmənt] *s.* abandono, abandonamiento; desamparo; desenvoltura, desembarazo.

abashed [əbǽʃt] *adj.* humillado, avergonzado.

abate [əbét] *v.* bajar, rebajar; disminuir; acabar con; mitigar(se); calmarse.

abatement [əbétmənt] *s.* diminución, merma; rebaja, descuento; mitigación.

abbey [ǽbɪ] *s.* abadía, monasterio.

abbot [ǽbət] *s.* abad.

abbreviate [əbrívɪet] *v.* abreviar, acortar, reducir.

abbreviation [əbrivɪéʃən] *s.* abreviación, abreviatura.

abdicate [ǽbdəket] *v.* abdicar, renunciar.

abdomen [ǽbdəmən] *s.* abdomen; vientre.

abduct [æbdʌ́kt] *v.* secuestrar, raptar, *Am.* plagiar (*a alguien*).

abduction [æbdʌ́kʃən] *s.* rapto, robo, secuestro (*de una persona*).

aberration [æbəréʃən] *s.* aberración, extravío (*de la mente*).

abhor [əbhɔ́r] *v.* aborrecer, odiar, abominar.

abhorrence [əbhɔ́rəns] *s.* aborrecimiento, aversión.

abide [əbáɪd] *v.* quedar, permanecer; morar, habitar; aguardar; soportar, tolerar; **to — by** conformarse a; atenerse a.

ability [əbɪ́lətɪ] *s.* habilidad, capacidad.

abject [ǽbdʒɛkt] *adj.* abatido; vil.

able [ébl] *adj.* hábil, capaz; competente; **able-bodied** de cuerpo sano; **to be — to** poder; saber.

ably [ébli] *adv.* hábilmente.

abnormal [æbnɔ́rml] *adj.* anormal.

aboard [əbɔ́rd] *adv.* a bordo; en el tren; **to go — embarcarse; all — !** ¡viajeros al tren!; *Am.* ¡vámonos!

abode [əbód] *s.* morada, domicilio, casa; *pret. & p.p. de* **to abide.**

abolish [əbálɪʃ] *v.* abolir; anular.

abolition [æbəlíʃən] *s.* abolición.

abominable [əbámnəbl] *adj.* abominable, aborrecible.

abortion [əbɔ́rʃən] *s.* aborto.

abound [əbáʊnd] *v.* abundar; **to — with** abundar en.

about [əbáʊt] *prep.* acerca de; tocante a; cerca de; alrededor de; por; *adv.* casi, poco más o menos; **at — ten o'clock** a eso de las diez; **to be — one's business** atender a su negocio; **to be — to** estar para, estar a punto de; **to face —** dar media vuelta; **to have no money — one's person** no llevar dinero consigo.

above [əbʌ́v] *prep.* por encima de; sobre; *adv.* arriba; **— all** sobre todo; **abovementioned** susodicho, ya mencionado; **from —** de arriba; del cielo, de Dios.

abridge [əbrídʒ] *v.* abreviar; compendiar, condensar; privar (*a uno de sus derechos*).

abroad [əbrɔ́d] *adv.* en el extranjero; fuera de casa; **to go —** ir al extranjero; **to spread —** divulgar o publicar por todas partes.

abrupt [əbrʌ́pt] *adj.* repentino; precipitado; áspero, brusco; escarpado; **-ly** *adv.* de repente; bruscamente.

abscess [ǽbsɛs] *s.* absceso.

absence [ǽbsns] *s.* ausencia; falta; **— of mind** abstracción; **leave of —** licencia (*para ausentarse*).

absent [ǽbsnt] *adj.* ausente; abstraído, distraído; **absent-minded** absorto, abstraído; [æbsént] *v.* **to — oneself** ausentarse.

absolute [ǽbsəlut] *adj.* absoluto; **the — lo** absoluto; **-ly** *adv.* absolutamente; en absoluto.

absolution [æbsəlúʃən] *s.* absolución.

absolve [æbsálv] *v.* absolver, remitir; perdonar, alzar la pena o el castigo.

absorb [əbsɔ́rb] *v.* absorber.

absorbent [əbsɔ́rbənt] *adj. & s.* absorbente.

absorption [əbsɔ́rpʃən] *s.* absorción; abstracción, embebecimiento.

abstain [əbstén] *v.* abstenerse, privarse.

abstinence [ǽbstənəns] *s.* abstinencia.

abstract [ǽbstrækt] *adj.* abstracto; *s.* sumario; extracto; **in the —** en abstracto; [æbstrǽkt] *v.* abstraer; considerar aisladamente; separar, retirar; resumir, compendiar.

abstraction [æbstrǽkʃən] *s.* abstracción; idea abstracta.

absurd [əbsə́d] *adj.* absurdo; insensato; ridículo, disparatado.

absurdity [əbsə́dətɪ] *s.* absurdo, disparate.

abundance [əbʌ́ndəns] *s.* abundancia, copia.

abundant [əbʌ́ndənt] *adj.* abundante, copioso.

1

abuse [əbjús] *s.* abuso; maltrato; ultraje; [əbjúz] *v.* abusar de; maltratar; injuriar; ultrajar.

abusive [əbjúsɪv] *adj.* abusivo; insultante, injurioso.

abyss [əbɪ́s] *s.* abismo; sima.

academic [ækədémɪk] *adj.* académico; escolar.

academy [əkǽdəmɪ] *s.* academia; colegio, instituto; escuela preparatoria.

accede [æksíd] *v.* acceder, consentir.

accelerate [ækséləret] *v.* acelerar(se).

acceleration [ækscləréʃən] *s.* aceleración.

accelerator [ækséləretə] *s.* acelerador.

accent [ǽksent] *s.* acento; [æksént] *v.* acentuar; recalcar.

accentuate [ækséntʃʊet] *v.* acentuar; recalcar; realzar.

accept [əksépt] *v.* aceptar; admitir; acoger; aprobar.

acceptable [əkséptəbl] *adj.* aceptable; grato; acepto.

acceptance [əkséptəns] *s.* aceptación; aprobación; buena acogida, recibimiento.

access [ǽksɛs] *s.* acceso; ataque (*de una enfermedad*); arrebato (*de furia*).

accessible [æksésəbl] *adj.* accessible; asequible, obtenible.

accessory [æksésərɪ] *adj.* accesorio; adjunto; *s.* accesorio; cómplice; **accessories** cosas accesorias, adornos, adminículos.

accident [ǽksədənt] *s.* accidente; percance, contratiempo; **by —** por casualidad.

accidental [æksədéntl] *adj.* accidental; casual; **-ly** *adv.* accidentalmente; por casualidad.

acclaim [əklém] *v.* aclamar, aplaudir; *s.* aclamación, aplauso.

acclamation [ækləméʃən] *s.* aclamación, aplauso.

acclimatize [əkláɪmətaɪz] *v.* aclimatar(se).

accommodate [əkɑmədét] *v.* acomodar, ajustar; ayudar, hacer un favor; hospedar, alojar; tener cabida para; **to — oneself** conformarse, adaptarse.

accommodation [əkɑmədéʃən] *s.* favor, ayuda; conveniencia; alojamiento (*en un hotel, casa, etc.*); cabida; adaptación; ajuste.

accompaniment [əkʌ́mpənɪmənt] *s.* acompañamiento.

accompanist [əkʌ́mpənɪst] *s.* acompañador, acompañante.

accompany [əkʌ́mpənɪ] *v.* acompañar.

accomplice [əkɑ́mplɪs] *s.* cómplice.

accomplish [əkɑ́mplɪʃ] *v.* cumplir; completar; lograr, conseguir; realizar, efectuar.

accomplished [əkɑ́mplɪʃt] *adj.* cumplido; realizado; consumado; establecido; diestro; perfecto.

accomplishment [əkɑ́mplɪʃmənt] *s.* cumplimiento; logro, realización; habilidad; perfección; mérito, proeza.

accord [əkɔ́rd] *s.* acuerdo, convenio; armonía, concierto; **of one's own —** voluntariamente; espontáneamente; **in — with** de acuerdo con; **with one —** unánimemente; *v.* otorgar, conceder, dar; concordar.

accordance [əkɔ́rdns] *s.* conformidad, acuerdo; **in — with** de acuerdo con, de conformidad con.

according [əkɔ́rdɪŋ]: **— to** según; conforme a; de acuerdo con; **— as** según (que), a medida que.

accordingly [əkɔ́rdɪŋlɪ] *adv.* en conformidad; así; como tal; por lo tanto; por consiguiente.

accost [əkɔ́st] *v.* abordar (*a alguien*) en la calle, acosar; molestar, perseguir.

account [əkáʊnt] *s.* cuenta; computación; relato; **on — of** a causa de; con motivo de; por; **on my —** por mí; **on my own —** por mi propia cuenta; **on no —** de ninguna manera; **of no —** de ningún valor o importancia; **to turn to —** aprovechar, hacer útil o provechoso; *v.* dar cuenta (a); considerar, tener por; **to — for** dar cuenta o razón de; explicar; **how do you — for that?** ¿cómo se explica eso?

accountable [əkáʊntəbl] *adj.* responsable; explicable.

accountant [əkáʊntənt] *s.* contador, tenedor de libros.

accounting [əkáʊntɪŋ] *s.* contabilidad, contaduría.

accredit [əkrédɪt] *v.* acreditar.

accrue [əkrú] *v.* acumular(se).

accumulate [əkjúmjəlet] *v.* acumular(se), juntar(se), amontonar(se).

accumulation [əkjumjəléʃən] *s.* acumulación, amontonamiento.

accuracy [ǽkjərəsɪ] *s.* precisión, exactitud, esmero.

accurate [ǽkjərɪt] *adj.* preciso, exacto; correcto; esmerado; cierto; certero; **-ly** *adv.* con exactitud; correctamente; con esmero.

accursed [əkɜ́st] *adj.* maldito; infame.

accusation [əkjɔzéʃən] *s.* acusación.

accuse [əkjúz] *v.* acusar; denunciar.

accuser [əkjúzə] *s.* acusador; delator, denunciador.

accustom [əkʌ́stəm] v. acostumbrar; **to — oneself** acostumbrarse; **to be -ed to** tener la costumbre de, acostumbrar, soler; estar acostumbrado a, estar hecho a.

ace [es] s. as; as, el mejor de su clase (*como un aviador excelente*); **within an — of** a punto de; muy cerca de.

ache [ek] s. dolor; **tooth—** dolor de muelas; v. doler.

achieve [ətʃív] v. acabar, llevar a cabo; realizar; conseguir, lograr; alcanzar.

achievement [ətʃívmənt] s. logro, realización; proeza, hazaña.

acid [ǽsɪd] adj. ácido; agrio; s. ácido.

acidity [əsídətɪ] s. acidez.

acknowledge [əknálɪdʒ] v. reconocer, admitir; confesar; **to — receipt** acusar recibo.

acknowledgement [əknálɪdʒmənt] s. reconocimiento, expresión de gratitud; confesión, admisión; **— of receipt** acuse de recibo.

acorn [ékɔrn] s. bellota.

acoustics [əkústɪks] s. acústica.

acquaint [əkwént] v. enterar, informar; dar a conocer; familiarizar; **to — oneself with** ponerse al corriente de; enterarse de; **to be -ed with** conocer a (*una persona*); estar enterado de (*algo*); conocer (*una ciudad, un país, etc.*).

acquaintance [əkwéntəns] s. conocimiento; conocido; -s amistades.

acquiesce [ækwɪés] v. asentir; consentir, quedar conforme.

acquiescence [ækwɪésn̩s] s. asentimiento, consentimiento; conformidad.

acquire [əkwáɪr] v. adquirir; obtener, conseguir; contraer (*costumbres, vicios*).

acquisition [ækwəzíʃən] s. adquisición.

acquit [əkwít] v. absolver, exonerar; pagar, redimir, librar de (*una obligación*); **to — oneself well** quedar bien; portarse bien.

acquittal [əkwít] s. absolución.

acre [ékə] s. acre (*medida de superficie*).

acrobat [ǽkrəbæt] s. acróbata.

across [əkrɔ́s] prep. a través de; al otro lado de; por; por en medio de; adv. a través, de través; **to go —** atravesar; **to come —, run —** encontrarse con; tropezar con.

act [ækt] s. acto; acción, hecho; v. hacer, desempeñar (*un papel*); representar (*en el teatro*); obrar; actuar; portarse; funcionar; **to — as** servir de, estar de.

acting [ǽktɪŋ] s. representación, desempeño (*de un papel dramático*); acción, actuación; adj. interino, suplente.

action [ǽkʃən] s. acción; acto; actuación;

funcionamiento.

active [ǽktɪv] adj. activo.

activity [æktívətɪ] s. actividad.

actor [ǽktə] s. actor.

actress [ǽktrɪs] s. actriz.

actual [ǽktʃʊəl] adj. verdadero, real; actual (*lo que realmente es*), existente; **-ly** adv. realmente, en realidad; de hecho, efectivamente.

acumen [əkjúmɪn] s. caletre, tino, perspicacia.

acute [əkjút] adj. agudo; perspicaz; penetrante.

adamant [ǽdəmænt] adj. duro; firme, inflexible.

adapt [ədǽpt] v. adaptar; **to — oneself** adaptarse, acomodarse.

adaptation [ædæptéʃən] s. adaptación.

add [æd] v. sumar; añadir, agregar.

addict [ǽdɪkt] s. adicto (*persona adicta al uso de narcóticos*); **drug —** morfinómano.

addicted [ədíktɪd] adj. adicto, dado, entregado, habituado.

addition [ədíʃən] s. adición; suma; añadidura, aditamento; **in — to** además de.

additional [ədíʃən] adj. adicional.

address [ədrés] s. dirección, domicilio; señas; sobrescrito; discurso, arenga; destreza; **form of —** tratamiento; v. dirigir, poner la dirección, señas o sobrescrito a; hablar, dirigir la palabra a; dirigirse a; **to — oneself to a task** aplicarse a una tarea.

addressee [ədresí] s. destinatario.

adequate [ǽdəkwɪt] adj. adecuado; proporcionado; suficiente.

adhere [ədhír] v. adherirse; pegarse.

adherence [ədhírəns] s. adherencia.

adhesion [ədhíʒən] s. adhesión.

adhesive [ədhísɪv] adj. adhesivo; pegajoso; **— tape** tela adhesiva, esparadrapo.

adjacent [ədʒésn̩t] adj. adyacente, contiguo.

adjective [ǽdʒɪktɪv] s. adjetivo.

adjoin [ədʒɔ́ɪn] v. estar contiguo o adyacente a, lindar con.

adjourn [ədʒɜ́n] v. aplazar, diferir; **to — the meeting** suspender o levantar la sesión; **meeting -ed** se levanta la sesión.

adjournment [ədʒɜ́nmənt] s. aplazamiento, levantamiento (*de una sesión*).

adjunct [ǽdʒəŋkt] s. adjunto, aditamento, añadidura; asociado, acompañante; adj. adjunto, unido, subordinado.

adjust [ədʒʌ́st] v. ajustar; acomodar; arreglar; graduar; **to — oneself** adap-

3

tarse, conformarse.

adjustment [ədʒʌstmənt] *s.* ajuste; ajustamiento; arreglo; regulación.

administer [ədmínəstə] *v.* administrar; dirigir, regir, gobernar; aplicar (*remedio, castigo, etc.*); to — an oath tomar juramento.

administration [ədmɪnəstréʃən] *s.* administración; dirección, gobierno; gerencia; manejo.

administrative [ədmínəstretɪv] *adj.* administrativo;ejecutivo;gubernativo.

administrator [ədmínəstretə] *s.* administrador.

admirable [ǽdmərəbl̩] *adj.* admirable; **admirably** *adv.* admirablemente.

admiral [ǽdmərəl] *s.* almirante.

admiration [ædməréʃən] *s.* admiración.

admire [ədmáɪr] *v.* admirar; estimar.

admirer [ədmáɪrə] *s.* admirador; pretendiente.

admission [ədmíʃən] *s.* admisión; confesión; acceso, entrada; precio de entrada o de ingreso.

admit [ədmɪt] *v.* admitir; aceptar; confesar,reconocer;conceder;dar entrada.

admittance [ədmítn̩s] *s.* entrada; derecho de entrar; admisión.

admonish [ədmúnɪʃ] *v.* amonestar.

admonition [ædmənʃən] *s.* amonestación, consejo.

ado [ədú] *s.* actividad; bulla; disturbio.

adobe [ədóbɪ] *s.* adobe; casa de adobe.

adolescence [ædlésn̩s] *s.* adolescencia.

adolescent [ædlésn̩t] *adj. & s.* adolescente.

adopt [ədápt] *v.* adoptar.

adoption [ədápʃən] *s.* adopción.

adoration [ædəréʃən] *s.* adoración.

adore [ədór] *v.* adorar.

adorn [ədórn] *v.* adornar; ornar; embellecer.

adornment [ədórnmənt] *s.* adorno.

adrift [ədríft] *adj. & adv.* a la deriva, flotando, flotante.

adroit [ədróɪt] *adj.* hábil, diestro.

adult [ədʌlt] *adj. & s.* adulto.

adulterate [ədʌltəret] *v.* adulterar.

adulterer [ədʌltərə] *s.* adúltero.

adultery [ədʌltərɪ] *s.* adulterio.

advance [ədvǽns] *v.* avanzar, progresar; adelantar; acelerar; promover; proponer; anticipar, pagar por adelantado; encarecer, subir (*precios*); *s.* avance; progreso; adelanto, anticipo; alza, aumento de precio; -s requerimientos, pretensiones, insinuaciones; in — por adelantado, con anticipación.

advanced [ədvǽnst] *adj.* avanzado; adelantado; — in years entrado en años,

viejo, anciano.

advancement [ədvǽnsmənt] *s.* adelantamiento, mejora, progreso; promoción.

advantage [ədvǽntɪdʒ] *s.* ventaja; beneficio, provecho; to have the — over llevar ventaja a; to take — of aprovecharse de; to take — of a person abusar de la confianza o paciencia de alguien.

advantageous [ædvəntédʒəs] *adj.* ventajoso; provechoso.

advent [ǽdvent] *s.* advenimiento; venida.

adventure [ədvéntʃə] *s.* aventura; riesgo.

adventurer [ədvéntʃərə] *s.* aventurero.

adventurous [ədvéntʃərəs] *adj.* aventurero; atrevido; aventurado, arriesgado.

adverb [ǽdvɜb] *m.* adverbio.

adversary [ǽdvəserɪ] *s.* adversario, antagonista, contrario.

adverse [ədvɜs] *adj.* adverso; opuesto, contrario; hostil; desfavorable.

adversity [ədvɜsətɪ] *s.* adversidad; infortunio.

advertise [ǽdvətaɪz] *v.* anunciar; avisar, dar aviso.

advertisement [ædvətáɪzmənt] *s.* anuncio, aviso.

advertiser [ǽdvətaɪzə] *s.* anunciador, anunciante.

advertising [ǽdvətaɪzɪŋ] *s.* anuncios; arte o negocio de anunciar.

advice [ədváɪs] *s.* aviso, advertencia; consejo; noticia.

advisable [ədváɪzəbl̩] *adj.* conveniente; prudente; recomendable.

advise [ədváɪz] *v.* aconsejar; avisar, advertir; informar; to — with consultar con; aconsejarse con.

adviser, advisor [ədváɪzə] *s.* consejero, aconsejador.

advocate [ǽdvəkɪt] *s.* abogado; defensor, intercesor; partidario; [ǽdvəket] *v.* abogar por; defender.

aerial [ériəl] *adj.* aéreo; *s.* antena.

aeroplane [éraplen] = **airplane.**

aesthetic [esθétɪk] *adj.* estético; -s *s.* estética.

afar [əfár] *adv.* lejos; from — desde lejos.

affable [ǽfəbl̩] *adj.* afable, amable.

affair [əfér] *s.* asunto; negocio; lance; función, tertulia, convite; cosa; love — amorío.

affect [əfékt] *v.* afectar; conmover; fingir; hacer ostentación de.

affectation [æfɪktéʃən] *s.* afectación.

affected [əféktɪd] *adj.* afectado; conmovido, enternecido; fingido; artificioso.

affection [əfékʃən] *s.* afecto, cariño; inclinación; afección, dolencia.

affectionate [əfékʃənɪt] *adj.* afectuoso, cariñoso.

affiliate [əfílɪet] *v.* afiliar; afiliarse, unirse, asociarse.

affinity [əfínɪtɪ] *s.* afinidad.

affirm [əfɔ́m] *v.* afirmar, asegurar, aseverar.

affirmative [əfɔ́mətɪv] *adj.* afirmativo; *s.* afirmativa.

affix [əfíks] *v.* fijar, pegar; **to — one's signature** poner su firma, firmar.

afflict [əflíkt] *v.* afligir; **to be -ed with** padecer de, sufrir de, adolecer de.

affliction [əflíkʃən] *s.* aflicción; pena, dolor; achaque; angustia; infortunio.

afford [əfɔ́rd] *v.* proveer, proporcionar; **I cannot — that expense** no puedo hacer ese gasto; **he cannot — to waste time** no le conviene perder el tiempo; no tiene tiempo que perder; **I cannot — that risk** no puedo (*o* no quiero) exponerme a ese riesgo.

affront [əfrʌ́nt] *s.* afrenta, agravio, ultraje; *v.* afrentar, agraviar, ultrajar.

afire [əfáɪr] *adj.* ardiendo, quemándose.

afloat [əflót] *adj. & adv.* flotante; flotando; a flote; a flor de agua; a bordo; inundado; a la deriva, sin rumbo; **the rumor is —** corre la voz.

afoot [əfút] *adv.* a pie; en marcha, en movimiento.

aforesaid [əfɔ́rsɛd] *adj.* susodicho, ya dicho.

afraid [əfréd] *adj.* miedoso, medroso; atemorizado, amedrentado; **to be —** temer, tener miedo.

afresh [əfréʃ] *adv.* de nuevo, desde el principio.

African [ǽfrɪkən] *adj. & s.* africano; negro.

after [ǽftə] *prep.* después de; tras, tras de; detrás de; en busca de; por; según; *adv.* después; detrás; *conj.* después (de) que; *adj.* subsiguiente; siguiente; **— all** después de todo; de todos modos; **day — tomorrow** pasado mañana; **after-dinner** de sobremesa; **—effect** consecuencia, resultado; **—math** consecuencias, resultados (*usualmente desastrosos*); **—thought** idea tardía.

afternoon [ǽftənún] *s.* tarde.

aftertaste [ǽfətest] *s.* dejo, dejillo (*sabor que queda en la boca*).

afterwards [ǽftəwədz] *adv.* después.

again [əgén] *adv.* otra vez, de nuevo; además; por otra parte; **— and —** repetidas veces; **never —** nunca jamás; **to come —** volver; **to do it —** volver a hacerlo.

against [əgénst] *prep.* contra; frente a; en contraste con; **— the grain a** contrapelo, a redopelo; **— a rainy day** para cuando llueva.

age [edʒ] *s.* edad; época; siglo; generación; **of — mayor de edad; old —** vejez, ancianidad; **to become of —** llegar a mayor de edad; **under —** menor de edad; *v.* envejecer(se).

aged [édʒɪd, édʒd] *adj.* viejo, anciano; añejo; envejecido; **— forty years de** cuarenta años; **— in wood** añejado en toneles o barriles (*dícese del vino*).

agency [édʒənsɪ] *s.* agencia; medio, intermedio.

agent [édʒənt] *s.* agente; intermediario, representante; apoderado.

aggrandize [ǽgrəndaɪz] *v.* engrandecer, agrandar.

aggravate [ǽgrəvet] *v.* agravar, empeorar; irritar, exasperar.

aggregate [ǽgrɪgɪt] *s.* agregado, conjunto, colección; *adj.* agregado, unido; **in the —** en conjunto.

aggression [əgréʃən] *s.* agresión.

aggressive [əgrésɪv] *adj.* agresivo; emprendedor.

aggressor [əgrésə] *s.* agresor.

aghast [əgǽst] *adj.* espantado, pasmado.

agile [ǽdʒəl] *adj.* ágil.

agility [ədʒílətɪ] *s.* agilidad.

agitate [ǽdʒətet] *v.* agitar; turbar, perturbar; alborotar; discutir acaloradamente; maquinar, tramar.

agitation [ædʒətéʃən] *s.* agitación; alboroto.

agitator [ǽdʒətetə] *s.* agitador, alborotador, revoltoso.

ago [əgó] *adj. & adv.* pasado; en el pasado; **many years —** hace muchos años; muchos años ha, mucho tiempo ha; **long —** hace mucho tiempo; ha mucho.

agonize [ǽgənaɪz] *v.* agonizar; sufrir angustiosamente; retorcerse de dolor; luchar.

agony [ǽgənɪ] *s.* agonía; angustia; tormento; dolor; lucha.

agree [əgrí] *v.* acordar, concordar, convenir; consentir; estar de acuerdo; ponerse de acuerdo; sentarle bien a uno (*dícese del clima, del alimento, etc.*).

agreeable [əgríəbl] *adj.* agradable, afable; complaciente; conveniente; satisfactorio.

5

agreement [əgrímənt] *s.* acuerdo, convenio; concordancia, concordia; conformidad; **to be in** — estar de acuerdo; **to come to an** — ponerse de acuerdo.

agricultural [ægrɪkʌ́ltʃərəl] *adj.* agrícola.

agriculture [ǽgrɪkʌ́ltʃə] *s.* agricultura.

agriculturist [ægrɪkʌ́ltʃərɪst] *s.* agricultor.

ahead [əhéd] *adv.* delante, al frente; adelante; — **of time** adelantado; antes de tiempo; **to go** — ir adelante; **to get** — adelantar(se).

aid [ed] *s.* ayuda, auxilio, socorro; ayudante, auxiliar; *v.* ayudar, auxiliar, socorrer.

ail [el] *v.* adolecer, padecer; **what -s you?** ¿qué tienes? ¿qué te aflige?

ailment [élmənt] *s.* achaque, dolencia.

aim [em] *s.* puntería; tino; fin, objeto; proposición; *v.* apuntar (*un arma*); dirigir, asestar; dirigir la puntería; aspirar (a); **to — to please** proponerse (o tratar de) agradar.

aimless [émlɪs] *adj.* sin propósito, sin objeto.

air [er] *s.* aire; brisa; tonada; **in the** — en el aire; indeciso, incierto; **in the open** — al raso, al aire libre; **to be on the** — emitir, radiodifundir; **to put on -s** darse tono; *adj.* de aire; aéreo; — **brake** freno neumático; — **line** línea aérea; ruta aérea; **by —mail** por correo aéreo, por vía aérea, por avión; **air-conditioned** de aire acondicionado; *v.* airear; orear; ventilar; publicar, pregonar; ostentar.

aircraft [érkræft] *s.* avión, aeroplano; aeronave; aviones.

airplane [érplen] *s.* aeroplano, avión; — **carrier** portaaviones.

airport [érport] *s.* aeropuerto, aeródromo.

airship [érʃɪp] *s.* aeronave.

airtight [értáit] *adj.* hermético.

airy [éri] *adj.* airoso; aireado, ventilado; ligero; tenue.

aisle [ail] *s.* pasillo, pasadizo; nave (*de una iglesia*).

ajar [ədʒár] *adj.* entreabierto, entornado.

alarm [əlárm] *s.* alarma; rebato; inquietud; — **clock** despertador; *v.* alarmar; inquietar.

alcohol [ǽlkəhɑl] *s.* alcohol.

alcoholic [ælkəhɔ́lɪk] *adj.* alcohólico.

alcove [ǽlkov] *s.* alcoba.

alderman [ɔ́ldəmən] *s.* concejal, regidor.

ale [el] *s.* cerveza.

alert [əlɜ́t] *adj.* alerto, vigilante; despierto; vivo; listo; *s.* alarma, rebato; **to be on the** — estar alerta.

alfalfa [ælfǽlfə] *s.* alfalfa.

algebra [ǽldʒəbrə] *s.* álgebra.

alien [éljən] *s.* extranjero; residente extranjero; *adj.* extraño, ajeno.

alienate [éljənet] *v.* enajenar; apartar, alejar (*a una persona de otra*).

alienist [éljənɪst] *s.* alienista, psiquiatra.

alight [əláit] *v.* apearse, desmontarse, bajar(de); posarse (*dícese de pájaros, mariposas, etc.*).

alike [əláik] *adj.* semejante; parecido; **to be** — parecerse, asemejarse; ser iguales; *adv.* del mismo modo.

alive [əláiv] *adj.* vivo; con vida; viviente; activo; — **with** lleno de.

all [ɔl] *adj.* todo (el); todos (los); *s.* todo; todo el mundo, todos; *adv.* enteramente; — **at once** de una vez; de un tirón; de repente; — **right** bueno; bien; — **the worse** tanto peor; **not at** — de ninguna manera; no hay de qué; **nothing at** — nada en absoluto; — **told** (o **in** —) en conjunto; todo (and) **for** — por última vez; una vez por todas; **to be — in** estar agotado, estar rendido de fatiga; **it is — over** se acabó, ha terminado todo.

allay [əlé] *v.* aliviar; calmar.

allegation [æləgéʃən] *s.* alegación, alegato; aseveración.

allege [əlédʒ] *v.* alegar; declarar; sostener, asegurar.

allegiance [əlídʒəns] *s.* lealtad, fidelidad; homenaje.

allergy [ǽlədʒɪ] *s.* alergia (*sensibilidad anormal a ciertos alimentos o sustancias*).

alleviate [əlíviet] *v.* aliviar.

alley [ǽli] *s.* callejón; callejuela; **blind** — callejón sin salida; **bowling** — boliche, *Am.* bolera.

alliance [əláiəns] *s.* alianza.

allied [əláid] *adj.* aliado; relacionado.

alligator [ǽləgetə] *s.* lagarto; caimán; — **pear** aguacate.

allot [əlát] *v.* asignar; repartir.

allow [əláu] *v.* permitir, dejar; conceder; admitir; asignar; abonar; **to — for certain errors** tener en cuenta ciertos errores.

allowable [əláuəbl] *adj.* permisible, admisible, lícito.

allowance [əláuəns] *s.* asignación; abono, pensión; ración, rebaja, descuento; permiso; concesión; **monthly** — mesada, mensualidad; **to make — for** tener en cuenta.

alloy [ǽlɔi] *s.* aleación, liga, mezcla (*de*

dos o *más metales*); [əlɔ́ɪ] *v.* alear, ligar, mezclar (*metales*).

allude [əlúd] *v.* aludir.

allure [əlúr] *v.* seducir, cautivar; atraer, halagar.

allurement [əlúrmənt] *s.* seducción, tentación; atractivo; halago.

alluring [əlúrɪŋ] *adj.* seductivo, halagüeño, encantador.

allusion [əlúʒən] *s.* alusión; indirecta, insinuación.

ally [əláɪ] *v.* unir; aliarse; **to — oneself (itself) with** aliarse con, unirse con; [ǽlaɪ] *s.* aliado.

almanac [ɔ́lmənæk] *s.* almanaque, calendario.

almighty [ɔlmáɪtɪ] *adj.* todopoderoso, omnipotente.

almond [ámənd] *s.* almendra; **— tree** almendro.

almost [ɔ́lmost] *adv.* casi; **I — fell down** por poco me caigo.

alms [ɑmz] *s.* limosna; **— box** cepo o cepillo, alcancía (*para limosnas*).

aloft [əlɔ́ft] *adv.* en alto; arriba.

alone [əlón] *adj.* solo; solitario; único; *adv.* sólo, solamente; **all — a solas;** completamente solo; solito; **to let —** no tocar; no molestar; dejar en paz; no hacer caso de.

along [əlɔ́ŋ] *prep.* a lo largo de; por; al lado de; **— with** junto con; en compañía de; **all —** todo el tiempo; de un extremo a otro; **all — the coast** por toda la costa; **to carry — with one** llevar consigo; **to go — with** acompañar; **to get —** ir bien; **to get — with** llevarse bien con; **get —!** ¡vete! ¡váyase! ¡largo de aquí!

alongside [əlɔ́ŋsáɪd] *prep.* & *adv.* al lado (de); al costado (de); lado a lado.

aloof [əlúf] *adj.* aislado, apartado, retirado; huraño; reservado; *adv.* aparte, lejos.

aloofness [əlúfnɪs] *s.* alejamiento, desapego, aislamiento.

aloud [əláud] *adv.* alto, recio, fuerte, en voz alta.

alphabet [ǽlfəbɛt] *s.* alfabeto.

already [ɔlrédɪ] *adv.* ya.

also [ɔ́lso] *adv.* también, además, igualmente.

altar [ɔ́ltə] *s.* altar; **high — altar** mayor; **—piece** retablo.

alter [ɔ́ltə] *v.* alterar; cambiar; variar.

alteration [ɔltəréʃən] *s.* alteración, cambio; mudanza; modificación.

alternate [ɔ́ltənɪt] *adj.* alternativo alterno; alternado; *s.* suplente; **-ly** *adv.* alternativamente, por turno;

[ɔ́ltənet] *v.* alternar; variar; turnar.

alternative [ɔltə́nətɪv] *adj.* alternativo; *s.* alternativa.

although [ɔlðó] *conj.* aunque, si bien, bien que.

altitude [ǽltətjud] *s.* altitud, altura, elevación.

altogether [ɔltəgéðə] *adv.* del todo, completamente; en conjunto.

aluminum [əlúmɪnəm] *s.* aluminio.

alumnus [ələ́mnəs] *s.* graduado, exalumno.

always [ɔ́lwɪz] *adv.* siempre.

am [æm] *1ª persona del presente de indic. del verbo* **to be:** soy, estoy.

amalgamate [əmǽlgəmet] *v.* amalgamar; combinar, unir.

amass [əmǽs] *v.* amontonar, acumular, apilar, *Am.* amasar.

amateur [ǽmətʃur] *s.* aficionado; novicio, principiante.

amaze [əméz] *v.* pasmar, maravillar, asombrar.

amazement [əmézmənt] *s.* pasmo, admiración, asombro.

amazing [əmézɪŋ] *adj.* pasmoso, asombroso, maravilloso.

ambassador [æmbǽsədə] *s.* embajador.

amber [ǽmbə] *s.* ámbar; color de ámbar; *adj.* ambarino; de ámbar.

ambiguity [æmbɪgjúətɪ] *s.* ambigüedad.

ambiguous [æmbígjuəs] *adj.* ambiguo.

ambition [æmbíʃən] *s.* ambición; aspiración.

ambitious [æmbíʃəs] *adj.* ambicioso.

amble [ǽmbl] *v.* andar, vagar.

ambulance [ǽmbjələns] *s.* ambulancia.

ambush [ǽmbuʃ] *s.* emboscada; celada; acecho; **to lie in —** estar emboscado, estar al acecho; *v.* emboscar; poner celada a.

amend [əménd] *v.* enmendar; rectificar; **-s** *s. pl.* satisfacción, compensación; **to make — for** resarcir, dar satisfacción por, compensar por.

amendment [əméndmənt] *s.* enmienda.

American [əmérəkən] *adj.* & *s.* americano; norteamericano.

amethyst [ǽməɪst] *s.* amatista.

amiable [émɪəbl] *adj.* amable, afable, amistoso.

amicable [ǽmɪkəbl] *adj.* amigable, amistoso.

amid [əmíd] *prep.* en medio de; entre; **amidst** [əmídst] = **amid.**

amiss [əmís] *adj.* errado, equivocado; impropio; *adv.* mal; fuera de lugar, impropiamente; **to take —** llevar a mal.

7

ammonia [əmónjə] s. amoníaco.

ammunition [æmjəníʃən] s. munición.

amnesty [æmnɛstɪ] s. amnestía.

among [əmʌ́ŋ] prep. entre, en medio de; **amongst** [əmʌ́ŋst] = among.

amorous [æmərəs] adj. amoroso.

amount [əmáunt] s. suma; cantidad; total; importe; valor; v. montar, subir, importar, ascender (a); valer; that **-s to stealing** eso equivale a robar.

amphitheater [æmfəθɪətə] s. anfiteatro.

ample [æmpl] adj. amplio; abundante; bastante, suficiente.

amputate [æmpjətet] v. amputar.

amuse [əmjúz] v. divertir, entretener, distraer; **to — oneself** divertirse.

amusement [əmjúzmənt] s. diversión, entretenimiento, pasatiempo, recreo, distracción.

amusing [əmjúzɪŋ] adj. divertido, entretenido; gracioso, chistoso.

an [ən, æn] art. indef. un, una.

analagous [ənǽləgəs] adj. análogo.

analogy [ənǽlədʒɪ] s. analogía, semejanza.

analysis [ənǽləsɪs] s. análisis.

analyze [ǽnlaɪz] v. analizar.

anarchy [ǽnəkɪ] s. anarquía.

anatomy [ənǽtəmɪ] s. anatomía.

ancestor [ǽnsɛstə] s. antepasado; **-s** abuelos, antepasados.

ancestral [ænsɛ́strəl] adj. solariego, de los antepasados; hereditario.

ancestry [ǽnsɛstrɪ] s. linaje, abolengo, ascendencia.

anchor [ǽŋkə] s. ancla; **to drop —** anclar, echar anclas, dar fondo, fondear; **to weigh —** levar el ancla; v. anclar; echar anclas; fijar, asegurar.

anchovy [ǽntʃovɪ] s. anchoa, anchova.

ancient [énʃənt] adj. antiguo; vetusto; **the -s** los antiguos; la antigüedad.

and [ənd, ænd] conj. y; e (delante de i o hi); **— so forth** etcétera; y así sucesivamente; **let us try — do it** tratemos de hacerlo; **let us go — see him** vamos a verle.

Andalusian [ændəlúʒən] adj. andaluz.

anecdote [ǽnɪkdot] s. anécdota.

anesthetic [ænəsɛtík] adj. & s. anestésico.

anew [ənjú] adv. otra vez, de nuevo; nuevamente.

angel [éndʒəl] s. ángel.

angelic [ændʒélɪk] adj. angélico.

anger [ǽŋgə] s. enojo, enfado, ira, cólera; v. enojar, enfadar, encolerizar.

angina [ændʒáɪnə] s. angina; **— pectoris** angina de pecho.

angle [ǽŋgl] s. ángulo; rincón; esquina;

punto de vista, aspecto; v. pescar.

Anglo-Saxon [ǽŋglosǽksṇ] adj. & s. anglosajón.

angry [ǽŋgrɪ] adj. enojado; colérico.

anguish [ǽŋgwɪʃ] s. angustia, ansia, pena, dolor.

angular [ǽŋgjələ] adj. angular; anguloso.

animal [ǽnəml] s. & adj. animal.

animate [ǽnəmɪt] adj. animado, viviente; [ǽnəmet] v. animar; alentar.

animation [ænəméʃən] s. animación; viveza.

animosity [ænəmásətɪ] s. animosidad, ojeriza, inquina, rencor.

ankle [ǽŋkl] s. tobillo.

annals [ǽnlz] s. pl. anales.

annex [ǽnɛks] s. anexo; añadidura, aditamento; ala de un edificio; [ənɛ́ks] v. anexar.

annexation [ænɛkséʃən] s. anexión.

annihilate [ənáɪəlet] v. aniquilar; anonadar.

anniversary [ænəvɪ́sərɪ] s. & adj. aniversario.

annotate [ǽnotet] v. anotar.

annotation [ænotéʃən] s. anotación, acotación, nota.

announce [ənáuns] v. anunciar; proclamar.

announcement [ənáunsmənt] s. anuncio; aviso; noticia.

announcer [ənáunsə] s. anunciador; **radio —** locutor.

annoy [ənɔ́ɪ] v. molestar; fastidiar; incomodar; enfadar.

annoyance [ənɔ́ɪəns] s. molestia; fastidio; enfado.

annual [ǽnjʊəl] adj. anual; s. anuario; planta anual; **-ly** adv. anualmente, cada año, todos los años.

annuity [ənúətɪ] s. anualidad, renta anual.

annul [ənʌ́l] v. anular; abolir.

anoint [ənɔ́ɪnt] v. ungir; untar; administrar la Extremaunción.

anon [ənán] adv. pronto, luego; otra vez.

anonymous [ənánəməs] adj. anónimo.

another [ənʌ́ðə] adj. & pron. otro; **one — uno a otro, unos a otros.

answer [ǽnsə] s. respuesta, contestación; réplica; solución; v. responder; contestar; replicar; **to — for** ser responsable de (o por); responder de; ser (salir) fiador de; **to — the purpose** ser adecuado, servir para el objeto.

ant [ænt] s. hormiga; **—-eater** oso hormiguero; **— hill** hormiguero.

antagonism [æntǽgənɪzəm] s. antagonismo, oposición, antipatía.

antagonist [æntǽgənɪst] s. antagonista,

adversario.

antagonize [æntǽgənaɪz] v. contrariar, oponerse a, hostilizar.

antecedent [æntəsídņt] adj. & s. antecedente.

antelope [ǽntɪop] s. antílope.

antenna [æntǽnə] (pl. **antennae** [ænténi]) s. antena.

anterior [æntírɪə] adj. anterior; delantero.

anteroom [ǽntɪrum] s. antecámara; sala de espera.

anthem [ǽnθəm] s. himno.

anthracite [ǽnθrəsaɪt] s. antracita.

antiaircraft [æntɪérkræft] adj. antiaéreo.

anticipate [æntísəpet] v. anticipar(se); prever; esperar.

anticipation [æntɪsəpéʃən] s. anticipación; expectación; previsión.

antics [ǽntɪks] s. pl. travesuras, cabriolas.

antidote [ǽntɪdot] s. antídoto.

antipathy [æntípəɵɪ] s. antipatía, repugnancia.

antiquated [ǽntəkwetɪd] adj. anticuado; desusado.

antique [æntík] adj. antiguo; anticuado; s. antigualla.

antiquity [æntíkwətɪ] s. antigüedad; vejez, ancianidad.

antiseptic [æntəséptɪk] adj. & s. antiséptico.

antisocial [æntɪsóʃəl] adj. antisocial.

antler [ǽntlə] s. asta, cuerno (del venado, ciervo, etc.).

anvil [ǽnvɪl] s. yunque.

anxiety [æŋzáɪətɪ] s. ansiedad, zozobra; ansia, anhelo, afán.

anxious [ǽŋkʃəs] adj. ansioso; inquieto, preocupado; anheloso, deseoso; **-ly** adv. con ansiedad, con ansia, ansiosamente.

any [énɪ] adj. & pron. cualquier(a), cualesquier(a); alguno, algunos; **in — case** de todos modos, en todo caso; **I have not — bread** no tengo pan; **she does not sing — more** ya no canta; **he does not want to work — more** no quiere trabajar más.

anybody [énɪbadɪ] pron. alguien, alguno; cualquiera; **not . . . — no . . . nadie**, no . . . ninguno; **he does not know — no conoce a nadie**.

anyhow [énɪhaʊ] adv. de todos modos; de cualquier modo.

anyone [énɪwʌn] pron. = **anybody**.

anything [énɪθɪŋ] pron. alguna cosa; cualquier cosa; algo; **not . . . — no . . . nada**; **not to know — no saber nada**; **— you wish** todo lo que quiera Vd.

anyway [énɪwe] adv. de todos modos; en cualquier caso.

anywhere [énɪhwɛr] adv. dondequiera; en cualquier parte o lugar; en todas partes; **not . . . — no . . . en (o a) ninguna parte**; **not to go — no ir a ninguna parte**.

apart [əpárt] adv. aparte; separadamente; a un lado; adj. aislado, separado; **to take — desarmar, desmontar; to tear — despedazar, hacer pedazos**.

apartment [əpártmənt] s. departamento, piso, apartamento; vivienda, habitación.

apathy [ǽpəθɪ] s. apatía, indiferencia, indolencia.

ape [ep] s. mono; v. remedar, imitar.

aperture [ǽpətʃə] s. abertura.

apex [épɛks] s. ápice, cumbre.

apiece [əpís] adv. cada uno, a cada uno, por persona.

apologetic [əpɑlədʒétɪk] adj. que se excusa o disculpa.

apologize [əpáɪədʒaɪz] v. disculparse, excusarse.

apology [əpálədʒɪ] s. apología; excusa, disculpa, justificación, satisfacción.

apoplexy [ǽpəplɛksɪ] s. apoplejía.

apostle [əpásḷ] s. apóstol.

apostolic [æpəstálɪk] adj. apostólico.

appall [əpɔ́l] v. aterrorizar, aterrar; asombrar, espantar.

appalling [əpɔ́lɪŋ] adj. aterrador; espantoso, asombroso.

apparatus [æpərétəs] s. aparato; aparejo.

apparel [əpǽrəl] s. ropa; ropaje; vestidos.

apparent [əpǽrənt] adj. aparente; visible; claro, evidente; patente; **heir — heredero presunto; -ly adv.** aparentemente, al parecer, por lo visto.

apparition [æpəríʃən] s. aparición; aparecido, espectro, fantasma.

appeal [əpíl] s. apelación; recurso; súplica; atracción; atractivo; llamamiento; v. apelar; recurrir, acudir; atraer, despertar interés o simpatía; llamar la atención.

appear [əpír] v. aparecer(se); parecer; comparecer.

appearance [əpírəns] s. apariencia, semblante; porte, facha; aparición.

appease [əpíz] v. apaciguar, aplacar; pacificar; conciliar; sosegar.

appeasement [əpízmənt] s. apaciguamiento; conciliación.

appendix [əpéndɪks] s. apéndice.

appertain [æpətén] v. pertenecer.

appetite [ǽpətaɪt] s. apetito; gana, deseo.

9

appetizer [ǽpətaɪzə] *s.* aperitivo.
appetizing [ǽpətaɪzɪŋ] *adj.* apetecible; apetitoso.
applaud [əplɔ́d] *v.* aplaudir.
applause [əplɔ́z] *s.* aplauso.
apple [ǽpl] *s.* manzana; — **tree** manzano; Adam's — nuez (*de la garganta*); *Am.* manzana; — **of my eye** niña de mis ojos.
applesauce [ǽplsɔs] *s.* compota de manzana.
appliance [əplάɪəns] *s.* utensilio, instrumento; herramienta.
applicant [ǽpləkənt] *s.* solicitante, aspirante, candidato.
application [ǽpləkéʃən] *s.* aplicación; solicitud, petición, memorial; *Am.* ocurso.
applicable [ǽplɪkəbl] *adj.* aplicable.
applied [əplάɪd] *adj.* & *p.p.* aplicado; — **for** pedido, solicitado.
apply [əplάɪ] *v.* aplicar(se); **to** — **to** dirigirse a, acudir a, recurrir a; **to** — **for** solicitar, pedir; **to** — **oneself** aplicarse, dedicarse; **to** — **on account** acreditar en cuenta.
appoint [əpɔ́ɪnt] *v.* nombrar; designar; señalar; equipar, amueblar; **a well -ed house** una casa bien amueblada.
appointment [əpɔ́ɪntmənt] *s.* nombramiento; designación; cita, compromiso; **-s** mobiliario, mueblaje; accesorios.
apportion [əpɔ́rʃən] *v.* repartir proporcionadamente, prorratear.
apportionment [əpɔ́rʃənmənt] *s.* prorrateo, distribución, repartimiento.
appraisal [əpréz] *s.* tasa, valuación.
appraise [əpréz] *v.* avaluar, valuar, tasar.
appreciable [əpríʃɪəbl] *adj.* apreciable, perceptible.
appreciate [əpríʃɪet] *v.* apreciar; estimar; agradecer; **to** — **in value** subir de valor.
appreciation [əpriʃɪéʃən] *s.* apreciación; aprecio; valuación; agradecimiento; aumento, alza, subida (*de precio*).
apprehend [æprɪhénd] *v.* aprehender, asir, prender; comprender; percibir.
apprehension [æprɪhénʃən] *s.* aprehensión, aprensión; recelo, desconfianza, presentimiento; captura.
apprehensive [æprɪhénsɪv] *adj.* aprensivo.
apprentice [əpréntɪs] *s.* aprendiz; novicio, principiante; *v.* poner de aprendiz.
apprenticeship [əpréntɪsʃɪp] *s.* aprendizaje.
approach [əprótʃ] *s.* acercamiento; aproximación; acceso, entrada; **meth-**

od of — técnica o modo de plantear (*un problema*); *v.* acercarse, aproximarse; abordar (*a alguien*).
approbation [æprəbéʃən] *s.* aprobación.
appropriate [əprópriɪt] *adj.* apropiado, propio, apto, conveniente, a propósito; [əprópriet] *v.* apropiarse, apoderarse de; asignar (*una suma de dinero*).
appropriation [əpropriéʃən] *s.* apropiación; asignación, suma asignada.
approval [əprúvl] *s.* aprobación; asentimiento.
approve [əprúv] *v.* aprobar; asentir a.
approximate [əpráksəmɪt] *adj.* aproximado; aproximativo; **-ly** *adv.* aproximadamente, casi, poco más o menos; [əpráksəmet] *v.* aproximar; aproximarse, acercarse.
apricot [épɪkət] *s.* albaricoque; *Am.* chabacano.
April [éprəl] *s.* abril.
apron [éprən] *s.* delantal.
apropos [æprəpó] *adv.* a propósito; *adj.* oportuno; pertinente; — **of** a propósito de.
apt [æpt] *adj.* apto, capaz; pertinente, a propósito; — **to** propenso a.
aptitude [ǽptətjud] *s.* aptitud, capacidad; habilidad.
aquarium [əkwérɪəm] *s.* acuario; pecera.
aquatic [əkwǽtɪk] *adj.* acuático.
aqueduct [ǽkwɪdʌkt] *s.* acueducto.
Arab [ǽrəb] *adj.* & *s.* árabe.
Aragonese [ǽrəgəniz] *adj* &. *s.* aragonés.
arbiter [árbɪtə] *s.* árbitro, arbitrador, juez árbitro.
arbitrary [árbətrerɪ] *adj.* arbitrario; despótico.
arbitrate [árbətret] *v.* arbitrar; decidir; someter al arbitraje.
arbitration [arbətréʃən] *s.* arbitraje, arbitración.
arbitrator [árbətretə] *s.* arbitrador, árbitro; medianero.
arbor [árbə] *s.* emparrado, enramada, glorieta.
arc [ark] *s.* arco; — **lamp** lámpara de arco.
arcade [arkéd] *s.* arcada; galería; soportal.
arch [artʃ] *s.* arco; bóveda; **semicircular** — arco de medio punto; — **enemy** enemigo acérrimo; *v.* arquear(se); enarcar(se).
archaic [arkéɪk] *adj.* arcaico, desusado, anticuado.
archbishop [ártʃbʃəp] *s.* arzobispo.
archipelago [arkəpéləgo] *s.* archipiélago.
architect [árkətɛkt] *s.* arquitecto.

architectural [ɑrkətéktʃərəl] *adj* arquitectónico.

architecture [árkətektʃə] *s.* arquitectura.

archway [ártʃwe] *s.* pasadizo (*bajo un arco*); arcada, galería abovedada.

arctic [árktɪk] *adj.* ártico.

ardent [árdṇt] *adj.* ardiente; apasionado.

ardor [árdə] *s.* ardor; enardecimiento; fervor.

arduous [árdʒuəs] *adj.* arduo, trabajoso.

are [ɑr] 2ª *persona y pl. del presente de indic. del verbo* to be: eres, estás; somos, estamos; sois, estáis; son, están.

area [érɪə] *s.* área, superficie; espacio; región.

arena [ərína] *s.* arena, redondel, plaza.

Argentine [árdʒəntin] *adj* & *s.* argentino.

argue [árgjʊ] *v.* argüir; debatir; altercar; to — into persuadir a.

argument [árgjəmənt] *s.* argumento; razonamiento; sumario, resumen.

arid [ǽrɪd] *adj.* árido.

arise [əráɪz] *v.* levantarse; elevarse; surgir; provenir.

arisen [ərízṇ] *p.p. de* to arise.

aristocracy [ǽrəstákrəsɪ] *s.* aristocracia.

aristocrat [ərístəkræt] *s.* aristócrata.

aristocratic [ərɪstəkrǽtɪk] *adj.* aristocrático.

arithmetic [ərɪfəmətɪk] *s.* aritmética.

ark [ɑrk] *s.* arca; — of the covenant arca del testamento; Noah's — arca de Noé.

arm [ɑrm] *s.* brazo; arma, — in — de bracete, de bracero; *Am.* de brazo, de brazos; at -'s length a una brazada; with open -s con los brazos abiertos; *v.* armar(se).

armada [ɑrmádə] *s.* armada, flota.

armament [árməmənt] *s.* armamento.

armature [ármətʃə] *s.* armadura.

armchair [ármtʃer] *s.* silla de brazos, sillón, butaca.

armful [ármfʊl] *s.* brazada.

armistice [árməstɪs] *s.* armisticio.

armor [ármə] *s.* armadura, blindaje; coraza; arnés; *v.* blindar, acorazar.

armored [árməd] *p.p.* blindado, acorazado.

armory [árməri] *s.* armería; arsenal.

armpit [ármpɪt] *s.* sobaco.

army [ármɪ] *s.* ejército; muchedumbre; — doctor médico militar; regular — tropa de línea.

aroma [ərómə] *s.* aroma; fragancia.

aromatic [ærəmǽtɪk] *adj.* aromático.

arose [əróz] *pret. de* to arise.

around [əráund] *adv.* alrededor; en re-dor; a la redonda; en torno; en derredor; cerca; all — por todos lados; *prep.* alrededor de; cerca de; — here por aquí; to go — in circles dar vueltas, to go — the world dar la vuelta al mundo.

arouse [əráuz] *v.* despertar, *Am.* recordar (*al dormido*); excitar; promover.

arraign [ərén] *v* acusar; procesar (*a un criminal*).

arrange [əréndʒ] *v.* arreglar; disponer, colocar; acomodar, hacer arreglos (para), hacer planes (para)

arrangement [əréndʒmənt] *s.* arreglo; disposición; colocación, orden; convenio.

array [əré] *s.* arreglo, formación, orden; orden (*de batalla*), pompa; gala, atavío, *v.* formar (*tropas*); poner en orden; ataviar, adornar.

arrears [ərírz] *s. pl.* atrasos, pagos o rentas vencidos y no cobrados; in — atrasado (*en el pago de una cuenta*).

arrest [ərést] *s.* arresto, captura, aprensión; detención; *v.* aprehender o prender, arrestar; detener; llamar, atraer (*la atención*).

arrival [əráɪv[] *s.* llegada; arribo; venida; the new -s los recién llegados.

arrive [əráɪv] *v.* llegar; arribar; to — at a result lograr (*o conseguir*) un resultado.

arrogance [ǽrəgəns] *s.* arrogancia.

arrogant [ǽrəgənt] *adj.* arrogante.

arrow [ǽro] *s.* saeta, flecha.

arsenal [ársṇ̩l] *s.* arsenal.

arsenic [ársṇ̩k] *s.* arsénico.

art [ɑrt] *s.* arte, destreza; astucia; fine -s bellas artes, master of -s licenciado en letras, maestro en artes.

artery [ártərɪ] *s.* arteria.

artful [ártfəl] *adj.* artero, mañero, ladino.

artichoke [ártɪtʃok] *s.* alcachofa.

article [ártɪk] *s.* artículo; — of clothing prenda de vestir; — of merchandise mercancía, mercadería.

articulate [artíkjəlɪt] *adj.* articulado, claro, inteligible; capaz de hablar; [artíkjəlet] *v.* articular; enunciar; enlazar.

articulation [artɪkjəléʃən] *s.* articulación; coyuntura.

artifice [ártəfɪs] *s.* artificio; ardid.

artificial [artəfíʃəl] *adj.* artificial; postizo; afectado, artificioso.

artillery [ɑrtílərɪ] *s.* artillería; — man artillero.

artisan [ártəzṇ] *s.* artesano; artífice.

artist [ártɪst] *s.* artista.

11

artistic [ɑrtístɪk] *adj.* artístico; **-ally** *adv.* artísticamente.

as [əz] *adv., conj., prep.* como; mientras; a medida que, según; en el momento en que; — **far** — hasta, hasta donde; — **for** (— **to**) en cuanto a; — **if** como si; — **it were** por decirlo así; — **large** — tan grande como; — **much** — tanto como, — well tan bien; también; — **yet** hasta ahora, todavía; — **long** — you wish todo el tiempo que Vd. quiera; **strong** — **he is** aunque es tan fuerte, **the same** — lo mismo que.

ascend [əsénd] *v.* ascender; subir; elevarse.

ascension [əsénʃən] *s.* ascensión, subida.

ascent [əsént] *s.* ascenso; subida; ascensión.

ascertain [æsətén] *v.* averiguar, indagar.

ascribe [əskráɪb] *v.* atribuir, imputar, achacar

ash [æʃ] *s.* ceniza, — **tray** cenicero; — **tree** fresno; **Ash Wednesday** miércoles de ceniza; **ash-colored** *adj.* ceniciento, cenizo.

ashamed [əʃémd] *adj.* avergonzado, corrido; **to be** — tener vergüenza; avergonzarse.

ashore [əʃór] *adv.* a tierra; en tierra; **to go** — desembarcar.

Asiatic [eʒɪǽtɪk] *adj.* & *s.* asiático.

aside [əsáɪd] *adv.* aparte; a un lado; al lado; *s.* aparte (*en un drama*).

ask [æsk] *v.* preguntar; pedir; rogar; solicitar; invitar, **to** — **for** pedir; **to** — **for (about, after)** preguntar por; **to** — **a question** hacer una pregunta.

askance [əskǽns] *adv.* de soslayo; con recelo, recelosamente; **to look** — mirar con recelo; no aprobar.

asleep [əslíp] *adj.* dormido; **to fall** — dormirse; **my arm is** — se me ha dormido (entumecido *o* entumido) el brazo.

asparagus [əspǽrəgəs] *s.* espárrago.

aspect [ǽspekt] *s.* aspecto.

asphalt [ǽsfɔlt] *s.* asfalto.

aspiration [æspəréʃən] *s.* aspiración; anhelo.

aspire [əspáɪr] *v.* aspirar; anhelar, ambicionar.

ass [æs] *s.* asno, burro; pollino.

assail [əsél] *v.* asaltar, acometer, agredir.

assailant [əsélənt] *s.* asaltador, agresor.

assassin [əsǽsɪn] *s.* asesino.

assassinate [əsǽsŋet] *v.* asesinar.

assassination [əsæsŋéʃən] *s.* asesinato.

assault [əsɔlt] *s.* asalto, acometida, ataque; *v* asaltar, acometer, atacar; violar

assay [əsé] *v.* ensayar (*metales*); analizar, examinar; contrastar (*pesas, moneda*); *s.* ensaye (*de metales*); contraste (*de pesas, moneda*).

assemble [əsémbl] *v.* reunir(se), congregar(se), juntar(se); convocar; armar, montar (*maquinaria*).

assembly [əsémblɪ] *s.* asamblea; reunión; montaje (*de maquinaria*); — **hall** salón de sesiones; paraninfo.

assent [əsént] *s.* asentimiento; consentimiento; *v.* asentir; consentir.

assert [əsɜt] *v.* aseverar, asegurar, afirmar; **to** — **oneself** hacerse valer; obrar con firmeza; vindicarse.

assertion [əsɜʃən] *s.* aserción, aserto, afirmación.

assess [əsés] *v.* avaluar; tasar; asignar, imponer (*impuestos, multas, contribuciones, etc.*).

assessment [əsésmənt] *s.* avaluación, tasación; imposición (*de contribuciones, multas, etc.*); contribución, impuesto.

asset [ǽset] *s.* cualidad, ventaja; **-s** capital, fondos, caudal; haber, activo; **personal -s** bienes muebles.

assiduous [əsídʒʊəs] *adj.* asiduo, diligente.

assign [əsáɪn] *v.* asignar; señalar, designar; traspasar, ceder a favor de.

assignment [əsáɪnmənt] *s.* asignación; designación; cesión (*de bienes*); tarea (*asignada*); lección (*señalada*).

assimilate [əsímlet] *v.* asimilar(se), absorber(se).

assist [əsíst] *v.* asistir, ayudar.

assistance [əsístəns] *s.* asistencia, ayuda.

assistant [əsístənt] *s.* asistente; ayudante; auxiliar; *adj.* subordinado, auxiliar.

associate [əsóʃɪɪt] *adj.* asociado; *s.* asociado; socio; compañero; colega; [əsóʃɪet] *v.* asociar(se); relacionar.

association [əsosɪéʃən] *s.* asociación; sociedad; conexión, relación.

assorted [əsórtɪd] *adj.* surtido, mezclado, variado, de todas clases.

assortment [əsórtmənt] *s.* variedad; clasificación; surtido; colección, grupo.

assume [əsúm] *v.* asumir; tomar; dar por sentado, dar por supuesto; arrogarse, apropiarse.

assumption [əsámpʃən] *s.* suposición; toma, apropiación; presunción; asunción (*de la Virgen*).

assurance [əʃúrəns] *s.* seguridad, certeza; convicción; confianza; **life** — seguro de vida. *Véase* **insurance**.

assure [əʃúr] *v.* asegurar; afirmar; infundir confianza.

assuredly [əʃúrɪdlɪ] *adv.* seguramente;

sin duda, con seguridad.

asterisk [ǽstərɪsk] *s.* asterisco.

astonish [əstánɪʃ] *v.* asombrar, pasmar, espantar.

astonishing [əstánɪʃɪŋ] *adj.* asombroso, pasmoso, maravilloso.

astonishment [əstánɪʃmənt] *s.* asombro, pasmo, sorpresa.

astound [əstáund] *v.* pasmar; aterrar, aturdir.

astray [əstré] *adv.* fuera de camino; *adj.* desviado, extraviado, descaminado; **to go — perderse**; errar el camino; extraviarse; **to lead —** desviar, extraviar; llevar por mal camino; seducir.

astride [əstráid] *adv.* a horcajadas.

astronomer [əstránəmə] *s.* astrónomo.

astronomy [əstránəmɪ] *s.* astronomía.

Asturian [æstjúrɪən] *adj. & s.* asturiano.

astute [əstjút] *adj.* astuto, sagaz.

asunder [əsʌ́ndə] *adj.* separado; **to cut — separar**, apartar; dividir en dos.

asylum [əsáɪləm] *s.* asilo; hospicio, **orphan —** orfanato, casa de huérfanos, *Am.* orfanatorio.

at [æt] *prep.* a; en; en (la) casa de; **— last** por fin, al fin; **— once** al punto; **to be — work** estar trabajando; **to enter — that door** entrar por aquella puerta.

ate [et] *pret. de* **to eat.**

atheist [éɵɪst] *s.* ateo.

athlete [ǽolɪt] *s.* atleta.

athletic [æolétɪk] *adj.* atlético.

athletics [æolétɪks] *s.* gimnasia; atletismo; deportes.

Atlantic [ətlǽntɪk] *adj.* atlántico; *s.* el Atlántico.

atlas [ǽtləs] *s.* atlas.

atmosphere [ǽtməsfɪr] *s.* atmósfera; ambiente.

atmospheric [ætməsférɪk] *adj.* atmosférico.

atom [ǽtəm] *s.* átomo; **— bomb** bomba atómica.

atomic [ətámɪk] *adj.* atómico.

atone [ətón] *v.* expiar, purgar; reparar.

atonement [ətónmənt] *s.* expiación; reparación.

atrocious [ətróʃəs] *adj.* atroz.

atrocity [ətrásətɪ] *s.* atrocidad; maldad.

attach [ətǽtʃ] *v.* unir, juntar; sujetar, pegar, adherir; poner (*sello o firma*); embargar (*bienes*); asignar; atribuir.

attachment [ətǽtʃmənt] *s.* adhesión; apego, afición, cariño; embargo (*de bienes*); accesorio.

attack [ətǽk] *s.* ataque, asalto; acceso; *v.* atacar; acometer, embestir.

attain [ətén] *v.* lograr, conseguir, alcanzar; llegar a.

attainment [əténmənt] *s.* logro, consecución; adquisición; dote habilidad.

attempt [ətémpt] *s.* tentativa; prueba, ensayo; esfuerzo; atentado; *v.* tentar, intentar; procurar, tratar (de), probar; **to — the life of** atentar contra la vida de.

attend [əténd] *v.* atender, cuidar, mirar por; asistir a; acompañar.

attendance [əténdəns] *s.* asistencia; presencia; concurrencia.

attendant [əténdənt] *s.* acompañante; sirviente, servidor; asistente; *adj.* acompañante.

attention [əténʃən] *s.* atención; cuidado; fineza; urbanidad; **to pay —** hacer caso, prestar atención.

attentive [əténtɪv] *adj.* atento; cortés.

attest [ətést] *v.* atestiguar, atestar; certificar; dar fe.

attic [ǽtɪk] *s.* desván.

attire [ətáɪr] *s.* atavío; vestidura; vestido, traje; *v.* ataviar, adornar.

attitude [ǽtətjud] *s.* actitud; postura.

attorney [ətɔ́nɪ] *s.* abogado; procurador; apoderado; **— general** fiscal (*de una nación o estado*); **district —** fiscal de distrito; **power of —** procuración, poder.

attract [ətrǽkt] *v.* atraer; cautivar; **to — attention** llamar la atención.

attraction [ətrǽkʃən] *s.* atracción; atractivo; **-s** diversiones; lugares o sitios de interés.

attractive [ətrǽktɪv] *adj.* atractivo; seductor; simpático.

attractiveness [ətrǽktɪvnɪs] *s.* atracción; atractivo.

attribute [ǽtrəbjut] *s.* atributo; propiedad; [ətríbjʊt] *v.* atribuir, achacar.

auction [ɔ́kʃən] *s.* subasta, almoneda, remate, *Am.* vendutta; *v.* subastar; rematar.

audacious [ɔdéʃəs] *adj.* audaz, atrevido, osado.

audacity [ɔdǽsətɪ] *s.* audacia, osadía, descaro.

audible [ɔ́dəbl] *adj.* audible.

audience [ɔ́dɪəns] *s.* audiencia; auditorio, público, concurrencia.

audit [ɔ́dɪt] *v.* intervenir (*cuentas*); asistir a (*una clase*) de oyente; *s.* intervención, comprobación de cuentas.

auditor [ɔ́dɪtə] *s.* interventor (*de cuentas*); oyente.

auditorium [ɔdətórɪəm] *s.* salón de conferencias o conciertos; paraninfo.

auger [ɔ́gə] *s.* taladro, barrena.

aught [ɔt] *s.* algo.

augment [əgmént] *v.* aumentar

augur [ɔ́gə] s. agorero, v. augurar, pronosticar. **to — well** (o ill) ser de buen (o mal) agüero

August [ɔ́gəst] s. agosto.

aunt [ænt] s. tía.

auspices [ɔ́spɪsɪz] s. pl. auspicios, protección.

auspicious [ɔspʃəs] adj. propicio, favorable.

austere [ɔstɪ́r] adj austero, adusto, severo.

austerity [ɔstérətɪ] s. austeridad, severidad

Austrian [ɔ́strɪən] adj. & s. austríaco.

authentic [ɔəéntɪk] adj auténtico.

author [ɔ́ɔə] s. autor; escritor

authoritative [əɔ́rətetɪv] adj. autorizado, que tiene autoridad, autoritario.

authority [əɔ́rətɪ] s. autoridad; facultad. **to have on good** — saber de buena tinta.

authorize [ɔ́ɔəraɪz]-v autorizar

auto [ɔ́to] s. auto, automóvil.

automatic [ɔtəmǽtɪk] adj. automático; **-ally** adv automáticamente.

automobile [ɔ́təməbil] s. automóvil.

autonomy [ɔtánəmɪ] s. autonomía.

autumn [ɔ́təm] s. otoño.

autumnal [ɔtʌ́mnl] adj. otoñal.

auxiliary [ɔgzɪ́ljərɪ] adj. & s. auxiliar

avail [əvél] v aprovechar, beneficiar, **to — oneself of** aprovecharse de, s. provecho, ventaja, **of no —** de ninguna utilidad o ventaja.

available [əvéləbl] adj. disponible; aprovechable, obtenible.

avalanche [ǽvlæntʃ] s. alud, torrente.

avarice [ǽvərɪs] s. avaricia.

avaricious [ævərʃəs] adj. avaro, avariento.

avenge [əvéndʒ] v. vengar; vindicar

avenger [əvéndʒə] s. vengador.

avenue [ǽvənu] s. avenida.

aver [əvɜ́] v afirmar, asegurar.

average [ǽvrɪdʒ] s. promedio, término medio, **on an —** por término medio, adj. medio, mediano, ordinario; v. promediar, calcular o sacar el promedio, **to — a loss** prorratear una pérdida; **he -s 20 miles an hour** avanza o recorre un promedio de 20 millas por hora.

averse [əvɜ́s] adj. adverso, renuente.

aversion [əvɜ́ʒən] s. aversión; malquerencia, inquina.

avert [əvɜ́t] v apartar, desviar, evitar, impedir.

aviation [evɪéʃən] s. aviación.

aviator [évɪetə] s. aviador.

avocado [ɑvəkádo] s. aguacate.

avoid [əvɔ́ɪd] v evitar, eludir

avow [əváu] v confesar, reconocer, admitir

avowal [əváuəl] s. confesión, admisión.

await [əwét] v. esperar, aguardar

awake [əwék] adj despierto; alerto, **wide-awake** muy despierto, avispado; v. despertar(se)

awaken [əwékən] v despertar(se)

award [əwɔ́rd] s. premio; decisión, sentencia, v asignar, otorgar; conferir, adjudicar (un premio, medalla, etc.)

aware [əwér] adj consciente, enterado, sabedor, cauto, sobre aviso

away [əwé] adv lejos, fuera; adj ausente, **right —** ahora mismo, ahorita, **two miles —** a diez millas de aquí, **to give —** regalar **to go —** irse: **to take —** quitar

awe [ɔ] s. pavor, pasmo, **to stand in —** quedarse, o estar, pasmado; pasmarse; v. atemorizar, infundir pavor, maravillar

awful [ɔ́ful] adj terrible, horroroso; tremendo, impresionante; **-ly** adv. terriblemente, horrorosamente; muy.

awhile [əhwáɪl] adv (por) un rato, (por) algún tiempo.

awkward [ɔ́kwəd] adj torpe, desmañado, molesto, embarazoso; incómodo; inconveniente.

awl [ɔl] s. lezna, punzón.

awning [ɔ́nɪŋ] s. toldo.

awoke [əwók] pret. & p.p. de **to awake**.

ax, axe [æks] s hacha.

axis [ǽksɪs] (pl. **axes** [ǽksɪz]) s. eje.

axle [ǽks] s. eje (de una rueda), **front —** eje delantero, **rear —** eje trasero

aye [e] adv. sí; s. voto afirmativo.

Aztec [ǽztɛk] adj & s. azteca.

azure [ǽʒə] adj azul, s azur, azul celeste.

B

babble [bǽbl] s. balbuceo, parloteo, charla, v. balbucear, parlotear, charlar

babe [beb] = **baby**.

baboon [bæbún] s. mandril (especie de mono).

baby [bébɪ] s. nene, bebé, criatura, adj infantil; de niño; — **girl** nena; v mimar.

bachelor [bǽtʃələ] s. bachiller; soltero.

bacillus [bəsfləs] s. bacilo.

back [bæk] s espalda; lomo; revés, respaldo (de silla), espaldar; **behind one's —** a espaldas de uno, a espaldas vueltas; **in —** of detrás de, tras; **to fall on one's —** caer de espaldas, caer boca arriba. **to turn one's —**

volver las espaldas; *adj.* posterior; trasero; retrasado, atrasado, rezagado; — **pay** sueldo atrasado; — **yard** patio interior; corral; *adv.* atrás, detrás; — **and forth** de aquí para allá; **to come** — volver, regresar, **to give** — devolver; *v.* respaldar, endosar; sostener, apoyar; retroceder; hacer retroceder; **to** — **down** hacerse (para) atrás; retractarse.

backbone [bǽkbón] *s.* espinazo, espina dorsal; firmeza; apoyo, sostén.

backer [bǽkə] *s.* fiador; sostenedor, defensor.

background [bǽkgraʊnd] *s.* fondo; educación; experiencia; **to keep in the** — dejar en último término; quedarse en último término; mantenerse retirado.

backhand [bǽkhǽnd] *s.* revés; escritura inclinada a la izquierda, **-ed stroke** revés; **a -ed remark** una ironía; una indirecta.

backing [bǽkɪŋ] *s.* apoyo, garantía, endose, endoso; respaldo.

backward [bǽkwəd] *adj.* atrasado, retrasado, retrógrado; lerdo, tardo; huraño, tímido, esquivo; *adv.* = **backwards.**

backwardness [bǽkwədnɪs] *s.* torpeza, atraso; timidez.

backwards [bǽkwədz] *adv.* hacia (*o* para) atrás; de espaldas; **to go** — retroceder, andar hacia (*o* para) atrás.

bacon [békən] *s.* tocino.

bacteria [bæktíriə] *s. pl.* bacterias.

bacteriology [bæktɪriɑ́lədʒɪ] *s.* bacteriología.

bad [bæd] *adj.* malo; perverso, dañoso; podrido; **to go from** — **to worse** ir de mal en peor; **to look** — tener mal cariz, tener mala cara o mal aspecto; **-ly** *adv.* mal, malamente.

bade [bæd] *pret. de* **to bid.**

badge [bædʒ] *s.* insignia, divisa, distintivo.

badger [bædʒə] *s.* tejón; *v.* atormentar, acosar, molestar.

badness [bǽdnɪs] *s.* maldad.

baffle [bǽfl] *v.* desconcertar, confundir, frustrar, impedir.

bag [bæg] *s.* saco, bolsa, talega, costal, maleta; zurrón, morral; — **pipe** gaita gallega; *v.* ensacar; cazar; agarrar; adueñarse de; inflarse, abolsarse.

baggage [bǽgɪdʒ] *s.* equipaje; bagaje; — **car** furgón, vagón de equipajes; — **check** talón, contraseña de equipajes; — **tag** marbete, etiqueta.

bail [bel] *s.* fianza, caución, **to let out on** — poner en libertad bajo fianza, *v.* dar fianza; salir fiador; achicar (*agua*), vaciar; **to** — **out of a plane** tirarse (*con paracaídas*) de un aeroplano.

bait [bet] *s.* cebo; atractivo, aliciente; *v.* tentar, atraer; cebar; acosar, perseguir.

bake [bek] *v.* hornear, cocer al horno; calcinar.

baker [békə] *s.* panadero, pastelero, hornero.

bakery [békərɪ] *s.* panadería, pastelería, tahona.

baking [békɪŋ] *s.* hornada; cocimiento; — **powder** levadura.

balance [bǽləns] *s.* balanza, balance; equilibrio, saldo (*de una cuenta*); contrapeso; — **of trade** balanza comercial; — **of power** equilibrio político; **to lose one's** — perder el equilibrio; *v.* contrapesar; pesar; balancear(se); equilibrar, saldar (*una cuenta*).

balcony [bǽlkənɪ] *s.* balcón, galería (*de teatro*).

bald [bɔld] *adj.* calvo; pelado, sin vegetación; escueto, sin adornos; — **spot** calva.

bale [bel] *s.* bala, fardo (*de mercancías*), *v.* embalar, enfardar, empacar.

balk [bɔk] *v.* oponerse, rebelarse, resistirse; pararse de repente; negarse a seguir; encabritarse; **to** — **someone's plans** frustrar los planes de alguien.

ball [bɔl] *s.* bola, pelota; ovillo (*de estambre, etc.*); bala (*de cañón*); baile; — **bearing** cojinete de bolas; — **game** juego de pelota; beisbol; *v.* ovillar; **to** — **up** enredar, confundir

ballad [bǽləd] *s.* romance, copla, canción, balada.

ballast [bǽləst] *s.* lastre, grava (*usada en terraplenes, caminos, etc.*); *v.* lastrar, poner el lastre a (*una embarcación*).

balloon [bəlún] *s.* globo (*aerostático*).

ballot [bǽlət] *s.* balota, *Am.* boleta, cédula para votar; voto; — **box** urna electoral; *v.* balotar, votar.

balm [bɑm] *s.* bálsamo.

balmy [bámɪ] *adj.* balsámico, fragante, refrescante, suave; algo loco, chiflado.

balsam [bɔ́lsəm] *s.* bálsamo; especie de abeto.

bamboo [bæmbú] *s.* bambú.

ban [bæn] *s.* bando, proclama, excomunión; prohibición, **marriage -s** (*o* **banns**) amonestaciones; *v.* proscribir, prohibir; condenar.

banana [bænǽnə] *s.* banana; plátano; — **tree** banano; plátano.

band [bænd] *s.* banda; faja, lista, tira;

cinta; partida, pandilla, cuadrilla; **rubber** — liga de goma; *v.* unir, juntar; atar, ligar; **to** — **together** confederarse, juntarse.

bandage [bǽndɪdʒ] *s.* venda, vendaje; *v.* vendar.

bandit [bǽndɪt] *s.* bandido, bandolero.

bang [bǽŋ] *s.* golpe, golpazo; estallido; fleco (*de pelo*); **with a** — de golpe, de golpazo, de repente; con estrépito, — ! ¡pum!; *v.* golpear; hacer estrépito; cortar (*el pelo*) en fleco; **to** — **the door** dar un portazo

banish [bǽnɪʃ] *v.* proscribir, desterrar; **to** — **fear** desechar el temor.

banishment [bǽnɪʃmənt] *s.* proscripción; destierro.

banister [bǽnɪstə] *s.* balaustre; barandilla, barandal, pasamano.

bank [bǽŋk] *s.* banco, banca; orilla, banda, ribera; montón (*de tierra, etc.*); cuesta, escarpa; bajío, banco de arena; **savings** — caja de ahorros; *adj.* bancario; de banco; *v.* depositar en un banco; amontonar (*tierra o arena*); cubrir con cenizas, **tapar** (*el fuego*); ladear (*un aeroplano*); **to** — **upon** (*o* **on**) contar con

bankbook [bǽŋkbʊk] *s.* libreta de banco.

banker [bǽŋkə] *s.* banquero.

banking [bǽŋkɪŋ] *s.* **transacciones bancarias**, banca; *adj.* bancario, de banca; — **house** banca, casa de banca.

banknote [bǽŋknot] *s.* billete de banco.

bankrupt [bǽŋkrʌpt] *adj.* en quiebra, arruinado, insolvente; *v.* quebrar, arruinar.

bankruptcy [bǽŋkrʌptsɪ] *s.* bancarrota, quiebra; **to go into** — declararse insolvente; quebrar, hacer bancarrota.

banner [bǽnə] *s.* bandera, estandarte, pendón; *adj.* primero, principal, sobresaliente.

banquet [bǽŋkwɪt] *s.* banquete; *v.* banquetear.

baptism [bǽptɪzəm] *s.* bautismo; bautizo.

Baptist [bǽptɪst] *s.* bautista.

baptize [bǽptáɪz] *v.* bautizar.

bar [bɑr] *s.* barra; barrote, tranca, barrera, obstáculo; barra (*de jabón*); pastilla (*de chocolate*); tribunal; foro; cuerpo de abogados; mostrador de taberna; cantina, taberna; **sand** — banco de arena; **-s reja**; **to be admitted to the** — recibirse de abogado; *v.* atrancar (*la puerta*); estorbar, prohibir; excluir.

barb [bɑrb] *s.* púa.

barbarian [barbérɪən] *s. & adj.* bárbaro,

salvaje.

barbarous [bárbərəs] *adj.* bárbaro; salvaje; inculto.

barbecue [bárbɪkju] *s. Am.* barbacoa; *Am.* churrasco; *v.* hacer barbacoa; *Am.* churrasquear.

barbed [barbd] *adj.* con púas; — **wire** alambre de púas.

barber [bárbə] *s.* barbero; peluquero.

barbershop [bárbəʃap] *s.* barbería; peluquería.

bard [bard] *s.* bardo, vate, poeta.

bare [ber] *adj.* desnudo; descubierto; pelado; manifiesto, patente, vacío, desamueblado; — **majority** mayoría escasa; **to lay** — poner de manifiesto, hacer patente, revelar; **to ride** —**back** montar en pelo.

barefoot [bérfʊt] *adj.* descalzo, con los pies desnudos, -**ed** [bérfʊtɪd] = **barefoot.**

bareheaded [bérhédɪd] *adj.* descubierto, sin sombrero.

barelegged [bérlégɪd] *adj.* con las piernas desnudas; sin medias.

barely [bérlɪ] *adv.* apenas; escasamente; — **three pounds** tres libras escasas.

bareness [bérnɪs] *s.* desnudez.

bargain [bárgɪn] *s.* convenio, pacto, negocio, trato; ganga; — **sale** ganga, *Am.* barata; **into the** — por añadidura; de ganancia; **to make a** — cerrar un convenio; *v.* regatear; negociar; **to** — **for** regatear; contar con, esperar.

barge [bardʒ] *s.* lanchón, barca.

bark [bark] *s.* ladrido; corteza (*de árbol*), barco velero; *v.* ladrar; descortezar, quitar la corteza.

barley [bárlɪ] *s.* cebada.

barn [barn] *s.* establo, cuadra, granero, troje; pajar; **streetcar** — cobertizo para tranvías.

barnyard [bárnjard] *s.* corral; — **fowl** aves de corral.

barometer [bərámətə] *s.* barómetro.

baron [bǽrən] *s.* barón.

barracks [bǽrəks] *s. pl.* cuartel.

barrel [bǽrəl] *s.* barril, barrica, tonel, cuba; cañón (*de fusil, pistola, etc.*); *v.* embarrilar (*meter en barril*).

barren [bǽrən] *adj.* árido; estéril.

barrenness [bǽrənnɪs] *s.* aridez; esterilidad.

barrette [bərét] *s.* broche, prendedor (*para sujetar el pelo*).

barricade [bǽrəkéd] *s.* barricada, barrera; *v.* poner barricadas; obstruir el paso con barricadas.

barrier [bǽrɪə] *s.* barrera, valla, obstá-

culo.
barter [bártə] *v.* permutar, trocar, cambiar; *s.* permuta, trueque, cambio.
base [bes] *s.* base; basa; fundamento; *adj.* bajo, vil, ruin; inferior; *v.* basar, fundar; establecer.
baseball [bésból] *s.* baseball o beisbol.
basement [bésmənt] *s.* sótano.
baseness [bésnɪs] *s.* bajeza, ruindad, vileza.
bashful [bǽʃəl] *adj.* tímido, encogido, vergonzoso.
bashfulness [bǽʃəlnɪs] *s.* timidez, vergüenza, cortedad, apocamiento.
basic [bésɪk] *adj.* básico; fundamental.
basin [bésṇ] *s.* palangana, jofaina; lebrillo; tazón (*de fuente*); estanque, depósito de agua; **river** — cuenca de río.
basis [bésɪs] (*pl.* **bases** [bésiz]) *s.* base, fundamento.
bask [bæsk] *v.* calentarse (*al sol*); asolearse, tomar el sol.
basket [bǽskɪt] *s.* cesta, cesto, canasta.
basketball [bǽskɪtbɑl] *s.* basquetbol.
bass [bes] *s.* bajo (*en música*); *adj.* bajo, grave; — **drum** tambora, bombo; — **horn** tuba.
bastard [bǽstəd] *s. & adj.* bastardo.
baste [best] *v.* hilvanar; pringar (*empapar la carne con grasa*); apalear.
bat [bæt] *s.* palo, *Am.* bate (*de beisbol*); garrote; golpe, garrotazo; murciélago; *v.* apalear; dar palos; *Am.* batear; **not to — an eye** no pestañear.
batch [bætʃ] *s.* hornada; colección, grupo, conjunto.
bath [bæθ] *s.* baño.
bathe [beθ] *v.* bañar(se).
bather [béθə] *s.* bañista.
bathhouse [bǽθhaʊs] *s.* casa de baños; bañadero.
bathrobe [bǽθrob] *s.* bata de baño.
bathroom [bǽθrum] *s.* baño, cuarto de baño.
bathtub [bǽθtʌb] *s.* bañera, tina.
battalion [bətǽljən] *s.* batallón.
batter [bǽtə] *s.* batido, masa; *Am.* bateador (*de beisbol*); *v.* golpear; **to — down** demoler.
battery [bǽtərɪ] *s.* batería; acumulador; asalto.
battle [bǽtḷ] *s.* batalla, lucha, combate; *v.* batallar, luchar, combatir.
battlefield [bǽtḷfild] *s.* campo de batalla.
battleship [bǽtḷʃɪp] *s.* buque de guerra, acorazado.
bawl [bɔl] *s.* aullido, grito, *v.* aullar; gritar; pregonar; **to — out** regañar, reprender.

bay [be] *s.* bahía; ladrido, balido, aullido; — **rum** ron de laurel; — **tree** laurel; — **window** ventana saliente, mirador; **to hold at** — tener a raya; *adj.* bayo; *v.* dar aullidos, ladridos o balidos.
bayonet [béənɪt] *s.* bayoneta; *v.* traspasar; herir con bayoneta.
bazaar [bəzár] *s.* bazar; feria.
be [bi] *v.* ser; estar; quedar(se); hallarse, verse, encontrarse; — **that as it may** sea como sea; **to — cold** (**warm, hungry, right**, *etc.*) tener frío (calor, hambre, razón, *etc.*); **to — in a hurry** tener prisa; **he is to** — ha de ser; va a ser; **it is cold** (**hot, windy**, *etc.*) hace frío (calor, viento, *etc.*).
beach [bitʃ] *s.* playa, ribera; *v.* varar, poner en seco (*una embarcación*), encallar.
beacon [bíkən] *s.* faro, fanal; boya luminosa; señal.
bead [bid] *s.* cuenta (*de rosario, collar, etc.*); abalorio; glóbulo; gota (*de sudor*); -**s** rosario; collar de cuentas; *v.* adornar con abalorios o cuentecitas.
beak [bik] *s.* pico (*de ave*); espolón (*de nave*).
beam [bim] *s.* rayo (*de luz o de calor*); sonrisa; viga; vigueta; brazo (*de balanza*); **radio** — línea de radiación, radiofaro; *v.* emitir (*luz, rayos*); brillar; sonreír, estar radiante de alegría; radiar, transmitir por radio.
beaming [bímɪŋ] *adj.* radiante, resplandeciente; sonriente.
bean [bin] *s.* judía, habichuela; *Am.* frijol; *Am.* poroto; **coffee** — grano de café; **Lima** — haba; **string** — judía o habichuela verde, *Am.* ejote, poroto.
bear [ber] *s.* oso, osa, bajista (*el que hace bajar los valores en la Bolsa*), *v.* soportar; llevar; sobrellevar; tolerar, aguantar; producir; parir, dar a luz; **to — down** deprimir; apretar; **to — a grudge** guardar rencor; **to — in mind** tener en cuenta, **to — on a subject** tener relación con un asunto, **to — oneself with dignity** portarse con dignidad; **to — out** confirmar; **to — testimony** dar testimonio.
beard [bɪrd] *s.* barba, barbas; aristas (*de trigo o maíz*); -**ed** *adj.* barbado, barbudo.
bearer [bérə] *s.* portador; mensajero.
bearing [bérɪŋ] *s.* porte, presencia, relación, conexión; rumbo, orientación, **ball** — cojinete de bolas; **beyond** — inaguantable, insufrible, **to lose one's** -**s** perder el rumbo, desorientarse, **fruit-bearing** *adj.* fructífero.

beast [bist] *s.* bestia, animal.
beat [bit] *s.* golpe; toque (*de tambor*); latido, palpitación; compás; ronda (*que hace el policía*); *v.* batir; golpear; azotar; vencer, ganar; marcar (*el compás*); pulsar, latir; sonar (*tambores*); **to — around the bush** andarse por las ramas; valerse de rodeos; *pret. & p.p. de* **to beat.**
beaten [bítṇ] *p.p. de* **to beat** & *adj.* batido; vencido; fatigado; **— path** camino trillado.
beater [bítə] *s.* batidor; molinillo; golpeador; **egg —** batidor de huevos.
beating [bítɪŋ] *s.* paliza, tunda, zurra; latido, pulsación.
beatitude [bɪætətjud] *s.* beatitud, bienaventuranza; **the Beatitudes** las bienaventuranzas.
beau [bo] *s.* galán, pretendiente.
beauteous [bjútɪəs] *adj.* bello, hermoso.
beautiful [bjútəfəl] *adj.* bello, hermoso.
beautify [bjútəfaɪ] *v.* hermosear, embellecer.
beauty [bjúti] *s.* belleza, hermosura; beldad; **— parlor** salón de belleza.
beaver [bívə] *s.* castor; **— board** cartón para tabiques.
became [bɪkém] *pret. de* **to become.**
because [bɪkɔ́z] *conj.* porque; **— of** *prep.* por, a causa de.
beckon [békən] *s.* seña, llamada; *v.* llamar a señas.
become [bɪkʌ́m] *v.* sentar bien a, quedar bien a; convenir a; hacerse; ponerse; llegar a ser; convertirse en; **to — crazy** volverse loco; enloquecer; **to — angry** enojarse; **to — frightened** asustarse; **to — old** envejecer(se); **what has — of him?** ¿qué ha sido de él?; ¿qué se ha hecho él?; *p.p. de* **to become.**
becoming [bɪkʌ́mɪŋ] *adj.* propio, conveniente; decente, decoroso; **that dress is — to you** le sienta bien ese traje.
bed [bed] *s.* cama, lecho; cauce (*de un río*); fondo (*de lago o mar*); yacimiento (*mineral*); **to go to —** acostarse; **to put to —** acostar.
bedbug [bédbʌg] *s.* chinche.
bedclothes [bédkloz] *s. pl.* ropa de cama.
bedding [bédɪŋ] **= bedclothes.**
bedroom [bédrum] *s.* cuarto de dormir, alcoba, *Am.* recámara.
bedside [bédsaɪd]: **at the —** al lado de la cama; **— table** velador, mesilla de noche.

bedspread [bédspred] *s.* colcha, sobrecama.
bedtime [bédtaɪm] *s.* hora de acostarse, hora de dormir.
bee [bi] *s.* abeja; reunión (*para trabajar o competir*); **to have a — in one's bonnet** tener una idea metida en la cabeza.
beech [bitʃ] *s.* haya; **—nut** nuez de haya, hayuco.
beef [bif] *s.* carne de vaca o toro; vaca, toro (*engordados para matar*); **roast —** rosbif.
beefsteak [bífstek] *s.* bistec, biftec o bisté.
beehive [bíhaɪv] *s.* colmena; abejera.
been [bɪn, ben] *p.p. de* **to be.**
beer [bɪr] *s.* cerveza; **— tavern** cervecería.
beet [bit] *s.* remolacha, *Am.* betabel.
beetle [bítl] *s.* escarabajo.
befall [bɪfɔ́l] *v.* sobrevenir, acaecer, suceder.
befallen [bɪfɔ́lən] *p.p. de* **to befall.**
befell [bɪfél] *pret. de* **to befall.**
befit [bɪfít] *v.* convenir.
before [bɪfór] *adv.* antes; delante; al frente; *prep.* antes de; delante de; enfrente de; ante; *conj.* antes (de) que.
beforehand [bɪfórhænd] *adv.* de antemano, por adelantado, con antelación, con anticipación.
befriend [bɪfrénd] *v.* ofrecer o brindar amistad a; favorecer; amparar.
beg [beg] *v.* rogar, suplicar, pedir; mendigar, pordiosear; **to — the question** dar por sentado lo mismo que se arguye.
began [bɪgǽn] *pret. de* **to begin.**
beget [bɪgét] *v.* engendrar; causar, producir.
beggar [bégə] *s.* mendigo, pordiosero; pobre; infeliz, miserable.
begin [bɪgín] *v.* comenzar, empezar, principiar.
beginner [bɪgínə] *s.* principiante; novicio.
beginning [bɪgínɪŋ] *s.* principio; comienzo, empiezo; origen; **— with** comenzando con (*o* por); a partir de; **at the —** al principio.
begot [bɪgát] *pret. & p.p. de* **to beget**
begotten [bɪgátṇ] *p.p. de* **to beget.**
beguile [bɪgáɪl] *v.* engañar; defraudar; seducir.
begun [bɪgʌ́n] *p.p. de* **to begin.**
behalf [bɪhǽf]: **in (on) — of** por; en nombre de; a favor de; en defensa de; **in my —** en mi nombre; a mi favor; por mí.

behave [bɪhév] *v* portarse, conducirse, obrar, proceder (*bien o mal*); — **yourself!** ¡pórtate bien!

behavior [bɪhévjə] *s.* comportamiento, proceder, conducta; funcionamiento; reacción.

behead [bɪhéd] *v* decapitar, degollar, descabezar.

beheld [bɪhéld] *pret.* & *p.p. de* to **behold.**

behind [bɪháɪnd] *adv.* detrás, atrás, a la zaga, en zaga; *prep.* detrás de, tras; — **one's back** a espaldas de uno; — **time** atrasado, retrasado; **from** — por detrás, **to arrive ten minutes** — **time** llegar con diez minutos de retraso, **to fall** — atrasarse; retrasarse.

behold [bɪhóld] *v.* contemplar, mirar; —! ¡he aquí!

behoove [bɪhúv] *v.* serle necesario a uno, corresponderle a uno; atañerle a uno.

being [bíɪŋ] *s.* ser; ente, esencia, existencia, *ger. de* to be siendo, **for the time** — por ahora; por el momento.

belated [bɪlétɪd] *adj.* tardío; atrasado.

belch [bɛltʃ] *v* eructar, **to** — **forth** echar, arrojar, vomitar, *s* eructo.

Belgian [béldʒɪən] *adj* & *s.* belga.

belief [bəlíf] *s.* creencia, fe, convicción, opinión

believable [bəlívəbl] *adj* creíble

believe [bəlív] *v* creer, pensar, **to** — **in** creer en, tener fe en, confiar en.

believer [bəlívə] *s* creyente, fiel.

belittle [bɪlítl] *v* menospreciar, apocar, empequeñecer; dar poca importancia a.

bell [bɛl] *s.* campana, campanilla, **cow** — cencerro, esquila, **call** — timbre; **jingle** — cascabel, —**flower** campanilla, campánula.

bellboy [bélbɔɪ] *s* mozo de hotel, botones

belle [bɛl] *s* beldad, mujer bella.

belligerent [bəlídʒərənt] *adj* & *s.* beligerante.

bellow [bélo] *s.* bramido, rugido, *v.* rugir, bramar, berrear; gritar.

bellows [béloz] *s.* (*sing.* & *pl.*) fuelle.

belly [béli] *s.* barriga, panza, vientre, estómago.

belong [bəlɔ́ŋ] *v.* pertenecer, corresponder, **it does not** — **here** está fuera de su sitio, está mal colocado.

belongings [bəlɔ́ŋɪŋz] *s. pl.* posesiones, bienes, efectos, cosas.

beloved [bɪlʌ́vɪd] *adj* querido, amado

below [bəló] *adv* abajo, bajo; debajo, **here** — aquí abajo, en este mundo, de tejas abajo, *prep.* bajo, debajo de.

belt [bɛlt] *s.* cinturón, cintó; correa, zona; s**word** — talabarte; *v* ceñir, fajar.

bemoan [bɪmón] *v* lamentarse de, quejarse de.

bench [bɛntʃ] *s.* banco, banca; tribunal.

bend [bɛnd] *s.* curva; vuelta, recodo; *v.* encorvar(se), doblar(se), *Am.* enchuecar(se); inclinar(se); someter(se), ceder; **to** — **one's efforts** esforzarse (por), dirigir sus esfuerzos.

beneath [bɪníθ] *prep.* debajo de, bajo; indigno de; inferior a.

benediction [bɛnədíkʃən] *s.* bendición.

benefactor [bénəfæktə] *s.* benefactor, bienhechor; patrón.

beneficent [bənéfəsnt] *adj.* benéfico.

beneficial [bɛnəfíʃəl] *adj* benéfico; ventajoso, provechoso.

benefit [bénəfɪt] *s.* beneficio; provecho, ventaja; — **performance** función de beneficio, *v* beneficiar; hacer bien, **to** — **by** the advice aprovecharse del consejo, **he** -**ed by the medicine** le hizo bien la medicina.

benevolence [bənévələns] *s* benevolencia.

benevolent [bənévələnt] *adj.* benévolo.

benign [bɪnáɪn] *adj.* benigno, afable.

bent [bɛnt] *s.* inclinación; tendencia, propensión, *pret.* & *p.p* de to **bend**; *adj.* encorvado, inclinado, doblado; corvo, gacho, **to be** — **on** estar resuelto a.

bequeath [bɪkwíθ] *v.* heredar, legar, dejar en testamento

bequest [bɪkwést] *s* legado, donación.

berate [bɪrét] *v.* regañar, reñir, reprender

berry [béri] *s.* baya (*como mora, fresa, etc.*), grano (*de café*)

berth [bɜə] *s.* litera (*de un camarote*); **to give a wide** — **to** sacarle el cuerpo a, hacerse a un lado para dejar pasar.

beseech [bɪsítʃ] *v.* suplicar, rogar

beset [bɪsét] *v.* atacar; rodear; acosar; *pret.* & *p.p. de* to **beset.**

beside [bɪsáɪd] *prep.* al lado de, cerca de; además de; fuera de, **to be** — **oneself** estar fuera de sí, estar loco, **that is** — **the question** eso no hace al caso; no se trata de eso, *adv* además.

besides [bɪsáɪdz] *adv* además; *prep.* además de.

besiege [bɪsídʒ] *v* sitiar, cercar, acosar, importunar.

besought [bɪsɔ́t] *pret.* & *p.p. de* to **beseech.**

best [bɛst] *adj* mejor, *adv* mejor más, **the** — el mejor, lo mejor, — **girl**

novia, querida; — **man** padrino de boda; **at** — a lo más, cuando más, **to do one's** — hacer todo lo posible; **to get the** — **of a person** vencer o ganarle a una persona; **to make the** — **of** sacar el mejor partido de.

bestow [bıstó] v. otorgar, conferir; **to** — **gifts upon** hacer regalos (o dádivas) a; **time well -ed** tiempo bien empleado.

bet [bet] s. apuesta; v. apostar, pret. & p.p. de **to bet**.

betake [bıték] v. **to** — **oneself** encaminarse, dirigirse.

betaken [bıtékən] p.p. de **to betake**.

betook [bıtúk] pret. de **to betake**.

betray [bıtré] v. traicionar, vender, hacer traición; revelar, no guardar (un secreto); **to** — **one's ignorance** hacer patente su ignorancia.

betrayer [bıtréə] s. traidor, traicionero.

betrothal [bıtróəəl] s. esponsales, compromiso, mutua promesa de matrimonio.

betrothed [bıtróet] s. prometido, desposado, novio, novia.

better [bétə] adj. mejor, adv mejor, más, — **half** cara mitad; **so much the** — tanto mejor, **to be** — **off** estar mejor así; estar en mejores condiciones, **to change for the** — mejorar(se), **to get** — mejorar(se), restablecerse, aliviarse, v mejorar, **to** — **oneself** mejorarse, mejorar de situación.

betterment [bétəmənt] s. mejoramiento, mejora, mejoría.

between [bətwín] prep. entre, en medio de, adv en medio.

beverage [bévrıdʒ] s. bebida.

bewail [bıwél] v. lamentar; quejarse de.

beware [bıwér] v. guardarse (de), cuidarse (de), — ! ¡cuidado! ¡guárdese!

bewilder [bıwíldə] v. confundir, turbar, perturbar, dejar perplejo, **to be -ed** estar turbado o perplejo, estar desorientado.

bewilderment [bıwíldəmənt] s. perplejidad, aturdimiento.

bewitch [bıwítʃ] v. hechizar, aojar, encantar, cautivar.

beyond [bıjánd] adv. más allá, más lejos; prep. allende, más allá de, fuera de; — **my reach** fuera de mi alcance.

bias [báıəs] s. prejuicio; inclinación, tendencia, sesgo, oblicuidad; **on the** — sesgado, al sesgo, de lado; adj. sesgado, oblicuo; v. predisponer, inclinar, influir en.

bib [bıb] s. babero, pechera (de delantal)

Bible [báıbļ] s. Biblia.

biblical [bıblıkļ] adj. bíblico.

bicker [bíkə] v. disputar, reñir.

bicycle [báısıkļ] s. bicicleta; v. andar en bicicleta.

bid [bıd] s. postura, oferta, envite (en naipes), turno (para envidar), invitación; v. ofrecer (precio); mandar; invitar, convidar; rogar; envidar (en naipes), **to** — **fair** parecer muy probable, **to** — **good-bye** decir adiós; despedirse, **to**—**up** alzar, pujar (la oferta en una subasta), pret. & p.p. de **to bid**.

bidden [bídn] p.p. de **to bid** & **to bide**.

bide [baıd] v. aguardar; **to** — **one's time** esperar una buena oportunidad.

bier [bır] s. féretro.

big [bıg] adj. grande; importante; imponente; — **Dipper Osa Mayor**; — **game** caza mayor; — **sister** hermana mayor; — **with child** encinta, **to talk** — darse bombo, Am. darse corte; **big-bellied** panzudo, panzón, barrigón, **big-hearted** magnánimo

bigamy [bígəmı] s. bigamía.

bigot [bígət] s. fanático.

bigotry [bígətrı] s. fanatismo, intolerancia.

bile [baıl] s. bilis, hiel, cólera, mal humor

bill [bıl] s. cuenta, factura, proyecto de ley, cartel, anuncio; programa (de teatro), billete de banco; pico (de ave), — **of exchange** libranza, letra de cambio; — **of fare** lista de platos; — **of lading** conocimiento de embarque, — **of rights** declaración de derechos, — **of sale** escritura o acta de venta, v cargar en cuenta, enviar una cuenta a, **to** — **and coo** acariciarse y arrullar (como las palomas).

billboard [bílbord] s. cartelera.

billfold [bílfold] s. cartera.

billiards [bíljədz] s. billar.

billion [bíljən] s. billón, millón de millones, mil millones (en los Estados Unidos y Francia).

billow [bílo] s. oleada; ola grande, v alzarse en olas.

bin [bın] s. arcón, depósito, **coal** — carbonera, **grain** — granero.

bind [baınd] v. unir, juntar, ligar; amarrar, vendar, ceñir, restringir; obligar, compeler, encuadernar, empastar; ribetear (con cinta o banda).

binding [báındıŋ] s. encuadernación, ribete, cinta, **cloth** — encuadernación en tela, **paper** — encuadernación en rústica; adj. obligatorio.

biography [baıágrəfı] s. biografía.

biology [baıálədʒı] s. biología.

birch [bɜtʃ] s. abedul.
bird [bɜd] s. ave; pájaro; persona extraña o mal vista; — **of prey** ave de rapiña; — **seed** alpiste; — **shot** perdigones.
birth [bɜθ] s. nacimiento; parto; linaje; origen, principio; — **certificate** certificado (o fe) de nacimiento; — **control** control de la natalidad; limitación de partos; — **rate** natalidad; **to give** — dar a luz, parir.
birthday [bɜθde] s. cumpleaños, natalicio.
birthplace [bɜθples] s. lugar de nacimiento, suelo natal.
birthright [bɜθraɪt] s. derechos naturales o de nacimiento; naturalidad; primogenitura.
biscuit [bískɪt] s. bizcocho; galleta; panecillo.
bishop [bíʃəp] s. obispo; alfil (en ajedrez).
bison [báɪsn] s. bisonte, búfalo.
bit [bɪt] s. pedacito, trocito; pizca, miaja, migaja; poquito; bocado (del freno); taladro; **I don't care a** — no me importa un ardite; pret. & p.p. de **to bite**.
bitch [bɪtʃ] s. perra; ramera, prostituta.
bite [baɪt] s. mordedura, mordisco; bocado, bocadito; picadura (de insecto); v. morder; mordiscar; picar.
bitten [bítn] p.p. de **to bite**.
bitter [bítə] adj. amargo; agrio, acre; áspero; mordaz; **to fight to the — end** luchar hasta morir; **-s** s. pl. amargo; **-ly** adv. amargamente; con amargura.
bitterness [bítənɪs] s. amargura, amargor; rencor; aspereza.
black [blæk] adj. negro; obscuro; sombrío; **black-and-blue** amoratado, lleno de moretones; — **mark** mancha, estigma, marca de deshonra; s. negro; luto; **—out** obscurecimiento; **to put down in — and white** poner por escrito v. teñir de negro; embetunar, dar bola o betún a (los zapatos).
blackberry [blǽkberɪ] s. zarzamora, mora.
blackbird [blǽkbɜd] s. mirlo.
blackboard [blǽkbord] s. encerado; pizarrón; pizarra.
blacken [blǽkən] v. ennegrecer; obscurecer; teñir de negro: denigrar.
blackhead [blǽkhed] s. espinilla.
blackish [blǽkɪʃ] adj. negruzco.
blackmail [blǽkmel] s. chantaje, extorsión; v. ejercer el chantaje, extorsionar.
blackness [blǽknɪs] s. negrura; obscuridad.

blacksmith [blǽksmɪθ] s. herrero; **-'s shop** herrería.
bladder [blǽdə] s. vejiga.
blade [bled] s. hoja (de navaja, cuchillo, etc.); hoja (de hierba); espada; pala (de remo); aspa (de hélice); **shoulder** — espaldilla o paletilla.
blame [blem] s. culpa; v. culpar, echar la culpa a; **to be to** — tener la culpa.
blameless [blémlɪs] adj. inculpable.
blanch [blæntʃ] v. blanquear; palidecer; escaldar (almendras).
bland [blænd] adj. blando, suave.
blank [blæŋk] adj. en blanco; vacío; aturdido; — **cartridge** cartucho vacío; — **face** cara sin expresión; — **form** blanco, forma en blanco, Am. esqueleto; — **verse** verso suelto o libre; s. blanco; vacío; hueco, intermedio; papel en blanco; forma en blanco; **application** — forma (o blanco) para memorial o solicitud.
blanket [blǽŋkɪt] s. manta; frazada; cobertor; Am. cobija; Am. sarape, poncho; adj. general, inclusivo, que abarca un grupo o clase.
blare [blɛr] s. fragor; son de trompetas; clarinada; v. trompetear, proclamar; sonar (las trompetas); hacer estruendo.
blaspheme [blæsfím] v. blasfemar.
blasphemy [blǽsfɪmɪ] s. blasfemia.
blast [blæst] s. ráfaga de viento, golpe de viento; soplo repentino; trompetazo, sonido (de trompeta); silbido; explosión, detonación; carga de dinamita; — **furnace** alto horno; v. volar (con dinamita, etc.); destruir.
blaze [blez] s. llama, llamarada, incendio; resplandor; — **of anger** arranque de ira; v. arder; resplandecer; **to — a trail** abrir (o marcar) una senda.
bleach [blitʃ] s. blanqueador; blanqueo; v. blanquear(se); desteñir(se).
bleachers [blítʃəz] s. pl. graderías, Am. glorietas.
bleak [blik] adj. yermo, desierto; helado.
blear [blɪr] v. nublar (los ojos).
bleary [blírɪ] adj. nublado, inflamado, lagrimoso, lagañoso.
bleat [blit] s. balido; v. balar.
bled [bled] pret. & p.p. de **to bleed**.
bleed [blid] v. sangrar; desangrar; extorsionar.
blemish [blémɪʃ] s. mancha, tacha, defecto; v. manchar; empañar.
blend [blend] s. mezcla, entremezcla; gradación (de colores, sonidos, etc.); v. mezclar, entremezclar; graduar (colores o sonidos); entremezclarse, fundirse;

armonizar.

bless [blɛs] v. bendecir; **God — you!** ¡que Dios te bendiga!

blessed [blésɪd] adj. bendito; santo, beato; bienaventurado; **the whole — day** todo el santo día; [blɛst] pret. & p.p. de **to bless.**

blessing [blésɪŋ] s. bendición; gracia, don, beneficio.

blest blest] adj. = **bléssed.**

blew [blu] pret. de **to blow.**

blight [blaɪt] s. pulgón (parásito); tizón (honguillo parásito); quemadura (enfermedad de las plantas); roña (de las plantas); malogro; ruina; v. destruir, arruinar; frustrar (esperanzas).

blind [blaɪnd] adj. ciego; tapado, oculto; hecho a ciegas; **— alley** callejón sin salida; **— choice** selección hecha a ciegas; **— flying** vuelo ciego, vuelo a ciegas; **—man** ciego; **—man's buff** juego de la gallina ciega; s. persiana, cortinilla; biombo; venda (para los ojos); anteojera (para resguardar los ojos del caballo); **to be a — for some-one** ser tapadera de alguien; v. cegar; ofuscar; encubrir, tapar.

blinder [bláɪndə] s. anteojera, Am. visera (para caballos de tiro).

blindfold [bláɪndfold] v. vendar (los ojos); adj. vendado (de ojos); s. venda (para los ojos).

blindly (bláɪndlɪ] adv. ciegamente; a ciegas.

blindness [bláɪndnɪs] s. ceguera, cegue-dad.

blink [blɪŋk] s. pestañeo; parpadeo; guiño; guiñada; v. pestañear; par-padear; guiñar.

bliss [blɪs] s. beatitud, bienaventuranza, gloria; felicidad.

blister [blístə] s. ampolla, vejiga (en la piel o en cualquier superficie); v. am-pollar, levantar ampollas; ampollarse.

blizzard [blízəd] s. ventisca; v. ventis-car.

bloat [blot] v. inflar(se); abotagarse.

block [blɑk] s. bloque, trozo de piedra; zoquete; manzana (de casas), Am. cuadra; horma (para sombrero); estor-bo, obstáculo; grupo, sección; **— pulley** polea; **chopping —** tajo; v. estorbar; tapar; bloquear; planchar (sobre horma); parar (una pelota, una jugada); **to — out** esbozar, bosquejar; **to — the door** impedir el paso; **to — up a door** tapiar una puerta.

blockade [blɑkéd] s. bloqueo; obstruc-ción; v. bloquear.

blockhead [blákhɛd] s. zoquete, tonto,

zopenco.

blond(e) [bland] adj. & s. rubio, blondo; Am. huero, güero.

blood [blʌd] s. sangre; **— count** análi-sis cuantitativo de la sangre; **— pud-ding** (o **— sausage**) morcilla; **— relative** pariente consanguíneo; **— vessel** vena; arteria; **in cold —** en sangre fría.

bloodshed [blʌdʃed] s. matanza; derra-me, derramiento o efusión de sangre.

bloodshot [blʌdʃɑt] adj. inyectado de sangre.

bloodthirsty [blʌdθɜstɪ] adj. sangui-nario.

bloody [blʌdɪ] adj. sangriento; ensan-grentado; sanguinario, feroz.

bloom [blum] s. flor; florecimiento, floración; lozanía; color rosado (en las mejillas) v. florecer, Am. florear.

blooming [blúmɪŋ] adj. floreciente; fresco, lozano, vigoroso.

blossom [blásəm] s. flor; floración, flore-cimiento; v. florecer.

blot [blat] s. mancha, borrón; tacha; v. manchar; borrar; secar (con papel secante); emborronar, echar manchas o borrones; **to — out** borrar, tachar; destruir; **this pen -s** esta pluma echa borrones; **blotting paper** papel se-cante.

blotch [blatʃ] v. emborronar o borronear, manchar, cubrir con manchas; s. man-cha, borrón.

blotter [blátə] s. papel secante; libro borrador.

blouse [blaʊs] s. blusa.

blow [blo] s. golpe; porrazo; sorpresa, choque, desastre; soplo, soplido; fan-farrón; **to come to -s** venir a las manos; v. soplar; ventear; resoplar; sonar (una trompeta); fanfarronear; **to — a fuse** quemar un fusible; **to — one's nose** sonarse; **to — one's brains out** levantarse la tapa de los sesos; **to — open** abrirse; **to — out** apagar(se); estallar, reventar(se) (un neumático); **to—over** pasar; disiparse; **to — up** inflar, hinchar; volar (con dinamita); estallar, reventar.

blower [blóə] s. soplador; fuelle; ven-tilador, aventador.

blown [blon] p.p. de **to blow** & adj. soplado; inflado; **full-blown rose** rosa abierta.

blowout [blóaʊt] s. reventón (de neu-mático); escape violento de gas, aire, etc.

blowpipe [blópaɪp] s. soplete.

blue [blu] adj. azul; triste, melancólico;

s. azul; **the -s** melancolía, morriña, murria; *v.* azular, teñir de azul.

bluebell [blúbel] *s.* campanilla azul *(flor).*

bluebird [blúbɜd] *s.* pájaro azul, *Am.* azulejo.

bluejay [blúdʒe] *s.* gayo, especie de azulejo *(pájaro).*

bluff [blʌf] *s.* acantilado, escarpa, risco; fanfarronada; fanfarrón, farsante; *v.* fanfarronear; alardear, hacer alarde; echar bravatas; embaucar.

bluffer [blʌfə] *s.* farsante, fanfarrón.

bluing [blúɪŋ] *s.* añil *(para ropa blanca).*

bluish [blúɪʃ] *adj.* azulado, azulejo.

blunder [blʌndə] *s.* disparate, desatino; despropósito; *v.* disparatar, desatinar; equivocarse.

blunt [blʌnt] *adj.* despuntado, embotado; brusco, grosero, *Am.* claridoso; *v.* despuntar, embotar.

blur [blɜ] *s.* mancha; tacha; nube, cosa obscura o confusa; *v.* empañar, borronear, manchar; nublar, ofuscar; empañarse, nublarse.

blush [blʌʃ] *s.* sonrojo; rubor; *v.* sonrojarse, ruborizarse, ponerse colorado.

bluster [blʌstə] *v.* ventear o soplar recio *(el viento);* fanfarronear; *s.* ventolera, ventarrón, fuerte golpe de viento; jactancia, fanfarronada.

blustering [blʌstɜrɪŋ] *adj.* fanfarrón, jactancioso; — **wind** ventarrón.

boar [bor] *s.* jabalí.

board [bord] *s.* tabla, tablero; mesa; comidas; junta, consejo; cartón; **the -s** las tablas, el teatro; — **and room** cuarto y comida, pensión completa, asistencia; — **of directors** junta directiva; **bulletin** — tablilla para anuncios; **free on** — (f.o.b.) franco a bordo; **on** — a bordo; en el tren; **to go by the** — caer en el mar; perderse; ser descartado; *v.* ir a bordo; subir *(al tren);* entablar, cubrir con tablas; tomar a pupilaje, dar asistencia, pensión o pupilaje; residir o comer *(en casa de huéspedes).*

boarder [bórdə] *s.* huésped, pupilo, pensionista.

boardinghouse [bórdɪŋhaʊs] *s.* casa de huéspedes, pensión.

boast [bost] *s.* jactancia; alarde; bravata; gloria, orgullo; *v.* jactarse, alardear; hacer alarde de; ostentar.

boastful [bóstfəl] *adj.* jactancioso.

boastfulness [bóstfəlnɪs] *s.* jactancia; ostentación.

boat [bot] *s.* bote; barco, buque; lancha, chalupa.

boathouse [bóthaʊs] *s.* casilla o cobertizo para botes.

boating [bótɪŋ] *s.* paseo en lancha o bote; **to go** — pasear en bote.

boatman [bótmən] *(pl.* **boatmen** [bótmɛn]) *s.* barquero.

bob [bab] *s.* meneo, sacudida; pesa *(de metal);* **to wear a** — llevar el pelo corto *(o en melena); v.* menearse; **to** — **one's hair** cortarse el pelo en melena; **to** — **up** aparecer de repente; **to** — **up and down** saltar, brincar; cabecear *(dícese de una embarcación).*

bobwhite [bábhwáit] *s.* cordorniz.

bode [bod] *pret. & p.p. de* **to bide.**

bodice [bádɪs] *s.* corpiño, jubón.

bodily [bádlɪ] *adj.* corpóreo; corporal; *adv.* todos juntos, colectivamente; **they rose** — se levantaron todos a una, se levantaron todos juntos.

body [bádɪ] *s.* cuerpo; agregado, conjunto; gremio; carrocería *(de automóvil);* fuselaje *(de aeroplano);* — **of water** extensión de agua; — **politic** grupo político; estado.

bog [bag] *s.* pantano; tremedal; *v.* hundir(se); atascarse.

Bohemian [bohímɪən] *adj. & s.* bohemio.

boil [bɔɪl] *s.* hervor; tumorcillo; **to come to a** — soltar el hervor, hervir; *v.* hervir; cocer; bullir; **to** — **down** hervir hasta evaporar; abreviar.

boiler [bɔ́ɪlə] *s.* caldera, marmita; caldera de vapor; calorífero central.

boisterous [bɔ́ɪstərəs] *adj.* bullicioso; estrepitoso, ruidoso; tumultuoso.

bold [bold] *adj.* atrevido, osado; arriesgado; audaz; insolente; claro, bien delineado; — **cliff** risco escarpado; **bold-faced** descarado; **bold-faced type** negritas.

boldness [bóldnɪs] *s.* atrevimiento; osadía; audacia; descaro, insolencia.

bologna [bəlóni] *s.* especie de embutido.

Bolshevik [bólʃəvɪk] *adj. & s.* bolchevique.

bolster [bólstə] *s.* travesaño, almohada larga *(para la cabecera de la cama);* refuerzo, sostén, soporte; *v.* sostener, apoyar; apuntalar; **to** — **someone's courage** infundirle ánimo a alguien.

bolt [bolt] *s.* pestillo, cerrojo; perno, tornillo grande; salida de repente; rollo *(de paño, de papel);* **thunder** — rayo; *v.* cerrar con cerrojo; tragar, engullir; romper con *(un partido político);* echarse a correr, lanzarse de repente; caer como rayo; **to** — **out** salir de golpe.

bomb [bam] *s.* bomba; *v.* bombardear.

bombard [bɑmbárd] *v.* bombardear, cañonear.

bombardier [bɑmbədír] *s.* bombardero.

bombardment [bɑmbárdmənt] *s.* bombardeo, cañoneo.

bombastic [bɑmbǽstɪk] *adj.* ampuloso, altisonante.

bomber [bámə] *s.* bombardero, avión de bombardeo.

bonbon [bánban] *s.* bombón, confite.

bond [band] *s.* lazo, vínculo; ligadura; fianza, vale; obligación, bono.

bondage [bándɪdʒ] *s.* servidumbre, esclavitud.

bondsman [bándzmən] *s.* fiador.

bone [bon] *s.* hueso; espina (*de pez*); **-s** restos; osamenta; — **of contention** materia de discordia; **to make no -s about it** no pararse en pelillos; obrar francamente; *v.* deshuesar, quitar los huesos o espinas.

bonfire [bánfaɪr] *s.* hoguera, fogata.

bonnet [bánɪt] *s.* gorra; sombrero (*de mujer*).

bonus [bónəs] *s.* prima, premio, gratificación.

bony [bóni] *adj.* huesudo.

boo [bu] *v.* mofarse, burlarse (*a gritos*); — ! *interj.* ¡bu!; **-s** *s. pl.* rechifla, gritos de mofa.

booby [búbi] *s.* bobo, bobalicón.

book [buk] *s.* libro; **The Book** la Biblia; **cash** — libro de caja; **memorandum** — libreta; **on the -s** cargado en cuenta; **to keep -s** llevar los libros o la contabilidad; *v.* inscribir, asentar (*en un libro*); **to** — **passage** reservar pasaje.

bookcase [búkkes] *s.* estante, estantería, armario para libros.

bookkeeper [búkkipə] *s.* tenedor de libros, contador.

bookkeeping [búkkipɪŋ] *s.* teneduría de libros, contabilidad; **double entry** — partida doble.

booklet [búklɪt] *s.* librillo, librito, cuaderno, folleto.

bookseller [búkselə] *s.* librero.

bookshelf [búkʃelf] *s.* estante, repisa para libros.

bookshop [búkʃap] *s.* librería.

bookstore [búkstor] *s.* librería.-

boom [bum] *s.* estampido; alza, auge (*en el mercado o bolsa*); bonanza, prosperidad momentánea; *v.* rugir, resonar, hacer estampido; prosperar, medrar, florecer, estar en bonanza; fomentar.

boon [bun] *s.* don; bendición, gracia, favor; *adj.* jovial, congenial.

boor [bur] *s.* patán, hombre zafio o grosero.

boorish [búriʃ] *adj.* grosero, zafio.

boost [bust] *s.* empuje, empujón (*de abajo arriba*); — **in prices** alza o auge de precios; *v.* empujar, alzar, levantar; hacer subir.

boot [but] *s.* bota, calzado; **to** — por añadidura, de ganancia, *Am.* de pilón, *Am.* de ñapa; *v.* dar un puntapié; **to** — **out** echar a puntapiés, echar a patadas.

bootblack [bútblæk] *s.* limpiabotas.

booth [buθ] *s.* casilla, puesto.

bootlegger [bútlegə] *s.* contrabandista (*de licores*).

bootlicker [bútlɪkə] *s.* servilón, zalamero.

booty [búti] *s.* botín, saqueo.

border [bórdə] *s.* borde, margen, orilla; orla, franja; ribete; frontera; *v.* ribetear, guarnecer (*el borde*); orlar; **to** — **on** (*o* **upon**) lindar con, confinar con; rayar en; **it -s on madness** raya en locura.

bore [bor] *s.* taladro, barreno; agujero (*hecho con taladro*); calibre (*de un cañón, cilindro, etc.*); persona o cosa aburrida; *v.* taladrar, horadar, barrenar; aburrir, fastidiar; *pret. de* **to bear**.

bored [bord] *adj.* cansado, aburrido; *p.p. de* **to bore**.

boredom [bórdəm] *s.* aburrimiento, tedio, hastío, fastidio.

boring [bórɪŋ] *adj.* aburrido, fastidioso, tedioso.

born [born] *p.p. de* **to bear** & *adj.* nacido; innato; **to be** — nacer.

borne [born] *p.p. de* **to bear**.

borough [bɝo] *s.* villa; distrito de municipio.

borrow [bɝo] *v.* pedir prestado; tomar prestado; tomar fiado.

borrower [bɝəwə] *s.* el que pide prestado.

bosom [búzəm] *s.* seno, pecho, corazón; pechera (*de camisa*); **in the** — **of the family** en el seno de la familia; *adj.* querido; — **friend** amigo íntimo.

boss [bɔs] *s.* jefe; patrón; mayoral, capataz; **political** — cacique político; *v.* mandar, dominar, dirigir.

bossy [bɔsi] *adj.* mandón, autoritario.

botany [bátnɪ] *s.* botánica.

both [boθ] *adj. & pron.* ambos, entrambos, los dos; — **this and that** tanto esto como aquello; — **of them** ambos, ellos dos, los dos; — (**of**) **his friends** sus dos amigos, ambos amigos.

bother [báðə] *s.* molestia; fastidio; incomodidad; enfado; *v.* molestar(se); fastidiar, enfadar; incomodar; estorbar.

bothersome [báðəsəm] *adj.* molesto.

bottle [bátl] *s.* botella; *v.* embotellar.

bottom [bátəm] *s.* fondo; base; fundamento; asiento (*de silla*); **to be at the — of the class** ser el último de la clase; **what is at the — of all this?** ¿qué hay en el fondo de todo esto?

boudoir [budwár] *s.* tocador

bough [baʊ] *s.* rama.

bought [bɔt] *pret. & p.p. de* **to buy.**

boulder [bóldə] *s.* peña, roca, guijarro grande, pedrusco.

boulevard [búləvard] *s.* bulevar

bounce [baʊns] *s.* bote, rebote (*de una pelota*); salto, brinco; *v.* hacer saltar; saltar, brincar; botar; echar, arrojar (*a alguien*); echar, despedir de un empleo.

bound [baʊnd] *s.* salto, brinco; bote, rebote; límite, confín; *adj.* ligado; confinado; obligado; ceñido; encuadernado; **to be — for** ir para, ir con rumbo a; **to be — up in one's work** estar absorto en su trabajo; **it is — to happen** es seguro que sucederá; **I am — to do it** estoy resuelto a hacerlo; *v.* botar, resaltar, saltar, brincar; limitar, ceñir, cercar; *pret. & p.p. de* **to bind.**

boundary [báʊndərɪ] *s.* límite, linde; confín; frontera.

boundless [báʊndlɪs] *adj.* ilimitado, sin límite, sin término.

bountiful [báʊntəfəl] *adj.* generoso, liberal; abundante.

bounty [báʊntɪ] *s.* largueza, generosidad; don, favor, gracia; premio, recompensa.

bouquet [buké] *s.* ramillete, ramo de flores; aroma, fragancia.

bourgeois [bʊrʒwá] *adj. & s.* burgués.

bout [baʊt] *s.* combate, lucha, contienda, asalto; **a — of pneumonia** un ataque de pulmonía.

bow [baʊ] *s.* saludo, reverencia, inclinación; proa; *v.* hacer una reverencia, inclinarse (*para saludar*); someterse; **to — one's head** inclinar la cabeza **-ed down** agobiado.

bow [bo] *s.* arco (*para tirar flechas*); arco (*de violín*); curva; lazo, moño (*de cintas*); **bow-legged** *adj.* patizambo, patituerto; *v.* arquear; tocar (*un instrumento*) con arco.

bowels [báʊəlz] *s. pl.* intestinos; entrañas; tripas.

bower [báʊə] *s.* enramada, ramada, glorieta.

bowl [bol] *s.* cuenco; tazón; jícara; boliche, bola; **wash — palangana, lavamanos; -s** juego de bolos; *v.* bolear, jugar a los bolos, jugar al boliche.

box [baks] *s.* caja; estuche; palco de teatro; casilla; compartimiento; bofetada; **—car** furgón; **— office** taquilla; *v.* encajonar; meter en una caja; abofetear; boxear.

boxer [báksə] *s.* boxeador, pugilista.

boxing [báksɪŋ] *s.* boxeo, pugilato.

boy [bɔɪ] *s.* niño; muchacho; mozo.

boycott [bóɪkət] *v.* boycotear; *s.* boycoteo.

boyhood [bóɪhʊd] *s.* niñez; mocedad, juventud.

boyish [bóɪʃ] *adj.* pueril; juvenil; aniñado.

brace [bres] *s.* traba; tirante; apoyo, refuerzo; corchete (|̲ |̲); **carpenter's —** berbiquí; *v.* trabar; apoyar, reforzar; asegurar; estimular, fortalecer; **to — up** animarse, cobrar ánimo.

bracelet [bréslɪt] *s.* brazalete, pulsera.

bracket [brǽkɪt] *s.* ménsula, soporte, sostén; repisa; **-s** paréntesis cuadrados; *v.* colocar entre paréntesis; unir; agrupar.

brag [brǽg] *s.* jactancia; *v.* jactarse (de); hacer alarde de.

braggart [brǽgət] *adj. & s.* jactancioso, fanfarrón.

braid [bred] *s.* trenza; galón, trencilla; *v.* trenzar; galonear, guarnecer con galones.

brain [bren] *s.* cerebro; seso; **to rack one's -s** devanarse los sesos, romperse la cabeza; *v.* saltar la tapa de los sesos.

brake [brek] *s.* freno, *Am.* retranca, *Am.* garrote; **— lining** forro de freno; **to apply the -s** frenar; *v.* frenar, enfrenar, *Am.* retrancar, *Am.* dar garrote.

brakeman [brékmən] *s.* guardafrenos, *Am.* retranquero, *Am.* garrotero.

bramble [brǽmbl] *s.* zarza, breña.

bran [brǽn] *s.* salvado.

branch [brǽntʃ] *s.* rama (*de árbol*); ramo (*de la ciencia*); sucursal; bifurcación; sección; tributario (*de un río*); ramificación; **— railway** ramal; *v.* ramificarse; bifurcarse.

brand [brǽnd] *s.* marca; marca de fábrica; hechura; hierro, *Am.* fierro (*de marcar*); estigma; **brand-new** nuevecito, flamante, acabado de hacer o comprar; *v.* marcar; herrar, marcar (*con hierro candente*); difamar; **to — as** motejar de.

brandish [brǽndɪʃ] *v.* blandir; *s.* floreo, molinete.

25

brandy [brǽndɪ] *s.* aguardiente; coñac.
brass [bræs] *s.* latón, bronce; desfachatez, descaro; **-es** utensilios de latón. instrumentos músicos de metal; — **band** banda, murga.
brassière [brǝzíɾ] *s.* corpiño, sostén (*para ceñir los pechos*).
brat [bræt] *s.* mocoso.
bravado [brǝvádo] *s.* bravata; jactancia.
brave [brev] *adj.* bravo, valiente, valeroso; *v.* arrostrar; desafiar, hacer frente a.
bravery [brévǝrɪ] *s.* valor, valentía.
brawl [brɔl] *v.* reyerta, pendencia, riña; alboroto; *v.* armar una pendencia, alborotar, reñir.
bray [bre] *s.* rebuzno; *v.* rebuznar.
brazen [brézn̩] *adj.* bronceado; de bronce; de latón; descarado, desvergonzado.
breach [britʃ] *s.* brecha, abertura; violación, infracción; rompimiento; — **of faith** abuso de confianza; — **of promise** violación de un compromiso; *v.* abrir brecha.
bread [bred] *s.* pan; —**box** caja para pan; *Am.* empanizar.
breadth [bredθ] *s.* anchura, ancho; extensión; amplitud.
break [brek] *s.* rompimiento; rotura; interrupción, pausa; bajón (*en la bolsa o mercado*); **to have a bad (good)** — tener mala (buena) suerte; **to make a bad** — cometer un disparate; *v.* romper(se), quebrantar(se), quebrar(se); amansar, domar; arruinar; **to** — **away** fugarse, escaparse; **to** — **into** forzar la entrada en, allanar (*una morada*); **to** — **loose** escaparse, desprenderse, soltarse; **to** — **out** estallar (*una guerra*); **to** — **out of prison** escaparse de la cárcel; **to** — **a promise** faltar a la palabra; **to** — **up** desmenuzar, despedazar; disolver; perturbar.
breakable [brékǝbl] *adj.* quebradizo.
breaker [brékǝ] *s.* rompiente (*ola*); **law** — infractor.
breakfast [brékfǝst] *s.* desayuno; **to eat** — tomar el desayuno; *v.* desayunarse.
breakwater [brékwǝtǝ] *s.* rompeolas, malecón.
breast [brest] *s.* pecho; seno; teta; pechuga (*de ave*); **to make a clean** — **of it** confesarlo todo.
breath [breθ] *s.* aliento; resuello; respiro; soplo, hálito; **in the same** — al mismo instante, con el mismo aliento; **out of** — sin aliento, jadeante; **under one's** — en voz baja, entre dientes.
breathe [brið] *v.* respirar; resollar; tomar aliento; exhalar; **to** — **into** infundir;

he -ed his last exhaló el último suspiro; **he did not** — **a word** no dijo palabra.
breathless [bréǝlɪs] *adj.* jadeante; sin aliento.
bred [bred] *pret. & p.p. de* **to breed.**
breeches [brítʃɪz] *s. pl.* bragas, calzones; **riding** — pantalones de montar.
breed [brid] *s.* casta, raza; ralea, especie; *v.* criar; procrear, engendrar; educar; producirse; multiplicarse.
breeder [brídǝ] *s.* criador; animal de cría.
breeding [brídɪŋ] *s.* cría, crianza; educación, modales.
breeze [briz] *s.* brisa, vientecillo.
breezy [brízɪ] *adj.* airoso, ventilado; refrescado (*por la brisa*); animado, vivaz; **it is** — hace brisa.
brethren [bréðrɪn] *s. pl.* hermanos (*los fieles de una iglesia o los miembros de una sociedad*).
brevity [brévǝtɪ] *s.* brevedad.
brew [bru] *s.* cerveza; mezcla; *v.* fermentar, hacer (*licores*); preparar (*té*); fomentar, tramar; fabricar cerveza; amenazar (*una tormenta, calamidad etc.*).
brewery [brúǝrɪ] *s.* cervecería, fábrica de cerveza.
briar, brier [bráɪǝ] *s.* zarza; rosal silvestre.
bribe [braɪb] *s.* soborno, cohecho; *v.* sobornar, cohechar.
bribery [bráɪbǝrɪ] *s.* soborno, cohecho.
brick [brɪk] *s.* ladrillo; ladrillos; *v.* enladrillar.
brickbat [brɪkbæt] *s.* pedazo de ladrillo; insulto.
bridal [bráɪdl] *adj.* nupcial; de bodas; de novia; — **dress** vestido de novia.
bride [braɪd] *s.* novia, desposada.
bridegroom [bráɪdgrum] *s.* novio, desposado.
bridesmaid [bráɪdzmed] *s.* madrina de boda.
bridge [brɪdʒ] *s.* puente; caballete de la nariz; **draw**— puente levadizo; **suspension** — puente colgante; *v.* tender un puente; **to** — **a gap** llenar un vacío.
bridle [bráɪdl] *s.* brida, freno de caballo, freno, restricción; — **path** camino de herradura; *v.* embridar, enfrenar; reprimir, subyugar; erguirse, erguir la cabeza.
brief [brif] *adj.* breve, corto, conciso; *s.* sumario, resumen; informe, memorial; breve apostólico; **to hold a** — **for** abogar por; **-ly** *adv.* brevemente; en resumen, en breve.

briefcase [brífkes] s. portapapeles, cartera grande.

brigade [brɪgéd] s. brigada.

bright [braɪt] adj. brillante, claro, luciente; radiante; alegre; listo, vivo, ' inteligente; — **color** color subido.

brighten [bráɪtn̩] v. abrillantar, pulir, dar lustre; avivar(se); alegrar(se); animar(se); aclararse, despejarse (el cielo).

brightness [bráɪtnɪs] s. brillo, lustre, esplendor; claridad; viveza, agudeza, inteligencia.

brilliance [bríljəns] s. brillantez, brillo; lustre; resplandor.

brilliant [bríljənt] adj. brillante; resplandeciente; espléndido; talentoso; s. brillante; diamante.

brim [brɪm] s. borde, margen, orilla; ala (de sombrero); **to fill to the** — llenar o arrasar hasta el borde; **to be filled to the** — estar hasta los topes; estar de bote en bote; v. **to** — **over** rebosar.

brine [braɪn] s. salmuera.

bring [brɪŋ] v. traer; llevar; ocasionar, causar; **to** — **about** producir, efectuar, ocasionar; **to** — **down** bajar; **to** — **forth** dar a luz; producir; **to** — **to** resucitar; **to** — **up** criar, educar; **to** — **up a subject** traer a discusión un asunto.

brink [brɪŋk] s. borde, orilla, margen; **on the** — **of** al borde de.

brisk [brɪsk] adj. vivo, animado; fuerte; rápido; **-ly** adv. aprisa; fuerte.

bristle [brɪ́s] s. cerda; v. erizar(se); **to** — **with** estar erizado (o lleno) de.

bristly [brɪ́slɪ] adj. cerdoso; erizado.

British [brɪ́tɪʃ] adj. británico; **the** — los ingleses.

brittle [brɪ́tl̩] adj. quebradizo; frágil.

broach [brotʃ] v. traer a colación, comenzar a hablar de (un asunto).

broad [brɔd] adj. ancho; amplio, vasto, extenso; tolerante; — **hint** insinuación clara; **in** — **daylight** en pleno día; **broad-minded** tolerante; de amplias miras.

broadcast [brɔ́dkæst] s. radiodifusión, difusión, emisión; transmisión; v. difundir; radiodifundir, radiar, emitir.

broadcloth [brɔ́dklɔə] s. paño fino de algodón o de lana.

brocade [brokéd] s. brocado.

broil [brɔɪl] v. asar(se).

broke [brok] pret. de **to break**; adj. quebrado, arruinado; pelado, sin dinero; **to go** — quebrar, arruinarse.

broken [brókən] p.p. de **to break** & adj. roto; rompido; quebrado; quebrantado; arruinado; abatido; — **English** inglés champurrado o champurreado; inglés mal pronunciado.

broker [brókɚ] s. corredor, agente; bolsista; **money** — cambista, corredor de cambio.

bronchitis [brankáɪtɪs] s. bronquitis.

bronco, broncho [bráŋko] s. potro o caballo bronco, Am. redomón; — **buster** domador.

bronze [branz] s. bronce; color de bronce; v. broncear.

brooch [brotʃ] s. broche (alfiler de pecho).

brood [brud] s. pollada; nidada; cría; casta; v. empollar; **to** — **over** cavilar.

brook [brʊk] s. arroyuelo, riachuelo, Am. quebrada; v. tolerar, aguantar.

broom [brum] s. escoba; retama (arbusto); —**stick** palo o mango de escoba.

broth [brɔə] s. caldo.

brother [bráðɚ] s. hermano; cofrade.

brotherhood [bráðɚhud] s. hermandad; fraternidad; cofradía.

brother-in-law [bráðɚrɪnlə] s. cuñado.

brotherly [bráðɚlɪ] adj. fraternal.

brought [brɔt] pret. & p.p. de **to bring**.

brow [braʊ] s. ceja; frente.

brown [braʊn] adj. moreno; café; castaño; pardo oscuro; tostado; v. tostar(se).

browse [braʊz] v. hojear; ramonear, pacer, pastar (el ganado).

bruise [bruz] s. magulladura, cardenal, contusión; v. magullar(se); estropear(se).

brunet, brunette [brunét] adj. moreno, trigueño.

brunt [brʌnt] s. fuerza (de un golpe o ataque); **the** — **of the battle** lo más reñido del combate.

brush [brʌʃ] s. cepillo; brocha; pincel; matorral; roce; encuentro; v. cepillar, acepillar; rozar; **to** — **aside** desechar, echar a un lado; **to** — **up** cepillarse; repasar (una materia, una técnica, etc.).

brushwood [brʌ́ʃwʊd] s. broza; maleza, matorral, zarzal.

brusque [brʌsk] adj. brusco.

brutal [brútl̩] adj. brutal, bruto.

brutality [brutǽlətɪ] s. brutalidad.

brute [brut] s. bruto, bestia; adj. bruto, brutal; bestial.

bubble [bʌ́b] s. burbuja; borbollón; ampolla; v. borbotar; hacer espuma; bullir; **to** — **over with joy** rebosar de gozo.

buck [bʌk] s. macho cabrío, cabrón; gamo; macho (del ciervo, antílope, etc.); corveta, respingo (de un caballo); embestida; — **private** soldado raso; **to**

pass the — *Am.* pasar el fardo; *v.* cabriolear, respingar; embestir; encabritarse; bregar con (*el viento*); **to** — **up** cobrar ánimo; **the horse -ed the rider** el caballo tiró al jinete.

bucket [bÁkɪt] *s.* cubo, cubeta, balde.

buckle [bÁkl] *s.* hebilla; *v.* abrochar con hebilla; doblarse; abollarse; **to** — **down to** aplicarse con empeño a; **to** — **with** luchar con.

buckshot [bÁkʃat] *s.* posta, perdigón.

buckwheat [bÁkhwit] *s.* trigo sarraceno.

bud [bʌd] *s.* botón, yema; capullo, pimpollo; retoño; *v.* echar botones o retoños; florecer.

buddy [bÁdɪ] *s.* camarada, compañero.

budge [bʌdʒ] *v.* mover(se), menear(se), bullir.

budget [bÁdʒɪt] *s.* presupuesto.

buff [bʌf] *s.* piel de ante o búfalo; color de ante; pulidor; **blindman's** — juego de la gallina ciega; *v.* pulir, pulimentar.

buffalo [bÁflo] *s.* búfalo.

buffet [bʌfé] *s.* aparador; repostería; mostrador para refrescos; fonda de estación.

buffoon [bʌfún] *s.* bufón; payaso.

bug [bʌg] *s.* insecto; bicho; microbio.

buggy [bÁgɪ] *s.* cochecillo.

bugle [bjúgl] *s.* clarín; corneta; trompeta.

build [bɪld] *s.* estructura; talle, forma, hechura; *v.* edificar, construir; fabricar; **to** — **up one's health** reconstituir su salud.

builder [bÍldə] *s.* constructor.

building [bÍldɪŋ] *s.* edificio; construcción.

built [bɪlt] *pret. & p.p. de* **to build.**

bulb [bʌlb] *s.* bulbo (*de la cebolla y otras plantas*); planta bulbosa; **electric light** — bombilla, bujía eléctrica, ampolla, *Am.* foco, bombita.

bulge [bʌldʒ] *s.* bulto; protuberancia; panza; *v.* abultar; combarse.

bulgy [bÁldʒɪ] *adj.* abultado.

bulk [bʌlk] *s.* bulto, volumen; masa; **the** — **of the army** el grueso del ejército.

bulky [bÁlkɪ] *adj.* abultado, voluminoso, grueso.

bull [bʊl] *s.* toro; alcista (*el que hace subir los valores en la bolsa*); disparate, error; **Papal** — bula; —**fight** corrida de toros; —**fighter** torero; **bull's-eye** centro del blanco; tiro perfecto.

bulldog [bÚldɔg] *s.* perro dogo, perro de presa.

bullet [bÚlɪt] *s.* bala.

bulletin [bÚlətɪn] *s.* boletín; — **board** tablilla para fijar anuncios o avisos.

bullfrog [bÚlfrɑg] *s.* rana grande.

bullion [bÚljən] *s.* oro (*o* plata) en barras; metálico; lingotes de oro o plata.

bully [bÚlɪ] *s.* pendenciero, valentón, fanfarrón, matón; *adj.* excelente, magnífico; *v.* intimidar; echar bravatas.

bulwark [bÚlwək] *s.* baluarte; defensa.

bum [bʌm] *s.* holgazán, vagabundo; gorrón; borracho; **to go on a** — irse de juerga; *adj.* malo, mal hecho, de ínfima calidad; inútil, inservible; **to feel** — estar indispuesto, *v.* holgazanear; vivir de gorra.

bumblebee [bÁmblbi] *s.* abejorro, abejón.

bump [bʌmp] *s.* tope, choque; golpe; chichón; abolladura; hinchazón; joroba, protuberancia; *v.* topar, topetear; chocar; abollar; **to** — **along** zarandearse, ir zarandeándose; **to** — **off** derribar; matar.

bumper [bámpə] *s.* parachoques, defensa; tope; *adj.* grande, excelente; — **crop** cosecha abundante.

bun [bʌn] *s.* bollo (*de pan*).

bunch [bʌntʃ] *s.* manojo, puñado; racimo (*de uvas, plátanos, etc.*); grupo; — **of flowers** ramillete de flores; *v.* juntar(se), agrupar(se).

bundle [bÁndl] *s.* lío, bulto, fardo, hato; haz; paquete; *v.* liar, atar; envolver; **to** — **up** abrigarse, taparse bien.

bungalow [bÁŋgəlo] *s.* casita de un piso.

bungle [bÁŋgl] *v.* chapucear; estropear; echar a perder.

bunion [bÁnjən] *s.* juanete.

bunk [bʌŋk] *s.* litera, camilla (*fija en la pared*); embuste, tontería, paparrucha, papa.

bunny [bÁnɪ] *s.* conejito.

buoy [bɔɪ] *s.* boya; *v.* boyar, mantener a flote; **to** — **up** sostener, apoyar.

buoyant [bɔɪənt] *adj.* boyante, flotante; vivaz, animado, alegre.

burden [bɜ́dɳ] *s.* carga, peso; cuidado; gravamen; *v.* cargar; agobiar.

burdensome [bɜ́dɳsəm] *adj.* gravoso; pesado.

bureau [bjúro] *s.* oficina; despacho; división, ramo; cómoda; **travel** — oficina de turismo; **weather** — oficina de meteorología, observatorio meteorológico.

burglar [bɜ́glə] *s.* ladrón (*que se mete en casa ajena*).

burglary [bɜ́glərɪ] *s.* robo.

burial [bɛ́rɪəl] *s.* entierro; — **place** cementerio.

burlap [bɜ́læp] *s.* arpillera, tela burda de cáñamo.

burly [bɔ́lı] *adj.* corpulento, voluminoso, grandote.

burn [bɔn] *s.* quemadura; *v.* quemar(se); incendiar; arder; abrasar(se).

burner [bɔ́nə] *s.* quemador; mechero; hornilla.

burnish [bɔ́nıʃ] *v.* bruñir; pulir; *s.* bruñido, pulimento.

burnt [bɔnt] *pret. & p.p. de* **to burn.**

burrow [bɔ́o] *s.* madriguera, conejera; *v.* hacer madrigueras en; escarbar; socavar, minar; esconderse.

burst [bɔst] *s.* reventón, explosión; estallido; — **of laughter** carcajada; *v.* reventar(se); abrirse; estallar; **to — into** entrar de repente; **to — into tears** prorrumpir en lágrimas; **to — with laughter** estallar o reventar de risa; *pret. & p.p. de* **to burst.**

bury [béri] *v.* enterrar; sepultar; **to be buried in thought** estar absorto, meditabundo o pensativo.

bus [bʌs] *s.* autobús, ómnibus, *Am.* camión o camioneta, *Am.* guagua.

bush [buʃ] *s.* arbusto; mata; matorral, breñal; **rose —** rosal; **to beat around the —** andarse por las ramas.

bushel [búʃəl] *s.* fanega (*medida de áridos*).

bushy [búʃı] *adj.* matoso, espeso; lleno de arbustos.

busily [bízlı] *adv.* diligentemente.

business [bíznıs] *s.* negocio; ocupación; comercio; asunto; — **house** casa de comercio, establecimiento mercantil; — **transaction** negocio, transacción comercial; **to do —** **with** negociar con, comerciar con; **he has no — doing** it no tiene derecho a hacerlo; **not to be one's —** no concernirle a uno, no importarle a uno; **to make a — deal** hacer un trato.

businesslike [bíznıslaık] *adj.* eficaz, eficiente, práctico; formal.

businessman [bíznısmæn] *s.* hombre de negocios, comerciante.

bust [bʌst] *s.* busto; pecho (*de mujer*); **to go out on a —** salir o ir de parranda; *v.* reventar; quebrar; domar (*un potro*).

bustle [bʌ́st] *s.* bulla, bullicio, trajín, alboroto; polisón (*para abultar las caderas*); *v.* bullir(se); menearse; trajinar.

busy [bízı] *adj.* ocupado; activo; —**body** entremetido; — **street** calle de mucho tráfico; *v.* **to — oneself** ocuparse.

but [bʌt] *conj., prep. & adv.* pero, mas; sino; menos, excepto; sólo, no . . . más que; — **for you** a no ser por Vd.; **not**

only . . . — also no sólo . . . sino (que) también; **I cannot help —** no puedo menos de; **she is — a child** no es más que una niña.

butcher [bútʃə] *s.* carnicero; -**'s shop** carnicería; *v.* matar (*reses*); hacer una matanza o carnicería; destrozar.

butchery [bútʃrı] *s.* carnicería, matanza.

butler [bátlə] *s.* despensero, mayordomo; -**'s pantry** despensa.

butt [bʌt] *s.* culata (*de rifle*); colilla (*de cigarro*); tope, topetazo; cabezada; **the — of ridicule** el blanco de las burlas; *v.* topetear, embestir; **to — in** entremeterse; **to — into a conversation** meter baza, *Am.* meter su cuchara.

butter [bátə] *s.* manteca, mantequilla; *v.* enmantecar, untar con manteca o mantequilla.

buttercup [bátəkʌp] *s.* botón de oro (*flor*).

butterfly [bátəflaı] *s.* mariposa.

buttermilk [bátəmılk] *s.* suero de mantequilla.

butterscotch [bátəskátʃ] *s.* confite o jarabe de azúcar y mantequilla.

buttocks [bátəks] *s. pl.* nalgas, asentaderas.

button [bátn̩] *s.* botón; —**hook** abotonador; *v.* abotonar(se).

buttonhole [bátnhol] *s.* ojal; *v.* hacer ojales; **to — someone** detener, demorar a uno (*charlando*).

buttress [bátrıs] *s.* contrafuerte; refuerzo, sostén; *v.* sostener, reforzar, poner contrafuerte.

buy [baı] *v.* comprar; **to — off** sobornar; **to — up** acaparar.

buyer [báıə] *s.* comprador.

buzz [bʌz] *s.* zumbido; murmullo; *v.* zumbar; murmurar; **to — the bell** tocar el timbre.

buzzard [bázəd] *s.* buitre, *Am.* aura, *Am.* zopilote, *Am.* carancho.

by [baı] *prep.* por; cerca de; al lado de; junto a; según; — **and —** luego, pronto; — **dint of** a fuerza de; — **far** con mucho; — **night** de noche; — **the way** de paso; a propósito; entre paréntesis; — **this time** ya; a la hora de ésta; — **two o'clock** para las dos; **days gone —** días pasados.

bygone [báıgɔn] *adj.* pasado; **let -s be -s** lo pasado pasado, lo pasado pisado.

bylaw [báılɔ] *s.* estatuto; reglamento.

bypath [báıpæθ] *s.* atajo, vereda.

by-product [báıprɑdəkt] *s.* producto secundario o accesorio.

bystanders [báıstændəz] *s.* circunstantes, presentes; mirones.

29

C

cab [kæb] s. coche de alquiler; taxímetro, taxi; casilla (*de una locomotora*); — **driver** cochero; chófer.

cabbage [kǽbɪdʒ] s. col, repollo, berza.

cabin [kǽbɪn] s. cabaña, choza, bohío, barraca; camarote (*de buque*); **airplane** — cabina de aeroplano.

cabinet [kǽbənɪt] s. gabinete; armario; escaparate, vitrina.

cable [kébl] s. cable, amarra; cablegrama; — **address** dirección cablegráfica; v. cablegrafiar.

cablegram [kéb|græm] s. cablegrama.

cabman [kǽbmən] s. cochero; chófer.

cackle [kǽkl] s. cacareo; charla; risotada; v. cacarear; parlotear, charlar.

cactus [kǽktəs] (*pl.* **cacti** [kǽktaɪ]) s. cacto.

cad [kæd] s. canalla (*m.*); malcriado.

cadence [kédns] s. cadencia.

cadet [kədét] s. cadete.

café [kəfé] s. café, restaurante.

cafeteria [kæfətírɪə] s. restaurante (*en donde se sirve uno mismo*).

caffein [kǽfiɪn] s. cafeína.

cage [kedʒ] s. jaula; v. enjaular.

cake [kek] s. pastel; bizcocho; bollo; torta; *Am.* panqué; pastilla (*de jabón*); — **of ice** témpano de hielo; v. apelmazarse, formar masa compacta.

calamity [kəlǽmətɪ] s. calamidad.

calcium [kǽlsɪəm] s. calcio.

calculate [kǽlkjəlet] v. calcular; **to** — **on** contar con.

calculation [kælkjəléʃən] s. cálculo; cómputo, cuenta.

calculus [kǽlkjələs] s. cálculo.

calendar [kǽləndər] s. calendario, almanaque; — **year** año corriente.

calf [kæf] (*pl.* **calves** [kævz]) s. ternero, ternera, becerro, becerra; pantorrilla (*de la pierna*); —**skin** piel de becerro o becerrillo.

caliber [kǽləbər] s. calibre.

calico [kǽləko] s. calicó (*tela de algodón*).

call [kɔl] s. llamada; llamamiento; visita; demanda, pedido; **within** — al alcance de la voz; v. llamar; gritar; hacer una visita; pasar (*lista*); **to** — **at a port** hacer escala en un puerto; **to** — **for** ir por; demandar, pedir; **to** — **on** visitar a; acudir a (*en busca de auxilio*); **to** — **to order a meeting** abrir la sesión; **to** — **together** convocar; **to** — **up on the phone** llamar por teléfono.

caller [kɔ́lə] s. visita, visitante; llamador (*el que llama*).

callous [kǽləs] adj. calloso; duro.

callus [kǽləs] s. callo.

calm [kɑm] s. calma; sosiego; adj. calmo, tranquilo, quieto, sosegado; v. calmar, tranquilizar, sosegar; **to** — **down** calmarse; —**ly** adv. tranquilamente, con calma.

calmness [kámnɪs] s. calma, sosiego, tranquilidad.

calorie [kǽlɔrɪ] s. caloría.

calumny [kǽləmnɪ] s. calumnia.

came [kem] pret. de to come.

camel [kǽml] s. camello.

camera [kǽmərə] s. cámara fotográfica.

camouflage [kǽməflɑʒ] s. camuflaje; disfraz; v. encubrir, disfrazar.

camp [kæmp] s. campo, campamento; — **chair** silla de tijera; **political** — partido político; v. acampar.

campaign [kæmpén] s. campaña; v. hacer campaña; hacer propaganda.

camphor [kǽmfə] s. alcanfor.

campus [kǽmpəs] s. campo (*de una universidad*).

can [kæn] s. lata, bote, envase; — **opener** abrelatas; v. envasar, enlatar; v. defect. y aux. (*usado sólo en las formas* **can** y **could**) poder, saber.

Canadian [kənédɪən] adj. & s. canadiense.

canal [kənǽl] s. canal; **irrigation** — acequia.

canary [kənérɪ] s. canario.

cancel [kǽnsl] v. cancelar; anular; revocar; tachar.

cancellation [kænsléʃən] s. cancelación; anulación; revocación.

cancer [kǽnsə] s. cáncer.

candid [kǽndɪd] adj. cándido, franco, sincero.

candidacy [kǽndədəsɪ] s. candidatura.

candidate [kǽndədet] s. candidato; aspirante.

candle [kǽndl] s. candela, vela; bujía; cirio; — **power** potencia lumínica (*en bujías*).

candlestick [kǽndlstɪk] s. candelero; palmatoria.

candor [kǽndə] s. candor, sinceridad.

candy [kǽndɪ] s. dulce, confite, bombón; — **shop** confitería, dulcería; v. confitar, azucarar; almibarar, garapiñar; cristalizarse (*el almíbar*); **candied almonds** almendras garapiñadas.

cane [ken] s. caña; — **plantation** (o —**field**) cañaveral; — **chair** silla de bejuco; **sugar** — caña de azúcar; **walking** — bastón; **to beat with a** — bastonear, apalear.

canine [kénaɪn] adj. canino, perruno.

canned [kænd] adj. enlatado, envasado,

conservado (*en lata o en vidrio*); — **goods** conservas alimenticias.

cannery [kǽnəri] *s.* fábrica de conservas alimenticias.

cannibal [kǽnəb]] *s.* caníbal.

cannon [kǽnən] *s.* cañón.

cannonade [kænənéd] *s.* cañoneo; *v.* cañonear.

cannot [kǽnɒt] = **can not** no puedo, no puede, no podemos, etc.

canoe [kənú] *s.* canoa, *Am.* piragua, *Am.* chalupa.

canon [kǽnən] *s.* canon; ley, regla; criterio, norma; canónigo.

canopy [kǽnəpɪ] *s.* dosel, pabellón.

cantaloupe [kǽnt]op] *s.* melón.

canteen [kæntín] *s.* cantina; cantimplora.

canton [kǽntən] *s.* cantón, región, distrito.

canvas [kǽnvəs] *s.* lona; lienzo; toldo; cañamazo.

canvass [kǽnvəs] *s.* inspección; escrutinio; indagación, encuesta, pesquisa; solicitación (*de votos*); *v.* examinar, escudriñar; recorrer (*un distrito solicitando algo*); hacer una encuesta; solicitar votos o pedidos comerciales.

canyon [kǽnjən] *s.* cañón, garganta.

cap [kæp] *s.* gorro, gorra; boina; tapa, tapón; cima, cumbre; **percussion —** cápsula fulminante; *v.* tapar, poner tapón a; **that -s the climax** eso es el colmo.

capability [kepəbílətɪ] *s.* capacidad, aptitud.

capable [képəb]] *adj.* capaz; hábil; competente.

capacious [kəpéʃəs] *adj.* capaz, amplio, espacioso.

capacity [kəpǽsətɪ] *s.* capacidad; cabida; habilidad; aptitud; **in the — of a teacher** en calidad de maestro.

cape [kep] *s.* capa; capote; cabo, promontorio.

caper [képə] *s.* cabriola; voltereta, brinco; **to cut -s** cabriolar, retozar, hacer travesuras; *v.* cabriolar, retozar, juguetear, brincar.

capital [kǽpət]] *s.* capital (*f.*), ciudad principal; capital (*m.*), caudal; chapitel (*de una columna*); letra mayúscula; **to make — of** sacar partido de, aprovecharse de; *adj.* capital; principal; excelente; **— punishment** pena capital, pena de muerte.

capitalism [kǽpət]ɪzəm] *s.* capitalismo.

capitalist [kǽpət]ɪst] *s.* capitalista; **-ic** *adj.* capitalista.

capitalization [kæpət]əzéʃən] *s.* capitalización.

capitalize [kǽpət]aɪz] *v.* capitalizar; sacar provecho (de); escribir con mayúscula.

capitol [kǽpət]] *s.* capitolio.

caprice [kəprís] *s:* capricho.

capricious [kəpríʃəs] *adj.* caprichoso.

capsize [kæpsáɪz] *v.* zozobrar, volcar(se).

capsule [kǽps]] *s.* cápsula.

captain [kǽptɪn] *s.* capitán; *v.* capitanear, mandar; servir de capitán.

captivate [kǽptəvet] *v.* cautivar.

captive [kǽptɪv] *s.* & *adj.* cautivo, prisionero.

captivity [kæptívətɪ] *s.* cautiverio, prisión.

captor [kǽptə] *s.* aprehensor o aprensor.

capture [kǽptʃə] *s.* captura; aprensión; presa; toma; *v.* capturar; prender; tomar (*una ciudad*).

car [kar] *s.* coche, automóvil, auto, *Am.* carro; vagón (*de ferrocarril*); camarín (*de ascensor*), ascensor, *Am.* elevador; **dining —** coche comedor; **freight —** furgón, vagón de carga.

caramel [kǽrəm]] *s.* caramelo.

carat [kǽrət] *s.* quilate.

caravan [kǽrəvæn] *s.* caravana.

carbolic [karbálɪk] *adj.* carbólico.

carbon [kárbən] *s.* carbono; **— copy** copia en papel carbón; **— paper** papel carbón; **— monoxide** monóxido de carbón.

carburetor [kárbəretə] *s.* carburador.

carcass [kárkəs] *s.* esqueleto; cuerpo descarnado, despojo; res (*muerta*); casco (*de un buque*).

card [kard] *s.* tarjeta; naipe, carta; carda (*para cardar lana*); — **index** índice de fichas; fichero; **—sharp** fullero; **file —** ficha, papeleta; **post —** tarjeta postal; **pack of -s** baraja, naipes; **to play -s** jugar a la baraja, jugar a los naipes; *v.* cardar (*lana*).

cardboard [kárdbord] *s.* cartón; **fine —** cartulina.

cardinal [kárdnəl] *adj.* cardinal; principal, fundamental; rojo, bermellón; **— number** número cardinal; *s.* cardenal (*dignatario eclesiástico*); **— bird** cardenal.

care [ker] *s.* cuidado; aflicción; ansiedad; cautela; esmero; cargo, custodia; **to take — of** cuidar de; *v.* tener interés (por); **to — about** tener interés en (*o por*); preocuparse de; importarle a uno; **to — for** cuidar de; estimar, tenerle cariño a; gustarle a uno; simpatizarle a uno (*una persona*); **to — to** querer, desear, tener ganas de;

what does he — ? ¿a él qué le importa?

career [kərír] s. carrera, profesión.

carefree [kérfri] adj. libre de cuidado, sin cuidados, despreocupado.

careful [kérfəl] adj. cuidadoso; esmerado; cauteloso; **to be —** tener cuidado; **-ly** adv. cuidadosamente, con cuidado; con esmero.

carefulness [kérfəlnɪs] s. cuidado; esmero; cautela.

careless [kérlɪs] adj. descuidado; negligente; indiferente; **-ly** adv. sin cuidado; sin esmero; descuidadamente.

carelessness [kérlɪsnɪs] s. descuido; falta de esmero; desaliño; negligencia.

caress [kərés] s. caricia; v. acariciar.

caretaker [kértekə] s. cuidador, guardián, vigilante, celador.

carfare [kárfɛr] s. pasaje de tranvía.

cargo [kárgo] s. carga, cargamento; flete.

caricature [kǽrɪkətʃə] s. caricatura; v. caricaturar o caricaturizar.

carload [kárlod] s. furgonada, vagonada, carga de un furgón o vagón.

carnal [kárnl] adj. carnal.

carnation [karnéʃən] s. clavel; color encarnado o rosado.

carnival [kárnəvl] s. carnaval; fiesta, holgorio; feria, verbena.

carnivorous [karnívərəs] adj. carnívoro, carnicero.

carol [kǽrəl] s. villancico; **Christmas —** villancico de Navidad; v. cantar villancicos; celebrar con villancicos.

carouse [kəráuz] v. andar de parranda, Am. andar de farra; embriagarse.

carpenter [kárpəntə] s. carpintero.

carpentry [kárpəntrɪ] s. carpintería.

carpet [kárpɪt] s. alfombra; **small —** tapete.

carriage [kǽrɪdʒ] s. carruaje, coche; acarreo, transporte; porte; **— paid** porte pagado; **good —** buen porte, garbo, manera airosa.

carrier [kǽrɪə] s. portador; mensajero; carretero, trajinante; transportador; Am. cargador; **airplane —** portaaviones; **disease —** transmisor de gérmenes contagiosos; **mail —** cartero.

carrot [kǽrət] s. zanahoria.

carry [kǽrɪ] v. llevar; acarrear, transportar; Am. cargar; sostener (una carga); traer consigo; ganar, lograr (una elección, un premio, etc.); **to — away** llevarse; cargar con; entusiasmar, encantar; **to — on** continuar; no parar; **to — oneself well** andar derecho, airoso, garboso; **to — out** llevar a cabo, realizar; sacar.

cart [kart] s. carro, carreta, vagoncillo; v. acarrear.

cartage [kártɪdʒ] s. carretaje, acarreo.

carter [kártə] s. carretero; acarreador.

carton [kártn] s. caja de cartón.

cartoon [kartún] s. caricatura.

cartoonist [kartúnɪst] s. caricaturista.

cartridge [kártrɪdʒ] s. cartucho; **— belt** cartuchera, canana; **— box** cartuchera; **— shell** cápsula.

carve [karv] v. tallar; labrar; cincelar; esculpir; trinchar, tajar (carne).

carver [kárvə] s. trinchador; trinchante (cuchillo); entallador, escultor.

carving [kárvɪŋ] s. talla, obra de escultura, entalladura; **— knife** trinchante.

cascade [kæskéd] s. cascada, salto de agua.

case [kes] s. caso; caja; funda, cubierta, vaina; **window —** marco de ventana; **in — that** caso que, en caso de que, dado que; **in any —** en todo caso; **just in —** por si acaso.

casement [késmənt] s. puerta ventana.

cash [kæʃ] s. dinero contante; **— box** cofre; **— payment** pago al contado; **— on delivery** (c.o.d.) contra reembolso, cóbrese al entregar; **— register** caja registradora (de dinero); **to pay —** pagar al contado; v. cambiar, cobrar (un cheque).

cashier [kæʃír] s. cajero.

cask [kæsk] s. tonel, barril, cuba.

casket [kǽskɪt] s. ataúd; **jewel —** joyero, cofrecillo.

casserole [kǽsarol] s. cacerola.

cassock [kǽsək] s. sotana.

cast [kæst] s. tirada (al pescar); molde, matiz; apariencia; defecto (del ojo); reparto (de papeles dramáticos); actores; **— iron** hierro fundido o colado; v. echar; tirar; arrojar; lanzar; moldear; repartir (papeles dramáticos); escoger (para un papel dramático); **to — a ballot** votar; **to — a statue in bronze** vaciar una estatua en bronce; **to — about** buscar; hacer planes; **to — aside** desechar; **to — lots** echar suertes; **to be — down** estar abatido; pret. & p.p. de **to cast**.

castanets [kǽstənɛts] s. pl. castañuelas.

caste [kæst] s. casta; **to lose —** perder el prestigio social.

Castilian [kæstíljən] s. & adj. castellano.

castle [kǽsl] s. castillo; alcázar; fortaleza; torre, roque (en ajedrez).

castor oil [kǽstə ɔɪl] s. aceite de ricino.

casual [kǽʒʊəl] adj. casual; accidental.

casualty [kǽʒʊəltɪ] s. baja o pérdida (en el ejército); accidente.

cat [kæt] *s.* gato; gata.
catalogue [kǽtlɔg] *s.* catálogo; *v.* catalogar.
cataract [kǽtərækt] *s.* catarata.
catarrh [kətúr] *s.* catarro.
catastrophe [kətǽstrəfɪ] *s.* catástrofe.
catch [kætʃ] *s.* presa; botín; pesca; pestillo (*de la puerta*); trampa; cogida (*de la pelota*); — **phrase** frase llamativa; — **question** pregunta tramposa; **he is a good** — es un buen partido; **to play** — jugar a la pelota; *v.* coger; prender; asir; alcanzar; enganchar; comprender; ser contagioso, pegarse; **to** — **a glimpse of** vislumbrar; **to** — **cold** coger un resfriado, resfriarse; **to** — **on** comprender, caer en la cuenta; **to** — **one's eye** llamarle a uno la atención; **to** — **sight of** avistar; **to** — **unaware** sorprender, coger desprevenido; **to** — **up with** alcanzar a, emparejarse con.
catcher [kǽtʃə] *s.* cogedor, agarrador; parador, cácher o receptor (*en beisbol*).
catching [kǽtʃɪŋ] *adj.* pegajoso, contagioso; atractivo.
catechism [kǽtəkɪzəm] *s.* catecismo.
category [kǽtəgorɪ] *s.* categoría.
cater [kétə] *v.* surtir, abastecer, proveer los alimentos (*para banquetes, fiestas, etc.*) **to** — **to proveer a las necesidades o al gusto de; to** — **to the taste of** halagar el gusto de.
caterpillar [kǽtəpɪlə] *s.* oruga; — **tractor** tractor.
cathedral [kəéɪdrəl] *s.* catedral.
Catholic [kǽəəlɪk] *s.* & *adj.* católico.
Catholicism [kəéúləsɪzəm] *s.* catolicismo.
catsup [kǽtsəp] *s.* salsa de tomate.
cattle [kǽtl] *s.* ganado, ganado vacuno; — **raiser** ganadero, *Am.* estanciero; — **raising** ganadería; — **ranch** hacienda de ganado, *Am.* rancho, *Am.* estancia.
caught [kɔt] *pret.* & *p.p.* de **to catch.**
cauliflower [kɔ́ləflauə] *s.* coliflor.
cause [kɔz] *s.* causa; *v.* causar; originar; **to** — **to hacer; inducir a.
caution [kɔ́ʃən] *s.* precaución, cautela; aviso, advertencia; —! ¡cuidado! ¡atención!; *v.* prevenir, avisar, advertir.
cautious [kɔ́ʃəs] *adj.* cauto, cauteloso, cuidadoso; precavido.
cavalier [kævəlfr] *s.* caballero; galán; *adj.* orgulloso, altivo, desdeñoso.
cavalry [kǽv|rɪ] *s.* caballería.
cave [kev] *s.* cueva; caverna; *v.* **to** — **in** hundirse; desplomarse.
cavern [kǽvən] *s.* caverna.
cavity [kǽvətɪ] *s.* cavidad, hueco.

caw [kɔ] *s.* graznido; *v.* graznar.
cease [sis] *v.* cesar; parar, desistir; dejar de.
ceaseless [síslɪs] *adj.* incesante.
cedar [sídə] *s.* cedro.
cede [sid] *v.* ceder.
ceiling [síliŋ] *s.* techo (*interior*); cielo máximo *(en aviación)*; altura máxima (*en aviación*); — **price** precio máximo.
celebrate [séləbret] *v.* celebrar.
celebrated [séləbretɪd] *adj.* célebre, renombrado.
celebration [seləbréʃən] *s.* celebración; fiesta.
celebrity [səlébrətɪ] *s.* celebridad; renombre.
celery [sélərɪ] *s.* apio.
celestial [səléstʃəl] *adj.* celestial, celeste.
cell [sɛl] *s.* celda; célula; pila eléctrica.
cellar [sélə] *s.* bodega, sótano.
celluloid [séljəlɔɪd] *s.* celuloide.
cement [səmént] *s.* cemento; **reinforced** — cemento armado; *v.* unir, cementar, pegar con cemento; cubrir con cemento.
cemetery [sémətɛrɪ] *s.* cementerio.
censor [sénsə] *s.* censor; censurador, crítico; *v.* censurar (*cartas, periódicos, etc.*).
censorship [sénsəʃɪp] *s.* censura.
censure [sénʃə] *s.* censura, crítica, reprobación; *v.* censurar, criticar, reprobar.
census [sénsəs] *s.* censo.
cent [sent] *s.* centavo (*de peso o dólar*); **per** — por ciento.
centennial [senténɪəl] *adj.* & *s.* centenario.
center [séntə] *s.* centro; *v.* centrar; colocar en el centro; concentrar(se).
centigrade [séntəgred] *adj.* centígrado.
centipede [séntəpid] *s.* ciempiés, cientopiés.
central [séntrəl] *adj.* central; céntrico; *s.* (la) central de teléfonos.
centralize [séntrəlaɪz] *v.* centralizar.
century [séntʃərɪ] *s.* siglo.
cereal [sírɪəl] *adj.* cereal; *s.* cereal; grano.
ceremonial [serəmónɪəl] *adj.* ceremonial; *s.* ceremonial; rito.
ceremonious [serəmónɪəs] *adj.* ceremonioso.
ceremony [sérəmonɪ] *s.* ceremonia; ceremonial.
certain [sɝ́tn] *adj.* cierto, seguro; **-ly** *adv.* ciertamente; por cierto; de cierto; seguramente; de seguro.
certainty [sɝ́tntɪ] *s.* certeza; certidumbre; seguridad.
certificate [sɝtɪ́fəkɪt] *s.* certificado; documento; testimonio; — **of stock**

bono, obligación; **birth** — partida de nacimiento; **death** — partida (*o* certificado) de defunción.

certify [sə́tıfaı] *v.* certificar; dar fe, atestiguar.

cessation [sesés͡ən] *s.* suspensión, paro.

cesspool [séspul] *s.* cloaca, rezumadero.

chafe [t͡ʃef] *s.* rozadura; irritación, molestia; *v.* rozar(se); frotar; irritar(se).

chaff [t͡ʃæf] *s.* hollejo, cáscara; *v.* embromar, bromear.

chagrin [ʃəgrín] *s.* mortificación, desazón, pesar; **-ed** *p.p.* mortificado, afligido.

chain [t͡ʃen] *s.* cadena; — **of mountains** cordillera; — **store** tienda sucursal (*una entre muchas de una misma empresa*); *v.* encadenar.

chair [t͡ʃer] *s.* silla; cátedra; presidencia; **arm** — sillón (de brazos); **easy** — butaca, poltrona; **folding** — silla de tijera; **rocking** — mecedora.

chairman [t͡ʃérmən] *s.* presidente (*de una junta*).

chairmanship [t͡ʃérmənʃıp] *s.* presidencia (*de una junta*).

chalice [t͡ʃǽlıs] *s.* cáliz (*vaso sagrado*).

chalk [t͡ʃɔk] *s.* tiza, yeso; greda; *v.* enyesar; marcar con tiza o yeso; **to** — **down** apuntar con tiza o yeso (*en el pizarrón*); **to** — **out** bosquejar, esbozar con tiza.

chalky [t͡ʃɔ́kı] *adj.* yesoso; blanco.

challenge [t͡ʃǽlındʒ] *s.* desafío; reto; demanda; *v.* desafiar, retar; disputar, poner a prueba; dar el quienvive.

chamber [t͡ʃémbə] *s.* cámara; aposento.

chambermaid [t͡ʃémbəmed] *s.* camarera, sirvienta.

chamois [ʃǽmı] *s.* gamuza.

champion [t͡ʃǽmpıən] *s.* campeón; defensor; *v.* defender.

championship [t͡ʃǽmpıənʃıp] *s.* campeonato.

chance [t͡ʃæns] *s.* oportunidad, ocasión; probabilidad, posibilidad; suerte, fortuna; casualidad, azar; riesgo; billete de rifa o lotería; **by** — por casualidad; **game of** — juego de azar; **to run a** — correr riesgo; *adj.* casual, accidental; *v.* arriesgar; **to** — **to** acertar a, hacer (*algo*) por casualidad.

chancellor [t͡ʃǽnsələ] *s.* canciller; primer ministro; magistrado; rector de universidad.

chandelier [ʃænd]ír] *s.* araña de luces, *Am.* candil.

change [t͡ʃendʒ] *s.* cambio; mudanza; alteración; vuelta (*dinero devuelto*), *Am.* vuelto; suelto, moneda suelta; muda de ropa; **the** — **of life** la menopausia; *v.* cambiar; mudar; alterar; **to** — **clothes** mudar de ropa; **to** — **trains** transbordar(se), cambiar de tren.

changeable [t͡ʃéndʒəbl] *adj.* mudable, variable; inconstante; — **silk** seda tornasolada.

channel [t͡ʃǽnl] *s.* canal; cauce.

chant [t͡ʃænt] *s.* canto llano o gregoriano; sonsonete; *v.* cantar (*psalmos, himnos, etc.*).

chaos [kéəs] *s.* caos; desorden.

chaotic [keátık] *adj.* caótico.

chap [t͡ʃæp] *s.* grieta, raja, rajadura (*en la piel*); chico; **what a fine** — **he is!** ¡qué buen tipo (*o* sujeto) es!; *v.* agrietarse, rajarse (*la piel*).

chapel [t͡ʃǽpl] *s.* capilla.

chaperon(e) [ʃǽpərən] *s.* acompañante, persona de respeto; **to go along as a** — *Am.* ir de moscón; *v.* acompañar, servir de acompañante.

chaplain [t͡ʃǽplın] *s.* capellán; **army** — capellán castrense.

chapter [t͡ʃǽptə] *s.* capítulo; cabildo (*de una catedral*).

char [t͡ʃɑr] *v.* requemar, carbonizar.

character [kǽrıktə] *s.* carácter; personaje.

characteristic [kærıktərístık] *adj.* característico; típico; *s.* característica, rasgo característico; distintivo; peculiaridad.

characterize [kǽrıktəraız] *v.* caracterizar.

charcoal [t͡ʃárkol] *s.* carbón; carboncillo (*para dibujar*); — **drawing** dibujo al carbón.

charge [t͡ʃɑrdʒ] *s.* carga; peso; embestida, asalto, ataque; cargo, acusación; cuidado, custodia; encargo; mandato; precio, coste; — **account** cuenta abierta; — **prepaid** porte pagado; **under my** — a mi cargo; **to be in** — of estar encargado de; *v.* cargar; cargar en cuenta; cobrar (*precio*); mandar; exhortar; atacar, embestir, asaltar; **to** — **with murder** acusar de homicidio.

charger [t͡ʃárdʒə] *s.* cargador (*de batería*); caballo de guerra, corcel.

chariot [t͡ʃérıət] *s.* carroza; carruaje.

charitable [t͡ʃérətəbl] *adj.* caritativo.

charity [t͡ʃérıtı] *s.* caridad; limosna; beneficencia.

charlatan [ʃárlətn] *s.* charlatán; farsante.

charm [t͡ʃɑrm] *s.* encanto; atractivo; hechizo; talismán; **watch** — dije; *v.* encantar; cautivar; hechizar.

charming [t͡ʃármıŋ] *adj.* encantador,

atractivo.

chart [tʃɑrt] *s.* carta (*hidrográfica o de navegar*); mapa; gráfica, representación gráfica; *v.* cartografiar, delinear mapas o cartas; **to — a course** trazar o planear una ruta o derrotero.

charter [tʃɑrtə] *s.* carta constitucional, constitución, código; título; carta de privilegio; **— member** socio fundador; *v.* fletar (*un barco*); alquilar (*un ómnibus*).

chase [tʃes] *s.* caza; persecución; *v.* cazar; perseguir; **to — away** ahuyentar.

chasm [kæzəm] *s.* abismo; vacío.

chaste [tʃest] *adj.* casto; honesto; puro.

chastise [tʃæstáiz] *v.* castigar.

chastisement [tʃæstáizmənt] *s.* castigo, escarmiento.

chastity [tʃǽstəti] *s.* castidad; honestidad; pureza.

chat [tʃæt] *s.* charla, plática; *v.* charlar, platicar.

chattels [tʃǽt|z] *s. pl.* enseres, bienes muebles.

chatter [tʃǽtə] *s.* charla, parloteo; castañeteo (*de los dientes*); chirrido (*de aves*); *v.* charlar, parlotear, cotorrear; castañetear (*los dientes*).

chauffeur [ʃófə] *s.* chófer, cochero de automóvil.

cheap [tʃip] *adj.* barato; cursi, de mal gusto; **to feel —** sentir vergüenza; **-ly** *adv.* barato, a poco precio.

cheapen [tʃípən] *v.* abaratar.

cheapness [tʃípnɪs] *s.* baratura; cursilería.

cheat [tʃit] *s.* fraude, engaño; trampa; trampista, tramposo; estafador; embaucador; *v.* engañar; trampear; embaucar; estafar.

check [tʃek] *s.* cheque (*de banco*); talón, marbete, contraseña (*de equipajes, etc.*); marca, señal; cuenta (*de restaurante*); restricción, represión; cuadro (*de un tejido o tela*); comprobación; jaque (*en ajedrez*); **—room** vestuario; depósito de equipajes, *Am.* consigna; *v.* refrenar, reprimir, restringir; facturar, depositar (*equipajes*); inspeccionar; confrontar, comprobar; marcar (*con una señal*); dar jaque (*en ajedrez*); **to — out of a hotel** desocupar el cuarto o alojamiento de un hotel.

checkbook [tʃékbʊk] *s.* libreta de cheques; libro talonario.

checker [tʃékə] *s.* cuadro; casilla (*de un tablero de ajedrez, etc.*); pieza (*del juego de damas*); comprobador; inspector; **-s** juego de damas; **—board** tablero; *v.* cuadricular, marcar con cuadritos.

-ed career vida azarosa, vida llena de variedad; **-ed cloth** paño o tela a cuadros.

cheek [tʃik] *s.* mejilla, carrillo; cachete; descaro, desfachatez; **fat —** mejilla gorda, moflete; **— bone** pómulo.

cheer [tʃɪr] *s.* alegría; buen ánimo, jovialidad; consuelo; **-s** aplausos, vivas; *v.* alegrar, alentar, animar; aplaudir, vitorear; **to — up** alentar, dar ánimo; cobrar ánimo, animarse.

cheerful [tʃírfəl] *adj.* animado, alegre, jovial; **-ly** *adv.* alegremente, con alegría, con júbilo; de buena gana, de buen grado.

cheerfulness [tʃírfəlnɪs] *s.* jovialidad, alegría; buen humor.

cheerily [tʃírəli] = **cheerfully**.

cheerless [tʃírlɪs] *adj.* abatido, desalentado, desanimado; triste, sombrío.

cheery [tʃírɪ] = **cheerful**.

cheese [tʃiz] *s.* queso; **cottage —** requesón.

chemical [kémɪk|] *adj.* químico; *s.* producto químico.

chemist [kémɪst] *s.* químico.

chemistry [kémɪstrɪ] *s.* química.

cherish [tʃérɪʃ] *v.* acariciar, abrigar (*una esperanza, un ideal, etc.*); apreciar.

cherry [tʃérɪ] *s.* cereza; **— tree** cerezo.

chess [tʃes] *s.* ajedrez; **—board** tablero de ajedrez.

chest [tʃest] *s.* cofre, arca; caja; pecho; **— of drawers** cómoda.

chestnut [tʃésnət] *s.* castaña; **— tree** castaño; *adj.* castaño; **— horse** caballo zaino.

chew [tʃu] *s.* mascada, mordisco, bocado; *v.* mascar, masticar.

chewing gum [tʃúɪŋ gʌm] *s.* goma de mascar; *Am.* chicle.

chick [tʃɪk] *s.* polluelo, pollito; pajarito; **chick-pea** garbanzo.

chicken [tʃɪkɪn] *s.* pollo; polluelo; **— pox** viruelas locas; **chicken-hearted** cobarde, gallina.

chide [tʃaɪd] *v.* regañar, reprender, reprobar.

chief [tʃif] *s.* jefe, caudillo; cacique (*de una tribu*); **commander in —** comandante en jefe; *adj.* principal; **— clerk** oficial mayor; **— justice** presidente de la corte suprema; **-ly** *adv.* principalmente, mayormente; sobre todo.

chiffon [ʃɪfán] *s.* gasa.

chilblain [tʃílblen] *s.* sabañón.

child [tʃaɪld] *s.* niño, niña; hijo, hija; **-'s play** cosa de niños; **to be with —** estar encinta.

childbirth [tʃáɪldbɜθ] *s.* parto, alumbramiento.

childhood [tʃáɪldhʊd] s. niñez, infancia.

childish [tʃáɪldɪʃ] *adj.* pueril; infantil; — **action** niñería, niñada.

childless [tʃáɪldlɪs] *adj.* sin hijos.

childlike [tʃáɪldlaɪk] *adj.* como niño, aniñado, pueril.

children [tʃíldrən] *pl. de* child.

Chilean [tʃílɪən] *adj. & s.* chileno.

chili [tʃílɪ] s. *Am.* chile, *Am.* ají.

chill [tʃɪl] s. frío, resfrío; enfriamiento; escalofrío, calofrío; -s **and fever** escalofríos; *adj.* frío; *v.* resfriar(se); enfriar(se); **to become** -ed resfriarse, escalofriarse.

chilly [tʃílɪ] *adj.* frío; friolento.

chime [tʃaɪm] s. repique, campaneo; -s órgano de campanas, juego de campanas; *v.* repicar, campanear; tocar, sonar, tañer (*las campanas*); **to —** **with** estar en armonía con.

chimney [tʃímnɪ] s. chimenea; **lamp —** tubo de lámpara, *Am.* bombilla.

chin [tʃɪn] s. barba.

china [tʃáɪnə] s. loza de china, porcelana, loza fina; vajilla de porcelana; — **closet** chinero.

chinaware [tʃáɪnəwer] = **china.**

Chinese [tʃaɪníz] *adj.* chino; s. chino; idioma chino.

chink [tʃɪŋk] s. grieta, hendidura.

chip [tʃɪp] s. astilla, brizna; fragmento; desconchadura; desportilladura; ficha (*de pócar*); *v.* astillar; desconchar(se); descascarar(se); desportillar(se); picar, tajar (*con cincel o hacha*); **to — in** contribuir con su cuota.

chipmunk [tʃípmʌŋk] s. especie de ardilla.

chirp [tʃɜrp] s. chirrido; pío; gorjeo; *v.* chirriar; piar; pipiar; gorjear.

chisel [tʃízļ] s. cincel; *v.* cincelar; sisar, estafar.

chivalrous [ʃívļrəs] *adj.* caballeresco, caballeroso, galante, cortés.

chivalry [ʃívļrɪ] s. caballería; caballerosidad.

chlorine [klórin] s. cloro.

chloroform [klórəform] s. cloroformo.

chocolate [tʃókļɪt] s. chocolate; — **pot** chocolatera.

choice [tʃɔɪs] s. selección; preferencia; escogimiento; cosa elegida; favorito, preferido; alternativa; **to have no other —** no tener otra alternativa; *adj.* selecto; bien escogido; excelente.

choir [kwaɪr] s. coro.

choke [tʃok] s. sofoco, ahogo; tos ahogada; estrangulación; estrangulador, obturador (*de automóvil*) *v.* sofocar(se),

---

ahogar(se); estrangular(se); obstruir, tapar; regularizar (*el motor*).

cholera [kálərə] s. cólera (*m.*).

choose [tʃuz] *v.* escoger; elegir, seleccionar; **to — to** optar por; preferir; **I do not — to do it** no se me antoja (o no es mi gusto) hacerlo.

chop [tʃap] s. chuleta, costilla, tajada (*de carne*); -s quijadas (*usualmente de animal*); *v.* tajar, cortar; picar, desmenuzar (*carne*).

choppy [tʃápɪ] *adj.* picado, agitado.

choral [kórəl] *adj.* coral.

chord [kɔrd] s. cuerda; acorde.

chore [tʃor] s. tarea; quehacer.

chorus [kórəs] s. coro; *v.* cantar o hablar en coro; contestar a una voz.

chose [tʃoz] *pret. de* to choose.

chosen [tʃózṇ] *p.p. de* to choose.

christen [krísṇ] *v.* bautizar.

christening [krísṇɪŋ] s. bautizo, bautismo.

Christian [krístʃən] s. & *adj.* cristiano; — **name** nombre de pila o bautismo.

Christianity [krɪstʃiǽnɪtɪ] s. cristiandad, cristianismo.

Christmas [krísməs] s. Navidad, Pascua de Navidad; — **Eve** Nochebuena; — **gift** regalo de Navidad; aguinaldo; **Merry —!** ¡Felices Navidades! ¡Felices Pascuas!

chronic [kránɪk] *adj.* crónico.

chronicle [kránɪkļ] s. crónica; *v.* relatar; escribir la crónica de.

chronicler [kránɪklə] s. cronista.

chronological [kranəládʒɪk!] *adj.* cronológico.

chronometer [krənámətə]s. cronómetro.

chrysanthemum [krɪsǽnθəməm] s. crisantema, crisantemo.

chubby [tʃʌ́bɪ] *adj.* rechoncho; gordiflón.

chuck [tʃʌk] s. mamola, golpecito, caricia (*debajo de la barba*); *v.* echar, tirar (*lo que no sirve*); **to — under the chin** hacer la mamola.

chuckle [tʃʌ́kl] s. risita; *v.* reír entre dientes.

chum [tʃʌm] s. compañero, camarada, compinche.

chunk [tʃʌŋk] s. trozo; zoquete.

church [tʃɜrtʃ] s. iglesia.

churchman [tʃɜ́rtʃmən] s. clérigo, eclesiástico, sacerdote.

churchyard [tʃɜ́rtʃjard] s. patio de iglesia; camposanto, cementerio.

churn [tʃɜrn] s. mantequera (*para hacer manteca*); *v.* batir (*en una mantequera*); agitar, revolver.

cider [sáɪdə] s. sidra.

cigar [sɪgár] s. cigarro, puro; — **store**

tabaquería, estanquillo.

cigarette [sɪgərét] s. cigarrillo, pitillo, *Am.* cigarro; **— case** cigarrera, pitillera; **— holder** boquilla; **— lighter** encendedor.

cinch [sɪntʃ] s. cincha; ganga, cosa fácil; *v.* cinchar; apretar.

cinder [síndə] s. ceniza; carbón, brasa, ascua; **-s** cenizas; rescoldo.

cinnamon [sínəmən] s. canela; **— tree** canelo.

cipher [sáɪfə] s. cifra; número; cero.

circle [sɔ́kl] s. círculo; cerco, rueda; *v.* cercar, circundar; circular, dar vueltas.

circuit [sɔ́kɪt] s. circuito; rodeo, vuelta.

circular [sɔ́kjələ] *adj.* circular; redondo; s. circular; hoja volante.

circulate [sɔ́kjələt] *v.* circular; poner en circulación.

circulation [sɔkjəléʃən] s. circulación.

circumference [səkámfərəns] s. circunferencia.

circumlocution [sɔkəmlokjúʃən] s. circunlocución, rodeo.

circumscribe [sɔkəmskráɪb] *v.* circunscribir, limitar.

circumspect [sɔ́kəmspɛkt] *adj.* circunspecto; prudente.

circumspection [sɔkəmspékʃən] s. circunspección, miramiento, prudencia.

circumstance [sɔ́kəmstæns] s. circunstancia; incidente; ceremonia, pompa.

circus [sɔ́kəs] s. circo.

cistern [sístən] s. cisterna.

citadel [sítəd]] s. ciudadela.

citation [saɪtéʃən] s. citación; cita; mención.

cite [saɪt] *v.* citar; citar a juicio; mencionar.

citizen [sítəzn] s. ciudadano, paisano.

citizenship [sítəznʃɪp] s. ciudadanía.

citron [sítrən] s. acitrón.

city [sítɪ] s. ciudad, población; municipio; *adj.* municipal; urbano; **— council** ayuntamiento; **— hall** ayuntamiento, casa municipal.

civic [sívɪk] *adj.* cívico.

civics [sívɪks] s. derecho político.

civil [sívl] *adj.* civil; cortés; **— engineer** ingeniero civil.

civilian [səvíljən] s. paisano (*persona no militar*).

civility [səvílətɪ] s. civilidad, cortesía, urbanidad.

civilization [sɪvləzéʃən] s. civilización.

civilize [sívlaɪz] *v.* civilizar.

civilized [sívlaɪzd] *adj.* civilizado.

clad [klæd] *pret. & p.p.* de **to clothe.**

claim [klem] s. demanda; reclamación, reclamo; derecho, título; pretensión;

miner's — denuncia.; *v.* reclamar; demandar; pedir, exigir; afirmar, sostener; **to — a mine** denunciar una mina; **to — to be** pretender ser.

claimant [klémənt] s. reclamante o reclamador; pretendiente (*a un trono*).

clairvoyant [klervóɪənt] *adj.* clarividente.

clam [klæm] s. almeja.

clamber [klǽmbə] *v.* trepar, encaramarse, subir a gatas, subir gateando.

clamor [klǽmə] s. clamor; clamoreo; gritería, vocería; *v.* clamar; vociferar, gritar.

clamorous [klǽmərəs] *adj.* clamoroso.

clamp [klæmp] s. grapa; tornillo de banco; *v.* afianzar, sujetar; pisar recio.

clan [klæn] s. clan; tribu.

clandestine [klændéstɪn] *adj.* clandestino.

clang [klæŋ] s. tantán, retintín; campanada, campanillazo; **—! —!** ¡tan! ¡tan!; *v.* sonar, repicar (*una campana o timbre*); hacer sonar, tocar fuerte.

clap [klæp] s. palmada; golpe seco; **— of thunder** trueno; *v.* palmear, palmotear, aplaudir, dar palmadas; cerrar de golpe (*un libro*); dar una palmada, *Am.* palmear (*sobre la espalda*); **to — in jail** meter (*o encajar*) en la cárcel.

clarify [klǽrəfaɪ] *v.* aclarar.

clarinet [klǽrənét] s. clarinete.

clarity [klǽrətɪ] s. claridad, luz.

clash [klæʃ] s. choque, encontrón, colisión; riña, conflicto; estruendo; *v.* chocar; darse un encontrón; hacer crujir; oponerse, estar en conflicto.

clasp [klæsp] s. broche; hebilla; cierre; traba; apretón, apretón de manos; *v.* abrochar; asir, agarrar; sujetar, asegurar; abrazar; apretar (*la mano*).

class [klæs] s. clase; *v.* clasificar.

classic [klǽsɪk] *adj. & s.* clásico; **— scholar** humanista, erudito clásico.

classical [klǽsɪkl] *adj.* clásico.

classification [klæsəfəkéʃən] s. clasificación.

classify [klǽsəfaɪ] *v.* clasificar.

classmate [klǽsmet] s. compañero de clase, condiscípulo.

classroom [klǽsrum] s. clase, aula.

clatter [klǽtə] s. estrépito, boruca; traqueteo; bullicio; alboroto; *v.* hacer estrépito o boruca; traquetear; meter bulla o alboroto.

clause [klɔz] s. cláusula.

claw [klɔ] s. garra; zarpa; uña; pinza (*de langosta, cangrejo, etc.*); orejas (*de un martillo*); arañazo; *v.* desgarrar; arañar; rasgar.

clay [kle] s. barro; arcilla, greda.

clean [klin] adj. limpio; puro; adv. limpiamente; clean-cut bien tallado, de buen talle, de buen parecer; v. limpiar; asear; to — up limpiar(se), asear(se).

cleaner [klína] s. limpiador; quitamanchas.

cleanliness [klénlɪnɪs] s. limpieza; aseo.

cleanly [klénlɪ] adj. limpio; aseado; [klínlɪ] adv. limpiamente.

cleanness [klínnɪs] s. limpieza; aseo.

cleanse [klenz] v. limpiar; asear; purificar, depurar.

cleanser [klénzə] s. limpiador.

clear [klɪr] adj. claro; patente, manifiesto; límpido; despejado; libre (de culpa, estorbos, deudas, etc.); — profit ganancia neta; to pass — through atravesar, traspasar de lado a lado; to be in the — estar sin deudas; estar libre de culpa; v. aclarar(se); despejar(se); clarificar; quitar (estorbos); desmontar (un terreno); salvar, saltar por encima de; librar (de culpa, deudas, etc.); sacar (una ganancia neta); pasar (un cheque) por un banco de liquidación; liquidar (una cuenta); to — the table levantar la mesa; to — up aclarar(se).

clearance [klírəns] s. espacio (libre entre dos objetos) ; despacho de aduana; — sale saldo, venta (de liquidación). Am. barata.

clearing [klírɪŋ] s. aclaramiento; claro; terreno desmontado o desarbolado; liquidación de balances; —house banco de liquidación.

clearness [klírnɪs] s. claridad.

cleave [kliv] v. hender(se); tajar; rajar, partir.

cleaver [klívə] s. cuchilla o hacha (de carnicero).

clef [klef] s. clave (en música).

cleft [kleft] s. grieta, hendedura; adj. hendido, partido, rajado; pret. & p.p. de to cleave.

clemency [klémənsɪ] s. clemencia.

clement [klémənt] adj. clemente.

clench [klentʃ] s. agarro, agarrada, agarrón; apretón; v. agarrar, asir; apretar; apretar (los dientes, el puño).

clergy [klɜ́dʒɪ] s. clero.

clergyman [klɜ́dʒɪmən] s. clérigo, eclesiástico, pastor, sacerdote.

clerical [klérɪk] adj. clerical, eclesiástico; oficinesco, de oficina; de dependientes.

clerk [klɜrk] s. dependiente; empleado (de oficina); escribiente; archivero (de municipio); law — escribano; v. estar de dependiente.

clever [klévə] adj. diestro, hábil; listo;

talentoso; mañoso; '-ly adv. hábilmente; con destreza; con maña.

cleverness [klévənɪs] s. destreza, habilidad, maña; talento.

clew [klu] s. indicio (que indica el camino para resolver un misterio o problema).

click [klɪk] s. golpecito; chasquido (de la lengua); gatillazo (sonido del gatillo de una pistola); taconeo (sonido de tacones); v. sonar (un pestillo, un broche, un gatillo, etc.); chasquear (la lengua); to — the heels cuadrarse (militarmente); taconear.

client [kláɪənt] s. cliente.

clientele [klaɪəntél] s. clientela.

cliff [klɪf] s. risco, precipicio, peñasco, escarpa.

climate [kláɪmɪt] s. clima.

climax [kláɪmæks] s. clímax, culminación; v. culminar; llegar al clímax.

climb [klaɪm] s. subida, ascenso; v. subir; trepar; encaramarse; to — down bajar a gatas; desprenderse (de un árbol).

climber [kláɪmə] s. trepador; enredadera, planta trepadora.

clime [klaɪm] s. clima.

clinch [klɪntʃ] v. remachar, redoblar (un clavo); afianzar, sujetar, asegurar bien; cerrar (un trato); abrazarse fuertemente; s. remache; abrazo; agarrón; to be in a — estar agarrados o abrazados.

cling [klɪŋ] v. pegarse, adherirse.

clinic [klínɪk] s. clínica.

clip [klɪp] s. broche, presilla; tijeretada (corte con tijeras); trasquila, trasquiladura; paper — sujetapapeles; to go at a good — ir a paso rápido; andar de prisa; v. recortar; cortar; trasquilar (el pelo o lana de los animales); to — together sujetar.

clipper [klípə] s. clíper (velero o avión de gran velocidad); trasquilador; recortador; -s tijeras; maquinilla (para recortar el pelo).

clipping [klípɪŋ] s. recorte.

cloak [klok] s. capa; manto; v. tapar, embozar, encubrir.

cloakroom [klókrum] s. guardarropa, vestuario.

clock [klɑk] s. reloj; alarm — despertador.

clockwork [klɑ́kwɜrk] s. maquinaria de reloj; like — con precisión, puntualmente; sin dificultad.

clod [klɑd] s. terrón; tonto, necio.

clog [klɑg] s. estorbo, obstáculo; zueco (zapato de suela gruesa o de madera); — dance zapateado; v. estorbar, embarazar; obstruir, atorar, tapar; obstruirse, atascarse, azolvarse (*Am.* enzolvarse), atorarse (*un caño, acequia, etc.*).

cloister [klóɪstə] *s.* claustro; monasterio; convento; *v.* enclaustrar.

close [kloz] *s.* fin, terminación, conclusión; *v.* cerrar(se); concluir; **to — an account** saldar una cuenta; **to — in upon** cercar, rodear; **to — out** liquidar, vender en liquidación.

close [klos] *adj.* cercano, próximo; aproximado; íntimo; estrecho, ajustado; cerrado; mezquino, tacaño; sofocante, opresivo; mal ventilado; **— attention** suma atención; **— questioning** interrogatorio detallado o minucioso; **— translation** traducción fiel; **at — range** de cerca; *adv.* cerca; **-ly** *adv.* aproximadamente; estrechamente; apretadamente; con sumo cuidado a atención.

closeness [klósnɪs] *s.* cercanía, proximidad; aproximación; estrechez; intimidad; tacañería, avaricia; mala ventilación, falta de aire; fidelidad (*de una traducción*).

closet [klázɪt] *s.* ropero; alacena, armario; gabinete, retrete, excusado; *v.* encerrar en un cuarto (*para una entrevista secreta*); **to — oneself (themselves)** encerrarse.

clot [klɑt] *v.* coagular(se), cuajar(se); *s.* coágulo, cuajarón.

cloth [klɔθ] *s.* tela, paño, género; trapo; *adj.* de paño; **— binding** encuadernación en tela.

clothe [kloð] *v.* vestir; cubrir; revestir; investir.

clothes [kloz] *s. pl.* ropa; ropaje, vestidos; **suit of —** terno, traje, *Am.* flux; **—line** tendedero; **—pin** pinzas, gancho (*para tender la ropa*).

clothier [klóðjə] *s.* comerciante en ropa o paño; ropero, pañero.

clothing [klóðɪŋ] *s.* ropa; ropaje, vestidos.

cloud [klaʊd] *s.* nube; **storm —** nubarrón; *v.* nublar(se), anublar(se); obscurecer; manchar.

cloudless [kláʊdlɪs] *adj.* claro, despejado; sin nubes.

cloudy [kláʊdɪ] *adj.* nublado; nubloso; sombrío.

clove [klov] *s.* clavo (*especia*); **— of garlic** diente de ajo.

clover [klóvə] *s.* trébol; **to be in —** estar o vivir en la abundancia; sentirse próspero.

clown [klaʊn] *s.* payaso, bufón; *v.* payasear, bufonear, hacer el payaso.

cloy [klɔɪ] *v.* empalagar; hastiar.

club [klʌb] *s.* club, círculo; casino; garrote, porra; palo; basto (*de la baraja*); *v.* golpear, aporrear, apalear; **to — together** formar club; escotar, pagar la cuota que le toca a cada uno, *Am.* cotizar.

clubhouse [klʌbhaʊs] *s.* club, casino.

cluck [klʌk] *s.* cloqueo; *v.* cloquear.

clue = **clew**.

clump [klʌmp] *s.* terrón; pisada fuerte; **— of bushes** matorral; **— of trees** grupo de árboles, arboleda; *v.* apiñar, amontonar; **to — along** andar pesadamente.

clumsy [klʌmzɪ] *adj.* torpe, desmañado; incómodo; difícil de manejar; mal hecho.

clung [klʌŋ] *pret.* & *p.p. de* to cling.

cluster [klʌstə] *s.* racimo; grupo; *v.* agrupar(se); arracimarse (*formar racimo*).

clutch [klʌtʃ] *s.* apretón fuerte; agarro, agarrón; embrague (*de automóvil*); **-es** garras; uñas; **— pedal** palanca del embrague; **to step on the —** pisar el embrague; desembragar, soltar el embrague; **to throw in the —** embragar; *v.* agarrar, asir; apretar.

clutter [klʌtə] *v.* obstruir; atestar (*de cosas*); poner en desorden; *s.* desorden, confusión.

coach [kotʃ] *s.* coche; entrenador (*en deportes*); maestro particular; *v.* aleccionar; guiar, adiestrar, *Am.* entrenar; **to — with** ser instruido o entrenado por.

coachman [kótʃmən] *s.* cochero.

coagulate [koǽgjəlet] *v.* coagular(se), cuajar(se).

coal [kol] *s.* carbón; ascua, brasa; **hard —** carbón de piedra, antracita; **soft —** hulla; **— bin** carbonera; **— dealer** carbonero; **— oil** kerosina; *v.* cargar de carbón, echar carbón; proveer(se) de carbón.

coalition [koəlíʃən] *s.* coalición.

coarse [kors] *adj.* tosco; burdo, basto; áspero; rudo; grosero; vulgar; **— sand** arena gruesa.

coarseness [kórsnɪs] *s.* tosquedad; vulgaridad, grosería, rudeza.

coast [kost] *s.* costa, litoral; **— guard** guardacostas, guarda de costas; *v.* costear, navegar por la costa; deslizar(se), resbalar(se) cuesta abajo.

coastal [kóstl] *adj.* costero, costanero, de la costa.

coastline [kóstlaɪn] *s.* costa, litoral.

coat [kot] *s.* chaqueta, *Am.* saco; lana, pelo (*de un animal*); **lady's —** abrigo de señora; **— hanger** colgador; **— of arms** escudo de armas; **— of paint**

capa de pintura; v. cubrir; revestir, dar una mano (de pintura); to — with sugar azucarar, bañar en azúcar.

coattail [kóttel] s. faldón.

coax [koks] v. rogar o persuadir con halagos, halagar, tentar.

cob [kab] s. carozo, zuro (de la mazorca del maíz), Am. tusa, Am. olote.

cobbler [kábla] s. remendón (zapatero); pudín de bizcocho y fruta.

cobweb [kábweb] s. telaraña.

cocaine [kokén] s. cocaína.

cock [kak] s. gallo; macho de ave; espita, grifo; martillo (de armas de fuego); —sure muy seguro de sí mismo; v. amartillar (un arma de fuego); ladear (la cabeza), ladearse (el sombrero).

cockroach [kákrotʃ] s. cucaracha.

cocktail [káktel] s. coctel; aperitivo (de ostras, almejas, frutas, etc.).

cocky [káki] adj. arrogante, Am. retobado.

cocoa [kóko] s. cacao; bebida de cacao, chocolate.

coconut [kókonət] s. coco (fruta).

cocoon [kəkún] s. capullo (del gusano de seda, etc.).

cod [kad] s. bacalao, abadejo; cod-liver oil aceite de hígado de bacalao.

coddle [kádl] v. mimar, consentir.

code [kod] s. código; clave; — message comunicación en clave; signal — código de señales.

codfish [kádfiʃ] = cod.

coerce [koás] v. forzar, obligar.

coffee [kófi] s. café; — shop café; — tree cafeto; black — café solo.

coffeepot [kófipat] s. cafetera.

coffer [kófə] s. cofre, arca.

coffin [kófin] s. ataúd, féretro.

coherent [kohírənt] adj. coherente; conexo.

cohesion [kohíʒən] s. cohesión.

coiffure [kwafjúr] s. tocado, peinado.

coil [koil] s. rollo; rosca; espiral de alambre; electric — bobina; v. arrollar(se), enrollar(se); enroscar(se).

coin [koin] s. moneda; v. acuñar; inventar, forjar (una frase o palabra).

coinage [kóinidʒ] s. acuñación; sistema monetario; moneda, monedas; invención (de una palabra o frase).

coincide [koinsáid] v. coincidir.

coincidence [kóinsədəns] s. coincidencia; casualidad.

coke [kok] s. cok, coque (combustible).

cold [kold] adj. frío; — cream crema cosmética; — meat fiambre; to be — tener frío; it is — today hace frío hoy; s. frío; catarro, resfriado; to catch a

— resfriarse, acatarrarse.

coldness [kóldnis] s. frialdad; indiferencia, despego.

collaborate [kəlǽbəret] v. colaborar.

collaboration [kəlæbəréʃən] s. colaboración.

collapse [kəlǽps] s. desplome, derrumbe, derrumbamiento; hundimiento; postración; v. doblar(se), plegar(se); contraer (el volumen); hundirse, derrumbarse, desplomarse; sufrir una postración.

collar [kálə] s. collar; cuello (de vestido, camisa, etc.); collera (para mulas o caballos de tiro); v. acollarar, poner collar a; coger o agarrar por el cuello; prender.

collateral [kəlǽtərəl] adj. colateral; auxiliar, subsidiario, accesorio; s. garantía (para un préstamo bancario)

colleague [kálig] s. colega.

collect [kəlékt] v. recoger; coleccionar; cobrar; recaudar (impuestos); reunir(se); congregarse; to — oneself calmarse; sosegarse, reportarse.

collection [kəlékʃən] s. colección; agrupación (de gente); recolección, cobranza, cobro, recaudación; colecta.

collective [kəléktiv] adj. colectivo.

collector [kəléktə] s. colector; coleccionista (de sellos, objetos artísticos, etc.); cobrador (de billetes, deudas, etc.); recaudador (de impuestos).

college [kálidʒ] s. colegio; medical — colegio o escuela de medicina.

collide [kəláid] v. chocar; estar en conflicto, oponerse.

collie [káli] s. perro de pastor.

collision [kəlíʒən] s. choque, colisión; oposición, pugna (de intereses, ideas, etc.).

colloquial [kəlókwiəl] adj. familiar; — expression locución o frase familiar.

colon [kólən] s. colon (del intestino); dos puntos (signo de puntuación).

colonel [kźnl] s. coronel.

colonial [kəlóniəl] adj. colonial.

colonist [kálənist] s. colono, colonizador.

colonization [kalənəzéʃən] s. colonización.

colonize [kálənaiz] v. colonizar; establecerse en colonia.

colony [káləni] s. colonia.

color [kʌlə] s. color; colorido; the —s la bandera; v. colorar; colorear; dar colorido; pintar; teñir; iluminar (una fotografía, grabado, etc.); ruborizarse.

colored [kʌləd] adj. colorado, teñido, colorido, pintado; de color; coloreado; — person persona de color.

colorful [kÁləfəl] *adj.* lleno de color; colorido; vistoso; vívido; pintoresco.

coloring [kÁlərɪŋ] *s.* colorido; coloración; colorante.

colorless [kÁləlɪs] *adj.* incoloro; descolorido.

colossal [kəlásl] *adj.* colosal.

colt [kolt] *s.* potro.

Columbian [kəlÁmbɪən] *adj.* colombiano, de Colombia; colombino, referente a Cristóbal Colón.

column [káləm] *s.* columna.

comb [kom] *s.* peine; peineta (*de mujer*); cresta (*de gallo*); rastrillo, carda (*para lana*); almohaza (*para caballos*); panal (*de miel*); *v.* peinar; rastrillar, cardar (*lana*); escudriñar; **to — one's hair** peinarse.

combat [kámbæt] *s.* combate, pelea; *v.* combatir.

combatant [kámbətənt] *adj. & s.* combatiente.

combination [kambənéʃən] *s.* combinación.

combine [kəmbáɪn] *v.* combinar(se), unir(se).

combustible [kəmbÁstəbl] *adj. & s.* combustible.

combustion [kəmbÁstʃən] *s.* combustión.

come [kʌm] *v.* venir; llegar; provenir; **to — about** suceder; **to — again** volver, volver a venir; **to — back** volver, regresar; **to — downstairs** bajar; **to — in** entrar; **to — out** salir; **to — of age** llegar a mayor edad; **to — off** soltarse, zafarse; **to — to** volver en sí; **to — to terms** ponerse de acuerdo, ajustarse; **to — up** subir; surgir (*una cuestión*); *p.p. de* **to come.**

comedian [kəmídɪən] *s.* cómico, comediante.

comedy [kámədɪ] *s.* comedia.

comely [kámlɪ] *adj.* agradable a la vista, gentil, bien parecido.

comet [kámɪt] *s.* cometa.

comfort [kÁmfət] *s.* comodidad; bienestar; alivio, consuelo; *v.* consolar, confortar, aliviar.

comfortable [kÁmfətəbl] *adj.* cómodo; confortable; **— life** vida holgada; **— income** un buen pasar, renta suficiente; **comfortably** *adv.* cómodamente; con comodidad; holgadamente.

comforter [kÁmfətə] *s.* consolador; edredón, cobertor acolchado.

comfortless [kÁmfətlɪs] *adj.* incómodo; desconsolado.

comic [kámɪk] *adj.* cómico; chistoso; gracioso; **-s** *s. pl.* caricaturas, historietas cómicas.

comical [kámɪkl] *adj.* cómico, gracioso.

coming [kÁmɪŋ] *adj.* que viene, que llega; próximo; venidero; *s.* venida, llegada; **— of Christ** advenimiento de Cristo.

comma [káme] *s.* coma.

command [kəmænd] *s.* mando; mandato, orden; mandamiento; comandancia; comando; dominio; **at your —** a la orden de Vd., a la disposición de Vd.; **he has a good — of English** domina bien el inglés; *v.* mandar; ordenar; dominar; comandar; **to — respect** inspirar respeto, imponerse.

commander [kəmǽndə] *s.* jefe; comandante; teniente de navío; comendador (*de ciertas órdenes*); **— in chief** comandante en jefe; general en jefe.

commandment [kəmǽndmənt] *s.* mandamiento; mandato, orden.

commemorate [kəmǽmərət] *v.* conmemorar.

commence [kəméns] *v.* comenzar.

commencement [kəménsmənt] *s.* comienzo, principio; acto de distribución de diplomas.

commend [kəménd] *v.* alabar, elogiar; encomendar, encargar; recomendar.

commendation [kaməndéʃən] *s.* encomio, alabanza.

comment [káment] *s.* comentario, observación, nota; *v.* comentar; hacer observaciones; hacer comentarios.

commentary [káməntərɪ] *s.* comentario.

commentator [kámentetə] *s.* comentador; comentarista; **radio —** comentarista radial.

commerce [káməs] *s.* comercio.

commercial [kəmɝʃəl] *adj.* comercial.

commiseration [kəmɪzəréʃən] *s.* compasión.

commissary [káməsɛrɪ] *s.* comisario.

commission [kəmíʃən] *s.* comisión; encargo; junta; nombramiento; **to put out of —** inutilizar; descomponer, quebrar; retirar del servicio (*un navío*); *v.* comisionar; encargar; nombrar; poner en servicio (*un navío*); **-ed officer** oficial comisionado (*alférez u oficial superior a éste*).

commissioner [kəmíʃənə] *s.* comisionado; comisario; **police —** comisario de policía.

commit [kəmít] *v.* cometer; encargar; **to — to memory** aprender de memoria; **to — to prison** encarcelar; **to — oneself** dar o expresar su opinión, expresarse abiertamente, comprometerse.

committee [kəmítɪ] *s.* comité; comisión.

junta; — of one comisionado o delegado único.

commodity [kəmádətɪ] s. mercancía; género, mercadería, artículo de comercio, producto.

common [kámən] adj. común; general; corriente; vulgar, ordinario; público; — law derecho consuetudinario; — sense sentido común; — soldier soldado raso; -s s. pl. refectorio (de un colegio o universidad); ejido, campo común; -ly adv. comúnmente, por lo común.

commonness [kámənnɪs] s. vulgaridad, ordinariez; frecuencia.

commonplace [kámənples] adj. común, trivial; s. lugar común.

commonwealth [kámənwɛlθ] s. estado; república; pueblo, colectividad.

commotion [kəmóʃən] s. conmoción; tumulto; bullicio; levantamiento.

commune [kəmjún] v. comunicarse (con); comulgar.

communicate [kəmjúnəket] v. comunicar(se); transmitir.

communication [kəmjunəkéʃən] s. comunicación.

communicative [kəmjúnəketɪv] adj. comunicativo.

communion [kəmjúnjən] s. comunión.

communism [kámjʊnɪzəm] s. comunismo.

communist [kámjʊnɪst] s. & adj. comunista.

community [kəmjúnətɪ] s. comunidad; sociedad; vecindario, barrio; — chest caja de beneficencia, fondos de beneficencia.

compact [kəmpǽkt] adj. compacto; denso; apretado; conciso, sucinto; [kámpækt] s. pacto, trato, convenio; polvera.

compactness [kəmpǽktnɪs] s. solidez; densidad; concisión.

companion [kəmpǽnjən] s. compañero; acompañante.

companionship [kəmpǽnjənʃɪp] s. compañerismo, camaradería; compañía.

company [kámpənɪ] s. compañía; sociedad; visita; ship's — tripulación; to keep — with acompañar a; cortejar a; tener relaciones con, frecuentar la compañía de.

comparable [kámpərəbl] adj. comparable.

comparative [kəmpǽrətɪv] adj. comparativo.

compare [kəmpér] v. comparar; cotejar; confrontar; contrastar; beyond — incomparable, sin par, sin igual, sin

comparación.

comparison [kəmpǽrəsn̩] s. comparación; símil; beyond — incomparable, sin comparación; in — with comparado con.

compartment [kəmpártmənt] s. compartimiento, sección, división; departamento.

compass [kámpəs] s. compás (para dibujar); brújula; área, ámbito; alcance.

compassion [kəmpǽʃən] s. compasión, lástima.

compassionate [kəmpǽʃənɪt] adj. compasivo, misericordioso.

compatible [kəmpǽtəbl] adj. compatible.

compatriot [kəmpétrɪət] s. compatriota.

compel [kəmpél] v. compeler, obligar; exigir.

compensate [kámpənset] v. compensar; recompensar; remunerar.

compensation [kampənséʃən] s. compensación; recompensa; remuneración.

compete [kəmpít] v. competir.

competence [kámpətəns] s. competencia, aptitud, capacidad.

competent [kámpətənt] adj. competente; calificado; capaz.

competition [kampətíʃən] s. competencia; concurso, certamen; contienda.

competitive [kəmpétətɪv] adj. en competencia; — examination oposición, concurso.

competitor [kəmpétətə] s. competidor; rival; opositor.

compile [kəmpáɪl] v. compilar, recopilar.

complacency [kəmplésnsɪ] s. complacencia, contentamiento.

complacent [kəmplésn̩t] adj. complaciente, satisfecho.

complain [kəmplén] v. quejarse; querellarse.

complaint [kəmplént] s. queja; quejido, lamento; dolencia, enfermedad; to lodge a — hacer una reclamación.

complement [kámpləmənt] s. complemento; [kámpləmənt] v. complementar, completar.

complete [kəmplít] adj. completo; v. completar; terminar; -ly adv. completamente, por completo.

completeness [kəmplítnɪs] s. perfección; minuciosidad; lo completo; lo cabal; lo acabado.

completion [kəmplíʃən] s. completamiento; terminación, conclusión; cumplimiento.

complex [kámpleks] s. complejo; [kəmpléks] adj. complejo; compuesto;

complicado.

complexion [kəmplékʃən] s. cutis, tez; aspecto.

complexity [kəmpléksətɪ] s. complejidad.

compliance [kəmplái̯əns] s. complacencia; condescendencia; conformidad; cumplimiento; **in — with** en conformidad con; **de acuerdo con,** conforme a.

complicate [kámpləket] v. complicar.

complicated [kámpləketɪd] adj. complicado.

complication [kampləkéʃən] s. complicación.

compliment [kámpləmənt] s. cumplido, cumplimiento; requiebro, lisonja, galantería; **to send one's -s** enviar saludos; [kámpləmənt] v. cumplimentar; requebrar; lisonjear; alabar.

comply [kəmplái̯] v. consentir, conformarse (con), obrar de acuerdo (con); cumplir (con).

component [kəmpónənt] adj. & s. componente.

compose [kəmpóz] v. componer; **to — oneself** sosegarse, serenarse, calmarse.

composed [kəmpózd] adj. compuesto; tranquilo, sereno, sosegado; **to be — of** estar compuesto de, componerse de, constar de.

composer [kəmpózə] s. compositor; autor.

composite [kəmpázɪt] adj. compuesto; s. compuesto; mezcla.

composition [kampəzíʃən] s. composición; arreglo; compuesto.

composure [kəmpóʒə] s. compostura, calma, serenidad.

compound [kámpau̯nd] adj. & s. compuesto; [kampáu̯nd] v. componer; mezclar, combinar; **to — interest** calcular el interés compuesto.

comprehend [kamprɪhénd] v. comprender; abarcar, abrazar, incluir.

comprehensible [kamprɪhénsəbl] adj. comprensible, inteligible.

comprehension [kamprɪhénʃən] s. comprensión.

comprehensive [kamprɪhénsɪv] adj. comprensivo; inclusivo.

compress [kámprɛs] s. compresa; [kamprés] v. comprimir, apretar, condensar.

compression [kəmpréʃən] s. compresión.

comprise [kəmprái̯z] v. comprender, abarcar, incluir, abrazar; constar de.

compromise [kámprəmai̯z] s. compromiso; arreglo; avenencia; término medio; v. comprometer; avenirse, transigir, Am. transar.

comptroller [kəntrólə] s. interventor, Am. contralor.

compulsion [kəmpʌlʃən] s. compulsión, coacción.

compulsory [kəmpʌlsərɪ] adj. obligatorio.

computation [kampjətéʃən] s. cómputo, cálculo.

compute [kəmpjút] v. computar.

comrade [kámræd] s. camarada, compañero.

concave [kankév] adj. cóncavo.

conceal [kənsíl] v. encubrir, ocultar, esconder.

concealment [kənsílmənt] s. encubrimiento.

concede [kənsíd] v. conceder; otorgar; admitir, reconocer.

conceit [kənsít] s. presunción, amor propio, vanagloria; concepto, agudeza.

conceited [kənsítɪd] adj. presuntuoso, presumido, vanidoso, engreído.

conceivable [kənsívəbl] adj. concebible, imaginable, comprensible.

conceive [kənsív] v. concebir; imaginar.

concentrate [kánsntret] v. concentrar(se), reconcentrar(se).

concentration [kansntréʃən] s. concentración; reconcentración.

concept [kánsept] s. concepto, idea; opinión.

conception [kənsépʃən] s. concepción; concepto, idea.

concern [kənsɝn] s. compañía, negociación; negocio, ocupación; establecimiento mercantil; interés; cuidado, preocupación; **to be of no — no ser de consecuencia;** v. concernir, importar, interesar; preocupar; **in all that -s him** en cuanto le atañe, en cuanto le concierne.

concerned [kənsɝnd] adj. interesado; preocupado, intranquilo, inquieto, ansioso; **to be — about** interesarse por, preocuparse por; **as far as I am —** por lo que me concierne, por lo que me toca, en cuanto a mí me atañe.

concerning [kənsɝnɪŋ] prep. tocante a, respecto a, acerca de.

concert [kánsɝt] s. concierto; [kənsɝt] v. concertar, arreglar (un plan).

concession [kənséʃən] s. concesión.

conciliate [kənsílɪet] v. conciliar, poner en armonía; ganar la voluntad de.

concise [kənsáɪs] adj. conciso, sucinto.

conciseness [kənsáɪsnɪs] s. concisión, brevedad.

conclude [kənklúd] v. concluir; acabar, terminar; deducir; decidir.

conclusion [kənklúʒən] s. conclusión.

conclusive [kənklúsɪv] *adj.* conclusivo, concluyente.

concoct [kənkákt] *v.* confeccionar; preparar (*combinando diversos ingredientes*); inventar, urdir.

concoction [kənkákʃən] *s.* cocimiento, menjurje; mezcla.

concord [kánkərd] *s.* concordia, conformidad, acuerdo; convenio, pacto.

concrete [kánkrít] *adj.* concreto; de hormigón, de cemento; *s.* hormigón, cemento, *Am.* concreto.

concur [kənkə́] *v.* estar de acuerdo, ser del mismo parecer; unirse.

condemn [kəndém] *v.* condenar; **to — a building** condenar un edificio.

condemnation [kandemnéʃən] *s.* condenación.

condensation [kandenséʃən] *s.* condensación; resumen, compendio.

condense [kəndéns] *v.* condensar(se).

condescend [kandɪsénd] *v.* condescender.

condescension [kandɪsénʃən] *s.* condescendencia.

condiment [kándəmənt] *s.* condimento.

condition [kəndíʃən] *s.* condición; estado; nota o calificación provisional; **on — that** a condición de que, con tal que; *v.* acondicionar; poner en buena condición; estipular; reprobar provisionalmente (*a un estudiante*).

conditional [kəndíʃənl] *adj.* condicional.

condole [kəndól] *v.* condolerse; **to — with** dar el pésame a; consolar a.

condolence [kəndóləns] *s.* pésame.

conduce [kəndjús] *v.* conducir.

conducive [kəndjúsɪv] *adj.* conducente.

conduct [kándʌkt] *s.* conducta; comportamiento, proceder; dirección, manejo; [kəndʌ́kt] *v.* conducir; dirigir, manejar; **to — oneself well** portarse bien.

conductor [kəndʌ́ktə] *s.* conductor; guía; **orchestra —** director de orquesta; **train —** revisor; cobrador, *Am.* conductor.

conduit [kándɪt] *s.* conducto; caño; cañería, tubería.

cone [kon] *s.* cono; **paper —** cucurucho; **pine —** piña.

confection [kənfékʃən] *s.* confección; confitura; confite, dulce.

confectionery [kənfékʃənɛrɪ] *s.* confitería; dulcería; confites, dulces.

confederacy [kənfédərəsɪ] *s.* confederación.

confederate [kənfédərɪt] *adj. & s.* confederado; [kənfédəret] *v.* confederar(se).

confederation [kənfedəréʃən] *s.* confederación.

confer [kənfə́] *v.* conferir, conceder; conferenciar, consultar.

conference [kánfərəns] *s.* conferencia; consulta, junta, sesión.

confess [kənfés] *v.* confesar(se); reconocer, admitir.

confession [kənféʃən] *s.* confesión.

confessional [kənféʃənl] *s.* confesionario.

confessor [kənfésə] *s.* confesor.

confidant [kɑnfədǽnt] *s.* confidente.

confide [kənfáɪd] *v.* confiar; fiar.

confidence [kánfədəns] *s.* confianza; confidencia; **— game** estafa; **— man** estafador.

confident [kánfədənt] *adj.* confiado; seguro, cierto; **-ly** *adv.* confiadamente, con toda seguridad.

confidential [kɑnfədénʃəl] *adj.* confidencial; íntimo; secreto; **-ly** *adv.* en confianza.

confine [kánfaɪn] *s.* confín; [kənfáɪn] *v.* confinar; encerrar; **to — oneself to** limitarse a; **to be -ed in bed** estar encamado, guardar cama.

confinement [kənfáɪnmənt] *s.* encerramiento; encierro; prisión, encarcelación.

confirm [kənfə́m] *v.* confirmar.

confirmation [kɑnfəméʃən] *s.* confirmación.

confiscate [kánfɪsket] *v.* confiscar.

conflagration [kɑnfləgréʃən] *s.* conflagración, incendio.

conflict [kánflɪkt] *s.* conflicto, oposición, choque; lucha, combate; [kənflíkt] *v.* chocar, oponerse, estar en conflicto.

conform [kənfɔ́rm] *v.* conformar(se).

conformity [kənfɔ́rmətɪ] *s.* conformidad.

confound [kənfáund] *v.* confundir, perturbar, desconcertar, aturdir; **— it!** ¡caramba!

confront [kənfrʌ́nt] *v.* confrontar; carear, poner cara a cara (*a dos reos*); encararse con, afrontar, hacer frente a, arrostrar.

confuse [kənfjúz] *v.* confundir; trastornar; embrollar; desconcertar.

confused [kənfjúzd] *adj.* confuso; revuelto; desconcertado, perplejo; **to become —** confundirse; desconcertarse.

confusing [kənfjúzɪŋ] *adj.* confuso, revuelto; desconcertante.

confusion [kənfjúʒən] *s.* confusión; desorden; tumulto; perplejidad.

congeal [kəndʒíl] *v.* congelar(se), helar(se), cuajar(se).

congenial [kəndʒínjəl] *adj.* congenial;

simpático; **to be — with** congeniar con, simpatizar con.

congestion [kəndʒéstʃən] s. congestión; aglomeración.

conglomeration [kənglɑməréʃən] s. aglomeración.

congratulate [kəngrǽtʃəlet] v. congratular, felicitar, dar el parabién.

congratulation [kəngrǽtʃəléʃən] s. congratulación, felicitación, parabién, enhorabuena.

congregate [kángrɪget] v. congregar(se), juntar(se), reunir(se).

congregation [kɑŋgrɪgéʃən] s. congregación; asamblea, reunión; colección, agregado; fieles, feligreses (de una iglesia).

congress [kángrəs] s. congreso; asamblea.

congressional [kəngréʃənl] adj. perteneciente al congreso.

congressman [kángrəsmən] s. congresista, diputado, representante.

conjecture [kəndʒéktʃə] s. conjetura, suposición; v. conjeturar, suponer.

conjugate [kándʒəget] v. conjugar.

conjugation [kandʒəgéʃən] s. conjugación.

conjunction [kəndʒʌ́ŋkʃən] s. conjunción.

conjure [kʌ́ndʒə] v. conjurar; **to — up** evocar; [kəndʒúr] rogar, implorar.

connect [kənékt] v. conectar; unir(se), juntar(se); enlazar(se); relacionar(se); acoplar.

connection [kənékʃən] s. conexión; enlace; vínculo, unión; relación; -s parientes; amigos, amistades.

conniption [kənípʃən] s. pataleta; **to have a —** darle a uno una pataleta.

connive [kənáɪv] v. conspirar; disimular; hacerse cómplice.

connoisseur [kanəsɜ́] s. conocedor, perito.

conquer [kánkə] v. conquistar; vencer.

conqueror [kánkərə] s. conquistador; vencedor.

conquest [kánkwest] s. conquista.

conscience [kánʃəns] s. conciencia.

conscientious [kanʃiénʃəs] adj. concienzudo.

concious [kánʃəs] adj. consciente; sabedor; **-ly** adv. conscientemente; a sabiendas.

consciousness [kánʃəsnɪs] s. consciencia, estado consciente; **to lose —** perder el sentido o conocimiento.

conscript [kənskrɪpt] v. reclutar; [kánskrɪpt] s. recluta.

consecrate [kánsɪkret] v. consagrar; dedicar.

consecration [kansɪkréʃən] s. consagración; dedicación.

consecutive [kənsékjətɪv] adj. consecutivo.

consent [kənsént] s. consentimiento; permiso, asentimiento; v. consentir; permitir, asentir.

consequence [kánsəkwens] s. consecuencia.

consequent [kánsəkwent] adj. consecuente; consiguiente; s. consecuente, consiguiente, consecuencia; **-ly** adv. por consiguiente, por consecuencia.

conservation [kansəvéʃən] s. conservación; preservación.

conservative [kənsɜ́vətɪv] adj. conservador; conservativo; s. conservador.

conservatory [kənsɜ́vətorɪ] s. conservatorio; invernadero.

conserve [kənsɜ́v] s. conserva, dulce; v. conservar; preservar.

consider [kənsídə] v. considerar.

considerable [kənsídərəbl] adj. considerable; cuantioso; considerably adv. considerablemente; considerably older bastante más viejo.

considerate [kənsídərɪt] adj. considerado.

consideration [kənsɪdəréʃən] s. consideración; respeto; importancia; remuneración; **in — of** en atención a, teniendo en cuenta, en razón de, en vista de.

considering [kənsídərɪŋ] prep. en razón de, en vista de; en atención a, en consideración de.

consign [kənsáɪn] v. consignar; enviar; entregar.

consist [kənsíst] v. consistir (en); constar (de).

consistency [kənsístənsɪ] s. consecuencia; consistencia, firmeza, solidez.

consistent [kənsístənt] adj. consecuente, lógico; compatible; consistente, coherente.

consolation [kansəléʃən] s. consolación; consuelo.

console [kənsól] v. consolar.

consolidate [kənsálədet] v. consolidar(se); unir(se), combinar(se).

consonant [kánsənənt] adj. consonante; conforme; s. consonante.

consort [kánsɔrt] s. consorte; [kənsɔ́rt] v. **to — with** asociarse con.

conspicuous [kənspíkjuəs] adj. conspicuo, notorio; manifiesto, sobresaliente.

conspiracy [kənspírəsɪ] s. conspiración, conjuración.

conspirator [kənspírətə] s. conspirador,

conjurado.

conspire [kənspáɪr] v. conspirar; tramar, maquinar.

constable [kánstəb]] s. alguacil, policía; condestable (título).

constancy [kánstənsɪ] s. constancia.

constant [kánstənt] adj. constante; s. constante, cantidad constante; **-ly** adv. constantemente, continuamente, siempre; a menudo.

constellation [kɑnstəléʃən] s. constelación.

consternation [kɑnstənéʃən] s. consternación.

constipate [kánstəpet] v. estreñir.

constipation [kɑnstəpéʃən] s. estreñimiento.

constituent [kənstítʃʊənt] adj. constituyente; constitutivo; componente; s. componente, elemento; elector, votante.

constitute [kánstətjut] v. constituir; componer; establecer.

constitution [kɑnstətjúʃən] s. constitución.

constitutional [kɑnstətjúʃən]] adj. constitucional; s. paseo a pie, caminata (para hacer ejercicio).

constrain [kənstrén] v. constreñir; obligar, forzar; apretar, comprimir.

construct [kənstrʌkt] v. construir, fabricar.

construction [kənstrʌktʃən] s. construcción; estructura; interpretación.

constructive [kənstrʌktɪv] adj. constructivo; de utilidad positiva; provechoso.

construe [kənstrú] v. interpretar, explicar.

consul [káns]] s. cónsul.

consulate [káns]ɪt] s. consulado.

consult [kəns\ʌlt] v. consultar.

consultation [kɑns]téʃən] s. consulta.

consume [kənsúm] v. consumir; gastar; perder (el tiempo).

consumer [kənsúmə] s. consumidor.

consummate [kánsəmet] v. consumar, completar; [kəns\ʌmɪt] adj. consumado, perfecto, completo.

consumption [kəns\ʌmpʃən] s. consumo, gasto; consunción; tisis, tuberculosis.

consumptive [kəns\ʌmptɪv] adj. tísico.

contact [kántækt] s. contacto; v. tocar; poner(se) en contacto con; estar en contacto con.

contagion [kəntédʒən] s. contagio.

contagious [kəntédʒəs] adj. contagioso.

contain [kəntén] v. contener; encerrar; tener cabida para; reprimir, refrenar; **to — oneself** centenerse, refrenarse.

container [kənténə] s. envase, caja, recipiente.

contaminate [kəntǽmənet] v. contaminar, viciar, inficionar.

contemplate [kántəmplet] v. contemplar; meditar; tener la intención de; proyectar.

contemplation [kɑntəmpléʃən] s. contemplación; meditación; intención, propósito.

contemporary [kəntémpərerɪ] adj. contemporáneo; coetáneo.

contempt [kəntémpt] s. desdén, menosprecio; desprecio; **— of court** contumacia.

contemptible [kəntémptəb]] adj. despreciable, vil.

contemptuous [kəntémptʃʊəs] adj. desdeñoso.

contend [kənténd] v. contender; competir; argüir; altercar; sostener, afirmar.

content [kántənt] s. contenido; sustancia; capacidad, volumen; **-s** contenido; **table of -s** tabla de materias, índice general.

content [kəntént] adj. contento; satisfecho; s. contento; satisfacción; **to one's heart's —** a pedir de boca; hasta saciarse; **a su entera satisfacción**; v. contentar; satisfacer.

contented [kənténtɪd] adj. contento, satisfecho.

contention [kənténʃən] s. contención, contienda, disputa, controversia; tema, argumento; aseveración.

contentment [kənténtmənt] s. contentamiento, contento.

contest [kántest] s. concurso, certamen; debate; contienda; torneo; [kəntést] v. contender; disputar; luchar por; **to — with** competir con.

context [kántekst] s. contexto.

contiguous [kəntígjʊəs] adj. contiguo; adyacente.

continent [kántənənt] s. continente; adj. continente, casto, moderado.

continental [kɑntənéntl] adj. & s. continental.

contingency [kəntíndʒənsɪ] s. contingencia, eventualidad.

contingent [kəntíndʒənt] adj. & s. contingente.

continual [kəntínjʊəl] adj. continuo; frecuente; **-ly** adv. de continuo, continuamente, frecuentemente.

continuance [kəntínjʊəns] s. continuación; aplazamiento.

continuation [kəntɪnjʊéʃən] s. continuación.

continue [kəntínjʊ] v. continuar.

continuity [kəntənúətı] s. continuidad.
continuous [kəntínjʊəs] adj. continuo, sin parar, sin cesar.
contortion [kəntɔ́rʃən] s. contorsión.
contour [kántʊr] s. contorno; perímetro.
contraband [kántrəbænd] s. contrabando.
contract [kántrækt] s. contrato, pacto, convenio; contrata; **marriage — es**ponsales; [kəntrǽkt] v. contratar; contraer(se), encoger(se); **to — an ill**ness contraer una enfermedad; **to —** the brows fruncir las cejas.
contraction [kəntrǽkʃən] s. contracción.
contractor [kəntrǽktə] s. contratista.
contradict [kɑntrədíkt] v. contradecir; contrariar.
contradiction [kɑntrədíkʃən] s. contradicción; contrariedad.
contradictory [kɑntrədíktərı] adj. contradictorio; opuesto, contrario.
contrary [kántrerı] adj. contrario; opuesto; testarudo, obstinado; s. contrario; **on the —** al contrario.
contrast [kántræst] s. contraste; [kəntrǽst] v. contrastar.
contribute [kəntríbjʊt] v. contribuir.
contribution [kɑntrəbjúʃən] s. contribución; aportación; cuota; dádiva.
contributor [kəntríbjətə] s. contribuidor; colaborador.
contrite [kántraıt] adj. contrito.
contrivance [kəntráıvəns] s. traza, maquinación; artificio, invención; designio; artefacto, aparato, máquina.
contrive [kəntráıv] v. tramar, maquinar; inventar, idear; proyectar; **to — to** buscar el medio de, tratar de, procurar.
control [kəntról] s. mando, manejo, dirección; freno, restricción; regulador; Am. control; **-s** mandos, controles; — **stick** palanca (de un aeroplano); **to lose — of one's temper** perder la paciencia; v. gobernar, manejar, Am. controlar; regular, regularizar; restringir; contener, reprimir; tener a raya; **to — oneself** contenerse, dominarse.
controller [kəntrólə] s. interventor, registrador, Am. contralor, Am. controlador; regulador; aparato de manejo y control.
controversy [kántrəvɜsı] s. controversia, debate, disputa.
conundrum [kənándrəm] s. adivinanza, acertijo.
convalesce [kɑnvəlés] v. convalecer.
convene [kənvín] v. juntar, convocar; reunirse.
convenience [kənvínjəns] s. conveniencia, comodidad; **at one's —** cuando

le convenga a uno, cuando tenga oportunidad, cuando buenamente pueda.
convenient [kənvínjənt] adj. conveniente; oportuno; cómodo; a propósito; **-ly** adv. convenientemente, cómodamente.
convent [kánvent] s. convento.
convention [kənvénʃən] s. convención; congreso, asamblea; convenio; costumbre, regla.
conventional [kənvénʃənl] adj. convencional; tradicional.
converge [kənvɜ́dʒ] v. converger o convergir.
conversant [kánvəsnt] : **— with** versado en.
conversation [kɑnvəséʃən] s. conversación.
converse [kənvɜ́s] v. conversar, hablar, platicar.
conversion [kənvɜ́ʃən] s. conversión.
convert [kánvɜt] s. converso, persona convertida; catecúmeno (converso reciente); [kənvɜ́t] v. convertir(se).
convex [kɑnvéks] adj. convexo.
convey [kənvé] v. llevar; transportar; transferir, traspasar; transmitir; comunicar; **to — thanks** expresar agradecimiento, dar las gracias.
conveyance [kənvéəns] s. vehículo; transporte; transmisión; entrega; comunicación; traspaso; escritura de propiedad o traspaso.
convict [kánvıkt] s. presidiario; reo; [kənvíkt] v. convencer (de un delito), declarar culpable; probar la culpabilidad de.
conviction [kənvíkʃən] s. convicción; convencimiento; prueba de culpabilidad.
convince [kənvíns] v. convencer.
convincing [kənvínsıŋ] adj. convincente.
convocation [kɑnvəkéʃən] s. convocación; asamblea.
convoke [kənvók] v. convocar.
convoy [kánvɔı] s. convoy, escolta, guardia; [kənvɔ́ı] v. convoyar.
convulsion [kənvʌ́lʃən] s. convulsión, agitación.
coo [ku] s. arrullo; v. arrullar.
cook [kʊk] s. cocinero, cocinera; v. cocinar, guisar; cocer; **to — up a plan** urdir un plan.
cookery [kúkərı] s. cocina, arte de cocinar.
cookie, cooky [kúkı] s. bizcochito, bollito.
cooking [kúkıŋ] s. cocina, arte culinaria; **— stove** cocina de gas, cocina eléctrica, estufa; **— utensils** batería de

cocina, trastos de cocina.
cool [kul] *adj.* fresco; frío, indiferente; calmo, sereno; *s.* fresco, frescura; *v.* refrescar; enfriar; templar, calmar; **to — off** enfriarse; calmarse.
coolness [kúlnɪs] *s.* fresco, frescura; frialdad, indiferencia.
coon [kun] *s.* coatí (*cuadrúpedo carnívoro*); negro; **a -'s age** una eternidad, mucho tiempo.
coop [kup] *s.* jaula; **chicken —** gallinero; *v.* enjaular; **to — up** encerrar.
cooperate [koápəret] *v.* cooperar.
cooperation [koapəréʃən] *s.* cooperación.
cooperative [koápəretɪv] *adj.* cooperativo; *s.* cooperativa, sociedad cooperativa.
coördinate [koórdnet] *v.* coordinar; [koórdnɪt] *adj.* coordinado.
coördination [koordnéʃən] *s.* coordinación.
cop [kap] *s.* polizonte, policía.
cope [kop] *v.* **to — with** tener suficiente fuerza para; **I cannot — with this** no puedo con esto, no puedo dar abasto a esto.
copious [kópɪəs] *adj.* copioso, abundante.
copper [kápə] *s.* cobre; polizonte, policía; **— coin** moneda de cobre, centavo; **— kettle** marmita o caldera de cobre; *adj.* cobrizo.
copy [kápɪ] *s.* copia; ejemplar (*de un libro*); manuscrito (*para el impresor*); *v.* copiar; imitar; remedar.
copyright [kápɪraɪt] *s.* derecho de propiedad literaria; *v.* registrar, obtener patente de propiedad literaria.
coquette [kokét] *s.* coqueta.
coral [kórəl] *s.* coral; *adj.* coralino, de coral.
cord [kord] *s.* cuerda; cordón, cordel; cuerda (*medida de leña*); tendón; **— pantalones de pana; spinal —** espinazo, espina dorsal.
cordial [kórdʒəl] *adj. & s.* cordial.
corduroy [kórdərɔɪ] *s.* pana; **-s pantalones de pana; — road** camino de troncos o maderos.
core [kor] *s.* corazón, centro; núcleo; esencia; *v.* cortar el centro o corazón de; despepitar (*una manzana*).
cork [kork] *s.* corcho; tapón; **— tree** alcornoque; *v.* tapar con corcho.
corkscrew [kórkskru] *s.* tirabuzón, sacacorchos; *adj.* espiral, de forma espiral.
corn [korn] *s.* maíz; grano, cereal; callo (*de los pies o manos*); **— bread** pan de maíz; **— meal** harina de maíz; *v.* salar, curar, acecinar.

corned beef [kórnd bif] *s.* carne de vaca curada (*en salmuera y salitre*).
corner [kórnə] *s.* rincón; ángulo; esquina; rinconada; monopolio; **—stone** piedra angular; **— table** (**— shelf, — bracket**) rinconera; *v.* arrinconar; acorralar; acaparar, monopolizar.
cornet [kornét] *s.* corneta.
cornfield [kórnfild] *s.* maizal, *Am.* milpa.
cornice [kórnɪs] *s.* cornisa.
coronation [korənéʃən] *s.* coronación.
coronet [kórənɪt] *s.* coronilla, guirnalda.
corporal [kórpərəl] *adj.* corporal; corpóreo; *s.* cabo (*militar*).
corporation [korpəréʃən] *s.* corporación; sociedad mercantil.
corps [kor] *s.* cuerpo (*grupo organizado*); **air —** cuerpo de aviación; **army —** cuerpo de ejército.
corpse [korps] *s.* cadáver.
corpulent [kórpjələnt] *adj.* corpulento.
corpuscle [kórpəsl] *s.* corpúsculo.
corral [kəræl] *s.* corral; *v.* acorralar.
correct [kərékt] *v.* corregir; *adj.* correcto; **it is — está** bien; **-ly** *adv.* correctamente; **-ly done** bien hecho.
correction [kərékʃən] *s.* corrección.
correctness [kəréktnɪs] *s.* corrección.
corrector [kəréktə] *s.* corregidor, corrector.
correlate [kórəlet] *v.* correlacionar.
correspond [kərespánd] *v.* corresponder; corresponderse, cartearse, escribirse.
correspondence [kərespándəns] *s.* correspondencia.
correspondent [kərespándənt] *adj.* correspondiente; *s.* correspondiente; corresponsal.
corresponding [kərespándɪŋ] *adj.* correspondiente; conforme.
corridor [kórədə] *s.* corredor, pasillo, pasadizo.
corroborate [kəráboret] *v.* corroborar.
corrode [kəród] *v.* corroer(se).
corrupt [kərʌ́pt] *adj.* corrompido; perverso, depravado; **to become — corromperse;** *v.* corromper; pervertir; sobornar.
corruption [kərʌ́pʃən] *s.* corrupción; soborno; descomposición.
corset [kórsɪt] *s.* corsé.
cosmetic [kazmétɪk] *adj. & s.* cosmético.
cosmopolitan [kazməpálətn] *adj.* cosmopolita.
cost [kost] *s.* coste, costa o costo; **at all -s** a toda costa; **to sell at — vender** al costo; *v.* costar; *prét. & p.p. de* **to cost.**
costly [kóstlɪ] *adj.* costoso.
costume [kástjum] *s.* vestuario, traje,

48

vestido; atavío; indumentaria.

cot [kɑt] *s.* catre; **folding — catre de tijera.**

cottage [kátɪdʒ] *s.* casita, caseta; casa de campo; **— cheese** requesón.

cotton [kátŋ] *s.* algodón; **—seed** semilla de algodón; **— wool** algodón en rama; **— yarn** hilaza.

couch [kautʃ] *s.* canapé, diván; *v.* expresar; estar escondido o en acecho; **-ed in difficult language** expresado en lenguaje difícil.

cough [kɔf] *s.* tos; **— drop** pastilla para la tos; **whooping —** tos ferina; *v.* toser; **to — up** expectorar.

could [kʊd] *pret. del. v. defect.* **can.**

council [káunsl] *s.* concilio; consejo; **city —** consejo muncipal.

councilman [káunslmən] *s.* concejal.

councilor [káunslə] *s.* concejal.

counsel [káunsl] *s.* consejo; parecer, dictamen; abogado consultor; *v.* aconsejar; recomendar.

counselor [káunslə] *s.* consejero; abogado consultor.

count [kaunt] *s.* cuenta, cálculo; cómputo; cargo, acusación; conde; *v.* contar; valer, tener importancia; **to — on** contar con, confiar en.

countenance [káuntənəns] *s.* semblante, aspecto; **to give — to** favorecer, apoyar; aprobar; *v.* aprobar; favorecer, apoyar; tolerar.

counter [káuntə] *s.* contador; mostrador; tablero; ficha; *adj.* contrario, opuesto; *adv.* al contrario; **to run — to** ser contrario a, oponerse a; *v.* oponerse; contradecir; **to — a blow** devolver un golpe.

counteract [kauntəækt] *v.* contrarrestar, neutralizar.

counterbalance [kauntəbæləns] *v.* contrapesar; equilibrar; [káuntəbæləns] *s.* contrapeso.

counterfeit [káuntəfɪt] *s.* falsificación; *adj.* falso; falsificado, falseado; contrahecho; **— money** moneda falsa; *v.* contrahacer, falsificar, falsear.

countermand [káuntəmænd] *s.* contraorden, contramando, revocación, cancelección; [kauntəmænd] *v.* contramandar, revocar, cancelar.

counterpart [káuntəpart] *s.* contraparte.

counterpoise [káuntəpɔɪz] *s.* contrapeso; *v.* contrapesar.

countess [káuntɪs] *s.* condesa.

countless [káuntlɪs] *adj.* incontable, innumerable.

country [kántrɪ] *s.* país; tierra; patria; campo; *adj.* campestre; rural; rústico;

campesino.

countryman [kántrɪmən] *s.* compatriota, paisano; campesino, *Am.* ranchero, *Am.* jíbaro, *Am.* guajiro.

countryside [kántrɪsaɪd] *s.* campiña, campo.

county [káuntɪ] *s.* condado (*división de un estado*).

coupé [kupé, kup] *s.* cupé.

couple [kápl] *s.* par; pareja; *v.* parear; unir; acoplar.

couplet [káplɪt] *s.* copla, versos pareados.

coupling [káplɪŋ] *s.* unión, conexión; acoplamiento; enganche.

coupon [kúpan] *s.* cupón; talón.

courage [kɜ́ɪdʒ] *s.* coraje, ánimo, valor.

courageous [kərédʒəs] *adj.* valeroso, valiente, animoso.

courier [kʊ́rɪə] *s.* mensajero.

course [kors] *s.* curso; rumbo, trayecto; marcha, progreso; método; asignatura; plato (*de una comida*); **— of conduct** conducta, proceder; **golf —** campo o cancha de golf; **race —** hipódromo, pista; **in the — of a year** en el transcurso de un año; **of —** claro, por supuesto; **to follow a straight —** seguir una línea recta.

court [kort] *s.* patio; plazuela, plazoleta; juzgado, tribunal de justicia; corte; **tennis —** cancha para tenis; **— plaster** tela adhesiva, tafetán inglés, esparadrapo; **to pay — to** hacer la corte a, cortejar, galantear; *v.* cortejar; galantear; buscar; **to — danger** exponerse al peligro.

courteous [kɜ́tɪəs] *adj.* cortés.

courtesy [kɜ́təsɪ] *s.* cortesía; fineza, atención; reverencia.

courtier [kórtɪə] *s.* cortesano, palaciego.

court-martial [kórtmárʃəl] *s.* consejo de guerra; *v.* someter a consejo de guerra.

courtship [kórtʃɪp] *s.* cortejo, galanteo.

courtyard [kórtjard] *s.* patio.

cousin [kázn] *s.* primo, prima; **first — primo hermano, primo carnal.**

cove [kov] *s.* cala, ensenada.

covenant [kávənənt] *s.* convenio, pacto; contrato.

cover [kávə] *s.* cubierta, tapa, tapadera; cobija; cobertor; encuadernación; envoltura; funda; albergue, abrigo; **table — tapete; to send under separate — enviar por separado;** *v.* cubrir; tapar; encubrir; abrigar, proteger; abarcar; **to — a distance** recorrer una distancia.

covering [kávrɪŋ] *s.* cubierta, cobertura; envoltura; cobija, abrigo.

covet [kávɪt] *v.* codiciar; ambicionar.

covetous [kávɪtəs] *adj.* codicioso.

cow [kaʊ] s. vaca; hembra (de elefante y otros cuadrúpedos); v. atemorizar, acobardar.

coward [káʊəd] adj. & s. cobarde.

cowardice [káʊədɪs] s. cobardía.

cowardliness [káʊədlɪnɪs] s. cobardía.

cowardly [káʊədlɪ] adj. cobarde; adv. cobardemente.

cowboy [káʊbɔɪ] s. vaquero, Am. gaucho.

cower [káʊə] v. agacharse (de miedo o vergüenza), achicarse, encogerse (de miedo), acobardarse.

cowhide [káʊhaɪd] s. cuero de vaca, vaqueta.

cowl [kaʊl] s. capucha.

coy [kɔɪ] adj. recatado, esquivo, modesto; tímido; gazmoño.

coyote [káɪot, kaɪótɪ] s. coyote.

cozy [kózɪ] adj. cómodo y abrigado; cómodo y agradable.

crab [kræb] s. cangrejo; cascarrabias (persona de mal genio); — apple manzana silvestre.

crack [kræk] s. raja, grieta, rendija; crujido; estallido; trueno, estampido; golpe; pulla, chanza; at the — of dawn al romper el alba; adj. excelente; v. rajar(se), hender(se), agrietarse; crujir; estallar; to — a joke soltar un chiste; to — nuts cascar nueces.

cracked [krækt] adj. agrietado, rajado; quebrado; chiflado, loco.

cracker [krǽkə] s. galleta.

crackle [krǽkl] v. crujido; crepitación; chasquido; v. crujir, crepitar.

cradle [krédl] s. cuna.

craft [kræft] s. maña, destreza; astucia, artificio, cautela; arte, oficio; embarcación; embarcaciones.

craftsman [krǽftsmən] s. artesano, artífice.

crafty [krǽftɪ] adj. mañoso, astuto, cauteloso, taimado.

crag [kræg] s. risco, peñasco.

cram [kræm] v. rellenar; atestar; atracar(se), hartar(se); engullir.

cramp [kræmp] s. calambre; grapa; v. comprimir, apretar, estrechar; afianzar, sujetar (con grapa).

cranberry [krǽnbɛrɪ] s. arándano.

crane [krɛn] s. grulla (ave); grúa (máquina para levantar pesos); v. to — one's neck estirar el cuello.

cranium [krénɪəm] s. cráneo.

crank [kræŋk] s. cigüeña, manubrio, manija, manivela; he is a — es un maniático; v. voltear el manubrio o la cigüeña.

cranky [krǽŋkɪ] adj. cascarrabias; maniático; enojadizo.

cranny [krǽnɪ] s. grieta, rendija.

crape [krep] s. crespón; crespón negro.

crash [kræʃ] s. estallido, golpazo, estruendo; choque; fracaso; quiebra, bancarrota; v. estrellar(se); estallar; chocar; to — an airplane aterrizar de golpe un aeroplano; to — into chocar con, estrellarse contra.

crate [kret] s. canasto, cesta, jaula (para el transporte de mercancías, etc.); Am. huacal; v. embalar en jaula.

crater [krétə] s. cráter.

cravat [krəvǽt] s. corbata.

crave [krev] v. ansiar, anhelar, apetecer; to — mercy (pardon) pedir misericordia (perdón).

crawl [krɔl] s. marcha lenta; natación a la marinera; v. arrastrarse; gatear, andar a gatas; marchar lentamente; to be -ing with ants hormiguear, estar lleno de hormigas.

crayon [kréən] s. lápiz de color, Am. creyón; pastel; tiza, yeso.

craze [krez] s. manía, locura; moda; antojo; v. enloquecer.

crazy [krézɪ] adj. loco; trastornado; to go — volverse loco, perder el juicio.

creak [krik] s. crujido, rechino, rechinamiento; v. crujir, rechinar.

cream [krim] s. crema; nata; — of tomato soup puré de tomate; cold — crema cosmética; ice — helado; v. desnatar; batir, mezclar (azúcar y mantequilla); preparar (legumbres) con salsa de crema.

creamery [krímərɪ] s. lechería, quesería, Am. mantequillería.

creamy [krímɪ] adj. natoso; lleno de crema o nata.

crease [kris] s. pliegue; arruga; v. plegar, hacer pliegues; arrugar.

create [kriét] v. crear.

creation [kriéʃən] s. creación; obra.

creative [kriétɪv] adj. creativo, creador.

creator [kriétə] s. creador.

creature [krítʃə] s. criatura; ser viviente; animalejo.

credence [krídns] s. creencia, crédito.

credentials [krɪdénʃəlz] s. pl. credenciales.

credible [krédəbl] adj. creíble.

credit [krédɪt] s. crédito; buena fama; — and debit haber y deber; activo y pasivo; on — a crédito, al fiado, a plazo; to give — dar crédito, creer; acreditar, abonar; that does him — eso le acredita; v. acreditar; abonar en cuenta; creer, dar crédito; atribuir.

creditable [krédɪtəbl] adj. loable.

creditor [krédɪtə] s. acreedor.

credulous [krédʒələs] *adj.* crédulo.

creed [krid] *s.* credo; creencia.

creek [krik, krɪk] *s.* riachuelo, arroyo.

creep [krip] *v.* arrastrarse; gatear, andar a gatas; trepar (*las plantas*); andar lentamente; deslizarse; sentir hormigueo (*en el cuerpo*); *s. pl.* hormigueo; aprensión, horror.

creeper [krípə] *s.* enredadera, planta trepadora.

crepe [krep] = **crape**.

crept [krept] *pret. & p.p. de* **to creep**.

crescent [krésṇt] *adj.* creciente; *s.* luna creciente; media luna (*emblema de turcos y mahometanos*).

crest [krest] *s.* cresta; penacho; copete; cima, cumbre; timbre (*de un escudo de armas*).

crestfallen [kréstfolən] *adj.* cabizbajo, alicaído, abatido.

cretonne [krɪtán] *s.* cretona.

crevice [krévɪs] *s.* grieta, hendedura.

crew [kru] *s.* tripulación; cuadrilla (*de obreros*); *pret. de* **to crow**.

crib [krɪb] *s.* camita de niño; pesebre; granero, arcón; armazón (*usado en la construcción de edificios*); traducción o clave fraudulenta (*en un examen*); *v.* enjaular; usar traducción o clave fraudulenta (*en un examen*).

cricket [krɪkɪt] *s.* grillo; vilorta (*juego*).

crime [kraɪm] *s.* crimen.

criminal [krímənḷ] *adj. & s.* criminal.

crimp [krɪmp] *v.* rizar; *s.* rizo.

crimson [krímzṇ] *adj. & s.* carmesí.

cripple [krípḷ] *s.* cojo, manco; tullido; baldado, inválido; *v.* estropear; mutilar, derrengar; baldar; incapacitar.

crisis [kráɪsɪs] *s.* crisis.

crisp [krɪsp] *adj.* crespo, encrespado; tieso; bien tostado; quebradizo; — **answer** contestación aguda; — **wind** brisa refrescante; *v.* encrespar.

criterion [kraɪtírɪən] *s.* criterio.

critic [krítɪk] *s.* crítico; criticón.

critical [krítɪkḷ] *adj.* crítico; criticador, criticón.

criticism [krítəsɪzəm] *s.* crítica; criticismo.

criticize [krítəsaɪz] *v.* criticar; censurar.

croak [krok] *v.* croar; graznar; *s.* canto de ranas; graznido.

crochet [kroʃé] *s.* labor de gancho; — **hook** aguja de gancho; *v.* hacer labor de gancho.

crock [krak] *s.* vasija de loza, jarra.

crockery [krákorɪ] *s.* loza.

crocodile [krákədaɪl] *s.* cocodrilo, *Am.* caimán.

crony [krónɪ] *s.* compadre, compinche,

camarada, compañero.

crook [krʊk] *s.* falsario; estafador, maleante, pícaro; curva, vuelta; recodo; gancho; **shepherd's** — cayado; *v.* torcer(se); **to** — **one's arm** doblar el brazo o codo.

crooked [krʊkɪd] *adj.* torcido; curvo, encorvado, *Am.* chueco; falso, fraudulento.

croon [krun] *v.* cantar "tristes" (*con exagerado patetismo*).

crop [krap] *s.* cosecha; buche (*de ave*); látigo, *Am.* cuarta; — **of hair** cabellera; *v.* segar; recortar; rapar; **to** — **out** aparecer, asomar; **to** — **up** brotar, manifestarse inesperadamente.

cross [kros] *s.* cruz; cruce; cruzamiento (*de razas*); mezcla; *v.* cruzar(se); atravesar(se); santiguar(se); encontrarse; contrariar; *adj.* en cruz, cruzado, transversal; malhumorado; **cross-country** a campo traviesa; **cross-examine** *v.* interrogar, repreguntar; **cross-eyed** bizco; **word puzzle** crucigrama.

crossbar [krósbar] *s.* travesaño.

crossing [krósɪŋ] *s.* cruce; cruzamiento; encrucijada, crucero; travesía; **railroad** — cruce; **river** — vado.

crossroad [krósrod] *s.* vía transversal, encrucijada, crucero.

crouch [krautʃ] *v.* agacharse, agazaparse.

crow [kro] *s.* cuervo; canto del gallo; **crow's-foot** pata de gallo (*arrugas en el rabo del ojo*); *v.* cantar (*el gallo*); cacarear; jactarse, hacer alarde.

crowbar [króbar] *s.* barra, palanca de hierro.

crowd [kraʊd] *s.* muchedumbre; gentío, gente; cuadrilla, pandilla; grupo; *v.* agolparse, apiñar(se); estrujar, empujar.

crowded [kráʊdɪd] *adj.* atestado, lleno, apiñado.

crown [kraʊn] *s.* corona; copa (*de sombrero*); cima; *v.* coronar.

crucible [krúsəbḷ] *s.* crisol.

crucifix [krúsəfɪks] *s.* crucifijo.

crucify [krúsəfaɪ] *v.* crucificar.

crude [krud] *adj.* basto, tosco, rudo; inculto; — **oil** petróleo crudo; — **sugar** azúcar bruto, azúcar crudo.

cruel [krúəl] *adj.* cruel.

cruelty [krúəltɪ] *s.* crueldad.

cruet [krúɪt] *s.* ampolla (*pequeña vasija de cristal*); vinajera (*para servir vino en la misa*); **oil** — aceitera; **vinegar** — vinagrera.

cruise [kruz] *s.* travesía, viaje por mar; excursión; *v.* navegar.

cruiser [krúzə] *s.* crucero (*buque*).

crumb [krʌm] s. migaja; miga; mendrugo; v. desmenuzar, desmigajar.

crumble [krʌmbl] v. desmenuzar(se); desmoronarse.

crumple [krʌmpl] v. arrugar(se); ajar, apabullar.

crunch [krʌntʃ] v. crujir; mascullar.

crusade [krvséd] s. cruzada; v. hacer una campaña; hacer una cruzada.

crusader [krvsédə] s. cruzado.

crush [krʌʃ] s. compresión, presión; estrujamiento, apiñamiento de gente; v. estrujar; aplastar; majar; subyugar; **to — stone** moler piedra.

crust [krʌst] s. corteza (de pan, queso, etc.); costra; mendrugo; v. encostrarse, cubrir(se) de costra.

crusty [krʌstɪ] adj. costroso.

crutch [krʌtʃ] s. muleta.

cry [kraɪ] s. grito; lloro, lamento; **a far — from** muy distante de, muy lejos de; v. gritar; llorar; clamar; exclamar; vocear; **to — for help** pedir socorro.

crystal [krístl] s. cristal; **— clear** cristalino.

crystalline [krístlɪn] adj. cristalino.

crystallize [krístlaɪz] v. cristalizar(se).

cub [kʌb] s. cachorro (de oso, tigre, lobo, león); **— reporter** reportero novato.

Cuban [kjúbən] adj. & s. cubano.

cube [kjub] s. cubo; **— root** raíz cúbica.

cubic [kjúbɪk] adj. cúbico.

cuckoo [kúku] s. cuco, cuclillo; adj. tocado, chiflado, medio loco.

cucumber [kjúkʌmbə] s. pepino.

cud [kʌd] s. rumia; **to chew the —** rumiar.

cuddle [kádl] v. abrazar, tener en brazos; estar abrazados.

cudgel [kádʒəl] s. garrote; porra; v. aporrear, apalear.

cue [kju] s. señal, indicación; pie (últimas palabras de un parlamento que sirven de señal en el teatro); **billiard — taco** de billar.

cuff [kʌf] s. puño (de camisa o de vestido); doblez (del pantalón); bofetada; v. abofetear, dar de bofetadas.

culminate [kálmənet] v. culminar.

culprit [kálprɪt] s. reo, delincuente, culpable.

cult [kʌlt] s. culto; secta religiosa.

cultivate [káltəvet] v. cultivar; labrar, barbechar.

cultivated [káltəvetɪd] adj. cultivado; culto.

cultivation [kʌltəvéʃən] s. cultivación, cultivo; cultura.

cultivator [káltəvetə] s. cultivador; máquina cultivadora.

culture [káltʃə] s. cultura; cultivo.

cultured [káltʃəd] adj. culto; cultivado.

cumbersome [kámbəsəm] adj. engorroso, embarazoso, incómodo.

cunning [kánɪŋ] adj. astuto, socarrón, sagaz, taimado; diestro; cuco, mono, gracioso; s. astucia, maña, sagacidad.

cup [kʌp] s. taza, pocillo; copa (trofeo).

cupboard [kábəd] s. armario, aparador; alacena.

cur [kɜ] s. perro mestizo, Am. perro chusco; villano, vil, cobarde.

curate [kjúrɪt] s. cura.

curb [kɜb] s. reborde, encintado (de la acera), Am. cordón de la acera; freno, restricción; barbada (del freno de un caballo); brocal de pozo; v. refrenar, reprimir.

curd [kɜd] s. cuajada; v. cuajar(se), coagular(se).

curdle [kɜdl] v. cuajar(se), coagular(se).

cure [kjʊr] s. cura, curación; remedio; v. curar(se); sanar.

curio [kjúrɪo] s. curiosidad, objeto raro y curioso.

curiosity [kjʊrɪásətɪ] s. curiosidad; rareza.

curious [kjúrɪəs] adj. curioso; extraño, raro.

curl [kɜl] s. rizo, bucle; espiral (de humo); v. rizar(se); ensortijar(se); enroscar(se); retorcerse, alzarse en espirales (el humo).

curly [kɜlɪ] adj. rizo, rizoso, rizado, crespo, Am. chino.

currant [kɜənt] s. grosella; **— bush** grosellero.

currency [kɜənsɪ] s. moneda corriente; circulación; **paper —** papel moneda.

current [kɜənt] adj. corriente; común, prevaleciente, en boga; s. corriente.

curse [kɜs] s. maldición; calamidad; v. maldecir.

cursed [kɜst] adj. maldito.

curt [kɜt] adj. corto, brusco.

curtail [kɜtél] v. cercenar; acortar; restringir, reducir.

curtain [kɜtn] s. cortina; telón (de teatro); v. poner cortinas.

curvature [kɜvətʃə] s. curvatura.

curve [kɜv] s. curva; v. encorvar(se), torcer(se); doblar(se).

curved [kɜvd] adj. encorvado; torcido; curvo, corvo, Am. chueco.

cushion [kúʃən] s. cojín; almohadilla, almohadón; amortiguador (para amortiguar un sonido o golpe); v. acojinar; amortiguar (un choque).

custard [kástəd] s. flan, natillas.

custody [kástədɪ] s. custodia, cargo,

cuidado; **to hold in** — custodiar.
custom [kástəm] *s.* costumbre, hábito, uso, usanza; **-s** derechos de aduana; **— made** hecho a la medida; **— tailor** maestro sastre.
customary [kástəmerɪ] *adj.* acostumbrado, habitual, usual, de costumbre.
customer [kástəmə] *s.* parroquiano, cliente, marchante.
customhouse [kástəmhaʊs] *s.* aduana; **— official** aduanero; **— mark** marchamo.
cut [kʌt] *s.* corte (*m.*); cortadura, *Am.* cortada; rebanada, tajada; rebaja, reducción (*de precios, sueldos*); hechura (*de un traje*); ausencia (*de la clase*); grabado; **short** — atajo, camino corto; *v.* cortar; tajar; labrar, tallar; segar; rebajar, reducir (*precios, sueldos*); negar el saludo a; alzar (*los naipes*); **to** — **across** cruzar, atravesar; **to** — **capers** hacer cabriolas, cabriolar; **to** — **class** faltar a la clase; **to** — **out** recortar; excluir; **to be** — **out** for estar hecho para, tener vocación para; *pret.& p.p. de* **to cut.**
cute [[kjut] *adj.* mono, cuco, astuto.
cuticle [kjútɪk]] *s.* cutícula.
cutlery [kátlərɪ] *s.* cuchillería; cuchillos.
cutlet [kátlɪt] *s.* chuleta.
cutter [kátə] *s.* cortador; máquina para cortar; trineo; **wood** — leñador; **coast guard** — barco guardacostas.
cutting [kátɪŋ] *adj.* cortante; penetrante; mordaz, sarcástico.
cycle [sáɪk]] *s.* ciclo.
cyclone [sáɪklon] *s.* ciclón; huracán.
cylinder [sílɪndə] *s.* cilindro.
cylindrical [sɪlíndrɪk]] *adj.* cilíndrico.
cymbal [símb]] *s.* címbalo, platillo; **to play the -s** tocar los platillos.
cynic [sínɪk] *s.* cínico.
cynical [sínɪk]] *adj.* cínico.
cynicism [sínəsɪzəm] *s.* cinismo.
cypress [sáɪprəs] *s.* ciprés.

D

dad [dæd] *s.* papá, tata; **daddy** *s.* papaíto o papacito, tata, tatita, *Am.* taita.
daffodil [dǽfədɪl] *s.* narciso.
dagger [dǽgə] *s.* daga; puñal; **to look -s at** traspasar con la mirada.
daily [délɪ] *adj.* diario; *adv.* diariamente; *s.* diario, periódico.
dainty [déntɪ] *adj.* delicado, fino, primoroso, exquisito; *s.* golosina, manjar exquisito.
dairy [dérɪ] *s.* lechería, vaquería; quesería, quesera.
daisy [dézɪ] *s.* margarita, maya.

dale [del] *s.* cañada.
dally [dǽlɪ] *v.* juguetear; holgazanear; entretenerse, tardar; malgastar el tiempo.
dam [dæm] *s.* presa, represa; *v.* represar, estancar.
damage [dǽmɪdʒ] *s.* daño; perjuicio; avería; **to pay for -s** indemnizar, pagar los daños y perjuicios; *v.* dañar(se); averiar(se).
dame [dem] *s.* dama, señora; **old —** vieja.
damn [dæm] *v.* maldecir; condenar; blasfemar; **— it!** ¡maldito sea!
damnation [dæmnéʃən] *s.* condenación, perdición.
damp [dæmp] *adj.* húmedo; mojado; *s.* humedad; *v.* humedecer, mojar.
dampen [dǽmpən] *v.* mojar, humedecer; desalentar; amortiguar.
dampness [dǽmpnɪs] *s.* humedad.
damsel [dǽmz]] *s.* damisela.
dance [dæns] *s.* baile; danza; **— music** música de baile; *v.* bailar; danzar.
dancer [dǽnsə] *s.* bailador; bailarín, bailarina; danzante.
dandelion [dǽnd]aɪən] *s.* diente de león.
dandruff [dǽndrəf] *s.* caspa.
dandy [dǽndɪ] *s.* currutaco, majo, afectado; chulo; *adj.* elegante, excelente.
danger [déndʒə] *s.* peligro, riesgo.
dangerous [déndʒərəs] *adj.* peligroso; arriesgado; **-ly** *adv.* peligrosamente; **-ly ill** gravemente enfermo.
dangle [dǽŋg]] *v.* pender, colgar, bambolear(se) (*en el aire*).
dapple(d) [dǽp](d)] *adj.* rodado, con manchas (*dícese de los caballos*); **dapple-grey** rucio rodado, tordo, tordillo.
dare [der] *s.* desafío, reto, provocación; **— devil** atrevido, osado; *v.* atreverse, osar; desafiar.
daring [dérɪŋ] *s.* atrevimiento, osadía; *adj.* osado, atrevido, arrojado.
dark [dark] *adj.* obscuro; sombrío; **— horse** caballo desconocido (*que gana inesperadamente la carrera*); candidato nombrado inesperadamente; **— secret** secreto profundo; enigma; **dark-skinned** moreno, trigueño; *s.* obscuridad; sombra.
darken [dárkən] *v.* obscurecer(se); nublarse.
darkness [dárknɪs] *s.* obscuridad; tinieblas; sombra.
darky [dárkɪ] *s.* negro (*persona*).
darling [dárlɪŋ] *adj. & s.* amado, querido; **my —** vida mía (o mi vida), amor mío.
darn [darn] *s.* zurcido; **it is not worth**

a — no vale un comino, no vale un pito; *v.* zurcir;—! ¡caramba! ¡canastos!; -ing needle aguja de zurcir.

dart [dɑrt] *s.* dardo, flecha; sisa (*en un vestido*); movimiento rápido; *v.* lanzar(se); flechar; **to — out** salir como una flecha; **to — in and out** entrar y salir precipitadamente.

dash [dæʃ] *s.* raya; carrera corta; ímpetu; garbo; pizca (*de sal, azúcar, etc.*); rociada (*de agua*); —**board** tablero de instrumentos; **with a — of the pen** de una plumada; *v.* lanzar(se); echar(se); estrellar(se); salpicar; frustrar (*esperanzas*); **to — by** pasar corriendo; **to — out** salir a la carrera; **to — off a letter** escribir de prisa una carta.

data [détə] *s. pl.* datos.

date [det] *s.* fecha; data; cita, compromiso; dátil; **out of** — anticuado, desusado; fuera de moda; **up to — al día, moderno; up to this** — hasta ahora, hasta la fecha; *v.* fechar; **to — from** datar de; remontarse a.

daub [dɔb] *v.* embarrar, untar; pintarrajear.

daughter [dótə] *s.* hija; **daughter-in-law** nuera.

daunt [dɔnt] *v.* intimidar, asustar, espantar; desanimar.

dauntless [dóntlis] *adj.* denodado, intrépido.

davenport [dǽvənport] *s.* sofá.

dawn [dɔn] *s.* alba; amanecer, madrugada; *v.* amanecer; alborear, rayar (*el día*); **it just -ed upon me** acabo de darme cuenta.

day [de] *s.* día; **— after tomorrow** pasado mañana; **— before yesterday** anteayer o antier; **— laborer** jornalero; **by — de día; by the — por día; eight-hour — jornada de ocho horas; to win the —** ganar la jornada, triunfar.

daybreak [débrek] *s.* amanecer, alba, **at — al** amanecer, al romper el día, al rayar el día.

daylight [délait] *s.* luz del día.

daytime [détaim] *s.* día (*tiempo de luz natural*); **in the — durante el día. de día.

daze [dez] *s.* aturdimiento; deslumbramiento; **to be in a — estar aturdido, *v.* aturdir; ofuscar; deslumbrar.

dazzle [dǽz|] *s.* brillantez; *v.* deslumbrar, ofuscar.

deacon [díkən] *s.* diácono.

dead [ded] *adj.* muerto; — **air** aire viciado o estancado; — **letter** carta no reclamada; — **loss** pérdida absoluta,

adv. completamente, absolutamente; sumamente, muy; — **sure** completamente seguro; — **tired** muerto de cansancio; *s.* the — los muertos; **in the — of the night** en el sigilo de la noche; **in the — of winter** en lo más crudo del invierno.

deaden [dédŋ] *v.* amortiguar.

deadly [dédli] *adj.* mortal; fatal; como la muerte, cadavérico; *adv.* mortalmente; — **dull** sumamente aburrido.

deaf [def] *adj.* sordo; **deaf-mute** *s.* & *adj.* sordomudo.

deafen [défən] *v.* ensordecer; amortiguar, apagar (*un sonido*).

deafening [défəniŋ] *adj.* ensordecedor, estruendoso.

deafness [défnis] *s.* sordera.

deal [dil] *s.* trato, negocio; mano (*en el juego de naipes*); distribución, reparto (*de los naipes*); **a great** — of una gran cantidad de, mucho; **to give a square — tratar con equidad; *v.* tallar (*en juegos de naipes*); distribuir, repartir; dar (*un golpe*); **to — in** comerciar en; **to — with** tratar de (*un asunto*); tratar con; negociar con.

dealer [dílə] *s.* negociante, comerciante; tratante; tallador (*en el juego de naipes*).

dealings [dílinz] *s. pl.* relaciones (*comerciales o amistosas*); comercio, tratos; negocios.

dealt [delt] *pret. & p.p. de* to deal.

dean [din] *s.* deán (*dignidad eclesiástica*); decano (*de universidad*).

dear [dir] *adj.* querido, amado; caro, costoso; *adv.* caro; — me! ¡Dios mío!; **oh —! ¡ay!; my — querido mío; Dear Sir** Muy señor mío; -ly *adv.* cariñosamente; a precio alto; **my -ly beloved** muy amado mío; muy amados míos.

dearth [dɜə] *s.* escasez, carestía, insuficiencia.

death [deə] *s.* muerte; mortandad; — **rate** mortalidad.

deathbed [déəbed] *s.* lecho de muerte.

debase [dibés] *v.* rebajar el valor de; degradar, humillar, envilecer.

debatable [dibétəb|] *adj* discutible, disputable.

debate [dibét] *s.* debate, discusión; *v.* debatir, discutir; considerar; deliberar.

debit [débit] *s.* débito, adeudo, cargo, debe (*de una cuenta*); pasivo (*en contabilidad*); *v.* adeudar, cargar en cuenta.

debris [dəbrí] *s.* escombros; ruinas.

debt [det] *s.* deuda; adeudo; débito; **bad — cuenta incobrable; to run into — adeudarse, entramparse, cargarse de deudas.

debtor [détə] *s.* deudor.

debut [díbjú] *s.* estreno; **to make a —** debutar, estrenarse.

decade [déked] *s.* década, decenio.

decadence [díkédns] *s.* decadencia.

decanter [díkæntə] *s.* garrafa; **large —** garrafón.

decay [díké] *s.* decaimiento; decadencia, ruina; podredumbre; caries (*de la dentadura*); *v.* decaer; venir a menos; pudrir(se) o podrir(se).

decease [dísís] *s* muerte, fallecimiento; *v.* morir, fallecer.

deceased [dísíst] *adj. & s.* muerto, difunto.

deceit [dísít] *s.* engaño; fraude; trampa.

deceitful [dísítfəl] *adj.* engañador; tramposo; engañoso.

deceive [dísív] *v.* engañar.

December [dísémbə] *s.* diciembre.

decency [dísnsı] *s.* decencia.

decent [dísŋt] *adj.* decente; decoroso.

decide [dísáɪd] *v.* decidir, resolver, determinar; **to —** to resolverse a, decidirse a.

decided [dísáɪdɪd] *adj.* decidido, resuelto.

decimal [désəml] *adj.* decimal; *s.* decimal, fracción decimal.

decipher [dísáɪfə] *v.* descifrar.

decision [dísíʒən] *s.* decisión, resolución.

decisive [dísáɪsɪv] *adj.* decisivo; terminante.

deck [dek] *s.* cubierta (*de un buque*); baraja; *v.* cubrir; ataviar; **to — oneself out** emperifollarse.

declaration [dekləréʃən] *s.* declaración.

declare [dɪklǽr] *v.* declarar; afirmar.

decline [dɪkláɪn] *s.* declinación; decadencia; mengua; baja (*de precios*); *v.* declinar; decaer; rehusar; **to — to do something** negarse a hacer algo.

declivity [dɪklívətɪ] *s.* declive.

decompose [dikəmpóz] *v.* descomponer(se); corromper(se), pudrir(se).

decorate [dékəret] *v.* decorar, adornar; condecorar.

decoration [dekəréʃən] *s.* decoración; adorno; insignia, condecoración.

decorative [dékəretɪv] *adj.* decorativo; ornamental.

decorum [dɪkórəm] *s.* decoro; circunspección.

decoy [dɪkóɪ] *s.* reclamo, señuelo, figura de ave (*que sirve para atraer aves*); cebo (*artificio para atraer con engaño*); trampa, lazo; *v.* atraer con señuelo o engaño.

decrease [díkrıs] *s.* disminución o diminución; merma; mengua; [dɪkrís] *v.*

---

disminuir(se); mermar; menguar.

decree [dɪkrí] *s.* decreto; *v.* decretar; mandar.

decrepit [dɪkrépɪt] *adj.* decrépito.

dedicate [dédəket] *v.* dedicar.

dedication [dedəkéʃən] *s.* dedicación; dedicatoria.

deduce [dɪdjús] *v.* deducir, inferir.

deduct [dɪdʌkt] *v.* deducir, descontar, rebajar.

deduction [dɪdʌkʃən] *s.* deducción; rebaja, descuento.

deed [did] *s.* hecho, acción, acto; hazaña; escritura (*de venta o compra*).

deem [dim] *v.* juzgar, creer, considerar.

deep [dip] *adj.* hondo; profundo; obscuro; bajo, grave; **— in debt** cargado de deudas; **— in thought** absorto; **— mourning** luto riguroso; **to go off the — end** echarse a pique; caer en el abismo; **— into the night** en las tinieblas de la noche; *s.* the **—** el mar; **-ly** *adv.* profundamente, hondamente; intensamente.

deepen [dípən] *v.* ahondar, profundizar.

deer [dɪr] *s.* ciervo, venado; **—skin** piel o cuero de venado.

deface [dɪfés] *v.* desfigurar, estropear, mutilar.

defame [dɪfém] *v.* difamar, calumniar, denigrar.

default [dɪfólt] *s.* falla, falta, negligencia (*de un deber, pago, obligación*); deficiencia; *v.* fallar, faltar (*en el cumplimiento de un deber, pago, obligación*); no comparecer a la cita de un tribunal.

defeat [dɪfít] *s.* derrota, vencimiento; frustración (*de un plan*); *v.* vencer, derrotar; frustrar.

defect [dɪfékt] *s.* defecto.

defective [dɪféktɪv] *adj.* defectuoso; incompleto; subnormal, falto de inteligencia; **— verb** verbo defectivo.

defend [dɪfénd] *v.* defender.

defendant [dɪféndənt] *s.* acusado, demandado, procesado.

defender [dɪféndə] *s.* defensor; abogado defensor.

defense [dɪféns] *s.* defensa.

defenseless [dɪfénslıs] *adj.* indefenso, inerme.

defensive [dɪfénsɪv] *adj.* defensivo; *s.* defensiva.

defer [dɪfɜ́] *v.* diferir, posponer, aplazar; **to — to another's opinion** remitirse o ceder al dictamen de otro.

defiance [dɪfáɪəns] *s.* reto, desafío, provocación; oposición; **in — of** en abierta oposición con, a despecho de.

deficiency [dɪfíʃənsı] *s.* deficiencia; defecto; déficit.

deficient [dɪffʃənt] *adj.* deficiente; defectuoso.

deficit [défəsɪt] *s.* déficit.

defile [dɪfáɪl] *v.* viciar, corromper; profanar; manchar, ensuciar.

define [dɪfáɪn] *v.* definir.

definite [défənɪt] *adj.* definido; claro, preciso; fijo; — article artículo determinado o definido; -ly *adv.* definidamente; claramente; -ly not terminantemente no.

definition [defənʃʃən] *s.* definición.

definitive [dɪfínətɪv] *adj.* definitivo.

deform [dɪfórm] *v.* deformar; desfigurar, afear.

deformed [dɪfórmd] *adj.* deforme, disforme; deformado; desfigurado.

deformity [dɪfórmɪtɪ] *s.* deformidad; deformación.

defraud [dɪfród] *v.* defraudar.

defray [dɪfré] *v.* sufragar, costear, pagar (*gastos*).

deft [deft] *adj.* diestro, ágil.

defy [dɪfáɪ] *v.* desafiar; retar; oponerse a, resistirse a.

degenerate [dɪdʒénərɪt] *adj. & s.* degenerado; [dɪdʒénəret] *v.* degenerar.

degradation [degrədéʃən] *s.* degradación; envilecimiento.

degrade [dɪgréd] *v.* degradar; envilecer, rebajar.

degree [dɪgrí] *s.* grado; rango; by -s gradualmente; to get a — graduarse.

deign [den] *v.* dignarse, condescender.

deity [díətɪ] *s.* deidad.

dejected [dɪdʒéktɪd] *adj.* abatido.

dejection [dɪdʒékʃən] *s.* abatimiento, melancolía, depresión.

delay [dɪlé] *s.* demora, tardanza, dilación, retraso; *v.* demorar; retardar, dilatar; diferir; tardarse.

delegate [déləget] *s.* delegado, representante; *v.* delegar, diputar.

delegation [deləgéʃən] *s.* delegación, diputación.

deliberate [dɪlíbərɪt] *adj.* deliberado; premeditado; cauto, prudente; lento; -ly *adv.* deliberadamente; con premeditación; [dɪlíbəret] *v.* deliberar.

deliberation [dɪlibəréʃən] *s.* deliberación.

delicacy [déləkəst] *s.* delicadeza; sensibilidad; finura; golosina.

delicate [déləkət] *adj.* delicado; frágil; exquisito.

delicatessen [deləkətésn] *s.* tienda de fiambres, queso, ensaladas, etc.

delicious [dɪlíʃəs] *adj.* delicioso.

delight [dɪláɪt] *s.* deleite; delicia; *v.*

deleitar(se); encantar; agradar; to — in gozarse en, deleitarse en.

delighted [dɪláɪtɪd] *adj.* encantado; to be — to alegrarse de, tener mucho gusto en (*o* de).

delightful [dɪláɪtfəl] *adj.* deleitoso; delicioso; ameno, agradable.

delineate [dɪlíniet] *v.* delinear, trazar.

delinquent [dɪlíŋkwənt] *adj. & s.* delincuente.

delirious [dɪlírɪəs] *adj.* delirante; to be — delirar, desvariar.

delirium [dɪlírɪəm] *s.* delirio, desvarío.

deliver [dɪlívə] *v.* entregar; librar, libertar; pronunciar (*un discurso*); dar (*un golpe*).

deliverance [dɪlívərəns] *s.* liberación, rescate.

deliverer [dɪlívərə] *s.* libertador; portador, mensajero.

delivery [dɪlívərɪ] *s.* entrega; liberación; parto; elocuencia, manera de pronunciar un discurso; — service servicio de entrega; — truck camión (*o* camioneta) de reparto; mail — reparto de correo.

dell [del] *s.* cañada, hondonada.

delude [dɪlúd] *v.* engañar.

deluge [déljudʒ] *s.* diluvio; *v.* inundar; abrumar.

delusion [dɪlúʒən] *s.* ilusión; engaño, error.

demand [dɪmænd] *s.* demanda; exigencia; solicitud; on — a solicitud; *v.* demandar, reclamar; exigir.

demanding [dɪmændɪŋ] *adj.* exigente.

demeanor [dɪmínə] *s.* conducta, comportamiento, proceder.

demented [dɪméntɪd] *adj.* demente.

demobilize [dɪmóblaɪz] *v.* demovilizar.

democracy [dəmákrəsɪ] *s.* democracia.

democrat [déməkræt] *s.* demócrata.

democratic [deməkrætɪk] *adj.* democrático.

demolish [dɪmálɪʃ] *v.* demoler.

demon [dímən] *s.* demonio.

demonstrate [démənstret] *v.* demostrar.

demonstration [demənstréʃən] *s.* demostración; prueba.

demonstrative [dɪmánstrətɪv] *adj.* demostrativo; efusivo.

den [den] *s.* guarida; escondrijo; cueva, lugar de retiro.

denial [dɪnáɪəl] *s.* negación; negativa; self-denial abnegación.

denomination [dɪnɑmənéʃən] *s.* denominación; nombre, título, designación; secta religiosa.

denote [dɪnót] *v.* denotar.

denounce [dɪnáʊns] *v.* denunciar; delatar, acusar.

dense [dɛns] *adj.* denso; espeso, apretado; estúpido.

density [dénsətɪ] *s.* densidad; estupidez.

dent [dent] *s.* abolladura; mella; *v.* abollar; mellar.

dental [dént‖] *adj.* dental; *s.* dental, consonante dental.

dentist [déntɪst] *s.* dentista.

denunciation [dɪnʌnsɪéʃən] *s.* denuncia, acusación.

deny [dɪnáɪ] *v.* negar; rehusar; **to —** **oneself** sacrificarse, abnegarse; **to —** **oneself to callers** negarse a recibir visitas.

depart [dɪpárt] *v.* partir, salir, irse; desviarse, apartarse.

departed [dɪpártɪd] *adj.* ido; ausente; difunto.

department [dɪpártmənt] *s.* departamento; distrito; ramo, división; **—** **store** almacén.

departure [dɪpártʃə] *s.* salida, partida; desviación.

depend [dɪpénd] *v.* depender; **to — on** depender de; contar con, confiar en.

dependable [dɪpéndəb‖] *adj.* seguro, fidedigno, digno de confianza.

dependence [dɪpéndəns] *s.* dependencia; confianza.

dependency [dɪpéndənsɪ] *s.* dependencia; sucursal.

dependent [dɪpéndənt] *adj.* dependiente; subordinado; *s.* dependiente, familiar.

depict [dɪpíkt] *v.* pintar, describir; representar.

deplete [dɪplít] *v.* agotar; vaciar.

deplorable [dɪplórəb‖] *adj.* deplorable, lamentable.

deplore [dɪplór] *v.* deplorar.

deport [dɪpórt] *v.* deportar; **to — one-** **self well** portarse bien.

deportment [dɪpórtmənt] *s.* comportamiento, conducta.

depose [dɪpóz] *v.* deponer; declarar, atestiguar.

deposit [dɪpázɪt] *s.* depósito; *v.* depositar.

deposition [depəzíʃən] *s.* deposición; declaración.

depositor [dɪpázɪtə] *s.* depositador.

depot [dípo] *s.* depósito; almacén; estación de ferrocarril.

depreciate [dɪpríʃɪet] *v.* depreciar; bajar de precio; abaratar(se); menospreciar.

depress [dɪprés] *v.* deprimir; abatir; desanimar; depreciar, rebajar el valor de.

depressed [dɪprést] *adj.* abatido, decaído.

depressing [dɪprésɪŋ] *adj.* deprimente.

depression [dɪpréʃən] *s.* depresión; de-

caimiento, abatimiento; rebaja (*de precios*).

deprive [dɪpráɪv] *v.* privar.

depth [depθ] *s.* profundidad; hondura; fondo; longitud (*de un solar*); gravedad (*de los sonidos*); viveza (*de los colores*); **in the — of the night** en las tinieblas de la noche; **in the — of winter** en lo más crudo del invierno.

deputation [depjətéʃən] *s.* diputación, delegación; comisión.

depute [dɪpjút] *v.* diputar, delegar.

deputy [dépjətɪ] *s.* diputado; agente; delegado.

derange [dɪréndʒ] *v.* trastornar, desordenar.

derby [dɜ́bɪ] *s.* sombrero hongo, *Am.* sombrero de bola.

deride [dɪráɪd] *v.* escarnecer, ridiculizar, mofarse de, burlarse de.

derision [dɪríʒən] *s.* mofa, escarnio.

derive [dəráɪv] *v.* derivar(se); provenir; sacar (*provecho*); recibir (*placer*).

derrick [dérɪk] *s.* grúa; armazón (*para la explotación del petróleo*).

descend [dɪsénd] *v.* descender; bajar; **to** **— upon** caer sobre, acometer.

descendant [dɪséndənt] *adj.* & *s.* descendiente.

descent [dɪsént] *s.* descenso; bajada; descendencia, linaje; descendimiento; declive.

describe [dɪskráɪb] *v.* describir; trazar.

description [dɪskrípʃən] *s.* descripción; **of all -s** de todas clases.

descriptive [dɪskríptɪv] *adj.* descriptivo.

desert [dézət] *adj.* desierto, despoblado; estéril; *s.* desierto, yermo; páramo; [dɪzɜ́t] *v.* abandonar, desamparar; desertar.

deserter [dɪzɜ́tə] *s.* desertor.

desertion [dɪzɜ́ʃən] *s.* deserción, abandono, desamparo.

deserve [dɪzɜ́v] *v.* merecer.

deserving [dɪzɜ́vɪŋ] *adj.* meritorio; merecedor.

design [dɪzáɪn] *s.* designio, propósito, intención; plan, proyecto, diseño, dibujo; *v.* diseñar, trazar; proyectar; idear.

designate [dézɪgnet] *v.* designar; señalar, indicar, nombrar.

designer [dɪzáɪnə] *s.* diseñador; dibujante; proyectista; intrigante.

desirability [dɪzaɪrəbílətɪ] *s.* conveniencia, utilidad.

desirable [dɪzáɪrəb‖] *adj.* deseable; agradable; conveniente.

desire [dɪzáɪr] *s.* deseo; anhelo, ansia; *v.* desear; anhelar, ansiar.

desirous [dɪzáɪrəs] *adj.* deseoso.

desist [dɪzíst] *v.* desistir.

desk [dɛsk] *s.* escritorio, bufete, pupitre, mesa de escribir.

desolate [dés]ɪt] *adj.* desolado; despoblado, desierto; solitario; [dés]et] *v.* desolar; asolar, arrasar; despoblar.

desolation [dɛs]éʃən] *s.* desolación; soledad.

despair [dɪspér] *s.* desesperación; desesperanza; *v.* desesperarse, perder la esperanza.

despairing [dɪspérɪŋ] *adj.* desesperado, sin esperanza.

despatch [dɪspǽtʃ] = **dispatch.**

desperate [désprɪt] *adj.* desesperado; arriesgado, temerario; **— illness** enfermedad gravísima; **-ly** *adv.* desesperadamente; **-ly ill** gravísimamente enfermo.

desperation [dɛspəréʃən] *s.* desesperación; temeridad.

despise [dɪspáɪz] *v.* despreciar; desdeñar; menospreciar.

despite [dɪspáɪt] *s.* despecho; *prep.* a despecho de, a pesar de.

despoil [dɪspóɪl] *v.* despojar.

despondency [dɪspándənsɪ] *s.* abatimiento, desaliento, descaecimiento o decaimiento del ánimo.

despondent [dɪspándənt] *adj.* abatido, descaecido o decaído de ánimo, desalentado, desesperanzado.

despot [déspət] *s.* déspota.

despotic [dɪspátɪk] *adj.* despótico.

despotism [déspətɪzəm] *s.* despotismo.

dessert [dɪzэ́t] *s.* postre.

destination [dɛstənéʃən] *s.* destinación, destino; paradero.

destine [déstɪn] *v.* destinar; **-ed for** con rumbo a, con destinación a; destinado a.

destiny [déstənɪ] *s.* destino, sino, hado.

destitute [déstətjut] *adj.* destituido, necesitado; falto, desprovisto.

destroy [dɪstróɪ] *v.* destruir.

destroyer [dɪstróɪə] *s.* destruidor; destructor, cazatorpedero, destroyer.

destruction [dɪstrʌ́kʃən] *s.* destrucción; ruina.

destructive [dɪstrʌ́ktɪv] *adj.* destructivo.

detach [dɪtǽtʃ] *v.* separar, despegar, desprender; destacar (*una porción de tropa*).

detachment [dɪtǽtʃmənt] *s.* separación; desprendimiento; desapego, despego, alejamiento; destacamento (*militar*).

detail [dítel] *s.* detalle; pormenor; destacamento (*militar*); **to go into — de-**

tallar, pormenorizar; [dɪtél] *v.* detallar; pormenorizar; destacar, asignar.

detain [dɪtén] *v.* detener; entretener, demorar, retardar.

detect [dɪtékt] *v.* descubrir.

detective [dɪtéktɪv] *s.* detective, detectivo, policía secreto.

detention [dɪténʃən] *s.* detención.

deteriorate [dɪtíríəret] *v.* deteriorar(se).

deterioration [dɪtɪrɪəréʃən] *s.* deterioro.

determination [dɪtэ̀mənéʃən] *s.* determinación; decisión; resolución, firmeza.

determine [dɪtэ́mɪn] *v.* determinar; decidir; **to — to** determinarse a, decidirse a, resolverse a.

determined [dɪtэ́mɪnd] *adj.* determinado, decidido, resuelto.

detest [dɪtést] *v.* detestar, aborrecer.

detour [dítʊr] *s.* rodeo, desvío, desviación, vuelta; *v.* dar o hacer un rodeo.

devastate [dévəstet] *v.* devastar, arruinar, asolar.

develop [dɪvéləp] *v.* desarrollar(se); desenvolver(se); revelar (*una película o placa fotográfica*); explotar (*una mina*).

development [dɪvéləpmənt] *s.* desarrollo; desenvolvimiento; crecimiento; fomento; explotación; revelamiento (*de una película*).

deviate [dívɪet] *v.* desviar(se).

deviation [dívɪéʃən] *s.* desviación; desvío, extravío.

device [dɪváɪs] *s.* artificio; mecanismo, aparato; ardid, recurso; divisa; **left to one's own -s** abandonado a sus propios recursos.

devil [dévḷ] *s.* diablo; demonio.

devilish [dévlɪʃ] *adj.* diabólico; endiablado; travieso.

deviltry [dévḷtrɪ] *s.* diablura.

devious [dívɪəs] *adj.* desviado; tortuoso; indirecto.

devise [dɪváɪz] *v.* idear, trazar, urdir.

devoid [dɪvóɪd] *adj.* exento, libre, falto, privado, desprovisto.

devote [dɪvót] *v.* dedicar; consagrar; **to — oneself to** dedicarse a, consagrarse a, aplicarse a.

devoted [dɪvótɪd] *adj.* dedicado, consagrado; apegado; **— friend** amigo fiel o leal.

devotion [dɪvóʃən] *s.* devoción; piedad; afecto; lealtad.

devour [dɪváʊr] *v.* devorar.

devout [dɪváʊt] *adj.* devoto, piadoso; sincero.

dew [dju] *s.* rocío, sereno; *v.* rociar; caer (*el rocío*).

dewdrop [djúdrɑp] *s.* gota de rocío.

dewy [djúɪ] *adj.* rociado, húmedo de

rocío.

dexterity [dɛkstérətɪ] *s.* destreza.

dexterous [dékstrəs] *adj.* diestro.

diadem [dáɪədɛm] *s.* diadema.

diagnose [daɪəgnós] *v.* diagnosticar.

diagonal [daɪægən̩l] *adj.* diagonal, oblicuo; *s.* diagonal.

diagram [dáɪəgræm] *s.* diagrama.

dial [dáɪəl] *s.* esfera; muestra *(del reloj)*, *Am.* carátula; — **telephone** teléfono automático; *v.* sintonizar o captar *(una estación radiotelefónica)*.

dialect [dáɪəlɛkt] *s.* dialecto.

dialogue [dáɪəlɒg] *s.* diálogo; *v.* dialogar.

diameter [daɪǽmətə] *s.* diámetro.

diamond [dáɪmənd] *s.* diamante; rombo *(figura geométrica)*.

diaper [dáɪəpə] *s.* pañal.

diarrhea [daɪəríə] *s.* diarrea.

diary [dáɪərɪ] *s.* diario.

dice [daɪs] *s. pl. de* **die** dados; *v.* cuadricular, cortar en cuarterones o cubos.

dictate [dɪktet] *s.* dictado, precepto; *v.* dictar.

dictation [dɪktéʃən] *s.* dictado; mando absoluto; **to take —** escribir al dictado.

dictator [dɪktetə] *s.* dictador.

dictatorship [dɪktétəʃɪp] *s.* dictadura.

diction [dɪkʃən] *s.* dicción.

dictionary [dɪkʃənɛrɪ] *s.* diccionario.

did [dɪd] *pret. de* **to do**.

die [daɪ] *s.* *(pl. dice)* dado *(para jugar)*; *(pl. dies)* matriz, molde; cuño *(sello para acuñar moneda)*.

die [daɪ] *v.* morir(se); marchitarse, secarse *(las flores, plantas, etc.)*; **to — out** morirse, extinguirse, apagarse.

diet [dáɪət] *s.* dieta; régimen; **to be on a — estar a dieta; to put on a —** adietar, poner a dieta; *v.* ponerse a dieta; estar a dieta.

differ [dɪfə] *v.* diferir, diferenciarse, distinguirse; disentir; **to — with** no convenir con, no estar de acuerdo con.

difference [dɪfrəns] *s.* diferencia; distinción; discordia, controversia; **it makes no —** no importa, es igual, da lo mismo.

different [dɪfrənt] *adj.* diferente; distinto.

differentiate [dɪfərénʃɪet] *v.* diferenciar(se); distinguir(se).

difficult [dɪfəkʌlt] *adj.* difícil; dificultoso, trabajoso, penoso.

difficulty [dɪfəkʌltɪ] *s.* dificultad; apuro, aprieto.

diffidence [dɪfədəns] *s.* timidez; desconfianza de sí propio.

diffident [dɪfədənt] *adj.* huraño; tímido.

diffuse [dɪfjús] *adj.* difuso; prolijo; [dɪf-

júz] *v.* difundir.

diffusion [dɪfjúʒən] *s.* difusión; diseminación.

dig [dɪg] *v.* cavar; excavar; ahondar; escarbar; trabajar duro; **to — under** socavar; **to — up** desenterrar; *s.* piquete; pulla, sarcasmo.

digest [dáɪdʒɛst] *s.* sumario, compendio; recopilación; código; [dədʒést] *v.* digerir; recopilar.

digestible [dədʒéstəbl̩] *adj.* digestible, digerible.

digestion [dədʒéstʃən] *s.* digestión.

digestive [dədʒéstɪv] *adj.* digestivo.

dignified [dɪgnəfaɪd] *adj.* digno, mesurado; serio, grave.

dignitary [dɪgnətɛrɪ] *s.* dignatario.

dignity [dɪgnətɪ] *s.* dignidad.

digress [dəgrés] *v.* divagar.

digression [dəgréʃən] *s.* digresión, divagación.

dike [daɪk] *s.* dique, represa; zanja.

dilate [daɪlét] *v.* dilatar(se), extender(se), ensanchar(se).

diligence [dɪlədʒəns] *s.* diligencia; aplicación, esmero.

diligent [dɪlədʒənt] *adj.* diligente, activo, aplicado.

dilute [dɪlút] *v.* diluir, desleír; aguar; *adj.* diluido.

dim [dɪm] *adj.* penumbroso, obscuro; nublado; confuso; indistinto; deslustrado, sin brillo; *v.* obscurecer; anublar, ofuscar; atenuar.

dime [daɪm] *s.* moneda de diez centavos.

dimension [dəménʃən] *s.* dimensión.

diminish [dəmínɪʃ] *v.* disminuir; rebajar.

diminution [dɪmənjúʃən] *s.* diminución, mengua.

diminutive [dəmínjətɪv] *adj.* diminutivo; diminuto; *s.* diminutivo.

dimness [dɪmnɪs] *s.* semi-obscuridad, penumbra; ofuscamiento.

dimple [dɪmpl̩] *s.* hoyuelo.

din [dɪn] *s.* estruendo, fragor, estrépito.

dine [daɪn] *v.* comer; festejar u obsequiar con una comida.

diner [dáɪnə] *s.* coche-comedor; comensal *(persona que come a la mesa)*.

dingy [dɪndʒɪ] *adj.* negruzco; manchado, sucio.

dining [dáɪnɪŋ] *ger. de* **to dine**; **— car** coche-comedor; **— room** comedor.

dinner [dɪnə] *s.* comida; **— coat** smoking o esmoquin.

dint [dɪnt]: **by — of** a fuerza de.

dip [dɪp] *s.* zambullida; inmersión; bajada; declive; depresión; *v.* meter(se); zambullirse; mojar *(la pluma en el tintero)*; teñir; agachar *(la cabeza)*; saludar (con la bandera); inclinarse (un camino); dar un bajón (un avión); hundirse (el sol en el horizonte); **to — out** vaciar (con cucharón o cazo).

diphtheria [dɪfɵírɪə] s. difteria.

diploma [dɪplómə] s. diploma.

diplomacy [dɪplómǝsɪ] s. diplomacia.

diplomat [dɪploməæt] s. diplomático.

diplomatic [dɪpləmǽtɪk] adj. diplomático.

dipper [dɪpǝ] s. cucharón, cazo; **the Big Dipper** la Osa Mayor.

dire [daɪr] adj. extremo; horrendo; fatal, de mal agüero.

direct [dǝrékt] adj. directo; derecho, en línea recta; inmediato; **— current** corriente continua; **— object** acusativo; adv. directamente; **-ly** adv. directamente; inmediatamente; en seguida; v. dirigir; guiar; encaminar; dar direcciones ú ordenes.

direction [dǝrékʃǝn] s. dirección; administración; gerencia; rumbo.

directive [dǝréktɪv] adj. directivo; s. orden, mandato.

directness [dǝréktnɪs] s. derechura; franqueza; lo directo; **with —** sin rodeos.

director [dǝréktǝ] s. director; gerente.

directory [dǝréktǝrɪ] s. directorio; junta directiva; **telephone —** guía telefónica.

dirigible [dírǝdʒǝbl] adj. & s. dirigible.

dirt [dɜrt] s. suciedad; mugre; tierra, polvo, lodo.

dirty [dɜrtɪ] adj. sucio; mugriento; cochino; enlodado; manchado; v. ensuciar; manchar; enlodar.

disable [dɪsébl] v. incapacitar.

disadvantage [dɪsǝdvǽntɪdʒ] s. desventaja; **to be at a —** estar en una situación desventajosa.

disagree [dɪsǝgrí] v. diferir, disentir; no convenir, no estar de acuerdo; no sentarle a uno bien (el clima, la comida, etc.).

disagreeable [dɪsǝgríǝbl] adj. desagradable; áspero, de mal genio.

disagreement [dɪsǝgrímǝnt] s. desavenencia, desacuerdo; disensión; discordia; discordancia.

disappear [dɪsǝpír] v. desaparecer.

disappearance [dɪsǝpírǝns] s. desaparición.

disappoint [dɪsǝpóɪnt] v. chasquear; contrariar; decepcionar; faltar a lo prometido; desilusionar; **to be -ed** estar desilusionado o decepcionado; estar desengañado; quedar contrariado.

disappointing [dɪsǝpóɪntɪŋ] adj. desilusionante, desengañador, decepcionante.

disappointment [dɪsǝpóɪntmǝnt] s. desilusión, desengaño, decepción; chasco; contrariedad.

disapproval [dɪsǝprúvl] s. desaprobación.

disapprove [dɪsǝprúv] v. desaprobar.

disarm [dɪsárm] v. desarmar(se).

disarmament [dɪsármǝmǝnt] s. desarme.

disarray [dɪsǝré] s. desarreglo, confusión, desorden; v. desarreglar, desordenar.

disaster [dɪzǽstǝ] s. desastre.

disastrous [dɪzǽstrǝs] adj. desastroso.

disband [dɪsbǽnd] v. dispersar; licenciar (las tropas); desbandarse.

disbelieve [dɪsbǝlív] v. descreer, no creer.

disburse [dɪsbɜs] v. desembolsar.

disbursement [dɪsbɜsmǝnt] s. desembolso; gasto.

disc [dɪsk] = disk.

discard [dískǝrd] s. descarte; desecho, cosa desechada; [dɪskárd] v. descartar; desechar.

discern [dɪsɜn] v. discernir, distinguir; percibir.

discernment [dɪsɜnmǝnt] s. discernimiento.

discharge [dɪstʃárdʒ] s. descarga (de artillería); descargo (de una obligación); desempeño (de un deber); exoneración; despedida; licencia (militar); pago (de una deuda); derrame, desagüe; supuración; v. descargar; exonerar; poner en libertad; despedir, echar, deponer; dar de baja (a un soldado); pagar (una deuda); arrojar, supurar; desaguar.

disciple [dɪsáɪpl] s. discípulo.

discipline [dísǝplɪn] s. disciplina; v. disciplinar.

disclose [dɪsklóz] v. descubrir; revelar.

discolor [dɪskÁlǝ] v. descolorar(se), desteñir(se).

discomfort [dɪskÁmfǝt] s. incomodidad; malestar.

disconcert [dɪskǝnsɜt] v. desconcertar.

disconnect [dɪskǝnékt] v. desconectar; desunir, separar.

disconnected [dɪskǝnéktɪd] p.p. & adj. desconectado; desunido; inconexo, incoherente.

disconsolate [dɪskánslɪt] adj. desconsolado.

discontent [dɪskǝntént] s. descontento; v. descontentar.

discontented [dɪskǝnténtɪd] adj. descontento; descontentadizo.

discontinue [dɪskǝntínju] v. descontinuar; parar; suspender, interrumpir; abandonar.

discord [dískɔrd] s. discordia; disonancia, discordancia; desavenencia.

discount [dískaunt] s. descuento; rebaja; — **rate** tipo de descuento; v. descontar; rebajar.

discourage [dískɔ́ɪdʒ] v. desanimar, desalentar, abatir; **to — from** disuadir de.

discouragement [dískɔ́ɪdʒmənt] s. desaliento, abatimiento.

discourse [dískors] s. discurso; conversación; [dískórs] v. disertar, discurrir, hablar.

discourteous [dískɔ́tɪəs] adj. descortés, desatento.

discourtesy [dískɔ́təsɪ] s. descortesía, desatención.

discover [dískʌ́və] v. descubrir.

discoverer [dískʌ́vərə] s. descubridor.

discovery [dískʌ́vrɪ] s. descubrimiento.

discredit [dískrédɪt] s. descrédito; deshonra; v. desacreditar; deshonrar; no creer.

discreet [dískrít] adj. discreto, prudente.

discrepancy [dískrépənsɪ] s. discrepancia, diferencia; variación.

discretion [dískréʃən] s. discreción; prudencia; **at one's own —** a discreción.

discriminate [dískrímənet] v. discernir, distinguir; hacer distinciones, hacer favoritismos; **to — against** hacer favoritismos en perjuicio de.

discuss [dískʌ́s] v. discutir.

discussion [dískʌ́ʃən] s. discusión.

disdain [dísdén] s. desdén, menosprecio; v. desdeñar, menospreciar; desdeñarse de.

disdainful [dísdénfəl] adj. desdeñoso.

disease [dízíz] s. enfermedad.

diseased [dízízd] adj. enfermo.

disembark [dísɪmbárk] v. desembarcar.

disentangle [dísɪntǽŋgl] v. desenredar, desenmarañar, deshacer (una maraña o enredo).

disfigure [dísfígjə] v. desfigurar; afear.

disgrace [dísgrés] s. ignominia, deshonra; vergüenza; **to be in —** estar desacreditado, haber perdido la gracia o el favor; v. deshonrar; degradar; desacreditar; avergonzar.

disgraceful [dísgrésfəl] adj. vergonzoso.

disguise [dísgáɪz] s. disfraz; v. disfrazar.

disgust [dísgʌ́st] s. asco; repugnancia; disgusto; v. disgustar, dar asco; repugnar.

disgusted [dísgʌ́stɪd] adj. disgustado; descontento; asqueado.

disgusting [dísgʌ́stɪŋ] adj. asqueroso,

repugnante.

dish [dɪʃ] s. plato; manjar, vianda; **-es** vajilla; v. servir.

dishearten [dɪshártŋ] v. desalentar, desanimar, descorazonar.

disheveled [dɪʃévld] adj. desgreñado; desaliñado, desaseado.

dishonest [dísánɪst] adj. engañoso, falso, tramposo, falto de honradez, fraudulento.

dishonesty [dísánɪstɪ] s. fraude, falta de honradez.

dishonor [dísánə] s. deshonra; afrenta; v. deshonrar; recusar (un giro o cheque).

dishonorable [dísánərəbl] adj. deshonroso; infame.

disillusion [dísɪlúʒən] s. desilusión, decepción, desengaño; v. desilusionar, decepcionar, desengañar.

disinfect [dísɪnfékt] v. desinfectar.

disinfectant [dísɪnféktənt] s. desinfectante.

disinterested [dísíntərəstɪd] adj. desinteresado..

disk [dɪsk] s. disco.

dislike [dísláɪk] s. antipatía, aversión; v. sentir o tener aversión por; **I — it** me repugna, no me gusta, me desagrada.

dislocate [dísloket] v. dislocar, descoyuntar.

dislodge [díslɑ́dʒ] v. desalojar.

disloyal [díslɔ́ɪəl] adj. desleal.

dismal [dízml] adj. lúgubre, sombrío, tétrico.

dismantle [dísmǽntl] v. desmantelar; desmontar, desarmar.

dismay [dísmé] s. desmayo, desaliento, pavor; v. desalentar, desanimar; atemorizar.

dismiss [dísmɪs] v. despedir, expulsar, destituir; desechar; licenciar, dar de baja; dar por terminado (un pleito o caso jurídico); **to — the meeting** disolver la junta, levantar la sesión.

dismissal [dísmɪsl] s. despedida, expulsión, destitución (de un cargo).

dismount [dísmáunt] v. desmontar; apear(se); desarmar (un cañón, una máquina); desengastar (joyas).

disobedience [dísəbídɪəns] s. desobediencia.

disobedient [dísəbídɪənt] adj. desobediente.

disobey [dísəbé] v. desobedecer.

disorder [dísórdə] s. desorden; trastorno; confusión; enfermedad; v. desordenar; trastornar; desarreglar.

disorderly [dísórdəlɪ] adj. desordenado; desarreglado; revoltoso; escandaloso;

adv. desordenadamente.

disown [dɪsón] *v.* repudiar; desconocer, negar.

dispassionate [dɪspǽʃənɪt] *adj.* desapasionado.

dispatch [dɪspǽtʃ] *s.* despacho; envío; parte (*m.*), comunicación, mensaje; prontitud, expedición; *v.* despachar; enviar, expedir; matar.

dispel [dɪspél] *v.* disipar; dispersar.

dispensary [dɪspénsərɪ] *s.* dispensario.

dispensation [dɪspɒnséʃən] *s.* dispensa, exención; dispensación; distribución.

dispense [dɪspéns] *v.* dispensar, dar; repartir, distribuir; administrar (*la justicia*); despachar (*recetas, medicamentos*); **to — from** eximir de, dispensar de; **to — with** omitir; pasarse sin, prescindir de.

dispersal [dɪspə́sl] *s.* dispersión; desbandada.

disperse [dɪspə́s] *v.* dispersar(se), disipar(se), esparcir(se).

displace [dɪsplés] *v.* desalojar; desplazar; poner fuera de su lugar; suplantar.

display [dɪsplé] *s.* manifestación, exhibición; ostentación; *v.* exhibir; mostrar; manifestar; desplegar.

displease [dɪsplíz] *v.* desagradar; disgustar, fastidiar.

displeasure [dɪspléʒə] *s.* desagrado, disgusto, descontento.

disposal [dɪspózl] *s.* disposición; arreglo; venta (*de bienes*).

dispose [dɪspóz] *v.* disponer; arreglar; influir; **to — of** deshacerse de.

disposition [dɪspəzíʃən] *s.* disposición; arreglo; aptitud, inclinación; venta; **good (bad) —** buen (mal) genio.

disprove [dɪsprúv] *v.* refutar.

dispute [dɪspjút] *s.* disputa; *v.* disputar.

disqualify [dɪskwǽləfaɪ] *v.* inhabilitar, incapacitar, descalificar.

disregard [dɪsrɪgárd] *s.* desatención, falta de atención, negligencia, descuido; falta de respeto o consideración; *v.* desatender, no hacer caso de, desentenderse de.

disrespect [dɪsrɪspékt] *s.* desacato, falta de respeto.

disrespectful [dɪsrɪspéktfəl] *adj.* irrespetuoso.

dissatisfied [dɪssǽtɪsfaɪd] *adj.* descontento, malcontento, mal satisfecho.

dissatisfy [dɪssǽtɪsfaɪ] *v.* descontentar, no satisfacer.

dissect [dɪsɛ́kt] *v.* disecar, hacer una disección; analizar.

dissemble [dɪsɛ́mbl] *v.* disimular, fingir.

dissension [dɪsɛ́nʃən] *s.* disensión, discordia.

dissent [dɪsɛ́nt] *v.* disentir; *s.* desacuerdo; disensión, desavenencia.

dissimulation [dɪsɪmjəléʃən] *s.* disimulo.

dissipate [dɪsəpet] *v.* disipar(se).

dissipation [dɪsəpéʃən] *s.* disipación.

dissolute [dɪsəlut] *adj.* disoluto.

dissolution [dɪsəlúʃən] *s.* disolución.

dissolve [dɪzólv] *v.* disolver(se); anular.

dissuade [dɪswéd] *v.* disuadir.

distaff [dɪstæf] *s.* rueca.

distance [dɪstəns] *s.* distancia; lejanía; alejamiento; **in the — a lo lejos**, en lontananza.

distant [dɪstənt] *adj.* distante; apartado, lejano, remoto; esquivo; **to be — from** distar de; **-ly** *adv.* de lejos; remotamente; a distancia; en lontananza.

distaste [dɪstést] *s.* disgusto, aversión, repugnancia.

distasteful [dɪstéstfəl] *adj.* desagradable, repugnante.

distend [dɪsténd] *v.* dilatar, ensanchar.

distil [dɪstíl] *v.* destilar.

distillation [dɪstɪléʃən] *s.* destilación.

distillery [dɪstílərɪ] *s.* destilería.

distinct [dɪstíŋkt] *adj.* distinto, claro; diferente; **-ly** *adv.* distintamente, claramente, con claridad.

distinction [dɪstíŋkʃən] *s.* distinción.

distinctive [dɪstíŋktɪv] *adj.* distintivo.

distinguish [dɪstíŋgwɪʃ] *v.* distinguir; discernir.

distinguished [dɪstíŋgwɪʃt] *adj.* distinguido.

distinguishing [dɪstíŋgwɪʃɪŋ] *adj.* distintivo, característico.

distort [dɪstórt] *v.* desfigurar, deformar, torcer, falsear; tergiversar.

distract [dɪstrǽkt] *v.* distraer; perturbar.

distraction [dɪstrǽkʃən] *s.* distracción, diversión; perturbación; **to drive to — volver loco.**

distress [dɪstrés] *s.* angustia, aflicción, congoja; dolor; **to be in — tener una aflicción**; estar apurado; estar en zozobra (*un navío*); *v.* angustiar, acongojar, afligir; **to be -ed estar afligido o apurado.**

distribute [dɪstríbjʊt] *v.* distribuir, repartir.

distribution [dɪstrəbjúʃən] *s.* distribución; repartimiento.

distributor [dɪstríbjətə] *s.* distribuidor.

district [dɪstrɪkt] *s.* distrito; **— attorney** fiscal de distrito.

distrust [dɪstrʌ́st] *s.* desconfianza; recelo; *v.* desconfiar; recelar.

distrustful [dɪstrʌ́stfəl] *adj.* desconfiado, sospechoso, receloso.

disturb [dɪstɔ́b] v. turbar, perturbar, inquietar; desarreglar; incomodar, molestar; **don't — yourself!** ¡no se moleste Vd.!

disturbance [dɪstɔ́bɔns] s. disturbio; perturbación; desorden; alboroto; molestia.

disuse [dɪsjús] s. desuso; **to fall into —** caer en desuso; caducar.

ditch [dɪtʃ] s. zanja; foso; **irrigation —** acequia; v. zanjar, abrir zanjas; meter en la zanja; **to — someone** deshacerse de alguien.

ditto [dɪ́to] s. ídem, lo mismo.

divan [dáɪvæn] s. diván.

dive [daɪv] s. zambullida (echándose de cabeza), buceada, chapuz; picada (descenso rápido de un avión); garito, leonera; v. echarse de cabeza; zambullirse (de cabeza); bucear; sumergirse (un submarino); **to — into someone** abalanzarse sobre alguien.

diver [dáɪvɔ] s. buzo; zambullidor.

diverge [dɔvɔ́dʒ] v. divergir, irse apartando, separarse; diferir.

divergence [dɔvɔ́dʒɔns] s. divergencia; diferencia (de opiniones).

divers [dáɪvɔz] adj. diversos, varios.

diverse [dɔvɔ́s] adj. diverso, diferente.

diversion [dɔvɔ́ʒɔn] s. diversión, recreo; desviación.

diversity [dɔvɔ́sɔtɪ] s. diversidad, diferencia, variedad.

divert [dɔvɔ́t] v. divertir, entretener; distraer; desviar, apartar.

divide [dɔváɪd] v. dividir(se); partir.

dividend [dɪ́vɔdend] s. dividendo.

divine [dɔváɪn] adj. divino; v. adivinar.

divinity [dɔvɪ́nɔtɪ] s. divinidad; deidad; teología.

division [dɔvɪ́ʒɔn] s. división.

divorce [dɔvɔ́rs] s. divorcio; v. divorciar(se).

divulge [dɔváldʒ] v. divulgar.

dizziness [dɪ́zɪnɪs] s. vahido o vaguido, desvanecimiento, mareo, vértigo.

dizzy [dɪ́zɪ] adj. desvanecido, mareado, confuso; aturdido; **— speed** velocidad vertiginosa.

do [du] v. hacer; **to — away with** deshacerse de; prescindir de; **to — a lesson** estudiar una lección; **to — one's hair** peinarse, arreglarse el pelo; **to — the dishes** lavar los platos; **to — up** envolver; limpiar, arreglar; lavar o planchar; **to — well in business** prosperar en los negocios; **to — without** pasarse sin; **to have nothing to — with** no tener nada que ver con; **that**

will — basta, bastará; **that won't —** eso no sirve; eso no resultará bien; **this will have to —** habrá que conformarse con esto; **how — you — ?** ¿cómo está Vd.?; **— you hear me?** ¿me oye Vd.?; **yes, I — sí**, le oigo; **I — say it** sí lo digo.

docile [dás]] adj. dócil.

dock [dak] s. muelle, desembarcadero; dársena; dique de carena; v. entrar en el muelle; atracar, meter (una embarcación) en el muelle o dique; **to — the wages** rebajar la paga.

doctor [dáktɔ] s. doctor; médico, facultativo; v. medicinar, curar; **to — oneself** medicinarse, tomar medicinas.

doctrine [dáktrɪn] s. doctrina.

document [dákjɔmɔnt] s. documento; [dákjɔment] v. documentar.

dodge [dadʒ] s. evasión, evasiva; v. evadir(se); escabullirse; hurtar el cuerpo; **to — around a corner** dar un esquinazo.

doe [do] s. cierva; hembra (del antílope, del gamo, de la liebre).

dog [dɔg] s. perro, perra; can; **hot —** salchicha caliente, Am. perro caliente; **to put on a lot of —** emperifollarse; darse mucho tono, Am. darse mucho corte; v. seguir la pista de, perseguir, acosar; adv. sumamente, completamente; **dog-tired** cansadísimo.

dogma [dɔ́gmɔ] s. dogma.

dogmatic [dɔgmǽtɪk] adj. dogmático.

doily [dɔ́ɪlɪ] s. mantelito (para platos, vasos, lámparas, etc.).

doings [dúɪŋz] s. pl. hechos, acciones, acontecimientos; **great — mucha** actividad, fiesta, función.

dole [dol] s. reparto gratuito (de dinero o alimento); ración, limosna; v. repartir gratuitamente.

doleful [dólfɔl] adj. lúgubre, triste, lastimoso.

doll [dal] s. muñeca, muñeco; v. **to — up** emperifollarse, ataviarse; **dolly** s. muñequita.

dollar [dálɔ] s. dólar.

domain [domén] s. dominio; heredad.

dome [dom] s. cúpula; media naranja (de iglesia).

domestic [dɔméstɪk] adj. doméstico; hogareño; nacional, del país, Am. criollo; s. criado, sirviente.

dominant [dámɔnɔnt] adj. dominante.

dominate [dámɔnet] v. dominar.

domination [damɔné(ʃɔn)] s. dominación, dominio.

domineer [damɔnɪr] v. dominar, señorear.

domineering [damənírɪŋ] *adj.* dominador, mandón, imperioso, tiránico.

dominion [dəmínjən] *s.* dominio.

domino [dáməno] *s.* dominó, traje de máscara; disfraz; ficha (*de dominó*); **dominoes** dominó (*juego*).

don [dan] *s.* don (*título*); caballero; *v.* ponerse, vestirse.

donate [dónet] *v.* donar, regalar, hacer donación.

donation [donéʃən] *s.* donación; regalo, dádiva.

done [dʌn] *p.p. de* to do hecho; terminado, acabado; **to be —** in estar rendido de cansancio; **the meat is well —** está bien asada la carne.

donkey [dáŋkɪ] *s.* burro, asno.

doom [dum] *s.* hado, sino, destino; mala suerte, perdición, ruina; **the day of —** el día del juicio final; *v.* condenar, sentenciar; predestinar; **to be -ed to failure** estar predestinado al fracaso.

door [dor] *s.* puerta; entrada.

doorbell [dórbel] *s.* campanilla o timbre (*de llamada*).

doorknob [dórnab] *s.* tirador de puerta, perilla, manija.

doorman [dórmæn] *s.* portero.

doorstep [dórstep] *s.* escalón de la puerta; umbral.

doorway [dórwe] *s.* puerta, entrada; vano (*de la puerta*).

dope [dop] *s.* opio; narcótico; droga, menjurje, medicamento; información; **— fiend** morfinómano; **he is a —** es un zoquete; *v.* narcotizar; **to — out** adivinar, conjeturar; **to — oneself up** medicinarse demasiado.

dormitory [dórmətorɪ] *s.* dormitorio.

dose [dos] *s.* dosis; *v.* medicinar; **to — oneself** medicinarse.

dot [dat] *s.* punto; **on the —** en punto; *v.* marcar con puntos; poner el punto (*sobre la* i).

dotage [dótɪdʒ] *s.* chochez; **to be in one's —** chochear.

dote [dot] *v.* chochear; **to — on** estar loco por.

double [dʌbl] *adj.* doble; doblado; **— boiler** baño de María; **— deal** trato doble; *s.* doble; **-s** juego de dobles (*en tenis*); *adv.* doblemente; **double-breasted** cruzado; **double-faced** de dos caras; *v.* doblar(se); duplicar(se); **to — up** doblarse; **doubly** *adv.* doblemente; por duplicado.

doubt [daut] *s.* duda; *v.* dudar.

doubtful [dáutfəl] *adj.* dudoso; dudable.

doubtless [dáutlɪs] *adj.* indudable, cierto,

seguro; *adv.* sin duda; indudablemente; probablemente.

douche [duʃ] *s.* ducha; jeringa.

dough [do] *s.* pasta, masa; dinero.

doughnut [dónət] *s.* bollito o buñuelo en rosca.

dove [dʌv] *s.* paloma.

dove [dov] *pret. de* to dive.

down [daun] *adv.* abajo, hacia abajo; **— to** hasta; **— East** en el este; **— the street** calle abajo; **to cut — prices** reducir o rebajar precios; **to get — to work** aplicarse; **to go** (*o* **come**) **—** bajar; **to pay —** pagar al contado; **to put —** poner; anotar, apuntar, poner por escrito; *adj.* abatido, descorazonado; **— grade** declive, pendiente; **prices are —** han bajado los precios; **to be — on someone** tenerle ojeriza a alguien; **— plumón**; vello; pelusa; *v.* echar por tierra, derribar; rebajar (*precios*).

downcast [dáunkæst] *adj.* cabizbajo, abatido; **with — eyes** con los ojos bajos.

downfall [dáunfɔl] *s.* caída; ruina.

downpour [dáunpor] *s.* aguacero, chaparrón.

downright [dáunrait] *adj.* claro, positivo, categórico, absoluto; **— foolishness** solemne disparate; *adv.* enteramente; absolutamente.

downstairs [dáunstérz] *adv.* abajo; en el piso bajo; *adj.* del piso bajo; *s.* piso bajo, piso inferior.

downstream [dáunstrím] *adv.* río abajo, aguas abajo; con la corriente.

downtown [dáuntáun] *adv.* al centro, en el centro (*de una población*); *adj.* del centro; *s.* centro.

downward [dáunwəd] *adj.* descendente; inclinado; *adv.* (= **downwards**) hacia abajo.

downy [dáuni] *adj.* suave, blando; velloso; plumoso.

dowry [dáuri] *s.* dote.

doze [doz] *s.* siestecita, sueño ligero; *v.* dormitar.

dozen [dʌzn] *s.* docena.

drab [dræb] *adj.* pardo, pardusco; monótono.

draft [dræft] *s.* corriente de aire; trago; libranza, letra de cambio, giro bancario; trazado; plan; leva (*militar*), conscripción; tiro (*de estufa, hogar, etc.*); calado (*de un barco*); **— beer** cerveza de barril; **— horse** caballo de tiro; **rough — croquis, borrador; *v.* trazar, dibujar, delinear; reclutar, echar leva; redactar (*un documento*).

draftsman [drǽftsmən] *s.* dibujante.

drag [dræg] *s.* rastra; traba, obstáculo; **to have a — with someone** tener buenas aldabas con alguien; *v.* arrastrar(se); rastrear; moverse despacio; **to — on and on** prolongarse demasiado, prolongarse hasta el fastidio.

dragon [drǽgən] *s.* dragón.

drain [dren] *s.* desagüe; desaguadero, conducto; agotamiento; consumo; *v.* desaguar(se); apurar (*un vaso*); agotar, consumir; escurrir(se), secar(se); desecar (*un terreno*), *Am.* drenar.

drainage [drénɪdʒ] *s.* desagüe, *Am.* drenaje; desaguadero; sistema de desaguaderos; desecamiento, desecación (*de un terreno, laguna, etc.*).

drake [drek] *s.* pato.

drama [drámə] *s.* drama.

dramatic [drəmǽtɪk] *adj.* dramático.

dramatist [drámətɪst] *s.* dramaturgo, dramático.

dramatize [drǽmətaɪz] *v.* dramatizar.

drank [dræŋk] *pret. de* **to drink**.

drape [drep] *s.* colgadura, cortina, tapiz; *v.* colgar, entapizar, adornar con tapices; cubrir, revestir.

drapery [drépərɪ] *s.* tapicería, colgaduras, cortinas; pañería, paños, géneros.

drastic [drǽstɪk] *adj.* extremo, fuerte, violento; **to take — steps** tomar medidas enérgicas.

draught [dræft] *véase* **draft**.

draw [drɔ] *v.* tirar; estirar; jalar (halar); atraer; sacar; dibujar, trazar; girar, librar (*una libranza*); hacer (*una comparación*); correr (*la cortina*); **to — aside** apartar(se); **to — a breath** aspirar, tomar aliento; **to — lots** echar suertes, sortear; **to — near** acercarse; **to — out** sacar; sonsacar (*a una persona*); alargar, prolongar; **to — up** acercar(se); redactar (*un documento*); *s.* empate (*en deportes o juegos*); número sacado (*en una rifa*); atracción; **—bridge** puente levadizo.

drawback [drɔ́bæk] *s.* desventaja; obstáculo, inconveniente.

drawer [drɔr] *s.* cajón, gaveta; **-s** calzoncillos.

drawer [drɔ́ə] *s.* librador, girador; dibujante.

drawing [drɔ́ɪŋ] *s.* dibujo; delineación, trazado; sorteo; **— paper** papel de dibujo; **— room** sala de recibo, recibidor, recibimiento.

drawn [drɔn] *p.p. de* **to draw**.

dread [drɛd] *s.* pavor, temor, aprensión; *adj.* terrible; temido; *v.* temer; sentir aprensión de.

dreadful [drédfəl] *adj.* horrendo; espantoso.

dream [drim] *s.* sueño; ensueño; *v.* soñar; **to — of** soñar con, soñar en.

dreamer [drímə] *s.* soñador.

dreamland [drímlænd] *s.* tierra del ensueño; región de los sueños.

dreamt [drɛmpt] = **dreamed**.

dreamy [drímɪ] *adj.* soñoliento; soñador; melancólico; como un sueño; **a — recollection** un vago recuerdo.

dreary [drírɪ] *adj.* sombrío; melancólico.

dredge [drɛdʒ] *s.* draga; *v.* dragar.

dregs [drɛgz] *s. pl.* heces, sedimento.

drench [drɛntʃ] *s.* mojada, mojadura, empapada; *v.* empapar; mojar; remojar.

dress [drɛs] *s.* vestido, traje; vestidura, ropaje, atavío; **— rehearsal** ensayo general y último (*antes de una función*); **— suit** traje de etiqueta; *v.* vestir(se); arreglarse, componerse; aderezar; adobar (*carne o pieles*); curar (*heridas*); alinear, formar (*las tropas*); **to — down** reprender, regañar; **to — up** emperifollarse, acicalarse, ataviarse.

dresser [drésə] *s.* tocador, cómoda (*con espejo*); **she is a good —** viste con elegancia o buen gusto.

dressing [drésɪŋ] *s.* aderezo; salsa (*para ensaladas*); relleno (*para carne, pollo, etc.*); medicamento, vendajes (*para heridas*); **a — down** regaño; **— gown** bata; **— room** tocador; **— table** tocador.

dressmaker [drésmekə] *s.* modista.

drew [dru] *pret. de* **to draw**.

dribble [dríbl] *v.* gotear; dejar caer en gotas; babear; *s.* goteo; chorrito.

driblet [dríblɪt] *s.* gota, gotita; **in -s** gota a gota; en pequeñas cantidades.

dried [draɪd] *pret. & p.p. de* **to dry**; *adj.* seco; paso; **— fig** higo paso.

drift [drɪft] *s.* dirección, rumbo, tendencia; montón, amontonameinto (*de arena, nieve, etc.*); deriva, desvío (*de un barco o avión*); **to get the — of a conversation** enterarse a medias de una conversación; *v.* flotar; ir(se) a la deriva; dejarse llevar por la corriente; amontonarse (*la nieve, la arena*); esparcirse (*la arena, la nieve, las nubes*).

driftwood [drɪftwʊd] *s.* madera o leña flotante; madera de playa.

drill [drɪl] *s.* taladro, barrena; ejercicio; adiestramiento, *Am.* entrenamiento; disciplina; dril (*tela*); *v.* taladrar, barrenar, perforar; hacer ejercicio; aleccionar; disciplinar (*un ejército*); adiestrar(se), *Am.* entrenar(se).

drily [dráɪlɪ] *adv.* secamente.

drink [drɪŋk] s. bebida; trago; v. beber; **to —** a toast to beber a la salud de, brindar por; **— it down!** ¡bébaselo! ¡trágueselo!

drinkable [drɪŋkəbl] adj. potable.

drip [drɪp] s. goteo; v. gotear, caer gota a gota; dejar caer gota a gota.

drive [draɪv] s. paseo en coche o automóvil; calzada, carretera; campaña; empuje; tiro, tirada (de una pelota); v. impulsar, impeler, empujar; arrear (animales); conducir, guiar o manejar (un auto); forzar; encajar, clavar (una estaca, cuña, o clavo); tirar, lanzar (una pelota); dar un paseo en auto; llevar (a alguien) en auto; cavar (un pozo, túnel, etc.); **to — away** ahuyentar; **to — a good bargain** hacer un buen trato; **to — mad** volver loco; **what are you driving at?** ¿qué quieres decir con eso?

drivel [drɪvl] s. baba; ñoñería, tontería; v. babear; chochear, decir ñoñerías.

driveling [drɪvlɪŋ] adj. baboso.

driven [drɪvən] p.p. de to drive.

driver [draɪvɚ] s. cochero, chófer, mecánico, conductor (de automóvil); arriero (de animales); uno de los palos de golf; **pile —** martinete (para clavar pilotes); **slave —** mandón, tirano; **truck —** carretero, camionero.

driveway [draɪvwe] s. calzada de entrada, carretera de entrada.

drizzle [drɪzl] v. lloviznar; s. llovizna.

drone [dron] s. zángano; holgazán; zumbido; v. zumbar; hablar con monotonía; holgazanear, perder el tiempo.

droop [drup] v. doblarse, andar o estar alicaído; estar abatido; languidecer; marchitarse; bajar (los hombros, los párpados); his shoulders — tiene los hombros caídos; **-ing eyelids** párpados caídos.

drop [drɑp] s. gota; declive; baja; caída; **cough —** pastilla para la tos; **letter —** buzón; **— curtain** telón (de teatro); **— hammer** martinete; v. dejar caer, soltar; gotear; caer; dejar (un asunto, una amistad); **to — a line** poner unos renglones; **to — asleep** quedarse dormido, dormirse; **to — behind** dejar atrás; quedarse atrás; **to — in** hacer una visita inesperada, Am. descolgarse; **to — in a mailbox** echar al buzón; **to — out** retirarse; desaparecer; **to — the curtain** bajar el telón.

drought [draʊt] s. sequía.

drove [drov] s. manada, recua, rebaño; tropel; pret. de to drive.

drown [draʊn] v. ahogar(se), anegar(se);

apagar, ahogar (un sonido).

drowse [draʊz] v. dormitar, estar amodorrado.

drowsiness [draʊzɪnɪs] s. modorra, somnolencia.

drowsy [draʊzɪ] adj. soñoliento; adormilado, amodorrado; **to become —** amodorrarse.

drudge [drʌdʒ] v. afanarse, atarearse; s. trabajador, esclavo del trabajo.

drug [drʌg] s. droga, narcótico; **to be a — on the market** ser invendible (una mercancía); v. jaropar (administrar drogas en demasía); narcotizar.

druggist [drʌgɪst] s. boticario, droguista, droguero, farmacéutico.

drugstore [drʌgstor] s. botica, droguería, farmacia.

drum [drʌm] s. tambor; tímpano (del oído); barril, tonel; **bass —** tambora, bombo; **—stick** bolillo de tambor; v. tocar el tambor; tamborilear; **to — a lesson into someone** meterle a uno la lección en la cabeza; **to — up trade** solicitar o fomentar ventas.

drummer [drʌmɚ] s. tambor, tamborilero; viajante de comercio, agente.

drunk [drʌŋk] p.p. de to drink; adj. borracho, ebrio, emborrachado, bebido; **to get —** emborracharse, embriagarse.

drunkard [drʌŋkɚd] s. borracho, borrachón, beodo, bebedor.

drunken [drʌŋkən] adj. borracho, ebrio.

drunkenness [drʌŋkənnɪs] s. borrachera, embriaguez.

dry [draɪ] adj. seco; árido; **a — book** un libro aburrido; **— cleaner** quitamanchas; tintorero; **— cleaning** lavado o limpieza al seco; **— goods** lencería, géneros, tejidos, telas; **— measure** medida para áridos; v. secar(se); enjugar; **to — up** secarse, resecarse.

dryness [draɪnɪs] s. sequedad; aridez.

dubious [djubɪəs] adj. dudoso.

duchess [dʌtʃɪs] s. duquesa.

duck [dʌk] s. pato, pata; ánade; dril (género); zambullida, chapuz; agachada rápida (para evitar un golpe); v. zambullir(se), chapuzar(se); agachar(se); agachar (la cabeza).

duckling [dʌklɪŋ] s. patito, anadeja.

due [dju] adj. debido; vencido, pagadero; **in — time** a su debido tiempo; **the bill is —** se ha vencido la cuenta; **the train is — at two o'clock** el tren debe llegar a las dos; adv. directamente; **— east** hacia el este, rumbo al oriente; s. derecho, privilegio; **-s** cuota.

duel [djúəl] *s.* duelo, desafío, combate; *v.* batirse en duelo.

duet [djuét] *s.* duo, dueto.

dug [dʌg] *pret. & p.p. de* to dig.

duke [djuk] *s.* duque.

dukedom [djúkdəm] *s.* ducado.

dull [dʌl] *adj.* opaco, empañado, mate; sin brillo; aburrido; embotado, sin punta, sin filo; torpe, tardo; — **pain** dolor sordo; — **sound** sonido sordo o apagado; *v.* embotar(se); empañar(se); ofuscar; amortiguar (*un dolor o sonido*).

dullness [dʌ́lnɪs] *s.* falta de brillo; estupidez, torpeza; falta de punta o filo; aburrimiento; embotamiento (*de los sentidos o inteligencia*); pesadez.

duly [djúlɪ] *adv.* debidamente.

dumb [dʌm] *adj.* mudo; silencioso, callado; estúpido, torpe; — **creature** animal.

dumbness [dʌ́mnɪs] *s.* mudez; mutismo; estupidez.

dummy [dʌ́mɪ] *s.* maniquí, figurón, muñeco; zoquete, tonto; *adj.* falso, fingido.

dump [dʌmp] *s.* montón (*de tierra, carbón, etc.*); terrero, vaciadero, escorial; **garbage** — muladar; basurero; **to be in the -s** estar abatido; *v.* echar, vaciar, descargar; echar a la basura.

dunce [dʌns] *s.* zopenco, zoquete, tonto.

dune [djun] *s.* duna o médano.

dung [dʌŋ] *s.* boñiga, estiércol.

dungeon [dʌ́ndʒən] *s.* mazmorra, calabozo.

dunghill [dʌ́ŋhɪl] *s.* muladar, estercolero.

dupe [djup] *s.* inocentón, incauto, victima (*de un engaño*); *v.* embaucar.

duplicate [djúpləkɪt] *adj. & s.* doble, duplicado; [djúpləket] *v.* duplicar, copiar.

duplicity [djuplísətɪ] *s.* duplicidad, doblez.

durable [djúrəbl] *adj.* durable, duradero.

duration [djuréʃən] *s.* duración.

during [djúrɪŋ] *prep.* durante.

dusk [dʌsk] *s.* crepúsculo (*vespertino*), anochecida, caída de la tarde; sombra, oscuridad; **at** — al atardecer.

dusky [dʌ́skɪ] *adj.* obscuro, negruzco; sombrío.

dust [dʌst] *s.* polvo; tierra; **cloud of** — polvareda; *v.* sacudir el polvo, desempolvar, quitar el polvo; empolvar, llenar de polvo; espolvorear.

duster [dʌ́stə] *s.* limpiador; quitapolvo; **feather** — plumero.

dusty [dʌ́stɪ] *adj.* polvoriento; empolvado, lleno de polvo.

Dutch [dʌtʃ] *adj. & s.* holandés; — **treat** convite a escote.

Dutchman [dʌ́tʃmən] *s.* holandés.

duty [djútɪ] *s.* deber, obligación; derechos aduanales; impuesto; — **free** libre de derechos aduanales.

dwarf [dworf] *s. & adj.* enano; *v.* achicar, empequeñecer; impedir el desarrollo o crecimiento de.

dwell [dwel] *v.* residir, morar, habitar vivir; **to** — **on a subject** espaciarse o dilatarse en un asunto.

dweller [dwélə] *s.* habitante, morador.

dwelling [dwélɪŋ] *s.* morada, habitación, domicilio.

dwelt [dwelt] *pret. & p.p. de* to dwell.

dwindle [dwíndl] *v.* menguar, mermar; disminuir(se); gastarse.

dye [daɪ] *s.* tinte, tintura; *v.* teñir, tinturar.

dyer [dáɪə] *s.* tintorero; -**'s shop** tintorería.

dying [dáɪŋ] *adj.* moribundo; agonizante.

dynamic [daɪnǽmɪk] *adj.* dinámico; enérgico; -**s** *s.* dinámica.

dynamite [dáfnəmaɪt] *s.* dinamita; *v.* dinamitar, volar con dinamita.

dynamo [dáɪnəmo] *s.* dínamo.

dynasty [dáɪnəstɪ] *s.* dinastía.

dysentery [dísn̩terɪ] *s.* disentería.

E

each [itʃ] *adj.* cada; *pron.* cada uno; — **other** el uno al otro, uno(s) a otro(s).

eager [ígə] *adj.* anhelante, ansioso, deseoso; -**ly** *adv.* con anhelo; con ahinco; ansiosamente.

eagerness [ígənɪs] *s.* anhelo, ansia, deseo vehemente; ahinco; ardor.

eagle [ígl] *s.* águila.

ear [ɪr] *s.* oreja; oído; — **drum** tímpano; — **muff** orejera; — **of corn** mazorca; — **of wheat** espiga; **by** — de oído; **within** — **shot** al alcance del oído.

earl [ɜl] *s.* conde.

early [ɜ́lɪ] *adv.* temprano; *adj.* temprano; primitivo, remoto; — **riser** madrugador, tempranero, mañanero; **at an** — **date** en fecha próxima.

earn [ɜn] *v.* ganar; merecer.

earnest [ɜ́nɪst] *adj.* serio, formal; ardiente; **in** — en serio, con toda formalidad; de buena fe; -**ly** *adv.* seriamente; con ahinco; encarecidamente, ansiosamente.

earnestness [ɜ́nɪstnɪs] *s.* seriedad; celo; solicitud; sinceridad; **in all** — con todo ahinco; con toda formalidad; con toda sinceridad.

earnings [ɜ́nɪŋz] s. ganancias; sueldo, salario, paga.

earring [íːrɪŋ] s. arete, zarcillo, pendiente, arracada.

earth [ɜ́θ] s. tierra; suelo.

earthen [ɜ́θən] adj. de tierra; de barro.

earthenware [ɜ́θənwɛr] s. loza de barro; trastos, cacharros.

earthly [ɜ́θlɪ] adj. terrenal, terrestre, mundano; terreno; **to be of no — use** no servir para nada.

earthquake [ɜ́θkwek] s. terremoto, temblor de tierra.

earthworm [ɜ́θwɜm] s. lombriz.

ease [iz] s. facilidad; naturalidad; soltura; comodidad; tranquilidad; **at —** tranquilo; cómodo; v. facilitar; aliviar; mitigar; tranquilizar; aligerar (el peso); aflojar.

easel [ízl] s. caballete (de pintor).

easily [ízəlɪ] adv. fácilmente; sin dificultad; cómodamente.

east [ist] s. este; oriente, levante; adj. del este, oriental; adv. al este, hacia el este; en el este.

Easter [ístə] s. Pascuas, Pascua Florida; **— Sunday** Domingo de Resurrección o de Pascuas.

eastern [ístən] adj. oriental; del este.

eastward [ístwəd] adv. & adj. hacia el este u oriente.

easy [ízɪ] adj. fácil; cómodo; dócil; tranquilo; **— chair** silla cómoda, poltrona, butaca; **easy-going** man hombre cachazudo o calmo; **at an — pace** a paso moderado; **within — reach** al alcance; a la mano.

eat [it] v. comer; **to — away** corroer, destruir; **to — breakfast** desayunarse, tomar el desayuno; **to — dinner** tomar la comida, comer; **to — supper** tomar la cena, cenar; **to — one's heart out** sufrir en silencio; **to — one's words** retractarse.

eaten [ítn] p.p. de **to eat.**

eaves [ivz] s. pl. alero (de un tejado).

ebb [eb] s. reflujo; decadencia; **— tide** marea menguante; **to be at a low —** estar decaído; v. menguar, decaer.

ebony [ébənɪ] s. ébano.

eccentric [ɪkséntrɪk] adj. & s. excéntrico.

ecclesiastic [ɪklɪzɪǽstɪk] adj. & s. eclesiástico.

echo [éko] s. eco; v. hacer eco, repetir; resonar, repercutir.

eclipse [ɪklíps] s. eclipse; v. eclipsar.

economic [ikənámɪk] adj. económico.

economical [ikənámɪkl] adj. económico.

economics [ikənámɪks] s. economía política.

economist [ikánəmɪst] s. economista.

economize [ikánəmaɪz] v. economizar.

economy [ikánəmɪ] s. economía; parsimonia.

ecstasy [ékstəsɪ] s. éxtasis.

eddy [édɪ] s. remolino; v. arremolinarse.

Eden [ídn] s. Edén; paraíso.

edge [edʒ] s. orilla, borde; filo; **to be on — estar** nervioso.

edgewise [édʒwaɪz] adv. de lado; de filo.

edible [édəbl] adj. & s. comestible.

edifice [édəfɪs] s. edificio.

edify [édəfaɪ] v. edificar (moral y espiritualmente).

edit [édɪt] v. redactar; preparar o corregir (un manuscrito) para la imprenta; cuidar (una edición).

edition [ɪdíʃən] s. edición.

editor [édɪtə] s. redactor; director de un periódico; revisor (de manuscritos).

editorial [edətóriəl] adj. editorial; s. editorial (m.), artículo de fondo.

educate [édʒəket] v. educar; instruir.

education [edʒəkéʃən] s. educación; crianza; instrucción, enseñanza; pedagogía.

educational [edʒəkéʃənl] adj. educativo, docente; pedagógico.

educator [édʒəketə] s. educador.

eel [il] s. anguila.

effect [əfékt] s. efecto; **-s** bienes, efectos; **to go into —** hacerse vigente, ponerse en operación (una ley); v. efectuar; ejecutar; realizar.

effective [əfɛ́ktɪv] adj. efectivo, eficaz; vigente (una ley); **-ly** adv. eficazmente.

effectual [əféktʃʋəl] adj. eficaz.

effeminate [əfémənɪt] adj. afeminado.

efficacy [éfəkəsɪ] s. eficacia.

efficiency [əfíʃənsɪ] s. eficiencia; eficacia.

efficient [əfíʃənt] adj. eficiente; eficaz.

effort [éfət] s. esfuerzo; empeño.

effrontery [əfrántərɪ] s. descaro, desvergüenza, desfachatez.

effusive [əfjúsɪv] adj. efusivo, demostrativo, expansivo.

egg [eg] s. huevo; **fried — huevo** frito o estrellado; **hard-boiled — huevo** cocido, huevo duro; **scrambled -s** huevos revueltos; **soft-boiled — huevo** pasado por agua; v. **to — on** incitar.

eggplant [égplænt] s. berenjena.

egotism [ígətɪzəm] s. egotismo; egoísmo.

Egyptian [ɪdʒípʃən] adj. & s. egipcio.

either [íðə] adj. & pron. uno u otro; **— of the two** cualquiera de los dos; **in — case** en ambos casos; adv. tampoco; **nor I —** ni yo tampoco; conj. o.

eject [ɪdʒékt] v. echar, arrojar, expulsar.

elaborate [ɪlǽbərɪt] adj. elaborado, primoroso; esmerado; [ɪlǽbəret] v. elaborar.

elapse [ɪlǽps] v. transcurrir, pasar.

elastic [ɪlǽstɪk] adj. elástico; s. elástico; goma elástica; cordón elástico; liga elástica.

elasticity [ɪlæstísətɪ] s. elasticidad.

elated [ɪlétɪd] adj. exaltado, gozoso, alborozado.

elbow [élbo] s. codo; recodo, ángulo; **to be within — reach** estar a la mano; v. codear, dar codazos; **to — one's way through** abrirse paso a codazos.

elder [éldə] adj. mayor, más grande, más viejo, de más edad; s. mayor; anciano; dignatario (*en ciertas iglesias*); **our -s** nuestros mayores; nuestros antepasados.

elderly [éldəlɪ] adj. viejo, anciano.

eldest [éldɪst] adj. mayor.

elect [ɪlékt] adj. & s. electo; elegido; v. elegir.

election [ɪlékʃən] s. elección.

elector [ɪléktə] s. elector.

electoral [ɪléktərəl] adj. electoral.

electric [ɪléktrɪk] adj. eléctrico; **— meter** electrómetro, contador eléctrico; **— storm** tronada, tempestad; s. tranvía o ferrocarril eléctrico.

electrical [ɪléktrɪkl] adj. eléctrico; **— engineering** electrotecnia, ingeniería eléctrica; **— engineer** ingeniero electricista; electrotécnico.

electrician [ɪlektrʃən] s. electricista.

electricity [ɪlektrísətɪ] s. electricidad.

electrify [ɪléktrəfaɪ] v. electrizar; electrificar.

electrocute [ɪléktrəkjut] v. electrocutar.

elegance [éləgəns] s. elegancia.

elegant [éləgənt] adj. elegante.

element [éləmənt] s. elemento.

elemental [eləmént] adj. elemental.

elementary [eləméntərɪ] adj. elemental.

elephant [éləfənt] s. elefante.

elevate [éləvet] v. elevar; alzar, levantar.

elevation [eləvéʃən] s. elevación; altura; exaltación.

elevator [éləvetə] s. ascensor, *Am.* elevador; **grain —** almacén de granos.

elicit [ɪlísɪt] v. extraer, sonsacar; **to — admiration** despertar admiración; **to — applause** suscitar el aplauso o los aplausos.

eligible [élɪdʒəbl] adj. elegible.

eliminate [ɪlímənet] v. eliminar.

elimination [ɪlɪmənéʃən] s. eliminación.

elk [ɛlk] s. ante.

elm [ɛlm] s. olmo.

elope [ɪlóp] v. fugarse (*con su novio*).

eloquence [éləkwəns] s. elocuencia.

eloquent [éləkwənt] adj. elocuente.

else [ɛls] adj. & adv. otro (*úsase sólo en ciertas combinaciones*); más, además; **or —** de otro modo; si no; **nobody —** ningún otro; **nothing —** nada más; **somebody —** algún otro, otra persona; **what — ?** ¿qué más?

elsewhere [élshwer] adv. en otra parte, a otra parte.

elucidate [ɪlúsədet] v. elucidar, esclarecer, aclarar, clarificar.

elucidation [ɪlusədéʃən] s. elucidación, esclarecimiento, explicación.

elude [ɪlúd] v. eludir, evadir.

emaciated [ɪméʃɪetɪd] adj. demacrado, escuálido, macilento.

emanate [émənet] v. emanar, brotar.

emanation [emənéʃən] s. emanación; efluvio.

emancipate [ɪmǽnsəpet] v. emancipar.

emancipation [ɪmænsəpéʃən] s. emancipación.

embalm [ɪmbám] v. embalsamar.

embankment [ɪmbǽŋkmənt] s. terraplén; dique.

embargo [ɪmbárgo] s. embargo; prohibición; **to put an — on** embargar.

embark [ɪmbárk] v. embarcar(se).

embarrass [ɪmbǽrəs] v. turbar, desconcertar; apenar; avergonzar; embarazar; **to be financially -ed** encontrarse escaso de fondos.

embarrassing [ɪmbǽrəsɪŋ] adj. embarazoso, penoso; desconcertante; angustioso.

embarrassment [ɪmbǽrəsmənt] s. turbación, vergüenza, desconcierto; aprieto, apuro, dificultad; estorbo, embarazo.

embassy [émbəsɪ] s. embajada.

embellish [ɪmbélɪʃ] v. embellecer, hermosear.

ember [émbə] s. ascua; **-s** ascuas, rescoldo.

embezzle [ɪmbézl] v. desfalcar.

embezzlement [ɪmbézlmənt] s. desfalco, peculado.

embitter [ɪmbítə] v. amargar.

emblem [émbləm] s. emblema.

embody [ɪmbádɪ] v. encarnar, dar cuerpo a; incorporar, abarcar.

emboss [ɪmbós] v. realzar, grabar en relieve.

embrace [ɪmbrés] s. abrazo; v. abrazar(se); abarcar.

embroider [ɪmbrɔ́ɪdə] v. bordar; recamar; ornar, embellecer.

embroidery [ɪmbrɔ́ɪdərɪ] s. bordado; bordadura; recamo.

emerald [émərəld] s. esmeralda.

emerge [ɪmɜ́dʒ] v. emerger; surtir.

emergency [ɪmɜ́dʒənsɪ] s. caso fortuito; aprieto; urgencia; emergencia.

emigrant [émɔgrənt] adj. & s. emigrante.

emigrate [émɔgret] v. emigrar.

emigration [emɔgréʃən] s. emigración.

eminence [émənəns] s. eminencia.

eminent [émənənt] adj. eminente.

emit [ɪmít] v. emitir; exhalar, arrojar; despedir (olor, humo, etc.).

emotion [ɪmóʃən] s. emoción.

emotional [ɪmóʃən̩] adj. emocional; emotivo; sentimental; sensible.

emperor [émpərə] s. emperador.

emphasis [émfəsɪs] s. énfasis.

emphasize [émfəsaɪz] v. dar énfasis; hacer hincapié en; subrayar, recalcar; acentuar.

emphatic [ɪmfǽtɪk] adj. enfático; recalcado; -ally adv. enfáticamente.

empire [émpaɪr] s. imperio.

employ [ɪmplóɪ] v. emplear; dar empleo a; ocupar; to be in his — ser su empleado; trabajar a sus órdenes.

employee [ɪmplóɪí] s. empleado.

employer [ɪmplóɪə] s. patrón, amo, principal.

employment [ɪmplóɪmənt] s. empleo; ocupación.

empower [ɪmpáʊə] v. autorizar; apoderar (dar poder a un abogado).

empress [émprɪs] s. emperatriz.

emptiness [émptɪnɪs] s. vaciedad; futilidad, vanidad.

empty [émptɪ] adj. vacío; vacante, desocupado; vano; v. vaciar; desaguar, desembocar.

enable [ɪnébḷ] v. capacitar, hacer capaz; habilitar, dar poder; facilitar; hacer posible.

enact [ɪnǽkt] v. decretar, promulgar; hacer el papel de.

enamel [ɪnǽm̩l] s. esmalte; v. esmaltar.

enamor [ɪnǽmə] v. enamorar, mover a amar; encantar; to be -ed of estar enamorado de.

encamp [ɪnkǽmp] v. acampar.

enchant [ɪntʃǽnt] v. encantar; embelesar; hechizar.

enchanter [ɪntʃǽntə] s. encantador; hechichero, mago, brujo.

enchantment [ɪntʃǽntmənt] s. encanto; encantamiento; hechicería.

enchantress [ɪntʃǽntrɪs] s. encantadora; hechicera, bruja.

encircle [ɪnsɜ́kḷ] v. cercar, rodear, ceñir.

enclose [ɪnklóz] v. encerrar; cercar, rodear, circundar; incluir.

enclosure [ɪnklóʒə] s. recinto, cercado, vallado; remesa, lo remitido (dentro de una carta), lo adjunto; encerramiento.

encompass [ɪnkʌ́mpəs] v. abarcar; encuadrar; rodear, ceñir, circundar.

encounter [ɪnkáʊntə] s. encuentro; combate; v. encontrar(se); encontrarse con; tropezar con.

encourage [ɪnkɜ́ɪdʒ] v. alentar, animar; fomentar.

encouragement [ɪnkɜ́ɪdʒmənt] s. aliento, ánimo; estímulo; fomento.

encroach [ɪnkrótʃ] v. to — upon usurpar, invadir, meterse en, quitar (el tiempo).

encyclopedia [ɪnsaɪkləpídɪə] s. enciclopedia.

end [end] s. fin; cabo; término; extremo; no — of things un sin fin de cosas; odds and -s retazos; on — de punta; to put an — to acabar con, poner fin a; v. acabar; terminar; concluir, dar fin.

endanger [ɪndéndʒə] v. poner en peligro, arriesgar.

endear [ɪndir] v. hacer amar, hacer querer; to — oneself hacerse querer.

endeavor [ɪndévə] s. esfuerzo, empeño; tentativa; tarea; v. procurar, tratar de, intentar; esforzarse por o en.

ending [éndɪŋ] s. final; terminación; conclusión.

endless [éndlɪs] adj. sin fin, interminable, inacabable; eterno.

endorse = indorse.

endorsement = indorsement.

endow [ɪndáʊ] v. dotar.

endowment [ɪndáʊmənt] s. dotación; dote, don.

endurance [ɪndjúrəns] s. resistencia; aguante; paciencia; duración.

endure [ɪndjúr] v. aguantar, soportar, sufrir; durar, perdurar.

enema [énəmə] s. lavativa.

enemy [énəmɪ] s. enemigo.

energetic [enədʒétɪk] adj. enérgico.

energy [énədʒɪ] s. energía.

enervate [énəvet] v. enervar, debilitar.

enfold = infold.

enforce [ɪnfórs] v. dar fuerza a; hacer cumplir (una ley); to — obedience hacer obedecer, imponer obediencia.

enforcement [ɪnfórsmənt] s. coacción; cumplimiento forzoso (de una ley).

engage [ɪngédʒ] v. ocupar; emplear, contratar; atraer (la atención); alquilar; engranar, acoplar; to — in battle trabar batalla; to — (oneself) to do it comprometerse a hacerlo; to be -ed in something estar ocupado en algo; to be -ed to be married estar comprometido para casarse.

70

engagement [ɪngédʒmənt] *s.* compromiso; cita; noviazgo; convenio, contrato; pelea; traba, engrane, acoplamiento (*de maquinaria*).

engender [ɪndʒéndə] *v.* engendrar, producir.

engine [éndʒən] *s.* máquina; motor; locomotora.

engineer [endʒənfr] *s.* ingeniero; maquinista (*de locomotora*); *v.* dirigir, planear.

engineering [endʒənfrɪŋ] *s.* ingeniería; manejo, planeo.

English [ínglɪʃ] *adj.* inglés; *s.* inglés, idioma inglés; **the —** los ingleses.

Englishman [ínglɪʃmən] *s.* inglés.

engrave [ɪngrév] *v.* grabar, esculpir.

engraving [ɪngrévɪŋ] *s.* grabado; estampa, lámina; **wood —** grabado en madera.

engrossed [ɪngróst] *adj.* absorto, ensimismado.

engulf [ɪngʌ́lf] *v.* engolfar, absorber, tragar.

enhance [ɪnhǽns] *v.* realzar; engrandecer.

enigma [ɪnfgmə] *s.* enigma.

enjoin [ɪndʒɔ́ɪn] *v.* mandar, ordenar; **to — from** prohibir, vedar.

enjoy [ɪndʒɔ́ɪ] *v.* gozar de; disfrutar de; **to — oneself** divertirse, gozar, deleitarse; **to — the use of** usufructuar.

enjoyable [ɪndʒɔ́ɪəbl] *adj.* agradable, deleitable.

enjoyment [ɪndʒɔ́ɪmənt] *s.* placer, goce; disfrute; usufructo.

enlarge [ɪnlárdʒ] *v.* agrandar(se); ensanchar; ampliar; **to — upon** explayarse en, extenderse en; comentar.

enlighten [ɪnláɪtn] *v.* alumbrar; iluminar; ilustrar, instruir.

enlist [ɪnlíst] *v.* alistar(se); sentar plaza (*de soldado*); reclutar.

enlistment [ɪnlístmənt] *s.* reclutamiento; alistamiento.

enliven [ɪnláɪvən] *v.* avivar, animar, alegrar.

enmity [énmətɪ] *s.* enemistad.

ennoble [ɪnóbl] *v.* ennoblecer.

enormous [ɪnɔ́rməs] *adj.* enorme.

enough [ɪnʌ́f] *adj. & adv.* bastante; *s.* lo bastante, lo suficiente; **that is —** eso basta, con eso basta; **—!** ¡basta!.

enquire = **inquire.**

enrage [ɪnrédʒ] *v.* enrabiar, hacer rabiar; enfurecer.

enrapture [ɪnrǽptʃə] *v.* extasiar, embelesar, enajenar.

enrich [ɪnrítʃ] *v.* enriquecer.

enroll [ɪnról] *v.* alistar(se); matricular(se); inscribir(se); hacerse miembro.

enrollment [ɪnrólmənt] *s.* alistamiento; registro, matrícula.

ensign [énsn] *s.* alférez (*de la marina*); [énsaɪn] bandera; insignia.

enslave [ɪnslév] *v.* esclavizar.

ensnare [ensnér] *v.* enredar, entrampar, embaucar.

ensue [ensú] *v.* sobrevenir, seguir(se), resultar.

entail [ɪntél] *v.* envolver, ocasionar; vincular (*una herencia*).

entangle [ɪntǽŋgl] *v.* enredar, enmarañar, embrollar.

enter [éntə] *v.* entrar en; ingresar en; asentar (*una partida, cantidad, etc.*); registrar; salir (*al escenario*).

enterprise [éntəpraɪz] *s.* empresa.

enterprising [éntəpraɪzɪŋ] *adj.* emprendedor.

entertain [entətén] *v.* divertir; agasajar; obsequiar; banquetear; acariciar (*una idea*); abrigar (*una esperanza, un rencor*); **she -s a great deal** es muy fiestera u obsequiosa.

entertaining [entəténɪŋ] *adj.* entretenido, divertido, chistoso.

entertainment [entəténmənt] *s.* entretenimiento; pasatiempo; diversión; fiesta; convite.

enthusiasm [ɪnθjúzɪæzəm] *s.* entusiasmo.

enthusiast [ɪnθjúzɪæst] *s.* entusiasta.

enthusiastic [ɪnθjuzɪǽstɪk] *adj.* entusiasta, entusiástico; **to be —** estar estusiasmado.

entice [ɪntáɪs] *v.* atraer, tentar, seducir, halagar.

entire [ɪntáɪr] *adj.* entero, cabal; **the — world** todo el mundo; **-ly** *adv.* enteramente, por entero.

entirety [ɪntáɪrtɪ] *s.* totalidad, entereza; conjunto; todo.

entitle [ɪntáɪtl] *v.* titular, intitular; autorizar, dar derecho.

entity [éntətɪ] *s.* entidad; ente, ser.

entrails [éntrəlz] *s. pl.* entrañas; tripas.

entrance [éntrəns] *s.* entrada; ingreso.

entreat [ɪntrít] *v.* suplicar, rogar; instar.

entreaty [ɪntrítɪ] *s.* súplica, ruego; instancia.

entrench = **intrench.**

entrust [ɪntrʌ́st] *v.* confiar; depositar; entregar.

entry [éntrɪ] *s.* entrada; ingreso; partida, registro, anotación; **double —** partida doble (*en teneduría*).

enumerate [ɪnjúməret] *v.* enumerar.

enunciate [ɪnʌ́nsɪet] *v.* articular; enunciar, declarar.

envelop [ɪnvéləp] *v.* envolver.

ENV—EVE

envelope [énvəlop] *s.* sobre, cubierta (*de una carta*).
enviable [énvɪəbl] *adj.* envidiable.
envious [énvɪəs] *adj.* envidioso.
environment [ɪnváɪrənmənt] *s.* ambiente, medio ambiente.
environs [ɪnváɪrənz] *s. pl.* cercanías, contornos, alrededores.
envoy [énvɔɪ] *s.* enviado.
envy [énvɪ] *s.* envidia; *v.* envidiar.
epic [épɪk] *s.* epopeya, poema épico; *adj.* épico.
epidemic [epədémɪk] *s.* epidemia; peste; *adj.* epidémico.
episode [épəsod] *s.* episodio.
epistle [ɪpísl] *s.* epístola, carta.
epitaph [épətæf] *s.* epitafio.
epoch [épək] *s.* época.
equal [íkwəl] *adj.* igual; **to be — to a task** ser competente (*o* tener suficientes fuerzas) para una tarea; *s.* igual; cantidad igual; *v.* igualar; ser igual a; **-ly** *adv.* igualmente; por igual.
equality [ɪkwúlətɪ] *s.* igualdad.
equalize [íkwəlaɪz] *v.* igualar; emparejar; equilibrar; nivelar.
equation [ɪkwéʒən] *s.* ecuación.
equator [ɪkwétə] *s.* ecuador.
equilibrium [ikwəlíbrɪəm] *s.* equilibrio.
equip [ɪkwíp] *v.* equipar; proveer; habilitar.
equipment [ɪkwípmənt] *s.* equipo; aparatos; avíos; habilitación.
equity [ékwətɪ] *s.* equidad; justicia.
equivalent [ɪkwívələnt] *adj. & s.* equivalente.
equivocal [ɪkwívəkl] *adj.* equívoco, ambiguo.
era [írə] *s.* era, época.
eradicate [ɪrǽdɪket] *v.* desarraigar; extirpar.
erase [ɪrés] *v.* borrar; tachar.
eraser [ɪrésə] *s.* goma, *Am.* borrador; **blackboard —** cepillo.
erasure [ɪréʒə] *s.* borradura, raspadura.
ere [ɛr] *prep.* antes de; *conj.* antes (de) que.
erect [ɪrékt] *adj.* erguido; derecho; levantado; *Am.* parado; *v.* erigir; levantar, alzar.
ermine [ə́mɪn] *s.* armiño.
erosion [ɪróʒən] *s.* erosión; desgaste.
err [ɜ] *v.* errar; equivocarse; descarriarse.
errand [érənd] *s.* mandado, recado, encargo; **— boy** mandadero.
errant [érənt] *adj.* errante; **knight-errant** caballero andante.
erroneous [ərónɪəs] *adj.* erróneo, errado.
error [érə] *s.* error.
erudition [erʊdíʃən] *s.* erudición.

eruption [ɪrápʃən] *s.* erupción.
escapade [éskəped] *s.* trapisonda, travesura.
escape [əskép] *s.* escape; fuga, huída; escapada; escapatoria; *v.* escapar(se), fugarse; huir(se); eludir, evadir; **it -s me** se me escapa.
escort [éskɔrt] *s.* escolta; acompañante; convoy; [ɪskɔ́rt] *v.* escoltar; convoyar; acompañar.
escutcheon [ɪskátʃən] *s.* escudo de armas, blasón.
especial [əspéʃəl] *adj.* especial; **-ly** *adv.* especialmente.
espionage [éspɪənɪdʒ] *s.* espionaje.
essay [ése] *s.* ensayo; [esé] *v.* ensayar.
essence [ésŋs] *s.* esencia.
essential [əsénʃəl] *adj.* esencial.
establish [əstǽblɪʃ] *v.* establecer.
establishment [əstǽblɪʃmənt] *s.* establecimiento.
estate [əstét] *s.* hacienda, heredad; bienes, propiedades; estado, condición; **country —** finca rural.
esteem [əstím] *s.* estima, estimación, aprecio; *v.* estimar, apreciar; considerar, juzgar.
estimable [éstəməbl] *adj.* estimable.
estimate [éstəmɪt] *s.* tasa, cálculo aproximado; presupuesto; opinión; [éstəmet] *v.* estimar, tasar, calcular aproximadamente; hacer un presupuesto; juzgar, opinar.
estimation [estəméʃən] *s.* juicio, opinión; estima; estimación.
estuary [éstʃʊerɪ] *s.* estuario o estero, desembocadura de un río.
etch [etʃ] *v.* grabar al agua fuerte.
etching [étʃɪŋ] *s.* agua fuerte, grabado al agua fuerte.
eternal [ɪtɜ́nl] *adj.* eterno.
eternity [ɪtɜ́nətɪ] *s.* eternidad.
ether [íθə] *s.* éter.
ethereal [ɪθírɪəl] *adj.* etéreo.
ethical [éɔɪkl] *adj.* ético, moral.
ethics [éɛɪks] *s.* ética, moral.
etiquette [étɪkɛt] *s.* etiqueta (*regla de conducta social*).
etymology [etəmálədʒɪ] *s.* etimología.
eucalyptus [jukəlíptəs] *s.* eucalipto.
European [jʊrəpíən] *adj. & s.* europeo.
evacuate [ɪvǽkjuet] *v.* evacuar; desocupar.
evade [ɪvéd] *v.* evadir.
evaluate [ɪvǽljuet] *v.* valorar, avaluar.
evaporate [ɪvǽpəret] *v.* evaporar(se).
evaporation [ɪvæpəréʃən] *s.* evaporación.
evasion [ɪvéʒən] *s.* evasión, evasiva.
evasive [ɪvésɪv] *adj.* evasivo.
eve [iv] *s.* víspera, vigilia; **Christmas**

72

Eve Nochebuena; **New Year's Eve** víspera del.Año Nuevo; **on the — of** en vísperas de.

even [ívən] *adj.* liso, plano, llano; igual; parejo; a nivel; uniforme; **— dozen** docena cabal; **— number** número par; **— temper** genio apacible; **to be — with someone** estar mano a mano (*o* estar a mano) con alguien; **to get — with someone** desquitarse de alguien; *adv.* aun, hasta; **— if** (*o* **— though**) aun cuando; **— so** aún así; **not —** ni siquiera, ni aun; *v.* allanar; nivelar(se); igualar(se); emparejar; **-ly** *adv.* igualmente; de un modo igual; con uniformidad; con suavidad.

evening [ívnɪŋ] *s.* tarde; noche (*las primeras horas*); **— gown** vestido de etiqueta; **— star** estrella vespertina, lucero de la tarde.

evenness [ívənnɪs] *s.* lisura; igualdad; **— of temper** apacibilidad o suavidad de genio.

event [ivént] *s.* suceso, acontecimiento; incidente, evento; resultado, consecuencia; **in any —** en todo caso; **in the — of** en caso de.

eventful [ivéntfəl] *adj.* lleno de sucesos; importante, memorable.

eventual [ivéntʃuəl] *adj.* eventual; último, final, terminal; **-ly** *adv.* finalmente, por fin, con el tiempo; eventualmente.

ever [évə] *adv.* siempre; jamás; alguna vez; **— so much** muchísimo; **for — and —** por (*o* para) siempre jamás; **hardly —** casi nunca, apenas; **if —** si alguna vez; **more than —** más que nunca; **the best friend I — had** el mejor amigo que en mi vida he tenido.

evergreen [évəgrin] *s.* siempreviva, sempiterna; *adj.* siempre verde.

everlasting [evəlǽstiŋ] *adj.* sempiterno, eterno, perpetuo; duradero; *s.* eternidad; sempiterna (*planta*); siempreviva; perpetua, flor perpetua.

evermore [evəmór] *adv.* para siempre; **for —** para siempre jamás.

every [évrɪ] *adj.* cada; todo; todos los, todas las; **— bit of it** todo, todito; **— day** todos los días; **— once in a while** de vez en cuando; **— one of them** todos ellos; **— other day** cada dos días, un día sí y otro no.

everybody [évrɪbadɪ] *pron.* todos, todo el mundo.

everyday [évrɪdé] *adj.* diario, cuotidiano, de todos los días; ordinario.

everyone [évrɪwʌn] *pron.* todos; todo el mundo; cada uno.

everything [évrɪθɪŋ] *pron.* todo.

everywhere [évrɪhwer] *adv.* por (*o* en) todas partes; a todas partes.

evict [ivíkt] *v.* desalojar; expulsar.

evidence [évədəns] *s.* evidencia; prueba; demostración, señal; testimonio; **to be in —** mostrarse; *v.* hacer evidente, evidenciar; patentizar, revelar, mostrar.

evident [évədənt] *adj.* evidente, patente.

evil [ívl] *adj.* malo, malvado, maligno; aciago, de mal agüero; **to cast the — eye** aojar; **the Evil One** el Diablo; *s.* mal; maldad; *adv.* mal.

evildoer [ivldúə] *s.* malhechor.

evoke [ivók] *v.* evocar; **to — laughter** provocar a risa.

evolution [evəlúʃən] *s.* evolución.

evolve [iválv] *v.* desarrollar(se), desenvolver(se); urdir; evolucionar.

ewe [ju] *s.* oveja.

exact [ɪgzǽkt] *adj.* exacto; *v.* exigir; **-ly** *adv.* exactamente; en punto.

exacting [ɪgzǽktɪŋ] *adj.* exigente.

exaggerate [ɪgzǽdʒəret] *v.* exagerar.

exalt [ɪgzɔ́lt] *v.* exaltar, ensalzar.

exaltation [egzɔltéʃən] *s.* exaltación.

examination [ɪgzæmənéʃən] *s.* examen; reconocimiento (*médico*).

examine [ɪgzǽmɪn] *v.* examinar; reconocer (*dícese del médico*).

example [ɪgzǽmpl] *s.* ejemplo.

exasperate [ɪgzǽspəret] *v.* exasperar, irritar.

excavate [ékskəvet] *v.* excavar.

exceed [iksíd] *v.* exceder; sobrepasar; propasarse.

exceedingly [iksídɪŋlɪ] *adv.* sumamente, extremamente; **— well** extremamente bien.

excel [iksél] *v.* sobresalir (en *o* entre); sobrepugar (a).

excellence [éksləns] *s.* excelencia.

excellency [éks[ə]nsɪ] *s.* excelencia.

excellent [ékslənt] *adj.* excelente.

except [iksépt] *prep.* excepto, menos; *v.* exceptuar.

excepting [ikséptɪŋ] *prep.* excepto, salvo, menos, exceptuando.

exception [iksépʃən] *s.* excepción; objeción; **with the — of** a excepción de, con excepción de; **to take —** objetar; ofenderse.

exceptional [iksépʃən[l]] *adj.* excepcional.

excess [iksés] *s.* exceso; sobrante; **— baggage (weight)** exceso de equipaje (de peso); **to drink to —** beber en exceso.

excessive [iksésiv] *adj.* excesivo; **-ly** *adv.* excesivamente, en exceso, demasiado.

exchange [ikstʃéndʒ] *s.* cambio; trueque;

intercambio, canje (de publicaciones, prisioneros); lonja, bolsa; **rate of —** cambio, Am. tipo de cambio; **telephone —** central de teléfonos; v. cambiar; trocar; canjear (publicaciones, prisioneros); **to — greetings** saludarse; mandarse felicitaciones.

excite [ɪksáɪt] v. excitar; acalorar; agitar.

excited [ɪksáɪtɪd] adj. excitado, acalorado; animado; **to get — entusiasmarse; sobreexcitarse; acalorarse; -ly** adv. acaloradamente, agitadamente.

excitement [ɪksáɪtmənt] s. excitación; acaloramiento; agitación, alboroto; animación.

exciting [ɪksáɪtɪŋ] adj. excitante, excitador; estimulante.

exclaim [ɪksklém] v. exclamar.

exclamation [ɛkskləméʃən] s. exclamación; — **point** punto de admiración.

exclude [ɪksklúd] v. excluir.

exclusion [ɪksklúʒən] s. exclusión.

exclusive [ɪksklúsɪv] adj. exclusivo; privativo; — **of** sin contar.

excommunicate [ɛkskəmjúnəket] v. excomunicar.

excommunication [ɛkskəmjunəkéʃən] s. excomunión.

excrement [ɛ́kskrɪmənt] s. excremento.

excursion [ɪkskɝ́ʒən] s. excursión; correría; expedición.

excusable [ɪkskjúzəbl] adj. excusable, disculpable.

excuse [ɪkskjús] s. excusa; disculpa; [ɪkskjúz] v. excusar; disculpar; perdonar, dispensar; eximir; — **me!** ¡dispense Vd.!; ¡ perdone Vd.!

execute [ɛ́ksɪkjut] v. ejecutar; ajusticiar; llevar a cabo.

execution [ɛksɪkjúʃən] s. ejecución; desempeño.

executioner [ɛksɪkjúʃənə] s. verdugo.

executive [ɪgzékjʊtɪv] adj. ejecutivo; s. ejecutivo, poder ejecutivo; gerente, administrador.

executor [ɪgzékjətə] s. albacea, ejecutor testamentario; [ɛ́ksɪkjutə] ejecutor.

exemplary [ɪgzémpləri] adj. ejemplar.

exempt [ɪgzémpt] adj. exento, libre; v. eximir, exentar.

exemption [ɪgzémpʃən] s. exención.

exercise [ɛ́ksəsaɪz] s. ejercicio; v. ejercitar(se); ejercer (poder o autoridad); hacer ejercicio, hacer gimnasia; **to be -d about something** estar preocupado o sobreexcitado por algo.

exert [ɪgzɝ́t] v. ejercer; **to — oneself** esforzarse, hacer esfuerzos, empeñarse.

exertion [ɪgzɝ́ʃən] s. ejercicio; esfuerzo, empeño.

exhale [ɛkshél] v. exhalar, emitir; espirar; soplar.

exhaust [ɪgzɔ́st] s. escape (de gas o vapor); v. agotar; consumir; debilitar, fatigar, **I am -ed** no puedo más; **estoy** agotado.

exhaustion [ɪgzɔ́stʃən] s. agotamiento; fatiga, postración.

exhibit [ɪgzíbɪt] v. exhibir; mostrar, exponer.

exhibition [ɛksəbíʃən] s. exhibición; exposición, manifestación.

exhilarate [ɪgzíləret] v. alborozar, excitar, animar, entusiasmar.

exhort [ɪgzɔ́rt] v. exhortar.

exile [égzaɪl] s. destierro, exilio; desterrado; v. desterrar; expatriar.

exist [ɪgzíst] v. existir.

existence [ɪgzístəns] s. existencia.

existent [ɪgzístənt] adj. existente.

exit [ɛ́gzɪt] s. salida; salida (del foro); v. vase o vanse (un personaje o personajes al fin de una escena).

exodus [ɛ́ksədəs] s. éxodo.

exonerate [ɪgzánəret] v. exonerar.

exorbitant [ɪgzɔ́rbətənt] adj. exorbitante.

exotic [ɪgzátɪk] adj. exótico; raro, extraño.

expand [ɪkspǽnd] v. ensanchar(se); dilatar(se); extender(se); agrandar(se); desarrollar (una ecuación).

expanse [ɪkspǽns] s. espacio, extensión.

expansion [ɪkspǽnʃən] s. expansión; ensanche; desarrollo (de una ecuación).

expansive [ɪkspǽnsɪv] adj. expansivo; efusivo.

expect [ɪkspékt] v. esperar; contar con; **I — so** supongo que sí.

expectation [ɛkspɛktéʃən] s. expectación; expectativa; esperanza.

expectorate [ɪkspéktəret] v. expectorar, desgarrar.

expedient [ɪkspídɪənt] adj. conveniente, oportuno; ventajoso; prudente; s. expediente, medio.

expedition [ɛkspɪdíʃən] s. expedición.

expeditionary [ɛkspɪdíʃənɛrɪ] adj. expedicionario.

expel [ɪkspél] v. expeler; expulsar.

expend [ɪkspénd] v. gastar; consumir.

expenditure [ɪkspéndɪtʃə] s. gasto; desembolso.

expense [ɪkspéns] s. gasto; coste, costa o costo.

expensive [ɪkspénsɪv] adj. costoso.

expensiveness [ɪkspénsɪvnɪs] s. precio subido, coste elevado.

experience [ɪkspíriəns] s. experiencia; aventura, lance; v. experimentar; pasar *(penas, sufrimientos)*; sentir.

experienced [ɪkspfrɪənst] *adj.* experimentado; ducho, perito, experto.

experiment [ɪkspérəmənt] *s.* experimento, prueba; *v.* experimentar, hacer un experimento.

experimental [ɪkspɛrəméntl] *adj.* experimental.

expert [ékspɔt] *s.* experto, perito; [ɪkspát] *adj.* experto, perito, experimentado.

expiration [ɛkspəréʃən] *s.* terminación; vencimiento *(de un plazo)*; espiración *(del aire)*.

expire [ɪkspáɪr] *v.* expirar, morir; acabar; vencerse *(un plazo)*; expeler *(el aire aspirado)*.

explain [ɪksplén] *v.* explicar.

explainable [ɪksplénəbl] *adj.* explicable.

explanation [ɛksplənéʃən] *s.* explicación.

explanatory [ɪksplǽnətorɪ] *adj.* explicativo.

explode [ɪksplód] *v.* estallar, hacer explosión, *Am.* explotar; reventar; volar *(con dinamita)*; desacreditar *(una teoría)*.

exploit [éksplɔɪt] *s.* hazaña, proeza; [ɪksplɔ́ɪt] *v.* explotar; sacar partido de, abusar de.

exploitation [ɛksplɔɪtéʃən] *s.* explotación.

exploration [ɛksploréʃən] *s.* exploración.

explore [ɪksplór] *v.* explorar.

explorer [ɪksplórə] *s.* explorador.

explosion [ɪksplóʒən] *s.* explosión, estallido.

explosive [ɪksplósɪv] *adj.* & *s.* explosivo.

export [éksport] *s.* exportación; artículo exportado, mercancía exportada; [ɪkspórt] *v.* exportar.

exportation [ɛksportéʃən] *s.* exportación.

expose [ɪkspóz] *v.* exponer; exhibir, mostrar, poner a la vista; revelar; desenmascarar.

exposition [ɛkspəzíʃən] *s.* exposición; exhibición.

exposure [ɪkspóʒə] *s.* exposición; revelación; **to die of** — morir a efecto de la intemperie.

expound [ɪkspáund] *v.* exponer, explicar.

express [ɪksprés] *adj.* expreso; explícito, claro; — **company** compañía de expreso; expreso, *Am.* exprés; — **train** tren expreso; *adv.* por expreso, por exprés; *s.* expreso; tren expreso, *Am.* exprés; *v.* expresar; enviar por expreso *(o por exprés)*.

expression [ɪkspréʃən] *s.* expresión.

expressive [ɪksprésɪv] *adj.* expresivo.

expulsion [ɪkspʌ́lʃən] *s.* expulsión.

exquisite [ɛkskwízɪt] *adj.* exquisito.

exquisiteness [ɪkskwízɪtnɪs] *s.* exquisitez; primor.

extant [ɪkstǽnt] *adj.* existente.

extend [ɪksténd] *v.* extender(se); tender; prolongar(se); alargar(se); agrandar; dilatar, prorrogar *(un plazo)*; dar *(el pésame, el parabién, ayuda, etc.)*.

extended [ɪksténdɪd] *adj.* extenso; prolongado; extendido.

extension [ɪksténʃən] *s.* extensión; prolongación; prórroga *(de un plazo)*; añadidura, anexo.

extensive [ɪksténsɪv] *adj.* extenso, ancho, dilatado; extensivo; **-ly** *adv.* extensamente, por extenso; extensivamente; **-ly** used de uso general o común.

extent [ɪkstént] *s.* extensión; grado; **to a great** — en gran parte, generalmente; **to such an** — **that** a tal grado que; **to the** — **of one's ability** en proporción a su habilidad; **up to a certain** — hasta cierto punto.

extenuate [ɪksténjuet] *v.* atenuar, mitigar.

exterior [ɪkstfrɪə] *adj.* exterior; externo; *s.* exterioridad; exterior, porte, aspecto.

exterminate [ɪkstə́mənet] *v.* exterminar, destruir por completo, extirpar.

extermination [ɪkstəmənéʃən] *s.* exterminio.

external [ɪkstə́nl] *adj.* externo; exterior; *s.* exterioridad; lo externo.

extinct [ɪkstíŋkt] *adj.* extinto; extinguido, apagado.

extinguish [ɪkstíŋgwɪʃ] *v.* extinguir; apagar.

extol [ɪkstól] *v.* enaltecer; ensalzar.

extort [ɪkstórt] *v.* obtener por fuerza o amenaza, exigir *(dinero, promesa, etc.)*, *Am.* extorsionar.

extortion [ɪkstórʃən] *s.* extorsión.

extra [ékstrə] *adj.* extraordinario; de sobra, de más, adicional; suplementario; — **tire** neumático de repuesto o de recambio; — **workman** obrero supernumerario; *adv.* extraordinariamente; *s.* extra; extraordinario *(de un periódico)*; suplemento; gasto extraordinario; recargo *(cargo adicional)*; actor suplente o supernumerario.

extract [ékstrækt] *s.* extracto; cita, trozo *(entresacado de un libro)*; resumen; [ɪkstrǽkt] *v.* extraer; seleccionar; citar.

extraordinary [ɪkstrórdnɛrɪ] *adj.* extraordinario; **extraordinarily** *adv.* extraordinariamente; de manera extraordinaria.

extravagance [ɪkstrǽvəgəns] *s.* despilfarro, derroche, gasto excesivo; lujo excesivo; extravagancia, capricho.

extravagant [ɪkstrǽvəgənt] *adj.* gastador, despilfarrado; extravagante, disparatado; **— praise** elogios excesivos; **— prices** precios exorbitantes.

extreme [ɪkstrím] *adj.* extremo; último; más remoto; excesivo; riguroso; radical; **— opinions** opiniones extremadas; *s.* extremo; cabo; **to go to -s** extremar, exagerar; hacer extremos; tomar las medidas más extremas; **-ly** *adv.* extremamente, en extremo.

extremity [ɪkstrémətɪ] *s.* extremidad, extremo; medida extrema; **in —** en gran peligro; en un apuro.

exuberant [ɪgzjúbərənt] *adj.* exuberante.

exult [ɪgzʌ́lt] *v.* alborozarse, regocijarse.

eye [aɪ] *s.* ojo; **— shade** visera; **in a twinkling of an —** en un abrir y cerrar de ojos; **hook and —** macho y hembra; **to catch one's —** llamar la atención; **to have good -s** tener buena vista; **to have before one's -s** tener a (*o* tener ante) la vista; **to keep an — on** cuidar, vigilar; **to see — to —** estar completamente de acuerdo; *v.* mirar, observar.

eyeball [áɪbɔl] *s.* globo del ojo.

eyebrow [áɪbraʊ] *s.* ceja.

eyeglass [áɪglæs] *s.* lente, cristal (*de anteojo*); ocular (*de microscopio o telescopio*); **-es** lentes, anteojos.

eyelash [áɪlæʃ] *s.* pestaña.

eyelid [áɪlɪd] *s.* párpado.

eyesight [áɪsaɪt] *s.* vista; **poor —** mala vista.

F

fable [fébl] *s.* fábula.

fabric [fǽbrɪk] *s.* género, tela; tejido; textura; estructura.

fabulous [fǽbjələs] *adj.* fabuloso.

façade [fəsád] *s.* fachada.

face [fes] *s.* cara, rostro; fachada, frente (*m.*); haz, superficie; muestra (*de reloj*), *Am.* carátula; **— value** valor nominal; **in the —of** en presencia de, ante, frente a; **to lose —** perder prestigio; **to make -s** hacer muecas o gestos; **to save one's —** salvar el amor propio; *v.* encararse con; enfrentarse con; hacer frente a; mirar hacia; forrar; **to — about** volverse, *Am.* voltearse; **to — danger** afrontar o arrostrar el peligro; **to — with marble** revestir de mármol; **it -s the street** da a la calle.

facilitate [fəsílətet] *v.* facilitar.

facility [fəsílətɪ] *s.* facilidad.

fact [fækt] *s.* hecho; dato; verdad, realidad; **in —** de hecho; en realidad.

faction [fǽkʃən] *s.* facción, bando, partido, pandilla.

factor [fǽktə] *s.* factor; elemento; agente; *v.* descomponer en factores.

factory [fǽktrɪ] *s.* fábrica.

faculty [fǽkltɪ] *s.* facultad.

fad [fæd] *s.* novedad; manía; moda.

fade [fed] *v.* descolorar(se), desteñir(se); marchitar(se); apagarse (*un sonido*); desvanecerse.

fagged [fægd] *adj.* agotado, rendido de cansancio.

fail [fel] *v.* faltar; fallar; fracasar; decaer; debilitarse; quebrar, hacer bancarrota; no tener éxito; **to — in an examination** fallar en un examen, salir mal en un examen; **to — a student** reprobar o suspender a un estudiante; **to — to do it** dejar de hacerlo, no hacerlo; **don't — to come** no deje Vd. de venir; **without —** sin falta.

failure [féljə] *s.* fracaso; malogro; falta, descuido, negligencia; quiebra, bancarrota; debilitamiento.

faint [fent] *adj.* débil; lánguido; casi imperceptible, tenue, vago, indistinto; **to feel —** sentirse desvanecido; **—hearted** tímido, cobarde; *s.* desmayo; *v.* desmayarse; languidecer; **-ly** *adv.* débilmente; lánguidamente; indistintamente, vagamente, tenuemente; apenas.

faintness [féntnɪs] *s.* languidez, debilidad, desfallecimiento; falta de claridad; vaguedad.

fair [fer] *adj.* justo, recto, honrado; imparcial; equitativo; regular, mediano; rubio, blondo; bello; despejado, claro; **— chance of success** buena probabilidad de éxito; **— complexion** tez blanca; **— hair** pelo rubio; **— name** reputación sin mancilla; **— play** juego limpio; **— sex** sexo bello; **— weather** buen tiempo, tiempo bonancible; **to act —** obrar con imparcialidad (*o* con equidad); **to play —** jugar limpio; *s.* feria; mercado; exposición; **-ly** *adv.* justamente; imparcialmente; medianamente; **-ly difficult** medianamente difícil; **-ly well** regular, bastante bien.

fairness [férnɪs] *s.* justicia, equidad, imparcialidad; blancura (*de la tez*); belleza.

fairy [férɪ] *s.* hada; **— godmother** hada madrina; **— tale** cuento de hadas.

fairyland [férɪlænd] *s.* tierra de las hadas.

faith [feθ] *s.* fe; fidelidad; **in good —** de buena fe; **to have — in** tener fe o confianza en; **to keep —** cumplir con la palabra.

faithful [féefəl] *adj.* fiel; leal; **-ly** *adv.* fielmente; con fidelidad; puntualmente; **-ly yours** suyo afectísimo; siempre suyo.

faithfulness [féefəlnɪs] *s.* fidelidad; lealtad; exactidud.

faithless [féelɪs] *adj.* infiel; sin fe; desleal; falso.

fake [fek] *s.* fraude, trampa; falsedad; embustero; *adj.* falso, fingido; *v.* falsear; fingir; simular.

falcon [fólkən] *s.* halcón.

fall [fɔl] *s.* caída; bajada; ruina; baja (*de precios*); otoño; **-s** cascada, catarata, salto de agua; *v.* caer(se); decaer; bajar; **to — asleep** dormirse, quedarse dormido; **to — back** retroceder; **to — behind** atrasarse, rezagarse, quedarse atrás; **to — in love** enamorarse; **to — out with** reñir con, enemistarse con; **to — to** one tocarle a uno, corresponderle a uno; **his plans fell through** fracasaron (*o* se malograron) sus planes.

fallen [fólən] *p.p. de* to fall.

fallow [fǽlo] *adj.* baldío; *s.* barbecho, *v.* barbechar.

false [fɔls] *adj.* falso; postizo (*dientes, barba, etc.*); fingido, simulado.

falsehood [fólshʊd] *s.* falsedad, mentira.

falseness [fólsnɪs] *s.* falsedad.

falsify [fólsəfaɪ] *v.* falsificar, falsear; mentir.

falsity [fólsətɪ] *s.* falsedad; mentira.

falter [fóltə] *v.* vacilar; titubear; tambalearse; bambolearse; **to — an excuse** balbucear una excusa; *s.* temblor, vacilación.

fame [fem] *s.* fama.

famed [femd] *adj.* afamado, famoso, renombrado.

familiar [fəmfljə] *adj.* familiar, íntimo; confianzudo; **to be — with a subject** conocer bien, estar versado en oser conocedor de una materia; *s.* familiar.

familiarity [fəmɪliǽrətɪ] *s.* familiaridad; confianza, franqueza.

family [fǽmlɪ] *s.* familia; **— name** apellido; **— tree** árbol genealógico; **to be in the — way** estar encinta.

famine [fǽmɪn] *s.* hambre; escasez, carestía.

famished [fǽmɪʃt] *adj.* hambriento, muerto de hambre; **to be —** morirse de hambre.

famous [féməs] *adj.* famoso.

fan [fæn] *s.* abanico; aventador; ventilador; aficionado (*a deportes*); admirador; *v.* abanicar; ventilar.

fanatic [fənǽtɪk] *adj. & s.* fanático.

fanaticism [fənǽtəsɪzəm] *s.* fanatismo.

fanciful [fǽnsɪfəl] *adj.* fantástico; caprichoso; imaginario.

fancy [fǽnsɪ] *s.* fantasía, antojo, capricho; imaginación; afición, gusto; **to have a — for** tener afición a; **to strike one's —** antojársele a uno; **to take a — to a person** caerle a uno bien (*o* simpatizarle a uno) una persona; *adj.* fantástico, de fantasía; de adorno; elegante; **— ball** baile de fantasía o disfraces; **— free** libre de cuidados; **—work** labor; bordado fino; *v.* imaginar(se); fantasear; forjar, concebir (*una idea*); **to — oneself** imaginarse; **just — the ideal** ¡figúrate qué idea! **I don't — the idea of** no me gusta la idea de.

fang [fæŋ] *s.* colmillo (*de ciertos animales*).

fantastic [fæntǽstɪk] *adj.* fantástico; extravagante.

fantasy [fǽntəsɪ] *s.* fantasía.

far [far] *adv.* lejos; **— away** muy lejos; **— and wide** por todas partes; **—** mucho mejor; **— off** muy lejos; a lo lejos; **by —** con mucho; **as — as** hasta; **in cuanto a**; **as — as I know** según parece; a lo que parece; que yo sepa; **so —** hasta ahora; hasta aquí; hasta entonces; **how — ?** ¿hasta dónde?; *adj.* lejano, distante, remoto; **— journey** largo viaje; **it is a — cry from** dista mucho de.

faraway [fárəwé] *adj.* muy lejano, distante, remoto; abstraído.

farce [fars] *s.* farsa.

fare [fer] *s.* pasaje, tarifa de pasajes; pasajero; comida, alimento; *v.* pasarla (*bien o mal*); irle a uno (*bien o mal*); **to — forth** salir.

farewell [ferwél] *s.* despedida, adiós; **to bid — to** despedirse de; **—!** ¡adiós!

farfetched [fárfétʃt] *adj.* traído de muy lejos; forzado; traído por los cabellos; que no hace al caso; improbable, poco creíble.

farm [farm] *s.* hacienda, granja, *Am.* estancia, *Am.* rancho; **— hand** peón; **— produce** productos agrícolas; *v.* cultivar, labrar (*la tierra*); **to — out** dar en arriendo; repartir.

farmer [fármə] *s.* labrador; granjero; agricultor; *Am.* ranchero, *Am.* estanciero, *Am.* hacendado.

farmhouse [fármhaʊs] *s.* alquería, finca.

farming [fármɪŋ] *s.* labranza, agricultura, cultivo de los campos; *adj.* agrícola.

farmyard [fármjard] *s.* corral (*de una*

alquería).

far-off [fárɔ́f] *adj.* distante, remoto.

farther [fárðə] *adv.* más lejos; más; — on más adelante; *adj.* más remoto, más lejano.

farthest [fárðɪst] *adj.* más lejano; más remoto; *adv.* más lejos.

fascinate [fǽsn̩et] *v.* fascinar.

fascination [fæsn̩éʃən] *s.* fascinación.

fashion [fǽʃən] *s.* moda, boga; estilo; manera; — plate figurín; the latest — la última moda (*o* novedad); after a — medianamente, no muy bien; to be in — estar de moda; estilarse; *v.* forjar, hacer, formar; idear.

fashionable [fǽʃnəbl] *adj.* de moda; de buen tono; elegante.

fast [fæst] *adj.* rápido, veloz; adelantado (*dícese del reloj*); firme; fiel (*amigo*); fijo; disipado, disoluto; *adv.* aprisa, de prisa; firmemente, fijamente; — asleep profundamente dormido; *s.* ayuno; *v.* ayunar.

fasten [fǽsn̩] *v.* fijar(se); sujetar(se), asegurar(se); atar, unir; abrochar(se).

fastener [fǽsn̩ə] *s.* broche; abrochador.

fastidious [fæstídɪəs] *adj.* melindroso.

fat [fæt] *adj.* gordo; grasiento; mantecoso; — profits ganancias pingües; *s.* grasa, manteca; gordura; the — of the land lo mejor y más rico de la tierra.

fatal [fétl] *adj.* fatal.

fatality [fətǽlətɪ] *s.* fatalidad; muerte.

fate [fet] *s.* hado, sino, destino; fortuna, suerte.

father [fáðə] *s.* padre.

fatherhood [fáðəhud] *s.* paternidad.

father-in-law [fáðərɪnlɔ] *s.* suegro.

fatherland [fáðəlænd] *s.* patria.

fatherly [fáðəlɪ] *adv.* paternal.

fathom [fǽðəm] *v.* sondar, sondear; penetrar; *s.* braza (*medida de profundidad*).

fathomless [fǽðəmlɪs] *adj.* insondable.

fatigue [fətíg] *s.* fatiga, cansancio; *v.* fatigar(se), cansar(se).

fatness [fǽtnɪs] *s.* gordura.

fatten [fǽtn̩] *v.* engordar.

faucet [fɔ́sɪt] *s.* grifo, llave, espita, canilla, *Am.* bitoque.

fault [fɔlt] *s.* falta; defecto, tacha; culpa; falla (*grieta o quiebra geológica*); to a — excesivamente; to be at — ser culpable; to find — with criticar a.

faultfinder [fɔ́ltfaɪndə] *s.* criticón, criticador.

faultless [fɔ́ltlɪs] *adj.* intachable, sin tacha, perfecto.

faulty [fɔ́ltɪ] *adj.* defectuoso, imperfecto.

favor [févə] *s.* favor; your — of the . . . su grata (carta) del . . . ; *v.* favorecer.

favorable [févrəbl] *adj.* favorable; favorably *adv.* favorablemente.

favorite [févrɪt] *adj.* & *s.* favorito.

favoritism [févrɪtɪzəm] *s.* favoritismo.

fawn [fɔn] *s.* cervato; color de cervato; *v.* adular; halagar.

fear [fɪr] *s.* temor, miedo; pavor; *v.* temer.

fearful [fírfəl] *adj.* terrible, espantoso; temible, temeroso; miedoso.

fearless [fírlɪs] *adj.* sin temor, intrépido, atrevido, arrojado.

fearlessness [fírlɪsnɪs] *s.* intrepidez, arrojo, osadía, atrevimiento.

feasible [fízəbl] *adj.* factible, hacedero, dable.

feast [fist] *s.* fiesta; festín, banquete; *v.* festejar, obsequiar; banquetear; to — one's eyes on deleitar la vista en.

feat [fit] *s.* proeza, hazaña; acto de destreza; suerte (*en el circo*).

feather [féðə] *s.* pluma; -s plumaje; a — in one's cap un triunfo para uno; — weight de peso mínimo; *v.* emplumar.

feathery [féðərɪ] *adj.* plumoso; ligero, como una pluma.

feature [fítʃə] *s.* facción, rasgo distintivo; película principal (*en el cine*); -s facciones (*de la cara*); — article artículo sobresaliente o principal; *v.* destacar, hacer sobresalir; dar realce a; mostrar, exhibir (*como cosa principal*), hacer resaltar.

February [fébrʊerɪ] *s.* febrero.

fed [fed] *pret.* & *p. p. de* to feed; to be — up estar harto; estar hasta la coronilla, estar hasta el copete.

federal [fédərəl] *adj.* federal.

federation [fedəréʃən] *s.* federación, confederación, liga.

fee [fi] *s.* honorario (honorarios); derechos; cuota; admission — derechos de entrada; precio de entrada.

feeble [fíbl] *adj.* débil, endeble; feebly *adv.* débilmente.

feed [fid] *s.* forraje, pasto, pienso (*para los caballos*); comida; *v.* alimentar(se); dar de comer; pacer, pastar; to — coal echar carbón.

feel [fil] *v.* sentir; tocar, tentar; palpar; to — better (sad, happy, *etc.*) sentirse mejor (triste, feliz, *etc.*); to — one's way tantear el camino; to — for someone compadecer a alguien; it -s soft está suave; it -s hot in here se siente calor aquí; *s.* tacto, sentido del tacto; this cloth has a nice — esta tela es suave al tacto.

feeler [fílə] *s.* tentáculo, antena (*de los*

insectos); tiento; propuesta (*para averiguar la inclinación o pensamiento de alguien*).

feeling [fílɪŋ] *s.* sensación; tacto; sentimiento; emoción; pasión; compasión; ternura; **to hurt someone's -s** ofender la sensibilidad de alguien: *adj.* sensible, compasivo.

feet [fit] *pl. de* **foot.**

feign [fen] *v.* fingir.

fell [fel] *v.* derribar, echar abajo; cortar (*un árbol*); *pret. de* **to fall.**

fellow [félo] *s.* socio, miembro (*de una sociedad, colegio, etc.*); becario (*estudiante que disfruta una beca*); camarada; compañero; individuo, tipo, sujeto, hombre; — **citizen** conciudadano; — **man** prójimo; — **member** consocio; colega; — **student** condiscípulo.

fellowship [féloʃɪp] *s.* compañerismo; unión; confraternidad; sociedad; beca; **to get a** — obtener una beca.

felony [félənɪ] *s.* crimen.

felt [fɛlt] *s.* fieltro; *adj.* de fieltro; *pret. & p.p. de* **to feel.**

female [fímel] *s.* hembra; *adj.* hembra; femenino, mujeril, de la mujer; — **cat** (**dog,** *etc.*) gata (perra, *etc.*); — **screw** tuerca, hembra de tornillo.

feminine [fémənɪn] *adj.* femenino, femenil.

fence [fɛns] *s.* cerca, valla, vallado; receptor de cosas robadas; **to be on the** — estar indeciso; *v.* esgrimir; **to** — **in** cercar, rodear con cerca.

fencing [fénsɪŋ] *s.* esgrima; cercado.

fender [féndə] *s.* guardabarros, guardafango; *Am.* trompa (*de locomotora*).

ferment [fɜ́ment] *s.* fermento; fermentación; [fəmént] *v.* fermentar; hacer fermentar.

fermentation [fɜ̀mənté ʃən] *s.* fermentación.

fern [fɜn] *s.* helecho.

ferocious [fəróʃəs] *adj.* feroz, fiero.

ferocity [fərásətɪ] *s.* ferocidad, fiereza.

ferret [férɪt] *v.* **to** — **out** buscar, cazar; escudriñar, indagar.

ferry [férɪ] *s.* barca de pasaje (*a través de un río o bahía*); embarcadero; *v.* transportar de una orilla a otra; atravesar (*un río*) en barca de pasaje.

fertile [fɜ́tl] *adj.* fértil; fecundo.

fertility [fɜtílətɪ] *s.* fertilidad.

fertilize [fɜ́tlaɪz] *v.* fertilizar; abonar; fecundar.

fertilizer [fɜ́tlaɪzə] *s.* abono (*para la tierra*).

fervent [fɜ́vənt] *adj.* ferviente; fervoroso.

fervor [fɜ́və] *s.* fervor; ardor.

fester [féstə] *v.* supurar; enconarse (*una llaga*); *s.* llaga, úlcera.

festival [féstəvl] *s.* fiesta.

festive [féstɪv] *adj.* festivo; alegre.

festivity [festívətɪ] *s.* júbilo, regocijo; festividad.

fetch [fetʃ] *v.* ir a buscar; coger; traer.

fete [fet] *s.* fiesta; *v.* festejar; agasajar.

fetter [fétə] *v.* engrillar, meter en grillos, encadenar; **-s** *s. pl.* grillos, cadenas, trabas.

feud [fjud] *s.* riña, pelea, contienda; **old** — enemistad antigua (*entre dos personas o familias*).

feudal [fjúdl] *adj.* feudal.

fever [fívə] *s.* fiebre, calentura.

feverish [fívərɪʃ] *adj.* calenturiento, febril.

feverishness [fívərɪʃnɪs] *s.* calentura; agitación febril.

few [fju] *adj. & pron.* pocos; **a** — unos pocos, unos cuantos.

fiancé [fiɑnsé] *s.* novio; **fiancée** *f.* novia.

fib [fɪb] *s.* bola, mentirilla, paparrucha; papa; *v.* echar papas, decir o contar paparruchas.

fibber [fíbə] *s.* paparruchero, cuentero, mentirosillo.

fiber [fáɪbə] *s.* fibra.

fibrous [fáɪbrəs] *adj.* fibroso.

fickle [fɪkl] *adj.* inconstante, voluble, veleidoso, mudable.

fiction [fíkʃən] *s.* ficción.

fictional [fíkʃənl] *adj.* novelesco; ficticio.

fictitious [fɪktíʃəs] *adj.* ficticio.

fiddle [fídl] *s.* violín; *v.* tocar el violín; **to** — **around** malgastar el tiempo; juguetear.

fidelity [faɪdélətɪ] *s.* fidelidad.

fidget [fídʒɪt] *v.* estar inquieto; agitarse, menearse nerviosamente.

field [fild] *s.* campo; campo o cancha (*de deportes*); — **artillery** artillería de campaña; — **glasses** anteojos de larga vista.

fiend [find] *s.* demonio, diablo; **dope** — morfinómano.

fiendish [fíndɪʃ] *adj.* diabólico.

fierce [fɪrs] *adj.* feroz, fiero; furioso, espantoso.

fierceness [fírsnɪs] *s.* ferocidad; fiereza; vehemencia.

fiery [fáɪrɪ] *adj.* fogoso; ardiente; vehemente.

fig [fɪg] *s.* higo; — **tree** higuera.

fight [faɪt] *s.* lucha; pelea; riña, pleito; **he has a lot of** — **left** le sobra fuerza para luchar; *v.* luchar (con); pelear;

combatir; reñir; batirse; **to — it out** decidirlo a golpes o con argumentos; **to — one's way through** abrirse camino a la fuerza.

fighter [fáɪtə] s. luchador; combatiente; guerrero; **— airplane** aeroplano de combate.

fighting [fáɪtɪŋ] s. lucha, combate, pelea; adj. combatiente; luchador.

figure [fígjə] s. figura; forma; talle (de una persona); cifra, número; valor, precio; **-s** cuentas, cálculos; **— of speech** figura de dicción; **to be good at -s** saber hacer bien las cuentas; ser listo en aritmética; **to cut a poor —** tener mala facha, hacer el ridículo; v. figurar; imaginarse, figurarse; adornar con dibujos; calcular; **to — on** contar con, confiar en; tener la intención de, proponerse; tomar en cuenta; **to — out** descifrar, resolver.

filament [fíləmənt] s. filamento.

file [faɪl] s. fichero; archivo; registro, lista; guardapapeles; fila; lima (para cortar o pulir); **— card** ficha, papeleta; v. archivar; guardar en el fichero; registrar, asentar en el registro; limar; desfilar, marchar en fila.

filial [fílɪəl] adj. filial.

fill [fɪl] v. llenar(se); ocupar (un puesto); empastar (un diente); servir, atender, despachar (un pedido); inflar (un neumático); tapar (un agujero); **to — out a blank** llenar un formulario (forma o esqueleto).

fillet [fɪlé] s. filete; [fílɪt] cinta, lista de adorno.

filling [fílɪŋ] s. relleno; empaste (dental); **gold —** orificación.

filly [fílɪ] s. potranca.

film [fɪlm] s. película; membrana; tela (formada sobre la superficie de un liquido); nube (en el ojo); v. filmar (cinematografiar); **her eyes -ed with tears** se le arrasaron los ojos de lágrimas.

filter [fíltə] s. filtro; v. filtrar(se).

filth [fɪlθ] s. suciedad; porquería; mugre.

filthiness [fílθɪnɪs] s. suciedad, porquería.

filthy [fílθɪ] adj. sucio, puerco, cochino; mugriento.

fin [fɪn] s. aleta (de pez).

final [fáɪnl] adj. final; terminante; definitivo; **-ly** adv. finalmente; en fin, por fin.

finance [fənǽns] s. teoría bancaria, Am. finanza; **-s** fondos, recursos monetarios; negocios bancarios, Am. finanzas; v. hacer operaciones bancarias; fomentar (un negocio o empresa), Am. finan-

ciar.

financial [fənǽnʃəl] adj. financiero; monetario.

financier [fɪnənsír] s. financiero, Am. financista.

financing [fənǽnsɪŋ] s. Am. financiamiento.

find [faɪnd] v. hallar; encontrar; declarar; **to — fault with** criticar a, censurar a; **to — guilty** declarar o encontrar culpable; **to — out** descubrir; averiguar; s. hallazgo.

finding [fáɪndɪŋ] s. descubrimiento; hallazgo; fallo, decisión; **-s** resultados, datos (de una investigación).

fine [faɪn] adj. fino; perfecto, excelente; superior; primoroso; **— arts** bellas artes; **— sand** arena fina o menuda; **— weather** tiempo claro o despejado; **to feel —** sentirse muy bien de salud; **to have a — time** pasar un rato muy divertido; **fine-looking** bien parecido, guapo; s. multa; **in —** finalmente, en fin, en resumen; v. multar; **-ly** adv. finamente; con primor; excelentemente; muy bien, perfectamente.

fineness [fáɪnnɪs] s. finura; fineza; primor; excelencia, perfección.

finery [fáɪnərɪ] s. galas; atavíos, adornos.

finger [fíŋgə] s. dedo (de la mano); **—print** impresión digital; **the little —** el dedo meñique; **middle —** dedo del corazón, dedo de enmedio; **ring —** dedo anular; v. tocar; manosear.

fingernail [fíŋgənel] s. uña.

finicky [fínɪkɪ] adj. melindroso.

finish [fínɪʃ] s. fin, término, conclusión; pulimento; **to have a rough —** estar sin pulir, sin pulimento o al natural; v. acabar, acabar con, terminar, finalizar; pulir, pulimentar.

finished [fínɪʃt] adj. acabado; pulido, pulimentado; excelente.

fir [fɜ] s. abeto.

fire [faɪr] s. fuego; lumbre; quemazón; incendio; ardor; **— alarm** alarma de incendios; **— department** cuerpo o servicio de bomberos; servicio de incendios **— engine** bomba (para incendios); **— escape** escalera de salvamento; **— insurance** seguro contra incendios; **to be on —** estar ardiendo, estar quemándose; **to catch —** incendiarse, quemarse; **to set on —** pegar fuego, incendiar; **to be under enemy —** estar expuesto al fuego del enemigo; v. incendiar; pegar fuego; inflamar; disparar; **to — an employee** despedir (o expulsar) a un empleado.

firearm [fáɪrɑrm] s. arma de fuego.

firebrand [fáɪrbrænd] s. tizón; pavesa.

firecracker [fáɪrkrækǝ] s. triquitraque.

firefly [fáɪrflaɪ] s. luciérnaga.

fireman [fáɪrmǝn] s. bombero; fogonero.

fireplace [fáɪrples] s. chimenea, hogar.

fireproof [fáɪrpruf] adj. incombustible; a prueba de incendio; v. hacer incombustible.

fireside [fáɪrsaɪd] s. hogar.

firewood [fáɪrwʊd] s. leña.

fireworks [fáɪrwɔks] s. fuegos artificiales.

firm [fɜm] adj. firme; fijo; estable; s. firma, razón social (nombre de una casa comercial); compañía (comercial o industrial); **-ly** adv. firmemente, con firmeza.

firmament [fɜ́mǝmǝnt] s. firmamento.

firmness [fɜ́mnɪs] s. firmeza, estabilidad.

first [fɜst] adj. primero; adv. primero, en primer lugar, al principio; **from the —** desde el principio; **first-born** primogénito; **first-class** de primera clase; **first-cousin** primo hermano; **first-rate** de primera clase; muy bien; **—hand** de primera mano.

fish [fɪʃ] s. pez; pescado; **— market** pescadería; **— story** patraña, cuento extravagante o increíble; **neither — nor fowl** ni chicha ni limonada; v. pescar.

fisher [fɪʃǝ] s. pescador.

fisherman [fɪʃǝrmǝn] s. pescador.

fishery [fɪʃǝrɪ] s. pesquera; pesquería, pesca.

fishhook [fɪʃhʊk] s. anzuelo.

fishing [fɪʃɪŋ] s. pesca, pesquería, **— rod** caña de pescar; **— tackle** avíos o enseres de pescar; **to go —** ir de pesca.

fissure [fɪʃǝ] s. grieta, hendedura, Am. rajadura.

fist [fɪst] s. puño; **to shake one's — at** amenazar con el puño.

fit [fɪt] adj. apto; a propósito, propio, conveniente; capaz; sano, de buena salud, en buen estado; **— to be tied** frenético; **not to see — to do it** no tener a bien hacerlo; s. talle (de un traje); ajuste; encaje (de una pieza en otra); ataque, convulsión; **— of anger** acceso, arrebato o arranque de cólera; **by -s and starts** espasmódicamente; **that suit is a good —** ese traje le entalla (o le viene) bien; v. ajustar(se); adaptar; encajar(se), caber (en); acomodar; entallar (un vestido); venir bien (un vestido, zapatos, sombrero, etc.); ser a propósito para, ser propio para; capacitar, preparar; **to — in with** armonizar con; llevarse bien con; **to — out** equipar, proveer; **it does not**

— the facts no está de acuerdo con los hechos; no hace al caso.

fitness [fítnɪs] s. aptitud; capacidad; conveniencia; propiedad (de una idea, de una palabra, etc.); **physical —** buena salud.

fitting [fítɪŋ] adj. propio, apropiado; a propósito, conveniente; s. ajuste; **dress —** prueba de un traje o vestido; **-s** avíos, guarniciones, accesorios.

fix [fɪks] v. fijar; asegurar; arreglar; ajustar; remendar; componer; reparar; **to — up** arreglar(se); componer(se); s. apuro, aprieto.

fixed [fɪkst] adj. fijo, firme.

fixture [fíkstʃǝ] s. accesorio fijo; persona firmemente establecida (en un sitio o empleo); **electric light -s** instalaciones eléctricas (como brazos de lámparas, arañas).

flabby [flǽbɪ] adj. blanducho.

flag [flæg] s. bandera; banderola; **— lily** flor de lis; **—stone** losa; v. hacer señas con banderola; adornar con banderas; decaer, debilitarse, menguar, flaquear.

flagrant [flégrǝnt] adv. flagrante, notorio, escandaloso.

flagstaff [flǽgstæf] s. asta de bandera.

flair [flɛr] s. instinto, penetración, cacumen, disposición o aptitud natural.

flake [flek] s. copo (de nieve); escama; hojuela; **corn -s** hojuelas de maíz; v. descostrarse, descascararse.

flame [flem] s. llama; flama; v. llamear, flamear, echar llamas; inflamar(se); enardecer(se).

flaming [flémɪŋ] adj. llameante; flameante; encendido; ardiente, apasionado; **— red** rojo encendido.

flank [flæŋk] s. flanco; costado; lado; ijar (de un animal); v. flanquear; rodear.

flannel [flǽnl] s. franela.

flap [flæp] s. aleta; cubierta (de bolsillo); golpeteo; aleteo; v. golpetear; aletear, batir (las alas); hojear con violencia (las páginas).

flare [flɛr] s. llamarada; llama; arranque (de ira); vuelo (de una falda); v. llamear, echar llamaradas; tener vuelo (una falda); **to — up** enfurecerse; encenderse; **the illness -ed up** recrudeció la enfermedad.

flash [flæʃ] s. rayo; destello, llamarada; fogonazo; **— of hope** rayo de esperanza; **— of lightning** relámpago; **— of wit** agudeza; **in a —** en un instante; **news —** última noticia (enviada por radio o telégrafo); v. relampaguear; destellar; brillar; centellear; radiar o telegrafiar (*noticias*); **to — by** pasar como un relámpago.

flashing [flǽʃɪŋ] *s.* relampagueo, centelleo; *adj.* relumbrante; flameante.

flashlight [flǽʃlaɪt] *s.* linterna eléctrica.

flashy [flǽʃɪ] *adj.* relumbrante; llamativo, de relumbrón, ostentoso; chillante, chillón (*dícese de los colores*).

flask [flæsk] *s.* frasco.

flat [flæt] *adj.* plano, llano; chato; aplastado; insípido; monótono; desinflado; **— denial** negativa terminante; **— note** nota desentonada; **— rate** precio o número redondo; **D —** re bemol (*nota musical*); **—car** vagón de plataforma; **to be — broke** estar completamente pelado, estar sin dinero; **to fall — caer** de plano; caer mal (*un discurso, chiste, etc.*); **to sing —** desafinarse, cantar desentonadamente; **to refuse -ly** negarse absolutamente; *s.* plano; palma (*de la mano*); apartamento, departamento, piso; bemol (*en música*).

flatiron [flǽtaɪən] *s.* plancha.

flatness [flǽtnɪs] *s.* llanura; lisura; insipidez; desafinamiento (*en música*).

flatten [flǽtn] *v.* aplastar(se); aplanar(se); allanar(se).

flatter [flǽtə] *v.* lisonjear; adular.

flatterer [flǽtərə] *s.* lisonjero, adulador.

flattering [flǽtərɪŋ] *adj.* lisonjero, halagüeño, adulador.

flattery [flǽtərɪ] *s.* lisonja, halago; adulación.

flavor [flévə] *s.* sabor; gusto; condimento; *v.* sazonar; dar sabor a; condimentar.

flavorless [flévəlɪs] *adj.* insípido, sin sabor.

flaw [flɔ] *s.* defecto; falta; tacha; imperfección.

flawless [flɔlɪs] *adj.* sin tacha; intachable, irreprochable; perfecto.

flax [flæks] *s.* lino.

flay [fle] *v.* desollar.

flea [fli] *s.* pulga.

fled [fled] *pret. & p.p. de* **to flee.**

flee [fli] *v.* huir; huir de.

fleece [flis] *s.* vellón, lana; *v.* trasquilar, esquilar; despojar, estafar, defraudar.

fleet [flit] *s.* flota; armada; *adj.* veloz.

fleeting [flitɪŋ] *adj.* fugaz, transitorio, pasajero, efímero.

Flemish [flémɪʃ] *adj.* flamenco; *s.* flamenco, idioma flamenco; **the —** los flamencos.

flesh [fleʃ] *s.* carne; **— and blood** carne y hueso; **— color** color encarnado; **in the —** en persona.

fleshy [fléʃɪ] *adj.* carnoso; gordo, gordiflón.

flew [flu] *pret. de* **to fly.**

flexibility [fleksəbílətɪ] *s.* flexibilidad.

flexible [fléksəbl] *adj.* flexible.

flicker [flíkə] *s.* titilación, parpadeo, luz trémula; temblor momentáneo (*de emoción*); aleteo; especie de pájaro carpintero; *v.* titilar; temblar; parpadear; vacilar; aletear; **to — one's eyelash** pestañear.

flier [fláɪə] *s.* volador; aviador; tren rápido.

flight [flaɪt] *s.* vuelo; bandada (*de pájaros*); escuadrilla (*de aviones*); fuga, huída; **— of stairs** tramo de escalera; **to put to —** poner en fuga.

flimsy [flímzɪ] *adj.* endeble, débil; tenue; quebradizo; frágil; baladí; **a — excuse** una excusa baladí.

fling [flɪŋ] *v.* arrojar(se), lanzar(se); tirar; echar; **to — open (shut)** abrir (cerrar) de golpe; *s.* tiro; tirada, lanzamiento; tentativa; **to go out on a —** irse a echar una cana al aire.

flint [flɪnt] *s.* pedernal.

flip [flɪp] *v.* arrojar, lanzar al aire; sacudir; dar un dedazo.

flappancy [flǽpənsɪ] *s.* ligereza; frivolidad; impertinencia; petulancia.

flippant [flípənt] *adj.* ligero (*en sus acciones y modales*), ligero de cascos; frívolo; impertinente; petulante.

flirt [flɜt] *s.* coqueta; coquetón, coquetona; *v.* coquetear.

flirtation [flɜtéʃən] *s.* coquetería; **to carry on a —** coquetear.

flit [flɪt] *v.* pasar velozmente; volar; revolotear.

float [flot] *s.* boya; cosa flotante, flotador; corcho (*de una caña de pescar*); balsa; carro o carroza (*de procesiones, fiestas, etc.*); *v.* flotar; sobrenadar; boyar; poner a flote; lanzar al mercado (*una nueva emisión de valores, bonos, etc.*).

flock [flak] *s.* bandada (*de pájaros, niños, etc.*); rebaño, grey; manada (*de animales*); grupo; **— of people** gentío, muchedumbre; *v.* agruparse, congregarse; **to — to** acudir juntos (*o en bandadas*) a; **to — together** andar juntos, volar en bandadas, ir en grupo.

flog [flag] *v.* azotar.

flood [flʌd] *s.* inundación; diluvio; avenida (*de agua*), crecida; creciente; torrente; **—gate** compuerta (*de una presa*); esclusa (*de un canal*); **— light** reflector; proyector de luz; **— tide** flujo (*o marea ascendente*); *v.* inundar.

floor [flor] *s.* suelo; piso; plan, fondo (*de un buque*); fondo (*del mar*); **to have the —** tener la palabra; *v.* solar; entarimar, enladrillar, enlosar; echar al suelo, derribar; asombrar.

flop [flɑp] *v.* caer o colgar flojamente; aletear; menearse (*una cosa*) de uno a otro lado; echar, lanzar, dejar caer; fracasar, fallar; **to — down** dejarse caer; desplomarse, tumbarse; **to — over** voltear(se); dar vueltas; *s.* fracaso.

florist [flórɪst] *s.* florero, florera; **—'s shop** florería.

floss [flɔs] *s.* seda floja; pelusa; fibra sedosa; **dental —** seda dental.

flounder [fláʊndə] *v.* patalear (*en el lodo, nieve, etc.*); forcejear (*por salir del lodo, nieve, o cualquier aprieto*); revolcarse; tropezar, cometer errores; *s.* lenguado (*pez*).

flour [flaʊr] *s.* harina.

flourish [flɔ́ɪʃ] *v.* florecer, prosperar, medrar; blandir (*una espada o bastón*); agitar en el aire; *s.* floreo; adorno o rasgo caprichoso; ostentación.

floury [fláʊrɪ] *adj.* harinoso.

flow [flo] *s.* flujo; corriente; **— of words** torrente de palabras; *v.* fluir; correr; flotar, ondear; **to — into** desembocar en; **to be -ing with riches** nadar en la abundancia.

flower [fláʊə] *s.* flor; **— bed** cuadro de jardín; **— vase** florero; *v.* florecer, *Am.* florear.

flowerpot [fláʊrpat] *s.* tiesto, maceta.

flowery [fláʊrɪ] *adj.* florido.

flowing [flóɪŋ] *adj.* flúido, corriente, fluente; suelto, ondeante.

flown [flon] *p.p.* de **to fly**.

flu [flu] *s.* influenza, gripe.

fluctuate [flʌ́ktʃuet] *v.* fluctuar.

fluctuation [flʌktʃuéʃən] *s.* fluctuación.

flue [flu] *s.* cañón (*de chimenea*); tubo de escape.

fluency [flúənsɪ] *s.* fluidez; labia.

fluent [flúənt] *adj.* fluente, flúido; **to speak -ly** hablar con facilidad.

fluff [flʌf] *v.* mullir; esponjar.

fluffy [flʌ́fɪ] *adj.* mullido, suave, blando; cubierto de vello o plumón; **— hair** pelo esponjado o esponjoso.

fluid [flúɪd] *adj.* & *s.* flúido.

flung [flʌŋ] *pret.* & *p.p.* de **to fling**.

flunk [flʌŋk] *s.* reprobación (*en un examen o asignatura*); *v.* reprobar, suspender (*en un examen*); salir mal, fracasar o fallar (*en un examen*).

flunky [flʌ́ŋkɪ] *s.* lacayo; ayudante servil; zalamero, persona servil.

flush [flʌʃ] *s.* sonrojo, rubor; bochorno;

flujo rápido; flux (*de naipes*) *adj.* lleno; rico; parejo, al mismo nivel; **— with** a flor de, a ras de; *v.* sonrojar(se), ruborizar(se), poner(se) colorado; hacer rebosar (*de agua*); **to — out** vaciar (*un depósito*), enjuagar.

flute [flut] *s.* flauta; estría (*de una columna*); *v.* acanalar, estriar (*una columna*).

flutter [flʌ́tə] *s.* aleteo; agitación; alboroto; vuelco (*del corazón*); *v.* aletear; revolotear; agitar(se); palpitar; menear(se); tremolar (*una bandera*).

flux [flʌks] *s.* flujo.

fly [flaɪ] *s.* mosca; pliegue (*para cubrir botones*); bragueta (*abertura de los pantalones*); **on the —** al vuelo; **to hit a —** pegar una planchita o elevar una palomita (*en beisbol*); *v.* volar; pasar velozmente; huir; ondear; enarbolar (*una bandera*); **to — at** lanzarse sobre; **to — away** volar, irse, escaparse; **to — off the handle** perder los estribos (*o la paciencia*); **to — open (shut)** abrirse (cerrarse) de repente; **to — up in anger** montar en cólera.

flyer = **flier**.

flyleaf [fláɪlif] *s.* guarda (*hoja en blanco al principio y al fin de un libro*).

foam [fom] *s.* espuma; *v.* espumar, hacer espuma.

focus [fókəs] *s.* foco; distancia focal; *v.* enfocar(se).

fodder [fádə] *s.* forraje.

foe [fo] *s.* enemigo.

fog [fag] *s.* niebla, neblina, bruma; velo, nube (*en una película o fotografía*); **—horn** sirena; *v.* anublar, ofuscar, obscurecer; ponerse brumoso; velar(se) (*una película*).

foggy [fági] *adj.* brumoso, nublado; obscuro, confuso.

foil [fɔɪl] *s.* oropel, hojuela, laminita de metal; florete (*de esgrima*); realce, contraste; **tin —** hojuela de estaño; *v.* frustrar.

fold [fold] *s.* pliegue, doblez; redil; grey; **three—** tres veces; **hundred—** cien veces; *v.* doblar(se), plegar(se); envolver; **to — one's arms** cruzarse de brazos.

folder [fóldə] *s.* folleto, circular; papelera; plegador (*el que pliega*); plegadera (*máquina para plegar*).

folding [fóldɪŋ] *adj.* plegadizo; **— chair** silla plegadiza, silla de tijera; **— machine** plegadora, máquina plegadora; **— screen** biombo.

foliage [fólɪɪdʒ] *s.* follaje, fronda.

folio [fólɪo] *s.* folio; infolio, libro en folio; pliego; **— edition** edición en folio.

folk [fok] *s.* gente; pueblo; **-s** parientes, allegados; familia; personas; amigos (*vocativo familiar*); *adj.* popular, del pueblo; **— dance** danza o baile tradicional; **—lore** folklore; cuentos, leyendas y tradiciones populares; **— song** canción popular, canción típica o tradicional.

follow [dálo] *v.* seguir; ejercer (*un oficio o profesión*); seguir el hilo de (*un argumento*); seguirse (*como consecuencia*); **to — suit** jugar el mismo palo (*en naipes*); seguir el ejemplo, imitar.

follower [fáləwə] *s.* seguidor; imitador; partidario.

following [fáləwɪŋ] *s.* séquito, comitiva, partidarios; *adj.* siguiente; subsiguiente.

folly [fálɪ] *s.* locura; necedad, tontería; desatino.

foment [fomént] *v.* fomentar.

fond [fɑnd] *adj.* aficionado (a); amigo (de), amante (de), encariñado (con); cariñoso, afectuoso; tierno; **to be — of** querer a (*una persona*); estar encariñado con, ser aficionado a; gustar de (*algo*); **-ly** *adv.* cariñosamente, afectuosamente.

fondle [fándl] *v.* acariciar.

fondness [fándnɪs] *s.* cariño, afecto; afición.

font [fɑnt] *s.* pila bautismal; fuente.

food [fud] *s.* alimento, sustento; comida.

foodstuff [fúdstʌf] *s.* alimento; producto alimenticio; comestibles.

fool [ful] *s.* tonto, necio, zonzo; payaso; **to play the —** payasear, hacer el payaso; *v.* chasquear, chancear(se); bromear, embromar; engañar; **to — away time** malgastar el tiempo.

foolish [fúlɪʃ] *adj.* tonto; necio, bobo, zonzo.

foolishness [fúlɪʃnɪs] *s.* tontería, necedad, bobería.

foot [fut] *s.* pie; pata (*de animal*); **on —** a pie; **— soldier** soldado de infantería; **to put one's — in it** meter la pata; *v.* andar a pie; **to — it** andar a pie; **to — the bill** pagar la cuenta; sufragar los gastos.

football [fútbɔl] *s.* futbol, football.

footing [fútɪŋ] *s.* base; posición firme; **to be on a friendly — with** tener relaciones amistosas con; **to lose one's —** perder pie.

footlights [fútlaɪts] *s. pl.* candilejas (*del teatro*); tablas, teatro.

footman [fútmən] *s.* lacayo.

footnote [fútnot] *s.* nota al pie de una página.

footpath [fútpæə] *s.* vereda, senda, trocha (*para gente de a pie*).

footprint [fútprɪnt] *s.* huella, pisada.

footstep [fútstɛp] *s.* pisada, paso, huella; **to follow in the -s of** seguir las pisadas o huellas de.

footstool [fútstul] *s.* banquillo, taburete, escabel.

fop [fɑp] *s.* currutaco.

for [fɔr] *prep.* por; para; **— all of her intelligence** a pesar de su inteligencia; **— fear that** por miedo (de) que; **— the present** por el presente, por ahora; **as — him** en cuanto a él; **to know — a fact** saber de cierto, saber de hecho; **to pay him — it** pagárselo; **to thank him — it** agradecérselo; *conj.* porque, pues.

forage [fɔrɪdʒ] *s.* forraje; *v.* forrajear; dar forraje a.

foray [fɔre] *s.* correría, incursión; saqueo; *v.* pillar, saquear.

forbade [fəbæd] *pret. de* **to forbid.**

forbear [fɔrbér] *s.* antepasado; [fɔrbér] *v.* abstenerse de; tener paciencia.

forbid [fəbíd] *v.* prohibir; vedar.

forbidden [fəbídn] *adj.* prohibido; vedado; *p.p. de* **to forbid.**

forbidding [fəbídɪŋ] *adj.* austero, reservado; pavoroso; impenetrable.

forbore [fɔrbór] *pret. de* **to forbear.**

forborne [fɔrbórn] *p.p. de* **to forbear.**

force [fɔrs] *s.* fuerza; cuerpo (*de policía, de empleados, etc.*) in **— en** vigor, vigente; **armed -s** fuerzas armadas; *v.* forzar, obligar; **to — one's way** abrirse paso por fuerza; **to — out** echar por fuerza, echar a la fuerza.

forced [fɔrst] *adj.* forzado.

forceful [fórsfəl] *adj.* vigoroso; enérgico.

forceps [fórsəps] *s.* gatillo (*tenazas para sacar muelas*); pinzas.

forcible [fórsəbl] *adj.* fuerte, enérgico; potente; violento; eficaz; hecho a la fuerza; **forcibly** *adv.* fuertemente; con energía; forzosamente; por fuerza.

ford [fɔrd] *s.* vado; *v.* vadear.

fore [fɔr] *adj.* anterior, delantero; de proa; *s.* frente; puesto delantero; *adv.* delante, hacia adelante; *interj.* ¡cuidado! (*dícese en el campo de golf*).

forearm [fórarm] *s.* antebrazo.

forebode [fɔrbód] *v.* presagiar; presentir.

foreboding [fɔrbódɪŋ] *s.* presentimiento; presagio.

forecast [fórkæst] *s.* pronóstico; [fɔrkǽst] *v.* pronosticar; predecir; *pret & p.p. de* **to forecast.**

forefather [fórfaðə] *s.* antepasado.

forefinger [fórfɪŋgə] *s.* (dedo) índice.

forefoot [fórfʌt] s. pata delantera, mano (*de cuadrúpedo*).

forego [forgó] v. abstenerse de.

foregone [forgón] p.p. de to forego; a — **conclusion** una conclusión inevitable.

foreground [fórgraund] s. frente, primer plano, primer término.

forehead [fórɪd] s. frente (*f.*).

foreign [fórɪn] adj. extranjero; foráneo; extraño; — **to his nature** ajeno a su índole; — **office** ministerio de relaciones exteriores; departamento de negocios extranjeros; — **trade** comercio exterior; **foreign-born** extranjero de nacimiento.

foreigner [fórɪnə] s. extranjero; forastero.

forelock [fórlak] s. guedeja.

foreman [fórmən] s. capataz; presidente (*de un jurado*); *Am.* caporal (*de un rancho o hacienda*).

foremost [fórmost] adj. primero; delantero; principal, más notable, más distinguido.

forenoon [fornún] s. (la) mañana.

forerunner [forrʌnə] s. precursor; presagio.

foresaw [forsó] pret. de to foresee.

foresee [forsí] v. prever.

foreseen [forsín] p.p. de to foresee previsto.

foresight [fórsaɪt] s. previsión.

forest [fórɪst] s. bosque, selva; — **ranger** guardabosques; v. arbolar, plantar de árboles.

forester [fórɪstə] s. guardabosques; silvicultor; habitante de un bosque.

forestry [fórɪstrɪ] s. silvicultura.

foretell [fortél] v. predecir, pronosticar, presagiar.

foretold [fortóld] pret. & p.p. de to foretell.

forever [fɔ́ɛvə] adv. por (*o* para) siempre.

forfeit [fórfɪt] s. multa; pena; prenda perdida; **game of -s** juego de prendas; v. perder, perder el derecho a.

forgave [fəgév] pret. de to forgive.

forge [fordʒ] s. fragua; forja; v. fraguar; forjar; falsear, falsificar; **to — ahead** abrirse paso; avanzar.

forgery [fórdʒərɪ] s. falsificación.

forget [fəgét] v. olvidar; olvidarse de; **to — oneself** cometer un desmán impensadamente; perder el tino o la paciencia.

forgetful [fəgétfəl] adj. olvidadizo; negligente.

forgetfulness [fəgétfəlnɪs] s. olvido; negligencia.

forget-me-not [fəgétmɪnat] s. nomeol-

vides.

forgive [fəgív] v. perdonar.

forgiven [fəgívən] p.p. de to forgive.

forgiveness [fəgívnɪs] s. perdón.

forgiving [fəgívɪŋ] adj. perdonador, misericordioso, de buen corazón.

forgot [fəgát] pret. & p.p. de to forget.

forgotten [fəgátṇ] p.p. de to forget.

fork [fork] s. tenedor, *Am.* trinche; horquilla (*para heno*); horcón; bifurcación; v. bifurcarse; levantar o arrojar (*heno*) con horquilla.

forlorn [fəlórn] adj. desamparado, desdichado.

form [form] s. forma; condición, estado; **blank —** blanco, forma en blanco, *Am.* esqueleto; v. formar(se).

formal [fórml] adj. formal, perteneciente a la forma; convencional; ceremonioso; — **party** reunión de etiqueta; **-ly** adv. formalmente, con ceremonia, solemnemente.

formality [formǽlətɪ] s. formalidad, ceremonia; formalismo.

formation [forméʃən] s. formación.

former [fórmə] adj. primero, precedente, anterior; antiguo; **in — times** en otro tiempo, en días de antaño, antiguamente, anteriormente; **the —** aquél (aquélla, aquéllos, aquéllas); **-ly** adv. anteriormente; antes, en tiempos pasados.

formidable [fórmɪdəbl] adj. formidable.

formula [fórmjələ] s. fórmula.

formulate [fórmjəlet] v. formular.

forsake [fəsék] v. desamparar; abandonar.

forsaken [fəsékən] p.p. de to forsake & adj. desamparado, abandonado.

forsook [fəsúk] pret. de to forsake.

fort [fort] s. fuerte, fortín, fortaleza.

forth [forθ] adv. adelante; hacia adelante; **to go —** salir; **and so —** etcétera, y así sucesivamente.

forthcoming [fórəkʌmɪŋ] adj. venidero, próximo; **funds will not be — until** no habrá fondos disponibles hasta.

forthwith [forewfə] adv. en seguida, pronto, al punto.

fortification [fortəfəkéʃən] s. fortificación.

fortify [fórtəfaɪ] v. fortificar; fortalecer.

fortitude [fórtətjud] s. fortaleza.

fortnight [fórtnaɪt] s. quincena, quince días, dos semanas.

fortress [fórtrɪs] s. fortaleza, fuerte.

fortuitous [fortjúətəs] adj. fortuito; inopinado, inesperado.

fortunate [fórtʃənɪt] adj. afortunado; **-ly** adv. afortunadamente, por fortuna.

fortune [fórtʃən] s. fortuna; **—teller**

agorero, adivino.

forum [fórəm] s. foro; tribunal.

forward [fórwəd] adj. delantero; precoz; progresista; atrevido; descarado; adv. adelante, hacia adelante; v. transmitir; despachar; reenviar; **to — a plan** fomentar un plan.

fossil [fásl] adj. fósil; anticuado; s. fósil.

foster [fóstə] v. criar, nutrir; fomentar, promover; adj. putativo; adoptivo.

fought [fot] pret. & p.p. de **to fight**.

foul [faul] adj. sucio; asqueroso; puerco, cochino; fétido; vil; injusto; **— air** aire viciado; **— ball** pelota foul (en beisbol); **—mouthed** mal hablado, obsceno; **— play** juego sucio; fraude; violencia; **— weather** mal tiempo; s. mala jugada (contraria a las reglas del juego), trampa, Am. chapuza, foul; v. ensuciar; violar (las reglas de un juego); Am. pegar un foul (en beisbol).

found [faund] v. fundar, establecer; pret. & p.p. de **to find**.

foundation [faundéʃən] s. fundación; base, fundamento; dotación.

founder [fáundə] s. fundador; fundidor (de metales); v. zozobrar, irse a pique; fracasar; tropezar; hacer zozobrar.

foundry [fáundrɪ] s. fundición.

fountain [fáuntn̩] s. fuente; manantial; **— pen** pluma (de) fuente, pluma estilográfica.

fourscore [fórskór] adj. cuatro veintenas, ochenta.

fourth [forθ] adj. cuarto; s. cuarto, cuarta parte; **the — of July** el cuatro de julio.

fowl [faul] s. ave; gallo, gallina; pollo.

fox [fáks] s. zorra; zorro; persona astuta.

foxy [fáksɪ] adj. zorro, zorruno, astuto.

fraction [frǽkʃən] s. fracción; quebrado.

fracture [frǽktʃə] s. fractura; quiebra; rotura; v. fracturar; quebrar, romper.

fragile [frǽdʒəl] adj. frágil.

fragment [frǽgmənt] s. fragmento.

fragrance [frégrəns] s. fragancia.

fragrant [frégrənt] adj. fragante, oloroso.

frail [frel] adj. frágil; endeble, débil.

frailty [frélti] s. debilidad, flaqueza.

frame [frem] s. armazón, armadura, esqueleto; estructura; marco (de un cuadro, ventana, puerta, etc.); disposición (de ánimo); **embroidery —** bastidor para bordar; **— house** casa con armazón de madera; v. formar, forjar; fabricar; enmarcar (poner en marco); inventar; **to — someone** conspirar contra una persona; **to — up a charge** forjar un cargo o acusación.

framework [frémwɜk] s. armazón, es-

queleto; estructura.

franc [fræŋk] s. franco (moneda francesa).

franchise [frǽntʃaɪz] s. franquicia; derecho o privilegio político; sufragio, voto.

frank [fræŋk] adj. franco, sincero; **very — francote**; s. sello de franqueo; franquicia de correos; v. franquear, despachar, enviar (carta) exenta de franqueo.

frankfurter [frǽŋkfətə] s. salchicha.

frankness [frǽŋknɪs] s. franqueza, sinceridad.

frantic [frǽntɪk] adj. frenético; **-ally** adv. frenéticamente.

fraternal [frətɜ́n̩l] adj. fraternal.

fraternity [frətɜ́nətɪ] s. fraternidad; confraternidad.

fraud [frɔd] s. fraude, engaño; trampa, Am. chapuza; trampista, tramposo.

fraudulent [frɔ́dʒələnt] adj. fraudulento.

fray [fre] s. reyerta, riña, pelea, alboroto; raedura; v. raer(se); deshilacharse.

frayed [fred] adj. raído, deshilachado.

freak [frik] s. capricho; rareza, hombre o cosa rara; monstruosidad, fenómeno.

freckle [frékl̩] s. peca; v. ponerse pecoso.

freckled [frékld] adj. pecoso.

freckly [fréklɪ] adj. pecoso.

free [fri] adj. libre; suelto; gratuito; exento; liberal, generoso; **— of charge** gratis; **— on board (f.o.b.)** libre a bordo; **— port** puerto franco; **postage — franco de porte; to give someone a hand** dar rienda suelta o libertad de acción a una persona; **—hand drawing** dibujo a pulso, dibujo a mano; adv. libremente; gratis, de balde; v. librar; libertar; soltar; eximir; **-ly** adv. libremente; con soltura.

freedom [frídəm] s. libertad; libre uso; exención.

freeze [friz] v. helar(se); congelar(se).

freezing [frízɪŋ] adj. helado, glacial; **— point** punto de congelación.

freight [fret] s. flete; carga; **— train** tren de carga, tren de mercancías; **by — por carga; v. fletar, cargar; enviar por carga.

French [frɛntʃ] adj. francés; **to take — leave** marcharse a la francesa, irse sin despedirse; s. francés, idioma francés; **the —** los franceses.

Frenchman [frɛ́ntʃmən] s. francés.

frenzy [frénzɪ] s. frenesí.

frequency [fríkwənsɪ] s. frecuencia.

frequent [fríkwənt] adj. frecuente; v. frecuentar; **-ly** adv. frecuentemente, a menudo.

fresh [frɛʃ] adj. fresco; reciente; nuevo; impertinente, entremetido; **— water**

agua dulce; **-ly** *adv.* frescamente; con frescura; nuevamente, recientemente; **-ly painted** recién pintado, acabado de pintar.

freshen [fréʃən] *v.* refrescar(se).

freshman [fréʃmən] *s.* novato, novicio, estudiante del primer año.

freshness [fréʃnɪs] *s.* frescura; frescor, fresco; descaro.

fret [frɛt] *v.* irritar(se); apurarse; estar nervioso; agitarse; *s.* agitación, apuro, preocupación; traste (*de guitarra, mandolina, etc.*); **—work** calado.

fretful [frétfəl] *adj.* descontentadizo, malhumorado, enojadizo; nervioso.

friar [fráɪə] *s.* fraile.

friction [fríkʃən] *s.* fricción; rozamiento; frotación; desavenencia.

Friday [fráɪdɪ] *s.* viernes.

fried [fraɪd] *adj.* frito; freído; *p.p. de* **to fry**.

friend [frɛnd] *s.* amigo, amiga.

friendless [fréndlɪs] *adj.* sin amigos, solo.

friendliness [fréndlɪnɪs] *s.* afabilidad; amistad.

friendly [fréndlɪ] *adj.* amistoso, afable, amigable; propicio, favorable; *adv.* amistosamente.

friendship [frénʃɪp] *s.* amistad.

frigate [frígɪt] *s.* fragata.

fright [fraɪt] *s.* espanto, susto; terror; espantajo, **she is a —** es un adefesio.

frighten [fráɪtn] *v.* espantar, asustar, atemorizar; **to — away** espantar, ahuyentar; **to get -ed** espantarse, asustarse.

frightened [fráɪtnd] *adj.* espantado, asustado.

frightful [fráɪtfəl] *adj.* espantoso, terrible, horroroso.

frigid [frídʒɪd] *adj.* frígido, frío.

fringe [frɪndʒ] *s.* fleco; flequillo; orla; *v.* adornar con fleco; orlar.

frippery [frípərɪ] *s.* perifollos, moños, perejiles; cursilería.

frisk [frɪsk] *v.* retozar, cabriolar, saltar, brincar; registrar (*los bolsillos*), *Am.* esculcar.

frisky [frískɪ] *adj.* retozón, juguetón.

fritter [frítə] *s.* fritura, fruta de sartén; *v.* **to — away** malgastar, desperdiciar poco a poco.

frivolity [frɪválətɪ] *s.* frivolidad.

frivolous [frívələs] *adj.* frívolo.

fro [fro] : **to and —** de una parte a otra; de aquí para allá.

frock [frɑk] *s.* vestido (*de mujer*); **— coat** levita.

frog [frɑg] *s.* rana; broche (*de cordoncillos o galones*); **— in the throat** gallo en la garganta.

frolic [frálɪk] *s.* retozo, juego; holgorio, diversión; *v.* retozar, travesear, juguetear.

from [frɑm, frʌm] *prep.* de; desde; **to take something away — a person** quitarle algo a una persona.

front [frʌnt] *s.* frente (*m.*); fachada; frontispicio; **in — of** enfrente de; delante de; **shirt —** pechera; *adj.* delantero; frontal; frontero; *v.* hacer frente a; **to — towards** mirar hacia; dar a, caer a.

frontier [frʌntír] *s.* frontera; *adj.* fronterizo.

frost [frɔst] *s.* escarcha; helada; *v.* escarchar; helar; cubrir de escarcha.

frosting [frɔstɪŋ] *s.* escarcha, confitura (*para cubrir un pastel*); helado.

frosty [frɔstɪ] *adj.* escarchado, cubierto de escarcha; helado.

froth [frɔθ] *s.* espuma; *v.* espumar, hacer espuma; echar espuma o espumarajos; **to — at the mouth** echar espumarajos por la boca; enfurecerse.

frown [fraʊn] *s.* ceño; entrecejo; *v.* fruncir el ceño o las cejas; **to — at** mirar con ceño; desaprobar (*algo*).

froze [froz] *pret. de* **to freeze**.

frozen [frózn] *p.p. de* **to freeze**.

frugal [frúgl] *adj.* frugal.

fruit [frut] *s.* fruto (*en general*); fruta (*comestible*); **to eat —** comer fruta; **— tree** árbol frutal; *v.* fructificar, producir frutas.

fruitful [frútfəl] *adj.* fructuoso; productivo; provechoso.

fruitless [frútlɪs] *adj.* infructuoso, improductivo, estéril.

frustrate [frʌstret] *v.* frustrar.

frustration [frʌstréʃən] *s.* frustración.

fry [fraɪ] *v.* freír(se); *s.* fritada; **small —** pececillos; gente menuda; **French fries** patatas fritas a la francesa; **-ing pan** sartén.

fudge [fʌdʒ] *s.* dulce (*usualmente de chocolate y nueces*).

fuel [fjúəl] *s.* combustible; incentivo.

fugitive [fjúdʒətɪv] *adj.* fugitivo; transitorio; *s.* fugitivo, prófugo.

fulfill [fʊlfíl] *v.* cumplir; cumplir con; realizar; llevar a cabo; llenar (*un requisito*).

fulfillment [fʊlfílmənt] *s.* cumplimiento.

full [fʊl] *adj.* lleno; completo; harto; pleno; **— dress** traje de etiqueta; **— moon** plenilunio, luna llena; **— skirt** falda de vuelo entero; **— of fun** muy divertido, muy chistoso; **at — speed** a toda velocidad; **in — completamente;**

por completo; **to the —** por completo, por entero, totalmente; *adv.* completamente, enteramente; **to know — well** saber perfectamente, saber a ciencia cierta; **full-blooded** de raza pura; **full-fledged** hecho y derecho; maduro; completo; **-y** *adv.* completamente, enteramente, por completo.

fullness [fʌlnɪs] *s.* plenitud; llenura.

fumble [fʌmbl] *v.* tentalear, buscar a tientas; chapucear, no coger la pelota o soltarla al correr.

fume [fjum] *v.* exhalar vapor o gas; rabiar; **-s** *s. pl.* vapores, emanaciones, gases.

fumigate [fjúməget] *v.* fumigar, sahumar, *Am.* humear.

fun [fʌn] *s.* diversión; burla, broma, chanza, *Am.* choteo; **for —** en (o de) broma; de chanza; de chiste; **full of —** muy divertido; **to have —** divertirse; **to make — of** burlarse de, chancearse con, *Am.* chotear, chotearse con.

function [fʌŋkʃən] *s.* función; *v.* funcionar.

fund [fʌnd] *s.* fondo, caudal; **-s** fondos, recursos; *v.* consolidar (*una deuda*); prorrogar el plazo de (*una deuda*).

fundamental [fʌndəméntl] *adj.* fundamental; *s.* fundamento, principio.

funeral [fjúnərəl] *adj.* funeral, fúnebre; *s.* funeral, exequias, funerales.

fungus [fʌŋgəs] *s.* hongo; fungosidad.

funnel [fʌnl] *s.* embudo; humero (*cañón de chimenea*).

funny [fʌnɪ] *adj.* chistoso, cómico, gracioso, divertido; extraño, raro; **the funnies** la sección cómica (*de un periódico*).

fur [fɜ] *s.* piel (*de animales peludos o lanudos*); sarro (*en la lengua*); **— coat** abrigo de pieles; *v.* forrar, cubrir o adornar con pieles.

furious [fjúrɪəs] *adj.* furioso.

furl [fɜl] *v.* arrollar, enrollar; plegar.

furlough [fɜlo] *s.* licencia militar; *v.* dar licencia militar.

furnace [fɜnɪs] *s.* horno.

furnish [fɜnɪʃ] *v.* proveer, suministrar, surtir; equipar; proporcionar; **to — a room** amueblar un cuarto.

furniture [fɜnɪtʃə] *s.* muebles, mobiliario, moblaje, mueblaje.

furrow [fɜo] *s.* surco, arruga; *v.* surcar, arar.

further [fɜðə] *adj.* adicional; más lejano, más remoto; *adv.* además; más; más lejos; *v.* promover, fomentar, adelantar.

furthermore [fɜðəmor] *adv.* además.

furthest [fɜðɪst] *adj.* (el) más lejano, (el) más remoto; *adv.* más lejos.

furtive [fɜtɪv] *adj.* furtivo.

fury [fjúrɪ] *s.* furia; frenesí.

fuse [fjuz] *s.* fusible; mecha; *v.* fundir(se).

fuselage [fjúzlɪdʒ] *s.* fuselaje.

fuss [fʌs] *s.* melindre, preocupación inútil; bulla innecesaria; **to make a — over someone** darle a alguien demasiada importancia, desvivirse por alguien; *v.* hacer melindres, inquietarse (*por bagatelas*).

fussy [fʌsɪ] *adj.* melindroso; minucioso (*en demasía*); inquieto, nervioso; **— dress** vestido con demasiados adornos.

futile [fjútl] *adj.* fútil; vano.

future [fjútʃə] *adj.* futuro; *s.* futuro; porvenir.

fuzz [fʌz] *s.* vello; pelusa.

fuzzy [fʌzɪ] *adj.* velloso; cubierto de plumón fino; cubierto de pelusa.

G

gab [gæb] *v.* charlar, parlotear; *s.* charla; **gift of —** labia, facundia.

gabardine [gébədin] *s.* gabardina (*paño*).

gabble [gæbl] *s.* charla, cotorreo; *v.* charlar, cotorrear.

gable [gébl] *s.* gablete (*de un tejado*); **— roof** tejado de caballete o de dos aguas; **— window** ventana con gablete.

gad [gæd] *v.* vagar, callejear; andar de aquí para allá.

gadget [gædʒɪt] *s.* adminículo, artefacto, chisme.

gag [gæg] *s.* mordaza; broma, burla; morcilla, chiste (*improvisado por un actor*); *v.* amordazar; dar náuseas, hacer vomitar, basquear; interpolar chistes (*en la escena*).

gage *véase* **gauge**.

gaiety [géətɪ] *s.* alegría, viveza, alborozo.

gaily [gélɪ] *adv.* alegremente; vistosamente.

gain [gen] *s.* ganancia, provecho; *v.* ganar.

gait [get] *s.* paso, andadura, marcha.

gale [gel] *s.* ventarrón; **— of laughter** risotada, carcajada, risada.

gall [gɔl] *s.* bilis, hiel; amargura; odio; descaro; **— bladder** vejiga de la bilis; *v.* irritar.

gallant [gælənt] *adj.* valiente; noble; vistoso; [gəlént] *adj.* galante, atento, cortés; galanteador; *s.* galán.

gallantry [gæləntrɪ] *s.* galantería; gallardía, valor.

gallery [gælərɪ] *s.* galería; paraíso, gallinero (*del teatro*).

galley [gælɪ] *s.* galera; cocina (*de un*

buque); — **proof** galerada; — **slave** galeote.

gallon [gǽlən] *s.* galón (*aproximadamente cuatro litros*).

gallop [gǽləp] *s.* galope; *v.* galopar, galopear; ir a galope.

gallows [gǽloz] *s.* horca.

galoshes [gəlɔ́ʃız] *s. pl.* chanclos, zapatos fuertes, zapatones.

gamble [gǽmbl] *v.* jugar, apostar, aventurar (*algo*) en el juego; **to — away** perder en el juego; **to — everything** jugar el todo por el todo; arriesgarlo todo; *s.* jugada (*en juegos de azar*), apuesta; riesgo.

gambol [gǽmbəl] *v.* retozar; cabriolar; juguetear; *s.* retozo, cabriola.

game [gem] *s.* juego; deporte; caza (*animales de caza y su carne*); **to make —** of mofarse de, burlarse de; *adj.* valiente, atrevido; resuelto; **— bird** ave de caza.

gander [gǽndə] *s.* ánsar, ganso.

gang [gæŋ] *s.* cuadrilla; pandilla; juego (*de herramientas o máquinas*); *v.* agruparse); **to — up against** conspirar contra.

gangplank [gǽŋplæŋk] *s.* plancha, pasamano (*de un buque*), pasarela.

gangrene [gǽŋgrin] *s.* gangrena; *v.* gangrenar(se).

gangster [gǽŋstə] *s.* bandolero, bandido, maleante, atracador.

gangway [gǽŋwe] *s.* paso, pasadizo; plancha, pasamano; portalón (*de un barco*); — ¡a un lado! ¡ábranse!

gantlet = **gauntlet**.

gap [gæp] *s.* brecha, abertura; boquete; hueco; intervalo.

gape [gep] *s.* brecha, abertura; bostezo; boqueada; *v.* boquear, abrir la boca; estar boquiabierto (*mirando*); estar embobado; bostezar.

garage [gərɑ́ʒ] *s.* garaje.

garb [gɑrb] *s.* vestido; vestidura; aspecto, apariencia; *v.* vestir, ataviar.

garbage [gɑ́rbɪdʒ] *s.* desperdicios, basura.

garden [gɑ́rdn] *s.* jardín; huerta; huerto; *v.* cultivar un jardín.

gardener [gɑ́rdnə] *s.* jardinero, hortelano; horticultor.

gargle [gɑ́rgl] *s.* gargarismo, *Am.* gárgaras; *v.* gargarizar, hacer gárgaras, *Am.* gargarear.

garland [gɑ́rlənd] *s.* guirnalda.

garlic [gɑ́rlɪk] *s.* ajo.

garment [gɑ́rmənt] *s.* prenda (*de vestir*).

garnish [gɑ́rnɪʃ] *s.* aderezo; adorno; *v.* aderezar; adornar, guarnecer.

garret [gǽrɪt] *s.* desván, buhardilla.

garrison [gǽrəsn] *s.* guarnición; *v.* guarnecer o guarnicionar (*una fortaleza*).

garter [gɑ́rtə] *s.* liga (*para sujetar las medias*); *v.* sujetar con liga.

gas [gæs] *s.* gas; gasolina; **— burner** mechero; — stove estufa o cocina de gas; **tear —** gas lacrimante o lacrimógeno; *v.* asfixiar con gas; envenenar con gas.

gaseous [gǽsɪəs] *adj.* gaseoso.

gash [gæʃ] *s.* cuchillada, herida, incisión; *v.* dar una cuchillada, acuchillar.

gasoline [gǽslɪn] *s.* gasolina.

gasp [gæsp] *s.* boqueada; grito sofocado; *v.* boquear; jadear; sofocarse; abrir la boca (*de asombro*).

gate [get] *s.* portón, entrada; puerta; *Am.* tranquera (*puerta de trancas*).

gateway [gétwe] *s.* paso, entrada.

gather [gǽðə] *v.* recoger; coger; reunir(se), juntar(se); deducir, colegir; fruncir (*en pliegues*); cobrar (*fuerzas*); **to — dust** llenarse de polvo, empolvarse; *s.* pliegue.

gathering [gǽðrɪŋ] *s.* asamblea, reunión; muchedumbre; pliegue.

gaudy [gɔ́dɪ] *adj.* vistoso, llamativo, chillón, chillante.

gauge [gedʒ] *s.* calibrador; indicador; instrumento para medir; medida; calibre (*de un cañón, pistola, etc.*); ancho (*del ferrocarril*), *Am.* trocha; *v.* medir; calibrar; estimar, calcular.

gaunt [gɔnt] *adj.* macilento, demacrado, flaco.

gauntlet [gɔ́ntlɪt] *s.* guantelete; manopla; **to throw down the —** retar, desafiar.

gauze [gɔz] *s.* gasa; cendal.

gave [gev] *pret. de* to give.

gawk [gɔk] *v.* bobear, mirar embobado; *s.* simplón, bobo.

gawky [gɔ́kɪ] *adj.* torpe, desmañado, bobo.

gay [ge] *adj.* alegre; vivo; vistoso; festivo.

gayety *véase* gaiety.

gaze [gez] *s.* mirada (fija); *v.* contemplar, mirar con fijeza, clavar la mirada.

gazette [gəzét] *s.* gaceta.

gear [gɪr] *s.* aperos; herramientas; aparejo; equipo; rueda dentada; engranaje (*de ruedas dentadas*); **foot—** calzado; **low —** primera velocidad; **steering —** mecanismo de dirección; **to be in —** estar engranado; **to shift —** cambiar de engrane o velocidad; **to throw in —** engranar; **to throw out of —** desengranar; **—shift lever** palanca de engrane, palanca de cambios; *v.* engranar.

geese [gis] *pl. de* **goose.**

gelatin [dʒélətṇ] *s.* gelatina, jaletina.

gem [dʒɛm] *s.* gema, piedra preciosa; joya, alhaja; panecillo, bollo.

gender [dʒéndə] *s.* género.

general [dʒénərəl] *adj. & s.* general; **in — en** general, por lo común, por lo general.

generality [dʒɛnərǽlətɪ] *s.* generalidad.

generalize [dʒénərəlaɪz] *v.* generalizar.

generate [dʒénəret] *v.* engendrar; producir; originar.

generation [dʒenəréʃən] *s.* generación; producción.

generosity [dʒenərɑ́sətɪ] *s.* generosidad.

generous [dʒénərəs] *adj.* generoso; magnánimo, liberal; amplio; abundante.

genial [dʒínjəl] *adj.* genial, afable.

genius [dʒínjəs] *s.* genio; ingenio, talento.

genteel [dʒɛntíl] *adj.* gentil, cortés; elegante; gallardo.

gentile [dʒéntaɪl] *adj. & s.* gentil.

gentle [dʒénṭl] *adj.* suave; afable; apacible; manso; gentil.

gentleman [dʒéntlmən] *s.* caballero; **gentlemen** *pl.* caballeros; señores.

gentlemanly [dʒéntlmənlɪ] *adj.* caballeroso, caballero, cortés.

gentleness [dʒéntlnɪs] *s.* suavidad, dulzura, apacibilidad; mansedumbre.

gently [dʒéntlɪ] *adv.* suavemente; despacio; dulcemente; con ternura; mansamente.

genuine [dʒénjuɪn] *adj.* genuino; sincero.

geographical [dʒiəgrǽfɪk̩l] *adj.* geográfico.

geography [dʒiágrəfɪ] *s.* geografía.

geological [dʒiəládʒɪk̩l] *adj.* geológico.

geology [dʒiáládʒɪ] *s.* geología.

geometric [dʒiəmétrɪk] *adj.* geométrico.

geometry [dʒiámətrɪ] *s.* geometría.

geranium [dʒərénɪəm] *s.* geranio.

germ [dʒɜm] *s.* germen; microbio.

German [dʒɜ́mən] *adj. & s.* alemán.

germinate [dʒɜ́mənet] *v.* germinar.

gesticulate [dʒɛstíkjəlet] *v.* gesticular, hacer gestos o ademanes, accionar, manotear.

gesture [dʒést͡ʃə] *s.* gesto; ademán; **a mere —** una pura formalidad; *v.* gesticular, hacer gestos.

get [get] *v.* obtener, adquirir, lograr, conseguir; recibir, ganar; llegar (a); traer; coger, atrapar; preparar (*la lección, la comida, etc.*); **to — along** llevarse bien (*con alguien*); ir pasándolo (*o* ir pasándola); **to — angry** ponerse enojado, enojarse; **to — away** escaparse; irse; **to — down** bajar; **to — ill** ponerse

enfermo, enfermar(se); **to — in** entrar; meter(se); llegar; **to — married** casarse; **to — off the train** bajar del tren; apearse del tren; **to — old** envejecer(se); **to — on** subir a; montar; **to — out** salir; irse; sacar; divulgarse (*un secreto*); **to — over** pasar por encima de; recuperarse de (*una enfermedad*); olvidar (*una ofensa*); pasársele a uno (*el susto*); **to — ready** preparar(se); alistar(se); **to — rich** enriquecerse, hacerse rico; **to — rid of** deshacerse de, desprenderse de; **to — through** pasar; terminar; **to — together** juntar(se), reunir(se); ponerse de acuerdo; **to — up** levantarse; **I got him to do it** le persuadí a que lo hiciese; **I (have) got to do it** tengo que hacerlo; **I don't — it** no lo comprendo; **that's what -s me** (*or* **-s my goat**) eso es lo que me irrita.

ghastly [gǽstlɪ] *adj.* horrible; pálido, lívido, cadavérico.

ghost [gost] *s.* espectro, fantasma; **the Holy Ghost** el Espíritu Santo; **not to have the — of a notion** de no tener la más remota idea de.

ghostly [góstlɪ] *adj.* como un espectro; de espectros, de aparecidos.

giant [dʒáɪənt] *s.* gigante; *adj.* gigantesco; enorme.

giddy [gídɪ] *adj.* ligero de cascos, frívolo; voluble, inconstante; desvanecido; **— speed** velocidad vertiginosa.

gift [gɪft] *s.* regalo; dádiva; don; dote, talento, prenda; donación.

gifted [gíftɪd] *adj.* talentoso, de talento.

gigantic [dʒaɪgǽntɪk] *adj.* gigantesco.

giggle [gíg̩l] *s.* risita, risilla; risa falsa; *v.* reírse falsamente; reírse sofocando la voz; reír con una risilla afectada.

gild [gɪld] *v.* dorar.

gill [gɪl] *s.* agalla (*de pez*).

gilt [gɪlt] *adj. & s.* dorado; *pret. & p.p. de* **to gild.**

gin [dʒɪn] *s.* ginebra (*licor*).

ginger [dʒíndʒə] *s.* jengibre; **— ale** cerveza de jengibre.

gingerbread [dʒíndʒəbred] *s.* pan de jengibre; ornato de mal gusto.

gingham [gíŋəm] *s.* guinga (*tela de algodón*).

gipsy *véase* **gypsy.**

giraffe [dʒərǽf] *s.* jirafa.

gird [gɜd] *v.* ceñir; rodear; **to — oneself** for prepararse para.

girdle [gɜ́d̩l] *s.* ceñidor; cinto; faja; *v.* ceñir; fajar; cercar.

girl [gɜl] *s.* niña; muchacha; joven; chica, moza; criada.

girlhood [gɜ́lhʊd] *s.* niñez; mocedad, juventud.

girlish [gɜ́lɪʃ] *adj.* pueril; de niña, de muchacha; juvenil.

girt [gɜt] *pret. & p.p. de* to gird; *v. véase* gird.

girth [gɜθ] *s.* circunferencia; cincha (*para caballos*); faja; *v.* cinchar; ceñir.

gist [dʒɪst] *s.* substancia, esencia.

give [gɪv] *v.* dar; regalar; ceder, dar de sí; to — away regalar; entregar; revelar (*un secreto*); to — back devolver; to — birth dar a luz, parir; to — in ceder; darse por vencido; to — off emitir; to — out divulgar; repartir; agotarse; to — up abandonar; desistir; renunciar a; perder la esperanza; rendir(se); ceder, darse por vencido; *s.* elasticidad.

given [gɪ́vən] *p.p. de* to give; *adj.* dado; regalado; adicto, entregado; dispuesto, inclinado; — name nombre de pila, nombre de bautismo; — time hora determinada;—that dado que, supuesto que.

giver [gɪ́və] *s.* dador, donador.

glacial [gléʃəl] *adj.* glacial.

glacier [gléʃə] *s.* glaciar, helero.

glad [glæd] *adj.* alegre; contento; to be — to alegrarse de, tener mucho gusto en (*o de*); -ly *adv.* alegremente; con mucho gusto; de buena gana.

gladden [glǽdn] *v.* regocijar, alegrar.

glade [gled] *s.* claro herboso (*en un bosque*).

gladness [glǽdnɪs] *s.* alegría, gozo.

glamour [glǽmə] *s.* encanto, hechizo; fascinación, embrujo; — girl niña hechicera.

glamorous [glǽmərəs] *adj.* fascinador, hechicero.

glance [glæns] *s.* mirada, vistazo, ojeada; vislumbre; *v.* echar (*o dar*) un vistazo; vislumbrar; pegar de soslayo; to — off rebotar de soslayo (*o de lado*).

gland [glænd] *s.* glándula.

glare [gler] *s.* resplandor, relumbre; mirada furiosa; *v.* resplandecer, relumbrar; to — at mirar enfurecido a.

glass [glæs] *s.* vidrio; cristal; vaso; copa (*de cristal*); lente; looking — espejo; -es anteojos, lentes, gafas; *adj.* de vidrio; — blower vidriero, soplador de vidrio; — case escaparate.

glassware [glǽswer] *s.* vajilla de cristal, cristalería; — shop cristalería.

glassy [glǽsɪ] *adj.* vidrioso.

glaze [glez] *s.* vidriado; lustre; superficie lustrosa o glaseada; *v.* vidriar; glasear; lustrar; poner vidrios a.

glazier [gléʒə] *s.* vidriero.

gleam [glim] *s.* destello, rayo, fulgor, viso; *v.* destellar, fulgurar, centellear.

glean [glin] *v.* recoger; espigar.

glee [gli] *s.* regocijo; júbilo; — club orfeón, masa coral.

glib [glɪb] *adj.* locuaz; de mucha labia; — excuse excusa fácil.

glide [glaɪd] *s.* deslizamiento; ligadura (*en música*); planeo (*de un aeroplano*); *v.* deslizarse; resbalarse; planear (*un aeroplano*).

glider [gláɪdə] *s.* deslizador, planeador (*aeroplano*).

glimmer [glɪ́mə] *s.* vislumbre; viso; titileo; — of hope rayo de esperanza; *v.* titilar, centellear.

glimpse [glɪmps] *s.* vislumbre; vistazo, ojeada; to catch a — of vislumbrar; *v.* vislumbrar.

glint [glɪnt] *s.* fulgor, rayo, destello.

glisten [glɪ́sn] *v.* relucir, brillar.

glitter [glɪ́tə] *s.* lustre, brillo, resplandor; *v.* relumbrar, relucir, brillar.

gloat [glot] *v.* gozarse (en), deleitarse (en); relamerse (*de gusto*).

globe [glob] *s.* globo; esfera.

gloom [glum] *s.* lobreguez, sombra; abatimiento, tristeza, melancolía.

gloomy [glúmɪ] *adj.* lóbrego, sombrío; triste, melancólico; abatido.

glorify [glórəfaɪ] *v.* glorificar.

glorious [glórɪəs] *adj.* glorioso; espléndido.

glory [glórɪ] *s.* gloria; *v.* gloriarse; vanagloriarse.

gloss [glɔs] *s.* lustre, brillo; pulimento; glosa, comentario; *v.* lustrar, dar brillo a; pulir; glosar, comentar; to — over encubrir, dar colorido de bueno (*a algo que no lo es*).

glossary [glásərɪ] *s.* glosario.

glossy [glɔ́sɪ] *adj.* lustroso; pulido.

glove [glʌv] *s.* guante; *v.* enguantar, poner guantes.

glow [glo] *s.* incandescencia; brillo (*de un ascua*); calor vivo; fosforescencia *v.* lucir, brillar (*como un ascua*); fosforecer; estar encendido o enardecido.

glowing [glóɪŋ] *adj.* encendido, ardiente.

glowworm [glów3m] *s.* luciérnaga.

glue [glu] *s.* cola (*para pegar*); *v.* encolar, pegar (*con cola*).

glutton [glʌ́tn] *s.* glotón.

gluttonous [glʌ́tnəs] *adj.* glotón; goloso.

gluttony [glʌ́tnɪ] *s.* gula, glotonería.

gnarled [nɑrld] *adj.* nudoso, torcido.

gnash [næʃ] *v.* crujir, rechinar (*los dientes*).

gnat [næt] *s.* jején (*insecto*).

gnaw [nɔ] v. roer.

go [go] v. ir(se); andar; marchar, funcionar; acudir; **to — around** andar alrededor de; dar vueltas; **to — away** irse; **to — back on one's word** faltar a la palabra; **to — by** pasar por; guiarse por (una regla); **to — down** bajar; **to — insane** volverse loco; **to — into** entrar en; investigar; caber en; **to — off** hacer explosión; dispararse; irse, salir disparado; **to — on** proseguir, continuar; **to — out** salir; apagarse; **to — over** pasar por encima de; examinar con cuidado; releer; repasar; recorrer; **to — to sleep** dormirse; **to — under** ir o pasar por debajo de; hundirse; **to — up** subir; **to let —** soltar; **there is not enough to — around** no hay (bastante) para todos; s. empuje, energía; **it is a —** trato hecho; **to be on the —** estar en continuo movimiento.

goad [god] s. aguijón; v. aguijonear; aguijar, incitar.

goal [gol] s. meta; fin, objetivo.

goat [got] s. cabra; **male — macho** cabrío; **to be the —** ser la víctima, pagar el pato.

goatee [gotí] s. perilla.

gobble [gábl] v. tragar, engullir; **to — up** engullirse.

gobbler [gáblə] s. pavo.

go-between [góbətwin] s. medianero.

goblet [gáblɪt] s. copa grande.

goblin [gáblɪn] s. duende.

god [gad] s. dios; God Dios.

godchild [gádtʃaɪld] s. ahijado, ahijada.

goddess [gádɪs] s. diosa.

godfather [gádfaðə] s. padrino.

godless [gádlɪs] adj. impío, ateo.

godlike [gádlaɪk] adj. como Dios; divino.

godly [gádlɪ] adj. pío, devoto; divino.

godmother [gádmʌðə] s. madrina.

goggles [gáglz] s. pl. antiparras, gafas.

going [góɪŋ] ger. & adj. que anda, marcha o funciona bien; **to be —** ir, irse; s. ida, partida; **comings and -s** idas y venidas.

goiter [gɔ́ɪtə] s. papera, Am. buche.

gold [gold] s. oro; **— standard** patrón de oro.

golden [góldn] adj. de oro; áureo; dorado.

goldfinch [góldfɪntʃ] s. jilguero amarillo.

goldfish [góldfɪʃ] s. carpa dorada.

goldsmith [góldsmɪθ] s. orfebre.

golf [galf] s. golf.

gondola [gándələ] s. góndola; cabina (de una aeronave); **— car** vagón de mer-

cancías (sin techo), Am. jaula.

gone [gɔn] p.p. de to go & adj. ido; perdido; **he is —** se fué; **it is all —** se acabó; ya no hay más.

gong [gɔŋ] s. gong, batintín.

good [gud] adj. bueno; válido; valedero; **— afternoon** buenas tardes; **— day** buenos días; adiós; **— evening** buenas noches; **— morning** buenos días; **— night** buenas noches; **Good Friday** Viernes Santo; **for —** para siempre, permanentemente; **to have a — time** pasar un buen rato; divertirse; **to make —** pagar, compensar; cumplir (una promesa); salir bien, tener buen éxito; s. bien; beneficio, provecho, ventaja; **-s** bienes, efectos; mercancías.

good-bye [gudbáɪ] s. & interj. adiós.

good-looking [gúdlúkɪŋ] adj. bien parecido, guapo.

goodly [gúdlɪ] adj. grande, considerable; de buena apariencia.

good-natured [gúdnétʃəd] adj. de buen genio, bonachón, afable.

goodness [gúdnɪs] s. bondad; **—!** ¡Dios mío! ¡cielos!

goody [gúdɪ] s. golosina, bonbón, dulce; interj. ¡qué gusto!; **goody-goody** beatuco (el que afecta virtud), papanatas.

goose [gus] s. ganso; bobo, tonto; **— flesh** carne de gallina.

gooseberry [gúsbɛrɪ] s. grosella; grosellero (arbusto).

gopher [gófə] s. roedor semejante a la ardilla.

gore [gor] s. cuajarón de sangre; cuchillo (Am. cuchilla), sesga (tira de lienzo en figura de cuchilla); v. acornear, herir con los cuernos; hacer una sesga en (un traje).

gorge [gɔrdʒ] s. cañada, barranco, barranca; v. engullir(se), atracarse.

gorgeous [gɔ́rdʒəs] adj. primoroso, vistoso, hermosísimo.

gorilla [gərílə] s. gorila.

gory [górɪ] adj. sangriento, ensangrentado.

gospel [gáspl] s. evangelio; **it is the — truth** es la pura verdad.

gossip [gásɪp] s. chisme, chismería; murmuración; habilla; murmurador, chismero o chismoso; v. chismear, murmurar.

gossipy [gásəpɪ] adj. chismero, chismoso.

got [gat] pret. & p.p. de to get.

Gothic [gáɪk] adj. gótico; s. gótico (idioma de los godos); estilo gótico.

gotten [gátn] p.p. de to get.

gouge [gaʊdʒ] s. gubia (especie de for-

món o escoplo curvo); *v.* excavar con gubia, formón o escoplo; **to — someone's eyes out** sacarle los ojos a alguien.

gourd [gord] *s.* calabaza.

gout [gaʊt] *s.* gota (*enfermedad*).

govern [gʌ́vən] *v.* gobernar; regir.

governess [gʌ́vənɪs] *s.* institutriz.

government [gʌ́vəmənt] *s.* gobierno.

governmental [gʌvəmǽntl] *adj.* gubernativo.

governor [gʌ́vənə] *s.* gobernador; regulador (*de una máquina*).

gown [gaʊn] *s.* vestido (*de mujer*); toga (*de un juez, profesor, etc.*); **dressing —** bata.

grab [grǽb] *v.* agarrar, asir; arrebatar; *s.* arrebatiña; agarro, agarrón; presa.

grace [gres] *s.* gracia; favor; donaire, garbo; **to say —** bendecir la mesa, dar gracias; **to be in the good -s of someone** gozar del favor de uno; *v.* agraciar, adornar.

graceful [grésfəl] *adj.* gracioso, agraciado, garboso; **-ly** *adv.* graciosamente, con gracia, con garbo.

gracefulness [grésfəlnɪs] *s.* gracia, donaire, gallardía, garbo.

gracious [gréʃəs] *adj.* afable; cortés; **—!** ¡válgame Dios!

gradation [gredéʃən] *s.* graduación; gradación; grado.

grade [gred] *s.* grado; nota, calificación; cuesta, declive, pendiente, *Am.* gradiente; **— crossing** cruce a nivel (*de un ferrocarril con una carretera*); **the -s** la escuela primaria; *v.* graduar, clasificar; calificar, dar una calificación; nivelar (*un camino*).

gradual [grǽdʒʊəl] *adj.* gradual; **-ly** *adv.* gradualmente, poco a poco.

graduate [grǽdʒʊɪt] *adj.* graduado, que ha recibido un grado académico; **to do — work** cursar asignaturas superiores (*al bachillerato*); *s.* estudiante graduado (*que estudia para licenciado o doctor*); [grǽdʒʊet] *v.* graduar(se).

graduation [grædʒʊéʃən] *s.* graduación.

graft [grǽft] *s.* injerto; tejido injertado; sisa, malversación (*de caudales públicos*); ganancia ilegal, *Am.* mordida; *v.* injertar; malversar fondos ajenos; sisar, exigir pago ilegal, *Am.* morder.

grafter [grǽftə] *s.* malversador (*de fondos públicos*), estafador, *Am.* coyote, *Am.* mordelón.

grain [gren] *s.* grano; fibra (*de la madera*), veta (*del mármol o madera*); **against the —** a (*o* al) redopelo, a contrapelo.

gram [grǽm] *s.* gramo.

grammar [grǽmə] *s.* gramática; **— school** escuela primaria.

grammatical [grəmǽtɪkl] *adj.* gramatical, gramático.

granary [grǽnərɪ] *s.* granero.

grand [grǽnd] *adj.* grande; grandioso, admirable; magnífico.

grandchild [grǽntʃaɪld] *s.* nieto.

grandchildren [grǽntʃɪldrən] *s. pl.* nietos.

granddaughter [grǽndɔtə] *s.* nieta.

grandeur [grǽndʒə] *s.* grandeza, grandiosidad; majestad.

grandfather [grǽnfaðə] *s.* abuelo.

grandiose [grǽndɪos] *adj.* grandioso, magnífico.

grandma [grǽnma] *s.* abuela, abuelita, *Am.* mamá grande.

grandmother [grǽnmʌðə] *s.* abuela.

grandness [grǽndnɪs] *s.* grandeza; grandiosidad; magnificencia.

grandpa [grǽnpa] *s.* abuelo, abuelito, *Am.* papá grande.

grandparent [grǽnperənt] *s.* abuelo, abuela; **-s** abuelos.

grandson [grǽnsʌn] *s.* nieto.

grandstand [grǽnstænd] *s.* andanada, gradería cubierta.

grange [grendʒ] *s.* granja; asociación de agricultores.

granite [grǽnɪt] *s.* granito (*roca*).

granny [grǽnɪ] *s.* abuelita; viejecita, viejita.

grant [grǽnt] *s.* concesión; subvención; donación; transferencia de propiedad (*mediante escritura*); *v.* conceder; otorgar; ceder, transferir (*derechos, propiedad, etc.*); **to take for -ed** dar por supuesto, dar por sentado.

granulate [grǽnjəlet] *v.* granular(se).

grape [grep] *s.* uva.

grapefruit [grépfrut] *s.* toronja.

grapevine [grépvaɪn] *s.* vid; parra.

graph [grǽf] *s.* diagrama, gráfica; *v.* hacer una gráfica o diagrama.

graphic [grǽfɪk] *adj.* gráfico.

graphite [grǽfaɪt] *s.* grafito.

grapple [grǽpl] *v.* luchar, pelear cuerpo a cuerpo; aferrar, agarrar.

grasp [grǽsp] *v.* agarrar; asir; apretar; abarcar; comprender; *s.* agarro, asimiento; apretón de manos; **to be within one's —** estar al alcance de uno; **to have a good — of a subject** estar fuerte en una materia, saber a fondo una materia.

grass [grǽs] *s.* hierba; césped; pasto.

grasshopper [grǽshapə] *s.* saltamontes, saltón, *Am.* chapulín.

grassy [grǽsɪ] *adj.* herboso, *Am.* pastoso.

grate [gret] *s.* reja, verja, enrejado; parrilla, brasero; *v.* enrejar, poner enrejado; crujir, rechinar (*los dientes*); rallar (*queso*); **to — on** molestar, irritar.

grateful [grétfəl] *adj.* agradecido; grato, agradable.

grater [grétə] *s.* rallador.

gratify [grǽtəfaɪ] *v.* complacer, dar gusto, agradar; satisfacer.

grating [grétɪŋ] *s.* reja, enrejado, verja; *adj.* rechinante; molesto, áspero.

gratis [grétɪs] *adv.* gratis, de balde.

gratitude [grǽtətjud] *s.* gratitud.

gratuitous [grətjúətəs] *adj.* gratuito; sin fundamento; **— statement** afirmación arbitraria.

grave [grev] *adj.* grave; serio; *s.* tumba, sepulcro, sepultura; acento grave; **—stone** losa o lápida sepulcral.

gravel [grǽvl] *s.* grava, guijo, cascajo; cálculos (*en los riñones, la vejiga, etc.*); mal de piedra; *v.* cubrir con grava.

graveyard [grévjard] *s.* cementerio.

gravity [grǽvətɪ] *s.* gravedad; seriedad.

gravy [grévɪ] *s.* salsa; jugo (*de carne*).

gray [gre] *adj.* gris; cano; entrecano (*que empieza a encanecer*); **— horse** rucio, tordo, tordillo; **— matter** seso; **gray-headed** canoso; *s.* gris, color gris; *v.* encanecer; poner(se) gris.

grayish [gréɪʃ] *adj.* grisáceo, pardusco; **— hair** pelo entrecano.

grayness [grénɪs] *s.* grisura, gris, calidad de gris; encanecimiento.

graze [grez] *v.* pacer, apacentar, *Am.* pastear, pastar; rozar; raspar; *s.* roce, rozón, raspadura.

grease [gris] *s.* grasa; *v.* engrasar; untar; lubricar; **to — the palm** untar la mano, sobornar.

greasy [grísɪ] *adj.* grasiento, grasoso.

great [gret] *adj.* gran(de); eminente; magnífico, excelente; **a — deal una gran cantidad; muchos; mucho; a — many muchos; a — while un largo rato o tiempo; -ly *adv.* grandemente; mucho; muy; en gran parte; sobremanera.

great-grandchild [grétgrǽntʃaɪld] *s.* biznieto.

great-grandfather [grétgrǽnfaðə] *s.* bisabuelo.

great-grandmother [grétgrǽnmʌðə] *s.* bisabuela.

greatness [grétnɪs] *s.* grandeza.

Grecian [gríʃən] *adj. & s.* griego.

greed [grid] *s.* codicia; avaricia; gula.

greedily [grídɪlɪ] *adv.* vorazmente; con avaricia; con gula.

greediness [grídɪnɪs] *s.* codicia; avaricia; gula; voracidad.

greedy [grídɪ] *adj.* codicioso; avaro; goloso; voraz.

Greek [grik] *adj. & s.* griego.

green [grin] *adj.* verde; novato, inexperto; **to grow —** verdear; **the fields look —** verdean los campos; *s.* verde, verdor; césped, prado; campo de golf; **-s** verduras, hortalizas.

greenhouse [grínhaʊs] *s.* invernáculo, invernadero.

greenish [grínɪʃ] *adj.* verdoso.

greenness [grínnɪs] *s.* verdor, verdura; inmadurez; falta de experiencia, impericia.

greet [grit] *v.* saludar; **to — each other** saludarse.

greeting [grítɪŋ] *s.* saludo; salutación; **-s** ¡salud! ¡saludos!

grenade [grinéd] *s.* granada, bomba pequeña.

grew [gru] *pret. de* **to grow.**

grey = **gray.**

greyish = **gray.**

greyness = **grayness.**

greyhound [gréhaʊnd] *s.* lebrel, galgo.

griddle [grídl] *s.* tartera; plancha (*para tapar el hornillo*).

grief [grif] *s.* dolor, pesar; **to come to —** sobrevenirle a uno una desgracia; fracasar.

grievance [grívəns] *s.* queja; resentimiento; motivo de queja, injusticia, ofensa.

grieve [griv] *v.* afligir(se); lamentar(se), acongojar(se).

grievous [grívəs] *adj.* doloroso, penoso; grave, atroz.

grill [grɪl] *s.* parrilla; **men's —** restaurante para hombres; *v.* asar en parrillas; interrogar (*a un sospechoso*).

grim [grɪm] *adj.* austero, áspero; fiero; torvo, siniestro.

grimace [grimés] *s.* mueca, gesto; *v.* hacer muecas o gestos.

grime [graɪm] *s.* mugre; *v.* ensuciar.

grimy [gráɪmɪ] *adj.* mugriento.

grin [grɪn] *s.* sonrisa abierta; sonrisa maliciosa; sonrisa canina; *v.* sonreír (*mostrando mucho los dientes*).

grind [graɪnd] *v.* moler; machacar; afilar, amolar; afanarse demasiado, estudiar con desmasiado empeño, machacar la lección; **to — a hand organ** tocar el organillo; **to — one's teeth** rechinar los dientes; *s.* molienda; faena, trabajo penoso; estudiante tesonero; **the daily —** la rutina diaria.

grinder [gráɪndə] *s.* moledor; molinillo *(para moler café);* amolador, afilador; muela *(piedra para afilar);* muela *(diente molar).*

grip [grɪp] *v.* agarrar; asir; apretar; impresionar, conmover; *s.* agarro; asimiento; apretón; asidero, asa; valija, maletín, saco de mano; **to have a — on someone** tener agarrado a alguien.

grippe [grɪp] *s.* gripe, influenza.

grit [grɪt] *s.* arenilla, arena; piedra arenisca; firmeza, tesón; **-s** maíz, avena, o trigo a medio moler; *v.* rechinar, crujir.

gritty [grítɪ] *adj.* arenoso; valeroso, firme.

grizzly [grízlɪ] *adj.* grisáceo, pardusco; **— bear** oso pardo.

groan [gron] *s.* gemido, quejido; *v.* gemir; quejarse; crujir *(por exceso de peso).*

grocer [grósə] *s.* abacero, *Am.* abarrotero, *Am.* bodeguero.

grocery [grósərɪ] *s.* abacería, tienda de comestibles, *Am.* abarrotería, *Am.* tienda de abarrotes; *Am.* bodega; **groceries** comestibles, *Am.* abarrotes.

groom [grum] *s.* novio; caballerizo, mozo de caballeriza; establero; *v.* almohazar, limpiar con la almohaza *(a los caballos),* cuidar *(a los caballos);* **to —** oneself asearse, peinarse, componerse; **well-groomed** bien vestido, aseado, limpio.

groove [gruv] *s.* estría, ranura, acanaladura; surco *(en un camino);* muesca, encaje; *v.* acanalar, estriar.

grope [grop] *v.* tentalear, tentar, andar a tientas; **to — for** buscar tentando, buscar a tientas.

gross [gros] *adj.* grueso; burdo; tosco; grosero; **— earnings** ganancias totales; **— ignorance** ignorancia crasa; **— weight** peso bruto; *s.* grueso, totalidad; gruesa *(doce docenas).*

grotesque [grotésk] *adj. & s.* grotesco.

grotto [grúto] *s.* gruta.

grouch [ɡraʊtʃ] *s.* mal humor; gruñón, refunfuñón, cascarrabias; **to have a — against** someone tenerle ojeriza *(o mala voluntad)* a una persona; guardarle rencor a alguien; *v.* gruñir, refunfuñar; estar de mal humor.

grouchy [gráʊtʃɪ] *adj.* gruñón, refunfuñón, malhumorado, cascarrabias.

ground [graʊnd] *s.* suelo, tierra; terreno; motivo, razón; fundamento, base; **-s** heces, desperdicios, sedimento; **— floor** piso bajo, planta baja; **to break —** ro-

turar, arar; cavar; **to give —** retroceder, ceder; **to hold one's —** mantenerse firme; *v.* conectar *(un alambre)* con la tierra; encallar *(una embarcación);* aterrizar *(un aeroplano);* **to be well -ed** poseer las bases o principios fundamentales; *pret. & p.p. de* **to grind.**

groundless [gráʊndlɪs] *adj.* infundado.

group [grʊp] *s.* grupo; *v.* agrupar.

grove [grov] *s.* arboleda, bosquecillo.

grow [gro] *v.* crecer; brotar; cultivar; criar; producir; **to — angry** ponerse enojado o enfadado, enfadarse, enojarse; **to — better** ponerse mejor, mejorar; **to — difficult** dificultarse, hacerse difícil; **to — late** hacerse tarde; **to — old** ponerse viejo, envejecer; **to — out of a habit** perder la costumbre; **to — pale** ponerse pálido, palidecer; **to — tired** cansarse.

growl [graʊl] *s.* gruñido; *v.* gruñir.

growler [gráʊlə] *s.* gruñón; regañón.

grown [gron] *p.p. de* **to grow** & *adj.* crecido; desarrollado; **— man** hombre maduro, hombre hecho; **— with trees** poblado de árboles.

grown-up [grónʌp] *adj.* crecido, adulto; *s.* adulto.

growth [groθ] *s.* crecimiento, acrecentamiento; aumento; desarrollo; vegetación; tumor, lobanillo, excrecencia.

grudge [grʌdʒ] *s.* inquina, rencor, resentimiento, mala voluntad; *v.* tener inquina, envidia o mala voluntad; dar de mala gana.

gruff [grʌf] *adj.* áspero, rudo; grosero.

grumble [grʌ́mbl] *s.* refunfuño, gruñido, queja; *v.* refunfuñar, gruñir, quejarse.

grumbler [grʌ́mblə] *s.* gruñón; regañón.

grumpy [grʌ́mpɪ] *adj.* malhumorado; gruñón.

grunt [grʌnt] *s.* gruñido, *Am.* pujido; *v.* gruñir, *Am.* pujar.

guarantee [gærəntí] *s.* garantía; fianza; fiador; *v.* garantizar; dar fianza; salir fiador de.

guarantor [gærəntə] *s.* fiador.

guaranty [gǽrəntɪ] *s.* garantía; fianza; fiador; *v. véase* **guarantee.**

guard [gɑrd] *s.* guarda; guardia; resguardo; **to be on —** estar alerta; estar en guardia; **to keep —** vigilar; *v.* guardar; resguardar; vigilar; **to — (oneself) against** guardarse de.

guardian [gárdɪən] *s.* guardián, custodio; tutor; **— angel** ángel custodio, ángel de la guarda.

guardianship [gárdɪənʃɪp] *s.* tutela; guarda, custodia.

Guatemalan [gwɑtəmálən] *adj. & s.*

guatemalteco.

guess [gɛs] *s.* conjetura, suposición; adivinación; *v.* adivinar; suponer, creer.

guest [gɛst] *s.* convidado; visita; huésped, pensionista, inquilino.

guffaw [gʌfɔ́] *s.* risotada, carcajada.

guidance [gáɪdn̩s] *s.* guía, dirección.

guide [gaɪd] *s.* guía.

guidebook [gáɪdbʊk] *s.* guía del viajero; **railway** — guía de ferrocarriles.

guild [gɪld] *s.* gremio; cofradía; asociación.

guile [gaɪl] *s.* engaño, astucia.

guilt [gɪlt] *s.* culpa, delito; culpabilidad.

guiltless [gɪ́ltlɪs] *adj.* libre de culpa; inocente.

guilty [gɪ́ltɪ] *adj.* culpable; reo, delincuente.

guise [gaɪz] *s.* aspecto, apariencia; modo; **under the** — of so capa de; disfrazado de.

guitar [gɪtár] *s.* guitarra.

gulf [gʌlf] *s.* golfo; abismo.

gull [gʌl] *s.* gaviota.

gullet [gʌ́lɪt] *s.* gaznate.

gully [gʌ́lɪ] *s.* barranco, barranca; hondonada.

gulp [gʌlp] *s.* trago; *v.* tragar; engullir; **to — it down** tragárselo.

gum [gʌm] *s.* goma; encía; **chewing —** goma de mascar, *Am.* chicle; **— tree** árbol gomífero, *Am.* gomero; *v.* engomar, pegar con goma.

gun [gʌn] *s.* arma de fuego; cañón; fusil, escopeta; pistola, revólver; **a 21 — salute** una salva de 21 cañonazos.

gunboat [gʌ́nbot] *s.* cañonero, lancha cañonera.

gunner [gʌ́nə] *s.* artillero, cañonero; ametrallador.

gunpowder [gʌ́npaʊdə] *s.* pólvora.

gurgle [gɝ́gl̩] *v.* borbotar, hacer borbollones; *s.* borbollón, borbotón.

gush [gʌʃ] *s.* chorro; borbollón, borbotón; efusión (*de cariño o entusiasmo*); *v.* chorrear, borbotar, borbollar, borbollonear; brotar; ser demasiado efusivo.

gust [gʌst] *s.* ráfaga, ventolera.

gut [gʌt] *s.* tripa, intestino; cuerda de tripa; **to have -s** tener agallas (*ánimo*).

gutter [gʌ́tə] *s.* arroyo (*de la calle o de un camino*); gotera (*del techo*); zanja.

guy [gaɪ] *s.* sujeto, tipo, individuo; tirante, alambre, cadena (*para sostener algo*); *v.* sostener (*algo*) con tirantes; burlarse de, mofarse de.

gymnasium [dʒɪmnéʒɪəm] *s.* gimnasio.

gymnastics [dʒɪmnǽstɪks] *s. pl.* gimnasia.

gypsy [dʒípsɪ] *s. & adj.* gitano.

H

habit [hǽbɪt] *s.* hábito; costumbre; **drinking —** vicio de la bebida; **riding —** traje de montar.

habitual [həbítʃʊəl] *adj.* habitual; acostumbrado.

hack [hæk] *s.* tajo; tos seca; caballo de alquiler; rocín; escritor mercenario; *v.* tajar, picar; toser con tos seca.

hackneyed [hǽknɪd] *adj.* trillado, muy común.

had [hæd] *pret. & p.p. de* to have; **you — better do it** es bueno que Vd. lo haga; sería bueno que Vd. lo hiciese; **I — rather go than stay** preferiría irme a quedarme.

hag [hæg] *s.* hechicera, bruja; viejota.

haggard [hǽgəd] *adj.* macilento, flaco.

haggle [hǽgl̩] *v.* regatear.

hail [hel] *s.* granizo; saludo; llamada, grito; **Hail Mary** Ave María; *interj.* ¡saludo!; ¡salve!; *v.* granizar; saludar; llamar; aclamar; **to — from** proceder de, ser oriundo de.

hailstorm [hélstɔrm] *s.* granizada.

hair [her] *s.* pelo; cabello; vello; filamento (*de las plantas*); **— net** red para el cabello.

hairbrush [hérbrʌʃ] *s.* cepillo para el cabello.

haircut [hérkʌt] *s.* corte de pelo; **to have a —** hacerse cortar el pelo.

hairdo [hérdu] *s.* peinado.

hairdresser [hérdrɛsə] *s.* peluquero; peinadora.

hairless [hérlɪs] *adj.* sin pelo, pelado; lampiño.

hairpin [hérpɪn] *s.* horquilla, *Am.* gancho (*para el pelo*).

hairy [hérɪ] *adj.* peludo, cabelludo; hirsuto, velloso; velludo.

hale [hel] *adj.* sano, fuerte, robusto; *v.* llevar (*a una persona*) por fuerza.

half [hæf] *s.* mitad; **— an apple** media manzana; *adj.* medio; **— brother** hermanastro; **— cooked** a medio cocer, medio cocido; **half-past one** la una y media.

half-breed [hǽfbrid] *adj. & s.* mestizo.

half-hour [hæfáʊr] *s.* media hora; *adj.* de media hora.

half-mast [hǽfmæst] *s.* media asta; *v.* poner a media asta (*la bandera*).

half-open [hǽfópən] *adj.* entreabierto; medio abierto, entornado.

halfway [hǽfwe] *adj. & adv.* a medio camino; parcial, incompleto; **— between** equidistante de; **— finished** a medio acabar; **tó do something** — hacer algo a medias.

half-witted [hǽfwƀtɪd] *adj.* ímbécil, zonzo.

halibut [hǽləbət] *s.* mero, hipogloso *(pez)*.

hall [hɔl] *s.* salón *(para asambleas, funciones, etc.)*; edificio *(de un colegio o universidad)*; vestíbulo; corredor, pasillo; **town** — ayuntamiento.

hallo = **hello.**

hallow [hǽlo] *v.* santificar; consagrar.

Halloween [hæloín] *s.* víspera de Todos los Santos.

halo [hélo] *s.* halo; aureola.

halt [hɔlt] *s.* alto, parada; *v.* parar(se), detener(se); hacer alto; vacilar.

halter [hɔ́ltə] *s.* ronzal, cabestro.

halting [hɔ́ltɪŋ] *adj.* vacilante; **-ly** *adv.* con vacilación.

halve [hæv] *v.* partir por la mitad; partir en dos.

halves [hævz] *pl.* de **half; to go** — ir a medias.

ham [hæm] *s.* jamón.

hamburger [hǽmbɜgə] *s.* carne picada de vaca; bocadillo o emparedado de carne picada, *Am.* hamburguesa.

hamlet [hǽmlɪt] *s.* caserío, aldehuela.

hammer [hǽmə] *s.* martillo; martinete *(de piano)*; **sledge** — macho; *v.* martillar; machacar; clavar.

hammock [hǽmək] *s.* hamaca, *Am.* chinchorro.

hamper [hǽmpə] *s.* canasto, cesto grande, cuévano; *v.* estorbar, impedir, embarazar.

hand [hænd] *s.* mano; manecilla *(de reloj)*; obrero; letra *(modo de escribir)*; — **and glove** uña y carne; — **in** — (cogidos) de la mano; **at** — a la mano, cerca; **made by** — hecho a mano; **on** — disponible; en existencia; listo; **a la mano**, presente; **on the other** — en cambio, por otra parte; **to have one's -s full** estar ocupadísimo; *v.* entregar, dar; **to** — **down** bajar *(una cosa para dársela a alguien)*; transmitir *(de una a otra generación)*; pronunciar *(un fallo)*; **to** — **in** entregar; **to** — **over** entregar.

handbag [hǽndbæg] *s.* bolsa o bolso; saco de noche, maletín.

handball [hǽndbɔl] *s.* pelota; juego de pelota.

handbill [hǽndbɪl] *s.* hoja volante *(anuncio)*.

handcuff [hǽndkʌf] *v.* maniatar; **-s** *s. pl.* esposas, manillas de hierro.

handful [hǽndfəl] *s.* manojo, puñado.

handicap [hǽndɪkæp] *s.* desventaja, es-

torbo, impedimento, obstáculo; ventaja o desventaja *(impuesta en ciertas contiendas)*; — **race** carrera de handicap; *v.* estorbar, poner trabas a.

handiwork [hǽndɪwɜk] *s.* labor, trabajo hecho a mano; artefacto.

handkerchief [hǽŋkətʃɪf] *s.* pañuelo.

handle [hǽndl] *s.* mango, asa; tirador *(de puerta o cajón)*; puño *(de espada)*; manubrio *(de bicicleta, organillo, etc.)*; *v.* manejar; manipular; manosear, tocar; comerciar en; **-s easily** se maneja con facilidad, es muy manuable.

handmade [hǽndméd] *adj.* hecho a mano.

handsaw [hǽndsɔ] *s.* serrucho.

handshake [hǽndʃek] *s.* apretón de manos.

handsome [hǽnsəm] *adj.* hermoso, guapo, bien parecido; generoso; **a** — **sum** una suma considerable.

handwriting [hǽndrɑɪtɪŋ] *s.* letra *(modo de escribir)*, escritura.

handy [hǽndɪ] *adj.* a la mano, próximo; hábil, diestro; manuable, fácil de manejar.

hang [hæŋ] *v.* colgar; suspender; ahorcar; inclinar *(la cabeza)*; **sentenced to** — condenado a la horca; **to** — **around** andar holgazaneando por un sitio; rondar; esperar sin hacer nada; **to** — **on** colgarse de; depender de; estar pendiente de; persistir; **to** — **paper on a wall** empapelar una pared; **to** — **with tapestries** entapizar; *s.* modo de caerle la ropa a una persona; modo de manejar *(un mecanismo)*; modo de resolver *(un problema)*; significado *(de un argumento)*; **I don't care a** — no me importa un ardite.

hangar [hǽŋə] *s.* hangar, cobertizo.

hanger [hǽŋə] *s.* colgadero; percha, clavijero; **paper** — empapelador.

hanging [hǽŋɪŋ] *s.* muerte en la horca; **-s** colgaduras; *adj.* colgante; colgado.

hangman [hǽŋmən] *s.* verdugo.

hangnail [hǽŋnel] *s.* padrastro *(pedacito de pellejo que se levanta junto a las uñas)*.

hang-over [hǽŋovə] *s.* sobrante, remanente, resto; **to have a** — *Am.* tener un ratón o estar enratonado *(tras una borrachera)*, *Am.* estar crudo o tener una cruda.

haphazard [hæphǽzəd] *adv.* al azar, al acaso, a la ventura, a la buena de Dios; *adj.* casual; impensado.

haphazardly [hæphǽzədlɪ] *adv.* = **haphazard.**

hapless [hǽplɪs] *adj.* desventurado, desgraciado.

97

happen [hǽpən] v. suceder, pasar, acontecer, sobrevenir, acaecer; **to — to hear** (do, be, etc.) oír (hacer, estar, etc.) por casualidad; **to — to pass by** acertar a pasar; **to — on** (upon) encontrarse con, tropezar con.

happening [hǽpənɪŋ] s. acontecimiento, suceso.

happily [hǽplɪ] adv. felizmente; afortunadamente.

happiness [hǽpɪnɪs] s. felicidad, dicha, contento.

happy [hǽpɪ] adj. feliz; dichoso, alegre; afortunado; **to be —** to alegrarse de.

harangue [hərǽŋ] s. arenga, perorata; v. arengar, perorar.

harass [hǽrəs] v. acosar, hostigar, molestar.

harbor [hárbə] s. puerto; asilo, refugio, abrigo; v. abrigar; hospedar; albergar.

hard [hard] adj. duro; tieso; arduo, difícil; **— cash** dinero contante y sonante, metálico; **— coal** antracita; **— liquor** licor espiritoso (aguardiente, ron, etc.); **— luck** mala suerte; **— of hearing** medio sordo; **— water** agua cruda; adv. fuerte, recio, con fuerza; con empeño, con ahínco; **— by** muy cerca; **—hearted** de corazón duro; **hardworking** muy trabajador, industrioso, aplicado.

harden [hárdṇ] v. endurecer(se).

hardening [hárdṇɪŋ] s. endurecimiento.

hardly [hárdlɪ] adv. apenas; a duras penas; difícilmente; duramente, con aspereza; probablemente no.

hardness [hárdnɪs] s. dureza; aspereza; dificultad.

hardship [hárdʃɪp] s. apuro, aflicción; trabajo, penalidad.

hardware [hárdwɛr] s. quincalla, quincallería; **— shop** quincallería, ferretería.

hardy [hárdɪ] adj. robusto, fuerte, recio; atrevido.

hare [hɛr] s. liebre.

harebrained [hérbrénd] adj. atolondrado, ligero de cascos.

harlot [hárlət] s. ramera, prostituta.

harm [harm] s. daño; mal; perjuicio; v. dañar; hacer mal, hacer daño; perjudicar.

harmful [hármfəl] adj. dañoso; dañino, nocivo, perjudicial.

harmless [hármlɪs] adj. innocuo; inofensivo; no dañoso, inocente.

harmlessness [hármlɪsnɪs] s. innocuidad; inocencia, falta de malicia.

harmonic [harmánɪkl] adj. armónico.

harmonious [harmónɪəs] adj. armonioso.

harmonize [hármənaɪz] v. armonizar; concordar; congeniar.

harmony [hármənɪ] s. armonía.

harness [hárnɪs] s. guarniciones (de caballerías); jaez, aparejo; **to get back in —** volver al servicio activo, volver a trabajar; volver a la rutina; v. enjaezar, poner guarniciones a (un caballo, mula, etc.).

harp [harp] s. arpa; v. tocar el arpa; **to — on** repetir constantemente (una nota, palabra, tema, etc.); porfiar en.

harpoon [harpún] s. arpón; v. arponear, pescar con arpón.

harrow [hǽro] s. rastro, rastrillo, grada; v. rastrear, rastrillar; atormentar; horrorizar.

harrowing [hǽrəwɪŋ] adj. horrendo, horripilante, que pone los cabellos de punta.

harry [hǽrɪ] v. acosar, molestar; asolar.

harsh [harʃ] adj. tosco, áspero; severo, austero.

harshness [hárʃnɪs] s. aspereza; tosquedad; severidad.

harvest [hárvɪst] s. cosecha; siega, agosto; recolección; v. cosechar; segar.

hash [hæʃ] s. picadillo.

haste [hest] s. prisa; apresuramiento; **in — de** prisa; **to make —** darse prisa, apresurarse.

hasten [hésṇ] v. apresurar(se), precipitar(se); darse prisa.

hastily [héstɪlɪ] adv. aprisa, de prisa, apresuradamente, precipitadamente.

hasty [héstɪ] adj. apresurado; precipitado.

hat [hæt] s. sombrero.

hatch [hætʃ] v. empollar; criar pollos; idear, maquinar; s. cría, nidada, pollada; escotillón, trampa (puerta en el suelo); **—way** escotilla.

hatchet [hǽtʃɪt] s. hacha; **to bury the —** echar pelillos a la mar, olvidar rencores o enemistades.

hate [het] s. odio, aborrecimiento; v. odiar; aborrecer; detestar.

hateful [hétfəl] adj. odioso, aborrecible.

hatred [hétrɪd] s. odio, aversión.

haughtily [hɔ́tɪlɪ] adv. con altivez, altaneramente, arrogantemente.

haughtiness [hɔ́tɪnɪs] s. altanería, altivez.

haughty [hɔ́tɪ] adj. altivo, altanero, arrogante.

haul [hɔl] v. acarrear, transportar; jalar (halar); tirar de; arrastrar; **to — down the flag** arriar (o bajar) la bandera; s. acarreo; transporte; tirón, estirón; buena pesca; ganancia, botín.

haunch [hɔntʃ] s. anca.
haunt [hɔnt] v. frecuentar a menudo; andar por, vagar por (como fantasma o espectro); **that idea -s me** me persigue esa idea; **-ed house** casa de espantos, fantasmas o aparecidos; s. guarida.
have [hæv] v. tener; poseer; haber (v. aux.); **to — a suit made** mandar hacer un traje; **to — a look at** dar un vistazo a, echar una mirada a; **to — to** tener que; deber; **I'll not — it** so no lo toleraré, no lo permitiré; **what did she — on?** ¿qué vestido llevaba (puesto)?
haven [hévən] s. asilo, abrigo, refugio; puerto.
havoc [hævək] s. estrago, estropicio, ruina; **to cause —** hacer estragos.
hawk [hɔk] s. halcón; v. pregonar (mercancías).
hawthorn [hɔθɔorn] s. espino.
hay [he] s. heno, paja, hierba seca; **— fever** catarro asmático.
hayloft [hélɔft] s. henil, pajar.
haystack [héstæk] s. montón de heno o paja.
hazard [hǽzəd] s. azar; riesgo, peligro; estorbo, obstáculo (en el campo de golf); v. arriesgar, aventurar.
hazardous [hǽzədəs] adj. peligroso.
haze [hez] s. bruma, neblina, niebla; v. atormentar, hostigar (con bromas estudiantiles).
hazel [hézl] s. avellano; **—nut** avellana; adj. de avellano; avellanado, color de avellana.
hazy [hézɪ] adj. nublado, brumoso; confuso.
he [hi] pron. pers. él; **— who** el que, quien; **he-goat** macho cabrío.
head [hɛd] s. cabeza; cabecera (de cama); jefe; **— of hair** cabellera; **game of -s or tails** juego de cara y cruz, juego de las chapas, Am. juego de cara y sello; **to be out of one's —** delirar, estar delirante; **to come to a — ** madurar; supurar (un absceso); **to keep one's —** conservar la calma, no perder la cabeza; **it goes to his —** le desvanece; se le sube a la cabeza; adj. principal, primero; de proa, de frente; **head-on** de frente; v. encabezar; ir a la cabeza de; acaudillar; mandar, dirigir; **to — off** atajar; detener, refrenar; **to — towards** dirigirse a, encaminarse a.
headache [hédek] s. dolor de cabeza.
headdress [héddrɛs] s. tocado, adorno para la cabeza.

headgear [hédgir] s. sombrero, gorro, gorra; tocado, toca (de mujer); cabezada (de guarnición para caballo).
heading [hédɪŋ] s. encabezamiento, título.
headland [hédlənd] s. cabo, promontorio.
headlight [hédlaɪt] s. linterna delantera, faro delantero.
headline [hédlaɪn] s. título, encabezado.
headlong [hédlɔ́ŋ] adv. de cabeza; precipitadamente.
headquarters [hédkwɔ́rtəz] s. cuartel general; jefatura; oficina principal.
headstrong [hédstrɔŋ] adj. testarudo, porfiado, obstinado.
headway [hédwe] s. progreso, avance; **to make —** avanzar, adelantar, progresar.
heal [hil] v. curar; sanar; cicatrizar.
health [hɛlə] s. salud; sanidad; salubridad.
healthful [hélfəl] adj. sano; salubre; saludable.
healthfulness [hélfəlnɪs] s. salubridad; sanidad.
healthy [hélɪ] adj. sano; saludable.
heap [hip] s. montón; pila; v. amontonar; apilar.
hear [hɪr] v. oír; escuchar; tener noticias; **to — about someone** oír hablar de alguien; **to — from someone** tener noticias de alguien; **to — of** saber de, tener noticias de, oír hablar de; **I -d that . . .** oí decir que . . .
heard [hɜd] pret. & p.p. de **to hear**.
hearer [híɾə] s. oyente.
hearing [hírɪŋ] s. oído; audiencia; examen de testigos; **hard of —** medio sordo, algo sordo; **within —** al alcance del oído.
hearsay [hírse] s. hablilla, rumor; **by —** de oídas.
hearse [hɜs] s. carroza fúnebre.
heart [hɑrt] s. corazón; ánimo; **at —** en realidad, en el fondo; **from the bottom of one's —** de corazón, con toda el alma; con toda sinceridad; **to learn by —** aprender de memoria; **to take — ** cobrar ánimo; **to take to —** tomar en serio; tomar a pechos.
heartache [hártek] s. dolor del corazón; angustia, pesar, congoja.
heartbroken [hártbrokən] adj. traspasado de dolor, acongojado, angustiado; desengañado.
hearten [hártn] v. animar.
heartfelt [hártfelt] adj. sentido, cordial, sincero; **my — sympathy** mi más sentido pésame.
hearth [hɑrθ] s. hogar; fogón.

99

heartily [hártⱼlⱼ] *adv.* de corazón; cordialmente; de buena gana; **to eat** — comer con apetito; comer bien (*o* mucho).

heartless [hártlⱼs] *adj.* de mal corazón; cruel; insensible.

heart-rending [hártrendⱼɳ] *adj.* angustioso; agudo.

hearty [hártⱼ] *adj.* sincero, cordial; sano, fuerte; — **food** alimento nutritivo; **a** — **laugh** una buena carcajada; — **meal** comida abundante.

heat [hit] *s.* calor; ardor; vehemencia; celo (*ardor sexual de la hembra*); calefacción (*para las habitaciones*); corrida, carrera (*de prueba*); *v.* calentar(se); acalorar(se).

heater [hítə] *s.* calentador; calorífero.

heathen [híðən] *s.* pagano, gentil, idólatra; paganos; *adj.* pagano; irreligioso.

heating [hítⱼɳ] *s.* calefacción.

heave [hiv] *v.* levantar, alzar (*con esfuerzo*); arrojar, lanzar; exhalar (*un suspiro*); jalar (*un cable*); jadear; basquear, hacer esfuerzos por vomitar.

heaven [hévən] *s.* cielo.

heavenly [hévənlⱼ] *adj.* celeste; celestial; divino.

heavily [hévⱼⱼ] *adv.* pesadamente, lentamente; copiosamente, excesivamente.

heaviness [hévⱼnⱼs] *s.* pesadez, pesantez; opresión, abatimiento.

heavy [hévⱼ] *adj.* pesado; grueso; burdo; oprisivo; — **rain** aguacero recio o fuerte; **with a** — **heart** abatido, acongojado.

hectic [héktⱼk] *adj.* febril; inquieto.

hedge [hedʒ] *s.* seto; vallado, barrera; *v.* cercar; poner valla o seto a; evitar o evadir contestaciones.

hedgehog [hédʒhag] *s.* erizo.

heed [hid] *v.* atender; hacer caso; prestar atención; *s.* atención, cuidado; **to pay** — prestar atención a; hacer caso de.

heedless [hídlⱼs] *adj.* descuidado; desatento.

heel [hil] *s.* talón (*del pie o de una media*); tacón (*del zapato*); **head over** —**s** patas arriba; *v.* poner tacón a; poner talón a.

heifer [héfə] *s.* novilla, vaquilla.

height [haⱼt] *s.* altura; elevación; — **of folly** colmo de la locura.

heighten [háⱼtɳ] *v.* avivar; aumentar(se); realzar.

heinous [hénəs] *adj.* aborrecible, odioso; malvado.

heir [ɛr] *s.* heredero.

heiress [érⱼs] *s.* heredera.

held [held] *pret. & p.p. de* **to hold.**

hell [hel] *s.* infierno.

hello [heló] *interj.* ¡hola!; ¡halo!.

helm [helm] *s.* timón.

helmet [hélmⱼt] *s.* yelmo.

help [help] *s.* ayuda; auxilio; remedio; alivio; criado o criados, sirviente o sirvientes; empleado o empleados; *v.* ayudar, asistir; auxiliar; remediar; servir (*algo de comer*); **to** — **down** ayudar a bajar — **yourself** sírvase Vd. (*de comer o beber*); tómelo Vd., está a la disposición de Vd.; **he cannot** — **it** no puede evitarlo; **he cannot** — **doing it** no puede menos de hacerlo; **he cannot** — **but come** no puede menos de venir.

helper [hélpə] *s.* ayudante, asistente.

helpful [hélpfəl] *adj.* útil, servicial; provechoso.

helping [hélpⱼɳ] *s.* ayuda; porción (*que se sirve en la mesa*).

helpless [hélplⱼs] *adj.* desamparado; desvalido; imposibilitado; incapaz; perplejo, indeciso (*sin saber qué hacer*); **a** — **situation** una situación irremediable.

helplessness [hélplⱼsnⱼs] *s.* incapacidad; incompetencia; impotencia, debilidad; abandono, desamparo.

hem [hem] *s.* dobladillo, bastilla; *v.* dobladillar, bastillar, hacer dobladillos en (*la ropa*); **to** — **in** rodear, cercar; **to** — **and haw** toser y retoser (*fingidamente*); tartamudear, vacilar.

hemisphere [héməsfⱼr] *s.* hemisferio.

hemlock [hémlak] *s.* cicuta (*hierba venenosa*); abeto americano.

hemp [hemp] *s.* cáñamo, *Am.* sisal.

hemstitch [hémstⱼtʃ] *s.* dobladillo de ojo; *v.* hacer (*o echar*) dobladillo de ojo

hen [hen] *s.* gallina; ave hembra.

hence [hens] *adv.* de (*o* desde) aquí; desde ahora; por lo tanto, por consiguiente; **a week** — de hoy en ocho días; de aquí a una semana.

henceforth [hensfórⱼ] *adv.* de aquí en adelante; de hoy en adelante; desde ahora.

her [hɜ] *pron.* la; le, a ella; ella (*con preposición*); *adj.* su (sus), de ella.

herald [hérəld] *s.* heraldo; anunciador, proclamador; precursor; *v.* anunciar, proclamar, publicar.

herb [ɜb] *s.* hierba (yerba).

herd [hɜd] *s.* hato, rebaño; ganado; manada; tropel, muchedumbre; **the common** — el populacho, la chusma; *v.* reunir, juntar (*el ganado*); ir en manadas, ir juntos.

herdsman [hɜdzmən] *s.* vaquero, vaquerizo; pastor.

here [hɪr] *adv.* aquí; aeá; — **it is** aquí está, helo aquí, aquí lo tiene Vd.; — **is to you!** ¡a la salud de Vd.!; **that is neither — nor there** eso nc. viene al caso.

hereafter [hɪréftə] *adv.* de aquí (o de hoy) en adelante; desde ahora en adelante; en lo futuro; *s.* **the —** la otra vida.

hereby [hɪrbáɪ] *adv.* por este medio; mediante la presente, por la presente; con estas palabras.

hereditary [hɑrédətərɪ] *adj.* hereditario.

heredity [hərédətɪ] *s.* herencia.

herein [hɪrín] *adv.* aquí dentro; en esto.

heresy [hérəsɪ] *s.* herejía.

heretic [hérətɪk] *s.* hereje.

heretofore [hɪrtəfór] *adv.* hasta ahora, hasta el presente.

herewith [hɪrwfə] *adv.* aquí dentro, con esto, adjunto, incluso.

heritage [hérətɪdʒ] *s.* herencia.

hermit [hɔ́mɪt] *s.* ermitaño.

hernia [hɔ́nɪə] *s.* hernia, ruptura, relajamiento.

hero [híro] *s.* héroe; protagonista.

heroic [hɪróɪk] *adj.* heroico.

heroine [héroɪn] *s.* heroína.

heroism [héroɪzəm] *s.* heroísmo.

heron [hérən] *s.* garza.

herring [hérɪŋ] *s.* arenque.

hers [hɜz] *pron. pos.* suyo (suya, suyos, suyas), de ella; el suyo (la suya, los suyos, las suyas); el (la, los, las) de ella; **a friend of —** un amigo suyo.

herself [hɔsélf] *pron.* ella misma; se (*como reflexivo*); **by —** sola; por sí (sola); **she — did it** ella misma lo hizo; **she talks to —** ella habla para sí, habla consigo misma, habla para sus adentros, habla sola.

hesitant [hézətənt] = **hesitating.**

hesitate [hézətet] *v.* vacilar; titubear; dudar.

hesitating [hésətetɪŋ] *adj.* vacilante; indeciso; irresoluto; **-ly** *adv.* con vacilación.

hesitation [hezətéʃən] *s.* vacilación; titubeo, duda.

hew [hju] *v.* tajar, cortar; picar (*piedra*); labrar (*madera, piedra*).

hewn [hjun] *p.p. de* **to hew.**

hey [he] *interj.* ¡he!; ¡oiga!; ¡oye!

hiccup, hiccough [híkʌp] *s.* hipo; *v.* hipar, tener hipo.

hickory [híkərɪ] *s.* nogal americano; — **nut** nuez (*del nogal americano*).

hid [hɪd] *pret. & p.p. de* **to hide.**

hidden [hídn] *p.p. de* **to hide;** *adj.* oculto, escondido.

hide [haɪd] *v.* ocultar(se); esconder(se); **to — from** esconderse de, recatarse de; *s.* cuero, piel; **to play — and seek** jugar al escondite.

hideous [hídɪəs] *adj.* horrendo, horripilante, feote.

high [haɪ] *adj.* alto; — **altar** altar mayor; — **and dry** enjuto; en seco; solo, abandonado; — **antiquity** antigüedad remota; — **explosive** explosivo de gran potencia; — **tide** pleamar; — **wind** ventarrón, viento fuerte; in — **gear** en directa, en tercera velocidad; **two feet —** dos pies de alto; **it is — time** that ya es hora de que; **to be in — spirits** estar muy animado; *adv.* alto; a precio subido; en alto; **to look — and low** buscar por todas partes; **high-grade** de calidad superior; **high-handed** arbitrario, despótico; **high-minded** magnánimo, orgulloso; **high-sounding** altisonante, rimbombante; **high-strung** muy tenso.

highland [háɪlənd] *s.* tierra montañosa; **the Highlands** las montañas de Escocia.

highly [háɪlɪ] *adv.* altamente; sumamente, muy; — **paid** muy bien pagado.

highness [háɪnɪs] *s.* altura; elevación; **Alteza** (*título*).

highway [háɪwe] *s.* camino real; carretera, calzada.

highwayman [háɪwemən] *s.* forajido, salteador de caminos, bandido.

hike [haɪk] *s.* caminata, paseo largo, *Am.* andada; *v.* dar (o echar) una caminata.

hill [hɪl] *s.* colina, collado, cerro; montoncillo de tierra; **ant —** hormiguero; **down—** cuesta abajo; **up—** cuesta arriba.

hillock [hílək] *s.* collado, otero, montecillo.

hillside [hílsaɪd] *s.* ladera.

hilltop [híltap] *s.* cumbre, cima (*de una colina*).

hilly [hílɪ] *adj.* montuoso; accidentado.

hilt [hɪlt] *s.* empuñadura, puño (*de una espada o daga*).

him [hɪm] *pron.* le; lo; él (*con preposición*).

himself [hɪmsélf] *pron.* él mismo; se (*como reflexivo*); a sí mismo; *véase* **herself.**

hind [haɪnd] *adj.* trasero; posterior; *s.* cierva; — **most** *adj.* último, postrero.

hinder [híndə] *v.* estorbar, impedir, obstruir.

hindrance [híndrəns] *s.* estorbo, obstáculo, impedimento.

hinge [hɪndʒ] *s.* gozne; bisagra; *v.* engoznar, poner goznes; **to — on** girar sobre; depender de.

hint [hɪnt] *s.* indirecta, insinuación; sugestión; **not to take the —** no darse por entendido; *v.* insinuar, intimar, sugerir indirectamente.

hip [hɪp] *s.* cadera.

hippopotamus [hɪpəpátəməs] *s.* hipopótamo.

hire [haɪr] *s.* alquiler; paga, sueldo; *v.* alquilar; emplear, dar empleo, *Am.* enganchar, *Am.* conchabar; **to — out** alquilarse, ponerse a servir a otro.

his [hɪz] *pron. pos.* suyo (suya, suyos, suyas), de él; el suyo (la suya, los suyos, las suyas); el (la, los, las) de él; **a friend of —** un amigo suyo; *adj.* su (sus), de él.

hiss [hɪs] *s.* silbido, chiflido; siseo; *v.* sisear, silbar, chiflar.

historian [hɪstɔ́rɪən] *s.* historiador.

historic [hɪstɔ́rɪk] *adj.* histórico.

historical [hɪstɔ́rɪk]] *adj.* histórico.

history [hɪ́stɪɪ] *s.* historia.

hit [hɪt] *v.* pegar, golpear; dar (*un golpe*); dar en (*o* con); chocar; **they — it off well** se llevan bien, congenian; **to — the mark** acertar, atinar, dar en el blanco; **to — upon** dar con; encontrarse con, encontrar por casualidad; *pret. & p.p. de* **to hit**; *s.* golpe; choque; golpe de fortuna; pulla, dicharacho; **to be a great —** ser un gran éxito; **to make a — with someone** caerle en gracia a una persona.

hitch [hɪtʃ] *v.* atar, amarrar; enganchar; uncir (*bueyes*); dar un tirón; **to — one's chair nearer** to acercar su silla a; *s.* tirón; obstáculo, impedimento, tropiezo; enganche, enganchamiento.

hitchhike [hɪ́tʃhaɪk] *v.* viajar de gorra (*en automóvil*), *Am.* irse *o* viajar de mosca.

hither [hɪ́ðə] *adv.* acá; **— and thither** acá y allá.

hitherto [hɪðətú] *adv.* hasta aquí, hasta ahora, hasta hoy.

hive [haɪv] *s.* colmena; enjambre; **-s** ronchas (*de la piel*).

hoard [hord] *s.* tesoro escondido; acumulamiento secreto de provisiones; *v.* atesorar, guardar (*con avaricia*); acumular secretamente.

hoarse [hors] *adj.* bronco, áspero, ronco.

hoarseness [hórsnɪs] *s.* ronquera; carraspera.

hoary [hórɪ] *adj.* cano, encanecido, canoso.

hobble [hábl] *v.* cojear, renquear; maniatar *o* manear (*un animal*); impedir,

estorbar; *s.* cojera; traba, maniota *o* manea (*cuerda con que se atan las manos de una bestia*).

hobby [hábɪ] *s.* afición; trabajo hecho por afición (*no por obligación*).

hobo [hóbo] *s.* vagabundo.

hodgepodge [hádʒpɑdʒ] *s.* mezcolanza, baturrillo.

hoe [ho] *s.* azada, azadón; *v.* cavar, escardar, limpiar con azadón.

hog [hɑg] *s.* puerco, cerdo, cochino; *v.* apropiárselo todo.

hoist [hɔɪst] *v.* alzar, levantar; izar (*la bandera, las velas*); *s.* elevador, *Am.* malacate.

hold [hold] *v.* tener(se); retener; detener; tener cabida para; sostener; mantener(se); opinar; celebrar (*una reunión, etc.*); ocupar (*un puesto*); ser válido (*un argumento o regla*); **to — back someone** detener (*o* refrenar) a alguien; **to — forth** perorar, hablar largamente; **to — in place** sujetar; **to — off** mantener(se) a distancia; mantenerse alejado; **to — on** agarrar(se); asir(se); persistir; **— on!** ¡agárrese bien!; ¡deténgase! ¡pare!; **to — someone responsible** hacerle a uno responsable; **to — someone to his word** obligar a uno a cumplir su palabra; **to — oneself erect** tenerse *o* andar derecho; **to — one's own** mantenerse firme; **to — one's tongue** callarse; **to — out** continuar, durar; mantenerse firme; **to — over** aplazar; durar; continuar en un cargo; **to — still** estarse quieto *o* callado; **to — tight** apretar; **to — to one's promise** cumplir con la promesa; **to — up** levantar, alzar; detener; asaltar, atracar (*para robar*); **how much does it — ?** ¿cuánto le cabe? *s.* agarro; dominio; influencia; autoridad; bodega (*de un barco*); cabina de carga (*de un aeroplano*); **to get — of** asir, agarrar; atrapar; **to take — of** coger, agarrar, asir.

holder [hóldə] *s.* tenedor, posesor; receptáculo; cojinillo (*para coger un trasto caliente*); **cigarette —** boquilla; **pen—** portaplumas.

holdup [hóldʌp] *s.* asalto, atraco.

hole [hol] *s.* agujero; abertura; hoyo, hueco, cavidad; bache (*de un camino*); **swimming —** charco, remanso; **to be in a —** hallarse en un apuro *o* aprieto.

holiday [hálədе] *s.* día de fiesta, día festivo, festividad; **-s** días de fiesta, vacaciones.

holiness [hólɪnɪs] *s.* santidad.

hollow [hálo] *adj.* hueco; vacío; cóncavo; hundido; falso; *s.* hueco; hoyo; cavidad; concavidad; depresión; cañada, hondonada; *v.* ahuecar; excavar; ahondar.

holly [háli] *s.* agrifolio, acebo.

holster [hólstə] *s.* pistolera, funda (*de pistola*).

holy [hóli] *adj.* santo; sagrado, sacro; — **water** agua bendita.

homage [hámidʒ] *s.* homenaje; reverencia, acatamiento; **to do** — acatar, rendir homenaje, honrar.

home [hom] *s.* casa, hogar; habitación, domicilio; **at** — en casa; *adj.* doméstico; casero; — **office** oficina matriz o central; — **rule** autonomía; — **run** *Am.* jonrón (*en beisbol*); — **stretch** último trecho (*de una carrera*); *adv.* a casa; en casa; **to strike** — herir en lo vivo; dar en el clavo o en el blanco.

homeland [hómlænd] *s.* tierra natal, suelo patrio.

homeless [hómlɪs] *adj.* sin casa; destituido.

homelike [hómlaɪk] *adj.* hogareño, cómodo.

homely [hómlɪ] *adj.* feo; llano, sencillo; casero, doméstico.

homemade [hómméd] *adj.* hecho en casa; doméstico, nacional, del país.

homesick [hómsɪk] *adj.* nostálgico.

homesickness [hómsɪknɪs] *s.* nostalgia.

homestead [hómstɛd] *s.* heredad; casa y terrenos adyacentes.

homeward [hómwəd] *adv.* a casa; hacia la patria; — **voyage** retorno, viaje de vuelta.

homework [hómwɜk] *s.* trabajo de casa; trabajo hecho en casa.

homicide [háməsaɪd] *s.* homicidio; homicida, asesino.

homogeneous [homədʒíniəs] *adj.* homogéneo.

hone [hon] *v.* amolar, asentar, afilar; *s.* piedra de afilar.

honest [ánɪst] *adj.* honrado, recto; genuino; — **goods** mercancías genuinas; **-ly** *adv.* honradamente; de veras.

honesty [ánɪstɪ] *s.* honradez, rectitud.

honey [hánɪ] *s.* miel; dulzura; querido, querida.

honeycomb [hánɪkom] *s.* panal.

honeyed [hánɪd] *adj.* meloso; dulce; melifluo.

honeymoon [hánɪmun] *s.* luna de miel; viaje de novios, viaje de bodas; *v.* pasar la luna de miel.

honeysuckle [hánɪsʌk] *s.* madreselva.

honk [hɔŋk] *s.* pitazo (*de automóvil*);

graznido (*voz del ganso*); *v.* sonar la bocina; graznar.

honor [ánə] *s.* honor; honra; señoría (*título*); **upon my** — sobre mi palabra; *v.* honrar; dar honra.

honorable [ánərəbl] *adj.* honorable; honroso; honrado.

honorary [ánərɛrɪ] *adj.* honorario, honorífico.

hood [hʊd] *s.* capucha, caperuza; capirote, cubierta (*del motor*); *v.* encapuchar, encapirotar.

hoof [hʊf] *s.* casco, pezuña; pata (*de caballo, toro, etc.*).

hook [hʊk] *s.* gancho, garfio; anzuelo (*para pescar*); — **and eye** corchete; macho y hembra, **by** — **or crook** por la buena o por la mala, por angas o por mangas; **on his own** — por su propia cuenta; *v.* enganchar(se); abrochar(se); pescar, coger con anzuelo; robar, hurtar.

hooky [húkɪ] : **to play** — hacer novillos, *Am.* capear la escuela, *Am.* pintar venado, *Am.* jubilarse.

hoop [hʊp] *s.* aro; argolla; *v.* poner aro a; ceñir, cercar.

hoot [hut] *v.* ulular (*dícese del buho, lechuza, etc.*); rechiflar, ridiculizar; *s.* alarido, chillido.

hooting [hútɪŋ] *s.* grita, rechifla.

hop [hap] *s.* salto, brinco; baile; *v.* saltar; brincar.

hope [hop] *s.* esperanza; *v.* esperar; **to** — **for** esperar; **to** — **against** — esperar desesperando; esperar lo que no puede ser, esperar lo imposible.

hopeful [hópfəl] *adj.* esperanzado, lleno de esperanza; **a young** — un joven prometedor; **-ly** *adv.* con esperanza; con ansia; lleno de esperanza.

hopeless [hóplɪs] *adj.* sin esperanza, falto de esperanza, desesperanzado; desesperado; irremediable; — **cause** causa perdida; — **illness** enfermedad incurable; **it is** — no tiene remedio; **-ly** *adv.* sin esperanza, sin remedio.

hopelessness [hóplɪsnɪs] *s.* falta de esperanza; falta de remedio; desesperanza, desaliento.

horde [hɔrd] *s.* horda; muchedumbre, gentío; enjambre.

horizon [həráɪzn] *s.* horizonte.

horizontal [horəzántl] *adj.* horizontal.

horn [hɔrn] *s.* cuerno; asta; bocina, trompa (*de un automóvil*); corneta; trompeta; — **of plenty** cuerno de la abundancia; *v.* acornear, dar cornadas; **to** — **in** entremeterse.

hornet [hórnɪt] *s.* avispón; **-'s nest** avispero.

pero.

horrible [hɔ́rəbl] *adj.* horrible; **horribly** *adv.* horriblemente.

horrid [hɔ́rɪd] *adj.* horrendo, horrible.

horrify [hɔ́rəfaɪ] *v.* horrorizar, aterrorizar, espantar.

horror [hɔ́rə] *s.* horror.

horse [hɔrs] *s.* caballo; caballete (*de madera*), borriquete (*de carpinteros*); **saddle —** caballo de silla; **— dealer** chalán; **— race** carrera de caballos; **— sense** sentido común.

horseback [hɔ́rsbæk] *s.* lomo de caballo; **to ride —** montar a caballo, cabalgar, jinetear.

horsefly [hɔ́rsflaɪ] *s.* tábano, mosca de caballo.

horselaugh [hɔ́rslæf] *s.* carcajada, risotada.

horseman [hɔ́rsmən] *s.* jinete.

horsemanship [hɔ́rsmənʃɪp] *s.* equitación.

horsepower [hɔ́rspauə] *s.* caballo de fuerza.

horseradish [hɔ́rsrædɪʃ] *s.* rábano picante.

horseshoe [hɔ́rʃʃu] *s.* herradura.

hose [hoz] *s.* medias; manga o manguera (*para regar*); **men's —** calcetines.

hosiery [hóʒrɪ] *s.* medias; calcetines; calcetería (*negocio*); **— shop** calcetería.

hospitable [háspɪtəbl] *adj.* hospitalario.

hospital [háspɪtl] *s.* hospital.

hospitality [hɑspɪtǽlətɪ] *s.* hospitalidad.

host [host] *s.* huésped (*el que hospeda*), anfitrión (*el que convida*); hospedero, mesonero; hueste; ejército, multitud; hostia; **sacred —** hostia consagrada.

hostage [hástɪdʒ] *s.* rehén (*persona que queda como prenda en poder del enemigo*).

hostess [hóstɪs] *s.* huéspeda (*la que hospeda o convida*).

hostile [hástl] *adj.* hostil.

hostility [hastílətɪ] *s.* hostilidad.

hot [hɑt] *adj.* caliente; caluroso; cálido; picante (*como el pimentón, chile, ají, etc.*); furioso; fresco, reciente; **—bed** semillero; **hot-headed** enojadizo, impetuoso; exaltado; **— house** invernáculo, invernadero; **it is — today** hace calor hoy.

hotel [hotél] *s.* hotel.

hotel-keeper [hotélkípə] *s.* hotelero.

hotly [hátlɪ] *adv.* calurosamente, con vehemencia.

hound [haund] *s.* perro de busca, lebrel, galgo, sabueso, podenco; *v.* acosar, perseguir; azuzar, incitar.

hour [aur] *s.* hora; **— hand** horario.

hourly [áurlɪ] *adv.* por horas; **a cada hora**; a menudo; *adj.* frecuente; por horas.

house [haus] *s.* casa; cámara, asamblea legislativa; **country —** casa de campo; **a full —** un lleno completo (*en el teatro*); [hauz] *v.* alojar; hospedar.

household [háushold] *s.* casa, familia; *adj.* casero; doméstico.

housekeeper [háuskipə] *s.* casera; ama de llaves; **to be a good —** ser una mujer hacendosa.

housekeeping [háuskipɪŋ] *s.* gobierno de casa; quehaceres domésticos.

housetop [háustɑp] *s.* techumbre, tejado.

housewife [háuswaɪf] *s.* mujer de su casa; madre de familia.

housework [háuswək] *s.* trabajo de casa; quehaceres domésticos.

hove [hov] *pret. & p.p. de* **to heave**.

hovel [hávl] *s.* choza, cabaña, *Am.* bohío, *Am.* jacal; cobertizo.

hover [hávə] *v.* cernerse (*como un pájaro*); vacilar; **to — around** revolotear; rondar.

how [hau] *adv.* cómo; **— beautiful!** ¡qué hermoso!; **— early (late, soon)?** ¿cuándo? ¿a qué hora?; **— far is it?** ¿a qué distancia está? ¿cuánto dista de aquí?; **— long?** ¿cuánto tiempo?; **— many?** ¿cuántos? **— much is it?** ¿cuánto es? ¿a cómo se vende? ¿cuál es el precio?; **— old are you?** ¿cuántos años tiene Vd.? **no matter — much** por mucho que; **he knows — difficult it is** él sabe lo difícil que es; él sabe cuán difícil es.

however [hauévə] *adv. & conj.* sin embargo, no obstante, con todo, empero; **— difficult it may be** por muy difícil que sea; **— much** por mucho que.

howl [haul] *s.* aullido, alarido, chillido, grito; *v.* aullar; chillar, dar alaridos; gritar.

hub [hʌb] *s.* cubo (*de una rueda*); eje, centro de actividad.

hubbub [hʌ́bʌb] *s.* ajetreo; barullo.

huckster [hʌ́kstə] *s.* vendedor ambulante.

huddle [hʌ́dl] *s.* montón, confusión, tropel; **to be in a —** estar agrupados (*en futbol para planear una jugada*); **to get in a —** agruparse (*para aconsejarse o planear algo*); *v.* amontonar(se); acurrucarse.

hue [hju] *s.* tinte, matiz.

huff [hʌf] *s.* enojo, rabieta; **to get into a —** enojarse.

hug [hʌg] *v.* abrazar, estrechar; **to — the coast** costear; *s.* abrazo fuerte.

huge [hjudʒ] *adj.* enorme; descomunal.

hull [hʌl] *s.* casco (*de una nave*); armazón (*de una aeronave*); vaina, hollejo (*de ciertas legumbres*); *v.* mondar, pelar, desvainar, deshollejar.

hum [hʌm] *v.* canturrear (*o* canturriar), tararear; zumbar (*dícese de insectos, máquinaria, etc.*); *to* — *to sleep* arrullar; *s.* canturreo, tarareo; zumbido; *interj.* ¡hum!; ¡ejém!

human [hjúmən] *adj.* humano; *s.* ser humano.

humane [hjumén] *adj.* humano; humanitario.

humanitarian [hjumænətériən] *adj.* humanitario; *s.* filántropo.

humanity [hjumǽnətɪ] *s.* humanidad.

humble [hʌmbl] *adj.* humilde; *v.* humillar; **humbly** *adv.* humildemente, con humildad.

humbleness [hʌmblnɪs] *s.* humildad.

humid [hjúmɪd] *adj.* húmedo.

humidity [hjumídətɪ] *s.* humedad.

humiliate [hjumílɪet] *v.* humillar.

humiliation [hjumɪlɪéʃən] *s.* humillación.

humility [hjumílətɪ] *s.* humildad.

hummingbird [hʌmɪŋbɜd] *s.* colibrí, pájaro mosca, *Am.* chuparrosa, *Am.* chupaflor, *Am.* guainumbí.

humor [hjúmə] *s.* humor, humorismo, gracia; capricho; *out of* — de mal humor, malhumorado, disgustado; *v.* seguir el humor (*a una persona*), complacer; mimar.

humorous [hjúmərəs] *adj.* humorístico, gracioso, cómico, chistoso.

hump [hʌmp] *s.* joroba, corcova, giba; *v.* encorvarse.

humpback [hʌmpbæk] = **hunchback.**

hunch [hʌntʃ] *s.* joroba, corcova, giba; presentimiento, corazonada; *v.* encorvar (*la espalda*).

hunchback [hʌntʃbæk] *s.* joroba; jorobado.

hundred [hʌndrəd] *adj.* cien(to); *s.* ciento; -*s* centenares, cientos.

hundredth [hʌndrədθ] *adj.* centésimo.

hung [hʌŋ] *pret. & p.p. de* to hang.

hunger [hʌŋgə] *s.* hambre; *v.* tener hambre, estar hambriento; *to* — *for* ansiar, anhelar.

hungrily [hʌŋgrɪlɪ] *adv.* con hambre, hambrientamente.

hungry [hʌŋgrɪ] *adj.* hambriento; *to be* — tener hambre.

hunk [hʌŋk] *s.* pedazo grande; mendrugo (*de pan*).

hunt [hʌnt] *v.* cazar; perseguir; buscar; escudriñar; *to* — *down* dar caza a;

seguir la pista de; *to* — *for* buscar; *s.* caza, cacería; busca, búsqueda; perseguimiento.

hunter [hʌntə] *s.* cazador; buscador; perro de caza, perro de busca.

huntsman [hʌntsmən] *s.* cazador.

hurl [hɜl] *v.* arrojar, lanzar.

hurrah [hər ó] *interj.* ¡hurra! ¡viva!; *v.* vitorear.

hurricane [hɜ́ɪken] *s.* huracán.

hurried [hɜ́ɪd] *adj.* apresurado; -**ly** *adv.* de prisa, apresuradamente, a escape.

hurry [hɜ́ɪ] *v.* apresurar(se); precipitar(se); dar(se) prisa; apurarse; correr; *to* — *in* (*out*) entrar (salir) de prisa; *to* — *up* apresurar(se); dar(se) prisa; *s.* prisa; precipitación; *to be in a* — tener prisa, ir de prisa, estar de prisa.

hurt [hɜt] *v.* hacer daño; dañar; perjudicar; herir; lastimar; doler; *to* — *one's feelings* darle a uno que sentir; lastimar a uno; *my tooth* -*s me duele la muela; *pret. & p.p. de* to hurt; *s.* daño; herida; lesión; dolor.

husband [hʌzbənd] *s.* marido, esposo.

hush [hʌʃ] *v.* acallar, aquietar; callar(se); —! ¡chitón! ¡silencio! ¡cállese! ¡quieto!; *to* — *up a scandal* encubrir un escándalo; *s.* silencio, quietud.

husk [hʌsk] *s.* cáscara, hollejo, vaina; *v.* mondar, pelar, deshollejar.

husky [hʌskɪ] *adj.* ronco; forzudo, fuerte; cascarudo.

hustle [hʌsl] *v.* apresurar(se); apurarse; menear(se); atropellar; *s.* prisa, apresuramiento, meneo; actividad; — *and bustle* vaivén.

hut [hʌt] *s.* choza, cabaña, *Am.* bohío.

hyacinth [háɪəsɪnə] *s.* jacinto.

hybrid [háɪbrɪd] *adj.* híbrido.

hydraulic [haɪdrɔ́lɪk] *adj.* hidráulico.

hydrogen [háɪdrədʒən] *s.* hidrógeno.

hydroplane [háɪdrəplen] *s.* hidroplano, hidroavión.

hygiene [háɪdʒɪn] *s.* higiene.

hymn [hɪm] *s.* himno.

hyphen [háɪfən] *s.* guión.

hypocrisy [hɪpákrəsɪ] *s.* hipocresía.

hypocrite [hípəkrɪt] *s.* hipócrita.

hypocritical [hɪpəkrítɪkl] *adj.* hipócrita.

hypothesis [haɪpáəəsɪs] *s.* hipótesis.

hysterical [hɪstérɪk] *adj.* histérico.

I

I [aɪ] *pron. pers.* yo.

Iberian [aɪbɪ́rɪən] *adj.* ibérico, ibero.

ice [aɪs] *s.* hielo; helado, sorbete; — *cream* helado; *ice-cream parlor Am.* heladería; — **skates** patines de cuchilla; — *water* agua helada; *v.* helar;

escarchar, alfeñicar, cubrir con escarcha (*un pastel*).

iceberg [áısbɜg] *s.* montaña de hielo, témpano.

icebox [áısbɑks] *s.* nevera, *Am.* refrigerador.

iceman [áısmæn] *s.* vendedor de hielo.

icicle [áısɪk]] *s.* carámbano.

icy [áısı] *adj.* helado, frío; congelado; cubierto de hielo.

idea [aıdíə] *s.* idea.

ideal [aıdíəl] *adj.* & *s.* ideal.

idealism [aıdíəlɪzəm] *s.* idealismo.

idealist [aıdíəlɪst] *s.* idealista.

idealistic [aıdíəlístɪk] *adj.* idealista.

identical [aıdéntɪk]] *adj.* idéntico.

identify [aıdéntəfaı] *v.* identificar.

identity [aıdéntətı] *s.* identidad.

idiom [ídıəm] *s.* modismo, idiotismo.

idiot [ídɪət] *s.* idiota.

idiotic [ıdıátık] *adj.* idiota.

idle [áıd]] *adj.* ocioso; perezoso, holgazán; vano; desocupado; *v.* holgazanear; perder el tiempo; funcionar (*el motor solo, sin engranar*); **idly** *adv.* ociosamente; inútilmente; perezosamente.

idleness [áıd]nıs] *s.* ociosidad; ocio, desocupación; pereza, holgazanería.

idler [áıdlə] *s.* holgazán, haragán.

idol [áıd]] *s.* ídolo.

idolatry [aıdúlətrı] *s.* idolatría.

idolize [áıd]aız] *v.* idolatrar.

idyl [áıd]] *s.* idilio.

if [ıf] *conj.* si.

ignite [ıgnáıt] *v.* encender(se), inflamar(se); prender, pegar fuego a.

ignition [ıgníʃən] *s.* ignición, encendido (*de un motor*); — switch interruptor de encendido, *Am.* switch de ignición.

ignoble [ıgnób]] *adj.* innoble; bajo, vil.

ignorance [ígnərəns] *s.* ignorancia.

ignorant [ígnərənt] *adj.* ignorante.

ignore [ıgnór] *v.* no hacer caso de, desatender; desairar.

ill [ıl] *adj.* enfermo; malo; — **nature** mal genio, mala índole; — **will** mala voluntad, ojeriza, inquina; *s.* mal; enfermedad; calamidad, infortunio; *adv.* mal, malamente; — **at ease** inquieto, intranquilo; **ill-bred** mal criado; **ill-clad** mal vestido; **ill-humored** malhumorado; **ill-mannered** descortés, grosero; **ill-natured** de mala índole, *Am.* mal genioso.

illegal [ılígl] *adj.* ilegal; ilícito.

illegitimate [ılıdʒítəmıt] *adj.* ilegítimo; bastardo.

illicit [ılísıt] *adj.* ilícito.

illiteracy [ılítərəsı] *s.* analfabetismo.

illiterate [ılítərıt] *adj.* & *s.* analfabeto.

illness [ílnıs] *s.* mal, enfermedad.

illuminate [ılúmənet] *v.* iluminar; alumbrar; esclarecer.

illumination [ılumənéʃən] *s.* iluminación; alumbrado.

illusion [ılúʒən] *s.* ilusión.

illusive [ılúsıv] *adj.* ilusorio, ilusivo, falaz.

illusory [ılúsərı] *adj.* ilusorio, ilusivo, engañoso.

illustrate [ıləstrét] *v.* ilustrar; esclarecer.

illustration [ıləstréʃən] *s.* ilustración; grabado, estampa; aclaración, esclarecimiento.

illustrator [íləstretə] *s.* ilustrador.

illustrious [ılástrıəs] *adj.* ilustre.

image [ímıdʒ] *s.* imagen.

imagery [ímıdʒrı] *s.* conjunto de imágenes, figuras; fantasía.

imaginary [ımǽdʒənerı] *adj.* imaginario.

imagination [ımædʒənéʃən] *s.* imaginación; imaginativa.

imaginative [ımǽdʒənetıv] *adj.* imaginativo.

imagine [ımǽdʒın] *v.* imaginar(se); figurarse.

imbecile [ímbəsıl] *adj.* & *s.* imbécil.

imbibe [ımbáıb] *v.* embeber, absorber; beber.

imbue [ımbjú] *v.* imbuir, infundir; impregnar, empapar.

imitate [ímətet] *v.* imitar; remedar.

imitation [ımətéʃən] *s.* imitación; remedo; *adj.* imitado, de imitación.

imitator [ímətetə] *s.* imitador; remedador.

immaculate [ımǽkjəlıt] *adj.* inmaculado, sin mancha.

immaterial [ımətírıəl] *adj.* inmaterial, espiritual; **it is** — **to me** me es indiferente.

immediate [ımídıɪt] *adj.* inmediato; próximo; **-ly** *adv.* inmediatamente; en seguida; al punto, en el acto, al instante.

immense [ıméns] *adj.* inmenso.

immensity [ıménsətı] *s.* inmensidad.

immerse [ımɜ́s] *v.* sumergir, sumir.

immigrant [íməgrənt] *adj.* & *s.* inmigrante.

immigrate [íməgret] *v.* inmigrar.

immigration [ıməgréʃən] *s.* inmigración.

imminent [ímənənt] *adj.* inminente.

immodest [ımádıst] *adj.* deshonesto, impúdico, indecente.

immoral [ımárəl] *adj.* inmoral; licencioso.

immorality [ımərǽlətı] *s.* inmoralidad.

immortal [ımɔ́rtl] *adj.* & *s.* inmortal.

immortality [ımɔrtǽlətı] *s.* inmortalidad.

immovable [ımúvəbl] *adj.* inmovible (*o* inamovible); inmóvil; inmutable.

immune [ımjún] *adj.* inmune.

immunity [ımjúnətı] *s.* inmunidad.

imp [ımp] *s.* diablillo.

impair [ımpér] *v.* dañar, perjudicar, menoscabar, desvirtuar, debilitar.

impairment [ımpérmənt] *s.* menoscabo; perjuicio; deterioro.

impart [ımpárt] *v.* impartir, dar, comunicar.

impartial [ımpárʃəl] *adj.* imparcial.

impartiality [ımparʃǽlətı] *s.* imparcialidad.

impassible [ımpǽsəbl] *adj.* impasible.

impassioned [ımpǽʃənd] *adj.* apasionado, vehemente, ardiente.

impassive [ımpǽsıv] *adj.* impasible.

impatience [ımpéʃəns] *s.* impaciencia.

impatient [ımpéʃənt] *adj.* impaciente.

impeach [ımpítʃ] *v.* demandar o acusar formalmente (*a un alto funcionario de gobierno*); **to — a person's honor** poner en tela de juicio el honor de uno.

impede [ımpíd] *v.* impedir, estorbar, obstruir.

impediment [ımpédəmənt] *s.* impedimento, obstáculo, estorbo; traba.

impel [ımpél] *v.* impeler, impulsar.

impending [ımpéndıŋ] *adj.* inminente, amenazador.

imperative [ımpérətıv] *adj.* imperativo; imperioso, urgente; *s.* imperativo.

imperceptible [ımpəséptəbl] *adj.* imperceptible.

imperfect [ımpə́fıkt] *adj.* imperfecto; defectuoso; *s.* imperfecto (*tiempo del verbo*).

imperial [ımpírıəl] *adj.* imperial.

imperil [ımpérəl] *v.* poner en peligro, arriesgar.

imperious [ımpírıəs] *adj.* imperioso; urgente.

impersonal [ımpə́snl] *adj.* impersonal.

impersonate [ımpə́snet] *v.* representar (*un personaje*); remedar, imitar; fingirse otro, pretender ser otro.

impertinence [ımpə́tnəns] *s.* impertinencia; insolencia, descaro.

impertinent [ımpə́tnənt] *adj.* impertinente; insolente, descarado.

impervious [ımpə́vıəs] *adj.* impermeable; impenetrable; **— to reason** refractario, testarudo.

impetuous [ımpétʃuəs] *adj.* impetuoso.

impetus [ímpətəs] *s.* ímpetu.

impious [ímpıəs] *adj.* impío.

implacable [ımplékəbl] *adj.* implacable.

implant [ımplǽnt] *v.* implantar, plantar; inculcar, infundir.

implement [ímpləmənt] *s.* herramienta, instrumento; **-s** utensilios, aperos, enseres.

implicate [ímplıket] *v.* implicar, envolver, enredar.

implore [ımplór] *v.* implorar, rogar; suplicar.

imply [ımplái] *v.* implicar; querer decir; insinuar.

impolite [ımpəláıt] *adj.* descortés.

import [ímport] *s.* significado, significación, sentido; importancia; **-s** artículos importados; [ımpórt] *v.* importar; significar, querer decir.

importance [ımpórtns] *s.* importancia.

important [ımpórtnt] *adj.* importante.

impose [ımpóz] *v.* imponer; **to — upon** abusar de (*la amistad, hospitalidad, confianza de alguien*); engañar.

imposing [ımpózıŋ] *adj.* imponente; impresionante.

imposition [ımpəzíʃən] *s.* imposición; carga, impuesto; abuso (*de confianza*).

impossibility [ımpasəbflətı] *s.* imposibilidad.

impossible [ımpásəbl] *adj.* imposible.

impostor [ımpástə] *s.* impostor, embaucador.

imposture [ımpástʃə] *s.* impostura, fraude, engaño.

impotence [ímpətəns] *s.* impotencia.

impotent [ímpətənt] *adj.* impotente.

impoverish [ımpávərıʃ] *v.* empobrecer.

impregnate [ımprégnet] *v.* impregnar; empapar; empreñar.

impress [ímpres] *s.* impresión, marca, señal, huella; [ımprés] *v.* imprimir, estampar, marcar, grabar; impresionar.

impression [ımpréʃən] *s.* impresión; marca.

impressive [ımprésıv] *adj.* impresionante; imponente.

imprint [ímprınt] *s.* impresión; pie de imprenta; [ımprínt] *v.* imprimir; estampar.

imprison [ımprísn] *v.* aprisionar, encarcelar.

imprisonment [ımpríznmənt] *s.* prisión, encarcelación o encarcelamiento.

improbable [ımprábəbl] *adj.* improbable.

improper [ımprápə] *adj.* impropio.

improve [ımprúv] *v.* mejorar(se); **to — upon** mejorar; **to — one's time** aprovechar el tiempo.

improvement [ımprúvmənt] *s.* mejoramiento; mejora; progreso, adelanto; mejoría (*de una enfermedad*).

improvise [ímprəvaız] *v.* improvisar.

imprudent [ɪmprúdn̩t] *adj.* imprudente.

impudence [ímpjədəns] *s.* impudencia, descaro, insolencia.

impudent [ímpjədənt] *adj.* impudente, descarado, insolente.

impulse [ímpʌls] *s.* impulso; ímpetu; inclinación; **to act on** — obrar impulsivamente.

impunity [ɪmpjúnətɪ] *s.* impunidad, falta o exención de castigo.

impure [ɪmpjúr] *adj.* impuro; sucio; adulterado.

impurity [ɪmpjúrətɪ] *s.* impureza.

impute [ɪmpjút] *v.* imputar, achacar, atribuir.

in [ɪn] *prep.* en; dentro de; de (*después de un superlativo*); — **haste** de prisa; — **the morning** por (*o* en) la mañana; — **writing** por escrito; **at two** — **the morning** a las dos de la mañana; **dressed** — **white** vestido de blanco; **the tallest** — **his class** el más alto de su clase; **to come** — **a week** venir de hoy en ocho días, venir dentro de ocho días; *adv.* dentro; adentro; **en casa; to be** — **and out** estar entrando y saliendo; **to be all** — no poder más, estar rendido de cansancio; **to be** — **with someone** estar asociado con alguien; disfrutar el aprecio de una persona; **to come** — entrar; **to have it** — **for someone** tenerle ojeriza a una persona; **to put** — meter; **is the train** — ? ¿ha llegado el tren?

inability [ɪnəbílətɪ] *s.* inhabilidad, incapacidad.

inaccessible [ɪnəksésəbl̩] *adj.* inaccesible; inasequible.

inaccurate [ɪnǽkjərɪt] *adj.* inexacto, impreciso, incorrecto.

inactive [ɪnǽktɪv] *adj.* inactivo; inerte.

inactivity [ɪnæktívətɪ] *s.* inactividad, inacción, inercia.

inadequate [ɪnǽdəkwɪt] *adj.* inadecuado; insuficiente.

inadvertent [ɪnədvə́tn̩t] *adj.* inadvertido; descuidado; **-ly** *adv.* inadvertidamente; descuidadamente.

inanimate [ɪnǽnəmɪt] *adj.* inanimado.

inasmuch [ɪnəzmʌ́tʃ] : — **as** visto que, puesto que; en cuanto.

inattentive [ɪnəténtɪv] *adj.* desatento.

inaugurate [ɪnɔ́gjəret] *v.* inaugurar, iniciar; investir de una dignidad o cargo.

inauguration [ɪnɔgjəréʃən] *s.* inauguración.

inborn [ínbórn] *adj.* innato, connatural.

incandescent [ɪnkəndésn̩t] *adj.* incandescente, candente.

incapable [ɪnképəbl̩] *adj.* incapaz.

incense [ínsens] *s.* incienso; [ɪnséns] *v.* inflamar, exasperar.

incentive [ɪnséntɪv] *s.* incentivo, estímulo.

incessant [ɪnsésn̩t] *adj.* incesante, continuo.

inch [ɪntʃ] *s.* pulgada (2.54 *centímetros*); **by -es** poco a poco, gradualmente; **every** — **a man** nada menos que todo un hombre; **to be within an** — **of** estar a dos pulgadas de, estar muy cerca de; *v.* avanzar muy despacio (*por pulgadas*).

incident [ínsədənt] *s.* incidente, suceso, acontecimiento.

incidental [ɪnsədént̩l] *adj.* incidental; accidental; contingente; **-s** *s. pl.* gastos imprevistos; **-ly** *adv.* incidentalmente; de paso.

incision [ɪnsíʒən] *s.* incisión.

incite [ɪnsáɪt] *v.* incitar.

inclination [ɪnklənéʃən] *s.* inclinación.

incline [ínklaɪn] *s.* declive, pendiente, cuesta; [ɪnkláɪn] *v.* inclinar(se).

inclose = **enclose**.

inclosure = **enclosure**.

include [ɪnklúd] *v.* incluir, encerrar; abarcar.

inclusive [ɪnklúsɪv] *adj.* inclusivo; **from Monday to Friday** — del lunes al viernes inclusive.

incoherent [ɪnkohírənt] *adj.* incoherente, inconexo.

income [ínkʌm] *s.* renta, rédito, ingreso, entrada; — **tax** impuesto sobre rentas.

incomparable [ɪnkɔ́mpərəbl̩] *adj.* incomparable, sin par, sin igual.

incompatible [ɪnkəmpǽtəbl̩] *adj.* incompatible.

incompetent [ɪnkɔ́mpətənt] *adj.* incompetente.

incomplete [ɪnkəmplít] *adj.* incompleto.

incomprehensible [ɪnkɑmprɪhénsəbl̩] *adj.* incomprensible.

inconsiderate [ɪnkənsídərɪt] *adj.* inconsiderado, falto de miramiento.

inconsistency [ɪnkənsístənsɪ] *s.* inconsecuencia; falta de uniformidad (*en la aplicación de una regla o principio*).

inconsistent [ɪnkənsístənt] *adj.* inconsecuente; falto de uniformidad.

inconstancy [ɪnkɔ́nstənsɪ] *s.* inconstancia, mudanza.

inconstant [ɪnkɔ́nstənt] *adj.* inconstante, mudable, voluble.

inconvenience [ɪnkənvínjəns] *s.* inconveniencia; molestia; *v.* incomodar; molestar.

inconvenient [ɪnkənvínjənt] *adj.* inconveniente; inoportuno.

incorporate [ɪnkɔ́rpərɪt] *adj.* incorporado; asociado; [ɪnkɔ́rpəret] *v.* incorporar; incorporarse, asociarse *(para formar un cuerpo)*.

incorrect [ɪnkərékt] *adj.* incorrecto.

increase [ínkrɪs] *s.* aumento; acrecentamiento; crecimiento; incremento; [ɪnkrís] *v.* aumentar(se); acrecentar(se), crecer.

increasingly [ɪnkrísɪŋlɪ] *adv.* más y más; cada vez más.

incredible [ɪnkrédəbl] *adj.* increíble.

incredulity [ɪnkrədúlətɪ] *s.* incredulidad.

incredulous [ɪnkrédʒələs] *adj.* incrédulo, descreído.

inculcate [ɪnkʌ́lket] *v.* inculcar, infundir.

incur [ɪnkɜ́] *v.* incurrir en.

incurable [ɪnkjúrəbl] *adj.* incurable, irremediable; *s.* incurable.

indebted [ɪndétɪd] *adj.* adeudado, endeudado; obligado, agradecido.

indebtedness [ɪndétɪdnɪs] *s.* deuda; obligación.

indecency [ɪndísnsɪ] *s.* indecencia.

indecent [ɪndísnt] *adj.* indecente.

indeed [ɪndíd] *adv.* en verdad, a la verdad; de veras; realmente.

indefinite [ɪndéfənɪt] *adj.* indefinido.

indelible [ɪndéləbl] *adj.* indeleble.

indelicate [ɪndéləkət] *adj.* indelicado, indecoroso.

indemnify [ɪndémnəfaɪ] *v.* indemnizar.

indemnity [ɪndémnətɪ] *s.* indemnización.

indent [ɪndént] *v.* dentar, endentar; sangrar *(comenzar un renglón más adentro que los otros)*.

independence [ɪndɪpéndəns] *s.* independencia.

independent [ɪndɪpéndənt] *adj.* independiente.

indescribable [ɪndɪskráɪbəbl] *adj.* indescriptible.

index [índeks] *s.* índice; *v.* alfabetizar, ordenar alfabéticamente; poner en un índice.

Indian [índɪən] *adj.* & *s.* indio; — **Ocean** Océano Indico.

indicate [índəket] *v.* indicar.

indication [ɪndəkéʃən] *s.* indicación.

indicative [ɪndíkətɪv] *adj.* & *s.* indicativo.

indict [ɪndáɪt] *v.* procesar, demandar *(ante un juez)*; enjuiciar, formar causa a.

indictment [ɪndáɪtmənt] *s.* acusación *(hecha por el Gran Jurado)*, denuncia, proceso judicial.

indifference [ɪndífrəns] *s.* indiferencia; apatía.

indifferent [ɪndífrənt] *adj.* indiferente; apático.

indigenous [ɪndídʒənəs] *adj.* indígena, autóctono, nativo.

indigestion [ɪndədʒéstʃən] *s.* indigestión.

indignant [ɪndígnənt] *adj.* indignado; **-ly** *adv.* con indignación.

indignation [ɪndɪgnéʃən] *s.* indignación.

indignity [ɪndígnətɪ] *s.* indignidad, afrenta.

indigo [índɪgo] *s.* índigo, añil; — **blue** azul de añil.

indirect [ɪndərékt] *adj.* indirecto.

indiscreet [ɪndɪskrít] *adj.* indiscreto.

indiscretion [ɪndɪskréʃən] *s.* indiscreción.

indispensable [ɪndɪspénsəbl] *adj.* indispensable.

indispose [ɪndɪspóz] *v.* indisponer.

indisposed [ɪndɪspózd] *adj.* indispuesto

indisposition [ɪndɪspəzíʃən] *s.* indisposición; malestar.

indistinct [ɪndɪstíŋkt] *adj.* indistinto.

individual [ɪndəvídʒʊəl] *adj.* individual; *s.* individuo, sujeto, persona.

individuality [ɪndəvɪdʒuǽlətɪ] *s.* individualidad; individuo, persona.

indivisible [ɪndəvízəbl] *adj.* indivisible.

indoctrinate [ɪndáktrɪnet] *v.* adoctrinar.

indolence [índələns] *s.* indolencia, desidia, apatía.

indolent [índələnt] *adj.* indolente, desidioso, apático.

indomitable [ɪndámətəbl] *adj.* indomable.

indoor [índor] *adj.* interior, de casa.

indoors [índórz] *adv.* dentro, en casa; adentro; **to go —** entrar; ir adentro.

indorse [índɔ́rs] *v.* endosar; respaldar; apoyar, garantizar.

indorsement [índɔ́rsmənt] *s.* endose, endoso; respaldo; garantía, apoyo.

indorser [índɔ́rsə] *s.* endosante.

induce [ɪndjús] *v.* inducir.

inducement [ɪndjúsmənt] *s.* aliciente, incentivo.

induct [ɪndʌ́kt] *v.* introducir; iniciar; instalar *(en un cargo)*.

induction [ɪndʌ́kʃən] *s.* inducción; instalación *(en un cargo)*.

indulge [ɪndʌ́ldʒ] *v.* gratificar, complacer; seguir el humor a *(una persona)*; mimar, consentir *(a un niño)*; **to — in** darse a, entregarse a *(un placer)*; darse el lujo de, permitirse el placer de.

indulgence [ɪndʌldʒəns] *s.* indulgencia; complacencia (*en el vicio o placer*).
indulgent [ɪndʌldʒənt] *adj.* indulgente.
industrial [ɪndʌstrɪəl] *adj.* industrial.
industrialist [ɪndʌstrɪəlɪst] *s.* industrial; fabricante.
industrious [ɪndʌstrɪəs] *adj.* industrioso, aplicado, diligente.
industry [índəstrɪ] *s.* industria; aplicación, diligencia.
ineffable [ɪnéfəbl] *adj.* inefable.
ineffective [ɪnəféktɪv] *adj.* inefectivo, ineficaz.
inequality [ɪnɪkwálətɪ] *s.* desigualdad; disparidad.
inert [ɪnə́t] *adj.* inerte.
inertia [ɪnə́ʃə] *s.* inercia.
inestimable [ɪnéstəməbl] *adj.* inestimable.
inevitable [ɪnévətəbl] *adj.* inevitable.
inexhaustible [ɪnɪgzɔ́stəbl] *adj.* inagotable.
inexpensive [ɪnɪkspénsɪv] *adj.* económico, barato.
inexperience [ɪnɪkspfrɪəns] *s.* inexperiencia, falta de experiencia.
inexperienced [ɪnɪkspfrɪənst] *adj.* inexperto, falto de experiencia.
inexplicable [ɪnéksplɪkəbl] *adj.* inexplicable.
inexpressible [ɪnɪksprésəbl] *adj.* inexpresable, indecible, inefable.
infallible [ɪnfǽlɪbl] *adj.* infalible.
infamous [ɪnfəməs] *adj.* infame, ignominioso.
infamy [ɪnfəmɪ] *s.* infamia.
infancy [ɪnfənsɪ] *s.* infancia.
infant [ɪnfənt] *s.* infante, bebé, criatura, nene.
infantile [ɪnfəntaɪl] *adj.* infantil.
infantry [ɪnfəntrɪ] *s.* infantería.
infect [ɪnfékt] *v.* infectar, inficionar; contagiar; contaminar.
infection [ɪnfékʃən] *s.* infección; contagio.
infectious [ɪnfékʃəs] *adj.* infeccioso; contagioso.
infer [ɪnfɜ́] *v.* inferir, deducir, colegir.
inference [ɪnfərəns] *s.* inferencia, deducción.
inferior [ɪnffrɪə] *adj. & s.* inferior.
inferiority [ɪnfɪrɪɔ́rətɪ] *s.* inferioridad.
infernal [ɪnfɜ́nəl] *adj.* infernal.
inferno [ɪnfɜ́no] *s.* infierno.
infest [ɪnfést] *v.* infestar, plagar.
infidel [ɪnfədl] *adj. & s.* infiel.
infinite [ɪnfənɪt] *adj. & s.* infinito.
infinitive [ɪnfínətɪv] *adj. & s.* infinitivo.
infinity [ɪnfínətɪ] *s.* infinidad; infinito.
infirm [ɪnfɜ́m] *adj.* enfermizo, achacoso,

débil.
infirmary [ɪnfɜ́mərɪ] *s.* enfermería.
infirmity [ɪnfɜ́mətɪ] *s.* enfermedad, achaque; flaqueza.
inflame [ɪnflém] *v.* inflamar(se); enardecer(se).
inflammation [ɪnfləméʃən] *s.* inflamación.
inflate [ɪnflét] *v.* inflar; hinchar.
inflation [ɪnfléʃən] *s.* inflación; hinchazón.
inflection [ɪnflékʃən] *s.* inflexión.
inflict [ɪnflíkt] *v.* infligir, imponer.
influence [ɪnflʊəns] *s.* influencia, influjo; *v.* influir en; ejercer influencia o influjo sobre.
influential [ɪnflʊénʃəl] *adj.* influyente.
influenza [ɪnflʊénzə] *s.* influenza, gripe.
influx [ɪnflʌks] *s.* entrada, afluencia (*de gente*).
infold [ɪnfóld] *v.* envolver; abrazar; abarcar.
inform [ɪnfɔ́rm] *v.* informar; enterar; avisar; **to — against** delatar a, denunciar a.
informal [ɪnfɔ́rml] *adj.* informal, sin ceremonia; **— visit** visita de confianza; **-ly** *adv.* informalmente, sin ceremonia, de confianza.
information [ɪnfəméʃən] *s.* información; informe; noticias; conocimientos, saber.
infringe [ɪnfríndʒ] *v.* infringir, violar; **to — upon** violar.
infuriate [ɪnfjʊ́rɪet] *v.* enfurecer.
infuse [ɪnfjúz] *v.* infundir; inculcar.
ingenious [ɪndʒínjəs] *adj.* ingenioso.
ingenuity [ɪndʒənúətɪ] *s.* ingeniosidad.
ingratitude [ɪngrǽtətjud] *s.* ingratitud.
ingredient [ɪngrídɪənt] *s.* ingrediente.
inhabit [ɪnhǽbɪt] *v.* habitar, vivir en, residir en.
inhabitant [ɪnhǽbətənt] *s.* habitante.
inhale [ɪnhél] *v.* inhalar, aspirar, inspirar.
inherent [ɪnhfrənt] *adj.* inherente.
inherit [ɪnhérɪt] *v.* heredar.
inheritance [ɪnhérətəns] *s.* herencia.
inhibit [ɪnhfbɪt] *v.* inhibir, cohibir, refrenar, reprimir; impedir.
inhibition [ɪnɪbíʃən] *s.* inhibición, cohibición; prohibición, restricción.
inhospitable [ɪnháspɪtəbl] *adj.* inhospitalario.
inhuman [ɪnhjúmən] *adj.* inhumano.
inimitable [ɪnímətəbl] *adj.* inimitable.
iniquity [ɪnfkwətɪ] *s.* iniquidad, maldad.
initial [ɪnfʃəl] *adj. & s.* inicial; *v.* marcar o firmar con iniciales.
initiate [ɪnfʃɪet] *v.* iniciar.

initiative [ɪnˈʃɪetɪv] s. iniciativa.

inject [ɪndʒékt] v. inyectar; injerir, introducir.

injection [ɪndʒékʃən] s. inyección.

injunction [ɪndʒʌ́ŋkʃən] s. mandato, orden; entredicho.

injure [ínдʒə] v. dañar; herir, lesionar; lastimar.

injurious [ɪndʒúrɪəs] adj. dañoso, dañino, perjudicial.

injury [ínдʒərɪ] s. daño; herida, lesión; perjuicio.

injustice [ɪndʒʌ́stɪs] s. injusticia.

ink [ɪŋk] s. tinta; v. entintar; teñir o manchar con tinta.

inkling [íŋklɪŋ] s. indicación, indicio, idea, sospecha, noción vaga.

inkstand [íŋkstænd] s. tintero.

inkwell [íŋkwɛl] s. tintero.

inlaid [ɪnléd] adj. incrustado, embutido; — work embutido, incrustación; pret. & p.p. de to inlay.

inland [ínlənd] s. interior (de un país); adj. interior, del interior de un país; adv. tierra adentro.

inlay [ɪnlé] v. incrustar, embutir; [ínle] s. embutido.

inmate [ínmét] s. residente, asilado (de un hospicio, asilo, casa de corrección, etc.); presidiario; hospiciano.

inmost [ínmost] adj. más interior, más íntimo, más secreto o recóndito; más profundo.

inn [ɪn] s. posada, mesón, fonda.

innate [ɪnét] adj. innato, connatural.

inner [ínə] adj. interior; íntimo, recóndito; —most = inmost.

inning [ínɪŋ] s. entrada, cuadro (en beisbol); turno (del bateador en beisbol y otros juegos).

innkeeper [ínkipə] s. ventero, mesonero, posadero.

innocence [ínəsŋs] s. inocencia.

innocent [ínəsŋt] adj. & s. inocente.

innocuous [ɪnákjʊəs] adj. innocuo, inofensivo.

innovation [ɪnəvéʃən] s. innovación.

innuendo [ɪnjʊéndo] s. insinuación, indirecta.

innumerable [ɪnjúmərəbļ] adj. innumerable.

inoculate [ɪnákjələt] v. inocular; contaminar.

inoffensive [ɪnəfénsɪv] adj. inofensivo.

inopportune [ɪnapətjún] adj. inoportuno.

inquire [ɪnkwáɪr] v. inquirir, indagar; preguntar; to — about preguntar por; to — into indagar, investigar.

inquiry [ɪnkwáɪrɪ] s. indagación; investigación; pregunta; interrogatorio.

inquisition [ɪnkwəzíʃən] s. inquisición; indagación.

inquisitive [ɪnkwízətɪv] adj. inquisitivo, investigador; preguntón; curioso.

inroad [ínrod] s. incursión, invasión, ataque; to make -s upon atacar; mermar.

insane [ɪnsén] adj. insano, loco; — asylum manicomio, casa de locos.

insanity [ɪnsǽnətɪ] s. locura.

insatiable [ɪnséʃɪəbļ] adj. insaciable.

inscribe [ɪnskráɪb] v. inscribir.

inscription [ɪnskrípʃən] s. inscripción; letrero.

insect [ínsekt] s. insecto.

insecure [ɪnsɪkjúr] adj. inseguro.

insensible [ɪnsénsəbļ] adj. insensible.

insensitive [ɪnsénsətɪv] adj. insensible.

inseparable [ɪnsépərəbļ] adj. inseparable.

insert [ínsɝt] s. inserción; intercalación; hoja (insertada en un libro); circular, folleto (insertado en un periódico); [ɪnsɝ́t] v. insertar; intercalar; encajar; meter.

insertion [ɪnsɝ́ʃən] s. inserción; introducción.

inside [ɪnsáɪd] s. interior; -s entrañas; adj. interior, interno; secreto; adv. dentro; adentro; to turn — out volver(se) al revés; prep. dentro de.

insight [ínsaɪt] s. penetración, discernimiento; intuición; perspicacia; comprensión.

insignia [ɪnsígnɪə] s. pl. insignias.

insignificant [ɪnsɪgnífəkənt] adj. insignificante.

insinuate [ɪnsínjʊet] v. insinuar.

insinuation [ɪnsɪnjʊéʃən] s. insinuación; indirecta.

insipid [ɪnsípɪd] adj. insípido.

insist [ɪnsíst] v. insistir en; empeñarse (en); porfiar, persistir.

insistence [ɪnsístəns] s. insistencia, empeño, porfía.

insistent [ɪnsístənt] adj. insistente; porfiado, persistente.

insolence [ínsələns] s. insolencia.

insolent [ínsələnt] adj. insolente.

inspect [ɪnspékt] v. inspeccionar; examinar, registrar.

inspection [ɪnspékʃən] s. inspección; registro.

inspector [ɪnspéktə] s. inspector.

inspiration [ɪnspəréʃən] s. inspiración.

inspire [ɪnspáɪr] v. inspirar.

install [ɪnstɔ́l] v. instalar.

installation [ɪnstəléʃən] s. instalación.

installment, instalment [ɪnstɔ́lmənt]

s. instalación; abono (*pago*); entrega o continuación (*semanal o mensual de una novela*); **to pay in -s** pagar por plazos; pagar en abonos.

instance [ínstəns] *s.* ejemplo, caso; vez, ocasión; instancia; **for —** por ejemplo.

instant [ínstənt] *s.* instante; *adj.* inmediato; urgente; **the 10th —** el 10 del (mes) corriente; **-ly** *adv.* al instante, inmediatamente.

instantaneous [ɪnstənténɪəs] *adj.* instantáneo.

instead [ɪnstéd] *adv.* en lugar de ello (eso, él, ella, *etc.*); **— of** en lugar de, en vez de.

instep [ínstɛp] *s.* empeine (*del pie, del zapato*).

instigate [ínstəget] *v.* instigar.

instill [ɪnstíl] *v.* inculcar, infundir.

instinct [ínstɪŋkt] *s.* instinto.

instinctive [ɪnstíŋktɪv] *adj.* instintivo.

institute [ínstətjut] *s.* instituto; *v.* instituir.

institution [ɪnstətjúʃən] *s.* institución.

instruct [ɪnstrʌ́kt] *v.* instruir; dar instrucciones.

instruction [ɪnstrʌ́kʃən] *s.* instrucción; enseñanza; **lack of —** falta de saber o conocimientos; **-s** órdenes, instrucciones.

instructive [ɪnstrʌ́ktɪv] *adj.* instructivo.

instructor [ɪnstrʌ́ktə] *s.* instructor.

instrument [ínstrəmənt] *s.* instrumento.

instrumental [ɪnstrəméntl] *adj.* instrumental; **to be — in** ayudar a, servir de instrumento para.

insufferable [ɪnsʌ́frəbl] *adj.* insufrible, inaguantable.

insufficiency [ɪnsəffʃənsɪ] *s.* insuficiencia; incompetencia; falta, escasez.

insufficient [ɪnsəffʃənt] *adj.* insuficiente; inadecuado.

insulate [ínsəlet] *v.* aislar.

insulation [ɪnsəléʃən] *s.* aislamiento; aislación.

insulator [ínsəletə] *s.* aislador.

insult [ínsʌlt] *s.* insulto; [ɪnsʌ́lt] *v.* insultar.

insurance [ɪnʃúrəns] *s.* aseguramiento; seguro; prima, premio (*de una póliza de seguro*); **— agent** agente de seguros; **— company** compañía de seguros; **— policy** póliza de seguro; **accident —** seguro contra accidentes; **fire —** seguro contra incendios; **life —** seguro sobre la vida.

insure [ɪnʃúr] *v.* asegurar; asegurarse de.

insurgent [ɪnsʌ́dʒənt] *adj. & s.* insurgente, insurrecto.

insurmountable [ɪnsəmáʊntəbl] *adj.* insuperable.

insurrection [ɪnsərékʃən] *s.* insurrección, rebelión, alzamiento.

intact [ɪntǽkt] *adj.* intacto.

integral [íntəɡrəl] *adj.* integral; integrante; *s.* integral.

integrity [ɪntéɡrətɪ] *s.* integridad, entereza.

intellect [íntlɛkt] *s.* intelecto; entendimiento.

intellectual [ɪntléktʃʊəl] *adj. & s.* intelectual.

intelligence [ɪntélədʒəns] *s.* inteligencia; información, noticias; **policía secreta.**

intelligent [ɪntélədʒənt] *adj.* inteligente.

intemperance [ɪntémpərəns] *s.* intemperancia.

intend [ɪnténd] *v.* intentar, pensar, tener la intención de; proponerse; destinar; **to — to do it** pensar hacerlo.

intense [ɪnténs] *adj.* intenso.

intensity [ɪnténsətɪ] *s.* intensidad.

intensive [ɪnténsɪv] *adj.* intenso; intensivo.

intent [ɪntént] *s.* intento, intención, propósito; significado; **to all -s and purposes** en todo caso, en todos sentidos; en realidad; *adj.* atento; **— on** absorto en, reconcentrado en; resuelto a, decidido a.

intention [ɪnténʃən] *s.* intención.

intentional [ɪnténʃənl] *adj.* intencional; **-ly** *adv.* intencionalmente, adrede, a propósito.

inter [ɪntə́] *v.* enterrar, sepultar.

intercede [ɪntəsíd] *v.* interceder.

intercept [ɪntəsépt] *v.* interceptar; atajar.

interception [ɪntəsépʃən] *s.* intercepción.

intercession [ɪntəséʃən] *s.* intercesión.

interchange [ɪntətʃendʒ] *s.* intercambio; cambio, trueque; [ɪntətʃéndʒ] *v.* cambiar, trocar; permutar; alternar.

intercourse [íntəkors] *s.* comunicación; comercio, trato; intercambio (*de ideas, sentimientos, etc.*).

interest [íntərɪst] *s.* interés; rédito; participación (*en un negocio*); *v.* interesar.

interested [íntərɪstɪd] *adj.* interesado; **to be** (*o* **become**) **— in** interesarse en (*o* por).

interesting [íntərɪstɪŋ] *adj.* interesante.

interfere [ɪntəfír] *v.* intervenir; interponerse, entremeterse; estorbar; **to — with** estorbar, frustrar; dificultar.

interference [ɪntəffrəns] *s.* intervención; obstáculo; interferencia (*en la radio*).

interior [ɪntíɾɪə] *adj.* interior; interno; *s.* interior.

interjection [ɪntədʒékʃən] *s.* interjección, exclamación; intercalación.

interlace [ɪntəlés] *v.* entrelazar, enlazar, entretejer.

interlock [ɪntəlák] *v.* entrelazar(se); trabar(se).

intermediate [ɪntəmídɪɪt] *adj.* intermedio.

interminable [ɪntɜ́mɪnəbl] *adj.* interminable, inacabable.

intermingle [ɪntəmíŋgl] *v.* entremezclar(se), entreverar(se); mezclar(se).

intermission [ɪntəmíʃən] *s.* intermisión, intermedio, entreacto.

intermittent [ɪntəmítnt] *adj.* intermitente.

intern [ɪntɜ́n] *v.* internar, confinar, encerrar; [ɪntɜn] *s.* practicante (*de medicina en un hospital*).

internal [ɪntɜ́n] *adj.* interno; interior.

international [ɪntənǽʃənl] *adj.* internacional.

interoceanic [ɪntəoʃɪǽnɪk] *adj.* interoceánico.

interpose [ɪntəpóz] *v.* interponer(se).

interpret [ɪntɜ́prɪt] *v.* interpretar.

interpretation [ɪntɜprɪtéʃən] *s.* interpretación.

interpreter [ɪntɜ́prɪtə] *s.* intérprete.

interrogate [ɪntéɾəget] *v.* interrogar.

interrogation [ɪnterəgéʃən] *s.* interrogación.

interrogative [ɪntəɾágətɪv] *adj.* interrogativo; *s.* pronombre o palabra interrogativa.

interrupt [ɪntəɾʌ́pt] *v.* interrumpir.

interruption [ɪntəɾʌ́pʃən] *s.* interrupción.

intersect [ɪntəsékt] *v.* cortar(se); cruzar(se).

intersection [ɪntəsékʃən] *s.* intersección; **street** — bocacalle.

intersperse [ɪntəspɜ́s] *v.* entremezclar, esparcir.

intertwine [ɪntətwáɪn] *v.* entrelazar, entretejer, trenzar.

interval [ɪntəvl] *s.* intervalo.

intervene [ɪntəvín] *v.* intervenir; interponerse; mediar.

intervention [ɪntəvénʃən] *s.* intervención.

interview [ɪntəvju] *s.* entrevista; *v.* entrevistar, entrevistarse con.

intestine [ɪntéstɪn] *s.* intestino; *adj.* intestino, interno.

intimacy [ɪntəməsɪ] *s.* intimidad.

intimate [ɪntəmɪt] *adj.* íntimo; *s.* amigo íntimo; [ɪntəmet] *v.* intimar, insinuar;

indicar, dar a entender.

intimation [ɪntəméʃən] *s.* intimación, insinuación.

intimidate [ɪntímədet] *v.* intimidar, acobardar, infundir miedo.

into [íntʊ, íntə] *prep.* en; dentro de; hacia el interior.

intolerable [ɪntálərəbl] *adj.* intolerable, inaguantable.

intolerance [ɪntáləɾəns] *s.* intolerancia.

intolerant [ɪntáləɾənt] *adj.* intolerante.

intonation [ɪntonéʃən] *s.* entonación.

intoxicate [ɪntáksəket] *v.* embriagar; emborrachar.

intoxication [ɪntaksəkéʃən] *s.* embriaguez; envenenamiento, intoxicación (*estado tóxico o envenenamiento parcial*).

intravenous [ɪntɾəvínəs] *adj.* intravenoso.

intrench [ɪntɾéntʃ] *v.* atrincherar; **to —** **oneself** atrincherarse; **to — upon** **another's rights** infringir los derechos ajenos; **to be -ed** estar atrincherado; estar firmemente establecido.

intrepid [ɪntɾépɪd] *adj.* intrépido.

intricate [ɪntɾɪkɪt] *adj.* intrincado, enredado.

intrigue [ɪntɾíg] *s.* intriga; enredo; trama; lío, embrollo; *v.* intrigar; tramar, maquinar.

intriguer [ɪntɾíɡə] *s.* intrigante.

introduce [ɪntɾədjús] *v.* introducir; presentar.

introduction [ɪntɾədʌ́kʃən] *s.* introducción; presentación.

intrude [ɪntɾúd] *v.* entremeterse (*o entrometerse*); introducir, meter.

intruder [ɪntɾúdə] *s.* intruso, entremetido.

intrusion [ɪntɾúʒən] *s.* intrusión, entremetimiento.

intrusive [ɪntɾúsɪv] *adj.* intruso.

intrust = **entrust**.

intuition [ɪntʊʃən] *s.* intuición.

inundate [ínəndet] *v.* inundar.

inure [ɪnjúɾ] *v.* habituar, acostumbrar.

invade [ɪnvéd] *v.* invadir.

invader [ɪnvédə] *s.* invasor.

invalid [ɪnvǽlɪd] *adj.* inválido (*que no vale*), nulo, de ningún valor.

invalid [ínvəlɪd] *adj.* inválido, enfermizo, achacoso; **— diet** dieta para inválidos; *s.* inválido.

invaluable [ɪnvǽljebl] *adj.* de gran precio o valor, inapreciable, inestimable.

invariable [ɪnvéɾɪəbl] *adj.* invariable; **invariably** *adv.* invariablemente; sin falta, sin excepción.

invasion [ɪnvéʒən] *s.* invasión.

invent [ɪnvént] v. inventar.
invention [ɪnvénʃən] s. invención; invento; inventiva, facultad para inventar.
inventive [ɪnvéntɪv] adj. inventivo.
inventiveness [ɪnvéntɪvnɪs] s. inventiva.
inventor [ɪnvéntə] s. inventor.
inventory [ínvəntorɪ] s. inventario; v. inventariar.
inverse [ɪnvə́s] adj. inverso.
invert [ɪnvə́t] v. invertir; trastrocar; volver al revés.
invest [ɪnvést] v. invertir, colocar (fondos); investir (de una dignidad o cargo); revestir (de autoridad); sitiar.
investigate [ɪnvéstəget] v. investigar, indagar.
investigation [ɪnvestəgéʃən] s. investigación; indagación.
investigator [ɪnvéstəgetə] s. investigador; indagador.
investment [ɪnvéstmənt] s. inversión (de fondos).
investor [ɪnvéstə] s. el que invierte fondos.
invigorate [ɪnvígəret] v. vigorizar, fortalecer.
invincible [ɪnvínsəbl] adj. invencible.
invisible [ɪnvízəbl] adj. invisible.
invitation [ɪnvətéʃən] s. invitación.
invite [ɪnváɪt] v. invitar; convidar.
inviting [ɪnváɪtɪŋ] adj. atractivo; seductivo, tentador.
invoice [ínvɔɪs] s. factura; envío, mercancías enviadas; v. facturar.
invoke [ɪnvók] v. invocar.
involuntary [ɪnvɑ́ləntɛrɪ] adj. involuntario.
involve [ɪnvɑ́lv] v. complicar, enredar; envolver; implicar; comprometer; **to get -d in difficulties** embrollarse, meterse en embrollos.
inward [ínwəd] adj. interior; interno; secreto; adv. hacia el interior; hacia dentro, adentro, para dentro; **-s** adv. = inward.
iodine [áɪədaɪn] s. yodo.
ire [aɪr] s. ira.
iridescent [ɪrədésn̩t] adj. iridiscente, tornasolado, irisado.
iris [áɪrɪs] s. iris; arco iris; flor de lis.
Irish [áɪrɪʃ] adj. irlandés; s. irlandés, idioma irlandés; **the —** los irlandeses.
irksome [ə́ksəm] adj. fastidioso, engorroso, molesto, tedioso.
iron [áɪən] s. hierro; plancha (de planchar ropa); adj. férreo, de hierro; **—work** herraje, trabajo en hierro; **—works** herrería; fábrica de hierro;

v. planchar; **to — out a difficulty** allanar una dificultad.
ironical [aɪránɪk] adj. irónico.
ironing [áɪənɪŋ] s. planchado.
irony [áɪrənɪ] s. ironía.
irregular [ɪrégjələ] adj. irregular.
irrelevant [ɪrélǝvənt] adj. fuera de propósito, inaplicable al caso, inoportuno, que no viene (o no hace) al caso.
irreligious [ɪrɪlídʒəs] adj. irreligioso, impío.
irremediable [ɪrɪmídɪəbl] adj. irremediable; incurable.
irreproachable [ɪrɪprótʃəbl] adj. irreprochable, intachable.
irresistible [ɪrɪzístəbl] adj. irresistible.
irresolute [ɪrézəlut] adj. irresoluto, indeciso.
irreverence [ɪrévərəns] s. irreverencia, desacato.
irreverent [ɪrévərənt] adj. irreverente.
irrigate [írəget] v. regar; irrigar, bañar.
irrigation [ɪrəgéʃən] s. riego; irrigación; **— canal** acequia, canal de irrigación.
irritable [írətəbl] adj. irritable; colérico.
irritate [írətet] v. irritar.
irritating [írətetɪŋ] adj. irritante.
irritation [ɪrətéʃən] s. irritación.
island [áɪlənd] s. isla.
islander [áɪləndə] s. isleño.
isle [aɪl] s. isla, ínsula.
isolate [áɪslet] v. aislar.
isolation [aɪsléʃən] s. aislamiento.
isolationism [aɪsléʃənɪzəm] s. aislamiento.
issue [íʃʊ] s. tirada, impresión; emisión (de valores, acciones, etc.); problema, argumento; resultado, consecuencia; **without —** sin prole, sin sucesión; **to take — with** disentir o diferir de; v. publicar, dar a luz; promulgar (un decreto); emitir (valores, acciones, etc.); emanar; fluir; salir; brotar; provenir.
isthmus [ísməs] s. istmo.
it [ɪt] pron. neutro lo, la (acusativo); ello, él, ella (después de una preposición); por lo general no se traduce cuando es sujeto del verbo: **— is there** está allí; **— is I** soy yo; **— is raining** llueve, está lloviendo **what time is — ?** ¿qué hora es?; **— is two o'clock** son las dos; **how goes — ?** ¿qué tal?
Italian [ɪtǽljən] adj. & s. italiano.
italic [ɪtǽlɪk] adj. itálico; **-s** s. letra bastardilla.
italicize [ɪtǽləsaɪz] v. poner en letra bastardilla.
itch [ɪtʃ] s. comezón; picazón; sarna (enfermedad de la piel); v. picar, darle a uno comezón; sentir comezón; **to be**

-ing to tener ansias de.

itchy [ítʃɪ] *adj.* sarnoso, *Am.* sarniento; **to feel —** sentir comezón.

item [áitəm] *s.* artículo; detalle; noticia, suelto (*de un periódico*); partida (*de una lista*).

itemize [áitəmaɪz] *v.* pormenorizar, detallar; hacer una lista de.

itinerary [aɪtínərɛrɪ] *s.* itinerario; ruta; guía de viajeros.

its [ɪts] *pos. neutro* su (sus), de él, de ella, de ello.

itself [ɪtsélf] *pron. neutro* mismo, misma; **by —** por sí, de por sí, por sí solo; solo, aislado; **in —** en sí.

ivory [áɪvrɪ] *s.* marfil.

ivy [áɪvɪ] *s.* hiedra (yedra).

J

jab [dʒæb] *v.* picar; pinchar; *s.* piquete, pinchazo.

jack [dʒæk] *s.* gato (*para alzar cosas pesadas*); sota (*en naipes*); macho (*del burro y otros animales*); bandera de proa; **— of all trades** aprendiz de todo y oficial de nada; **— pot** premio gordo, premio mayor; **— rabbit** liebre americana; *v.* **to — up** solevantar, alzar con gato (*un objeto pesado*).

jackass [dʒǽkæs] *s.* asno, burro.

jacket [dʒǽkɪt] *s.* chaqueta; envoltura; forro (*de un libro*); hollejo (*de la patata*).

jackknife [dʒǽknaɪf] *s.* navaja.

jagged [dʒǽgɪd] *adj.* serrado, dentado.

jail [dʒel] *s.* cárcel; *v.* encarcelar.

jailer [dʒélə] *s.* carcelero.

jam [dʒæm] *v.* estrujar, apachurrar; atorar(se); obstruir(se); atascar(se); apiñar(se), agolpar(se); **to — on the brakes** frenar de golpe; **to — one's fingers** machucarse los dedos; **to — through** forzar por, meter a la fuerza; *s.* conserva, compota; apretura; atascamiento; **traffic —** aglomeración de transeúntes o automóviles, *Am.* bola; **to be in a —** estar en un aprieto.

janitor [dʒǽnətə] *s.* conserje; portero; casero (*encargado de un edificio*).

January [dʒǽnjuɛrɪ] *s.* enero.

Japanese [dʒæpəníz] *adj. & s.* japonés.

jar [dʒɑr] *s.* jarra, jarro; tarro; choque; sacudida; trepidación, vibración; **large earthen —** tinaja; *v.* trepidar; hacer vibrar; hacer temblar; menear; **to — on one's nerves** ponerle a uno los nervios de punta.

jargon [dʒárgən] *s.* jerga, jerigonza.

jasmine [dʒǽzmɪn] *s.* jazmín.

jasper [dʒǽspə] *s.* jaspe.

jaunt [dʒɔnt] *s.* caminata, excursión; *v.* dar un paseíto, hacer una corta caminata.

jaw [dʒɔ] *s.* quijada, mandíbula, *Am.* carretilla; **-s grapa** (*de herramienta*).

jawbone [dʒɔbón] *s.* mandíbula, quijada.

jay [dʒe] *s.* grajo; rústico, bobo; **blue —** azulejo; **—walker** el que cruza las bocacalles descuidadamente.

jazz [dʒæz] *s.* jazz (*cierta clase de música sincopada*); *v.* tocar el jazz; bailar el jazz; **to — up** sincopar; animar, alegrar.

jealous [dʒéləs] *adj.* celoso; envidioso; **to be — of someone** tener celos de una persona, tenerle celos a una persona.

jealousy [dʒéləsɪ] *s.* celos; envidia.

jeer [dʒɪr] *s.* mofa, befa, escarnio, *Am.* choteo; *v.* mofar, befar, *Am.* chotear; **to — at** mofarse de.

jelly [dʒélɪ] *s.* jalea; *v.* convertir(se) en jalea, hacer(se) gelatinoso.

jerk [dʒɜk] *s.* tirón; sacudida, *Am.* jalón; espasmo muscular; *v.* sacudir(se); dar un tirón; atasajar (*la carne*); **to — out** sacar de un tirón; **-ed beef** tasajo, *Am.* charqui.

jersey [dʒɜzɪ] *s.* tejido de punto, tejido elástico, *Am.* jersey; chaqueta, blusa, camisa (*de punto*), *Am.* jersey.

jest [dʒɛst] *s.* broma; chanza; chiste; *v.* bromear; chancearse.

jester [dʒéstə] *s.* chancero, burlón; bufón.

Jesuit [dʒéʒuɪt] *s.* jesuíta.

jet [dʒɛt] *s.* chorro; surtidor (*de fuente*); azabache; **gas —** mechero de gas; *adj.* de azabache; **jet-black** negro como el azabache; *v.* chorrear, salir en chorro.

Jew [dʒu] *s.* judío.

jewel [dʒúəl] *s.* joya, alhaja; gema; **— box** estuche, joyero.

jeweler [dʒúələ] *s.* joyero; **-'s shop** joyería.

jewelry [dʒúəlrɪ] *s.* joyas, alhajas, pedrería; **— store** joyería.

Jewish [dʒúíʃ] *adj.* judío.

jiffy [dʒífɪ] *s.* instante; **in a —** en un instante, en dos paletas, en un decir Jesús, en un santiamén.

jig [dʒɪg] *s.* jiga (*música y baile*); **— saw** sierra mecánica (*para recortar figuras*); **—saw puzzle** rompecabezas (*de recortes*); *v.* tocar una jiga; bailar una jiga; bailotear; menear(se).

jiggle [dʒígl̩] *v.* zangolotear(se), zarandear(se), menear(se); *s.* zarandeo, meneo, zangoloteo.

jilt [dʒɪlt] *v.* desairar, dar calabazas, dejar plantado.

jingle [dʒíŋgl̩] *s.* retintín; verso o rima infantil; **— bell** cascabel; *v.* hacer retintín.

job [dʒɑb] *s.* tarea, faena; trabajo; empleo, ocupación; **to be out of a —** estar sin trabajo; estar desocupado.

jockey [dʒákɪ] *s.* jockey; *v.* maniobrar (*para sacar ventaja o ganar un puesto*).

join [dʒɔɪn] *v.* juntar(se); enlazar(se); acoplar; unirse a, asociarse a.

joint [dʒɔɪnt] *s.* juntura, coyuntura, articulación; conexión; bisagra; garito (*casa de juego*); fonducho, restaurante de mala muerte; **out of —** descoyuntado; desunido; *adj.* unido, asociado; copartícipe; colectivo; **— account** cuenta en común; **— action** acción colectiva; **— committee** comisión mixta; **— creditor** acreedor copartícipe; **— heir** coheredero; **— session** sesión plena; **-ly** *adv.* juntamente, juntos, unidamente, colectivamente.

joke [dʒok] *s.* broma; chiste, chanza; *v.* bromear; chancear(se), *Am.* chotear.

joker [dʒókə] *s.* bromista, chancero, guasón, *Am.* choteador; naipe especial (*que no pertenece a ningún palo*).

jokingly [dʒókɪŋlɪ] *adv.* en (o de) chanza, en (o de) broma; de chiste.

jolly [dʒálɪ] *adj.* jovial; alegre; festivo; *v.* bromear, chancearse.

jolt [dʒolt] *s.* sacudida; sacudimiento; choque; *v.* sacudir.

jostle [dʒásl] *v.* rempujar o empujar, dar empellones; codear; *s.* rempujón, empujón, empellón.

jot [dʒɑt] *v.* to **— down** apuntar, tomar apuntes; *s.* jota, pizca.

journal [dʒɜnl] *s.* diario; periódico; revista; acta (*de una junta o concilio*).

journalism [dʒɜnlɪzəm] *s.* periodismo.

journalist [dʒɜnlɪst] *s.* periodista.

journalistic [dʒɜnlístɪk] *adj.* periodístico.

journey [dʒɜnɪ] *s.* viaje; jornada; *v.* viajar.

joy [dʒɔɪ] *s.* júbilo, regocijo; alegría, gusto, deleite; felicidad.

joyful [dʒɔ́ɪfəl] *adj.* regocijado, jubiloso; alegre; **-ly** *adv.* con regocijo, regocijadamente, con júbilo, alegremente.

joyous [dʒɔ́ɪəs] *adj.* jubiloso, alegre, gozoso.

jubilant [dʒúblənt] *adj.* jubiloso, alegre.

jubilee [dʒúblɪ] *s.* jubileo; júbilo.

judge [dʒʌdʒ] *s.* juez; **— advocate** auditor de un consejo militar; *v.* juzgar.

judgment [dʒʌ́dʒmənt] *s.* juicio; sentencia, fallo; opinión; discernimiento; **— day** día del juicio final.

judicial [dʒudfʃəl] *adj.* judicial.

judicious [dʒudfʃəs] *adj.* juicioso, cuerdo.

jug [dʒʌg] *s.* cántaro; jarro, jarra; botija; chirona (*cárcel*) *Am.* chirola.

juggle [dʒʌ́gl] *v.* hacer juegos de manos; hacer suertes; **to — the accounts** barajar (*o* manipular) las cuentas; *s.* juego de manos, suerte; trampa.

juggler [dʒʌ́glə] *s.* prestidigitador, malabarista.

juice [dʒus] *s.* jugo; zumo.

juiciness [dʒúsɪnɪs] *s.* jugosidad.

juicy [dʒúsɪ] *adj.* jugoso, zumoso; suculento; **a — story** un cuento picante.

July [dʒulái] *s.* julio.

jumble [dʒʌ́mbl] *v.* revolver(se), barajar, mezclar(se); *s.* mezcolanza, revoltijo; confusión.

jump [dʒʌmp] *v.* saltar; brincar; salvar (*de un salto*); hacer saltar; comerse una pieza (*en el juego de damas*); **to — at the chance** asir o aprovechar la oportunidad; **to — bail** perder la fianza por evasión; **to — over** saltar por encima de, salvar de un salto; **to — the track** descarrilarse; **to — to conclusions** hacer deducciones precipitadas; *s.* salto; brinco; subida repentina (*del precio*); **to be always on the —** andar siempre de aquí para allá; trajinar, trafagar, ser muy activo.

jumper [dʒʌ́mpə] *s.* saltador; chaquetón holgado (*de obrero*); vestido sin mangas (*puesto sobre la blusa de mujer*); **-s** traje de juego (*para niños*).

jumpy [dʒʌ́mpɪ] *adj.* saltón; asustadizo, nervioso.

junction [dʒʌ́ŋkʃən] *s.* unión, juntura; confluencia (*de dos ríos*); empalme (*de ferrocarriles*).

juncture [dʒʌ́ŋktʃə] *s.* juntura; coyuntura; **at this —** a esta sazón, en esta coyuntura.

June [dʒun] *s.* junio.

jungle [dʒʌ́ŋgl] *s.* selva; matorral; *Am.* jungla; *Am.* manigua.

junior [dʒúnjə] *adj.* menor, más joven; **— college** colegio para los dos primeros años del bachillerato; **John Smith, Junior (Jr.)** John Smith, hijo; *s.* estudiante del tercer año (*en escuela superior, colegio o universidad*).

junk [dʒʌŋk] *s.* basura, desperdicios; trastos viejos; cosa inservible; **Chinese —** junco chino (*embarcación pequeña*); *v.* desechar, echar a la basura.

jurisdiction [dʒurɪsdíkʃən] *s.* jurisdicción.

jurisprudence [dʒurɪsprúdns] *s.* jurisprudencia, derecho.

juror [dʒúrə] *s.* jurado, miembro de un jurado.

jury [dʒúri] *s.* jurado; **grand — jurado** de acusación.

just [dʒʌst] *adj.* justo; recto; exacto; *adv.* ni más ni menos, exactamente, justamente; precisamente; sólo, no más, nada más; apenas; **— now** ahora mismo; **he — left** acaba de salir, *Am.* salió recién; **she is — a little girl** no es más que una niña, es una niña no más; **to have —** acabar de.

justice [dʒʌstis] *s.* justicia; juez; magistrado.

justification [dʒʌstəfəkéʃən] *s.* justificación.

justify [dʒʌstəfai] *v.* justificar.

justly [dʒʌstli] *adv.* justamente; con razón.

jut [dʒʌt] *v.* sobresalir, proyectarse, extenderse; *s.* salidizo, proyección.

juvenile [dʒúvənl] *adj.* juvenil.

K

kangaroo [kæŋgərú] *s.* canguro.

keel [kil] *s.* quilla; *v.* dar de quilla (*voltear un barco*); **to —** over volcar(se); zozobrar; caerse patas arriba, desplomarse.

keen [kin] *adj.* agudo; afilado; perspicaz; ansioso.

keenness [kínnis] *s.* agudeza, perspicacia; anhelo, ansia.

keep [kip] *v.* guardar; tener guardado; tener; retener; conservar(se); preservar(se); mantener(se); **to — accounts** llevar las cuentas; **to — at it** persistir, seguir dale que dale; **to — away** mantener(se) alejado; **to — back** tener a raya; detener; reprimir, restringir; **to — from** impedir; guardar(se) de; abstenerse de; **to — going** seguir andando, seguir adelante; seguir viviendo; **to — off** no arrimarse, no acercarse; no entrar; mantener(se) a distancia; **to — one's hands off** no tocar; **to — one's temper** contenerse, refrenarse, reprimirse; **to — quiet** estarse quieto o callado; **to — something up** seguir o continuar haciendo algo; **to — to the right** seguir a la derecha, mantenerse a la derecha; **to — track of** llevar la cuenta de; no perder de vista; *s.* manutención, subsistencia; **for -s** para siempre; para guardar; dado, no prestado.

keeper [kípɚ] *s.* guardián, custodio; **jail — carcelero.**

keeping [kípɪŋ] *s.* custodia; mantenimiento; preservación, conservación; **in — with** en armonía con.

keepsake [kípsek] *s.* prenda, recuerdo, regalo.

keg [kɛg] *s.* tonel, barril.

kennel [kénl] *s.* perrera.

kept [kɛpt] *pret. & p.p. de* to keep.

kerchief [kɝtʃif] *s.* pañuelo, pañolón.

kernel [kɝnl] *s.* simiente; grano (*de trigo o maíz*); meollo (*de ciertas frutas como la nuez*); núcleo.

kerosene [kérəsin] *s.* kerosina, petróleo para lámparas.

kettle [kétl] *s.* caldera; **—drum** tímpano; **tea—** marmita, tetera, *Am.* pava (*para el mate*).

key [ki] *s.* llave; clave; tecla (*de piano, órgano o máquina de escribir*); cayo, isleta; **— ring** llavero; **to be in —** estar a tono, estar templado; estar en armonía; *v.* poner a tono, afinar, templar (*con llave*); armonizar; **to — up** elevar el tono de; **to be all -ed up** estar sobreexcitado, estar en tensión nerviosa.

keyboard [kíbord] *s.* teclado.

keyhole [kíhol] *s.* ojo de la cerradura.

keynote [kínot] *s.* nota tónica; idea o principio fundamental.

keystone [kíston] *s.* clave (*de un arco*); base, fundamento principal.

khaki [káki] *s.* kaki, caqui; *adj.* de kaki.

kick [kɪk] *s.* coz; patada; puntapié; queja; protesta; fuerza (*de una bebida*); estímulo; **to have a —** *Am.* patear (*dícese del licor*); *v.* cocear; dar coces o patadas; dar puntapiés; patear; quejarse, protestar; **to — out** echar a patadas; echar, expulsar; **to — the bucket** estirar la pata, morir, *Am.* patear el balde; **to — up a lot of dust** levantar una polvareda.

kid [kɪd] *s.* cabrito; cabritilla (*piel curtida de cabrito*); niño, niña; **— gloves** guantes de cabritilla; *v.* bromear, embromar; chancearse con, *Am.* chotear.

kidnap [kídnæp] *v.* secuestrar, raptar.

kidnapper [kídnæpɚ] *s.* secuestrador; robachicos, ladrón de niños.

kidnapping [kídnæpɪŋ] *s.* rapto, secuestro.

kidney [kídni] *s.* riñón; **— bean** judía, frijol; **— stones** cálculos.

kill [kɪl] *v.* matar; destruir; amortiguar; parar (*el motor*); *s.* animal o animales matados (*en la caza*).

killer [kílɚ] *s.* matador; asesino.

kiln [kɪln] *s.* horno.

kilo [kílo], **kilogram** [kíləgræm] *s.* kilo, kilogramo.

kilometer [kíləmitɚ] *s.* kilómetro.

kimono [kɪmónə] *s.* quimono; bata.

kin [kɪn] *s.* parentela, parientes, familia; **to notify the nearest of —** avisar al pariente o deudo más cercano.

kind [kaɪnd] *adj.* bondadoso; benévolo; amable; **to send one's — regards to** enviar afectuosos saludos a**; kind-hearted** de buen corazón; **— of tired** algo cansado; *s.* clase, especie, género; **to pay in —** pagar en especie; pagar en la misma moneda.

kindergarten [kíndəgartn] *s.* escuela de párvulos.

kindle [kíndl] *v.* encender(se); inflamar(se); incitar; prender (*el fuego*).

kindling [kíndrɪd] *s.* encendimiento; leña ligera, astillas, *Am.* charamuscas.

kindly [káɪndlɪ] *adj.* bondadoso; benigno; benévolo; amable, apacible; *adv.* bondadosamente, amablemente; con benevolencia; por favor; **not to take — to criticism** no aceptar de buen grado las correcciones.

kindness [káɪndnɪs] *s.* bondad, amabilidad; gentileza; benevolencia; favor.

kindred [kíndrɪd] *adj.* emparentado; allegado; semejante; **— facts** hechos relacionados; **— spirits** espíritus afines.

king [kɪŋ] *s.* rey; rey (*en ajedrez*); dama (*en el juego de damas*).

kingdom [kíŋdəm] *s.* reino.

kingly [kíŋlɪ] *adj.* regio, real; majestuoso; *adv.* regiamente; majestuosamente.

kinky [kíŋkɪ] *adj.* crespo, ensortijado, *Am.* grifo.

kinship [kínʃɪp] *s.* parentesco; afinidad; semejanza.

kinsman [kínzmən] *s.* pariente, deudo.

kiss [kɪs] *s.* beso; *v.* besar.

kit [kɪt] *s.* estuche, caja de herramientas; saco, envoltura (*para guardar instrumentos, herramientas, etc.*); gatito; **medicine —** botiquín; **soldier's —** mochila.

kitchen [kítʃɪn] *s.* cocina; **—ware** trastos de cocina.

kite [kaɪt] *s.* cometa (*f.*), *Am.* papalote; milano (*pájaro*).

kitten [kítn] *s.* gatito.

kitty [kítɪ] *s.* gatito, minino.

knack [næk] *s.* destreza, maña, habilidad.

knapsack [næpsæk] *s.* mochila, morral, alforja.

knave [nev] *s.* bribón, bellaco, pícaro; sota (*de naipes*).

knead [nid] *v.* amasar, sobar.

knee [ni] *s.* rodilla; **knee-deep** hasta la rodilla; metido hasta las rodillas.

kneel [nil] *v.* arrodillarse; hincarse.

knell [nɛl] *s.* doble (*toque de campanas por los difuntos*); *v.* doblar, tocar a muerto.

knelt [nɛlt] *pret.* & *p.p.* de **to kneel.**

knew [nju] *pret.* de **to know.**

knickknack [níknæk] *s.* chuchería, baratija, chisme.

knife [naɪf] *s.* cuchillo; cuchilla; **carving —** trinchante; **pocket —** cortaplumas; navaja; *v.* acuchillar.

knight [naɪt] *s.* caballero; campeón; caballo (*en ajedrez*); **— errant** caballero andante; *v.* armar caballero.

knighthood [náɪthʊd] *s.* caballería, orden de la caballería.

knit [nɪt] *v.* tejer (*a punto de aguja*); hacer calceta o malla; enlazar; soldarse (*un hueso*); **to — one's brow** fruncir las cejas, arrugar la frente; *pret.* & *p.p.* de **to knit.**

knitting [nítɪŋ] *s.* labor de punto; **— needle** aguja de media.

knives [naɪvz] *pl.* de **knife.**

knob [nab] *s.* perilla, botón, tirador (*de puerta, cajón, etc.*); protuberancia.

knock [nak] *v.* golpear; golpetear; llamar o tocar a la puerta; criticar, censurar; hablar mal de; **to — down** derribar; desmontar (*una máquina o aparato*); **to — off** suspender (*el trabajo*); rebajar (*del precio*); derribar, echar abajo; **to — out** aplastar de un golpe, poner fuera de combate; dejar sin sentido; *s.* golpe; golpeteo; toque, llamada, aldabonazo; crítica, censura; **knock-kneed** zambo, patizambo.

knocker [nákə] *s.* llamador, aldaba, aldabón; criticón, murmurador.

knoll [nol] *s.* colina, loma; eminencia.

knot [nat] *s.* nudo; lazo; *v.* anudar(se).

knotty [nátɪ] *adj.* nudoso; dificultoso, enredado.

know [no] *v.* conocer; saber; reconocer; distinguir; **to — how to swim** saber nadar; **to — of** saber de; tener conocimiento de; tener noticias de; estar enterado de.

knowingly [nóɪŋlɪ] *adv.* a sabiendas; adrede.

knowledge [nálɪdʒ] *s.* conocimiento; saber, sabiduría; pericia; **not to my — no** que yo sepa.

known [non] *p.p.* de **to know.**

knuckle [nʌkl] *s.* nudillo; coyuntura, articulación; *v.* someterse; **to — down** someterse; aplicarse con empeño al trabajo.

L

label [lébl] *s.* marbete, etiqueta, rótulo; *v.* marcar, rotular; apodar, llamar.

labor [lébə] *s.* trabajo; labor; obra; mano de obra; la clase obrera; **— union**

unión de obreros; **to be in** — estar de parto; v. trabajar; afanarse; estar de parto; elaborar (un punto).

laboratory [lǽbrətorɪ] s. laboratorio.

laborer [lébərə] s. trabajador, obrero; jornalero, peón.

laborious [ləbóriəs] adj. laborioso, trabajoso, penoso; industrioso.

labyrinth [lǽbərɪnɵ] s. laberinto.

lace [les] s. encaje; cordón, cordoncillo, cinta (de zapato, de corsé, etc.); **gold** — galón de oro (para guarnecer uniformes); v. atar con cinta o córdón; guarnecer con encajes; enlazar, entrelazar.

lack [læk] s. falta; escasez, carencia; deficiencia; v. carecer de, faltarle a uno; necesitar; **he** -**s courage** le falta ánimo.

lacking [lǽkɪŋ] adj. falto, carente.

lacquer [lǽkə] s. laca; v. barnizar con laca.

lad [læd] s. rapaz, chico.

ladder [lǽdə] s. escalera de mano.

laden [lédn] adj. cargado; agobiado, abrumado; v. cargar; agobiar.

ladies [lédɪz] pl. de **lady.**

ladle [lédl] s. cucharón; v. servir (sopa) con cucharón.

lady [lédɪ] s. señora; dama; —**like** como señora, muy fina, elegante; —**love** amada, querida.

lag [læg] v. rezagarse, quedarse atrás, atrasarse; andar lentamente; s. retardo o retardación, retraso.

lagoon [ləgún] s. laguna.

laid [led] pret. & p.p. de **to lay; to be** — **up** estar incapacitado o estropeado.

lain [len] p.p. de **to lie.**

lair [ler] s. guarida; cueva de fieras.

lake [lek] s. lago.

lamb [læm] s. cordero; —**kin** corderito.

lame [lem] adj. cojo; lisiado, estropeado; — **excuse** disculpa falsa; v. hacer cojo; estropear, incapacitar.

lament [ləmént] s. lamento; v. lamentar(se).

lamentable [lǽməntəbl] adj. lamentable; doloroso.

lamentation [læməntéʃən] s. lamentación, lamento.

lamp [læmp] s. lámpara; linterna; farol; —**post** poste (de farol); —**shade** pantalla de lámpara.

lance [læns] s. lanza; v. alancear, lancear, herir con lanza; picar con bisturí.

land [lænd] s. tierra; terreno; suelo; v. desembarcar; aterrizar (un avión); llegar; coger (un pez); **to** — **a job** conseguir una colocacion, lograr un

empleo.

landholder [lǽndholdə] s. terrateniente, propietario, hacendado.

landing [lǽndɪŋ] s. desembarco, desembarque; aterrizaje (de un avión); desembarcadero; descanso (de escalera); — **field** campo de aterrizaje; aeropuerto; — **strip** pista de aterrizaje.

landlady [lǽndledɪ] s. patrona, casera, dueña (de la casa).

landlord [lǽndlɔrd] s. amo, patrón, propietario, dueño; casero.

landmark [lǽndmark] s. mojón, señal (para fijar los confines); marca; suceso culminante.

landowner [lǽndonə] s. terrateniente, propietario, hacendado.

landscape [lǽndskep] s. paisaje.

landslide [lǽndslaɪd] s. derrumbe, derrumbamiento, desplome; gran mayoría de votos.

lane [len] s. senda, vereda; callejuela; ruta, derrotero (de vapores o aviones).

language [lǽŋgwɪdʒ] s. lengua; idioma; lenguaje.

languid [lǽŋgwɪd] adj. lánguido.

languish [lǽŋgwɪʃ] v. languidecer.

languor [lǽŋgə] s. languidez.

lank [læŋk] adj. alto y delgado, largucho.

lanky [lǽŋkɪ] adj. largucho, zancón, zancudo.

lantern [lǽntən] s. linterna; farol.

lap [læp] s. falda, regazo; aleta; etapa, trecho (de una carrera); v. lamer; **to** — **over** cruzar(se) sobre, entrecruzar-(se).

lapel [ləpél] s. solapa.

lapse [læps] s. lapso; transcurso; desliz, error; v. deslizarse; pasar, transcurrir; caer en un desliz; decaer (el entusiasmo, el interés, etc.); caducar (un plazo, un contrato, etc.).

larboard [lúrbəd] s. babor; adj. de babor; — **side** banda de babor.

larceny [lársnɪ] s. latrocinio, hurto; ratería.

lard [lard] s. lardo, manteca de puerco; v. mechar.

large [lardʒ] adj. grande; **at** — suelto, libre; sin trabas; en general; -**ly** adv. grandemente, en gran parte.

lariat [lǽrɪət] s. reata.

lark [lark] s. alondra; diversión, holgorio, jarana; **to go on a** — ir o andar de jarana.

larva [lárvə] s. larva.

larynx [lǽrɪŋks] s. laringe.

lascivious [ləsívɪəs] adj. lascivo.

lash [læʃ] s. látigo; azote, latigazo; pestaña; v. fustigar; azotar; censurar, reprender; amarrar.

lass [læs] *s.* moza, muchacha, doncella.

lassitude [lǽsətjud] *s.* dejadez, flojedad, decaimiento de fuerzas.

lasso [lǽso] *s.* lazo, reata, mangana, *Am.* guaso; *v.* lazar, *Am.* enlazar.

last [læst] *adj.* último; final; pasado; — **night** anoche; — **year** el año pasado; **at** — por fin, finalmente, al fin; **next to the** — penúltimo; **to arrive** — llegar el último; *s.* fin, término; horma (*de zapato*); *v.* durar; perdurar; **-ly** *adv.* finalmente, en conclusión.

lasting [lǽstɪŋ] *adj.* duradero; perdurable.

latch [lætʃ] *s.* pestillo, picaporte, aldaba, cerrojo; *v.* cerrar con aldaba.

late [let] *adj.* tardío; tardo; reciente; último; —**comer** recién llegado; rezagado; **a** — **hour** una hora avanzada; **the** — **Mr. X** el finado (o difunto) Sr. X; **to have a** — **supper** cenar tarde; *adv.* tarde; — **in the night a una hora** avanzada de la noche; — **into the night a deshoras de la noche;** — **in the week a fines de la semana; of** — últimamente, recientemente; hace poco; **to be** — ser tarde; llegar tarde; estar atrasado, venir o llegar con retraso (*el tren*); **the train was ten minutes** — el tren llegó con diez minutos de retraso; **-ly** últimamente, recientemente; hace poco, poco ha.

latent [létn̩t] *adj.* latente.

later [létə] *adv. & adj.* (*comp. de* late) más tarde; después; luego; más reciente; posterior.

lateral [lǽtərəl] *adj.* lateral.

latest [létɪst] *adv. & adj.* (*superl. de* late) más tarde; más reciente, más nuevo; último; **the** — **fashion** la última moda, las últimas novedades; **the**—**news** las últimas novedades, las noticias más recientes; **at the** — a más tardar.

lathe [leð] *s.* torno (*de carpintero o mecánico*).

lather [lǽðə] *s.* jabonadura, espuma de jabón; *v.* jabonar, enjabonar; espumar, hacer espuma.

Latin [lǽtn̩] *adj.* latino; *s.* latín.

latitude [lǽtətjud] *s.* latitud; libertad; amplitud.

latter [lǽtə] *adj.* último; **towards the** — **part of the week a** (o hacia) fines de la semana; **the** — éste (ésta, esto, *etc.*).

lattice [lǽtɪs] *s.* celosía; enrejado, rejilla.

laud [lɔd] *v.* loar, encomiar, alabar.

laudable [lɔ́dəbl̩] *adj.* laudable, loable.

laugh [læf] *v.* reír(se); **to** — **at** reírse de;

to — **loudly** reírse a carcajadas; **to** — **in one's sleeve** reírse para sus adentros; **she -ed in his face** se rió en sus barbas; *s.* risa; **loud** — risotada, carcajada, risada.

laughable [lǽfəbl̩] *adj.* risible; ridículo.

laughter [lǽftə] *s.* risa.

launch [lɔntʃ] *v.* botar o echar (*un barco*) al agua; lanzar; empezar; poner en operación; **to** — **forth** lanzarse; **to** — **forth on a journey** emprender un viaje; *s.* lancha.

launder [lɔ́ndə] *v.* lavar y planchar (*la ropa*).

laundress [lɔ́ndrɪs] *s.* lavandera.

laundry [lɔ́ndrɪ] *s.* lavandería; lavado; ropa (lavada).

laurel [lɔ́rəl] *s.* laurel; gloria, honor.

lava [lávə] *s.* lava.

lavatory [lǽvətorɪ] *s.* lavabo; lavamanos; lavatorio.

lavender [lǽvəndə] *s.* espliego, lavándula; *adj.* lila, morado claro.

lavish [lǽvɪʃ] *adj.* gastador, pródigo, dadivoso; abundante, copioso; profuso; lujoso; *v.* prodigar; malgastar, despilfarrar; **to** — **praise upon** colmar de alabanzas a; **-ly** pródigamente; copiosamente; lujosamente.

law [lɔ] *s.* ley; derecho, jurisprudencia; regla; — **student** estudiante de leyes, estudiante de derecho; **law-abiding** observante de la ley.

lawbreaker [lɔ́brekə] *s.* infractor, transgresor.

lawful [lɔ́fəl] *adj.* legal; lícito; válido; permitido.

lawless [lɔ́lɪs] *adj.* sin ley; ilegal; desenfrenado; revoltoso; licencioso.

lawmaker [lɔ́mekə] *s.* legislador.

lawn [lɔn] *s.* césped, prado; linón (*tela de hilo o algodón*); — **mower** cortadora de césped.

lawsuit [lɔ́sut] *s.* pleito, litigio.

lawyer [lɔ́jə] *s.* abogado, jurisconsulto.

lax [læks] *adj.* flojo; suelto; relajado.

laxative [lǽksətɪv] *adj. & s.* laxante, purgante.

laxity [lǽksətɪ] *s.* flojedad, flojera; relajamiento (*de una regla, ley, etc.*).

lay [le] *pret. de* lie.

lay [le] *v.* colocar; poner; tender, extender; poner (*huevos*); echar (*la culpa*); atribuir (*la responsabilidad*); presentar, exponer; asentar (*el polvo*); **to** — **a wager** apostar; **to** — **aside** poner a un lado; ahorrar; **to** — **away** (o by) guardar; **to** — **bare** revelar; exponer; **to** — **down** poner, colocar; rendir (*las armas*); **to** — **down the law** mandar, dictar; **to — hold of** asir, agarrar; **to — off** a workman suspender a un obrero; **to — open** exponer a la vista; **to — out** a plan trazar un plan; **to — up** almacenar; guardar, ahorrar; **to be laid up** estar incapacitado c estropeado; **to — waste** asolar; *s.* lay, balada, canción; situación, orientación (*del terreno*); *adj.* lego, laico; profano (*no iniciado en una ciencia*).

layer [léə] *s.* capa; estrato; gallina ponedora.

layman [lémən] *s.* lego, seglar, laico.

lazily [lézɪlɪ] *adv.* perezosamente.

laziness [lézɪnɪs] *s.* pereza.

lazy [lézɪ] *adj.* perezoso, holgazán.

lead [lɛd] *s.* plomo; plomada, pesa de plomo.

lead [lid] *v.* guiar, dirigir; llevar; conducir; mandar (*un ejército*); ir a la cabeza de; sobresalir entre; ser mano (*en el juego de naipes*); **to — an orchestra** dirigir una orquesta, llevar la batuta; **to — astray** llevar por mal camino, extraviar, descarriar; **to — the way** ir por delante, mostrar el camino; *s.* delantera, primer lugar; mando, dirección; indicio; papel principal; primer actor.

leaden [lɛdṇ] *adj.* plomizo; aplomado, color de plomo; pesado.

leader [lídə] *s.* jefe, caudillo, *Am.* líder; director; guía; caballo delantero; **-s** puntos suspensivos.

leadership [lídəʃɪp] *s.* dirección, mando; iniciativa.

leading [lídɪŋ] *adj.* principal; delantero; **— man** primer actor.

leaf [lif] *s.* hoja; *v.* echar hojas (*un árbol*), cubrirse de hojas; **to — through a book** hojear un libro.

leafless [líflɪs] *adj.* sin hojas, deshojado.

leaflet [líflɪt] *s.* hojilla; folleto, hoja volante, papel volante, circular.

leafy [lífɪ] *adj.* frondoso.

league [lig] *s.* liga, confederación; sociedad; legua; *v.* asociar(se); ligarse, coligarse.

leak [lik] *s.* gotera (*en un techo*); agujero, grieta (*por donde se escapa el agua o el gas*); escape (*de gas, vapor, electricidad, etc.*); *v.* gotear(se); rezumar(se); hacer agua (*dícese de un barco*); salirse, escaparse (*el gas, el vapor, etc.*).

lean [lin] *v.* inclinar(se); recostar(se), reclinar(se), apoyar(se); *adj.* magro, flaco; **— year** año estéril, año improductivo.

leant [lɛnt] = **leaned.**

leap [lip] *v.* saltar; brincar; *s.* salto, brin-

co; **— year** año bisiesto.

leapt [lɛpt] *pret. & p.p. de* **to leap.**

learn [lɜn] *v.* aprender; saber, averiguar, enterarse de.

learned [lɜ́nɪd] *adj.* erudito; docto.

learner [lɜ́nə] *s.* aprendedor; estudiante, estudioso.

learning [lɜ́nɪŋ] *s.* erudición, saber; aprendizaje.

learnt [lɜnt] *pret. & p.p. de* **to learn.**

lease [lis] *v.* arrendar, dar o tomar en arriendo; *s.* arriendo, contrato de arrendamiento.

least [list] *adj.* (el) mínimo, (el) más pequeño; *adv.* menos; **at —** al menos, a lo menos, por lo menos; **the —** lo (el, la) menos.

leather [léðə] *s.* cuero, piel; *adj.* de cuero, de piel; **— strap** correa.

leave [liv] *v.* dejar; abandonar; salir (de); partir; irse; **to — out** dejar fuera; omitir; *s.* permiso, licencia; **— of absence** licencia; **to take — of** despedirse de.

leaven [lévən] *s.* levadura, fermento; *v.* fermentar (*la masa*).

leaves [livz] *pl. de* **leaf.**

leavings [lívɪŋz] *s.* sobras, desperdicios.

lecture [léktʃə] *s.* conferencia, discurso; reprensión; *v.* dar una conferencia; explicar; reprender.

lecturer [léktʃərə] *s.* conferenciante; lector (*de universidad*).

led [lɛd] *pret. & p.p. de* **to lead.**

ledge [lɛdʒ] *s.* borde; salidizo.

ledger [lédʒə] *s.* libro mayor (*en contabilidad*).

leech [litʃ] *s.* sanguijuela.

leer [lɪr] *s.* mirada de soslayo, mirada lujuriosa; *v.* mirar de soslayo; mirar con lujuria.

left [lɛft] *pret. & p.p. de* **to leave; I have two books —** me quedan dos libros; *adj.* izquierdo; *s.* izquierda; mano izquierda; **at (on, to) the —** a la izquierda.

left-handed [léfthændɪd] *adj.* zurdo; a la izquierda; torpe; malicioso, insincero; **— compliment** alabanza irónica.

leftist [léftɪst] *s.* izquierdista.

leftover [léftovə] *adj.* sobrante; **-s** *s. pl.* sobras.

leg [lɛg] *s.* pierna; pata (*de animal, mesa, etc.*); pie o pata (*de banquillo, silla, etc.*); etapa, trecho (*de una carrera o viaje*); **to be on one's last -s** estar en las últimas.

legacy [légəsɪ] *s.* legado, herencia.

legal [lígḷ] *adj.* legal; lícito.

legalize [líglaɪz] *v.* legalizar; sancionar,

autorizar.
legate [légɪt] *s.* legado; delegado.
legation [lɪgéʒən] *s.* legación; embajada.
legend [lédʒənd] *s.* leyenda; letrero, inscripción.
legendary [lédʒəndɛrɪ] *adj.* legendario.
leggings [légɪŋz] *s. pl.* polainas.
legion [lídʒən] *s.* legión.
legislate [lédʒɪslet] *v.* legislar.
legislation [ledʒɪsléʃən] *s.* legislación.
legislative [lédʒɪslɛtɪv] *adj.* legislativo.
legislator [lédʒɪsletə] *s.* legislador.
legislature [lédʒɪsletʃə] *s.* legislatura, asamblea legislativa.
legitimate [lɪdʒítəmɪt] *adj.* legítimo.
leisure [líʒə] *s.* ocio; — hours horas de ocio; **to be at** — estar ocioso; estar libre o desocupado; **do it at your** — hágalo Vd. cuando pueda o le convenga; hágalo Vd. en sus ratos de ocio.
leisurely [líʒəlɪ] *adj.* lento, deliberado, pausado; *adv.* sin prisa, despacio, a sus (mis, tus, *etc.*) anchas.
lemon [lémən] *s.* limón; — **tree** limonero; *adj.* de limón; — **color** cetrino.
lemonade [lemənéd] *s.* limonada.
lend [lend] *v.* prestar.
lender [léndə] *s.* prestador; **money** — prestamista.
length [leŋkə] *s.* largo, largor, largura, longitud; duración; cantidad (*de una sílaba*); **at** — largamente, detenidamente; **al fin; to go to any** — hacer cuanto esté de su parte.
lengthen [léŋkeən] *v.* alargar(se); prolongar(se).
lengthwise [léŋkəwaɪz] *adv.* a lo largo; longitudinalmente; *adj.* longitudinal.
lengthy [léŋkɔɪ] *adj.* largo, prolongado.
lenient [líniənt] *adj.* indulgente, clemente, poco severo.
lens [lenz] *s.* lente; cristalino (*del ojo*).
lent [lent] *pret. & p.p. de* **to lend**.
Lent [lent] *s.* cuaresma.
leopard [lépəd] *s.* leopardo.
less [les] *adj.* menor; *adv. & prep.* menos; — **and** — cada vez menos.
lessen [lésn] *v.* aminorar(se), disminuir(se), reducir(se); mermar.
lesser [lésə] *adj.* menor, más pequeño.
lesson [lésn] *s.* lección.
lest [lest] *conj.* no sea que, por miedo de que.
let [let] *v.* dejar, permitir; alquilar, arrendar; — **us** (*o* **let's**) **do it** vamos a hacerlo, hagámoslo; — **him come** que venga; **to** — **be** no molestar, dejar en paz; no tocar; **to** — **down** bajar; desilusionar; **to** — **go** soltar; **to** — **in** dejar entrar, admitir; **to** —

know avisar, enterar, hacer saber; **to** — **off** soltar; dejar libre; **to** — **through** dejar pasar; **to** — **up** disminuir; *pret. & p.p. de* **to let**.
lethargy [léəədʒɪ] *s.* letargo; **to fall into a** — aletargarse.
letter [létə] *s.* letra; carta; — **box** buzón; — **carrier** cartero; —**head** membrete; *v.* rotular, hacer a mano letras de molde.
lettuce [létɪs] *s.* lechuga.
level [lévl] *adj.* llano, plano; a nivel; igual; parejo; **level-headed** bien equilibrado, sensato; *adv.* a nivel; a ras; *s.* nivel; **to be on the** — obrar rectamente, obrar sin engaño; ser o decir la pura verdad; *v.* nivelar; igualar; allanar; apuntar, asestar (*un arma*); **to** — **to the ground** arrasar, echar por tierra.
lever [lévə] *s.* palanca; **control** — palanca de mando.
levy [lévɪ] *s.* imposición, recaudación (*de tributos, impuestos, etc.*); leva, enganche, reclutamiento; embargo (*de propiedad*); *v.* imponer, exigir, recaudar (*tributos o multas*); reclutar; **to** — **on someone's property** embargar la propiedad de alguien.
lewd [lud] *adj.* lujurioso, lascivo, deshonesto.
lewdness [lúdnɪs] *s.* lascivia, lujuria.
liability [laɪəbflɑtɪ] *s.* responsabilidad; obligación; desventaja; **liabilities** obligaciones, deudas; pasivo.
liable [láɪəbl] *adj.* responsable, obligado; sujeto, expuesto; propenso; probable.
liar [láɪə] *s.* mentiroso, embustero.
libel [láɪbl] *s.* libelo; difamación; *v.* difamar.
liberal [lɪbərəl] *adj. & s.* liberal.
liberality [lɪbərǽlətɪ] *s.* liberalidad; largueza, generosidad.
liberate [lɪbəret] *v.* libertar, librar; soltar.
liberation [lɪbəréʃən] *s.* liberación.
liberator [lɪbəretə] *s.* libertador.
libertine [lɪbətin] *adj. & s.* libertino.
liberty [lɪbətɪ] *s.* libertad; **at** — libre.
librarian [laɪbrérɪən] *s.* bibliotecario.
library [láɪbrɛrɪ] *s.* biblioteca.
lice [laɪs] *pl. de* **louse**.
license, licence [láɪsns] *s.* licencia; permiso; título; **driver's** — licencia (pase, certificado o patente) de chófer; título de conductor; licencia para manejar; — **plate** placa (*o* chapa) de numeración, chapa de circulación, chapa de matrícula; *v.* licenciar, dar licencia a; permitir, autorizar.

licentious [laɪsénʃəs] *adj.* licencioso, disoluto.

lick [lɪk] *v.* lamer; dar una tunda o zurra; vencer; **to — someone's boots** adular a uno con servilismo; **to — the dust** morder el polvo; adular; *s.* lamedura, *Am.* lamida; lengüetada; **salt —** lamedero (*lugar salino donde lame el ganado*); **not to do a — of work** no hacer absolutamente nada.

licking [líkɪŋ] *s.* zurra, tunda.

lid [lɪd] *s.* tapadera, tapa; **eye—** párpado.

lie [laɪ] *s.* mentira; embuste; **to give the — to** desmentir, dar un mentís; *v.* mentir (*pret. & p.p.* lied); tenderse, acostarse; yacer; estar; estar situado; consistir (en); **to — back** recostarse, echarse hacia atrás; **to — down** acostarse, echarse, tenderse; **to — in wait** acechar, espiar.

lieutenant [luténənt] *s.* teniente; **second —** subteniente.

life [laɪf] *s.* vida; **from — del natural; still — naturaleza muerta; —boat** bote de salvamento, lancha salvavidas; **— imprisonment** prisión perpetua; **— insurance** seguro sobre la vida; **— pension** pensión vitalicia; **— preserver** salvavidas, cinto o chaqueta de salvamento.

lifeless [laɪflɪs] *adj.* sin vida; muerto; exánime; inanimado; desanimado.

lifelessness [láɪflɪsnɪs] *s.* falta de vida; inercia; falta de animación.

lifelike [láɪflaɪk] *adj.* como la vida; natural, que parece vivo.

lifelong [láɪflɔ́ŋ] *adj.* perpetuo, de toda la vida.

lifetime [láɪftaɪm] *s.* vida, transcurso de la vida.

lift [lɪft] *v.* levantar; alzar; elevar; disiparse (*las nubes, la niebla, las tinieblas*); **to — one's hat** quitarse el sombrero (*para saludar*); *s.* elevación; exaltación de ánimo; alzamiento, levantamiento; carga; ayuda (*para levantar una carga*); alza (*de un zapato*); ascensor, *Am.* elevador; **to give someone a — in a car** llevar a alguien en el auto.

light [laɪt] *s.* luz; lumbre; **tail — Am.** farito trasero, *Am.* farol de cola, *Am.* calavera; *adj.* claro; con luz; de tez blanca; ligero; leve; frívolo; **— drink** bebida suave; **—headed** frívolo, ligero de cascos; **—hearted** alegre; **— opera** opereta; **to make — of** dar poca importancia a; *v.* encender(se); iluminar, alumbrar; **to — upon** caer

sobre; posarse en (*dícese de los pájaros, mariposas, etc.*).

lighten [láɪtn] *v.* aligerar; iluminar; aclarar; relampaguear; alegrar.

lighter [láɪtə] *s.* encendedor.

lighthouse [láɪthaus] *s.* faro.

lighting [láɪtɪŋ] *s.* iluminación; alumbrado.

lightly [láɪtlɪ] *adv.* ligeramente; levemente; frívolamente; sin seriedad.

lightness [láɪtnɪs] *s.* ligereza; frivolidad; claridad.

lightning [láɪtnɪŋ] *s.* relampagueo; relámpago; **— rod** pararrayos.

likable [láɪkəbl] *adj.* agradable, simpático, placentero.

like [laɪk] *adv. & prep.* como; del mismo modo que; semejante a; *adj.* semejante, parecido; **in — manner** de manera semejante, del mismo modo; **to feel — going** tener ganas de ir; **to look — someone** parecerse a alguien; **it looks — rain** parece que va a llover, quiere llover; *s.* semejante, igual; **-s** gustos; preferencias; *v.* gustarle a uno; **he -s books** le gustan los libros; **do whatever you —** haz lo que gustes.

likely [láɪklɪ] *adj.* probable, creíble; prometedor; **— place** lugar a propósito; **it is — to happen** es probable que suceda; *adv.* probablemente.

liken [láɪkən] *v.* asemejar, comparar.

likeness [láɪknɪs] *s.* semejanza; parecido; retrato.

likewise [láɪkwaɪz] *adv.* igualmente, asimismo; del mismo modo; también.

liking [láɪkɪŋ] *s.* simpatía; afición; preferencia, gusto.

lilac [láɪlək] *s.* lila; *adj.* lila, morado claro.

lily [lílɪ] *s.* lirio; azucena.

limb [lɪm] *s.* rama (*de árbol*); miembro (*del cuerpo*), pierna, brazo.

limber [límbə] *adj.* flexible; ágil; *v.* hacer flexible; **to — up** agilitar(se), hacer(se) flexible.

lime [laɪm] *s.* cal; lima (*fruta*); liga (*para cazar pájaros*).

limelight [láɪmlaɪt] *s.* luz de calcio; proscenio; **to be in the —** estar a la vista del público.

limestone [láɪmston] *s.* piedra caliza.

limit [límɪt] *s.* límite; confín; *v.* limitar.

limitation [lɪmɪtéʃən] *s.* limitación; restricción.

limited [límɪtɪd] *adj.* limitado; restringido.

limitless [límɪtlɪs] *adj.* ilimitado, sin límites.

limp [lɪmp] *s.* cojera; *v.* cojear; renquear;

adj. flojo; flexible.

limpid [límpɪd] *adj.* límpido; claro, transparente.

line [laɪn] *s.* línea; renglón; raya; cuerda; ramo, giro *(de negocios);* especialidad; — **of goods** surtido, línea (*Am.* renglón) de mercancías; **branch railway** — ramal; **pipe** — cañería, tubería; **to bring into** — alinear; obligar a proceder de acuerdo con un plan; poner de acuerdo; **to get in** — meterse en fila, hacer (*o* formar) cola; *v.* linear, rayar; alinear; forrar; **to** — **up** alinear(se); formarse, formar fila.

lineage [línɪɪdʒ] *s.* linaje.

linear [línɪə] *adj.* lineal.

lined [laɪnd] *adj.* rayado; forrado.

linen [línɪn] *s.* lino; ropa blanca.

liner [láɪnə] *s.* vapor, buque; **air** — avión, transporte aéreo.

linger [língə] *v.* tardar(se), demorarse, dilatarse; andar ocioso, vagar; perdurar; prolongarse.

lingerie [lænʒəri] *s.* ropa interior de mujer.

lining [láɪnɪŋ] *s.* forro.

link [lɪŋk] *s.* eslabón; enlace; **cuff** —**s** gemelos; *v.* eslabonar(se); enlazar(se).

linnet [línɪt] *s.* jilguero.

linoleum [lɪnólɪəm] *s.* linóleo (*tela impermeable para cubrir el suelo*).

linseed [línsid] *s.* linaza; — **oil** aceite de linaza.

lint [lɪnt] *s.* hilas; hilachas.

lion [láɪən] *s.* león.

lioness [láɪənɪs] *s.* leona.

lip [lɪp] *s.* labio.

lipstick [lípstɪk] *s.* lápiz para los labios.

liquid [líkwɪd] *adj.* líquido; — **assets** valores líquidos (*o* realizables); — **measure** medida para líquidos; *s.* líquido.

liquidate [líkwɪdet] *v.* liquidar, saldar (*cuentas*); poner término a.

liquidation [lɪkwɪdéʃən] *s.* liquidación; saldo de cuentas.

liquor [líkə] *s.* licor; bebida espiritosa (*como aguardiente, ron, etc.*).

lisp [lɪsp] *s.* ceceo; *v.* cecear; balbucir.

list [lɪst] *s.* lista; registro; escora (*inclinación de un barco*); *v.* alistar, registrar, poner o apuntar en una lista; hacer una lista de; escorar, inclinarse a la banda.

listen [lísn̩] *v.* escuchar; atender, dar oídos, prestar atención; — ! ¡oye! ¡escucha!; ¡oiga! ¡escuche!; **to** — **in** escuchar por radio; escuchar a hurtadillas (*una conversación*).

listener [lísn̩ə] *s.* escuchador, oyente;

radio — radioescucha, radioyente.

listless [lístlɪs] *adj.* abstraído; indiferente; indolente; desatento.

listlessness [lístlɪsnɪs] *s.* indiferencia, inatención, abstracción.

lit [lɪt] *pret. & p.p. de* **to light;** *adj.* alumbrado; algo borracho.

literal [lítərəl] *adj.* literal; **-ly** *adv.* al pie de la letra, literalmente.

literary [lítərɛrɪ] *adj.* literario.

literature [lítərətʃur] *s.* literatura; impresos, folletos, circulares.

litigation [lɪtɪgéʃən] *s.* litigio, pleito.

litter [lítə] *s.* camada, cría; litera; canilla; cama de paja (*para animales*); cosas esparcidas en desorden; desorden, revoltillo; *v.* desarreglar, revolver, esparcir cosas por.

little [lítl̩] *adj.* pequeño; poco; — **Bear** Osa Menor; **a** — **coffee** un poco de café; **a** — **while** un ratito (*o* ratico), un poco; *adv. & s.* poco; — **by** — poco a poco.

live [lɪv] *v.* vivir; **to** — **down** hacer olvidar, borrar (*el pasado*); **to** — **up to** vivir en conformidad con, vivir de acuerdo con.

live [laɪv] *adj.* vivo; enérgico, activo; — **coal** ascua encendida; — **oak** encina: — **question** cuestión palpitante, cuestión de actualidad; — **wire** alambre cargado; persona muy activa.

livelihood [láɪvlɪhʌd] *s.* vida, alimento, subsistencia, manutención.

liveliness [láɪvlɪnɪs] *s.* viveza, animación; agilidad.

lively [láɪvlɪ] *adj.* vivo; vivaz; animado, alegre; airoso; — **horse** caballo brioso; *adv.* vivamente; de prisa.

liver [lívə] *s.* hígado; vividor.

livery [lívərɪ] *s.* librea; caballeriza (*para caballos de alquiler*); **auto** — **garage** para autos de alquiler.

lives [laɪvz] *pl. de* **life.**

livestock [láɪvstak] *s.* ganado.

livid [lívɪd] *adj.* lívido; amoratado.

living [lívɪŋ] *s.* vida; manutención, subsistencia; *adj.* vivo; viviente; — **room** sala; — **wage** sueldo suficiente para vivir; **the** — los vivos.

lizard [lízəd] *s.* lagarto; **small** — lagartija.

load [lod] *s.* carga; **ship** — cargamento; **-s of** gran cantidad de; montones de; *v.* cargar; agobiar; colmar.

loaf [lof] *s.* hogaza de pan; **sugar** — azúcar de pilón; *v.* holgazanear, haraganear.

loafer [lófə] *s.* holgazán, haragán, zángano.

loan [lon] *s.* préstamo; empréstito; — **shark** usurero; *v.* prestar (*dinero*).

loath [loθ] *adj.* maldispuesto, renuente; **to be — to** repugnarle a uno.

loathe [loð] *v.* repugnarle a uno; abominar.

loathsome [lóðsəm] *adj.* repugnante, asqueroso; aborrecible.

loaves [lovz] *pl. de* **loaf.**

lobby [lábɪ] *s.* vestíbulo; antecámara; salón de entrada; camarilla (*que busca ventajas ante un cuerpo legislativo*); **hotel —** vestíbulo o patio del hotel; *v.* cabildear (*procurar ventajas o partidarios en una asamblea*).

lobster [lábstə] *s.* langosta de mar.

local [lókl] *adj.* local; — **train** tren ordinario.

locality [lokǽlətɪ]*s.* localidad; comarca.

localize [lóklaɪz] *v.* localizar.

locate [lóket] *v.* situar, establecer; localizar, averiguar la posición de; avecindarse, radicarse, establecerse.

location [lokéʃən] *s.* situación; sitio, localidad.

lock [lak] *s.* cerradura; esclusa (*de un canal*); llave (*de un arma de fuego*); guedeja (*de pelo*); bucle, rizo; *v.* cerrar con llave; trabar(se), juntar(se); entrelazar(se); **to — in** encerrar; **to — out** cerrar la puerta (*a alguien*), dejar afuera; **to — up** encerrar; encarcelar.

locket [lákɪt] *s.* guardapelo.

lockout [lákaʊt] *s.* paro (*suspensión del trabajo por parte de los empresarios*); cierre de fábrica.

locksmith [láksmɪə] *s.* cerrajero.

locomotive [lokəmótɪv] *s.* locomotora; — **engineer** maquinista.

locust [lókəst] *s.* langosta, saltamontes; cigarra; — **tree** algarrobo; acacia falsa.

lodge [ladʒ] *s.* logia; casita accesoria; casa de campo; *v.* alojar(se); hospedar(se); colocar; **to — a complaint** presentar una queja.

lodger [ládʒə] *s.* huésped, inquilino.

lodging [ládʒɪŋ] *s.* alojamiento, hospedaje; vivienda.

loft [lɔft] *s.* desván; galería, balcón interior (*de un templo*); **choir —** coro; **hay —** pajar.

lofty [lɔ́ftɪ] *adj.* elevado; sublime; altivo.

log [lag] *s.* leño, troza, tronco aserrado; corredera (*aparato para medir las millas que anda la nave*); diario de navegación; — **cabin** cabaña de troncos; *v.* cortar (*árboles*); cortar leños y transportarlos; registrar (*en el diario de navegación*).

logic [ládʒɪk] *s.* lógica.

logical [ládʒɪkl] *adj.* lógico.

loin [lɔɪn] *s.* ijada, ijar, lomo.

loiter [lɔ́ɪtə] *v.* holgazanear, vagar, malgastar el tiempo; **to — behind** rezagarse.

loll [lal] *v.* arrellanarse o repantigarse, recostarse con toda comodidad.

lone [lon] *adj.* solo, solitario.

loneliness [lónlɪnɪs] *s.* soledad.

lonely [lónlɪ] *adj.* solo, solitario; triste, desamparado.

lonesome [lónsəm] *adj.* solo, solitario; triste, nostálgico.

long [lɔŋ] *adj.* largo; **the whole day —** todo el santo día; **three feet —** tres pies de largo; **to be — in coming** tardar en venir; *adv.* mucho, mucho tiempo; — **ago** hace mucho tiempo; **as** (*o* **so**) — as en tanto que, mientras que; **how — is it since . . . ?** ¿cuánto tiempo hace que . . . ?; **so — !** ¡hasta luego! ¡adiós!; **long-suffering** sufrido, paciente; **long-winded** prolijo, largo (*en hablar*); *v.* anhelar; ansiar; **to — for** anhelar; suspirar por.

longer [lɔ́ŋɡə] *adj.* más largo; *adv.* más, más tiempo; **no —** ya no; **not . . . any —** ya no; no . . . más.

longevity [landʒévətɪ] *s.* longevidad.

longing [lɔ́ŋɪŋ] *s.* anhelo, añoranza, nostalgia; *adj.* anhelante, anheloso, nostálgico; **-ly** *adv.* con anhelo anhelosamente, con ansia.

longitude [lándʒətjud] *s.* longitud.

longshoreman [lɔ́ŋʃormən] *s.* estibador (*de barco o muelle*), cargador.

look [lʊk] *v.* mirar; parecer; **it -s well on you** le cae (*o* le sienta) bien; **to — after** atender, cuidar; **to — alike** parecerse; asemejarse; **to — down on a person** mirar con desprecio (*o* menospreciar) a alguien; **to — for** buscar; esperar; **to — forward to** anticipar con placer; **to — into** examinar, investigar; — **out!** ¡cuidado!; ¡tenga cuidado!; **to — out of** asomarse a; **to — over** examinar; dar un vistazo a; **to — up** levantar la vista; buscar; **to — up to** admirar, mirar con respeto; *s.* mirada, vistazo; **-s** apariencia, aspecto; **to have good -s** ser bien parecido.

looking glass [lʊ́kɪŋɡlæs] *s.* espejo.

lookout [lʊ́kaʊt] *s.* vigía; atalaya; mirador; vista, perspectiva; **that is your —** ¡eso a usted!; **to be on the —** estar alerta.

loom [lum] *s.* telar; *v.* destacarse, descollar; asomar(se), aparecer.

loop [lup] *s.* lazo, gaza, presilla; vuelta, curva; circuito; *v.* hacer una gaza (con o en); atar con gaza o presilla; hacer un circuito.

loophole [lúphol] *s.* agujero, abertura; salida; escapatoria.

loose [lus] *adj.* suelto; flojo; holgado; desatado; disoluto; — **change** suelto, moneda suelta; **to let** — soltar; *v.* soltar; desatar; aflojar; -**ly** *adv.* sueltamente; flojamente; con poca exactitud, sin fundamento.

loosen [lúsn] *v.* soltar(se); aflojar(se); desatar(se); **to** — **one's hold** desasirse, soltarse.

looseness [lúsnɪs] *s.* soltura; flojedad, flojera; holgura; relajación; flujo (*de vientre*).

loot [lut] *s.* botín, pillaje, saqueo; *v.* saquear, pillar, robar.

lop [lɑp] *v.* tronchar, desmochar (*Am.* mochar).

loquacious [lokwéʃɔs] *adj.* locuaz, hablador, lenguaraz.

lord [lɔrd] *s.* señor; dueño, amo; lord; **Lord's Prayer** Padre Nuestro; **Our Lord** Nuestro Señor; *v.* señorear, mandar; **to** — **it over** señorear, dominar.

lordly [lɔ́rdlɪ] *adj.* señoril; noble; altivo; despótico; *adv.* altivamente, imperiosamènte.

lordship [lɔ́rdʃɪp] *s.* señoría (*título*); señorío, dominio.

lose [luz] *v.* perder; **to** — **sight of** perder de vista.

loss [lɔs] *s.* pérdida; **to be at a** — estar perplejo; no saber qué hacer; **to sell at a** — vender con pérdida.

lost [lɔst] *pret. & p.p. de* **to lose**; *adj.* perdido; extraviado; — **in thought** absorto, abstraído; **to get** — perderse, extraviarse.

lot [lɑt] *s.* lote; parte, porción; suerte; solar, porción de terreno; **a** — **of** (o -**s of**) una gran cantidad de; mucho; muchos; **to draw -s** echar suertes; **to fall to one's** — tocarle a uno, caerle en suerte; *adv.* mucho; **a** — **better** mucho mejor.

lotion [lóʃən] *s.* loción.

lottery [látərɪ] *s.* lotería.

loud [laud] *adj.* ruidoso; recio, fuerte; chillón (*dícese también de los colores*); *adv.* ruidosamente, fuerte, recio; alto, en voz alta.

loud-speaker [láudspíkə] *s.* altavoz, altoparlante.

lounge [laundʒ] *s.* sala de descanso; sofá, diván, canapé; *v.* arrellanarse,

repantigarse, recostarse cómodamente; sestear; holgazanear.

louse [laus] *s.* piojo.

lousy [láuzɪ] *adj.* piojoso; asqueroso.

lovable [lávəbl] *adj.* amable.

love [lʌv] *s.* amor; cariño; afición; — **affair** amorío; **to be in** — estar enamorado; **to fall in** — with enamorarse de; **to make** — **to** enamorar a; *v.* amar, querer; gustar mucho de, gustarle a uno mucho; encantarle a uno algo.

loveliness [lávlɪnɪs] *s.* belleza, hermosura; amabilidad.

lovely [lávlɪ] *adj.* amable; lindo, bello; exquisito; encantador; ameno.

lover [lávə] *s.* amante; **music** — aficionado a (o amante de) la música.

loving [lávɪŋ] *adj.* amante, amoroso, cariñoso, afectuoso; -**ly** *adv.* cariñosamente, afectuosamente.

low [lo] *adj.* bajo; vil; humilde; abatido; débil; gravemente enfermo; deficiente; — **comedy** farsa, sainete; — **gear** primera velocidad; — **Mass** misa rezada; **dress with a** — **neck** vestido escotado (o con escote); **to be** — **on something** estar escaso de algo; **to be in** — **spirits** estar abatido o desanimado; *adv.* bajo; en voz baja, quedo, quedito; con bajeza, a precio bajo vilmente; *s.* mugido; *v.* mugir.

lower [lóə] *adj.* más bajo; inferior; — **case letter** letra minúscula; — **classman** estudiante de los dos primeros años; — **house** cámara de diputados; *v.* bajar; disminuir; rebajar; abatir; humillar.

lowland [lólænd] *s.* tierra baja.

lowliness [lólɪnɪs] *s.* bajeza; humildad.

lowly [lólɪ] *adj.* bajo, humilde; inferior; *adv.* humildemente.

lowness [lónɪs] *s.* bajeza; humildad; abatimiento; gravédad (*de tono*); debilidad (*de un sonido*); baratura.

loyal [lɔ́iəl] *adj.* leal, fiel.

loyalty [lɔ́iəltɪ] *s.* lealtad, fidelidad.

lubricant [[lúbrɪkənt] *adj. & s.* lubricante.

lubricate [lúbrɪket] *v.* lubricar.

lucid [lúsɪd] *adj.* lúcido; claro; luciente.

luck [lʌk] *s.* suerte; fortuna; **in** — de buena suerte; **in bad** — de mala suerte.

luckily [lákɪlɪ] *adv.* afortunadamente, por fortuna.

lucky [lákɪ] *adj.* afortunado, feliz; **to be** — tener suerte, tocarle a uno la suerte.

lucrative [lúkrətɪv] *adj.* lucrativo.

ludicrous [lúdɪkrəs] *adj.* ridículo.

lug [lʌg] *v.* llevar, traer, *Am.* cargar; **to — away** cargar con, llevarse (*una cosa pesada*).

luggage [lʌ́gɪdʒ] *s.* equipaje.

lukewarm [lúkwórm] *adj.* tibio, templado; indiferente.

lull [lʌl] *v.* arrullar; sosegar; calmar(se); *s.* calma, momento de calma.

lullaby [lʌ́labaɪ] *s.* arrullo, canción de cuna.

lumber [lʌ́mbə] *s.* madera, maderaje; **—man** maderero, negociante en madera; **—yard** depósito de maderas; *v.* cortar y aserrar madera; explotar los bosques; moverse pesadamente.

luminous [lúmənəs] *adj.* luminoso.

lump [lʌmp] *s.* terrón; bulto; hinchazón, chichón; protuberancia; **— of sugar** terrón de azúcar; *v.* amontonar; consolidar (*gastos*); apelotonarse, aterronarse, formar terrones.

lumpy [lʌ́mpɪ] *adj.* aterronado.

lunatic [lúnətɪk] *adj.* & *s.* lunático, loco.

lunch [lʌntʃ] *s.* almuerzo; merienda; *Am.* lonche; **—room** merendero, *Am.* lonchería; *v.* almorzar; merendar; *Am.* tomar el lonche.

luncheon [lʌ́ntʃən] *s.* almuerzo; merienda.

lung [lʌŋ] *s.* pulmón.

lurch [lɜtʃ] *s.* sacudida; tambaleo repentino; **to give a — tambalearse; to leave someone in the —** dejar a uno plantado, dejar a uno a buenas noches; *v.* tambalearse; dar un tambaleo repentino.

lure [lur] *s.* aliciente, atractivo; tentación; cebo o reclamo (*para atraer*); *v.* atraer; seducir; atraer (*con cebo o reclamo*).

lurk [lɜk] *v.* estar oculto; estar en acecho; moverse furtivamente.

luscious [lʌ́ʃəs] *adj.* exquisito, delicioso, sabroso.

lust [lʌst] *s.* lujuria; deseo vehemente; codicia; *v.* **to — after** codiciar.

luster [lʌ́stə] *s.* lustre, brillo.

lustrous [lʌ́strəs] *adj.* lustroso.

lusty [lʌ́stɪ] *adj.* vigoroso, fornido, robusto.

lute [lut] *s.* laúd.

luxuriant [lʌgʒúrɪənt] *adj.* lozano, frondoso, exuberante.

luxurious [lʌgʒúrɪəs] *adj.* lujoso; dado al lujo; frondoso.

luxury [lʌ́kʃərɪ] *s.* lujo.

lye [laɪ] *s.* lejía.

lying [láɪɪŋ] *ger. de* to lie; *adj.* mentiroso; **lying-in hospital** casa de maternidad.

lynch [lɪntʃ] *v.* linchar.

lynx [lɪŋks] *s.* lince.

lyre [laɪr] *s.* lira.

lyric [lɪ́rɪk] *s.* poema lírico; *adj.* lírico.

lyrical [lɪ́rɪk]] *adj.* lírico.

lyricism [lɪ́rəsɪzəm] *s.* lirismo.

M

macaroni [mækəróni] *s.* macarrón o macarrones.

macaroon [mækərún] *s.* macarrón, almendrado, bollito de almendra.

machine [məʃín] *s.* máquina; automóvil; **— gun** ametralladora; **— made** hecho a máquina; **political —** camarilla política; **sewing —** máquina para coser.

machinery [məʃínərɪ] *s.* maquinaria.

machinist [məʃínɪst] *s.* mecánico, maquinista.

mackerel [mǽkərəl] *s.* escombro, caballa (*pez*).

mad [mæd] *adj.* loco; rabioso; furioso, enojado; **to drive —** enloquecer, volver loco; **to get —** encolerizarse; **to go —** volverse loco, enloquecerse; **-ly** *adv.* locamente.

madam, madame [mǽdəm] *s.* madama, señora.

madcap [mǽdkæp] *s.* calavera (*m.*), *adj.* temerario; temerario; atolondrado.

madden [mǽdn] *v.* enloquecer(se).

made [med] *pret.* & *p.p. de* to make; **to be — of** estar hecho de; ser de; **to have something — mandar hacer** algo; **made-up** fingido, falso; artificial, pintado (*con afeites*).

madman [mǽdmæn] *s.* loco.

madness [mǽdnɪs] *s.* locura; rabia.

magazine [mǽgəzín] *s.* revista; almacén (*especialmente para provisiones militares*); **powder —** polvorín.

magic [mǽdʒɪk] *s.* magia; *adj.* mágico.

magician [mədʒíʃən] *s.* mágico; brujo.

magistrate [mǽdʒɪstret] *s.* magistrado.

magnanimous [mægnǽnəməs] *adj.* magnánimo.

magnet [mǽgnɪt] *s.* imán.

magnetic [mægnétɪk] *adj.* magnético.

magnificence [mægnífəsns] *s.* magnificencia.

magnificent [mægnífəsnt] *adj.* magnífico.

magnify [mǽgnəfaɪ] *v.* agrandar, engrandecer; amplificar; exagerar.

magnitude [mǽgnətjud] *s.* magnitud.

magpie [mǽgpaɪ] *s.* urraca; cotorra, hablador, habladora.

mahogany [məhógənɪ] *s.* caoba.

maid [med] *s.* criada, sirvienta, camarera, *Am.* recamarera, *Am.* mucama; doncella; **— of honor** doncella de honor; old — solterona.

maiden [médn] *s.* doncella; virgen; mozuela; soltera; — **lady** mujer soltera; — **voyage** primer viaje (*de un vapor*).

mail [mel] *s.* correo; correspondencia; **air** — correo aéreo; **coat of** — malla; —**bag** valija; — **train** tren correo; *v.* echar al correo.

mailbox [mélbɑks] *s.* buzón.

mailman [mélmæn] *s.* cartero.

maim [mem] *v.* mutilar, estropear.

main [men] *adj.* principal, mayor, de mayor importancia; *s.* tubería, cañería principal (*de agua o gas*); alta mar, océano; **in the** — en su mayor parte; en general, en conjunto; **-ly** *adv.* principalmente.

mainland [ménlænd] *s.* continente, tierra firme.

maintain [mentén] *v.* mantener; sostener, afirmar; guardar.

maintenance [méntənəns] *s.* mantenimiento; sustento; manutención; sostén, sostenimiento.

maize [mez] *s.* maíz.

majestic [mədʒéstɪk] *adj.* majestuoso.

majesty [médʒɪstɪ] *s.* majestad.

major [médʒə] *adj.* mayor, más grande; principal; — **key** tono mayor; *s.* comandante; mayor, mayor de edad; curso o asignatura de especialización (*en la universidad*); *v.* especializarse (*en un curso de estudios*).

majority [mədʒórətɪ] *s.* mayoría; mayor edad.

make [mek] *v.* hacer; fabricar; formar; pronunciar (*un discurso*); **to — a clean breast of** confesar; **to — a train** alcanzar un tren; **to — a turn** dar vuelta; **to — away with** llevarse, robar; matar; **to — fast** asegurar, afianzar; **to — headway** progresar, adelantar, avanzar; **to — much of** dar mucha importancia a; **to — neither head nor tail of** no comprender nada de; **to — nothing out of** no comprender nada de, no sacar nada en limpio; **to — out in the distance** distinguir a lo lejos; **to — over** rehacer, alterar (*un traje*); **to — sure** asegurarse; **to — toward** dirigirse a, encaminarse a; **to — up a story** inventar un cuento; **to — up after a quarrel** hacer las paces; **to — up for a loss** compensar por una pérdida; **to — up one's face** pintarse la cara; **to — up one's mind** resolverse, decidirse; *s.* hechura, forma; marca (*de fábrica*); manufactura.

maker [méka] *s.* hacedor; fabricante; artífice.

make-up [mékʌp] *s.* compostura, composición, hechura; naturaleza, carácter; **facial** — afeite, cosmético.

malady [mælədɪ] *s.* mal, enfermedad.

malaria [mælériə] *s.* malaria, fiebre palúdica, paludismo.

malcontent [mælkəntent] *adj.* & *s.* malcontento.

male [mel] *adj.* macho; varón; masculino; varonil; de hombres, de varones; *s.* macho; varón; hombre.

malice [mælɪs] *s.* malicia.

malicious [məlíʃəs] *adj.* malicioso, perverso, malévolo.

malign [məláɪn] *v.* calumniar, difamar; *adj.* maligno; pernicioso.

malignant [məlígnənt] *adj.* maligno; malévolo.

mallet [mælɪt] *s.* mazo, maceta.

malt [mɔlt] *s.* malta; **-ed milk** leche malteada.

mama, mamma [mámə] *s.* mamá.

mammal [mæml] *s.* mamífero.

mammoth [mæməə] *adj.* gigantesco, enorme.

mammy [mæmɪ] *s.* mamita; niñera negra; criada negra.

man [mæn] *s.* hombre; varón; pieza (*de ajedrez*); — **and wife** marido y mujer; **to a** — unánimemente, todos a una; **officers and men** oficiales y soldados; **man-of-war** buque de guerra; — **cook** cocinero; *v.* armar, proveer de gente armada; guarnecer (*una fortaleza*); tripular (*una embarcación*).

manage [mænɪdʒ] *v.* manejar; gobernar, dirigir; gestionar; **to — to do something** arreglárselas para hacer algo.

manageable [mænɪdʒəbl] *adj.* manejable; domable, dócil.

management [mænɪdʒmənt] *s.* manejo; dirección; gobierno, administración; gerencia.

manager [mænɪdʒə] *s.* gerente; director, administrador; empresario.

mandate [mændet] *s.* mandato; *v.* asignar por mandato.

mane [men] *s.* melena (*del león*), crin (*del caballo*).

maneuver [mənúvə] *s.* maniobra; gestión; *v.* maniobrar; manipular, manejar.

manful [mænfəl] *adj.* varonil; viril.

manganese [mæŋgənis] *s.* manganeso.

mange [mendʒ] *s.* sarna, roña.

manger [méndʒə] *s.* pesebre.

mangle [mæŋgl] *v.* magullar, mutilar, destrozar, estropear; planchar en máquina de planchar; *s.* planchadora (*máquina de planchar*).

mangy [méndʒi] *adj.* sarnoso, *Am.* sarniento.

manhood [mǽnhʊd] *s.* virilidad; edad viril; hombres.

mania [méniə] *s.* manía.

manicure [mǽnɪkjʊr] *s.* manicura; *v.* manicurar;

manifest [mǽnəfɛst] *adj.* manifiesto; *s.* manifiesto (*lista de la carga de un buque*); *v.* manifestar; poner de manifiesto; declarar.

manifestation [mænəfɛstéʃən] *s.* manifestación.

manifesto [mænɪfésto] *s.* manifiesto, bando, proclama.

manifold [mǽnəfold] *adj.* múltiple; numeroso, diverso.

manikin [mǽnəkin] *s.* maniquí; muñeco; hombrecillo.

manila [mənílə] *s.* abacá (*cáñamo de Manila*); — **paper** papel de Manila.

manipulate [mənípjəlet] *v.* manipular; manejar.

manipulation [mənɪpjəléʃən] *s.* manipulación.

mankind [mænkáɪnd] *s.* humanidad, género humano; los hombres.

manly [mǽnlɪ] *adj.* varonil, viril; *adv.* varonilmente.

manner [mǽnə] *s.* manera; modo; género; aire, ademán; -s maneras, modales; costumbres; **after the — of** a la manera de; **by no — of means de** ningún modo.

mannish [mǽnɪʃ] *adj.* hombruno.

manoeuvre = maneuver.

manor [mǽnə] *s.* solar, casa solariega.

mansion [mǽnʃən] *s.* mansión; palacio.

manslaughter [mǽnslɔtə] *s.* homicidio impremeditado o casual.

mantel [mǽntl] *s.* manto (*de una chimenea*); repisa de chimenea.

mantle [mǽntl] *s.* manto; capa.

manual [mǽnjʊəl] *adj.* manual; — **training school** escuela de artes y oficios; *s.* manual; teclado de órgano.

manufacture [mænjəfǽktʃə] *s.* fabricación; manufactura; *v.* fabricar, manufacturar.

manufacturer [mænjəfǽktʃərə] *s.* fabricante.

manufacturing [mænjəfǽktʃərɪŋ] *s.* fabricación; *adj.* fabril, manufacturero.

manure [mənúr] *s.* estiércol; abono; *v.* estercolar, abonar (*la tierra*).

manuscript [mǽnjəskript] *adj. & s.* manuscrito.

many [ménɪ] *adj.* muchos; — **a time**

muchas veces; **a great —** muchísimos; **as — as** tantos como; cuantos; **as — as five** hasta cinco; **how — ?** ¿cuántos?; **three books too —** tres libros de más; **too —** demasiados.

map [mæp] *s.* mapa; *v.* trazar un mapa de; **to — out** proyectar, planear.

maple [mépl] *s.* arce, *Am.* meple.

mar [mɑr] *v.* desfigurar, estropear.

marble [márbl] *s.* mármol; canica (*para jugar*); **to play -s** jugar a las canicas; *adj.* de mármol; marmóreo.

march [mɑrtʃ] *s.* marcha; *v.* marchar, caminar; hacer marchar; **to — in** entrar marchando; **to — out** marcharse; salirse marchando.

March [mɑrtʃ] *s.* marzo.

mare [mɛr] *s.* yegua.

margin [márdʒin] *s.* margen; orilla; sobrante; reserva (*fondos*).

marginal [márdʒɪnl] *adj.* marginal; — **note** nota marginal, acotación.

marigold [mǽrəgold] *s.* caléndula, maravilla.

marine [mərín] *adj.* marino; marítimo; — **corps** cuerpo de marinos; *s.* marino; soldado de marina; **merchant —** marina mercante.

mariner [mǽrənə] *s.* marinero.

maritime [mǽrətaɪm] *adj.* marítimo.

mark [mɑrk] *s.* marca; señal, seña; nota, calificación; **question —** punto de interrogación; **to come up to the —** alcanzar la norma requerida; **to hit the —** dar en el blanco; **to make one's —** distinguirse; **to miss one's —** fallar; errar el tiro; fracasar; *v.* marcar; señalar; notar; observar; calificar; — **my words!** ¡advierte lo que te digo!; **to — down** anotar, apuntar; rebajar el precio de.

marker [márkə] *s.* marcador; marca, señal; jalón.

market [márkɪt] *s.* mercado, plaza; — **place** mercado, plaza; — **price** precio corriente; **meat —** carnicería; **stock —** mercado de valores, bolsa; *v.* vender; vender o comprar en el mercado; **to go -ing** ir de compras.

marmalade [márməled] *s.* mermelada.

maroon [mərún] *s. & adj.* rojo obscuro.

marooned [mərúnd] *adj.* abandonado (*en lugar desierto*) aislado; **to get —** encontrarse aislado, perdido o incomunicado.

marquis [márkwɪs] *s.* marqués.

marquise [márkiz] *s.* marquesa.

marriage [mǽrɪdʒ] *s.* matrimonio; casamiento, boda; unión, enlace; — **license** licencia para casarse.

married [mǽrɪd] *adj.* casado; conyugal. — **couple** matrimonio, cónyuges; pareja de casados; **to get** — casarse.

marrow [mǽro] *s.* meollo, tuétano, medula (*de los huesos*).

marry [mǽrɪ] *v.* casar; casarse; casarse con.

marsh [mɑrʃ] *s.* pantano; ciénaga.

marshal [mɑ́rʃəl] *s.* mariscal; alguacil; jefe de policía (*en ciertas regiones*); maestro de ceremonia; **fire** — jefe de bomberos; *v.* ordenar, arreglar; guiar, conducir con ceremonia.

marshmallow [mɑ́rʃmælo] *s.* pastilla o bombón de altea.

marshy [mɑ́rʃɪ] *adj.* pantanoso, cenagoso.

mart [mɑrt] *s.* mercado.

martial [mɑ́rʃəl] *adj.* marcial; — **law** estado-de guerra.

martin [mɑ́rtɪn] *s.* avión (*pájaro*).

martyr [mɑ́rtə] *s.* mártir; *v.* martirizar, torturar, atormentar.

martyrdom [mɑ́rtədəm] *s.* martirio.

marvel [mɑ́rvl] *s.* maravilla; *v.* maravillarse.

marvelous [mɑ́rvləs] *adj.* maravilloso.

masculine [mǽskjəlɪn] *adj.* masculino; varonil; hombruno.

mash [mæʃ] *v.* majar, amasar; machacar, magullar; **-ed potatoes** puré de papas (*o patatas*); patatas majadas.

mask [mæsk] *s.* máscara; disfraz; careta; *v.* disfrazar, enmascarar; encubrir; **-ed ball** baile de máscaras.

mason [mésn̩] *s.* albañil; **Mason** masón; francmasón.

masonry [mésn̩rɪ] *s.* albañilería; mampostería; **Masonry** masonería, francmasonería.

masquerade [mæskəréd] *s.* mascarada; disfraz, máscara; *v.* enmascararse, disfrazarse; andar disfrazado.

mass [mæs] *s.* masa; montón; mole; mayoría, mayor parte; misa; — **meeting** mitin popular; **the -es** las masas, el pueblo; *v.* juntar(se) en masa.

massacre [mǽsəkə] *s.* hecatombe, matanza, carnicería, destrozo; *v.* hacer matanza o hecatombe, destrozar.

massage [məsáʒ] *v.* friccionar, dar masaje; *s.* masaje.

massive [mǽsɪv] *adj.* sólido, macizo; voluminoso, imponente.

mast [mæst] *s.* mástil, palo.

master [mǽstə] *s.* amo, dueño, señor; maestro; patrón, experto, perito; **band** — director de la banda; — **of arts** maestro en artes, licenciado; **-'s degree** licenciatura, grado de licencia-

do; *adj.* maestro; — **builder** maestro de obras; — **key** llave maestra; *v.* dominar; domar; gobernar; **to** — **a language** dominar un idioma.

masterful [mǽstəfəl] *adj.* magistral; dominante.

masterly [mǽstəlɪ] *adj.* magistral; *adv* magistralmente.

masterpiece [mǽstəpis] *s.* obra maestra.

mastery [mǽstəri] *s.* maestría, arte, destreza; dominio.

mastiff [mǽstɪf] *s.* mastín, alano.

mat [mæt] *s.* estera; esterilla, felpudo, tapete; colchoncillo (*de gimnasia*); borde de cartón (*para hacer resaltar una pintura*).

match [mætʃ] *s.* fósforo, cerilla *Am.* cerillo; pareja; partida, contienda, juego; **he has no** — no tiene igual; **he is a good** — es un buen partido; **the hat and coat are a good** — el abrigo y el sombrero hacen juego; *v.* igualar; aparear; hacer juego, armonizar; **to** — **one's strength** medir uno sus fuerzas; **these colors do not** — **well** estos colores no casan bien.

matchless [mǽtʃlɪs] *adj.* sin par, sin igual, incomparable.

mate [met] *s.* compañero, compañera; consorte; macho o hembra (*entre animales o aves*); piloto (*el segundo de un buque mercante*); oficial subalterno (*en la marina*); *v.* aparear(se).

material [mətíriəl] *adj.* material; esencial; *s.* material; tejido, género; materia; **raw** — materia prima.

maternal [mətɜ́nl̩] *adj.* maternal, materno.

maternity [mətɜ́nətɪ] *s.* maternidad.

mathematical [mæθəmǽtɪkl̩] *adj.* matemático.

mathematician [mæθəmətíʃən] *s.* matemático.

mathematics [mæθəmǽtɪks] *s.* matemáticas.

matinée [mætɪné] *s.* función de la tarde, *Am.* matiné.

matriculate [mətríkjəlet] *v.* matricular(se).

matriculation [mətrɪkjəléʃən] *s.* matriculación, matrícula.

matrimony [mǽtrəmonɪ] *s.* matrimonio, casamiento.

matrix [métrɪks] *s.* matriz; molde.

matron [métrən] *s.* matrona, madre de familia; ama de llaves; vigilante, cuidadora (*de un asilo, cárcel para mujeres, etc.*).

matter [mǽtə] *s.* materia; material; sustancia; asunto, cuestión; cosa; pus;

— **for complaint** motivo de queja; — **of two minutes** cosa de dos minutos; **as a** — **of fact** de hecho; en verdad, en realidad; **business -s** negocios; **printed** — impresos; **serious** — cosa seria; **it is of no** — no tiene importancia; **to do something as a** — **of course** hacer algo por rutina; **what is the** — ? ¿qué pasa?; ¿qué tiene Vd.?; **matter-of-fact person** persona de poca imaginación; v. importar; supurar; **it does not** — 'no importa, no le hace.

mattress [mǽtrɪs] s. colchón; **spring** — colchón de muelles.

mature [mǝtjúr] adj. maduro; .a — note un pagaré vencido; v. madurar(se); vencerse, hacerse cobrable o pagadero (*un pagaré, una deuda*).

maturity [mǝtjúrǝtɪ] s. madurez; vencimiento (*de una deuda u obligación*).

maul [mɔl] v. magullar; maltratar; manejar rudamente; golpear.

maxim [mǽksɪm] s. máxima.

maximum [mǽksǝmǝm] adj. & s. máximo.

may [me] v. irr y defect. poder; tener permiso para, serle permitido a uno; ser posible; — **I sit down?** ¿puedo sentarme?; — **you have a good time** que se divierta Vd.; **it** — **be that** puede ser que, tal vez sea que; **it** — **rain** puede (ser) que llueva, es posible que llueva; **she** — **be late** puede (ser) que llegue ella tarde.

May [me] s. mayo, mes de mayo; — **Day** primero de mayo; —**pole** mayo; — **Queen** maya (*reina de la fiesta del primero de mayo*).

maybe [mébɪ] adv. quizás, tal vez, acaso.

mayonnaise [meǝnéz] s. mayonesa.

mayor [méǝ] s. alcalde, alcalde mayor.

maze [mez] s. laberinto; confusión; **to be in a** — estar confuso o perplejo.

me [mi] pron. pers. me; mí (*después de preposición*); **give it to** — démelo (a mí); **for** — para mí; **with** — conmigo.

meadow [médo] s. pradera, prado; — **lark** alondra de los prados.

meager [mígǝ] adj. escaso, insuficiente; magro, flaco.

meal [mil] s. comida; harina (*a medio moler*); **corn** — harina de maíz; —**time** hora de comer.

mean [min] adj. ruin, bajo, humilde; vil; mezquino, tacaño; de mal genio; malo, indispuesto; mediano; medio; intermedio; — **distance** distancia media; s. medio; término medio; **-s** medios; recursos; **a man of -s** un hombre

pudiente o rico; **by -s of** por medio de; **by all -s** de todos modos; **a toda costa**; por supuesto; **by no -s** de ningún modo; v. querer decir, significar; pensar, proponerse, tener la intención de; intentar; destinar; **he -s well** tiene buenas intenciones.

meaning [mínɪŋ] s. significado, sentido; significación; propósito, intención; adj. significativo; **well-meaning** bien intencionado.

meaningless [mínɪŋlɪs] adj. sin sentido, vacío de sentido.

meanness [mínnɪs] s. ruindad, vileza, bajeza; mezquindad.

meant [ment] pret. & p.p. de **to mean**.

meantime [míntaɪm] adv. mientras tanto, entretanto; s. ínterin, entretanto; **in the** — en el ínterin, mientras tanto.

meanwhile [mínhwaɪl] = **meantime**.

measles [mízlz] s. sarampión.

measurable [méʒrǝbl] adj. medible, mensurable; **measurably** adv. marcadamente.

measure [méʒǝ] s. medida; compás (*de música*); cadencia, ritmo; proyecto de ley; ley; **beyond** — sobremanera; **con exceso**; **dry** — medida para áridos; **in large** — en gran parte, en gran manera; v. medir.

measured [méʒǝd] adj. medido; moderado; acompasado.

measurement [méʒǝmǝnt] s. medida; dimensión; tamaño; medición.

meat [mit] s. carne; meollo, sustancia; — **ball** albóndiga; — **market** carnicería; **cold** — fiambre.

meaty [mítɪ] adj. carnoso; sustancioso.

mechanic [mǝkǽnɪk] adj. & s. mecánico; **-s** s. mecánica.

mechanical [mǝkǽnɪkl] adj. mecánico; maquinal.

mechanism [mékǝnɪzǝm] s. mecanismo.

medal [médl] s. medalla.

meddle [médl] v. entrometerse o entremeterse; meterse.

meddler [médlǝ] s. entremetido.

meddlesome [médlsǝm] adj. entremetido.

median [mídɪǝn] adj. mediano, del medio; s. punto, línea o número del medio; mediana.

mediate [mídɪet] v. mediar; intervenir; arbitrar.

mediation [midié√ǝn] s. mediación, intervención, intercesión.

mediator [mídɪetǝ] s. mediador, medianero, árbitro.

medical [médɪkl] adj. médico; — **school**

escuela de medicina.

medicine [médəsn] *s.* medicina; medicamento; — **ball** pelota grande de cuero; — **cabinet** botiquín; — **man** curandero indio.

medieval [midíɪvl] *adj.* medioeval o medieval.

mediocre [midíókə] *adj.* mediocre, mediano; ordinario.

mediocrity [midiákrətɪ] *s.* mediocridad, medianía.

meditate [médətet] *v.* meditar.

meditation [medətéʃən] *s.* meditación.

medium [mídɪəm] *s.* medio; medio ambiente; *adj.* mediano; intermedio; a medio cocer, a medio asar.

medley [médlɪ] *s.* baturrillo, mezcla, mezcolanza.

meek [mik] *adj.* manso, dócil, paciente, sufrido.

meekness [míknɪs] *s.* mansedumbre, docilidad.

meet [mit] *v.* encontrar(se); reunirse; conocer (*personalmente*), ser presentado a; ir a esperar (*un tren, vapor, o a alguien*); satisfacer (*deseos, requisitos, etc.*); pagar (*una deuda*); sufragar (*gastos*); responder a (*una acusación*); **to — in battle** trabar batalla; **to — with** encontrarse con; tropezar con; topar con; reunirse con; *s.* concurso, contienda (*tratándose de deportes*); **track —** competencia de atletas.

meeting [mítɪŋ] *s.* reunión; mitin; sesión; asamblea; encuentro.

megaphone [mégəfon] *s.* megáfono, portavoz, bocina.

melancholy [mélənkəlɪ] *s.* melancolía; *adj.* melancólico.

mellow [mélo] *adj.* maduro, sazonado; dulce, blando, suave; *v.* madurar(se), sazonar(se); ablandar(se), suavizar(se).

melodious [məlódɪəs] *adj.* melodioso.

melody [mélədɪ] *s.* melodía.

melon [mélən] *s.* melón.

melt [melt] *v.* derretir(se); disolver(se); fundir(se).

member [mémbə] *s.* miembro; socio.

membership [mémbəʃɪp] *s.* número de miembros o socios; asociación; (*los*) miembros (*de un club o sociedad*).

membrane [mémbren] *s.* membrana.

memento [mɪménto] *s.* memento, memoria, recuerdo.

memoir [mémwɑr] *s.* memoria, apuntaciones; -**s** memorias; autobiografía.

memorable [mémərəbl] *adj.* memorable.

memorandum [memərændəm] *s.* memorándum; memoria, apunte; —

book memorándum, librito de apuntes, memorial.

memorial [məmórɪəl] *s.* monumento conmemorativo; obra o fiesta conmemorativa; memorial, petición; *adj.* conmemorativo.

memorize [méməraɪz] *v.* aprender de memoria.

memory [mémərɪ] *s.* memoria; recuerdo.

men [men] *pl. de* **man.**

menace [ménɪs] *s.* amenaza; *v.* amenazar.

mend [mend] *v.* remendar; reparar, componer; enmendar; **to — one's ways** enmendarse, reformarse; *s.* remiendo; reparación; **to be on the —** ir mejorando.

menial [mínɪəl] *adj.* servil, bajo.

menstruation [menstruéʃən] *s.* menstruo o menstruación.

mental [méntl] *adj.* mental.

mentality [mentælətɪ] *s.* mentalidad, ingenio.

mention [ménʃən] *s.* mención; alusión. *v.* mencionar, mentar; **don't — it** no hay de qué (*contestación a* "thank you").

menu [ménju] *s.* menú, lista de platos.

meow [mjaʊ] = **mew.**

mercantile [mʒkəntɪl] *adj.* mercantil.

mercenary [mʒsnɛrɪ] *adj.* mercenario.

merchandise [mʒtʃəndaɪz] *s.* mercancías, mercaderías; **piece of —** mercancía.

merchant [mʒtʃənt] *s.* comerciante; negociante; mercader; *adj.* mercante, mercantil; **— marine** marina mercante.

merciful [mʒsɪfəl] *adj.* misericordioso, piadoso.

merciless [mʒsɪlɪs] *adj.* sin piedad, despiadado, incompasivo.

mercury [mʒkjərɪ] *s.* mercurio; azogue.

mercy [mʒsɪ] *s.* merced; favor, gracia; misericordia, piedad, compasión; **to be at the — of** estar a merced de.

mere [mɪr] *adj.* mero; simple, puro; **a — formality** una pura formalidad, no más que una formalidad, una formalidad no más; **a — trifle** una nonada; **-ly** *adv.* meramente; sólo, solamente; simplemente.

merge [mʒdʒ] *v.* combinar(se), unir(se); absorber(se); fundirse.

meridian [mərídɪən] *adj. & s.* meridiano.

merit [mérɪt] *s.* mérito; *v.* merecer.

meritorious [mérətórɪəs] *adj.* meritorio.

merrily [mérəlɪ] *adv.* alegremente, con regocijo.

merriment [mérɪmənt] *s.* alegría, regocijo, júbilo.

merry [mérɪ] *adj.* alegre; jovial; divertido; festivo; — **Christmas** Felices Navidades, Felices Pascuas; **to make** — divertirse.

merry-go-round [mérɪgəraund] *s.* tío vivo, *Am.* los caballitos.

merrymaker [mérɪmekə] *s.* fiestero; juerguista.

merrymaking [mérɪmekɪŋ] *s.* regocijo; jaleo, juerga, jolgorio; *adj.* regocijado, alegre, festivo, fiestero.

mesh [mɛʃ] *s.* malla; red; -es red, redes; *v.* enredar, coger con red; **to** — **gears** engranar.

mess [mɛs] *s.* rancho, comida (*en el ejército o la marina*); lío, confusión; suciedad; — **of fish** plato o ración de pescado; **to make a** — **of** revolver, confundir; ensuciar; echar a perder; *v.* revolver, confundir; ensuciar, echar a perder (*generalmente:* **to** — **up**); **to** — **around** revolver o mezclar las cosas; entrometerse; **messy** [mésɪ] *adj.* desordenado, desarreglado; sucio.

message [mésɪdʒ] *s.* mensaje; parte (*m.*), comunicación; recado.

messenger [mésṇdʒə] *s.* mensajero; mandadero.

met [mɛt] *pret. & p.p. de* **to meet**.

metal [métḷ] *s.* metal; *adj.* de metal, metálico.

metallic [mətálɪk] *adj.* metálico.

metallurgy [métḷɜdʒɪ] *s.* metalurgia.

metaphor [métəfə] *s.* metáfora.

meteor [mítɪə] *s.* meteoro; estrella fugaz.

meteorological [mitɪərəládʒɪkḷ] *adj.* meteorológico.

meteorology [mitɪərálədʒɪ] *s.* meteorología.

meter [mítə] *s.* metro; contador (*de gas, agua, electricidad, etc.*).

method [méθəd] *s.* método; técnica.

methodical [məθádɪkḷ] *adj.* metódico.

metre = **meter**.

metric [métrɪk] *adj.* métrico.

metropolis [mətrápḷɪs] *s.* metrópoli.

metropolitan [metrəpálətṇ] *adj.* metropolitano.

mettle [métḷ] *s.* temple, brío, ánimo, valor.

mew [mju] *s.* maullido, maúllo, miau; *v.* maullar.

Mexican [méksɪkən] *adj. & s.* mejicano o mexicano.

mezzanine [mézənin] *s.* entresuelo.

mice [maɪs] *pl. de* **mouse**.

microbe [máɪkrob] *s.* microbio.

microphone [máɪkrəfon] *s.* micrófono.

microscope [máɪkrəskop] *s.* microscopio.

microscopic [maɪkrəskápɪk] *adj.* microscópico.

mid [mɪd] *adj.* medio (*úsase por lo general en composición*); **in** — **air** en el aire; *prep.* en medio de, entre.

midday [mɪdde] *s.* mediodía; *adj.* del mediodía.

middle [mɪdḷ] *adj.* medio; intermedio; **Middle Ages** Edad Media; — **finger** dedo de en medio, dedo del corazón; — **size** tamaño mediano; *s.* medio, centro, mitad; **in the** — **of** en medio de, a la mitad de; **towards the** — **of the month** a mediados del mes.

middle-aged [mɪdḷédʒd] *adj.* de edad mediana, de edad madura.

middleman [mɪdḷmæn] *s.* revendedor; medianero, corredor, agente.

middle-sized [mɪdḷsáɪzd] *adj.* de mediano tamaño, de mediana estatura.

middy [mɪdɪ] *s.* guardiamarina (*m.*); — **blouse** blusa a la marinera.

midget [mɪdʒɪt] *s.* enanillo.

midnight [mɪdnaɪt] *s.* medianoche; *adj.* de (la) medianoche; — **blue** azul oscuro; — **Mass** misa del gallo.

midshipman [mɪdʃɪpmən] *s.* guardiamarina (*m.*)

midst [mɪdst] *s.* medio, centro; **in the** — **of** en medio de, entre; **in our** — entre nosotros.

midstream [mɪdstrim] *s.* el medio (*o* el centro) de la corriente.

midsummer [mɪdsʌ́mə] *s.* pleno verano, solsticio estival, la mitad del verano.

midterm [mɪdtɜm]; — **examination** examen a mitad del curso.

midway [mɪdwé] *adj.* situado a medio camino; equidistante; *adv.* a medio camino; en medio del camino.

midwife [mɪdwaɪf] *s.* partera, comadrona.

mien [min] *s.* facha, aspecto.

might [maɪt] *imperf. de* **may** podía; podría; pudiera, pudiese; *s.* poder, poderío, fuerza.

mighty [máɪtɪ] *adj.* poderoso, potente, fuerte; *adv.* muy, sumamente.

migrate [máɪgret] *v.* emigrar.

migration [maɪgréʃən] *s.* migración.

mike [maɪk] = **microphone**.

mild [maɪld] *adj.* suave; blando; apacible; templado, moderado.

mildness [máɪldnɪs] *s.* suavidad; mansedumbre; apacibilidad; templanza, dulzura.

mile [maɪl] *s.* milla; —**stone** mojón.

mileage [máɪlɪdʒ] *s.* millaje, número de millas; recorrido (*en millas*). *Compárese* kilometraje, número de kiló-

133

metros.

military [mílɔterɪ] *adj.* militar; de guerra; *s.* the — el ejército; los militares.

militia [mɔlíʃɔ] *s.* milicia.

milk [mɪlk] *s.* leche; — **diet** régimen lácteo; *v.* ordeñar.

milkmaid [mílkmed] *s.* lechera.

milkman [mílkmɔn] *s.* lechero, *Am.* vaquero.

milky [mílkɪ] *adj.* lácteo; lechoso; **Milky Way** Vía Láctea.

mill [mɪl] *s.* molino; fábrica; la milésima parte de un dólar; **saw—** aserradero; **spinning** — hilandería; **sugar** — ingenio de azúcar; **textile** — fábrica de tejidos; *v.* moler; aserrar (*madera*); fabricar; acordonar (*el canto de la moneda*); **to** — **around** arremolinarse (*una muchedumbre*).

miller [mílɔ] *s.* molinero; mariposa nocturna.

milliner [mílɔnɔ] *s.* modista (*de sombreros para señoras*).

millinery [mílɔnerɪ] *s.* sombreros de señora; artículos para sombreros de señora; oficio de modista; — **shop** sombrerería.

million [míljɔn] *s.* millón; **a** — **dollars** un millón de dólares.

millionaire [mɪljɔnér] *adj.* & *s.* millonario.

millionth [míljɔnɵ] *adj.* & *s.* millonésimo.

millstone [mílston] *s.* muela o piedra de molino; carga pesada.

mimic [mímɪk] *adj.* mímico, imitativo; — **battle** simulacro; *s.* imitador, remedador; *v.* imitar, remedar.

mince [mɪns] *v.* picar, desmenuzar; **not to** — **words** hablar con toda franqueza.

mincemeat [mínsmit] *s.* picadillo (*especialmente el de carne, pasas, manzanas y especias*).

mind [maɪnd] *s.* mente; pensamiento; inteligencia; ánimo, espíritu; propósito, intención; parecer, opinión; **to be out of one's** — estar loco, haber perdido el juicio; **to change one's** — cambiar de parecer; **to give someone a piece of one's** — cantarle a alguien la verdad; echarle a alguien un buen regaño; **to have a** — **to** estar por, sentir ganas de; **to make up one's** — decidirse, resolverse; **to my** — a mi modo de ver; **to speak one's** — **freely** hablar con toda franqueza; *v.* cuidar; atender a, hacer caso de, obedecer; **I don't** — no tengo inconveniente en ello; **never** — no importa; no se

preocupe; no se moleste; no haga Vd. caso; **to** — **one's own business** atender a lo suyo, no meterse en lo ajeno.

mindful [máɪndfɔl] *adj.* atento (a); cuidadoso (de).

mine [maɪn] *pron. pos.* mío (mía, míos, mías); el mío (la mía, los míos, las mías); **a book of** — un libro mío.

mine [maɪn] *s.* mina; — **sweeper** dragaminas; *v.* minar; explotar (*una mina*); extraer (*mineral*).

miner [máɪnɔ] *s.* minero.

mineral [mínɔrɔl] *adj.* & *s.* mineral.

mingle [míŋgl] *v.* mezclar(se); entremezclar(se); confundir(se); juntarse.

miniature [mínɪtʃɔ] *s.* miniatura; *adj.* en miniatura; diminuto.

minimize [mínɔmaɪz] *v.* empequeñecer.

minimum [mínɔmɔm] *adj.* & *s.* mínimo.

mining [máɪnɪŋ] *s.* minería, explotación de minas; *adj.* minero; — **engineer** ingeniero de minas.

minister [mínɪstɔ] *s.* ministro; pastor, clérigo; *v.* ministrar; atender; proveer, socorrer.

ministry [mínɪstrɪ] *s.* ministerio; socorro, ayuda.

mink [mɪŋk] *s.* visón.

minnow [míno] *s.* pececillo de río.

minor [máɪnɔ] *adj.* menor; de menor edad; secundario; — **key** tono menor; *s.* menor de edad; premisa menor (*de un silogismo*); tono menor; curso o asignatura menor.

minority [mɔnɔ́rɔtɪ] *s.* minoría; minoridad, menor edad; menor parte.

minstrel [mínstrɔl] *s.* trovador; bardo, vate; actor cómico que remeda al negro norteamericano.

mint [mɪnt] *s.* menta, hierbabuena (yerbabuena); pastilla o bombón de menta; casa de moneda; **a** — **of money** un montón de dinero, la mar de dinero; *v.* acuñar.

minuet [mɪnjʊét] *s.* minué.

minus [máɪnɔs] *adj.* negativo; sin, falto de; **seven** — **four** siete menos cuatro; *s.* menos, signo menos.

minute [mínɪt] *s.* minuto; **-s** acta (*de una junta*); — **hand** minutero.

minute [mɔnjút] *adj.* menudo, diminuto; minucioso, detallado.

miracle [mírɔkl] *s.* milagro.

miraculous [mɔrækjɔlɔs] *adj.* milagroso.

mirage [mɔráɜ] *s.* espejismo.

mire [maɪr] *s.* cieno, fango, lodo; *v.* atascar(se) en el fango; enlodar(se).

mirror [mírɔ] *s.* espejo; *v.* reflejar.

mirth [mɜ˞θ] s. júbilo, regocijo, alegría.
mirthful [mɜ˞θfəl] adj. jubiloso, regocijado, gozoso, alegre.
miry [máɪrɪ] adj. cenagoso, fangoso, lodoso.
misbehave [mɪsbɪhév] v. portarse mal, obrar mal.
miscarriage [mɪskǽrɪdʒ] s. aborto, malparto; mal éxito; extravío (de una carta, papel, etc.).
miscarry [mɪskǽrɪ] v. malograrse, frustrarse; abortar; extraviarse (una carta).
miscellaneous [mɪslénɪəs] adj. misceláneo, diverso.
mischief [mɪstʃɪf] s. travesura; diablura; mal, daño; diablillo, persona traviesa.
mischievous [mɪstʃɪvəs] adj. travieso; malicioso; dañino.
misconduct [mɪskándʌkt] s. mala conducta; mala administración; [mɪskəndʌkt] v. maladministrar, manejar mal; **to — oneself** portarse mal, conducirse mal.
misdeed [mɪsdíd] s. fechoría, mala acción.
misdemeanor [mɪsdɪmínə] s. mal comportamiento; fechoría.
miser [máɪzə] s. avaro, avariento.
miserable [mízrəbl] adj. miserable; infeliz, desdichado.
miserly [máɪzəlɪ] adj. avariento, avaro; tacaño, mezquino.
misery [mízrɪ] s. miseria, desgracia; estrechez, pobreza; dolor.
misfortune [mɪsfɔ́rtʃən] s. infortunio, desgracia, desastre.
misgiving [mɪsgívɪŋ] s. mal presentimiento, aprensión, recelo, temor.
mishap [mɪshǽp] s. desgracia, contratiempo, accidente.
mislaid [mɪsléd] pret. & p.p. de to mislay.
mislay [mɪslé] v. extraviar, perder; poner fuera de su sitio, colocar mal; traspapelar (una carta, documento, etc.).
mislead [mɪslíd] v. guiar por mal camino; extraviar, descarriar; engañar.
misled [mɪsléd] pret. & p.p. de to mislead.
misplace [mɪsplés] v. extraviar, poner fuera de su sitio, colocar mal; traspapelar (una carta, documento, etc.).
misprint [mɪsprínt] s. errata, error tipográfico, error de imprenta.
misrepresent [mɪsreprɪzént] v. falsear, falsificar; tergiversar.
miss [mɪs] v. errar, no acertar; fallar; equivocar; perder (una oportunidad, un tren, etc.); faltar a; echar de menos,

Am. extrañar; **he just -ed being killed** por poco le matan; s. error; falla, falta.
miss [mɪs] s. señorita; **Miss Smith** la señorita Smith.
missile [mɪsl] s. proyectil; arma arrojadiza; adj. arrojadizo, que se puede arrojar o tirar.
missing [mɪsɪŋ] adj. ausente; perdido; **one book is —** falta un libro.
mission [mɪʃən] s. misión.
missionary [mɪʃənerɪ] adj. & s. misionero.
misspell [mɪsspél] v. escribir con mala ortografía, deletrear mal.
mist [mɪst] s. neblina, niebla; llovizna, Am. garúa; v. lloviznar; anublar.
mistake [məsték] s. error, yerro, equivocación; errata (de imprenta); **to make a —** equivocarse; v. equivocar.
mistaken [məstékən] p.p. de to mistake & adj. equivocado; errado; erróneo, incorrecto; **to be —** estar equivocado, equivocarse, errar.
mister [mɪstə] s. señor.
mistook [mɪstʊk] pret. de to mistake.
mistreat [mɪstrít] v. maltratar.
mistress [mɪstrɪs] s. señora; ama, dueña; querida, amante; **school—** maestra.
mistrust [mɪstrʌst] s. desconfianza; v. desconfiar de.
mistrustful [mɪstrʌstfəl] adj. desconfiado, sospechoso, receloso.
misty [mɪstɪ] adj. brumoso; nublado; empañado; vago, indistinto.
misunderstand [mɪsʌndəstǽnd] v. comprender mal; entender mal; interpretar mal; no comprender.
misunderstanding [mɪsʌndəstǽndɪŋ] s. equivocación; mala interpretación, mala inteligencia; desavenencia.
misunderstood [mɪsʌndəstúd] pret. & p.p. de to misunderstand.
misuse [mɪsjús] s. abuso; mal uso; malversación (de fondos); [mɪsjúz] v. abusar de; maltratar; usar o emplear mal; malversar (fondos).
mite [maɪt] s. óbolo, friolera, pequeñez; criatura.
miter [máɪtə] s. mitra; dignidad de obispo.
mitigate [mítəget] v. mitigar.
mitten [mítn] s. mitón (guante de una pieza y sin dedos).
mix [mɪks] v. mezclar(se); unir(se), juntar(se), asociar(se); **to — someone up** confundir a uno; s. mezcla; confusión, lío.
mixture [mɪkstʃə] s. mezcla; mezcolanza.

moan [mon] s. quejido, gemido; v. gemir; quejarse; lamentar(se).

moat [mot] s. foso.

mob [mab] s. populacho; muchedumbre, gentío, *Am.* bola (*de gente*); v. atropellar; apiñarse o agolparse alrededor de.

mobile [móbl] adj. móvil; movible; movedizo.

mobilization [mobləzéʃən] s. movilización.

mobilize [móblaɪz] v. movilizar.

moccasin [mákəsn] s. *Am.* mocasín (*zapato burdo de cuero*); *Am.* mocasín (*víbora venenosa*).

mock [mok] v. mofar, mofarse de; remedar, imitar; to — at mofarse de; burlarse de; s. mofa, burla, escarnio; mímica; remedo; adj. falso, ficticio, imitado; — battle simulacro, batalla fingida.

mockery [mókərɪ] s. burla, mofa, escarnio; remedo.

mode [mod] s. modo; manera; moda.

model [mádl] s. modelo; patrón; figurín, maniquí; adj. ejemplar, modelo; — school escuela modelo; v. modelar; moldear, formar; posar, servir de modelo.

moderate [mádərɪt] adj. moderado; templado; módico; [mádəret] v. moderar(se); templar(se).

moderation [madəréʃən] s. moderación; templanza.

modern [mádən] adj. moderno.

modernize [mádənaɪz] v. modernizar.

modest [mádɪst] adj. modesto.

modesty [mádəstɪ] s. modestia.

modification [madəfəkéʃən] s. modificación.

modify [mádəfaɪ] v. modificar.

modulate [mádʒəlet] v. modular.

Mohammedan [mohǽmədən] adj. & s. mahometano.

moist [mɔɪst] adj. húmedo; mojado.

moisten [mɔ́ɪsn] v. humedecer, mojar.

moisture [mɔ́ɪstʃə] s. humedad.

molar [mólə] adj. molar; s. muela.

molasses [məlǽsɪz] s. melaza, miel de caña.

mold [mold] s. molde, matriz; moho; tierra vegetal; v. moldear, amoldar; modelar; enmohecer(se), cubrir(se) de moho.

molder [móldə] v. desmoronarse.

molding [móldɪŋ] s. moldura; moldeamiento.

moldy [móldɪ] adj. mohoso.

mole [mol] s. lunar; topo (*animal*); dique, malecón, rompeolas.

molecule [máləkjul] s. molécula.

molest [məlést] v. molestar.

molten [móltn] adj. derretido, fundido, en fusión.

moment [mómənt] s. momento; importancia, consecuencia.

momentary [mómənterɪ] adj. momentáneo.

momentous [moméntəs] adj. importante.

momentum [moméntəm] s. momento (*de una fuerza*); ímpetu.

monarch [mánək] s. monarca.

monarchy [mánəkɪ] s. monarquía.

monastery [mánəsterɪ] s. monasterio.

Monday [mándɪ] s. lunes.

monetary [mánəterɪ] adj. monetario.

money [mánɪ] s. dinero; — changer cambista; — order giro postal; paper — papel moneda; silver — moneda de plata; money-making lucrativo, provechoso, ganancioso.

mongrel [máŋgrəl] adj. & s. mestizo, mixto, cruzado, *Am.* chusco (*perro*).

monk [mʌŋk] s. monje.

monkey [máŋkɪ] s. mono; —shine monada, monería; — wrench llave inglesa; v. juguetear; hacer monerías; payasear; entremeterse; to — with juguetear con; meterse con.

monogram [mánəgrǽm] s. monograma.

monologue [mánlɔg] s. monólogo, soliloquio.

monopolize [mənápǝlaɪz] v. monopolizar, acaparar.

monopoly [mənáplɪ] s. monopolio.

monosyllable [mánəsɪləbl] s. monosílabo.

monotonous [mənátn̩əs] adj. monótono.

monotony [mənátnɪ] s. monotonía.

monster [mánstə] s. monstruo; adj. enorme.

monstrosity [manstrásətɪ] s. monstruosidad; monstruo.

monstrous [mánstrəs] adj. monstruoso.

month [mʌnθ] s. mes.

monthly [mánlɪ] adj. mensual; s. publicación mensual; adv. mensualmente.

monument [mánjəmənt] s. monumento.

monumental [manjəméntl] adj. monumental; colosal, grandioso.

moo [mu] s. mugido; v. mugir.

mood [mud] s. humor, disposición de ánimo; modo (*del verbo*); to be in a good — estar de buen humor; to be in the — to estar dispuesto a, tener gana de.

moody [múdɪ] adj. caprichoso, voluble, mudable; melancólico, mohino.

moon [mun] s. luna; mes lunar; once

in a blue — de Pascuas a San Juan, muy rara vez, *Am.* por campanada de vacante, *Am.* a cada muerte de (*o* por la muerte de un) obispo.

moonlight [múnlaɪt] *s.* luz de la luna; **— dance** baile a la luz de la luna; **— night** noche de luna.

moor [mʊr] *v.* amarrar, atracar (*un buque*); anclar; estar anclado; *s.* terreno inculto o baldío.

Moor [mʊr] *s.* moro.

Moorish [múríʃ] *adj.* morisco, moro.

mop [map] *s.* trapeador; **dust —** limpiapolvo; **— of hair** greñas, cabellera abundante; *v.* limpiar (*el suelo*), *Am.* trapear; **to —** one's brow limpiarse (*o* secarse) la frente; **to — up** limpiar; vencer; acabar con.

mope [mop] *v.* andar quejumbroso o abatido.

moral [mórəl] *adj.* moral; **— philosophy** ética, moral; *s.* moraleja; **-s** moral, ética.

morale [mərǽl] *s.* moral, entereza de ánimo.

moralist [mórəlɪst] *s.* moralista.

morality [mərǽlətɪ] *s.* moralidad.

moralize [mórəlaɪz] *v.* moralizar.

morbid [mórbɪd] *adj.* mórbido, morboso; malsano.

more [mor] *adj. & adv.* más; **— and —** cada vez más, más y más; **— or less** poco más o menos; **there is no —** no hay más, ya no hay; se acabó.

moreover [moróvə] *adv.* además.

morning [mórnɪŋ] *s.* mañana; **good —** ! ¡buenos días!; **tomorrow —** mañana por la mañana; *adj.* de la mañana; matutino, matinal; **morning-glory** dondiego de día; **— star** lucero del alba.

morphine [mórfin] *s.* morfina.

morrow [móro] : **on the —** el día de mañana; mañana.

morsel [mórsl] *s.* bocado; manjar sabroso.

mortal [mórtl] *adj. & s.* mortal.

mortality [mortǽlətɪ] *s.* mortalidad; mortandad.

mortar [mórtə] *s.* mortero; argamasa, mezcla; **metal —** almirez.

mortgage [mórgɪdʒ] *s.* hipoteca, gravamen; *v.* hipotecar.

mortify [mórtəfaɪ] *v.* mortificar; avergonzar.

mosaic [mozéɪk] *adj. & s.* mosaico.

mosquito [məskíto] *s.* mosquito; **— net** mosquitero.

moss [mɔs] *s.* musgo; **moss-grown** musgoso, cubierto de musgo; anticua-

do.

mossy [mɔsɪ] *adj.* musgoso.

most [most] *adv.* más; sumamente, muy; *s.* la mayoría, la mayor parte, el mayor número o cantidad; los más; **— people** la mayoría (*o* la mayor parte) de la gente; **at the —** a lo más, a lo sumo; **for the —** part por la mayor parte; generalmente, mayormente; **the — that I can do** lo más que puedo hacer; **the — votes** el mayor número de votos, los más votos.

mostly [móstlɪ] *adv.* por la mayor parte; mayormente, principalmente.

moth [mɔθ] *s.* polilla; mariposa nocturna; **— ball** bolita de naftalina; **moth-eaten** apolillado.

mother [mʌðə] *s.* madre; **mother-of-pearl** madreperla, nácar; *adj.* de madre; materno, maternal; nativo, natal; **— country** madre patria; país natal; **— Superior** superiora; **— tongue** lengua materna; *v.* servir de madre a, cuidar de.

motherhood [mʌðəhʊd] *s.* maternidad.

mother-in-law [mʌðərɪnlɔ] *s.* suegra.

motherly [mʌðəlɪ] *adj.* maternal, materno.

motif [motíf] *s.* motivo, tema.

motion [móʃən] *s.* moción; movimiento; ademán; señal, seña; *v.* hacer una seña o señas; indicar.

motionless [móʃənlɪs] *adj.* inmóvil, inmoble.

motion picture [móʃənpíktʃə] *s.* cine o cinematógrafo; película; fotografía cinematográfica; **motion-picture** *adj.* cinematográfico.

motive [mótɪv] *s.* motivo; tema; *adj.* motriz.

motley [mátlɪ] *adj.* abigarrado, multicolor, de diversos colores; variado, mezclado; *s.* mezcla, mezcolanza.

motor [mótə] *s.* motor; automóvil; *v.* pasear o ir en automóvil.

motorboat [mótəbot] *s.* autobote, lancha de gasolina, bote de motor.

motorcar [mótəkar] *s.* automóvil.

motorcoach [mótəkotʃ] *s.* autobús, ómnibus, *Am.* camión, *Am.* guagua.

motorcycle [mótəsaɪkl] *s.* motocicleta.

motorist [mótərɪst] *s.* motorista, automovilista.

motorman [mótəmən] *s.* motorista.

mottled [mátld] *adj.* moteado, jaspeado, manchado.

motto [máto] *s.* mote, divisa, lema.

mould = **mold**.

moulder = **molder**.

moulding = **molding**.

mouldy = moldy.

mound [maʊnd] s. montecillo, montículo, montón de tierra.

mount [maʊnt] s. monte; montura, cabalgadura, caballo; v. montar; montar a caballo; subir, ascender; armar (*una máquina*); engastar (*joyas*).

mountain [máʊntɪn] s. montaña; adj. montañés; de montaña; — **goat** cabra montés; — **lion** puma; — **range** cordillera, cadena de montañas.

mountaineer [maʊntɪnír] s. montañés.

mountainous [máʊntɪnəs] adj. montañoso.

mourn [morn] v. lamentar; deplorar; **to — for** llorar a; estar de duelo por.

mournful [mórnfəl] adj. fúnebre; lúgubre; lastimero; triste.

mourning [mórnɪŋ] s. luto; duelo; lamentación; **to be in** — estar de luto, estar de duelo; adj. de luto.

mouse [maʊs] s. ratón; — **trap** ratonera.

moustache = mustache.

mouth [maʊθ] s. boca; abertura; desembocadura, embocadura (*de un río*).

mouthful [máʊθfəl] s. bocado.

mouthpiece [máʊθpis] s. boquilla (*de un instrumento de viento*); portavoz.

movable [múvəbl] adj. móvible, móvil; **—s** s. pl. muebles, bienes muebles.

move [muv] v. mover(se); mudarse, mudar de casa; menear(se); conmover; inducir; proponer, hacer la moción de (*en una asamblea*); andar; hacer una jugada (*en ajedrez o damas*); — **away** irse; alejarse; apartarse; **to — forward** avanzar; **to — on** seguir adelante, caminar; **to — out** irse, mudarse, mudar de casa; s. movimiento; mudanza (*de una casa a otra*); paso, trámite (*para conseguir algo*); jugada, turno (*en juegos*); **get a — on there!** ¡ande! ¡dése prisa! *Am.* ¡ándele!

movement [múvmənt] s. movimiento; maniobra; meneo; acción; mecanismo, movimiento (*de un reloj*); evacuación (*del vientre*).

movie [múvɪ] s. cine, película; **—s** cine.

mow [mo] v. segar; cortar (*césped*).

mower [móə] s. segador; segadora, cortadora mecánica; máquina segadora.

mown [mon] adj. & p.p. segado.

Mr. [místə] Sr., señor; **Mrs.** [mísɪz] Sra., señora.

much [mʌtʃ] adj., adv. & s. mucho; — **the same** casi lo mismo; **as — as** tanto como; **how —?** ¿cuánto?; **not — of a book** un libro de poco valor; **not — of a poet** un poetastro; **so —**

that tanto que; **too —** demasiado; **very —** muchísimo; **to make — of** dar mucha importancia a.

muck [mʌk] s. estiércol húmedo; cieno; porquería, suciedad.

mucous [mjúkəs] adj. mucoso; — **membrane** membrana mucosa.

mud [mʌd] s. lodo, fango, cieno; — **wall** tapia.

muddle [mʌdl] v. enturbiar; confundir; embrollar; s. confusión, embrollo, lío, desorden.

muddy [mʌdɪ] adj. fangoso, lodoso; turbio; confuso; v. enlodar, ensuciar; enturbiar.

muff [mʌf] s. manguito (*para las manos*); falla, error (*en ciertos juegos*); v. no coger, dejar escapar (*la pelota*).

muffin [mʌfɪn] s. bollo, panecillo.

muffle [mʌfl] v. embozar; tapar; apagar, amortiguar (*un sonido*).

muffler [mʌflə] s. bufanda; silenciador (*para maquinaria*).

mug [mʌg] s. pichel, vaso con asa.

mulatto [məlǽto] s. mulato.

mulberry [mʌlberɪ] s. mora; — **tree** moral.

mule [mjul] s. mulo, mula; **muleteer** [mjulətír] s. arriero.

mull [mʌl] v. meditar, ponderar, revolver en la mente; calentar (*vino, sidra, etc.*) con azúcar y especias.

multiple [mʌltəpl] s. múltiplo; adj. múltiple.

multiplication [mʌltəpləkéʃən] s. multiplicación; — **table** tabla de multiplicar.

multiplicity [mʌltəplísətɪ] s. multiplicidad.

multiply [mʌltəplaɪ] v. multiplicar(se).

multitude [mʌltətjud] s. multitud.

mum [mʌm] adj. callado, silencioso; **to keep —** estarse (o quedarse) callado.

mumble [mʌmbl] v. murmurar, hablar entre dientes; mascullar; s. murmullo; **to talk in a —** mascullar las palabras, hablar entre dientes.

mummy [mʌmɪ] s. momia.

mumps [mʌmps] s. parótidas, paperas.

munch [mʌntʃ] v. mascar ruidosamente, mascullar.

municipal [mjunísəpl] adj. municipal.

municipality [mjunɪsəpǽlətɪ] s. municipio; municipalidad.

munition [mjuníʃən] s. munición; — **plant** fábrica de municiones, arsenal; v. guarnecer, abastecer de municiones.

mural [mjúrəl] adj. & s. mural.

murder [mɜ́də] s. asesinato, homicidio; v. asesinar.

murderer [mɔ́dərə] s. asesino, homicida.

murderess [mɔ́dəris] s. asesina, homicida.

murderous [mɔ́dərəs] adj. asesino, homicida.

murmur [mɔ́mə] s. murmullo; susurro; queja; v. murmurar; susurrar; quejarse.

muscle [mʌ́sl] s. músculo.

muscular [mʌ́skjələ] adj. muscular; musculoso.

muse [mjuz] v. meditar; s. meditación; Muse musa.

museum [mjuzɔ́əm] s. museo.

mush [mʌʃ] s. potaje espeso de maíz; masa de maíz; cualquier masa blanda; sentimentalismo.

mushroom [mʌ́ʃrum] s. seta, hongo.

music [mjúzik] s. música; — stand atril.

musical [mjúzikl] adj. musical, músico; melodioso; armonioso; aficionado a la música; — comedy zarzuela, comedia musical.

musician [mjuzíʃən] s. músico.

muskmelon [mʌ́skmelən] s. melón.

muskrat [mʌ́skræt] s. almizclera (roedor semejante a la rata).

muslin [mʌ́zlin] s. muselina.

muss [mʌs] v. desarreglar, desordenar; arrugar.

must [mʌst] v. defect. (por lo general se usa sólo en el presente) deber; deber de, haber de; tener que.

mustache [mʌ́stæʃ] s. bigote, mostacho.

mustard [mʌ́stəd] s. mostaza; — plaster sinapismo.

muster [mʌ́stə] v. pasar lista o revista; juntarse para una formación militar; reunir(se); to — out dar de baja; to — up one's courage cobrar valor o ánimo; s. revista (de soldados o marinos); to pass — pasar lista o revista; ser aceptable (en una inspección).

musty [mʌ́sti] adj. mohoso; rancio, añejo.

mute [mjut] adj. mudo; s. mudo; letra muda; sordina (de violín).

mutilate [mjútlet] v. mutilar.

mutiny [mjútni] s. motín; v. amotinarse.

mutter [mʌ́tə] v. murmurar, refunfuñar; hablar entre dientes; s. murmullo, refunfuño.

mutton [mʌ́tn] s. carne de carnero; — chop chuleta de carnero.

mutual [mjútʃul] adj. mutuo.

muzzle [mʌ́zl] s. hocico; bozal (para el hocico); boca (de arma de fuego); v. abozalar, poner bozal a; amordazar; hacer callar.

my [mai] adj. mi (mis).

myriad [mɪ́riəd] s. miríada, diez mil; millares, gran cantidad.

myrtle [mɔ́tl] s. mirto, arrayán.

myself [məsélf] pron. yo mismo; me (como reflexivo); a mí mismo; by — solo; I — did it yo mismo lo hice; I talk to — hablo conmigo mismo, hablo para mis adentros.

mysterious [mistíriəs] adj. misterioso.

mystery [místri] s. misterio.

mystic [místik] adj. & s. místico.

mystical [místikl] adj. místico.

myth [miɵ] s. mito, fábula.

mythology [miɵálədʒi] s. mitología.

N

nab [næb] v. agarrar, coger; arrestar.

nag [næg] s. rocín, caballejo, jaco; v. importunar, irritar (con repetidos regaños).

nail [nel] s. clavo; uña (del dedo); — file lima (para las uñas); v. clavar; clavetear; agarrar, atrapar.

naive [naív] adj. simple, ingenuo, cándido.

naked [nékid] adj. desnudo.

nakedness [nékidnis] s. desnudez.

name [nem] s. nombre; renombre, fama; —sake tocayo; by the — of nombrado, llamado; apellidado; family — apellido; to call someone -s motejar o decirle groserías a uno; ponerle apodos a uno; to make a — for oneself ganar fama; what is your — ? ¿cómo se llama Vd.?; v. nombrar; mentar, mencionar; llamar.

nameless [némlis] adj. sin nombre; anónimo.

namely [némli] adv. a saber, esto es, es decir.

nap [næp] s. siesta; pelo (de un tejido); to take a — echar un sueño, echar una siesta; v. dormitar; echar un sueño; sestear.

nape [nep] s. nuca, cogote.

naphtha [nǽpɵə] s. nafta.

napkin [nǽpkin] s. servilleta.

narcissus [narsísəs] s. narciso.

narcotic [narkátik] adj. & s. narcótico.

narrate [nærét] v. narrar.

narration [næréʃən] s. narración.

narrative [nǽrətiv] adj. narrativo; s. narración; narrativa; relato.

narrow [nǽro] adj. estrecho; angosto; limitado; intolerante; — escape trance difícil, escapada difícil; — search búsqueda esmerada; narrow-minded fanático, intolerante; -s s. pl. desfiladero, paso; estrecho o estrechos;

v. angostar(se), estrechar(se); limitar, restringir, reducir; -ly *adv.* estrechamente; he -ly escaped por poco no se escapa.

narrowness [nǽrənɪs] *s.* estrechez, estrechura, angostura; limitación; intolerancia.

nasal [nézl] *adj.* nasal.

nastiness [nǽstɪnɪs] *s.* suciedad, porquería; grosería.

nasturtium [nəstɔ́ʃəm] *s.* mastuerzo.

nasty [nǽstɪ] *adj.* sucio, asqueroso; feo; indecente; grosero; a — fall una caída terrible; a — disposition un genio horrible.

nation [néʃən] *s.* nación.

national [nǽʃənl] *adj.* nacional; *s.* nacional, ciudadano.

nationality [næʃənǽlətɪ] *s.* nacionalidad.

native [nétɪv] *adj.* nativo; natal; natural; indígena; del país, *Am.* criollo; — of oriundo de, natural de; *s.* nativo, natural, indígena; habitante.

nativity [nətívətɪ] *s.* nacimiento; natividad *(de la Vírgen María);* the Nativity la Navidad.

natural [nǽtʃərəl] *adj.* natural; sencillo, sin afectación; *s.* becuadro *(signo musical);* he is a — for that job tiene aptitud natural para ese puesto; -ly *adv.* naturalmente; con naturalidad.

naturalism [nǽtʃərəlɪzəm] *s.* naturalismo.

naturalist [nǽtʃərəlɪst] *s.* naturalista.

naturalization [nætʃərələzéʃən] *s.* naturalización.

naturalize [nǽtʃərəlaɪz] *v.* naturalizar.

naturalness [nǽtʃərəlnɪs] *s.* naturalidad.

nature [nétʃə] *s.* naturaleza; natural, genio, índole; instinto; especie; to copy from — copiar del natural.

naught [nɔt] *s.* cero; nada.

naughty [nɔ́tɪ] *adj.* malo, desobediente; travieso, pícaro; malicioso.

nausea [nɔ́zɪə] *s.* náusea.

nauseate [nɔ́zɪet] *v.* dar náuseas, dar bascas, asquear, dar asco; sentir náusea; to be -ed tener náuseas.

nauseating [nɔ́zɪetɪŋ] *adj.* nauseabundo, asqueroso.

naval [névl] *adj.* naval; — officer oficial de marina.

nave [nev] *s.* nave *(de una iglesia).*

navel [névl] *s.* ombligo; — orange naranja california *(sin semillas).*

navigable [nǽvəgəbl] *adj.* navegable.

navigate [nǽvəget] *v.* navegar.

navigation [nævəgéʃən] *s.* navegación;

náutica.

navigator [nǽvəgetə] *s.* navegador, navegante.

navy [névɪ] *s.* marina de guerra; armada; — blue azul marino; — yard astillero, arsenal.

nay [ne] *adv.* no; no sólo . . . sino (que) también; *s.* no, voto negativo.

near [nɪr] *adv.* cerca; casi; — at hand cerca, a la mano; I came — forgetting to do it por poco se me olvida hacerlo; to come (go, draw) — acercarse; —sighted miope; *prep.* cerca de; — the end of the month hacia fines del mes; *adj.* cercano, próximo; estrecho, íntimo; — silk seda imitada; I had a — accident por poco me sucede un accidente; *v.* acercarse (a).

near-by [nírbáɪ] *adv.* cerca, a la mano; *adj.* cercano, próximo.

nearly [nírlɪ] *adv.* casi, cerca de; aproximadamente, próximamente; I — did it estuve al punto de hacerlo, estuve para hacerlo.

nearness [nírnɪs] *s.* cercanía, proximidad.

neat [nit] *adj.* pulcro, aseado, limpio; ordenado; esmerado; hábil, diestro; -ly *adv.* aseadamente; esmeradamente; ordenadamente; hábilmente.

neatness [nítnɪs] *s.* pulcritud, aseo; limpieza; esmero; claridad.

necessarily [nésəsərəlɪ] *adv.* necesariamente.

necessary [nésəserɪ] *adj.* necesario; **necessaries** *s. pl.* necesidades, requisitos.

necessitate [nəsésətet] *v.* necesitar, precisar.

necessity [nəsésətɪ] *s.* necesidad.

neck [nɛk] *s.* cuello; pescuezo; garganta; — of land istmo; low — escote; — and — parejos *(en una carrera).*

necklace [néklɪs] *s.* collar; gargantilla.

necktie [néktaɪ] *s.* corbata.

need [nid] *s.* necesidad; pobreza; for — of por falta de; if — be si fuere menester, en caso de necesidad; *v.* necesitar; tener necesidad de; hacerle falta a uno; tener que.

needful [nídfəl] *adj.* necesario; necesitado.

needle [nídl] *s.* aguja.

needless [nídlɪs] *adj.* innecesario, inútil.

needlework [nídlwɔk] *s.* labor, bordado; costura.

needy [nídɪ] *adj.* necesitado, menesteroso.

ne'er [nɛr] *adv. contr. de* never; **ne'er-**

do-well *s.* persona incompetente; haragán.

negation [nɪgéʃən] *s.* negación; negativa.

negative [négətɪv] *adj.* negativo; *s.* negativa; negación, partícula o voz negativa; negativa (*de una fotografía*).

neglect [nɪglékt] *s.* negligencia; descuido; abandono; *v.* descuidar; desatender; abandonar; **to — to** dejar de, olvidar, olvidarse de.

neglectful [nɪgléktfəl] *adj.* negligente, descuidado.

negligence [néglədʒəns] *s.* negligencia.

negligent [néglədʒənt] *adj.* negligente, descuidado.

negotiate [nɪgóʃɪet] *v.* negociar; agenciar; vencer (*un obstáculo o dificultad*), dar cima a.

negotiation [nɪgoʃɪéʃən] *s.* negociación.

negro [nígro] *s.* & *adj.* negro.

neigh [ne] *s.* relincho; *v.* relinchar.

neighbor [nébə] *s.* vecino; prójimo; *adj.* vecino; cercano.

neighborhood [nébəhud] *s.* vecindad; vecindario; inmediación; **in the — of** a hundred dollars cerca de cien dólares.

neighboring [nébərɪŋ] *adj.* vecino; cercano; colindante.

neither [níðə] *pron.* ninguno, ni (el) uno ni (el) otro; **— of the two** ninguno de los dos; *adj.* ninguno; **— one of us** ninguno de nosotros; *conj.* ni; **— ... nor ni ... ni; — will I** tampoco yo, ni yo tampoco.

nephew [néfju] *s.* sobrino.

nerve [nɜv] *s.* nervio; valor, ánimo; audacia; descaro; -s nervios; nerviosidad; **to strain every —** esforzarse hasta más no poder, poner el mayor empeño posible.

nervous [nɜvəs] *adj.* nervioso.

nervousness [nɜvəsnɪs] *s.* nerviosidad; agitación.

nest [nest] *s.* nido; nidada; **— egg** nidal; ahorros; **— of baskets** (boxes, tables) juego graduado de cestas (cajas, mesitas); **wasp's —** avispero; *v.* anidar.

nestle [nésl] *v.* acurrucarse; abrigar(se); anidar.

net [net] *s.* red; malla; tejido de mallas; *adj.* de mallas, de punto de malla; *v.* redar, enredar, coger con red; cubrir con una red.

net [net] *adj.* neto; **— price** precio neto; **— profit** ganancia neta o líquida; *v.* producir una ganancia neta o líquida; obtener una ganancia líquida.

nettle [nétl] *s.* ortiga; *v.* picar, irritar, enfadar.

network [nétwɜk] *s.* red; malla; **radio —** red de estaciones radiofónicas.

neuter [njútə] *adj.* neutro.

neutral [njútrəl] *adj.* neutral; neutro.

neutrality [njutrǽlətɪ] *s.* neutralidad.

neutralize [njútrəlaɪz] *v.* neutralizar.

never [névə] *adv.* nunca, jamás; **— mind** no importa; no haga Vd. caso; **no se moleste** Vd.; **never-ending** perpetuo, eterno; de nunca acabar.

nevertheless [nevə∂olés] *adv.* & *conj.* sin embargo, no obstante, con todo, empero.

new [nju] *adj.* nuevo; reciente; moderno; fresco; *adv.* recién; **—born baby** criatura recién-nacida.

newcomer [njúkʌmə] *s.* recién llegado.

newly [njúlɪ] *adv.* nuevamente, recientemente; **— arrived** recién llegado; **— wed** recién casado.

newness [njúnɪs] *s.* novedad, calidad de nuevo.

news [njuz] *s.* noticias, nuevas; novedades; **piece of —** noticia, nueva; **—boy** vendedor de periódicos; **—reel** película noticiera; película de noticias mundiales; **—stand** puesto de periódicos.

newsmonger [njúzmʌŋgə] *s.* chismoso, chismero, gacetilla.

newspaper [njúzpepə] *s.* periódico.

next [nekst] *adj.* próximo; entrante, que viene; siguiente; contiguo; **in the —** life en la otra vida; **to be —** in turn tocarle a uno, ser su turno; *adv.* después, luego; **— best** segundo en cualidad o importancia; *prep.*; **— to** junto a; al lado de; después de.

nibble [nɪbl] *s.* mordisco; *v.* mordiscar, mordisquear; picar, morder.

nice [naɪs] *adj.* fino; bueno; amable, simpático; lindo; primoroso; refinado, esmerado; preciso, exacto; **-ly** *adv.* con esmero; con finura o primor; sutilmente, con delicadeza; amablemente; bien; **to get along -ly with** llevarse bien con.

nicety [náɪsətɪ] *s.* fineza, finura; delicadeza; exactitud.

niche [nɪtʃ] *s.* nicho.

nick [nɪk] *s.* mella, desportilladura; **in the — of time** en el momento crítico; *v.* mellar, desportillar.

nickel [nɪkl] *s.* níquel; moneda de cinco centavos; **nickel-plated** niquelado.

nickname [nɪknem] *s.* mote, apodo; *v.* apodar, poner apodo a.

niece [nis] *s.* sobrina.

niggardly [nígədlɪ] *adj.* mezquino, ruin, tacaño; *adv.* mezquinamente, ruinmente.

night[naɪt] *s.* noche; **good — !** ¡buenas noches!; **tomorrow —** mañana por la noche; *adj.* nocturno; de noche; **— owl** buho; trasnochador; **— watchman** sereno, vigilante nocturno.

nightfall [náɪtfɔl] *s.* anochecer, caída de la tarde, anochecida.

nightgown [náɪtgaʊn] *s.* camisa de dormir, camisa de noche; *Am.* camisón.

nightingale [náɪtŋgel] *s.* ruiseñor.

nightly [náɪtlɪ] *adv.* cada noche, todas las noches; *adj.* nocturno, de noche.

nightmare [náɪtmɛr] *s.* pesadilla.

nimble [nímbl] *adj.* ágil, ligero; listo.

nip [nɪp] *v.* pellizcar; mordiscar; marchitar, helar *(por la acción del frío)*; **to — in the bud** cortar en germen, destruir al nacer; **— off** despuntar; podar; *s.* pellizco; mordisco; trago.

nipple [nípl] *s.* teta, tetilla, pezón; pezón de goma.

nitrate [náɪtret] *s.* nitrato.

nitrogen [náɪtrədʒən] *s.* nitrógeno.

no [no] *adv.* no; **— longer** ya no; **there is — more** no hay más; *adj.* ningun(o); **— matter how much** por mucho que; **— one** ninguno, nadie; **— smoking** se prohibe fumar; **I have — friend** no tengo ningún amigo; **of — use** inútil, sin provecho; *s.* no, voto negativo.

nobility [nobílətɪ] *s.* nobleza.

noble [nóbl] *s.* & *adj.* noble.

nobleman [nóblmən] *s.* noble.

nobleness [nóblnɪs] *s.* nobleza.

nobly [nóblɪ] *adv.* noblemente.

nobody [nóbadɪ] *pron.* nadie, ninguno.

nod [nad] *v.* inclinar la cabeza *(para hacer una seña, saludar, o asentir)*; cabecear, dar cabezadas *(dormitando)*; *s.* inclinación de cabeza, saludo; señal de asentimiento *(con la cabeza)*.

noise [nɔɪz] *s.* ruido; barullo; sonido; *v.* divulgar; **it is being -d about** that corre el rumor que.

noiseless [nɔ́ɪzlɪs] *adj.* sin ruido, silencioso, quieto; **-ly** *adv.* sin ruido, silenciosamente.

noisily [nɔ́ɪzɪlɪ] *adv.* ruidosamente.

noisy [nɔ́ɪzɪ] *adj.* ruidoso.

nominal [námənl] *adj.* nominal.

nominate [námənet] *v.* nombrar, designar.

nomination [namənéʃən] *s.* nombramiento, nominación.

none [nʌn] *pron.* ninguno; ningunos; nada; **I want — of that** no quiero nada de eso; **that is — of his business** no le importa a él eso; *adv.* no, de ningún modo; **— the less** no menos; **to be — the happier for** that no estar por eso más contento.

nonentity [nanɛ́ntətɪ] *s.* nulidad, persona o cosa inútil.

nonsense [nánsɛns] *s.* tontería, necedad; disparate, desatino.

noodle [núdl] *s.* tallarín, fideo, pasta *(para sopa)*.

nook [nʊk] *s.* rincón; **breakfast —** desayunador.

noon [nun] *s.* mediodía.

noonday [núnde] *s.* mediodía; *adj.* meridiano, de mediodía; **— meal** comida de mediodía.

noontide [núntaɪd] *s.* mediodía.

noontime [núntaɪm] *s.* mediodía.

noose [nus] *s.* dogal; lazo, nudo corredizo, *Am.* gaza; *v.* lazar, coger con lazo; hacer un lazo corredizo en.

nor [nɔr] *conj.* ni; **neither . . . —** ní . . . ni.

norm [nɔrm] *s.* norma.

normal [nɔ́rml] *adj.* normal; *s.* norma; normal, línea perpendicular.

north [nɔrθ] *s.* norte; *adj.* septentrional; norteño; del norte; **— pole** polo norte, polo ártico; **— wind** cierzo, norte; **North American** norteamericano; *adv.* al norte, hacia el norte.

northeast [nɔrɛíst] *adj.* & *s.* nordeste; *adv.* hacia el nordeste, rumbo al nordeste.

northeastern [nɔrɛístən] *adj.* del nordeste, nordeste.

northern [nɔ́rðən] *adj.* septentrional; norteño; del norte; hacia el norte; **— lights** aurora boreal.

northerner [nɔ́rðənə] *s.* norteño, habitante del norte.

northward [nɔ́rɛwəd] *adv.* hacia el norte, rumbo al norte.

northwest [nɔrɛwɛ́st] *adj.* & *s.* noroeste; *adv.* hacia el noroeste.

northwestern [nɔrɛwɛ́stən] *adj.* noroeste del noroeste.

Norwegian [nɔrwídʒən] *adj.* & *s.* noruego.

nose [noz] *s.* nariz; proa *(de un barco)*; **— dive** picada *(de un avión)*; *v.* olfatear; **to — around** husmear, curiosear.

nostalgia [nastǽldʒɪə] *s.* nostalgia, añoranza.

nostrils [nástrəlz] *s. pl.* narices, ventanas de la nariz.

not [nat] *adv.* no; **— at all** de ningún modo; de nada *(contestación a "thank* you"); — **at all sure** nada seguro; — **even a word** ni siquiera una palabra.

notable [nótəbl] *adj.* notable.

notary [nótərɪ] *s.* notario.

notation [notéʃən] *s.* notación; apunte; anotación.

notch [nɑtʃ] *s.* muesca, ranura; hendidura; *v.* ranurar, hacer una ranura en.

note [not] *s.* nota; apunte, apuntación; **bank —** billete de banco; **promissory —** pagaré, abonaré; *v.* notar, observar, reparar; **to — down** apuntar.

notebook [nótbʊk] *s.* libreta; cuaderno, libro de apuntes.

noted [nótɪd] *adj.* notable, célebre, famoso.

noteworthy [nótwɜ̄ðɪ] *adj.* notable, célebre.

nothing [nʌθɪŋ] *s.* nada; cero; **for —** por nada; inútilmente; de balde, gratis.

notice [nótɪs] *s.* noticia; aviso, advertencia, anuncio; mención; **to give a short —** avisar a última hora; **to take —** of hacer caso de, prestar atención a; *v.* notar, observar; prestar atención a; hacer caso a (o de); notificar.

noticeable [nótɪsəbl] *adj.* notable; conspicuo; perceptible.

notify [nótəfaɪ] *v.* notificar, avisar.

notion [nóʃən] *s.* noción; idea; capricho; **-s** mercería, artículos menudos (*como alfileres, botones, etc.*), chucherías.

notorious [notórɪəs] *adj.* notorio.

notwithstanding [nɑtwɪɛstǽndɪŋ] *prep.* a pesar de; *adv. & conj.* no obstante, sin embargo; **— that** a pesar (de) que.

nought = naught.

noun [naʊn] *s.* nombre, sustantivo.

nourish [nɜ́rɪʃ] *v.* nutrir, alimentar.

nourishing [nɜ́rɪʃɪŋ] *adj.* nutritivo, alimenticio.

nourishment [nɜ́rɪʃmənt] *s.* nutrimento, sustento, alimento; nutrición.

novel [návl] *s.* novela; *adj.* novel, nuevo; raro, original.

novelist [návlɪst] *s.* novelista.

novelty [návltɪ] *s.* novedad; innovación; **novelties** novedades.

November [novémbə] *s.* noviembre.

novice [návɪs] *s.* novicio; novato, principiante.

now [naʊ] *adv.* ahora; ya; **— . . . —** ya . . . ya, ora . . . ora; **— and then** de vez en cuando, de cuando en cuando; **— that** ahora que; **— then** ahora bien; **he left just —** salió hace poco,

Am. salió recién.

nowadays [náʊədez] *adv.* hoy día.

nowhere [nóhwer] *adv.* en ninguna parte, a ninguna parte.

noxious [nákʃəs] *adj.* nocivo.

nucleus [njúklɪəs] *s.* núcleo.

nude [njud] *adj.* desnudo.

nudge [nʌdʒ] *v.* codear, tocar con el codo; *s.* codazo ligero.

nuisance [njúsns] *s.* molestia; lata, fastidio; persona o cosa fastidiosa.

null [nʌl] *adj.* nulo; **— and void** nulo e inválido.

numb [nʌm] *adj.* entumecido o entumido, aterido; **to become —** entumecerse, entumirse, aterirse; *v.* entumecer.

number [nʌmbə] *s.* número; *v.* numerar; ascender a (*cierto número*); **to — him among one's friends** contarle entre sus amigos.

numberless [nʌmbəlɪs] *adj.* innumerable, sin número.

numeral [njúmrəl] *s.* número, cifra; guarismo; *adj.* numeral.

numerical [njumérɪkl] *adj.* numérico.

numerous [njúmrəs] *adj.* numeroso; numerosos, muchos.

nun [nʌn] *s.* monja.

nuptial [nʌpʃəl] *adj.* nupcial; **-s** *s. pl.* nupcias, bodas.

nurse [nɜs] *s.* enfermera, enfermero; niñera, aya, *Am.* nana, *Am.* manejadora, *Am.* pilmama; **wet —** nodriza, ama de cría; *v.* criar, amamantar, dar de mamar, lactar; mamar; cuidar (*a un enfermo*); abrigar (*rencor*).

nursery [nɜ́srɪ] *s.* cuarto para niños; criadero, semillero (*de plantas*); **day —** sala donde se cuida y divierte a los niños.

nurture [nɜ́tʃə] *s.* crianza; nutrimento; *v.* criar; nutrir; cuidar; fomentar.

nut [nʌt] *s.* nuez (*nombre genérico de varias frutas como la almendra, la castaña, la avellana, etc.*); tuerca; loco, tipo raro o extravagante.

nutcracker [nʌtkrækə] *s.* cascanueces.

nutmeg [nʌtmeg] *s.* nuez moscada.

nutrition [njutrɪʃən] *s.* nutrición; nutrimento, alimento.

nutritious [njutrɪʃəs] *adj.* nutritivo, alimenticio.

nutritive [njútrɪtɪv] *adj.* nutritivo.

nutshell [nʌtʃel] *s.* cáscara de nuez (*o de otro fruto semejante*); **in a — en suma, en breve, en pocas palabras.

nymph [nɪmf] *s.* ninfa.

143

O

oak [ok] s. roble; encina; — **grove** robledo o robledal; **live** — encina siempreverde.

oar [or] s. remo; v. remar, bogar.

oasis [oésis] s. oasis.

oat [ot] s. avena (planta); -s avena, granos de avena.

oath [oθ] s. juramento; blasfemia, reniego.

oatmeal [ótmil] s. harina de avena; gachas de avena.

obedience [əbídɪəns] s. obediencia.

obedient [əbídɪənt] adj. obediente.

obesity [obísəti] s. obesidad, gordura.

obey [əbé] v. obedecer.

object [ábdʒɪkt] s. objeto; cosa; complemento (del verbo); [əbdʒékt] v. objetar; oponerse; tener inconveniente.

objection [əbdʒékʃən] s. objeción, reparo; inconveniente.

objective [əbdʒéktɪv] adj. objetivo; — **case** caso complementario; s. objetivo; fin, propósito.

obligate [ábləget] v. obligar, constreñir, comprometer.

obligation [abləgéʃən] s. obligación; deber; deuda; **to be under — to estar** obligado a; estar agradecido a, deber favores a.

obligatory [əblígətorɪ] adj. obligatorio.

oblige [əbláɪdʒ] v. obligar; complacer; **much -ed!** ¡muchas gracias! ¡muy agradecido!; **to be very much -ed to someone** quedar muy agradecido con alguien.

obliging [əbláɪdʒɪŋ] adj. complaciente, obsequioso, comedido, cortés.

oblique [əblík] adj. oblicuo.

obliterate [əblítəret] v. borrar; arrasar, destruir.

oblivion [əblívɪən] s. olvido.

oblivious [əblívɪəs] adj. olvidado, abstraído.

obnoxious [əbnákʃəs] adj. ofensivo; molesto; odioso.

obscene [əbsín] adj. obsceno.

obscenity [əbsénəti] s. obscenidad, indecencia.

obscure [əbskjúr] adj. obscuro; v. obscurecer; ofuscar.

obscurity [əbskjúrəti] s. obscuridad.

obsequies [ábsɪkwɪz] s. exequias, honras, funerales.

obsequious [əbsíkwɪəs] adj. obsequioso; servil, zalamero.

observance [əbzɔ́vəns] s. observancia; ceremonia, rito.

observant [əbzɔ́vənt] adj. observador; observante.

observation [abzɜvéʃən] s. observación.

observatory [əbzɔ́vətorɪ] s. observatorio; mirador.

observe [əbzɔ́v] v. observar; guardar (las fiestas religiosas); celebrar (una fiesta).

observer [əbzɔ́və] s. observador.

obsess [əbsés] v. obsesionar, causar obsesión.

obsession [əbséʃən] s. obsesión; idea fija.

obsolete [ábsəlit] adj. anticuado; desusado.

obstacle [ábstək!] s. obstáculo.

obstinacy [ábstənəsi] s. obstinación, terquedad, porfía.

obstinate [ábstənɪt] adj. obstinado, terco, porfiado.

obstruct [əbstrʌkt] v. obstruir.

obstruction [əbstrʌkʃən] s. obstrucción; impedimento, estorbo.

obtain [əbtén] v. obtener, conseguir, alcanzar, adquirir.

obtainable [əbténəb!] adj. obtenible, asequible.

obviate [ábviet] v. obviar; allanar (una dificultad).

obvious [ábvɪəs] adj. obvio, evidente.

occasion [əkéʒən] s. ocasión; oportunidad; causa, motivo; acontecimiento; v. ocasionar, causar.

occasional [əkéʒən!] adj. ocasional; infrecuente, poco frecuente; **-ly** adv. de vez en cuando, a veces.

occidental [aksədént!] adj. & s. occidental.

occupant [ákjəpənt] s. ocupante; inquilino.

occupation [akjəpéʃən] s. ocupación; trabajo, empleo, oficio.

occupy [ákjəpaɪ] v. ocupar.

occur [əkɔ́] v. ocurrir, suceder; **to — to one** ocurrírsele a uno, venirle a la mente.

occurrence [əkɔ́əns] s. ocurrencia, suceso, caso, acontecimiento.

ocean [óʃən] s. océano.

o'clock [əklák] contr. de of the clock; **it is two — son** las dos.

October [aktóbə] s. octubre.

oculist [ákjəlɪst] s. oculista.

odd [ad] adj. extraño, singular, raro; non o impar; — **change** suelto, cambio sobrante; — **moments** momentos libres, momentos de ocio; — **shoe** zapato suelto (sin compañero); — **volume** tomo suelto; **thirty —** treinta y tantos, treinta y pico; **-ly** adv. extrañamente, de un modo raro.

oddity [ádətɪ] *s.* rareza.

odds [adz] *s. pl. o sing.* diferencia, disparidad (*en apuestas*): ventaja, puntos de ventaja (*en apuestas*); — **and ends** retazos, trozos sobrantes, pedacitos varios; **the — are against me** la suerte me es contraria, estoy de mala suerte; **to be at -s with** estar reñido o enemistado con.

ode [od] *s.* oda.

odious [ódɪəs] *adj.* odioso.

odor [ódə] *s.* olor; **bad —** mal olor, hedor.

odorous [ódərəs] *adj.* oloroso.

o'er [or] *contr. de* over.

of [av, ʌv] *prep.* de; — **course** por supuesto, claro, ya se ve; — **late** últimamente; **a quarter —** five las cinco menos cuarto; **to smell —** oler a; **to taste —** saber a.

off [ɔf] *adv.* lejos, fuera, a distancia; (*equivale al reflexivo se en ciertos verbos*: marcharse, irse, *etc.*); — **and on** de vez en cuando; a intervalos; **ten cents —** rebaja de diez centavos; **ten miles —** a una distancia de diez millas; **to take a day —** ausentarse por un día; descansar por un día; *adj.* ausente; distante, más remoto; quitado; **the — side** el lado más remoto; **with his hat —** con el sombrero quitado; **the electricity is —** está cortada la electricidad; **to be —** in one's accounts estar errado en sus cuentas; **to be —** to war haberse ido a la guerra; **to be well —** ser persona acomodada, estar en buenas circunstancias; *prep.* lejos de; **off-color** de mal color; verde (*indecente*); — **shore** a vista de la costa; — **standard de** calidad inferior; — **the road** desviado, descarriado; a un lado del camino; **to be —** duty no estar de turno; estar libre.

offend [əfénd] *v.* ofender.

offender [əféndə] *s.* ofensor; transgresor, delincuente.

offense [əféns] *s.* ofensa; agravio; delito, culpa; **no —** was meant lo hice (*o* lo dije) sin malicia; **weapon of —** arma ofensiva.

offensive [əfénsɪv] *adj.* ofensivo; *s.* ofensiva.

offer [ɔfə] *v.* ofrecer; **to — to do it** ofrecerse a hacerlo; *s.* oferta; ofrecimiento; promesa; propuesta.

offering [ɔfərɪŋ] *s.* ofrenda; oferta, ofrecimiento.

offhand [ɔfhǽnd] *adv.* de improviso, por el momento, sin pensarlo, impensadamente; *adj.* impensado, hecho de improviso; **in an — manner** con indiferencia; descuidadamente; sin plan.

office [ɔfɪs] *s.* oficio; cargo; función; oficina, despacho; — **building** edificio para oficinas; **post —** correo; **box —** taquilla, *Am.* boletería; **through the good -s of** por el intermedio de.

officer [ɔfəsə] *s.* oficial; funcionario; policía, agente de policía; *v.* comandar, dirigir (*como oficial*); proveer de oficiales.

official [əffʃəl] *adj.* oficial; *s.* oficial, funcionario; empleado público.

officiate [əffʃɪet] *v.* oficiar.

officious [əffʃəs] *adj.* oficioso, intruso, entremetido.

offset [ɔfsét] *v.* compensar por; contrapesar.

offspring [ɔfsprɪŋ] *s.* prole, hijos, descendientes; hijo, vástago; resultado, consecuencia.

oft [ɔft] = **often.**

often [ɔfən] *adv.* muchas veces, con frecuencia, frecuentemente, a menudo; **how —** ? ¿cuántas veces?; ¿cada cuándo?

ogre [ógə] *s.* ogro, gigante, monstruo.

oil [ɔɪl] *s.* aceite; óleo; petróleo; — **can** alcuza; — **painting** pintura al óleo; — **well** pozo de petróleo; **motor —** aceite para motores; *v.* aceitar, engrasar, lubricar; untar.

oilcloth [ɔɪlklɔθ] *s.* hule, tela de hule.

oily [ɔɪlɪ] *adj.* aceitoso, oleoso; grasiento.

ointment [ɔɪntmənt] *s.* ungüento.

O.K. [óké] *adj.* bueno; corriente, convenido; *adv.* bien; **it's —** está bien; **to give one's —** dar el Vº. Bº. (visto bueno); *v.* dar el Vº. Bº., aprobar.

old [old] *adj.* viejo; antiguo; añejo; — **maid** solterona; — **man** anciano, viejo; — **wine** vino añejo; **days of —** días de antaño; **how — are you?** ¿cuántos años tiene Vd.? ¿qué edad tiene Vd.?; **to be — enough to . . .** tener bastante edad para . . . ; **to be an —** **hand at** ser ducho en, ser muy perito o experto en.

olden [óldn] *adj.* viejo, antiguo, de antaño.

old-fashioned [óldfǽʃənd] *adj.* pasado de moda; anticuado; chapado a la antigua.

old-time [óldtáɪm] *adj.* vetusto, de tiempos antiguos; de antaño.

old-timer [óldtáɪmə] *s.* antiguo residente.

olive [álɪv] *s.* oliva, aceituna; — **grove** olivar; — **oil** aceite de oliva; — **tree** olivo; *adj.* aceitunado, verde aceituna.

omelet [ámlɪt] *s.* tortilla de huevos.

omen [ómən] *s.* agüero, presagio.

ominous [ámənəs] *adj.* siniestro, de mal agüero, amenazador.

omission [omíʃən] *s.* omisión.

omit [omít] *v.* omitir; dejar de.

omnipotent [amnípotənt] *adj.* omnipotente, todopoderoso.

on [αn] *prep.* en; a; sobre, encima de; — **all sides** por todos lados; — **arriving** al llegar; — **board** a bordo; en el tren; — **condition that** con la condición de que; — **credit** al fiado; — **foot** a pie; — **horseback** a caballo; — **Monday** el lunes; — **purpose** a propósito, adrede; — **sale** de venta; — **time** a tiempo; a plazo; *adv.* adelante; **farther** — más adelante; **later** — después; **and** — sin parar, sin cesar, continuamente; *adj.* puesto; **his hat is** — lleva puesto el sombrero; **the light is** — está encendida la luz.

once [wʌns] *adv.* una vez; en otro tiempo; — **and for all** una vez por todas, definitivamente; — **in a while** de vez en cuando; — **upon a time** érase que se era; en otro tiempo; **at** — al punto; a un mismo tiempo; **just this** — siquiera esta vez, sólo esta vez; *conj.* una vez que, cuando; luego que.

one [wʌn] *adj.* un, uno; — **hundred** cien, ciento; — **thousand** mil; **his** — **chance** su única oportunidad; **the** — **and only** el único; **one-armed** manco; **one-eyed** tuerto; **one-sided** de un solo lado; unilateral; parcial; desigual; *s. & pron.* uno; — **another** uno a otro; — **by** — uno a uno; uno por uno; **the** — **who** el que, la que; **the green** — el verde; **this** — éste, ésta.

oneself [wʌnsélf] *pron.* se (*reflexivo*); **to speak to** — hablar consigo mismo; **by** — solo; por sí, por sí solo.

onion [ánjən] *s.* cebolla.

onlooker [ánlʊkə] *s.* espectador, mirón.

only [ónlɪ] *adj.* solo, único; *adv.* sólo, solamente; *conj.* sólo que.

onset [ánset] *s.* embestida, ataque; impulso inicial, primer ímpetu; arranque.

onto [ántu] *prep.* a; sobre.

onward [ánwəd] *adv.* adelante; hacia adelante.

ooze [uz] *v.* rezumar(se), escurrir(se).

opal [ópl] *s.* ópalo.

opaque [opék] *adj.* opaco; mate.

open [ópən] *v.* abrir(se); **to** — **into** comunicarse con, tener paso a; **to** — **onto** dar a, caer a, mirar a; *adj.* abierto; franco, sincero; expuesto (a); — **country** campo raso, campo abierto;

— **question** cuestión discutible; — **to temptation** expuesto a caer en la tentación; — **winter** invierno sin nieve; **in the** — **air** al (*o* en el) aire libre; **open-minded** receptivo; de amplias miras; **—mouthed** boquiabierto, con la boca abierta; *s.* campo raso, aire libre.

opening [ópənɪŋ] *s.* abertura; apertura, comienzo; claro (*en un bosque*); puesto vacante; oportunidad; *adj.* primero; — **night of a play** estreno de una comedia; **the** — **number** el primer número (*de un programa*).

opera [ápərə] *s.* ópera; — **glasses** gemelos; — **house** ópera, teatro de la ópera; **comic** — ópera cómica, zarzuela.

operate [ápəret] *v.* operar; funcionar; obrar; maniobrar; manejar; **to** — **on a person** operar a una persona.

operation [apəréʃən] *s.* operación; funcionamiento; manipulación; manejo; maniobra; **to be in** — funcionar, estar funcionando.

operator [ápəretə] *s.* operador, cirujano; maquinista, mecánico, operario; especulador (*en la Bolsa*); **mine** — explotador de minas; **telegraph** — telegrafista; **telephone** — telefonista.

operetta [apərétə] *s.* opereta, zarzuela.

opinion [əpínjən] *s.* opinión, parecer.

opium [ópɪəm] *s.* opio.

opponent [əpónənt] *s.* contrario, adversario, antagonista.

opportune [apətjún] *adj.* oportuno; a propósito.

opportunity [apətjúnətɪ] *s.* oportunidad; ocasión.

oppose [əpóz] *v.* oponer(se); oponerse a.

opposing [əpózɪŋ] *adj.* opuesto, contrario.

opposite [ápəzɪt] *adj.* opuesto; contrario; frontero, de enfrente; — **to** frente a; *prep.* frente a, en frente de; *s.* contrario; **the** — lo opuesto, lo contrario.

opposition [apəzíʃən] *s.* oposición; resistencia.

oppress [əprés] *v.* oprimir; agobiar.

oppression [əpréʃən] *s.* opresión.

oppressive [əprésɪv] *adj.* opresivo; abrumador; gravoso; bochornoso, sofocante.

oppressor [əprésə] *s.* opresor.

optic [áptɪk] *adj.* óptico; **-s** *s.* óptica.

optical [áptɪk] *adj.* óptico.

optician [aptíʃən] *s.* óptico.

optimism [áptəmɪzəm] *s.* optimismo.

optimist [áptəmɪst] *s.* optimista.

optimistic [aptəmfstɪk] *adj.* optimista.
option [ápʃən] *s.* opción, derecho de escoger; alternativa.
optional [ápʃən‖] *adj.* discrecional.
opulence [ápjələns] *s.* opulencia, riqueza, abundancia.
opulent [ápjələnt] *adj.* opulento, rico; abundante.
or [ɔr] *conj.* o, u (*delante de* o, ho).
oracle [ɔ́rək‖] *s.* oráculo.
oral [ɔ́rəl] *adj.* oral; bucal.
orange [ɔ́rɪndʒ] *s.* naranja; — **blossom** azahar; — **grove** naranjal; — **tree** naranjo; *adj.* de naranja; anaranjado.
orangeade [ɔrɪndʒéd] *s.* naranjada.
oration [oréʃən] *s.* discurso, peroración, arenga.
orator [ɔ́rətə] *s.* orador.
oratory [ɔ́rətorɪ] *s.* oratoria, elocuencia; oratorio, capilla.
orb [ɔrb] *s.* orbe.
orbit [ɔ́rbɪt] *s.* órbita.
orchard [ɔ́rtʃəd] *s.* huerto.
orchestra [ɔ́rkɪstrə] *s.* orquesta; — **seat** butaca, luneta, *Am.* platea (*de orquesta*).
orchid [ɔ́rkɪd] *s.* orquídea.
ordain [ɔrdén] *v.* ordenar; decretar.
ordeal [ɔrdíl] *s.* prueba penosa.
order [ɔ́rdə] *s.* orden; pedido; clase; **holy -s** órdenes sagradas; **in — en** orden; **en buen estado; en regla; in — to** para, a fin de; **in — that** para que, a fin de que; **made to — mandado hacer, hecho a la medida; to be out of — estar** descompuesto; estar desordenado; no estar en regla; *v.* ordenar, mandar; arreglar; pedir (*hacer un pedido*); **to — away** echar, despedir, expulsar.
orderly [ɔ́rdəlɪ] *adj.* ordenado; en orden, bien arreglado; bien disciplinado; *s.* ordenanza (*soldado*); asistente de hospital.
ordinance [ɔ́rdnəns] *s.* ordenanza, ley, reglamento.
ordinarily [ɔ́rdnɛrəlɪ] *adv.* ordinariamente, por lo común.
ordinary [ɔ́rdnɛrɪ] *adj.* ordinario.
ore [ɔr] *s.* mineral.
organ [ɔ́rgən] *s.* órgano; **hand — organillo.
organic [ɔrgǽnɪk] *adj.* orgánico; constitutivo, fundamental.
organism [ɔ́rgənɪzəm] *s.* organismo.
organist [ɔ́rgənɪst] *s.* organista.
organization [ɔrgənəzéʃən] *s.* organización; organismo; entidad; sociedad.
organize [ɔ́rgənaɪz] *v.* organizar(se).
organizer [ɔ́rgənaɪzə] *s.* organizador.

orgy [ɔ́rdʒɪ] *s.* orgía.
orient [ɔ́rɪent] *s.* oriente; *v.* orientar.
oriental [orɪéntl] *adj.* & *s.* oriental.
orientate [ɔ́rɪentet] *v.* orientar.
orifice [ɔ́rəfɪs] *s.* orificio.
origin [ɔ́rədʒɪn] *s.* origen.
original [ərídʒən‖] *adj.* & *s.* original; **-ly** *adv.* originalmente, originariamente; en el principio, al principio.
originality [ərɪdʒənǽlətɪ] *s.* originalidad.
originate [ərídʒənet] *v.* originar(se).
oriole [ɔ́rɪol] *s.* oriol (*pájaro*).
ornament [ɔ́rnəmənt] *s.* ornamento, adorno; [ɔ́rnəment] *v.* ornamentar, adornar, ornar.
ornamental [ɔrnəméntl] *adj.* ornamental, de adorno, decorativo.
ornate [ɔrnét] *adj.* ornado, adornado en exceso; — **style** estilo florido.
orphan [ɔ́rfən] *adj.* & *s.* huérfano; — **asylum** hospicio, orfanato, asilo de huérfanos; *v.* dejar huérfano a.
ostentation [astəntéʃən] *s.* ostentación, boato.
ostentatious [astəntéʃəs] *adj.* ostentoso.
ostrich [ɔ́strɪtʃ] *s.* avestruz.
other [ʌ́ðə] *adj.* & *s.* otro; — **than** otra cosa que; **más que; every — day** cada dos días, un día sí y otro no; **some — day** otro día.
otherwise [ʌ́ðəwaɪz] *adv.* de otro modo; en otros respetos; *adj.* otro, diferente.
otter [átə] *s.* nutria; piel de nutria.
ought [ɔt] *v. defect.* (*por lo general se traduce por el presente y el condicional de* deber) debo, debes, etc.; debería, deberías, etc.; debiera, debieras, etc.
ounce [auns] *s.* onza.
our [aur] *adj.* nuestro (nuestra, nuestros, nuestras).
ours [aurz] *pron. pos.* nuestro (nuestra, nuestros, nuestras); el nuestro (la nuestra, los nuestros, las nuestras); **a friend of — un** amigo nuestro.
ourselves [aursélvz] *pron.* nosotros mismos; nos (*reflexivo*); a nosotros mismos; **we — nosotros mismos; by — solos; por nosotros; *véase* herself.
oust [aust] *v.* echar, expulsar.
out [aut] *adv.* fuera; afuera; hacia fuera; — **of fear** por miedo, de miedo; — **of humor** malhumorado; — **of money** sin dinero; — **of print** agotado; — **of touch with** aislado de, sin contacto con; — **of tune** desentonado; **made — of** hecho de; **to fight it — decidirlo** luchando; **to have it — with** habérselas con; **to speak — hablar** francamente; *adj.* ausente; apagado; — **and — criminal** crimi-

nal empedernido; — and — **refusal** una negativa redonda; — **size** tamaño poco común o extraordinario; **before the week is** — antes de que termine la semana; **the book is just** — acaba de publicarse el libro; **the secret is** — se ha divulgado el secreto.

outbreak [áutbrek] s. erupción; ataque, arranque (de ira); motín, insurrección, tumulto; **at the** — **of the war** al estallar la guerra.

outburst [áutbɜst] s. explosión; estallido; arranque (de pasión); erupción.

outcast [áutkæst] adj. excluido, desechado; desterrado; s. paria (persona excluida de la sociedad).

outcome [áutkʌm] s. resultado, consecuencia.

outcry [áutkraı] s. grito; clamor.

outdoor [áutdor] adj. externo, fuera de la casa; — **games** juegos al aire libre.

outdoors [autdórz] adv. puertas afuera, fuera de casa, al aire libre, al raso; s. aire libre, campo raso, campiña.

outer [áutə] adj. exterior, externo.

outfit [áutfɪt] s. equipo; pertrechos; v. equipar, habilitar, aviar.

outing [áutıŋ] s. excursión, gira (jira), caminata.

outlaw [áutlɔ] s. forajido, bandido; prófugo, fugitivo; v. proscribir; declarar ilegal.

outlay [áutle] s. gasto, desembolso; [autlé] v. gastar, desembolsar.

outlet [áutlɛt] s. salida; desaguadero, desagüe.

outline [áutlaın] s. bosquejo, esbozo; contorno; v. bosquejar, esbozar; delinear.

outlive [autlɪv] v. sobrevivir.

outlook [áutluk] s. vista; perspectiva.

outlying [áutlaııŋ] adj. circundante, exterior, remoto (del centro).

out-of-date [áutəvdét] adj. fuera de moda, anticuado.

outpost [áutpost] s. avanzada.

output [áutput] s. rendimiento; producción total.

outrage [áutredʒ] s. ultraje; v. ultrajar.

outrageous [autrédʒəs] adj. afrentoso; atroz.

outran [autrǽn] pret. de **to outrun**.

outrun [autrʌ́n] v. aventajar (en una carrera); dejar atrás; p.p. de **to outrun**.

outset [áutsɛt] s. comienzo, principio.

outshine [autʃáın] v. eclipsar, sobrepasar (en brillo o lucidez).

outshone [autʃón] pret. & p.p. de **to outshine**.

outside [áutsáıd] adj. exterior, externo; foráneo; adv. fuera, afuera; fuera de casa; prep. fuera de; s. exterior, parte exterior; superficie; lado de afuera; **in a week, at the** — en una semana, a lo sumo; **to close on the** — cerrar por fuera.

outsider [autsáıdə] s. foráneo, persona de fuera; extraño.

outskirts [áutskɜts] s. pl. alrededores, arrabales, cercanías.

outspoken [áutspókən] adj. franco, francote, Am. claridoso.

outstanding [áutstǽndıŋ] adj. sobresaliente; destacado, notable; — **bills** cuentas por cobrar; — **debts** deudas por pagar.

outstretched [autstrétʃt] adj. extendido; **with** — **arms** con los brazos abiertos.

outward [áutwəd] adj. exterior, externo; aparente; superficial; adv. fuera, hacia fuera; — **bound** que sale, de salida; para fuera, para el extranjero; **-ly** adv. exteriormente; por fuera; aparentemente.

outweigh [autwé] v. exceder en peso o valor; sobrepujar.

oval [óvl] adj. oval, ovalado; s. óvalo.

ovation [ovéʃən] s. ovación.

oven [ʌ́vən] s. horno.

over [óvə] prep. sobre; por; por encima de; encima de; a través de; al otro lado de; más de; — **night** por la noche, durante la noche; (véase **overnight**); — **to** a; **all** — **the city** por toda la ciudad; adv. encima; al otro lado; otra vez, de nuevo; — **again** otra vez, de nuevo; — **against** en contraste con; — **and** — una y otra vez, repetidas veces; —**curious** demasiado curioso; —**generous** demasiado generoso; — **here** acá, aquí; — **there** allá, allí; **two years and** — más de dos años; **to do it** — hacerlo otra vez, volver a hacerlo; adj. excesivo; **it is all** — ya se acabó, se ha acabado; ha pasado.

overalls [óvəɔlz] s. pl. Am. overol, overoles (pantalones de trabajo).

overate [ovəét] pret. de **to overeat**.

overboard [óvəbord] adv. al mar, al agua.

overcame [ovəkém] pret. de **to overcome**.

overcast [óvəkæst] adj. encapotado, nublado; **to become** — encapotarse, nublarse; [ovəkǽst] v. nublar o anublar; sobrehilar (dar puntadas sobre el borde de una tela); pret. & p.p. de **to**

overcast.

overcoat [óvəkot] s. sobretodo, abrigo.

overcome [ovəkʌm] v. vencer; rendir; *p.p. & adj.* vencido; rendido; agobiado; **to be — by weariness** estar rendido de fatiga.

overeat [ovəít] v. hartarse.

overeaten [ovəítn̩] *p.p. de* to overeat.

overexcite [óvərɪksáɪt] v. sobreexcitar.

overflow [óvəflo] s. derramə, desbordamiento; inundación; superabundancia; [ovəfló] v. derramarse, desbordarse; rebosar; inundar.

overgrown [óvəgrón] *adj.* denso, frondoso, poblado (*de follaje, herbaje, etc.*); — **boy** muchachón, muchacho demasiado crecido para su edad.

overhang [ovəhǽŋ] v. colgar por encima de; proyectarse o sobresalir por encima de; adornar con colgaduras; amenazar (*dícese de un desastre o calamidad*).

overhaul [ovəhól] v. reparar (*de cabo a rabo*); remendar; alcanzar (*en una carrera*).

overhead [óvəhɛd] s. gastos generales (*renta, seguro, alumbrado, calefacción, etc.*); *adj.* de arriba; elevado; — **expenses** gastos generales; [óvəhɛ́d] *adv.* encima de la cabeza, arriba; en lo alto.

overhear [ovəhír] v. oír por casualidad, alcanzar a oír, acertar a oír.

overheard [ovəhɜ́d] *pret. & p.p. de* to overhear.

overheat [óvəhít] v. recalentar(se); calentar(se) demasiado.

overhung [ovəhʌ́ŋ] *pret. & p.p. de* to overhang.

overland [óvəlænd] *adv. & adj.* por tierra.

overload [ovəlód] v. sobrecargar; [óvəlod] s. sobrecarga.

overlook [ovəlúk] v. mirar a (*desde lo alto*); dar a, tener vista a; pasar por alto, omitir; perdonar (*faltas*); descuidar, no notar; inspeccionar, examinar.

overly [óvəlɪ] *adv.* excesivamente.

overnight [óvənáɪt] *adv.* durante la noche; toda la noche; *adj.* de noche; nocturno; — **bag** saco de noche; — **trip** viaje de una noche.

overpower [ovəpáuə] v. subyugar, abrumar, vencer.

overran [ovərǽn] *pret. de* to overrun.

overrun [ovərʌ́n] v. desbordarse, inundar; sobrepasar; infestar, invadir; *p.p. de* to overrun.

overseas [óvəsíz] *adv.* en ultramar, allende los mares; *adj.* de ultramar.

oversee [ovəsí] v. dirigir; vigilar.

overseer [óvəsɪr] s. sobrestante, capataz; inspector, superintendente.

overshoe [óvəʃu] s. chanclo; zapato de goma, caucho o hule.

oversight [óvəsaɪt] s. inadvertencia, negligencia, descuido.

overstep [ovəstɛ́p] v. sobrepasarse, propasarse; traspasar; **to — the bounds** traspasar los límites; propasarse.

overtake [ovəték] v. alcanzar.

overtaken [ovətékən] *p.p. de* to overtake.

overthrew [ovəərú] *prét. de* to overthrow.

overthrow [óvəəro] s. derrocamiento, derrota, destrucción; caída; [ovəəró] v. derrocar; derribar, echar abajo, volcar; destronar.

overthrown [ovəərón] *p.p. de* to overthrow.

overtime [óvətaɪm] *adv. & adj.* en exceso de las horas estipuladas; — **pay** sobresueldo.

overtook [ovətúk] *pret. de* to overtake.

overture [óvətʃə] s. obertura, preludio; propuesta, proposición.

overturn [ovətɜ́n] v. volcar(se); trastornar; derribar; echar abajo.

overwhelm [ovəhwélm] v. abrumar, agobiar; oprimir; arrollar.

overwhelming [ovəhwélmɪŋ] *adj.* abrumador; opresivo; arrollador, irresistible, poderoso.

overwork [óvəwɜ́k] v. atarearse, afanarse más de lo debido, trabajar demasiado; s. exceso de trabajo.

owe [o] v. deber, adeudar.

owing [óɪŋ] *adj.* debido; — **to** debido a.

owl [aul] s. lechuza, buho, *Am.* tecolote.

own [on] *adj.* propio; **a house of his —** una casa suya; **his — people** los suyos; **to be on one's —** no estar a merced ajena; trabajar por su propia cuenta; **to come into one's —** entrar en posesión de lo suyo; **to hold one's —** mantenerse firme; v. poseer, tener; admitir, reconocer; **to — to** confesar; **to — up** confesar.

owner [ónə] s. dueño, amo; propietario; poseedor.

ownership [ónʃɪp] s. posesión, propiedad.

ox [aks] (pl. **oxen** [áksn̩]) s. buey.

oxygen [áksədʒən] s. oxígeno.

oyster [ɔ́ɪstə] s. ostra, ostión.

P

pace [pes] s. paso; v. pasear, andar; andar al paso; marchar; medir a pasos.

pacific [pəsífɪk] *adj.* pacífico.
pacify [pǽsəfaɪ] *v.* pacificar, apaciguar; calmar.
pack [pæk] *s.* fardo, lío, carga; manada (*de lobos*); cuadrilla, pandilla (*de ladrones*); jauría (*de perros*); muchedumbre; baraja (*de naipes*); — **animal** acémila, bestia de carga; *v.* empacar, empaquetar; embalar; enlatar; envasar; apiñar(se); cargar (*una bestia*); hacer (*el baúl, la maleta*); **to — off** despedir de repente; echar a la calle; largarse, irse.
package [pǽkɪdʒ] *s.* paquete; fardo, bulto; cajetilla (*de cigarrillos*).
packer [pǽkə] *s.* empacador; embalador, envasador.
packet [pǽkɪt] *s.* paquetillo; cajetilla.
packing [pǽkɪŋ] *s.* embalaje; envase; relleno; — **box** caja para embalar o empacar; — **house** establecimiento frigorífico, fábrica para envasar o enlatar comestibles.
pact [pækt] *s.* pacto, convenio.
pad [pæd] *s.* almohadilla, cojincillo; tableta, bloc de papel; *v.* rellenar; forrar; acolchar.
padding [pǽdɪŋ] *s.* relleno (*de pelo, algodón, paja, etc.*), *Am.* guata; ripio, palabras o frases inútiles.
paddle [pǽdl] *s.* pala; remo de canoa; — **wheel** rueda de paleta; *v.* remar con pala; apalear; chapotear (*en el agua*).
padlock [pǽdlɑk] *s.* candado; *v.* cerrar con candado.
pagan [pégən] *s.* & *adj.* pagano.
paganism [pégənɪzəm] *s.* paganismo.
page [pedʒ] *s.* página; paje; "botones" (*de hotel*), mensajero; *v.* paginar; vocear, llamar a voces.
pageant [pǽdʒənt] *s.* manifestación, desfile, procesión, pompa; representación al aire libre.
paid [ped] *pret.* & *p.p. de* **to pay.**
pail [pel] *s.* balde, cubo, cubeta.
pain [pen] *s.* dolor; sufrimiento; **-s** esmero; **on** (**under**) — **of** so pena de; **to be in** — estar sufriendo, tener dolores; **to take -s** esmerarse, extremarse; *v.* doler; causar dolor; afligir.
painful [pénfəl] *adj.* doloroso; penoso; arduo.
painless [pénlɪs] *adj.* sin dolor; libre de dolor.
painstaking [pénztekɪŋ] *adj.* esmerado, cuidadoso; aplicado.
paint [pent] *s.* pintura, color; colorete; *v.* pintar; pintarse (*la cara*); **to — the town red** irse de juerga o de parranda,

Am. irse de farra.
paintbrush [péntbrʌʃ] *s.* pincel; brocha.
painter [péntə] *s.* pintor.
painting [péntɪŋ] *s.* pintura.
pair [per] *s.* par; pareja; **a — of scissors** unas tijeras; *v.* aparear(se); hacer pareja, hacer pares; **to — off** aparear(se).
pajamas [pədʒǽməz] *s. pl.* pijama.
pal [pæl] *s.* compañero, camarada.
palace [pǽlɪs] *s.* palacio.
palate [pǽlɪt] *s.* paladar.
pale [pel] *adj.* pálido; descolorido; *v.* palidecer, ponerse pálido o descolorido.
paleness [pélnɪs] *s.* palidez.
palisade [pæləséd] *s.* palizada, estacada; **-s** riscos, acantilados.
pall [pɔl] *v.* empalagar; aburrir; **it -s on me** me empalaga; me aburre; *s.* paño de ataúd; palia (*lienzo que se pone encima del cáliz*).
pallid [pǽlɪd] *adj.* pálido.
pallor [pǽlə] *s.* palidez.
palm [pɑm] *s.* palma; palmera; — **Sunday** Domingo de Ramos; — **tree** palma, palmera; *v.* **to — something off on someone** pasar o dar algo indeseable a una persona (*sin que se dé cuenta de ello*).
palpable [pǽlpəbl] *adj.* palpable, tangible; evidente.
palpitate [pǽlpətet] *v.* palpitar, latir.
palpitation [pælpətéʃən] *s.* palpitación; latido.
paltry [póltrɪ] *adj.* mezquino, miserable, despreciable, insignificante.
pamper [pǽmpə] *v.* mimar, consentir (*a un niño*).
pamphlet [pǽmflɪt] *s.* folleto, *Am.* panfleto.
pan [pæn] *s.* cazuela, cacerola; cazo; platillo (*de balanza*); **dish —** cazo para lavar platos; **frying —** sartén; *v.* **to — out** (**well**) salir bien, dar buen resultado.
Pan-American [pǽnəmérəkən] *adj.* panamericano.
pancake [pǽnkek] *s.* tortita de harina, *Am.* panqué.
pander [pǽndə] *s.* alcahuete, encubridor; *v.* alcahuetear, servir de alcahuete.
pane [pen] *s.* vidrio, cristal (*de ventana o puerta*); cuadro (*de vidrio*).
panel [pǽnl] *s.* panel, tablero; cuarterón (*de puerta, ventana, etc.*); tabla (*doble pliegue de una falda o vestido*); **jury —** jurado; *v.* proveer de (*o adornar con*) paneles.
pang [pæŋ] *s.* dolor agudo; angustia,

tormento.

panic [pǽnɪk] *adj. & s.* pánico; **panic-stricken** sobrecogido de pánico.

pansy [pǽnzɪ] *s.* pensamiento (*flor*).

pant [pænt] *v.* jadear; palpitar; **to —for** anhelar, ansiar.

panther [pǽneə] *s.* pantera.

panting [pǽntɪŋ] *s.* jadeo, palpitación; *adj.* jadeante.

pantry [pǽntrɪ] *s.* despensa.

pants [pænts] *s. pl.* pantalones.

papa [pápə] *s.* papá.

papal [pépl] *adj.* papal.

paper [pépə] *s.* papel; periódico; tema, ensayo; -**s** papeles, documentos, credenciales; **naturalization** -**s** carta de naturaléza, certificado de ciudadanía; **— of pins** cartón de alfileres; **on —** escrito; por escrito; *adj.* de papel; para papel; **— doll** muñeca de papel; **— money** papel moneda; **—weight** pisapapeles; *v.* empapelar.

paprika [pəpríka] *s.* pimentón.

par [par] *s.* paridad, igualdad; valor nominal; **— value** valor a la par; **above —** sobre par, a premio, con prima; **at —** a la par; **below —** bajo par, a descuento; **on a — with** al par de, al nivel de, igual a; **to feel above —** sentirse mejor que de ordinario; **to feel below —** sentirse menos bien que de ordinario.

parable [pǽrəbl] *s.* parábola (*alegoría bíblica*).

parachute [pǽrəʃut] *s.* paracaídas.

parachutist [pǽrəʃutɪst] *s.* paracaidista.

parade [pəréd] *s.* parada, desfile, procesión; paseo; **— ground** campo de maniobras; **to make a — of** ostentar, hacer ostentación de; *v.* desfilar, pasar en desfile; marchar en parada; hacer ostentación de.

paradise [pǽrədaɪs] *s.* paraíso.

paradox [pǽrədaks] *s.* paradoja.

paraffin [pǽrəfɪn] *s.* parafina.

paragraph [pǽrəgræf] *s.* párrafo; *v.* dividir en párrafos.

Paraguayan [pærəgwáɪən] *adj. & s.* paraguayo.

parallel [pǽrəlɛl] *adj. & s.* paralelo; *v.* ser (*o correr*) paralelo a; comparar, cotejar.

paralysis [pərǽləsɪs] *s.* parálisis.

paralyze [pǽrəlaɪz] *v.* paralizar.

paramount [pǽrəmaʊnt] *adj.* importantísimo, superior, supremo, máximo.

parapet [pǽrəpɪt] *s.* parapeto.

parasite [pǽrəsaɪt] *s.* parásito.

parasol [pǽrəsɔl] *s.* parasol, sombrilla.

parcel [pársl] *s.* paquete; parcela, porción, lote (*de terreno*); **— post** paquete postal; *v.* parcelar, dividir en porciones o parcelas; hacer paquetes; **to — out** repartir.

parch [partʃ] *v.* resecar(se); tostar(se).

parchment [pártʃmənt] *s.* pergamino.

pardon [párdn] *s.* perdón; indulto; **I beg your —** perdone Vd.; dispense Vd.; *v.* perdonar; dispensar; indultar.

pare [pɛr] *v.* mondar, pelar (*manzanas, patatas, etc.*); cortar, recortar; **to — down expenditures** reducir gastos.

parent [pérənt] *s.* padre, madre; origen; -**s** padres.

parentage [pérəntɪdʒ] *s.* linaje; padres.

parenthesis [pərénəəsɪs] (*pl.* parentheses [pərénəəsɪz]) *s.* paréntesis.

parish [pǽrɪʃ] *s.* parroquia.

parishioner [pərʃənə] *s.* parroquiano, feligrés; -**s** fieles, feligreses.

park [park] *s.* parque; *v.* estacionar, dejar (*un automóvil*); estacionarse; -**ing lot** *Am.* playa de estacionamiento; -**ing space** sitio o lugar para estacionarse; **free -ing** estacionamiento gratis; **no -ing** se prohíbe estacionarse; no estacionarse.

parley [párlɪ] *s.* parlamento, discusión, conferencia; *v.* parlamentar, discutir.

parliament [párləmənt] *s.* parlamento.

parliamentary [parləméntərɪ] *adj.* parlamentario.

parlor [párlə] *s.* sala, salón; sala de recibo; **— car** coche salón; **beauty —** salón de belleza.

parochial [pərókɪəl] *adj.* parroquial.

parody [pǽrədɪ] *s.* parodia; *v.* parodiar.

parole [pəról] *s.* palabra de honor; **to put on —** dejar libre (*a un prisionero*) bajo palabra de honor; *v.* dejar libre bajo palabra de honor.

parrot [pǽrət] *s.* cotorra, loro, perico, papagayo; *v.* remedar, repetir como loro.

parry [pǽrɪ] *v.* parar, quitar o reparar (*un golpe*); *s.* quite, reparo.

parsley [pársIɪ] *s.* perejil.

parsnip [pársnəp] *s.* chirivía (*legumbre*).

parson [pársn] *s.* pastor, clérigo.

part [part] *s.* parte (*f.*); papel (*dramático*); raya (*del cabello*); **— and parcel** parte esencial o inherente; **— owner** condueño, dueño en parte; **— time** parte del tiempo; **in foreign -s** en el extranjero, en países extranjeros; **spare -s** piezas accesorias, piezas de repuesto (*o de refacción*); **do your —** haga Vd. cuanto esté de su parte; *v.* partir(se); separar(se); **to — company** separarse; **to — from** separarse de, despedirse de; **to —** one's hair hacerse la raya; **to —** with separarse de, despedirse de, deshacerse de.

partake [pərtέk] v. tomar parte, tener parte, participar.

partaken [pərtékən] p.p. de **to partake.**

partial [pár∫əl] adj. parcial; **-ly** adv. parcialmente, en parte; con parcialidad.

partiality [par∫ǽlɪtɪ] s. parcialidad.

participant [pətɪsəpənt] adj. & s. participante, partícipe, copartícipe.

participate [pətɪsəpet] v. participar.

participation [pətɪsəpé∫ən] s. participación.

participle [pártəsəpl] s. participio; **present —** gerundio.

particle [pártɪkl] s. partícula.

particular [pətɪkjələ] adj. particular; peculiar; esmerado, exacto; escrupuloso; quisquilloso; exigente; s. particular, detalle, circunstancia; **in —** en particular, especialmente; **-ly** adv. particularmente, en particular.

parting [pártɪŋ] s. despedida; separación; bifurcación; **the —** of the ways encrucijada, bifurcación, cruce de caminos; adj. de despedida, último.

partisan [pártəzn] adj. partidario; parcial; s. partidario; secuaz, seguidor.

partition [pətɪ∫ən] s. partición; división, separación; tabique, Am. medianía; v. partir, dividir; repartir.

partly [pártlɪ] adv. en parte.

partner [pártnə] s. socio, consocio; compañero; **dancing —** pareja de baile.

partnership [pártnə∫ɪp] s. sociedad, compañía.

partook [pərtúk] pret. de **to partake.**

partridge [pártrɪdʒ] s. perdiz.

party [pártɪ] s. tertulia, reunión, fiesta; grupo, partida (de gente) parte (en un pleito, contrato); **hunting —** partida de caza; **political —** partido político.

pass [pǽs] s. paso; pase, permiso de entrar; aprobación (en un examen); trance, situación; **— key** llave maestra; **to come to —** suceder; v. pasar; pasar por; pronunciar (sentencia), dar (un juicio o parecer); aprobar (a un estudiante); adoptar (una ley); ser aprobado en (un examen); **to — away** pasar a mejor vida, morir; desaparecer; pasar (el tiempo).

passable [pǽsəbl] adj. pasable, transitable; pasadero, regular, mediano.

passage [pǽsɪdʒ] s. pasaje; paso, tránsito; transcurso (del tiempo); pasillo, pasadizo; travesía, viaje por mar; aprobación (de un proyecto de ley); adopción (de una ley).

passenger [pǽsndʒə] s. pasajero; **the -s** los pasajeros; el pasaje.

passer-by [pǽsəbáɪ] s. transeúnte, viandante.

passion [pǽ∫ən] s. pasión; **Passion play** drama de la Pasión; **to fly into a —** montar en cólera, encolerizarse.

passionate [pǽ∫ənɪt] adj. apasionado.

passive [pǽsɪv] adj. pasivo; s. voz pasiva.

passport [pǽsport] s. pasaporte.

password [pǽsw3d] s. consigna, contraseña, santo y seña.

past [pǽst] adj. pasado; último; **— master** perito; **the — president** el expresidente, el último presidente; **— tense** tiempo pasado; pretérito; **for some time —** desde hace algún tiempo, de poco tiempo a esta parte; prep. **— bearing** insoportable; **— understanding** incomprensible; **half — two** las dos y media; **woman — forty** cuarentona, mujer de más de cuarenta años; **to go — the house** pasar por (o por enfrente de) la casa; s. pasado; pretérito; pretérito imperfecto; **man with a —** hombre de dudosos antecedentes.

paste [pest] s. pasta; engrudo; v. pegar (con engrudo).

pasteboard [péstbord] s. cartón; **— box** caja de cartón.

pasteurize [pǽstəraɪz] v. pasterizar (o pasteurizar).

pastime [pǽstaɪm] s. pasatiempo.

pastor [pǽstə] s. pastor, clérigo, cura.

pastoral [pǽstərəl] adj. pastoril; pastoral; s. pastoral, carta pastoral; égloga; pastorela, idilio.

pastry [péstrɪ] s. pastelería, pasteles; **— cook** pastelero; **— shop** pastelería.

pasture [pǽst∫ə] s. pastura, pasto; dehesa; v. pastar, pacer; apacentar(se).

pat [pǽt] adj. apto, oportuno; **to have a lesson —** saber al dedillo la lección; **to stand —** mantenerse firme; adv. a propósito; oportunamente; de molde; s. palmadita, caricia, golpecito; **— of butter** cuadrito de mantequilla; v. dar palmaditas a; acariciar; pasar la mano (para alisar o acariciar).

patch [pǽt∫] s. remiendo; parche; mancha; pedazo (de terreno); sembrado; v. remendar; **to — up a quarrel** hacer las paces.

pate [pet] s. coronilla (de la cabeza); **bald —** calva.

patent [pétnt] adj. patente, evidente, manifiesto; de patente; **— leather** charol; **— medicine** medicina de

patente; — **right** patente; s..patente;
v. patentar.
paternal [pətə́rnl] adj. paternal, paterno.
paternity.[pətə́nətı] s. paternidad.
path [pæθ] s. senda, sendero; vereda;
ruta; tráyectoria (de una bala).
pathetic [pəθétɪk] adj. patético.
pathos [péθas] s. patetismo, cualidad
patética.
pathway [pǽθwe] s. senda, vereda, vía.
patience [péʃəns] s. paciencia.
patient [péʃənt] adj. paciente; pacienzudo; s. paciente, enfermo.
patriarch [pétrɪɑrk] s. patriarca.
patriarchal [petrɪárkl] adj. patriarcal.
patrimony [pǽtrəmonɪ] s. patrimonio.
patriot [pétrɪət] s. patriota.
patriotic [petrɪátɪk] adj. patriótico.
patriotism [pétrɪotɪzəm] s. patriotismo.
patrol [pətról] s. patrulla; ronda; v.
patrullar, rondar.
patron [pétrən] s. patrón, patrono; benefactor; cliente, parroquiano; —
saint santo patrón.
patronage [pétrənɪdʒ] s. patrocinio,
amparo; clientela; condescendencia;
political — control de nombramien-
tos políticos.
patroness [pétrənɪs] s. patrona, pro-
tectora.
patronize [pétrənaɪz] v. patrocinar, amparar; tratar con condescendencia;
favorecer, ser parroquiano de.
patter [pǽtə] v. golpetear ligeramente;
talonear; charlar, parlotear; s. golpeteo; golpecitos; taloneo; charla, parloteo.
pattern [pǽtən] s. modelo; dechado;
muestra; ejemplo; patrón, molde;
diseño, dibujo (en tejidos, telas, etc.);
v. **to** — **oneself after** seguir el
ejemplo de; **to** — **something after**
(on, upon) forjar o modelar algo a
imitación de.
paunch [pɔntʃ] s. panza, barriga.
pause [pɔz] s. pausa; v. pausar, hacer
pausa; detenerse, parar.
pave [pev] v. pavimentar; **to** — **the
way for** preparar o abrir el camino
para; **to** — **with bricks** enladrillar;
to — **with flagstones** enlosar.
pavement [pévmənt] s. pavimento;
brick — enladrillado.
pavilion [pəvíljən] s. pabellón.
paw [pɔ] s. garra, zarpa; v. echar la
zarpa; arañar; manosear; **to** — **the
ground** patear la tierra (dícese del
caballo).
pawn [pɔn] s. prenda, empeño; peón
(de ajedrez); —**broker** prestamista,

prendero; —**shop** empeño, casa de
empeños, montepío; **in** — en prenda;
v. empeñar, dejar en prenda.
pay [pe] v. pagar; costear; ser provechoso; valer la pena; **to** — **attention**
prestar atención; **to** — **back** restituir, devolver; **to** — **court** hacer la
corte; **to** — **down** pagar al contado;
to — **homage** hacer o rendir homenaje; **to** — **one's respects** presentar
sus respetos; **to** — **a visit** hacer una
visita; s. pago; recompensa; paga;
sueldo; —**day** día de pagos, Am. día
de raya; —**master** pagador, Am.
rayador; —**roll** nómina.
payable [péəbl] adj. pagadero.
payment [pémənt] s. pago; paga; — **in
full** pago total.
pea [pi] s. guisante, chícharo; **sweet** —
guisante de olor.
peace [pis] s. paz.
peaceable [písəbl] adj. pacífico, tranquilo.
peaceful [písfəl] adj. pacífico; tranquilo,
quieto, sosegado.
peach [pitʃ] s. melocotón, durazno; persona bella o admirable; — **tree** durazno, duraznero, melocotonero.
peacock [píkak] s. pavón, pavo real;
to act like a — pavonearse, hacer
ostentación.
peak [pik] s. pico, cumbre, cima; cúspide; punto máximo.
peal [pil] s. repique (de campanas); —
of laughter carcajada, risotada; —
of thunder trueno; v. repicar (las
campanas).
peanut [pínət] s. cacahuate, Am. maní.
pear [per] s. pera; — **tree** peral; **alligator** — aguacate, Am. palta (variedad
sudamericana).
pearl [pɜl] s. perla; — **necklace** collar
de perlas; **mother-of-pearl** nácar,
madreperla.
pearly [pɜ́lɪ] adj. perlino; nacarado;
aperlado.
peasant [pézn̩t] adj. & s. campesino,
rústico, Am. jíbaro, Am. guajiro.
pebble [pébl] s. guija, china, guijarro,
piedrecilla.
peck [pɛk] v. picar, picotear; s. picotazo,
picotada; medida de áridos (aproximadamente 9 litros); **a** — **of trouble**
la mar de disgustos o molestias.
peculiar [pɪkjúljə] adj. peculiar; raro,
singular, extraño.
peculiarity [pɪkjulɪǽrətɪ] s. peculiaridad; particularidad; rareza.
pedagogue [pédəgag] s. pedagogo, dómine.

pedal [pédl] *s.* pedal; *v.* pedalear, mover los pedales.

pedant [pédņt] *s.* pedante.

pedantic [pɪdǽntɪk] *adj.* pedante, pedantesco.

peddle [pédl] *v.* ir vendiendo de puerta en puerta; **to — gossip** chismear

peddler [pédlə] *s.* buhonero, vendedor ambulante.

pedestal [pédɪstl] *s.* pedestal.

pedestrian [padéstrɪən] *s.* peatón, transeúnte, viandante; *adj.* pedestre.

pedigree [pédəgri] *s.* linaje, genealogía.

peek [pik] *v.* atisbar, espiar; *s.* atisbo.

peel [pil] *s* corteza, cáscara (*de algunas frutas*); pellejo (*de patatas*); *v.* pelar(se), descortezar(se), deshollejar(se); **to keep one's eye -ed** tener los ojos muy abiertos, estar alerta.

peep [pip] *v.* atisbar, espiar; asomar(se); pipiar, piar; *s.* atisbo; ojeada; pío (*de pollo o ave*).

peer [pɪr] *s.* par, igual; noble; *v.* mirar con atención, atisbar; asomar; **to — into other people's business** fisgar, curiosear.

peeve [piv] *v.* irritar, poner de mal humor; **to get -d** amoscarse, ponerse de mal humor.

peevish [pívɪʃ] *adj.* enojadizo; malhumorado.

peg [pɛg] *s.* espiga, clavo de madera, estaquilla; clavija (*de violín*); **to take a person down a —** rebajar o humillar a alguien; *v.* clavar, clavetear; poner estaquillas; **to — along** atarearse, trabajar con tesón.

pellet [pélɪt] *s.* pelotilla; píldora; bola.

pell-mell [pélmél] *adj.* confuso, tumultuoso; *adv.* a trochemoche, atropelladamente, en tumulto.

pelt [pɛlt] *s.* zalea, cuero (*especialmente de oveja*); piel; *v.* golpear; **to — with stones** apedrear, arrojar piedras a.

pen [pɛn] *s.* pluma (*para escribir*); corral; redil; **—holder** mango de pluma, portaplumas; **— name** nombre de pluma; **fountain —** pluma fuente, pluma estilográfica; **pig —** pocilga; *v.* escribir (*con pluma*); acorralar, encerrar.

penal [pínl] *adj.* penal.

penalty [pénltɪ] *s.* pena, castigo; multa.

penance [pénəns] *s.* penitencia.

pencil [pénsl] *s.* lápiz; lapicero; **— sharpener** tajalápiz.

pendant [péndənt] *s.* pendiente (*adorno que cuelga*); *adj.* pendiente.

pending [péndɪŋ] *adj.* pendiente; colgado; *prep.* durante.

pendulum [péndзələm] *s.* péndulo.

penetrate [pénətret] *v.* penetrar.

penetrating [pénətretɪŋ] *adj.* penetrante.

penetration [penətréʃən] *s.* penetración.

peninsula [pənínsələ] *s.* península.

penitent [pénətənt] *adj.* arrepentido, penitente; *s.* penitente.

penitentiary [penəténʃərɪ] *s.* penitenciaría, presidio.

penknife [pénnaɪf] *s.* cortaplumas; navaja.

penmanship [pénmənʃɪp] *s.* escritura, caligrafía.

pennant [pénənt] *s.* banderola, gallardete.

penniless [pénɪlɪs] *adj.* pobre, sin dinero.

penny [pénɪ] *s.* centavo (*de dólar*); **to cost a pretty —** costar un ojo de la cara, costar un dineral.

pension [pénʃən] *s.* pensión; retiro (*de un militar*); *v.* pensionar.

pensive [pénsɪv] *adj.* pensativo.

pent [pɛnt] *adj.* encerrado; acorralado; **pent-up emotions** sentimientos reprimidos.

people [pípl] *s.* gente; pueblo; *v.* poblar.

pepper [pépə] *s.* pimienta; **— plant** pimentero; **— shaker** pimentero; **green -s** pimientos verdes; **red —** pimentón, chile. *Am.* ají; *v.* sazonar con pimienta; **to — with bullets** acribillar a balazos.

peppermint [pépəmɪnt] *s.* menta; pastilla o bombón de menta.

per [pɚ] *prep.* por; **— capita** por cabeza; **— cent** por ciento; **— year** al año; **ten cents — dozen** diez centavos por docena (o diez centavos la docena).

percale [pəkél] *s.* percal.

perceive [pəsív] *v.* percibir.

percentage [pəséntɪdʒ] *s.* porcentaje, tanto por ciento.

perceptible [pəséptəbl] *adj.* perceptible.

perception [pəsépʃən] *s.* percepción.

perch [pɝtʃ] *s.* percha (*para pájaros*); perca (*pez*); *v.* encaramar(se); posarse (*en una percha o rama*).

perchance [pətʃǽns] *adv.* por ventura, acaso, quizás, tal vez.

percolate [pɝkəlet] *v.* filtrar(se), colar(se); rezumarse; penetrar.

perdition [pədíʃən] *s.* perdición.

perennial [pəréniəl] *adj.* perenne; continuo; perpetuo.

perfect [pɝfɪkt] *adj.* perfecto; completo; *s.* tiempo perfecto (*del verbo*); [pəfékt]

v. perfeccionar.
perfection [pəfékʃən] *s.* perfección.
perfidious [pəfídɪəs] *adj.* pérfido.
perfidy [pɜ́fɪdɪ] *s.* perfidia.
perforate [pɜ́faret] *v.* perforar.
perform [pəfɔ́rm] *v.* ejecutar; llevar a cabo, cumplir, hacer; funcionar (*una máquina*); desempeñar o representar un papel.
performance [pəfɔ́rməns] *s.* ejecución; desempeño, cumplimiento; funcionamiento (*de una máquina o motor*); función, representación; acto, acción.
perfume [pɜ́fjum] *s.* perfume; [pəfjúm] *v.* perfumar.
perfumery [pəfjúmərɪ] *s.* perfumería; perfumes.
perhaps [pəhǽps] *adv.* acaso, tal vez, quizá (*o* quizás), puede ser.
peril [pérəl] *s.* peligro; riesgo, *v.* poner en peligro.
perilous [pérələs] *adj.* peligroso.
perimeter [pərímətə] *s.* perímetro.
period [pírɪəd] *s.* período; punto final; fin, término.
periodic [pɪrɪádɪk] *adj.* periódico.
periodical [pɪrɪádɪkl] *adj.* periódico; *s.* revista, publicación periódica.
perish [pérɪʃ] *v.* perecer.
perishable [pérɪʃəbl] *adj.* perecedero; deleznable.
perjure [pɜ́dʒə] *v.* to — oneself perjurar.
perjury [pɜ́dʒrɪ] *s.* perjurio, juramento falso.
permanence [pɜ́mənəns] *s.* permanencia.
permanent [pɜ́mənənt] *adj.* permanente; duradero.
permeate [pɜ́mɪet] *v.* penetrar, saturar; difundirse por, filtrarse por.
permissible [pəmísəbl] *adj.* lícito.
permission [pəmíʃən] *s.* permiso, licencia.
permit [pɜ́mɪt] *s.* permiso, pase; licencia; [pəmít] *v.* permitir.
pernicious [pəníʃəs] *adj.* pernicioso.
perpendicular [pɜpəndíkjələ] *adj.* & *s.* perpendicular.
perpetrate [pɜ́pətret] *v.* perpetrar, cometer.
perpetual [pəpétʃʊəl] *adj.* perpetuo.
perpetuate [pəpétʃʊet] *v.* perpetuar.
perplex [pəpléks] *v.* confundir, turbar, aturdir.
perplexed [pəplékst] *adj.* perplejo, confuso.
perplexity [pəpléksətɪ] *s.* perplejidad, confusión.
persecute [pɜ́sɪkjut] *v.* perseguir, aco-

sar.
persecution [pɜsɪkjúʃən] *s.* persecución.
persecutor [pɜ́sɪkjutə] *s.* perseguidor.
perseverance [pɜsəvírəns] *s.* perseverancia.
persevere [pɜsəvír] *v.* perseverar; persistir.
persist [pəzíst] *v.* persistir; porfiar.
persistence [pəzístəns] *s.* persistencia; porfía.
persistent [pəzístənt] *adj.* persistente; porfiado.
person [pɜ́sn̩] *s.* persona.
personage [pɜ́sn̩ɪdʒ] *s.* personaje.
personal [pɜ́sn̩l] *adj.* personal; en persona.
personality [pɜsn̩ǽlətɪ] *s.* personalidad; persona, personaje; alusión personal.
personnel [pɜsn̩él] *s.* personal.
perspective [pəspéktɪv] *s.* perspectiva; — drawing dibujo en perspectiva
perspiration [pɜspəréʃən] *s.* sudor.
perspire [pəspáɪr] *v.* sudar.
persuade [pəswéd] *v.* persuadir.
persuasion [pəswéʒən] *s.* persuasión; creencia.
persuasive [pəswésɪv] *adj.* persuasivo.
pert [pɜt] *adj.* insolente, descarado, atrevido, *Am.* retobado.
pertain [pətén] *v.* pertenecer; atañer.
pertinent [pɜ́tn̩ənt] *adj.* pertinente, a propósito, al caso.
perturb [pətɜ́b] *v.* perturbar.
peruse [pərúz] *v.* leer con cuidado.
Peruvian [pərúvɪən] *adj.* & *s.* peruano.
pervade [pəvéd] *v.* llenar, penetrar, difundirse por.
perverse [pəvɜ́s] *adj.* perverso; terco, obstinado.
pervert [pəvɜ́t] *v.* pervertir; falsear; [pɜ́vɜt] *s.* perverso.
pessimism [pésəmɪzəm] *s.* pesimismo.
pessimist [pésəmɪst] *s.* pesimista; -ic *adj.* pesimista.
pest [pɛst] *s.* peste, plaga; pestilencia.
pester [péstə] *v.* importunar, molestar.
pestilence [péstl̩əns] *s.* pestilencia.
pet [pet] *s.* animal mimado, animal casero o doméstico; niño mimado; favorito; *adj.* favorito; mimado; — name nombre de cariño (*por lo general diminutivo*); *v.* mimar, acariciar.
petal [pétl̩] *s.* pétalo.
petition [pətíʃən] *s.* petición, súplica; instancia, memorial, solicitud, *Am.* ocurso; *v.* solicitar, pedir, dirigir una instancia o memorial a; suplicar, rogar.
petroleum [pətrólɪəm] *s.* petróleo.

petticoat [pétɪkot] *s.* enaguas.
petty [pétɪ] *adj.* insignificante, pequeño; mezquino; inferior, subordinado; — **cash** fondos para gastos menores; — **larceny** ratería; — **officer** oficial subordinado (*en la marina*); — **treason** traición menor.
pew [pju] *s.* banco de iglesia.
phantom [fǽntəm] *s.* fantasma.
pharmacist [fɑ́rməsɪst] *s.* farmacéutico, boticario.
pharmacy [fɑ́rməsɪ] *s.* farmacia, botica.
phase [fez] *s.* fase.
phenomena [fənámənə] *pl. de* **phenomenon.**
phenomenon [fənámənan] *s.* fenómeno.
philosopher [fəlásəfə] *s.* filósofo.
philosophical [fɪləsáfɪkḷ] *adj.* filosófico.
philosophy [fəlásəfɪ] *s.* filosofía.
phone [fon] *s.* teléfono; *v.* telefonear.
phonetics [fonétɪks] *s.* fonética.
phonograph [fónəgræf] *s.* fonógrafo.
phosphate [fásfet] *s.* fosfato.
phosphorus [fásfərəs] *s.* fósforo (*elemento químico*).
photo [fóto] *s.* fotografía, retrato.
photograph [fótəgræf] *s.* fotografía, retrato; *v.* fotografiar, retratar.
photographer [fətágrəfə] *s.* fotógrafo.
photography [fətágrəfɪ] *s.* fotografía.
phrase [frez] *s.* frase; expresión, locución; *v.* frasear; expresar, formular.
physic [fízɪk] *s.* purga, purgante; *v.* purgar.
physical [fízɪkḷ] *adj.* físico.
physician [fəzíʃən] *s.* médico.
physicist [fízəsɪst] *s.* físico.
physics [fízɪks] *s.* física.
physiological [fɪzɪəládʒɪkḷ] *adj.* fisiológico.
physiology [fɪzɪálədʒɪ] *s.* fisiología.
physique [fɪzík] *s.* físico, constitución física, talle, cuerpo.
piano [pɪǽno] *s.* piano; — **bench** banqueta de piano; — **stool** taburete de piano; **grand** — piano de cola; **upright** — piano vertical.
picaresque [pɪkərésk] *adj.* picaresco.
pick [pɪk] *v.* escoger; coger; picar; mondarse, limpiarse (*los dientes*); desplumar (*un ave*); roer (*un hueso*); falsear (*una cerradura*); armar (*una pendencia*); **to** — **flaws** criticar, censurar; **to** — **out** escoger; **to** — **pockets** ratear; **to** — **up** recoger; **to** — **up speed** acelerar la marcha; *s.* pico (*herramienta*); selección; lo selecto, lo mejor; recolección, cosecha; **ice** — punzón para romper hielo; **tooth**— mondadientes, palillo de dientes.

pickaxe [pɪ́kæks] *s.* pico, zapapico.
picket [pɪ́kɪt] *s.* piquete (*estaca o palo clavado en la tierra*); piquete (*vigilante huelguista*); piquete de soldados; *v.* estacionar piquetes cerca de (*una fábrica, campamento, etc.*); vigilar (*por medio de piquetes*); estar de guardia.
pickle [pɪ́kḷ] *s.* encurtido; **to be in a** — hallarse en un aprieto; *v.* encurtir, escabechar; **-ed cucumbers** pepinillos encurtidos; **-ed fish** escabeche, pescado en escabeche.
pickpocket [pɪ́kpɑkɪt] *s.* rata (*m.*), ratero.
picnic [pɪ́knɪk] *s.* partida de campo, día de campo, comida campestre, *Am.* picnic; *v.* hacer una comida campestre; ir a un picnic.
picture [pɪ́ktʃə] *s.* cuadro, pintura; retrato; fotografía; lámina, grabado; película; — **frame** marco; — **gallery** museo o galería de pinturas; *v.* pintar, dibujar; describir; imaginar(se).
picturesque [pɪktʃərésk] *adj.* pintoresco.
pie [paɪ] *s.* pastel; empanada.
piece [pis] *s.* pieza; pedazo; trozo; parte, sección; — **of advice** consejo; — **of land** parcela; — **of money** moneda; — **of news** noticia; — **of nonsense** tontería; —**meal** en pedazos, a pedazos, por partes; *v.* remendar; **to** — **between meals** comer a deshoras; **to** — **on** to juntar a, pegar a; **to** — **together** unir, pegar, juntar.
pier [pɪr] *s.* muelle, embarcadero; rompeolas; pilar (*de puente o arco*).
pierce [pɪrs] *v.* atravesar, traspasar; taladrar; agujerear, perforar.
piety [páɪətɪ] *s.* piedad, religiosidad.
pig [pɪg] *s.* puerco, cerdo, cochino; — **iron** hierro en lingotes; —**headed** cabezón, testarudo; **guinea** — conejillo de Indias.
pigeon [pɪ́dʒən] *s.* pichón; paloma.
pigeonhole [pɪ́dʒənhol] *s.* casilla; *v.* encasillar.
pigment [pɪ́gmənt] *s.* pigmento, color.
pike [paɪk] *s.* pica, lanza; lucio (*pez*).
pile [paɪl] *s.* pila, montón; pelo (*de ciertos tejidos*); pilote; **-s** almorranas (*enfermedad*); — **driver** martinete (*para clavar pilotes*); *v.* apilar(se), amontonar(se); acumular(se).
pilfer [pɪ́lfə] *v.* pillar, ratear, hurtar, sisar.
pilgrim [pɪ́lgrɪm] *s.* peregrino, romero.
pilgrimage [pɪ́lgrəmɪdʒ] *s.* peregrinación, romería.
pill [pɪl] *s.* píldora; persona fastidiosa.
pillage [pɪ́lɪdʒ] *v.* pillar, saquear; *s.* pillaje, saqueo.

pillar [pʹlə] *s.* pilar, columna; **to go from — to post** ir de Ceca en Meca.

pillow [pʹlo] *s.* almohada; cojín.

pillowcase [pʹlokes] *s.* funda de almohada.

pilot [pʹɪlət] *s.* piloto; guía; **— light** (*o* **— burner**) mechero, encendedor (*de una cocina o estufa de gas*); **harbor —** práctico de puerto; *v.* pilotar o pilotear; dirigir, guiar.

pimple [pʹɪmpl] *s.* grano, barro.

pin [pɪn] *s.* alfiler; prendedor; espiga; bolo (*del juego de bolos*); **— money** dinero para alfileres; **— wheel** molinete, *Am.* remolino; **breast —** broche; *v.* prender (*con alfiler*); asegurar, fijar, clavar; **to — down** fijar, inmovilizar; hacer dar una contestación definitiva; **to — one's hope to** poner toda su esperanza en; **to — up** prender con alfileres; colgar (*un dibujo o retrato*), fijar con tachuelas.

pincers [pʹɪnsəz] *s. pl.* pinzas; tenazas; **small —** tenacillas.

pinch [pɪntʃ] *v.* pellizcar; apretar; escatimar, economizar; prender, arrestar; **to — one's finger in the door** machucarse el dedo en la puerta; *s.* pellizco; pizca, porción pequeña; punzada, dolor agudo; aprieto, apuro; **— hitter** suplente, sustituto.

pinchers [pʹɪntʃəz] = **pincers.**

pine [paɪn] *s.* pino; **— cone** piña; **— grove** pinar; **— nut** piñón; *v.* languidecer; **to — away** consumirse; **to — for** anhelar, suspirar por.

pineapple [pʹaɪnæpl] *s.* piña, ananá o ananás.

pink [pɪŋk] *s.* clavel; color de rosa; **in the — of condition** en la mejor condición; *adj.* rosado, color de rosa.

pinnacle [pʹɪnəkl] *s.* pináculo, cumbre.

pint [paɪnt] *s.* pinta (*aproximadamente medio litro*).

pioneer [paɪənʹɪr] *s.* explorador, colonizador; fundador, iniciador, precursor; *v.* explorar, colonizar; fundar, promover.

pious [pʹaɪəs] *adj.* pío, piadoso.

pipe [paɪp] *s.* pipa (*de fumar*); tubo; caño; cañón (*de órgano*); caramillo, flauta; **— line** cañería, tubería; *v.* conducir por cañerías; desaguar por cañería; proveer de tuberías o cañerías; chillar; **to — down** bajar la voz.

piper [pʹaɪpə] *s.* gaitero, flautista.

piping [pʹaɪpɪŋ] *s.* cañería, tubería; cordoncillo (*de adorno para costuras*); chillido, silbido; *adj.* agudo, chillón; **— hot** muy caliente; hirviendo.

pippin [pʹɪpɪn] *s.* camuesa.

pique [pik] *s.* enojo, resentimiento; *v.* picar, excitar; enojar, irritar; **to — oneself on** picarse de, preciarse de.

pirate [pʹaɪrət] *s.* pirata; *v.* piratear; plagiar.

pistol [pʹɪstl] *s.* pistola; revólver.

piston [pʹɪstn] *s.* pistón, émbolo; **— ring** aro de pistón; **— rod** vástago del émbolo.

pit [pɪt] *s.* hoyo; foso; hueso (*de ciertas frutas*); **— of the stomach** boca del estómago.

pitch [pɪtʃ] *s.* tiro, lanzamiento (*de una pelota*); cabezada (*de un barco*); diapasón, tono; grado, declive, grado de inclinación; pez (*f.*), brea; resina; **— dark** oscurísimo; *v.* tirar, lanzar, arrojar; cabecear (*un barco*); graduar el tono de (*un instrumento o voz*); echarse de cabeza; inclinarse; **to — a tent** armar una tienda de campaña; acampar; **to — into** arremeter contra; reprender, regañar; **— in!** ¡manos a la obra!

pitcher [pʹɪtʃə] *s.* cántaro, jarro o jarra; tirador, lanzador (*en beisbol*).

pitchfork [pʹɪtʃfɔrk] *s.* horca, horquilla (*para hacinar las mieses, levantar la paja, etc.*).

piteous [pʹɪtɪəs] *adj.* lastimero, lastimoso.

pith [pɪθ] *s.* meollo, médula; esencia, sustancia.

pitiful [pʹɪtɪfəl] *adj.* lastimoso; lamentable; miserable.

pitiless [pʹɪtɪlɪs] *adj.* despiadado, incompasivo, cruel.

pity [pʹɪtɪ] *s.* piedad; lástima; compasión; **for -'s sake** por piedad, por Dios; **what a — !** ¡qué lástima!; *v.* compadecer; tener lástima por; apiadarse de, tener piedad de.

placard [plæʹkɑrd] *s.* letrero, cartel; *v.* fijar carteles.

place [ples] *s.* lugar, sitio; puesto; empleo; posición; localidad; **— of business** oficina; despacho; **— of worship** templo, iglesia; **market —** plaza, mercado; **in — of** en lugar de, en vez de; **it is not my — to do it** no es mi deber hacerlo, no me toca a mí hacerlo; *v.* colocar; situar; poner; acomodar, dar empleo a.

placid [plæʹsɪd] *adj.* plácido, apacible, sosegado.

plague [pleg] *s.* plaga; peste, pestilencia; calamidad; *v.* plagar, infestar; importunar.

plaid [plæd] *s.* tartán, tela a cuadros; manta escocesa a cuadros; diseño a cuadros; *adj.* a cuadros.

plain [plen] *adj.* llano, sencillo, claro; franco; ordinario; — **fool** tonto de capirote; — **woman** mujer sin atractivo; **in** — **sight** en plena vista, **plain-clothes man** detectivo; *adv.* claramente; — **stupid** completamente estúpido, **plain-spoken** franco, francote, sincero, *s* llano, llanura.

plaintiff [pléntıf] *s.* demandante.

plaintive [pléntıv] *adj.* lastimero, triste.

plan [plæn] *s.* plan; proyecto; plano (*dibujo o mapa*), *v.* planear; proyectar, idear; pensar, proponerse.

plane [plen] *s.* plano, superficie plana; aeroplano; cepillo (*de carpintero*); *adj.* plano, llano; — **tree** plátano falso; *v.* acepillar, alisar con cepillo (*la madera o los metales*).

planet [plǽnıt] *s.* planeta.

plank [plæŋk] *s.* tabla, tablón; principio, base (*del programa de un partido político*); *v.* entablar, entarimar, cubrir con tablas; asar (*carne*) en una tabla.

plant [plænt] *s.* planta; fábrica, taller; *v.* plantar; sembrar; implantar; establecer.

plantation [plæntéʃən] *s.* plantación; plantío; sembrado; **coffee** — cafetal; **cotton** — algodonal; **rubber** — cauchal, **sugar** — ingenio de azúcar.

planter [plǽntə] *s.* plantador, cultivador.

plaque [plæk] *s.* placa.

plasma [plǽzmə] *s.* plasma.

plaster [plǽstə] *s.* yeso; emplasto, — **of Paris** yeso, yeso mate; **court** — esparadrapo, tafetán inglés; **mustard** — sinapismo; *v.* enyesar; emplastar, poner emplastos a; pegar (*carteles, anuncios*); embarrar.

plastic [plǽstık] *adj.* plástico.

plat [plæt] *s.* plano; parcela, *v.* levantar o trazar un plano.

plate [plet] *s.* plato; placa; plancha; lámina, **dental** — dentadura postiza; *v.* platear; dorar: niquelar; blindar, proteger con planchas de metal.

plateau [plætó] *s.* altiplanicie, mesa, meseta.

plateful [plétful] *s.* plato, plato lleno.

platform [plǽtfɔrm] *s.* plataforma; tablado; programa de un partido político; **railway** — andén.

platinum [plǽtnəm] *s.* platino.

platitude [plǽtətjud] *s.* lugar común, perogrullada.

platter [plǽtə] *s.* platel, platón.

play [ple] *v.* jugar; juguetear; tocar

(*música*); representar; hacer, desempeñar (*un papel*); manipular (*un instrumento, radio, fonógrafo, etc.*); **to** — **a joke** hacer una broma, dar un chasco; **to** — **cards** jugar a los naipes, jugar a la baraja, **to** — **havoc** hacer estragos, causar daño; **to** — **tennis** jugar al tenis; **to** — **the fool** hacerse el tonto, fingirse tonto; **to be all -ed out** no poder más, estar agotado; *s.* juego; jugada (*acción, movimiento en un juego*); pieza, drama, comedia, representación; recreación, diversión; — **on words** juego de palabras, equívoco; **to give full — to** dar rienda suelta a.

player [pléə] *s.* jugador; músico; cómico, actor; — **piano** piano mecánico, pianola; **piano** — pianista; **violin** — violinista.

playful [pléfəl] *adj.* juguetón, retozón; bromista.

playground [plégraund] *s.* campo o patio de recreo.

playmate [plémet] *s.* compañero de juego.

plaything [pléʊıŋ] *s.* juguete.

playwright [pléraıt] *s.* dramático, dramaturgo.

plea [pli] *s.* súplica, ruego; alegato, defensa; pretexto; **on the** — **that** con el pretexto de que.

plead [plid] *v.* abogar; suplicar; argüir; alegar; defender (*una causa*); **to** — **guilty** declararse o confesarse culpable.

pleasant [pléznt] *adj.* grato; agradable; simpático.

pleasantry [plézntrı] *s.* chanza, broma, chiste, humorada.

please [pliz] *v.* agradar, gustar, dar gusto a; complacer; — **do it** haga Vd. el favor de hacerlo, tenga Vd. la bondad de hacerlo, sírvase hacerlo; **as you** — como Vd. quiera, como Vd. guste; **if you** — si me hace Vd. (el) favor; **to be -ed to** complacerse en, tener gusto en; alegrarse de; **to be -ed with** gustarle a uno, estar satisfecho de (*o con*).

pleasing [plízıŋ] *adj.* agradable.

pleasure [pléʒə] *s.* placer, gusto; deleite, alegría, gozo; — **trip** viaje de recreo; **what is your** — ? ¿qué deseaba Vd.? ¿en qué puedo servirle?

pleat [plit] *s.* pliegue, doblez; *v.* plegar, hacer pliegues (en).

plebeian [plıbíən] *adj. & s.* plebeyo.

pledge [plɛdʒ] *s.* promesa; prenda (*garantía*); fianza; **as a** — **of** en prenda de; *v.* prometer; empeñar, dar en prenda; hacer firmar una promesa; **to — one's word** empeñar (*o* dar) su palabra; **to — to secrecy** exigir promesa de sigilo.

plenipotentiary [plenəpəténʃərɪ] *adj.* & *s.* plenipotenciario.

plentiful [pléntɪfəl] *adj.* abundante, copioso.

plenty [pléntɪ] *s.* abundancia, copia; **— of time** bastante tiempo; **that is —** con eso basta; basta.

pliable [pláləbl] *adj.* flexible; manejable, dócil; transigente.

pliant [plálənt] *adj.* flexible; dócil, sumiso.

pliers [pláləz] *s. pl.* alicates, tenazas.

plight [plaɪt] *s.* apuro, aprieto, situación difícil.

plod [plɒd] *v.* bregar, trafagar, afanarse, trabajar asiduamente.

plot [plɒt] *s.* trama, enredo; complot, conspiración; parcela (*de tierra*), solar; plano, diagrama; *v.* tramar, urdir; maquinar, conspirar; hacer el plano o diagrama de; **to — a curve** hacer una gráfica.

plotter [plɒtə] *s.* conspirador; tramador; conjurado.

plough [plau] = **plow.**

plow [plau] *s.* arado; **—share** reja de arado; *v.* arar; surcar.

pluck [plʌk] *v.* coger; arrancar; desplumar (*un ave*); puntear (*las cuerdas de una guitarra*); **to — at** tirar de; **to — up** arrancar; cobrar ánimo; *s.* ánimo, valor; tirón.

plucky [plʌkɪ] *adj.* valeroso, animoso.

plug [plʌg] *s.* taco, tapón; caballejo, penco; elogio incidental (*de un producto comercial o de una persona*); **— of tobacco** tableta de tabaco; **electric —** clavija de conexión; **fire —** boca de agua para incendios; **spark —** bujía; *v.* tapar; **to — along** afanarse, atarearse; **to — in** enchufar, conectar; **to — up** tapar, obstruir.

plum [plʌm] *s.* ciruela; la cosa mejor; la mejor colocación; **— pudding** pudín inglés con pasas; **— tree** ciruelo.

plumage [plúmɪdʒ] *s.* plumaje.

plumb [plʌm] *s.* plomo, pesa de plomo; sonda; **out of —** no vertical; *adj.* vertical, a plomo, recto; **—bob** plomo, plomada; *adv.* a plomo, verticalmente; **— crazy** completamente loco; *v.* sondear; aplomar (*una pared*).

plumber [plʌmə] *s.* plomero.

plumbing [plʌmɪŋ] *s.* plomería; cañerías (*de un edificio*); oficio de plomero.

plume [plum] *s.* pluma; plumaje; penacho; *v.* adornar con plumas; **to — its wing** alisarse o componerse el plumaje del ala.

plump [plʌmp] *adj.* rechoncho, regordete, rollizo; *adv.* de golpe; *v.* **to — down** dejar(se) caer; desplomarse, sentarse de golpe.

plunder [plʌndə] *s.* pillaje, saqueo; botín; *v.* pillar; saquear.

plunge [plʌndʒ] *v.* zambullir(se), sumergir(se); hundir(se); lanzar(se), arrojar(se), precipitar(se); **to — headlong** echarse de cabeza; *s.* zambullida; salto (*de arriba abajo*).

plural [plúrəl] *adj.* & *s.* plural.

plus [plʌs] *s.* más, signo más; **— quantity** cantidad positiva; **two — three** dos más tres.

plush [plʌʃ] *s.* felpa; velludo.

ply [plaɪ] *v.* manejar con tesón (*un instrumento o herramienta*); importunar (*con preguntas*); hacer con regularidad un recorrido (*entre dos puntos*); **to — a trade** seguir o ejercer un oficio; **to — oneself with** saturarse de, rellenarse de; *s.* doblez, pliegue; capa (*de tejido, goma, etc.*).

pneumatic [njumǽtɪk] *adj.* neumático.

pneumonia [njumónjə] *s.* pulmonía.

poach [potʃ] *v.* escalfar (*huevos*); invadir (*un vedado*); cazar o pescar en vedado; robar caza o pesca (*de un vedado*).

pocket [pákɪt] *s.* bolsillo, faltriquera, *Am.* bolsa; tronera (*de billar*); cavidad; hoyo; *v.* embolsarse; apropiarse; ocultar (*el orgullo o rencor*); aguantar (*un insulto*).

pocketbook [pákɪtbuk] *s.* cartera; portamonedas; **woman's —** bolsa.

pocketknife [pákɪtnaɪf] *s.* navaja; cortaplumas.

pod [pɒd] *s.* vaina (*de guisante, frijol, etc.*).

poem [póɪm] *s.* poema, poesía.

poet [póɪt] *s.* poeta; vate.

poetess [póɪtɪs] *s.* poetisa.

poetic [poétɪk] *adj.* poético; **-s** *s.* arte poética, poética.

poetical [poétɪkl] *adj.* poético.

poetry [póɪtrɪ] *s.* poesía.

point [pɔɪnt] *s.* punto; punta (*de lápiz, espada, tierra, etc.*); **it is not to the —** no viene al caso; **not to see the —** no caer en la cuenta; no ver el chiste, propósito o intención; **on the — of** a punto de; *v.* apuntar; señalar; indicar; **to — out** señalar, mostrar, indicar.

pointed [póɪntɪd] *adj.* puntiagudo, agudo; satírico; apto, a propósito, al caso;

159

— arch arco apuntado, arco ojival.

pointer [pɔ́ɪntə] s. puntero; indicador, señalador; perro de punta y vuelta; indicación, consejo.

poise [pɔɪz] s. equilibrio; porte, compostura; v. equilibrar(se); balancear(se).

poison [pɔ́ɪzn] s. veneno; ponzoña; v. envenenar, emponzoñar.

poisonous [pɔ́ɪznəs] adj. venenoso, ponzoñoso.

poke [pok] v. atizar, remover (el fuego); picar (con el dedo o cualquier objeto puntiagudo); **to —** along andar perezosamente; **to — around** husmear, curiosear; **to — fun at** burlarse de; **to — into** meter en; **to — out** sacar; proyectarse; s. pinchazo; piquete; codazo; aguijonada; **slow —** tardón.

polar [pólə] adj. polar; **— bear** oso blanco.

pole [pol] s. poste; pértiga, palo largo; asta (de bandera); garrocha; polo; **Pole** polaco; **north —** polo norte, polo ártico; **south —** polo sur, polo antártico; **— vault** salto con garrocha.

police [pəlís] s. policía; v. vigilar; guardar el orden.

policeman [pəlísmən] s. policía (m.), guardia de policía, polizonte, Am. vigilante, Am. gendarme.

policy [pálɪsɪ] s. política; **insurance —** póliza de seguro.

Polish [pólɪʃ] adj. polaco; s. polaco, idioma polaco.

polish [pálɪʃ] s. pulimento; lustre, brillo; urbanidad, cultura; **shoe —** betún, bola; v. pulir, pulimentar; dar brillo o lustre a; embolar, dar bola o brillo a (zapatos).

polite [pəláit] adj. cortés, fino, urbano, político.

politeness [pəláitnɪs] s. cortesía; fineza, urbanidad.

politic [pálətɪk] adj. político, prudente; conveniente.

political [pəlíftɪkl] adj. político.

politician [palətfʃən] s. político; politicastro.

politics [pálətɪks] s. política.

poll [pol] s. votación; lista electoral; **-s** comicios; urnas electorales; casilla (donde se vota); **— tax** impuesto (de tanto por cabeza); v. registrar los votos de; votar; recibir (votos).

pollen [pálən] s. polen.

pomegranate [pʌ́mgrænit] s. granada; **— tree** granado.

pomp [pamp] s. pompa, boato.

pompous [pámpəs] adj. pomposo, os-

tentoso.

pond [pand] s. charca; estanque; **fish —** vivero.

ponder [pándə] v. ponderar, pesar, examinar; **to — over** reflexionar.

ponderous [pándərəs] adj. ponderoso; pesado.

pontoon [pantún] s. pontón, chata, barco chato; flotador (de hidroavión); **— bridge** pontón, puente flotante.

pony [póni] s. caballito, potrillo; clave o traducción (usada ilícitamente en un examen).

poodle [púdl] s. perro de lanas.

pool [pul] s. charco; charca; trucos (juego parecido al billar); polla o puesta (en ciertos juegos); fondos en común, combinación de fondos (para una empresa o para especular); "trust"; **swimming —** piscina; v. formar una polla; combinar fondos.

poor [pur] adj. pobre; malo; de mala calidad; **— student** estudiante pobre; mal estudiante; **— little thing** pobrecito; **the —** los pobres; **-ly** adv. pobremente; mal.

poorhouse [púrhaus] s. hospicio, casa de pobres.

pop [pap] s. tronido, trueno, estallido; detonación; **— of a cork** taponazo; **soda —** gaseosa; v. reventar, estallar; detonar; saltar (un tapón); **to — a question** espetar una pregunta; **to — corn** hacer palomitas de maíz, hacer rosetas de maíz; **to — in and out** entrar y salir de sopetón; **to — one's head out** sacar o asomar de repente la cabeza.

popcorn [pápkɔrn] s. rosetas, palomitas de maíz, Am. alborotos.

Pope [pop] s. Papa.

popeyed [pápaid] adj. de ojos saltones, Am. desorbitado.

poplar [páplə] s. álamo; **black —** chopo; **— grove** alameda.

poppy [pápi] s. amapola.

populace [pápjəlɪs] s. pueblo, populacho.

popular [pápjələ] adj. popular.

popularity [papjələǽrətɪ] s. popularidad.

populate [pápjələt] v. poblar.

population [papjəléʃən] s. población.

populous [pápjələs] adj. populoso.

porcelain [pɔ́rslɪn] s. porcelana.

porch [pɔrtʃ] s. pórtico, porche; galería.

porcupine [pɔ́rkjəpain] s. puerco espín.

pore [por] s. poro; v. **to — over a book** engolfarse en la lectura.

pork [pɔrk] s. puerco, carne de puerco; **— chop** chuleta de puerco; **salt —** tocino salado.

porous [pórəs] *adj.* poroso.
porridge [pórɪdʒ] *s.* potaje, gachas.
port [pɔrt] *s.* puerto; vino de Oporto; babor (*lado izquierdo de un barco*); —hole porta, portilla.
portable [pórtəbl] *adj.* portátil.
portal [pórtl] *s.* portal.
portent [pórtent] *s.* portento, presagio, agüero.
portentous [pɔrténtəs] *adj.* portentoso; prodigioso; de mal agüero.
porter [pórtə] *s.* mozo de cordel, *Am.* cargador; camarero (*en un coche-cama*); portero.
portfolio [pɔrtfólɪo] *s.* portafolio, cartera; carpeta; ministerio.
portion [pórʃən] *s.* porción; *v.* repartir.
portly [pórtlɪ] *adj.* corpulento.
portrait [pórtret] *s.* retrato.
portray [pɔrtré] *v.* retratar, pintar, dibujar, representar.
portrayal [pɔrtréəl] *s.* retrato, delineación, delineamiento, representación.
Portuguese [pórtʃəgiz] *adj.* & *s.* portugués.
pose [poz] *s.* postura, actitud; afectación; *v.* posar (*como modelo*); colocar(se) en cierta postura; afectar una actitud o postura; proponer, plantear (*una cuestión o problema*); **to — as** fingirse, hacerse pasar por.
position [pəzíʃən] *s.* posición; postura; situación, empleo, puesto.
positive [pázətɪv] *adj.* positivo; cierto, seguro; categórico; dogmático.
possess [pəzés] *v.* poseer.
possession [pəzéʃən] *s.* posesión.
possessive [pəzésɪv] *adj.* & *s.* posesivo.
possessor [pəzésə] *s.* poseedor, posesor, dueño.
possibility [pəsəbflətɪ] *s.* posibilidad.
possible [pásəbl] *adj.* posible; **possibly** *adv.* posiblemente; acaso, tal vez.
post [post] *s.* poste, pilar; puesto; empleo; **army —** guarnición militar; **—haste** por la posta, rápidamente; **— office** correo, casa de correos; **post-office box** apartado, casilla postal; **—paid** porte pagado, franco de porte; *v.* fijar (*anuncios, carteles*); anunciar; poner en lista; apostar, situar; echar al correo; **to — an entry** asentar o hacer un asiento (*en teneduría*); **to be well -ed** estar al corriente, estar bien enterado.
postage [póstɪdʒ] *s.* porte, franqueo; **— stamp** sello de correo, *Am.* estampilla, *Am.* timbre.
postal [póstl] *adj.* postal; **— card** tarjeta postal; **— money order** giro postal.

postcard [póstkard] *s.* tarjeta postal.
poster [póstə] *s.* cartel, cartelón; fijador de carteles.
posterior [pastfríə] *adj.* posterior; trasero.
posterity [pastérətɪ] *s.* posteridad.
posthumous [pástʃuməs] *adj.* póstumo.
postman [póstmən] *s.* cartero.
postmaster [póstmæstə] *s.* administrador de correos.
postpone [postpón] *v.* posponer; aplazar, diferir; postergar.
postponement [postpónmənt] *s.* aplazamiento.
postscript [pósskrɪpt] *s.* posdata.
posture [pástʃə] *s.* postura, actitud; posición; *v.* adoptar una postura.
posy [pózɪ] *s.* flor.
pot [pat] *s.* pote; olla, puchero, cacharro (*de cocina*); bacín, bacinica (*de cámara o recámara*); **flower —** tiesto, maceta; **—bellied** panzudo, barrigón.
potassium [pətǽsɪəm] *s.* potasio.
potato [pətéto] *s.* patata, papa; **sweet —** batata, *Am.* camote, *Am.* boniato.
potency [pótnsɪ] *s.* potencia, poder, fuerza.
potent [pótnt] *adj.* potente, poderoso, fuerte.
potential [pəténʃəl] *adj.* & *s.* potencial.
pottage [pátɪdʒ] *s.* potaje.
potter [pátə] *s.* alfarero, fabricante de vasijas o cacharros de barro; **-'s field** cementerio de pobres y desconocidos.
pottery [pátərɪ] *s.* cerámica, alfarería; vasijas de barro.
pouch [pautʃ] *s.* bolsa, saquillo; **mail —** valija; **tobacco —** tabaquera, petaca.
poultice [póltɪs] *s.* emplasto.
poultry [póltrɪ] *s.* aves de corral.
pounce [pauns] *s.* salto (*para agarrar*); zarpada; *v.* **to — into** entrar de sopetón; **to — upon** abalanzarse sobre, saltar sobre, agarrar.
pound [paund] *s.* libra; golpazo; **— sterling** libra esterlina; *v.* golpear; machacar, martillar.
pour [por] *v.* vaciar, verter; servir (*una taza de té*); fluir; llover a cántaros, llover recio.
pout [paut] *v.* hacer pucheros, lloriquear; poner cara de enfado; *s.* puchero, pucherito.
poverty [pávətɪ] *s.* pobreza.
powder [páudə] *s.* polvo; pólvora (*explosivo*); polvos (*de tocador*); **— compact** polvera; **— magazine** polvorín; **— puff** polvera, borla, *Am.* cisne, *Am.* mota; *v.* empolvar(se); polvorear, espolvorear; pulverizar(se); **to — one's face** empolvarse la cara, ponerse pol-

vos.

power [páuə] s. poder; poderío; potencia; fuerza; **motive —** fuerza motriz; **— of attorney** poder; **— plant** planta de fuerza motriz.

powerful [páuəfəl] adj. poderoso.

powerless [páuəlıs] adj. impotente.

practicable [prǽktɪkəbl] adj. practicable; factible, hacedero; práctico; **— road** camino transitable.

practical [prǽktɪkl] adj. práctico; **— joke** chasco, burla pesada; **-ly** adv. casi, virtualmente; realmente, en realidad; prácticamente.

practice [prǽktɪs] s. práctica; ejercicio (de una profesión); método; regla, costumbre; clientela; v. practicar; ejercer (una profesión); ejercitarse.

practiced [prǽktɪst] adj. práctico, experimentado; experto, perito.

prairie [préri] s. pradera, llanura.

praise [prez] s. alabanza; elogio; encomio; v. alabar; elogiar; encomiar.

praiseworthy [prézwɝðɪ] adj. laudable.

prance [præns] v. cabriolar, hacer cabriolas.

prank [præŋk] s. travesura, burla; **to play -s** hacer travesuras.

prate [pret] v. parlotear, charlar; s. parloteo, charla.

prattle [prǽtl] v. parlotear, charlar; s. parloteo, charla.

pray [pre] v. orar, rezar; rogar, suplicar; **— tell me** dígame por favor, le ruego que me diga.

prayer [prɛr] s. oración, rezo; ruego, súplica; **— book** devocionario; **Lord's —** Padre Nuestro.

preach [pritʃ] v. predicar; sermonear.

preacher [prítʃə] s. predicador.

preaching [prítʃɪŋ] s. predicación; sermón; sermoneo.

preamble [príæmbl] s. preámbulo.

prearranged [priərǽndʒd] adj. arreglado de antemano.

precarious [prɪkɛ́rɪəs] adj. precario; inseguro.

precaution [prɪkɔ́ʃən] s. precaución.

precede [prɪsid] v. preceder.

precedence [prɪsídns] s. precedencia; prioridad.

precedent [présədənt] s. precedente.

preceding [prɪsídɪŋ] adj. precedente, anterior.

precept [prísɛpt] s. precepto.

precinct [prísɪŋkt] s. distrito; recinto; **-s** límites, inmediaciones.

precious [préʃəs] adj. precioso; querido, amado, caro; **— little** poquísimo, muy poco.

precipice [présəpɪs] s. precipicio.

precipitate [prɪsífpətet] v. precipitar(se); adj. precipitado, apresurado, atropellado; s. precipitado.

precipitation [prɪsɪpətéʃən] s. precipitación; lluvia (o nieve, rocío, granizo, etc.); cantidad de agua pluvial.

precipitous [prɪsífpətəs] adj. precipitoso, escarpado; precipitado.

precise [prɪsáɪs] adj. preciso, exacto.

precision [prɪsíʒən] s. precisión, exactitud.

preclude [prɪklúd] v. excluir; impedir.

precocious [prɪkóʃəs] adj. precoz.

predecessor [prɛdɪsésə] s. predecesor.

predestine [prɪdéstɪn] v. predestinar.

predicament [prɪdfkəmənt] s. aprieto, apuro, dificultad.

predicate [prédɪkɪt] adj. & s. predicado.

predict [prɪdfkt] v. predecir, vaticinar.

prediction [prɪdfkʃən] s. predicción, pronóstico, vaticinio.

predilection [prɪdɪlékʃən] s. predilección, preferencia.

predispose [prɪdɪspóz] v. predisponer.

predominance [prɪdámənəns] s. predominio; ascendiente.

predominant [prɪdámənənt] adj. predominante.

predominate [prɪdámənet] v. predominar.

preface [préfɪs] s. prefacio; prólogo; v. prologar.

prefer [prɪfɝ́] v. preferir; **to — a claim** presentar una demanda.

preferable [préfɝəbl] adj. preferible; preferente; **preferably** adv. preferiblemente; preferentemente, de preferencia.

preference [préfɝəns] s. preferencia.

preferred [prɪfɝ́d] p.p. & adj. preferido; **— shares** acciones preferentes.

prefix [prífɪks] s. prefijo; [prifíks] v. prefijar, anteponer.

pregnancy [prégnənsɪ] s. preñez, embarazo.

pregnant [prégnənt] adj. preñado; lleno, repleto; encinta.

prejudice [prédʒədɪs] s. prejuicio, prevención; daño; v. predisponer, prevenir; perjudicar.

prelate [prélɪt] s. prelado.

preliminary [prɪlímɪnɛrɪ] adj. & s. preliminar.

prelude [préljud] s. preludio; v. preludiar.

premature [primətjúr] adj. prematuro.

premeditated [prɪmédətetɪd] adj. premeditado.

premier [prímɪə] s. primer ministro;

adj. primero; principal.

premise [prémɪs] *s.* premisa; **-s** terrenos; local.

premium [prímɪəm] *s.* premio; **at a —** muy escaso, muy caro; **insurance —** prima de seguro.

preoccupy [priókjəpaɪ] *v.* preocupar; ocupar de antemano.

prepaid [pripéd] *adj.* pagado de antemano; **to send —** enviar porte pagado, enviar franco de porte.

preparation [prepəréʃən] *s.* preparación; preparativo.

preparatory [pripǽrətorɪ] *adj.* preparatorio.

prepare [pripér] *v.* preparar(se).

preparedness [pripérɪdnɪs] *s.* preparación, prevención.

preposition [prepəzíʃən] *s.* preposición.

preposterous [pripástrəs] *adj.* absurdo, insensato.

prerequisite [prirékwəzɪt] *s.* requisito previo.

prerogative [prirágətɪv] *s.* prerrogativa.

presage [présɪdʒ] *s.* presagio; [prisédʒ] *v.* presagiar.

prescribe [priskráɪb] *v.* prescribir; recetar.

prescription [priskrípʃən] *s.* receta; prescripción, precepto, mandato.

presence [prézn̩s] *s.* presencia; **— of mind** aplomo, serenidad.

present [préznt] *s.* presente; regalo; **at — al** presente, ahora; **for the — por** ahora; *adj.* presente; corriente, actual; **— company excepted** mejorando lo presente; **— participle** gerundio; **to be —** asistir, estar presente; [prizént] *v.* presentar; regalar, obsequiar.

presentation [prezn̩téʃən] *s.* presentación; regalo, obsequio.

presentiment [prizéntəmənt] *s.* presentimiento; corazonada.

presently [prézntlɪ] *adv.* luego, pronto, dentro de poco.

preservation [prezəvéʃən] *s.* preservación; conservación.

preserve [prizɜ́v] *v.* preservar, guardar; conservar; mantener; *s.* conserva, compota; **forest —** vedado.

preside [prizáɪd] *v.* presidir; **to — at (— over) a meeting** presidir una junta.

presidency [prézədənsɪ] *s.* presidencia.

president [prézədənt] *s.* presidente.

presidential [prezədénʃəl] *adj.* presidencial.

press [pres] *v.* prensar; apretar; comprimir; planchar (*ropa*); forzar; apremiar; urgir; empujar; **to — forward**

empujar hacia adelante; avanzar, ganar terreno; **to — one's point** porfiar; insistir en su árgumento; **to — through the crowd** abrirse paso por entre la multitud; **to be hard -ed by work** estar abrumado de trabajo; **to be hard -ed for money** estar escaso de fondos; *s.* prensa; imprenta.

pressing [présɪŋ] *adj.* apremiante, urgente.

pressure [préʃə] *s.* presión; apremio, urgencia; **— cooker** cocinilla de presión; **— gauge** manómetro.

prestige [prestíʒ] *s.* prestigio.

presumable [prisúməbl] *adj.* presumible, probable.

presume [prizúm] *v.* presumir; suponer; **to — on (upon)** abusar de; **to — to** atreverse a.

presumption [prizámpʃən] *s.* presunción; pretensión; suposición.

presumptuous [prizámptʃʊəs] *adj.* presuntuoso, pretencioso, presumido.

presuppose [prisəpóz] *v.* presuponer.

pretend [priténd] *v.* pretender; fingir.

pretense [priténs] *s.* pretensión; presunción; ostentación; apariencia; pretexto; **under — of** so pretexto de.

pretension [priténʃən] *s.* pretensión; pretexto.

pretext [prítekst] *s.* pretexto.

prettily [prítɪlɪ] *adv.* lindamente; agradablemente.

prettiness [prítɪnɪs] *s.* lindeza, gracia.

pretty [prítɪ] *adj.* lindo, bonito, bello, *Am.* chulo; *adv.* medianamente; bastante; un poco, algo; **— well** regular, así así; bastante bien, medianamente.

prevail [privél] *v.* prevalecer; **to — on (upon)** persuadir.

prevailing [privélɪŋ] *adj.* predominante; en boga.

prevalent [prévələnt] *adj.* prevaleciente; común, corriente.

prevent [privént] *v.* prevenir, evitar; impedir; estorbar.

prevention [privénʃən] *s.* prevención; precaución.

previous [prívɪəs] *adj.* previo; **-ly** *adv.* previamente; antes; de antemano.

prey [pre] *s.* presa; víctima; **birds of — aves** de rapiña; *v.* **to — on** cazar; rapiñar, pillar; robar; **it -s upon my mind** me tiene preocupado, me tiene en zozobra.

price [praɪs] *s.* precio; valor; costo (coste *o* costa); **at any —** a toda costa, a todo trance; *v.* apreciar, valuar, fijar el precio de; averiguar el precio de.

priceless [práɪslɪs] *adj.* sin precio, inapreciable.

prick [prɪk] v. picar; pinchar; punzar; sentir comezón; sentir picazón; **to** — **up one's ears** aguzar las orejas; s. picadura; punzada; pinchazo; piquete; aguijón; púa.

prickly [prɪklɪ] adj. espinoso, lleno de espinas; lleno de púas; — **heat** picazón causada por el calor; — **pear** tuna (de nopal).

pride [praɪd] s. orgullo; soberbia; v. **to** — **oneself on (upon)** enorgullecerse de, preciarse de.

priest [prist] s. sacerdote.

priesthood [prísthud] s. sacerdocio.

prim [prɪm] adj. remilgado; repulido; peripuesto; estirado.

primarily [praɪmérəlɪ] adv. primariamente, principalmente; en primer lugar.

primary [práɪmerɪ] adj. primario; primero; fundamental; principal; — **colors** colores elementales; — **election** elección primaria; — **school** escuela primaria.

prime [praɪm] adj. primero; principal; primario; selecto, de primera calidad; — **minister** primer ministro; — **number** número primo; s. flor (de la vida o de la edad); la flor y nata (lo mejor); plenitud; número primo; **to be in one's** — estar en la flor de la edad; v. preparar, informar, instruir de antemano; cebar (un carburador, bomba o arma de fuego).

primer [prímə] s. abecedario, cartilla de lectura; compendio.

primeval [praɪmívl] adj. primitivo.

primitive [prímətɪv] adj. primitivo.

primness [prímnɪs] s. remilgo, tiesura, demasiada formalidad; dengue, afectación.

primp [prɪmp] v. acicalar(se), adornar(se), arreglar(se).

primrose [prímroz] s. prímula o primavera (flor); color amarillo pálido.

prince [prɪns] s. príncipe.

princely [prínslɪ] adj. noble, regio, magnífico, propio de un príncipe.

princess [prínsɪs] s. princesa.

principal [prínsəpl] adj. principal; s. principal, capital; principal, jefe, director.

principle [prínsəpl] s. principio; regla; ley; fundamento, base.

print [prɪnt] s. tipo, letra de molde; estampa; lámina, grabado; estampado (tejido estampado); diseño (estampado); impresión; **in** — impreso, publicado; **out of** — agotado; v. imprimir; estam-

par; escribir en letra de molde; **-ed fabric** estampado.

printer [prínta] s. impresor.

printing [príntɪŋ] s. imprenta; impresión; tipografía; — **office** imprenta; — **press** prensa.

prior [práɪə] adj. previo, anterior, precedente; — **to** anterior a, con antelación a; s. prior (de un monasterio).

priority [praɪɔ́rətɪ] s. prioridad, precedencia, antelación.

prism [prízəm] s. prisma.

prison [prízn] s. prisión, cárcel; v. encarcelar.

prisoner [prízna] s. prisionero, preso.

privacy [práɪvəsɪ] s. secreto, reserva; retiro; **to have no** — carecer de sitio privado; estar a la vista del público.

private [práɪvɪt] adj. privado; personal; particular; secreto; confidencial; **a** — **citizen** un particular; — **school** escuela particular; s. soldado raso; **in** — en secreto; a solas, privadamente.

privation [praɪvéʃən] s. privación.

privilege [prívlɪdʒ] s. privilegio.

privileged [prívlɪdʒd] adj. privilegiado; **to be** — **to** tener el privilegio de.

prize [praɪz] s. premio, galardón; presa, botín de guerra; — **fight** boxeo público, pugilato; — **fighter** boxeador, pugilista; — **medal** medalla de premio; v. apreciar, estimar, tener en gran estima.

probability [prɑbəbílətɪ] s. probabilidad.

probable [prɑ́bəbl] adj. probable; **probably** adv. probablemente.

probation [probéʃən] s. probación; noviciado; prueba; **to put a prisoner on** — poner a un prisionero en libertad bajo la vigilancia de un juez.

probe [prob] v. tentar, reconocer, sondear (una herida); escudriñar, examinar a fondo; indagar; s. tienta (instrumento de cirujano); indagación.

problem [prɑ́bləm] s. problema.

procedure [prəsídʒə] s. procedimiento; proceder.

proceed [prəsíd] v. proceder; proseguir; seguir adelante; **to** — **to** proceder a, comenzar a, ponerse a.

proceeding [prəsídɪŋ] s. procedimiento; transacción; -s transacciones; actas; proceso.

proceeds [prósidz] s. pl. producto, ganancia.

process [práses] s. proceso; procedimiento; método; **in** — **of time** con el transcurso del tiempo, con el tiempo, andando el tiempo; **in the** — **of being made** en vía de preparación; v.

preparar mediante un procedimiento especial, someter a un procedimiento; procesar (*ante un juez*).

precession [prəsέʃən] *s.* procesión; desfile; **funeral** — cortejo fúnebre.

proclaim [proklém] *v.* proclamar; promulgar.

proclamation [prakləméʃən] *s.* proclamación; proclama.

procure [prokjúr] *v.* procurar, conseguir, obtener.

prod [prad] *v.* aguijonear; picar.

prodigal [prádɪgl] *adj.* & *s.* pródigo, gastador.

prodigious [prədídʒəs] *adj.* prodigioso.

prodigy [prádədʒɪ] *s.* prodigio.

produce [prádjus] *s.* producto; productos agrícolas; [prədjús] *v.* producir.

producer [prədjúsə] *s.* productor; **theatrical** — empresario.

product [prádəkt] *s.* producto.

production [prədΛkʃən] *s.* producción; producto; obra, composición; representación teatral.

productive [prədΛktɪv] *adj.* productivo.

profanation [prəfənéʃən] *s.* profanación, desacato.

profane [prəfén] *adj.* profano; *v.* profanar.

profess [prəfés] *v.* profesar; pretender.

profession [prəféʃən] *s.* profesión.

professional [prəféʃənl] *adj.* profesional; *s.* profesional, *Am.* profesionista.

professor [prəfésə] *s.* profesor, catedrático.

proffer [práfə] *s.* oferta, propuesta; *v.* ofrecer, proponer.

proficiency [prəfíʃənsɪ] *s.* pericia, destreza.

proficient [prəfíʃənt] *adj.* proficiente, perito, experto.

profile [prófaɪl] *s.* perfil; contorno.

profit [práfɪt] *s.* provecho, utilidad, beneficio; ganancia; lucro; — **and loss** pérdidas y ganancias; **net** — ganancia neta o líquida; *v.* aprovechar; ganar, sacar provecho; **.to** — **by** aprovecharse de, sacar provecho de.

profitable [práfɪtəbl] *adj.* provechoso; lucrativo.

profiteer [prəfətír] *s.* extorsionista, carero, explotador, logrero; *v.* extorsionar, explotar, cobrar más de lo justo.

profound [prəfáund] *adj.* profundo.

profuse [prəfjús] *adj.* profuso, abundante; pródigo.

progeny [prádʒənɪ] *s.* prole.

program [prógræm] *s.* programa; plan.

progress [prágrɛs] *s.* progreso; [prəgrés] *v.* progresar.

progressive [prəgrésɪv] *adj.* progresivo; progresista; *s.* progresista.

prohibit [prohíbɪt] *v.* prohibir; vedar.

prohibition [proəbíʃən] *s.* prohibición.

project [prádʒɛkt] *s.* proyecto, plan; [prədʒékt] *v.* proyectar(se); extenderse, sobresalir.

projectile [prədʒéktl] *s.* proyectil; *adj.* arrojadizo; — **weapon** arma arrojadiza.

projection [prədʒékʃən] *s.* proyección; saliente, salidizo.

proletarian [prolətériən] *adj.* & *s.* proletario.

proletariat [prolətériət] *s.* proletariado.

prologue [prólɔg] *s.* prólogo.

prolong [prəlɔ́ŋ] *v.* prolongar.

prolongation [prolɔŋgéʃən] *s.* prolongación.

promenade [prɑmənéd] *s.* paseo; baile (*usualmente* prom); *v.* pasearse.

prominent [prámənənt] *adj.* prominente; notable; saliente; conspicuo.

promiscuous [prəmískjuəs] *adj.* promiscuo.

promise [prámɪs] *s.* promesa; *v.* prometer; **Promised Land** Tierra de Promisión.

promising [prámɪsɪŋ] *adj.* prometedor.

promissory [práməsorɪ] *adj.* promisorio; — **note** pagaré.

promontory [práməntorɪ] *s.* promontorio.

promote [prəmót] *v.* promover; fomentar; explotar; adelantar, ascender; elevar (*a un empleo o dignidad superior*).

promoter [prəmótə] *s.* promotor, promovedor.

promotion [prəmóʃən] *s.* promoción; ascenso; adelantamiento.

prompt [prampt] *adj.* pronto, puntual; listo, presto; *v.* mover, incitar, inducir; apuntar (*servir de apuntador en el teatro*); soplar (*sugerir a otro lo que debe decir en una clase o junta*).

promptly [prámptlɪ] *adv.* pronto, prontamente, presto; puntualmente; con prontitud, con presteza.

promptness [prámptnɪs] *s.* prontitud, presteza; puntualidad.

promulgate [prəmΛlget] *v.* promulgar.

prone [pron] *adj.* inclinado; propenso, dispuesto; boca abajo; postrado.

prong [prɔŋ] *s.* púa, punta.

pronoun [prónaun] *s.* pronombre.

pronounce [prənáuns] *v.* pronunciar; declarar.

pronounced [prənáunst] *adj.* pronunciado, marcado; — **opinions** opiniones decididas.

pronunciation [prənʌnsɪéʃən] *s.* pronunciación.

proof [pruf] *s.* prueba; comprobación; *adj.* impenetrable, resistente; **— against** a prueba de; **—reader** corrector de pruebas de imprenta; **— sheet** prueba, pliego de prueba; **galley —** galerada; **bomb—** a prueba de bomba; **fire —** a prueba de incendios; **water—** impermeable.

prop [prɑp] *s.* puntal; sostén, apoyo; *v* apuntalar, sostener.

propaganda [prɑpəgǽndə] *s.* propaganda.

propagate [prɑpəget] *v.* propagar(se).

propagation [prɑpəgéʃən] *s.* propagación; diseminación.

propel [prəpél] *v.* propulsar, impeler.

propeller [prəpélə] *s.* hélice (*de un buque o avión*); propulsor, impulsor.

proper [prɑpə] *adj.* propio; conveniente, a propósito; justo; correcto; **— noun** nombre propio; **-ly** *adv.* propiamente; con propiedad, correctamente.

property [prɑpətɪ] *s.* propiedad; posesión; posesiones, bienes.

prophecy [prɑfəsɪ] *s.* profecía.

prophesy [prɑfəsaɪ] *v.* profetizar, predecir, pronosticar, augurar.

prophet [prɑfɪt] *s.* profeta.

prophetic [prəfétɪk] *adj.* profético.

propitious [prəpíʃəs] *adj.* propicio, favorable.

proportion [prəpórʃən] *s.* proporción; **out of—** desproporcionado; *v.* proporcionar; **well -ed** bien proporcionado.

proposal [prəpóz] *s.* propuesta; proposición; declaración (*de amor*).

propose [prəpóz] *v.* proponer; declararse, hacer propuesta de matrimonio; **to — to do something** proponerse hacer algo.

proposition [prɑpəzíʃən] *s.* proposición; propuesta; asunto.

proprietor [prəpráɪətə] *s.* propietario, dueño.

propriety [prəpráɪətɪ] *s.* propiedad, corrección; decoro.

prorate [prorét] *v.* prorratear, repartir proporcionalmente.

prosaic [prozéɪk] *adj.* prosaico.

prose [proz] *s.* prosa; *adj.* prosaico.

prosecute [prásɪkjut] *v.* procesar, enjuiciar, demandar ante un juez; llevar adelante (*un negocio, empresa, demanda, etc.*).

prosecution [prɑsɪkjúʃən] *s.* prosecución, seguimiento; parte acusadora (*en un pleito*).

prosecutor [prásɪkjutə] *s.* fiscal; acusador.

prospect [práspekt] *s.* perspectiva, vista; esperanza; espectativa; cliente (candidato o comprador) probable; probabilidad de éxito (*para un negocio, empleo, etc.*); *v.* explorar, andar en busca de.

prospective [prəspéktɪv] *adj.* probable, posible, esperado; presunto.

prospector [prəspéktə] *s.* explorador, buscador (*de minas, petróleo, etc.*).

prosper [práspə] *v.* prosperar, medrar.

prosperity [prɑspérətɪ] *s.* prosperidad.

prosperous [práspərəs] *adj.* próspero.

prostitute [prástɑtjut] *s.* ramera, prostituta; *v.* prostituir.

prostrate [prástret] *adj.* postrado; abatido; *v.* postrar; abatir.

protect [prətékt] *v.* proteger.

protection [prətékʃən] *s.* protección; amparo.

protective [prətéktɪv] *adj.* protector; **— tariff** tarifa proteccionista.

protector [prətéktə] *s.* protector.

protectorate [prətéktrɪt] *s.* protectorado.

protégé [prótəge] *s.* protegido.

protein [prótiin] *s.* proteína.

protest [prótest] *s.* protesta, protestación; [prətést] *v.* protestar.

protestant [prátɪstənt] *adj. & s.* protestante.

protestation [prɑtəstéʃən] *s.* protestación, protesta.

protoplasm [prótəplæzəm] *s.* protoplasma.

protract [protrǽkt] *v.* alargar, extender, prolongar.

protrude [protrúd] *v.* sobresalir; resaltar; proyectar(se).

protuberance [protjúbərəns] *s.* protuberancia.

proud [praud] *adj.* orgulloso; soberbio.

prove [pruv] *v.* probar; demostrar; comprobar; resultar.

proverb [právзb] *s.* proverbio; refrán.

provide [prəváɪd] *v.* proveer; abastecer; suplir; estipular; **to — for** hacer provisión para; **to — with** proveer de.

provided [prəváɪdɪd] *conj.* con tal (de) que, a condición (de) que; **— that** con tal (de) que.

providence [právədəns] *s.* providencia.

providential [prɑvədénʃəl] *adj.* providencial.

provider [prəváɪdə] *s.* proveedor.

province [právɪns] *s.* provincia; jurisdicción; **it isn't within my — no** está dentro de mi jurisdicción; **no es**

de mi incumbencia.

provincial [prəvínʃəl] *adj.* provincial; s. provinciano.

provision [prəvíʒən] *s.* provisión; abastecimiento; estipulación; -s provisiones; víveres; **to make the necessary -s** tomar las medidas (o precauciones) necesarias.

proviso [prəváizo] *s.* condición, estipulación.

provocation [pravəkéʃən] *s.* provocación.

provoke [prəvók] *v.* provocar; irritar; enfadar.

prow [prau] *s.* proa.

prowess [práuis] *s.* proeza.

prowl [praul] *v.* rondar en acecho; fisgonear.

proximity [praksímətɪ] *s.* proximidad.

proxy [práksɪ] *s.* apoderado, substituto, delegado; **by —** mediante apoderado.

prude [prud] *s.* mojigato, persona gazmoña.

prudence [prúdṇs] *s.* prudencia.

prudent [prúdṇt] *adj.* prudente.

prudery [prúdərɪ] *s.* mojigatería, gazmoñería, remilgo.

prudish [prúdɪʃ] *adj.* gazmoño, remilgado.

prune [prun] *s.* ciruela; ciruela pasa; *v.* podar, recortar.

pry [praɪ] *v.* atisbar, espiar; fisgar, fisgonear; curiosear; **to — a secret out** extraer (o arrancar) un secreto; **to — apart** separar por fuerza; **to — into other people's affairs** entremeterse en lo ajeno; **to — open** abrir a la fuerza; **to — up** levantar con una palanca.

psalm [sam] *s.* salmo.

pseudonym [sjúdnim] *s.* seudónimo.

psychiatrist [saɪkáɪətrɪst] *s.* psiquiatra, alienista.

psychiatry [saɪkáɪətrɪ] *s.* psiquiatría.

psychological [saɪkəládʒɪk] *adj.* psicológico.

psychologist [saɪkálədʒɪst] *s.* psicólogo.

psychology [saɪkálədʒɪ] *s.* psicología.

public [páblɪk] *adj.* público; **— prosecutor** fiscal; *s.* público.

publication [pablɪkéʃən] *s.* publicación.

publicity [pablísətɪ] *s.* publicidad, propaganda.

publish [páblɪʃ] *v.* publicar; editar; **-ing house** editorial o editora.

publisher [páblɪʃə] *s.* publicador; editor.

pucker [páka] *v.* fruncir.

pudding [púdɪŋ] *s.* budín, pudín.

puddle [pádḷ] *s.* charco.

puff [páf] *s.* resoplido; bocanada (de

humo, vapor, *etc.*); bullón (*de vestido*); **— of wind** ráfaga, soplo; **— paste** hojaldre; **cream —** bollo de crema; **powder —** polvera, borla, *Am.* mota; *v.* resoplar, jadear; echar bocanadas; **to — up** inflar(se); ahuecar(se); hinchar(se).

pug [pag] *s.* perro dogo; **— nose naris** chata, ñata o respingada.

pull [pul] *v.* tirar de; jalar (halar); sacar; arrancar; estirar; **to — apart** desgarrar; despedazar; descomponer; desmontar; **to — down the curtain** bajar la cortinilla; **to — oneself together** componerse, serenarse; **to — over to the right** hacerse a la derecha, desviarse hacia la derecha; **to — up** arrancar; parar (*un caballo, un auto*); parar, hacer alto; **to — through** salir de un apuro; sacar (*a alguien*) de un apuro; **the train —ed into the station** el tren llegó a la estación; *s.* tirón; estirón; ascenso difícil; esfuerzo (*para subir*); **to have —** tener buenas aldabas, tener influencia.

pullet [púlɪt] *s.* polla.

pulley [púlɪ] *s.* polea; garrucha.

pulp [palp] *s.* pulpa.

pulpit [púlpɪt] *s.* púlpito.

pulsate [pálset] *v.* pulsar, latir.

pulse [pals] *s.* pulso; pulsación.

pulverize [pálvəraɪz] *v.* pulverizar.

pumice [pámɪs] *s.* piedra pómez.

pump [pamp] *s.* bomba (*para sacar agua*); zapatilla; **gasoline —** bomba de gasolina; **hand —** bomba de mano; **tire —** bomba para neumáticos; *v.* manejar la bomba, *Am.* bombear; inflar (*un neumático*); **to — someone** sacarle (o sonsacarle) a una persona la verdad o un secreto.

pumpkin [pámpkɪn] *s.* calabaza.

pun [pan] *s.* equívoco, retruécano, juego de palabras; *v.* decir retruécanos o equívocos, jugar del vocablo.

punch [pantʃ] *s.* puñetazo, puñada; ponche (*bebida*); punzón, sacabocados; empuje, fuerza, vitalidad; **— bowl** ponchera; *v.* dar un puñetazo, dar una puñada; punzar, horadar, perforar; **to — a hole** hacer un agujero o perforación.

punctual [páŋktʃuəl] *adj.* puntual.

punctuality [paŋktʃuélətɪ] *s.* puntualidad.

punctuate [páŋktʃuet] *v.* puntuar.

punctuation [paŋktʃuéʃən] *s.* puntuación.

puncture [páŋktʃə] *v.* picar, punzar, pinchar; agujerear, perforar; **-d tire**

neumático picado; *s.* picadura; pinchazo; perforación; **to have a tire —** teñer un neumático picado, tener una llanta o goma picada.

punish [pʌnɪʃ] *v.* castigar.

punishment [pʌnɪʃmənt] *s.* castigo.

puny [pjúnɪ] *adj.* endeble, débil, flaco, enfermizo; insignificante.

pup [pʌp] *s.* cachorro.

pupil [pjúpl] *s.* discípulo; **— of the eye** pupila, niña del ojo.

puppet [pʌpɪt] *s.* títere, muñeco, monigote; **— show** títeres.

puppy [pʌpɪ] *s.* cachorrito.

purchase [pɔ́tʃəs] *v.* comprar; mercar; *s.* compra; merca; **to get a — upon** agarrarse fuerte a.

purchaser [pɔ́tʃəsə] *s.* comprador, marchante.

pure [pjur] *adj.* puro; **-ly** *adv.* puramente; meramente.

purée [pjuré] *s.* puré.

purgative [pɔ́gətɪv] *adj.* purgante; *s.* purga, purgante.

purgatory [pɔ́gətɔrɪ] *s.* purgatorio.

purge [pɔdʒ] *v.* purgar(se); limpiar; purificar(se); *s.* purga, purgante.

purify [pjúrəfaɪ] *v.* purificar(se); depurar.

purity [pjúrətɪ] *s.* pureza.

purple [pɔ́pl] *s.* púrpura; *adj.* purpúreo, morado.

purport [pɔ́port] *s.* significado; tenor, sustancia; [pəpórt] *v.* pretender, aparentar.

purpose [pɔ́pəs] *s.* propósito, intención; fin, objeto; **for no —** sin objeto, inútilmente, en vano, para nada; **on —** adrede, de propósito; *v.* proponerse.

purr [pɔ] *s.* ronroneo (*del gato*); zumbido (*del motor*); *v.* ronronear (*el gato*).

purse [pɔs] *s.* bolsillo, portamonedas, bolsa; *v.* **to — one's lips** fruncir los labios.

pursue [pəsú] *v.* perseguir; seguir; dedicarse a (*una carrera, un estudio*).

pursuer [pəsúə] *s.* perseguidor.

pursuit [pəsút] *s.* perseguimiento; busca; ocupación; ejercicio (*de una profesión, cargo, etc.*); **in — of** a caza de, en seguimiento de, en busca de.

pus [pʌs] *s.* pus, podre.

push [puʃ] *v.* empujar; fomentar, promover; apresurar; **to — aside** hacer a un lado, rechazar, apartar; **to — forward** empujar, abrirse paso; avanzar; **to — through** encajar (*por un agujero o rendija*); abrirse paso a empujones; *s.* empuje; empujón, empellón; **— button** botón eléctrico.

pushcart [púʃkart] *s.* carretilla de mano.

pussy [púsɪ] *s.* minino, gatito; **— willow** especie de sauce americano.

put [put] *v.* poner; colocar; **to — a question** hacer una pregunta; **to — across an idea** darse a entender bien; hacer aceptar una idea; **to — away** apartar; guardar; **to — before** poner delante, anteponer; proponer ante; **to — by money** ahorrar o guardar dinero; **to — down** apuntar, anotar; sofocar (*una revolución*); rebajar (*los precios*); **to — in words** expresar; **to — in writing** poner por escrito; **to — off** aplazar, posponer; diferir; **to — on** ponerse (*ropa*); **to — on airs** darse tono o ínfulas; **to — on weight** engordar; **to — out** apagar, extinguir; **to — someone out** echar o expulsar a alguien; molestar o incomodar a alguien; **to — to shame** avergonzar; **to — up** enlatar, envasar (*frutas, legumbres*); apostar (*dinero*); alojar(se); erigir; **to — up for sale** poner de venta; **to — up with** aguantar, tolerar; *pret. & p.p.* **de to put.**

putrefy [pjútrəfaɪ] *v.* podrir (*o pudrir*), corromper.

putrid [pjútrɪd] *adj.* putrefacto, podrido.

putter [pʌtə] *v.* trabajar sin orden ni sistema; ocuparse en cosas de poca monta; malgastar el tiempo.

putty [pʌtɪ] *s.* masilla; *v.* tapar o rellenar con masilla.

puzzle [pʌzl] *s.* rompecabezas, acertijo; enigma; **crossword —** crucigrama; *v.* embrollar, poner perplejo, confundir; **to — out** desenredar, descifrar; **to — over** ponderar; tratar de resolver o descifrar; **to be -d** estar perplejo.

pyramid [pírəmɪd] *s.* pirámide.

Q

quack [kwæk] *s.* graznido (*del pato*); curandero, matasanos, medicastro; charlatán; *adj.* falso; *v.* graznar.

quagmire [kwǽgmaɪr] *s.* tremedal, cenagal.

quail [kwel] *s.* codorniz.

quaint [kwent] *adj.* raro, extraño; pintoresco.

quake [kwek] *s.* temblor; terremoto; *v.* temblar.

qualification [kwɑləfəkéʃən] *s.* calificación; cualidad, calidad; requisito; aptitud.

qualify [kwɑ́ləfaɪ] *v.* calificar; capacitar; **to — for a position** estar capacitado para una posición; **his studies —**

him for the job sus estudios le capacitan para el puesto.

quality [kwáləti] s. cualidad; calidad.

qualm [kwɑm] s. escrúpulo.

quantity [kwántəti] s. cantidad.

quarantine [kwɔ́rəntin] s. cuarentena; v. poner en cuarentena, aislar.

quarrel [kwɔ́rəl] s. riña, reyerta, pendencia; querella; v. reñir; pelear, disputar.

quarrelsome [kwɔ́rəlsəm] adj. reñidor, pendenciero.

quarry [kwɔ́ri] s. cantera; presa, caza (animal perseguido); v. explotar (una cantera); trabajar en una cantera.

quart [kwɔrt] s. cuarto de galón (0.9463 de un litro).

quarter [kwɔ́rtə] s. cuarto, cuarta parte; moneda de 25 centavos; trimestre (cuarta parte de un año); barrio, distrito; -s morada, vivienda, alojamiento; **from all -s** de todas partes; **to give no — to the enemy** no dar cuartel al enemigo; adj. cuarto; v. cuartear, dividir en cuartos; descuartizar; acuartelar, acantonar, alojar (tropas).

quarterly [kwɔ́rtəli] adv. trimestralmente, por trimestres; adj. trimestral; s. publicación trimestral.

quartet [kwɔrtét] s. cuarteto.

quartz [kwɔrts] s. cuarzo.

quaver [kwévə] v. temblar; s. temblor; trémolo (de la voz); calmar.

quay [ki] s. muelle, embarcadero.

queen [kwin] s. reina.

queer [kwir] adj. raro, extraño, singular; excéntrico; **to feel —** sentirse raro, no sentirse bien; v. poner en ridículo, comprometer; **to — oneself with** quedar mal con, ponerse mal con.

quell [kwel] v. reprimir; sofocar (una revuelta); calmar.

quench [kwentʃ] v. apagar (el fuego, la sed); reprimir, sofocar, ahogar, templar el ardor de.

query [kwíri] s. pregunta; interrogación, signo de interrogación; duda; v. preguntar, expresar duda; marcar con signo de interrogación.

quest [kwest] s. busca; pesquisa.

question [kwéstʃən] s. pregunta; cuestión; problema; duda; proposición; **— mark** signo de interrogación; **beyond — fuera de duda; that is out of the — ¡imposible!; ¡ ni pensar en ello!;** v. preguntar; interrogar; dudar.

questionable [kwéstʃənəbl] adj. dudoso; discutible.

questioner [kwéstʃənə] s. interrogador,

preguntador.

questioning [kwéstʃənɪŋ] s. interrogatorio; adj. interrogador.

questionnaire [kwestʃənér] s. cuestionario, lista de preguntas, interrogatorio.

quibble [kwíbl] v. sutilizar, valerse de argucias o sutilezas; andar en dimes y diretes; s. sutileza, argucia.

quick [kwɪk] adj. pronto, presto, listo; rápido, veloz; agudo; **— temper** genio violento; **— wit** mente aguda; adv. rápidamente, de prisa, con prisa, pronto; s. carne viva; **to cut to the —** herir en lo vivo, herir en el alma.

quicken [kwíkən] v. acelerar(se); avivar(se); aguzar (la mente, el entendimiento).

quickly [kwíklɪ] adv. pronto, presto, de prisa, aprisa, rápidamente.

quickness [kwíknɪs] s. rapidez; presteza, prontitud; viveza; agudeza (de ingenio).

quicksand [kwíksænd] s. arena movediza.

quicksilver [kwíksɪlvə] s. mercurio, azogue.

quiet [kwáɪət] adj. quieto; callado; tranquilo; en calma; reposado; s. quietud; sosiego, reposo; calma; silencio; v. aquietar; sosegar; calmar, tranquilizar; **to — down** aquietarse; calmarse; **-ly** adv. quietamente, con quietud; calladamente; tranquilamente.

quietness [kwáɪətnɪs] s. quietud; sosiego, calma.

quill [kwɪl] s. pluma; cañón (de pluma de ave); púa (de puerco espín).

quilt [kwɪlt] s. colcha; v. acolchar.

quince [kwɪns] s. membrillo.

quinine [kwáɪnaɪn] s. quinina.

quip [kwɪp] s. pulla, dicharacho; agudeza.

quirk [kwɜk] s. chifladura, extravagancia, capricho; peculiaridad mental.

quit [kwɪt] v. dejar, abandonar; irse; parar, cesar; **to — doing something** dejar de hacer algo; **-s** adj. desquitado; **we are -s** no nos debemos nada, estamos desquitados; Am. estamos a mano; pret. & p.p. de **to quit**.

quite [kwaɪt] adv. bastante; del todo, enteramente; **— a person** una persona admirable; **— so** así es, en efecto; **it's — the fashion** está muy en boga.

quitter [kwftə] s. el que deja fácilmente lo empezado, el que se da fácilmente por vencido; evasor; desertor.

quiver [kwívə] v. temblar; estremecerse;

s. temblor; estremecimiento.

quiz [kwɪz] s. examen; interrogatorio; cuestionario; v. examinar, interrogar, hacer preguntas.

quota [kwóta] s. cuota.

quotation [kwotéʃən] s. citación, cita; cotización (de precios); — marks comillas.

quote [kwot] v. citar; cotizar (precios); to — from citar a, entresacar una cita de; s. cita, citación; -s comillas; in -s entre comillas.

quotient [kwóʃənt] s. cociente.

R

rabbi [rǽbaɪ] s. rabí, rabino.

rabbit [rǽbɪt] s. conejo.

rabble [rǽbl] s. populacho, plebe; canalla.

rabies [rébɪz] s. rabia, hidrofobia.

raccoon [rækún] s. Am. mapache.

race [res] s. raza; corrida, carrera; contienda; — track (o — course) pista; boat — regata; v. correr; competir en una carrera; ir corriendo; regatear (competir en una regata); acelerar (un motor).

racer [résə] s. corredor; caballo de carrera; auto de carrera.

racial [réʃəl] adj. racial.

rack [ræk] s. percha, colgadero, clavijero; potro de tormento; baggage — red; towel — toallero; to fall into — and ruin caer en un estado de ruina total; v. atormentar; to — one's brain devanarse los sesos, quebrarse uno la cabeza.

racket [rǽkɪt] s. raqueta (de tenis); boruca, estrépito, baraúnda; bullicio; trapacería.

racketeer [rækɪtír] s. trapacista, trapacero, extorsionista; v. trapacear, extorsionar.

radiance [rédɪəns] s. resplandor, brillo.

radiant [rédɪənt] adj. radiante; resplandeciente, brillante.

radiate [rédɪet] v. irradiar; radiar.

radiator [rédɪetə] s. radiador; calorífero.

radical [rǽdɪk] adj. & s. radical.

radio [rédɪo] s. radio (m. o f.); radiotelefonía; radiotelegrafía; — commentator comentarista radial; — listener radioescucha, radioyente; — program programa radiofónico; by — por radio; v. radiar, emitir, transmitir, radiodifundir o difundir.

radish [rǽdɪʃ] s. rábano.

radium [rédɪəm] s. radio (elemento químico).

radius [rédɪəs] s. radio (de un círculo).

raffle [rǽfl] s. rifa, sorteo; v. rifar, sortear.

raft [ræft] s. balsa; a — of things un montón (o la mar) de cosas.

rafter [rǽftə] s. viga (del techo).

rag [ræg] s. trapo; harapo, andrajo, Am. hilacho; — doll muñeca de trapo; to be in -s estar hecho andrajos, Am. estar hecho tiras.

ragamuffin [rǽgəmʌfɪn] s. pelagatos, golfo; granuja, pilluelo.

rage [redʒ] s. rabia, furor; ira; to be all the — estar en boga, estar de moda; v. rabiar; enfurecerse; estar enfurecido; bramar; to — with anger bramar de ira.

ragged [rǽgɪd] adj. andrajoso, haraposo, harapiento, desharrapado, roto; — edge borde raído o deshilachado; to be on the — edge estar al borde del precipicio; estar muy nervioso.

raid [red] s. incursión, invasión repentina; allanamiento (de un local); air — ataque aéreo, bombardeo aéreo; v. hacer una incursión; invadir de repente; caer sobre; allanar (un local); entrar a la fuerza.

rail [rel] s. riel, carril; ferrocarril; barandal, barandilla; — fence empalizada, estacada; by — por ferrocarril.

railing [rélɪŋ] s. baranda, barandilla; pasamano (de escalera), balaustrada, barrera; rieles.

railroad [rélrod] s. ferrocarril; adj. ferroviario; de ferrocarril.

railway [rélwe] s. ferrocarril; adj. ferroviario; de ferrocarril; — crossing cruce, crucero.

raiment [rémənt] s. vestidura, ropaje.

rain [ren] s. lluvia; — water agua llovediza; v. llover; — or shine que llueva o no; llueva o truene; a todo trance.

rainbow [rénbo] s. arco iris.

raincoat [rénkot] s. impermeable; Am. capa de agua, Am. manga o capa de hule.

raindrop [réndrap] s. gota de agua.

rainfall [rénfɔl] s. lluvia, lluvias; cantidad de agua pluvial; aguacero.

rainy [rénɪ] adj. lluvioso.

raise [rez] v. levantar, alzar; subir; erigir; criar; cultivar; reunir (dinero); reclutar (un ejército); fermentar; to — a question hacer una observación o suscitar una duda; to — a racket armar un alboroto; s. aumento de sueldo.

raisin [rézn] s. pasa, uva seca.

rake [rek] s. rastro, rastrillo; libertino, perdulario; v. rastrear, rastrillar (la tierra); raspar; barrer (con rastrillo);

atizar (*el fuego*).

rally [rǽlɪ] *v.* juntar(se); recobrarse; mejorar (*de salud*); fortalecerse; revivir; tomar nueva vida; **to — to the side of** acudir al lado de; *s.* junta popular, junta libre; recuperación.

ram [rǽm] *s.* carnero; ariete o martillo hidráulico; espolón de buque; **battering — ariete**; *v.* apisonar, aplanar a golpes; aplastar de un choque; rellenar, atestar; **to — a boat** chocar con un barco; arremeter contra un barco.

ramble [rǽmbl] *v.* vagar; divagar; callejear; *s.* paseo, andanza.

rampart [rǽmpart] *s.* baluarte, muralla.

ran [rǽn] *pret. de* to run

ranch [rǽntʃ] *s.* hacienda, *Am.* rancho; **cattle — hacienda** de ganado, *Am.* rancho, *Am.* estancia.

rancid [rǽnsɪd] *adj.* rancio, acedo.

rancor [rǽŋkə] *s.* rencor, encono.

random [rǽndəm] *adj.* impensado; fortuito, al azar; **at — al azar, a la ventura.**

rang [rǽŋ] *pret. de* to ring.

range [rendʒ] *v.* alinear; poner en fila; arreglar; rondar, vagar por; fluctuar; **to — ten miles** tener un alcance de diez millas (*un arma de fuego*); *s.* fila, hilera; alcance; extensión; fluctuación, variación (*dentro de ciertos* límites); distancia; pastizal, *Am.* pastal; estufa; **gas — cocina de gas; — of mountains** cordillera, cadena de montañas; **— of vision** campo de visión; **in — with** en línea con; **shooting — campo** de práctica para tirar.

rank [rǽŋk] *s.* rango, categoría; orden; calidad; grado; fila; línea, hilera; the **— and file** el pueblo, la gente ordinaria; la tropa; *v.* poner en fila; ordenar, arreglar; clasificar; **to — above** sobrepasar a; ser de grado superior a; **to — high** tener un alto rango, categoría o renombre; ser tenido en alta estima; **to — second** tener el segundo lugar; **to — with** estar al nivel de, tener el mismo grado que; **he -s high.** in athletics sobresale en los deportes.

ransack [rǽnsæk] *v.* escudriñar; saquear.

ransom [rǽnsəm] *s.* rescate; *v.* rescatar; redimir.

rant [rǽnt] *v.* desvariar; disparatar; gritar necedades.

rap [rǽp] *v.* golpear, dar un golpe; criticar, censurar; **to — on the door** llamar o tocar a la puerta; *s.* golpe; **not to care a — no importarle a uno** un ardite.

rapacious [rəpéʃəs] *adj.* rapaz.

rape [rep] *s.* estupro, violación (*de una mujer*); *v.* forzar, violar (*a una mujer*).

rapid [rǽpɪd] *adj.* rápido; **-s** *s. pl.* raudal, rápidos (*de un río*).

rapidity [rəpídətɪ] *s.* rapidez, velocidad.

rapt [rǽpt] *adj.* extasiado; absorto.

rapture [rǽptʃə] *s.* éxtasis, rapto.

rare [rɛr] *adj.* raro; precioso; extraordinario, extraño; a medio asar, a medio freír, medio crudo; **-ly** *adv.* rara vez, raras veces; raramente; extraordinariamente.

rarity [rɛrətɪ] *s.* rareza; enrarecimiento (*de la atmósfera*).

rascal [rǽskl] *s.* bribón, bellaco, pícaro.

rash [rǽʃ] *adj.* temerario, atrevido; precipitado; imprudente; *s.* salpullido, erupción (*de la piel*).

rashness [rǽʃnɪs] *s.* temeridad.

rasp [rǽsp] *v.* chirriar; irritar; *s.* chirrido, sonido áspero; ronquera, carraspera.

raspberry [rǽzberɪ] *s.* frambuesa; **— bush** frambueso.

raspy [rǽspɪ] *adj.* ronco; áspero.

rat [rǽt] *s.* rata; postizo (*para el pelo*).

rate [ret] *s.* proporción; porcentaje, tanto por ciento, *Am.* tipo (*de interés*); tarifa; precio; **— of exchange** cambio, *Am.* tipo de cambio; **— of increase** incremento proporcional; **— of increase** incremento proporcional; **at any — en todo caso, de todos modos; at that — a ese paso; en esa proporción; at the — of** a razón de; **first — de primera clase o calidad; muy bien; v. calificar, clasificar, considerar; tasar, valuar; he -s as the best** se le considera como el mejor; **he -s high** se le tiene en alta estima.

rather [rǽðə] *adv.* algo, un poco, un tanto; más bien; mejor; mejor dicho; **— than** más bien que; **I would — die than** prefiero antes la muerte que; **I would — not go** preferiría no ir.

ratify [rǽtəfaɪ] *s.* ratificar.

rating [rétɪŋ] *s.* clasificación; rango, grado; clase.

ratio [réʃo] *s.* razón, proporción; relación.

ration [réʃən] *s.* ración; *v.* racionar.

rational [rǽʃənl] *adj.* racional.

rationing [réʃənɪŋ] *s.* racionamiento.

rattle [rǽtl] *v.* traquetear; golpetear; sacudir ruidosamente; confundir, desconcertar; **to — off** decir de corrido (*o decir muy aprisa*); *s.* traqueteo; golpeteo; **child's — sonaja, sonajero; death — estertor de la muerte.**

rattlesnake [rǽtlsnek] *s.* culebra de

cascabel, *Am.* cascabel o cascabela.

raucous [rɔ́kəs] *adj.* ronco; estentóreo.

ravage [rǽvɪdʒ] *s.* estrago, ruina, destrucción, asolamiento; saqueo, pillaje; *v.* asolar, arruinar; pillar, saquear.

rave [rev] *v.* desvariar, delirar, disparatar; bramar; to — about someone deshacerse en elogios de alguien.

raven [révən] *s.* cuervo; *adj.* negro lustroso.

ravenous [rǽvənəs] *adj.* voraz; devorador; to be — tener un hambre canina.

ravine [rəvín] *s.* quebrada, hondonada, barranco (o barranca).

ravish [rǽvɪʃ] *v.* encantar; arrebatar; violar (*a una mujer*).

raw [rɔ] *adj.* crudo; áspero; pelado, descarnado; inexperto, nuevo; — material materia prima; — recruit recluta nuevo; — silk seda en rama, seda cruda; — sugar azúcar bruto, azúcar crudo.

rawhide [rɔ́haɪd] *s.* cuero crudo; — whip rebenque.

ray [re] *s.* rayo; raya (*especie de pez*).

rayon [réan] *s.* rayón, seda artificial.

raze [rez] *v.* arrasar, asolar.

razor [rézə] *s.* navaja de afeitar; — blade hoja de afeitar; safety — navaja de seguridad.

reach [ritʃ] *v.* llegar a; alcanzar; tocar; extenderse; to — for tratar de coger; echar mano a; to — into meter la mano en; penetrar en; to — out one's hand alargar o tender la mano; *s.* alcance; extensión; beyond his — fuera de su alcance; within his — a su alcance.

react [rɪǽkt] *v.* reaccionar.

reaction [rɪǽkʃən] *s.* reacción.

reactionary [rɪǽkʃənɛrɪ] *adj.* & *s.* reaccionario.

read [rid] *v.* leer; indicar (*dícese de un contador, termómetro, etc.*); to — law estudiar derecho; it -s thus dice así, reza así; it -s easily se lee fácilmente o sin esfuerzo.

read [red] *pret.* & *p.p. de* to read.

reader [rídə] *s.* lector; libro de lectura.

readily [rédɪlɪ] *adv.* pronto, con presteza; fácilmente, sin esfuerzo.

readiness [rédɪnɪs] *s.* prontitud, presteza, facilidad; buena disposición; to be in — estar preparado, estar listo.

reading [rídɪŋ] *s.* lectura; indicación (*de un barómetro, termómetro, etc.*); — room sala o salón de lectura.

readjust [riadʒʌ́st] *v.* reajustar, ajustar de nuevo; arreglar de nuevo; readjustar.

readjustment [riadʒʌ́stmənt] *s.* reajuste; readaptación; nuevo arreglo.

ready [rédɪ] *adj.* pronto, listo; preparado; propenso; dispuesto; — cash fondos disponibles; dinero a la mano.

ready-made [rédɪméd] *adj.* hecho, ya hecho.

real [rɪəl] *adj.* real, verdadero; — estate bienes raíces, bienes inmuebles; -ly *adv.* realmente, verdaderamente.

realism [rɪəlɪzəm] *s.* realismo.

realist [rɪəlɪst] *s.* realista; -ic *adj.* realista, vivo, natural.

reality [rɪǽlətɪ] *s.* realidad.

realization [rɪələzéʃən] *s.* realización; comprensión.

realize [rɪəlaɪz] *v.* darse cuenta de, hacerse cargo de; realizar, efectuar; convertir en dinero.

realm [rɛlm] *s.* reino; dominio, región.

reap [rip] *v.* segar; cosechar; recoger; obtener, sacar (*provecho, fruto, etc.*).

reaper [rípə] *s.* segador; segadora, máquina segadora.

reappear [riəpír] *v.* reaparecer.

rear [rɪr] *adj.* trasero, posterior; de atrás; — admiral contraalmirante; — guard retaguardia; *s.* espalda, parte de atrás; trasero; fondo (*de una sala, salón, etc.*); cola (*de una fila*); in the — detrás, atrás, a la espalda; *v.* criar, educar; encabritarse, empinarse (*el caballo*).

reason [rízn] *s.* razón; causa, motivo; by — of a causa de; it stands to — es razonable; *v.* razonar; to — out discurrir, razonar.

reasonable [ríznəbl] *adj.* razonable, justo; racional; módico, moderado; reasonably *adv.* razonablemente; con razón; bastante.

reasoning [ríznɪŋ] *s.* razonamiento, raciocinio.

reassure [riəʃúr] *v.* tranquilizar, restaurar la confianza a; asegurar de nuevo.

rebate [ríbet] *s.* rebaja (*de precio*); *v.* rebajar (*precio*).

rebel [rébl] *s.* & *adj.* rebelde; [rɪbél] *v.* rebelarse.

rebellion [rɪbéljən] *s.* rebelión.

rebellious [rɪbéljəs] *adj.* rebelde.

rebirth [ribɝ́θ] *s.* renacimiento.

rebound [rɪbáund] *v.* rebotar; repercutir; [ríbaund] *s.* rebote; on the — de rebote.

rebuff [rɪbʌ́f] *s.* desaire; repulsa; *v.* desairar; rechazar.

rebuild [ribɪ́ld] *v.* reconstruir, reedificar.

rebuilt [ribílt] *pret. & p.p. de* **to rebuild.**

rebuke [ribjúk] *s.* reprensión, reproche, reprimenda, repulsa; *v.* reprender, reprochar.

recall [rikɔ́l] *s.* llamada, aviso (*para hacer volver*); retirada (*de un diplomático*); revocación; [rikɔ́l] *v.* recordar; retirar; revocar.

recede [risíd] *v.* retroceder; retirarse.

receipt [risít] *s.* recibo; fórmula, receta; -s entradas, ingresos; **on — of** al recibo de; **we are in — of your kind letter** ... obra en nuestro poder su grata ... ; *v.* sellar (*con el recibí*), dar recibo.

receive [risív] *v.* recibir.

receiver [risívə] *s.* receptor; recibidor, depositario, síndico; recipiente, receptáculo.

recent [rísnt] *adj.* reciente; **-ly** *adv.* recientemente, *Am.* recién (*como en* salió recién); **-ly married** recién casados.

receptacle [riséptəkl] *s.* receptáculo.

reception [risépʃən] *s.* recepción; recibimiento; acogida, acogimiento.

recess [risés] *s.* nicho, hueco; tregua, intermisión; hora de recreo o asueto; **in the -es of** en lo más recóndito de; *v.* suspender el trabajo; levantar (*por corto tiempo*) una sesión; hacer un hueco o nicho en (*la pared*).

recipe [résəpi] *s.* receta, fórmula.

recipient [risípiənt] *s.* recipiente, recibidor; *adj.* receptivo.

reciprocal [risíprəkl] *adj.* recíproco, mutuo.

reciprocate [risíprəket] *v.* corresponder.

recital [risáitl] *s.* recitación; relación; narración; recital (*músico*).

recitation [resətéʃən] *s.* recitación.

recite [risáit] *v.* recitar; relatar; decir o dar la lección.

reckless [réklis] *adj.* temerario, atrevido; precipitado; descuidado; **— with one's money** derrochador.

recklessness [réklisnis] *s.* temeridad, osadía, descuido.

reckon [rékən] *v.* contar, computar, calcular; juzgar; suponer; **to — on** contar con.

reckoning [rékəniŋ] *s.* cuenta; ajuste de cuentas; cálculo; **the day of —** el día del juicio.

reclaim [riklém] *v.* recobrar, aprovechar (*tierras baldías*); aprovechar o utilizar (*el hule usado*); pedir la devolución de, tratar de recobrar.

recline [rikláin] *v.* reclinar(se), recostar(se).

recluse [riklús] *adj.* recluso, solitario; *s.* recluso, solitario, ermitaño.

recognition [rɛkəgníʃən] *s.* reconocimiento.

recognize [rékəgnaiz] *v.* reconocer.

recoil [rikɔ́il] *v.* recular, *Am.* patear (*un arma de fuego*); retroceder, retirarse; *s.* reculada; rebote.

recollect [rɛkəlékt] *v.* recordar; [rikəlékt] recobrar, volver a cobrar; recoger, reunir.

recollection [rɛkəlékʃən] *s.* recuerdo.

recommend [rɛkəménd] *v.* recomendar.

recommendation [rɛkəmɛndéʃən] *s.* recomendación.

recompense [rékəmpɛns] *v.* recompensar; *s.* recompensa.

reconcile [rékənsail] *v.* reconciliar; ajustar, conciliar; **to — oneself to** resignarse a, conformarse con.

reconciliation [rɛkənsiliéʃən] *f.* reconciliación; ajuste, conciliación; conformidad, resignación.

reconnoiter [rikənɔ́itə] *v.* reconocer, explorar; hacer un reconocimiento o exploración.

reconsider [rikənsídə] *v.* reconsiderar.

reconstruct [rikənstrákt] *v.* reconstruir, reedificar.

reconstruction [rikənstrákʃən] *s.* reconstrucción.

record [rékəd] *s.* registro; copia oficial de un documento; memoria; historial (*de una persona*), hoja de servicios; disco (*fonográfico*); record (*en deportes*); **to break the speed —** batir el record de velocidad; **an off-the-record remark** una observación que no ha de constar en el acta; observación hecha en confianza; *adj.* notable, extraordinario; sobresaliente; [rikɔ́rd] *v.* registrar; asentar, apuntar; inscribir; grabar en disco fonográfico.

recount [rikáunt] *s.* recuento, segunda cuenta; [rikáunt] *v.* contar, narrar, relatar, referir; [rikáunt] recontar, volver a contar.

recourse [ríkors] *s.* recurso, refugio, auxilio; **to have — to** recurrir a.

recover [rikávə] *v.* recobrar(se), recuperar(se); recobrar la salud; reponerse; [rikávə] volver a cubrir.

recovery [rikávri] *s.* recobro; recuperación; cobranza.

recreation [rɛkriéʃən] *s.* recreación, recreo.

recruit [rikrút] *v.* reclutar; alistar; *s.* recluta; novato, nuevo miembro (*de una organización*).

rectangle [réktæŋgl] *s.* rectángulo.

rectify [réktəfaɪ] v. rectificar.
rector [réktə] s. rector.
rectum [réktəm] s. recto.
recuperate [rɪkjúpəret] v. recuperar, recobrar; recobrar la salud.
recur [rɪkɜ́] v. volver a ocurrir; repetirse; **to — to a matter** volver a un asunto.
red [rɛd] adj. rojo; colorado, encarnado; **red-hot** candente; enfurecido, furioso; muy caliente; **— tape** formalismo, trámites enojosos; **— wine** vino tinto; **to see —** enfurecerse; s. color rojo; rojo.
redden [rédn̩] v. enrojecer(se); ruborizarse, ponerse rojo; teñir de rojo.
reddish [rédɪʃ] adj. rojizo.
redeem [rɪdím] v. redimir; rescatar; desempeñar (una prenda); cumplir (una promesa).
redeemer [rɪdímə] s. salvador, redentor; **the Redeemer** el Redentor.
redemption [rɪdémpʃən] s. redención; rescate; **— of a note** pago de una obligación.
redness [rédnɪs] s. rojez o rojura; inflamación.
redouble [rɪdʌ́bl̩] v. redoblar; repetir; repercutir.
redress [rídrɛs] s. reparación, enmienda; compensación; desagravio; [rɪdrɛ́s] v. enmendar, rectificar, remediar, reparar; desagraviar.
reduce [rɪdjús] v. reducir; mermar; rebajar; adelgazar(se); subyugar.
reduction [rɪdʌ́kʃən] s. reducción; merma; rebaja.
redwood [rédwʊd] s. Am. secoya o secuoya (árbol gigantesco de California); madera roja de la secoya.
reed [rid] s. caña; junco, junquillo; lengüeta, boquilla (de ciertos instrumentos de viento); caramillo.
reef [rif] s. arrecife, escollo; banco de arena (en el mar).
reek [rik] v. exhalar, echar (vaho o vapor); heder, oler mal; s. hedor, mal olor.
reel [ril] s. carrete; carretel; cinta cinematográfica; v. aspar, enredar (en carretel); bambolearse, tambalearse; **to — off stories** ensartar cuento tras cuento.
re-elect [riəlékt] v. reelegir.
re-election [riəlékʃən] s. reelección.
re-enter [riéntə] v. volver a entrar.
re-establish [riəstǽblɪʃ] v. restablecer.
refer [rɪfɜ́] v. referir; transmitir, remitir; dejar al juicio o decisión de; referirse, aludir; acudir, recurrir (a un tratado, diccionario, etc.).

referee [rɛfərí] s. árbitro; v. arbitrar.
reference [réfrəns] s. referencia; mención, alusión; fiador, el que recomienda a otro; **— book** libro de referencia, libro de consulta; **commercial -s** fiadores, referencias comerciales; **letter of —** carta de recomendación; **with — to** con respecto a, respecto de, en cuanto a.
refill [rifíl] v. rellenar.
refine [rɪfáɪn] v. refinar, purificar; pulir; perfeccionar.
refined [rɪfáɪnd] adj. refinado; pulido, fino, culto.
refinement [rɪfáɪnmənt] s. refinamiento, finura; buena crianza; refinación, purificación; perfeccionamiento.
refinery [rɪfáɪnərɪ] s. refinería.
reflect [rɪflékt] v. reflejar (luz, calor); reflexionar; meditar; **to — on one's character** desdecir del carácter de uno.
reflection [rɪflékʃən] s. reflexión; reflejo, imagen, tacha, discrédito; **on —** después de reflexionarlo.
reflex [rífleks] adj. reflejo; s. reflejo; acción refleja.
reflexive [rɪfléksɪv] adj. reflexivo.
reform [rɪfɔ́rm] v. reformar(se); s. reforma.
reformation [rɛfəméʃən] s. reforma.
reformer [rɪfɔ́rmə] s. reformador; reformista.
refraction [rɪfrǽkʃən] s. refracción.
refractory [rɪfrǽktərɪ] adj. refractario; terco, obstinado, rebelde.
refrain [rɪfrén] v. refrenarse, abstenerse; s. estribillo.
refresh [rɪfréʃ] v. refrescar(se); renovar.
refreshing [rɪfréʃɪŋ] adj. refrescante; renovador, que renueva; placentero.
refreshment [rɪfréʃmənt] s. refresco.
refrigeration [rɪfrɪdʒəréʃən] s. refrigeración, enfriamiento.
refrigerator [rɪfrɪdʒəretə] s. nevera, Am. refrigerador.
refuge [réfjudʒ] s. refugio, asilo, amparo.
refugee [réfjʊdʒí] s. refugiado.
refund [rɪfʌ́nd] s. reembolso, reintegro; [rɪfʌ́nd] v. reembolsar, restituir, reintegrar; [rifʌ́nd] consolidar (una deuda).
refusal [rɪfjúzl̩] s. negativa; desaire; opción (derecho de recusar un convenio provisional).
refuse [rɪfjúz] v. rehusar; negar; desechar; rechazar; **to — to** rehusarse a, negarse a.
refuse [réfjus] s. desechos, basura, sobras, desperdicios.
refute [rɪfjút] v. refutar.

regain [rɪgén] v. recobrar; ganar de nuevo.

regal [rígl] adj. regio, real.

regale [rɪgél] v. regalar, agasajar; recrear.

regalia [rɪgélɪə] s. pl. galas, decoraciones, insignias.

regard [rɪgárd] v. mirar; considerar; juzgar; estimar; as -s this tocante a esto, en cuanto a esto; por lo que toca a esto; s. miramiento, consideración; respeto; estima; mirada; -s recuerdos, memorias; in (o with) — to con respecto a, tocante a, respecto de.

regarding [rɪgárdɪŋ] prep. tocante a, con respecto a, respecto de, relativo a.

regardless [rɪgárdlɪs]: — of sin hacer caso de, prescindiendo de.

regent [rídʒənt] s. regente.

regime [rɪʒím] s. régimen.

regiment [rédʒəmənt] s. regimiento.

region [rídʒən] s. región.

register [rédʒɪstə] s. registro; matrícula; archivo; lista; contador, indicador; registro (del órgano, de la voz); cash — caja registradora; v. registrar; matricular(se); inscribir(se); marcar, indicar; mostrar, manifestar; certificar (una carta).

registrar [rédʒɪstrɑr] s. registrador, archivero.

registration [redʒɪstréʃən] s. registro; asiento (en un libro); matrícula; inscripción.

regret [rɪgrét] s. pesadumbre, dolor; sentimiento, remordimiento; to send -s enviar sus excusas (al rehusar una invitación); v. sentir, lamentar; arrepentirse de.

regrettable [rɪgrétəbl] adj. lamentable.

regular [régjələ] adj. regular; metódico, ordenado; a — fool un verdadero necio, un tonto de capirote; — price precio corriente; — soldier soldado de línea.

regularity [regjəlǽrətɪ] s. regularidad.

regulate [régjəlet] v. regular, regularizar.

regulation [regjəléʃən] s. regulación; regla, orden; -s reglamento; — uniform uniforme de regla, uniforme de ordenanza.

regulator [régjələtə] s. regulador; registro (de reloj).

rehearsal [rɪhɔ́sl] s. ensayo (de un drama, concierto, etc.); enumeración, repetición.

rehearse [rɪhɔ́s] v. ensayar; repetir, repasar.

reign [ren] s. reino, reinado; v. reinar.

reimburse [riːɪmbɔ́s] v. reembolsar.

reimbursement [riːɪmbɔ́smənt] s. reembolso, reintegro.

rein [ren] s. rienda; v. guiar, gobernar; refrenar (un caballo).

reindeer [réndɪr] s. reno (especie de ciervo).

reinforce [riːɪnfɔ́rs] v. reforzar.

reinforcement [riːɪnfɔ́rsmənt] s. refuerzo.

reiterate [riˈɪtəret] v. reiterar, repetir.

reject [rɪdʒékt] v. rechazar; desechar; descartar; rehusar.

rejoice [rɪdʒɔ́ɪs] v. regocijar(se).

rejoicing [rɪdʒɔ́ɪsɪŋ] s. regocijo, júbilo.

rejoin [rɪdʒɔ́ɪn] v. reunirse con; volver(se) a unir; [rɪdʒɔ́ɪn] replicar.

rejuvenate [rɪdʒúvənet] v. rejuvenecer.

relapse [rɪlǽps] s. recaída; v. recaer, reincidir.

relate [rɪlét] v. relatar, narrar; relacionar; it -s to se relaciona con, se refiere a.

related [rɪlétɪd] adj. relatado, narrado; relacionado; to become — by marriage emparentar; we are — somos parientes; estamos emparentados.

relation [rɪléʃən] s. relación; narración; parentesco; pariente; -s parientes, parentela; with — to con relación a, con respecto a, tocante a.

relationship [rɪléʃənʃɪp] s. relación; parentesco.

relative [rélətɪv] adj. relativo; s. relativo, pronombre relativo; pariente, deudo; — to relativo a; tocante a; referente a.

relax [rɪlǽks] v. relajar; aflojar; mitigar(se); esparcirse, recrearse.

relaxation [rilækséʃən] s. esparcimiento, expansión, solaz, recreo, recreación; aflojamiento o relajamiento (de músculos); — of discipline relajación de la disciplina; — of one's mind esparcimiento del ánimo.

relay [rílé] s. relevo, remuda; — race carrera de relevo; electric — relevador; [rílé] v. transmitir, despachar; hacer cundir (una noticia); to — a broadcast reemitir (o redifundir) un programa de radio.

release [rɪlís] v. soltar; librar; poner en libertad; relevar; aliviar; to — a piece of news hacer pública una nueva; to — from blame exonerar; s. liberación; alivio; exoneración; escape.

relegate [réləget] v. relegar; to — to a corner arrinconar, arrumbar.

relent [rɪlént] v. mitigar(se); ceder; aplacarse.

relentless [rɪléntlɪs] adj. implacable.

reliability [rɪlaɪəbílətɪ] s. formalidad; puntualidad; integridad.

reliable [rɪláɪəbl] *adj.* formal; puntual; digno de confianza.

reliance [rɪláɪəns] *s.* confianza; **self-reliance** confianza en sí, confianza en sus propias fuerzas.

relic [rélɪk] *s.* reliquia.

relief [rɪlíf] *s.* alivio; descanso, consuelo; ayuda, socorro; relieve, realce; **low —** bajo relieve; **to be on —** recibir manutención gratuita; **to put in —** realzar, poner en relieve.

relieve [rɪlív] *v.* relevar; librar; ayudar; aliviar; mitigar.

religion [rɪlíɡʒən] *s.* religión.

religious [rɪlíɡʒəs] *adj.* & *s.* religioso.

relinquish [rɪlíŋkwɪʃ] *v.* abandonar, dejar.

relish [rélɪʃ] *s.* buen sabor; gusto; apetito; goce; condimento; entremés (*aceitunas, encurtidos, etc.*); *v.* saborear, paladear; gustarle a uno, agradarle a uno.

reluctance [rɪláktəns] *s.* repugnancia, renuencia, aversión, desgana.

reluctant [rɪláktənt] *adj.* renuente, refractario, opuesto; **-ly** *adv.* renuentemente, con renuencia, de mala gana, a redopelo.

rely [rɪláɪ] *v.* **to — on** contar con, confiar en, fiarse de.

remain [rɪmén] *v.* quedar(se), permanecer, estarse, restar, faltar.

remainder [rɪméndə] *s.* resto; restante; residuo.

remains [rɪménz] *s. pl.* restos; reliquias; sobras.

remake [rimék] *v.* rehacer, hacer de nuevo.

remark [rɪmárk] *s.* observación, nota, reparo; *v.* notar, observar; **to — on** comentar; aludir a.

remarkable [rɪmárkəbl] *adj.* notable; extraordinario; **remarkably** *adv.* notablemente; extraordinariamente.

remedy [rémədɪ] *s.* remedio; cura; *v.* remediar; curar.

remember [rɪmémbə] *v.* recordar; acordarse; **— me to him** déle Vd. recuerdos (o memorias) de mi parte.

remembrance [rɪmémbrəns] *s.* recuerdo; recordación; memoria; **-s** recuerdos, saludos.

remind [rɪmáɪnd] *v.* recordar.

reminder [rɪmáɪndə] *s.* recordatorio, recordativo, memorándum, memoria; advertencia.

reminiscence [remənísɪns] *s.* reminiscencia, memoria, recuerdo.

remiss [rɪmís] *adj.* descuidado, negligente.

remission [rɪmíʃən] *s.* remisión, perdón.

remit [rɪmít] *v.* remitir; remesar, enviar una remesa; perdonar, absolver.

remittance [rɪmítns] *s.* remisión, envío, remesa (*de fondos*).

remnant [rémnənt] *s.* resto; residuo; retazo (*de tela, paño, etc.*); vestigio.

remodel [rimádl] *v.* rehacer, reconstruir; modelar de nuevo.

remorse [rɪmɔ́rs] *s.* remordimiento.

remote [rɪmót] *adj.* remoto; lejano.

removal [rɪmúvl] *s.* mudanza, traslado; deposición (*de un empleo*); eliminación; extracción; alejamiento.

remove [rɪmúv] *v.* remover; mudar(se), trasladar(se); quitar; eliminar; extirpar; sacar, extraer; deponer (*de un empleo*); apartar; alejar.

removed [rɪmúvd] *adj.* remoto, distante.

renaissance [renəzáns] *s.* renacimiento.

renascence [rɪnǽsns] *s.* renacimiento.

rend [rend] *v.* desgarrar, rasgar; rajar.

render [réndə] *v.* dar; entregar; hacer; ejecutar, interpretar (*música o un papel dramático*); traducir; **to — an account of** rendir o dar cuenta de; **to — homage** rendir homenaje; **to — thanks** rendir gracias, dar las gracias; **to — useless** inutilizar, incapacitar.

renew [rɪnjú] *v.* renovar; restaurar; reanudar; prorrogar (*un préstamo*).

renewal [rɪnjúəl] *s.* renovación; reanudación; prórroga.

renounce [rɪnáuns] *v.* renunciar.

renovate [rénəvet] *v.* renovar.

renown [rɪnáun] *s.* renombre.

renowned [rɪnáund] *adj.* renombrado.

rent [rent] *s.* alquiler; renta, arrendamiento; **it is for —** se alquila, se arrienda; *v.* alquilar, arrendar.

rent [rent] *pret.* & *p.p.* de **to rend**; *s.* grieta, hendidura; rasgadura, rotura.

rental [réntl] *s.* renta, alquiler.

reopen [riópən] *v.* reabrir(se), volver a abrir(se).

repair [rɪpér] *v.* reparar; remendar; componer; restaurar; **to — to** dirigirse a; *s.* reparo, reparación; remiendo; postura; **in —** en buen estado; compuesto.

reparation [repəréʃən] *s.* reparación; desagravio.

repay [rɪpé] *v.* resarcir; compensar; reembolsar; pagar.

repayment [rɪpémənt] *s.* reintegro, pago, devolución, restitución.

repeal [rɪpíl] *v.* derogar, abrogar, revocar, abolir (*una ley*); *s.* abrogación, derogación, revocación, abolición (*de una ley*).

repeat [rɪpít] v. repetir; s. repetición.
repeated [rɪpítɪd] adj. repetido; **-ly** adv. repetidamente; repetidas veces, una y otra vez.
repel [rɪpél] v. repeler; rechazar; repugnar; **that idea -s me** me repugna (o me es repugnante) esa idea.
repent [rɪpént] v. arrepentirse (de).
repentance [rɪpéntəns] s. arrepentimiento.
repentant [rɪpéntənt] adj. arrepentido; penitente.
repetition [repɪtíʃən] s. repetición.
replace [rɪplés] v. reponer, volver a colocar; reemplazar; restituir; remudar.
replaceable [rɪplésəbl] adj. reemplazable; substituible.
replacement [rɪplésmənt] s. reposición; reemplazo; devolución, restitución; substitución.
replenish [rɪpléniʃ] v. reabastecer; rellenar, llenar.
replete [rɪplít] adj. repleto, atestado.
replica [réplɪkə] s. reproducción, copia exacta.
reply [rɪplái] v. replicar, contestar, responder; s. réplica, contestación, respuesta.
report [rɪpórt] v. dar cuenta de; avisar; informar; presentar un informe; rendir informe; hacer un reportaje, Am. reportar; denunciar, delatar; presentarse; **to — for duty** presentarse; **it is -ed that** dizque, se dice que, corre la voz que; s. noticia, reporte; informe; memorial; relación; rumor; estallido, disparo; **news —** reportaje.
reporter [rɪpórtə] s. reportero, repórter.
repose [rɪpóz] v. reposar, descansar; **to — one's confidence in** confiar en; depositar su confianza en; s. reposo.
represent [reprɪzént] v. representar.
representation [reprɪzentéʃən] s. representación.
representative [reprɪzéntətɪv] adj. representativo; representante; típico; s. representante; delegado, diputado.
repress [rɪprés] v. reprimir; refrenar, restringir; cohibir.
repression [rɪpréʃən] s. represión.
reprimand [réprəmænd] v. reprender, regañar; s. reprimenda, reprensión, regaño.
reprisal [rɪpráɪzl] s. represalia.
reproach [rɪprótʃ] v. reprochar; censurar, criticar; echar en cara; s. reproche, reprimenda; censura.
reproduce [riprədjús] v. reproducir.
reproduction [riprədʌkʃən] s. reproduc-

ción.
reproof [rɪprúf] s. reprensión, reproche, regaño.
reprove [rɪprúv] v. reprobar, reprénder, censurar.
reptile [réptl] s. reptil.
republic [rɪpʌblɪk] s. república.
republican [rɪpʌblɪkən] adj. & s. republicano.
repudiate [rɪpjúdɪet] v. repudiar.
repugnance [rɪpʌgnəns] s. repugnancia; aversión.
repugnant [rɪpʌgnənt] adj. repugnante; antipático.
repulse [rɪpʌls] v. repulsar, repeler; rechazar; s. repulsa; desaire.
repulsive [rɪpʌlsɪv] adj. repulsivo, repugnante.
reputable [répjətəbl] adj. de buena reputación.
reputation [repjətéʃən] s. reputación, renombre.
repute [rɪpjút] v. reputar; estimar, considerar; s. reputación; renombre, fama; **of ill —** de mala fama.
request [rɪkwést] s. solicitud, petición, demanda; súplica, ruego; **at the — of** a solicitud de, a instancias de; v. solicitar, pedir, rogar, suplicar.
require [rɪkwáir] v. requerir; exigir, demandar.
requirement [rɪkwáirmənt] s. requerimiento, requisito; exigencia; necesidad.
requisite [rékwəzɪt] s. requisito; adj. requerido, necesario.
requisition [rekwəzíʃən] s. requisición, demanda, orden; v. demandar, pedir, ordenar.
rescue [réskjʊ] v. rescatar; librar; salvar; s. rescate, salvamento, salvación, socorro; **to go to the — of** acudir al socorro de, ir a salvar a.
research [rísɚtʃ] s. rebusca, búsqueda, investigación; [rɪsɚtʃ] v. rebuscar, investigar.
resemblance [rɪzémbləns] s. semejanza, parecido.
resemble [rɪzémbl] v. asemejarse a, semejar, parecerse a.
resent [rɪzént] v. resentirse de, sentirse de, darse por agraviado de.
resentful [rɪzéntfəl] adj. resentido; rencoroso.
resentment [rɪzéntmənt] s. resentimiento.
reservation [rezəvéʃən] s. reservación; reserva.
reserve [rɪzɚv] v. reservar; s. reserva.
reservoir [rézəvɔr] s. depósito (de agua,

aceite, gas, provisiones, etc.); receptáculo; **water** — alberca, aljibe, tanque, estanque.

reside [rɪzáɪd] v. residir, vivir.

residence [rézədəns] s. residencia; domicilio.

resident [rézədənt] adj. & s. residente.

residue [rézədjʊ] s. residuo; resto.

resign [rɪzáɪn] v. renunciar; dimitir; **to — oneself to** resignarse a.

resignation [rɛzɪgnéʃən] s. renuncia, dimisión; resignación.

resin [rézɪ] s. resina.

resist [rɪzíst] v. resistir; oponerse, resistirse a.

resistance [rɪzístəns] s. resistencia.

resistant [rɪzístənt] adj. resistente.

resolute [rézəlʊt] adj. resuelto.

resolution [rɛzəlúʃən] s. resolución; acuerdo.

resolve [rɪzálv] v. resolver(se); **to — into** resolverse en, reducirse a, transformarse en; **to —. to** acordar; proponerse, resolverse a.

resort [rɪzɔ́rt] v. recurrir, acudir; **to — to force** recurrir a la fuerza; s. refugio; morada; **as a last —** como último recurso; **summer —** lugar de veraneo; **vice —** garito; casa de mala fama; **to have — to** recurrir a.

resorter [rɪzɔ́rtə] s. **summer —** veraneante.

resound [rɪzáʊnd] v. resonar; repercutir; retumbar.

resource [rɪsɔ́rs] s. recurso; **natural -s** recursos o riquezas naturales.

respect [rɪspékt] v. respetar; **as -s** por lo que respecta a, por lo que toca a, tocante a; s. respeto; consideración; **with — to** (con) respecto a, respecto de; por lo que atañe a.

respectable [rɪspéktəb] adj. respetable.

respectful [rɪspéktfəl] adj. respetuoso.

respecting [rɪspéktɪŋ] prep. con respecto a, tocante a.

respective [rɪspéktɪv] adj. respectivo.

respiration [rɛspəréʃən] s. respiración, respiro.

respite [réspɪt] s. tregua, pausa, descanso; intervalo; prórroga.

resplendent [rɪspléndənt] adj. resplandeciente.

respond [rɪspánd] v. responder; corresponder; reaccionar.

response [rɪspáns] s. respuesta, contestación; reacción.

responsibility [rɪspɑnsəbflətɪ] s. responsabilidad.

responsible [rɪspánsəbl̩] adj. responsable; formal, digno de confianza.

rest [rɛst] s. descanso; reposo; quietud; tregua; pausa; apoyo; **at —** èn paz; en reposo; tranquilo; **the —** el resto; los demás; v. descansar; reposar; apoyar; **to — on** descansar sobre; apoyar(se) en; basar(se) en; contar con, confiar en, depender de.

restaurant [réstərənt] s. restaurante, Am. restorán.

restful [réstfəl] adj. reposado, sosegado, tranquilo.

restitution [rɛstətjúʃən] s. restitución; devolución.

restless [réstlɪs] adj. inquieto, intranquilo.

restlessness [réstlɪsnɪs] s. inquietud, desasosiego, intranquilidad.

restoration [rɛstəréʃən] s. restauración; restitución; renovación.

restore [rɪstór] v. restaurar; renovar; restituir; restablecer.

restrain [rɪstrén] v. refrenar, contener, cohibir, reprimir, coartar; restringir.

restraint [rɪstrént] s. restricción; reserva, circunspección; moderación; cohibición.

restrict [rɪstríkt] v. restringir, limitar.

restriction [rɪstríkʃən] s. restricción.

result [rɪzʌ́lt] v. resultar; **to — from** resultar de; **to — in** parar en; causar; dar por resultado; s. resulta, resultado; **as a —** de resultas, como resultado.

resume [rɪzúm] v. reasumir, volver a tomar; recomenzar; reanudar, continuar.

résumé [rèzumé] s. resumen, sumario.

resuscitate [rɪsʌ́sətet] v. resucitar; revivir.

retail [rítel] s. venta al por menor; **at — al por menor**; **— merchant** detallista, comerciante al por menor; **— price** precio al por menor; v. detallar; vender al menudeo (o vender al por menor), Am. menudear.

retailer [rítélə] s. detallista, revendedor, comerciante al por menor.

retain [rɪtén] v. retener; emplear.

retaliate [rɪtǽliet] v. desquitarse, vengarse.

retaliation [rɪtæliéʃən] s. desquite; desagravio; represalia, venganza.

retard [rɪtárd] v. retardar, retrasar, atrasar.

retinue [rétnju] s. comitiva, séquito, acompañamiento.

retire [rɪtáɪr] v. retirar(se); jubilar(se); acostarse; apartarse.

retirement [rɪtáɪrmənt] s. retiro; jubilación.

retort [rɪtórt] v. replicar; redargüir; s.

réplica.

retouch [rɪtʌtʃ] v. retocar; s. retoque.

retrace [rɪtrés] v. repasar; volver a trazar; **to — one's steps** volver sobre sus pasos, retroceder.

retract [rɪtrǽkt] v. retractar, retractarse de; desdecirse (de); retraer.

retreat [rɪtrít] s. retiro, refugio, asilo; retirada; retreta (toque de retirada); v. retirarse; retroceder.

retrench [rɪtréntʃ] v. cercenar, reducir, disminuir; economizar.

retrieve [rɪtrív] v. cobrar (la caza); recobrar, recuperar; reparar (una pérdida).

return [rɪtə́n] v. volver, regresar; retornar; devolver; replicar; redituar; producir; restar (la pelota en tenis); **to — a favor** corresponder a un favor; **to — a report** rendir un informe; s. vuelta, regreso; retorno; recompensa; restitución, devolución; réplica; resto (en un juego de pelota); rédito, ganancia; informe; **— game** desquite, juego de desquite; **— ticket** boleto de vuelta; **by — mail** a vuelta de correo; **election -s** reportaje de elecciones; **in — en** cambio; **in — for** a cambio de, a trueque de; **income tax —** declaración de rentas; **many happy -s** muchas felicidades (en su día).

reunion [rijúnjən] s. reunión; junta.

reunite [rijunáɪt] v. reunir(se), volver a unirse; reconciliar(se).

reveal [rɪvíl] v. revelar.

revel [révl] v. deleitarse, gozarse; parrandear, Am. farrear; andar de parranda, Am. andar de farra; s. parranda, juerga, jarana.

revelation [rɛvléʃən] s. revelación; **Revelation(s)** Apocalipsis.

revelry [révlrɪ] s. jaleo, juerga, jarana.

revenge [rɪvéndʒ] v. vengar, vindicar; s. venganza; desquite.

revengeful [rɪvéndʒfəl] adj. vengativo.

revenue [révənju] s. renta; rédito; rentas públicas, ingresos.

revere [rɪvír] v. venerar.

reverence [révrəns] s. reverencia; veneración; v. reverenciar, venerar.

reverend [révrənd] adj. reverendo; venerable.

reverent [révrənt] adj. reverente.

reverie, revery [révərɪ] s. ensueño; arrobamiento.

reverse [rɪvə́s] adj. inverso, invertido; contrario, opuesto; s. revés; reverso, dorso; lo contrario; contratiempo; v. invertir; voltear; revocar (una sentencia).

revert [rɪvə́t] v. revertir, volver atrás, retroceder.

review [rɪvjú] v. repasar; revisar; revistar, pasar revista a (las tropas); reseñar, hacer una reseña de (un libro); s. revista; repaso; reseña, crítica (de un libro, drama, etc.); revisión (de un caso jurídico, sentencia, etc.).

revile [rɪváɪl] v. vilipendiar, vituperar, denigrar.

revise [rɪváɪz] v. revisar, repasar, releer (para corregir); corregir, enmendar.

revision [rɪvíʒən] s. revisión; enmienda; edición enmeudada o mejorada.

revival [rɪváɪvl] s. renovación; revivificación; renacimiento; nueva presentación (de una pieza u obra); **— meeting** junta para revivir el fervor religioso; **religious —** despertamiento (o nuevo fervor) religioso.

revive [rɪváɪv] v. revivir, resucitar; volver en sí; renacer; reavivar, reanimar(se); avivar.

revoke [rɪvók] v. revocar, abrogar, anular; renunciar (en los juegos de naipes).

revolt [rɪvólt] s. revuelta, rebelión, sublevación; v. rebelarse, sublevarse; **it -s me** me da asco, me repugna.

revolution [rɛvəlúʃən] s. revolución; vuelta (que da una rueda).

revolutionary [rɛvəlúʃənɛrɪ] adj. & s. revolucionario.

revolutionist [rɛvəlúʃənɪst] s. revolucionario.

revolve [rɪválv] v. girar, dar vueltas; rodar; voltear, dar vueltas a; **to — in one's mind** revolver en la mente, ponderar, reflexionar.

revolver [rɪválvə] s. revólver.

reward [rɪwɔ́rd] v. premiar; recompensar; s. premio, gratificación, recompensa, galardón; albricias (por haber hallado algún objeto perdido).

rewrite [rɪráɪt] v. volver a escribir; refundir (un escrito).

rhetoric [rétərɪk] s. retórica.

rheumatism [rúmətɪzəm] s. reumatismo, reuma.

rhinoceros [raɪnásərəs] s. rinoceronte.

rhubarb [rúbarb] s. ruibarbo.

rhyme [raɪm] s. rima; **without — or reason** sin ton ni son; v. rimar.

rhythm [rɪ́ðəm] s. ritmo.

rhythmical [rɪ́ðmɪkl] adj. rítmico, acompasado, cadencioso.

rib [rɪb] s. costilla; varilla (de paraguas); cordoncillo (de ciertos tejidos).

ribbon [rɪ́bən] s. cinta; listón, banda; tira.

rice [raɪs] s. arroz; **— field** arrozal.

rich [rɪtʃ] adj. rico; costoso, suntuoso; sabroso; — color color vivo; — food alimento muy mantecoso o dulce.

riches [rɪtʃɪz] s. pl. riqueza, riquezas.

rickety [rɪkɪtɪ] adj. desvencijado; raquítico.

rid [rɪd] v. librar, desembarazar; to get — of librarse de, deshacerse de, desembarazarse de; pret. & p.p. de to rid.

ridden [rɪdn] p.p. de to ride.

riddle [rɪdl] s. acertijo, adivinanza, enigma; v. acribillar, perforar; to — with bullets acribillar a balazos.

ride [raɪd] v. cabalgar, montar; pasear (en automóvil, a caballo); ir en tranvía, automóvil, tren, etc.; to — a bicycle andar o montar en bicicleta; to — a horse montar un caballo; to — horseback montar a caballo; to — over a country pasar o viajar por un país (en auto, a caballo o por tren); to — someone dominar a alguien; burlarse de alguien; s. paseo (a caballo o en automóvil); viaje (a caballo, en automóvil, por ferrocarril, etc.).

rider [raɪdə] s. jinete; pasajero (de automóvil); biciclista; motociclista; aditamento, cláusula añadida (a un proyecto de ley).

ridge [rɪdʒ] s. espinazo; lomo (entre dos surcos); arista, intersección (de dos planos); cordillera; cerro; caballete (de tejado); cordoncillo (de ciertos tejidos).

ridicule [rɪdɪkjul] s. ridículo; burla, mofa; v. ridiculizar, poner en ridículo.

ridiculous [rɪdɪkjələs] adj. ridículo.

rifle [raɪfl] s. rifle; v. pillar, robar; despojar.

rig [rɪg] v. aparejar, equipar; enjarciar (un barco de vela); to — oneself up emperifollarse, ataviarse; s. aparejo, equipo; aparato; atavío, traje.

rigging [rɪgɪŋ] s. jarcia, aparejo.

right [raɪt] adj. derecho; diestro; recto; justo; propio; adecuado; correcto; — angle ángulo recto; — side lado derecho; derecho (de un tejido, traje, etc.); it is — that está bien que, es justo que; to be — tener razón; to be all — estar bien; estar bien de salud; to be in one's — mind estar, estar en sus cabales; adv. derecho, directamente; rectamente; justamente; bien; correctamente; a la derecha; —aboutface media vuelta; — hungry muy hambriento; — now ahora mismo, inmediatamente; — there allí mismo, Am. allí mero; go — home! ¡vete derechito a casa!; it is — where you

left it está exactamente (o en el mero lugar) donde lo dejaste; to hit — in the eye dar de lleno en el ojo, Am. dar en el mero ojo; s. derecho; autoridad; privilegio; — of way derecho de vía; by — (by -s) justamente, con justicia; según la ley; from — to left de derecha a izquierda; to the — a la derecha; to be in the — tener razón; v. enderezar; corregir.

righteous [raɪtʃəs] adj. recto, justo, virtuoso.

righteousness [raɪtʃəsnɪs] s. rectitud, virtud.

rightful [raɪtfəl] adj. justo; legítimo.

right-hand [raɪthænd] adj. derecho, de la mano derecha; — man brazo derecho.

rightist [raɪtɪst] s. derechista.

rightly [raɪtlɪ] adv. con razón; justamente, rectamente; propiamente, aptamente, debidamente.

rigid [rɪdʒɪd] adj. rígido.

rigidity [rɪdʒɪdətɪ] s. rigidez; tiesura.

rigor [rɪgə] s. rigor; rigidez; severidad.

rigorous [rɪgəəs] adj. rigoroso (o riguroso), severo.

rim [rɪm] s. borde, orilla; aro.

rime = **rhyme**.

rind [raɪnd] s. corteza, cáscara.

ring [rɪŋ] s. anillo, sortija; argolla; aro; círculo; arena (de un circo); campo de combate; pista (de un hipódromo); toque; tañido; repique; sonido metálico; —leader cabecilla; — of defiance tono de reto; — of shouts gritería; — of a telephone llamada de teléfono; ring-shaped en forma de anillo, anular; key—llavero; sarcastic—retintín; v. tocar (un timbre, una campanilla o campana); sonar; tañer, repicar; resonar; zumbar (los oídos); to — for something llamar para pedir algo; to — the nose of an animal ponerle una argolla en la nariz a un animal; to — up on the phone llamar por teléfono.

ringlet [rɪŋlɪt] s. rizo, bucle; pequeña sortija.

rink [[rɪŋk] s. patinadero (cancha para patinar).

rinse [rɪns] v. enjuagar; lavar; aclarar (la ropa); s. enjuague.

riot [raɪət] s. motín, desorden, alboroto, tumulto, Am. bola; — color riqueza o exceso de colores chillantes; v. amotinarse, alborotar, armar un tumulto.

rip [rɪp] v. rasgar(se), romper(se); descoser(se); to — off rasgar, arrancar, cortar; **to — out a seam** descoser una costura; s. rasgón, rasgadura, rotura; descosido.

ripe [raɪp] *adj.* maduro, sazonado; **en sazón; — for** maduro para, sazonado para; bien preparado para, listo para.

ripen [ráɪpən] *v.* madurar(se), sazonar-(se).

ripeness [ráɪpnɪs] s. madurez, sazón.

ripple [rípl] *v.* rizar(se), agitar(se), ondear, temblar (*la superficie del agua*); murmurar (*un arroyo*); s. onda, temblor, ondulación (*en la superficie del agua*); murmullo (*de un arroyo*).

rise [raɪz] *v.* subir; ascender; alzarse, levantarse; elevarse; surgir; salir (*el sol, la luna, un astro*); hincharse (*la masa del pan*); **to — up in rebellion** sublevarse, levantarse, alzarse (en rebelión); *s.* subida; ascenso; pendiente; elevación; salida (*del sol, de la luna, etc.*); subida, alza (*de precios*).

risen [rízn] *p.p. de* to rise.

risk [rɪsk] *s.* riesgo; *v.* arriesgar, aventurar, poner en peligro; exponerse a; **to — defeat** correr el riesgo de perder, exponerse a perder.

risky [rískɪ] *adj.* arriesgado, peligroso, aventurado.

rite [raɪt] *s.* rito, ceremonia.

ritual [rítʃʊəl] *adj. & s.* ritual, ceremonial.

rival [ráɪvl] *s.* rival, competidor, émulo; *adj.* competidor; **the — party** el partido opuesto; *v.* rivalizar con, competir con.

rivalry [ráɪvlrɪ] *s.* rivalidad.

river [rívə] *s.* río.

rivet [rívɪt] *s.* remache; *v.* remachar; fijar.

rivulet [rívjəlɪt] *s.* riachuelo, arroyuelo.

road [rod] *s.* camino; carretera; vía.

roadside [ródsaɪd] *s.* borde del camino.

roadway [ródwe] *s.* camino, carretera.

roam [rom] *v.* vagar, errar, andar errante.

roar [ror] *v.* rugir, bramar; **to — with laughter** reír a carcajadas; *s.* rugido, bramido; **— of laughter** risotada, carcajada.

roast [rost] *v.* asar(se); tostar (*café, maíz, etc.*); ridiculizar, criticar; *s.* asado, carne asada; *adj.* asado; **— beef** rosbif, rosbí.

rob [rɑb] *v.* robar, hurtar; **to — some-one of something** robarle algo a alguien.

robber [rábə] *s.* ladrón; **highway —** salteador.

robbery [rábrɪ] *s.* robo, hurto.

robe [rob] *s.* manto, traje talar, túnica, toga (*de un juez, letrado, etc.*); bata; **automobile —** manta de automóvil.

robin [rábɪn] *s.* petirrojo.

robust [róbʌst] *adj.* robusto, fuerte.

rock [rɑk] *s.* roca, peña; peñasco; **— crystal** cristal de roca; **— salt** sal de piedra, sal gema o sal mineral; **to go on the -s** tropezar en un escollo, *Am.* escollar; *v.* mecer(se), balancear(se); bambolear(se); estremecer; **to — to sleep** adormecer (*meciendo*), arrullar.

rocker [rákə] *s.* mecedora; arco de una mecedora o cuna.

rocket [rákit] *s.* cohete.

rocking [rákɪŋ] *s.* balanceo; *adj.* oscilante **— chair** silla mecedora.

rocky [rákɪ] *adj.* roqueño, rocoso, rocalloso, peñascoso; pedregoso; movedizo; tembloroso: débil desvanecido.

rod [rɑd] *s.* vara, varilla; medida de longitud (*aproximadamente 5 metros*); **fishing —** caña de pescar.

rode [rod] *pret. de* to ride.

rogue [rog] *s.* pícaro, bribón, tunante, pillo; **-s' gallery** colección policíaca de retratos de criminales.

roguish [rógɪʃ] *adj.* pícaro, pillo, picaresco; travieso.

role [rol] *s.* papel, parte.

roll [rol] *v.* rodar; girar; balancearse (*un barco*); bambolearse; ondular, retumbar (*el trueno, un cañón*); aplanar, alisar con rodillo; arrollar, enrollar, hacer un rollo o bola; envolver; redoblar (*un tambor*); pronunciar (*la rr doble*); **to — over in the snow** revolverse o revolcarse en la nieve; **to — up** arrollar, enrollar, envolver; *s.* rollo (*de papel, paño, tela, etc.*); balanceo (*de un barco*); retumbo (*del trueno, de un cañón*); redoble (*de un tambor*); lista; ondulación; oleaje; bollo, rosca, panecillo; **to call the —** pasar lista.

roller [rólə] *s.* rodillo, cilindro (*para aplanar o alisar*); rollo (*rodillo de pastelero*); oleada; **— coaster** montaña rusa; **— skate** patín de ruedas.

Roman [rómən] *adj. & s.* romano; **— nose** nariz aguileña.

romance [rómæns] *s.* romance; novela (*de caballerías o de aventuras*); cuento, fábula; aventura romántica; amorío, lance amoroso; *v.* contar o fingir fábulas; andar en amoríos o aventuras; **Romance** *adj.* romance, románico, neolatino.

romantic [rómæntɪk] *adj.* romántico; novelesco.

romanticism [rómæntəsɪzəm] *s.* romanticismo.

romanticist [romántəsıst] *s.* romántico, escritor romántico.

romp. [ramp] *v.* triscar, juguetear, retozar, travesear.

roof [ruf] *s.* techo, techumbre, techado; tejado; — **garden** azotea-jardín; — **of the mouth** paladar; **flat** — azotea; *v.* techar.

room [rum] *s.* cuarto, pieza, sala, habitación; espacio; lugar, sitio; **there is no** — **for** more no cabe(n) más, no hay lugar o cabida para más; **to make** — hacer lugar; —**mate** compañero de cuarto; *v.* vivir, hospedarse, alojarse.

roomer [rúmə] *s.* inquilino.

roominess [rúmınıs] *s.* holgura.

roomy [rúmı] *adj.* espacioso, amplio, holgado.

roost [rust] *s.* gallinero; percha de gallinero; *v.* acurrucarse (*las aves en la percha*); pasar la noche.

rooster [rústə] *s.* gallo.

root [rut] *s.* raíz; *v.* arraigar(se); echar raíces; hocicar, hozar (*dícese de los cerdos*); **to** — **for** vitorear, aclamar; **to** — **out** (*o* — **up**) desarraigar, arrancar de raíz; **to become -ed** arraigarse.

rope [rop] *s.* soga, cuerda; reata, lazo; **to be at the end of one's** — haber agotado el último recurso; estar (*o* andar) en las últimas; no saber qué hacer; **to know the -s** saber todas las tretas de un asunto o negocio; *v.* amarrar, lazar, enlazar; **to** — **off** acordelar, poner cuerdas tirantes alrededor de (*un sitio*); **to** — **someone in** embaucar a alguien.

rosary [rózərı] *s.* rosario.

rose [roz] *pret. de* to rise.

rose [roz] *s.* rosa; color de rosa; —**bush** rosal; — **window** rosetón.

rosebud [rózbʌd] *s.* capullo o botón de rosa, yema, pimpollo.

rosette [rozét] *s.* roseta; rosetón.

rostrum [rústrəm] *s.* tribuna.

rosy [rózı] *adj.* rosado; color de rosa; alegre, risueño; — **future** porvenir risueño.

rot [rɑt] *v.* pudrir(se); corromperse; *s.* podre, podredumbre, putrefacción.

rotary [rótərı] *adj.* rotatorio, giratorio, rotativo.

rotate [rótet] *v.* girar, dar vueltas; hacer girar; turnarse; cultivar en rotación.

rotation [rotéʃən] *s.* rotación, vuelta; — **of crops** rotación de cultivos.

rote [rot] *s.* rutina, repetición maquinal; **by** — maquinalmente.

rotten [rátņ] *adj.* podrido, putrefacto;

hediondo; corrompido, corrupto.

rouge [ruʒ] *s.* colorete; *v.* pintar(se), poner(se) colorete.

rough [rʌf] *adj.* áspero; tosco; brusco; grosero; fragoso, escabroso; borrascoso, tempestuoso; — **diamond** diamante en bruto; — **draft** borrador; bosquejo; — **estimate** cálculo aproximativo, tanteo; — **ground** terreno escabroso; — **idea** idea aproximada; — **sea** mar picado; — **weather** tiempo borrascoso; *adv. véase* roughly; *v.* **to** — **it** vivir sin lujos ni comodidades, hacer vida campestre.

roughen [rʌfən] *v.* hacer o poner áspero; picar, rascar (*una superficie*); rajarse, agrietarse (*la piel*)r

roughly [rʌflı] *adv.* ásperamente; groseramente, rudamente; aproximadamente; **to estimate** — tantear.

roughness [rʌfnıs] *s.* aspereza; escabrosidad; rudeza; tosquedad; **the** — **of the sea** lo picado del mar; **the** — **of the weather** lo borrascoso del tiempo.

round [raund] *adj.* redondo; rotundo; circular; — **trip** viaje redondo, viaje de ida y vuelta; **round-trip ticket** boleto (*o* billete) de ida y vuelta; *s.* vuelta, rotación, revolución; ronda; vuelta (*en el juego de naipes*); tanda, turno (*en ciertos deportes*); escalón, travesaño (*de escalera de mano*); danza en rueda; — **of ammunition** carga de municiones; descarga; — **of applause** explosión de aplausos; — **of pleasures** sucesión de placeres; **to make the -s** rondar; *prep. & adv. véase* around; — **about** a la redonda; por todos lados; **round-shouldered** cargado de espaldas; **to come** — **again** volver otra vez; **to go** — **a corner** doblar una esquina; *v.* redondear; dar vuelta a; **to** — **a corner** doblar una esquina; **to** — **out** redondear; completar; **to** — **up cattle** juntar el ganado, *Am.* rodear el ganado.

roundabout [ráundəbaut] *adj.* indirecto.

roundup [ráundʌp] *s.* rodeo (*de ganado*).

rouse [rauz] *v.* despertar(se), *Am.* recordar; excitar; incitar, provocar; levantar (*la caza*).

rout [raut] *s.* derrota, fuga desordenada; *v.* derrotar; poner en fuga; **to** — **out** echar, hacer salir a toda prisa.

route [rut] *s.* ruta, camino, vía; itinerario; *v.* dirigir o enviar por cierta ruta.

routine [rutín] *s.* rutina.

rove [rov] *v.* vagar, errar, andar errante.

rover [róvə] *s.* vagabundo.

row [rau] *s.* riña, pelea, pelotera; *v.* pelearse, reñir, armar una riña o pelotera.

row [ro] *s.* fila, hilera; paseo en lancha;
v. remar, bogar; llevar en lancha o bote.

rowboat [róbot] *s.* bote de remos, lancha.

rower [róə] *s.* remero.

royal [rótəl] *adj.* real, regio.

royalist [rótəlɪst] *s.* realista.

royalty [rótəltɪ] *s.* realeza, soberanía real;
persona o personas reales; derechos
(*pagados a un autor o inventor*).

rub [rʌb] *v.* frotar; restregar; fregar;
raspar; irritar; **to — out** borrar; **to —
someone the wrong way** irritar,
contrariar, llevarle a uno la contraria;
s. fricción, friega, frotación; roce; sarcasmo; **there is the —** allí está la
dificultad.

rubber [rʌbə] *s.* caucho, goma, *Am.* hule;
goma elástica; goma de borrar; partida
(*en ciertos juegos de naipes*); jugada
decisiva (*en ciertos juegos de naipes*);
-s chanclos, zapatos de goma o hule;
adj. de caucho, de goma, *Am.* de hule;
— band faja o banda de goma; —
plantation cauchal; **— tree** *Am.*
caucho, *Am.* gomero.

rubbish [rʌbɪʃ] *s.* basura, desechos, desperdicios; tonterías.

rubble [rʌbl] *s.* escombros; ripio, cascajo, fragmentos de ladrillos o piedras;
piedra en bruto, piedra sin labrar.

ruby [rúbɪ] *s.* rubí.

rudder [rʌdə] *s.* timón.

ruddy [rʌdɪ] *adj.* rojo; rojizo; rubicundo.

rude [rud] *adj.* rudo; grosero; áspero;
brusco; tosco.

rudeness [rúdnɪs] *s.* rudeza, grosería,
descortesía; tosquedad.

rueful [rúfəl] *adj.* triste; lastimoso, lamentable.

ruffian [rʌfɪən] *s.* rufián, hombre brutal.

ruffle [rʌfl] *v.* rizar, fruncir (*tela*); arrugar; desarreglar; rizar (*la superficie del
agua*); perturbar; molestar; *s.* volante
(*de un traje*); frunce, pliegue; ondulación (*en el agua*).

rug [rʌg] *s.* alfombra, tapete.

rugged [rʌgɪd] *adj.* escabroso, fragoso;
áspero; recio, robusto; tosco; borrascoso, tempestuoso.

ruin [rúɪn] *s.* ruina; **to go to —** arruinarse, caer en ruinas, venir a menos; *v.*
arruinar; echar a perder; estropear.

ruinous [rúɪnəs] *adj.* ruinoso; desastroso.

rule [rul] *s.* regla; reglamento; precepto;
gobierno, mando; **as a —** por regla general; *v.* regir, gobernar; mandar; dirigir,
guiar; dominar; fallar, decidir; rayar
(*con regla*); **to — out** excluir; **to —
over** regir, gobernar.

ruler [rúlə] *s.* gobernante; soberano;
regla (*para medir o trazar líneas*).

ruling [rúlɪŋ] *s.* fallo, decisión; gobierno;
adj. predominante, prevaleciente; principal.

rum [rʌm] *s.* ron.

rumble [rʌmbl] *v.* retumbar, hacer estruendo, rugir; *s.* retumbo, estruendo,
rumor, ruido sordo; **— seat** asiento
trasero (*de cupé*).

ruminate [rúmənet] *v.* rumiar; reflexionar, meditar.

rummage [rʌmɪdʒ] *v.* escudriñar revol-
viéndolo todo; *s.* búsqueda desordenada; **— sale** venta de prendas usadas
(*para beneficencia*).

rumor [rúmə] *s.* rumor; runrún; *v.* murmurar; **it is -ed that** corre la voz que.

rump [rʌmp] *s.* anca; trasero.

rumple [rʌmpl] *v.* estrujar, ajar; arrugar; *s.* arruga (*en un traje*).

rumpus [rʌmpəs] *s.* barullo, alharaca,
boruca, batahola.

run [rʌn] *v.* correr; andar (*una máquina,
un reloj, etc.*), funcionar, marchar;
fluir; chorrear; recorrer; dirigir, manejar (*un negocio, empresa, máquina,
casa, etc.*); extenderse (*de un punto a
otro*); correrse (*los colores*); ser candidato (*a un puesto político*); **to — a fever** tener calentura; **to — away** huir;
fugarse, escaparse; **to — across a person** encontrarse o tropezar con una
persona; **to — down** dejar de funcionar
(*una máquina, reloj, etc.*); aprehender a
(*un criminal*); hablar mal de; atropellar; **to get — down in health** que-
brantársele a uno la salud; **to — dry**
secarse; **to — into** tropezar con, encontrarse con; chocar con; **to — into
debt** adeudarse; **to — something
into** meter algo en, clavar algo en; **to
— out** salirse; **to — out of money**
acabársele a uno el dinero; **to — over**
derramarse (*un líquido*); atropellar, pasar por encima de; repasar, echar un
vistazo a (*la lección, un libro, etc.*); **to
— through a book** hojear un libro; **—
the play ran for three months** se
dió la comedia durante tres meses; *s.*
carrera, corrida; curso, marcha; recorrido; manejo; **— of good luck** serie
de repetidos éxitos; **— of perform-
ances** serie de representaciones; **— on
a bank** corrida, demanda extraordinaria de fondos bancarios; **in the long
—** a la larga; **stocking —** carrera; **the
common — of mankind** el común de
las gentes; **to have the — of** tener el
libre uso de; *p.p. de* to run.

runaway [rʌ́nəwe] *adj.* fugitivo; — **horse** caballo desbocado; — **marriage** casamiento de escapatoria; *s.* fugitivo; caballo desbocado; fuga.

rung [rʌŋ] *s.* barrote, travesaño (*de silla, escalera de mano, etc.*); *pret. & p.p. de* **to ring**.

runner [rʌ́nə]·*s.* corredor; tapete (*para un pasillo o mesa*), *Am.* pasillo; carrera (*en una media*); cuchilla (*de patín o de trineo*); contrabandista.

running [rʌ́nɪŋ] *s.* corrida, carrera; manejo, dirección; flujo; **to be out of the** — estar fuera de combate; *adj.* corriente; — **board** estribo; — **expenses** gastos corrientes; — **knot** nudo corredizo; — **water** agua corriente; **in** — **condition** en buen estado; **for ten days** — por diez días seguidos.

runt [rʌnt] *s.* enano; hombrecillo.

runway [rʌ́nwe] *s.* senda; vía; pista (*de aterrizaje*).

rupture [rʌ́ptʃə] *s.* ruptura; rompimiento, rotura, hernia; *v.* romper(se); reventar.

rural [rʊ́rəl] *adj.* rural, campestre.

rush [rʌʃ] *v.* lanzar(se), precipitar(se); apresurar(se); despachar con prontitud; abalanzarse; acometer; empujar; **to** — out salir a todo correr; **to** — **past** pasar a toda prisa; *s.* precipitación, prisa; acometida; junco; — **chair** silla de junco; — **of business** gran movimiento comercial; — **of people** tropel de gente; — **order** pedido urgente.

Russian [rʌ́ʃən] *adj. & s.* ruso.

rust [rʌst] *s.* moho, orín; tizón (*enfermedad de las plantas*); — **color** color rojizo; *v.* enmohecer(se), oxidar(se).

rustic [rʌ́stɪk] *adj. & s.* rústico, campesino.

rustle [rʌ́stl] *v.* susurrar, crujir; menear; **to** — **cattle** robar ganado; *s.* susurro, crujido.

rusty [rʌ́stɪ] *adj.* mohoso, cubierto de orín, oxidado; rojizo; entorpecido, falto de uso; falto de práctica.

rut [rʌt] *s.* rodada; rutina, método rutinario; **to be in a** — hacer una cosa por rutina, ser esclavo de la rutina.

ruthless [rúɵlɪs] *adj.* despiadado, cruel, brutal.

ruthlessness [rúɵlɪsnɪs] *s.* fiereza, falta de miramiento, truculencia, crueldad.

rye [raɪ] *s.* centeno.

S

saber [sébə] *s.* sable.

sabotage [sǽbətaʒ] *s.* sabotaje; *v.* sabo-

tear.

sack [sæk] *s.* saco; costal; saqueo, pillaje; *v.* ensacar, meter en un saco; saquear, pillar.

sacrament [sǽkrəmənt] *s.* sacramento.

sacred [sékrɪd] *adj.* sagrado, sacro.

sacredness [sékrɪdnɪs] *s.* santidad; lo sagrado.

sacrifice [sǽkrəfaɪs] *s.* sacrificio; **to sell** **at a** — vender con pérdida; *v.* sacrificar.

sacrilege [sǽkrəlɪdʒ] *s.* sacrilegio.

sacrilegious [sækrɪlídʒəs] *adj.* sacrílego.

sad [sæd] *adj.* triste.

sadden [sædn] *v.* entristecer(se).

saddle [sædl] *s.* silla de montar; silla de bicicleta o motocicleta; —**bag** alforja; — **horse** caballo de silla —**tree** arzón; *v.* ensillar; **to** — **someone with responsibilities** cargar a alguien de responsabilidades.

sadistic [sædístɪk] *adj.* sádico, cruel.

sadness [sædnɪs] *s.* tristeza.

safe [sef] *adj.* seguro; salvo; sin riesgo, sin peligro; digno de confianza; — **and** **sound** sano y salvo; **safe-conduct** salvoconducto; **to be** — no correr peligro, estar a salvo; *s.* caja fuerte; **-ly** *adv.* seguramente; con seguridad; sin peligro; **to arrive** **-ly** llegar bien, llegar sin contratiempo alguno.

safeguard [séfgard] *s.* salvaguardia; resguardo, defensa; *v.* resguardar, proteger, salvaguardar.

safety [séftɪ] *s.* seguridad; protección; **in** — con seguridad; sin peligro; *adj.* de seguridad; — **device** mecanismo de seguridad; — **pin** imperdible, alfiler de seguridad.

saffron [sǽfrən] *s.* azafrán; *adj.* azafranado, color de azafrán.

sag [sæg] *v.* combarse, pandearse; doblegarse; deprimirse, hundirse (*en el centro*); encorvarse; **his shoulders** — tiene las espaldas caídas; *s.* pandeo, flexión, depresión; concavidad.

sagacious [səgéʃəs] *adj.* sagaz, ladino, astuto.

sagacity [səgǽsətɪ] *s.* sagacidad; astucia.

sage [sedʒ] *adj.* sabio; cuerdo, prudente; *s.* sabio; salvia (*planta*).

said [sed] *pret. & p.p. de* **to say.**

sail [sel] *s.* vela (*de barco*); viaje o paseo en barco de vela; **under full** — a toda vela; **to set** — hacerse a la vela; *v.* navegar; hacerse a la vela; zarpar, salir (*un buque*); viajar, ir (*en barco, bote, etc.*); pasear en bote de vela; **to** — **a** **kite** volar una cometa o papalote; **to** — **along** deslizarse; navegar; ir bien;

to —. along the coast costear.

sailboat [sélbot] s. bote o barco de vela.

sailor [sélə] s. marinero; marino.

saint [sent] s. santo; *adj.* santo; san *(delante de nombres masculinos excepto: Santo Tomás, Santo Domingo, Santo Toribio)*; v. canonizar.

saintly [séntlɪ] *adj.* santo; pío, devoto.

sake [sek]: for the — of por; por amor a; por consideración a; for my — por mí; for pity's — por piedad.; ¡caramba!; for the — of argument por vía de argumento.

salad [séləd] s. ensalada; — dressing aderezo *(para ensalada).*

salary [sélərɪ] s. salario, sueldo.

sale [sel] s. venta; saldo, *Am.* barata; — by auction almoneda, subasta; -s tax impuesto sobre ventas; for (on) — de venta.

salesman [sélzmən] s. vendedor; dependiente *(de tienda)*; traveling — agente viajero, viajante de comercio.

saleswoman [sélzwʊmən] s. vendedora; dependienta *(de tienda).*

salient [sélɪənt] *adj.* saliente, sobresaliente; prominente.

saliva [səláɪvə] s. saliva.

sallow [sélo] *adj.* amarillento, pálido.

sally [sélɪ] s. salida; agudeza, chiste agudo; v. salir, hacer una salida; to — forth salir.

salmon [sémən] s. salmón.

saloon [səlún] s. salón *(de un vapor)*; taberna, *Am.* cantina; dining — of a ship salón-comedor de un vapor.

salt [sɔlt] s. sal; chiste, agudeza, smelling -s sales aromáticas; the — of the earth la flor y nata de la humanidad; *adj.* salado; salobre; —cellar salero; — mine salina; — pork tocino salado; — shaker salero; — water agua salada, agua de mar; v. salar; to — one's money away guardar o ahorrar su dinero.

saltpeter [sóltpítə] s. salitre, nitro; — mine salitral, salitrera.

salty [sóltɪ] *adj.* salado; salobre.

salutation [sæljətéʃən] s. salutación, saludo.

salute [səlút] s. saludo; gun — salva; v. saludar; cuadrarse *(militarmente).*

salvation [sælvéʃən] s. salvación.

salve [sæv] s. untura, ungüento; alivio; v. aliviar, aquietar, calmar; untar.

same [sem] *adj.* mismo; igual; idéntico; it is all the — to me me es igual, me da lo mismo; the — lo mismo; el mismo (la misma, los mismos, las mismas).

sample [sémpl] s. muestra, prueba; book of -s muestrario; v. probar; calar.

sanctify [sǽŋktəfaɪ] v. santificar.

sanction [sǽŋkʃən] s. sanción; aprobación, autorización; v. sancionar; ratificar; aprobar, autorizar.

sanctity [sǽŋktətɪ] s. santidad.

sanctuary [sǽŋktʃʊerɪ] s. santuario; asilo.

sand [sænd] s. arena; — pit arenal; v. enarenar, cubrir de arena; mezclar con arena; refregar con arena.

sandal [sǽndl] s. sandalia; alpargata; *Am.* guarache (huarache).

sandpaper [sǽndpepə] s. papel de lija; v. lijar, pulir o alisar con papel de lija.

sandstone [sǽndston] s. piedra arenisca.

sandwich [sǽndwɪtʃ] s. bocadillo, emparedado, sandwich; v. intercalar, meter (entre).

sandy [sǽndɪ] *adj.* arenoso; arenisco; — hair pelo rojizo.

sane [sen] *adj.* sano, sensato; cuerdo.

sang [sæŋ] *pret. de* to sing.

sanitarium [sænətérɪəm] s. sanatorio.

sanitary [sǽnəterɪ] *adj.* sanitario.

sanitation [sænətéʃən] s. saneamiento; salubridad.

sanity [sǽnətɪ] s. cordura.

sank [sæŋk] *pret. de* to sink.

sap [sæp] s. savia; tonto, bobo; v. agotar, debilitar, minar.

sapling [sǽplɪŋ] s. vástago, renuevo; arbolillo.

sapphire [sǽfaɪr] s. zafiro; color de zafiro.

sarcasm [sárkæzəm] s. sarcasmo.

sarcastic [sarkǽstɪk] *adj.* sarcástico.

sardine [sardín] s. sardina.

sash [sæʃ] s. faja *(cinturón de lana, seda o algodón)*; banda, cinta ancha; window— bastidor *(o marco)* de ventana.

sat [sæt] *pret. & p.p. de* to sit.

satchel [sǽtʃəl] s. valija, maletín, maleta, saco.

sate [set] v. saciar.

sateen [sætín] s. satén o rasete *(raso de inferior calidad).*

satellite [sǽtlaɪt] s. satélite.

satiate [séʃɪet] v. saciar, hartar.

satin [sǽtn] s. raso.

satire [sǽtaɪr] s. sátira.

satirical [sətírɪkl] *adj.* satírico.

satirize [sǽtəraɪz] v. satirizar.

satisfaction [sætɪsfǽkʃən] s. satisfacción.

satisfactorily [sætɪsfǽktrəlɪ] *adv.* satisfactoriamente.

satisfactory [sætɪsfǽktrɪ] *adj.* satisfactorio.

satisfied [sǽtɪsfaɪd] *adj.* satisfecho, contento.

satisfy [sǽtɪsfaɪ] *v.* satisfacer.

saturate [sǽtʃəret] *v.* saturar, empapar.

Saturday [sǽtədɪ] *s.* sábado.

sauce [sɔs] *s.* salsa; — **dish** salsera; *v.* aderezar con salsa; sazonar, condimentar; insolentarse con.

saucepan [sɔ́spæn] *s.* cacerola.

saucer [sɔ́sə] *s.* platillo.

sauciness [sɔ́sɪnɪs] *s.* descaro, insolencia.

saucy [sɔ́sɪ] *adj.* descarado, respondón, insolente, *Am.* retobado.

saunter [sɔ́ntə] *v.* pasearse, vagar.

sausage [sɔ́sɪdʒ] *s.* salchicha, salchichón; longaniza; chorizo.

savage [sǽvɪdʒ] *adj.* salvaje; fiero; bárbaro, brutal, feroz; *s.* salvaje.

savagery [sǽvɪdʒrɪ] *s.* salvajismo; crueldad, fiereza.

savant [səvǽnt] *s.* sabio.

save [sev] *v.* salvar; ahorrar; economizar; guardar; resguardar; **to — from** librar de; **to — one's eyes** cuidarse la vista; *prep.* salvo, menos, excepto.

saver [sévə] *s.* salvador; libertador; ahorrador; **life-** salvavidas.

saving [sévɪŋ] *adj.* salvador; ahorrativo, económico; frugal; *s.* ahorro, economía; **-s** ahorros; **-s bank** caja o banco de ahorros; *prep.* salvo, excepto, con excepción de.

savior [sévjə] *s.* salvador.

savor [sévə] *s.* sabor; dejo; *v.* saborear; sazonar; **to — of** saber a, tener el sabor de; **it -s of treason** huele a traición.

savory [sévərɪ] *adj.* sabroso.

saw [sɔ] *s.* sierra; **—horse** caballete; *v.* aserrar, serrar; **it -s easily** es fácil de aserrar; *pret. de* **to see.**

sawdust [sɔ́dʌst] *s.* aserrín, serrín.

sawmill [sɔ́mɪl] *s.* aserradero.

sawn [sɔn] *p.p. de* **to saw.**

Saxon [sǽksn] *adj. & s.* sajón.

saxophone [sǽksəfon] *s.* saxófono.

say [se] *v.* decir; declarar; **—!** ¡diga! ¡oiga usted!; **that is to** — es decir; **to — one's prayers** rezar, decir o recitar sus oraciones; **to — the least** por lo menos; **it is said that** dizque, se dice que, dicen que; *s.* afirmación, aserto; **the final** — la autoridad decisiva; **to have a — in** a matter tener voz y voto en un asunto; **to have one's —** expresarse, dar su opinión.

saying [séɪ] *s.* dicho, refrán; aserto; **as the —** goes como dice el refrán.

scab [skæb] *s.* costra (*de una herida*); roña; esquirol (*obrero que sustituye a un huelguista*); obrero que acepta un

jornal inferior; *v.* encostrarse (*una herida*), cubrirse de una costra.

scabbard [skǽbəd] *s.* vaina, funda (*de espada, puñal, etc.*).

scabby [skǽbɪ] *adj.* costroso; roñoso, sarnoso, tiñoso.

scabrous [skébrəs] *adj.* escabroso.

scaffold [skǽfld] *s.* andamio, tablado; patíbulo, cadalso.

scaffolding [skǽfldɪŋ] *s.* andamiada (*Am.* andamiaje), andamios.

scald [skɔld] *v.* escaldar; **to — milk** calentar la leche hasta que suelte el hervor; *s.* escaldadura, quemadura.

scale [skel] *s.* escala; platillo de balanza; balanza; escama (*de pez o de la piel*); costra; **pair of -s** balanza; **platform —** báscula; *v.* escalar; subir, trepar por; graduar (*a escala*); medir según escala; pesar; escamar, quitar las escamas a; pelarse, despellejarse; descostrar(se); **to — down prices** rebajar proporcionalmente los precios.

scallop [skúləp] *s.* onda, pico (*adorno*); molusco bivalvo; **-s** festón (*recortes en forma de ondas o picos*); *v.* festonear, recortar en forma de ondas o picos; asar con salsa o migas de pan.

scalp [skælp] *s.* cuero cabelludo; *v.* desollar el cráneo; revender (*boletos, billetes*) a precio subido.

scaly [skélɪ] *adj.* escamoso, lleno de escamas; **— with rust** mohoso.

scamp [skæmp] *s.* pícaro, bribón, bellaco.

scamper [skǽmpə] *v.* correr, escabullirse, escaparse; *s.* escabullida, carrera, corrida.

scan [skæn] *v.* escudriñar; examinar, mirar detenidamente; echar un vistazo a (*en el habla popular*); medir (*el verso*).

scandal [skǽndl] *s.* escándalo; maledicencia, murmuración.

scandalize [skǽndlaɪz] *v.* escandalizar, dar escándalo.

scandalous [skǽndləs] *adj.* escandaloso; difamatorio; vergonzoso.

scant [skænt] *adj.* escaso; corto, insuficiente; *v.* escatimar, limitar.

scanty [skǽntɪ] *adj.* escaso; insuficiente.

scar [skar] *s.* cicatriz; costurón; raya, marca (*en una superficie pulida*); *v.* marcar, rayar; hacer o dejar una cicatriz en.

scarce [skers] *adj.* escaso; raro, **-ly** *adv.* escasamente; apenas.

scarcity [skérsətɪ] *s.* escasez; carestía, insuficiencia.

scare [sker] *v.* espantar, asustar; alarmar; sobresaltar; **he -s easily** se asusta fácilmente; **to — away** ahuyentar, espantar; *s.* susto, sobresalto.

scarecrow [skérkro] *s.* espantajo; espantapájaros.

scarf [skɑrf] *s.* bufanda; mantilla; pañuelo (*para el cuello o la cabeza*); tapete (*para una mesa, tocador, etc.*).

scarlet [skárlɪt] *adj.* de color escarlata; — **fever** escarlata, escarlatina.

scary [skéri] *adj.* espantadizo, asustadizo, miedoso.

scatter [skǽtə] *v.* esparcir(se); desparramar(se); dispersar(se); —**brained** ligero de cascos, aturdido.

scene [sin] *s.* escena; escenario; decoración; vista; **to make a** — causar un escándalo.

scenery [sínərɪ] *s.* paisaje, vista; **stage** — decoraciones.

scent [sent] *s.* olor; perfume; pista, rastro; **to be on the** — **of** seguir el rastro de; **to have a keen** — tener buen olfato; *v.* oler, olfatear, ventear, husmear; perfumar.

scepter [séptə] *s.* cetro.

sceptic [sképtɪk] *adj. & s.* escéptico.

scepticism [sképtəsɪzəm] *s.* escepticismo.

schedule [skédʒʊl] *s.* horario; itinerario (*de trenes*); lista, inventario (*adjunto a un documento*); *v.* fijar el día y la hora (*para una clase, conferencia, etc.*); establecer el itinerario para (*un tren o trenes*).

scheme [skim] *s.* esquema, plan, proyecto; empresa; ardid, trama, maquinación; **color** — combinación de colores; **metrical** — sistema de versificación; *v.* proyectar, urdir; maquinar, intrigar, tramar.

schemer [skímə] *s.* maquinador, intrigante; proyectista.

scheming [skímɪŋ] *adj.* maquinador, intrigante; *s.* maquinación.

scholar [skálə] *s.* escolar, estudiante; becario (*el que disfruta una beca*); erudito, docto.

scholarly [skálərlɪ] *adj.* erudito, sabio, docto; *adv.* eruditamente, doctamente.

scholarship [skálərʃɪp] *s.* saber; erudición; beca; **to have a** — disfrutar una beca.

scholastic [skolǽstɪk] *adj.* escolástico; escolar.

school [skul] *s.* escuela; — **of fish** banco de peces; *adj.* de escuela; — **day** día de escuela; — **board** consejo de enseñanza; *v.* enseñar, educar, instruir, aleccionar.

schoolboy [skúlbɔɪ] *s.* muchacho de escuela.

schoolgirl [skúlgɜl] *s.* muchacha de escuela.

schoolhouse [skúlhaʊs] *s.* escuela.

schooling [skúlɪŋ] *s.* instrucción; enseñanza, educación.

schoolmaster [skúlmæstə] *s.* maestro de escuela.

schoolmate [skúlmet] *s.* condiscípulo, compañero de escuela.

schoolroom [skúlrum] *s.* clase, aula.

schoolteacher [skúltitʃə] *s.* maestro de escuela.

schooner [skúnə] *s.* goleta; vaso grande para cerveza; **prairie** — galera con toldo.

science [sáɪəns] *s.* ciencia.

scientific [saɪəntífɪk] *adj.* científico; -**ally** *adv.* científicamente.

scientist [sáɪəntɪst] *s.* científico, hombre de ciencia.

scion [sáɪən] *s.* vástago.

scissors [sízəz] *s. pl.* tijeras.

scoff [skɔf] *s.* mofa, burla, befa, escarnio; *v.* escarnecer; mofarse; **to** — **at** mofarse de, burlarse de, escarnecer a.

scold [skold] *v.* reñir, reprender, regañar; *s.* regañón, persona regañona.

scolding [skóldɪŋ] *s.* regaño, reprensión; *adj.* regañón.

scoop [skup] *s.* cuchara, cucharón; pala; palada, cucharada; buena ganancia; **newspaper** — primera publicación de una noticia; *v.* cavar, excavar; ahuecar; cucharear, sacar con cucharón o pala; achicar (*agua*); **to** — **in a good profit** sacar buena ganancia.

scoot [skut] *v.* escabullirse, correr, irse a toda prisa; —**!** ¡largo de aquí!

scope [skop] *s.* alcance, extensión; esfera, campo.

scorch [skɔrtʃ] *v.* chamuscar; resecar, agostar; *s.* chamusquina, *Am.* chamuscada o chamuscadura.

score [skor] *s.* cuenta; escor (*en el juego*), raya, línea; calificación (*expresada numéricamente*); veintena; **musical** — partitura; **on that** — a ese respecto; **on the** — **of** a causa de, con motivo de; **to keep the** — llevar el escor, llevar la cuenta; **to settle old** —**s** desquitarse; *v.* marcar el escor, señalar los tantos en un juego; calificar (*numéricamente*); instrumentar (*música*); rayar, marcar con rayas; **to** — **a point** ganar un punto o tanto; **to** — **a success** lograr éxito, obtener un triunfo.

scorn [skɔrn] *s.* desdén, menosprecio; *v.* desdeñar, menospreciar.

scornful [skɔ́rnfəl] *adj.* desdeñoso.

scorpion [skɔ́rpɪən] *s.* escorpión, alacrán.

Scotch [skɑtʃ] *adj.* escocés; **the —** los escoceses, el pueblo escocés.

scoundrel [skáundrəl] *s.* bellaco, bribón, pícaro.

scour [skaʊr] *v.* fregar, restregar, limpiar; pulir; **to — the country** recorrer la comarca (*en busca de algo*).

scourge [skɜdʒ] *s.* azote; *v.* azotar; castigar.

scout [skaʊt] *s.* explorador (*usualmente militar*); **a good —** un buen explorador; una buena persona, un buen compañero; *v.* explorar; reconocer.

scowl [skaʊl] *s.* ceño; *v.* fruncir el ceño, mirar con ceño; poner mala cara.

scramble [skrǽmbl] *v.* hacer un revoltillo de (*huevos*); revolver, mezclar confusamente; **to — for something** forcejear por coger algo; pelearse por coger algo; **to — up** trepar o subir a gatas (*una cuesta*); **-d eggs** revoltillo, huevos revueltos; *s.* revoltillo, confusión; pelea.

scrap [skræp] *s.* fragmento, pedacito; migaja; riña, reyerta; **-s** sobras; desperdicios; desechos; retales; **—book** álbum de recortes; **— iron** recortes o desechos de hierro, *v.* desechar; tirar a la basura; descartar; pelear, reñir.

scrape [skrep] *v.* raspar; rasguñar; rascar, raer; rozar; **to — along** ir tirando, ir pasándola; **to — together** recoger o acumular poco a poco; **to bow and —** ser muy servil; *s.* raspadura; rasguño; aprieto, dificultad, lío.

scraper [skrépə] *s.* raspador: persona ahorrativa y tacaña.

scratch [skrætʃ] *v.* arañar, rasguñar; rascar; raspar; rayar; escarbar; hacer garabatos, escribir mal; **to — out** borrar, tachar; sacar (*los ojos*) con las uñas; *s.* arañazo, araño, rasguño; raya, marca; **to start from —** empezar sin nada; empezar desde el principio; empezar sin ventaja.

scrawl [skrɔl] *s.* garabato; *v.* hacer garabatos, escribir mal.

scrawny [skrɔ́nɪ] *adj.* huesudo, flaco.

scream [skrim] *s.* chillido, alarido, grito; **he's a —** es muy cómico o chistoso; *v.* chillar, gritar.

screech [skritʃ] *s.* chillido; **— owl** lechuza; *v.* chillar.

screen [skrin] *s.* pantalla; mampara; biombo; resguardo; tamiz, cedazo; **— door** antepuerta de tela metálica; **motion-picture —** pantalla de cinematógrafo; **wire —** pantalla de tela metálica; *v.* tapar; resguardar, proteger con una pantalla o biombo; cerner;

proyectar sobre la pantalla, filmar; **to — windows** proteger las ventanas con tela metálica.

screw [skru] *s.* tornillo; **— eye** armella; **— nut** tuerca; **— propeller** hélice; **— thread** rosca; *v.* atornillar; torcer, retorcer; **to — a lid on** atornillar una tapa; **to — up one's courage** cobrar ánimo.

screwdriver [skrúdraɪvə] *s.* destornillador.

scribble [skríbl] *v.* garrapatear, hacer garabatos, borronear, escribir mal o de prisa; *s.* garabato.

script [skrɪpt] *s.* letra cursiva, escritura; manuscrito (*de un drama, de una película*).

scripture [skríptʃə] *s.* escritura sagrada; **the Scriptures** la Sagrada Escritura, la Biblia.

scroll [skrol] *s.* rollo de pergamino o papel; voluta, adorno en espiral; rúbrica (*de una firma*).

scrub [skrʌb] *v.* fregar; restregar; *s.* friega, fregado; *adj.* achaparrado; bajo, inferior; **— oak** chaparro; **— pine** pino achaparrado; **— team** equipo de jugadores suplentes o menos bien entrenados; **— woman** fregona.

scruple [skrúpl] *s.* escrúpulo; *v.* escrupulizar, tener escrúpulos.

scrupulous [skrúpjələs] *adj.* escrupuloso.

scrutinize [skrútɪnaɪz] *v.* escudriñar, escrutar

scrutiny [skrútɪnɪ] *s.* escrutinio.

scuff [skʌf] *v.* raspar; arrastrar los pies.

scuffle [skʌfl] *s.* refriega, riña, pelea; *v.* forcejear; luchar, pelear; arrastrar los pies.

sculptor [skʌ́lptə] *s.* escultor

sculpture [skʌ́lptʃə] *s.* escultura; *v.* esculpir, cincelar, tallar.

scum [skʌm] *s.* nata, capa, espuma, escoria; residuo, desechos; canalla, gente baja; *v.* espumar.

scurry [skɜ́ɪ] *v.* escabullirse; echar a correr; apresurarse; *s.* apresuramiento; corrida, carrera.

scuttle [skʌ́tl] *v.* echar a correr; barrenar (*un buque*); echar a pique; *s.* escotilla, escotillón; balde (*para carbón*).

scythe [saɪð] *s.* guadaña.

sea [si] *s.* mar; **to be at —** estar en el mar; estar perplejo o confuso; **to put to —** hacerse a la mar; *adj.* marino, marítimo, de mar; **— biscuit** galleta; **— green** verdemar; **— gull** gaviota; **— level** nivel del mar; **— lion** león marino, foca; **— power** potencia naval.

seaboard [síbord] *s.* costa, litoral; *adj.*

costanero, litoral.

seacoast [síkost] *s.* costa, litoral.

seal [sil] *s.* sello; timbre; foca, león marino; **to set one's — to** sellar; aprobar; *v.* sellar; estampar; cerrar; tapar; **to — in** encerrar, cerrar herméticamente; **to—with sealing wax** lacrar.

sealing wax [síliŋ wæks] *s.* lacre.

seam [sim] *s.* costura; juntura; cicatriz; filón, veta; *v.* echar una costura, coser.

seaman [símən] *s.* marino, marinero.

seamstress [símstrɪs] *s.* costurera.

seaplane [síplen] *s.* hidroavión.

seaport [síport] *s.* puerto de mar.

sear [sɪr] *v.* chamuscar(se), tostar(se); resecar(se); herrar, marcar con hierro candente; *adj.* reseco, marchito.

search [sɜtʃ] *v.* buscar; escudriñar; registrar; examinar; **to — a prisoner** registrar a un prisionero; **to — for something** buscar algo; **to — into** investigar, indagar; *s.* busca, búsqueda; registro, inspección; investigación, pesquisa, indagación; **— warrant** mandato judicial de practicar un registro; **in — of** en busca de.

seashore [síʃor] *s.* costa, playa, orilla o ribera del mar.

seasick [sísɪk] *adj.* mareado; **to get —** marearse.

seasickness [sísɪknɪs] *s.* mareo.

seaside [sísaɪd] *s.* costa, litoral; playa.

season [sízŋ] *s.* estación (*del año*); temporada; sazón, ocasión, tiempo; **— ticket** billete de abono; **Christmas —** navidades; **harvest —** siega, tiempo de la cosecha; **opera —** temporada de la ópera; **to arrive in good —** llegar en sazón, llegar a tiempo; *v.* sazonar; condimentar; aclimatar.

seasoning [sízŋ̩ŋ] *s.* condimento; salsa; desecación (*de la madera*).

seat [sit] *s.* asiento; silla; sitio; residencia; sede (*episcopal, del gobierno, etc*); nalgas; fondillos, parte trasera (*de los pantalones o calzones*); **— of learning** centro de estudios, centro de erudición; *v.* sentar; asentar; dar asiento a; **to — oneself** sentarse; **it -s a thousand people** tiene cabida para mil personas.

seaweed [síwid] *s.* alga marina.

secede [sisíd] *v.* separarse (*de una federación o unión*).

seclude [sɪklúd] *v.* recluir, apartar, aislar; **to — oneself from** recluirse de, apartarse de.

secluded [sɪklúdɪd] *adj.* apartado, aislado; solitario.

seclusion [sɪklúʒən] *s.* apartamiento, soledad, aislamiento; retiro.

second [sékənd] *adj.* segundo; inferior; **— hand** segundero (*de reloj*); **— lieutenant** subteniente; **second-rate** de segunda clase; mediocre, inferior; **on — thought** después de pensarlo bien; *s.* segundo; padrino (*en un desafío*); ayudante; mercancía de segunda calidad; mercancía defectuosa; *v.* secundar (*o segundar*), apoyar; apadrinar.

secondary [sékəndɛrɪ] *adj.* secundario; **— education** segunda enseñanza; **— school** escuela secundaria, escuela de segunda enseñanza.

second-hand [sékəndhænd] *adj.* de segunda mano; usado; indirecto, por intermedio de otro.

secondly [sékəndlɪ] *adv.* en segundo lugar.

secrecy [síkrəsɪ] *s.* secreto, sigilo, reserva.

secret [síkrɪt] *s.* secreto; *adj.* secreto; escondido, oculto; **— service** policía secreta; **-ly** *adv.* secretamente, en secreto.

secretary [sékrətɛrɪ] *s.* secretario; escritorio (*con estantes para libros*).

secrete [sɪkrít] *v.* secretar (*una secreción*); esconder, ocultar.

secretion [sɪkríʃən] *s.* secreción.

secretive [sɪkrítɪv] *adj.* reservado, callado; **— gland** glándula secretoria.

sect [sɛkt] *s.* secta.

section [sékʃən] *s.* sección; trozo; tajada; región; barrio; *v.* seccionar, dividir en secciones.

secular [sékjələ] *adj. & s.* secular.

secure [sɪkjúr] *adj.* seguro; firme; *v.* asegurar; afianzar; obtener; resguardar; **-ly** *adv.* seguramente, con seguridad; firmemente.

security [sɪkjúrətɪ] *s.* seguridad; fianza, garantía, prenda; resguardo, protección; **securities** bonos, obligaciones, acciones, valores.

sedan [sɪdǽn] *s.* sedán.

sedate [sɪdét] *adj.* sosegado; tranquilo; sereno; serio.

sedative [sédətɪv] *adj. & s.* calmante, sedativo.

sedentary [sédŋ̩tɛrɪ] *adj.* sedentario; inactivo.

sediment [sédəmənt] *s.* sedimento, heces, residuo.

sedition [sɪdíʃən] *s.* sedición.

seditious [sɪdíʃəs] *adj.* sedicioso.

seduce [sɪdjús] *v.* seducir.

seduction [sɪdʌ́kʃən] *s.* seducción.

see [si] *v.* ver; **— that you do it no** deje Vd. de hacerlo; tenga Vd. cuidado de hacerlo; **I'll — to it** me encargaré de ello; **let me — a** ver; **to — a person home** acompañar a una persona a casa; **to — a person off** ir a la estación para despedir a una persona; **to — a person through a difficulty** ayudar a una persona a salir de un apuro; **to — through a person** adivinar lo que piensa una persona, darse cuenta de sus intenciones; **to — to one's affairs** atender a sus asuntos; **to have seen military service** haber servido en el ejército; *s.* sede, silla; **Holy See Santa Sede.**

seed [sid] *s.* semilla, simiente; pepita; **to go to —** producir semillas; decaer, declinar; descuidar de su persona, andar desaseado; *v.* sembrar; despepitar, quitar las pepitas o semillas de; producir semillas.

seedling [sídlıŋ] *s.* planta de semillero; arbolillo (*de menos de tres pies de altura*).

seedy [sídı] *adj.* semilloso, lleno de semillas; raído; desaseado.

seek [sik] *v.* buscar; pedir, solicitar; **to — after** buscar; **to — to** tratar de, esforzarse por.

seem [sim] *v.* parecer; **it -s to me** me parece.

seemingly [símıŋlı] *adv.* aparentemente, en apariencia, al parecer.

seemly [símlı] *adj.* propio, decente, decoroso.

seen [sin] *p.p. de* **to see.**

seep [sip] *v.* escurrirse, rezumarse, colarse, filtrarse.

seer [sɪr] *s.* vidente, adivino, profeta.

seethe [sið] *v.* bullir, hervir; burbujear.

segment [ségmənt] *s.* segmento.

seize [siz] *v.* asir, coger, agarrar; apoderarse de; prender o aprehender; aprovecharse de (*una oportunidad*); embargar, secuestrar; **to — upon** asir; **to become -d with fear** sobrecogerse de miedo.

seizure [síʒə] *s.* cogida; captura; aprehensión (*de un criminal*); secuestro, embargo (*de bienes*); ataque (*de una enfermedad*).

seldom [séldəm] *adv.* rara vez, raras veces, raramente.

select [səlékt] *adj.* selecto, escogido; *v.* elegir, escoger; entresacar.

selection [səlékʃən] *s.* selección, elección.

self [self] : **by one —** por sí, por sí mismo; **for one —** para sí; **one's other —** su otro yo; **his wife and — su** esposa y él (*véase* **herself, himself, ourselves, themselves,** *etc.*); **self-centered** egoísta, egocéntrico; **self-conscious** cons-

ciente de sí, cohibido, tímido; **self-control** dominio de sí mismo (*o de sí propio*); **self-defense** defensa propia; **self-denial** abnegación; **self-evident** patente, manifiesto; **self-esteem** respeto de sí mismo; amor propio; **self-government** gobierno autónomo, autonomía; gobierno democrático; **self-interest** propio interés; egoísmo; **self-love** amor propio; **self-possessed** sereno, dueño de sí, tranquilo; **self-sacrifice** abnegación; **self-satisfied** pagado de sí, satisfecho de sí.

selfish [sélfıʃ] *adj.* egoísta; **-ly** *adv.* con egoísmo, por egoísmo.

selfishness [sélfıʃnıs] *s.* egoísmo.

selfsame [sélfsém] *adj.* mismo, idéntico, mismísimo.

sell [sel] *v.* vender; venderse, estar de venta; **to — at auction** vender en almoneda o subasta, subastar; **to — out** venderlo todo.

seller [séla] *s.* vendedor.

selves [selvz] *pl. de* **self.**

semblance [sémbləns] *s.* semejanza; apariencia.

semicircle [sémɔsɔkl̩] *s.* semicírculo.

semicolon [sémɔkolən] *s.* punto y coma.

seminary [sémɔnɛrı] *s.* seminario.

senate [sénɪt] *s.* senado.

senator [sénɪtə] *s.* senador.

send [send] *v.* enviar; mandar; despachar; remitir, expedir; lanzar (*una flecha, pelota, etc.*); **to — away** despedir, despachar; **to — forth** despachar, enviar; emitir; exhalar; echar; **to — someone up for 15 years** condenar a un reo a 15 años de prisión; **to — word** avisar, mandar decir, mandar recado.

sender [séndə] *s.* remitente; transmisor.

senile [sínaɪl] *adj.* senil, caduco; chocho.

senility [sɔnílɪtɪ] *s.* senectud; chochera o chochez.

senior [sínjə] *adj.* mayor, de más edad; más antiguo, superior en dignidad o rango; **— class** clase del cuarto año; *s.* persona o socio más antiguo; estudiante del último año; **to be somebody's — by two years** ser dos años mayor que alguien.

sensation [senséʃən] *s.* sensación.

sensational [senséʃən̩] *adj.* sensacional; emociante.

sense [sens] *s.* sentido; sentimiento; sensación; juicio, sensatez; significado; **common —** sentido común; **to make — tener** sentido; **to be out of one's -s** estar fuera de sí, estar loco; *v.* percibir, sentir; darse cuenta de.

senseless [sénslɪs] *adj.* sin sentido; insensato, absurdo; insensible, privado de sentido.

sensibility [sɛnsəbflətɪ] *s.* sensibilidad.

sensible [sénsəbl] *adj.* sensato, razonable, cuerdo; sensible, perceptible; **sensibly** *adv.* sensatamente, con sensatez, con sentido común; sensiblemente, perceptiblemente.

sensitive [sénsətɪv] *adj.* sensitivo; sensible; quisquilloso, susceptible.

sensitiveness [sénsətɪvnɪs] *s.* sensibilidad.

sensual [sénʃuəl] *adj.* sensual, carnal, lujurioso.

sensuality [sɛnʃʊælətɪ] *s.* sensualidad; lujuria.

sent [sent] *pret. & p.p. de* **to send.**

sentence [séntəns] *s.* sentencia, fallo, decisión; oración (*gramatical*); **death — pena capital;** *v.* sentenciar.

sentiment [séntəmənt] *s.* sentimiento; sentido.

sentimental [sentəméntl] *adj.* sentimental.

sentimentality [sentəmentǽlətɪ] *s.* sentimentalismo, sentimentalidad.

sentinel [séntənl] *s.* centinela.

sentry [séntrɪ] *s.* centinela.

separate [sépɪt] *adj.* separado; apartado, solitario; distinto, diferente; **-ly** *adv.* separadamente, por separado; aparte; [sépəret] *v.* separar(se); apartar(se).

separation [sepəréʃən] *s.* separación.

September [septémbə] *s.* septiembre.

sepulcher [sépḷkə] *s.* sepulcro, sepultura.

sequel [sɪkwəl] *s.* secuela; continuación, consecuencia; resultado.

sequence [sɪkwəns] *s.* secuencia, sucesión; serie, continuación; consecuencia, resultado; runfla (*serie de tres o más naipes de un mismo palo*).

serenade [serənéd] *s.* serenata; *v.* dar serenata a.

serene [sərín] *adj.* sereno; tranquilo; claro, despejado.

serenity [sɪrénətɪ] *s.* serenidad; calma.

sergeant [sárdʒənt] *s.* sargento; **— at arms** oficial que guarda el orden (*en un cuerpo legislativo*).

serial [sɪrɪəl] *s.* cuento o novela por entregas; *adj.* consecutivo, en serie; **— novel** novela por entregas.

series [sɪrɪz] *s.* serie; series.

serious [sɪrɪəs] *adj.* serio; grave; **-ly** *adv.* seriamente, con seriedad, en serio; gravemente.

seriousness [sɪrɪəsnɪs] *s.* seriedad; gravedad.

sermon [sɜ́mən] *s.* sermón.

serpent [sɜ́pənt] *s.* serpiente; sierpe.

serum [sɪrəm] *s.* suero.

servant [sɜ́vənt] *s.* sirviente; criado; servidor; **— girl** criada, *Am.* mucama.

serve [sɜv] *v.* servir; surtir, abastecer; **to — a term in prison** cumplir una condena; **to — a warrant** entregar una citación; **to — as** servir de; **to — for** servir de, servir para; **to — notice on** notificar, avisar, advertir; **to — one's purpose** servir para el caso o propósito; **it -s me right** bien me lo merezco; *s.* saque (*de la pelota en tenis*).

server [sɜ́və] *s.* servidor; saque (*el que saca la pelota en el juego de tenis*); bandeja; mesa de servicio.

service [sɜ́vɪs] *s.* servicio; saque (*de la pelota en tenis*); entrega (*de una citación judicial*); **at your — a** la disposición de Vd., servidor de Vd.; **funeral — honras fúnebres, funerales, exequias; mail — servicio de correos; table — servicio de mesa, vajilla; tea — juego o servicio de té; — entrance** entrada para el servicio; **— man** militar; **— station** estación de servicio; *v.* servir; reparar; surtir (*una tienda*).

serviceable [sɜ́vɪsəbḷ] *adj.* servible; útil; duradero.

servile [sɜ́vḷ] *adj.* servil.

servitude [sɜ́vətjud] *s.* servidumbre; esclavitud.

session [séʃən] *s.* sesión.

set [set] *v.* poner; colocar, asentar; fijar; establecer; ajustar; engastar (*piedras preciosas*); solidificar(se), endurecer(se) (*el cemento, yeso, etc.*); ponerse (*el sol, la luna*); empollar; **to — a bone** componer un hueso dislocado; **to — a trap** armar una trampa; **to — about** ponerse a; **to — an example** dar ejemplo; **to — aside** poner a un lado, poner aparte; apartar; ahorrar; **to — back** retrasar, atrasar; **to — forth** exponer, expresar; manifestar; **to — forth on a journey** ponerse en camino; **to — off** disparar, hacer estallar (*un explosivo*); hacer resaltar; salir; **to — on fire** pegar o poner fuego a, incendiar; **to — one's jaw** apretar las quijadas; **to — one's heart on** tener la esperanza puesta en; **to — one's mind on** resolverse a, aplicarse a; **to — out for** partir para, salir para; **to — out to** empezar a; **to — right** colocar bien; enderezar; rectificar; **to — sail** hacerse a la vela; **to — the**

191

brake frenar, apretar el freno; **to —
up** erigir, levantar; armar, montar
(*una máquina*); parar (*tipo de imprenta*); establecer, poner (*una tienda,
un negocio*); **to — upon someone**
acometer, asaltar a alguien; *pret. &
p.p. de* **to set**; *adj.* fijo; firme; sólido;
resuelto; rígido; puesto; establecido;
engastado; **— to go** listo para partir;
s. juego, colección; serie; grupo, clase;
partida (*de tenis*); **— of dishes** servicio de mesa, vajilla; **— of teeth**
dentadura; **radio —** radio, radiorre-
ceptor; **tea —** servicio para té.

setback [sétbæk] *s.* atraso, revés, retroceso inesperado.

settee [setí] *s.* canapé.

setting [sétɪŋ] *s.* engaste (*de una joya*);
escena, escenario; puesta (*del sol, de
un astro*); **— sun** sol poniente.

settle [sétl] *v.* colonizar, poblar; estable-
cer(se); fijar(se); asentar(se); arreglar,
poner en orden, ajustar (*cuentas*); zanjar (*una disputa*); pagar, liquidar, saldar; **to — down;** formalizarse; asen-
tarse; calmarse; poner casa; **to — on
a date** fijar o señalar una fecha; **to —
property on** (**upon**) asignar bienes o
propiedad a; **to — the matter** decidir
el asunto, concluir con el asunto.

settlement [sét]mənt] *s.* establecimiento; colonia; poblado; colonización;
asignación o traspaso (*de propiedad*);
ajuste, arreglo; pago; saldo, finiquito,
liquidación; **— house** casa de beneficencia; **marriage —** dote.

settler [sétlə] *s.* colono, poblador; **— of**
disputes zanjador de disputas.

sever [sévə] *v.* desunir(se), partir(se), di-
vidir(se), separar(se); cortar, romper.

several [sévrəl] *adj.* varios, diversos,
distintos, diferentes.

severe [səvír] *adj.* severo; áspero, austero; rígido; riguroso; grave; recio,
fuerte.

severity [səvérətɪ] *s.* severidad; austeridad; rigidez; gravedad; rigor.

sew [so] *v.* coser.

sewer [sjúə] *s.* albañal, cloaca.

sewing [sóɪŋ] *s.* costura; modo de coser;
— machine máquina de coser; **—
room** cuarto de costura.

sewn [son] *p.p. de* **to sew.**

sex [seks] *s.* sexo.

sexton [sékstən] *s.* sacristán.

sexual [sékʃʊəl] *adj.* sexual.

shabby [ʃǽbɪ] *adj.* raído, gastado; andrajoso; mal vestido; vil, injusto; **to treat
someone shabbily** tratar a alguien
injustamente o con menosprecio.

shack [ʃæk] *s.* cabaña, choza, *Am.* bohío,
Am. jacal.

shackle [ʃǽk] *v.* encadenar; trabar,
echar trabas a, poner grillos a; estorbar; **-s** *s. pl.* cadenas, trabas, grillos,
esposas; estorbo.

shade [ʃed] *s.* sombra; tinte, matiz;
visillo, cortinilla; pantalla (*de lámpara*), visera (*para los ojos*); **a —
longer** un poco más largo; **— of
meaning** matiz; **in the — of** a la
sombra de; *v.* sombrear; dar sombra;
resguardar de la luz; matizar.

shadow [ʃǽdo] *s.* sombra; obscuridad,
espectro; **under the —** al abrigo
de, a la sombra de; **without a — of
doubt** sin sombra de duda; *v.* sombrear; obscurecer; **to — someone**
espiarle a alguien los pasos, seguirle
por todas partes.

shadowy [ʃǽdəwɪ] *adj.* lleno de sombras;
tenebroso; vago, indistinto.

shady [ʃédɪ] *adj.* sombrío, sombreado,
umbrío; **— business** negocio sospechoso; **— character** persona de carácter dudoso, persona de mala fama.

shaft [ʃæft] *s.* pozo o tiro (*de mina, de
elevador*); cañón de chimenea; columna; eje, árbol (*de maquinaria*); flecha.

shaggy [ʃǽgɪ] *adj.* peludo, velludo; lanudo; desaseado; áspero.

shake [ʃek] *v.* menear(se); estremecer-
(se); temblar; sacudir(se); agitar(se);
titubear, vacilar; hacer vacilar; dar,
estrechar (*la mano*); **to — hands** dar
un apretón de manos, darse la mano;
to — one's head mover o menear
la cabeza; cabecear, **to — with cold**
tiritar de frío, estremecerse de frío;
to — with fear temblar de miedo,
estremecerse de miedo; *s.* sacudida,
sacudimiento; estremecimiento; temblor, apretón (*de manos*); **hand—**
apretón de manos.

shaken [ʃékən] *p.p. de* **to shake.**

shaky [ʃékɪ] *adj.* tembloroso; vacilante.

shall [ʃæl] *v. aux. del futuro del indicativo
en las primeras personas* (**I, we**); *en
las demás expresa mayor énfasis, mandato u obligación,* **he — not ¹do it**
no lo hará, no ha de hacerlo; **thou
shalt not steal** no hurtarás.

shallow [ʃǽlo] *adj.* bajo, poco profundo;
superficial; ligero de cascos.

shallowness [ʃǽlonɪs] *s.* poca hondura,
poca profundidad; superficialidad; ligereza de juicio.

sham [ʃæm] *s.* fingimiento, falsedad,
farsa; *adj.* fingido, simulado; falso; **—
battle** simulacro, batalla fingida; *v.*

fingir, simular.

shame [ʃem] s. vergüenza; deshonra; — **on you!** ¡qué vergüenza!; **it is a** — es una vergüenza; es una lástima; **to bring** — **upon** deshonrar; v. àvergonzar; deshonrar.

shameful [ʃémfəl] adj. vergonzoso.

shameless [ʃémlɪs] adj. desvergonzado, descarado.

shamelessness [ʃémlɪsnɪs] s. desvergüenza; descaro, desfachatez.

shampoo [ʃæmpú] s. champú, lavado de la cabeza; v. dar un champú, lavar (la cabeza).

shamrock [ʃǽmrɑk] s. trébol.

shank [ʃæŋk] s. canilla (parte inferior de la pierna); zanca.

shanty [ʃǽntɪ] s. choza, cabaña, casucha.

shape [ʃep] s. forma; figura; estado, condición; **to be in a bad** — estar mal; **to put into** — arreglar, poner en orden, ordenar; v. formar, dar forma a; tomar forma; **to** — **one's life** dar forma a, ajustar o disponer su vida; **his plan is shaping well** va desarrollándose bien su plan.

shapeless [ʃéplɪs] adj. informe, sin forma.

share [ʃɛr] s. porción, parte; participación; acción (participación en el capital de una compañía); v. compartir; repartir; participar; **to** — **in** participar en, tener parte en; **to** — **a thing with** compartir una cosa con.

shareholder [ʃérholdə] s. accionista.

shark [ʃɑrk] s. tiburón; estafador; perito, experto; **loan** — usurero; **to be a** — **at** ser un águila (o ser muy listo) para.

sharp [ʃɑrp] adj. agudo; puntiagudo: cortante; punzante; mordaz; picante; astuto; claro, distinto, bien marcado; repentino; — **curve** curva abrupta, curva pronunciada o muy cerrada; — **ear** oídofino;—**features** facciones bien marcadas; — **struggle** lucha violenta; — **taste** sabor acre; — **temper** genio áspero; — **turn** vuelta repentina; s. sostenido (en música); **card**— tahur, fullero; adv. véase **sharply**; **at ten o'clock** — a las diez en punto.

sharpen [ʃárpən] v. afilar(se); sacar punta a; aguzar(se); amolar.

sharply [ʃárplɪ] adv. agudamente; mordazmente, ásperamente; repentinamente; claramente; **to arrive** — llegar en punto.

sharpness [ʃárpnɪs] s. agudeza; sutileza; mordacidad; rigor; aspereza; acidez.

shatter [ʃǽtə] v. estrellar(se), astillar(se), hacer(se) añicos; quebrar(se), romper(se); **to** — **one's hopes** frustrar

sus esperanzas; **his health was** -**ed** se le quebrantó la salud; -**s** s. pl. pedazos, trozos, añicos, fragmentos; **to break into** — hacer(se) añicos.

shave [ʃev] v. afeitar(se), rasurar(se); rapar(se); acepillar (madera); s. rasura, Am. afeitada; **he had a close** — por poco no se escapa; se salvó por milagro.

shaven [ʃévən] p.p. de to **shave**; **clean-shaven** bien afeitado.

shaving [ʃévɪŋ] s. rasura, Am. afeitada; — **wood** -**s** virutas; — **brush** brocha de afeitar; — **soap** jabón de afeitar.

shawl [ʃɔl] s. mantón, chal.

she [ʃi] pron. pers. ella; — **who** la que; s. hembra; **she-bear** osa; **she-goat** cabra.

sheaf [ʃif] s. haz, gavilla, manojo; lío; v. hacer gavillas.

shear [ʃɪr] v. trasquilar, esquilar (las ovejas); cortar (con tijeras grandes).

shears [ʃɪrz] s. pl. tijeras grandes.

sheath [ʃie] s. vaina; funda, envoltura.

sheathe [ʃið] v. envainar.

sheaves [ʃivz] pl. de **sheaf**.

shed [ʃed] s. cobertizo; tejadillo; Am. galpón (de una estancia); v. derramar; difundir; esparcir; mudar (de piel, plumas, etc.); ser impermeable (un paño, abrigo, sombrero, etc.); **to** — **leaves** deshojarse; pret. & p.p. de **to shed**.

sheen [ʃin] s. lustre, viso.

sheep [ʃip] s. oveja; carnero; ovejas; — **dog** perro de pastor; —**fold** redil; —**skin** zalea; badana; pergamino; diploma (de pergamino).

sheepish [ʃípɪʃ] adj. vergonzoso, encogido, tímido.

sheer [ʃɪr] adj. puro; completo; fino, delgado, transparente, diáfano; escarpado, cortado a pico; **by** — **force** a pura fuerza.

sheet [ʃit] s. sábana; hoja, pliego (de papel); lámina (de metal); extensión (de agua, hielo); — **lightning** relampagueo.

shelf [ʃelf] s. estante, anaquel; repisa; saliente de roca.

shell [ʃel] s. concha; cáscara (de huevo, nuez, etc.); vaina (de guisantes, frijoles, garbanzos, etc.); casco (de una embarcación); armazón (de un edificio); granada, bomba; cápsula (para cartuchos); v. cascar (nueces); desvainar, quitar la vaina a, pelar; desgranar (maíz, trigo, etc.); bombardear.

shellac [ʃəlǽk] s. laca; v. barnizar con laca.

shellfish [ʃélfɪʃ] s. marisco; mariscos.

shelter [ʃéltə] s. abrigo, refugio, asilo;

resguardo, protección; **to take** — refugiarse, abrigarse; v. abrigar, refugiar, guarecer; proteger, amparar.

shelve [ʃelv] v. poner o guardar en un estante; poner a un lado, arrinconar, arrumbar.

shelves [ʃelvz] s. pl. estantes, anaqueles; estantería.

shepherd [ʃépəd] s. pastor; zagal; — **dog** perro de pastor.

sherbet [ʃə́bɪt] s. sorbete.

sheriff [ʃérɪf] s. alguacil mayor (de un condado en los Estados Unidos).

sherry [ʃérɪ] s. jerez, vino de Jerez.

shield [ʃild] s. escudo, rodela, broquel; resguardo, defensa; v. escudar, resguardar, proteger.

shift [ʃɪft] v. cambiar; mudar(se); alternar(se); variar; desviar(se); trasladar, transferir; **to** — **for oneself** valerse o mirar por sí mismo; **to** — **gears** cambiar de marcha; **to** — **the blame** echar a otro su propia culpa; s. cambio; desvío, desviación; tanda, grupo de obreros; turno; **gear** — cambio de marcha.

shiftless [ʃíftlɪs] adj. negligente; holgazán.

shilling [ʃílɪŋ] s. chelín.

shin [ʃɪn] s. espinilla (de la pierna); v. **to** — **up** trepar.

shine [ʃaɪn] v. brillar, resplandecer, lucir; pulir; dar brillo, lustre o bola, embolar (zapatos); s. brillo, lustre, resplandor; **rain or** — llueva o truene; **to give a shoe** — dar bola (brillo o lustre) a los zapatos; embolar o embetunar los zapatos; limpiar el calzado.

shingle [ʃíŋgl] s. ripia, tabla delgada, Am. tejamanil o tejamaní; pelo corto escalonado; letrero de oficina; **-s** zona (erupción de la piel); v. cubrir con tejamaniles; techar con tejamaniles.

shining [ʃáɪnɪŋ] adj. brillante; resplandeciente.

shiny [ʃáɪnɪ] adj. brillante; lustroso.

ship [ʃɪp] s. buque, barco, navío, nave; aeronave, avión; —**builder** ingeniero naval, constructor de buques; —**mate** camarada de a bordo; —**yard** astillero; **on** —**board** a bordo; v. embarcar(se); despachar, enviar; remesar; transportar; alistarse como marino.

shipment [ʃípmənt] s. embarque; cargamento; despacho, envío; remesa.

shipper [ʃípə] s. embarcador; remitente.

shipping [ʃípɪŋ] s. embarque; despacho, envío; —**charges** gastos de embarque; —**clerk** dependiente de muelle; dependiente encargado de embarques.

shipwreck [ʃíprek] s. naufragio; v. echar a pique, hacer naufragar; naufragar, irse a pique.

shirk [ʃɜk] v. evadir, evitar.

shirt [ʃɜt] s. camisa; —**waist** blusa; **in** — **sleeves** en camisa, en mangas de camisa.

shiver [ʃívə] v. tiritar; temblar; estremecerse; s. escalofrío, temblor, estremecimiento.

shoal [ʃol] s. bajío, banco de arena; banco (de peces).

shock [ʃak] s. choque; sacudida; sacudimiento; golpe; sobresalto; — **absorber** amortiguador; — **of grain** hacina o gavilla de mieses; — **of hair** guedeja, greña; — **troops** tropas de asalto; v. chocar, ofender; escandalizar; causar fuerte impresión; horrorizar; sacudir; conmover; hacinar, hacer gavillas de (mieses).

shocking [ʃákɪŋ] adj. chocante, ofensivo, repugnante; espantoso, escandaloso.

shod [ʃad] pret. & p.p. de **to shoe**.

shoe [ʃu] s. zapato; botín; **brake** — zapata de freno; **horse**— herradura; — **blacking** betún, bola; — polish brillo, lustre, bola; — **store** zapatería, Am. peletería; v. calzar; herrar (un caballo).

shoeblack [ʃúblæk] s. limpiabotas.

shoehorn [ʃúhɔrn] s. calzador.

shoelace [ʃúles] s. lazo, cinta, cordón de zapato.

shoemaker [ʃúmekə] s. zapatero.

shoestring [ʃústrɪŋ] s. lazo, cinta, cordón de zapato.

shone [ʃon] pret. & p.p. de **to shine**.

shook [ʃuk] pret. de **to shake**.

shoot [ʃut] v. tirar, disparar, descargar; hacer fuego; fusilar; dar un balazo; lanzar; disparar (una instantánea); fotografiar, filmar (una escena); echar (los dados); brotar (las plantas); **to** — **by** pasar rápidamente; **to** — **forth** brotar, salir; germinar; lanzarse; **to** — **it out with someone** pelearse a balazos; **to** — **up a place** entrarse a balazos por un lugar; s. vástago, retoño, renuevo; **to go out for a** — salir a tirar; ir de caza.

shooter [ʃútə] s. tirador.

shooting [ʃútɪŋ] s. tiroteo; — **match** certamen de tiradores (o de tiro al blanco); — **pain** punzada, dolor agudo; — **star** estrella fugaz.

shop [ʃap] s. tienda; taller; —**window** escaparate, vitrina, aparador, Am. vidriera; **barber**— barbería; **beauty** — salón de belleza; **to talk** — hablar uno de su oficio o profesión; *v.* ir de tiendas; ir de compras, comprar.

shopkeeper [ʃápkipə] *s.* tendero.

shopper [ʃápə] *s.* comprador.

shopping [ʃápiŋ] *s.* compra, compras; **to go —** ir de compras, ir de tiendas.

shore [ʃor] *s.* costa, playa, orilla, ribera; puntal; **ten miles off —** a diez millas de la costa; *v.* **to — up** apuntalar, poner puntales.

shorn [ʃorn] *p.p.* de **to shear.**

short [ʃɔrt] *adj.* corto; breve; bajo, *Am.* chaparro; escaso; brusco; **— cut** atajo; método corto; **short-legged** de piernas cortas; **— loan** préstamo a corto plazo; **for —** para abreviar; **in —** en resumen, en suma, en conclusión; **in — order** rápidamente, prontamente; **in a — time** en poco tiempo; al poco tiempo; **to be —** of estar falto o escaso de; **to cut —** acortar, abreviar, terminar de repente; **to run —** of something acabársele (írsele acabando) a uno algo; **to stop —** parar de repente, parar en seco.

shortage [ʃɔrtidʒ] *s.* escasez, carestía; déficit; falta.

shortcoming [ʃɔrtkʌmiŋ] *s.* falta, defecto.

shorten [ʃɔrtn] *v.* acortar(se), abreviar(se), disminuir(se).

shortening [ʃɔrtniŋ] *s.* manteca, grasa (*para hacer pasteles*); acortamiento; abreviación.

shorthand [ʃɔrthænd] *s.* taquigrafía.

shortly [ʃɔrtli] *adv.* brevemente; en breve; al instante, pronto, luego; bruscamente, secamente.

shortness [ʃɔrtnis] *s.* cortedad; brevedad; pequeñez; escasez, deficiencia.

shorts [ʃɔrts] *s. pl.* calzoncillos, calzones cortos.

shortsighted [ʃɔrtsáitid] *adj.* miope; corto de vista.

shot [ʃat] *pret. & p.p.* de **to shoot;** *s.* tiro; disparo; balazo; cañonazo; bala; balas; inyección; tirada (*en ciertos juegos*); **— of liquor** trago de aguardiente; **buck—** municiones, postas; **not by a long —** ni con mucho, ni por pienso, nada de eso; **he is a good —** es buen tirador, tiene buen tino; **to take a — at** disparar un tiro a; hacer una tentativa de; **within rifle —** a tiro de rifle.

shotgun [ʃátgʌn] *s.* escopeta.

should [ʃud] *v. aux.* del *condicional en las primeras personas* (I, we) : **I said that I — go** dije que iría; *equivale al imperfecto de subjuntivo:* **if it — rain**

si lloviera; *se usa con la significación de deber:* **you — not do it** no debiera (o no debería) hacerlo.

shoulder [ʃóldə] *s.* hombro; lomo, pernil (*de puerco, cordero*); borde, saliente (*de un camino*); **-s** espalda, espaldas; **— blade** espaldilla, paletilla; **straight from the —** con toda franqueza; **to turn a cold —** to volver las espaldas a, tratar fríamente; *v.* cargar al hombro, echarse sobre las espaldas; cargar con, asumir; empujar con el hombro.

shout [ʃaut] *v.* gritar; vocear; *s.* grito.

shove [ʃʌv] *v.* empujar, dar empellones; **to — aside** echar a un lado, rechazar; **to — off** partir, zarpar (*un buque*); salir, irse; *s.* empujón, empellón; empuje.

shovel [ʃʌvl] *s.* pala; *v.* traspalar.

show [ʃo] *v.* mostrar; enseñar; exhibir; probar, demostrar; indicar; verse; asomarse; **— him in** que pase, hágale entrar; **to — off** alardear, hacer ostentación de; lucirse; **to — up** aparecer, presentarse; **to — someone up** hacer subir a alguien; mostrarle el camino (*para subir*); desenmascarar a alguien, poner a alguien en la evidencia; *s.* exhibición; demostración; ostentación; espectáculo; representación, función; apariencia; **— window** escaparate, vitrina, aparador, *Am.* vidriera; **to go to the —** ir al teatro, ir al cine; **to make a — of oneself** exhibirse, hacer ostentación.

showcase [ʃókes] *s.* vitrina, aparador.

shower [ʃáuə] *s.* aguacero, chubasco, chaparrón, lluvia; ducha, baño de ducha; **bridal —** tertulia para obsequiar a una novia; *v.* llover; caer un aguacero.

shown [ʃon] *p.p.* de **to show.**

showy [ʃói] *adj.* ostentoso; vistoso; chillón.

shrank [ʃræŋk] *pret.* de **to shrink.**

shred [ʃred] *s.* tira, triza; andrajo; fragmento; pizca; **to be in -s** estar raído; estar andrajoso; estar hecho trizas; **to tear to -s** hacer trizas; *v.* desmenuzar; hacer trizas, hacer tiras; *pret. & p.p. de* **to shred.**

shrew [ʃru] *s.* arpía, mujer brava, mujer de mal genio.

shrewd [ʃrud] *adj.* astuto, sagaz, agudo.

shriek [ʃrik] *v.* chillar, gritar; *s.* chillido, grito.

shrill [ʃril] *adj.* agudo, penetrante, chillón; *v.* chillar.

shrimp [ʃrimp] *s.* camarón; hombrecillo insignificante.

195

shrine [ʃraɪn] s. santuário; altar; lugar venerado.

shrink [ʃrɪŋk] v. encoger(se); contraer-(se); disminuir; **to — back** retroceder; **to — from** retroceder ante, apartarse de; huir de, rehuir.

shrinkage [ʃrínkɪdʒ] s. encogimiento; contracción; merma.

shrivel [ʃrívl] v. encoger(se); fruncir(se), marchitar(se); disminuir(se).

shroud [ʃraʊd] s. mortaja; v. amortajar; cubrir, ocultar.

shrub [ʃrʌb] s. arbusto.

shrubbery [ʃrʌ́bərɪ] s. arbustos.

shrug [ʃrʌg] v. encogerse de hombros; s. encogimiento de hombros.

shrunk [ʃrʌŋk] pret. & p.p. de to shrink.

shrunken [ʃrʌ́ŋkən] p.p. de to shrink.

shudder [ʃʌ́də] v. temblar, estremecerse; s. temblor, estremecimiento.

shuffle [ʃʌ́fl] v. barajar; revolver, mezclar; arrastrar (los pies); **to — along** ir arrastrando los pies; s. mezcla, confusión; evasiva; **— of feet** arrastramiento de pies; **it is your — a** Vd. le toca barajar.

shun [ʃʌn] v. esquivar, evadir, rehuir, evitar.

shut [ʃʌt] v. cerrar(se); **to — down** parar el trabajo; cerrar (una fábrica); **to — in** encerrar; **to — off** cortar (el gas, la electricidad, el agua, etc.); **to — off from** incomunicar, aislar de, cortar la comunicación con; excluir; **to — out** impedir la entrada de; cerrar la puerta a; **to — up** cerrar bien; tapar; encerrar; tapar la boca, hacer callar; callarse; pret. & p.p. de **to shut**; adj. cerrado.

shutter [ʃʌ́tə] s. contraventana; postigo (de ventana); cerrador; obturador (de una cámara fotográfica).

shuttle [ʃʌ́tl] s. lanzadera; v. ir y venir acompasadamente (como una lanzadera).

shy [ʃaɪ] adj. tímido, apocado, vergonzoso; asustadizo; esquivo; **to be — on** estar escaso de; **to be — two cents** fáltarle a uno dos centavos; v. esquivarse, hacerse a un lado; asustarse; **to — at something** retroceder ante algo; respingar (un caballo) al ver algo; espantarse con algo; **to — away** esquivarse de repente; respingar (un caballo); desviarse, apartarse.

shyness [ʃáɪnɪs] s. apocamiento, timidez, vergüenza.

shyster [ʃáɪstə] s. leguleyo, abogadillo tramposo, picapleitos.

sick [sɪk] adj. enfermo, malo; nauseado;

angustiado; **— leave** licencia por enfermedad; **to be — for** languidecer por, suspirar por; **to be — of** estar cansado de; estar harto de; **to be — to** (o at) one's stomach tener náuseas; **to make —** enfermar; dar pena, dar lástima; s. **the —** los enfermos; v. incitar, azuzar (a un perro) **— him** ¡síguele!

sicken [sɪ́kən] v. enfermar(se), poner(se) enfermo; dar asco; tener asco; sentir náuseas.

sickening [síkniŋ] adj. nauseabundo, repugnante; lastimoso.

sickle [sɪ́kl] s. hoz.

sickly [sɪ́klɪ] adj. enfermizo; achacoso, enclenque; malsano.

sickness [sɪ́knɪs] s. enfermedad; malestar; náusea.

side [saɪd] s. lado; cara; costado; ladera, falda (de una colina); partido, facción; **— by — lado a lado; by his — a su** lado; **by the — of** al lado de; **on all -s** por todos lados; **to take -s with** ser partidario de, ponerse al lado de; adj. lateral; de lado; oblicuo; incidental; secundario, de menos importancia; **— glance** mirada de soslayo, de través o de reojo; **— issue** cuestión secundaria; **— light** luz lateral; noticia, detalle o ilustración incidental; **v. to — with** estar por, ser partidario de, apoyar a, opinar con.

sideboard [sáɪdbɔrd] s. aparador.

sidetrack [sáɪdtræk] v. desviar; echar a un lado.

sidewalk [sáɪdwɔk] s. acera, Am. banqueta, Am. vereda.

sideways [sáɪdwez] adv. de lado, de costado; oblicuamente; hacia un lado; adj. lateral, de lado, oblicuo.

siege [sidʒ] s. cerco, sitio, asedio; **to lay — to** sitiar, cercar.

sieve [sɪv] s. tamiz, cedazo; criba; v. véase **sift**.

sift [sɪft] v. cerner, tamizar; cribar.

sigh [saɪ] v. suspirar; s. suspiro.

sight [saɪt] s. vista; visión; espectáculo, escena; mira (de un arma de fuego); **in — of** a vista de; **payable at —** pagadero a la vista; **he is a —** es un adefesio o mamarracho; **this room is a —** este cuarto es un horror; **to catch — of** vislumbrar, avistar; **to know by — conocer de vista; to lose — of** perder de vista; **to see the -s** ver o visitar los puntos de interés; v. avistar; ver.

sightseeing [sáɪtsiŋ] s. turismo; **— tour** paseo en auto para ver puntos de interés.

196

sign [saɪn] *s.* signo; seña, señal; muestra, letrero; —**board** cartel; tablero (*para fijar anuncios*); *v.* firmar; contratar, hacer firmar; **to — over property** ceder una propiedad mediante escritura, hacer cesión legal de propiedad; **to — up for a job** firmar el contrato para un empleo; contratar para un empleo.

signal [sígnl] *s.* señal, seña; *v.* señalar, indicar, hacer seña, dar la señal; *adj.* señalado, notable; extraordinario; — **beacon** faro; — **code** código de señales.

signature [sígnətʃə] *s.* firma.

signer [sáɪnə] *s.* firmante.

significance [sɪgnífəkəns] *s.* significación; significado.

significant [sɪgnífəkənt] *adj.* significativo.

signify [sígnəfaɪ] *v.* significar.

silence [sáɪləns] *s.* silencio; *v.* acallar; apagar (*un sonido*); aquietar, sosegar.

silent [sáɪlənt] *adj.* silencioso; callado; tácito; — **partner** socio comanditario (*que no tiene voz ni voto*).

silhouette [sɪluét] *s.* silueta; *v.* perfilar; **to be -d against** perfilarse contra.

silk [sɪlk] *s.* seda; *adj.* de seda; — **industry** industria sedera; — **ribbon** cinta de seda.

silken [sɪlkən] *adj.* sedoso; de seda.

silkworm [sɪlkwɜm] *s.* gusano de seda.

silky [sɪlkɪ] *adj.* sedoso, sedeño; de seda.

sill [sɪl] *s.* umbral; **window —** antepecho de ventana.

silly [sɪlɪ] *adj.* necio, tonto, bobo, simple; absurdo, insensato.

silver [sɪlvə] *s.* plata; vajilla de plata; color de plata; *adj.* de plata; plateado; argentino; — **wedding** bodas de plata; *v.* platear; argentar; **to — a mirror** azogar un espejo.

silversmith [sɪlvəsmɪθ] *s.* platero.

silverware [sɪlvəwɛr] *s.* vajilla de plata, vajilla plateada; cuchillos, cucharas y tenedores (*por lo general de plata o plateados*).

silvery [sɪlvərɪ] *adj.* plateado; argentino.

similar [sɪmələ] *adj.* semejante; **-ly** *adv.* semejantemente; de la misma manera.

similarity [sɪmələrətɪ] *s.* semejanza, parecido.

simile [sɪməlɪ] *s.* símil.

simmer [sɪmə] *v.* hervir a fuego lento.

simple [sɪmpl] *adj.* simple; sencillo; llano; tonto, mentecato; **simple-minded** ingenuo, simple, simplón; *s.* simple.

simpleton [sɪmpltən] *s.* simplón, papanatas, papamoscas.

simplicity [sɪmplísətɪ] *s.* sencillez; simplicidad; simpleza; ingenuidad.

simplify [sɪmpləfaɪ] *v.* simplificar.

simply [sɪmplɪ] *adv.* simplemente; sencillamente; solamente.

simultaneous [saɪmˈténɪəs] *adj.* simultáneo.

sin [sɪn] *s.* pecado, culpa; *v.* pecar.

since [sɪns] *conj.* desde que; después (de) que; puesto que, como, visto que; dado que; *prep.* desde, despues de; *adv.* desde entonces; **ever —** desde entonces; **he died long —** murió hace mucho tiempo; **we have been here — five** estamos aquí desde las cinco.

sincere [sɪnsír] *adj.* sincero.

sincerity [sɪnsérətɪ] *s.* sinceridad.

sinecure [sɪnɪkjur] *s.* sinecura (*trabajo fácil y bien pagado*).

sinew [sɪnju] *s.* tendón; fibra, vigor.

sinewy [sɪnjəwɪ] *adj.* nervudo, nervioso o nervoso; fuerte, vigoroso.

sinful [sɪnfəl] *adj.* pecaminoso; pecador.

sing [sɪŋ] *v.* cantar; **to — out of tune** desentonar(se), desafinar; **to — to sleep** arrullar.

singe [sɪndʒ] *v.* chamuscar; *s.* chamusquina, *Am.* chamuscada, *Am.* chamuscadura.

singer [sɪŋə] *s.* cantor; cantora, cantatriz.

single [sɪŋgl] *adj.* solo; individual; particular; soltero; — **entry bookkeeping** teneduría por partida simple; — **room** cuarto para uno; — **woman** mujer soltera; **not a — word** ni una sola palabra; *s.* billete de un dólar; *v.* **to — out** singularizar, distinguir, escoger; entresacar.

singlehanded [sɪŋglhǽndɪd] *adj.* solo, sin ayuda.

singsong [sɪŋsɔŋ] *s.* sonsonete, cadencia monótona.

singular [sɪŋgjələ] *adj.* singular; raro, extraordinario; *s.* singular, número singular.

sinister [sɪnɪstə] *adj.* siniestro, aciago, funesto.

sink [sɪŋk] *v.* hundir(se); sumir(se), sumergir(se); echar a pique; irse a pique, naufragar; cavar (*un pozo*); enterrar, clavar (*un puntal o poste*); **to — into one's mind** grabarse en la memoria; **to — one's teeth into** clavar el diente en; **to — to sleep** caer en el sueño; *s.* sumidero; fregadero.

sinner [sɪnə] *s.* pecador.

sinuous [sɪnjuəs] *adj.* sinuoso, tortuoso; con vueltas y rodeos.

sinus [sáɪnəs] *s.* seno, cavidad (*en un*

hueso); **frontal** — seno frontal.

sip [sɪp] *v.* sorber; chupar; *s.* sorbo.

siphon [sáɪfən] *s.* sifón; *v.* sacar (*agua*) con sifón.

sir [sɜ] *s.* señor.

siren [sáɪrən] *s.* sirena.

sirloin [sɜ́lɔɪn] *s.* solomillo, solomo.

sirup [sírəp] *s.* jarabe.

sissy [sísɪ] *adj.* & *s.* afeminado, maricón.

sister [sístə] *s.* hermana; **Sister Mary** Sor María.

sister-in-law [sístərɪnlɔ] *s.* cuñada, hermana política.

sit [sɪt] *v.* sentar(se); colocar, asentar; posarse (*un pájaro*); estar sentado; estar situado; empollar (*las gallinas*); apoyarse; reunirse, celebrar sesión (*un cuerpo legislativo, un tribunal*); sentar, venir o caer (*bien o mal un traje*); **to — down** sentarse; **to — out a dance** quedarse sentado durante una pieza de baile; **to — still** estarse quieto; **to — tight** mantenerse firme en su puesto; **to — up** incorporarse; **to — up all night** velar toda la noche; **to — up and take notice** despabilarse.

site [saɪt] *s.* sitio, local, situación.

sitting [sítɪŋ] *s.* sesión (*de un cuerpo legislativo, tribunal, etc.*); sentada; **at one** — de una sentada; *adj.* sentado; **— hen** gallina ponedora; **— room** sala (de descanso); sala de espera; antesala.

situated [sítʃvetɪd] *adj.* situado, sito, ubicado, colocado.

situation [sɪtʃuéʃən] *s.* situación; colocación, empleo; posición.

size [saɪz] *s.* tamaño; medida; *v.* clasificar según el tamaño; **to — up** tantear, formarse una idea de, juzgar.

sizzle [sízl] *v.* chirriar (*aplícase al sonido que hace la carne al freírse*); *s.* chirrido (*de la carne al freírse*).

skate [sket] *s.* patín; **ice** — patín de hielo, patín de cuchilla; **roller** — patín de ruedas; *v.* patinar.

skein [sken] *s.* madeja.

skeleton [skélətn] *s.* esqueleto; armazón; **— key** llave maestra.

skeptic = sceptic.

sketch [sketʃ] *s.* boceto; diseño; croquis, esbozo; *v.* bosquejar; delinear; esbozar, dibujar.

ski [ski] *s.* esquí; *v.* esquiar, patinar con esquís.

skid [skɪd] *v.* patinar, resbalar(se); patinar (*una rueda*); deslizarse.

skill [skɪl] *s.* destreza, maña, habilidad, pericia.

skilled [skɪld] *adj.* experto, práctico, ex-

perimentado, hábil.

skillet [skɪlɪt] *s.* sartén; cacerola.

skillful, skilful [skílfəl] *adj.* experto, diestro, ducho, hábil, perito.

skim [skɪm] *v.* desnatar, quitar la nata a; espumar, quitar la espuma a; leer superficialmente; **to — over the surface** rozar la superficie.

skimp [skɪmp] *v.* escatimar; economizar; ser tacaño; hacer (*las cosas*) con descuido.

skimpy [skímpɪ] *adj.* escaso; tacaño.

skin [skɪn] *s.* piel; cutis; pellejo; cuero; cáscara, hollejo; **to save one's** — salvar el pellejo; **skin-deep** superficial; *v.* desollar; pelar; **to — someone (out of his money)** desplumar a una persona, quitarle a uno el dinero.

skinny [skínɪ] *adj.* flaco; descarnado.

skip [skɪp] *v.* saltar; brincar; saltarse (*unos renglones, un párrafo, etc.*), omitir; saltar por encima de, salvar de un brinco; **to — out** salir a escape, escabullirse, escaparse; *s.* salto, brinco; omisión.

skipper [skípə] *s.* patrón (*de barco*); capitán; saltador, brincador.

skirmish [skɜ́mɪʃ] *s.* escaramuza; *v.* escaramuzar, sostener una escaramuza.

skirt [skɜt] *s.* falda, *Am.* pollera; orilla, borde; **under—** enaguas; *v.* bordear, orillar, ir por la orilla de; circundar; **to — along a coast** costear.

skit [skɪt] *s.* parodia, juguete o paso cómico; boceto satírico o burlesco.

skull [skʌl] *s.* cráneo; calavera.

skunk [skʌŋk] *s. Am.* zorrillo o zorrino, *Am.* mapurite.

sky [skaɪ] *s.* cielo; **— blue** azul celeste.

skylark [skáɪlark] *s.* alondra, calandria.

skylight [skáɪlaɪt] *s.* claraboya, tragaluz.

skyrocket [skáɪrakɪt] *s.* cohete.

skyscraper [skáɪskrepə] *s.* rascacielos.

slab [slæb] *s.* tabla, plancha, losa; tajada gruesa; **marble** — losa de mármol.

slack [slæk] *adj.* flojo; tardo, lento; inactivo; **— season** temporada inactiva; *s.* flojedad, flojera; inactividad; **to take up the** — apretar, estirar; **-s** pantalones anchos con pliegues, *v.* véase **slacken**.

slacken [slákən] *v.* aflojar(se); flojear; retardar(se); disminuir.

slag [slæg] *s.* escoria.

slain [slen] *p.p. de* **to slay.**

slam [slæm] *v.* cerrar(se) de golpe; dejar caer de golpe; **to — someone** decirle a alguien una claridad o grosería; **to — the door** dar un portazo; *s.* golpazo; claridad, grosería; **— of a door**

portazo; **to make a grand —** ganar todas las bazas (*en el juego de bridge*).

slander [slǽndə] *s.* calumnia, maledicencia; *v.* calumniar.

slanderous [slǽndərəs] *adj.* calumnioso.

slang [slæŋ] *s.* jerga, jerigonza; vulgarismo.

slant [slænt] *s.* sesgo; inclinación; punto de vista; *adj.* sesgado; inclinado; oblicuo; *v.* sesgar; inclinar(se); ladear.

slap [slæp] *s.* palmada, manazo, manotada; insulto, desaire; *v.* dar una palmada a, dar un manazo a.

slash [slæʃ] *v.* acuchillar; dar cuchilladas o tajos; cortar; hacer fuerte rebaja de (*precios, sueldos*); *s.* cuchillada; tajo, tajada, cortadura.

slat [slæt] *s.* tabla, tablilla.

slate [slet] *s.* pizarra; color de pizarra; lista de candidatos; **— pencil** pizarrín.

slaughter [slɔ́tə] *s.* carnicería, matanza, *Am.* carneada; **—house** matadero, *Am.* matanza; *v.* matar; *Am.* carnear; hacer una matanza; destrozar.

slave [slev] *s.* esclavo; **— driver** capataz de esclavos; persona que agobia de trabajo a otra; **— labor** trabajo de esclavos; trabajadores forzados; *v.* trabajar como esclavo.

slaver [slǽvə] *s.* baba; *v.* babosear, babear.

slavery [slévrɪ] *s.* esclavitud.

slavish [slévɪʃ] *adj.* servil.

slay [sle] *v.* matar.

sled [slɛd] *s.* trineo, rastra.

sleek [slik] *adj.* liso; pulido, resbaloso; suave; artero, mañoso; *v.* alisar; pulir.

sleep [slip] *v.* dormir; **to — it off** dormir la mona; **to — off a headache** curarse con sueño un dolor de cabeza; **to — on it** consultarlo con la almohada; *s.* sueño; **to go to —** dormirse, quedarse dormido; **to put to —** adormecer; arrullar (*al nene*).

sleeper [slípə] *s.* durmiente; coche-cama, coche-dormitorio.

sleepily [slípɪlɪ] *adv.* con somnolencia.

sleepiness [slípɪnɪs] *s.* sueño, modorra, somnolencia.

sleeping [slípɪŋ] *adj.* durmiente; dormido; **— car** coche-cama, coche-dormitorio; **— pills** píldoras para dormir; **— sickness** encefalitis letárgica.

sleepless [slíplɪs] *adj.* desvelado, insomne, sin sueño.

sleepy [slípɪ] *adj.* soñoliento; amodorrado; **to be —** tener sueño.

sleet [slit] *s.* cellisca; *v.* cellisquear.

sleeve [sliv] *s.* manga.

sleigh [sle] *s.* trineo; **— bell** cascabel; *v.* pasearse en trineo.

sleight [slaɪt] : **— of hand** juego de manos; prestidigitación, escamoteo.

slender [sléndə] *adj.* delgado; tenue; escaso, insuficiente.

slept [slɛpt] *pret. & p.p. de* **to sleep.**

sleuth [sluə] *s.* detective (*o* detectivo).

slew [slu] *pret. de* **to slay.**

slice [slaɪs] *s.* rebanada, tajada; lonja; *v.* rebanar, tajar; cortar.

slick [slɪk] *v.* alisar; pulir; **to — up** alisar bien, pulir bien; pulirse, acicalarse, componerse; *adj.* liso; meloso, suave; aceitoso; astuto, mañoso.

slicker [slíkə] *s.* impermeable de hule (*o* de caucho); embaucador.

slid [slɪd] *pret. & p.p. de* **to slide.**

slidden [slídn̩] *p.p. de* **to slide.**

slide [slaɪd] *v.* resbalar(se); deslizar(se); hacer resbalar; patinar; **to — into** meter(se) en; **to — out** (*o* **— away**) deslizarse, colarse, escabullirse, escaparse; **to let something —** dejar pasar algo; no hacer caso de algo; *s.* resbalón; resbaladero, lugar resbaladizo; ligado (*en música*); *véase* **landslide**; **— cover** tapa corrediza; **— rule** regla de cálculo; **microscope —** platina.

slight [slaɪt] *s.* desaire, menosprecio, desdén, desatención; *v.* desairar, menospreciar; descuidar, desatender; *adj.* delgado; delicado; leve, ligero; pequeño; insignificante; escaso; **-ly** *adv.* escasamente; ligeramente; un poco, apenas.

slim [slɪm] *adj.* delgado; esbelto; escaso.

slime [slaɪm] *s.* limo, cieno, fango; baba, secreción viscosa.

slimy [sláɪmɪ] *adj.* viscoso, mucoso, fangoso; baboso.

sling [slɪŋ] *s.* honda (*para tirar piedras*); cabestrillo (*para sostener el brazo*); eslinga (*maroma provista de ganchos para levantar pesos*); **—shot** tirador de goma o hule; *v.* tirar, arrojar; **to — a rifle over one's shoulder** echarse el rifle al hombro.

slink [slɪŋk] *v.* andar furtivamente, **to — away** escurrirse, escabullirse, deslizarse.

slip [slɪp] *v.* deslizar(se); resbalar(se); cometer un desliz; equivocarse; **to — away** escaparse, escabullirse, escurrirse; **to — in** meter(se); **to — one's dress on** ponerse de prisa el vestido; **to — out** salirse; sacar a hurtadillas; **to — out of joint** dislocarse, *Am.* zafarse (*un hueso*); **to — something**

off quitar(se) algo; **to let an opportunity** — dejar pasar una oportunidad; **it slipped my mind so me olvidó, se me pasó; it slipped off se zafó**; s. desliz; resbalón; error, equivocación; funda (de muebles, de almohada); combinación-enagua; pedazo (de papel), papeleta; embarcadero; guía, sarmiento (para transplantar); — **knot** nudo corredizo.

slipper [slípə] s. zapatilla; babucha; pantufla.

slippery [slíprɪ] adj. resbaloso, resbaladizo; evasivo.

slit [slɪt] v. cortar, hacer una rendija, abertura o incisión; **to — into strips** cortar en tiras; pret. & p.p. de to slit; s. abertura, hendedura, rendija; cortada, incisión.

slobber [slábə] s. baba; v. babosear, babear.

slobbering [slábərɪŋ] adj. baboso.

slogan [slógən] s. lema, mote.

sloop [slup] s. chalupa.

slop [slɑp] v. ensuciar, salpicar; derramar(se); s. fango, suciedad; **-s** lavazas, agua sucia; desperdicios.

slope [slop] v. inclinar(se); s. inclinación; declive; falda, ladera; cuesta, bajada; vertiente.

sloppy [slápɪ] adj. puerco, sucio, cochino; desaseado; mal hecho.

slot [slɑt] s. abertura, hendedura, ranura (en que se introduce una moneda); — **machine** máquina automática que funciona por medio de una moneda, "traganíqueles", "tragamonedas"; v. hacer una abertura o hendedura.

sloth [sloθ] s. pereza; perezoso (cuadrúpedo).

slouch [slautʃ] s. persona perezosa o desaseada; postura muy relajada o floja; — **hat** sombrero gacho; **to walk with a —** andar con los hombros caídos y la cabeza inclinada; v. andar agachado; andar caído de hombros; andar alicaído; arrellanarse, repantigarse (en una silla).

slovenliness [slávənlɪnɪs] s. desaseo, desaliño; suciedad.

slovenly [slávənlɪ] adj. desaseado, desaliñado; desarreglado.

slow [slo] adj. lento, despacioso; tardo; atrasado; lerdo, torpe; adv. lentamente, despacio; v. **to — down (o — up)** retardar, disminuir (el paso, la marcha, la velocidad); aflojar el paso; **-ly** adv. despacio, lentamente.

slowness [slónɪs] s. lentitud; torpeza; cachaza.

slug [slʌg] s. bala; porrazo, puñetazo; babosa (molusco sin concha); haragán; trago (de aguardiente); lingote (de imprenta); v. aporrear, abofetear, dar puñetazos.

sluggard [slʌgəd] s. holgazán, haragán.

sluggish [slʌgɪʃ] adj. tardo; inactivo.

sluice [slus] s. compuerta; caño, canal; **—gate** compuerta.

slum [slʌm] s. barrio bajo; v. visitar los barrios bajos.

slumber [slʌmbə] v. dormitar; dormir; s. sueño, sueño ligero.

slump [slʌmp] v. hundirse; desplomarse; bajar repentinamente (los precios o valores); s. desplome, hundimiento, bajón, baja repentina (de precios, valores, etc.).

slung [slʌŋ] pret. & p.p. de to sling.

slunk [slʌŋk] pret. & p.p. de to slink.

slush [slʌʃ] s. nieve a medio derretir; lodazal, fango; sentimentalismo; desperdicios.

sly [slaɪ] adj. astuto, socarrón, zorro, taimado; **on the —** a hurtadillas, a escondidas.

slyness [slaɪnɪs] s. disimulo, astucia.

smack [smæk] s. sabor, dejo; beso ruidoso; chasquido (de látigo); palmada, manotada; **a —** of something una pizca de algo; v. dar un beso ruidoso; chasquear (un látigo); dar un manazo; **to —** of saber a, tener el sabor de; oler a; **to — one's lips** chuparse los labios, saborearse, rechuparse, relamerse.

small [smɔl] adj. pequeño, chico; bajo; insignificante; mezquino; — **change** dinero menudo, suelto; — **hours** primeras horas de la mañana; — **letters** letras minúsculas; — **talk** conversación insubstancial, charladuría; — **voice** vocecita; **to feel —** sentirse pequeño o insignificante.

smallness [smólnɪs] s. pequeñez; bajeza.

smallpox [smólpɑks] s. viruelas.

smart [smart] adj. listo, vivo, inteligente; ladino; astuto; agudo; elegante; — **remark** observación aguda o penetrante; — **set** gente de buen tono; s. escozor, Am. ardor; v. picar, escocer, Am. arder.

smash [smæʃ] v. quebrantar, quebrar; romper; destrozar; aplastar; **to — into** chocar con; topar con, darse un tope contra; s. quebrazón, quiebra; fracaso; choque o tope violento; derrota completa.

smattering [smætərɪŋ] s. conocimiento superficial y rudimental.

smear [smɪr] v. embarrar, untar, manchar; to — with paint pintorrear, pintarrajear; s. mancha.

smell [smel] v. oler; to — of oler a; s. olor; olfato; — of olor a; to take a — oler.

smelly [smέlɪ] adj. oloroso; hediondo.

smelt [smelt] v. fundir (metales); pret. & p.p. de to smell.

smile [smaɪl] v. sonreír(se); s. sonrisa.

smiling [smáɪlɪŋ] adj. risueño, sonriente; -ly adv. sonriendo, con cara risueña.

smite [smaɪt] v. golpear; herir; castigar; afligir; véase smitten.

smith [smɪθ] s. forjador; véase blacksmith, goldsmith, silversmith.

smithy [smɪθɪ] s. herrería, fragua, forja.

smitten [smɪtŋ] p.p. de to smite & adj. afligido; castigado; enamorado; to be — with a disease darle a uno una enfermedad.

smock [smak] s. bata corta, batín.

smoke [smok] s. humo; **cloud of —** humareda; to have a — dar una fumada, fumar; v. fumar, Am. chupar (un cigarro); humear; ahumar; to — out ahuyentar o echar fuera con humo.

smoker [smókə] s. fumador; vagón de fumar; reunión o tertulia de fumadores.

smokestack [smókstæk] s. chimenea.

smoking [smókɪŋ] adj. humeante; de fumar; para fumadores; — car vagón de fumar; — room fumadero, cuarto de fumar.

smoky [smókɪ] adj. humeante; humoso, lleno de humo; ahumado.

smooth [smuð] adj. liso; terso; igual, parejo; plano, llano; suave; tranquilo; sagaz; — disposition genio afable; — manners maneras o modales afables; — style estilo fluido y fácil; — talker hablador melifluo y sagaz; v. alisar; allanar; pulir; emparejar; to — over allanar, alisar, arreglar; -ly adv. suavemente; blandamente; fácilmente, con facilidad.

smoothness [smúðnɪs] s. lisura; igualdad, uniformidad; suavidad; afabilidad; tranquilidad; facilidad, fluidez.

smote [smot] pret. de to smite.

smother [smʌ́ðə] v. ahogar(se); sofocar(se); asfixiar(se).

smudge [smʌdʒ] v. tiznar, manchar o ensuciar con tizne; ahumar; s. tiznón, mancha (hecha con tizne); humareda, nube espesa de humo.

smuggle [smʌ́gl̩] v. contrabandear, hacer contrabando; to — in meter de contrabando; to — out sacar de contra-

bando.

smuggler [smʌ́glə] s. contrabandista.

smut [smʌt] s. tizne; suciedad, mancha; obscenidad, dicho obsceno o indecente; tizón (enfermedad de ciertas plantas); v. tiznar; ensuciar, manchar.

smutty [smʌ́tɪ] adj. tiznado, manchado de tizne; sucio.

snack [snæk] s. bocado, bocadillo, tentempié, bocadito; merienda, comida ligera.

snag [snæg] s. tocón (tronco cortado casi a flor de tierra); raigón; tropiezo, obstáculo; to hit a — tropezar con un obstáculo; v. rasgar; enredar.

snail [snel] s. caracol.

snake [snek] s. culebra, víbora; v. culebrear.

snap [snæp] v. chasquear, dar un chasquido; estallar; quebrar(se); fotografiar instantáneamente; his eyes — le chispean los ojos; to — at echar una mordida o mordisco a; dar una tarascada a, morder; asir (una oportunidad); to — back at tirar una mordida a; dar una respuesta grosera a; to — off soltarse, saltar; quebrar(se); to — one's fingers tronar los dedos, castañetear con los dedos; to — shut cerrar(se) de golpe; to — together apretar, abrochar; to — up agarrar, asir; morder; s. chasquido; estallido; mordida, mordisco, dentellada; broche de presión; energía, vigor; galleta; cosa fácil, ganga; cold — nortazo; repentino descenso de temperatura; not to care a — no importarle a uno un ardite o un comino; adj. hecho de prisa, impensado; instantáneo; — fastener broche de presión; — judgment decisión atolondrada; — lock cerradura de golpe.

snappy [snǽpɪ] adj. mordedor, Am. mordelón; enojadizo, Am. enojón; violento, vivo; elegante; — cheese queso acre o picante; — eyes ojos chispeantes.

snapshot [snǽpʃat] s. instantánea, fotografía instantánea; v. sacar una instantánea.

snare [sner] s. trampa, lazo; acechanza; red; v. enredar; atrapar, coger con trampa; tender lazos a.

snarl [snarl] v. gruñir; enmarañar(se), enredar(se); s. gruñido; maraña, enredo; pelo enmarañado.

snatch [snætʃ] v. arrebatar; agarrar; to — at tratar de asir o agarrar; s. arrebatiña, arrebatamiento; trozo, pedacito; to make a — at tratar de arrebatar, tratar de agarrarse a.

sneak [snik] *v.* andar furtivamente; obrar solapadamente; **to — in** meter(se) a escondidas; colarse; **to — out** escurrirse, salirse a hurtadillas; sacar, llevarse (*algo*) a escondidas; *s.* persona solapada.

sneer [snir] *v.* sonreír con sorna; hacer un gesto de desdén; mofarse; **to — at** mofarse de; *s.* sorna, mofa, rechifla; gesto desdeñoso.

sneeze [sniz] *v.* estornudar; *s.* estornudo.

sniff [snif] *v.* husmear, olfatear; sorber (*por las narices*); resollar para adentro; **to — at** husmear; menospreciar; *s.* husmeo, olfateo; sorbo (*por las narices*).

sniffle [snifl] *v.* sorber por las narices.

snip [snip] *v.* tijeretear; **to — off** cortar de un tijeretazo, recortar; *s.* tijeretada, tijeretazo; pedacito, recorte.

snipe [snaip] *v.* tirar, disparar desde un escondite.

snitch [snitʃ] *v.* arrebatar; ratear; hurtar.

snoop [snup] *v.* fisgar, fisgonear, curiosear; *s.* curioso, fisgón.

snooze [snuz] *v.* dormitar, sestear; *s.* siestecita, siestita; **to take a —** echar un sueñecito o siestita; descabezar el sueño.

snore [snor] *v.* roncar; *s.* ronquido.

snort [snort] *v.* resoplar; bufar; *s.* resoplido, bufido.

snout [snaut] *s.* hocico, jeta.

snow [sno] *s.* nieve; *v.* nevar; **to be -ed under** estar totalmente cubierto por la nevada.

snowball [snóbɔl] *s.* bola de nieve; *v.* tirar bolas de nieve.

snowdrift [snódrift] *s.* ventisca, ventisquero, montón de nieve.

snowfall [snófɔl] *s.* nevada.

snowflake [snóflek] *s.* copo de nieve.

snowstorm [snóstorm] *s.* fuerte nevada, nevasca.

snowy [snói] *adj.* nevado; níveo, blanco como la nieve.

snub [snʌb] *v.* desairar, menospreciar; *s.* desaire; **snub-nosed** chato, *Am.* ñato.

snuff [snʌf] *v.* olfatear, husmear, ventear; aspirar (*por la nariz*); despabilar (*una candela*); **to — at** olfatear, ventear; **to — out** apagar, extinguir; **to — up** sorber (*por las narices*); *s.* sorbo (*por la nariz*); rapé, tabaco en polvo; pabilo, mecha quemada (*de una vela*).

snug [snʌg] *adj.* apretado; ajustado; compacto; abrigado; cómodo.

so [so] *adv.* así; tan, muy; tanto; **so-so** regular; **so-and-so** Fulano (de tal); **— as to** para; **— far** tan lejos; hasta ahora, hasta aquí; **— many** tantos; **— much** tanto; **— much for that** basta por ese lado; **— much the better** tanto mejor; **— that** de modo que; para que; a fin de que; de suerte que; **— then** conque, pues bien, así pues; **and — forth** etcétera; y así sucesivamente; **I believe —** así lo creo; **is that — ?** ¿de veras? ¿de verdad?; ¡no diga!; **ten minutes or —** poco más o menos diez minutos, como diez minutos.

soak [sok] *v.* remojar(se); empapar(se); **to — up** absorber, embeber; chupar; **to be -ed through** estar empapado; estar calado hasta los huesos; *s.* remojo, mojada; borrachín; golpe, puñetazo.

soap [sop] *s.* jabón; **— bubble** pompa de jabón, *Am.* bombita; burbuja de jabón; **— dish** jabonera; **soft —** jabón blando; lisonja, adulación; *v.* enjabonar.

soapy [sópi] *adj.* lleno de jabón.

soar [sor] *v.* remontarse; encumbrarse; subir muy alto; remontar el vuelo.

sob [sab] *v.* sollozar; *s.* sollozo.

sober [sóbə] *adj.* sobrio; moderado, templado; serio, grave; cuerdo, sensato; tranquilo, sereno; **to be —** estar en su juicio; no estar borracho; *v.* **to — down** sosegar(se), calmar(se); formalizarse; **to — up** desembriagarse, desemborracharse; bajársele a uno la borrachera.

soberly [sóbəli] *adv.* sobriamente; cuerdamente, con sensatez; seriamente.

soberness [sóbənis] *s.* sobriedad; seriedad.

sobriety [sɔbráiəti] *s.* sobriedad; cordura.

so-called [sókɔld] *adj.* así llamado, llamado.

sociable [sóʃəbl] *adj.* sociable, social; tratable.

social [sóʃəl] *adj.* social; sociable; tratable, de buen trato; *s.* reunión social; tertulia.

socialism [sóʃəlizəm] *s.* socialismo.

socialist [sóʃəlist] *adj. & s.* socialista.

society [səsáiəti] *s.* sociedad; compañía.

sociology [soʃiálədʒi] *s.* sociología.

sock [sak] *s.* calcetín; porrazo, golpe; *v.* pegar, apalear, golpear; *Am.* batear (*una pelota*).

socket [sákit] *s.* cuenca (*del ojo*); portalámparas, enchufe, *Am.* sóquet.

sod [sad] *s.* césped; terrón (*de tierra*

sembrada de césped); *v.* cubrir de césped.

soda [sódə] *s.* soda, sosa; **— fountain** *Am.* fuente de soda; **— water** agua gaseosa; **baking —** bicarbonato de sodio.

sodium [sódɪəm] *s.* sodio.

sofa [sófə] *s.* sofá.

soft [sɔft] *adj.* blando; muelle; suave; tierno; dulce; **soft-boiled eggs** huevos pasados por agua; **— coal** carbón bituminoso; **— drink** bebida no alcohólica; **— metal** metal dulce, metal maleable; **— soap** jabón blando; adulación; **— water** agua dulce; *adv. véase* **softly.**

soften [sófən] *v.* ablandar(se); suavizar(se); enternecer(se); templar(se); **to — one's voice** bajar la voz, hablar quedo (*o* quedito).

softly [sóftlɪ] *adv.* blandamente; suavemente; quedo, quedito.

softness [sóftnɪs] *s.* blandura; molicie; suavidad; ternura; dulzura.

soil [sɔɪl] *s.* suelo; terreno, tierra; mancha; *v.* ensuciar(se); manchar(se).

sojourn [sódʒɜn] *s.* estada, estancia, permanencia, *Am.* estadía; [sodʒɜ́n] *v.* permanecer; estarse, residir por una temporada.

solace [sálɪs] *s.* solaz; *v.* solazar.

solar [sólə] *adj.* solar, del sol.

sold [sold] *pret. & p.p. de* **to sell; to be — on an idea** estar bien convencido de una idea.

solder [sádə] *v.* soldar; *s.* soldadura.

soldier [sóldʒə] *s.* soldado.

sole [sol] *adj.* solo, único; exclusivo; *s.* suela (*del zapato*); planta (*del pie*); lenguado (*pez*); *v.* solar, echar suelas a; **to half-sole** echar o poner medias suelas a.

solely [sóllɪ] *adv.* sólamente, únicamente.

solemn [sáləm] *adj.* solemne.

solemnity [səlémnətɪ] *s.* solemnidad.

solicit [səlísɪt] *v.* solicitar.

solicitor [səlísətə] *s.* solicitador, agente.

solicitous [səlísɪtəs] *adj.* solícito.

solicitude [səlísətjud] *s.* solicitud, cuidado.

solid [sálɪd] *s.* sólido; *adj.* sólido; firme; macizo; sensato; unánime; **— blue** todo azul; **— gold** oro puro; **for one — hour** por una hora entera, por una hora sin parar; **the country is — for** el país está firmemente unido en favor de.

solidarity [salədǽrətɪ] *s.* solidaridad.

solidify [səlídəfaɪ] *v.* solidificar(se).

solidity [səlídətɪ] *s.* solidez.

soliloquy [səlíləkwɪ] *s.* soliloquio.

solitary [sálətɛrɪ] *adj.* solitario; solo; *s.* solitario, ermitaño.

solitude [sálətjud] *s.* soledad.

solo [sólo] *s.* solo.

soloist [sóloɪst] *s.* solista.

soluble [sáljəbl] *adj.* soluble, que se disuelve fácilmente.

solution [səlúʃən] *s.* solución.

solve [salv] *v.* resolver; explicar, aclarar, desenredar.

somber [sámbə] *adj.* sombrío.

some [sʌm] *adj.* algún, alguno; algunos, unos; algo de, un poco de; **— one** alguien, alguno; **— twenty people** unas veinte personas; *pron.* algunos, unos; algo, un poco; una parte.

somebody [sʌ́mbadɪ] *pron.* alguien; **a — un** personaje de importancia.

somehow [sʌ́mhaʊ] *adv.* de algún modo, de alguna manera; **— or other** de una manera u otra; por alguna razón.

someone [sʌ́mwʌn] *pron.* alguno, alguien.

somersault [sʌ́mərsɔlt] *s.* voltereta; *v.* dar una voltereta.

something [sʌ́meɪŋ] *s.* algo, alguna cosa; un poco; **— else** alguna otra cosa, otra cosa.

sometime [sʌ́mtaɪm] *adv.* algún día; alguna vez, en algún tiempo; **-s** *adv.* a veces, algunas veces, de vez en cuando.

somewhat [sʌ́mhwat] *s.* algo, alguna cosa, un poco; *adv.* algo, un tanto.

somewhere [sʌ́mhwɛr] *adv.* en alguna parte; **— else** en alguna otra parte.

son [sʌn] *s.* hijo.

song [sɔŋ] *s.* canción, canto; **the Song of Songs** el Cantar de los Cantares; **— bird** ave canora, pájaro cantor; **to buy something for a —** comprar algo muy barato.

son-in-law [sʌ́nɪnlɔ] *s.* yerno, hijo político.

sonnet [sánɪt] *s.* soneto.

sonorous [sənórəs] *adj.* sonoro.

soon [sun] *adv.* pronto, presto; luego; **— after** poco después (de); al poco tiempo; **as — as** tan pronto como; luego que, así que; **how — ?** ¿cuándo?

soot [sʊt] *s.* hollín; tizne.

soothe [suð] *v.* calmar, sosegar; aliviar.

soothsayer [súesɛə] *s.* adivino.

sooty [sútɪ] *adj.* tiznado, cubierto de hollín.

sop [sap] *v.* empapar; **to — up** absorber; **to be sopping wet** estar hecho una sopa; *s.* sopa (*pan u otra cosa empapada en leche, caldo, etc.*); soborno, regalo (*para* *acallar, conciliar, o sobornar*).

sophomore [sáfəmor] s. estudiante de segundo año.

soprano [səpræno] s. soprano; **high —** tiple; **— voice** voz de soprano.

sorcerer [sórsərə] s. brujo, hechicero.

sordid [sórdɪd] adj. sórdido; vil, indecente; mezquino.

sore [sor] adj. dolorido; inflamado, enconado; afligido, apenado; lastimado, ofendido, picado; **— eyes** mal de ojos; **to be — at** estar enojado con; **to have a — throat** tener mal de garganta, dolerle a uno la garganta; s. úlcera, llaga; inflamación; lastimadura; pena, aflicción; **-ly** adv. dolorosamente, penosamente; **to be -ly in need of** necesitar con urgencia.

soreness [sórnɪs] s. dolor, dolencia; inflamación.

sorrel [sórəl] adj. alazán (*rojo canela*); s. color alazán; caballo alazán.

sorrow [sáro] s. dolor, pena, pesar; pesadumbre; arrepentimiento; v. apenarse, afligirse, sentir pena.

sorrowful [sórəfəl] adj. pesaroso, doloroso, lastimoso, afligido; **-ly** adv. tristemente, dolorosamente, con pena, desconsoladamente.

sorry [sórɪ] adj. triste, pesaroso, afligido, arrepentido; lastimoso; **I am —** lo siento; me pesa; **I am — for her** la compadezco.

sort [sort] s. suerte, clase, especie; **— of** tired algo cansado, un tanto cansado; **all -s** of toda suerte de, toda clase de; **out of - s** de mal humor, malhumorado; indispuesto; v. clasificar, ordenar, arreglar; **to — out** separar, clasificar; entresacar; escoger.

sought [sot] pret. & p.p. de **to seek.**

soul [sol] s. alma; **not a — nadie, ni un alma.

sound [saʊnd] adj. sano; cuerdo; sensato; firme, sólido; ileso; **a — beating** una buena zurra o tunda; **—business** buen negocio, negocio bien organizado; **— reasoning** raciocinio sólido; **— sleep** sueño profundo; **— title** título válido o legal; **of — mind** en su juicio cabal; **safe and — sano y salvo; **to sleep — dormir profundamente; s. son, sonido; tono; brazo de mar; **— wave** onda sonora; v. sonar, tocar; sondear; tantear; auscultar (*el pecho, los pulmones*); cantar, entonar (*alabanzas*); **to — out** tantear, sondear.

soundness [sáʊndnɪs] s. solidez; cordura, buen juicio; rectitud; validez; **— of body** buena salud corporal.

soup [sup] s. sopa.

sour [saʊr] adj. agrio; desabrido; acre; ácido; rancio; malhumorado; **— milk** leche cortada; v. agriar(se); cortarse (*la leche*); fermentar; poner(se) de mal humor.

source [sors] s. origen; manantial, fuente.

sourness [sáʊrnɪs] s. acidez, agrura, desabrimiento.

south [saʊθ] s. sur, sud; adj. meridional; del sur; austral; **South American** sudamericano, suramericano; **— pole** polo sur, polo antártico; adv. hacia el sur.

southeast [saʊθíst] s. & adj. sudeste; adv. hacia el sudeste.

southeastern [saʊθístən] adj. del sudeste, sudeste.

southern [sʌðən] adj. meridional, del sur, austral, sureño; **— Cross** Cruz del Sur.

southerner [sʌðənə] s. sureño, meridional, habitante del sur.

southward [sáʊθwəd] adv. hacia el sur, rumbo al sur.

southwest [saʊθwést] s. & adj. sudoeste (*o suroeste*); adv. hacia el sudoeste.

southwestern [saʊθwéstən] adj. sudoeste (*o suroeste*), del sudoeste.

souvenir [suvənír] s. recuerdo, memoria.

sovereign [sávrɪn] s. & adj. soberano.

sovereignty [sávrɪntɪ] s. soberanía.

soviet [sóvɪɪt] s. sóviet; adj. soviético.

sow [saʊ] s. puerca.

sow [so] v. sembrar.

sown [son] p.p. de **to sow.**

space [spes] s. espacio; v. espaciar.

spacious [spéʃəs] adj. espacioso; dilatado, vasto.

spade [sped] s. azada, azadón; espada (*del juego de naipes*); v. cavar con la azada.

span [spæn] s. palmo; espacio; tramo; arco u ojo (*de puente*); envergadura (*de un aeroplano*); **— of life** longevidad; v. medir a palmos; atravesar.

spangle [spæŋgl] s. lentejuela; v. adornar con lentejuelas; brillar, centellear; **-d with stars** estrellado, sembrado (*o tachonado*) de estrellas.

Spaniard [spænjəd] s. español.

spaniel [spænjəl] s. perro de aguas.

Spanish [spænɪʃ] adj. español; s. español, idioma español.

spank [spæŋk] v. zurrar, dar una tunda, dar nalgadas; s. palmada, nalgada.

spanking [spæŋkɪŋ] s. zurra, tunda, nalgadas.

spare [spɛr] v. ahorrar; evitar (*molestias, trabajo, etc.*); perdonar; **I cannot**

— **another dollar** no dispongo de otro dólar, no tengo más dinero disponible; **I cannot** — **the car today** no puedo pasarme hoy sin el automóvil; **to** — **no expense** no escatimar gastos; **to** — **the enemy** usar de clemencia con el enemigo; **to have time to** — tener tiempo de sobra; *adj.* flaco, descarnado; escaso, frugal; mezquino; sobrante; de sobra; de repuesto; — **cash** dinero disponible o de sobra; — **time** tiempo libre, tiempo disponible; — **tire** neumático de repuesto.

spark [spark] *s.* chispa; — **plug** bujía; *v.* chispear, echar chispas, chisporrotear.

sparkle [spárk]] *s.* chispa, centella; brillo, centelleo; viveza, animación; *v.* centellear; chispear; relucir, brillar.

sparkling [spárkliŋ] *adj.* centelleante; reluciente; chispeante; — **wine** vino espumoso.

sparrow [spáro] *s.* gorrión, pardal.

sparse [spars] *adj.* escaso; esparcido; poco denso, poco poblado; — **hair** pelo ralo.

spasm [spǽzəm] *s.* espasmo.

spat [spæt] *pret.* & *p.p. de* **to spit**; *v.* reñir, disputar; dar un manazo o sopapo; *s.* sopapo, manotada; riña, desavenencia; **-s** polainas cortas.

spatter [spǽtə] *v.* salpicar; rociar; manchar; *s.* salpicadura; rociada.

speak [spik] *v.* hablar; decir; recitar; — **to the point!** ¡vamos al grano!; **so to** — por decirlo así; **to** — **for** hablar por, hablar en nombre o en favor de; pedir, solicitar; apalabrar, reservar; **to** — **one's mind** hablar sin rodeos, decir claramente lo que se piensa; **to** — **out** (o — **up**) hablar claro; hablar con toda franqueza; hablar en voz alta.

speaker [spíkə] *s.* orador; conferenciante, conferencista; el que habla; — **of the House** presidente de la cámara de representantes; **loud-speaker** altavoz, altoparlante.

spear [spɪr] *s.* lanza; arpón (*para pescar*); brote, retoño, hoja (*de hierba*); *v.* alancear, lancear, herir con lanza.

spearmint [spírmɪnt] *s.* yerbabuena (hierbabuena), menta.

special [spéʃəl] *adj.* especial; particular; — **delivery** entrega especial de correo; *s.* tren o autobús especial; carta urgente, entrega especial; **-ly** *adv.* especialmente; en especial; sobre todo.

specialist [spéʃəlɪst] *s.* especialista.

specialize [spéʃəlaɪz] *v.* especializarse.

specialty [spéʃəltɪ] *s.* especialidad.

species [spíʃɪz] *s.* especie; especies.

specific [spɪsífɪk] *adj.* específico; peculiar, característico; — **gravity** peso específico; *s.* específico; **-ally** *adv.* específicamente; específicadamente; particularmente, en particular.

specify [spésəfaɪ] *v.* especificar; estipular.

specimen [spésəmən] *s.* espécimen, muestra, ejemplar.

speck [spek] *s.* mota; manchita; partícula; **not a** — ni pizca; *v. véase* **speckle**.

speckle [spék]] *s.* manchita; mota; *v.* motear, salpicar de motas o manchas; manchar.

speckled [spék]d] *adj.* moteado; — **with freckles** pecoso.

spectacle [spéktək]] *s.* espectáculo; **-s** gafas, anteojos; **to make a** — **of oneself** ponerse en la evidencia, ponerse en ridículo.

spectacular [spektǽkjələ] *adj.* espectacular, ostentoso, aparatoso.

spectator [spéktetə] *s.* espectador.

specter [spéktə] *s.* espectro, fantasma, aparecido.

spectrum [spéktrəm] *s.* espectro.

speculate [spékjəlet] *v.* especular; reflexionar.

speculation [spekjəléʃən] *s.* especulación; reflexión.

speculative [spékjələtɪv] *adj.* especulativo; teórico.

speculator [spékjələtə] *s.* especulador.

sped [sped] *pret.* & *p.p. de* **to speed.**

speech [spitʃ] *s.* habla; lenguaje, idioma; discurso, arenga; conferencia; parlamento (*de un actor*); **to make a** — pronunciar un discurso, hacer una perorata.

speechless [spítʃlɪs] *adj.* sin habla; mudo; estupefacto.

speed [spid] *s.* velocidad; rapidez; presteza, prontitud; — **limit** velocidad máxima; **at full** — a toda velocidad; *v.* apresurar(se), acelerar(se), dar(se) prisa; correr; ir con exceso de velocidad; despachar.

speedily [spídɪlɪ] *adv.* velozmente, rápidamente; a todo correr; de prisa, con prontitud.

speedometer [spidámətə] *s.* velocímetro.

speedy [spídɪ] *adj.* veloz, rápido.

spell [spel] *s.* hechizo, encanto; temporada, corto período; ataque (*de una enfermedad*); **to put under a** — aojar; hechizar, encantar; *v.* deletrear;

significar, indicar; **how is it -ed?** ¿cómo se escribe?

speller [spélə] s. silabario; deletreador.

spelling [spélɪŋ] s. ortografía; deletreo; **— book** silabario.

spelt [spɛlt] pret. & p.p. de to spell.

spend [spɛnd] v. gastar; usar, agotar, consumir; **to — a day** pasar un día.

spendthrift [spéndθrɪft] s. derrochador, gastador, pródigo.

spent [spɛnt] pret. & p.p. de to spend.

sphere [sfɪr] s. esfera; globo, orbe.

spherical [sférɪk] adj. esférico.

spice [spaɪs] s. especia; picante; aroma; v. condimentar, sazonar con especias.

spicy [spáɪsɪ] adj. sazonado con especias; picante; aromático.

spider [spáɪdə] s. araña; sartén; **— web** telaraña.

spigot [spígət] s. espita, grifo, canilla.

spike [spaɪk] s. espiga; perno; clavo largo; alcayata; pico; v. clavar; clavetear.

spill [spɪl] v. verter; derramar(se); desparramar(se); hacer caer (de un caballo); revelar (una noticia, un secreto); s. derrame, derramamiento; vuelco; caída (de un caballo).

spilt [spɪlt] pret. & p.p. de to spill.

spin [spɪn] v. hilar; girar, dar vueltas, rodar; bailar (un trompo); **to — out** prolongar, alargar; **to — yarns** contar cuentos; s. giro, vuelta; paseo (en automóvil, bicicleta, etc.); barrena (hablando de aeroplanos).

spinach [spínɪtʃ] s. espinaca.

spinal [spáɪnl] adj. espinal; **— column** columna vertebral, espina dorsal.

spindle [spíndl] s. huso; eje.

spine [spaɪn] s. espina; espinazo, espina dorsal, columna vertebral.

spinner [spínə] s. hilandero, hilandera; máquina de hilar.

spinning [spínɪŋ] s. hilandería, arte de hilar; **— machine** aparato para hilar, máquina de hilar; **— mill** hilandería; **— top** trompo; **— wheel** torno de hilar.

spinster [spínstə] s. soltera; solterona.

spiral [spáɪrəl] adj. espiral; **— staircase** caracol, escalera espiral; s. espiral.

spire [spaɪr] s. aguja, chapitel de torre; cúspide, ápice; punto más alto; **— of grass** brizna de hierba.

spirit [spírɪt] s. espíritu; temple; viveza, animación; ánimo; tono **-s** abatimiento; **to be in good -s** estar de buen humor; **to be out of -s** estar triste o abatido; v. **to — away** llevarse misteriosamente.

spirited [spírɪtɪd] adj. vivo, brioso, fogoso.

spiritual [spírɪtʃʊəl] adj. espiritual; s. espiritual (tonada religiosa de los negros del sur de los Estados Unidos).

spit [spɪt] v. escupir; expectorar; pret. & p.p. de to spit; s. esputo, saliva; asador.

spite [spaɪt] s. despecho, rencor, inquina, ojeriza; **in — of** a despecho de; a pesar de; **out of —** por despecho; v. picar, irritar, hacer rabiar.

spiteful [spáɪtfəl] adj. rencoroso.

splash [splæʃ] v. salpicar; rociar; enlodar, manchar; chapotear (en el agua); s. salpicadura; rociada; chapoteo.

spleen [splin] s. bazo; mal humor, rencor.

splendid [spléndɪd] adj. espléndido.

splendor [spléndə] s. esplendor; esplendidez.

splice [splaɪs] v. empalmar, unir, juntar; s. empalme; junta.

splint [splɪnt] s. tablilla; astilla; v. entablillar.

splinter [splíntə] s. astilla; raja; v. astillar(se), hacer(se) astillas; romper(se) en astillas.

split [splɪt] v. hender(se), rajar(se); resquebrajar(se); partir(se), dividir(se); **to — hairs** pararse en pelillos; **to — one's sides with laughter** desternillarse de risa, reventar de risa; **to — the difference** partir la diferencia; pret. & p.p. de to split; adj. partido, hendido, rajado; dividido; resquebrajado; s. raja, hendedura, grieta; cisma, rompimiento.

spoil [spɔɪl] v. dañar(se), echar(se) a perder, podrir(se) o pudrir(se), corromper(se); estropear(se); arruinar; consentir, mimar; s. botín, presa; **-s of war** botín o despojos de guerra.

spoke [spok] s. rayo (de rueda); pret. de to speak.

spoken [spókən] p.p. de to speak.

spokesman [spóksmən] s. portavoz, vocero.

sponge [spʌndʒ] s. esponja; gorrón, parásito; v. lavar o limpiar con esponja; vivir de gorra, vivir a costa ajena; **to — up** chupar, absorber.

spongecake [spʌndʒkek] s. bizcocho esponjoso.

sponger [spʌndʒə] s. esponja, gorrón, pegote, parásito, Am. pavo.

spongy [spʌndʒɪ] adj. esponjoso, esponjado.

sponsor [spánsə] s. padrino, madrina; patrón (el que patrocina una empresa); defensor; fiador; fomentador, promovedor; *v.* apadrinar; promover, fomentar; patrocinar; ser fiador de.

spontaneity [spɑntəníətɪ] *s.* espontaneidad.

spontaneous [spɑnténɪəs] *adj.* espontáneo.

spook [spuk] *s.* espectro, fantasma, aparecido.

spool [spul] *s.* carrete, carretel; *v.* devanar, enredar (*hilo*) en carrete.

spoon [spun] *s.* cuchara; *v.* cucharear, sacar con cuchara.

spoonful [spúnfəl] *s.* cucharada.

sport [sport] *s.* deporte; **in — en** broma, de burla; **to make — of** reírse de, burlarse de; **to be a good — ser** buen perdedor (*en el juego*); ser un buen compañero; *v.* jugar; divertirse; bromear, chancearse; **to — a new dress** lucir un traje nuevo; -(s) *adj.* deportivo; **— clothes** trajes deportivos.

sportsman [spórtsmən] *s.* deportista; jugador generoso, buen perdedor (*en deportes*).

spot [spɑt] *s.* mancha; mota; sitio, lugar; **in -s** aquí y allí; aquí y allá; **on the — allí** mismo; al punto; **to pay — cash** pagar al contado; *v.* manchar, ensuciar; motear; echar de ver, distinguir; avistar; localizar.

spotless [spɑ́tlɪs] *adj.* sin mancha, limpio.

spotted [spɑ́tɪd] *adj.* manchado; moteado.

spouse [spauz] *s.* esposo, esposa.

spout [spaut] *v.* chorrear; brotar; salir en chorro; emitir; declamar, perorar; hablar mucho; *s.* chorro; surtidor; pico (*de tetera, cafetera, jarra, etc.*); espita.

sprain [spren] *v.* torcer (*una coyuntura o músculo*); **to — one's ankle** torcerse el tobillo; *s.* torsión, torcedura.

sprang [spræŋ] *pret. de* **to spring.**

sprawl [sprɔl] *v.* despatarrarse; estar despatarrado; tenderse; **to — one's legs** abrir las piernas; *s.* postura floja (*abiertos los brazos y piernas*).

spray [spre] *s.* rocío, rociada; líquido para rociar; ramita; **sea — espuma** del mar; *v.* rociar.

spread [spred] *v.* extender(se); desparramar(se); esparcir(se); difundir(se), diseminar(se), dispersar(se); propalar(se) (*noticias, rumores, etc.*), propagar(se); **to — apart** abrir(se), separar(se); **to — butter on** poner mantequilla en; **to — out the tablecloth** tender el mantel; **to — paint on** dar una mano de pintura a; **to — with** cubrir de; untar con; *s.* extensión; amplitud, anchura; envergadura (*de un aeroplano*);

difusión; diseminación; propagación; cubierta, sobrecama; comilona, festín; mantequilla, queso, etc., que se le unta al pan; *pret. & p.p. de* **to spread.**

spree [spri] *s.* juerga, parranda, holgorio; **to go on a — andar** (*o* ir) de parranda o juerga, *Am.* ir de farra.

sprig [sprɪg] *s.* ramita.

sprightly [spráɪtlɪ] *adj.* vivo, animado, brioso; alegre.

spring [sprɪŋ] *v.* saltar, brincar; hacer saltar; **to — a leak** hacer agua (*un barco*); comenzar a gotear (*la cañería, el techo, etc.*); formarse una gotera; **to — a trap** hacer saltar una trampa; **to — at** abalanzarse sobre; **to — from** salir de, nacer de, brotar de; **to — news or a surprise** dar de sopetón una noticia o sorpresa; **to — something open** abrir algo a la fuerza; **to — to one's feet** levantarse de un salto; **to — up** brotar; surgir; crecer; levantarse de un salto; *s.* primavera; muelle (*de metal*); resorte; elasticidad; salto, brinco; manantial, fuente; origen; *adj.* primaveral; **— board** trampolín; **— mattress** colchón de muelles; **— water** agua de manantial.

springtime [sprɪ́ŋtaɪm] *s.* primavera.

sprinkle [sprɪ́ŋkl] *v.* rociar; regar; espolvorear; salpicar; lloviznar; *s.* rociada, rocío; llovizna; **— of salt** pizca de sal.

sprint [sprɪnt] *v.* echar una carrera; *s.* carrera, carrerilla, corrida corta.

sprout [spraut] *v.* brotar; retoñar, germinar; hacer germinar o brotar; *s.* retoño, renuevo; **Brussels -s** bretones, coles de Bruselas.

spruce [sprus] *s.* abeto; *adj.* pulcro, aseado, pulido; elegante; *v.* **to — up** asearse, componerse, emperifollarse.

sprung [sprʌŋ] *pret. & p.p. de* **to spring.**

spun [spʌn] *pret. & p.p. de* **to spin.**

spur [spɜ] *s.* espuela; acicate; aguijón, estímulo; espolón (*del gallo*); estribación (*de una montaña*); **— track** ramal corto (*de ferrocarril*); **on the — of the moment** impensadamente, sin la reflexión debida; por el momento; *v.* espolear, aguijar, picar, incitar; **to — on** animar, incitar a obrar o a seguir adelante.

spurn [spɜn] *v.* rechazar, desdeñar, menospreciar.

spurt [spɜt] *v.* salir a borbotones; chorrear; echar chorros; hacer un repentino esfuerzo (*para ganar una carrera*); *s.* borbotón, chorrazo, chorro repentino; esfuerzo repentino; — **of anger** arranque de ira; **-s of flame** llamaradas.

sputter [spʌ́tə] v. chisporrotear; refunfuñar; s. chisporroteo; refunfuño.

sputum [spjútəm] s. esputo.

spy [spaɪ] s. espía; v. espiar; acechar; atisbar; **to —** on esplar, atisbar.

spyglass [spáɪglæs] s. anteojo de larga vista.

squabble [skwábl] s. reyerta; v. reñir, disputar.

squad [skwad] s. escuadra, patrulla, partida.

squadron [skwádrən] s. escuadra; escuadrón.

squalid [skwálɪd] adj. escuálido.

squall [skwɔl] s. chubasco; chillido; v. chillar.

squander [skwándə] v. despilfarrar, derrochar, malgastar, disipar.

square [skwer] s. cuadro; cuadrado; plaza; manzana de casas; escuadra (de carpintero); casilla (de tablero de ajedrez, damas, etc.); **he is on the —** obra de buena fe; v. cuadrar; ajustar, arreglar, saldar (cuentas); justificar; cuadricular; **to — one's shoulders** enderezar los hombros; cuadrarse; **to — oneself with** sincerarse con, justificarse ante; **to — a person with another** poner bien a una persona con otra; adj. cuadrado, en cuadro, a escuadra, en ángulo recto; saldado; justo, recto, equitativo; franco; — **corner** esquina en ángulo recto; — **-dance** cuadrilla; — **meal** comida completa, comida en regla; — **mile** milla cuadrada; — **root** raíz cuadrada; **to be — with someone** estar en paz con alguien, no deberle nada, A m. estar a mano; adv. véase **squarely**.

squarely [skwérlɪ] adv. equitativamente, honradamente; firmemente; de buena fe; derecho, derechamente; **to hit the target — in the middle** pegar de lleno en el blanco.

squash [skwaʃ] s. calabaza; v. aplastar, despachurrar o apachurrar.

squat [skwat] v. agazaparse, sentarse én cuclillas; ocupar tierras baldías para ganar título de propietario; adj. agazapado, sentado en cuclillas; rechoncho, achaparrado, A m. chaparro.

squawk [skwɔk] v. graznar; chillar; quejarse; s. graznido; chillido; queja.

squeak [skwik] v. rechinar, chirriar; chillar; s. rechinamiento; chirrido, chillido.

squeal [skwil] v. chillar; quejarse, pro-

testar; soplar, delatar; s. chillido.

squeeze [skwiz] v. estrujar; despachurrar o apachurrar; exprimir; prensar; apretar; **to — into** meter(se) a estrujones, encajar(se) en; **to — out the juice** exprimir el jugo; **to — through a crowd** abrirse paso a estrujones por entre la muchedumbre; s. estrujón; apretón; abrazo fuerte; apretura.

squelch [skweltʃ] v. aplastar; acallar, imponer silencio; reprender; **to — a revolt** sofocar o apagar una revuelta.

squint [skwɪnt] v. mirar de través; mirar de soslayo; mirar achicando los ojos; mirar furtivamente; bizquear (mirar bizco); s. mirada de soslayo; mirada bizca; mirada furtiva; **squint-eyed** adj. bisojo o bizco.

squire [skwaɪr] s. escudero; v. acompañar, escoltar.

squirm [skwɜm] v. retorcerse; **to — out of a difficulty** forcejear para salir de un aprieto.

squirrel [skwɜ́əl] s. ardilla.

squirt [skwɜt] v. jeringar; echar un chisguete; salir a chorritos (o a chisguetes); s. jeringazo; chisguete.

stab [stæb] v. apuñalar, dar una puñalada, dar de puñaladas, acuchillar; pinchar; s. puñalada, cuchillada, estocada; pinchazo.

stability [stəbɪ́lətɪ] s. estabilidad.

stable [stébl] adj. estable; s. establo, cuadra, caballeriza; v. poner (los animales) en la caballeriza.

stack [stæk] s. pila, montón, rimero; hacina (de paja o heno); chimenea, cañón de chimenea; **library -s** estanterías o anaqueles de biblioteca; v. amontonar, apilar.

stadium [stédɪəm] s. estadio.

staff [stæf] s. báculo, cayado, bastón, vara; asta (de bandera, de lanza); cuerpo, consejo administrativo; — **of life** sostén de la vida; — **officer** oficial de estado mayor; **army —** estado mayor; **editorial —** redacción; **musical —** pentagrama; **teaching —** cuerpo docente; v. proveer de funcionarios y empleados (una organización).

stag [stæg] s. venado, ciervo; macho, hombre; — **dinner** banquete exclusivo para hombres.

stage [stedʒ] s. tablado; tablas, escenario; escena; teatro; etapa, tramo; período; parada; **—coach** ómnibus, autobús; **— hand** tramoyista; **by easy -s** por grados, gradualmente; v. representar, poner en escena; **to — a hold-up** hacer un asalto, atracar; **to — a**

STA—STA

surprise dar una sorpresa.

stagger[stǽgə] *v.* tambalearse, trastabillar, bambolearse; hacer tambalear; azorar, asombrar; **to — working hours** escalonar las horas de trabajo; *s.* tambaleo, bamboleo.

stagnant [stǽgnənt] *adj.* estancado; **to become —** estancarse.

staid [sted] *adj.* grave, serio.

stain [sten] *v.* manchar; teñir; colorar; **stained-glass window** vidriera de colores; *s.* mancha, mancilla; tinte, tintura; materia colorante.

stainless [sténlıs] *adj.* sin mancha, inmaculado, limpio; **— steel** acero inempañable o inoxidable.

stair [ster] *s.* peldaño, escalón; **-s** escalera.

staircase [stérkes] *s.* escalera.

stairway [stérwe] *s.* escalera.

stake [stek] *s.* estaca; puesta, apuesta; **his future is at —** su porvenir está en peligro o riesgo; **to die at the —** morir en la hoguera; **to have a — in the future of** tener interés en el porvenir de; **to have much at —** irle a uno mucho en una cosa; haber aventurado mucho; *v.* estacar; atar a una estaca; apostar; arriesgar, aventurar; **to — off** señalar con estacas (*un perímetro*).

stale [stel] *adj.* viejo; rancio; gastado, improductivo.

stalk [stɔk] *s.* tallo; caña.

stall [stɔl] *s.* casilla, puesto (*de un mercado o feria*); casilla o sección de un establo; *v.* encasillar, meter en casilla; atascarse (*un auto*); pararse (*el motor*); **he is -ing** está haciendo la pala; **to be -ed in the mud** estar atascado en el lodo.

stallion [stǽljən] *s.* caballo de cría, caballo padre, *Am.* padrillo, garañón.

stammer [stǽmə] *v.* tartamudear, balbucear; *s.* tartamudeo, balbuceo.

stammerer [stǽmərə] *s.* tartamudo.

stammering [stǽmərıŋ] *s.* tartamudeo; *adj.* tartamudo.

stamp [stæmp] *v.* sellar; timbrar; poner un sello a; estampar; imprimir; marcar, señalar; patear, patalear; **to — one's foot** dar patadas en el suelo; **to — out** extirpar, borrar; *s.* sello; timbre, estampilla; estampa; marca, impresión; patada (*en el suelo*); **postage —** sello, *Am.* estampilla, *Am.* timbre; **revenue —** timbre.

stampede [stæmpíd] *s.* estampida; huída en desorden; tropel; éxodo repentino; *v.* arrancar, huir en tropel; ir en tropel;

ahuyentar, hacer huir en desorden.

stanch [stɑntʃ] *v.* restañar, estancar; *adj.* fuerte, firme; leal, constante, fiel.

stand [stænd] *v.* poner derecho, colocar verticalmente, *Am.* parar; ponerse de pie, levantarse; estar de pie; estar (situado); pararse; aguantar, sufrir, tolerar; **to — a chance of** tener probabilidad de; **to — an expense** sufragar un gasto; **to — aside** apartarse; mantenerse apartado; **to — back of** colocarse detrás de; salir fiador de, garantizar a, respaldar a; **to — by** mantenerse a corta distancia; apoyar, defender; estar alerta; **to — for** significar; estar por, apoyar; tolerar; **to — in the way** estorbar; **to — on end** poner(se) de punta; erizarse (*el pelo*); **to — one's ground** mantenerse firme; **to — out** resaltar, destacarse; sobresalir; **to — six feet** tener seis pies de altura; **to — up for** apoyar, defender; **it -s to reason** es razonable, es lógico; *s.* puesto, mesilla; pedestal; posición; actitud; alto, parada (*para resistir*); quiosco; **grand —** andanada, gradería cubierta (*para espectadores*); **music —** atril; **umbrella —** paragüero.

standard [stǽndəd] *s.* norma; nivel normal; modelo, patrón, *Am.* estándar; criterio; base, sostén, pedestal; estandarte; **gold —** patrón de oro; **to be up to —** satisfacer las normas requeridas; *adj.* normal, que sirve de norma; de uso general; corriente; **standard-bearer** portaestandarte.

standardization [stændədəzéʃən] *s.* normalización, uniformación, igualación.

standardize [stǽndədaız] *v.* normalizar, uniformar, *Am.* estandardizar.

standing [stǽndıŋ] *s.* posición; reputación; **of long —** que ha prevalecido largo tiempo; muy antiguo; *adj.* derecho, en pie; de pie; establecido, permanente; **— water** agua estancada; **there is — room only** no quedan asientos.

standpoint [stǽndpoint] *s.* punto de vista.

standstill [stǽndstıl] *s.* alto; pausa; **to come to a —** pararse; hacer alto.

stank [stæŋk] *pret. de* **to stink.**

stanza [stǽnzə] *s.* estrofa.

staple [stépl] *s.* broche de alambre (*para sujetar papeles*); grapa, argolla, armella; artículo principal; **-s** artículos de necesidad prima; *adj.* principal; de uso corriente; indispensable; *v.* asegurar (*papeles*) con broche de alambre; sujetar con armellas.

209

star [star] s. estrella; asterisco; **star-spangled** estrellado; adj. sobresaliente, excelente; v. estrellar, adornar o señalar con estrellas; marcar con asterisco; presentar como estrella (a un actor); lucir(se) en las tablas o el cine, hacer el papel principal.

starboard [stárbord] s. estribor; adj. de estribor; — side banda de estribor; adv. a estribor.

starch [startʃ] s. almidón; fécula; v. almidonar.

stare [ster] v. mirar, mirar con fijeza o curiosidad; mirar azorado; clavar la mirada, fijar la vista; s. mirada fija, mirada persistente.

starfish [stárfiʃ] s. estrella de mar.

stark [stark] adj. tieso; escueto; — folly pura tontería; — in death tieso, muerto; — narrative narración escueta, sin adornos; adv. completamente, totalmente; — mad loco de remate; — naked enteramente desnudo, en cueros, Am. encuerado.

starlight [stárlaɪt] s. luz estelar, luz de las estrellas.

starry [stárɪ] adj. estrellado, sembrado de estrellas; como estrellas, brillante.

start [start] v. comenzar, empezar, principiar; poner(se) en marcha; partir, salir; dar un salto, sobresaltarse; the motor -s el motor arranca; to — after someone salir en busca de alguien; to — off salir, partir; dar principio a; to — out on a trip empezar una jornada, emprender un viaje; to — the motor hacer arrancar el motor; s. comienzo, empiezo, principio; sobresalto; respingo (de un caballo); arranque; ventaja (en una carrera).

starter [stártə] s. arranque, arrancador; iniciador; primero de una serie; self-starter arranque automático.

startle [stártl] v. asustar(se), sobresaltar(se), espantar(se).

startling [stártlɪŋ] adj. sobresaltante, pasmoso, asombroso, sorprendente.

starvation [starvéʃən] s. inanición, hambre.

starve [starv] v. morir(se) de hambre; hambrear; matar de hambre.

state [stet] s. estado; condición, situación; in great — con gran pompa; adj. de estado; del estado; de ceremonia; v. declarar, decir; expresar, exponer.

stately [stétlɪ] adj. majestuoso, imponente.

statement [stétmənt] s. declaración; exposición; informe, relato, cuenta,

estado de cuenta.

stateroom [stétrum] s. camarote (de un buque).

statesman [stétsmən] s. estadista, hombre de estado.

static [stǽtɪk] adj. estático; s. estática.

station [stéʃən] s. estación; paradero; puesto; estado, posición social; broadcasting — transmisora o emisora; v. estacionar, colocar, apostar.

stationary [stéʃənɛrɪ] adj. estacionario; fijo.

stationery [stéʃənɛrɪ] s. papelería.

statistics [stətístɪks] s. estadística; datos estadísticos.

statuary [stǽtʃuɛrɪ] s. estatuaria, arte de hacer estatuas; colección de estatuas.

statue [stǽtʃʊ] s. estatua.

stature [stǽtʃə] s. estatura.

status [stétəs] s. estado, condición; posición social o profesional.

statute [stǽtʃut] s. estatuto, ordenanza.

staunch = **stanch**.

stave [stev] s. duela de barril; v. poner duelas (a un barril); to — off mantener a distancia; evitar; rechazar.

stay [ste] v. quedarse, permanecer; parar(se); detener(se); hospedarse, alojarse; resistir; to — an execution diferir o aplazar una ejecución; to — one's hunger engañar el hambre; to — up all night velar toda la noche; s. estada, estancia, permanencia; suspensión; sostén, apoyo; varilla o ballena de corsé; to grant a — conceder una prórroga.

stead [sted] : in her (his) — en su lugar; to stand one in good — servirle a uno, ser de provecho para uno.

steadfast [stédfæst] adj. fijo, firme; constante.

steadily [stédɪlɪ] adv. constantemente; firmemente; sin parar, de continuo; sin vacilar.

steadiness [stédɪnɪs] s. firmeza; constancia; estabilidad.

steady [stédɪ] adj. firme; estable; invariable, constante; continuo; v. afianzar, mantener firme, asegurar; calmar (los nervios).

steak [stek] s. biftec o bisté; tajada (para asar o freír).

steal [stil] v. robar, hurtar; andar furtivamente; to — away colarse, escabullirse, escaparse; to — into a room meterse a hurtadillas en un cuarto; to — out of a room salirse a escondidas de un cuarto, colarse, escabullirse; s.,

robo, hurto.
stealth [stɛlθ] : **by** — a hurtadillas, a escondidas, con cautela.
stealthy [stɛlθɪ] *adj.* cauteloso, furtivo, secreto.
steam [stim] *s.* vapor; vaho; *adj.* de vapor; por vapor; — **engine** máquina de vapor; — **heat** calefacción por vapor; *v.* cocer al vapor; dar un baño de vapor; saturar de vapor; echar vapor; **to** — **into port** llegar a puerto (*un vapor*).
steamboat [stímbot] *s.* buque de vapor.
steamer [stímə] *s.* vapor, buque de vapor.
steamship [stímʃɪp] *s.* vapor, buque de vapor.
steed [stid] *s.* corcel, caballo de combate; caballo brioso.
steel [stil] *s.* acero; *adj.* acerado, de acero; *v.* acerar, revestir de acero; **to** — **oneself against** fortalecerse contra.
steep [stip] *adj.* empinado, escarpado, pendiente; muy alto; — **price** precio alto o excesivo; *v.* remojar, empapar; saturar; poner o estar en infusión.
steeple [stípl] *s.* aguja, chapitel; cúspide.
steepness [stípnɪs] *s.* inclinación abrupta; lo empinado, lo escarpado; altura (*de precios*).
steer [stɪr] *s.* novillo; buey; *v.* guiar, conducir, manejar, gobernar; timonear; **to** — **a course** seguir un rumbo; **the car** —**s easily** se maneja fácilmente el auto, es de fácil manejo.
stem [stɛm] *s.* tallo; tronco; pedúnculo (*de hoja, flor o fruto*); raíz (*de una palabra*); pie (*de copa*); cañón (*de pipa de fumar*); proa; *v.* estancar, represar; resistir, refrenar; contraponerse a; **to** — **from** provenir de.
stench [stɛntʃ] *s.* hedor, hediondez.
stenographer [stənágrəfə] *s.* estenógrafo, taquígrafo, mecanógrafo.
step [stɛp] *s.* paso; pisada; peldaño, escalón, grada; grado; gestión; — **by** — paso a paso; **to be in** — **with** marchar a compás con; estar de acuerdo con; **to take** —**s** dar pasos; tomar medidas; gestionar; *v.* andar, caminar; dar un paso; **to** — **aside** hacerse a un lado, apartarse; **to** — **back** dar un paso o pasos atrás; retroceder; **to** — **down** bajar; **to** — **off a distance** medir a pasos una distancia; **to** — **on** pisar, pisotear; **to** — **on the gas** pisar el acelerador; darse prisa; **to** — **out** salir; **to** — **up** subir; acelerar.
stepfather [stépfɑðə] *s.* padrastro.

stepmother [stépmʌðə] *s.* madrastra.
steppe [stɛp] *s.* estepa.
sterile [stérəl] *adj.* estéril.
sterility [stərílɪtɪ] *s.* esterilidad.
sterilize [stérəlaɪz] *v.* esterilizar.
sterling [stə́lɪŋ] *s.* vajilla de plata esterlina; *adj.* genuino; de ley; — **silver** plata de ley, plata esterlina; **pound** — libra esterlina.
stern [stɜn] *adj.* austero, severo; firme; *s.* popa.
sternness [stɜ́nnɪs] *s.* austeridad, severidad; firmeza.
stethoscope [stéθəskop] *s.* estetoscopio.
stevedore [stívədor] *s.* estibador, cargador.
stew [stju] *v.* estofar; preocuparse, apurarse; *s.* estofado, guisado; **to be in a** — estar preocupado o apurado.
steward [stjúwəd] *s.* mayordomo; camarero (*de buque o avión*).
stewardess [stjúwədɪs] *s.* camarera (*de buque o avión*).
stick [stɪk] *s.* palo; vara; garrote; raja de leña; — **of dynamite** barra de dinamita; **control** — palanca (*de aeroplano*); **walking** — bastón; **stick-up** atraco (*para robar*), asalto; *v.* pegar(se), adherir(se); permanecer; estar pegado; picar, pinchar; herir (*con cuchillo, puñal, etc.*); fijar (*con clavos, alfileres, tachuelas, etc.*); atascarse (*en el fango un carro, auto, etc.*); **to** — **something in** (o **into**) clavar o meter algo en; encajar en; **to** — **out** salir, sobresalir; proyectarse; **to** — **out one's head** asomar la cabeza; **to** — **out one's tongue** sacar la lengua; **to** — **to a job** perseverar (o persistir) en una tarea; **to** — **up** sobresalir, destacarse; estar de punta (*el pelo*); **to** — **one's hands up** alzar las manos; **to** — **someone up** asaltar o atracar a alguien (*para robar*); *véase* **stuck**.
sticker [stíkə] *s.* marbete engomado.
sticky [stíkɪ] *adk.* pegajoso.
stiff [stɪf] *adj.* tieso; rígido; entumido; duro; terco; fuerte; — **climb** subida ardua o difícil; — **price** precio alto o subido; **stiff-necked** terco, obstinado; **scared** — yerto, muerto de miedo; *s.* cadáver.
stiffen [stífən] *v.* atiesar(se), poner(se) tieso; entumir(se); endurecer(se); espesar(se); subir de punto, aumentar (*la resistencia*).
stiffness [stífnɪs] *s.* tiesura; rigidez; dureza; rigor; terquedad.
stifle [stáɪfl] *v.* ahogar(se), asfixiar(se), sofocar(se); apagar, extinguir.

stigma [stígmə] s. estigma; baldón.

still [stɪl] *adj.* quieto; callado, silencioso; tranquilo; inmóvil; **—born** nacido muerto; **—** life naturaleza muerta; *v.* aquietar; calmar; acallar; *adv.* todavía, aún; *conj.* empero, no obstante, sin embargo; *s.* destiladera, alambique; silencio.

stillness [stílnɪs] s. quietud, calma, silencio.

stilt [stɪlt] s. zanco; pilote, puntal, soporte.

stilted [stíltɪd] *adj.* tieso, afectado, pomposo.

stimulant [stímjələnt] *adj. & s.* estimulante.

stimulate [stímjəlet] *v.* estimular.

stimulation [stɪmjəléʃən] s. estimulación, estímulo.

stimulus [stímjələs] s. estímulo.

sting [stɪŋ] *v.* picar; pinchar, aguijonear; escocer (*Am.* arder); embaucar; *s.* picadura, piquete, mordedura, picazón; aguijón; escozor; **— of remorse** remordimiento.

stinginess [stíndʒɪnɪs] s. tacañería, mezquindad.

stingy [stíndʒɪ] *adj.* mezquino, ruin, tacaño; escaso.

stink [stɪŋk] *v.* heder, oler mal; apestar; *s.* hedor, mal olor, hediondez.

stint [stɪnt] *v.* escatimar; ser frugal o económico; **to — oneself** privarse de lo necesario, economizar demasiado; *s.* tarea, fæna; **without —** sin límite; sin escatimar; generosamente.

stipulate [stípjəlet] *v.* estipular.

stipulation [stɪpjəléʃən] s. estipulación, condición.

stir [stɝ] *v.* menear(se); mover(se), bullir(se); atizar (*el fuego*); incitar; conmover; perturbar; revolver; **to — up** incitar; conmover; revolver; suscitar (*un argumento, pelea, etc.*); *s.* meneo, agitación, movimiento; alboroto.

stirring [stɝɪŋ] *adj.* conmovedor.

stirrup [stɝəp] s. estribo.

stitch [stɪtʃ] *v.* coser; dar puntadas; *s.* puntada; punzada; **to be in -es** desternillarse de risa.

stock [stak] s. surtido; existencias, provisión; ganado; cepa, linaje, estirpe; acciones, valores; **in —** en existencia; **live—** ganado; **meat —** caldo de carne; *adj.* en existencia, existente, disponible; común, trivial; **— answer** contestación corriente, común o trivial; **— company** sociedad anónima, compañía teatral; **— exchange** bolsa; **— farm** hacienda de ganado, *Am.*

rancho, *Am.* estancia; **— market** mercado de valores, bolsa; **— room** almacén; **— size** tamaño ordinario (*regularmente en existencia*); **—yard** matadero; *v.* surtir, abastecer; tener en existencia (*para vender*); **to — a farm** surtir o proveer de ganado un rancho; **to — up with** surtirse de, acumular.

stockade [stakéd] s. estacada, empalizada; vallado; *v.* empalizar, rodear de empalizadas.

stockbroker [stákbrokə] s. bolsista, corredor de bolsa.

stockholder [stákholdə] s. accionista.

stocking [stákɪŋ] s. media.

stoic [stóɪk] *adj. & s.* estoico.

stoke [stok] *v.* atizar (*el fuego*); cebar, alimentar (*un horno*).

stole [stol] *pret. de* to steal.

stolen [stólən] *p.p. de* to steal.

stolid [stálɪd] *adj.* estólido, insensible.

stomach [stʌmək] s. estómago; *v.* aguantar, tolerar.

stone [ston] s. piedra; hueso (*de las frutas*); **within a -'s throw** a tiro de piedra; *adj.* pétreo, de piedra; **Stone Age** Edad de Piedra; **stone-deaf** totalmente sordo, sordo como una tapia; *v.* apedrear; deshuesar (*las frutas*).

stony [stónɪ] *adj.* pedregoso; pétreo, de piedra; duro.

stood [stʊd] *pret. & p.p. de* to stand.

stool [stul] s. taburete, banquillo; bacín, bacinica; excremento; **— pigeon** soplón (*el que delata a otro*).

stoop [stup] *v.* agacharse; doblarse, inclinarse; encorvarse; andar encorvado o caído de hombros; rebajarse, humillarse, abajarse; *s.* encorvamiento, inclinación (*de espaldas*); **to walk with a —** andar encorvado o caído de hombros; **stoop-shouldered** cargado de espaldas, encorvado.

stop [stap] *v.* parar(se), hacer alto, detener(se); acabar(se); cesar; parar de, dejar de; atajar; reprimir; suspender; obstruir, tapar; **to — at a hotel** hospedarse o alojarse en un hotel; **to — at nothing** no pararse en escrúpulos; **to — from** impedir; **to — over at** hacer escala en; **to — short** parar(se) de sopetón, parar(se) en seco; **to — up** tapar, obstruir; atascar; *s.* parada; alto, pausa; estada, estancia; detención; suspensión; llave (*de instrumento de viento*); traste (*de guitarra*); registro (*de órgano*); **— consonant** consonante explosiva.

stopover [stápovə] s. parada, escala; **to make a — in** hacer escala en.

stoppage [stápɪdʒ] s. detención; obstrucción; **work** — paro.

stopper [stápə] s. tapón.

storage [stórɪdʒ] s. almacenaje; — **battery** acumulador; **to keep in** — almacenar.

store [stor] s. tienda; almacén; depósito; acopio; **-s** provisiones; bastimentos; víveres; **department** —almacén; **dry-goods** — lencería, *Am.* mercería, *Am.* cajón de ropa; **fruit** — frutería; **hat** — sombrerería; **grocery** — abacería, tienda de comestibles, *Am.* tienda de abarrotes, *Am.* bodega; **shoe** — zapatería; **to have in** — tener guardado; *v.* almacenar; guardar; abastecer; **to** — **up** acumular.

storehouse [stórhaus] s. almacén, depósito.

storekeeper [stórkipə] s. tendero; almacenista; guardalmacén.

storeroom [stórrum] s. almacén; bodega; despensa.

stork [stork] s. cigüeña.

storm [storm] s. tormenta, tempestad, borrasca, temporal; tumulto; asalto; — **troops** tropas de asalto; **hail**—granizada; **snow**— nevasca; **wind**—vendaval; *v.* asaltar, atacar; rabiar; **it is -ing** hay tormenta, hay tempestad.

stormy [stórmɪ] *adj.* tempestuoso, borrascoso; turbulento.

story [stórɪ] s. cuento, historia, historieta; relato; chisme; rumor; argumento, trama; piso *(de un edificio)*; **newspaper** — artículo de periódico, gacetilla.

stout [staut] *adj.* corpulento, robusto, fornido; fuerte; firme; leal; valiente.

stove [stov] s. estufa; cocina de gas, cocina eléctrica; *pret. & p.p. de* **stave.**

stow [sto] *v.* meter, guardar; esconder; estibar, acomodar la carga de un barco; rellenar; **to** — **away on a ship** embarcarse clandestinamente, esconderse en un barco.

straddle [strædḷ] *v.* ponerse o estar a horcajadas; ponerse a caballo, cabalgar; favorecer ambos lados *(de un pleito, controversia, etc.).*

straggle [strǽgḷ] *v.* vagar, desviarse; extraviarse; andar perdido; dispersarse; **to** — **behind** rezagarse.

straight [stret] *adj.* recto; derecho; directo; honrado; franco; erguido; correcto; en orden; — **face** cara seria; — **hair** pelo lacio; — **hand of five cards** runfla de cinco naipes del mismo palo; — **rum** ron puro, sin mezcla; **for two hours** — por dos horas segui-

das, por dos horas sin parar; **to set a person** — dar consejo a una persona; mostrarle el camino, modo o manera de hacer algo; *adv.* directamente, derecho, en línea recta; francamente; honradamente; — **away** (o — **off** en seguida, al punto; **to talk** — **from the shoulder** hablar con toda franqueza o sinceridad.

straighten [strétn] *v.* enderezar(se); arreglar, poner en orden.

straightforward [stretfórwəd] *adj.* derecho, recto; honrado; franco, sincero; *adv.* directamente, en línea recta.

straightness [strétnɪs] s. derechura; rectitud; honradez.

straightway [strótwe] *adv.* luego, inmediatamente, en seguida.

strain [stren] *v.* estirar demasiado, hacer fuerza; poner tirante; violentar, forzar *(los músculos, los nervios, la vista, etc.)*; colar, tamizar; **to** — **one's wrist** torcerse la muñeca; *s.* tensión excesiva; tirantez; torcedura; esfuerzo excesivo; linaje, rasgo racial; aire, tonada.

strainer [strénə] s. coladera; cedazo.

strait [stret] s. estrecho; **-s** estrecho; aprieto, apuro; — **jacket** camisa de fuerza.

strand [strænd] *v.* encallar; dejar perdido *(sin medios de salir)*, dejar aislado, extraviar; **to be -ed** estar encallado; estar extraviada *(sin medios de salir)*, estar aislado, andar perdido; *s.* ribera, playa; ramal *(de cuerda, cable, etc.)*; hebra, hilo; — **of hair** guedeja; trenza; — **of pearls** hilera de perlas.

strange [strendʒ] *adj.* extraño; raro, singular; desconocido.

strangeness [stréndʒnɪs] s. extrañeza, rareza.

stranger [stréndʒə] s. extraño, desconocido; forastero.

strangle [strǽŋgḷ] *v.* estrangular(se).

strap [stræp] s. correa; tira de cuero o de tela; correón; tirante; **metal** — banda de metal; *v.* amarrar o atar con correas; azotar *(con correa)*; *véase* **strop.**

stratagem [strǽtədʒəm] s. estratagema.

strategic [strətídʒɪk] *adj.* estratégico.

strategy [strǽtədʒɪ] s. estrategia.

stratosphere [strǽtəsfɪr] s. estratosfera.

straw [strɔ] s. paja; **I don't care a** — no me importa un comino; *adj.* de paja; pajizo; **straw-colored** pajizo, color de paja; — **hat** sombrero de paja; — **vote** voto no oficial *(para averiguar la opinión pública).*

strawberry [stróberɪ] s. fresa.

213

stray [stre] *v.* extraviarse, descarriarse, desviarse; perderse, errar el camino; vagar; *adj.* extraviado, perdido; — **remark** observación aislada; *s.* animal perdido o extraviado.

streak [strik] *s.* raya, línea, lista; veta, vena; rasgo; rayo (*de luz*); — **of lightning** relámpago, rayo; *v.* rayar, *Am.* listar, hacer rayas o listas en.

stream [strim] *s.* corriente; chorro, río, arroyo, arroyuelo; — **of cars** desfile de autos; **down**— río abajo, agua abajo, con la corriente; **up**— río arriba, agua arriba, contra la corriente; *v.* correr (*el agua*), fluir; brotar, manar; derramarse; flotar (*en el viento*), ondear; **to**— **out** of salir a torrentes de.

streamer [strímə] *s.* banderola; gallardete; listón, cinta (*que flota en el aire*)

street [strit] *s.* calle.

streetcar [strítkɑr] *s.* tranvía.

strength [strɛŋkθ] *s.* fuerza; poder; potencia; fortaleza; **on the** — **of his promise** fundado en su promesa.

strengthen [strɛ́ŋkθən] *v* fortalecer(se), reforzar(se).

strenuous [strɛ́njuəs] *adj.* arduo; enérgico, vigoroso.

stress [strɛs] *s.* fuerza, esfuerzo; tensión, torsión, compresión; urgencia; énfasis; acento; *v.* acentuar; recalcar, dar énfasis a, hacer hincapié en.

stretch [strɛtʃ] *v.* estirar(se); alargar(se); tender(se); ensanchar; **to** — **oneself** estirarse, desperezarse; **to** — **out one's hand** tender o alargar la mano; *s.* trecho, distancia; extension; período de tiempo; elasticidad; tensión; esfuerzo (*de la imaginación*); estirón; **home** — último trecho (*de una carrera*).

stretcher [strɛ́tʃə] *s.* estirador, ensanchador, dilatador; camilla (*para los heridos*).

strew [stru] *v.* regar, esparcir.

strewn [strun] *p.p. de* **to strew**; — **with** regado de, cubierto de.

stricken [stríkən] *p.p. de* **to strike**, *adj.* herido; afligido; agobiado; atacado.

strict [strɪkt] *adj.* estricto; **in** — **confidence** en absoluta confianza, con toda reserva.

stridden [strídn] *p.p. de* **to stride**.

stride [straɪd] *v.* tranquear, caminar a paso largo, dar zancadas, andar a trancos; *s.* zancada, tranco, paso largo.

strife [straɪf] *s.* refriega, contienda, pleito.

strike [straɪk] *v.* dar, golpear, pegar; dar (*un golpe*); azotar; herir; atacar; chocar con; dar con, encontrar (*oro, pe-*

tróleo, etc.); ocurrírsele a uno (*una idea*); asumir, afectar (*una postura, una actitud*); dar (*la hora un reloj*); encender (*un fósforo*); acuñar (*moneda*); declararse o estar en huelga, **to** — **at** amagar; acometer; **to** — **off** borrar, tachar; cortar, **to** — **one's attention** atraer o llamar la atención; **to** — **one's fancy** antojársele a uno; **to** — **one's head against** darse un cabezazo contra; **to** — **out in a certain direction** tomar cierto rumbo, encaminarse o irse en cierta dirección; **to** — **someone for a loan** darle un sablazo a alguien, **to** — **up a friendship** trabar amistad, **to** — **with terror** sobrecoger de terror, **how does she** — **you?** ¿qué tal le parece?, ¿qué piensa Vd. de ella?, *s.* golpe, huelga, descubrimiento repentino (*de petróleo, de una mina, etc.*); —**breaker** esquirol (*obrero que sustituye a un huelguista*).

striker [stráɪkə] *s.* huelguista; golpeador.

striking [stráɪkɪŋ] *adj.* notable; llamativo; conspicuo, manifiesto; sorprendente; extraordinario, que está en huelga.

string [strɪŋ] *s.* cuerda; cordel, cinta, cordón; sarta (*de perlas, cuentas, etc.*); fibra (*de habichuelas, porotos, etc.*); fila, hilera; — **bean** habichuela, judía verde, *Am.* ejote, *Am.* poroto; — **of lies** sarta de mentiras; *v.* ensartar; tender (*un cable, un alambre*); desfibrar, quitar las fibras a; encordar (*una raqueta, un violín*); encordelar, atar con cordeles, lazos o cuerdas, tomar el pelo, engañar; **to** — **out** extender(se), prolongar(se); **to** — **up** colgar.

strip [strɪp] *v.* despojar; robar; desnudar(se); desvestir(se), desmantelar; **to** — **the gears** estropear el engranaje; **to** — **the skin from** desollar, pelar; *s.* tira, lista, listón; — **of land** faja de tierra.

stripe [straɪp] *s.* franja, raya, lista, tira; banda, galón; tipo, índole; *v.* rayar, *Am.* listar, adornar con listas.

striped [stráɪpɪd, straɪpt] *adj.* listado.

strive [straɪv] *v.* esforzarse; luchar, forcejear; hacer lo posible; **to** — **to** esforzarse por.

striven [strívən] *p.p. de* **to strive**.

strode [strod] *pret. de* **to stride**.

stroke [strok] *s.* golpe; ataque, apoplejía; — **of a bell** campanada; — **of a painter's brush** pincelada; — **of lightning** rayo; — **of the hand** caricia; — **of the pen** plumada; **at the** — **of ten** al dar las diez; *v.* frotar suavemente, pasar suavemente la mano, acariciar; alisar.

stroll [strol] *v.* dar un paseo, pasearse; vagar; **to — the streets** callejear; *s.* paseo, paseíto.

strong [strɔŋ] *adj.* fuerte; forzudo, fornido; vigoroso; recio; enérgico; firme; bien marcado; acérrimo; **— chance** buena probabilidad; **— coffee** café cargado; **— market** mercado firme; **strong-willed** de voluntad fuerte, decidido; *adv.* fuertemente; firmemente.

stronghold [strɔ́ŋhold] *s.* fuerte, plaza fuerte.

strop [strɔp] *v.* asentar (*navajas de afeitar*); *s.* asentador de navajas.

strove [strov] *pret. de* strive.

struck [strʌk] *pret. & p.p. de* to strike; **to be — with** a disease darle a uno una enfermedad; **to be — with terror** estar o quedar sobrecogido de terror.

structural [strʌ́ktʃərəl] *adj.* estructural, relativo a la estructura.

structure [strʌ́ktʃə] *s.* estructura; construcción; edificio.

struggle [strʌ́gl] *v.* bregar, luchar, pugnar; forcejear; esforzarse; *s.* esfuerzo; contienda; lucha, pugna.

strung [strʌŋ] *pret. & p.p. de* to string.

strut [strʌt] *v.* pavonearse, contonearse; *s.* contoneo; tirante, puntal.

stub [stʌb] *s.* trozo, fragmento, pedazo mochado; tocón (*de árbol*); talón (*de libro talonario, boleto, etc.*); **— book** libro talonario; **— pen** pluma de punta mocha; *v.* **to — one's foot** dar(se) un tropezón.

stubble [stʌ́bl] *s.* rastrojo; cañones (*de la barba*).

stubborn [stʌ́bən] *adj.* terco, testarudo, obstinado, porfiado, cabezón.

stubbornness [stʌ́bənnɪs] *s.* terquedad, testarudez, porfía, obstinación.

stucco [stʌ́ko] *s.* estuco; *v.* estucar, cubrir de estuco.

stuck [stʌk] *pret. & p.p. de* to stick pegado; atorado; atascado; **— full of holes** agujereado; **stuck-up** tieso, estirado, orgulloso.

stud [stʌd] *s.* tachón, tachuela de adorno; botón postizo para camisa; perno; **—horse** caballo padre; *v.* tachonar, clavetear.

student [stjúdṇt] *s.* estudiante.

studied [stʌ́dɪd] *adj.* estudiado.

studio [stjúdɪo] *s.* estudio, taller.

studious [stjúdɪəs] *adj.* estudioso; aplicado; estudiado.

study [stʌ́dɪ] *s.* estudio; cuidado, solici-

tud; gabinete de estudio; *v.* estudiar.

stuff [stʌf] *s.* materia; material; género; tela; cosa; cosas; menjurje, medicina; cachivaches, baratijas; **of good —** de buena estofa; *v.* rellenar; henchir; hartar(se), atracar(se), atiborrar(se).

stuffing [stʌ́fɪŋ] *s.* rellenó; material para rellenar.

stumble [stʌ́mbl] *v.* tropezar, dar(se) un tropezón; dar un traspié; hablar o recitar equivocándose a cada paso; **to — upon** tropezar con; *s.* tropiezo, tropezón, traspié.

stump [stʌmp] *s.* tocón (*tronco que queda de un árbol*); raigón (*de muela*); muñón (*de brazo o pierna cortada*); **— of a tail** rabo; **to be up a —** hallarse en un apuro, estar perplejo; *v.* trozar el tronco de (*un árbol*); renquear, cojear; dejar confuso, confundir; **to — the country** recorrer el país pronunciando discursos políticos.

stumpy [stʌ́mpɪ] *adj.* rechoncho, *Am.* chaparro; lleno de tocones.

stun [stʌn] *v.* aturdir, pasmar; atolondrar.

stung [stʌŋ] *pret. & p.p. de* to sting.

stunk [stʌŋk] *pret. & p.p. de* to stink.

stunning [stʌ́nɪŋ] *adj.* aplastante; elegante, bellísimo.

stunt [stʌnt] *v.* achaparrar, impedir el desarrollo de, no dejar crecer; hacer suertes; hacer piruetas; *s.* suerte; pirueta, suerte acrobática, maniobra gimnástica; hazaña sensacional.

stupefy [stjúpəfaɪ] *v.* atontar; entorpecer; aturdir, atolondrar, pasmar, dejar estupefacto.

stupendous [stjupéndəs] *adj.* estupendo.

stupid [stjúpɪd] *adj.* estúpido; atontado.

stupidity [stjupídətɪ] *s.* estupidez.

stupor [stjúpə] *s.* letargo, modorra; aturdimiento; **in a —** aletargado.

sturdy [stɔ́dɪ] *adj.* fornido, fuerte, robusto; firme.

stutter [stʌ́tə] *v.* tartamudear; *s.* tartamudeo; tartamudea.

stutterer [stʌ́tərə] *s.* tartamudo.

stuttering [stʌ́tərɪŋ] *adj.* tartamudo; *s.* tartamudeo.

sty [staɪ] *s.* pocilga; orzuelo (*en el párpado*), *Am.* perrilla.

style [staɪl] *s.* estilo; moda; **to be in —** estar de moda, estilarse; *v.* intitular, nombrar; **to — a dress** cortar un vestido a la moda.

stylish [staɪlɪʃ] *adj.* elegante; a la moda.

subdivision [sʌbdəvíʒən] *s.* subdivisión; parcelación de terrenos.

subdue [səbdjú] *v.* subyugar, someter;

215

sujetar, dominar; amansar, domar.

subdued [səbdjúd] *p.p. de* **to subdue;** *adj.* sumiso; sujeto; manso; suave; tenue; — **light** luz tenue.

subject [sábdʒıkt] *s.* súbdito; sujeto; asunto, tema, materia; *adj.* sujeto; sometido; inclinado, propenso; expuesto; [səbdʒékt] *v.* sujetar; someter; subyugar, sojuzgar.

subjection [səbdʒékʃən] *s.* sujeción; dominación; sumisión.

subjugate [sábdʒəget] *v.* subyugar, sojuzgar.

sublime [səbláım] *adj.* sublime.

submarine [sʌbmərín] *adj.* submarino; [sábmərın] *s.* submarino.

submerge [səbmɜ́dʒ] *v.* sumergir(se), hundir(se), sumir(se).

submission [səbmíʃən] *s.* sumisión, sometimiento.

submissive [səbmísıv] *adj.* sumiso.

submit [səbmít] *v.* someter; **to — a report** someter (presentar *o* rendir) un informe; **to — to punishment** someterse a un castigo.

subordinate [səbɔ́rdnıt] *adj. & s.* subordinado; subalterno; dependiente; [səbɔ́rdnet] *v.* subordinar.

subscribe [səbskráıb] *v.* subscribir(se); firmar; **to — five dollars** prometer una cuota *o* subscripción de cinco dólares; **to — for** subscribirse a, abonarse a; **to — to a plan** subscribirse a (*o* aprobar) un plan.

subscriber [səbskráıbə] *s.* suscritor, abonado; infrascrito (*que firma un documento*), firmante.

subscription [səbskrípʃən] *s.* subscripción, abono.

subsequent [sábsıkwent] *adj.* subsiguiente, subsecuente, posterior; -ly *adv.* después, posteriormente, subsiguientemente.

subservient [səbsɜ́vıent] *adj.* servil, servilón.

subside [səbsáıd] *v.* menguar, disminuir; bajar (*de nivel*); calmarse, aquietarse.

subsidize [sábsədaız] *v.* subvencionar.

subsidy [sábsədı] *s.* subvención.

subsist [səbsíst] *v.* subsistir.

substance [sábstəns] *s.* substancia (sustancia).

substantial [səbstǽnʃəl] *adj.* substancial, substancioso; sólido; considerable; importante; **to be in — agreement** estar en substancia de acuerdo.

substantive [sábstəntıv] *adj. & s.* sustantivo.

substitute [sábstətjut] *v.* sustituir (substituir); reemplazar; *s.* sustituto, su-

plente; reemplazo.

substitution [sʌbstətjúʃən] *s.* sustitución (substitución); reemplazo.

subterranean [sʌbtərénıən] *adj.* subterráneo.

subtle [sátl] *adj.* sutil.

subtlety [sátltı] *s.* sutileza; agudeza.

subtract [səbtrǽkt] *v.* sustraer (substraer); restar.

subtraction [səbtrǽkʃən] *s.* sustracción (substracción), resta.

suburb [sábɜb] *s.* suburbio, arrabal.

suburban [səbɜ́bən] *adj. & s.* suburbano.

subversive [səbvɜ́sıv] *adj.* subversivo (*en contra de la autoridad constituida*); trastornador, destructivo.

subway [sábwe] *s.* subterráneo, túnel; metro, ferrocarril subterráneo.

succeed [səksíd] *v.* suceder a; medrar, tener buen éxito, salir bien.

success [səksés] *s.* éxito, buen éxito; triunfo.

successful [səksésfəl] *adj.* afortunado; próspero; **to be — tener** buen éxito; -ly *adv.* con buen éxito, prósperamente.

succession [səkséʃən] *s.* sucesión.

successive [səksésıv] *adj.* sucesivo.

successor [səksésə] *s.* sucesor; heredero.

succor [sákə] *s.* socorro; *v.* socorrer.

succumb [səkám] *v.* sucumbir.

such [satʃ] *adj.* tal; semejante; — **a tal,** semejante; — **a good man** un hombre tan bueno; — **as tal** como, tales como; **at — an hour a tal** hora; **at — and — a place** en tal *o* cual lugar.

suck [sak] *v.* chupar; mamar; **to — up** chupar; sorber; *s.* chupada; mamada.

sucker [sákə] *s.* chupador; mamón, mamantón; dulce (*que se chupa*); primo (*persona demasiado crédula*).

suckle [sákl] *v.* mamar; amamantar, dar de mamar.

suction [sákʃən] *s.* succión; chupada, aspiración.

sudden [sádn] *adj.* súbito, repentino; precipitado; inesperado; **all of a — de** súbito, de repente, de sopetón; -ly *adv.* de súbito, de repente, de sopetón.

suddenness [sádnnıs] *s.* precipitación; rapidez.

suds [sadz] *s.* espuma, jabonadura.

sue [su] *v.* demandar; **to — for damages** demandar por daños y perjuicios; **to — for peace** pedir la paz.

suet [súıt] *s.* sebo, gordo, grasa.

suffer [sáfə] *v.* sufrir; padecer.

sufferer [sáfərə] *s.* sufridor.

suffering [sáfərıŋ] *s.* sufrimiento, padecimiento; *adj.* doliente; sufrido, paciente.

suffice [səfáɪs] v. bastar, ser bastante o suficiente.

sufficient [səffʃɔnt] adj. suficiente, bastante; **-ly** adv. suficientemente, bastante.

suffocate [sʌfɔket] v. sofocar(se), ahogar(se), asfixiar(se).

suffocation [sʌfɔkéʃən] s. asfixia, sofoco.

suffrage [sʌfrɪdʒ] s. sufragio; voto.

sugar [ʃúgə] s. azúcar; — **bowl** azucarera; — **cane** caña de azúcar; **lump of** — terrón de azúcar; v. azucarar; cristalizarse (el almíbar), Am. azucararse.

suggest [səgdʒést] v. sugerir, indicar.

suggestion [səgdʒéstʃən] s. sugestión, Am. sugerencia; indicación.

suggestive [səgdʒéstɪv] adj. sugestivo.

suicide [súosaɪd] s. suicidio; suicida; **to commit** — suicidarse.

suit [sut] s. traje, terno, Am. flux (o flus); palo (de la baraja); demanda, pleito; petición; galanteo; v. adaptar, acomodar; agradar; satisfacer; sentar bien, venir bien; caer bien; convenir; ser a propósito; — **yourself** haz lo que quieras, haga Vd. lo que guste.

suitable [sútəbl] adj. propio, conveniente, debido, a propósito, apropiado, adecuado.

suitably [sútəblɪ] adv. propiamente, adecuadamente, convenientemente.

suitcase [sútkes] s. maleta, valija.

suite [swit] s. serie; comitiva, acompañamiento; — **of rooms** vivienda, apartamento, habitación; **bedroom** — juego de muebles para alcoba.

suitor [sútə] s. pretendiente, galán; demandante (en un pleito).

sulk [salk] v. tener murria, estar hosco o malhumorado; s. murria.

sulky [sálkɪ] adj. malcontento, hosco, malhumorado; **to be** — tener murria.

sullen [sálɪn] adj. hosco, sombrío, tétrico; malhumorado, taciturno.

sully [sálɪ] v. manchar, ensuciar; empañar.

sulphate [sálfet] s. sulfato.

sulphide [sálfaɪd] s. sulfuro.

sulphur [sálfə] s. azufre.

sulphuric [sʌlfjúrɪk] adj. sulfúrico.

sultan [sáltn] s. sultán.

sultry [sáltrɪ] adj. bochornoso, sofocante;— **heat** bochorno, calor sofocante.

sum [sam] s. suma; cantidad; esencia, substancia; — **total** total; v. sumar; **to** — **up** resumir, recapitular.

summarize [sámraɪz] v. resumir, compendiar.

summary [sámrɪ] s. sumario, resumen;

compendio; adj. sumario; breve.

summer [sámə] s. verano; estío; adj. veraniego, estival, de verano; — **resort** balneario, lugar de veraneo; v. veranear.

summit [sámɪt] s. cima, cúspide, cumbre.

summon [sámən] v. citar; convocar, llamar; **-s** s. notificación; cita judicial, citación, emplazamiento.

sumptuous [sámptʃʊəs] adj. suntuoso.

sun [sʌn] s. sol; — **bath** baño de sol; — **porch** solana; v. asolear; **to** — **oneself** asolearse, tomar el sol.

sunbeam [sánbim] s. rayo de sol.

sunburn [sánbən] s. quemadura de sol, v. asolear(se); quemar(se) al sol, tostar(se) al sol.

Sunday [sándɪ] s. domingo.

sundial [sándaɪəl] s. cuadrante solar, reloj de sol.

sundown [sándaʊn] s. puesta del sol.

sundry [sándrɪ] adj. varios, diversos.

sunflower [sánflaʊə] s. girasol.

sung [sʌŋ] pret. & p.p. de **to sing**.

sunk [sʌŋk] pret. & p.p. de **to sink**.

sunken [sáŋkən] adj. hundido, sumido.

sunlight [sánlaɪt] s. luz del sol, luz solar.

sunny [sánɪ] adj. asoleado o soleado; alegre, risueño, resplandeciente; — **day** día de sol.

sunrise [sánraɪz] s. salida del sol, amanecer, amanecida.

sunset [sánsɛt] s. puesta del sol.

sunshine [sánʃaɪn] s. luz del sol, solana.

sunstroke [sánstrok] s. insolación.

sup [sʌp] v. cenar.

superb [supáb] adj. soberbio.

superficial [supəfíʃəl] adj. superficial.

superfluous [supáfluəs] adj. superfluo.

superhuman [supəhjúmən] adj. sobrehumano.

superintend [suprɪnténd] v. dirigir, inspeccionar, vigilar.

superintendent [suprɪnténdənt] s. superintendente; inspector; capataz.

superior [səpírɪə] adj. & s. superior.

superiority [səpɪrɪóratɪ] s. superioridad.

superlative [səpálətɪv] adj. & s. superlativo.

supernatural [supənǽtʃrəl] adj. sobrenatural; **the** — lo sobrenatural.

supersede [supəsíd] v. reemplazar.

superstition [supəstíʃən] s. superstición.

superstitious [supəstíʃəs] adj. supersticioso.

supervise [supəváɪz] v. dirigir, inspeccionar, vigilar.

supervision [supəvíʒən] s. inspección,

vigilancia.

supervisor [supəváizə] *s.* superintendente, inspector; interventor.

supper [sápə] *s.* cena.

supplant [səplǽnt] *v.* suplantar; reemplazar.

supple [sápl] *adj.* flexible; dócil.

supplement [sápləmənt] *s.* suplemento; apéndice; [sápləmənt] *v.* suplementar, completar.

suppliant [sáplɪənt] *adj. & s.* suplicante.

supplication [sʌplɪkéʃən] *s.* súplica, plegaria; ruego.

supply [səplái] *v.* proveer; abastecer, surtir; suplir; dar, suministrar; *s.* provisión, abastecimiento; bastimento; abasto; surtido; **supplies** provisiones; materiales; víveres; pertrechos; — **pipe** cañería o caño de abastecimiento, tubería o tubo de suministro.

support [səpórt] *v.* sostener; apoyar; mantener; sustentar; soportar, aguantar; *s.* apoyo; sostén, soporte, puntal; sustento, manutención; amparo.

supporter [səpórtə] *s.* defensor; partidario; mantenedor; sostén, apoyo; tirante *(para medias).*

suppose [səpóz] *v.* suponer.

supposed [səpózd] *adj.* supuesto; presunto; **-ly** *adv.* supuestamente.

supposition [sʌpəzíʃən] *s.* suposición.

suppress [səprés] *v.* suprimir; reprimir; parar, suspender; **to — a revolt** sofocar una revuelta o motín.

suppression [səpréʃən] *s.* supresión; represión.

supremacy [səprémʌsɪ] *s.* supremacía.

supreme [səprím] *adj.* supremo.

sure [ʃur] *adj.* seguro; cierto; estable; *adv. véase* **surely**; **be — and do it** hágalo sin falta, no deje Vd. de hacerlo; **-ly** *adv.* seguramente; ciertamente; con toda seguridad; sin falta.

surety [ʃúrtɪ] *s.* seguridad; garantía, fianza; fiador.

surf [sɜf] *s.* oleaje, rompientes; resaca.

surface [sɜ́fɪs] *s.* superficie; cara; *v.* alisar, allanar; poner superficie a.

surfeit [sɜ́fɪt] *s.* hastío, exceso; *v.* hastiar; empalagar.

surge [sɜdʒ] *s.* oleada, oleaje; *v.* agitarse, hinchar(se) *(el mar)*; surgir.

surgeon [sɜ́dʒən] *s.* cirujano.

surgery [sɜ́dʒərɪ] *s.* cirujía.

surgical [sɜ́dʒɪkl] *adj.* quirúrgico.

surly [sɜ́lɪ] *adj.* rudo, hosco, malhumorado.

surmise [səmáɪz] *v.* conjeturar, suponer, presumir; *s.* conjetura, suposición.

surmount [səmáunt] *v.* superar, vencer;

coronar.

surname [sɜ́nem] *s.* sobrenombre, apellido; *v.* apellidar, llamar.

surpass [səpǽs] *v.* sobrepasar, superar, sobrepujar, exceder, aventajar.

surpassing [səpǽsɪŋ] *adj.* sobresaliente, excelente.

surplus [sɜ́plʌs] *s.* sobra, sobrante, exceso, excedente; superávit; *adj.* sobrante, excedente, de sobra.

surprise [səpráɪz] *s.* sorpresa; *v.* sorprender.

surprising [səpráɪzɪŋ] *adj.* sorprendente.

surrender [səréndə] *v.* rendir(se), entregar(se), darse; ceder; *s.* rendición; entrega; cesión; sumisión.

surround [səráund] *v.* rodear, cercar, circundar.

surrounding [səráundɪŋ] *adj.* circundante, circunvecino, circunstante.

surroundings [səráundɪŋz] *s. pl.* alrededores, inmediaciones, cercanías; ambiente.

survey [sɜ́ve] *s.* examen, reconocimiento, inspección, estudio; medición, agrimensura *(de un terreno);* plano *(de un terreno);* bosquejo o esbozo general *(de historia, literatura, etc.);* — **course** curso general o comprensivo; [sɜvé] *v.* examinar, inspeccionar, reconocer medir *(un terreno),* levantar un plano *(el agrimensor).*

surveyor [sɜvéə] *s.* agrimensor.

survival [səváɪvl] *s.* supervivencia; sobreviviente; resto.

survive [səváɪv] *v.* sobrevivir; quedar vivo, salvarse.

survivor [səváɪvə] *s.* sobreviviente.

susceptible [səséptəbl] *adj.* susceptible; — **of proof** capaz de probarse; — **to** propenso a.

suspect [sáspɛkt] *s.* sospechoso; [səspɛ́kt] *v.* sospechar.

suspend [səspénd] *v.* suspender.

suspenders [səspéndəz] *s.* tirantes *(de pantalón).*

suspense [səspéns] *s.* suspensión, incertidumbre; ansiedad; **to keep in —** tener en suspenso, tener en duda.

suspension [səspénʃən] *s.* suspensión; — **bridge** puente colgante.

suspicion [səspíʃən] *s.* sospecha.

suspicious [səspíʃəs] *adj.* sospechoso; suspicaz.

sustain [səstén] *v.* sostener; mantener; sustentar; aguantar; sufrir *(un daño o pérdida);* apoyar, defender.

sustenance [sʌ́stənəns] *s.* sustento; subsistencia; alimentos; mantenimiento.

swagger [swǽgə] *v.* pavonearse, contonearse; fanfarronear; *s.* pavoneo, contoneo; fanfarronada.

swain [swen] *s.* galán.

swallow [swálo] *s.* golondrina; trago; *v.* tragar; deglutir.

swam [swæm] *pret. de* to swim.

swamp [swamp] *s.* pantano; ciénaga; — **land** cenagal, terreno pantanoso; *v.* inundar(se); sumergir(se); **to be -ed with work** estar abrumado de trabajo.

swampy [swámpɪ] *adj.* pantanoso, cenagoso, fangoso.

swan [swan] *s.* cisne.

swap [swap] *v.* cambalachear, cambiar, trocar; *s.* cambalache, cambio, trueque.

swarm [sworm] *s.* enjambre; *v.* pulular; bullir, hervir, hormiguear.

swarthy [swórðɪ] *adj.* trigueño, moreno, *Am.* prieto.

swat [swɑt] *v.* pegar, aporrear; aplastar de un golpe (*una mosca*); *s.* golpe.

sway [swe] *v.* mecer(se); cimbrar(se); balancearse; ladear(se); oscilar; tambalear; influir; *s.* oscilación; vaivén; balanceo; influjo, influencia; mando; predominio.

swear [swer] *v.* jurar; renegar, blasfemar, echar maldiciones; juramentar, tomar juramento; **to — by** jurar por; poner toda su confianza en; **to — in** juramentar; **to — off smoking** jurar no fumar más, renunciar al tabaco.

sweat [swet] *v.* sudar; trasudar; hacer sudar; *s.* sudor; trasudor.

sweater [swétə] *s. Am.* suéter; sudador, el que suda.

sweaty [swétɪ] *adj.* sudoroso.

Swede [swid] *s.* sueco.

Swedish [swídɪʃ] *adj.* sueco; *s.* sueco, idioma sueco.

sweep [swip] *v.* barrer; dragar (*puertos, ríos, etc.*); extenderse; **to — down upon** caer sobre; asolar; **to — everything away** barrer con todo; **she swept into the room** entró garbosamente en la sala; *s.* barrida; extensión; soplo (*del viento*).

sweeper [swípə] *s.* barrendero; **carpet —** escoba mecánica.

sweeping [swípɪŋ] *s.* barrido; **-s** basura; *adj.* abarcador, que lo abarca todo, vasto; asolador; — **victory** victoria completa.

sweet [swit] *adj.* dulce; oloroso; fresco; — **butter** mantequilla sin sal; — **corn** maíz tierno; — **milk** leche fresca; — **pea** guisante de olor; — **potato** batata, *Am.* camote, *Am.* boniato; **to have a — tooth** ser goloso, gustarle

a uno los dulces; *s.* dulce, golosina; **my —** mi vida, mi alma.

sweeten [swítn] *v.* endulzar(se), dulcificar(se); suavizar.

sweetheart [swíthart] *s.* querida, novia, prometida; amante, querido, galán, novio.

sweetmeat [swítmit] *s.* confite, confitura, dulce, golosina.

sweetness [swítnɪs] *s.* dulzura; melosidad; suavidad.

swell [swel] *v.* hinchar(se), henchir(se), inflar(se); dilatar(se); abultar(se); acrecentar; *s.* hinchazón; protuberancia; oleaje; *adj.* elegante; muy bueno, excelente, magnífico; **to have a — head** creerse gran cosa; ser vanidoso.

swelling [swélɪŋ] *s.* hinchazón; chichón, bulto; protuberancia.

swept [swept] *pret. & p.p. de* to sweep.

swerve [swɜv] *v.* desviar(se); torcer; cambiar repentinamente de rumbo; *s.* desvío brusco, cambio repentino de dirección; **to make a — to the right** torcer a la derecha.

swift [swɪft] *adj.* veloz, rápido.

swiftness [swíftnɪs] *s.* velocidad, rapidez, presteza, prontitud.

swim [swɪm] *v.* nadar; flotar; **to — across** pasar a nado, atravesar nadando; **my head is swimming** tengo vértigo, se me va la cabeza, estoy desvanecido; *s.* nadada; — **suit** traje de baño o natación.

swimmer [swímə] *s.* nadador.

swindle [swíndl] *v.* estafar; *s.* estafa.

swine [swaɪn] *s.* marrano, puerco, cerdo, cochino; marranos, puercos, cerdos.

swing [swɪŋ] *v.* columpiar(se), mecer(se), balancear(se); oscilar; hacer oscilar; blandir (*un bastón, espada, etc.*); colgar; girar; hacer girar; **to — a deal** llevar a cabo un negocio; **to — around** dar vuelta, girar; **to — one's arms** girar o menear los brazos; **to — open** abrirse de pronto (*una puerta*); *s.* columpio; hamaca; balanceo; vaivén; compás, ritmo; golpe, guantada, puñetazo; — **door** puerta giratoria; **in full —** en su apogeo, en pleno movimiento; **to give someone full —** darle a alguien completa libertad de acción.

swipe [swaɪp] *v.* hurtar, sisar.

swirl [swɜl] *v.* arremolinarse; girar, dar vueltas; *s.* remolino; torbellino; vuelta, movimiento giratorio.

Swiss [swɪs] *adj. & s.* suizo.

switch [swɪtʃ] *s.* látigo, azote, *Am.* chicote, *Am.* rebenque; latigazo; pelo postizo; cambio; **electric —** interruptor, conmutador; **railway** — aguja, cambio; **—man** guardagujas, *Am.* cambiavía; *v.* azotar; desviar(se); cambiar(se); **to** — **off** cortar (*la comunicación o la corriente eléctrica*); apagar (*la luz eléctrica*); **to** — **on the light** encender la luz.

switchboard [swítʃbɔrd] *s.* cuadro o tablero de distribución; cuadro conmutador.

swollen [swólən] *p.p. de* to swell.

swoon [swun] *v.* desvanecerse, desmayarse; *s.* desmayo.

swoop [swup] *v.* **to** — **down upon** caer de súbito sobre; abalanzarse sobre; acometer; **to** — **off** cortar de un golpe; **to** — **up** agarrar, arrebatar; *s.* descenso súbito; arremetida; **at one** — de un golpe.

sword [sord] *s.* espada; — **belt** talabarte.

swore [swor] *pret. de* to swear.

sworn [sworn] *p.p. de* to swear.

swum [swʌm] *p.p. de* to swim.

swung [swʌŋ] *pret. & p.p. de* to swing.

syllable [síləb] *s.* sílaba.

symbol [símbl] *s.* símbolo.

symbolic [símbálɪk] *adj.* simbólico.

symbolism [símbᴊɪzəm] *s.* simbolismo.

symmetrical [sɪmétrɪk] *adj.* simétrico.

symmetry [símɪtrɪ] *s.* simetría.

sympathetic [sɪmpəθétɪk] *adj.* simpático; que simpatiza o siente simpatía; compasivo; — **towards** favorablemente dispuesto a (o hacia).

sympathize [símpəθaɪz] *v.* simpatizar; compadecerse, condolerse.

sympathy [símpəθɪ] *s.* simpatía; armonía; lástima, compasión; **to extend one's** — dar el pésame.

symphony [símfənɪ] *s.* sinfonía; — **orchestra** orquesta sinfónica.

symptom [símptəm] *s.* síntoma.

syndicate [síndɪkɪt] *s.* sindicato; **newspaper** — sindicato periodístico; [síndɪket] *v.* sindicar, formar un sindicato; sindicarse, combinarse para formar un sindicato; vender (*un cuento, caricatura, serie de artículos, etc.*) a un sindicato.

synonym [sínənɪm] *s.* sinónimo.

synonymous [sɪnánəməs] *adj.* sinónimo.

syntax [síntæks] *s.* sintaxis.

synthesis [sínθəsɪs] *s.* síntesis.

synthetic [sɪnθétɪk] *adj.* sintético.

syringe [sírɪndʒ] *s.* jeringa.

syrup = **sirup.**

system [sístəm] *s.* sistema.

systematic [sɪstəmǽtɪk] *adj.* sistemático.

T

tabernacle [tǽbənæk] *s.* tabernáculo.

table [tébl] *s.* mesa; tabla (*de materias, de multiplicar, etc.*); — **cover** tapete, cubremesa; **—land** mesa, meseta; *v.* poner sobre la mesa; formar tabla o índice; **to** — **a motion** dar carpetazo a una moción, aplazar la discusión de una moción.

tablecloth [téblklɔə] *s.* mantel.

tablespoon [téblspun] *s.* cuchara grande.

tablespoonful [téblspunful] *s.* cucharada.

tablet [tæblɪt] *s.* tableta; tablilla, pastilla; bloc de papel; lápida, placa.

tableware [téblwɛr] *s.* vajilla, servicio de mesa.

tabulate [tæbjəlet] *v.* formar tablas o listas.

tacit [tǽsɪt] *adj.* tácito.

taciturn [tǽsətᴣn] *adj.* taciturno, silencioso.

tack [tæk] *s.* tachuela; hilván; virada o cambio de rumbo (*de una embarcación*); amura, jarcia (*para sostener el ángulo de una vela*); **to change** — cambiar de amura, cambiar de rumbo; *v.* clavetear con tachuelas; coser, hilvanar; pegar, clavar; juntar, unir; virar, cambiar de rumbo; zigzaguear (*un barco de vela*).

tackle [tæk] *s.* aparejo, equipo; enseres, avíos; agarrada (*en futbol*); atajador (*en futbol*); **fishing** — avíos de pescar; *v.* agarrar, asir, atajar (*en futbol*); atacar (*un problema*); acometer (*una empresa*).

tact [tækt] *s.* tacto, tino, tiento.

tactful [tǽktfl] *adj.* cauto, prudente, diplomático.

tactics [tǽktɪks] *s.* táctica.

tactless [tǽktlɪs] *adj.* falto de tacto o de tino; imprudente, incauto.

taffeta [tǽfɪtə] *s.* tafetán.

tag [tæg] *s.* marbete, etiqueta; cartela; pingajo, rabito, cabo; **to play** — jugar al tócame tú, jugar a la pega; *v.* pegar un marbete a, marcar; **to** — **after** seguir de cerca a, pisar los talones a; **to** — **something on to** juntar, añadir o agregar algo a.

tail [tel] *s.* cola, rabo; cabo, extremo, extremidad; — **light** farol trasero, farol de cola; — **spin** barrena.

tailor [télə] *s.* sastre.

taint [tent] *s.* tacha, mancha; corrupción; *v.* manchar; corromper(se), inficionar(se).

take [tek] *v.* tomar; coger; llevar; conducir; dar (*un paseo, vuelta, paso, salto*); hacer (*un viaje*); asumir; sacar o tomar (*una fotografía*); **to — a chance** aventurarse, correr un riesgo; **to — a fancy to** caerle en gracia a uno; aficionarse a; antojársele a uno; **to — a look at** mirar a, echar una mirada a; **to — a notion to** antojársele a uno; **to — after** salir a, parecerse a; seguir el ejemplo del; **to — amiss** interpretar mal, echar a mala parte; **to — an oath** prestar juramento; **to — apart** desarmar, desmontar; **to — away** llevarse; **to — back one's words** desdecirse, retractarse; **to — back to** devolver (*algo*) a; **to — by surprise** coger desprevenido, coger de sorpresa; **to — care of** cuidar de, atender a; **to — charge of** encargarse de; **to — cold** resfriarse, acatarrarse; **to — down in writing** poner por escrito, apuntar; **to — effect** surtir efecto, dar resultado; entrar en vigencia (*una ley*); **to — exercise** hacer ejercicio; hacer gimnasia; **to — from** quitar a; sustraer de, restar de; **to — in** meter en; recibir; abarcar; embaucar; reducir, achicar (*un vestido*); **to — leave** decir adiós, despedirse; **to — off** quitar; descontar, rebajar; despegar (*un aeroplano*); remedar, parodiar (*a alguien*); **to — offense** ofenderse, darse por ofendido; **to — on a responsibility** asumir una responsabilidad; **to — out** sacar; **to — place** tener lugar, suceder, ocurrir; **to — stock** hacer inventario; **to — stock in** creer, tener confianza en; **to — the floor** tomar la palabra; **to — to heart** tomar a pechos, tomar en serio; **to — to one's heels** poner pies en polvorosa; **to — to task** reprender, regañar; **to — up a matter** tratar un asunto; **to — up space** ocupar espacio; **I — it that** supongo que; *s.* toma; **take-off** despegue (*de un aeroplano*); remedo, parodia.

taken [tékən] *p.p. de* **to take**; **to be — ill** caer enfermo.

talcum [tǽlkəm] *s.* talco; **— powder** talco en polvo.

tale [tel] *s.* cuento, relato, fábula; chisme; **to tell -s** contar cuentos o chismes; chismear, murmurar.

talebearer [télbɛrə] *s.* soplón, chismoso.

talent [tǽlənt] *s.* talento.

talented [tǽləntid] *adj.* talentoso.

talk [tɔk] *v.* hablar; charlar, platicar, conversar; **to — into** inducir o persuadir a; **to — nonsense** decir tonterías, hablar disparates; **to — out of** disuadir de; **to — over** discutir; **to — up** alabar; hablar claro o recio, hablar en voz alta; *s.* charla, conversación, plática; habla; discurso; conferencia; rumor; **— of the town** comidilla, tema de murmuración.

talkative [tɔ́kətɪv] *adj.* hablador, locuaz, platicador.

talker [tɔ́kə] *s.* hablador; conversador; platicador; orador.

tall [tɔl] *adj.* alto; **— tale** cuento exagerado o increíble; **six feet —** seis pies de altura o de alto.

tallow [tǽlo] *s.* sebo.

tally [tǽlɪ] *s.* cuenta; **— sheet** plana para llevar la cuenta; *v.* llevar la cuenta; **to — up** contar, sumar; **to — with** coresponder con, concordar con.

tame [tem] *adj.* manso; dócil; **— amusement** diversión poco animada o desabrida; *v.* amansar, domar, domeñar; domesticar.

tamper [tǽmpə] *v.* **to — with** meterse con, juguetear con; falsificar (*un documento*); **to — with a lock** tratar de forzar una cerradura.

tan [tæn] *v.* curtir, adobar (*pieles*); zurrar, azotar; tostar(se), requemar(se); *adj.* tostado, requemado; color de canela; bayo, amarillento; *s.* color moreno, de canela o café con leche.

tangent [tǽndʒənt] *adj. & s.* tangente; **to go off at a —** salirse por la tangente.

tangerine [tǽndʒərin] *s.* naranja tangerina o mandarina.

tangible [tǽndʒəbl] *adj.* tangible, palpable; corpóreo.

tangle [tǽŋgl] *v.* enredar(se), enmarañar(se); confundir(se), embrollar(se); *s.* enredo, maraña, embrollo, confusión.

tank [tæŋk] *s.* tanque; depósito; **swimming —** piscina.

tanner [tǽnə] *s.* curtidor.

tannery [tǽnərɪ] *s.* curtiduría, tenería.

tantalize [tǽntlaɪz] *v.* molestar; hacer desesperar; exasperar.

tantrum [tǽntram] *s.* berrinche.

tap [tæp] *s.* palmadita; golpecito; espita, grifo; **— dance** zapateado, *Am.* zapateo; **—room** bar; **beer on —** cerveza del barril, cerveza de sifón; *v.* tocar, golpear ligeramente; dar una palmadita o golpecito; taladrar; extraer; **to — a tree** sangrar un árbol.

tape [tep] *s.* cinta, cintilla; **— measure** cinta para medir; **—worm** solitaria; **adhesive —** tela adhesiva, esparadrapo; v. atar o vendar con cinta; medir con cinta.

taper [tépə] s. velita, candela; adelgazamiento gradual (de un objeto); v. adelgazar, disminuir gradualmente; **to — off** ahusar(se), ir disminuyendo (hasta rematar en punta).

tapestry [tǽpɪstrɪ] s. tapiz, colgadura; tapicería; tela (para forrar muebles).

tapioca [tæpɪókə] s. tapioca.

tar [tɑr] s. alquitrán, brea, pez (f.); v. alquitranar, embrear, poner brea o alquitrán.

tardy [tárdɪ] adj. tardo, tardío, **to be — llegar tarde o retrasado.

target [tárgɪt] s. blanco; **— practice** tiro al blanco.

tariff [tǽrɪf] s. tarifa; arancel, impuesto.

tarnish [tárnɪʃ] v. empañar(se); manchar; perder el lustre; s. deslustre, falta de lustre, empañamiento; mancha.

tarry [tǽrɪ] v. demorarse, tardar(se).

tart [tɑrt] adj. acre, agridulce; agrio; picante; **— reply** respuesta mordaz o agria; s. tarta, torta rellena con dulce de frutas.

task [tæsk] s. faena, tarea, quehacer; **to take to —** reprender, regañar.

tassel [tǽsl] s. borla.

taste [test] v. gustar; probar, saborear, paladear; **to — of onion** saber a cebolla; **it -s sour** sabe agrio, tiene un sabor o gusto agrio; s. gusto; sabor, prueba; afición; **after—** dejo; **in good — de** buen gusto, **to take a — of** probar.

tasteless [téstlɪs] adj insípido; desabrido; de mal gusto.

tasty [téstɪ] adj. sabroso, gustoso; de buen gusto.

tatter [tǽtə] s. harapo, Am. hilacho.

tattered [tǽtəd] adj roto, harapiento, andrajoso.

tattle [tǽtl] v chismear, murmurar; s. habladuría, murmuración, hablilla; **—tale** chismoso, soplón.

taught [tɔt] pret. & p.p. de **to teach.**

taunt [tɔnt] v. mofarse de, echar pullas; reprochar; s. mofa, pulla.

tavern [tǽvən] s. taberna; posada.

tax [tæks] s. impuesto, contribución; esfuerzo; v. imponer contribuciones a; tasar; abrumar; reprender, reprobar; cobrar (un precio); **to — one's patience** abusar de la paciencia.

taxation [tækséʃən] s. impuestos, contribuciones; imposición de contribuciones.

taxi [tǽksɪ] s. taxímetro, taxi, automóvil de alquiler; v. ir en taxímetro; taxear

(un aeroplano).

taxicab [tǽksɪkæb] **= taxi.**

taxpayer [tǽkspeə] s. contribuyente.

tea [ti] s. té.

teach [titʃ] v. enseñar; instruir.

teacher [títʃə] s. maestro, maestra.

teaching [títʃɪŋ] s. enseñanza; instrucción; doctrina.

teacup [tíkʌp] s. taza para té.

teakettle [tíketl]· s. marmita, tetera, Am. pava (para el mate).

team [tim] s.˙ equipo (de jugadores); partido, grupo; tronco (de caballos, mulas, etc.); yunta (de bueyes); **—work** cooperación; v. uncir, enganchar; formar pareja; acarrear, transportar; **to — up** unirse, formar un equipo.

teamster [tímstə] s. carretero.

teapot [típɑt] s. tetera.

tear [tɪr] s. lágrima; **— gas** gas lacrimógeno o lacrimante; **to burst into -s** romper a llorar; deshacerse en lágrimas.

tear [ter] v. rasgar(se); desgarrar, romper; **to — along** ir a toda velocidad; andar aprisa, correr; **to — apart** desarmar, desmontar; separar, apartar; **to — away** arrancar; irse; **to — down** demoler, derribar (un edificio); desarmar, desmontar (una máquina), **to — off in a hurry** salir corriendo, salir a la carrera; **to — one's hair** mesarse los cabellos; s. desgarradura, rasgadura; rasgón, rotura, prisa; **wear and —** desgaste.

tearful [tírfəl] adj. lloroso.

tease [tiz] v. embromar; molestar; importunar.

teaspoon [tíspun] s. cucharilla, cucharita.

teaspoonful [tíspunfʊl] s. cucharadita.

teat [tit] s. teta.

technical [téknɪk] adj. técnico.

technician [teknɪʃən] s. técnico.

technique [tekník] s. técnica.

tedious [tídɪəs] adj. tedioso, pesado, aburrido, fastidioso.

tediousness [tídɪəsnɪs] s. tedio.

teem [tim] v. **to — with** abundar en, estar lleno de.

teens [tinz] s. pl. edad de trece a diecinueve años; números de trece a diecinueve; **to be in one's —** tener de trece a diecinueve años.

teeth [tie] s. pl. de **tooth; he escaped by the skin of his —** por poco no se escapa, se escapó por milagro.

telegram [téləgræm] s. telegrama.

telegraph [téləgræf] s. telégrafo; v. telegrafiar.

222

telegraphic [tɛləgrǽfɪk] *adj.* telegráfico.

telegraphy [təlégrəfɪ] *s.* telegrafía.

telephone [téləfon] *s.* teléfono; — **booth** casilla de teléfono; — **operator** telefonista; — **receiver** receptor telefónico; *v.* telefonear, llamar por teléfono.

telescope [téləskop] *s.* telescopio; *v.* enchufar(se), encajar(se) un objeto en otro.

television [télɛvɪʒən] *s.* televisión.

tell [tɛl] *v.* decir; contar; expresar; explicar; adivinar; decidir; **to — on someone** delatar a alguien, contar chismes de alguien; **to — someone off** decirle a alguien cuatro verdades; **his age is beginning to —** ya comienza a notársele la edad.

teller [télə] *s.* narrador, relator; pagador o recibidor (*de un banco*); escrutador de votos.

temerity [təmérətɪ] *s.* temeridad.

temper [témpə] *v.* templar; *s.* temple (*de un metal*); genio, temple, humor; mal genio; **to keep one's —** contenerse, dominarse; **to lose one's —** perder la calma, encolerizarse.

temperament [témprəmənt] *s.* temperamento; disposición; temple.

temperance [témprəns] *s.* templanza, sobriedad.

temperate [témprɪt] *adj.* templado, moderado; sobrio.

temperature [témprətʃə] *s.* temperatura; **to have a —** tener calentura o fiebre.

tempest [témpɪst] *s.* tempestad.

tempestuous [tɛmpésʧʊəs] *adj.* tempestuoso, borrascoso.

temple [témpl] *s.* templo; sien.

temporal [témpərəl] *adj.* temporal.

temporarily [témpərɛrəlɪ] *adv.* temporalmente.

temporary [témpərɛrɪ] *adj.* temporal, transitorio, provisorio; interino.

tempt [tɛmpt] *v.* tentar; incitar; provocar; atraer.

temptation [tɛmptéʃən] *s.* tentación.

tempter [témptə] *s.* tentador.

tempting [témptɪŋ] *adj.* tentador, atractivo.

tenacious [tɪnéʃəs] *adj.* tenaz, aferrado.

tenacity [tɪnǽsətɪ] *s.* tenacidad; aferramiento; tesón.

tenant [ténənt] *s.* inquilino, arrendatario.

tend [tɛnd] *v.* cuidar, vigilar, guardar; atender; tender, inclinarse.

tendency [téndənsɪ] *s.* tendencia; propensión.

tender [téndə] *adj.* tierno; delicado; sensible; **tender-hearted** de corazón tierno; *s.* oferta, ofrecimiento; ténder (*de un tren*); lancha (*de auxilio*); cuidador, vigilante; **legal —** moneda corriente; *v.* ofrecer.

tenderloin [téndələɪn] *s.* filete.

tenderness [téndənɪs] *s.* ternura, terneza; delicadeza.

tendon [téndən] *s.* tendón.

tendril [téndrɪl] *s.* zarcillo (*tallito de una planta trepadora*).

tenement [ténəmənt] *s.* casa de vecindad.

tennis [ténɪs] *s.* tenis; — **court** cancha de tenis.

tenor [ténə] *s.* tenor; significado; — **voice** voz de tenor.

tense [tɛns] *adj.* tenso; tirante; *s.* tiempo (*del verbo*).

tension [ténʃən] *s.* tensión; tirantez.

tent [tɛnt] *s.* tienda de campaña; pabellón; *v.* acampar.

tentacle [téntəkl] *s.* tentáculo.

tentative [téntətɪv] *adj.* tentativo.

tepid [tépɪd] *adj.* tibio.

term [tɜm] *s.* término; período; plazo; sesión; -s términos, expresiones, palabras; condiciones; **to be on good -s** estar en buenas relaciones; **not to be on speaking -s** no hablarse, no dirigirse la palabra; **to come to -s** ajustarse, ponerse de acuerdo; *v.* nombrar, llamar, denominar.

terminal [tɜmən] *adj.* terminal, final, último; *s.* término, fin; estación terminal; **electric —** toma de corriente; borne (*de aparato eléctrico*).

terminate [tɜmənet] *v.* terminar, acabar.

termination [tɜmənéʃən] *s.* terminación, fin; desinencia (*gramatical*).

terrace [térɪs] *s.* terraplén; terraza, terrado; *v.* terraplenar.

terrestrial [təréstrɪəl] *adj.* terrestre, terreno, terrenal.

terrible [térəbl] *adj.* terrible; **terribly** *adv.* terriblemente.

terrier [térɪə] *s.* perro de busca.

terrific [tərífɪk] *adj.* terrífico.

terrify [térəfaɪ] *v.* aterrar, aterrorizar.

territory [térətorɪ] *s.* territorio.

terror [térə] *s.* terror, espanto.

test [tɛst] *s.* prueba, ensayo, experimento; comprobación; examen; — **tube** probeta, tubo de ensayo; **to undergo a —** sufrir una prueba; *v.* probar, ensayar, comprobar, experimentar; poner a prueba; examinar.

testament [téstəmənt] *s.* testamento.

testify [téstəfaɪ] *v.* atestiguar, atestar.

testimony [téstəmonɪ] *s.* testimonio.

text [tɛkst] *s.* texto.

textbook [tékstbʊk] *s.* texto, libro de texto.

textile [tékstl] *adj.* textil; de tejidos; — mill fábrica de tejidos; *s.* tejido, materia textil.

texture [tékstʃə] *s.* textura, contextura; tejido.

than [ðæn] *conj.* que; **more — once** más de una vez; **more — he knows** más de lo que él sabe.

thank [θæŋk] *v.* dar gracias, agradecer; **— heaven!** ¡gracias a Dios!; **— you** gracias; **to.have oneself to — for** tener la culpa de; ser responsable de; **-s** *s. pl.* gracias.

thankful [θǽŋkfəl] *adj.* agradecido; **-ly** *adv.* agradecidamente, con agradecimiènto, con gratitud.

thankfulness [θǽŋkfəlnɪs] *s.* gratitud, agradecimiento.

thankless [θǽŋklɪs] *adj.* ingrato; — task tarea ingrata o infructuosa.

thanksgiving [θæŋksgívɪŋ] *s.* acción de gracias; **— Day** día de acción de gracias.

that [ðæt] *adj.* ese, esa, aquel, aquella; **— one** ése, ésa, aquél, aquélla; *pron.* ése, ésa, eso, aquél, aquélla, aquello; *pron. rel.* que; **— is** es decir; **— of** el de, la de, lo de; **— which** el que, la que, lo que; *conj.* que; para que, a fin de que; **so —** para que; de modo que, a fin de que, de suerte que, de tal manera que; *adv.* tan; **— far** tan lejos; hasta allá, hasta allí; **— long** así de largo; de este tamaño; tanto tiempo.

thatch [θætʃ] *s.* paja *(para techar)*; *v.* techar con paja; **-ed roof** techumbre o techo de paja.

thaw [θɔ] *v.* deshelar(se), derretir(se); volverse más tratable o amistoso; *s.* deshielo, derretimiento.

the [*delante de consonante* ðə; *delante de vocal* ðɪ] *art.* el, la; lo; los, las; *adv.* **— more . . . — less** cuanto más . . . tanto menos; mientras más . . . tanto menos.

theater [θíətə] *s.* teatro.

theatrical [ɒɪætrɪkl] *adj.* teatral.

thee [ðɪ] *pron.* te.

theft [θɛft] *s.* hurto, robo.

their [ðɛr] *adj.* su (sus), de ellos, de ellas.

theirs [ðɛrz] *pron. pos.* suyo (suya, suyos, suyas), de ellos, de ellas; el suyo (la suya, los suyos, las suyas); el (la, los, las) de ellos; **a friend of —** un amigo suyo, un amigo de ellos.

them [ðɛm] *pron.* los, las; les; ellos, ellas *(con preposición)*.

theme [θim] *s.* tema; ensayo.

themselves [ðəmsélvz] *pron.* ellos mismos, ellas mismas; se *(como reflexivo)*; **to — a sí mismos;** *véase* **herself.**

then [ðɛn] *adv.* entonces; en aquel tiempo; en aquella ocasión; después, luego, en seguida; *conj.* pues, en tal caso; **now —** ahora bien; **now and —** de vez en cuando, de cuando en cuando; **now . . . —** ora . . . ora; ya . . . ya; **well —** conque, pues entonces; ahora bien.

thence [ðɛns] *adv.* desde allí, de allí; desde entonces, desde aquel tiempo; por eso, por esa razón; **—forth** de allí en adelante, desde entonces.

theological [ɵɪəládʒɪk] *adj.* teológico; teologal.

theology [ɵiálədʒɪ] *s.* teología.

theoretical [ɵiərétɪk] *adj.* teórico.

theory [ɵíərɪ] *s.* teoría.

there [ðɛr] *adv.* allí, allá, ahí; **— is, — are** hay; **— followed an argument** siguió una disputa.

thereabouts [ðɛrəbáuts] *adv.* por allí, por ahí; aproximadamente.

thereafter [ðɛræftə] *adv.* después de eso, de allí en adelante.

thereby [ðɛrbái] *adv.* en relación con eso; así, de ese modo; por allí cerca.

therefore [ðɛrfor] *adv.* por eso, por consiguiente; por lo tanto.

therein [ðɛrín] *adv.* en eso, en ello; allí dentro.

thereof [ðɛráv] *adv.* de eso, de ello.

thereon [ðɛrán] *adv.* encima; encima de (o sobre) él, ella, ello, etc.

thereupon [ðɛrəpán] *adv.* luego, después, en eso, en esto; por consiguiente, por eso, por lo tanto; encima de (o sobre) él, ella, ello, etc.

therewith [ðɛrwɪθ] *adv.* con eso, con ello, con esto; luego, en seguida.

thermometer [ɵəmámətə] *s.* termómetro.

Thermos [ɵǝmǝs] *(marca de fábrica):* **— bottle** termos.

these [ðiz] *adj.* estos, estas; *pron.* éstos, éstas.

thesis [ɵísɪs] *s.* tesis.

they [ðe] *pron.* ellos, ellas.

thick [ɵɪk] *adj.* espeso; denso; tupido; grueso; torpe, estúpido; **— voice** voz ronca; **one inch —** una pulgada de espesor; *adv. véase* **thickly; thick-headed** cabezudo, testarudo; estúpido; **thick-set** grueso, rechoncho; **thick-skinned** insensible; que no se avergüenza fácilmente; *s.* espesor; densidad, lo más denso; **the — of the**

crowd lo más denso de la muchedumbre; **the — of the fight** lo más reñido del combate; **through — and thin** por toda suerte de penalidades.

thicken [θíkən] v. espesar(se); engrosar; **the plot -s** se complica el enredo.

thicket [θíkɪt] s. espesura, maleza, matorral, *Am.* manigua.

thickly [θíklɪ] adv. espesamente; densamente.

thickness [θíknɪs] s. espesor; espesura, grueso, grosor; densidad.

thief [θif] s. ladrón.

thieve [θiv] v. hurtar, robar.

thieves [θivz] pl. de **thief.**

thigh [θaɪ] s. muslo.

thimble [θímbl̩] s. dedal.

thin [θɪn] adj. delgado; flaco; ralo; escaso; tenue, fino; transparente; débil; aguado; **— broth** caldo aguado; **— hair** pelo ralo; v. adelgazar(se); enflaquecer; aguar (*el caldo*); **to — out** ralear (*el pelo*); ralear o aclarar (*un bosque*).

thine [ðaɪn] pron. pos. tuyo (tuya, tuyos, tuyas); el tuyo (la tuya, los tuyos, las tuyas); adj. tu, tus.

thing [θɪŋ] s. cosa; **no such —** nada de eso; **that is the — to do** eso es lo que debe hacerse; eso es lo debido.

think [θɪŋk] v. pensar; creer, juzgar; opinar; **to — it over** pensarlo; **to — of** pensar en; pensar de; **to — up an excuse** urdir una excusa; **to — well of** tener buena opinión de; **— nothing of it** no haga Vd. caso de ello, no le dé Vd. importancia; **what do you — of her?** ¿qué piensa Vd. de ella?; **to my way of -ing** a mi modo de ver.

thinker [θíŋkə] s. pensador.

thinly [θínlɪ] adv. delgadamente; escasamente.

thinness [θínnɪs] s. delgadez; flacura; raleza (*del cabello*); enrarecimiento (*del aire*).

third [θɜd] adj. tercero; s. tercio, tercera parte.

thirst [θɜst] s. sed; anhelo, ansia; v. tener sed; **to — for** tener sed de; anhelar, ansiar.

thirsty [θɜ́stɪ] adj. sediento; **to be —** tener sed.

this [ðɪs] adj. este, esta; pron. éste, ésta, esto.

thistle [θísl̩] s. abrojo; cardo.

thither [θíðə] adv. allá, hacia allá, para allá.

tho [ðo] = **though.**

thong [θɔŋ] s. correa, tira de cuero, *Am.* guasca.

thorn [θɔrn] s. espina, púa; espino; abrojo.

thorny [θɔ́rnɪ] adj. espinoso; arduo, difícil.

thorough [θə́ɹo] adj. completo, entero, cabal, cumplido, acabado; esmerado.

thoroughbred [θə́ɹobred] adj. de casta pura, de raza pura; bien nacido; s. animal o persona de casta; caballo de casta.

thoroughfare [θə́ɹofer] s. vía pública, carretera, camino real; pasaje.

thoroughly [θə́ɹolɪ] adj. completamente, enteramente, cabalmente; a fondo.

those [ðoz] adj. esos, esas, aquellos, aquellas; pron. ésos, ésas, aquéllos, aquéllas; **— of** los de, las de; **— which** los que, las que; **aquellos que; — who** los que, las que, quienes.

thou [ðaʊ] pron. tú.

though [ðo] conj. aunque, si bien, bien que; aun cuando; sin embargo; **as —** como si.

thought [θɔt] s. pensamiento; idea, intención; reflexión, meditación; consideración; cuidado; **to be lost in —** estar abstraído; **to give it no —** no pensar en ello, no darle importancia, no hacerle caso; pret. & p.p. de to **think.**

thoughtful [θɔ́tfəl] adj. pensativo; considerado; atento, solícito, cuidadoso; **to be — of others** pensar en los demás, tener consideración o solicitud por los demás; **-ly** adv. con reflexión; consideradamente, con consideración; con solicitud.

thoughtfulness [θɔ́tfəlnɪs] s. consideración, atención, cuidado, solicitud.

thoughtless [θɔ́tlɪs] adj. inconsiderado; descuidado; irreflexivo, atolondrado; **-ly** adv. inconsideradamente, sin consideración; sin reflexión; sin pensar; descuidadamente, irreflexivamente, atolondradamente.

thoughtlessness [θɔ́tlɪsnɪs] s. irreflexión, inadvertencia, descuido; atolondramiento.

thrash [θræʃ] v. trillar, desgranar (*las mieses*); zurrar, azotar; **to — around** revolcarse, agitarse, menearse; **to — out a matter** ventilar un asunto.

thread [θred] s. hilo; hebra, fibra; **screw —** rosca de tornillo; v. ensartar, enhebrar; **to — a screw** roscar un tornillo; **to — one's way through a crowd** colarse por entre la muchedumbre.

threadbare [θrédber] adj. raído, gastado.

threat [θrɛt] s. amenaza; amago.

threaten [θrétn̩] v. amenazar; amagar.

threatening [θrétnɪŋ] adj. amenazante, amenazador.

thresh [θreʃ] véase **thrash**.

threshold [θréʃold] s. umbral, entrada.

threw [θru] pret. de to **throw**.

thrice [θraɪs] adv. tres veces.

thrift [θrɪft] s. economía, frugalidad.

thrifty [θrɪftɪ] adj. económico, frugal; próspero.

thrill [θrɪl] v. emocionar(se), conmover-(se); estremecerse de emoción, sobre-excitarse; s. emoción viva, estreme-cimiento emotivo, sobreexcitación.

thrive [θraɪv] v. medrar, prosperar; flo-recer.

thriven [θrívən] p.p. de to **thrive**.

throat [θrot] s. garganta.

throb [θrab] v. latir, pulsar, palpitar; s. latido, palpitación.

throe [θro] s. agonía; congoja.

throne [θron] s. trono.

throng [θrɔŋ] s. muchedumbre, multi-tud, tropel, gentío; v. agolparse, api-ñarse; atestar.

throttle [θrátl] s. válvula reguladora, obturador, regulador; — **lever** palanca del obturador o regulador; v. ahogar; estrangular; to — **down** disminuir o reducir la velocidad.

through [θru] prep. por; a través de; por medio de; por conducto de; por entre; adv. de un lado a otro; de parte a parte, a través; de cabo a cabo; desde el principio hasta el fin; comple-tamente, enteramente; loyal — **and** — **leal** a toda prueba; to be **wet** — estar empapado; estar mojado hasta los tuétanos; to carry a plan — lle-var a cabo un plan; adj. directo, con-tinuo; — **ticket** billete (Am. boleto) directo; — **train** tren rápido, tren de servicio directo; to be — **with** haber acabado con; no querer ocuparse más de.

throughout [θruáut] prep. por todo; por todas partes de; desde el principio hasta el fin de; — **the year** durante todo el año; adv. por todas partes; en todas partes; en todo, en todos respe-tos; desde el principio hasta el fin.

throve [θrov] pret. de to **thrive**.

throw [θro] v. tirar, arrojar, lanzar; echar; to — **away** tirar, arrojar; mal-gastar; to — **down** arrojar, echar por tierra, derribar; to — **in gear** en-granar; to — **in the clutch** embra-gar; to — **off** a burden librarse o des-hacerse de una carga; to — **out** echar fuera; expeler; to — **out of gear** des-

engranar; to — **out of work** privar de trabajo, quitar el empleo a; to — **out the clutch** desembragar; to — **overboard** echar al agua; to — **up** vomitar; s. tiro, tirada.

thrown [θron] p.p. de to **throw**.

thrush [θrʌʃ] s. tordo, zorzal.

thrust [θrʌst] v. meter; hincar, clavar; encajar; empujar; to — **a task upon** **someone** imponer una tarea a una persona, obligar a alguien a desem-peñar un quehacer; to — **aside** echar o empujar a un lado; rechazar; to — **in** (o **into**) meter en, encajar en, inter-calar en; to — **out** sacar; echar fuera; to — **someone through with a** **sword** atravesar a alguien de parte a parte con la espada; pret. & p.p. de to **thrust**; s. estocada, cuchillada, puña-lada, lanzada; empuje, empujón o em-pellón; arremetida, acometida.

thud [θʌd] s. porrazo, golpazo, golpe sordo.

thug [θʌg] s. ladrón, salteador.

thumb [θʌm] s. pulgar; **under the** — of bajo el poder o influencia de; v. hojear (con el pulgar).

thumbtack [θʌ́mtæk] s. chinche.

thump [θʌmp] s. golpazo, porrazo, tras-tazo; golpe sordo; v. golpear, golpe-tear, aporrear, dar un porrazo.

thunder [θʌ́ndə] s. trueno; tronido; es-truendo; v. tronar.

thunderbolt [θʌ́ndəbolt] s. rayo.

thundering [θʌ́ndərɪŋ] adj. atronador.

thunderous [θʌ́ndərəs] adj. atronador, estruendoso.

thunderstorm [θʌ́ndəstɔrm] s. tronada, tormenta o tempestad de truenos.

Thursday [θɝ́zdɪ] s. jueves.

thus [ðʌs] adv. así; — **far** hasta aquí, hasta ahora, hasta hoy.

thwart [θwɔrt] v. frustrar; estorbar; im-pedir.

thy [ðaɪ] adj. tu, tus.

thyme [taɪm] s. tomillo.

thyself [ðaɪsélf] pron. tú mismo; a tí mismo; te (como reflexivo); véase her-self.

tick [tɪk] s. tic tac; funda (de colchón o almohada); garrapata (insecto pará-sito); v. hacer tic tac (como un reloj); latir (el corazón); to — **off** marcar.

ticket [tíkɪt] s. billete, Am. boleto; lista de candidatos (de un partido); balota (para votar); — **office** taquilla; des-pacho de boletos, Am. boletería.

tickle [tíkl] v. cosquillear, hacer cos-quillas; sentir o tener cosquillas; hala-gar, gustarle a uno; to be **-d to death**

morirse de gusto, estar muy contento; s. cosquilleo, cosquillas.

ticklish [tíklɪʃ] *adj.* cosquilloso; delicado, arriesgado, difícil.

tidbit [tídbɪt] *s.* bocado, bocadito, golosina.

tide [taɪd] *s.* marea; corriente; **Christmas —** navidades, temporada de navidad; *v.* **to — someone over a difficulty** ayudar a alguien durante una crisis o dificultad.

tidings [táɪdɪŋz] *s. pl.* noticias, nuevas.

tidy [táɪdɪ] *adj.* aseado, limpio, ordenado; **a — sum** una suma considerable; *v.* asear, arreglar, poner en orden; **to — oneself up** asearse.

tie [taɪ] *v.* atar, liar, ligar, amarrar; enlazar, vincular; empatar (*en juegos, carreras, etc.*); **to — tight** amarrar bien, apretar fuerte; **to — up the traffic** obstruir el tráfico; *s.* lazo, ligadura, atadura; enlace, vínculo; corbata; empate (*en carreras, juegos, etc.*); **railway —** traviesa, *Am.* durmiente o travesaño.

tier [tɪr] *s.* fila, hilera, ringlera.

tiger [táɪgə] *s.* tigre; **— cat** gato montés.

tight [taɪt] *adj.* apretado, ajustado, estrecho; hermético; firme, tieso, tirante; mezquino, tacaño; borracho; **to be in a — spot** estar en un aprieto; **to close —** apretar, cerrar herméticamente; **to hold on —** agarrarse bien; **it fits —** está muy estrecho o ajustado.

tighten [táɪtn] *v.* apretar; estrechar; estirar, poner tirante.

tightness [táɪtnɪs] *s.* estrechez; tirantez, tensión; mezquindad, tacañería.

tigress [táɪgrɪs] *s.* tigre hembra.

tile [taɪl] *s.* teja; baldosa, azulejo; **— roof** tejado; *v.* tejar, cubrir con tejas; cubrir con azulejos, embaldosar.

till [tɪl] *prep.* hasta; *conj.* hasta que; *v.* cultivar, labrar, arar; *s.* gaveta o cajón para el dinero.

tillage [tɪlədʒ] *s.* labranza, cultivo, labor.

tilt [tɪlt] *s.* ladeo, inclinación; declive; altercación, disputa; **at full — a** toda velocidad; *v.* ladear(se), inclinar(se).

timber [tímbə] *s.* madera de construcción; maderaje; madero; viga.

time [taɪm] *s.* tiempo; hora; vez; plazo; **at -s** a veces; **at one and the same — a** la vez; **at this —** ahora, al presente; **behind —** atrasado, retrasado; **from — to —** de vez en cuando; **in —** a tiempo; andando el tiempo; **on —** puntual; con puntualidad; **a** tiempo; a la hora debida; **several -s** varias veces; **to beat —** marcar el compás;

to buy on — comprar a plazo; **to have a good —** divertirse, pasar un buen rato; **what — is it?** ¿qué hora es?; *v.* cronometrar, medir el tiempo de; regular, poner en punto (*el reloj, el motor*); escoger el momento oportuno para.

timely [táɪmlɪ] *adj.* oportuno.

timepiece [táɪmpis] *s.* reloj; cronómetro.

timetable [táɪmtebl] *s.* itinerario, horario.

timid [tímɪd] *adj.* tímido.

timidity [tɪmídətɪ] *s.* timidez.

timorous [tímərəs] *adj.* timorato, tímido, miedoso.

tin [tɪn] *s.* estaño; hojalata, lata; cosa de hojalata; **— can** lata; **— foil** hoja de estaño; *v.* estañar, cubrir con estaño; enlatar.

tincture [tíŋktʃə] *s.* tintura; tinte; **— of iodine** tintura de yodo; *v.* tinturar, teñir.

tinder [tíndə] *s.* yesca.

tinge [tɪndʒ] *v.* teñir; matizar; *s.* tinte, matiz; dejo, saborcillo.

tingle [tíŋgl] *v.* hormiguear, sentir hormigueo; **to — with excitement** estremecerse de entusiasmo; *s.* hormigueo, picazón, comezón.

tinkle [tíŋkl] *v.* tintinear; hacer retintín; *s.* tintineo; retintín.

tinsel [tínsl] *s.* oropel; *adj.* de oropel.

tint [tɪnt] *s.* tinte, matiz; *v.* teñir, matizar.

tiny [táɪnɪ] *adj.* diminuto, menudo, chiquitico, chiquitín.

tip [tɪp] *s.* punta, extremo, extremidad; propina; noticia o aviso secreto; *v.* ladear(se), inclinar(se); dar propina (a); **to — a person off** dar aviso secreto a; **to — one's hat** tocarse el sombrero; **to — over** volcar(se), voltear(se).

tipsy [típsɪ] *adj.* alumbrado, algo borracho; ladeado.

tiptoe [típto] *s.* punta del pie; **on — de** puntillas; *v.* andar de puntillas.

tire [taɪr] *s.* llanta, neumático, goma; **flat —** llanta o goma reventada; *v.* cansar(se), fatigar(se).

tired [taɪrd] *adj.* cansado, fatigado; **— out** extenuado de fatiga, rendido.

tireless [táɪrlɪs] *adj.* incansable, infatigable.

tiresome [táɪrsəm] *adj.* cansado, aburrido, pesado.

tissue [tíʃʊ] *s.* tejido; **— paper** papel de seda.

tithe [taɪð] *s.* diezmo.

title [táɪtl] *s.* título; **— page** portada.

227

to [tu] *prep.* a; hasta; hacia; para; — **try** — tratar de; esforzarse por; **a quarter** — **five** las cinco menos cuarto; **bills** — **be paid** cuentas por pagar; **frightened** — **death** muerto de susto; **from house** — **house** de casa en casa; **he has** — **go** tiene que ir; **near** — cerca de; **not** — **my knowledge** no que yo sepa; *adv.* — **and fro** de acá para allá; **to come** — volver en sí.

toad [tod] *s.* sapo o escuerzo.

toast [tost] *v.* tostar(se); brindar por, beber a la salud de; *s.* tostada; brindis.

toaster [tóstə] *s.* tostador.

tobacco [təbǽko] *s.* tabaco.

today [tədé] *adv.* hoy; hoy día.

toe [to] *s.* dedo del pie; punta (*de la media, del zapato, etc.*); *v.* **to** — **in** andar con la punta de los pies para dentro.

toenail [tónel] *s.* uña del dedo del pie.

together [təgéðə] *adv.* juntamente; a un mismo tiempo, a la vez; juntos; — **with** junto con; **all** — juntos; en junto; **to call** — convocar, juntar; **to come** — juntarse, unirse; ponerse de acuerdo; **to walk** — andar juntos.

toil [tɔɪl] *v.* afanarse, trafagar, atarearse; *s.* esfuerzo, trabajo, faena, fatiga.

toilet [tɔ́ɪlɪt] *s.* retrete, excusado, común, *Am.* inodoro; — **articles** artículos de tocador; — **case** neceser; — **paper** papel de excusado, papel higiénico.

token [tókən] *s.* señal, símbolo; prenda; recuerdo; prueba, muestra; ficha (*de metal*); — **payment** pago nominal.

told [told] *pret. & p.p. de* **to tell**.

tolerance [tálərəns] *s.* tolerancia.

tolerant [tálərənt] *adj.* tolerante.

tolerate [táləret] *v.* tolerar.

toleration [taləréʃən] *s.* tolerancia.

toll [tol] *s.* doble, tañido (*de las campanas*); peaje; portazgo; — **bridge** puente de peaje; —**gate** barrera de peaje; **to pay** — pagar peaje o portazgo; *v.* tañer, doblar (*las campanas*).

tomato [təméto] *s.* tomate, *Am.* jitomate.

tomb [tum] *s.* tumba.

tombstone [túmston] *s.* lápida sepulcral.

tomcat [támkæt] *s.* gato.

tomorrow [təmóro] *adv.* mañana; — **morning** mañana por la mañana; — **noon** mañana al mediodía; **day after** — pasado mañana.

ton [tʌn] *s.* tonelada.

tone [ton] *s.* tono; sonido; timbre; *v.* dar tono a, modificar el tono de; **to** — **down** bajar de tono; suavizar; **to** — **down one's voice** moderar la voz; **to** — **in well with** armonizar con, entonar bien con; **to** — **up** subir de tono; tonificar, vigorizar.

tongs [tɔŋz] *s. pl.* tenazas.

tongue [tʌŋ] *s.* lengua; idioma; **to be tongue-tied** tener trabada la lengua.

tonic [tánɪk] *s. & adj.* tónico.

tonight [tənáɪt] *adv.* esta noche, a la noche.

tonnage [tʌ́nɪdʒ] *s.* tonelaje.

tonsil [táns]] *s.* amígdala.

tonsilitis [tans]áɪtɪs] *s.* amigdalitis.

too [tu] *adv.* también; demasiado; — **many** demasiados; — **much** demasiado; **it is** — **bad!** ¡es una lástima!

took [tʊk] *pret. de* **to take**.

tool [tul] *s.* instrumento; herramienta.

toot [tut] *v.* tocar o sonar la bocina; pitar; tocar (*un cuerno, trompa o trompeta*); **to** — **one's own horn** alabarse, cantar sus propias alabanzas; *s.* toque o sonido (*de bocina, trompeta, etc.*); silbido, pitido; pitazo (*de locomotora*).

tooth [tuθ] *s.* diente; muela; — **mark** dentellada; **to fight** — **and nail** luchar a brazo partido; **to have a sweet** — ser amigo de golosinas.

toothache [túeek] *s.* dolor de muelas.

toothbrush [túebrʌʃ] *s.* cepillo de dientes.

toothed [tuet] *adj.* dentado.

toothless [túelɪs] *adj.* desdentado.

toothpaste [túepest] *s.* pasta para los dientes, pasta dentífrica.

toothpick [túepɪk] *s.* mondadientes, palillo de dientes.

top [tap] *s.* cumbre, cima; copete; cúspide; tope; pináculo; remate; cabeza; superficie; copa (*de árbol*); tapa, cubierta; trompo; **at the** — **of his class** a la cabeza de su clase; **at the** — **of one's voice** a voz en cuello; **filled up to the** — lleno hasta el tope; **from** — **to bottom** de arriba abajo; **from** — **to toe** de pies a cabeza; **on** — **of** encima de, sobre; *adj.* superior; más alto; —**coat** abrigo, sobretodo; **at** — **speed** a velocidad máxima; *v.* coronar; exceder; sobresalir, sobrepujar; rematar; **to** — **off** rematar; terminar.

topaz [tópæz] *s.* topacio.

toper [tópə] *s.* bebedor, borrachín.

topic [tápɪk] *s.* tema, asunto, materia, tópico.

topmost [tápmost] *adj.* más alto; superior.

topple [tápl] *v.* echar abajo, derribar; volcar; **to** — **over** venirse abajo; volcarse.

topsy-turvy [tápsɪtɜ́vɪ] *adj. & adv.* patas arriba; en confusión; trastornado; enrevesado, al revés.

torch [tɔrtʃ] *s.* antorcha; **blow — soplete.**

tore [tor] *pret. de* to tear.

torment [tɔ́rment] *s.* tormento; [tɔrmént] *v.* atormentar; afligir.

torn [torn] *p.p. de* to tear roto, rompido, rasgado.

tornado [tɔrnédo] *s.* tornado.

torpedo [tɔrpído] *s.* torpedo; **— boat** torpedero; *v.* torpedear.

torrent [tɔ́rent] *s.* torrente.

torrid [tɔ́rid] *adj.* tórrido.

tortoise [tɔ́rtəs] *s.* tortuga.

tortuous [tɔ́rtʃʊəs] *adj.* tortuoso.

torture [tɔ́rtʃə] *s.* tortura, tormento; *v.* torturar, atormentar.

toss [tɔs] *v.* tirar, echar, arrojar, lanzar; menear(se); cabecear (*un buque*); **to — aside** echar a un lado; desechar; **to — up** echar para arriba; aventar; *s.* tiro, tirada; meneo, sacudida.

tot [tɔt] *s.* chiquitín, chiquitina, chiquitico, chiquitica, niñito, niñita, nene, nena.

total [tótl] *adj. & s.* total.

totalitarian [totælətériən] *adj.* totalitario.

totter [tátə] *v.* tambalear(se), bambolear(se); estar para desplomarse.

touch [tʌtʃ] *v.* tocar; palpar, tentar; conmover, enternecer; compararse con, igualar; **to — at a port** hacer escala en un puerto; **to — off an explosive** prender la mecha de un explosivo; **to — up** retocar; *s.* toque; tacto, sentido del tacto; tiento; **—stone** piedra de toque; **a — of fever** algo de calentura; **to keep in — with** mantener(se) en comunicación con.

touching [tʌ́tʃɪŋ] *adj.* conmovedor, enternecedor.

touchy [tʌ́tʃɪ] *adj.* quisquilloso, susceptible, sensible, sensitivo.

tough [tʌf] *adj.* correoso; fuerte; firme; duro; arduo, difícil; terco; empedernido, malvado.

toughen [tʌ́fn] *v.* curtir(se); endurecer(se), empedernir(se); hacer(se) correoso.

toughness [tʌ́fnɪs] *s.* dureza; correosidad; flexibilidad; tenacidad; resistencia; dificultad.

tour [tʊr] *s.* viaje, excursión; vuelta; jira; *v.* viajar por; recorrer; hacer una jira; hacer un viaje de turismo.

tourist [tʊ́rɪst] *s.* turista.

tournament [tɜ́nəmənt] *s.* torneo; certamen, concurso.

tow [to] *v.* remolcar; *s.* remolque; **—boat** remolcador; **—rope** cuerda de remolque; **to take in —** remolcar, llevar a remolque.

toward [tord] *prep.* hacia; rumbo a; alrededor de; para, para con; **— four o'clock** a eso de las cuatro.

towards [tordz] = **toward.**

towel [tʊ1] *s.* toalla.

tower [tʌ́ʊə] *s.* torre; torreón; **bell — campanario;** *v.* sobresalir, sobrepujar; destacarse, descollar; elevarse.

towering [tʌ́ʊrɪŋ] *adj.* encumbrado; elevado, muy alto; sobresaliente.

town [taʊn] *s.* población, ciudad, pueblo, aldea; municipio; **— hall** ayuntamiento.

township [tʌ́ʊnʃɪp] *s.* unidad primaria de gobierno local; sección de seis millas cuadradas (*en terrenos públicos*).

toxin [táksɪn] *s.* toxina.

toy [tɔɪ] *s.* juguete; *adj.* de juego, de juguete; pequeñito; *v.* jugar, juguetear.

trace [tres] *s.* señal, indicio, vestigio; huella, rastro; tirante (*de una guarnición*); *v.* trazar; calcar; rastrear, seguir la huella de; rebuscar, investigar; **to — the source of** remontarse al origen de, buscar el origen de.

trachea [trékɪə] *s.* tráquea.

track [træk] *s.* pista, huella, rastro; pisada; vereda, senda; vía; **— sports** deportes de pista; **race —** pista; **railroad — rieles,** vía del tren, vía férrea o ferrovía; **to be off the —** estar extraviado, estar descarrilado; **to be on the —** of rastrear, ir siguiendo la pista de; **to keep —** of llevar la cuenta de; no perder de vista; *v.* rastrear, seguir la huella de; **to — down** coger, atrapar; descubrir; **to — in** mud traer lodo en los pies, entrar con los pies enlodados.

tract [trækt] *s.* área; terreno; folleto; **digestive —** canal digestivo.

traction [trǽkʃən] *s.* tracción.

tractor [trǽktə] *s.* tractor.

trade [tred] *s.* comercio; trato, negocio; trueque, cambio; oficio; clientela, parroquianos; **— school** escuela de artes y oficios; **— union** gremio obrero o de obreros; *v.* comerciar, negociar, traficar, tratar; trocar, cambiar.

trademark [trédmark] *s.* marca de fábrica.

trader [trédə] *s.* mercader, comerciante, negociante, traficante.

tradesman [trédzmən] *s.* mercader, comerciante, traficante; tendero.

tradition [trədʃən] *s.* tradición.

traditional [trədʃənl] *adj.* tradicional.

traffic [trǽfɪk] *s.* tráfico; tráfago; tránsito; circulación; *v.* traficar, comerciar.

negociar.

tragedy [trǽdʒədɪ] *s.* tragedia.

tragic [trǽdʒɪk] *adj.* trágico.

trail [trel] *s.* pista, rastro, huella; senda, sendero, trocha, vereda; cola (*de vestido*); *v.* arrastrar(se); rastrear, seguir la pista de; andar detrás de; **to — be-hind** ir rezagado, rezagarse.

train [tren] *s.* tren; cola (*de vestido*); séquito, comitiva; *v.* amaestrar(se), ejercitar(se); adiestrar(se) o adestrar-(se), *Am.* entrenar(se); educar; disciplinar (*tropas*); apuntar (*un cañón*).

trainer [trénə] *s.* amaestrador; *Am.* entrenador.

training [trénɪŋ] *s.* adiestramiento, disciplina, *Am.* entrenamiento; educación; **— camp** campo de entrenamiento o práctica.

trait [tret] *s.* rasgo, característica; cualidad.

traitor [trétə] *s.* traidor.

tram [træm] *s.* vagoneta (*de una mina de carbón*).

tramp [træmp] *v.* pisotear; andar a pie; vagabundear; *s.* vago, vagabundo; caminata, marcha; pisadas.

trample [trǽmpl] *v.* pisar, hollar, pisotear; **to — on** pisotear, hollar; *s.* pisadas.

trance [træns] *s.* rapto, arrobamiento, enajenamiento, éxtasis; **to be in a —** estar arrobado, estar enajenado; estar distraído o ensimismado.

tranquil [trǽnkwɪl] *adj.* tranquilo.

tranquillity [trænkwílətɪ] *s.* tranquilidad.

transact [trænsǽkt] *v.* tramitar, despachar, llevar a cabo.

transaction [trænsǽkʃən] *s.* transacción, trato, negocio; trámite; negociación; **-s** actas; memorias.

transatlantic [trænsətlǽntɪk] *adj.* transatlántico.

transcend [trænsénd] *v.* trascender, ir más allá de.

transcontinental [trænskɑntɪnéntl] *adj.* transcontinental.

transcribe [trænskráɪb] *v.* transcribir.

transcript [trǽnskrɪpt] *s.* transcripción, copia.

transfer [trǽnsfə] *s.* transferencia; traslado; traspaso; trasbordo; **— of ownership** cesión o traspaso de propiedad; **streetcar —** transferencia, contraseña, cupón de trasbordo; [trænsfə́] *v.* transferir; trasbordar (*de un tren a otro*), cambiar (*de tren, de tranvía*); traspasar (*propiedad*), trasladar.

transfigure [trænsfígjə] *v.* transfigurar.

transform [trænsfórm] *v.* transformar-(se).

transformation [trænsfəméʃən] *s.* transformación.

transgress [trænsgrés] *v.* transgredir, violar, quebrantar (*una ley*); pecar; **to — the bounds of** traspasar los límites de.

transgression [trænsgréʃən] *s.* transgresión; violación de una ley; pecado.

transgressor [trænsgrésə] *s.* transgresor.

transient [trǽnʃənt] *s.* transeúnte; *adj.* transeúnte; transitorio, pasajero.

transit [trǽnsɪt] *s.* tránsito; **in —** en tránsito, de paso.

transition [trænzíʃən] *s.* transición; tránsito, paso.

transitive [trǽnsətɪv] *adj.* transitivo.

transitory [trǽnsətorɪ] *adj.* transitorio, pasajero.

translate [trænslét] *v.* traducir, verter; trasladar.

translation [trænsléʃən] *s.* traducción, versión; translación (*de un lugar a otro*).

translator [trænslétə] *s.* traductor.

translucent [trænslúsnt] *adj.* translúcido; **to be — traslucirse.

transmission [trænsmíʃən] *s.* transmisión; caja de velocidades.

transmit [trænsmít] *v.* transmitir; emitir.

transmitter [trænsmítə] *s.* transmisor; emisor.

transom [trǽnsəm] *s.* montante.

transparent [trænspérənt] *adj.* transparente.

transplant [trænsplǽnt] *v.* trasplantar.

transport [trǽnsport] *s.* transporte; acarreo; éxtasis; **— plane** aeroplano de transporte; [trænspórt] *v.* transportar; acarrear; **to be —ed with joy** estar enajenado de placer.

transportation [trænspətéʃən] *s.* transportación, transporte; boleto, pasaje.

transpose [trænspóz] *v.* transponer.

transverse [trænsvə́s] *adj.* transverso, transversal, puesto de través.

trap [træp] *s.* trampa, lazo, red; **— door** trampa; **mouse —** ratonera; *v.* entrampar, coger con trampa; atrapar.

trapeze [træpíz] *s.* trapecio.

trappings [trǽpɪŋz] *s. pl.* arreos, jaeces, guarniciones.

trash [træʃ] *s.* basura; hojarasca; cachivaches; gentuza, plebe.

travel [trǽvl] *v.* viajar; viajar por; recorrer; *s.* viaje; tráfico.

traveler [trǽvlə] *s.* viajero.

traveling [trǽvlɪŋ] *adj.* de viaje, para

viaje; — **expenses** gastos de viaje; — **salesman** agente viajero, viajante de comercio.

traverse [trǽvəs] v. atravesar, cruzar; recorrer; s. travesaño.

travesty [trǽvɪstɪ] s. parodia; v. parodiar, falsear.

tray [tre] s. bandeja; batea.

treacherous [trétʃərəs] adj. traicionero, traidor, alevoso.

treachery [trétʃərɪ] s. traición, perfidia, alevosía.

tread [tred] v. pisar, hollar; pisotear; andar a pie, caminar; s. paso; pisada, huella; Am. pise (de una rueda); **tire** — rodadura del neumático, Am. banda rodante.

treason [trízn̩] s. traición.

treasonable [tríznəbl̩] adj. traidor, traicionero.

treasure [tréʒə] s. tesoro; v. atesorar.

treasurer [tréʒərə] s. tesorero.

treasury [tréʒərɪ] s. tesorería; tesoro, erario; **Secretary of the Treasury** ministro de hacienda.

treat [trit] v. tratar; curar; convidar, invitar; s. obsequio, agasajo, convite; placer, gusto.

treatise [trítɪs] s. tratado.

treatment [trítmənt] s. trato; **medical** — tratamiento médico.

treaty [trítɪ] s. tratado, pacto, convenio.

treble [trébl̩] adj. triple; — **voice** voz atiplada; s. tiple; v. triplicar.

tree [tri] s. árbol; **apple** — manzano; **family** — árbol genealógico; **shoe** — horma de zapato; **to be up a** — estar subido a un árbol; estar en un gran aprieto; estar perplejo.

treeless [trílɪs] adj. pelado, sin árboles, despoblado de árboles.

treetop [trítɑp] s. copa de árbol.

trellis [trélɪs] s. emparrado, enrejado.

tremble [trémbl̩] v. temblar; estremecerse; s. temblor; estremecimiento.

tremendous [trɪméndəs] adj. tremendo.

tremor [trémə] s. temblor.

tremulous [trémjələs] adj. trémulo; tembloroso.

trench [trentʃ] s. trinchera; zanja, foso.

trend [trend] s. tendencia; rumbo, dirección.

trespass [tréspəs] v. invadir, traspasar; violar, infringir; pecar; **to — on property** meterse sin derecho en la propiedad ajena; **no -ing** prohibida la entrada; s. transgresión; pecado.

tress [tres] s. trenza; bucle.

trial [tráɪəl] s. ensayo, prueba; tentativa; aflicción; juicio, proceso; — **flight**

vuelo de prueba.

triangle [tráɪæŋgl̩] s. triángulo.

triangular [traɪǽŋgjələ] adj. triangular.

tribe [traɪb] s. tribu.

tribulation [trɪbjəléʃən] s. tribulación.

tribunal [trɪbjún̩] s. tribunal, juzgado.

tributary [trɪfbjətərɪ] adj. & s. tributario.

tribute [trɪfbjut] s. tributo; homenaje.

trick [trɪk] s. treta; suerte; maña, ardid, trampa; travesura; baza (en el juego de naipes); **to be up to one's old -s** hacer de las suyas; v. embaucar, trampear, hacer trampa; burlar; **to — oneself up** componerse, emperifollarse.

trickery [trɪfkərɪ] s. engaños, malas mañas, astucia.

trickle [trɪfkl̩] v. gotear; escurrir; s. goteo.

tricky [trɪfkɪ] adj. tramposo, Am. mañero; intrincado, complicado.

tried [traɪd] p.p. de **to try** & adj. probado.

trifle [tráɪfl̩] s. fruslería, friolera, nadería, nonada; bagatela; v. chancear(se), bromear; jugar, juguetear.

trigger [trígə] s. gatillo (de pistola, rifle, etc.).

trill [trɪl] v. trinar; **to — the r** pronunciar la erre doble; s. trino.

trim [trɪm] v. guarnecer, adornar; recortar; podar, mondar; despabilar (una vela); ganarle a uno (en el juego); **to — up** adornar, componer; adj. aseado, limpio, pulcro, acicalado; s. adorno, franja, ribete, guarnición; **to be in — for** estar en buena salud para; estar bien entrenado para.

trimming [trímɪŋ] s. adorno, aderezo, guarnición; orla, ribete, franja; paliza, zurra; -**s** adornos; accesorios; recortes.

trinket [tríŋkɪt] s. chuchería, baratija.

trip [trɪp] s. viaje; travesía; recorrido, jira; tropezón; v. tropezar; dar un traspié; equivocarse; hacer tropezar, hacer caer; saltar, brincar, corretear.

triple [trɪpl̩] adj. & s. triple; v. triplicar.

trite [traɪt] adj. trillado, trivial, vulgar.

triumph [tráɪəmf] s. triunfo; v. triunfar.

triumphal [traɪʌmfl̩] adj. triunfal.

triumphant [traɪʌmfənt] adj. triunfante; -**ly** adv. triunfantemente, en triunfo.

trivial [trɪfvjəl] adj. trivial, insignificante.

trod [trɑd] pret. & p.p. de **to tread.**

trodden [trɑdn̩] p.p. de **to tread.**

trolley [trɑlɪ] s. trole; tranvía de trole.

trombone [trɑmbon] s. trombón.

troop [trup] s. tropa; cuadrilla.

trophy [trófɪ] s. trofeo.

tropic [trɑpɪk] s. trópico; adj. tropical.

tropical [trópɪk] *adj.* tropical.

trot [trat] *v.* trotar; hacer trotar; *s.* trote.

trouble [trʌb] *v.* perturbar, turbar; molestar, incomodar; afligir; preocupar(se); **don't — to come no se moleste** Vd. en venir; *s.* pena, aflicción; inquietud, perturbación; dificultad; molestia; **panne**, avería, accidente (*a un mecanismo*); **heart — enfermedad del co-razón**; **to be in — estar en un aprieto o apuro**; **it is not worth the — no vale la pena.**

troublemaker [trʌb|mekə] *s.* agitador, alborotador, malcontento.

troublesome [trʌb|səm] *adj.* molesto, fastidioso, enfadoso, dificultoso; penoso

trough [trɔf] *s.* comedero; artesa; batea; **eaves — canal, gotera del tejado; drinking — abrevadero.**

trousers [tráuzəz] *s. pl.* pantalones.

trousseau [trúso] *s.* ajuar de novia.

trout [traut] *s.* trucha.

trowel [tráuəl] *s.* llana, *Am.* cuchara (*de albañil*).

truant [trúənt] *s.* novillero, holgazán (*que se ausenta de la escuela*); **to play — hacer novillos,** *Am.* capear la escuela, *Am.* pintar venado, *Am.* jubilarse; *adj.* vago, perezoso.

truce [trus] *s.* tregua.

truck [trʌk] *s.* camión; carretón; carreta; basura; baratijas; **garden — horta-lizas, legumbres y verduras; garden hortaliza, huerta de legumbres;** *v.* acarrear, transportar en camión o carretón.

trudge [trʌdʒ] *v.* caminar, caminar con esfuerzo; *s.* caminata.

true [tru] *adj.* verdadero; cierto; verí-dico; fiel; exacto, preciso; legítimo.

truly [trúlɪ] *adv.* verdaderamente, en verdad; en realidad; exactamente, co-rrectamente; fielmente; **very — yours su seguro servidor.**

trump [trʌmp] *s.* triunfo (*en el juego de naipes*); *v.* matar con un triunfo (*en el juego de naipes*); **to — up an excuse forjar o inventar una excusa.**

trumpet [trʌmpɪt] *s.* trompeta; clarín; **ear — trompetilla acústica;** *v.* trom-petear, tocar la trompeta; pregonar, divulgar.

trunk [trʌŋk] *s.* tronco; baúl; trompa (*de elefante*); **-s calzones cortos (*para deportes*); — line línea principal.**

trust [trʌst] *s.* confianza, fe; crédito; custodia; cargo; depósito; trust, sin-dicato o combinación monopolista; *v.* confiar; fiar en, tener confianza en, fiarse de; esperar; dar crédito a.

trustee [trʌstí] *s.* fideicomisario, depo-sitario; **university -s regentes uni-versitarios; board of -s patronato; consejo.**

trustful [trʌstfəl] *adj.* confiado.

trusting [trʌstɪŋ] *adj.* confiado.

trustworthy [trʌstwɜ̃ðɪ] *adj.* fidedigno, digno de confianza.

trusty [trʌstɪ] *adj.* fidedigno; honrado, leal; *s.* presidiario fidedigno (*a quien se le conceden ciertos privilegios*).

truth [truθ] *s.* verdad.

truthful [trúθfəl] *adj.* verdadero; verí-dico; veraz.

truthfulness [trúθfəlnɪs] *s.* veracidad.

try [traɪ] *v.* probar, ensayar; hacer la prueba; poner a prueba; intentar, pro-curar; procesar, enjuiciar, formar cau-sa (*a un acusado*); ver (*una causa*); **to — on a suit probarse un traje; to — one's luck probar fortuna; to — someone's patience poner a prue-ba la paciencia de alguien; to — to tratar de, procurar, intentar;** *s.* prue-ba, tentativa, ensayo.

trying [tráɪŋ] *adj.* molesto; penoso, irri-tante.

tub [tʌb] *s.* tina; bañera; baño; batea, cuba; *v.* lavar en tina o cuba.

tube [tjub] *s.* tubo; inner — cámara (*de un neumático*); **radio — lámpara o tubo de radio.**

tubercular [tjubɔ́kjələ] *adj.* tuberculoso, tísico.

tuberculosis [tjubɔkjəlósɪs] *s.* tubercu-losis.

tuck [tʌk] *v.* alforzar, hacer o echar al-forzas; **to — in meter en; to — in bed arropar; to — under one's arm meter bajo el brazo; to — up arre-mangar, recoger; to — up one's sleeves arremangarse;** *s.* alforza.

Tuesday [tjúzdɪ] *s.* martes.

tuft [tʌft] *s.* penacho, copete; borla; macizo (*de plantas*).

tug [tʌg] *v.* remolcar; jalar (halar); arrastrar; trabajar con esfuerzo; **to — at tirar de, jalar;** *s.* tirón, estirón, *Am.* jalón; remolcador; **—boat remolcador; — of war lucha a tirones de cuerda.**

tuition [tjuʃən] *s.* derechos de enseñan-za, *Am.* colegiatura.

tulip [tjúləp] *s.* tulipán.

tumble [tʌmbl] *v.* caer(se); voltear; dar volteretas; **to — down caerse; des-plomarse; to — into someone tro-pezar con alguien; to — over volcar, tumbar, derribar; venirse abajo;** *s.* caída, tumbo, vuelco, voltereta, *Am.* rodada; desorden.

tumbler [tʌmbləʳ] s. vaso (de mesa); acróbata.

tumor [tjúməʳ] s. tumor.

tumult [tjúmʌlt] s. tumulto.

tumultuous [tjumʌltʃuəs] adj. tumultuoso.

tuna [túnə] s. atún (pez).

tune [tjun] s. tonada; tono; armonía; **to be in —** estar a tono, estar afinado o templado; estar entonado; **to be out of —** estar desentonado o desafinado; desentonar; v. afinar, templar; armonizar; **to — in** sintonizar; **to — up** the motor poner al punto el motor.

tunic [tjúnɪk] s. túnica.

tunnel [tʌnl] s. túnel; socavón; v socavar; abrir un túnel.

turbulent [tɜ́bjələnt] adj. turbulento; revoltoso.

turf [tɜf] s. césped; terrón de tierra (con césped); hipódromo, pista (para carreras).

Turk [tɜk] s. turco.

turkey [tɜ́kɪ] s. pavo, Am. guajolote (o guajolote).

Turkish [tɜ́kɪʃ] adj. turco; s. turco, idioma turco.

turmoil [tɜ́mɔɪl] s. alboroto; confusión.

turn [tɜn] v. volver(se); voltear(se); girar, dar vueltas, rodar, virar; tornear, labrar al torno; ponerse (pálido, rojo, etc.); **to — back** volver atrás; volverse, retroceder; devolver; **to — down** an offer rechazar una oferta; **to — in** entregar; recogerse, acostarse; **to — inside out** voltear o volver al revés; **to — into** convertir(se) en; **to — off** apagar (la luz); cortar (el agua, el gas, etc.); **to — off the main road** salirse o desviarse de la carretera; **to — on** encender (la luz); abrir la llave (del gas, del agua); **to — on someone** volverse contra, acometer o caer sobre alguien; **to — out** apagar (la luz); echar, expulsar, arrojar; producir; **to — out well** salir o resultar bien; **to — over** volcar(se), voltear(se); doblar; revolver (en la mente); entregar; **to — over and over** dar repetidas vueltas; **to — sour** agriarse, fermentarse; **to — the corner** doblar la esquina; **to — to** acudir a; dirigirse a; convertir(se) en; **to — to the left** doblar o torcer a la izquierda; **to — up** aparecer; **to — up one's nose at** desdeñar; hacer ascos a; **to — up one's sleeves** arremangarse; **to — upside down** trastornar; volcar; **it -s my stomach** me da asco o náusea;

s. vuelta; revolución; giro; recodo (del camino); turno; virada, cambio de rumbo; **— of mind** actitud mental; **at every —** a cada paso; **to be one's —** tocarle a uno; **to do one a good —** hacerle a uno un favor; **to take -s** turnarse.

turnip [tɜ́nəp] s. nabo.

turnover [tɜ́novəʳ] s. vuelco (de un coche); cambio (de empleados); **business —** movimiento de mercancías, número de transacciones; **labor —** movimiento de obreros, cambio frecuente de trabajadores; **apple —** pastel de manzana; **— collar** cuello doblado.

turpentine [tɜ́pəntaɪn] s. trementina; aguarrás.

turpitude [tɜ́pətjud] s. torpeza, vileza.

turquoise [tɜ́kwɔɪz] s. turquesa.

turret [tɜ́rɪt] s. torrecilla; torre blindada; alminar.

turtle [tɜ́tl] s. tortuga; **—dove** tórtola.

tusk [tʌsk] s. colmillo.

tutor [tútəʳ] s. tutor, maestro particular; v. enseñar, instruir.

tuxedo [tʌksído] s. esmoquin.

twang [twæŋ] s. tañido (de una cuerda de guitarra); nasalidad, tonillo gangoso; v. puntear, tañer (una cuerda); hablar con voz nasal, hablar con tonillo gangoso.

twangy [twǽŋɪ] adj. gangoso, nasal.

tweed [twid] s. mezclilla de lana; **— suit** traje de mezclilla.

tweezers [twízəʳz] s. pl. pinzas, tenacillas.

twice [twaɪs] adv. dos veces.

twig [twɪg] s. ramita, varita.

twilight [twáɪlaɪt] s. crepúsculo; **at —** entre dos luces; adj. crepuscular.

twin [twɪn] adj. & s. gemelo, mellizo, Am. cuate.

twine [twaɪn] s. cuerda, cordel; v. enroscar(se), torcer(se), retorcer(se); entrelazar.

twinge [twɪndʒ] s. punzada (dolor agudo); v. punzar.

twinkle [twɪŋkl] v. titilar, parpadear, pestañear; chispear; s. titilación, parpadeo; pestañeo; guiño, guiñada; **in the — of an eye** en un abrir y cerrar de ojos.

twirl [twɜl] v. girar; dar vueltas; s. giro, vuelta; molinete, floreo.

twist [twɪst] v. torcer(se); retorcer(se), enroscar(se); s. torsión, torcedura; torzal, cordoncillo (hecho de varias hebras torcidas); curva, recodo, vuelta; rosca (de pan); **mental —** sesgo de la mente, sesgo mental.

twitch [twɪtʃ] v. crisparse, contraerse, torcerse convulsivamente (un músculo); temblar (los párpados); dar un tirón; s. temblor, ligera convulsión, contracción nerviosa; tirón.

twitter [twɪtə] v. gorjear (los pájaros); temblar; agitarse; s. gorjeo; agitación, estremecimiento nervioso.

twofold [túfóld] adj. doble.

type [taɪp] s. tipo; v. escribir a máquina.

typewrite [táɪpraɪt] v. escribir a máquina.

typewriter [táɪpraɪtə] s. máquina de escribir.

typewriting [táɪpraɪtɪŋ] s. mecanografía; trabajo de mecanógrafo.

typewritten [táipritn] adj. escrito a máquina.

typhoid [táɪfɔɪd] s. tifoidea, fiebre tifoidea.

typhus [táɪfəs] s. tifo.

typical [tɪ́pɪkl] adj. típico.

typist [táɪpɪst] s. mecanógrafo; mecanógrafa.

tyrannical [tɪrǽnɪkl] adj. tiránico, tirano.

tyranny [tɪ́rənɪ] s. tiranía.

tyrant [táɪrənt] s. tirano.

U

udder [ʌ́də] s. ubre.

ugliness [ʌ́glɪnɪs] s. fealdad; fiereza.

ugly [ʌ́glɪ] adj. feo; fiero; repugnante; de mal genio; desagradable.

ulcer [ʌ́lsə] s. úlcera.

ulterior [ʌltfrɪə] adj. ulterior.

ultimate [ʌ́ltəmɪt] adj. último; final; fundamental; -ly adv. finalmente, a la larga.

umbrella [ʌmbrélə] s. paraguas; sombrilla.

umpire [ʌ́mpaɪr] s. árbitro, arbitrador; v. arbitrar.

un- [ʌn-] prefijo negativo equivalente a: sin, no, in-, des-.

unable [ʌnébl] adj. incapaz, inhábil; **to be — to** come no poder venir.

unaccustomed [ʌnəkʌ́stəmd] adj. desacostumbrado; insólito, inusitado.

unaffected [ʌnəféktɪd] adj. inafectado, sin afectación, natural, sincero.

unalterable [ʌnɔ́ltərəbl] adj. inalterable.

unanimity [junənímətɪ] s. unanimidad.

unanimous [junǽnəməs] adj. unánime.

unarmed [ʌnɑ́rmd] adj. desarmado.

unavoidable [ʌnəvɔ́ɪdəbl] adj. inevitable, ineludible.

unaware [ʌnəwér] adj. desprevenido; inadvertido; ignorante; incauto; **-s** adv. inesperadamente, inopinadamen-

te; impensadamente.

unbalanced [ʌnbǽlənst] adj. desequilibrado; **— account** cuenta no saldada.

unbearable [ʌnbérəbl] adj. inaguantable, insoportable.

unbecoming [ʌnbɪkʌ́mɪŋ] adj. impropio; **an — dress** un vestido que no sienta bien o que cae mal.

unbelief [ʌnbəlíf] s. incredulidad.

unbelievable [ʌnbəlívəbl] adj. increíble.

unbeliever [ʌnbəlívə] s. descreído, incrédulo.

unbelieving [ʌnbəlívɪŋ] adj. descreído, incrédulo.

unbending [ʌnbéndɪŋ] adj. inflexible.

unbiased [ʌnbáɪəst] adj. imparcial, libre de prejuicio.

unbosom [ʌnbúzəm] v. revelar, confesar, descubrir (secretos); **to — oneself** desahogarse con alguien, revelarle sus más íntimos secretos.

unbound [ʌnbáund] adj. desencuadernado, no encuadernado; suelto, destado.

unbroken [ʌnbrókən] adj. intacto, entero; indómito; ininterrumpido, continuo.

unbutton [ʌnbʌ́tn] v. desabotonar, desabrochar.

uncanny [ʌnkǽnɪ] adj. extraño, raro, misterioso.

unceasing [ʌnsísɪŋ] adj. incesante.

uncertain [ʌnsə́tn] adj. incierto; dudoso; indeciso.

uncertainty [ʌnsə́tntɪ] s. incertidumbre; falta de certeza.

unchangeable [ʌntʃéndʒəbl] adj. inmutable, inalterable, invariable.

unchanged [ʌntʃéndʒd] adj. inalterado, igual.

uncharitable [ʌntʃǽrətəbl] adj. duro, falto de caridad.

uncle [ʌŋkl] s. tío.

unclean [ʌnklín] adj. inmundo, sucio; impuro.

uncomfortable [ʌnkʌ́mfətəbl] adj. incómodo; molesto.

uncommon [ʌ́nkɑmən] adj. poco común, insólito, raro.

uncompromising [ʌnkɑ́mprəmaɪzɪŋ] adj. intransigente; inflexible.

unconcern [ʌnkənsə́n] s. indiferencia.

unconditional [ʌnkəndʃənl] adj. incondicional, absoluto.

uncongenial [ʌnkəndʒínjəl] adj. que no congenia, incompatible.

unconquerable [ʌnkáŋkərəbl] adj. invencible, inconquistable.

unconquered [ʌnkáŋkəd] adj. no conquistado, no vencido.

unconscious [ʌnkánʃəs] adj. inconsciente; privado.

unconsciousness [ʌnkʌ́nʃəsnɪs] *s.* inconsciencia; insensibilidad.

uncontrollable [ʌnkəntróləbl] *adj.* irrefrenable, ingobernable.

unconventional [ʌnkənvénʃən] *adj.* despreocupado, libre de trabas o reglas.

uncouth [ʌnkúθ] *adj.* rudo, tosco, inculto, grosero; desmañado.

uncover [ʌnkʌ́və] *v.* descubrir(se); revelar; destapar(se); desabrigar(se).

unction [ʌ́ŋkʃən] *s.* unción; fervor; **Extreme Unction** Extremaunción.

unctuous [ʌ́ŋkʃəs] *adj.* untuoso.

uncultivated [ʌnkʌ́ltəvetɪd] *adj.* inculto; baldío.

uncultured [ʌnkʌ́ltʃəd] *adj.* inculto; grosero.

undecided [ʌndɪsáɪdɪd] *adj.* indeciso.

undeniable [ʌndɪnáɪəbl] *adj.* innegable.

under [ʌ́ndə] *prep.* bajo; debajo de; menos de; **— age** menor de edad; **— cover** a cubierto; **— the cover of** al abrigo de, al amparo de; **— pretense of** so pretexto de; **— twelve** menos de doce; **to be — obligation to** deber favores a; *adv.* debajo; abajo; menos; *adj.* inferior, de abajo (*en ciertas combinaciones*); **— dose** dosis escasa o corta; **— secretary** subsecretario; **— side** lado de abajo, lado inferior; **the —dogs** los de abajo.

underbrush [ʌ́ndəbrʌʃ] *s.* maleza.

underclothes [ʌ́ndəkloz] *s. pl.* ropa interior.

underestimate [ʌ́ndəéstəmet] *v.* menospreciar, apreciar en menos de lo justo; salir corto en un cálculo.

underfed [ʌ́ndəféd] *adj.* malnutrido.

undergo [ʌndəgó] *v.* sufrir, aguantar, padecer.

undergone [ʌndəgón] *p.p. de* **to undergo.**

undergraduate [ʌndəgrǽdʒuɪt] *s.* estudiante del bachillerato; **— course** cursos o asignaturas para el bachillerato.

underground [ʌ́ndəgraund] *adj.* subterráneo; *s.* subterráneo; *adv.* bajo tierra; en secreto; ocultamente.

underhanded [ʌ́ndəhǽndɪd] *adj.* socarrón, secreto, disimulado, clandestino.

underline [ʌ́ndəlaɪn] *v.* subrayar.

underlying [ʌndəláɪŋ] *adj.* fundamental.

undermine [ʌndəmáɪn] *v.* minar, socavar.

underneath [ʌndəníθ] *prep.* bajo, debajo de; *adv.* debajo.

underpay [ʌ́ndəpé] *v.* malpagar; escatimar la paga.

undersell [ʌndəsél] *v.* malbaratar; vender a menos precio que.

undershirt [ʌ́ndəshət] *s.* camiseta.

undersigned [ʌndəsáɪnd] *s.* firmante, infrascrito; **the —** el infrascrito, los infrascritos.

undersized [ʌndəsáɪzd] *adj.* achaparrado, de tamaño inferior al normal.

underskirt [ʌ́ndəskət] *s.* enaguas, refajo.

understand [ʌndəstǽnd] *v.* entender; comprender; sobrentender.

understandable [ʌndəstǽndəbl] *adj.* comprensible.

understanding [ʌndəstǽndɪŋ] *s.* comprensión; entendimiento, inteligencia; acuerdo; *adj.* comprensivo.

understood [ʌndəstúd] *pret. & p.p. de* **to understand**; *adj.* entendido; convenido; sobrentendido.

understudy [ʌ́ndəstʌdɪ] *s.* sobresaliente, actor suplente; *v.* servir de sobresaliente o actor suplente.

undertake [ʌndəték] *v.* emprender; tratar de, intentar; comprometerse a.

undertaken [ʌndətékən] *p.p. de* **to undertake.**

undertaker [ʌ́ndətekə] *s.* director de funeraria; embalsamador.

undertaking [ʌndətékɪŋ] *s.* empresa.

undertook [ʌndətúk] *pret. de* **to undertake.**

undertow [ʌ́ndəto] *s.* resaca.

underwear [ʌ́ndəwer] *s.* ropa interior.

underwent [ʌndəwént] *pret. de* **to undergo.**

underworld [ʌ́ndəwəld] *s.* hampa, bajos fondos de la sociedad; clase criminal.

undesirable [ʌndɪzáɪrəbl] *adj.* indeseable; inconveniente.

undid [ʌndíd] *pret. de* **to undo.**

undisturbed [ʌndɪstə́bd] *adj.* impasible; sereno, tranquilo; intacto.

undo [ʌndú] *v.* deshacer; desatar; desabrochar; desenredar; anular; **to — one's hair** soltarse el cabello.

undone [ʌndʌ́n] *p.p. de* **to undo;** inacabado, sin hacer; sin terminar; **it is still —** está todavía por hacer, está inacabado; **to come —** desatarse.

undoubtedly [ʌndáutɪdlɪ] *adv.* indudablemente, sin duda.

undress [ʌndrés] *v.* desnudar(se), desvestir(se).

undue [ʌndjú] *adj.* indebido; impropio; excesivo.

undulate [ʌ́ndjolet] *v.* ondular, ondear.

unduly [ʌndjúlɪ] *adv.* indebidamente.

undying [ʌndáɪɪŋ] *adj.* imperecedero, eterno.

unearth [ʌnɔ́θ] *v.* desenterrar.

uneasily [ʌnízlɪ] *adv.* intranquilamente, inquietamente, con inquietud; incómodamente.

uneasiness [ʌnízɪnɪs] *s.* malestar, inquietud, intranquilidad, desasosiego.

uneasy [ʌnízɪ] *adj.* ansioso, inquieto, intranquilo; cohibido; incómodo.

uneducated [ʌnédʒəketɪd] *adj.* inculto, indocto, falto de instrucción, ignorante.

unemployed [ʌnɪmplɔ́ɪd] *adj.* desocupado, desempleado, cesante; ocioso; — **funds** fondos no invertidos o inactivos.

unemployment [ʌnɪmplɔ́ɪmənt] *s.* desempleo, cesantía, falta de empleo, desocupación.

unending [ʌnéndɪŋ] *adj.* inacabable, interminable.

unequal [ʌníkwəl] *adj.* desigual; insuficiente, ineficaz.

uneven [ʌnívən] *adj.* desigual, desparejo; irregular, accidentado; — **numbers** números impares o nones.

unevenness [ʌnívənnɪs] *s.* desigualdad; desnivel; irregularidad, escabrosidad (*del terreno*).

unexpected [ʌnɪkspéktɪd] *adj.* inesperado; **-ly** *adv.* de improviso, inesperadamente.

unfailing [ʌnféliŋ] *adj.* que nunca falta, constante, indefectible; infalible.

unfair [ʌnfér] *adj.* injusto; tramposo; **to act -ly** obrar de mala fe.

unfaithful [ʌnféθfəl] *adj.* infiel; desleal.

unfamiliar [ʌnfəmíljə] *adj.* poco familiar; desconocido; **to be — with** no tener conocimiento de; no estar al tanto de, ignorar; no conocer bien.

unfasten [ʌnfǽsn] *v.* desabrochar; desatar; aflojar.

unfavorable [ʌnfévrəbl] *adj.* desfavorable, contrario, adverso.

unfeeling [ʌnfílɪŋ] *adj.* insensible; incompasivo.

unfinished [ʌnfínɪʃt] *adj.* inacabado, sin terminar, sin acabar; sin barnizar, sin pulir.

unfit [ʌnfít] *adj.* incompetente, inepto, incapaz; inservible; impropio; *v.* incapacitar.

unfold [ʌnfóld] *v.* desenvolver(se), desarrollar(se); desdoblar; revelar.

unforeseen [ʌnforsín] *adj.* imprevisto.

unforgettable [ʌnfəgétəbl] *adj.* inolvidable.

unfortunate [ʌnfórtʃənɪt] *adj.* desventurado, infeliz, desgraciado, desdichado; **-ly** *adv.* desgraciadamente, por desgracia.

unfriendly [ʌnfréndlɪ] *adj.* hostil, enemigo; poco amistoso; *adv.* hostilmente.

unfurl [ʌnfɔ́l] *v.* desplegar.

unfurnished [ʌnfɔ́nɪʃt] *adj.* desamueblado.

ungrateful [ʌngrétfəl] *adj.* ingrato, desagradecido.

unhappy [ʌnhǽpɪ] *adj.* infeliz; desgraciado, desventurado, desdichado.

unharmed [ʌnhármd] *adj.* sin daño, ileso.

unhealthy [ʌnhélθɪ] *adj.* malsano; insalubre; enfermizo.

unheard-of [ʌnhɔ́dəv] *adj.* inaudito; desconocido.

unhitch [ʌnhítʃ] *v.* desenganchar; desatar.

unhook [ʌnhúk] *v.* desenganchar; desabrochar.

unhurt [ʌnhɔ́t] *adj.* ileso.

uniform [júnəfɔrm] *adj.* & *s.* uniforme.

uniformity [junəfɔ́rmɪtɪ] *s.* uniformidad.

unify [júnəfaɪ] *v.* unificar, unir.

unimportant [ʌnɪmpɔ́rtṇt] *adj.* insignificante, poco importante.

union [júnjən] *s.* unión; — **leader** jefe de un gremio obrero; **trade-union** gremio obrero.

unique [juník] *adj.* único, singular.

unison [júnəzṇ] : **in —** al unísono (*en el mismo tono*); al compás.

unit [júnɪt] *s.* unidad.

unite [junáɪt] *v.* unir(se).

unity [júnətɪ] *s.* unidad; unión.

universal [junəvɔ́s̩l] *adj.* universal.

universe [júnəvɔs] *s.* universo.

university [junəvɔ́sətɪ] *s.* universidad.

unjust [ʌndʒʌ́st] *adj.* injusto.

unjustifiable [ʌndʒʌ́stəfaɪəbḷ] *adj.* injustificable, injustificado.

unkempt [ʌnkémpt] *adj.* desaseado, desaliñado; desgreñado.

unkind [ʌnkáɪnd] *adj.* falto de bondad; descortés; cruel.

unknown [ʌnnón] *adj.* desconocido; no sabido; ignoto; — **quantity** incógnita; **it is —** se ignora, no se sabe, se desconoce.

unlawful [ʌnlɔ́fəl] *adj.* ilegal, ilícito.

unless [ənlés] *conj.* a menos que, a no ser que.

unlike [ʌnláɪk] *adj.* desemejante, distinto, diferente; *prep.* a diferencia de.

unlikely [ʌnláɪklɪ] *adj.* improbable, inverosímil.

unlimited [ʌnlímɪtɪd] *adj.* ilimitado.

unload [ʌnlód] *v.* descargar; vaciar; deshacerse de (*acciones, mercancías*).

unlock [ʌnlák] *v.* abrir (*con llave*); soltar, destrabar; revelar, penetrar (*secretos*).

unlucky [ʌnlʌ́kɪ] *adj.* desdichado, desventurado, desgraciado, desafortunado; aciago, de mal agüero, funesto; **an — number** un número de mala suerte.

unmanageable [ʌnmǽnɪdʒəbl] *adj.* inmanejable, ingobernable, intratable, indomable.

unmarried [ʌnmǽrɪd] *adj.* soltero.

unmerciful [ʌnmɜ́sɪfəl] *adj.* despiadado, inclemente.

unmistakable [ʌnməstékəbl] *adj.* inequívoco, claro, inconfundible.

unmoved [ʌnmúvd] *adj.* fijo; inmutable, impasible; indiferente.

unnatural [ʌnnǽtʃərəl] *adj.* afectado, artificial; anormal; **an — mother** una madre desnaturalizada.

unnecessary [ʌnnésəsərɪ] *adj.* innecesario.

unnoticed [ʌnnótɪst] *adj.* inadvertido.

unobliging [ʌnəbláɪdʒɪŋ] *adj.* poco complaciente, descortés, descomedido.

unobserved [ʌnəbzɜ́vd] *adj.* inadvertido; sin ser visto.

unobtainable [ʌnəbténəbl] *adj.* inobtenible, inasequible, inaccesible.

unoccupied [ʌnákjəpaɪd] *adj.* desocupado; vacío; desalquilado.

unpack [ʌnpǽk] *v.* desempacar; desembalar.

unpaid [ʌnpéd] *adj.* no pagado; sin pagar; — **bills** cuentas por pagar.

unpleasant [ʌnpléʒn̩t] *adj.* desagradable.

unpleasantness [ʌnpléʒn̩tnɪs] *s.* manera desagradable; desazón; desavenencia; **the — of a situation** lo desagradable de una situación; **to have an — with** tener una desavenencia con.

unprecedented [ʌnprésədɛntɪd] *adj.* sin precedente; inaudito.

unprepared [ʌnprɪpérd] *adj.* desprevenido; no preparado; no listo.

unpublished [ʌnpʌ́blɪʃt] *adj.* inédito, no publicado.

unquenchable [ʌnkwéntʃəbl] *adj.* inapagable, inextinguible.

unquestionable [ʌnkwéstʃənəbl] *adj.* indisputable, indudable; irreprochable.

unravel [ʌnrǽvl] *v.* desenredar; desenmarañar; deshilachar(se); deshilar.

unreal [ʌnríəl] *adj.* irreal; ilusorio, imaginario.

unreasonable [ʌnríznəbl] *adj.* desrazonable, fuera de razón; irracional.

unrecognizable [ʌnrékəgnaɪzəbl] *adj.* irreconocible, no conocible, incapaz de reconocerse; desconocido.

unrefined [ʌnrɪfáɪnd] *adj.* no refinado; inculto, grosero.

unrest [ʌnrést] *s.* inquietud, desasosiego.

unroll [ʌnról] *v.* desenrollar(se), desenvolver(se).

unruly [ʌnrúlɪ] *adj.* indómito; indócil; desobediente.

unsafe [ʌnséf] *adj.* inseguro, peligroso.

unsalable [ʌnséləbl] *adj.* invendible.

unsatisfactory [ʌnsætɪsfǽktrɪ] *adj.* no satisfactorio, inaceptable.

unseen [ʌnsín] *adj.* no visto, oculto; invisible.

unselfish [ʌnsélfɪʃ] *adj.* desinteresado.

unselfishness [ʌnsélfɪʃnɪs] *s.* desinterés, abnegación.

unsettled [ʌnsétld] *adj.* desordenado, en desorden; turbio; inestable; incierto; indeciso; deshabitado; no establecido; — **bills** cuentas no liquidadas, cuentas pendientes; — **weather** tiempo variable; **an — liquid** un líquido revuelto o turbio.

unshaken [ʌnʃékən] *adj.* inmóvil, inmovible, firme.

unsightly [ʌnsáɪtlɪ] *adj.* feo, desagradable a la vista.

unskilled [ʌnskɪld] *adj.* inexperto.

unskillful [ʌnskɪlfəl] *adj.* inhábil, desmañado, inexperto.

unsociable [ʌnsóʃəbl] *adj.* insociable, huraño, intratable, arisco.

unspeakable [ʌnspíkəbl] *adj.* indecible; inefable; atroz.

unstable [ʌnstébl] *adj.* inestable.

unsteady [ʌnstédɪ] *adj.* inseguro, inestable; movedizo; variable, inconstante.

unsuccessful [ʌnsəksésfəl] *adj.* sin éxito; desafortunado; **to be — no tener éxito.

unsuitable [ʌnsútəbl] *adj.* impropio, inapropiado; inepto; inconveniente; incongruente; incompatible.

unsuspected [ʌnsəspéktɪd] *adj.* insospechado.

untidy [ʌntáɪdɪ] *adj.* desaliñado, desaseado; desarreglado, en desorden.

untie [ʌntáɪ] *v.* desatar(se); desamarrar; deshacer (*un nudo o lazo*).

until [ʌntfl] *prep.* hasta; *conj.* hasta que.

untimely [ʌntáɪmlɪ] *adj.* inoportuno; prematuro; *adv.* inoportunamente; fuera de sazón; demasiado pronto.

untiring [ʌntáɪrɪŋ] *adj.* incansable.

untold [ʌntóld] *adj.* indecible, innumerable, incalculable, inestimable.

untouched [ʌntʌ́tʃt] *adj.* intacto, no tocado, íntegro; impasible, no conmovido; **to leave** — no tocar, dejar intacto; dejar impasible, no conmover.

untried [ʌntráɪd] *adj.* no probado, no ensayado, no experimentado; — **law case** causa todavía no vista.

untroubled [ʌntrʌ́bld] *adj* sosegado, tranquilo, quieto.

untrue [ʌntrú] *adj.* falso; infiel; desleal; mentiroso.

untruth [ʌntrúə] *s.* falsedad; mentira.

untrained [ʌntrénd] *adj.* indisciplinado, falto de disciplina; sin educación; inexperto.

unused [ʌnjúzd] *adj.* no usado; desacostumbrado; — **to** no hecho a, desacostumbrado a.

unusual [ʌnjúʒʊəl] *adj.* inusitado, insólito; desusado; raro, extraño; extraordinario.

unveil [ʌnvél] *v.* quitar el velo a; revelar, descubrir.

unwary [ʌnwɛ́rɪ] *adj.* incauto.

unwashed [ʌnwɔ́ʃt] *adj.* no lavado, sin lavar; sucio.

unwelcome [ʌnwélkəm] *adj.* indeseable, no deseado; mal acogido, mal recibido, mal quisto.

unwholesome [ʌnhólsəm] *adj.* malsano; insalubre, dañino.

unwieldy [ʌnwíldɪ] *adj.* inmanejable, difícil de manejar, embarazoso, engorroso.

unwilling [ʌnwɪ́lɪŋ] *adj.* renuente, maldispuesto, reacio; **to be** — **to** no querer, no estar dispuesto a; **-ly** *adv.* de mala gana, sin querer.

unwillingness [ʌnwɪ́lɪŋnɪs] *s.* renuencia, falta de voluntad; mala gana.

unwise [ʌnwáɪz] *adj.* imprudente, indiscreto; necio.

unworthy [ʌnwʒ́ðɪ] *adj.* indigno.

unwrap [ʌnrǽp] *v.* desenvolver.

up [ʌp] *adv.* arriba, hacia arriba, en lo alto; de pie; *adj.* levantado; derecho, erecto; terminado, concluido; — **and down** de arriba abajo; de acá para allá; **-s and downs** altibajos; fluctuaciones, vaivenes; — **the river** río arriba; — **to now** hasta ahora; **his time is** — ha expirado su tiempo; se ha cumplido su plazo; **prices are** — los precios han subido; **that is** — **to you** queda a la discreción de Vd.; eso es cosa suya; **to be** — **against it** estar perplejo, no saber qué hacer; estar en un aprieto; **to be** — **on the news** estar al corriente (o al tanto) de las noticias); **to be** — **to one's old tricks**

hacer de las suyas; **to eat it** — comérselo; **what's** — ? ¿qué pasa?; *v.* levantar, alzar.

upbraid [ʌpbréd] *v.* reprender, regañar

upheld [ʌphéld] *pret.* & *p.p. de* **to uphold.**

uphill [ʌphíl] *adv.* cuesta arriba; *adj* ascendente; trabajoso, arduo.

uphold [ʌphóld] *v.* sostener; apoyar

upholster [ʌphólstə] *v.* entapizar y rellenar (*muebles*).

upholstery [ʌphólstrɪ] *s.* tapicería.

upkeep [ʌpkip] *s.* manutención.

upland [ʌplənd] *s.* altiplanicie, tierra alta.

uplift [ʌplɪft] *s.* elevación; edificación (*espiritual*); [ʌplɪft] *v.* elevar; edificar (*espiritualmente*).

upon [əpán] *prep.* en, sobre, encima de; — **arriving** al llegar.

upper [ʌ́pə] *adj.* superior; alto; — **berth** litera alta, cama alta (*de un coche dormitorio*); **to have the** — **hand** ejercer dominio o mando; llevar la ventaja; *s.* litera alta, cama alta; pala (*parte superior del calzado*).

upright [ʌ́praɪt] *adj.* recto; derecho; vertical; justo, honrado; — **piano** piano vertical; *s.* poste; puntal; piano vertical.

uprightness [ʌ́praɪtnɪs] *s.* rectitud.

uprising [ʌprálzɪŋ] *s.* alzamiento, levantamiento; revuelta.

uproar [ʌ́pror] *s.* tumulto, alboroto, bulla, gritería.

uproarious [ʌprórɪəs] *adj.* estruendoso, bullicioso, tumultuoso.

uproot [ʌprút] *v.* desarraigar, arrancar de raíz.

upset [ʌpsét] *v.* volcar; trastornar; tumbar; perturbar, turbar; **to become** — volcarse; turbarse; trastornársele a uno el estómago; *pret.* & *p.p. de* **to upset;** *adj.* indispuesto, descompuesto; desarreglado, trastornado; [ʌpsét] *s.* vuelco; trastorno; desorden; indisposición.

upshot [ʌ́pʃat] *s.* resultado, fin.

upside [ʌ́psáɪd] *s.* lado o parte superior; — **down** al revés; patas arriba; en desorden.

upstairs [ʌpstérz] *adv.* arriba, en el piso de arriba; *adj.* de arriba; *s.* piso (o pisos) de arriba.

upstart [ʌ́pstart] *s.* advenedizo, principiante presuntuoso.

up-to-date [ʌ́ptədét] *adj.* moderno; al corriente, al tanto.

upturn [ʌ́ptʒn] *s.* alza, subida (*de precios*); mejora.

upward [ʌ́pwəd] *adv.* arriba, para arriba,

hacia arriba; más; — **of** más de; *adj.*
ascendente, hacia arriba, para arriba.
upwards [ápwədz] *adv.* = **upward.**
urban [ə́bən] *adj.* urbano.
urchin [ə́tʃin] *s.* granuja, pilluelo; **sea —**
erizo de mar.
urge [ədʒ] *v.* urgir, instar; exhortar; recomendar o solicitar con instancia;
apremiar, incitar, estimular; *s.*impulso;
gana, ganas; estímulɔ.
urgency [ə́dʒənsɪ] *s.* urgencia; apremio.
urgent [ə́dʒənt]*adj.*urgente, apremiante.
urinate [júrənet] *v.* orinar.
urine [júrɪn] *s.* orina, (los) orines.
urn [ɜn] *s.* urna; **coffee —** cafetera.
us [ʌs] *pron.* nos; nosotros (*con preposición*).
usage [júsɪdʒ] *s.* usanza; uso; **hard —**
uso constante.
use [jus] *s.* uso; empleo; utilidad; **it is
of no —** es inútil; no sirve; **out of —**
desusado, ya no usado; pasado de
moda; **to have no further — for** ya
no necesitar, ya no tener necesidad de;
what is the — of it? ¿para qué
sirve?; ¿qué ventaja tiene?; ¿qué objeto tiene?; [jus] *v.* usar; emplear;
servirse de, hacer uso de; acostumbrar
soler, *Am.* saber; **— your judgment**
haz lo que te parezca; **— up** gastar,
agotar; consumir; **to be -d to** estar
hecho, acostumbrado o habituado a;
he -d to do it solía hacerlo, lo hacía.
useful [júsfəl] *adj.* útil.
usefulness [júsfəlnɪs] *s.* utilidad.
useless [júslɪs] *adj.* inútil; inservible.
uselessness [júslɪsnɪs] *s.* inutilidad.
usher [ʌ́ʃə] *s.* acomodador (*en un teatro
o iglesia*); ujier; *v.* conducir, llevar,
acompañar; introducir.
usual [júʒʊəl] *adj.* usual; corriente, común, general; **-ly** *adv.* usualmente,
generalmente, por lo general.
usurer [júʒərə] *s.* usurero.
usurp [juzə́p] *v.* usurpar.
usury [júʒərɪ] *s.* usura.
utensil [juténsl] *s.* utensilio.
uterus [jútərəs] *s.* útero.
utility [jutílətɪ] *s.* utilidad; servicio.
utilize [jútlaɪz] *v.* utilizar; aprovechar.
utmost [ʌ́tmost] *adj.* sumo, extremo;
más distante; más grande, mayor;
más alto; último; **he did his —** hizo
cuanto pudo; **to the —** hasta más no
poder.
utter [ʌ́tə] *v.* proferir; decir, expresar;
to — a cry dar un grito; *adj.* completo,
total; absoluto.
utterance [ʌ́tərəns] *s.* declaración; expresión; modo de hablar.

uttermost [ʌ́təmost] = **utmost.**
uvula [júvjələ] *s.* campanilla, galillo de
la garganta.

V

vacancy [vékənsɪ] *s.* vacante, empleo
vacante; vacío; habitación o apartamento desocupado.
vacant [vékənt] *adj.* vacante; vacío;
desocupado; libre.
vacate [véket] *v.* desocupar, dejar vacío;
dejar vacante.
vacation [vekéʃən] *s.* vacación; vacaciones.
vaccinate [væksnet] *v.* vacunar.
vaccination [væksnéʃən] *s.* vacunación.
vaccine [væksin] *s.* vacuna.
vacillate [væslet] *v.* vacilar.
vacuum [vækjʊəm] *s.* vacío; **— cleaner**
escoba eléctrica.
vagabond [vægəbɑnd] *adj.* & *s.* vagabundo.
vagrant [végrənt] *adj.* vago, vagabundo,
errante; *s.* vago, vagabundo.
vague [veg] *adj.* vago.
vain [ven] *adj.* vano; vanidoso; **in —**
en vano.
vainglory [venglórɪ] *s.* vanagloria.
vale [vel] *s.* valle; cañada.
valentine [væləntaɪn] *s.* tarjeta o regalo
del día de San Valentín (*el día de los
enamorados*); **to my —** a mi querido,
a mi querida.
valet [vælɪt] *s.* criado, camarero; plan-
chador de trajes.
valiant [væljənt] *adj.* valiente, valeroso.
valid [vælɪd] *adj.* válido; valedero.
validity [vəlɪdətɪ] *s.* validez.
valise [vəlís] *s.* valija, maleta, *Am.* velís,
Am. petaca.
valley [vælɪ] *s.* valle.
valor [vælə] *s.* valor, ánimo, valentía.
valorous [vælərəs] *adj.* valeroso, valiente.
valuable [væljəbl] *adj.* valioso; precioso;
preciado; **-s** *s. pl.* objetos de valor,
joyas, alhajas.
valuation [væljuéʃən] *s.* valuación, valoración; avalúo; tasa.
value [væljʊ] *s.* valor; precio; mérito;
estimación, aprecio; *v.* valorar, avaluar, valuar; apreciar, estimar.
valueless [væljʊlɪs] *adj.* sin valor.
valve [vælv] *s.* válvula; valva (*de los
moluscos*); **safety —** válvula de seguridad.
van [væn] *s.* camión (*para transportar
muebles*); **—guard** vanguardia.
vane [ven] *s.* veleta; aspa (*de molino de
viento*); paleta (*de hélice*).

239

vanilla [vənflə] s. vainilla.

vanish [vǽnɪʃ] v. desvanecerse, desaparecer(se).

vanity [vǽnətɪ] s. vanidad; — case neceser; — table tocador.

vanquish [vǽnkwɪʃ] v. vencer.

vantage [vǽntɪdʒ] s. ventaja; point of — lugar estratégico.

vapor [vépə] s. vapor; vaho.

variable [vérɪəbl] adj. & s. variable.

variance [vérɪəns] s. variación, cambio; desavenencia; to be at — estar desavenidos; no estar de acuerdo.

variation [verɪéʃən] s. variación; variedad.

varied [vérɪd] adj. variado, vario.

variegated [vérɪgetɪd] adj. abigarrado.

variety [vəráɪɪtɪ] s. variedad.

various [vérɪəs] adj. varios; diferentes, distintos.

varnish [vúrnɪʃ] s. barniz; v. barnizar.

vary [vérɪ] v. variar; cambiar.

vase [ves] s. vaso, jarrón.

vassal [vǽsl] adj. & s. vasallo.

vast [vǽst] adj. vasto; inmenso; anchuroso; -ly adv. vastamente, sumamente, muy.

vastness [vǽstnɪs] s. inmensidad.

vat [vǽt] s. tina, tanque.

vaudeville [vódəvɪl] s. vodevil, función de variedades.

vault [vɔlt] s. bóveda; tumba; bank — caja fuerte; depósito; pole — salto con garrocha; v. abovedar, edificar una bóveda; dar figura de bóveda; saltar con garrocha; saltar por encima de.

vaunt [vɔnt] v. jactarse; ostentar, alardear; s. jactancia.

veal [vil] s. carne de ternera; — cutlet chuleta de ternera.

veer [vɪr] v. virar; s. virada.

vegetable [védʒtəbl] s. vegetal, planta; legumbre; -s hortaliza, legumbres; green -s verduras; adj. vegetal; de legumbres, dè hortaliza; — garden hortaliza.

vegetate [védʒətet] v. vegetar.

vegetation [vedʒətéʃən] s. vegetación.

vehemence [víəməns] s. vehemencia.

vehement [víəmənt] adj. vehemente.

vehicle [vítkl] s. vehículo.

veil [vel] s. velo; v. velar; tapar, encubrir.

vein [ven] s. vena; veta, filón.

veined [vend] adj. veteado, jaspeado; venoso.

velocity [vəlúsətɪ] s. velocidad.

velvet [vélvɪt] s. terciopelo; velludo; adj. de terciopelo; aterciopelado.

velvety [vélvɪtɪ] adj. aterciopelado.

vendor [véndə] s. vendedor; buhonero, vendedor ambulante.

veneer [vənír] s. chapa; v. chapar o chapear, Am. enchapar.

venerable [vénərəbl] adj. venerable; venerando.

venerate [vénəret] v. venerar.

veneration [venəréʃən] s. veneración.

Venezuelan [venəzwílən] adj. & s. venezolano.

vengeance [véndʒəns] s. venganza; with a — con furia; con violencia.

venison [vénəzn] s. venado, carne de venado.

venom [vénəm] s. veneno, ponzoña.

venomous [vénəməs] adj. venenoso, ponzoñoso.

vent [vent] s. abertura; escape; desahogo; fogón (de arma de fuego); to give — to anger desahogar la ira, dar desahogo a la cólera; v. dar salida o desahogo; desahogar, descargar.

ventilate [véntlet] v. ventilar.

ventilation [ventléʃən] s. ventilación.

ventilator [véntletə] s. ventilador.

venture [véntʃə] s. ventura, riesgo; business — especulación; empresa o negocio arriesgado; v. aventurar, arriesgar; to — outside aventurarse a salir; to — to aventurarse a, atreverse a, osar.

venturous [véntʃərəs] adj. aventurado.

veranda [vərǽndə] s. galería; terraza; balcón corrido.

verb [vɜb] s. verbo.

verbal [vɜbl] adj. verbal; oral.

verbose [vəbós] adj. verboso; palabrero.

verdict [vɜdɪkt] s. veredicto; fallo, decisión, sentencia; — of "not guilty" veredicto de inculpabilidad.

verdure [vɜdʒə] s. verdura, verdor, verde.

verge [vɜdʒ] s. borde, margen, orilla; on the — of al borde de; a punto de; v. to — on rayar en, estar al margen de; to — toward tender a, inclinarse a.

verify [vérəfaɪ] v. verificar; comprobar.

verily [vérəlɪ] adv. en verdad.

veritable [vérətəbl] adj. verdadero.

verse [vɜs] s. verso.

versed [vɜst] adj. versado, experto, perito.

version [vɜʒən] versión.

vertical [vɜtɪkl] adj. vertical.

very [vérɪ] adv. muy; — much muchísimo; — many muchísimos; it is — cold today hace mucho frío hoy; adj. mismo; mismísimo; mero; the — man el mismísimo hombre; the — thought of la mera idea de.

vespers [véspəz] *s. pl.* vísperas.
vessel [vésl] *s.* vasija; vaso; barco, embarcación; **blood —** vaso, vena, arteria.
vest [vest[*s.* chaleco; *v.* conferir; **to — with power** revestir de autoridad, conferir poder a.
vestibule [véstəbjul] *s.* vestíbulo; zaguán.
vestige [véstɪdʒ] *s.* vestigio.
vestment [véstmənt] *s.* vestidura.
veteran [vétərən] *adj. & s.* veterano.
veterinary [vétrənerɪ] *s.* veterinario o albéitar.
veto [víto] *s.* veto; prohibición; *v.* vedar, prohibir; poner el veto a; negarse a aprobar.
vex [veks] *v.* molestar, hostigar; incomodar, enfadar; perturbar.
vexation [vekséʃən] *s.* molestia, incomodidad; enojo.
via [váɪə] *prep.* por, por la vía de.
viaduct [váɪədʌkt] *s.* viaducto.
vial [váɪəl] *s.* frasco, redoma; **small —** ampolleta.
viands [váɪəndz] *s. pl.* vianda, alimentos, comida.
vibrate [váɪbret] *v.* vibrar.
vibration [vaɪbréʃən] *s.* vibración.
vice [vaɪs] *s.* vicio; falta, defecto.
vice-president [váɪsprézədənt] *s.* vice-presidente.
viceroy [váɪsrɔɪ] *s.* virrey.
vice versa [váɪsɪvésə] viceversa.
vicinity [vəsɪnɪtɪ] *s.* vecindad; cercanía; inmediaciones.
vicious [víʃəs] *adj.* vicioso; malo; maligno; malicioso; **— dog** perro mordedor, perro bravo.
vicissitude [vəsísətjud] *s.* vicisitud, peripecia.
victim [víktɪm] *s.* víctima.
victor [víktə] *s.* vencedor.
victorious [vɪktórɪəs] *adj.* victorioso.
victory [víktrɪ] *s.* victoria.
victuals [vítlz] *s. pl.* vituallas, víveres.
vie [vaɪ] *v.* competir.
view [vju] *s.* vista; paisaje; parecer, opinión; inspección; mira, propósito; **in — of** en vista de; **to be within —** estar al alcance de la vista; **with a — to** con el propósito de; con la esperanza o expectación de; con la mira puesta en; *v.* mirar; examinar.
viewpoint [vjúpɔɪnt] *s.* punto de vista.
vigil [vídʒəl] *s.* vigilia, velada; **to keep — velar.**
vigilance [vídʒələns] *s.* vigilancia, desvelo.
vigilant [vídʒələnt] *adj.* vigilante.

vigor [vígə] *s.* vigor.
vigorous [vígərəs] *adj.* vigoroso.
vile [vaɪl] *adj.* vil, bajo, ruin; pésimo.
villa [vílə] *s.* quinta, casa de campo.
village [vílɪdʒ] *s.* villa, aldea.
villager [vílɪdʒə] *s.* aldeano.
villain [vílən] *s.* villano, malvado, bellaco.
villainous [vílənəs] *adj.* villano, ruin, vil, bellaco.
villainy [vílənɪ] *s.* villanía, vileza.
vim [vɪm] *s.* vigor, fuerza, energía.
vindicate [víndəket] *v.* vindicar, vengar.
vindictive [vɪndíktɪv] *adj.* vengativo.
vine [vaɪn] *s.* vid, parra; enredadera.
vinegar [vínɪgə] *s.* vinagre.
vineyard [vínjəd] *s.* viña, viñedo.
vintage [víntɪdʒ] *s.* vendimia; edad, época.
violate [váɪəlet] *v.* violar; infringir.
violation [vaɪəléʃən] *s.* violación; infracción.
violence [váɪələns] *s.* violencia.
violent [váɪələnt] *adj.* violento.
violet [váɪəlɪt] *s.* violeta; violado, **color** de violeta; *adj.* violado.
violin [vaɪəlín] *s.* violín.
violinist [vaɪəlínɪst] *s.* violinista.
viper [váɪpə] *s.* víbora.
virgin [vədʒɪn] *adj. & s.* virgen.
virginal [védʒɪnl] *adj.* virginal.
virtual [vétʃʊəl] *adj.* virtual; **-ly** *adv.* virtualmente.
virtue [vétʃʊ] *s.* virtud.
virtuous [vétʃʊəs] *adj.* virtuoso.
visa [vízə] *s.* visa, visado; *v.* visar, refrendar.
visé = visa.
vise [vaɪs] *s.* tornillo de banco.
visible [vízəbl] *adj.* visible.
vision [víʒən] *s.* visión; vista.
visionary [víʒənerɪ] *adj.* visionario; imaginario; *s.* visionario, iluso, soñador.
visit [vízɪt] *v.* visitar; **to — punishment upon** mandar un castigo a, castigar a; *s.* visita.
visitation [vɪzətéʃən] *s.* visitación, visita; castigo, calamidad.
visitor [vízɪtə] *s.* visita; visitador.
visor [váɪzə] *s.* visera.
vista [vístə] *s.* vista, paisaje.
vital [váɪtl] *adj.* vital.
vitality [vaɪtǽlətɪ] *s.* vitalidad.
vitamin [váɪtəmɪn] *s.* vitamina.
vivacious [vaɪvéʃəs] *adj.* vivaz, vivaracho, vivo, alegre, animado.
vivacity [vaɪvǽsɪtɪ] *s.* viveza, vivacidad.
vivid [vívɪd] *adj.* vívido, vivo; animado.
vocabulary [vəkǽbjələrɪ] *s.* vocabulario.
vocal [vókl] *adj.* vocal; oral; **to be**

— hablar, expresarse.

vocation [voké∫ən] s. vocación.

vogue [vog] s. boga, moda; **in —** en boga, de moda.

voice [vɔɪs] s. voz; habla; voto; v. expresar, decir; **-d consonant** consonante sonora.

voiceless [vɔ́ɪslɪs] adj. mudo; sin voz; **— consonant** consonante sorda.

void [vɔɪd] adj. vacío; nulo, inválido; **— of** falto de, desprovisto de; s. vacío; v. vaciar, evacuar; anular, invalidar.

volatile [vɑ́lətɪl] adj. volátil; inconstante.

volcanic [vɑlkǽnɪk] adj. volcánico.

volcano [vɑlkéno] s. volcán.

volition [volí∫ən] s. volición; voluntad.

volley [vɑ́lɪ] s. descarga, lluvia (de piedras, flechas, balas, etc.); voleo (de la pelota); v. descargar una lluvia de proyectiles; volear una pelota.

volt [volt] s. voltio.

voltage [vóltɪdʒ] s. voltaje.

volume [vɑ́ljəm] s. volumen; tomo; bulto; suma, cantidad.

voluminous [vəlʌ́mənəs] adj. voluminoso.

voluntary [vɑ́ləntɛrɪ] adj. voluntario.

volunteer [vɑləntír] s. voluntario; adj. voluntario; de voluntarios; v. ofrecer, dar voluntariamente; ofrecerse.

voluptuous [vəlʌ́pt∫ʊəs] adj. voluptuoso.

vomit [vɑ́mɪt] s. vómito; v. vomitar, Am. deponer.

voracious [vorέ∫əs] adj. voraz.

vote [vot] s. voto; votación; v. votar; votar por.

voter [vótə] s. votante, elector.

vouch [vaʊt∫] v. **to — for** dar fe de; garantizar, responder de; salir fiador de.

voucher [váʊt∫ə] s. comprobante, justificante; recibo; fiador.

vouchsafe [vaʊt∫séf] v. otorgar, conceder.

vow [vaʊ] s. voto; juramento; v. votar, jurar, hacer voto de.

vowel [váʊəl] s. & adj. vocal.

voyage [vɔ́ɪɪdʒ] s. viaje; travesía; v. viajar.

vulgar [vʌ́lgə] adj. soez, ordinario, grosero; vulgar.

vulture [vʌ́lt∫ə] s. buitre, Am. cóndor.

W

wabble [wɑ́bl] v. tambalear(se), bambolear(se); vacilar; temblar; s. tambaleo, bamboleo; balanceo.

wad [wɑd] s. taco; bodoque; pelotilla, bolita, rollo; **— of money** rollo de billetes (de banco); dinero; v. atacar (un arma de fuego); rellenar; hacer una pelotilla de.

waddle [wɑ́dl] v. anadear; contonearse; zarandearse (al andar); s. anadeo; zarandeo, contoneo.

wade [wed] v. vadear; chapotear; andar descalzo por la orilla del agua; **to — through a book** leer con dificultad un libro.

wafer [wéfə] s. oblea; hostia (consagrada).

waft [wæft] v. llevar en vilo, llevar por el aire; llevar a flote; s. ráfaga de aire; movimiento (de la mano).

wag [wæg] v. menear; sacudir; **to — the tail** colear, menear la cola; s. meneo; bromista, farsante.

wage [wedʒ] v. hacer (guerra); dar (batalla); s. (usualmente **wages**) paga, jornal; **— earner** jornalero, obrero; trabajador.

wager [wédʒə] s. apuesta; v. apostar.

wagon [wǽgən] s. carro, carreta; carretón.

wail [wel] v. gemir, lamentar; s. gemido, lamento.

waist [west] s. cintura; talle; blusa; **—band** pretina.

waistcoat [wéstkot] s. chaleco.

wait [wet] v. esperar, aguardar; servir; **to — for** esperar, aguardar; **to — on** (**upon**) servir a; atender a; **to — table** servir la mesa, servir de mozo o camarero (en un restaurante); s. espera; **to lie in — for** estar en acecho de.

waiter [wétə] s. mozo, camarero, sirviente, Am. mesero.

waiting [wétɪŋ] s. espera; **— room** sala de espera.

waitress [wétrɪs] s. camarera, moza, Am. mesera.

waive [wev] v. renunciar a; **to — one's right** renunciar voluntariamente a sus derechos.

wake [wek] v. despertar(se); **to — up** despertar(se); despabilarse; s. velatorio (acto de velar a un muerto), Am. velorio; estela (huella que deja un barco en el agua); **in the — of** después de, detrás de.

wakeful [wékfəl] adj. desvelado, despierto; insomne.

waken [wékən] v. despertar(se); Am. recordar (a una persona que está dormida).

walk [wɔk] v. andar, caminar, ir a pie; recorrer a pie; pasear; **to — away** irse, marcharse; **to — back home**

volverse a casa (a pie); **to — down** bajar; **to — in** entrar; **to — out** salirse, irse; parar el trabajo, declararse en huelga; **to — the streets** callejear; **to — up** subir; *s.* paseo; senda, vereda; acera; paso (*del caballo*); manera de andar; **— of life** vocación; **a ten minutes' —** una caminata de diez minutos.

wall [wɔl] *s.* pared; muro; muralla; **low mud — tapia; to drive to the —** poner entre la espada y la pared, poner en un aprieto.

wallet [wálɪt] *s.* cartera.

wallflower [wɔ́lflauə] *s.* alelí; **to be a — at a dance** comer pavo, *Am.* planchar el asiento.

wallop [wálǝp] *v.* pegar, zurrar, golpear; *s.* guantada, bofetón, golpazo.

wallow [wálo] *v.* revolcarse; chapalear o chapotear (*en el lodo*).

wallpaper [wɔ́lpepǝ] *s.* papel (de empapelar).

walnut [wɔ́lnǝt] *s.* nuez de nogal; nogal; **— tree** nogal.

waltz [wɔlts] *s.* vals; *v.* valsar, bailar el vals.

wan [wan] *adj.* pálido, enfermizo, enclenque; lánguido.

wand [wand] *s.* vara, varita; **magic —** varita de virtud.

wander [wándǝ] *v.* vagar, errar; **to — away** extraviarse; **to — away from** apartarse de, desviarse de; **my mind -s easily** me distraigo fácilmente.

wanderer [wándǝrǝ] *s.* vago, vagabundo.

wane [wen] *v.* menguar; decaer; *s.* mengua; diminución; **to be on the —** ir menguando; ir desapareciendo.

want [want] *v.* querer, desear; necesitar; *s.* falta; necesidad; escasez, carencia; **to be in —** estar necesitado.

wanting [wántɪŋ] *adj.* falto; deficiente; necesitado.

wanton [wántǝn] *adj.* desenfrenado, libre; licencioso; inconsiderado; temerario.

war [wɔr] *s.* guerra; *v.* guerrear, hacer guerra; **to — on** guerrear con.

warble [wɔ́rbl] *v.* gorjear; trinar; *s.* gorjeo; trino.

warbler [wɔ́rblǝ] *s.* cantor; pájaro gorjeador.

ward [wɔrd] *s.* pupilo, menor o huérfano (*bajo tutela*); cuadra (*de hospital, prisión, etc.*); distrito (*de una ciudad*); *v.* **to — off** resguardarse de; evitar; parar (*un golpe*).

warden [wɔ́rdn] *s.* guardián; alcaide; **prison —** alcaide de una prisión.

wardrobe [wɔ́rdrob] *s.* guardarropa, ropero, armario; vestuario; ropa.

warehouse [wérhaus] *s.* almacén, depósito.

wares [werz] *s. pl.* artículos, mercancías, mercaderías, efectos.

warfare [wɔ́rfer] *s.* guerra.

warlike [wɔ́rlaɪk] *adj.* guerrero, bélico.

warm [wɔrm] *adj.* caliente, cálido, caluroso; acalorado; cordial; reciente; **—hearted** de buen corazón; **he is —** tiene calor; **it is — today** hace calor hoy; *v.* calentar(se); **to — over** recalentar; **to — up** calentar(se); acalorarse; entusiasmarse.

warmth [wɔrmθ] *s.* calor; cordialidad.

warn [wɔrn] *v.* avisar, advertir, amonestar; prevenir, precaver.

warning [wɔ́rnɪŋ] *s.* aviso, advertencia, amonestación; escarmiento; **let that be a — to you** que te sirva de escarmiento.

warp [wɔrp] *s.* urdimbre (*de un tejido*); torcedura, deformación; comba; *v.* combar(se), deformar(se), torcer(se); urdir (*los hilos de un telar*).

warrant [wɔ́rent] *s.* autorización; garantía, justificación; comprobante; orden, mandato, citación (*ante un juez*); *v.* autorizar; garantizar; justificar.

warrior [wɔ́rɪǝ] *s.* guerrero.

warship [wɔ́rʃɪp] *s.* buque de guerra, acorazado.

wart [wɔrt] *s.* verruga.

wary [wérɪ] *adj.* cauteloso, cauto, precavido, prevenido; **to be — of** desconfiar de.

was [waz] *pret. de* **to be** (*primera y tercera persona del singular*).

wash [waʃ] *v.* lavar(se); **to — away** deslavar(se); **to be -ed away by the waves** ser arrastrado por las olas; *s.* lavado; lavadura; lavatorio; lavazas, agua sucia; **mouth —** enjuague o enjuagatorio; **—bowl** lavabo, palangana, lavamanos; **—cloth** paño para lavarse; **— dress** vestido lavable; **— room** lavabo, lavatorio.

washable [wáʃǝbl] *adj.* lavable.

washed-out [wáʃtáut] *adj.* desteñido; agotado, sin fuerzas.

washer [wáʃǝ] *s.* lavador; máquina de lavar; arandela (*para una tuerca*); **—woman** lavandera.

washing [wáʃɪŋ] *s.* lavado; ropa sucia o para lavar; ropa lavada; **— machine** lavadora, máquina de lavar.

wasp [wasp] *s.* avispa.

waste [west] *v.* gastar; desgastar; malgastar, desperdiciar, derrochar; disipar; **to — away** gastarse, consumirse; desgastarse; *s.* desperdicio; gasto inútil; desgaste; desechos, desperdicios; terreno baldío, desierto; *adj.* inútil, desechado; desierto; baldío, **— of time** pérdida de tiempo; **—basket** cesto para papeles; **— land** terreno baldío; **—paper** papeles inútiles, papel de desecho; **to go to —** gastarse, perderse; malgastarse, desperdiciarse; **to lay —** asolar, arruinar.

wasteful [wéstfəl] *adj.* despilfarrado, gastador; desperdiciado; inéconómico.

watch [watʃ] *v.* mirar, observar; vigilar; velar; cuidar; **— out!** ¡cuidado!; **to — out for** tener cuidado con; cuidar; vigilar; *s.* reloj (de bolsillo); vela, vigilia; guardia; centinela, vigilante; **— chain** cadena de reloj, *Am.* leontina; **— charm** dije; **wrist —** reloj de pulsera; **to be on the —** tener cuidado; estar alerta; **to keep — over** vigilar a.

watchful [wátʃfəl] *adj.* alerto, vigilante, despierto, atento.

watchman [wátʃmən] *s.* vigilante, guardia, sereno.

watchtower [wátʃtauə] *s.* atalaya, mirador.

watchword [wátʃwɜd] *s.* contraseña, santo y seña, consigna; lema.

water [wɔ́tə] *s.* agua; **— color** acuarela; color para acuarela; **— power** fuerza hidráulica; **—shed** vertiente; **— sports** deportes acuáticos; *v.* regar; aguar, diluir con agua; abrevar, dar de beber (*al ganado*); beber agua (*el ganado*); tomar agua (*un barco, locomotora, etc.*); **my eyes —** me lloran los ojos; **my mouth -s** se me hace agua la boca.

waterfall [wɔ́təfɔl] *s.* cascada, catarata, caída de agua.

watermelon [wɔ́təmɛlən] *s.* sandía.

waterproof [wɔ́təpruf] *adj. & s.* impermeable; *v.* hacer impermeable.

waterspout [wɔ́təspaut] *s.* surtidor; tromba, manga de agua.

waterway [wɔ́təwe] *s.* vía de agua, río navegable, canal.

watery [wɔ́tərɪ] *adj.* aguado; acuoso; mojado, húmedo.

wave [wev] *v.* ondear; ondular; agitar; blandir (*una espada, bastón, etc.*); **to — aside** apartar, rechazar; **to — good-bye** hacer una seña o ademán de despedida; **to — hair** ondular el pelo; **to — one's hand** hacer una seña o señas con la mano; mover la mano; *s.*

onda; ola; ondulación; **— of the hand** ademán, movimiento de la mano; **permanent —** ondulación permanente.

waver [wévə] *v.* oscilar; vacilar, titubear; tambalear(se); *s.* vacilación, titubeo.

wavy [wévɪ] *adj.* rizado, ondulado; ondulante.

wax [wæks] *s.* cera; **— candle** vela de cera; **— paper** papel encerado; *v.* encerar; pulir con cera; hacerse, ponerse; crecer (*la luna*).

way [we] *s.* vía; camino; ruta; senda; modo, manera; **— in** entrada; **— out** salida; **— through** paso, pasaje; **a long — off** muy lejos, a una larga distancia; **by — of** por, por vía de; **by — of comparison** a modo de comparación; **by the —** de paso; **in no — **de ningún modo; **on the — to** camino de, rumbo a; **out of the —** fuera del camino; apartado; a un lado; impropio; extraordinario; **to be in a bad —** hallarse en mal estado; **to be well under —** estar (*un trabajo*) ya bastante avanzado; **to give —** ceder; quebrarse; **to have one's —** hacer su capricho, salirse con la suya; **to make — for** abrir paso para.

waylay [welé] *v.* estar en acecho de (*alguien*); asaltar; detener (*a una persona*).

wayside [wésaɪd] *s.* borde del camino; **— inn** posada al borde del camino.

wayward [wéwəd] *adj.* voluntarioso, desobediente.

we [wi] *pron.* nosotros, nosotras.

weak [wik] *adj.* débil; flaco; endeble; **— market** mercado flojo; **weak-minded** de voluntad débil; simple; **— tea** té claro o suave.

weaken [wíkən] *v.* debilitar(se); desmayar, flaquear, perder ánimo.

weakly [wíklɪ] *adv.* débilmente; *adj.* enfermizo, débil, enclenque.

weakness [wíknɪs] *s.* debilidad; flaqueza.

wealth [wɛlθ] *s.* riqueza; copia, abundancia.

wealthy [wélθɪ] *adj.* rico.

wean [win] *v.* destetar; apartar gradualmente (*de un hábito, de una amistad*).

weapon [wépən] *s.* arma.

wear [wɛr] *v.* llevar, tener o traer puesto; usar; gastar, desgastar; **to — away** gastar(se); desgastar(se); consumir(se); **to — off** desgastar(se), gastar(se); borrarse; **to — out** gastar(se); desgastar(se), consumir(se); agotar; cansar; **it -s well** es duradero; dura mucho; **as the day wore on** a medida que pasaba el día; *s.* uso, gasto; durabilidad; **— and tear** desgaste; uso; **men's —** ropa para hombres; **clothes for summer —** ropa de verano.

wearily [wírɪlɪ] *adv.* penosamente, con cansancio, con fatiga, fatigadamente.

weariness [wírɪnɪs] *s.* cansancio, fatiga.

wearing [wérɪŋ] *adj.* cansado, aburrido, fastidioso.

wearisome [wírɪsəm] *adj.* fatigoso, molesto, fastidioso.

weary [wírɪ] *adj.* cansado, fatigado; aburrido; *v.* cansar(se), fatigar(se).

weasel [wízl̩] *s.* comadreja.

weather [wéðə] *s.* tiempo; **weatherbeaten** desgastado o curtido por la intemperie; **— bureau** oficina meteorológica; **— conditions** condiciones atmosféricas; **—vane** veleta; **it is fine — hace buen tiempo; to be under the —** estar enfermo; estar indispuesto; *v.* exponer a la intemperie; orear, secar al aire; **to — a storm** aguantar un chubasco; salir ileso de una tormenta.

weave [wiv] *v.* tejer, entretejer; urdir; **to — together** entretejer, entrelazar; combinar; *s.* tejido.

weaver [wívə] *s.* tejedor.

web [wɛb] *s.* tela; membrana *(entre los dedos de los pájaros acuáticos)*; **spider's — telaraña.**

wed [wɛd] *v.* casarse; casarse con; casar; *p.p. de* **to wed.**

wedded [wédɪd] *p.p. & adj.* casado; unido; **— to an idea** aferrado a una idea.

wedding [wédɪŋ] *s.* boda, casamiento, nupcias, enlace; **— day** día de bodas; **— trip** viaje de novios; **silver —** bodas de plata.

wedge [wɛdʒ] *s.* cuña; **entering —** cuña, entrada, medio de entrar, modo de penetrar; *v.* acuñar, meter cuñas; **to be -d between** estar encajado entre.

Wednesday [wénzdɪ] *s.* miércoles.

wee [wi] *adj.* diminuto, chiquitico, pequeñito.

weed [wid] *s.* cizaña, mala hierba; *v.* desherbar *(o desyerbar)*, quitar o arrancar la mala hierba; **to — a garden** desherbar un huerto; **to — out** escardar; eliminar, arrancar, entresacar.

weedy [wídɪ] *adj.* herboso, lleno de malas hierbas.

week [wik] *s.* semana; **—day** día de trabajo, día laborable, día hábil; **—end** fin de semana; **a — from today** de hoy en ocho días.

weekly [wíklɪ] *adj.* semanal, semanario; *adv.* semanalmente, por semana; *s.* semanario, periódico o revista semanal.

weep [wip] *v.* llorar.

weeping [wípɪŋ] *adj.* llorón; lloroso; **— willow** sauce llorón; *s.* llanto, lloro, lágrimas.

weevil [wívl̩] *s.* gorgojo.

weigh [we] *v.* pesar; ponderar, considerar; **to — anchor** zarpar, levar el ancla; **to — down** agobiar; abrumar; **to — on one's conscience** serle a uno gravoso, pesarle a uno.

weight [wet] *s.* peso; pesa *(de reloj o medida para pesar)*; carga; **paper—** pisapapeles; *v.* cargar, sobrecargar; añadir peso a; asignar un peso o valor relativo a.

weighty [wétɪ] *adj.* grave, ponderoso; de mucho peso; importante.

weird [wɪrd] *adj.* extraño, raro, misterioso, fantástico.

welcome [vélkəm] *s.* bienvenida; buena acogida; *adj.* grato, agradable; bien acogido, bien quisto; bien recibido; **— home!** ¡bienvenido!; **— rest** grato reposo o descanso; **you are —** no hay de qué, de nada *(para contestar a* "thank you"*)*; **you are — here** está Vd. en su casa; **you are — to use it** se lo presto con todo gusto; está a su disposición; *v.* dar la bienvenida a; acoger o recibir con gusto.

weld [wɛld] *v.* soldar(se); *s.* soldadura.

welfare [wélfɛr] *s.* bienestar; bien; felicidad; **— work** labor social o de beneficencia.

well [wɛl] *adv.* bien; **he is — over fifty** tiene mucho más de cincuenta años; **— then** pues bien, ahora bien, conque; **well-bred** bien criado; bien educado; **well-meaning** bien intencionado; **well-nigh** casi, muy cerca de; *adj.* bueno; bien de salud, sano; conveniente; **— and good** santo y muy bueno; **well-being** bienestar; **well-off** acomodado, adinerado; en buenas condiciones; **well-to-do** próspero, adinerado; **all is — no hay novedad, todo va bien; it is — to do it** conviene hacerlo, es conveniente hacerlo.

well [wɛl] *s.* pozo; cisterna; manantial; **artesian —** pozo artesiano; *v.* manar; **tears -ed up in her eyes** se le arrasaron los ojos de lágrimas.

welt [wɛlt] *s.* verdugo, verdugón, roncha.

went [wɛnt] *pret. de* **to go.**

wept [wɛpt] *pret. & p.p. de* **to weep.**

were [wɜ] *pret. de* **to be** *(en el plural y en la segunda persona del singular del* *indicativo; es además el imperfecto del subjuntivo);* if **I — you** si yo fuera Vd.; **there —** había, hubo.

west [wɛst] *s.* oeste, occidente, ocaso; *adj.* occidental, del oeste; **West Indies** Antillas; *adv.* hacia el oeste, al oeste; en el oeste.

western [wɛstən] *adj.* occidental, del oeste.

westerner [wɛstənə] *s.* natural del oeste, habitante del oeste, occidental.

westward [wɛstwəd] *adv.* hacia el oeste; *adj.* occidental, oeste.

wet [wɛt] *adj.* húmedo; mojado;— **nurse** nodriza, ama de leche; *s.* humedad; antiprohibicionista (*el que favorece la venta de bebidas alcohólicas*); *v.* mojar; humedecer; *pret. & p.p. de* **to wet.**

wetness [wɛtnɪs] *s.* humedad.

whack [hwæk] *v.* golpear, pegar; *s.* golpe; golpazo; tentativa, prueba.

whale [hwel] *s.* ballena; *v.* pescar ballenas.

wharf [hwɔrf] *s.* muelle, embarcadero.

what [hwɑt] *pron. interr.* qué; qué cosa; cuál; *pron. rel.* lo que; **— for?** ¿para qué? *adj.* qué; **— book?** ¿qué libro? **— a man!** ¡qué hombre!; **— happy children!** ¡qué niños más (*o* tan) felices!; **take — books you need** tome Vd. los libros que necesite.

whatever [hwɑtɛvə] *pron.* cualquiera cosa que, lo que, cuanto, todo lo que; **— do you mean?** ¿qué quiere Vd. decir?; **do it, — happens** hágalo suceda lo que suceda; *adj.* cualquiera; **any person —** una persona cualquiera; **no money —** nada de dinero.

whatsoever [hwɑtsoɛvə] = **whatever.**

wheat [hwit] *s.* trigo; **cream of —** crema de trigo.

wheel [hwil] *s.* rueda; rodaja; disco; bicicleta; timón; **— chair** silla rodante, silla de ruedas; **steering —** volante (*de automóvil*); rueda del timón; *v.* rodar; hacer rodar; girar; acarrear; andar en bicicleta; **to — around** dar una vuelta; girar sobre los talones; **to — the baby** pasear al bebé en su cochecito.

wheelbarrow [hwílbæro] *s.* carretilla.

when [hwɛn] *adv. & conj.* cuando; *adv. interr.* ¿cuándo?

whence [hwɛns] *adv.* de donde; de que.

whenever [hwɛnɛvə] *adj. & conj.* cuando, siempre que, cada vez que.

where [hwɛr] *adv.* donde; adonde; en donde; por donde; **—?** ¿dónde?; ¿adónde?

whereabouts [hwérəbaʊts] *s.* paradero;

adv. interr. ¿dónde?

whereas [hwɛræz] *conj.* mientras que, puesto que, visto que, considerando que.

whereby [hwɛrbái] *adv.* por donde, por lo cual; con lo cual.

wherefore [hwérfor] *adv.* por qué; por lo cual; por eso, por lo tanto.

wherein [hwɛrín] *adv.* en qué; en donde; en lo cual.

whereof [hwɛráv] *adv.* de que; de donde; de quien, de quienes.

whereupon [hwɛrəpán] *adv.* después de lo cual; entonces.

wherever [hwɛrɛvə] *adv.* dondequiera que, adondequiera que, por dondequiera que.

wherewithal [hwérwɪðɔl] *s.* medios, fondos; dinero.

whet [hwɛt] *v.* amolar, afilar; aguzar, estimular.

whether [hwɛðə] *conj.* si; ya sea que, sea que; **— we escape or not** ya sea que escapemos o no; **I doubt —** dudo (de) que.

which [hwɪtʃ] *pron. interr.* ¿cuál?; ¿cuáles?; *pron. rel.* que; el cual, la cual, los cuales, las cuales; el que, la que, los que, las que; *adj. interr.* ¿qué?; **— boy has it?** ¿cuál de los muchachos lo tiene? ¿qué muchacho lo tiene?; **— way did he go?** ¿por qué camino se fué?; ¿por dónde se fué?; **during —** time tiempo durante el cual.

whichever [hwɪtʃɛvə] *pron. & adj.* cualquiera (que), cualesquiera (que); el que, la que; **— road you take** cualquier camino que Vd. siga.

whiff [hwɪf] *s.* soplo; fumada, bocanada; repentino olor o hedor; *v* soplar; echar bocanadas.

while [hwaɪl] *s.* rato; tiempo, temporada, **a short —** un ratito; **a short — ago** hace poco, hace poco rato; **to be worth —** valer la pena; *conj.* mientras, mientras que; *v.* **to — away the time** pasar el tiempo.

whilst [hwaɪlst] *conj.* mientras, mientras que.

whim [hwɪm] *s.* capricho, antojo.

whimper [hwímpə] *v.* lloriquear, gimotear; quejarse; *s.* lloriqueo, gimoteo; quejido.

whimsical [hwímzɪkl] *adj.* caprichoso.

whine [hwaɪn] *v.* lloriquear; quejarse; *s.* gemido, quejido.

whiner [hwáɪnə] *s.* llorón, persona quejosa, *Am.* quejumbres.

whip [hwɪp] *v.* azotar, fustigar; zurrar, dar una paliza a, dar latigazos a;

batir (*crema, huevos*); vencer; **to —**
up batir; coger o asir de repente;
hacer de prisa; *s.* azote, látigo, fuete;
batido.

whipping [hwípɪŋ] *s.* tunda, zurra, paliza; **— cream** crema para batir.

whir [hwɜ] *v.* zumbar; *s.* zumbido.

whirl [hwɜl] *v.* girar, dar vueltas; arremolinarse; **my head -s** siento vértigo,
estoy desvanecido; *s.* giro, vuelta; remolino; espiral (*de humo*); confusión.

whirlpool [hwɜ́lpul] *s.* remolino, vorágine, vórtice.

whirlwind [hwɜ́lwɪnd] *s.* remolino, torbellino.

whisk [hwɪsk] *v.* barrer; desempolvar
(*con escobilla*); batir (*huevos*); **to —**
away barrer de prisa; llevarse de prisa, arrebatar; irse de prisa, escaparse;
to — something out of sight escamotear algo, esconder algo de prisa;
s. **— broom** escobilla; **with a — of**
the broom de un escobillazo.

whisker [hwískə] *s.* pelo de la barba;
-s barbas; patillas; bigotes (*del gato*).

whiskey [hwískɪ] *s.* whisky (*aguardiente*
de maíz, centeno, etc.).

whisper [hwíspə] *v.* cuchichear, hablar
en secreto; soplar, decir al oído; susurrar; secretearse; **it is -ed that** corre
la voz que; dizque, dicen que; *s.* cuchicheo, secreteo; susurro; murmullo;
to talk in a — hablar en secreto;
susurrar.

whistle [hwɪsl] *v.* silbar; chiflar; pitar;
to — for someone llamar a uno con
un silbido; *s.* silbido, chiflido; sibato,
pito.

whit [hwɪt] *s.* jota, pizca.

white [hwaɪt] *adj.* blanco; puro; inocente; honrado, recto; **—caps** cabrillas o
palomas (*olas con crestas blancas*); **—**
lead albayalde; **— lie** mentirilla, mentira venial; **white-livered** cobarde; **to**
show the — feather mostrar cobardía, portarse como cobarde; *s.* blanco; clara (*del huevo*).

whiten [hwáɪtn̩] *v.* blanquear; emblan-
quecer(se), poner(se) blanco.

whiteness [hwáɪtnɪs] *s.* blancura; palidez; pureza.

whitewash [hwáɪtwɑʃ] *v.* blanquear, enjalbegar; encubrir, disimular (*faltas,*
errores); absolver (*sin justicia*); *s.* lechada.

whither [hwíðə] *adv.* adonde; **—?** ¿a-
dónde?

whitish [hwáɪtɪʃ] *adj.* blancuzco, blanquecino, blanquizco.

whittle [hwɪtl̩] *v.* cortar, mondar, tallar;

tajar, sacar punta a (*un lápiz*); **to —**
down expenses cercenar o reducir los
gastos.

whiz [hwɪz] *v.* zumbar; *s.* zumbido, silbido; **to be a —** ser un águila, ser
muy listo.

who [hu] *pron. rel.* quien, quienes, que,
el que, la que, los que, las que; **he —**
el que, quien; *pron. interr.* ¿quién?;
¿quiénes?; **— is it?** ¿quién es?

whoever [huévə] *pron.* quienquiera que,
cualquiera que; el que.

whole [hol] *adj.* todo; entero; íntegro;
the — day todo el día; **—hearted**
sincero, cordial; **—heartedly** de todo
corazón; con todo ánimo; *s.* todo,
total, totalidad; **as a —** en conjunto;
on the — en general, en conjunto.

wholesale [hólsel] *s.* venta al por mayor,
Am. mayoreo; **by —** al por mayor;
adj. al por mayor; en grandes cantidades; **— dealer** comerciante al por
mayor, *Am.* mayorista; **— slaughter**
matanza; gran hecatombe; **— trade**
comercio al por mayor, *Am.* comercio
mayorista; *adv.* al por mayor, por
mayor; *v.* vender al por mayor, *Am.*
mayorear.

wholesome [hólsəm] *adj.* saludable,
sano; salubre; **— man** hombre normalmente bueno o de buena índole.

wholly [hólɪ] *adv.* enteramente, completamente, totalmente.

whom [hum] *pron. pers.* a quien, a
quienes; que; al que (a la que, a los
que, *etc.*); al cual (a la cual, a los
cuales, *etc.*); **for —** para quien; **— did**
you see? ¿a quién vió Vd.?

whoop [hup] *s.* grito, chillido, alarido;
respiro convulsivo (*que acompaña a la*
tos ferina); *v.* gritar, vocear, echar
gritos; respirar convulsivamente (*al*
toser); **to — it up** armar una gritería,
gritar; **whooping cough** tos ferina.

whore [hor] *s.* ramera, puta, prostituta.

whose [huz] *pron.* cuyo, cuya, cuyos,
cuyas; *pron. interr.* ¿de quién?; ¿de
quiénes?; **— book is this?** ¿de quién
es este libro?

why [hwaɪ] *adv.* ¿por qué?; **the reason**
— la razón por la que (o la cual); **—,**
of course! ¡sí, por supuesto!; ¡claro
que sí!; **—, that is not true!** ¡sí eso
no es verdad! *s.* porqué, causa, razón,
motivo.

wick [wɪk] *s.* mecha, pabilo.

wicked [wíkɪd] *adj.* malvado, malo, inicuo.

wickedness [wíkɪdnɪs] *s.* maldad, iniquidad, perversidad.

wicker [wíkə] s. mimbre; — **chair** silla de mimbre.

wicket [wíkɪt] s. postigo; ventanilla.

wide [waɪd] adj. ancho; amplio; vasto; extenso; — **apart** muy apartados; **wide-awake** muy despierto; alerta, vigilante; — **of the mark** muy lejos del blanco; — **open** muy abierto; abierto de par en par; **far and —** por todas partes, extensamente; **to open —** abrir mucho; abrir (la puerta) de par en par; **two feet —** dos pies de ancho (o de anchura).

widely [wáɪdlɪ] adv. ampliamente; extensamente; muy; mucho.

widen [wáɪdn] v. ensanchar(se), ampliar(se), dilatar(se).

widespread [wáɪdspréd] adj. muy esparcidə, muy extensivo; bien difundido; extendido; general, extendido por todas partes.

widow [wído] s. viuda.

widower [wídowə] s. viudo.

width [wíde] s. ancho, anchura.

wield [wild] v. manejar; esgrimir (la espada o la pluma); ejercer (el poder).

wife [waɪf] s. esposa.

wig [wɪg] s. peluca.

wiggle [wɪgl] v. menear(se); s. meneo.

wigwam [wígwɑm] s. choza de los indios norteños.

wild [waɪld] adj. salvaje; feroz, fiero; montaraz; silvestre; indómito; Am. cimarrón; impetuoso, desenfrenado; bullicioso; violento; loco; enojado; desatinado; ansioso; **to talk —** disparatar, desatinar; s. yermo, desierto, monte.

wildcat [wáɪldkæt] s. gato montés; — **scheme** empresa arriesgada.

wilderness [wíldənɪs] s. yermo, desierto, monte; inmensidad.

wildness [wáɪldnɪs] s. salvajez; ferocidad, fiereza; locura.

wile [waɪl] s. ardid, engaño; astucia.

wilful, willful [wílfəl] adj. voluntarioso, testarudo, caprichudo; intencional.

will [wɪl] v. querer, decidir; ordenar, mandar; legar; v. defect. y aux. querer; rigurosamente debe usarse para formar el futuro en las segundas y terceras personas : **she — go** ella irá; en las primeras personas indica voluntad o determinación : **I — not do it** no lo haré, no quiero hacerlo.

will [wɪl] s. voluntad; albedrío; testamento; **free —** libre albedrío; **ill —** mala voluntad, malquerencia.

willing [wílɪŋ] adj. bien dispuesto, deseoso, complaciente; voluntario; **-ly** adv. con gusto, de buena gana, de buena voluntad; voluntariamente.

willingness [wílɪŋnɪs] s. buena voluntad, buena gana.

willow [wílo] s. sauce; mimbrera; **weeping —** sauce llorón.

wilt [wɪlt] v. marchitar(se); ajar(se); desmayar; languidecer.

wily [wáɪlɪ] adj. astuto, artero.

win [wɪn] v. ganar; lograr, obtener; persuadir; alcanzar; **to — out** ganar, triunfar; salirse con la suya; **to — over** persuadir; atraer; alcanzar o ganar el favor de.

wince [wɪns] v. cejar (ante una dificultad o peligro); encogerse (de dolor, susto, etc.).

winch [wɪntʃ] s. malacate.

wind [wɪnd] s. viento, aire; resuello; — **instrument** instrumento de viento; **to get — of** barruntar; tener noticia de.

wind [waɪnd] v. enredar; devanar, ovillar; dar cuerda a (un reloj); serpentear (un camino); dar vueltas; **to — someone around one's finger** manejar fácilmente a alguien, gobernarle; **to — up one's affairs** terminar o concluir uno sus negocios; s. vuelta; recodo.

windbag [wíndbæg] s. fuelle, parlanchín, hablador.

windfall [wíndfɔl] s. golpe de fortuna, ganancia repentina, herencia inesperada.

winding [wáɪndɪŋ] adj. sinuoso, tortuoso, que da vueltas; — **staircase** escalera de caracol.

windmill [wínmɪl] s. molino de viento.

window [wíndo] s. ventana; **show —** escaparate, vitrina, aparador, Am. vidriera; — **shade** visillo, cortinilla; — **sill** antepecho, repisa de ventana.

windowpane [wíndopen] s. cristal de ventana, vidriera.

windpipe [wíndpaɪp] s. tráquea, gaznate.

windshield [wíndʃild] s. parabrisa, guardabrisa.

windy [wíndɪ] adj. airoso; ventoso; **it is —** hace aire, ventea, sopla el viento.

wine [waɪn] s. vino; — **cellar** bodega.

wing [wɪŋ] s. ala; bastidor (de escenario); **under the — of** bajo la tutela de; **to take —** levantar el vuelo.

winged [wɪŋd, wíŋɪd] adj. alado.

wink [wɪŋk] v. guiñar; pestañear, parpadear, s. guiño, guiñadaʼ **I didn't sleep a —** no pegué los ojos en toda la noche.

winner [wínə] s. ganador; vencedor; —

248

of a prize agraciado, premiado.

winning [wínɪŋ] *adj.* ganancioso; triunfante, victorioso; atractivo, encantador; **-s** *s. pl.* ganancias.

winsome [wínsəm] *adj.* simpático, atractivo, gracioso.

winter [wíntə] *s.* invierno; — **clothes** ropa de invierno; *v.* invernar, pasar el invierno.

wintry [wíntrɪ] *adj.* invernal, de invierno; frío, helado.

wipe [waɪp] *v.* secar; enjugar; limpiar; **to — away one's tears** limpiarse las lágrimas; **to — off** borrar; limpiar; **to — out a regiment** destruir o aniquilar un regimiento.

wire [waɪr] *s.* alambre; telegrama; **by —** por telégrafo; — **entanglement** alambrada; — **fence** alambrado; — **netting** tela metálica, alambrado; **to pull -s** mover los hilos; *v.* poner alambrado, instalar alambrado eléctrico; atar con alambre; telegrafiar.

wireless [wáɪrlɪs] *adj.* inalámbrico, sin hilos; — **telegraphy** radiotelegrafía; *s.* radio, radiotelegrafía; telegrafía sin hilos; radiotelefonía; radiograma.

wiry [wáɪrɪ] *adj.* de alambre; como alambre; nervudo.

wisdom [wízdəm] *s.* sabiduría, saber; cordura; prudencia; — **tooth** muela del juicio.

wise [waɪz] *adj.* sabio, cuerdo, sensato; discreto, prudente; **the Three Wise Men** los Tres Reyes Magos; **to get — to** darse cuenta de; *s.* modo, manera; **in no —** de ningún modo.

wisecrack [wáɪzkræk] *s.* bufonada, dicho agudo o chocarrero, dicharacho.

wish [wɪʃ] *v.* desear, querer; **to — for** desear; anhelar; **I — it were true!** ¡ojalá (que) fuera verdad!; *s.* deseo.

wistful [wístfəl] *adj.* anhelante, anheloso, ansioso; tristón, melancólico.

wit [wɪt] *s.* agudeza, sal, chiste; ingenio; hombre agudo o de ingenio; **to be at one's wit's end** haber agotado todo su ingenio; **to be out of one's -s** estar fuera de sí, estar loco; **to lose one's -s** perder el juicio; **to use one's -s** valerse de su industria o ingenio.

witch [wɪtʃ] *s.* hechicera; bruja.

witchcraft [wítʃkræft] *s.* hechicería.

with [wɪð, wɪθ] *prep.* con; para con; en compañía de; **filled —** lleno de; **ill —** enfermo de; **the one — the black hat** el del (o la del) sombrero negro.

withdraw [wɪðdrɔ́] *v.* retirar(se); apartar(se); separar(se); **to — a statement** retractarse.

withdrawal [wɪðdrɔ́əl] *s.* retirada, retiro.

withdrawn [wɪðdrɔ́n] *p.p. de* **to withdraw.**

withdrew [wɪðdrú] *pret. de* **to withdraw.**

wither [wíðə] *v.* marchitar(se); ajar(se); secar(se).

withheld [wɪðhéld] *pret. & p.p. de* **to withhold.**

withhold [wɪðhóld] *v.* retener; detener; **to — one's consent** negarse a dar su consentimiento.

within [wɪðín] *prep.* dentro de; — **call** al alcance de la voz; — **five miles a** poco menos de cinco millas; **it is — my power** está en mi mano; *adv.* dentro, adentro.

without [wɪðáut] *prep.* sin; — **my seeing him** sin que yo le viera; *adv.* fuera, afuera.

withstand [wɪðstǽnd] *v.* resistir; aguantar, padecer.

withstood [wɪðstúd] *pret. & p.p. de* **to withstand.**

witness [wítnɪs] *s.* testigo; testimonio; *v.* ver, presenciar; ser testigo de; atestiguar, dar fe de.

witticism [wítəsɪzəm] *s.* ocurrencia, agudeza, dicho agudo.

witty [wítɪ] *adj.* agudo, ocurrente, gracioso, divertido, chistoso; — **remark** dicho agudo, agudeza, ocurrencia.

wives [waɪvz] *s. pl. de* **wife.**

wizard [wízəd] *s.* genio, hombre de ingenio; mago, mágico.

woe [wo] *s.* miseria, aflicción, infortunio; — **is me!** ¡miserable de mí!

woke [wok] *pret. de* **to wake.**

wolf [wulf] (*pl.* **wolves** [wulvz]) *s.* lobo.

woman [wúmən] (*pl.* **women** [wímɪn]) *s.* mujer; — **writer** escritora.

womanhood [wúmənhud] *s.* estado de mujer; la mujer (las mujeres); integridad femenil; feminidad.

womankind [wúmənkaɪnd] *s.* la mujer, las mujeres, el sexo femenino.

womanly [wúmənlɪ] *adj.* femenil, mujeril, femenino; *adv.* femenilmente, como mujer.

womb [wum] *s.* vientre, entrañas; útero, matriz.

won [wʌn] *pret. & p.p. de* **to win.**

wonder [wʌ́ndə] *s.* maravilla; prodigio; admiración; **in — maravillado; no — that** no es mucho que; no es extraño que; *v.* asombrarse, maravillarse, pasmarse, admirarse; **to — at** admirarse de, maravillarse de; **I — what time it is** ¿qué hora será? **I — when he came** ¿cuándo vendría? **I should not — if** no me extrañaría que.

wonderful [wʌ́ndəfəl] *adj.* maravilloso, admirable; **-ly** *adv.* maravillosamente, admirablemente, a las mil maravillas: **-ly well** sumamente bien.

wondrous [wʌ́ndrəs] *adj.* maravilloso, pasmoso, extraño.

wont [wʌnt] *adj.* acostumbrado; **to be — to** soler, acostumbrar, *Am.* saber; *s.* costumbre, hábito, uso.

woo [wu] *v.* cortejar, enamorar, galantear.

wood [wud] *s.* madera, palo; leña, **-s** bosque; selva, **— engraving** grabado en madera, **—shed** leñera, cobertizo para leña; **fire—** leña; **piece of fire—** leño.

woodcutter [wúdkʌtə] *s.* leñador.

wooded [wúdid] *adj.* arbolado, poblado de árboles.

wooden [wúdn̩] *adj.* de madera, de palo; tieso.

woodland [wúdlænd] *s.* monte, bosque, selva.

woodman [wúdmən] *s.* leñador; habitante del bosque.

woodpecker [wúdpekə] *s.* pájaro carpintero.

woodwork [wúdwɜk] *s.* maderamen; labrado en madera; obra de carpintería.

woof [wuf] *s.* trama (*de un tejido*); tejido.

wool [wul] *s.* lana; *adj.* de lana, lanar; **wool-bearing** lanar; **— dress** vestido de lana.

woolen [wúlɪn] *adj.* de lana; lanudo; **— mill** fábrica de tejidos de lana; *s.* tejido de lana; género o paño de lana.

woolly [wúlɪ] *adj.* lanudo; de lana.

word [wɜd] *s.* palabra; vocablo, voz; noticia, aviso; mandato, orden; **pass— contraseña; by — of mouth** de palabra, verbalmente; *v.* expresar; redactar, formular.

wordy [wɜ́dɪ] *adj.* palabrero, verboso, ampuloso.

wore [wor] *pret. de* **to wear.**

work [wɜk] *s.* trabajo; obra; faena; tarea; empleo, ocupación; labor; **-s** taller, fábrica; maquinaria, mecanismo; **at —** trabajando; ocupado; *v.* trabajar; funcionar; obrar; surtir efecto; manejar, manipular; resolver (*un problema*); explotar (*una mina*); hacer trabajar; **to — havoc** hacer estropicios, causar daño; **to — loose** soltarse, aflojarse; **to — one's way through college** sufragar los gastos universitarios con su trabajo; **to — one's way up** subir por sus propios

esfuerzos; **to — out a plan** urdir un plan; **to be all -ed up** estar sobreexcitado; **it didn't — out** no dió resultado; **the plan -ed well** tuvo buen éxito el plan.

worker [wɜ́kə] *s.* trabajador; obrero; operario.

working [wɜ́kɪŋ] *s.* funcionamiento, operación; cálculo (*de un problema*); explotación (*de una mina*); *adj.* obrero, trabajador; **— class** clase obrera o trabajadora; **— hours** horas de trabajo; **a hard-working man** un hombre muy trabajador.

workingman [wɜ́kɪŋmæn] *s.* trabajador; obrero.

workman [wɜ́kmən] *s.* trabajador, obrero, operario.

workmanship [wɜ́kmənʃɪp] *s.* hechura; trabajo; mano de obra.

workshop [wɜ́kʃɑp] *s.* taller.

world [wɜld] *s.* mundo; **the World War** la Guerra Mundial.

worldly [wɜ́ldlɪ] *adj.* mundano, mundanal, terreno, terrenal.

worm [wɜm] *s.* gusano; lombriz; **worm-eaten** comido de gusanos; carcomido, apolillado; *v.* **to — a secret out of someone** extraerle o sonsacarle un secreto a una persona; **to — oneself into** insinuarse en, meterse en.

worn [worn] *p.p. de* **to wear**; **worn-out** gastado, roto; rendido de fatiga.

worry [wɜ́ɪ] *s.* inquietud, ansiedad, cuidado, preocupación, apuro, apuración; *v.* inquietar(se), preocupar(se), afligir(se), apurar(se).

worse [wɜs] *adj.* peor; más malo; *adv.* peor; **— and —** cada vez peor, **— than ever** peor que nunca; **from bad to —** de mal en peor; **so much the —** tanto peor; **to be — off** estar peor que antes; **to change for the —** empeorar(se); **to get —** empeorar(se).

worship [wɜ́ʃəp] *s.* adoración, culto, veneración; *v.* adorar; reverenciar.

worshiper [wɜ́ʃəpə] *s.* adorador; **the -s** los fieles.

worst [wɜst] *adj.* peor, *adv.* peor; **the —** el peor; la peor; lo peor; *v.* derrotar.

worth [wɜθ] *s.* valor, valía, mérito; precio; **ten cent's —** de diez centavos de; **to get one's money's — out of** sacar todo el provecho posible del dinero gastado en; *adj.* digno de; **— hearing** digno de oírse; **to be — valer; to be — doing** valer la pena de hacerse; **to be — while** valer la pena.

worthless [wɜ́θlɪs] *adj.* sin valor; inútil;

despreciable.

worthy [wʊ́ðɪ] *adj.* digno; valioso, apreciable; meritorio, merecedor; *s.* benemérito, hombre ilustre.

would [wʊd] *imperf. de indic. y de subj. del verbo defect.* **will: she — come every day** solía venir (*o* venía) todos los días; **if you — do it** si lo hiciera Vd.; *expresa a veces deseo:* — **that I knew it!** ¡quién lo supiera!; ¡ojalá que yo lo supiera!; *v. aux. del condicional* : **she said she — go** dijo que iría.

wound [wund] *s.* herida; llaga, lesión; *v.* herir; lastimar; agraviar.

wound [waʊnd] *pret. & p.p. de* **to wind**.

wove [wov] *pret. de* **to weave**.

woven [wóvən] *p.p. de* **to weave**.

wrangle [rǽŋgl] *v.* altercar, disputar, reñir; juntar, *Am.* rodear (*el ganado*); *s.* riña, pendencia.

wrap [ræp] *v.* envolver; enrollar, arrollar, **to — up** envolver(se); abrigar(se), tapar(se); **to be wrapped up in** estar envuelto en; estar absorto en; *s.* abrigo, manto.

wrapper [rǽpə] *s.* envoltura, cubierta; **woman's —** bata.

wrapping [rǽpɪŋ] *s.* envoltura; **— paper** papel de envolver.

wrath [ræθ] *s.* ira, cólera, rabia.

wrathful [rǽθfəl] *adj.* colérico, rabioso, iracundo.

wreath [riθ] *s.* guirnalda, corona; **— of smoke** espiral de humo.

wreathe [rið] *v.* hacer guirnaldas; adornar con guirnaldas; **-d in smiles** sonriente.

wreck [rɛk] *s.* ruina; destrucción; naufragio; accidente; destrozos, despojos (*de un naufragio*), *v.* arruinar; naufragar; echar a pique; destrozar, demoler; **to — a train** descarrilar un tren.

wrench [rɛntʃ] *v.* torcer, retorcer; arrancar, arrebatar; *s.* torcedura; torsión; tirón, arranque, *Am.* jalón; llave de tuercas; **monkey —** llave inglesa.

wrest [rɛst] *v.* arrebatar, arrancar, usurpar.

wrestle [résl] *v.* luchar a brazo partido; luchar; *s.* lucha a brazo partido.

wrestler [réslə] *s.* luchador (*a brazo partido*).

wretch [rɛtʃ] *s.* miserable, infeliz; villano.

wretched [rétʃɪd] *adj.* miserable; desdichado, infeliz; afligido; bajo, vil; malísimo; **a — piece of work** un trabajo pésimo o malísimo.

wriggle [rígl] *v.* menear(se), retorcer(se); **to — out of** salirse de, escaparse de; escabullirse de.

wring [rɪŋ] *v.* torcer, retorcer; exprimir, estrujar; **to — money from someone** arrancar dinero a alguien; **to — out** exprimir (*la ropa*).

wrinkle [rɪ́ŋkl] *s.* arruga; surco, **the latest — in style** la última novedad; *v.* arrugar(se).

wrist [rɪst] *s.* muñeca, **— watch** reloj de pulsera.

writ [rɪt] *s.* auto, orden judicial, mandato jurídico; **the Holy Writ** la Sagrada Escritura.

write [raɪt] *v.* escribir; **to — back** contestar por carta; **to — down** apuntar, poner por escrito, **to — off** cancelar (*una deuda*); **to — out** poner por escrito, escribir por entero; **to — up** relatar, describir; redactar.

writer [ráɪtə] *s.* escritor; autor.

writhe [raɪð] *v.* retorcerse.

writing [ráɪtɪŋ] *s.* escritura; escrito; composición literaria; forma o estilo literario; **hand— letra; — desk** escritorio; **— paper** papel de escribir; **to put in —** poner por escrito.

written [rítn] *p.p. de* **to write**.

wrong [rɔŋ] *adj.* falso, incorrecto, malo; injusto; equivocado; mal hecho; inoportuno; inconveniente; **the — side of a fabric** el envés o el revés de un tejido; **the — side of the road** el lado izquierdo o contrario del camino; **that is the — book** ése no es el libro, **it is in the — place** no está en su sitio, está mal colocado; *adv.* mal; **al revés; to go — extraviarse, descaminarse; resultar mal; *s.* mal, daño, perjuicio; injusticia, agravio; **to be in the —** no tener razón, estar equivocado; **to do —** hacer mal; *v.* perjudicar; agraviar; hacer mal a.

wrote [rot] *pret. de* **to write**.

wrought [rɔt] *pret. & p.p. irr. de* **to work**; *adj.* labrado; forjado; **— iron** hierro forjado, **— silver** plata labrada; **to be wrought-up** estar sobreexcitado.

wrung [rʌŋ] *pret. & p.p. de* **to wring**.

wry [raɪ] *adj.* torcido; **to make a — face** hacer una mueca.

Y

yacht [jɑt] *s.* yate, *v.* navegar en yate.

Yankee [jǽŋkɪ] *adj.* & *s.* yanqui.

yard [jɑrd] *s.* yarda (*medida de longitud*); patio; cercado; terreno (*adyacente a una casa*); **back — corral; barn—**

corral; **navy** — arsenal; ship— astillero.

yardstick [járdstɪk] s. yarda (*de medir*); medida (*metro, vara, etc.*); patrón, norma.

yarn [jarn] s. estambre; hilado, hilaza; cuento enredado y poco probable.

yawn [jɔn] v. bostezar; s. bostezo.

yea [je] adv. sí; s. sí, voto afirmativo.

year [jɪr] s. año, —**book** anuario; -'**s income** renta anual; **by the** — por año; **leap** — año bisiesto.

yearly [jírlɪ] adj. anual; adv. anualmente; una vez al año, cada año.

yearn [jɜn] v. anhelar, **to** — **for** anhelar; suspirar por.

yearning [jɜ́nɪŋ] s. anhelo.

yeast [jist] s. levadura, fermento.

yell [jɛl] v. gritar, dar gritos, vociferar; s. grito, alarido.

yellow [jélo] adj. amarillo; cobarde; — **fever** fiebre amarilla; s. amarillo; v. poner(se) amarillo.

yellowish [jéloɪʃ] adj. amarillento.

yelp [jelp] v. aullar, ladrar; s. aullido, ladrido.

yes [jɛs] adv. sí.

yesterday [jéstədɪ] adv. & s. ayer; **day before** — anteayer o antier.

yet [jet] adv. & conj. todavía, aún; con todo, sin embargo; no obstante; **as** — todavía, aún; **not** — todavía no.

yield [jíld] v. ceder, rendir, producir; someterse; **to** — **five percent** redituar el cinco por ciento; s. rendimiento, rendición; rédito.

yoke [jok] s. yugo, yunta (*de bueyes, mulas, etc.*); v. uncir; unir.

yolk [jok] s. yema (*de huevo*)

yonder [jándə] adj. aquel, aquella, aquellos, aquellas; adv. allá, allí, más allá, acullá.

yore [jor] : **in days of** — antaño, en días de antaño.

you [ju] pron. pers. tú, usted, vosotros, ustedes; te, le, lo, la, os, las, los; **to** — a tí, a usted, a vosotros, a ustedes; te, le, les; pron. impers. se, uno.

young [jʌŋ] adj. joven; nuevo; — **leaves** hojas tiernas; — **man** joven; her — **ones** sus niños, sus hijitos; **the** — **people** la gente joven, los jóvenes, la juventud; s. jóvenes; cría, hijuelos (*de los animales*).

youngster [jʌ́ŋstə] s. muchacho, niño, jovencito, chiquillo.

your [jʊr] adj. tu (tus), vuestro (vuestra, vuestros, vuestras), su (sus), de usted, de ustedes.

yours [jʊrz] pron. pos. tuyo (tuya, tuyos, tuyas); vuestro (vuestra, vuestros, vuestras); suyo (suya, suyos, suyas), de usted, de ustedes; el tuyo (la tuya, los tuyos, las tuyas); el suyo (la suya, los suyos, las suyas); el (la, los, las) de usted; el (la, los, las) de ustedes; **a friend of** — un amigo tuyo . un amigo vuestro; un amigo suyo, un amigo de usted o ustedes.

yourself [jʊrsélf] pron. te, se (*como reflexivo*); **to** — a tí mismo; a usted mismo; **you** — tú mismo; usted mismo; *véase* **herself**.

yourselves [jʊrsélvz] pron. os, se (*como reflexivo*); **to** — a vosotros mismos; a ustedes mismos; **you** — vosotros mismos; ustedes mismos.

youth [jue] s. joven; juventud; jóvenes.

youthful [júɵfəl] adj. joven; juvenil.

Yuletide [júltaɪd] s. Pascua de Navidad; Navidades.

Z

zeal [zil] s. celo, fervor, ardor, entusiasmo.

zealot [zélət] s. fanático.

zealous [zéləs] adj. celoso, ardiente, fervoroso.

zenith [zínɪɵ] s. cenit, cumbre.

zephyr [zéfə] s. céfiro.

zero [zíro] s. cero.

zest [zɛst] s. entusiasmo; buen sabor.

zigzag [zígzæg] s. zigzag; adj. & adv. en zigzag; v. zigzaguear, culebrear, andar en zigzag, serpentear.

zinc [zɪŋk] s. cinc (zinc).

zipper [zípə] s. cierre relámpago, abrochador corredizo o de corredera, *Am.* riqui.

zodiac [zódiæk] s. zodíaco.

zone [zon] s. zona; v. dividir en zonas.

zoo [zu] s. jardín zoológico.

zoological [zoalódʒɪkl] adj. zoológico.

zoology [zoálədʒɪ] s. zoología.

PART THREE / PARTE TERCERA
IDIOMS / EXPRESIONES IDIOMATICAS

PART THREE / PARTE TERCERA

EXPRESIONES IDIOMATICAS ESPAÑOLAS

SPANISH IDIOMS

A continuación.   Los detalles del viaje se dan *a continuación*.
The details of the trip are given below *as follows*.

A fin de cuentas.   *A fin de cuentas*, todo se resolvió sin dificultad.
At the end, everything was settled without difficulty.

A fines de.   Se marchan *a fines de* la semana que viene.
They are leaving *at the end of* next week.

A la larga.   Creo que *a la larga* nos convendrá el negocio.
I think that *in the long run* the proposition will be good for us.

A las mil maravillas.   Me siento ahora *a las mil maravillas*.
I feel *just wonderful* now.

A lo lejos.   *Allá a lo lejos* se divisa el Palacio Presidencial.
Way over there you can see the Presidential Palace.

A más tardar.   Debemos terminar el trabajo para el sábado, *a más tardar*.
We must finish the work by Saturday, *at the very latest*.

A mediados de.   La casa estará terminada *a mediados del* verano.
The house will be finished *around the middle of* summer.

A otro perro con ese hueso.   Vete *a otro perro con ese hueso*.
Tell it to the marines.

A principios de.   Llegaron a la ciudad *a principios de* marzo.
They reached the city *at the beginning of* March.

A propósito.   *A propósito*, ¿cómo sigue Juan de su enfermedad?
By the way, how is Juan recovering?

A tontas y a locas.   Esta fiesta se ha preparado *a tontas y a locas*.
This party was prepared *in a helter-skelter way*.

A troche y moche.   Ellos se comportaron cuando oyeron la noticia *a troche y moche*.
They were *in complete confusion* when they heard the news.

A ver.   *A ver* si podemos ir a Cuba este verano.
Let's see whether we can go to Cuba next summer.

1

Agarrarlo con las manos en la masa. Al ladrón *lo agarraron con las manos en la masa.*
They *caught* the thief *red-handed.*

Agotarle la paciencia. Juan *me está agotando la paciencia.*
Juan *is wearing out my patience.*

Al fin y al cabo. *Al fin y al cabo,* no se pudo hacer lo que querían.
When all was said and done, what they wanted was impossible.

Al parecer. *Al parecer* es un hombre muy culto.
Apparently he is a very cultivated man.

Al pie de la letra. Favor de copiar este documento *al pie de la letra.*
Please copy this document *word for word.*

Andar de boca en boca. La conducta de María *anda de boca en boca.*
Everybody's gossiping about Maria's behavior.

Andar de la Ceca a la Meca. Al fin encontré lo que quería, pero tuve que *andar de la Ceca a la Meca.*
At last I found what I wanted, but I had *to look high and low.*

Andar de mal en peor. Juan *anda de mal en peor.*
Juan *is getting worse and worse.*

Andarse con rodeos. Yo no *me ando con rodeos* en estos asuntos.
I don't *beat about the bush* in these matters.

Aquí hay gato encerrado. Me parece que *aquí hay gato encerrado.*
I think *I smell a rat.*

Así es la vida. ¿Qué te parece lo que le sucedió a él? ¡*Así es la vida!*
What do you think of what happened to him? *That's life for you!*

Buscar tres pies al gato. Tú le andas *buscando los pies al gato* y te va a pesar.
You're *looking for trouble* and you'll be sorry.

Camino de. Mañana estaremos en *camino de* Buenos Aires.
Tomorrow we'll be *on our way to* Buenos Aires.

Cargar con el muerto. No sé por qué yo siempre *cargo con el muerto.*
I don't know why I'm always *left holding the bag.*

Codearse con. Yo *me codeo con* la gente del gobierno.
I'm *intimate with* people in the government.

Como de costumbre. Lo encontramos, *como de costumbre*, en el Hotel Hilton.
We met him, *as usual*, at the Hilton Hotel.

Consultar con la almohada. Te recomiendo *consultes con tu almohada* antes de llegar a una decisión.
I advise you to *sleep on it* before reaching a decision.

Contar con. *Contamos con* tu presencia en nuestra fiesta del sábado.
We are counting on your coming to our party Saturday.

Costar trabajo. *Cuesta trabajo* hacerle venir a estas reuniones.
It is difficult to get him to come to these gatherings.

Creerse la gran cosa. Juan *se cree la gran cosa.*
Juan *thinks a lot of himself.*

Cueste lo que cueste. *Cueste lo que cueste,* nos vamos al Brasil este año.
At whatever cost, we're going to Brazil this year.

Cuidado con. *(Tenga) cuidado con* los carteristas en la ciudad.
Watch out for the pickpockets in the city.

Dar calabazas. Carmen le *dió calabazas* a Roberto.
Carmen *turned down* Roberto's proposal.

Dar de alta. Ya le *dieron de alta* en el hospital.
They have already *discharged* him from the hospital.

Dar de baja. Le van a *dar de baja* en el colegio por sus fracasos académicos.
They're going *to kick him out* of college because of his academic failures.

Dar de comer. Hay que *dar de comer* al enfermo a las seis de la tarde.
The patient must *be fed* at six P.M.

Dar en el clavo. Mario *dió en el clavo* con su conferencia pública ayer.
Mario *hit the nail on the head* in his public lecture yesterday.

Dar en qué pensar. Lo que ha hecho Mario me *da* mucho *en qué pensar.*
What Mario has done *gives* me *food for thought.*

Dar lata. Ellos *dan* mucha *lata.*
They're a pain in the neck.

Dar parte.　Hay que *dar parte* a la policía del robo de las prendas.
The police must *be informed* of the theft of the jewels.

Darle lo mismo.　*Me da lo mismo* este modelo que aquel.
It makes no difference to me whether it's one model or the other.

Darle un sablazo.　A Pedro *le dieron un sablazo* sus cuñados.
Pedro's brothers-in-law *put the touch on him.*

Darse bombo.　Esta gente *se da mucho bombo.*
These people *give themselves an air of importance.*

Darse con la puerta en las narices.　En este asunto *me di con la puerta en las narices.*
In this matter *I hit my head against a stone wall.*

Darse cuenta.　El (*no*) *se da cuenta* que está muy enfermo.
He *doesn't realize* that he is very sick.

Darse ínfulas.　Yo no sé por qué *se da tanta ínfula* este hombre.
I don't know why this fellow *is such a show-off.*

Darse por ofendido.　Juan *se ha dado por ofendido* porque no le invitaron.
Juan *has taken offense* because he was not invited.

Darse por vencido.　*Me doy por vencido*, no puedo arreglar este radio.
I give up, I can't fix this radio.

Darse tono.　Los Rodríguez *se dan* mucho *tono.*
The Rodriguezes *put on airs.*

Dárselas de.　El *se las da de* experto en la materia.
He *claims to be* an expert in the matter.

De buena gana.　Iremos a la conferencia *de buena gana.*
We'll *gladly* go to the lecture.

De buenas a primeras.　Se levantó *de buenas a primeras* y abandonó la reunión.
He got up *on the spur of the moment* and left the meeting.

De cabo a rabo.　Hemos recorrido la ciudad *de cabo a rabo.*
We've been through *every nook and corner* of the city.

De lo lindo.　Nos divertimos en el viaje *de lo lindo.*
We had *a great* time on the trip.

De mala gana.　Lo haré aunque *de mala gana.*
I'll do it, but *unwillingly.*

De nada.   Se puso bravo *de nada*.
He got excited *for no reason*.

De ninguna manera.   No permitiré *de ninguna manera* que
hagan lo que quieren.
I shall *absolutely* forbid them to do what they want.

De repuesto.   Tenemos material *de repuesto*.
We have material *to spare*.

De todos modos.   Nos veremos allí *de todos modos*.
At any rate, we'll see each other there.

De vez en cuando.   Viene por la biblioteca *de vez en cuando*.
He comes to the library *once in a while*.

Decirle cuatro verdades.   El se merece que *le digan cuatro
verdades*.
He deserves *to be told off*.

Decírselo en su cara.   Ya es hora de que *se lo digas en su cara*.
It's time *you told him right to his face*.

Dejarlo plantado.   Se fueron y *lo dejaron plantado*.
They went away and *left him flat*.

Dentro de poco.   Juan y María están por llegar *dentro de poco*.
Juan and Maria will be here *in a little while*.

Dormir a pierna suelta.   Juan *está durmiendo a pierna suelta*.
Juan *is sleeping like a top*.

Dormirse sobre sus laureles.   Ellos *se duermen sobre sus laureles*.
They are resting on their laurels.

Echar a perder.   El pastel se *echó a perder*.
The cake *was spoiled*.

Echar al correo.   Voy a *echar al correo* esta carta.
I'm going *to mail* this letter.

Echar de menos.   A él le *echan de menos* mucho.
They miss him very much.

Echar piropos.   A José le gusta *echar piropos* a las mujeres.
Jose likes *to flirt* with women.

Echar una cana al aire.   A todos nos gusta alguna vez *echar una
cana al aire*.
We all like *to go on a spree* once in a while.

Empinar el codo. Es lástima que le guste demasiado *empinar el codo.*
Too bad he likes *to drink* too much.

En el fondo. *En el fondo* hay mucha incomprensión mutua.
At bottom, there's considerable mutual misunderstanding.

En la actualidad. *En la actualidad* no hay mucha co-operación entre ellos.
At the present time there's not much co-operation among them.

En los quintos infiernos. Ellos viven *en los quintos infiernos.*
They are living *at the end of nowhere.*

En menos de lo que canta un gallo. Me trajo el encargo *en menos de lo que canta un gallo.*
He brought me the order *in no time at all.*

En otros términos. *En otros términos,* ya Ud. no desea adquirir la casa.
In other words, you no longer want to buy the house.

En pleno día. El robo ocurrió *en pleno día.*
The robbery took place *in broad daylight.*

En punto. La caravana saldrá a las seis de la tarde *en punto.*
The caravan will leave at six P.M. *sharp.*

En todas partes se cuecen habas. Esto te prueba que *en todas partes se cuecen habas.*
This proves to you that *it happens in the best of families.*

En un abrir y cerrar de ojos. Hizo lo que le mandaron *en un abrir y cerrar de ojos.*
He did what he was ordered *in a flash.*

En vigor. Esta ley todavía está *en vigor.*
This law is still *in force.*

Encontrarse con la horma de su zapato. Ahora sí que te *encontraste con la horma de tu zapato.*
Now *you've really met your match.*

Entrar como Pedro por su casa. Cuando llegó aquí, *entró como Pedro por su casa.*
When he got here, *he made himself at home.*

Es como hablarle a una pared. Cuando le mencionas este asunto, *es como hablarle a una pared.*
When you speak to him about that, *it is like talking to a wall.*

Escarmentar en cabeza ajena. Tu no *escarmientas en cabeza ajena.*
You don't *profit from the mistakes of others.*

Eso es harina de otro costal. Estás equivocado. *Eso es harina de otro costal.*
You are wrong. *That is a horse of another color.*

Eso nada más me faltaba. Después de todo lo ocurrido, *eso nada más me faltaba.*
After all that has happened, *that's all I needed!*

Estar al corriente. Ellos *están al corriente* de todo lo que está pasando.
They are informed about all that is happening.

Estar con un pie en la sepultura. He visto a Enrique y *está con un pie en la sepultura.*
I have seen Enrique and *he has one foot in the grave.*

Estar de acuerdo. *Estamos de acuerdo* en este asunto.
We are in agreement about this matter.

Estar de prisa. Aquí todo el mundo *está de prisa* siempre.
Here everybody *is* always *in a hurry.*

Estar de vacaciones. Los González *están de vacaciones* en Costa Rica.
The Gonzalezes *are taking a vacation* in Costa Rica.

Estar de vuelta. Ya *están de vuelta* de su viaje a Chile.
They are back from their trip to Chile.

Estar en ayunas. Sobre este asunto confieso que *estoy en ayunas.*
About that matter I admit *I am ignorant.*

Estar en la luna. Estas cosas le ocurren a José por *estar en la luna.*
These things happen to Jose because *he's always dreaming.*

Estar en las últimas. El pobre Jorge *está en las últimas.*
Poor Jorge *is on the point of death.*

Estar entre la espada y la pared. Te confieso que *estoy entre la espada y la pared.*
I confess to you that *I have my back to the wall.*

Estar hecho una sopa. ¿Qué te pasó? *Estás hecho una sopa.*
What happened to you? *You're soaking wet.*

Estirar la pata. Tuvo un accidente de automóvil y allí mismo *estiró la pata.*
He had an automobile accident and *he gave up the ghost* right there.

Faltar a su palabra. *Faltó a su palabra* más de una vez.
He broke his word more than once.

Faltar al respeto. El le *faltó al respeto.*
He treated him (her) *disrespectfully.*

Faltar poco. *Falta poco* para que salgamos de este lugar.
It's almost time for us to leave this place.

Ganarse la vida. Pedro *se gana la vida* pintando casas.
Pedro *makes his living* painting houses.

Hablar hasta por los codos. Le tengo temor a este señor porque *habla hasta por los codos.*
I'm afraid of that fellow because *he talks you deaf, dumb and blind.*

Hacer caso. Hay que *hacer caso* a las instrucciones que nos dan.
We (you) must *pay attention* to the instructions they are giving us.

Hacer castillos en el aire. El problema con Raúl es que pasa la mayor parte del tiempo *haciéndose castillos en el aire.*
The trouble with Raul is that he spends most of his time *building castles in Spain.*

Hacer de las suyas. José le *hizo* a María (*una*) *de las suyas.*
Jose *played* (*one*) *of his tricks* on Maria.

Hacer de tripas corazón. No queda más remedio que *hacer de tripas corazón.*
The only thing to do is *to pluck up your courage.*

Hacer escala. Vamos a *hacer escala en* varios puertos.
We're going *to call at* several ports.

Hacer falta. (*Me*) *hace falta* una capa de agua.
I need a raincoat.

Hacer gracia. (*No me*) *hace gracia* alguna lo que me acaba de decir.
I don't think what he has just told me is *funny.*

Hacer las paces. Te propongo que *hagas las paces* con tus vecinos.
I suggest *you make it up* with your neighbors.

Hacer pucheros. A la niña le gusta *hacer pucheros.*
The girl likes *to snivel.*

Hacer su agosto. En este negocio de libros *está haciendo su agosto.*
In this bookstore *he's raking it in.*

Hacer un papel. María *hizo un papel* muy bueno en la dramatización.
Maria *played a* good *role* in the performance.

Hacer un viaje. Vamos a *hacer un viaje* por el Caribe.
We're going *to make a trip* through the Caribbean.

Hacer una mala jugada. Le *hicieron una mala jugada* esta vez.
They played a nasty trick on him this time.

Hacerse de la vista gorda. Cuando le conviene, *se hace de la vista gorda.*
When it suits him, *he shuts his eyes.*

Hacerse de rogar. Rosario tiene el defecto que le gusta *hacerse de rogar.*
Rosario has the fault of *liking to be coaxed.*

Hacerse el sordo. En aquella ocasión Enrique *se hizo el sordo.*
In that moment, Enrique *turned a deaf ear.*

Hacerse entender. El *se hace entender* muy bien con lo que sabe del idioma.
He makes himself understood pretty well with what he knows of the language.

Hacérsele agua la boca. *Se me hace agua la boca* mirando este pastel.
My mouth waters when I look at this cake.

Hacérsele un nudo en la garganta. Tal fué la emoción que me causó que *se me hizo un nudo en la garganta.*
I was so moved *I had a lump in my throat.*

Hasta la coronilla. Juan me tiene *hasta la coronilla.*
I'm *absolutely fed up* with Juan.

Hay moros en la costa. Ten cuidado con lo que dices. *Hay moros en la costa.*
Be careful about what you are saying. *The coast is not clear.*

Ir a medias. Las cosas *van a medias.*
Things *are not too good.*

Ir al grano.   Prefiero *ir al grano* y dejar de hablar boberías.
I prefer *to come to the point* and stop talking nonsense.

Ir de compras.   Vamos a *ir de compras* hoy por la tarde.
We're *going shopping* this afternoon.

Ir de juerga.   Anoche *fuimos de juerga.*
Last night *we were out on a spree.*

Ir de vacaciones.   Vamos a *ir de vacaciones* en agosto.
We're going *to take a vacation* in August.

Ir por lana y salir trasquilado.   Juan se creyó una cosa y *fué*
por lana y salió trasquilado.
Juan thought a lot of himself, *went out to get the best of others*
and had the tables turned on him.

Irse para el otro mundo.   ¿Qué es de la vida de Fernando?
Fernando *se fué para el otro mundo.*
What's new with Fernando? Fernando *has kicked the bucket.*

Jugarle una mala partida.   A él *le jugaron una mala partida.*
They played a nasty trick on him.

La cosa está que arde.   Ten cuidado porque *la cosa está que arde.*
Be careful, *things are getting pretty hot.*

La verdad clara y desnuda.   Sobre este asunto ésta es *la verdad*
clara y desnuda.
This is *the whole truth* about this matter.

Lavarse las manos.   En este asunto *me lavo las manos.*
I wash my hands of this matter.

Llamar al pan pan, y al vino vino.   Yo acostumbro, Señor
García, *llamar al pan pan, y al vino vino.*
I am used *to calling a spade a spade,* Mr. Garcia.

Llegar a ser.   *Llegará a ser* un buen escultor.
He will become a good sculptor.

Llevar la batuta.   En este proyecto quien *lleva la batuta* es Rodríguez.
In this project it's Rodriguez who *is calling the tune.*

Llevarse bien.   *Se lleva bien* con todo el mundo.
He gets along well with everybody.

Llevarse la palma.   Carmela *se llevó la palma* en inglés.
Carmela *took first place* in English.

Llorar a moco tendido. El pobre José *lloraba a moco tendido.*
Poor Jose *was crying like a baby.*

Llover a cántaros. Está *lloviendo a cántaros.*
It's *raining cats and dogs.*

Lo que pasó, pasó. Bueno, Pedro y María, *lo que pasó, pasó.*
Well, Pedro and Maria, *let bygones be bygones.*

Más acá. Acerque la mesa *más acá.*
Bring the table *closer.*

Más allá. Ponga la mesa *más allá.*
Put the table *farther away.*

Meter gato por liebre. Cuando compré estos zapatos, *me metieron gato por liebre.*
When I bought these shoes, *they took me in.*

Meter la cuchara. Siempre *está metiendo la cuchara* en lo que no le importa.
He's always *butting in* where it's not his business.

Meter la nariz en todas partes. Esto te pasa por *meter la nariz en todas partes.*
That's what happens when you *stick your nose in where you don't belong.*

Meter la pata. Creo que *metiste la pata* en este asunto.
I think *you put your foot in it* in this matter.

Meterse a redentor. Por *meterte a redentor* te ha pasado todo esto.
That's what comes of *trying to save the world.*

Meterse en camisa de once varas. Te vas a *meter en camisa de once varas* si compras esta casa.
You're going *to get out of your depth* if you buy this house.

Meterse en honduras. Por no oír mis consejos *te has metido en honduras.*
You've gotten *into hot water* because you didn't follow my advice.

Meterse en un lío. Ellos *se metieron en un lío* tremendo.
They got into a tremendous *mess.*

Mirar de reojo. Me di cuenta que me *miraba de reojo.*
I realized that *he was looking* at me *out of the corner of his eye.*

Ni chicha ni limonada. Después de tanto hablar, *ni chicha ni limonada.*
After so much talk, *nothing happened.*

No atreverse a decir esta boca es mía.   Desde que ocurrió aquel incidente, *no se atreve a decir esta boca es mía.*
Since that incident, *he doesn't dare to open his mouth.*

No cabe duda.   *No cabe duda* que él no nos entendió.
There is no doubt that he did not understand us.

No caer bien.   El pescado *no (le) cae bien.*
The fish *doesn't agree (with him).*

No cantar victoria.   Espera un poco más. *No cantes victoria* todavía.
Wait a little longer. *Don't start crowing* yet.

No dar el brazo a torcer.   Creo que no podremos entendernos porque *no da su brazo a torcer.*
I think we won't be able to agree because *he is stubborn and won't give in.*

No dar pie con bola.   Está tan aturdido que *no da pie con bola.*
He's so hare-brained that *he makes a mess of things.*

No darse por entendido.   El *no se dió por entendido.*
He didn't take the hint.

No poder con.   Ellos *no pueden con* los hijos.
They can't handle their children.

No poder ver a (uno) ni en pintura.   Te confieso que *no puedo ver a (García) ni en pintura.*
I admit *I can't stand the sight of (García).*

No quisiera estar en su pellejo.   Después de lo que le ha ocurrido a Juan, *no quisiera estar en su pellejo.*
After what has happened to Juan, *I wouldn't like to be in his shoes.*

No saber en lo que se mete.   Ellos no tendrán éxito porque *no saben en lo que se meten.*
They won't succeed because *they don't know what they're getting into.*

No poder tragar a (uno).   Lo siento mucho, pero *no puedo tragar a* este hombre.
I'm sorry, but *I can't stomach* that man.

No tener donde caer muerto.   Su situación es tan mala que *no tiene donde caerse muerto.*
His situation is so bad, *he hasn't a corner to die in.*

No tener pelos en la lengua.   Diga Ud. lo que quiera, pero él *no tiene pelos en la lengua.*
Say what you want, *he speaks his mind freely.*

No viene al caso. Creo que esto *no viene al caso.*
I think this *has nothing to do with it.*

Pagar los platos rotos. Es injusto que ella tenga que *pagar los platos rotos.*
It is unjust that she should have *to pay the piper.*

Para siempre. Queremos vivir en este pueblo *para siempre.*
We'd like to live in this city *forever.*

Pasar las de Caín. La situación ha llegado hasta tal punto que *están pasando las de Caín.*
The situation has reached such a point *they are going through hell.*

Pasar las vacaciones. Vamos a *pasar las vacaciones* este año en México.
We're going *to spend our vacation* in Mexico this year.

Pedir prestado. Tengo que *pedir prestado* una escalera.
I have *to borrow* a ladder.

Perder la chaveta. *Perdió la chaveta* cuando le dieron la noticia del accidente.
He went out of his mind when they told him about the accident.

Perder los estribos. En este asunto especial te sugiero no *pierdas los estribos.*
In this special matter, I suggest that *you* don't *go to pieces.*

Poner el dedo en la llaga. Cuando le dije lo sucedido, me dí cuenta que le *puse el dedo en la llaga.*
When I told him what had happened, I realized *I had touched a sore spot.*

Poner el grito en el cielo. Cuando se enteró de lo que hizo el hijo, *puso el grito en el cielo.*
When he found out what his son had done, *he raised a terrible fuss.*

Poner los puntos sobre las íes. Le voy a *poner los puntos sobre las íes.*
I'm going *to make it absolutely clear to him.*

Poner por las nubes. Carolina te *puso por las nubes.*
Carolina *spoke very highly of* you.

Ponerlo a raya. Deja que venga a verme, lo voy a *poner a raya.*
Let him come and see me, I'll *put him in his place.*

Ponerlo en ridículo. Ella lo *puso en ridículo.*
She made a fool out of him.

Ponerse al corriente. Tengo que *ponerme al corriente* de los acontecimientos.
I must *catch up* on all the news.

Por lo pronto. *Por lo pronto* le enviamos la mitad del costo del viaje.
For the time being we are sending you half the expenses of the trip.

Por regla general. *Por regla general* nos vamos de la ciudad en el verano.
Generally speaking, we leave the city in the summer.

Por si acaso. *Por si acaso* no estás dispuesto a salir, llámame por teléfono.
Just in case you're not ready to leave, call me up.

Por término medio. *Por término medio*, vamos a verle tres veces al año.
On the average, we go to see him three times a year.

¿Qué mosca te ha picado? José, estás muy raro. *¿Qué mosca te ha picado?*
You're acting so funny, Jose. *What's eating you?*

¿Qué te parece? *¿Qué te parece* este traje que me compré?
How do you like this suit I bought?

Quedar en. *Quedó en* venir a buscarnos esta mañana.
He agreed to call for us this morning.

Quedarse con. Deseo *quedarme con* este vestido.
I'll take this dress.

Quedarse con un pie en el estribo. Por mi culpa *me quedé con un pie en el estribo.*
It was my own fault *I was left behind.*

Quedarse para vestir santos. Si no se enamora ahora, creo que se va a *quedar para vestir santos.*
If she doesn't fall in love now, I think she'll *be an old maid.*

Quemarse las pestañas. *Me estoy quemando las pestañas* en este curso de literatura española.
I'm burning the midnight oil over this Spanish literature course.

Querer decir. Lo que él *quiere decir* es que no nos entiende.
What *he means* is that he doesn't understand us.

Reír a mandíbula batiente. Cuando me hizo el cuento, *reí a mandíbula batiente.*
When he told me the story, *I nearly died laughing.*

Saber (de) al dedillo. (El) *sabe al dedillo* la lección de español.
He has the Spanish lesson *at the tip of his fingers.*

Saber de memoria. Hay que *saber de memoria* estas instrucciones
de viaje.
We must *memorize* these travel instructions.

Saber (uno) donde le aprieta el zapato. No te preocupes por
Juan, él *sabe donde le aprieta el zapato.*
Don't worry about Juan, *he knows when the shoe pinches.*

Sacar la cara por uno. No te preocupes, Juan, yo *saco la cara
por ti.*
Don't worry, Juan, *I'll go to bat for you.*

Sacar(lo) de quicio. A veces este hombre me *saca de quicio.*
Sometimes this man *drives* me *wild.*

Sacar(lo) de sus casillas. Cada vez que me encuentro con él *me
saca de mis casillas.*
Every time I'm with him, *he drives me crazy.*

Salir con el rabo entre las piernas. De tal manera lo vencieron
que *salió con el rabo entre las piernas.*
They gave him such a beating, *he left with his tail between his
legs.*

Salirle el tiro por la culata. El se creyó que iba a hacer lo que
quería, pero *le salió el tiro por la culata.*
He thought he could get away with it, but *it backfired on him.*

Salirse con la suya. Le gusta siempre *salirse con la suya.*
She always likes *to have her own way.*

Salirse por la tangente. *Te estás saliendo por la tangente.*
You are side-stepping the issue.

Se armó la de San Quintín. Anoche en la reunión sindical *se
armó la de San Quintín.*
Last night at the union meeting *there was a terrible row.*

Sea como fuere. *Sea como fuere*, no puedo seguir viviendo en este
hotel.
However it may be, I cannot go on living in this hotel.

Si mal no recuerdo. *Si mal no recuerdo*, hoy es cuando debemos
ir al médico.
If I remember right, today is when we're supposed to go to the
doctor.

Sondear el ambiente.   Antes de hacerlo, vamos a *sondear el ambiente.*
Before doing it, let's *get the lay of the land.*

Sudar la gota gorda.   Arreglar este lío le hará *sudar la gota gorda.*
He'll *go through plenty* trying to straighten out this mess.

Tarde o temprano.   *Tarde o temprano,* te casarás con él.
Sooner or later, you will marry him.

Tener al corriente.   Te *tendré al corriente* de todo lo que pase.
I'll keep you *informed* of whatever happens.

Tener años.   Mi hija *tiene seis años.*
My daughter *is six years old.*

Tener cuidado.   Cuando pases el puente, *ten cuidado* porque es viejo.
When you go over the bridge, *be careful* because it is old.

Tener ganas.   *Tengo ganas* de ir al teatro esta noche.
I feel like going to theater tonight.

Tener presente.   *Ten presente* estos detalles para que todo salga bien.
Keep these details *in mind* so that everything will come out right.

Tener prisa.   Juan siempre *tiene prisa* por irse a su casa.
Juan *is* always *in a hurry* to go home.

Tener que vérselas con uno.   Para eso *tienes que vértelas con él.*
If you do that, *you'll have to answer to him.*

Tener razón.   Ud. *tiene razón* en este caso.
In this case *you are right.*

Tenerlo entre ojos.   Por su culpa *lo tienen entre ojos.*
It's his own fault *they have a grudge against him.*

Tocarle en lo vivo.   Cuando me hablas de este asunto, *me tocas en lo vivo.*
When you speak to me about this, *you're touching an open wound.*

Todo el santo día.   Se pasó hablando con ella *todo el santo día.*
He spent *the whole blessed day* talking with her.

Tomar a pecho.   María, en cuanto a lo ocurrido, no lo *tomes a pecho.*
Don't *take* what's happened *to heart,* Maria.

Tomar el rábano por las hojas.   Creo que *tomaste el rábano por las hojas.*
I think *you've put the cart before the horse.*

Tomar las de Villadiego.   Cuando ocurrió el incidente *tomó las de Villadiego.*
When the incident occurred, *he took to his heels.*

Tomar por su cuenta.   No te preocupes, Juan, lo *tomaré por mi cuenta.*
Don't worry, Juan, *I'll take care of* it *personally.*

Tomarle el pelo.   Anoche *le tomaron el pelo* a Juan.
Last night *they were kidding* Juan *along.*

¡Trato hecho!   Te doy cien dólares por el televisor y *¡trato hecho!*
I'll give you a hundred dollars for the television set, and *it's a deal.*

Un día sí y un día no.   Venga a darme clases de español *un día sí y un día no.*
Come and teach me Spanish *every other day.*

Valer la pena.   *Vale la pena* ir al concierto de esta noche.
Tonight's concert *is worth while.*

Váyase con la música a otra parte.   Mire, María, le aconsejo *se vaya con la música a otra parte.*
Look, Maria, I advise you to *bark up another tree.*

Venga lo que venga.   *Venga lo que venga*, tendrá que contar conmigo primero.
Whatever happens, he will have to reckon with me first.

Venir a pedir de boca.   Este regalo *me viene (como) a pedir de boca.*
This gift *is just what I was hoping for.*

Venir al pelo.   Esta anécdota *viene al pelo.*
This story *fits the case to a T.*

Ver la paja en el ojo ajeno.   Tu siempre *ves la paja en el ojo ajeno.*
You always *see other people's faults.*

Viento en popa.   Sus negocios van *viento en popa.*
His business is *humming right along.*

Vivir de gorra.   Juan *vive de gorra* en casa de José.
Juan *is a hanger-on* at Jose's house.

Vivito y coleando.   Todavía me tienes *vivito y coleando.*
I'm still *alive and kicking.*

Volver en sí.   Después de un rato largo, *volvió en sí.*
After a long while, *he came to.*

EXPRESIONES IDIOMATICAS NACIONALES
NATIONAL IDIOMS

ARGENTINA

Afilar con.   Juan *está afilando con* la hija de Don José.
Juan *is flirting with* Jose's daughter.

Andar como bola sin manija.   Roberto está *andando como bola sin manija.*
Roberto is *going around in circles.*

Darse corte.   Este tipo se pasa la vida *dándose corte.*
That fellow spends his life *putting on airs.*

Estar en la vía.   Te confieso que ahora *estoy en la vía.*
I admit that now *I'm broke.*

Hacerle la pera.   Rosario le dió una cita, pero *le hizo la pera.*
Rosario made a date with her, but *she stood him up.*

Hacerse el chancho rengo.   El *se hizo el chancho rengo* cuando le presenté el problema.
He played dumb when I presented the problem to him.

Ir de farra.   Los muchachos universitarios *han ido de farra.*
The college boys *have gone out on a spree.*

Meterle la mula.   Estoy seguro que *me metieron la mula.*
I am sure *they cheated me.*

Ni por un Perú.   Lo que me propones no lo haría *ni por un Perú.*
I wouldn't do what you propose to me *for anything in the world.*

No tragarlo ni con bombilla de plata.   A Juan *no lo tragan ni con bombilla de plata.*
They can't stand Juan.

Pasar el fardo.   A José le *pasaron el fardo* en este asunto.
They passed the buck to Jose in this matter.

Quedarse sin el pan y sin la torta.   Al fin de la aventura, *se quedó sin el pan y sin la torta.*
At the end of the adventure, *he lost everything.*

BOLIVIA

Darse mucho pisto.   José y Pedro *se dan mucho pisto.*
Jose and Pedro *put on lots of airs.*

Hacerse el italiano.   No te empeñes en *hacerte el italiano.*
Don't keep on *playing dumb.*

Tener chaqui.   Después de la fiesta todo el mundo *tuvo chaqui.*
After the party, everyone *had a hangover.*

CHILE

Cuando la perdiz críe cola.   El pagará esa cuenta *cuando la perdiz críe cola.*
He'll pay the bill *when there are three Sundays in a week.*

Estar cufifo.   Ten paciencia con él porque *está cufifo.*
Be patient with him because *he's tipsy.*

Pololear con.   El joven americano *está pololeando con* la hija de Doña María.
The young American *is making out with* Maria's daughter.

Se armó la rosca.   Después de la reunión sindical, *se armó la rosca.*
After the union meeting, *there was a free-for-all.*

COLOMBIA

Estar como un gato en una pelea de perros.   Cada vez que voy a su casa *estoy como un gato en una pelea de perros.*
Every time I go to his house *I feel completely out of place.*

Estar enguayabado.   ¿Qué le pasa a nuestro amigo? *Está enguayabado.*
What's the matter with our friend? *He has a hangover.*

Farsear con.   A él le gusta *farsear con* las americanas que vienen a su tienda.
He likes *to flirt with* the Americans who come to his shop.

Hacerse el inglés.   El *se está haciendo el inglés.*
He's *playing dumb.*

Ponerse la leva.   ¿Dónde está el mensajero? *Se puso la leva.*
Where is the messenger boy? *He didn't come to work.*

COSTA RICA

Caerle como una bala. Juan González *me cae como una bala.*
Juan Gonzalez *gives me a pain in the neck.*

Comer cuento. Yo no soy un *come cuento.*
I'm not a *fall guy.*

Cortarle el rabo. La novia de José *le cortó el rabo.*
Jose's sweetheart *gave him the gate.*

Darse coba. Ten cuidado con él porque *se da mucha coba.*
Be careful because *he likes to act* very *important.*

Hacer película. Para *hacer película,* no hay otro como él.
For *showing off,* there's nobody like him.

Matar la culebra. *Matar la culebra* es un arte especial de algunas
personas.
Killing time is a special art some people have.

No poder bajarlo ni con aceite. Te confieso que *no puedo
bajarlo ni con aceite.*
I admit to you that *I can't stand the sight of him.*

Quedarse sin el santo y sin la limosna. Por meterse en ese
negocio, *se quedó sin el santo y sin la limosna.*
Because he went into that business, *he lost every penny he had.*

Tener cabanga por. *Tengo cabanga por* comerme un plato criollo.
I'm homesick for a creole dish.

¡Tumbe la vara! Mire, señor, *¡tumbe la vara!*
Look, mister, *lay off me, will you?*

CUBA

Coger un jalao. Anoche *cogí un jalao* en compañía de varios
amigos.
Last night *I got drunk* with several friends.

Darle cranque. A Juan siempre hay que *darle cranque.*
You've always got *to start* Juan *off.*

Darse lija. Este tipo *se da mucha lija.*
That guy *puts on* a lot of *airs.*

De Pascuas a San Juan.   El viene por aquí *de Pascuas a San Juan.*
He comes around *once in a blue moon.*

Donde el diablo dió los tres gritos.   Ellos viven *donde el diablo dió los tres gritos.*
They live *at the end of the world.*

Estar en la fuácata.   Ahora sí que *estoy en la fuácata.*
Now I'm flat as a pancake.

Ir de cumbancha.   El sábado vamos a *ir de cumbancha.*
Saturday we're going *to paint the town red.*

Irse de rumba.   Hoy *me voy de rumba.*
Today *I'm going on a spree.*

No tener ni un kilo.   Juan *no tiene ni un kilo* ahora.
Juan *is broke* now.

Pegar la gorra.   Juan y María, vengo a *pegar la gorra.*
Juan and Maria, I've come *to sponge on you.*

Saber nadar sin mojarse la ropa.   No te preocupes por él, porque *sabe nadar sin mojarse la ropa.*
Don't worry about him, *he knows his way around.*

Se formó el rollo.   Después del baile *se formó el rollo.*
After the dance *there was a free-for-all.*

Ser un buche y pluma.   No le creas lo que dice, él *es un buche y pluma.*
Don't believe a word he says, *he's a bluff.*

Vivir en las quimbambas.   Yo *vivo en las quimbambas.*
I live in the sticks.

ECUADOR

Armar broche.   Pedro *armó broche* en la fiesta.
Pedro *started a fight* at the party.

Chumarse.   Juan y yo *nos (vamos a) chumar* en la fiesta.
Juan and I *are going to get drunk* at the party.

Estar con chuchaqui.   Ellos *están* ahora *con chuchaqui.*
They have a hangover now.

Hacerle chino.   Trataron de *hacerle chino* anoche.
They tried *to fool him* last night.

EL SALVADOR

Caerle en la nuca.   Esta muchacha *me cae en la nuca*.
That girl *gives me a pain in the neck*.

Doblar el caite.   Ya José el ciego *dobló el caite*.
Jose the blind man *has kicked the bucket*.

Estar en la real quema.   *Estamos en la real quema* desde el mes
pasado.
We've been broke since last month.

Hacerse el papo.   Creo que *te estás haciendo el papo*.
I think *you're playing dumb*.

Sentirse como pollo comprado.   Cada vez que voy con él *me
siento como pollo comprado*.
Every time I go with him *I feel out of place*.

Tener cuello.   No te preocupes porque *tengo cuello*.
Don't worry, *I have pull*.

GUATEMALA

Agarrarlo con la gallina bajo el brazo.   Al ladrón *lo agarraron
con la gallina bajo el brazo*.
They caught the thief *red-handed*.

Darse paquete.   Este hombre *se da* mucho *paquete*.
That man *acts* very *important*.

Patear la cubeta.   Ana *está pateando la cubeta*.
Ana *is kicking the bucket*.

Quedarse sin el mico y sin la montera.   Después de pagar sus
deudas, *se quedó sin el mico y sin la montera*.
After paying his debts, *he was left penniless*.

HONDURAS

Caerle como píldoras.   Esta gente *me cae como píldoras*.
Those people *give me a pain*.

No pasarlo ni con candelas.   Lo siento mucho, pero *no lo paso
ni con candelas*.
I'm sorry, but *I can't stand the sight of him*.

Quedarse sin el plato y sin la cena.   Después de todo lo ocurrido,
se quedó sin el plato y sin la cena.
After it was all over, *he was left without a cent.*

Tener golilla.   Yo *tengo* mucha *golilla* con esta gente.
I have a lot of *pull* with those people.

MÉXICO

Caerle gordo.   Este señor *me cae gordo.*
That fellow *gives me a pain.*

Caerle sangrón.   Los Ramírez *me caen sangrones.*
The Ramirezes *are pests.*

Creerse la divina garza.   María González *se cree la divina garza.*
Maria Gonzalez *thinks she's hot stuff.*

Darle atole con el dedo.   *Me estás dando atole con el dedo.*
You're kidding me along.

Echar (a uno) de cabeza.   *A* (Juan) lo *echaron de cabeza.*
Someone gave (Juan) *away.*

Echarle la viga.   *Te (van a) echar la viga* cuando llegues a tu casa.
You're going to catch it when you get home.

Entre azul y buenas noches.   Se casan *entre azul y buenas noches.*
It is undecided when they are to get married.

Estar bruja.   Lo siento, Pedro, *estoy bruja.*
I'm sorry, Pedro, *I'm broke.*

Estar cuete.   No le hables porque *está cuete.*
Don't speak to him because *he's plastered.*

Estar en su mero mole.   Ahora sí que *estoy en mi mero mole.*
Now *I'm like a fish in water.*

Hacer (a uno) de chivo los tamales.   Juan (*me*) *hizo de chivo los
tamales.*
Juan *double-crossed* (*me*).

Hacer la barba.   Ten cuidado que le gusta *hacer la barba.*
Be careful, she likes *to play up to people.*

Hacerle la llorona.   No supiste *hacerle la llorona.*
You didn't know how *to give him a sob story.*

Hacerse guaje.   El sabe *hacerse guaje* cuando le conviene.
He knows how *to play dumb* when it suits him.

Hacerse para atrás.   Después de mucho hablar, *se hizo para atrás*.
After a lot of talking, *he backed out.*

Llevar gallo.   Le *estoy llevando gallo* todas las noches.
I serenade her every night.

Pintarle un violín.   Después de mucho hablarme, *me pintó un violín.*
After a lot of talk, *he didn't keep his word.*

Ponerle los ojos verdes.   No te dejes *poner los ojos verdes.*
Don't let them *pull the wool over your eyes.*

Quedarse sin Juan y sin las gallinas.   El pobre José *se ha quedado sin Juan y sin las gallinas.*
Poor Jose *was left flat broke.*

Ser un águila descalza.   El sí que *es un águila descalza.*
He certainly *knows what he's doing.*

NICARAGUA

Darle picones.   Juan *está dandole picones* a Pedro.
Juan *is making* Pedro *jealous.*

Dejarlo viendo para el icaco.   A María *la dejaron viendo para el icaco.*
Maria *was stood up.*

Estarle a uno arañando el tigre.   Es muy tarde y *me está arañando el tigre.*
It is late and *I'm as hungry as a wolf.*

Hacer de una aguja un machete.   Creo que *estás haciendo de una aguja un machete* en este asunto.
I think *you're making a mountain out of a mole hill* in this matter.

Pelar el ajo.   Juan *peló el ajo* ayer por la noche.
Juan *kicked the bucket* last night.

PANAMÁ

Comer del cuento.   ¡Puedes creer que Juan *comió del cuento!*
Can you believe that Juan *swallowed it hook, line and sinker!*

Estar en fuego.   Me parece que José *está en fuego.*
I think Jose *is drunk.*

Estar en la chirola.   ¿Dónde está Francisco? *Está en la chirola.*
Where is Francisco? *He's in the hoosegow.*

Estar limpio de bola.   Juan *está limpio de bola.*
Juan *is broke.*

Estar traqueado.   Creo que José *está traqueado.*
I think Jose *is plastered.*

Ir a la alemana.   Voy con la condición de *ir a la alemana.*
I'll go if we *go Dutch treat.*

Meterle un cují.   Creo que a Antonio *le metieron un cují.*
I think Antonio *was taken in.*

PARAGUAY

Caerle como un rayo.   Este hombre *me cae como un rayo.*
That man *gets on my nerves.*

En todas partes se queman las papas.   Esto te prueba que *en todas partes se queman las papas.*
This proves to you *it can happen anywhere.*

No poder ver (a uno) ni en caja de fósforos.   Te confieso que *a él no puedo verlo ni en caja de fósforos.*
I admit *I can't stand the sight of him.*

Ponerle el canasto.   A Pedro *le pusieron el canasto.*
They passed the buck to Pedro.

PERÚ

Cuando los pollos mamen.   Eso que me dices te lo creeré *cuando los pollos mamen.*
I'll believe that *when the moon is blue.*

Decirle vela verde.   No pude aguantar más y *le dije vela verde.*
I couldn't stand any more and *I told him off.*

Empavarse.   Cuando llegó el momento de darle un beso, *se empavó.*
When the time came to kiss her, *he blushed.*

Estar como gallina en corral ajeno.   Aquí *estoy como gallina en corral ajeno.*
I feel in the wrong pew here.

Estar con la perseguidora. No me hables mucho porque *estoy con la perseguidora.*
Don't talk so much. *I have a hangover.*

Estarle (a uno) corriendo el león. Ya es muy tarde y por eso *me está corriendo el león.*
It's late already and that's why *I'm as hungry as a wolf.*

Hacer teatro. Yo creo que ella *está haciendo teatro.*
I think *she's trying to appear important.*

Ir de jarana. Esta noche vamos a *ir de jarana.*
Tonight we're *going on a spree.*

Largarlo tieso. Apenas me dijo eso *lo largué tieso.*
As soon as he told me that, *I told him where to get off.*

Ser un "chicheñor." Ramón *es un "chicheñor."*
Ramon *is a yes-man.*

Sobarle la pantorrilla. Mira como *le soba la pantorrilla* al maestro.
Look how *she's polishing up* the teacher.

Tirar prosa. A este hombre le gusta *tirar prosa.*
That man likes *to act like a big wheel.*

URUGUAY

Tirársela de perro lanudo. Esta familia *se la tira de perro lanudo.*
That family *puts on the dog.*

VENEZUELA

Agarrarlo con el queso en la mano. A la criada *la agarraron con el queso en la mano.*
They caught the maid *red-handed.*

Estar en la carraplana. Por motivo de este accidente, *estoy en la carraplana.*
Because of this accident, *I'm in a tough spot.*

Hacerse el "musiú." Cuando le presenté la cuenta, *se hizo el "musiú."*
When I gave him the bill, *he changed the subject.*

Tener un ratón. Enrique *tiene un ratón.*
Enrique *has a hangover.*

U.S. IDIOMS

EXPRESIONES IDIOMATICAS DE LOS EE.UU.

A B C. He doesn't know the *A B C* of politics.
No sabe *los fundamentos* de la política.

A-1. He is an *A*-1 criminal lawyer.
El es un criminalista *de primera*.

About to. I was *about to* tell you everything.
Estuve *a punto* de decírtelo todo.

Aboveboard. This lawyer's dealings are all *aboveboard*.
Las relaciones del abogado son *honestas*.

According to Hoyle. What you did was not *according to Hoyle*.
Lo que hizo no fué *apropiado*.

Of age. She is *of age* but he is not yet twenty-one and is under age.
Ella es *mayor de edad*, pero él no tiene veintiún años todavía
y es menor de edad.

All along. We knew *all along* that he would be chosen.
Lo supimos *desde el principio* que él sería el escogido.

All at once. *All at once* he knew the solution.
De repente supo la solución.

All ears. When he heard his sweetheart's name, he was *all ears*.
Cuando oyó el nombre de su novia, se volvió *todo oídos*.

All in. After dancing all evening, she was *all in*.
Después de bailar toda la noche *se rindió de cansancio*.

All in all. *All in all*, it was a good piece of work.
En general, fué un buen trabajo.

All is up. He knows it *is all up* with him.
Sabe que ya *se le terminó* la oportunidad.

All over. When he got there, the excitement was *all over*.
Cuando él llegó, la agitación *había terminado*.

The news of the verdict was *all over*.
La noticia de la sentencia se supo *por todas partes*.

27

All right.   It is *all right* to go to the movies on Sunday.
Es correcto ir al cine los domingos.

All set.   They are *all set* to go on their trip.
Están listos para ir de viaje.

All the same.   He doesn't love her, but he'll marry her *all the same*.
No la ama, pero *a pesar de ello* se casará con ella.

All there.   Even though he's ninety, he's *all there*.
A pesar de los noventa años, *está muy bien*.

Allow for.   You must *allow for* contingencies in your estimate.
Debes *tener en cuenta* las contingencias en tu presupuesto.

Apple of one's eye.   She was the *apple of her parents' eye*.
Ella era *la preferida de sus padres*.

Apple-pie order.   The girls cleaned up and left their room in *apple-pie order*.
Las muchachas limpiaron y dejaron la casa *en orden*.

As a matter of fact.   *As a matter of fact*, he is entirely cured.
De seguro, él está completamente curado.

As yet.   *As yet* I have had no word from her.
Hasta ahora no he recibido noticias de ella.

At fault.   He was *at fault* in not coming to consult me.
Se equivocó en no venir a consultarme.

At first blush.   *At first blush* it seemed a wonderful idea to invest in the deal.
De primer momento pareció una buena idea invertir en el negocio.

At least.   She earns *at least* thirty-five dollars per week.
Gana *como mínimo* treinta y cinco dólares por semana.

At once.   Telephone her *at once*, as it is urgent.
Llámela *inmediatamente* por teléfono porque es urgente.

At one's fingertips.   He has all that information *at his fingertips*.
Tiene toda la información *en la punta de los dedos*.

At one's wit's end.   She is *at her wit's end* trying to think of a good excuse.
Está para volverse loca por encontrar una buena excusa.

At the top.   She was screaming *at the top* of her lungs.
Gritaba *con todos sus pulmones*.

At times. *At times* he even cried a little.
 A veces aun él lloró un poco.

Ax to grind. She always has an *ax to grind* when she comes to visit us.
 Siempre *se está quejando de algo* cuando viene a visitarnos.

Back number. We sell *back numbers* of magazines.
 Vendemos ejemplares *atrasados* de revistas.

Back out. We had a date for tonight, but she just *backed out*.
 Teníamos una cita esta noche, pero ella *se volvió atrás*.

Back up. The car *backed up*.
 El automóvil *dió marcha atrás*.

 The communist was *backed up* only by other communists.
 El comunista fué *respaldado* solamente por otros comunistas.

Bad blood. There was *bad blood* between the brothers.
 Había *enemistad* entre los hermanos.

Bad egg. That lazy boy is just a *bad egg*.
 Ese muchacho haragán es un *calavera*.

Bag and baggage. In five minutes she cleared out, *bag and baggage*, and he never saw her again.
 En cinco minutos se marchó *con todas sus pertenencias* y nunca la vió más.

Barge in. She *barged in* just as we got to the most important part of our discussion.
 Llegó inesperadamente cuando estábamos en la parte más importante de la discussión.

Bawl out. His father *bawled* him *out* for his bad behavior.
 Su padre le *regañó* por su mala conducta.

Bear out. My witness will *bear out* what I told you.
 Mi testigo *confirmará* lo que he dicho a Ud.

Bear up. She will have to learn to *bear up* under her sorrows.
 Ella tendrá que *resignarse* a sus penas.

Bear with. He will have to *bear with* her bad temper until she is well again
 El tendrá que *tener paciencia* con su genio hasta que ella se ponga bien.

Beard the lion.   He decided to *beard the lion* in his den and walked
into the boss's office to demand a raise.
Decidió *hacerle frente al león* en su jaula y entró en la oficina
del jefe y pidió un aumento de sueldo.

Beat about the bush.   Answer me directly instead of *beating about
the bush.*
Respóndeme directamente y no te *andes por las ramas.*

Beat it.   He said: "*Beat it,* here come the cops!"
El dijo: "*¡Pon los pies en polvorosa,* viene la policía!"

Beat one to it.   I wanted to ask her for a dance but he *beat me to
it.*
Quise bailar con ella, pero él *se me adelantó.*

Become of.   Poor orphan, I wonder what will *become of* him.
Pobre huérfano, me pregunto qué *será de* él.

Beeline.   He made a *beeline* for the drinks.
Se fué *derechito* a las bebidas.

Behind bars.   The judge gave him a year *behind bars.*
El juez lo metió *en la cárcel* por un año.

Behind one's back.   She made remarks about her friend *behind
her back.*
Ella habló mal de su amiga *en su ausencia.*

Below the belt.   That last remark hit him *below the belt.*
Lo último que dijo le hizo el efecto *de un golpe bajo.*

Beside oneself.   She was *beside herself* with rage.
Perdió el control y no pudo dominarse de rabia.

Beside the point.   Your answer to my question is entirely *beside
the point.*
Tu respuesta a mi pregunta *no viene al caso.*

Best man.   The bride's brother was the *best man.*
El hermano de la novia fué el *padrino de boda.*

Better half.   Is this beautiful woman your *better half?*
¿Es esta hermosa mujer tu *esposa?*

Better off.   He was *better off* in his daughter's home than living
alone.
Estaba *en mejores condiciones* en casa de su hija que viviendo
solo.

Between the devil and the deep sea.   He had to make a choice,
even though he was *between the devil and the deep sea.*
Tuvo que decidir a pesar de *estar entre la espada y la pared.*

Big hand. At every recital he got a *big hand.*
En cada recital recibió una *ovación.*

Big shot (big wheel; bigwig). He's a *big shot* in the labor organization.
Es *persona de influencia* en la organización obrera.

Birds of a feather. They're *birds of a feather*—that's why they're always together.
Siempre están juntos porque son *pájaros de la misma pluma.*

Bite one's head off. She was ready to *bite my head off* for teasing her.
Estaba *bravísima* por bromear con ella.

Black and white. Here's the whole story in *black and white.*
Esta es la historia en *todos sus detalles.*

Blind date. She doesn't want her friend to arrange a *blind date* for her.
Ella no quiere que su amiga le *concierte una cita con un desconocido.*

Blow off steam. The irate father calmed down quickly after *blowing off steam.*
El padre se calmó después de *desahogarse.*

Blow one's top. She *blew her top* when he came home drunk.
Ella *estalló* cuando él llegó borracho a la casa.

Blow over. When the storm *blows over* the temperature may drop.
Cuando *pase* la tormenta la temperatura bajará.

Blow up. The house *was blown up* by dynamite.
La casa *la volaron* con dinamita.

Bobby-soxer. The singer was surrounded by shrieking *bobby-soxers.*
El cantante fué rodeado por *jovencitas chillonas.*

Bone to pick. I have a *bone to pick* with you about your staying out so late.
Tengo que *vérmelas contigo* porque vuelves muy tarde a casa.

Bosom friends. They remained *bosom friends* in spite of the gossip.
Continuaron *amigos íntimos* a pesar de los chismes.

Bounce out. They *bounced* him *out* of the bar for using profane language.
Lo *echaron* de la barra por usar lenguaje profano.

Bound for. This tiny car from New York is *bound for* California.
Este automóvil pequeño de Nueva York *va para* California.

Bound to. A politician is *bound to* make promises at election time.
Un político *probablemente* hace promesas en época de elecciones.

Break away. A child must *break away* from overpossessive parents.
Un hijo debe *librarse* de padres demasiado amorosos.

Breakdown. She had a nervous *breakdown*.
Sufrió un *colapso* nervioso.

Break down. With one blow he *broke down* the door.
De un golpe *echó abajo* la puerta.

Their car *broke down* before they reached their destination.
Su auto *se descompuso* antes de llegar a su destino.

Break in. It took weeks to *break in* the new workers.
Duró semanas *enseñar* a los obreros nuevos.

She kept *breaking in* all the time the boss and I were talking.
Ella *se entrometía* cada vez que hablaba con el jefe.

Break out. Hostilities *broke out* again between the two armies.
Rompieron de nuevo las hostilidades entre los dos ejércitos.

Break the ice. That last joke *broke the ice* and everybody began chatting.
La última broma *rompió la seriedad* y todo el mundo empezó a hablar.

Break the news. She *broke the news* of her elopement to her family.
Ella *dió la noticia* de su fuga a su familia.

Break through. His objective was to *break through* the cordon.
Su objetivo fué *abrirse paso a través del* cordón.

Break up. To *break up* a marriage is sinful.
Destruir un matrimonio es pecado.

The party *broke up* at midnight.
La fiesta *terminó* a medianoche.

She will be *broken up* when she hears the sad news.
Ella *se pondrá muy triste* cuando oiga la noticia mala.

Break with. He *broke with* her and started to date her friend.
El *rompió con* ella y empezó a salir con la amiga de ella.

Bring about (bring on). Her breakdown was *brought about* by the tragic news.
Su colapso *fué causado* por las trágicas noticias.

Bring down. How can we make the landlords *bring down* the rents?
¿Cómo podemos hacer que los dueños *disminuyan* los alquileres?

Bring home. His absence *brought home* to us how much we missed him.
Su ausencia nos *demostró* cuánto lo extrañamos.

Bring home the bacon. In that family it was the mother who *brought home the bacon.*
En esa familia es la madre quien *sufragaba los gastos.*

Bring to light. The trial *brought to light* many secrets.
El juicio *reveló* muchos secretos.

Bring to mind. It *brought to mind* a similar trial presided over by this judge.
Nos recordó un juicio similar presidido por este juez.

Bring up. He is a difficult child to *bring up*.
El es un niño difícil de *educar*.

Broke. I spent all my money and am completely *broke*.
Gasté todo mi dinero y estoy *sin un centavo*.

Brush aside. She *brushed* her parents *aside* and rushed into her fiancé's arms.
No hizo caso de sus padres y corrió a los brazos de su novio.

Brush-off. He got a fast *brush-off* when he applied for the job.
Recibió un *rechazo* inmediato cuando solicitó el empleo.

Build-up. What a *build-up* they gave him to help him win!
¡Qué *propaganda* le hicieron para ayudarle a ganar!

Burn out. The fire *burned out* slowly.
El fuego *se consumió* poco a poco.

Burn the candle at both ends. If you *burn the candle at both ends*, you will not last long.
Si *te agotas*, no durarás mucho.

Burn the midnight oil. The students were advised not to *burn the midnight oil* before exams.
A los estudiantes se les aconsejó *no quedarse tarde estudiando* antes de los exámenes.

Burn up.   Chicago was *burned up* in the Great Fire.
Chicago fué *destruido totalmente* por el famoso incendio.

It *burns (me) up* to be called a liar.
(Me) enfurece que me llamen mentiroso.

Burning hot.   In the tropics the summers are *burning hot.*
En el trópico los veranos son *abrasadores.*

Burst into tears.   She *burst into tears* at the sad news.
Se echó a llorar al oír las tristes noticias.

Burst out laughing.   The child *burst out laughing* every time the clown appeared.
El niño *se echó a reír* cada vez que salía el payaso.

Bury the hatchet.   For a time the North and the South *buried the hatchet.*
Por un tiempo el Norte y el Sur *dejaron de pelear.*

Butt in.   She always *butts in*(to) our conversation.
Ella siempre *interrumpe* nuestra conversación.

Buy out.   The president of the stock company tried to *buy out* the other stockholders.
El presidente de la compañía de acciones trató de *comprar a* los otros accionistas.

Buy up.   He wanted to *buy up* all the land that remained.
Quiso *comprar todos* los terrenos que quedaron.

By accident.   We bumped into them *by accident* on the train.
Nos encontramos con ellos *inesperadamente* en el tren.

By all means.   *By all means,* we'll expect you for dinner tonight.
Sin falta te esperamos a comer esta noche.

By and large.   *By and large,* one would say the crowd was composed of teen-agers.
En general podría decirse que la mayoría de las personas eran jovencitos.

By oneself.   The baby is learning to eat *by himself.*
El niño está aprendiendo a comer *sin ayuda.*

The widower lives *by himself* since his wife died.
El viudo vive *solo* desde la muerte de su esposa.

By the skin of one's teeth.   The boy missed being run over by *the skin of his teeth.*
El muchacho no fué arrollado *por milagro.*

By the way. *By the way*, have you heard the latest gossip?
A propósito, ¿has oído el último chisme?

Call down. He was *called down* severely for being inattentive.
Le *reprendieron* severamente por estar distraído.

Call for. He *calls for* me early on Sunday.
Me *viene a buscar* temprano los domingos.

The Red Cross *called for* volunteers.
La Cruz Roja *pidió* más ayudantes.

Call in. *Call in* a specialist if you don't trust your doctor.
Consulta a un especialista si no confías en tu médico.

Call off. *Call off* the party if you don't know enough boys.
Cancela la fiesta si no conoces a suficientes jóvenes.

Call on. As soon as we found out where they lived, we *called on* them.
Tan pronto como supimos donde vivían *fuimos a visitar*les.

Call out. They *called out* to him from the window.
Le *llamaron* desde la ventana.

They *called out* the militia to stop the looting.
Requirieron la milicia para terminar el robo.

Call up. *Call us up* whenever you feel lonesome.
Llámanos por teléfono cuando estés triste.

Carry on. *Carry on* with your job until it is completed.
Sigue con tu trabajo hasta que lo completes.

Stop crying and *carrying on* like a child.
No llores más y no *sigas comportándote* como un niño.

Everybody talks about the way he is *carrying on* behind his wife's back.
Todos hablan de sus *amores ilícitos* que su esposa no sabe.

Carry out. He *carried out* all her commands.
El *llevó a cabo* todas las órdenes de ella.

Carry the ball. He *carries the ball* for the whole firm.
El *se encarga* de todo el negocio.

Catch fire. This log is too wet to *catch fire*.
Este leño está muy húmedo para *coger fuego*.

Catch hold of. The drowning man at last *caught hold of* the rope.
El hombre medio ahogado al fin *se agarró a* la soga.

Catch on. They may *catch on* if you keep on explaining.
Puede que *lo entiendan* si sigues explicando.

Catch one's eye. The girl's sensitive face *caught his eye*.
La cara sensitiva de la muchacha *le llamó la atención*.

Catch red-handed. They *caught* him *red-handed* with the stolen goods.
Lo *cogieron en flagrante* con las cosas robadas.

Catch up with. The second horse *caught up with* the first.
El segundo caballo *alcanzó* al primero.

Chain smoker. A *chain smoker* finds the cigarette habit hard to break.
Un *fumador empedernido* encuentra que es difícil dejar de fumar.

Chalk up. He *chalked up* the loss to lack of experience.
El *atribuyó* la pérdida a la falta de experiencia.

Change hands. This house has *changed hands* three times within the last year.
La casa *cambió de dueño* tres veces el año pasado.

Change one's mind. She *changed her mind* about the dress and bought it.
Cambió de parecer en cuanto al vestido y lo compró.

Check in. She *checked in* for work an hour late.
Llegó al trabajo con una hora de atraso.

Check out. Call me after you *check out* of your hotel.
Llámame cuando *te vayas* del hotel.

Checkup. A *checkup* is especially important in middle age.
Es especialmente importante tener *un examen médico* cuando se llega a los cuarenta.

Check up on. Her husband *checked up on* all her movements throughout the day.
Su esposo *investigó* todos sus actos durante el día.

Check with. The druggist *checked with* the doctor before filling the prescription.
El farmacéutico *consultó con* el médico antes de preparar la receta.

Chew the fat. Women can *chew the fat* all day without tiring.
Las mujeres pueden *chismear* todo el día sin cansarse.

37

Chicken feed. A dollar was just *chicken feed* to the millionaire.
Un peso fué una *migaja* para el millonario.

Chicken-hearted. He was too *chicken-hearted* to speak to the girl directly.
Fué muy *tímido* para hablar directamente a la muchacha.

Chicken out. He *chickened out* before the race got under way.
Se acobardó antes de empezar la carrera.

Child's play. It was *child's play* to win all his money.
Fué *muy fácil* ganarle todo su dinero.

Chip in. The children all *chipped in* and bought the teacher a watch.
Los muchachos *contribuyeron* y compraron un reloj para el maestro.

Chip off the old block. The son is a scientist too; just a *chip off the old block.*
El hijo es también un científico como el padre; *de tal palo tal astilla.*

Chips are down. When the *chips are down*, he always comes through with a winning idea.
Cuando la *situación es crítica* siempre presenta una idea feliz.

Close call. She didn't die, but she had a *close call.*
No murió, pero *por poco* se muere.

Cock and bull story. I never believed his *cock and bull stories.*
Nunca creí sus *cuentos increíbles.*

Coin money. The resort hotels *coin money.*
Los hoteles de veraneo *se enriquecen con rapidez.*

Come along. We want you to *come along* on this trip.
Queremos que nos *acompañes* en este viaje.

His book is *coming along* nicely.
Su libro *progresa* muy bien.

Come by. Where did she *come by* all that money?
¿Dónde *ganó* ella ese dinero?

Come down with. All winter he *came down with* colds regularly.
Durante todo el invierno *estuvo enfermo* con catarros.

Come in handy. Money always *comes in handy.*
El dinero *es* siempre *útil.*

Come on.   Will the acrobats *come on* again?
¿*Saldrán* de nuevo los acróbatas?

She feels a chill *coming on*.
Ella sienta que *le va a caer* un catarro.

Come out.   The picture will *come out* in November.
La película *aparecerá* en noviembre.

Everything that photographer snaps *comes out* well.
Cada fotografía que saca este fotógrafo *sale* bien.

Come out for.   The women *came out for* Roosevelt.
Las mujeres *apoyaron* a Roosevelt.

Come to.   The dinner and movies *came to* a lot of money.
El total de la comida y del teatro *fué* muy alto.

Come to one's senses.   When will you *come to your senses* and
begin to work?
¿Cuándo *recobrarás el sentido común* y empezarás a trabajar?

Come to terms.   They quickly *came to terms* and signed a contract.
Llegaron a un acuerdo en seguida firmaron un contrato.

Come to the point.   Please *come to the point* immediately.
Haga el favor de *ir al grano* en seguida.

Come true.   One by one her dreams *came true*.
Sus sueños *se realizaron* uno a uno.

Come upon.   When you *come upon* my name, let me know.
Cuando *llegues a* mi nombre avísame.

Cook one's goose.   She *cooked her* own *goose* when she insulted the
boss.
Arruinó su oportunidad cuando insultó a su jefe.

Cool as a cucumber.   She remained as *cool as a cucumber* when
they threatened her.
Permaneció *serena* cuando la amenazaron.

Cool one's heels.   As we were late for the opening, we had to
cool our heels outside.
Tuvimos que *esperar* por haber llegado tarde a la apertura.

Count one's chickens before they are hatched.   If you *count
your chickens before they are hatched*, you may be disappointed.
No cantes victoria antes de estar seguro.

Crack a joke.   He *cracked* (one) *joke* after another.
Dijo chistes uno tras otro.

Crack-up. He flunked the final exam and that caused his *crack-up*.
No pasó el examen final y eso lo *trastornó*.

Cream of the crop. These freshman are the *cream of the crop* of all schools.
Estos estudiantes de primer año son *la esperanza* de todas las escuelas.

Cry wolf. Don't *cry wolf* unless you're in real danger.
No *pidas auxilio* a no ser que estés en verdadero peligro.

Cut. The gangster wanted a good *cut* of the profits.
El bandido quiso una buena *porción* de las cosas robadas.

Cut down. She was overweight and tried to *cut down* on calories.
Pesaba mucho y trató de *reducir* las calorías.

Cut it out. She told him to *cut it out*, as he was annoying her with his teasing.
Le dijo que *no siguiera* molestándola con sus bromas.

Cut off. We were *cut off* in our telephone conversation.
Cortaron nuestra conversación por teléfono.

He *cut off* a huge slice of bread from the loaf.
Cortó un pedazo grande de la flauta de pan.

Cut out. She had to *cut out* the sweets in her diet, as she was overweight.
Tuvo que *eliminar* los dulces por pesar demasiado.

Cut out for. With so much dramatic talent, she is *cut out for* the stage.
Ella es *perfecta* para el teatro por su talento dramático.

Cut short. The card game was *cut short* when someone saw a policeman.
El juego de cartas *terminó de repente* cuando alguien vió al policía.

Dark horse. A *dark horse* won the nomination for president.
Un *candidato desconocido* ganó la nominación de presidente.

Dash off. He *dashed off* a quick note to his old friend.
Escribió rápidamente unas palabras a su viejo amigo.

Date. He asked if he could *date* her sometime.
Le preguntó si podría *invitarla* alguna vez.

Day in and day out. *Day in and day out*, he follows the same routine.
Sigue la misma rutina *día tras día*.

Dead as a doornail. Business is as *dead as a doornail*.
Los negocios están *paralizados*.

Die down. The noise did not *die down* till the car was out of sight.
El ruído no *se extinguió* hasta desaparecer la máquina.

Die out. The custom of curtseying is *dying out* completely.
La cortesía está *desapareciendo gradualmente*.

Dirty look. She gave you that *dirty look* for talking too loud.
Te *miró con desagrado* por hablar muy alto.

Do away with. After she jilted him he wanted to *do away with* himself.
Quiso *suicidarse* cuando ella lo dejó.

Do in. He was *done in* by the loan shark.
El prestamista lo *arruinó*.

Do over. You'll have to *do* that lesson *over*, because you don't know it.
Tienes que *hacer de nuevo* la lección por no saberla.

Do without. We can *do without* a maid in this tiny apartment.
No necesitamos una criada en este apartamento pequeño.

Dog-tired. He was too *dog-tired* to get undressed to go to sleep.
Estaba *muerto de cansancio* para desvestirse antes de ir a dormir.

Doll up. Are you all *dolled up* for a party?
¿Estás *engalanado* para una fiesta?

Done. The chicken isn't *done* yet.
El pollo no está *cocinado* todavía.

That isn't *done* in polite society.
Eso *no se hace* entre personas educadas.

Double-cross. His brother *double-crossed* him and took his money.
Su hermano le *engañó* y le llevó el dinero.

Down and out. That tramp certainly looks *down and out*.
Ese indigente está *sin dinero*.

Down in the mouth. She looks so *down in the mouth* because her husband is ill.
Ella luce *muy triste* por la enfermedad de su esposo.

Down to earth. She is very *down to earth* about sentimental matters.
Ella es muy *práctica* en asuntos sentimentales.

Draw the line. One or two drinks are reasonable, but there I *draw the line*.
Uno o dos tragos son suficientes, después *paro de beber*.

Draw up. His lawyer will *draw up* the will.
Su abogado *escribirá* su testamento.

Dress up. She got all *dressed up* before she met her fiancé for dinner.
Ella *se puso muy elegante* antes de ir a comer con su novio.

Drive someone mad. You'll *drive me mad* if you keep on beating those drums.
Me volverás loco si sigues tocando esos tambores.

Driving at. She asked so many questions I wondered what she was *driving at*.
Hizó tantas preguntas que yo no sabía *qué se propone*.

Drop by (drop in). I like to have my friends *drop by* on Sundays.
Deseo que mis amigos *me visiten* los domingos.

Drop in the bucket. What I spent today is just a *drop in the bucket* compared to what I usually spend.
Lo que gasté hoy es una *gota de agua* comparado con lo que suelo gastar.

Drop off. The leaves *dropped off* in bunches as the wind blew stronger.
Las hojas *se desprendían* a montones, a medida que aumentaba el viento.

Drop out of. People *dropped out of* the line because of the cold.
La gente *se retiró* de la línea de espera por el frío.

Drop someone a line. My children at college *drop me a line* twice a week.
Mis hijos en la escuela *me escriben* dos veces a la semana.

Drug on the market. This year portable radios are a *drug on the market*.
Este año *no se venden* los radios portátiles.

Dry up. "When are you going to *dry up?*" he shouted.
¿Cuándo te vas a *callar?*" gritó.

Dutch treat. She would only go to the movies with him if they went *Dutch treat*.
Sólo iba al cine con él si *cada cual se pagaba lo suyo*.

Eat one's cake and have it.   She'd like to divorce the millionaire and marry the young artist, but one cannot *eat one's cake and have it*.
Le gustaría divorciarse del millonario y casarse con el artista joven, pero las *cosas no siempre suceden a pedir de boca*.

Eat one's heart out.   She *eats her heart out* when she sees him with another girl.
Ella *sufre callada* cuando le ve con otra muchacha.

Eat one's words.   She was forced to *eat her words* about his honesty when he was convicted for fraud.
Tuvo que *retractarse* acerca de su honestidad cuando le sentenciaron por fraude.

Every so often.   *Every so often* throughout the night I thought I heard the rain.
De vez en cuando, durante la noche, creí haber oído la lluvia.

Face the music.   If your lie is found out, you must *face the music*.
Si se descubre tu mentira, *hazle frente a las consecuencias*.

Face up to.   You must *face up to* responsibilities instead of running away.
Debes *enfrentarte con* las responsabilidades y no huir de ellas.

Fair and square.   If you play the game *fair and square* you will always come out ahead.
Si eres *sincero y honesto* triunfarás en tus cosas.

Fall foul of.   Try not to *fall foul of* your mathematics teacher.
Procura no *perder la simpatía de* tu maestro de matemáticas.

Fall off.   The moment the star left the show, attendance *fell off*.
Desde el momento que el actor principal abandonó la obra, la asistencia *disminuyó*.

Fall out.   Let's not *fall out* about a silly letter.
No *nos desconcertemos* por una carta tonta.

Fall through.   If you don't side with us, the plan will *fall through*.
Si no estás con nosotros, el plan *fracasará*.

Far and wide.   *From far and wide* the children came running to follow the Pied Piper.
De todas partes vinieron corriendo los niños detrás del gaitero.

Far cry. It's a *far cry* from this to the stuff he used to write.
Hay una diferencia *como del día a la noche* entre esto y lo que escribía antes.

Farfetched. The plot of the novel was too *farfetched*.
El argumento de la novela fué muy *exagerado*.

Feather in one's cap. What a *feather in his cap* to be first in his class!
¡Qué *triunfo para él* ser el primero en su clase!

Feather one's nest. You must *feather your nest* while you are young and strong.
Debes *prepararte* para la vejez mientras eres joven y fuerte.

Fed up. He was *fed up* with his dull job.
Estaba *harto* de su oficio monótono.

Feel blue. I *feel blue* because he went away.
Me *siento triste* porque él se marchó.

Feel for. He really *felt for* her when he saw her blush with shame.
El *se condolió de* ella cuando la vió abochornada.

Feel it in one's bones. He could *feel it in his bones* that it would be an unlucky day.
Se lo dijo su corazón que sería un día fatal.

Feel like. I *feel like* having another cup of coffee.
Tengo ganas de tomar otra taza de café.

Feel one's way. I *felt my way* cautiously in the dark.
Procedí con cautela en la oscuridad.

Fellow travelers. The Communists and their *fellow travelers* voted against the government.
Los comunistas y sus *simpatizantes* votaron contra el gobierno.

Fence sitter. We never know whether he's a Democrat or a Republican, he's such a *fence sitter*.
Nunca sabemos si es demócrata o republicano porque *es un cambiacasaca*.

Few and far between. Good professors are *few and far between*.
Los profesores buenos son *escasos*.

Fifty-fifty. We'll share the expenses *fifty-fifty*.
Nos repartimos los gastos *a la mitad*.

Figure on. We *figure on* you to help drive.
Contamos con que tu manejes.

Figure out. A good mathematician can *figure out* the most complicated problems.
Un buen matemático puede *resolver* los problemas más complicados.

It wasn't long before he was able to *figure out* their plan.
No pasó mucho tiempo para que él pudiera *comprender* su plan.

Figure up. He quickly *figured up* the bill.
En seguida *calculó* la cuenta.

Fill in. *Fill in* all the blanks.
Llene los espacios en blanco.

He *filled* me *in* on all that had happened.
Me *informó* de todo lo sucedido.

Fill out. *Fill out* all the forms.
Complete todas las solicitudes.

Find fault with. They were constantly *finding fault with* one another.
Siempre estaban *criticándose*.

Find out. *Find out* what the pretty girl's name is.
Averigua el nombre de la muchacha bonita.

Firsthand. He got the news *firsthand* from the hero.
Averiguó las noticias *directamente* del héroe.

Fit as a fiddle. After his vacation he felt *fit as a fiddle*.
Volvió de sus vacaciones *en buena salud*.

Flash in the pan. His first novel was a *flash in the pan* but he never wrote another good one.
Su primera novela *fué un exito* pero nunca escribió otra buena.

Fly in the ointment. Having to take him along is the one *fly in the ointment*.
Tener que llevarlo a él es *el problema*.

Fool around. It has to be turned in shortly, so don't *fool around*.
Hay que terominarlo prnto, así que no *pierdas el tiempo*.

Foot the bill. Who will *foot the bill* for his education?
¿Quién *pagará los gastos* de su educación?

For a song. They bought the estate *for a song* because the owners went bankrupt.
Compraron la mansión *por casi nada* porque los dueños estaban en bancarrota.

For good. If he leaves now, it will be *for good*.
Si se va ahora, será *para siempre*.

For the time being. The money is sufficient *for the time being*.
El dinero es suficiente *por ahora*.

Forty winks. He looks refreshed because he had time to take *forty winks*.
Luce descansado porque tuvo tiempo de tomar una *siestecita*.

Free-lance. A *free-lance* writer must have a good agent.
Un escritor *independiente* tiene que tener un buen agente.

From A to Z. He knows the song *from A to Z*.
Se sabe la canción *del principio al fin*.

Game leg. He has a *game leg* from an automobile accident.
El *cojea* por causa de un accidente de automóvil.

Get about. He *gets about* with a cane since the accident.
Desde el accidente *se levanta y anda* con un bastón.

Get across. I couldn't *get* it *across* to him that something was wrong.
No pude *hacer* le *comprender* que algo anormal ocurría.

Get along. We barely *get along* on our combined salaries.
Con nuestros sueldos difícilmente *nos las arreglamos*.

It's late and he should be *getting along*.
Ya es tarde y él debe *marcharse*.

Mother-in-law and son-in-law *get along* well in our family.
La suegra y el yerno *se llevan* bien en nuestra familia.

Get at. The boy was trying to *get at* the freshly baked cookies.
El niño estaba tratando de *tocar* los panecitos.

What are you *getting at*, with that long story?
¿Qué *quieres conseguir* con esa historia larga?

Get away. The kidnaper *got away* without leaving a clue.
El secuestrador *se escapó* sin dejar rastro.

Get back. He just *got back* from two weeks in Florida.
Acaba de *regresar* de Florida donde estuvo por dos semanas.

He never *got* his money *back*.
Nunca pudo *recuperar* su dinero.

Get by. You'll never *get by* the first policeman.
No podrás *pasar sin ser visto* por el primer policía.

Get even with.   She'll *get even with* him for hurting her.
Ella *se vengará de* él por haberla ofendido.

Get going.   *Get going* before I hit you.
Ponte en marcha antes de que te pegue.

Get in.   She'll *get in* on the last train.
Llegará en el último tren.

It's a good business and we'll *get in*, too, before long.
Es un buen negocio y *entraremos en él* muy pronto.

As soon as they *get in* the newspapers, they sell them.
Tan pronto como *reciben* los periódicos los venden.

Get in one's hair.   She's a nuisance but don't let her *get in your hair*.
Ella es un estorbo, pero no te dejes *incomodar* por eso.

Get in touch with.   I'll *get in touch with* you the moment I see him.
*Me comunicaré con*tigo tan pronto le vea.

Get in with.   She wants to *get in with* the right people.
Ella quiere *asociarse con* la gente de importancia.

Get it.   You'll *get it* if you break that.
Recibirás un castigo si lo rompes.

Did you get what I said? Yes I *got it*.
¿Compraste lo que te pedí?—Sí, *lo compré.*

Get off.   They *got off* the train in a hurry.
Bajaron del tren rápidamente.

We'll *get off* a telegram to them.
Le *mandaremos* un telegrama a ellos.

Get on.   They *got on* the boat as it started.
Subieron al barco cuando empezaba a moverse.

Now that they've left, we can *get on* with the story.
Ahora que se fueron, podemos *continuar* con la historia.

Get on your hat and coat and leave.
Ponte el sombrero y el abrigo y márchate.

Get on one's nerves.   Her jokes *get on my nerves*.
Sus bromas *me desesperan.*

Get on the bandwagon.   Let's *get on the bandwagon* and celebrate with the rest.
Unámonos a la fiesta y celebremos con ellos.

Get out.   He wanted to *get out* his book by fall.
Quiso *publicar* su libro en el otoño.

Don't let that story *get out* until tomorrow.
Ne dejes que *se publique* esa historia hasta mañana.

Get out of hand.   The party *got out of hand* the moment the drinking started.
La fiesta *se descontroló* tan pronto empezaron a beber.

Get over.   He'll soon *get over* that love affair.
Pronto *olvidará* esa aventura de amor.

What time will you *get over* here?
¿A qué hora *llegarás* aquí?

Get over with.   I'll tell him now and *get* it *over with*.
Se lo diré y así *termino* este asunto.

Get ready.   See that she *gets ready* early.
Ocúpate de que ella *se prepare* temprano.

Get rid of.   I want to *get rid of* that old coat.
Quiero *disponer de* este abrigo viejo.

Get the better of.   He always *gets the better of* the bargain.
Siempre *sale ganando*.

Get the upper hand.   She *got the upper hand* in the affair by trickery.
Ella se *adueñó* del problema con triquiñuelas.

Get through.   I hope to *get through* with this lesson by noon.
Espero *terminar* esta lección al mediodía.

Get to.   When do we *get to* see you again?
¿Cuándo *volveremos* a verte otra vez?

Get together.   We'll *get together* after school in the drugstore.
Nos reuniremos en la farmacia después de la escuela.

They *got together* on the plan.
Se pusieron de acuerdo en el plan.

Get under one's skin.   She was so beautiful she began to *get under his skin*.
Era tan bonita que empezó a *conquistarle*.

Get wind of.   They *got wind of* our plans from our nosy maid.
Se enteraron de nuestros planes por nuestra criada habladora.

Ghost of a chance. She never had the *ghost of a chance* of marrying him.
Ella nunca tuvo *la menor probabilidad* de casarse con él.

Gift of gab. He can convince anybody of anything with that *gift of gab*.
Con *la labia* que *tiene* convence a cualquiera de cualquier cosa.

Gimmick. What's the *gimmick* in this wonderful deal?
¿Cuál es la *clave* en este gran negocio?

Give a buzz (give a call). *I'll give* you *a buzz* later and tell you about it.
Te llamaré por teléfono más tarde y te lo contaré.

Give a good account of. He *gave a good account of* himself in school.
Salió muy bien en la escuela.

Give a piece of one's mind. She *gave* him *a piece of her mind* about his drinking.
Ella le *dijo las verdades* acerca de sus borracheras.

Give a rap. You don't *give a rap* about my comfort.
No te importa un bledo mi comodidad.

Give-and-take. The *give-and-take* between the lawyers became very sharp.
El *toma y daca* entre los abogados se hizo muy evidente.

Give in. He *gave in* after prolonged pressure.
Se rindió después de prolongada presión.

Give off. The aroma the coffee *gave off* was delightful.
El aroma que *dió* el café era delicioso.

Give out. I'll *give out* the tickets for the concert.
Repartiré las entradas para el concierto.

The food *gave out* early in the day.
Los alimentos *se agotaron* temprano en el día.

Give rise to. Insecurity *gives rise to* many mental ills.
La inseguridad *produce* muchas preocupaciones mentales.

Give the cold shoulder. She *gave* me *the cold shoulder* for not calling her sooner.
Me *viró la espalda* por no haberla llamado antes.

Give up. They *gave up* hope of finding the lost child.
Perdieron la esperanza de encontrar al niño perdido.

Give way. The railing *gave way* under his weight.
La baranda *se rompió* bajo el peso de él.

Go-ahead. When he got the *go-ahead* from his lawyer, he talked.
Cuando su abogado *le avisó* él habló.

Go around. There were enough lollypops to *go around*.
Los caramelos *alcanzaron para todos*.

Go back on one's word. She was most unreliable, always *going back on her word*.
Siempre *faltaba a su palabra*, por eso no se podía confiar en ella.

Go for. She has *gone for* the priest.
Fué a *buscar* al cura.

John *went for* Betty the first time he saw her.
John *se enamoró de* Betty la primera vez que la vió.

Go-getter. The boss has succeeded because he is a *go-getter*.
El jefe ha triunfado porque es *ambicioso en su trabajo*.

Go in for. She *goes in for* the most advanced modern art.
Ella *se interesa en* el arte moderno más avanzado.

Go into. The professor will *go into* the fine points of the book tomorrow.
El profesor *discutirá* mañana la parte más importante del libro.

Go off. The fire-crackers *went off* with a bang.
Los voladores *se descargaron* con estruendo.

She was glad to *go off* by herself.
Ella se alegró de *irse* por sí misma.

The concert *went off* as scheduled.
El concierto *comenzó* a la hora acordada.

Go on. *Go on* and do it if you can.
Sigue y hazlo si puedes.

The lawyer had little information to *go on*.
El abogado tenía poca información para *iniciar el caso*.

Go out. The light in the window *went out*.
La luz en la ventana *se apagó*.

He often *went out* to dinner with her.
Salió a menudo a comer con ella.

Go out of one's way. I *go out of my way* to keep you happy.
Hago todo lo posible para hacerte feliz.

Go over. The lawyer *went over* the case once more.
El abogado *examinó* el caso una vez más.

They hope their candidate will *go over* with a bang.
Esperan que su candidato *tenga éxito.*

Go straight. Do you think he will *go straight* if the judge suspends
sentence?
¿Cree Ud. que él *viva honestamente* si el juez suspende la sentencia?

Go through. The heiress *went through* her fortune within the year.
La heredera *gastó* su fortuna en un año.

Go through with. The builders *went through with* their original
plans.
Los constructores *completaron* sus planes originales.

Go to bat for. He *went to bat for* his friend before the judge.
Ayudó a su amigo ante el juez.

Go to pot. The hotel has *gone to pot* since his wife died.
El hotel *quebró* después de la muerte de su esposa.

Go to the dogs. He drank heavily and quickly *went to the dogs.*
Bebía mucho y pronto se *arruinó.*

Go without saying. It *goes without saying* that the Philharmonic
is wonderful.
No hay que decirlo que la Filarmónica es magnífica.

Go wrong. Everything *went wrong* at that awful party.
Todo *salió mal* en esa fiesta desagradable.

He *went wrong* in his early youth.
Se descarrió en su juventud.

Half-baked. *Half-baked* ideas never succeed.
Las ideas *poco juiciosas* nunca triunfan.

Halfhearted. *Halfhearted* applause makes an actor furious.
Los aplausos *fríos* ponen al actor furioso.

Hand in. Students will *hand in* homework at nine o'clock.
Los estudiantes *presentarán* sus trabajos a las nueve.

Hand in hand (hand in glove). Husband and wife worked *hand
in hand.*
Los esposos trabajon *de acuerdo.*

Hand over. He *handed over* his money to her.
El le *entregó* su dinero a ella.

Hand to mouth. People think a poet lives from *hand to mouth*.
La gente se cree que un poeta vive *de un día para otro*.

Handle with kid gloves. The director *handled* the actress *with kid gloves*.
El director *trata* a la actriz *con sumo cuidado*.

Hang around. Don't let adolescents *hang around* saloons.
No permita a los adolescentes *reunirse en* los bares.

Hang on. *Hang on* to what you have while you're looking for more.
Agárrate a lo que tienes mientras buscas más.

Hang up. After a half hour of telephone conversation, he *hung up*.
Colgó el teléfono después de conversar por media hora.

Hard-boiled. The boy who set the fire is a *hard-boiled* character.
El muchacho que prendió el fuego tiene un carácter *cruel*.

Have a bone to pick. She always *has a bone to pick* with her poor husband.
Siempre *tiene algún asunto que aclarar* con su pobre esposo.

Have a chip on one's shoulder. He always *has a chip on his shoulder* and therefore is unhappy.
Siempre *es pendenciero* y por eso es infeliz.

Have a crush. The boy *has a crush* on his pretty classmate.
El muchacho *está enamorado* de su compañera bonita.

Have a day off. He works hard and only *has a day off* occasionally.
Trabaja mucho y pocas veces *tiene un día libre*.

Have a good time. They both *had a good time* at that gay gathering.
Los dos *se divertieron* en esa fiesta alegre.

Have a lot on the ball. She's very capable and *has a lot on the ball*.
Ella es muy capaz y *tiene mucha habilidad*.

Have a screw loose. She talks in such a queer fashion she must *have a screw loose*.
Habla en tal forma que debe *tener un tornillo flojo*.

Have cold feet. He *has cold feet* about getting up on a platform.
Tiene miedo de subir a la plataforma.

Have a drag.   If the owner of the car *has a drag* with the police-man, he'll not get a parking ticket.
Si el dueño del automóvil *tiene influencia* con el policía, no le pondrán una multa.

Have irons in the fire.   He always had a couple of *irons in the fire* as far as business went.
En cuanto a negocios siempre tenía *un par de ellos entre manos*.

Have it out.   The lawyers decided to *have it out* in the courtroom.
Los abogados decidieron *aclarar las cosas* en el juzgado.

Have one's hands full.   Mother *has her hands full* fixing three meals a day.
Mi madre *tiene mucho que hacer* preparando tres comidas al día.

Have one's heart in one's mouth.   As he climbed ever higher he *had his heart in his mouth*.
Mientras más subía más *tenía el alma en un hilo*.

Have one's heart set on.   The girl *had her heart set on* going to the dance.
La muchacha *estaba loca por* ir al baile.

Have one's own way.   His wife wanted to *have her own way* about everything.
Su esposa siempre quería *salirse cod la suya*.

Have pull.   The lawyer *had pull* with the judge, that's why he won the case.
El abogado *tenía influencia* con el juez, por eso ganó el pleito.

Have something on one's mind.   She's preoccupied because she *has something on her mind*.
Está preocupada porque *tiene muchos problemas*.

Have under one's thumb.   She's bossy and *has* her husband *under her thumb*.
Ella es mandona y al esposo lo *tiene en la mano*.

Head for.   She *headed for* the restroom to fix her make-up.
Fué al servicio de señoras a arreglarse la cara.

Head or tail.   I can't make *head or tail* of what she says.
No puedo *entender nada* de lo que dice.

Head over heels.   She fell *head over heels* for her handsome boss.
Se enamoró *locamente* de su jefe.

Hit.   The comedian was a *hit* in the play.
El cómico fué un *éxito* en la obra.

Hit it off. The two boys *hit it off* immediately and became great friends.
Los dos muchachos *simpatizaron* en seguida y se hicieron grandes amigos.

Hit the ceiling. When he lies to me I *hit the ceiling.*
Cuando me miente *me enfado.*

Hit the nail on the head. You *hit the nail on the head* when you said I was broke.
Tenías razón cuando dijiste que no tenía dinero.

Hold back. The lawyer *held back* the news I wanted most to hear.
El abogado *se reservó* lo que yo más quería oír.

Hold down. He *held down* an important job.
El *mantuvo* un empleo importante.

Hold forth. How long will he *hold forth* on that boring subject?
¿Cuándo terminará de *hablar* sobre este tema tan aburrido?

Hold good. The ban on liquor *held good* for a long time.
La Ley Seca *duró* mucho tiempo.

Hold on. The telephone operator told me to *hold on.*
La operadora de teléfono me dijo que *esperara.*

Hold on to. How do you expect to *hold on to* your maid if you don't treat her well?
¿Cómo esperas *retener* a tu criada si no la tratas bien?

Hold one's horses. *Hold your horses,* girls, the boys will soon arrive.
Cálmense, muchachas, los jóvenes llegarán pronto.

Hold one's tongue. Don't tell her the secret because she can't *hold her tongue.*
No le digas el secreto porque ella no puede *callarse.*

Hold out. He *held out* without food or water till they found him.
Pudo sobrevivir sin alimento o agua hasta que lo encontraron.

He *held out* despite the torture.
A pesar de la tortura *pudo resistir.*

Holdover. That law is a *holdover* from the last administration.
La ley *continúa* desde la otra administración.

Hold over. The movie *was held over* an extra day.
La película *se exhibió* un día más.

Hold the line. We must *hold the line* against inflation.
Debemos *hacer frente* a la inflación.

Hold up.   He was *held up* in the street and robbed.
Lo *asaltaron* y robaron en la calle.

His plane *was held up* by the violent storm.
Su avión *fué demorado* a causa de una tormenta violenta.

Hold water.   Her explanations could not *hold water.*
Sus explicaciones eran *ilógicas.*

Holding the bag.   I'll suffer severely if you run away and leave
me *holding the bag.*
Sufriré mucho si te vas y me dejas *con el problema en las manos.*

Hot air.   Don't believe the story because it's just a lot of *hot air.*
No creas la historia porque es *muy falsa.*

How come.   *How come* you don't want to see me any more?
¿*Cómo es* que no quieres verme más?

Hurry up.   Let's *hurry up* and finish the job.
Apurémonos y terminemos el trabajo.

In a body.   The police arrived *in a body* at the scene of the crime.
La policía llegó *de una vez* a la escena del crimen.

In a jam.   I'll be *in a* terrible *jam* if you don't lend me the money.
Si no me prestas el dinero me encontraré en un *compromiso
serio.*

In a jiffy.   When they smelled the food, they came *in a jiffy.*
Cuando olieron la comida vinieron *en seguida.*

In a nutshell.   This, *in a nutshell,* is all I have to say.
Esto es, *en pocas palabras,* todo lo que tengo que decir.

In a person's shoes.   I wouldn't want to be *in his shoes.*
No quisiera estar metido *en sus zapatos.*

In a way.   I'm sorry for him *in a way,* but he really deserves it.
Hasta cierto punto le compadezco, pero se lo merece.

In any event.   *In any event,* come see me when I get back.
De todos modos, ven a verme cuando regrese.

In clover.   Since the big boom in stocks he's been living *in clover.*
Desde que las acciones han subido está viviendo *como un rey.*

In dutch.   *He's* constantly *in dutch* with the police.
Siempre *tiene líos* con la policía.

In one's right mind.   How can one stay *in one's right mind* with
so much noise?
¿Cómo puede uno *estar tranquilo y no estar loco* con tanto ruido?

In order. The elevator was *in order* and we went upstairs in it.
El elevador estaba *arreglado* y subimos en él.

In plain English. I am telling you *in plain English* never to come around any more.
Sin miramientos te digo que no vuelvas más por aquí.

In the dark. We were kept *in the dark* about how he earned a living.
Nos quedamos *en ayunas* en cuanto a como se ganaba la vida.

In the doghouse. I'm always *in the doghouse* with my wife.
Siempre estoy *de malas* con mi esposa.

In the dumps. The boy has been *in the dumps* since his dog died.
El muchacho está *desconsalado* desde que murió su perro.

In the long run. *In the long run*, honesty always pays.
A la larga, la honestidad siempre recompensa.

In the nick of time. The firemen arrived *in the nick of time* and saved them all.
Los bomberos llegaron *en el último minuto* y los salvaron a todos.

In the same boat. We're all *in the same boat*, getting home late, and we'll all be punished.
Estamos *en las mismas circunstancias* por llegar tarde y nos castigarán a todos.

In the wind. It's *in the wind* that you're to be promoted.
Se dice que vas a ser ascendido.

Ins and outs. He knows the *ins and outs* of bureaucratic procedures.
Se sabe los *detalles* del procedimiento burocrático.

Iron out. Let's *iron out* this trouble now.
Vamos a *allanar* este problema ahora.

Jack up. I'm not going to buy here because the prices have been *jacked up*.
No compro aquí porque *han subido* los precios.

Jot down. I'll *jot down* your name and address in my book.
Anotaré tu nombre y dirección en mi libreta.

Jump at. She *jumped at* his invitation to the dance.
Se apresuró a aceptar su invitación al baile.

Jump the gun. We're going to *jump the gun* and leave right now.
Nos adelantamos y nos marchamos ahora mismo.

Jump to a conclusion. Don't *jump to the conclusion* that these pearls are real because I'm a millionaire.
Porque soy un millonario *no creas que* estas perlas son genuinas.

Keep a stiff upper lip. She *kept a stiff upper lip* throughout his illness.
Fué valiente durante toda su enfermedad.

Keep a straight face. He can't *keep a straight face* when he tells a joke.
No puede *permanecer serio (quedarse serio)* cuando dice una broma.

Keep abreast of. How can one *keep abreast of* all the scientific developments?
¿Cómo puede uno *estar al corriente de* todos los adelantos científicos?

Keep an eye on. *Keep an eye on* the cat while we're away.
Cuida al gato mientras no estamos aquí.

Keep company. The young man and women *kept company* for a year, then married.
El joven *cortejó* a la joven por un año, después se casaron.

Keep house. The elder girl *kept house* because there was no mother.
La mayor *se ocupó de la casa* al no haber madre.

Keep in hand. She was *kept in hand* by a stern father.
Ella fué *controlada* por un padre firme.

Keep in mind. *Keep in mind* your father's advice.
Ten presente los consejos de tu padre.

Keep in touch with. *Keep in touch with* your family, wherever the army may send you.
Comunícate con tu familia, no importa a donde te mande el ejército.

Keep on. *Keep on* writing daily.
Sigue escribiendo diariamente.

Keep one's chin up. She *kept her chin up* in the face of poverty.
A pesar de la pobreza ella *no se dejó vencer.*

Keep one's head. Even during the fire she *kept her head* and helped others.
Aun durante el fuego ella *no perdió el control* y ayudó a otros.

Keep one's shirt on. *Keep your shirt on* and listen to what I
have to say.
No te excites y oye lo que yo tengo que decir.

Keep one's temper. He *kept his temper* despite the insults.
No perdió la calma a pesar de los insultos.

Keep out. I told him to *keep out* of my affairs.
Le dije que *no se metiera* en mis asuntos.

Keep the ball rolling. It was a dull debate but he tried to *keep
the ball rolling* on both sides.
Fué un debate aburrido, pero él trató de *animarlo* por ambas
partes.

Keep the wolf from the door. The widow had to work hard to
keep the wolf from the door.
La viuda tuvo que trabajar mucho para *no pasar hambre*.

Keep track of. *Keep track of* all the money you spend by noting
it down in a little book.
Lleva la cuenta de todo el dinero que gastes en una libretica.

Keep up. If you *keep up* the good work, you'll succeed.
Si *sigues* trabajando bien tendrás éxito.

Keep up with. He *kept up with* the news by listening to the radio
broadcasts.
Se mantuvo al corriente de la noticias oyendo la radio.

Kick in. Everybody *kicked in* to buy the boss a present.
Todo el mundo *contribuyó* para hacerle un regalo al jefe.

Kick out. He was *kicked out* of school for drinking.
Lo *expulsaron* de la escuela por beber.

Kick the bucket. He'll be rich when his uncle *kicks the bucket*.
El será rico cuando *muera* su tío.

Kill time. I even read the comics at the dentist's to *kill time*.
Aun leí los muñequitos en el dentista para *matar el tiempo*.

Kill two birds with one stone. On this trip we expect to *kill
two birds with one stone*, by getting to Paris and buying a
Renault there.
En este viaje pensamos *matar dos pájaros de un tiro*, ir a París
y comprar un automóvil Renault allí.

Knock off. If you *knock off* now and rest, you'll be strong enough
to finish later.
Si *suspendes el trabajo* ahora y descansas, te sentirás más fuerte
para terminarlo luego.

Know-how. The college graduate doesn't have the *know-how* for this kind of job.
El recién graduado no tiene la *habilidad* necesaria para este empleo.

Know on which side one's bread is buttered. If he *knows on which side his bread is buttered*, he'll try to get along with his rich uncle.
Si él *sabe lo que le conviene*, tratará de llevarse bien con su tío rico.

Know one's stuff. When it comes to algebra, he *knows his stuff*.
Cuando se trata del álgebra, él *sabe lo que está haciendo*.

Know the ropes. To be a good director, you have to *know the ropes* about the acting profession.
Para ser un buen director hay que *estar al tanto de los detalles* de la profesión teatral.

Ladies' man. Don Juan was quite a *ladies' man*.
Don Juan fué un *gran galante*.

Laid up. She's been *laid up* with the flu for a week.
Está *recluída* por una semana a causa de la gripe.

Land-office business. They did a *land-office business* selling umbrellas during the rainy season.
Hicieron un *gran negocio* vendiendo paraguas en la estación de la lluvia.

Last straw. The bad news about his son was the *last straw* and hastened his death.
Las malas noticias acerca de su hijo fueron *el colmo* y apresuraron su muerte.

Laugh up one's sleeve. I *laughed up my sleeve* at his awful verses.
Me reí interiormente de sus pésimos versos.

Lay off. He was *laid off* because he drank.
Lo *dejaron cesante* por beber.

Lay off that subject; it's too controversial.
No toques ese tema; es muy controvertible.

Lead by the nose. It's pitiful the way she *leads* her husband *by the nose*.
Da lástima ver la forma en que ella *domina* a su esposo.

Leak out. Word about his nomination *leaked out* in spite of all the secrecy.
A pesar de todo el secreto *se supo* su nombramiento.

Leave flat. She *left* him *flat* at the altar.
Lo *dejó plantado* en el altar.

Leave in the lurch. When he gambled away the money, she *left* him *in the lurch*.
Ella lo *abandonó* cuando perdió el dinero en el juego.

Leave no stone unturned. *Leave no stone unturned* in your search for the kidnaper.
No dejes piedra sin mover en la búsqueda del raptor.

Leave out. Don't *leave out* my name when you tell about the discovery.
No omitas mi nombre cuando anuncies el descubrimiento.

Leave someone high and dry. At first they were inseparable, but then he *left her high and dry*.
Al principio ellos eran inseparables, pero después él la *abandonó*.

Leave word. I *left word* to give the baby his bottle at six.
Dejé dicho que le dieran el pomo al niñito a las seis.

Leave a person flat. He *left her flat* when the trip was over.
La dejó plantada cuando se terminó el viaje.

Left-handed compliment. It's a *left-handed compliment* to say she's beautiful for her age.
Es un *elogio mal intencionado* decir que ella está hermosa para su edad.

Leg to stand on. Despite his excuses, we know he didn't have a *leg to stand on*.
A pesar de sus excusas, sabemos que no tenía *razones en que apoyarse*.

Lend a hand. *Lend a hand*, please, or we'll never finish this job.
Ayúdanos, por favor, o no terminaremos el trabajo.

Let alone. *Let (me) alone* and go away.
Déjame en paz y vete.

Let bygones be bygones. We mean to be friends and *let bygones be bygones*.
Queremos ser amigos y *lo que pasó, pasó*.

Let down. Don't *let* me *down* now when I need your help.
No me *falles* ahora que necesito tu ayuda.

Let go. *Let (me) go* this time, and I won't do it again.
Déjame ir, no lo volveré a hacer.

Let go of me, you brute.
Suéltame, bruto.

Let in on.   She was the only one we *let in on* the secret.
Ella fué la única persona a quien le *dijimos* el secreto.

Let me out.   *Let me out* of here right now.
Déjeme salir de aquí ahora mismo.

Let off.   The policeman *let* her *off* with a warning.
La policía la *dejó en libertad*, pero con una amonestación.

Let on.   Don't *let on* that you know who I am.
No *reveles* que sabes quién soy.

Let one's hair down.   She *let her hair down* and told me all her troubles.
Se sintió en confianza y me contó todos sus problemas.

Let oneself go.   If she were to *let herself go*, she'd get fat.
Si ella *se descuidase*, se pondría gorda.

Let the cat out of the bag.   Don't *let the cat out of the bag* about their elopement.
No *descubras el secreto* acerca de la fuga de ellos.

Let up.   Why don't you *let up* on me and bother someone else?
¿Por qué no me *dejas tranquilo* y fastidias a otra persona?

Like a fish out of water.   The actress felt *like a fish out of water* among the housewives.
La actriz se sintió *como el pez fuera del aqua* entre las esposas.

Live up to.   It's hard to *live up to* the standards set by our parents.
Es difícil *vivir de acuerdo con* las normas que nuestros padres establecen.

Long face.   For a month after the funeral, he went around with a *long face*.
Por un mes después del entierro, él tenía *una cara muy triste*.

Look after.   The governess *looked after* the two children.
La institutriz *se ocupó de* los dos niños.

He *looked after* her as she walked down the street.
El la *siguió con la vista* cuando caminaba por la calle.

Look down on.   Don't *look down on* me because I'm a poor man.
No me *desprecie* porque soy un hombre pobre.

Look forward to.   We're *looking forward to* seeing you again.
Esperamos con placer verte otra vez.

Look high and low.   She *looked high and low* for the child's lost doll.
Buscó por todas partes la muñeca perdida de la niña.

Look into. The store promised to *look into* the matter of the overcharge.
La tienda prometió *investigar* el asunto de la cuenta errónea.

Look on. She *looks on* while the others work hard.
Ella *mira* mientras las otras trabajan duro.

Look out. *Look out* for temptations; they are hard to resist.
Cuídate de las tentaciones son difíciles de resistir.

Look out upon. Our apartment *looks out upon* the reservoir.
Nuestro apartamiento *mira* a la represa.

Look over. The boy *looked* the girl *over*.
El muchacho *observó* a la muchacha.

Look someone up. *Look me up* when you're in New York.
Ven a verme cuando estés en Nueva York.

Look up. Where could I *look up* the meaning of that expression?
¿Dónde puedo *encontrar* el significado de esta expresión?

Look up to. The priests *look up to* the Pope.
Los curas *miran con respeto* al Papa.

Lose one's mind. When she heard of his death she almost *lost her mind*.
Cuando supo de su muerte por poco *se vuelve loca*.

Lose one's shirt. He *lost his shirt* in the stock-market crash.
Perdió hasta la camisa en la baja de la Bolsa.

Lose one's temper. She *lost her temper* and hit him when he laughed at her.
Perdió el control y le pegó cuando se rió de ella.

Maiden name. Mrs. Smith denied that her *maiden name* had been Jones.
La Señora Smith negó que su *nombre de soltera* había sido Jones.

Make a beeline for. As it was cold, I *made a beeline for* the fireside.
Como hacía frío *fuí en seguida* al fuego.

Make a break. The two partners decided it was time to *make a clean break*.
Los dos compañeros de negocios decidieron que era hora de *descontinuar* el contrato en buena forma.

Make a clean breast. She *made a clean breast* of her behavior to her husband.
Ella *confesó* su conducta ante su esposo.

Make a face.   He *made a face* when I asked his girl for a dance.
Hizo una mueca cuando pedí a su compañera bailar conmigo.

Make a good living.   He *makes a good living* for such a young man
El *gana bastante dinero* para ser un hombre joven.

Make a killing.   He's rich because he *made a killing* in the stock market.
Está rico porque *tuvo suerte* en los negocios de la Bolsa.

Make a mess out of.   You'll *make a mess out of* your life if you divorce him.
Vas a *arruinar* tu vida si te divorcias de él.

Make a mountain out of a molehill.   No matter how small the task she *makes a mountain out of a molehill.*
Ella *exagera cualquier cosa* no importa lo insignificante que sea.

Make a play for.   That pretty secretary is *making a play for* the boss.
La secretaria está *tratando de conquistar* al jefe.

Make a racket.   Those children *make* such *a racket,* I can't sleep.
Esos muchachos *hacen* tanta *bulla* que no puedo dormir.

Make a train.   If we don't *make a* nine o'clock *train,* we'll be too late to see her.
Si no *salimos en el tren* de las nueve, no vamos a poder verla.

Make allowance for.   We have to *make allowance for* the fact that at least he tried.
Debemos *tener en cuenta* que por lo menos trató de hacerlo.

Make anything of it.   His argument is so complex I can't *make anything of it.*
Su argumento es tan complejo que no *lo entiendo nada.*

Make believe.   The soldier *made believe* he was dead.
El soldado *fingió* estar muerto.

Make ends meet.   With inflation it is difficult to *make ends meet.*
Con la inflación no se gana lo suficiente *para vivir.*

Make eyes at.   She *made eyes at* him because she was a flirt.
Le *miró amorosamente* porque ella era una coqueta.

Make for.   Let's *make for* home before this storm gets worse.
Vamos a casa antes de que la tormenta se ponga peor.

Make fun of.   His classmates *made fun of* the new boy.
Sus compañeros *se burlaron* del muchacho nuevo.

Make good. If you want to *make good*, work hard.
Si quieres *tener éxito*, trabaja duro.

Make good money. As president of the concern he *makes good money*.
Como presidente de la compañía *gana buen sueldo*.

Make good time. We *made good time* on our last trip.
Ganamos tiempo en el último viaje nuestro.

Make hay while the sun shines. Business is good and I'm *making hay while the sun shines*.
Los negocios están buenos y me *aprovecho de la ocasión*.

Make it snappy. Mother told me to *make it snappy* and get out of the rain.
Mi madre me dijo que *me apurara* y que saliera de la lluvia.

Make no bones about. She *made no bones about* wanting a raise.
No se anduvo con rodeos en cuanto a desear aumento de sueldo.

Make one's blood boil. It *made my blood boil* to hear him shout at her.
Me disgustó ver como él le gritaba a ella.

Make oneself scarce. Whenever the boss is here *make yourself scarce*.
Cada vez que el jefe esté aquí *váyase con disimulo*.

Make out. He *made out* a check for his son's music teacher.
Escribió un cheque para el maestro de música de su hijo.

She *made out* fine with her checking account.
Ella *se mantuvo bien* con su cuenta corriente de cheques.

Can you *make out* the items on this grocery list?
¿Puedes *identificar* los pedidos en esta lista de comestibles?

Make over. I'm going to *make over* that old dress into a blouse.
Voy a *convertir* ese vestido viejo en una blusa.

Make sure. *Make sure* you lock the door.
Esté seguro de cerrar la puerta.

Make the grade. You'll never *make the grade* if you don't work harder.
No *tendrás éxito* si no trabajas duro.

Make the most of. *Make the most of* your present leisure.
Aprovecha todo lo posible tus vacaciones.

Make up.   The counselors *made up* all the camp rules.
Los consejeros *hicieron* el reglamento del campamento de verano.

He *made up* a story to tell his teacher about his tardiness.
Inventó una historia para explicar su tardanza al maestro.

She *makes up* in her room before she comes down for coffee.
Ella *se hace el maquillaje* en su cuarto antes de bajar para tomar café.

The young couple finally *made up* after their quarrel.
La joven pareja *hizo* finalmente *las paces* después de la riña.

Make up for.   We'll *make up for* the extra time you put in with a big bonus.
Te *compensaremos* por haber trabajado extra con un bono grande.

Make up one's mind.   *Make up your mind* now whether you want to take the job.
Decide ahora si deseas aceptar el trabajo.

Make-up.   Her *make-up* was put on poorly.
Su *maquillaje* no estaba bien hecho.

Man in the street.   We must find out what the *man in the street* is thinking.
Debemos averiguar lo que el *ciudadano común* está pensando.

Mean well.   She made a mess out of the job, even though she *meant well*.
Hizo un lío del trabajo a pesar de *haber tenido buena intención*.

Meet halfway.   If you *meet* me *halfway*, we'll be able to conclude the deal.
Si *hacemos* el negocio *a la mitad*, lo podremos hacer.

Miss the point.   He *missed the point* of the story.
El *no comprendió el objetivo* del cuento.

Mixed-up.   How can we find it with such *mixed-up* directions?
¿Cómo podremos encontrarlo con direcciones tan *confusas?*

Monkey around with.   If you *monkey around with* that car you'll ruin the engine.
Si te *pones a jugar con* ese automóvil vas a arruinar el motor.

Narrow escape.   The child ran towards the train and had a *narrow escape*.
El niño corrió hacia el tren y se *salvó por un pelo*.

Near miss. The first bomb was a *near miss*.
La primera bomba por *poquito les cae*.

Neck and neck. It was *neck and neck* all the way through the race.
La carrera fué *lado a lado* todo el tiempo.

Never mind. *Never mind* the music and keep on studying.
No te ocupes de la música y sigue estudiando.

Nick of time. We caught the train in the *nick of time*.
Cogimos el tren en el *último minuto*.

Nip in the bud. The romance was *nipped in the bud* when her father sent her away.
El noviazgo fué *cortado de raiz* cuando el padre la mandó a otra parte.

No matter. *No matter* what you do I will always love you.
Hagas lo que hicieres, siempre te amaré.

Now and then. *Now and then* we visit the Murphys.
De vez en cuando visitamos a los Murphy.

Odds and ends. Out of *odds and ends* the boys built the boat.
Los muchachos construyeron el bote con *piezas de todas clases*.

Of age. At twenty-one a boy comes *of age*.
A los veinte y un años el joven llega a la *mayoría de edad*.

Of one's own accord. She went on to graduate school *of her own accord*.
Ella continuó los estudios post-graduados *voluntariamente*.

Off day. This is an *off day* for mother—that's why she's so cross
Hoy es un *día malo* para mamá—por eso está de mal humor.

Old Glory. *Old Glory* floats proudly atop the White House.
La bandera nacional flota orgullosa encima de la Casa Blanca

Old hand. I'm an *old hand* at children's games.
Tengo *mucha experiencia* con juegos de niños.

On a shoestring. He started his business *on a shoestring*.
Comenzó su negocio *con poco dinero*.

On edge. He was *on edge* all day as the stock market fell.
Estuvo *nervioso* todo el día por la baja de las acciones.

On its last legs. This old hat is *on its last legs*.
Este sombrero viejo está *ya que no sirve*.

On occasion.   *On occasion* she'd buy a new dress.
De vez en cuando ella compraba un vestido nuevo.

On one's toes.   If you're *on your toes,* they'll never fool you.
Si te *mantienes alerta* no podrán engañarte.

On purpose.   She tore her dress *on purpose* because she wanted another.
Rompió el vestido *adrede* porque quería otro.

On the air.   The Spanish language lesson goes *on the air* daily.
La lección de español está *en el aire* diariamente.

On the ball.   That bright teacher is certainly *on the ball.*
Ese maestro brillante es realmente *muy eficiente.*

On the carpet.   He was called *on the carpet* for his mistakes.
Le reprobaron por sus errores.

On the dot.   He was always *on the dot* for meals.
Siempre está *en punto* para las comidas.

On the go.   The child is *on the go* from morning till night.
El niño está *siempre activo* desde la mañana hasta la noche.

On the house.   The second drink will be *on the house.*
El segundo trago es *por cuenta del dueño.*

On the level.   I don't think his offer is *on the level.*
No creo que su oferta es *sincera.*

On the shelf.   I feel so old, I'm ready to be put *on the shelf.*
Me siento tan viejo que *no sirvo para nada.*

On the spot.   His last question put me *on the spot.*
Su última pregunta me puso *en aprietos.*

He made his decision *on the spot.*
Hizo su decisión *en seguida.*

On the square.   His fiancée felt that he was never *on the square* with her, and couldn't trust him.
Su novia pensó que él nunca fué *leal y honrado* con ella y por eso no pudo confiar en él.

On the whole.   *On the whole* his health has improved.
En general su salud ha mejorado.

On time.   Try to get here *on time* for meals.
Sé *puntual* en las comidas.

Once and for all. *Once and for all* I'm telling you to get out.
Definitivamente te digo que te marches.

Once in a blue moon. *Once in a blue moon* he comes to see his mother.
De tarde en tarde viene a ver a su madre.

Once in a while. It never snows there, but *once in a while* it rains.
Nunca nieva allí, pero *de vez en cuando* llueve.

Once-over. The boys gave the girl the *once-over*.
Los jóvenes le dieron un *vistazo rápido* a la muchacha.

One-horse town. She comes from a *one-horse town* of a thousand people.
Ella viene de un *pueblito sin importancia* de unos mil habitantes.

Out of date. The long skirt is again *out of date*.
La saya larga está otra vez *fuera de moda*.

Out of order. The radio was *out of order* so we couldn't hear the program.
El radio estaba *descompuesto* y no pudimos oír el programa.

Out of print. That book's been *out of print* for weeks.
Ese libro está *agotado* hace muchas semanas.

Out of step. He always thinks the other person's *out of step*.
Siempre piensa que la otra persona está *en desacuerdo*.

Out of the question. An interview with the president is *out of the question*.
Una entrevista con el presidente es *imposible*.

Over and over again. The parrot says the same thing *over and over again*.
La cotorra repite lo mismo *muchas veces*.

Over one's dead body. You'll get that whisky *over my dead body*.
Tendrás que pasar *sobre mi cadáver* para coger ese whiskey.

Pass away. He *passed away* before his wife could reach his bedside.
Falleció antes de que su esposa pudiera llegar a su lado.

Pass out. She *passed out* from the heat.
Se desmayó por el calor.

Pay through the nose. They *paid through the nose* for her furs.
Pagaron un precio exorbitante por sus pieles.

Pay up. I'll be grateful if you *pay up* now.
Estaré agradecido *si pagas lo que me debes* ahora.

Pick a quarrel. They *pick a quarrel* about the most picayune things.
Ellos *arman pendencias* por las cosas más insignificantes.

Pick off. He'll *pick off* those crows one by one.
Matará uno a uno esos cuervos *con su puntería.*

Pick on. We *picked on* the youngest child to portray him as a boy.
Seleccionamos al niño más joven para que representara al muchacho.

She always *picks on* her husband.
Siempre *molesta* a su esposo.

Pick up. She *picked up* that lamp in an antique shop.
Encontró esa lámpara en una tienda de antigüedades.

She *picked up* the French inflection easily.
Adquirió la inflección francesa fácilmente.

That car *picks up speed* without your being aware of it.
Ese automóvil *aumenta la velocidad* sin uno darse cuenta.

After that last illness he *picked up* quickly.
Después de esa última enfermedad *recobró* la salud rápidamente.

Pipe down. *Pipe down*, son. Your mother's complaining about the racket.
Disminuye el ruido, hijo. Tu madre se queja de la bulla.

Play around. If you *play around* instead of concentrating, you accomplish nothing.
Si te *diviertes* en vez de concentrarte, no podrás hacer nada.

Playboy. You can be a *playboy* forever, or settle down and work hard.
Tu puedes ser un *pisaverde* toda tu vida o un joven trabajador.

Play down. The student *played down* his failures.
El estudiante *no dió importancia a* sus fracasos.

Play hooky. They *played hooky* to go swimming.
No *fueron a la escuela* para ir a nadar.

Play into the hands of. The stupid soldier *played into the hands of* his captor.
El soldado *se dejó engañer por* el enemigo.

Play safe. He *played safe* and stayed on first base instead of stealing.
Fué cauteloso y se quedó en la primera base en vez de robar la segunda.

Play second fiddle. He *plays second fiddle* to his wife.
El *está subordinado* a su esposa.

Play the market. Not many a speculator *plays the market* successfully.
No muchos corredores de acciones *especulan* con éxito el mercado.

Play the ponies. Every Saturday night he *played the ponies.*
Todos los sábados por la noche *apostaba a los caballitos.*

Play up. The democrats *played up* their gubernatorial candidate.
Los demócratas *hicieron mucha propaganda por* su candidato gubernamental.

Play up to. The student *played up to* her professor to get a good grade.
El estudiante *alabó a* su profesor para conseguir una buena calificación.

Play with fire. To love him was to *play with fire.*
Amarle fué *jugar con candela.*

Played out. After that fast game of ball I'm all *played out.*
Después de ese partido de pelota tan rápido *estoy agotado.*

Point out. He *pointed out* the fine points of the game.
El *indicó* los puntos mejores del partido.

Polish off. He *polished off* three glasses of whisky.
De un golpe se bebió tres vasos de whisky.

Pop in. I just *popped in* to say hello.
Sólo *me detuve* para saludarte.

Pop the question. He *popped the question* as she stood under the mistletoe.
El *le propuso el matrimonio* cuando ella se detuvo bajo el muérdago.

Pull a boner. You *pulled a boner* when you said "no" to her.
Cometiste un error estúpido al decirle "no" a ella.

Pull a fast one. She *pulled a fast one* on the other girls, leaving the dirty dishes.
Ella *engañó* a las otras muchachas dejando los platos por lavar.

Pull down.　Don't *pull down* the tent till the rain stops.
No *desmontes* la tienda de campaña hasta que deje de llover.

The science professors *pull down* the best salaries.
Los profesores de ciencias *ganan* los sueldos mejores.

Pull in.　The train *pulled in* on time.
El tren *llegó* a su hora.

The bank robbers were *pulled in* by the police after a chase.
Los ladrones fueron *arrestados* por la policía después de perseguirlos.

Pull off.　*Pull off* that wet coat at once!
¡*Quítate* en seguida ese saco mojado!

Don't try to *pull off* another dirty trick.
No nos *hagas* otra broma pesada.

Pull one's leg.　He's always telling me how wonderful I am, but I know he's just *pulling my leg*.
Siempre me alaba, pero sé que *me* está *tomando el pelo*.

Pull oneself together.　She stopped crying and *pulled herself together*.
Dejó de llorar y *se controló*.

Pull out.　The car *pulled out* so quietly, we never heard it leave.
El automóvil *salió* tan silenciosamente que no lo vimos.

Pull over.　*Pull over* your car to our side of the road.
Arrima el automóvil al otro lado del camino.

Pull strings (pull wires).　Around politicians one has to *pull strings* to get anywhere.
Con los politiqueros hay que *usar influencias* para conseguir lo que se quiere.

Pull the wool over someone's eyes.　You aren't *pulling the wool over my eyes*, because I don't believe a word you're saying.
No me *engañas como un bobo*, porque no te creo una palabra de lo que estás diciendo.

Pull through.　You *pulled through* that illness in record time.
Saliste de la gravedad de tu enfermedad en breve tiempo.

Pull together.　If we *pull together* hard we can get that law passed.
Si *cooperamos* podemos hacer pasar esa ley.

Pull up.　He *pulled up* the weeds by the roots.
Arrancó la maleza de raíz.

Pull up to the curb and I'll get out.
Arrímate al contén y yo salgo.

Put away.   He *put away* a large meal.
El *comió* una comida grande.

Put away your coats and come into the living room.
Pongan los abrigos en el ropero y vengan a la sala.

Put down.   *Put down* your guns and surrender.
Suelten las pistolas y ríndanse.

The police helped *put down* the strike.
La policía ayudó a *sofocar* la huelga.

He *put* it *down* to her lack of experience.
El lo *atribuyó* a la falta de experiencia de ella.

Put heads together.   By *putting* their *heads together*, they found
a solution to the problem.
Consultándose encontraron la solución del problema.

Put off.   She was always *putting off* the job.
Siempre ella está *posponiendo* el trabajo.

Put on weight.   You can *put on weight* fast eating ice cream.
Puedes *aumentar de peso* pronto comiendo helados.

Put one's cards on the table.   She *put her cards on the table* and
told us she had never really had a singing lesson.
Fué franca y nos dijo que nunca había tomado una lección de
canto.

Put one's foot down.   Her father *put his foot down* when she
wanted to stay out past midnight.
Su padre *se opuso con energía* cuando ella quiso regresar después
de medianoche.

Put one's foot in it.   You *put your foot in it* telling her she re-
minded you of your wife.
Cometiste un error en decirle a ella que se parecía a tu esposa.

Put out.   *Put out* the light and go to bed.
Apaga la luz y acuéstate.

They *put* us *out* of the apartment so their daughter could move
in.
Nos *sacaron* del apartamento para que su hija pudiera mudarse
a él.

He's very much *put out* because of all the scandal.
El está muy *disgustado* a causa de todo el escándalo.

Put two and two together.   By *putting two and two together* she
surmised what was going on.
Atando cabos ella pudo darse cuenta de lo que estaba pasando.

Put up.   Within the hour they *put up* the sign.
En una hora *instalaron* el anuncio.

After the fire, they *put* us *up* at their place.
Después del fuego ellos nos *hospedaron* en su casa.

He *put up* the thousand dollars for bail.
El *dió* los mil pesos para la fianza.

Put up with.   We cannot *put up with* you any longer because of your outrageous behavior.
No podemos *aguantarte* más por tu conducta atroz.

Queer duck.   Your guardian's a *queer duck*. He does such eccentric things.
Tu guarda espaldas es *muy raro*. Hace cosas excéntricas.

Rain cats and dogs.   It was *raining cats and dogs*.
Llovía a cántaros.

Rain or shine.   *Rain or shine* our paper is delivered on time.
Con buen o mal tiempo el periódico es distribuído a tiempo.

Raise Cain.   Her father will *raise Cain* when he hears about the elopement.
Su padre *se pondrá bravísimo* cuando se entere de la fuga de ella.

Raw deal.   He got a *raw deal* when they made him cut his vacation short.
Fué injusto que le hicieran acortar sus vacaciones.

Red tape.   There is no *red tape* in getting a visa.
No hay *papeleo* en obtener una visa.

Rest on one's laurels.   He does nothing now but *rest on his laurels*.
Todo lo que hace ahora es *dormirse en sus laureles*.

Ride high.   They're *riding high* since they won all that cash.
Viven muy bien desde que ganaron tanto dinero.

Right away.   Come home *right away* because dinner is on the table.
Ven *en seguida* porque la comida está servida.

Right-hand man.   My husband is my *right-hand man* in this undertaking.
Mi esposo es mi *brazo derecho* en esta empresa.

Right now.   Finish your milk *right now*.
Toma la leche *ahora mismo*.

Ring a bell. What you say *rings a bell* in my mind.
Lo que dices *me recuerda algo que olvidé.*

Rough it. You'll learn to *rough it* in the African bush.
Aprenderás a *vivir con incomodidades* en el bosque africano.

Rules the roost. It's the wife who *rules the roost* in that family.
Es la esposa quien *lleva los pantalones* en esa familia.

Rub someone the wrong way. His inflection *rubs me the wrong way.*
Su inflección *me cae antipática.*

Run across. We Americans *run across* many compatriots abroad.
Los americanos *nos encontramos con* muchos compatriotas en el extranjero.

Run around with. He *ran around with* the same girl for a year.
Salió con la misma chica por un año.

Run down. Because he feels *run down* he wants a vacation.
Porque está *agotado* desea una vacación.

Don't *run down* the dog with your car.
No *arrolles* al perro con tu automóvil.

The old mill was too *run down* to work.
El viejo molino estaba muy *deteriorado* para usarlo.

He's always *running down* his associates.
El siempre *abusa de* sus compañeros.

He *ran down* the list of names.
Leyó la lista de nombres.

Run into. I *ran into* her at the Mardi gras.
Me *encontré* con ella en el Mardi gras.

Run off. We'll *run off* another edition of your book.
Publicaremos otra edición de su libro.

Run out. We *ran out* of gas on our trip.
Se nos *acabó* la gasolina en el viaje.

Run up. She *runs up* bills in every store.
Ella *acumula* cuentas en todas las tiendas.

Safe and sound. I found him *safe and sound* in his own bed.
Lo encontré *sano y salvo* en su cama.

Save face. In politics you must *save face* even in defeat.
En política hay que *simular buena cara* aunque se pierda.

Scare the daylights out of.   She *scared the daylights out of* me in that witch's costume.
Se me pararon los pelos cuando la ví vestida de bruja.

Scrape together.   We *scraped together* enough to pay off the mortgage.
Pudimos reunir suficiente dinero para pagar la hipoteca.

Second-hand.   That's a *second-hand* typewriter, but it works like a new one.
Es una máquina de escribir *de uso*, pero funciona como nueva.

Second-rate.   This wine is *second-rate* and sour.
Este vino es *de segunda clase* y agrio.

See about.   Please *see about* getting dinner ready because I'm starving.
Ponte a preparar la comida porque me muero de hambre.

See eye to eye.   We never *see eye to eye* on important matters.
Nunca *estamos de acuerdo* en asuntos importantes.

See off.   We *see* her *off* to Europe every summer.
La *despedimos* cada verano cuando sale para Europa.

See red.   I *see red* when he calls me names.
Me enfurece cuando me insulta.

See stars.   I *saw stars* when I fell down those stairs.
Ví estrellas cuando me caí en la escalera.

Sell down the river.   He'd *sell* his own brother *down the river* for money.
Traicionaría a su hermano por dinero.

Sell out.   The theater is *sold out* for the first performance.
El teatro *ha vendido todas las entradas* para la primera función.

Serve a term.   She *served a term* for forgery.
Estuvo en la cárcel por falsificadora.

Set in.   Frost *sets in* by mid-November.
La escarcha *comienza* a mediados de noviembre.

Set out.   He *set out* all the papers on the table.
El *colocó* todos los papeles en la mesa.

We *set out* for Chicago tomorrow.
Salimos para Chicago mañana.

Set up.   A monarchy was *set up* for the colony.
Una monarquía *fué establecida* para la colonia.

Settle down. He's wild, but will *settle down* later on.
El es loco, pero *se formalizará* más adelante.

Setup. We think it **is** a very attractive *setup* for a restaurant.
Creemos que es una *organización buena* para restaurante.

Shell out. We'll *shell out* for any worthy charity.
Nosotros *contribuiremos con dinero* a toda obra caritativa digna.

Shift for oneself. I've *shifted for myself* since ten years of age.
Yo *me las arreglo solo* desde la edad de diez años.

Short cut. There is no *short cut* to knowledge.
El saber no se adquiere *sin esfuerzo*.

Shorthanded. The hotel was *shorthanded* on New Year's Eve because of the strike.
El hotel tuvo *pocos sirvientes* en la víspera de Año Nuevo por la huelga.

Show up. He *shows up* regularly at cocktails.
El *asiste* regularmente a los cockteles.

Show-off. Joan is a *show-off* and always boasts about her clothes.
Joan es una *ostentadora* y siempre habla de su ropa.

Shut down. Let's *shut down* for the summer, even though it means losing business.
Vamos a *cerrar* por el verano, aunque perdamos dinero en el negocio.

Shut up. The boss told the foreman to *shut up* and stop complaining.
El jefe le dijo al capataz que *se callase* y dejase de quejarse.

Side with. The working men *sided with* the foreman against the boss.
Los obreros *se pusieron al lado del* capataz y en contra del jefe.

Sit in on. The journalists *sat in on* the conference between the Russians and the Americans.
Los periodistas *estuvieron presentes en* la conferencia ruso-americana.

Sit out. Let's *sit out* this dance and talk.
Vamos a *sentarnos durante* esta pieza y hablemos.

Six of one and a half dozen of the other. It's *six of one and a half dozen of the other*, so you can do whatever you want.
Lo mismo es lo uno que lo otro, así que puedes hacer lo que quieras.

Skate on thin ice. You're *skating on thin ice* when you discuss age with a woman.
Juegas con candela cuando discutes la edad con una mujer.

Slap down. Every time she spoke, he *slapped* her *down* with sharp sarcasm.
Cada vez que habló la *rebajó* con sarcasmo.

Sleep like a top. When one is young, one generally *sleeps like a top.*
Cuando joven se *duerme como un lirón.*

Sleep on. I'll *sleep on* your advice and let you know my decision soon.
Consideraré tu consejo y te diré mi decisión pronto.

Slip of the tongue. It was a *slip of the tongue* if I called you a name.
Lo que te dije lo *dije sin querer.*

Slip through one's fingers. That huge fortune *slipped through her fingers* in no time.
Esa inmensa fortuna *se le fué* en corto tiempo.

Slouch. He's no *slouch* at tennis—that's why his scores are invariably high.
El no es un *principiante* en tennis—por eso gana siempre.

Small fry. We take the *small fry* to see Santa every Christmas.
Llevamos a los *niños* a ver Santa Claus todas las Navidades.

The men in that business are *small fry;* it's the woman who's boss.
Es la mujer la jefe; los hombres ocupan un *segundo lugar* en ese negocio.

Smell a rat. The excuse was so phony I began to *smell a rat.*
La excusa era tan rara que comencé a *oler gato encerrado.*

Sneeze at. His offer is not to be *sneezed at*, it's such a good buy.
Su oferta no es de *despreciarse*, es una buena compra.

So long. *So long* now, we'll meet again at dinner.
Hasta luego, nos veremos otra vez en la comida.

Soft-soap. Don't *soft-soap* me, you old flatterer.
No me *lisonjees*, viejo piropeador.

Sow one's wild oats. He began *sowing his wild oats* in his early teens.
Se entregó *a los placeres* en su juventud.

Speak up. Always *speak up* when you believe you're in the right.
Habla siempre *que te oigan* cuando tienes razón.

Spick-and-span. She does all her own housework and keeps things *spick-and-span*.
Ella tiene siempre su casa *limpia y ordenada*.

Split hairs. Let's not *split hairs* over definitions.
No *nos disgustemos* por definiciones.

Split the difference. Let's *split the difference* between what you ask and what I offer.
Dividamos la diferencia entre lo que pides y lo que ofrezco.

Sponge on. Don't *sponge on* your friends or you'll soon lose them.
No *abuses de* tus amigos porque los perderás pronto.

Spread like wildfire. The rumor *spread like wildfire*.
El rumor *se propagó como reguero de pólvora*.

Square deal. Roosevelt believed in a *square deal* for everyone in the country.
Roosevelt creyó en *tratos justos* para cada cual en el país.

Stand a chance. He didn't *stand a chance* of winning the girl back.
No *tuvo chance alguno* de conquistar a la muchacha otra vez.

Stand aside. We all *stood aside* as he strode down the aisle.
Nos hicimos a un lado cuando él venía por el pasillo.

Stand by. We'll *stand by* you in joy and in sorrow.
Te *auxiliaremos* en cualquier situación feliz o triste.

Stand by until you get a signal to continue.
Quédate aquí hasta que recibas señal de seguir.

Stand for. He will not *stand for* intolerance.
El no *permitirá* la intolerancia.

Our flag *stands for* justice.
Nuestra bandera *representa* la justicia.

Stand one's ground. He *stands his ground* when he thinks he's right.
Cuando cree que tiene razón, *no cambia de opinión*.

Stand out. In that red dress you *stand out* like a beacon light.
Te *destaca notablemente* en ese vestido rojo.

Stand pat. In spite of any arguments he *stood pat* for his proposal.
A pesar de mis argumentos él *defendió* su proposición.

Stand to reason. It *stands to reason* that with his inheritance he won't work anymore.
Es lógico que con su herencia no trabaje más.

Stand up for. A judge *stands up for* an honest principle.
Un juez *sale en defensa de* un principio honesto.

Stay in. They *stay in* and watch television every single night.
Se quedan en casa y ven la televisión todas las noches.

Stay put. This golf ball will not *stay put.*
Esta bola de golfo no *se queda quieta.*

Steal a march. He *stole a march* on her when he asked her father first.
El *se adelantó* a ella al pedirle su mano al padre.

Step lively. We had to *step lively* to make our train.
Tuvimos que *darnos prisa* para coger nuestro tren.

Step on the gas. *Step on the gas* or we'll be late.
Acelera o llegaremos tarde.

Stew in his own juice. After the argument she left him to *stew in his own juice.*
Después del argumento ella lo dejó que *se quemara en su propia salsa.*

Stick out like a sore thumb. He *stuck out like a sore thumb* in his red overcoat.
El *sobresalía* en su abrigo rojo.

Stick up for. I always *stick up for* my brothers and sisters.
Siempre *defiendo* a mis hermanos y hermanas.

Stick-up. The *stick-up* by an armed burglar aroused the entire neighborhood.
El *asalto* por ladrón armado alarmó a todo los vecinos.

Straight from the horse's mouth. Coming *straight from the horse's mouth*, the communiqué frightened us.
El comunicado nos alarmó por venir *de buena fuente.*

Straight from the shoulder. This talk is *straight from the shoulder*, so listen carefully.
Esta conversación es *sin ambages ni rodeos*, así que escucha atentamente.

Stretch a point. They *stretched a point* when they admitted her to a grade-A college.
Hicieron una concesión cuando la admitieron en un college de primera clase.

Strike oil. We're looking for an idea that will really *strike oil*.
Buscamos una idea que tenga *éxito completo*.

Strike while the iron is hot. If we *strike while the iron is hot*, we'll get what we're demanding.
Si nos aprovechamos de la oportunidad, obtendremos lo que pedimos.

Stuck-up. What a *stuck-up*, arrogant man our boss is!
¡Qué hombre más *presumido* y arrogante es nuestro jefe!

Stuffed shirt. He's too much of a *stuffed shirt* to be likeable.
El es un tipo muy *almidonado* para ser simpático.

Suit to a T. This dress *suits* you *to a T*.
Este vestido te *sienta perfectamente*.

Switch on. *Switch on* the radio if you want to hear the news.
Pon el radio si quieres oír las noticias.

Tail end. I left at the *tail end* of the story and missed the point.
Salí al *final* de la historia y no pude saberla toda.

Take a break. Let's *take a* ten-minute *break* for coffee.
Vamos a *tomar un descanso* por diez minutos para tomar café.

Take after. The boy *takes after* his father in appearance.
El hijo *se parece mucho a* su padre en el físico.

Take apart. After he *took apart* his radio, he couldn't put it together again.
Después de *desarmar* su radio no pudo armarlo otra vez.

Take care. *Take care* of your health.
Cuida tu salud.

Take charge of. I'll *take charge of* the office while you're on vacation.
Me encargaré de la oficina mientras estás de vacaciones.

Take down. The stenographer *takes down* everything as it's dictated.
La estenógrafa *toma nota de* todo lo que le dictan.

Take down a peg. His unflattering remarks *took* her *down a peg*.
Sus palabras la *humillaron*.

Take for granted. I *took* it *for granted* that you wanted me to remain.
Di por sentado que querías que yo me quedara.

Take hold of. *Take hold of* yourself and face up to your troubles.
Contrólate y hazle frente a tus problemas.

Take in.   He was *taken in* by her wiles.
Fué engañado por sus trampas.

Did you *take in* a concert last night?
¿Fuiste a un concierto anoche?

They *took in* five thousand dollars that night.
Ganaron cinco mil dólares esa noche.

Take in one's stride.   She *took* her illness *in her stride.*
Tomó su enfermedad *sin mucha preocupación.*

Take it easy.   *Take it easy* after such a tiring night.
Descansa después de trabajar tanto esta noche.

Take off.   The plane *took off* smoothly.
El avión *levantó el vuelo* suavemente.

He *took off* his wet clothes.
Se quitó la ropa húmeda.

Take off one's hat.   I *take off my hat* to you for making a success
of that business.
Te *felicito* por el éxito que has tenido en ese negocio.

Take on.   They *take on* more workers in the spring.
Ellos *emplean* más obreros en la primavera.

Take one's time.   *Take your time* and think before speaking.
No te apures y piensa antes de hablar.

Take out.   He *takes* her *out* regularly to the movies.
El la *lleva* al cine regularmente.

He *took* the speck of dirt *out* of her eye.
El *extrajo* la basurita en el ojo de ella.

Take over.   Please *take over* whenever the boss has to leave.
Favor de *hacerte cargo del negocio* cada vez que el jefe tenga que
salir.

Take pains.   *Take pains* to do a good job.
Esmérate en hacer un buen trabajo.

Take place.   The birth *took place* at noon.
El nacimiento *tuvo lugar* al mediodía.

Take sick.   She *took sick* right after eating dinner.
Se enfermó inmediatamente después de comer.

Take someone's part (take someone's side).   I'm *taking your
part* in this dispute.
Estoy *a tu favor* en esta disputa.

Take something up with someone. I want to *take this matter up with you* to get your real opinion.
Quiero *discutir este asunto contigo* para saber tu opinión.

Take the bull by the horns. He *took the bull by the horns* and fired her.
El *se enfrentó al problema* y la despidió.

Take the floor. The lawyer *took the floor* when the prisoner sat down.
El abogado *tomó la palabra* cuando el prisionero se sentó.

Take the rap for. Are you going to *take the rap for* your brother?
¿Vas a *pagar las consecuencias por* tu hermano?

Take the words out of someone's mouth. You *took the words* right *out of my mouth* when you said that.
Me quitaste las palabras de la boca cuando dijiste eso.

Take time off. He *took time off* to rest up.
Se ausentó del trabajo para descansar.

Take time out. We *take time out* every afternoon for tea.
Suspendemos el trabajo cada tarde para tomar té.

Take to task. Her teacher *took* her *to task* over the poor examination.
Su maestro la *reprendió* por el examen tan pobre que hizo.

Take turns. The parents *took turns* feeding him.
Sus padres *se alternaron* para darle de comer.

Take up. He's going to *take up* golf this summer.
Va a *aprender* a jugar al golfo este verano.

He *takes up* all her free time.
El le *ocupa* todo el tiempo libre de ella.

Talk of the town. Her actions are the *talk of the town*.
Sus acciones son la *comidilla del pueblo*.

Talk shop. The men lunch together and *talk shop*.
Los hombres almuerzan juntos y *hablan de negocios*.

Talk through his hat. He is *talking through his hat* about things he doesn't understand.
El *habla disparates* acerca de cosas que no entiende.

Talk turkey. Let's *talk turkey* and conclude the deal.
Hablemos del negocio y concluyamos el contrato.

Tall story. That's a *tall story* if I ever heard one, and I don't believe a word of it.
Esa es la historia más fantástica que he oído y no creo una palabra de ella.

Tell it to the Marines. *Tell it to the marines* because we don't believe you.
Vete con el cuento a otra parte, no lo creemos.

Tell someone. *You're telling me!*
¿A mí me lo vas a decir?

Tell someone off. He *told* her *off* about gossiping all the time.
El la reprendió por chismear todo el tiempo.

Thank one's lucky stars. *I thank my lucky stars* I'm home again safely.
Gracias a mi estrella estoy otra vez salvo en casa.

Think better of it. She wanted to leave school, but *thought better of it.*
Quiso dejar la escuela, pero cambió de opinión.

Think little (highly) of. I *think little (highly) of* his last book.
Admiro poco (mucho) su último libro.

Think out. If we *think* this *out* together, we'll find the solution.
Si resolvemos esto juntos, encontraremos la solución.

Think over. I'll have to *think* it *over* before answering.
Tendré que pensarlo antes de dar una respuesta.

Think up. I must *think up* a good excuse for not going.
Debo buscar una buena excusa para no ir.

Through the grapevine. I heard *through the grapevine* that you were married.
He oído decir que te habías casado.

Through thick and thin. His fiancée stuck with him *through thick and thin.*
Su novia le acompañó a través de buenas y malas situaciones.

Throw (have) a fit. His parents *threw a fit* when he was expelled from school.
Sus padres se encolerizaron cuando lo expulsaron de la escuela.

Throw a party. They *threw a party* New Year's eve.
Dieron una fiesta en la víspera de Año Nuevo.

Throw in the sponge. He *threw in the sponge* after the blow that broke his nose.
Se dió por vencido cuando le rompieron la nariz.

Tip off. The Russian fled after he was *tipped off* by a fellow traveler.
El ruso se fué cuando fué *informado* por el simpatizador.

Tired (tuckered) out. I'm all *tired out* from playing tennis.
Estoy *agotado* por haber jugado al tenis.

Tom, Dick and Harry. Every *Tom, Dick and Harry* wants to be president.
Todo *Juan de los Palotes* quiere ser presidente.

Tooth and nail. He fought *tooth and nail* to win.
Peleó *denodadamente* para ganar.

Try on. *Try* it *on* and see if it is becoming.
Pruébatelo para ver si te queda bien.

Turn a deaf ear. She *turned a deaf ear* when he proposed marriage.
Ella *se hizo la sorda* cuando él le propuso el matrimonio.

Turn a hair. She didn't *turn a hair* when they made fun of her.
Ella no *se alteró* cuando se burlaron de ella.

Turn down. She *turned* him *down* when he proposed.
Ella le *rehusó* cuando él se le declaró.

Turn the radio *down* because it's too noisy.
Baja la radio porque está muy alta.

Turn in. I'll *turn in* at ten, as I do nightly.
Me acuesto a las diez, como hago todas las noches.

The pupil *turned in* his notebook.
El estudiante *entregó* su libreta.

Turn off. I *turned off* the radio.
Apagué la radio.

Turn on. I *turned on* my favorite television program.
Puse mi programa favorito de televisión.

Turn out. The day *turned out* sultry.
El día *resultó* bochornoso.

They all *turned out* to see the bride.
Todos ellos *fueron* a ver a la novia.

That university *turns out* some prominent scholars.
Esa universidad *produce* algunos eruditos prominentes.

Turn over.   I'll *turn over* the decision to my wife.
Dejaré la decisión en manos de mi esposa.

The motorcycle hit the curb and *turned over*.
La motorcicleta dió con el contén y *se volcó*.

Turn over a new leaf.   I'll *turn over a new leaf* with the new year.
Me enmendaré con el año nuevo.

Turn up.   The same blonde *turned up* at every cocktail party.
La misma rubia *apareció* en cada fiesta.

Turn up the radio. I can't hear the commentator.
Pon la radio *más alto*. No puedo oír al comentarista.

Twiddle one's thumbs.   Instead of doing her work, she *twiddled her thumbs*.
En vez de hacer su trabajo, *se puso a jugar*.

Two-faced.   You're *two-faced* and untrustworthy.
Eres *persona de dos caras* y no se puede confiar en tí.

Under one's breath.   If you mutter *under your breath*, nobody can understand you.
Si hablas *en voz baja*, nadie te puede entender.

Under the table.   They paid extra *under the table* for tickets to the game.
Pagaron extra *secretamente* para obtener los boletos para el juego.

Under someone's thumb.   He's *under his wife's thumb*, and she makes all the decisions.
El está *bajo el dominio de su esposa*, y ella hace todas las decisiones.

Under the weather.   I've been *under the weather* for a week with this cold.
Hace una semana que *me siento mal* por este catarro.

Up and about.   He was *up and about* a week after his appendectomy.
Una semana después de su apendiceptomía *andaba de arriba para abajo*.

Up to.   The boys must be *up to* mischief, the way they look.
Los muchachos deben estar *tramando* algo por como lucen.

It's *up to* you to make the decision.
Depende de tí hacer la decisión.

Up-to-date. This is an *up-to-date* list of the candidates.
Esta es una lista *completa hasta la fecha* de los candidatos.

Up-to-the-minute. He gave us an *up-to-the-minute* appraisal of the political situation.
Nos dió hasta el *último minuto* una interpretación de la situación política.

Upset the applecart. He *upset the applecart* by arriving too early.
Estropeó los planes por llegar demasiado temprano.

Wait up. They *waited up* for hours before she telephoned them.
Se desvelaron esperando por horas a que ella les telefonease.

Water wagon. I'm on the *water wagon* and drink only tea.
No bebo bebidas alcohólicas, solamente té.

Wear off. Your sorrow will *wear off* with time.
Tus penas *desaparecerán* con el tiempo.

Well-heeled. A woman who owns so many jewels must be *well-heeled.*
Una mujer que posee tantas prendas debe estar *bien de dinero.*

Well off. She had a rich husband who left her very *well off.*
Ella tuvo un esposo rico que le dejó *buena cantidad de dinero.*

You're certainly *well off* in that fine school.
En esa escuela tan buena *no tienes problemas.*

Well-to-do. He is looking for a *well-to-do* widow.
El busca a una viuda *adinerada.*

Wet blanket. At school she was always a *wet blanket*, never joining in the fun.
En la escuela ella fué una *aguafiestas*, nunca participó en ellas.

What's up? *What's up?* You all seem so irritated.
¿Qué pasa? Uds. todos parecen irritados.

White elephant. The factory was a *white elephant* and we tried to sell it.
La fábrica fué un *mal negocio* y tratamos de venderla.

Wild-goose chase. He led the police on a *wild-goose chase* looking for the kidnaper.
Dirigió a la policía en una *búsqueda infructuosa* del raptor.

Win hands down. The white horse *won* the race *hands down.*
El caballo blanco *ganó* la carrera *fácilmente.*

Wind up.   We'll be leaving as soon as we *wind up* our affairs.
Saldremos tan pronto *terminemos* nuestros asuntos.

With flying colors.   At exams she comes off *with flying colors* because she is so intelligent.
En los exámenes *sale muy bien* porque es muy inteligente.

Wolf.   Don't *wolf* your dinner down so fast.
No te *comas* la comida tan *de prisa.*

Work out.   He'll *work out* his problem if it takes him all night.
El *resolverá* su problema aunque le lleve toda la noche.

I'm confident that the French lessons will *work out* well.
Tengo confianza en que las lecciones de francés *saldrán bien.*

Work up.   We'll *work up* a new program of studies.
Prepararemos un nuevo programa de estudios.

Worn out.   The nurse was *worn out* by the cranky patient.
La enfermera estaba *rendida* por el paciente tan cascarrabias.

Wrap up.   We'll *wrap up* the deal tomorrow.
Concluiremos el negocio mañana.